Student Resources

The printed text is not all that you have to rely on in your study of money, banking, and financial markets. The following Web-based resources are also available to help you learn faster and more effectively:

Text Home Page
http://money.swcollege.com

■ ***Before the Test*** **Interactive Quizzes**
At the text's home page, you can take interactive quizzes on concepts covered in each chapter of the text.

■ **Chapter-Ending *Online Applications***
Each *Online Application* problem is an extensive Internet exercise that takes you to a particular URL to engage in an application. Every *Online Application* also includes a section entitled "For Group Study and Analysis."

■ ***"Link to..."*** **Web Resources**
Each *Link to...* feature includes Internet resources relating to the subject of the feature and the proposed research project. These are maintained and updated on the home page.

■ ***On the Web*** **Margin URLs**
These margin URLs are also included and updated at the text home page.

Money Xtra! Site
http://moneyxtra.swcollege.com

■ ***Another Perspective***
Readings on topics covered in each chapter, which are referenced in the margin of the book beside the most relevant text, are available at this site. Each *Another Perspective* reading includes quiz questions covering the reading's key points.

■ ***Online Case Study***
References to these case studies have been placed in the margin beside relevant text. Each *Online Case Study* includes interactive online quizzes that help you evaluate your understanding of how material covered in the text enables addressing the situations outlined in the case studies.

■ ***Economic Applications*** **Margin Features**
These features appear in margins alongside related text and direct you to the Money Xtra! site for links to *EconData* and *EconDebate* sites of South-Western that closely relate to concepts discussed in the text.

Money xtra!

CONGRATULATIONS!

Your purchase of this new textbook includes complimentary access to the Money Xtra! Web Site (http://moneyxtra.swcollege.com). Money Xtra! offers a variety of online learning enhancements, including:

ONLINE CASE STUDIES

Online Case Studies are related to chapter material. Each Online Case Study includes quiz questions that help you evaluate your understanding of how material covered in the text enables addressing the situations outlined in the case studies.

XTRA! QUIZZING

You can create and take randomly-generated quizzes on whichever chapter(s) you wish to test yourself, and endlessly practice for exams.

ANOTHER PERSPECTIVE

Another Perspective readings on topics covered in each chapter with associated quiz questions to test your comprehension of the reading.

ECONOMIC APPLICATIONS (e-con @pps)

EconNews Online, EconDebate Online, and EconData Online features help to deepen your understanding of theoretical concepts through hands-on exploration and analysis of the latest economic news stories, policy debates, and data.

Tear Out Card Missing?

If you did not buy a new textbook, the tear-out portion of this card may be missing, or the Access Code may not be valid. Access Codes can be used only once to register for access to **Money Xtra!**, and are not transferable. You can choose to either buy a new book or purchase access to the Money Xtra! site at http://moneyxtra.swcollege.com.

Copyright©2004 by South-Western, a division of Thomson Learning. Thomson Learning™ is a trademark used herein under license. ISBN: 0-324-27172-7

HOW TO REGISTER YOUR SERIAL NUMBER

STEP 1 Launch a Web browser and go to http://moneyxtra.swcollege.com

STEP 2 Click the "Register" button to enter your serial number.

STEP 3 Enter your serial number exactly as it appears here and create a unique User ID, or enter an existing User ID if you have previously registered for a different product via a serial number.

SERIAL NUMBER: SC-0001KHFK-MOXT

STEP 4 When prompted, create a password (or enter an existing password, if you have previously registered for a different product via a serial number). Submit the necessary information when prompted. Record your User ID and password in a secure location.

STEP 5 Once registered, follow the link to enter the product, or return to the URL above and select the "Enter" button. Note that the duration of your access

For technical support, contact 1-800-423-0563 or email support@thomsonlearning.com.

Money, Banking, and Financial Markets

Second Edition

Money, Banking, and Financial Markets

Second Edition

Roger LeRoy Miller
Institute for University Studies
Arlington, Texas

David VanHoose
Department of Economics
Baylor University

THOMSON
SOUTH-WESTERN

Australia · Canada · Mexico · Singapore · Spain · United Kingdom · United States

Money, Banking, and Financial Markets. Second Edition
Roger LeRoy Miller and David Van Hoose

Editor-in-Chief:
Jack Calhoun

Team Director:
Michael P. Roche

Publisher:
Michael B. Mercier

Acquisitions Editor:
Michael W. Worls

Sr. Developmental Editor:
Jan Lamar

Sr. Marketing Manager:
Lisa L. Lysne

Production Editor:
Ann Borman

Manufacturing Coordinator:
Sandee Milewski

Compositor:
Parkwood Composition

Printer:
Quebecor World

Internal Designer:
Ann Borman

Cover Designer:
Tippy McIntosh

Cover
Illustration:
PhotoDisc

Copyeditor:
Pat Lewis

Indexer:
Bob Marsh

COPYRIGHT © 2004 by South-Western, a division of Thomson Learning. Thomson Learning™ is a trademark used herein under license.

Printed in the United States of America
2 3 4 5 04 03

For more information contact South-Western, 5191 Natorp Boulevard, Mason, Ohio 45040.
Or you can visit our Internet site at:
http://www.swcollege.com

Dedications:

To Maya Miller-Wolf,

It is rare for an uncle
to have a niece who
understands the meaning
of money and business at
such a young age. Please
continue to amaze me!

RLM

For Michael.

DDV

Contents in Brief

Contents

Unit IV Central Banking, Monetary Policy, and the Federal Reserve System 367

Unit V Monetary Policy and the Economy 445

Unit VI Monetary Policy 617

Chapter 25 What Should the Fed Do?—Objectives and Targets of Monetary Policy 618

Chapter 26 Rules versus Discretion in Monetary Policy 645

Chapter 27 What the Fed Does—Interest Rate Targeting and Economic Activity 671

To the Instructor

A course in money, banking, and financial markets is challenging for both students and instructors. Our key objective in writing the first edition of *Money, Banking, and Financial Markets* was to provide the student reader with a sophisticated, yet accessible understanding of the subject matter while simultaneously providing the instructor with an up-to-date and sensibly organized presentation of the full range of topics appropriate for a thoroughly modern course. In this second edition, we have again made every effort to make this the most pedagogically sound text in the field. Toward this end, we have significantly enhanced the entire teaching-learning package:

- Web resources for the text have been significantly enhanced. In addition to resources available at the text's home page (**http://money.swcollege.com**), there is also a **MoneyXtra!** site (**http://moneyxtra.swcollege.com**) containing a number of learning tools.
- Available at the MoneyXtra! Web site are *Another Perspective* **readings** relevant to each chapter. References to these readings have been placed in the margin beside the relevant text. Accompanying each Internet-based reading are quiz questions that students can use to test their comprehension.
- Another Web-based feature relevant to each chapter that is available at the MoneyXtra! Web site is an ***Online Case Study.*** References to these case studies have been placed in the margin beside the relevant text. Each *Online Case Study* includes quiz questions that help students evaluate their understanding of how material covered in the text enables them to address the situations outlined in the case studies.
- Interactive *Before the Test* **online quizzes** covering the material in each chapter of the text are now available for students at the text's home page (**http://money.swcollege.com**).
- **PowerPoint slides** for all figures and tables are available to instructors.
- The *Instructor's Manual, Test Bank,* and *Study Guide* have all been updated and enhanced. Qualified instructors can now download the *Test Bank* via links available at the text's home page.
- We have developed 56 new learning-motivating ***Policy Focus, Global Focus,*** and ***Management Focus*** **features** that illustrate the applicability of text materials to up-to-date topics of current interest in the areas of money, banking, and financial markets.
- The opening to each chapter now introduces an issue that is addressed in a chapter-concluding feature—***Link to Policy, Link to the Global Economy,*** or ***Link to Management***—which provides an in-depth

illustration of policy, international, or management applications of concepts addressed within the chapter. Each of these features includes suggested research topics and Internet resources students can use to explore them.

- Also new to this edition are ***Economic Applications*** **margin features** that steer students, via the MoneyXtra! site, to *EconData* and *EconDebate* Web pages that are closely related to concepts discussed in the text.

Within the text, we have included several features that address fundamental issues that have emerged in recent years. These include:

- Fully integrated coverage of international financial markets and the global economy is a fundamental characteristic of the text.
- Cutting-edge developments in information technology and their economic and financial implications are examined throughout.
- Current-interest features underlining the real-world relevance of the study of money, banking, and financial markets appear in each chapter.
- Frequent margin references to Internet resources are included, along with end-of-chapter *Online Application* questions.
- The more than 175 graphs for this textbook are arguably the best in any text in this area. All lines and curves are color coded in a consistent manner, and we have provided full explanations underneath or alongside each graph or set of graphs.

Complete Coverage of Money, Banking, and Financial Markets

In this second edition, we have trimmed down the book while continuing to cover all of the essential elements of money, banking, and financial markets. These include:

- The forms, functions, and evolution of money and the emergence of digital cash
- Domestic and international financial markets and the role of electronic trading
- Interest rate risk, foreign exchange risk, and derivative securities
- Portfolio choice, international interest rate parities, and market efficiency
- Financial institutions, the economics of banking, and issues in bank management
- Depository institution regulation in a rapidly changing environment
- The money supply process and the implications of electronic money
- The Federal Reserve and its role in U.S. and global payment systems

- The linkage between day-to-day Federal Reserve policymaking and aggregate economic activity
- Intermediate monetary policy targets, rules versus discretion, and policy credibility
- Conducting monetary policy with an interest rate target
- International dimensions of monetary policy

Full Global Integration Throughout

Money, Banking, and Financial Markets is the first text in this field to fully integrate global economics and finance, starting from Chapter 1. The student is introduced to international issues in the field from the outset. Every chapter that follows continues this integration within whatever topic area the chapter addresses.

Of course, some chapters focus exclusive attention on international topics. Examples are Chapter 5: "A World Market?—International Financial Market Integration," Chapter 6: "Foreign Exchange Markets," and Chapter 28: "Policymaking in the World Economy—International Dimensions of Monetary Policy."

The Importance of New Information Technologies

Nearly forty years ago, banks and other financial institutions were among the first to perceive the dramatic cost efficiencies and potential revenue enhancements available from adopting information technologies. Only a few of the most significant uses of computers were readily noticeable to retail customers, however—automated teller machines networks, automated telephone account information and transfer services, and the like. The true banking information technology revolution took place largely out of sight to the general public, in the "back offices," as financial institutions increasingly became interconnected through automated clearing houses, large-value payment systems, and interbank funds markets.

Today, however, the information technologies in financial markets are visible to all. Internet brokers are transforming retail stock trading in the United States, and wireless online banking is now commonplace in several European nations. Students know these changes are under way, and they want to learn more about their potential effects. A fundamental objective of this text is to provide students with the background they need to understand the implications of emerging cybertechnologies for money, banking, and financial markets.

A Flexible Structure

Some instructors may find that there is more in this text than they wish to cover in a single semester. This is not an accident. In the end, the content of any economics course should reflect an instructor's professional decisions taking into account student backgrounds and departmental and college curricula. This is particularly true of a course within the broad field of money, banking, and financial markets. There are at least three separate types of courses that one could teach using this text:

1. **A Strongly Banking/Financial Markets-Oriented Course** (Core Units: 1, 2, 3, and 4). After covering the subjects in Unit 1, this course would include a detailed examination of all of the material in Units 2, 3, and 4. Material from Chapters 19 and 20 in Unit 5 would be covered. Depending on time constraints, the instructor could then touch on basic measurement issues and fundamental theories covered in Chapters 21 through 23, thereby providing students with sufficient background to touch on two or three selected chapters from Unit 6.

2. **A Strongly Money/Macro-Oriented Course** (Core Units: 1, 4, 5, and 6). After surveying all of Unit 1 and chapters 4, 6, and 9 in Unit 2, a course with this slant would cover the essential aspects of banking markets and regulation in Chapters 11, 12, and 14 in Unit 3. It would then cover the bulk of the chapters contained in Units 4, 5, and 6.

3. **A Middle-of-the-Road Course.** This course would attempt to strike a balance. It would cover both Units 1 and 2 and a more equalized (in terms of banking/financial markets versus macro-money content) sampling of selected chapters from remaining units of the text, depending on the specific objectives of the instructor.

Features That Teach and Reinforce

In our view, real-world applications should be a key aspect of a textbook on money, banking, and financial markets. To motivate student learning, in this edition we have included more than 80 new examples drawn from throughout the world. Five types of features are incorporated and referred to throughout the text.

Global Focus

Money, banking, and financial markets can no longer be considered a closed-economy subject. Events that affect the U.S. economy, banking system, and financial markets affect nations around the globe and vice versa. Global issues in money, banking, and financial markets are not only exciting to read about, but also important to understand. We have included among others the following:

- Stored Value and Debit Cards May Be the Ticket to Online Shopping in Russia
- In Japan, Corner Shops Become Web Banks—and Online-Commerce Package Pickup Centers
- Does Russia's Central Bank Really Need So Many Employees?
- Multilingual Monetary Musings in Europe
- Were Italian Lire Just Part of a Vast Central Banking Conspiracy?
- Is the ECB's "Complex Strategy for a Complex Region" Too Complicated?

Cyber Focus

The integration of emerging information technologies into banking and other financial services and the effects on financial markets dominate today's financial news. Understanding how these developments affect institutions and markets is now a central subject of the study of money, banking, and financial markets. A few of the topics covered include:

- Can Barter Make a Comeback on the Internet?
- The Growing Role of Electronic Communications Networks in U.S. Stock Markets
- Simplifying Cross-Border Retailing via Multicurrency Payment Processing
- Using the Web to Help Rich Clients Understand Their Portfolios
- Make Your Online Trades in Dollars and Leave the Hedging to Us
- Replacing Check Clearing with Interbank Internet Payments Networks

Policy Focus

Because policy is in the news so much, we felt it appropriate to include a special feature concerned with just policy issues. These features cover a wide variety of topics including:

- The Golden Dollar—A Botched Currency Reform, or Just Another "Loonie" Idea?
- Oh, Where Have All Those Dollars Gone?
- Confronting Counterfeit Currency
- What Would the Fed Do if Government Securities Were to Disappear?
- Can There Be Too Much Transparency in Monetary Policy?
- The Alphabet Soup of Price Indexes

Management Focus

Businesspeople and individuals managing their personal finances must keep abreast of the most recent developments in money, banking, and financial markets, which continually present both opportunities and challenges. To acquaint students with the variety of monetary, banking, and financial issues faced by managers, we have included features on topics such as the following:

- What Can Yields on Treasury Inflation-Indexed Securities Tell Us about U.S. Stock Prices?
- Making Islamic Financial Services Available on the Internet
- Brokered Deposits Catch On at Small Banks
- Banks Find a Creative Way to Comply with the Community Reinvestment Act
- Why Banks Charge Customers to Use Automated Teller Machines
- Can Firms Rely on Federal Funds Futures Prices to Predict Monetary Policy?

Link to . . . Features

New to this edition, these chapter-ending features provide an in-depth analysis of how concepts covered in the chapter relate to a topic in policy, management, or the global economy. Also included in every *Link to . . .* feature are a proposed research topic and Web resources (available at the MoneyXtra! Web site **http://money.swcollege.com**) that students can use to explore the topic area. These features include:

- **Link to Policy:** Does the Yield Curve Predict Recessions?
- **Link to Management:** Shifting Mortgages into Reverse Gear
- **Link to the Global Economy:** Will Stock Markets Outside the United States Ever Catch Up?
- **Link to Management:** Why Is Stockholding Still So Highly Concentrated Among the Rich?
- **Link to the Global Economy:** Excess Returns and Uncovered Interest Parity
- **Link to Management:** Will Credit Derivatives Allow Banks to Get Out of the Risk Business?
- **Link to Policy:** Federal Reserve Policy on and after September 11, 2001
- **Link to Management:** Inflation, Deflation, and Choosing between Debt and Equity Financing

Critical-Thinking Exercises

Critical thinking is an important aspect of every college student's education. We make sure that students are introduced to critical-thinking activities by ending each *Focus* and *Link to . . .* feature with critical-thinking questions called "For Critical Analysis." The suggested answers to these critical-thinking questions are included in the *Instructor's Manual.*

Internet Resources

Most students, particularly those taking intermediate-level economics courses, are familiar with how to use the Internet. We provide a number of important features for them:

1. **Alternative Perspectives** Readings on topics covered in each chapter, which are referenced in the margin of the book beside the most relevant text, are available at the MoneyXtra! Web site (**http://moneyxtra.swcollege.com**). Each *Alternative Perspective* reading includes quiz questions covering the reading's key points.

2. **Online Case Study** Case studies concerning the subject matter of each chapter, which are referenced in the margin beside the most relevant text, are also available at the MoneyXtra! Web site. Each *Online Case Study* has accompanying quiz questions addressing the key issues raised by the case study.

3. **Before the Test Interactive Quizzes** At the end of each chapter, students are directed to the text's home page (**http://money.swcollege.com**), where they can take interactive quizzes on concepts covered in each chapter of the text.

4. **Economic Applications Margin Features** These features appear in margins alongside related text and direct students to the MoneyXtra! site for links to *EconData* and *EconDebate* sites of South-Western College Publishing that closely relate to concepts discussed in the text.

5. **On the Web Margin URLs** New and updated *On the Web* features appear in the margins throughout the book. Each opens with a question linking the feature to the text material and provides brief guidance for navigating through the Web site.

6. **"Link to . . ." Web Resources** Each *Link to . . .* feature includes Internet resources relating to the subject of the feature and the proposed research project.

7. **Chapter-Ending Online Applications** All *Online Application* problems at the conclusion of each chapter have been updated or replaced. Each problem is an extensive Internet exercise that takes the student to a particular URL and then asks him or her to engage in an application. Every *Online Application* also includes a section entitled "For Group Study and Analysis."

Key Pedagogy

Learning cannot occur in a vacuum. We have made sure that students using this text have an ample number of pedagogical devices that will help them master the material.

Fundamental Issues and Answers within the Text of Each Chapter A unique feature of *Money, Banking, and Financial Markets* is the inclusion of **five to seven fundamental issues** at the beginning of each chapter. Within the text itself, but offset so as not to be a distraction from a student's reading, the fundamental issues are repeated with the **appropriate answers.** Students will find these questions and answers invaluable when reviewing the readings and studying for quizzes and examinations.

VOCABULARY IS EMPHASIZED Because vocabulary is often a stumbling block, we have **boldfaced** all important vocabulary terms within the text. Immediately in the margin these boldfaced terms are defined. They are further defined in the end-of-text glossary.

CHAPTER SUMMARY The chapter summary is presented in a numbered point-by-point format that corresponds to the chapter-opening fundamental issues, further reinforcing the full circular nature of the learning process for each chapter.

QUESTIONS AND PROBLEMS Each chapter ends with 10 questions and problems. Suggested answers are provided in the *Instructor's Manual.*

SELECTED REFERENCES AND FURTHER READING Appropriate references for materials in the chapter are given in this section.

The Supplements

Money, Banking, and Financial Markets is supported by the strongest set of supplements currently available.

STUDY GUIDE The *Study Guide,* which was written by Jim Lee of Texas A&M University at Corpus Christi, is designed to facilitate active learning by students. It provides summaries of chapter contents and key terms for students to look for and define in their own words as they read the text. To assist students in testing their understanding of the material, the *Study Guide* also includes 20 multiple-choice and 10 short-answer questions per chapter.

INSTRUCTOR'S MANUAL The *Instructor's Manual,* also written by Jim Lee, is designed to simplify the teaching tasks that instructors face. For each chapter it offers an overview of key concepts and objectives, a detailed outline built upon chapter headings in the text, and answers to end-of-chapter questions.

TEST BANK One of the most challenging aspects of teaching is evaluation of student performance. To assist instructors in this endeavor, a *Test Bank,* also written by Jim Lee, that includes between 20 and 40 multiple-choice questions per chapter, along with correct answers, is available to all adopters of *Money, Banking, and Financial Markets* via links from the text's home page (**http://money.swcollege.com**).

EXAMVIEW Computerized Testing Software contains all of the questions in the printed test bank. This program is an easy-to-use test creation software compatible with Microsoft Windows. Instructors can add or edit questions, instructions, and answers, and select questions by previewing them on the screen, selecting them randomly, or selecting them by number. Instructors can also create and administer quizzes online, whether over the Internet, a local area network (LAN), or a wide area network (WAN).

PowerPoint Slides For many instructors, multimedia presentations have become an indispensable part of the teaching-learning process. A complete set of PowerPoint slides is available for adopters of this text.

MoneyXtra! Free access to the MoneyXtra! Web site (a $25 value) is packaged with every new copy of the text. MoneyXtra! offers a variety of online learning enhancements, including "Another Perspective" features (reading on topics covered in each chapter with associated quiz questions); "Online Case Studies" (which also include quizzes); and links to "Economic Applications" (*EconData* and *EconDebate* online features that closely relate concepts discussed in the text to the latest contemporary applications). Icons throughout each chapter of the book alert students to an associated MoneyXtra! online enrichment activity anytime one is available to enhance the textual material. (Students purchasing a used book can buy access to MoneyXtra! online at **http://moneyxtra.swcollege.com**.)

Acknowledgments

We benefited from an extremely active and conscientious group of reviewers of the manuscript for this second edition of *Money, Banking, and Financial Markets*. At times they were tough and demanding, but the rewrites of the manuscript improved accordingly. To the following reviewers, we extend our sincere appreciation for the critical nature of your comments that we think helped make this a better text.

Burton Abrams University of Delaware	Pamela Labadie George Washington University
Harjit K. Arora LeMoyne College	Jim Lee Texas A&M University
Thomas J. Kopp Siena College	Jonas Prager New York University

Of course, no textbook project is done by the authors alone. We wish to thank our editor, Mike Worls, for his excellent guidance. In particular, we owe tremendous gratitude to our developmental editor, Jan Lamar, who has provided invaluable feedback and guidance. Our production team of Bill Stryker and Ann Borman put together an excellent design and never let us fall behind. The best copyeditor in the business, Pat Lewis, worked her magic to make the book read more smoothly. Peggy Buskey and Vicky True provided indispensable oversight of the process of developing the Internet resources for the text.

We anticipate revising this text for years to come and therefore welcome all comments and criticism from students and professors alike.

R.L.M.
D.D.V.

Unit 1 Introduction

CONTENTS

Chapter

1

Money—An Introduction

Fundamental Issues

1. How have financial globalization and cybertechnologies acted together to alter the economic roles of banking institutions and money?
2. What functions does money perform?
3. How has money evolved?
4. What are monetary aggregates, and how are they constructed?
5. How do changes in payments technologies affect our definitions of money?

What do Ithaca, New York, and La Plata, Argentina, most have in common? Residents of both cities have used local currencies alongside officially sanctioned national currencies. Some Ithaca residents can spend entire days without touching Federal Reserve notes, the U.S. government's authorized currency issued by the Federal Reserve System. In color combinations of maize yellow and acid green or pumpkin orange and powder blue, Ithaca hours *are currency notes "backed" by labor hours defined to be equal to ten dollars worth of Federal Reserve notes.*

Local currencies are used in about sixty other U.S. cities, including the bread *of Berkeley California, the* greenbacks *of Brooklyn, New York, and the* mo money *of New Orleans, Louisiana. These currencies, which are normally promoted by citizens' groups or chambers of commerce, circulate alongside the U.S. dollar. Some merchants accept them in payment for goods and services, but many others continue to accept only U.S. dollars. The Ithaca hour is more widely accepted than many other local currencies in the United States; nearly 500 businesses in Ithaca are willing to accept Ithaca hours in payment for goods or services.*

The local currency used in La Plata, Argentina, was issued by the provincial government to supplement the Argentine national currency. Although its formal name is "treasury letters in cancellation of obligations," in La Plata and elsewhere in the province, it is known as the patacón*—a slang term used by a character in a popular comic book. The* patacón *has not achieved widespread popularity. Following its introduction, protest marches by teachers, government employees, and hospital workers featured signs with slogans such as "Pay the foreign debt in* patacónes*" and "Full and timely payment in pesos."*

Why are people willing to accept some forms of money in exchange but not others? Why might different types of money circulate simultaneously? To consider the answers to these questions, you must first understand the functions of money.

Objectives of This Book and How They Relate to You

Not surprisingly, a key objective of this text is to help you understand the roles that money performs in the U.S. and world economies. To achieve this goal, however, you must also learn a substantial amount about banking and financial markets. As you will discover, these topics are closely related, because banks and other similar financial institutions issue checking deposits that are part of the quantity of money that circulates within the economy. This chapter explains the concept of money and discusses how money is measured in today's economy. Chapter 2 reviews the changes sweeping today's banking system, as banks, businesses, and households adopt sophisticated new information technologies in an increasingly interconnected world economy. Chapter 3 presents an overview of modern financial markets, instruments, and institutions. Together, these chapters provide essential background. By the time you have completed this book, you should have a clear understanding of why money is so important to society.

To be sure, if you continue your studies in the field of economics, you will find that knowledge of money, banking, and financial markets is critical to understanding macroeconomics and international trade and finance, as well as growth and development. If you choose a career in finance, the connection between this course and the rest of your courses is perhaps even more obvious. Indeed, one might say that a beginning course in money, banking, and financial markets is the basis of the field of finance. If you are going on to business and management in general, you will face a variety of problems throughout your studies and your business career, all of which will relate in some way to what you are going to learn in this text. After all, businesspersons must make decisions each day about how best to hold excess cash, how to pay for inventory, whether a potential investment should be undertaken, and so on. Managers everywhere face a dizzying array of choices about what kinds of technologies to apply to such tasks, and increasingly their concerns range beyond the borders of their home countries.

Finally, even students who go into other fields can benefit from a course in money, banking, and financial institutions. Virtually everyone uses a checking account, borrows to pay for a car or house, contemplates whether to allocate pension savings to an international asset portfolio, or evaluates the potential advantages of getting connected to a bank via the Internet. Money, banking, and financial markets affect us all.

The Globalization of Money, Banking, and Financial Markets

In years past, courses in money, banking, and financial markets typically covered U.S. banking, the Federal Reserve System, and the influence that each had—both independently and together—on the U.S. economy. This approach is no longer feasible. The U.S. banking system is now intricately linked to world financial markets. Financial booms and busts in such diverse locations as Mexico, the Philippines, Russia, and Argentina increasingly have direct effects on the bottom lines of major U.S. financial institutions.

One reason for this is that today many U.S. companies are multinational firms. These corporate clients of U.S. financial institutions are as likely to have a market presence in an Asian nation as they are to have business interests in Europe. Thus, when an economic downturn in Asia affects the fortunes of many U.S.-based companies, the performance of those companies' banks is also affected.

Another reason is that nowadays it is harder to determine where domestic U.S. financial markets end and the global marketplace begins. A major U.S. bank that hopes to make a big loan to a U.S.-based multinational construction company may face competition from banks located in Berlin or Hong Kong. The same bank may raise funds by issuing deposits to individuals or firms in Japan or Australia.

To read a detailed evaluation of dollarization around the globe and test your understanding of the concept, go to the Chapter 1 reading, entitled "Dollarization: A Scorecard," by Roberto Chang of the Federal Reserve Bank of Atlanta. http://moneyxtra.swcollege.com

At the same time, events in the United States have significant implications for other nations. People around the world scrutinize the nuances of Federal Reserve policy pronouncements for hints of how they may influence such far-flung locales as Hong Kong, Brazil, Croatia, and South Africa. If the Federal Reserve engages in policy actions that raise U.S. interest rates, savers worldwide may be inclined to sell bonds from these and other countries so that they can purchase U.S. Treasury bonds. In contrast, if the Federal Reserve enacts policies that reduce U.S. interest rates, firms and governments in these and other nations may be able to raise funds from around the world at lower interest rates, thereby improving their near-term growth prospects.

In the twenty-first century, the subject of money and banking is unavoidably *international.* This does not mean the subject is any harder to learn than it was in years past. Indeed, the globalization of money and banking in many ways makes it an even more diverse and fascinating area of study.

Money and Banking in the Digital Age

In some respects, the globalization of money and banking is a return to the past. Not until the late 1990s did the relative volumes of world trade—worldwide exports and imports in proportion to total production of goods and services—finally regain the levels they had achieved before the outbreak of World War I in 1914. Thus, the international dimension of money, banking, and financial markets is not entirely new. Where there is trade, there are banks and credit, so it is natural that money, banking, and financial market issues now span national borders.

Back to the Future

Undoubtedly, a "back to the future" component distinguishes today's globalization of money and banking from the experience of the late nineteenth and early twentieth centuries. Before cables were laid across the Atlantic Ocean, it took days for news of a European financial collapse to reach U.S. shores. Even after cables were in place, hours or even days might pass before U.S. savers responded to the news. Now, of course, satellites have reduced the informational delays to minutes or even seconds. Millions of people are on the Internet at any given instant, learning about the financial news literally as it happens. At the click of a button, many of these people can now adjust their own financial positions within seconds after they see the news on their screens.

Cybertechnologies: Technologies that connect savers, investors, traders, producers, and governments via computer linkages.

Cybertechnologies

In the area of money and banking, the development of **cybertechnologies,** which are computer-based techniques for linking savers, investors, traders, producers, and governments, has fundamentally altered the landscape. This has occurred most clearly in the international realm. Late-afternoon financial news in Paris is available instantly to those who are trading in the late morning in the New York financial markets. These individuals can react quickly using the same computers that give them the news, so the Paris and New York financial markets are linked more intimately than at any previous time in history. So, too, are the markets in London and Chicago and the markets in Philadelphia and Tokyo. Even in the absence of the boom in world trade in the latter part of the twentieth century, cybertechnologies would surely have produced nearly as much international financial interdependence as we see today. The growth in world trade has simply increased the volumes of financial flows across borders that cybertechnologies have made possible.

Implications for Banks and Their Customers As we shall discuss throughout this book, cybertechnologies promise to transform many aspects of the banking business. In fact, in many ways they already have. Most major banks commonly announce annual targets for growth in online accounts alongside traditional targets for asset growth and profitability. Banks and other providers of mortgage funds now post Web sites for Internet mortgage-loan shopping. Consortiums of banks currently are pursuing alternative cybertechnologies of the not-too-distant future. These include voice recognition systems for deposit withdrawals and software that permits borrowers to download consumer loans onto computer chips on their home personal computers. Then the borrowers can transfer the value of these loans to plastic cards to use when they go shopping. Furthermore, these new cybertechnologies provide the capability to purchase items over the Internet using electronic cash or checks.

Implications for Policymakers These developments make money and banking one of the most interesting subjects in economics for any student. As you will learn, they also promise to complicate the lives of policymakers. Previously, a policymaker who made a mistake could "weasel out of it" during the following days and weeks. Now, a big policy mistake can cause rapid market swings within hours or even minutes. On net, the new cybertechnologies promise many social gains. At the same time, however, they raise a number of important issues about monetary and financial policymaking. What is money? Should national and even international regulations, and the institutions that design and enforce those regulations, seek to determine what money will be like in the new world of banking? How will these decisions influence the world economy? These are themes that will surface throughout this text.

1. How have financial globalization and cybertechnologies acted together to alter the economic roles of banking institutions and money? Increased financial globalization has been an inevitable by-product of a significant growth in international trade. Nevertheless, the globalization of money and banking has been hastened by the advent of cybertechnologies that link financial institutions and markets without regard to national borders. In this respect, globalization and the development of cybertechnologies have worked hand in hand to bring about sweeping changes in money and banking.

Money: Its Functions, Forms, and Evolution

Any item that people are generally willing to accept in exchange for goods, services, and financial assets such as stocks or bonds is **money.** Many of us naturally think of money as coins or dollar bills. Most of what constitutes today's money, however, is in accounts in institutions such as banks, savings institutions, and credit unions.

Money's Functions

Money performs four key functions. It is a medium of exchange, a store of value, a unit of account, and a standard of deferred payment.

Money: Anything that functions as a medium of exchange, store of value, unit of account, and standard of deferred payment.

Medium of exchange: An attribute of money that permits it to be used as a means of payment.

Barter: The direct exchange of goods, services, and financial assets.

Store of value: An attribute of money that allows it to be held for future use without loss of value in the meantime.

Unit of account: An attribute of money that permits it to be used as a measure of the value of goods, services, and financial assets.

Standard of deferred payment: An attribute of money that permits it to be used as a means of valuing future receipts in loan contracts.

MEDIUM OF EXCHANGE The fundamental function of money is to serve as a **medium of exchange.** This means that people who trade goods, services, or financial assets are willing to accept money in exchange for these items. By using money, people avoid engaging in **barter,** or the direct exchange of goods, services, and financial assets. Barter is a very costly activity, because it requires finding others willing to exchange items directly. A key reason that people use money is to avoid this cost.

STORE OF VALUE Nevertheless, money has other important functions. One is its use as a **store of value.** An individual can set money aside today with an intent to purchase items at a later time. Meanwhile, money retains value that the individual can apply to those future purchases. For example, funds that a college student keeps in a checking account during summer months may be used to pay tuition or to purchase textbooks when the fall semester begins.

UNIT OF ACCOUNT Money also functions as a **unit of account,** which means that people maintain their financial accounts by using money to value goods, services, and financial assets. Households and businesses quote prices of goods, services, and financial assets in terms of money. For instance, retail stores throughout the United States express the prices of their goods in dollars.

STANDARD OF DEFERRED PAYMENT Finally, money serves as a **standard of deferred payment.** People agree to loan contracts that call for future repayments in terms of money. These contracts defer repayment of a loan until a later date. Parties to the contract agree to meet financial terms specified in units of money.

2. What functions does money perform? Money is a medium of exchange through which people make payments for goods, services, and financial assets. In addition, money is a store of value; that is, it is a repository of wealth across time. Money is also a unit of account, meaning that sellers quote prices in money terms. Finally, money is a standard of deferred payment, meaning that loans are extended and repaid using money.

Methods of Exchange and the Evolution of Money

The earliest economies relied on barter. A person who wished to exchange a good or service had to find a second individual willing to purchase that good or service. Yet that second person also had to possess a good or service that the first person desired as well. Thus, barter requires a **double coincidence of wants:** two individuals must simultaneously be willing and able to make a trade. (If the owners of some Web sites have their way, in future years it will be easier to find a double coincidence of wants; see on the next page *Cyber Focus: Can Barter Make a Comeback on the Internet?)*

The history of money began with a movement away from barter to **commodity moneys,** or physical goods with *both* nonmonetary *and* monetary uses. Societies then progressed from commodity moneys to **commodity standards,** or standardized tokens whose value is backed by the value of a physical monetary good, such as gold or silver. They then adopted **fiat moneys,** or forms of money not backed by anything except faith in its universal acceptance in trade. Today we are observing the continuation of this evolution, with the emergence of **electronic money** (or *e-money*), which is money that people can transfer directly via electronic impulses instead of via coins, paper currency, or checks.

Commodity Moneys and the Purchasing Power of Money Today's moneys are not linked to gold or other commodities. Nevertheless, we can learn much about the workings of any monetary economy from studying how a commodity money system functions. Table 1-1 on the next page lists some of the different types of commodity moneys that have existed throughout history. Any commodity money, such as tobacco, tortoise shells, goats, or a metal, typically has value in alternative uses. Metals such as gold or silver are especially easy to divide into smaller units, so they ultimately emerged as the most common type of commodity money. Gold and silver were portable, durable, very recognizable, and, most important, valued highly by nearly everyone because of their relative scarcity and intrinsic usefulness.

Since the beginnings of civilization, people have used gold to craft jewelry and other forms of ornamentation. Later, people learned how to use gold in manufacturing, finding it particularly useful for electrical connectors in devices such as stereo components and computer equipment. Whether used for monetary or other purposes, gold has a price. If gold is a commodity money, as it was in years past, then the price of gold is measured in terms of other goods and services that individuals must give up in exchange for gold. (Keep in mind that in a true gold

Double coincidence of wants: The situation when two individuals are simultaneously willing and able to make a trade; a requirement for barter.

Commodity money: A good with a nonmonetary value that is also used as money.

Commodity standard: A money unit whose value is fully or partially backed by the value of some other physical good such as gold or silver.

Fiat money: A token that has value only because it is accepted as money.

Electronic money (e-money): Money that people can transfer directly via electronic impulses.

GLOBAL POLICY **CYBER Focus** MANAGEMENT

Can Barter Make a Comeback on the Internet?

Completing any barter transaction requires a double coincidence of wants. Thus, those engaging in barter incur the high opportunity cost associated with finding others willing to exchange items directly. Normally, the costs of finding a partner to an exchange are prohibitively high—the traditional explanation for why societies past and present eventually opt to use money.

On the Internet, however, a would-be barterer can search for an exchange partner simply by meandering through Web *barter exchanges*. At these sites, people and companies can engage in bartering just as easily as they can transmit online bids at C2C sites such as eBay.com and QXL.com. At barter exchanges with names like Tradeaway.com and Bigvine.com, users simply sign up, agree to a credit check, and begin searching for trading partners. A company that operates an oil refinery can, for instance, obtain materials it requires to upgrade its operations by offering to refine an oil producer's petroleum without any cash trading hands. These are just two of the more than 400 regional barter exchanges in the United States, and they are also only two of the many exchanges that now offer their services online. On these exchanges, individuals and firms trade books for services such as tax advice, airline tickets for advertising space, and the like.

Apparently, the barter exchanges do not believe they will eventually drive money out of existence, however. Typically, the exchanges charge both sides of a barter transaction a fee of up to 4 percent of the amount traded—measured in dollars.

For Critical Analysis: Under what circumstances could barter transactions ever become more commonplace than exchanges settled with money?

commodity money system, there are no dollars, pesos, yen, and the like to use as units of account for pricing gold or any other goods and services.) Because the price of gold is measured in units of goods and services per unit of gold, it tells us how many units of goods and services a unit of gold can buy. Thus, the market price of gold measures the equilibrium **purchasing power of money,** or gold's value as a monetary good that people can use to purchase other goods and services.

Purchasing power of money: The value of money in terms of the amount of real goods and services it buys.

Table 1-1 Different Types of Money

Iron	Corn	Whale teeth	Round stones with centers removed
Copper	Salt	Boar tusks	Knives
Brass	Crystal salt bars	Red woodpecker scalps	Pots
Gold	Horses	Feathers	Boats
Silver	Sheep	Leather	Slaves
Wine	Goats	Pitch	Paper
Rum	Cows	Glass	Playing cards
Molasses	Tortoise shells	Polished beads (wampum)	Cigarettes
Tobacco	Snail shells	Agricultural implements	
Rice	Porpoise teeth		

A Commodity Standard A major drawback to using gold or silver as money is that lumps of gold or silver may have different market values because the purity or density of the metal in the lumps can vary. Before sellers accepted gold or silver in exchange, they typically had to verify the purity and weight of the metal that the buyer had offered. To avoid this costly and time-consuming process, people began to use *standardized* units of gold and silver. A monetary system in which the value of the medium of exchange depends on the value of gold is a **gold standard.** When silver served as the underlying commodity for the system, a *silver standard* was in force. Some nations have used both gold and silver as the basis for their monetary systems. A system in which the value of money depends on the values of two precious metals is a **bimetallic standard.**

With gold, silver, or bimetallic standards, people took gold or silver dust or nuggets to a goldsmith, who crafted the dust or nuggets into tokens of equal purity and weight. The goldsmith typically stamped the token to verify that this had been done. To make the tokens more portable and recognizable, they were often formed into flat, disk shapes that came to be called *coins*.

Proliferation of the Use of Coins Ultimately, coins became the main form of money for two reasons. One was that many shopkeepers would accept only coins validated by a goldsmith's stamp. The other was that governments got involved. In the eighth century, King Pepin the Short of France (the father of Charlemagne) introduced the first governmental system of coinage. He decreed that a pound of silver would be divided into 240 "pennies." Twelve pennies were equal to one-twentieth of a pound of silver, which in turn was exchangeable for a "solidus" of gold as defined by the Byzantine Empire during the third and fourth centuries. In England, a solidus was known as a "shilling," so twelve of the French silver coins were equal to an English shilling.

From the eighth century until our own time, commodity standards were the predominant type of monetary system. Governments either regulated or operated mints that produced coins. The rationale for government regulation of the minting process was to maintain public confidence in a nation's money. Many governments, however, got into the business of producing money for a more basic reason: they could profit from it. Mints owned and operated by rulers or their agents would purchase gold or silver in the form of dust or nuggets. Then they would produce coins that were issued at a face value that typically exceeded the value of the gold or silver content of the coins. The treasury would keep the difference, which was known as **seigniorage.** Seigniorage essentially amounted to a tax, because it was a transfer from citizens to the government.

Gold standard: A monetary system in which the value of money is linked to the value of gold.

Bimetallic standard: A monetary system in which the value of money depends on the values of two precious metals, such as gold and silver.

Seigniorage: The difference between the market value of money and the cost of its production, which is gained by the government that produces and issues the money.

Gold bullion: Within a gold standard, the amount of gold used as money.

Monetary base: A "base" amount of money that serves as the foundation for a nation's monetary system. Under a gold standard, the amount of gold bullion; in today's fiat money system, the sum of currency in circulation plus reserves of banks and other depository institutions.

The Economic Workings of a Commodity Standard For much of the world's financial history, gold was the centerpiece of the international monetary system. Under the gold standard, which functioned off and on from the early 1800s until the 1930s, the underpinning of a nation's monetary system was the quantity of gold. As in a gold commodity system, people used gold for both nonmonetary and monetary purposes. The quantity of gold devoted to monetary use was called **gold bullion.** Gold bullion functioned as the nation's **monetary base,** or the underlying, "base" amount of money that is the foundation for the entire monetary system.

Under a typical gold commodity standard, people no longer measure prices of goods and services in units of gold. Instead, they quote prices in *currency units* such as dollars per unit of goods and services. Thus, a currency, which may be in the form of coins and/or paper money, functions as the medium of exchange, unit of account, store of value, and standard of deferred payment. The currency's value, however, is linked directly to gold via a *rate of exchange* between the nation's currency and gold. In most historical instances, a "central bank," such as a private bank like the Bank of England (which was privately owned and operated from 1694 to 1946) or a government agency such as the Federal Reserve, has "pegged" the exchange rate of currency (pounds or dollars) for gold. Central banks accomplished this task by standing ready to buy or sell any amount of gold at the fixed rate of exchange, thereby ensuring that no one else would be able to buy gold for less or sell gold for more than that "pegged" currency price of gold. For example, in a situation where the central bank's gold bullion equals 1 million ounces and the governmentally established dollar-gold exchange rate is $30 per ounce of gold, the total *dollar value* of the gold bullion—the dollar value of the nation's monetary base—under the gold standard is equal to $30 per ounce times 1 million ounces of gold, or $30 million.

Once a central bank establishes the currency price of gold, it can influence the quantity of money by regulating the ratio of coins or notes that private mints or banks issue relative to the amounts of gold they hold as assets, or the *gold reserve ratio*. In this way, the central bank can influence the quantities of both coins (and/or notes) and gold bullion. That is, it can influence the total amount of money.

Seigniorage and Debasement under a Commodity Standard Because variations in the quantity of money typically affect an economy's price level, governments have had an incentive to become involved in the supervision of national monetary systems. Indeed, in the past many governments have required that their citizens use only government-produced money as the single, legal medium of exchange. If a government assumes this power—perhaps by operating the nation's central bank—it becomes a *monopoly producer* of money. In such an environment, the government is the only entity from which a nation's residents can obtain a legally recognized, widely accepted medium of exchange.

To maintain their positions as the sole producers of money, governments typically would impose stiff penalties for violating laws requiring the use of their coins in all exchanges. Because the governments profited from producing money, they had a clear motive for doing this: to keep up the demand for their coins. If a government were to permit its residents to use other types of money, then the willingness of the nation's citizens to use its coins might decline, reducing the government's seigniorage earnings. As a result, the government would have fewer resources to expend on governmentally sponsored activities, such as construction of plush government offices, maintenance of a national defense, or other endeavors.

Debasement: A reduction in the amount of precious metal in a coin that the government issues as money.

For centuries governments implemented commodity standards, including gold standards, almost solely through coinage. The idea was that the coins' metal content gave them inherent value. Eventually, however, governments mastered the trick of coin **debasement;** they reduced the gold base of the coins by mixing in other metals such as bronze or copper, thereby boosting seigniorage.

Once governments learned how to debase their coins, they quickly discovered other, even cheaper ways to make money production less expensive. After all, debasement effectively broke the link between the value of the money unit (the coin) and the value of the commodity standard (the gold or silver in the coin). To save themselves the trouble of melting down coins and debasing them, governments began such practices as "coin clipping," or physically cutting out a section—say, a fourth—of each coin and declaring that the value of the clipped coin was the same as before. They could then keep the clippings to mint additional coins. On net, coin production costs were reduced further, and governments earned more seigniorage.

The next step was paper money. Although some European nations experimented with paper money from time to time, American colonists were the first to accept the idea of paper-based commodity standards. Because gold and silver were particularly scarce in the first colonies, the colonial governments issued paper money backed by the value of European (typically English or Spanish) coins. Thus, colonial paper money was backed by European coins, which in turn were backed by gold or silver. This allowed the colonies to *indirectly* use a commodity standard.

Fiat Moneys The colonial governments quickly became frustrated with using an indirect approach to creating the money desired by residents of the growing North American economy. Despite efforts by the British Parliament in 1751 and 1764 to stop them, colonies began issuing paper moneys in the form of *bills of credit* that the governments promised to redeem at a future date. The colonial governments used these bills of credit to purchase items or construct public works projects. Those who obtained the bills of credit in exchange used them as media of exchange for other goods. As long as people believed that the governments could raise sufficient tax revenues to redeem the paper bills as promised, the bills circulated as money.

The First Federal Money Bills of credit were the first American paper moneys. They also were the first step toward today's fiat money system, because the values of the moneys that the colonial governments issued were no longer linked to commodities. Instead, the value of money depended on people's confidence in the taxing authority of the government. This was also true of the "Continentals" issued by the union of colonies during and after the American Revolution. Unfortunately for this paper money, however, people lost confidence in the taxing power of the confederation of colonies. The value of the Continental money plummeted, giving rise to the popular phrase "not worth a Continental."

From a Gold Standard to Fiat Money Throughout much of its history, the U.S. government sought to maintain a gold standard, although there were experiments with paper bills of credit from time to time. As the nation's banking system grew dramatically, banknotes and checking accounts became more widespread. Nevertheless, until 1971 the U.S. dollar was tied to gold in some fashion. In that year the United States renounced its commitment to the gold standard that was in place at the time. Under this gold standard, the U.S. government had formally tied the value of the dollar to a fixed amount of gold, and other nations in turn linked their currencies to the dollar. In 1971 the United States broke the dollar's ties to gold. And in 1973 most other developed nations agreed to allow their own currencies to "float" in value relative to the dollar. Effectively, the United States and other developed nations decided to experiment with a fiat money system. At present we are in the fourth decade of this "experiment."

In a fiat money system, money has value *only* because it is acceptable as a medium of exchange. In the past, governments issued fiat money in the form of paper currency or cheap metal coins. But the only paper money of the federal government (the U.S. Treasury) today consists of U.S. notes called "greenbacks" that were used to finance the Civil War and that technically are still in circulation (but held by collectors). Most paper money today is issued by central banks. For instance, look at the paper currency that you use. It is composed of "Federal Reserve notes" issued by the Federal Reserve System—an agency that functions as the central bank of the United States. In addition, many private financial institutions legally issue fiat money in the form of checkable deposits that we think of as "checking accounts." Banks, savings and loan associations, and credit unions are examples of such institutions. This is a key reason that we devote much discussion to these institutions in subsequent chapters.

E-Moneys Depository institutions remain central to the workings of today's fiat money economy. Nevertheless, their role will continue to evolve as a result of the growing use of e-money. A computer scientist calls e-money a form of "cryptographic algorithm," or secure programming placed upon a microchip embedded within a plastic card. This programming enables the microchip to communicate with similar chips located in electronic cash registers at retail outlets and automated teller machines operated by banks. The bearer of an e-money card can use such peripheral devices to authenticate the validity of the value stored on the card, transfer value from the card, or receive and store additional value.

E-money, therefore, is a new "token" that people today can use to engage in trade. As such, it may emerge as simply a modern elaboration of fiat money via a new technology, with government-issued currency residing primarily on microchips instead of paper printed by the Bureau of Engraving and Printing. As we shall discuss in more detail in the next chapter, however, the advent of e-money has the potential to more dramatically alter the nature of our fiat money system.

3. How has money evolved? The earliest system of exchange was barter, or the direct exchange of goods and services without the use of money. Barter suffers from the problem of double coincidence of wants, which the use of money helps to solve. Initially, people used commodity moneys that they could apply both for making exchanges and for nonmoney purposes. Later they adopted commodity standards by using tokens with values related to the value of a physical good such as gold. At this point governments often became involved in the production of money, because they could earn seigniorage by issuing units of money with a value exceeding the per-unit cost of production. Efforts to reduce the cost of producing money helped pave the way for the development of fiat money not backed by the value of any particular commodity and, today, for the potential emergence of e-money.

Defining and Measuring the Amount of Money in Circulation

Liquidity: The ease with which an asset can be sold or redeemed for a known amount of cash at short notice and at low risk of loss of nominal value.

Monetary aggregate: A grouping of assets sufficiently liquid to be defined as a measure of money.

Currency: Coins and paper money.

Students are often surprised to learn that economists have trouble agreeing about how to define and measure the amount of money in circulation. Some economists believe that what we call "money" should be whatever functions solely as an immediately available means of payment, such as paper currency and coins, checking accounts, and traveler's checks. Other economists, however, believe that this approach is too narrow, because money is also a store of value. They argue that other accounts, such as savings deposits and other easily redeemable assets, are so easy to convert into a medium of exchange that we should count them, too.

This dispute revolves around the notion of **liquidity,** or the ease with which an asset can be sold or redeemed for a known amount of cash at short notice and at low risk of loss of nominal value. To those who emphasize the medium-of-exchange approach to measuring money, money consists of currency and coins, checking accounts, and traveler's checks because they are the most obviously liquid of assets. They *already* are cash, so there is no "redeeming" to do. But those who emphasize money's function as a store of value point out that many assets in today's world are extremely liquid. Although they technically are not the medium of exchange, their owners can easily convert them for such use.

There is no simple solution to this dispute. Reasonable people on both sides can make good arguments. As we shall see, the Federal Reserve System—our central bank, commonly called "the Fed"—has sought to satisfy both groups by defining and measuring money in more than one way. The measures of money that the Fed reports are sums of various groupings of financial assets. For this reason, the Fed calls them **monetary aggregates.** These monetary aggregates differ according to the liquidity of the assets that are included or excluded.

The Monetary Base

The *monetary base,* which economists sometimes call "high-powered money," is the narrowest measure of money. In today's fiat money system, it is the amount of money produced directly by actions of the government or a central bank that acts on its behalf. The U.S. monetary base is the sum of currency *outside* the government, the Fed, and depository institutions plus reserves of depository institutions.

On the Web

How have depository institution reserves changed in recent months? Find out by viewing the Federal Reserve's H.3 *Statistical Release* at http://www.federalreserve.gov/releases/.

CURRENCY In the United States, **currency** has two main components. One is the dollar value of coins (mainly pennies, nickels, dimes, and quarters) minted by the U.S. Treasury and held *outside* the Treasury, the Federal Reserve banks, and depository institutions. The other is the dollar value of Federal Reserve notes issued by Federal Reserve banks. As stated earlier, some currency notes issued in the past by the U.S. Treasury remain in circulation, but they are a very small part of total currency. (Small-denomination paper currency is widely used in the United States, and efforts to introduce coins instead have so far fallen flat; see on the next page *Policy Focus: The Golden Dollar—A Botched Currency Reform, or Just Another "Loonie" Idea?*)

GLOBAL | POLICY Focus | CYBER | MANAGEMENT

The Golden Dollar—A Botched Currency Reform, or Just Another "Loonie" Idea?

When new European euro notes went into circulation in 2002, the smallest-denomination paper currency note was €5, which was worth just a little under $5. All smaller denominations of the euro circulate as coins. Worldwide, issuing small denominations as coins instead of paper currency is the norm. The United States is one of only a few nations still issuing a very small denomination unit of currency—namely, the dollar—in paper form.

A typical coin lasts about 30 years, whereas a typical dollar bill wears out in about 18 months. Thus, even though a dollar coin costs about 12 cents to produce, or more than three times the cost of producing a dollar bill, the total cost of producing and circulating currency is much lower for coins than for paper notes. For this reason, U.S. authorities have for some time expressed interest in switching to dollar coins.

Two Coins That Flopped

Since 1979, nearly 890 million Susan B. Anthony dollars—coins bearing the image of an early champion of women's right to vote—have been "in circulation" in the United States. Nevertheless, many U.S. residents who have memories extending back to 1979 have never even seen a Susan B. Anthony dollar. The coins do not really circulate; they are hoarded among the millions of private household collections of coins across the nation.

Starting in 2000, there has been another attempt to introduce a coin dollar, called the golden dollar because of its color (the coin contains no gold) and bearing the image of Sacagawea, the only woman to participate in the Lewis and Clark expedition. The first efforts to place this coin into circulation got off to a bad start when individuals found that they could obtain first issues of the coin at Wal-Mart outlets, but other businesses and financial institutions were initially unable to obtain the coins. In spite of a $45 million ad campaign, only half of the 1.1 billion coins produced by the end of 2000 had found their way into the hands of the public. This improved on the experience of the Susan B. Anthony dollar, but the problem was that the coin rarely appeared in day-to-day circulation.

Lessons from the "Loonie"

Well before the golden dollar was introduced, many economists had predicted that the coin would fail to gain rapid acceptance. The reason is that Federal Reserve banks issue currency to meet the public's demand, and most people find it more convenient to carry lightweight, silent paper currency instead of heavy, jingling coins. If U.S. authorities were really serious about reaping savings from introducing dollar coins, these economists argued, they should have withdrawn paper dollars from circulation as they introduced the golden dollar coins. Then individuals would have regarded the commitment to circulating coins as credible and adjusted to the coins.

Contrast the U.S. experience with that of Canada. When the Royal Canadian Mint introduced its dollar coin, popularly known as the "loonie" (from its image of a loon, a bird), in the summer of 1987, the eleven-sided, gold-colored coin initially was slow to catch on. When the Bank of Canada began withdrawing one-dollar bills from circulation two years later, however, individuals and firms learned to live with it. The loonie ultimately emerged as a circulating medium of exchange, and it continues to circulate today.

FOR CRITICAL ANALYSIS: Who ultimately bears the higher cost entailed in circulating paper dollar bills instead of dollar coins?

DEPOSITORY FINANCIAL INSTITUTION RESERVES Commercial banks, savings banks, savings and loan associations, and credit unions are **depository financial institutions** or, more simply, *depository institutions.* These institutions issue checking and savings deposits that are key components of broader measures of money. Depository institutions also must hold funds on deposit with Federal Reserve banks. These funds and the cash that the institutions hold in their vaults constitute the institutions' **reserves.** The source of these funds is the Fed itself, as we shall discuss in greater detail in Chapter 16.

Panel (a) of Figure 1-1 displays the relative sizes of these two components of the monetary base. The percentages shown here are typical figures that we would observe at any time. Currency normally is the bulk of the monetary base.

Depository financial institutions: Financial institutions that issue checking and savings deposits that are included in measures of money and that legally must hold reserves on deposit with Federal Reserve banks or in their vaults.

Reserves: Cash held by depository institutions in their vaults or on deposit with the Federal Reserve System.

M1: A Basic Definition of "Cash"

A broader definition of money, a monetary aggregate called **M1,** is shown in panel (b) of Figure 1-1. This measure of the quantity of money—which the *Wall Street Journal* and other publications often call "the money supply"—has three components: currency, traveler's checks issued by institutions other than depository institutions, and *transactions deposits* held at depository institutions.

M1: Currency plus transactions deposits.

Transactions deposits: Checking accounts.

Demand deposits: Non-interest-bearing checking accounts.

Negotiable-order-of-withdrawal (NOW) accounts: Interest-bearing checking deposits.

CURRENCY AND TRAVELER'S CHECKS The currency component of M1 is the same as that used to compute the monetary base. Only traveler's checks issued by nondepository institutions such as American Express and Thomas Cook are included in M1. The reason is that depository institutions place the funds that they use to redeem traveler's checks in special transactions deposit accounts that are already counted among transactions deposits.

TRANSACTIONS DEPOSITS Deposits at financial institutions from which holders may write checks for purchasing goods, services, or financial assets are **transactions deposits.** There are three types of transactions deposits. One is **demand deposits.** Demand deposits are non-interest-bearing checking deposits. Holders may convert funds in such deposits to currency "on demand" or write a check on these deposits to third parties, who then may access funds from the deposits "on demand." Another type of transactions deposit is a **negotiable-order-of-withdrawal, or NOW, account.** NOW accounts are interest-bearing

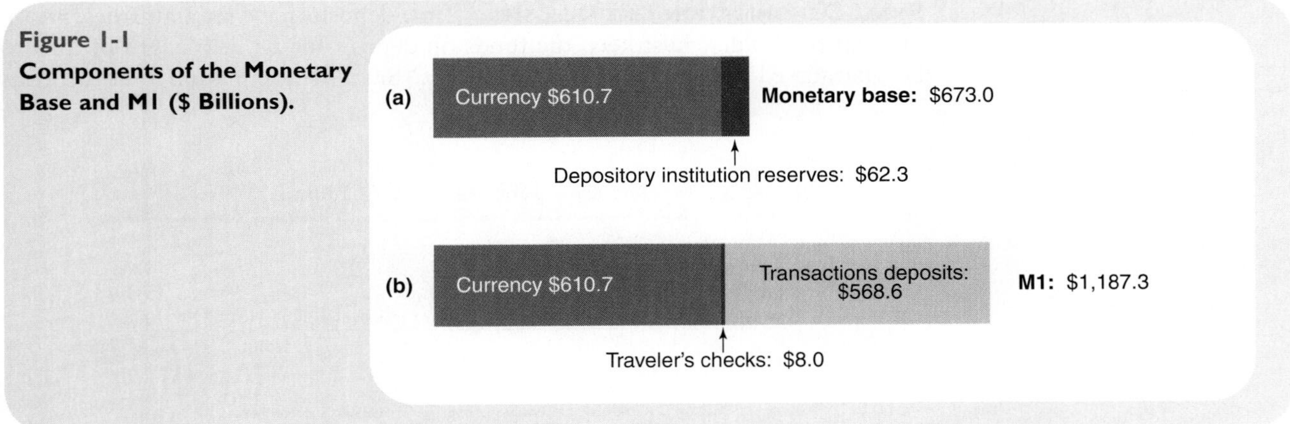

Figure 1-1
Components of the Monetary Base and M1 ($ Billions).

SOURCE: Board of Governors of the Federal Reserve System, H.6(508) *Statistical Release,* August 1, 2002.

Automated-transfer-system (ATS) account: A combined interest-bearing savings account and non-interest-bearing checking account in which the former is drawn on automatically when the latter is overdrawn.

M2: M1 plus savings and small-denomination time deposits and balances of individual and broker-dealer money market mutual funds.

Savings deposits: Interest-bearing savings accounts without set maturities.

Money market deposit accounts: Savings accounts with limited checking privileges.

Small-denomination time deposits: Deposits with set maturities and denominations of less than $100,000.

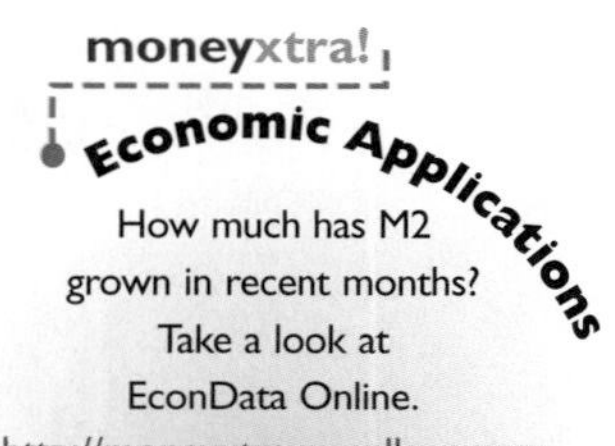

deposits that also offer checking privileges. The third type of transactions deposit is an **automatic-transfer-system,** or **ATS, account.** ATS accounts are combinations of interest-bearing savings accounts and non-interest-bearing demand deposits. Typically, holders of ATS accounts maintain small demand-deposit balances. Yet they may write sizable checks payable from their demand-deposit accounts, because funds are transferred automatically from their savings accounts to cover shortfalls.

As panel (b) of Figure 1-1 indicates, currency constitutes over half of M1. Transactions deposits account for most of the rest. Traveler's checks are a relatively insignificant component.

M2: Cash Plus Other Liquid Assets

The monetary base and M1 are alternative definitions of "cash money." The monetary base measures funds made available directly by the U.S. Treasury and the Federal Reserve System, while M1 measures funds more broadly available to the public at large. Both definitions of money include only highly liquid assets.

Yet other financial assets may also be converted very quickly into cash. **M2** is a broader definition of money that includes such assets. The monetary aggregate M2 is equal to M1 *plus* the following:

1. Savings deposits and money market deposit accounts at depository institutions.
2. Small-denomination time deposits at depository institutions.
3. Funds held by individuals, brokers, and dealers in money market mutual funds.

Table 1-2 lists recent dollar amounts of these components of M2.

SAVINGS DEPOSITS AND MONEY MARKET DEPOSIT ACCOUNTS **Savings deposits** are interest-bearing deposits without set maturities. **Money market deposit accounts** are savings accounts that permit limited checking privileges.

SMALL-DENOMINATION TIME DEPOSITS Time deposits have set maturities, meaning that the holder must keep the funds on deposit for a fixed length of time to be guaranteed a negotiated interest return. **Small-denomination time deposits**

Table 1-2 The Components of M2 ($ Billions)

M1	$1,187.3
Small-denomination time deposits	924.9
Savings deposits and money market deposits	2,511.4
Individual and broker-dealer money market mutual funds	944.6
M2	$5,568.2

SOURCE: Board of Governors of the Federal Reserve System, H.6(508) *Statistical Release*, August 1, 2002.

have denominations less than $100,000. A variety of small-denomination time deposits are available, including six-month money market certificates of deposit (CDs) and CDs with two to four years maturity.

Money market mutual funds: Pools of funds from savers that managing firms use to purchase short-term financial assets such as Treasury bills and commercial paper.

M3: M2 plus large-denomination time deposits, Eurodollars and repurchase agreements, and institution-only money market mutual funds.

Large-denomination time deposits: Deposits with set maturities and denominations greater than or equal to $100,000.

Repurchase agreement: A contract to sell financial assets with a promise to repurchase them at a later time.

Eurodollars: Dollar-denominated deposits located outside the United States.

MONEY MARKET MUTUAL FUNDS Many financial companies today offer **money market mutual funds,** which are pools of funds from savers that managing firms use to purchase short-term financial assets, such as Treasury bills and large CDs issued by depository financial institutions such as banks. Individuals, brokers, dealers, and larger institutions hold balances at money market mutual funds. The Fed has determined, however, that institutional balances at money market mutual funds typically are not very liquid. Therefore, the Fed includes only individual and broker-dealer holdings in M2. Institutional balances are included in a broader measure of money.

Figure 1-2 compares the monetary base, M1, and M2. Recently, M2 was over eight times larger than the monetary base and more than four times larger than M1. Indeed, savings and money market accounts together were twice as large as M1. The total amount of small-denomination time deposits was almost as large as M1. These comparisons are typical of those we would observe at any given time we might measure these definitions of money.

M3: The Broadest Monetary Aggregate

The Fed makes greatest use of the monetary base and M1 and M2 measures of money. Nevertheless, it also has a very broad money definition that it calls **M3.** This measure of money adds the following items to M2:

1. Large-denomination time deposits at depository institutions,
2. Term repurchase agreements and term Eurodollars.
3. Repurchase agreements at depository institutions and Eurodollar deposits held by U.S. residents (other than depository institutions) at foreign branches of U.S. depository institutions.
4. Institution-only money market mutual fund balances.

Table 1-3 on the next page lists the amounts of these components of M3.

Large-denomination time deposits are time deposits issued by depository institutions in amounts of $100,000 or more. A **repurchase agreement** is a contract to sell financial assets, such as U.S. Treasury bonds, with a promise to repurchase them at a later time, typically at a slightly higher price. This means that the original holder of financial assets who initiates the repurchase agreement effectively borrows funds for a time. A repurchase agreement permits the original holder to get access to funds for one or more days. Because funds are tied up in overnight repurchase agreements for such a short time, these are relatively liquid assets. For this reason, the Fed includes repurchase agreements in M3.

Eurodollars are dollar-denominated deposits in foreign depository institutions and in foreign branches of American depository institutions. Despite the name

Figure 1-2
Comparing the Monetary Base, M1, and M2 ($ Billions).

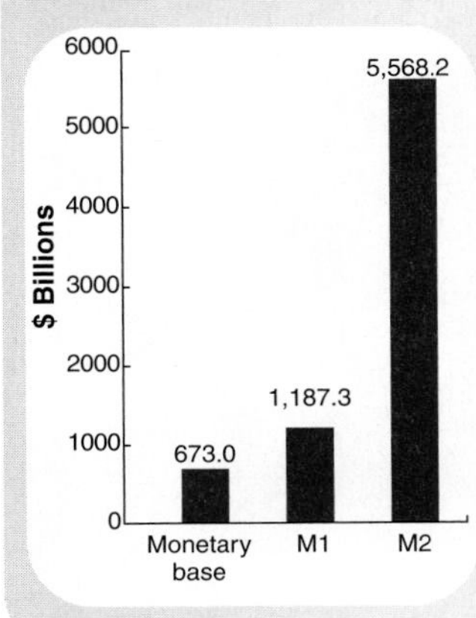

SOURCES: Board of Governors of the Federal Reserve System, H.6(508) *Statistical Release* and H.3(502) *Statistical Release*, August 1, 2002.

Table 1-3 The Components of M3 ($ Billions)

M2	$5,568.2
Large-denomination time deposits	810.6
Repurchase agreements and Eurodollar deposits	594.0
Institution-only money market mutual funds	1,180.8
M3	$8,153.6

SOURCE: Board of Governors of the Federal Reserve System, H.6(508) *Statistical Release*, August 1, 2002.

"Eurodollar," such deposits might, for instance, be in Japanese or Australian branches of U.S. banks. Given their short, one-day maturities, these dollar funds also are relatively liquid. Finally, *institution-only money market mutual fund balances* include mutual fund balances not held by individuals, brokers, and dealers.

The additional assets that M3 includes—large-denomination time deposits and so on—tend to be much less liquid than those that constitute M2. As a result, the Fed has tended to place less weight on M3 as a reliable measure of money. It also de-emphasizes the monetary base, because checking deposits are such an important means by which households and firms purchase goods, services, and financial assets. Therefore, the Fed has paid most attention to the M1 and M2 monetary aggregates.

On the Web
What are the latest trends in the monetary aggregates? To find out, go to the Federal Reserve's H.6 *Statistical Release* at http://www.federalreserve.gov/releases/.

Figure 1-3 shows annual percentage growth rates in M1 and M2 since 1970. As the figure indicates, these monetary aggregates have grown at different rates. Sometimes growth of one has declined while the other has grown more quickly. This has complicated the Fed's efforts to decide which of these aggregates is the more useful measure of money.

4. What are monetary aggregates, and how are they constructed?
Monetary aggregates are groupings of financial assets that are combined based on their degrees of liquidity into overall measures of money. The monetary base, M1, M2, and M3 are today's basic monetary aggregates. Of these, M1 and M2 are the most important to the Federal Reserve.

Can Money Be Defined in a Digital Economy?

History has taught us that money is not immune to technological change. For instance, private banknotes once were the most common form of money. Yet even when such notes were legal currency, technological improvements that made checks simpler and less costly to process gradually led to greater use of checking accounts.

Nonelectronic Payments

Today, currency, checks, and traveler's checks constitute the most widely used media of exchange. Other paper-based means of payment include credit-card transactions and money orders. As panel (a) of Figure 1-4 indicates, about 98

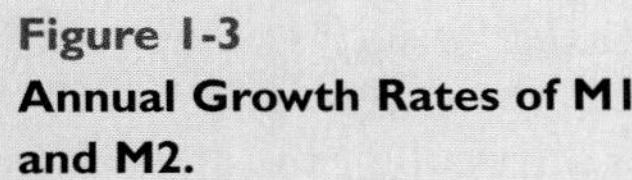

Figure 1-3
Annual Growth Rates of M1 and M2.

The Federal Reserve's two key monetary aggregates often grow at different rates.

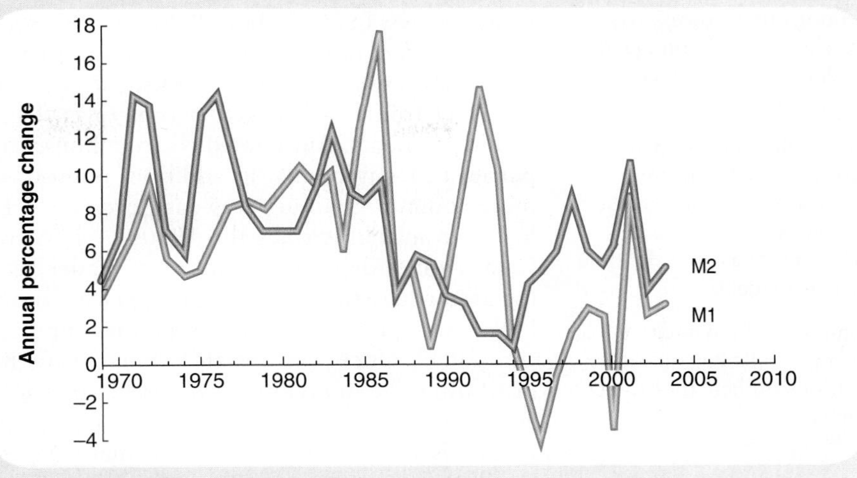

SOURCE: 2002 Economic Report of the President, *Economic Indicators,* various issues.

percent of all transactions in the United States for 2003 were made using these nonelectronic means of payment. Electronic means of payment such as **wire transfers**—payments made via telephone lines or through fiber-optic cables—accounted for only about 2 percent of total American transactions (*not* dollar volume, though).

Wire transfers: Payments made via telephone lines or through fiber-optic cables.

Electronic Payments

Ongoing improvements in information-processing technology have the potential to alter our conceptions of feasible means of payment. Panel (b) of Figure 1-4 shows why this is the case. Although nonelectronic means of payment will

Figure 1-4
Electronic versus Nonelectronic Payments.

As panel (a) indicates, nonelectronic transactions account for nearly all payments in the United States. Panel (b), however, shows that the bulk of the dollar value of exchanges is accomplished through electronic means of payment.

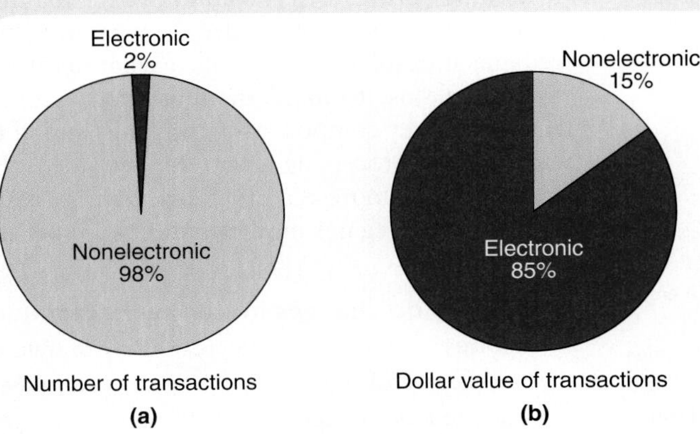

SOURCE: Authors' estimates.

Automated clearing houses: Institutions that process payments electronically on behalf of senders and receivers of those payments.

Point-of-sale (POS) transfer: Electronic transfer of funds from a buyer's account to the firm from which a good or service is purchased at the time the sale is made.

Automated bill payment: Direct payment of bills by depository institutions on behalf of their customers.

continue to account for the lion's share of the total number of *exchanges* in the United States, in 2003 about 85 percent of the *dollar value* of such exchanges was made by *electronic* means. Only about 15 percent of the dollar value of 2003 transactions was made with checks, currency, or other physical means of payment.

Direct transfers between parties of exchanges account for the bulk of electronic payments. **Automated clearing houses** also process payments on behalf of parties to transactions. In addition, **point-of-sale (POS) transfers** are becoming more common than in years past, even though the technology for POS transfers has been available since the 1960s. A POS transfer is an automatic transfer of funds from a deposit account to a retailer accomplished electronically from the location where the exchange takes place. For instance, a typical department store POS cash register essentially is a minicomputer that can communicate with other computers. Once appropriate arrangements have been made with a depository institution, an individual can use a plastic card with magnetically encoded account information to permit the department store POS cash register to transfer funds directly from the individual's deposit account to the account of the retailer.

Payment can also be made electronically through **automated bill payment.** With this payments technology, individuals arrange for depository institutions to pay some of their bills. The depository institutions automatically deduct funds from the individuals' accounts and transfer them electronically.

Computer Shopping

A number of firms are selling goods, services, and financial assets over the *Internet*—the electronic information system that links mainframe and personal computers around the United States and the rest of the world. Individuals most commonly use the Internet to send electronic mail or to access information from remote locations. Ever-increasing numbers of people and firms are arranging and executing financial transactions over the Internet, however. As we shall discuss in Chapter 2 and elsewhere in this book, many companies already have set up systems for such exchanges. These and other innovations in electronic payments technology promise to revolutionize the manner in which payments will be made.

Will they also revolutionize the meaning of money? The answer to this question remains unresolved at present. If what matters for measuring money are the items that people use to make the most transactions, then clearly checks and currency remain the key components of any measure of money. Yet it is undeniable that new information-processing technology broadens the liquidity of a number of assets by making them more readily convertible to cash. This indicates that in the future monetary aggregates may include even more items than they do at present.

moneyxtra!

Online Case Study

Put yourself in the place of a future Federal Reserve economist trying to evaluate the meaning of money in an economy with digital currency and deposits by going to the Chapter 1 Case Study, entitled "Internet Payments Meet Monetary Aggregates."
http://moneyxtra.swcollege.com

On the Web

Which banks offer the latest automated bill payment services? One place to check is the search engine offered by Banxquote at http://www.banx.com. At the opening page, select "Banking, Trading & Deposits." Go to the pull down menu and select "Online Banking, Bill Pay, and Trading."

5. How do changes in payments technologies affect our definitions of money? The more widespread ability to transfer funds electronically makes more assets convertible to money, thereby increasing their liquidity. This may induce central banks to include more assets in the monetary aggregates they use as indicators or targets of their monetary policies.

Link to the **Global Economy**

Is Dollarization the Answer in Argentina?

At the beginning of the twentieth century, Argentina was one of the most prosperous nations in the world. Although decades of economic decline followed, the nation's prospects had improved considerably by the 1990s. Many economists gave the credit for this improved performance to Argentina's efforts to maintain a stable value of its currency, the peso.

The Argentine Currency Board

Since 1991, Argentina had backed all pesos it issued with dollars. To oversee this arrangement, Argentina had a *currency board,* which is an institution that issues a national currency at a one-for-one rate of exchange with respect to the currency of another country. The first currency boards were established by nations that were members of the British Commonwealth, such as Hong Kong, the Cayman Islands, the Falkland Islands, and Gibraltar, which issued currency based on reserves of the British currency, the pound sterling. Singapore also has a currency-board system.

Argentina had hoped that its currency-board arrangement would link its financial markets to the more stable markets of the United States. Nevertheless, when the economy turned downward in the early 2000s, residents of Argentina began struggling to repay international debts. Foreign investors pulled $80 billion from the country's financial markets. Few foreign residents would consider buying securities issued by the government of Argentina, and the national government ultimately ended its currency-board arrangement.

Enter Provincial Currencies—and Dollarization?

The national government of Argentina was constrained by the currency-board arrangement it had adopted, because it could not simply create new pesos to pay wages to government workers or to purchase goods and services. Provincial governments did not face this constraint, however. In the summer of 2001, the Buenos Aires province, which includes the nation's capital city of Buenos Aires and towns such as La Plata, began paying its suppliers, employees, and retirees with *patacónes,* which were one-year bonds redeemable at an annual interest rate of 7 percent.

The provincial government issued *patacónes* in denominations ranging from one unit to one hundred units, which were officially valued at par with equivalent amounts of U.S. dollars. The *patacónes* were legal tender within the Buenos Aires province, but most businesses that accepted *patacónes* refused to accept them at par with the peso or the dollar. A La Plata McDonald's restaurant, for instance, began offering a special "Patacombo" meal that could be purchased with *patacónes.* This combo meal differed from a standard combo meal in one particular way: consumers had to pay one dollar more to obtain the meal with *patacónes.*

The *patacónes* and other experiments with provincial currencies complicated the monetary landscape in Argentina. Some economists believed that one possible solution to Argentina's problems might be *dollarization,* or the abandonment of all national and local currencies in favor of direct use of the U.S. dollar as a medium of exchange, unit of account, store of value, and standard of deferred payment. If it were to adopt dollarization, Argentina would be following the example of other nations, such as Panama and Ecuador, which have adopted the U.S. dollar as a circulating currency. The government would have to import sufficient U.S. currency for people to use in hand-to-hand transactions. Argentine residents would also have to convert remaining peso-denominated financial accounts and contracts to dollars—probably not a big task in light of estimates indicating that more than 90 percent of Argentine financial contracts are already dollar denominated.

Continued on next page

Link to the Global Economy, continued

Possible Implications of Dollarization for the United States

For the United States, both pros and cons would be associated with widespread dollarization by Argentina and other parts of Latin America. Dollarization would make it easier for U.S. companies to do business with Latin America, which accounts for about a fifth of U.S. trade. In addition, increased use of the dollar outside the United States could create a seigniorage windfall for the U.S. government. Argentina would pay for the stock of U.S. dollars it would need for hand-to-hand trade by its residents by giving the U.S. government interest-bearing securities. The U.S. government would then earn interest on those securities, but as usual it would not pay interest on its currency. Currently, worldwide seigniorage generates more than $15 billion a year for the U.S. Treasury. Dollarization by Argentina and other Latin American countries undoubtedly would increase U.S. seigniorage considerably.

At the same time, Fed and U.S. Treasury officials have expressed concerns about dollarization. If the Fed were to raise interest rates in an effort to contain U.S. inflation, its action might be inappropriate for a dollarized Latin American economy. Thus, the Fed action could have negative consequences outside the United States, fostering resentment and encouraging policymakers in dollarized countries to deflect blame for their economic problems onto U.S. policymakers. This could give governments of dollarized countries political cover for dodging tough decisions regarding appropriate policies for their own economies.

Research Project

What are the pros and cons of currency boards? Of dollarization? Why might a nation prefer to keep its own currency under a currency-board arrangement instead of dollarizing its economy?

Web Resources

1. What are the current status and future prospects of the world's currency boards? Explore this issue at Mark Bernkopf's Central Banking Resource Center at http://patriot.net/~bernkopf/, where you can click on "Currency Boards" for links to a number of resources relating to currency boards around the globe.

2. What do countries gain and lose from dollarization? For a review, see "The Dollarization Debate," by Andrew Berg and Eduardo Borensztein, *Finance and Development*, Vol. 37, No. 1, March 2000, at http://www.imf.org/external/pubs/ft/fandd/2000/03/berg.htm.

Does dollarization benefit developing countries? To review alternative perspectives on this debate and make your own judgment, go to EconDebate Online.
http://moneyxtra.swcollege.com

Chapter Summary

1. How Financial Globalization and Cybertechnologies Together Have Altered the Economic Roles of Banking Institutions and Money: Worldwide growth in international trade has contributed to the globalization of financial markets. At the same time, the development of cybertechnologies has linked financial institutions and markets within and across national borders, further enhancing global interdependence. These developments are forcing both financial institutions and monetary and financial policymakers to confront a number of profound issues about their roles in the new world of banking.

2. The Functions of Money: Money has four functions. It is a medium of exchange, which means that people use money to make payments for goods, services, and financial assets. It is also a store of value, so people can hold money for future use in exchange. In addition, money is a unit of account, meaning that prices are quoted in terms of money values. Furthermore, money is a standard of deferred payment, meaning that lenders make loans and buyers repay those loans with money.

3. The Evolution of Money: Early societies relied on barter, or the direct exchange of goods and services without the use of money, but barter poses the problem of double coincidence of wants. To address this problem, people initially facilitated exchanges by using commodity moneys that also had a value for other purposes. Over time, societies established commodity standards involving the use of tokens with values related to the value of a physical good such as gold. Governments often became involved in commodity standards, because they could earn seigniorage by issuing units of money with a value exceeding the per-unit cost of production. This practice ultimately provided the impetus for the development of fiat money not backed by the value of any particular commodity. Today society is contemplating the use of e-moneys in the form of cryptographic algorithms transferred in digital form.

4. Monetary Aggregates and Their Construction: Monetary aggregates are groupings of financial assets combined on the basis of their degrees of liquidity in an effort to measure the total quantity of money in circulation. Today's fundamental monetary aggregates are the monetary base, M1, M2, and M3. Of these, M1 and M2 traditionally have been the most important to the Federal Reserve System.

5. Payments Technologies and Definitions of Money: Technological changes in the processes by which payments are made can affect how we define money. Although nonelectronic payments continue to predominate in typical transactions, the bulk of dollars in transactions are transferred electronically. As such electronic transfers become more common, overall asset liquidity may increase, and new assets may gain sufficient liquidity to be classified as money.

Questions and Problems

(Answers to odd-numbered questions and problems may be found on the Web at http://money.swcollege.com under "Student Resources.")

1. If a money is a medium of exchange, must it be a store of value? Can you think of any real-world examples in which the two functions might be separated, with one money acting as the exchange medium but the other taking on the role of a store of value?

2. What are some advantages and disadvantages of the alternative forms of money: commodity moneys, commodity standards, and fiat moneys?

3. Based on your answer to question 2, is fiat money necessarily preferable to the other forms of money? Why or why not?

4. In a gold commodity money system, the price of gold recently fell from 2 units of goods and services per unit of gold to 1 unit of goods and services per unit of gold. What has happened to the purchasing power of money?

5. Suppose that a new method of making payments from savings accounts at depository institutions has induced U.S. residents to shift $100 billion from checking accounts to money market deposit accounts. What is the effect, if any, on

a. the monetary base?

b. M1?

c. M2?

6. A new means of drawing on checking accounts electronically to make payments over the Internet has induced U.S. residents to shift $200 billion from currency holdings to checking accounts. What is the effect, if any, on

a. the monetary base?

b. M1?

c. M2?

7. Using the following data ($ billions), calculate the amount of currency and the value of the M1 monetary aggregate:

Monetary base	500
Traveler's checks	15
Reserves of depository financial institutions	100
Demand deposits	435
Other checkable deposits	550

8. Consider the following data ($ billions), and calculate the monetary base, M1, and M2.

Currency	450
Savings deposits and money market deposit accounts	1,400
Small-denomination time deposits	1,000
Traveler's checks	10
Reserves of depository financial institutions	80
Total money market mutual funds	500
Institution-only money market mutual funds	200
Demand deposits	450
Other checkable deposits	490

9. Suppose that M1 is equal to $1,350 billion. The monetary base is equal to $500 billion, and transactions deposits (both demand deposits and other checkable deposits) and traveler's checks combined amount to $925 billion. What is the amount of reserves at depository financial institutions?

10. Explain in your own words why the growth in electronic means of payment might complicate the task of defining and measuring money.

Before the Test

Test your understanding of the material covered in this chapter by taking the Chapter 1 interactive quiz at http://money.swcollege.com.

Online Application

Internet URL: http://research.stlouis.org/fred

Title: FRED (Federal Reserve Economic Data)

Navigation: Go directly to the above URL. Under "Data Categories," click on "Index of All Data Series." Use the quick jump drop-down menu and click on "Monthly Monetary Data." Scroll down to file name DEMDEPNS (Demand Deposits at Commercial Banks NOT Seasonally Adjusted) or DEMDEPSL (Demand Deposits at Commercial Banks Seasonally Adjusted).

Application: Perform the following operations, and answer the following questions.

1. Select the data series for demand deposits (either seasonally or nonseasonally adjusted). Scan through the data. Do you notice any recent trend? [Hint: Compare the growth in the figures before 1993 with their growth after 1993.] In addition, take a look at the data series for currency and for other checkable deposits. Do you observe similar recent trends in these series?

2. Now go back to the original URL. Under "Data Categories," click on "Monetary Aggregates," and take a look at the M1 series (again, either seasonally or nonseasonally adjusted). Does it show any recent trend (pre-1993 versus post-1993)? Based on your answer to question 1, what appears to account for this behavior? [Note: We shall explain this recent behavior of M1 in Chapter 20.]

For Group Study and Analysis: FRED contains considerable financial data series. Assign individual members or groups of the class the task of examining data on assets included in M1, M2, and M3. Have each student or group of students look for big swings in the data. Then ask the groups to report back to the class as a whole. When did clear changes occur in various categories of the monetary aggregates? Were there times when people appeared to shift funds from one aggregate to another? Are there any other noticeable patterns that may have been related to economic events during various periods?

Selected References and Further Reading

Angell, Norman. *The Story of Money.* New York: Frederick A. Stokes Co., 1929.

Antinolfi, Gaetano, and Todd Keister. "Dollarization as a Monetary Arrangement for Emerging Market Economies." Federal Reserve Bank of St. Louis *Review* 83 (November/December 2001): 29–39.

Barro, Robert. "Money and the Price Level under the Gold Standard." *Economic Journal* 89 (March 1979): 13–33.

Clower, Robert. "Introduction." In *Monetary Theory: Selected Readings.* New York: Penguin Books, 1969.

Einzig, Paul. *Primitive Money.* 2d ed. New York: Oxford University Press, 1966.

Walter, John R. "Monetary Aggregates: A User's Guide." Federal Reserve Bank of Richmond *Economic Review* 75 (January/February 1989): 20–28.

MoneyXtra

moneyxtra! Log on to the MoneyXtra Web site now (**http://moneyxtra.swcollege.com**) for additional learning resources such as practice quizzes, case studies, readings, and additional economic applications.

Chapter 2

Banking in the New Cyberworld

Fundamental Issues

1. What is the difference between stored-value cards and smart cards?
2. Is digital cash less secure than physical cash?
3. What are the rationales for regulating cyberbanking?
4. Does e-money matter for monetary policy?

Electronic impulses can carry payment approval messages at nearly the speed of light, and telecommunications hardware can transmit instantaneously. Software programs residing on bank computers can then automatically authorize the transfer of funds from the account of the buyer of a good, service, or financial instrument to the account of the seller of the item.

One type of payment instrument that makes use of electronic payment authorizations and transfers is the increasingly popular debit card. By 2005, nearly 15 billion debit-card transactions will take place each year, yet in all likelihood, only about 6 billion of these transfers will take place instantaneously. Retailers that accept debit cards typically store the majority of debit-card payment messages for hours or even days before transmitting them for final settlement of transactions.

To proponents of electronic payments, there is something wrong with this picture. Even though debit cards have become a major success story in the annals of banking technology, individuals and firms typically are not using them to their fullest capabilities. This has led advocates of electronic banking and payments to urge that we make another technological leap by converting money to digital information. In this way, payment transmissions would always be instantaneous. In this chapter, you will learn about both debit cards and digital forms of money. You will also learn about the challenges that these and other developments pose for bank regulators.

E-Cash: The Future Is Now

According to the Bank for International Settlements, an institution that coordinates policymaking among the central banks of the world's most developed nations, U.S. residents make more than 300 billion cash transactions every year. Of these, 270 billion are in dollar amounts of less than $2. It is easy to see why people use paper currency and coins to purchase a soft drink, a candy bar, or a comic book. Why would they use electronic money, however, instead of currency and coins?

Stored-Value and Debit-Card Systems

To understand the incentives for using e-money instead of real cash, we must first contemplate exactly how e-money transactions take place. First, let's think about the simplest kind of e-money system, which is a **closed stored-value system.** In this type of system, cards containing prestored currency values entitle the bearer to purchase specific goods and services offered by the card issuer. For instance, many university libraries contain copy machines that faculty and students operate after inserting a plastic card that has a magnetic stripe on the back. Each time they make copies, the copy machine automatically deducts the per-copy fee. When the balance on a student's card runs low in the middle of copying an article, the student can replenish the balance by placing the card in a separate machine and inserting real cash. The machine stores the value of the cash on the card. Then the student can go back to the copy machine, reinsert the card, and finish copying the article.

Some closed stored-value cards are disposable, and the card owner throws away the card after spending the value placed on it. Cards with magnetic stripes or other means of electronic-data storage have a broad range of other uses, however. Banks and other issuers now can issue reusable cards for use in **open stored-value systems.** In these systems, there are a number of card issuers, acquirers, and merchants, and the bearer of a card may use it to purchase goods and services offered by any participating merchant.

Another type of card that functions in open systems is the **debit card,** which essentially adapts the technology used by stored-value cards to permit authorization of fund transfers between accounts of consumers and merchants. Figure 2-1 (p. 28) illustrates a sample transaction flow within a debit-card system. In this example, issuing banks, denoted Bank A and Bank B, provide cards to customers. These cardholders can use the cards to authorize transfers of funds from their checking or savings deposits at the banks so that they can buy goods and services from retailers that participate in the system. At the retail outlets, electronic cash-register terminals record the values of purchases and the routing numbers of issuing banks. At some point—either instantly or later in the day—the retailers submit the recorded transactions data to the banks where the retailers' own deposit accounts are located, denoted Bank C and Bank D. These banks then forward claims for funds to the system operator, which in turn transmits these claims to the issuing banks, Bank A and Bank B. Once Banks A and B honor their obligations to Banks C and D, the latter banks credit the deposit accounts of the retailers.

An important aspect of Figure 2-1 is that it could just as easily illustrate the workings of our current system of paper checks. Instead of using debit cards to buy goods and services from retailers, bank customers could have used checks to make their purchases. Then the retailers would send the checks on to their own banks, which would submit them to a check clearinghouse for payment. The clearinghouse then would process payments among the banks so that the retailers

Closed stored-value system: An e-money system in which consumers use cards containing prestored funds to buy specific goods and services offered by a single issuer of the cards.

Open stored-value system: An e-money system in which consumers buy goods and services using cards containing prestored funds that are offered by multiple card issuers and accepted by multiple retailers.

Debit card: A plastic card that allows the bearer to transfer funds to a merchant's account, provided that the bearer authorizes the transfer by providing personal identification.

Figure 2-1
A Debit-Card System.

Holders of cards issued by Bank A and Bank B can arrange for fund transfers from their accounts via card authorizations. Retailers in turn transmit claims to Bank C and Bank D. These banks then transmit their claims for funds to the operator of the system. The system operator transmits the claims to Bank A and Bank B and arranges account settlements among the four banks.

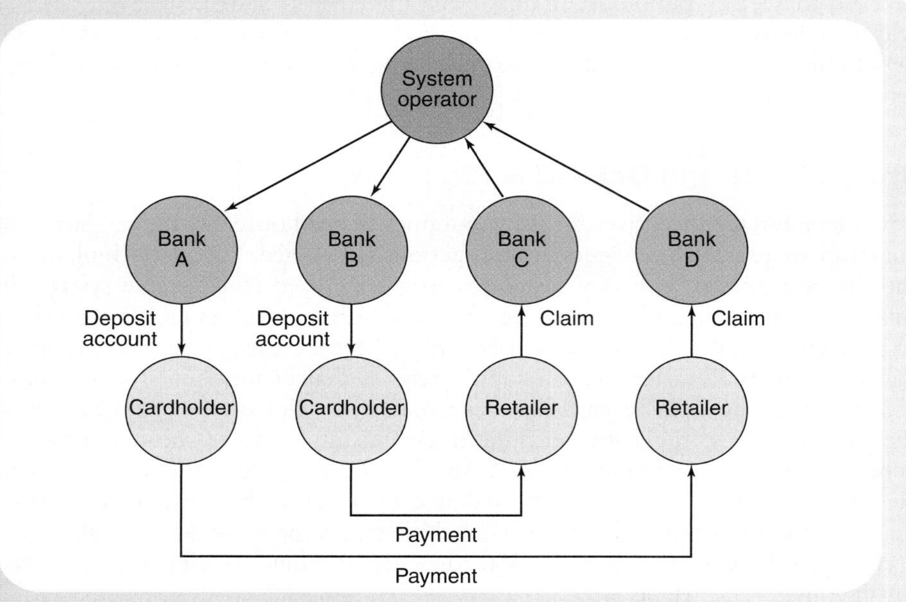

would receive final payment of funds. Thus, a debit-card system effectively amounts to electronic checking. As with standard paper check clearing, a number of clearinghouse transactions must take place behind the scenes to finalize a transaction. (In Russia, stored-value and debit cards have paved the way for Internet commerce; see *Global Focus: Stored-Value and Debit Cards May Be the Ticket to Online Shopping in Russia.)*

Smart Cards and Digital Cash

A more fundamental innovation has been the development of **smart cards,** which have embedded computer chips that can hold much more information than a magnetic stripe. The microchip on a smart card can do much more than maintain a running cash balance in its memory. These minute silicon chips function as microcomputers that can carry and process security programming.

Smart Cards This communications capability of smart cards gives them an advantage over the stored-value card's magnetic stripe that is swiped through a card reader. Magnetic stripe cards have a failure rate—a typical rate of failure to process a transaction correctly—of about 250 per million transactions. For smart cards, the failure rate is less than 100 per million transactions. Continuing improvements in microprocessor technology promise to push this failure rate even lower.

Smart card: A card containing a microprocessor that permits storage of funds via security programming, that can communicate with other computers, and that does not require online authorization for funds transfer to occur.

The microprocessors on smart cards can also authenticate the validity of transactions. When a cardholder initiates a transaction with a retailer, the chip in the retailer's electronic cash register confirms the authenticity of the smart card by examining a unique "digital signature" stored on the card's microchip. This dig-

GLOBAL Focus | POLICY | CYBER | MANAGEMENT

Stored-Value and Debit Cards May Be the Ticket to Online Shopping in Russia

Online commerce in Russia began to show progress for the first time in the early 2000s. According to some forecasts, Web-based retail transactions may account for as much as 1 percent of total Russian national expenditures by 2005—if Russian residents can find a way to pay for their online purchases.

The Russian Federation has a population of nearly 150 million people, yet there are only about 5 million active credit-card accounts. Even though a significant portion of the people holding these accounts are Internet users, many are so worried about fraud that they hesitate to use their credit cards to make online purchases.

One answer to this concern may be the STB debit card, which is issued by more than 100 banks. The heaviest users of the STB card are students, who already use the cards at cash machines and shops around the country. Now, through a Russian Internet payment system called Assist, STB cards can be used for Web purchases as well.

A 1998 financial crash wiped out big chunks of Russians' savings, however, and discouraged many people from using debit cards. For these people, a key alternative for online transactions is the old-fashioned stored-value card. For instance, a stand-alone Moscow-based payment-processing company called Avtocard issues the "e-port" card, which holders can use at a virtual mall composed of more than 100 Russian retailers.

For Critical Analysis: Why do you suppose that Russians are using stored-value cards on the Web, but relatively few U.S. residents do?

ital signature is generated by software called a *cryptographic algorithm,* which is a secure program loaded onto the microchip of the card. It guarantees to the retailer's electronic cash register that the smart card's chip is genuine and that it has not been tampered with by another party—such as a thief. Figure 2-2 on the next page illustrates how digital encryption helps to guarantee the security of electronic payments.

Thus, in an **open smart-card system** for e-money transfers, in which there are numerous smart-card issuers, holders, and participating retailers, a cardholder need not provide a personal identification number. Indeed, just as with physical cash, the user of a smart card can remain anonymous. There is also no need for online authorization using expensive telecommunication services. Each time a cardholder uses a smart card, the amount of the purchase is deducted automatically and credited to a retailer. The retailer, in turn, can store its electronic cash receipts in specially adapted point-of-sale terminals. The retailer can then transfer the accumulated balances to its bank at the end of the day by means of telephone links. This permits payments to be completed within just a few seconds.

Open smart-card system: An e-money system in which consumers use smart cards with embedded microprocessors, which may be issued by a number of institutions, to purchase goods and services offered by multiple retailers.

Digital Cash What does a smart card have that paper currency and coins do not? The answer is potentially even more convenience. Smart cards permit people to use **digital cash,** which consists of funds contained on the algorithms stored on microchips and other computer devices. Smart cards' microchips can communicate with any device equipped with appropriate software. In addition to

Digital cash: Funds contained on computer software, in the form of secure algorithms, that is stored on microchips and other computer devices.

Figure 2-2
Digital Encryption and Electronic Payment Security.

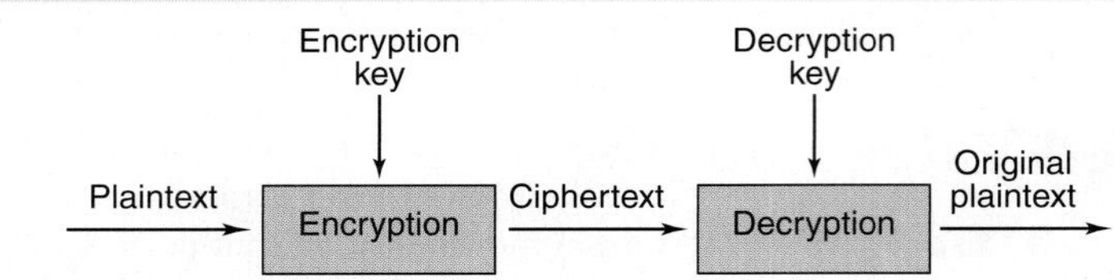

An electronic payment instruction starts out in a form readable by a human being, called "plaintext." When this instruction is entered into a computer, it is secured, or encrypted, using an "encryption key," which is a software code. In computer-readable form, the payment instruction is called "ciphertext," which the computer transmits to another location. A computer at the other location uses another software code, called a "decryption key," to read the data and turn the instruction back into a plaintext form that a human operator can read.

automated teller machines and electronic cash registers, such devices include any computer with sufficient memory and speed to operate the software, such as a personal computer.

On the Web
What are the latest developments in smart-card technology? Learn more about the evolution of and newest innovations in smart-card technology at http://www.smartcard.co.uk.

This means that unlike paper currency and coins, checks, and stored-value cards, which require physical space to process transactions, digital money stored on smart cards or other devices with smart-card-type microchips can be sent across cyberspace. Thus, an individual can use smart-card technology to purchase a service from an Internet-based retailer. Suppose that a rap-music enthusiast want to hear the latest rendition from a favorite performer. The enthusiast must have a smart-card-reading device connected to his personal computer—or have preloaded digital cash onto a program located on the hard drive of the computer. The performer's recording company must also have the necessary software. If both these conditions are met, then the rap-music enthusiast can enter a designated location on the recording company's Web site, point, click, and download the music as a digital file. His computer automatically sends digital cash as payment for this service. Then the enthusiast can listen to the latest release on his computer's speakers. (This example assumes no fraud.)

The Role of Payment Intermediaries Just because people have the capability to adopt a technology does not mean that they actually *do* implement it. The basic technology for stored-value cards has been available since the 1970s, but only recently have U.S. residents used the cards to buy such items as telephone calls. In many instances, a chicken-or-the-egg problem has been responsible for the delay. Retailers often do not want to install online systems for processing digital cash until more customers use it. But many customers will not use digital cash until more merchants are online and the customers are convinced that their payments are secure from transmission errors, fraud, and theft.

Payment intermediary: An institution that facilitates the transfer of funds between buyer and seller during the course of any purchase of goods, services, or financial assets.

The breakthrough in matching up retailers and their customers for online trading via smart cards and personal computers came when banks and financial software specialists teamed up to serve as **payment intermediaries,** or institutions that serve as go-betweens in processing the fund transferals that occur during the course of any purchase of goods, services, or financial assets. Banks traditionally have been key payment intermediaries. Since the Middle Ages, banks have served as storehouses for means of payment—gold, other precious metals, checking deposits—that people have accepted as money. The difference today is that banks now offer means of payment via cybertechnologies associated with the provision of digital cash. Banks are providing enhanced access to digital cash for good reason: they think that they can profit from the fees that they anticipate earning once e-money systems are broadly established, with themselves as payment intermediaries.

1. What is the difference between stored-value cards and smart cards? Stored-value cards are capable of storing computer-accessible data, including funds that the bearer of the card typically may spend on a specific good or service. Because they simply store information and do not process the data in any way, stored-value cards are most often used in closed systems operated by a single business or institution. Within open systems, debit cards may be used to transfer funds among accounts as long as the card user can provide authentication of the funds. By way of contrast, smart cards contain microprocessors that, in addition to tabulating data, can process security programs and communicate directly with other computers without need for authentication. This makes smart cards more flexible and secure for online transmission of payments within open systems linking many consumers, businesses, and financial institutions.

Online Banking

Banks everywhere expect to profit in several ways from widespread smart-card adoption. While customers have funds stored on their bank-issued smart cards, technically speaking those funds are still on deposit with their banks. Thus, banks can lend out unused balances on cards to other customers, most likely at a higher interest rate than the rate they pay on smart-card funds (we shall explain why this is so in Chapter 12). In addition, banks see the promise of fees that they will be able to charge retailers who accept the cards. They also anticipate getting to keep any spare change that customers leave on a card when they decide to throw it away. For instance, suppose that a bank finds that during a given week, a "typical" customer using a disposable smart card leaves 24 cents in "spare change" on the card when throwing it away because the customer does not think spending such a small amount is worth the effort. If 10,000 customers are "typical," then each week the bank will get to keep a total amount of $2,400. Over the course of a year, this "spare change" will accumulate to $124,800!

Many observers, however, feel that before most people become comfortable about cyberspace transmissions of digital cash, they must be certain that online dealings with their own banks are secure. This process is further along than the development of digital cash, so it will not be long before we can evaluate this view.

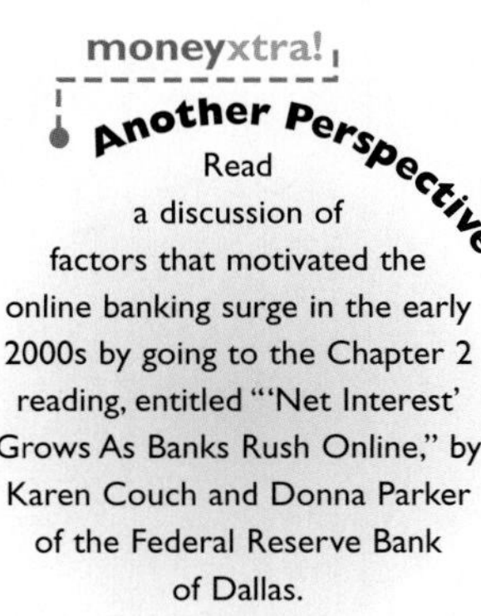

The Development of Online Banking Developers of home financial-management software initiated online banking in the United States. Wanting to include as many attractive features in their software packages as they could dream up, they started offering to help software users consolidate bills and initiate payments over the Internet via the software companies. To make this possible,

To think about whether the social gains from adopting e-money and online banking outweigh the private costs, go to the Chapter 2 Case Study, entitled "Investing in Digital Cash."
http://moneyxtra.swcollege.com

the software companies formed alliances with banks, because bill payments typically had to be issued from bank accounts.

Quickly, banks recognized that they might earn fee income by providing these services themselves. By 2000, 2,000 U.S. banks offered online banking services via the Internet. Today, more than 6,000 U.S. banks have developed some type of online banking, and most of the remainder are planning to offer such services.

Most bank customers who do online banking use three kinds of services. Bill consolidation and payment is one of the most popular. Another is transferring funds among accounts, thereby eliminating the need to make trips to a bank branch or automated teller machine (ATM) to conduct such transfers. The third is making initial applications for loans, which many banks now permit customers to do over the Internet. Although customers typically have to appear in person to finalize the terms of a loan, they can save some time and effort by starting the process at home.

A Chicken-or-the-Egg Problem? People still cannot engage in two important activities using online banking services: depositing and withdrawing funds. This, of course, is where smart cards should come into the picture. With smart cards, people could upload and download digital cash, thereby transforming their personal computers into home ATMs—which would give them more incentive to bank from home via the Internet. Yet, as noted above, many believe that online banking is the way to introduce people to e-money and thereby induce them to think about using smart cards. This raises the potential for a chicken-or-the-egg problem to develop: bank customers are waiting for widespread acceptability of smart cards before exploring home banking options, while banks are waiting for more customers to choose online banking before making big investments in smart-card technology.

Nevertheless, many bankers have decided that there are two very good reasons to promote online banking irrespective of smart cards. For one thing, once online banking is in place, it is less expensive for the bank, because the average cost of performing a transaction is lower. If customers interact directly with automated systems and computers that take only a few people to maintain, then the banks save the significant expense of opening and maintaining large systems of branch offices. Although the potential cost savings of online banking appear to be hard to quantify, this has not stopped some banks from adopting aggressive targets for converting their customers to Internet-based banking services. A number of banks have adopted explicit targets for the portions of their customers that they wish to convert to online banking services within the next few years.

Competitive Pressures for Online Banking Another key rationale that bankers everywhere have for developing online services is that if they do not, someone else may beat them to the punch and steal away their customers. Today a number of banks are already operating exclusively on the Internet. They have no physical branch offices, so they accept deposits through physical delivery systems, such as the U.S. Postal Service or Federal Express. This sharply reduces their costs, and these Internet-only banks promise to pass on part of the cost savings to customers in the form of lower fees and higher yields. Some even offer free checking with very low minimum deposits, such as $100, and no-fee money market accounts with average monthly balances of $2,500 or more.

These "virtual banks," as they have come to be known, are not the only potential source of competition faced by traditional banks. Today, there are several Internet loan brokers, such as QuickenMortgage, E-Loan, GetSmart, Lending Tree, and Microsoft's HomeAdviser. These broker systems use software that matches consumers with loans. The consumer supplies information to the program, which then searches among available loan products for the best fit. The loans are available from lenders with which the broker has a contractual relationship. (In Japan, traditional banks are losing out to convenience stores as Internet payment intermediaries; see on p. 34 *Global Focus: In Japan, Corner Shops Become Web Banks—and Online-Commerce Package Pickup Centers.*)

Internet loan brokers' biggest forays into banks' turf have been in the credit-card and mortgage markets. In the credit-card business, Internet brokers have been especially successful in providing credit-card debt consolidation services. They do not always compete with banks because often they act as marketers for traditional credit-card-issuing banks. The brokers receive fees for enrolling new customers for the credit-card issuers, which save the cost of developing lists of potential prospects and mailing card offers.

In the mortgage market, however, the competition is more direct. Indeed, Internet loan brokers often take the place of the traditional loan officer at a banking institution that makes mortgage loans. When mortgage rates fell in the late 1990s and again in the early 2000s, people who wished to refinance their houses flooded the telephone lines of traditional banking institutions, only to get lots of busy signals, long waits on hold, and slow responses from loan officers. This led many to turn on their computers and surf the Internet. Some real estate specialists now believe that in a few years at least 10 percent of U.S. mortgage-loan refinancings will be initiated through the Internet.

On the Web
Follow the latest mortgage market developments by visiting HSH Associates at http://www.hsh.com, the Microsoft Network at http://www.moneycentral.msn.com/loan/home.asp, the Mortgage Bankers Association at http://www.mbaa.org, or QuickenMortgage at http://quickenloans.quicken.com.

Regulatory Issues of Electronic Money

E-money makes some people nervous. Some are apprehensive about digital cash for the same kinds of reasons that have slowed adoption of any new technology. Until they have time to evaluate new technologies, people often begin by assuming the worst.

It remains to be seen whether people will find digital cash more convenient than other means of payment. As we have discussed above, there are reasons to think that many people ultimately will desire to use digital cash. The big issue in the minds of most potential users of cybermoney systems such as smart cards or online banking services is the *security* of e-money payments. For those who currently regulate banks, however, the development of a cybereconomy raises two key sets of issues. One involves the security of digital cash. The other relates to the potential for fraudulent banking.

The Security of Digital Cash

Just because smart cards will be equipped with authentication software does not mean they will be 100 percent secure. Ingenious criminals might pilfer digital cash in a number of ways.

GLOBAL Focus | POLICY | CYBER | MANAGEMENT

In Japan, Corner Shops Become Web Banks—and Online-Commerce Package Pickup Centers

In the United States, the widespread ownership of bank-issued credit cards has provided the foundation for most Internet payments. The United States also has a highly competitive market for package delivery services. In other countries, the lack of Internet payment options and well-developed delivery systems is holding up the growth of Web-facilitated commerce.

Paying in Cash at the Store Down the Street

Among the most important Japanese retailers are the *konbini,* which are discount convenience stores connected to high-tech information-processing networks. Several *konbini* chains have sought to establish a business that helps link buyers and sellers online.

Seven-Eleven, which operates 8,000 Japanese outlets, or almost three times the number of stores operated by Wal-Mart, has placed Internet kiosks in its stores so that customers can surf the Web and order products. To pay for goods ordered, consumers can use cash obtained from ATMs located in the stores. They hand the cash over to store clerks, who transmit the payment electronically to Internet sellers to complete the transactions. Thus, customers who rely on cash instead of credit cards can still shop online.

Furthermore, this service allows customers to bypass banks by effectively choosing Seven-Eleven as their payment intermediary. Some *konbini* are taking an additional step by applying for banking licenses permitting them to accept deposits and issue debit cards. This would save customers the trouble of getting cash from ATMs. It would also save store clerks the time and effort entailed in recycling cash back into the ATMs for other customers to withdraw.

Carrying the Goods Home

The entry of the *konbini* into the banking industry promises to make the Japanese banking system much more competitive. The *konbini* are also having an impact by simplifying the process of obtaining goods ordered online.

The Japanese system for delivering envelopes containing tickets ordered from an airline's Web site or packages of books purchased on the Internet is not very competitive. Market prices for deliveries are relatively high, which has discouraged online shopping. The *konbini,* however, permit consumers to pick up their envelopes and packages at the stores where they placed their Internet orders, thereby cutting out high-priced package delivery services.

For Critical Analysis: Some observers have speculated that the *konbini* might eventually begin making home deliveries of items that their customers order at Internet kiosks. What factors might limit the *konbini's* ability to compete with delivery companies as well as with banks?

Digital Counterfeiting One possible way that a crook could steal digital money is very old-fashioned but potentially very lucrative: counterfeiting. The most obvious way to counterfeit would be to produce smart cards that look, feel, and, most importantly, function just like legitimate smart cards.

Potential returns from smart-card counterfeiting might tempt well-trained engineers and computer scientists to form a counterfeiting ring. Such specialists potentially could analyze and "reverse-engineer" smart cards—that is, take apart cards and their software to determine how both are constructed. Then they could experiment with loading value onto fraudulent cards (or trying to fool computers into accepting fake cryptographic algorithms they have placed on the cards' microprocessors). If successful, they could spend the fraudulent digital funds.

Issuers of smart cards already have taken a number of defensive measures to limit the success of such counterfeiting efforts. To make counterfeit smart cards easier to recognize, issuers typically place holographic images on their own legitimate cards, just as credit-card issuers do. Issuers also design the computer code on the microprocessors so that data stored in memory cannot be accessed or changed except through predefined authorization and access software protocols. These software commands in turn are stored in a portion of the microprocessor's memory that can be changed only by altering its internal functions. To help prevent unauthorized reading of any data on the cards, smart cards are equipped with physical barriers intended to inhibit optical or electrical analysis or physical alteration of the microprocessor's memory. Most smart-card chips also are coated with several layers of wiring, installed in such a way that unauthorized removal of the chip is difficult to accomplish without damaging the chip beyond repair.

Swiping Digital Cash Offline and Online In recent years, a common type of bank robbery has the following *modus operandi:* two or three people drive a pickup truck through the front window of a bank branch or supermarket where an ATM is located, quickly lift the ATM onto the bed of the truck, drive to their hideout, and remove the cash in the ATM. An *offline theft* of digital cash is only slightly more sophisticated: thieves break into a merchant's establishment, physically remove the electronic devices used to store value from customers' smart cards, and download these funds onto their own cards.

More sophisticated thieves might attempt *online theft* by intercepting payment messages as they are transmitted from smart cards and other electronic-funds storage devices to host computers. For instance, if thieves learn the times of day that a large up-scale department store transmits its receipts to a central computer, they could try to tap into the transmission line and steal the funds. These kinds of online theft are most likely to be "inside jobs," in which employees commit *internal theft*—pilfering their own company's funds—using their knowledge of the company's systems for transmitting cybercash.

Could E-Money "Catch a Cold"? Counterfeiting, robbery, and internal theft are old problems. Stealing digital cash requires more technical ability than John Dillinger and Baby Face Nelson needed in the 1930s, but the crime is essentially the same. The dependence of digital cash on correctly functioning microprocessors and software, however, exposes e-money to special dangers.

In the classic James Bond movie *Goldfinger,* a supercriminal plots to blow up a small nuclear device inside Fort Knox, thereby making the gold stored there radioactive and, consequently, worthless. The supercriminal reasons that he will reap huge capital gains on his own hoards of accumulated gold. In a cybereconomy, it would be hard to profit financially from the wholesale destruction of outstanding stocks of digital cash. Not all crimes are committed for financial gain, however. A group of people who are fanatically wedded to some political or personal "cause" and who also happen to possess a talent for creating computer viruses potentially could transform themselves into superterrorists. A virus that damages the input-output mechanisms of smart-card microprocessors and other digital-cash storage and communications devices or that erases data stored on such e-money mechanisms potentially could create financial havoc, thereby attracting considerable attention to the terrorists' cause, whatever it might be.

MALFUNCTIONING MONEY Physical cash can wear out, and devices for scanning magnetic ink can misread checks. Nevertheless, people can still exchange physical units of money during electricity outages. Power failures or other equipment breakdowns, by way of contrast, can bring e-money transactions to a grinding halt.

Thus, consumers and retailers may face a trade-off in their use of digital cash. E-money systems are speedier, less costly, and more efficient than currency and checks. Just as air travel is on average the quickest and safest way to traverse a long distance, digital cash is a comparatively effective way to conduct transactions—when it works. Yet, when airplanes fail to operate correctly, the result can be spectacular crashes. Likewise, the gain from using cyberbanking technologies comes at the cost of exposure to new risks of loss.

2. Is digital cash less secure than physical cash? In some respects, the potential security problems of digital cash, such as counterfeiting and outright theft, are simply high-tech versions of security concerns people already experience when they use physical currency and coins. In other ways, however, digital cash has its own special security difficulties. Unlike physical money, digital cash potentially can be infected by computer viruses. In addition, during periods of hardware breakdowns or power failures, digital-cash transactions may be hindered, if not halted.

Bank Fraud: An Old Problem with a New Face

The security issues discussed above highlight potential problems that issuers and users of digital cash can face from external threats. Presumably, all parties normally wish to contain the scope of these problems. What happens, however, if payment intermediaries themselves—that is, bankers that issue smart cards, take in funds, and process payments—try to earn ill-gotten gains?

LESSONS FROM HISTORY: THE FREE-BANKING ERA During much of the nineteenth century, U.S. banks issued their own **banknotes,** which were privately issued paper moneys redeemable in gold. People learned to be wary of so-called wildcat banks, which set up gold-redemption offices in locales where wildcats, not the humans who might wish to redeem the banknotes, were located. Some of these banks were essentially fly-by-night operations that pocketed their customers' deposits of gold and other marketable assets and departed. Evidence now indicates that this practice was not as widespread as many historians initially believed, but there is no doubt that some wildcat banking occurred.

What made wildcat banking feasible was the enactment of so-called **free-banking laws** in many U.S. states after 1836. These laws permitted any group to secure a broad corporate charter allowing it to engage in banking practices. Prior to 1836, and in some states even after that date, a bank could be incorporated only if the state legislature gave permission. The requirements for obtaining a free-banking charter varied from state to state; Table 2-1 lists the states with and without free-banking laws by 1860.

Banknotes: Privately issued paper currency.

Free-banking laws: Laws in force in many U.S. states between 1837 and 1861 that allowed anyone to obtain a charter authorizing banking operations.

Table 2-1 States with Free-Banking Laws, 1837–1860

States with Free-Banking Laws	Year Law Passed	States without Free-Banking Laws
Michigan	1837[a]	Arkansas
Georgia	1838[b]	California
New York	1838	Delaware
Alabama	1849[b]	Kentucky
New Jersey	1850	Maine
Illinois	1851	Maryland
Massachusetts	1851[b]	Mississippi
Ohio	1851	Missouri
Vermont	1851[b]	New Hampshire
Connecticut	1852	North Carolina
Indiana	1852	Oregon
Tennessee	1852[b]	Rhode Island
Wisconsin	1852	South Carolina
Florida	1853[b]	Texas
Louisiana	1853	Virginia
Iowa	1858[b]	
Minnesota	1858	
Pennsylvania	1860[b]	

[a]Michigan prohibited free banking in 1840 and allowed it again in 1857.
[b]According to Rockoff, very little free banking was done under the laws in these states.

SOURCE: Reprinted from A. J. Rolnick and W. E. Weber, "Inherent Instability in Banking: The Free Banking Experience," *Cato Journal* 5 (Winter 1986). Their source was Hugh Rockoff, *The Free Banking Era: A Re-Examination* (New York: Arno Press, 1975).

Free banking was not truly "free." Most states required free banks to purchase and deposit state-issued bonds with state banking authorities. This meant that banks in some states were very risky propositions if the bonds issued by their state governments had uncertain prospects for full repayment or if the prices of the bonds fluctuated. Free-banking laws also required banks to pay gold or other specific assets in exchange for the banknotes they issued. Typically, free banks had to restrict their business to a single office; they could not open branches throughout states in which they were incorporated, nor could they branch across state lines.

Nevertheless, in many states free banks faced few other restrictions on their activities. Much recent research has shown that despite this relative lack of state oversight and the considerable latitude for entry into or exit from the industry, the notes of free banks generally were quite safe. Many free banks were long-lived institutions, and very few depositors actually experienced losses as a result of those free banks that closed down their operations at one time or another between 1837 and 1860. In addition, failures of free banks tended to be localized. They rarely led to failures of other banking institutions. Hence, the evidence indicates that most free banks were domesticated, conservative housecats, not fly-by-night wildcats.

In a cybereconomy, in which anyone in principle can post a Web site seeking deposits of funds and offering to pay depositors a rate of return, this nineteenth-century experience with free banking has some modern-day relevance. When contemplating the role of bank regulation in a world of digital cash, a big issue is whether cyberbanks are more likely to turn out to be housecats or wildcats.

WILDCAT BANKING, TWENTY-FIRST-CENTURY STYLE? In the summer of 1997, a newly formed company, based in a small North Carolina community, announced its intention to provide full-scale banking operations over the Internet. The company proclaimed its right to provide such services under U.S. constitutional law, and its Web site indicated that its deposits were backed by a policy issued by a major insurance company. The company had a "fax-on-demand telephone line" through which prospective customers could order an application to open an account. To attract deposits, the new virtual bank promised to pay annual interest rates up to 20 percent on savings accounts and 10 percent on checking accounts, at a time when most traditional banking institutions were offering deposit rates slightly above 5 percent. The virtual bank also said that it would offer small-business loans, "with no credit checks," at one to two percentage points above the prime rate.

Enforcement Limitations To the Office of the Comptroller of the Currency (OCC), the federal agency charged with regulating national banks, this essentially was a wildcat bank in the making. This seemed even more probable when it turned out that the "major insurance company" said to back the new bank's deposits announced it had never made such an arrangement. The OCC pointed out to the new company's owners that federal bank laws prevent institutions from accepting deposits without a formal bank charter. Nevertheless, the OCC had to turn to the Federal Trade Commission to enforce the law and stop the new company from opening its banking operations, because the OCC has power to enforce actions only against institutions that *do* have federal bank charters.

Web-Facilitated Risk Taking A year later, the Federal Deposit Insurance Corporation (FDIC), which administers federal deposit insurance (see Chapter 14) and regulates state-chartered banks, took control of a Kentucky-based banking institution called BestBank. The bank raised many of its deposits on the Internet. By the mid-1990s, its low-cost operations—the bank had only twenty-three employees at a single location—had permitted it to become five times more profitable than the average bank. What it wasn't telling its depositors, however, was that it was lending most of their funds to lower-income individuals via the issuance of a half-million credit cards with $600 borrowing limits. As a precondition for receipt, each cardholder had to join a Florida-based travel company at a fee of $543, which the bank charged to the cardholder's account before sending out the card, leaving only $57 of available credit. Many of the bank's credit-card customers, however, failed to pay off their loan balances. When the FDIC seized the bank, the bulk of the bank's cardholders had defaulted, and the bank was insolvent—its liabilities exceeded its assets by nearly $100 million.

These examples illustrate the dark side of cyberbanking. Certainly, the Internet can be a wonderful way to obtain information about potentially profitable business opportunities, and online banking and digital-cash transmission allow for speedier trading and quicker financial rewards. At the same time, however, these cybertechnologies can serve as a means for unscrupulous people to draw in funds that they plan to use in high-risk, or even fraudulent, ventures.

Regulating Cyberbanking

In light of the new risks—such as the potential for high-tech counterfeiting, system breakdowns or terrorist attacks, or online bank fraud—should governments step in and regulate cyberbanking? Before addressing this question, we first need to think about why governments might wish to regulate banking institutions.

THE RATIONALES FOR BANK REGULATION Banks have always faced considerable regulation. Since the earliest times, governments have sought to restrain or direct banking activities. The traditional justification for regulating banks has been that if the government were to leave them alone, socially "bad" outcomes might result. In the worst case of a banking panic, many customers might lose their life savings.

Certainly, in the broad sweep of world history many such events have occurred. In the United States between the 1830s and 1930s, national banking panics seemed to occur in nearly regular cycles of fifteen to twenty years, with significant panics taking place in 1837, 1857, 1873, 1893, 1907, and 1929–1933. The severity of the last of these panics motivated much of the federal regulation of depository institutions that exists today. It also lies behind some of the efforts to regulate the application of cyberbanking technologies.

Traditionally, governments have regulated banking institutions in an effort to pursue four essential goals:

1. **Maintaining depository institution liquidity.** A large portion of the liabilities of banking institutions are checking accounts and other types of deposits, which, as we discussed in Chapter 1, customers of the institutions have the legal right to access almost immediately. Any banking institution that finds itself without sufficient cash on hand to meet the needs of its depositors suffers from **illiquidity.** Such illiquidity inconveniences the institution's customers. If a large number of banks are illiquid simultaneously, however, then the result can be a serious disruption in the nation's flow of payments for goods and services, with potentially broader negative effects on the economy.

2. **Assuring bank solvency by limiting failures.** An overriding goal of bank regulation is to reduce the likelihood of widespread bank failures. Any business, including a bank, typically fails and declares bankruptcy when it reaches a point of *insolvency,* at which it is unable to pay debts as they mature. Although an insolvent business may have positive net worth, it is insolvent if it cannot meet its financial obligations. Because many of a bank's assets are financial instruments that are more liquid than most assets of nonfinancial businesses, the terms *bankruptcy* and *insolvency* are generally used synonymously. Consequently, a depository institution generally is considered to have reached a point of **insolvency** when the value of its assets falls below the value of its liabilities, so that the value of its *equity,* or net worth, is negative. A key aspect of the regulation of depository institutions typically is the

Illiquidity: A situation in which a banking institution lacks the cash assets required to meet requests for depositor withdrawals.

Insolvency: A situation in which the value of a bank's assets falls below the value of its liabilities.

periodic *examination* of their accounting ledgers to verify that the institutions are solvent. Another aspect normally is the *supervision* of these institutions via the publication and enforcement of rules and standards with which they must comply. A purpose of regulatory supervision is to make insolvency and failure a rare occurrence.

3. Promoting an efficient financial system. Another key rationale for bank regulation is to promote an environment in which banking institutions can provide their services at the lowest possible cost. Achieving cost efficiency minimizes the total resources that society expends on the services that banks provide, thereby freeing up the largest possible amount of remaining resources for other social uses.

4. Protecting consumers. Throughout history many leading Americans have mistrusted banks. Thomas Jefferson said that they were more dangerous than standing armies. When Andrew Jackson lost considerable personal wealth to banks from foreclosed loans after suffering big losses on land speculation, he made bank bashing a favorite political pastime. Members of Congress have heeded the calls of many of their constituents by passing legislation intended to protect consumers from possible misbehavior by bank managers. Hence, consumer protection is another fundamental goal of bank regulation.

DIFFICULTIES IN ATTAINING ALL REGULATORY GOALS Regulators of depository institutions struggle to achieve all four goals simultaneously. Typically, achieving one objective may entail sacrificing another. For instance, a problem that regulators often face is distinguishing illiquidity from insolvency. It is possible for a banking institution to be illiquid temporarily yet to be solvent otherwise, just as it is possible for an otherwise wealthy individual to experience temporary "cash flow" difficulties. Bank regulators, and particularly a central bank such as the Federal Reserve, can assist institutions suffering from short-term liquidity problems by extending them credit. The difficulty is that typically illiquidity is one symptom of pending insolvency. Extending such loans can keep otherwise insolvent institutions operating when they really ought to close. Efforts to promote liquidity of banks can thereby permit poorly managed, insolvent banks to run up even more debts, worsening the extent of their insolvency.

In addition, because earning high profits helps banks avoid liquidity and insolvency difficulties, government regulators often are tempted to find ways to protect banks from competition, which might hurt their profitability. At the same time, banks are more likely to operate as efficiently as possible when exposed to considerable rivalry from other financial institutions. Competition, however, drives down bank profitability; if profitability falls too low, unexpected shocks to the economy or financial system can cause banks to operate at significant losses, thereby threatening their liquidity and solvency levels.

INNOVATION MAY BE STIFLED Furthermore, laws designed to protect bank customers from potentially unscrupulous bank managers can interfere with the development of innovative banking practices that ultimately might improve overall customer service. For example, suppose that a reputable bank develops the ability to post an Internet Web site where a visitor can apply for a loan without having to drive to a bank and conduct a long-winded interview with a bank loan officer. The bank also gains because it reduces the amount of time that loan officers must allocate to such personal interviews. To prevent *un*scrupulous banks from taking advantage of unwary consumers on the Internet, however, government regulators may require this reputable bank to meet a number of standards in posting its Web site. They may also require the bank to file detailed reports about each application it receives. The costs of meeting the government's consumer protection regulations might very well offset the efficiency gains that the bank had hoped to achieve, inducing it to drop its plans to provide the new service. Thus, protecting consumers can reduce bank efficiency.

The Pros and Cons of Regulating Cyberbanking As we shall discuss in more detail in Chapter 14, a key issue of bank regulation is determining how best to trade off progress toward achieving one regulatory goal against sacrificing progress in accomplishing others. Undoubtedly, this will prove to be a challenge as money and banking continue to move across corridors within cyberspace.

On the one hand, for instance, a traditional way to limit banks' potential for insolvency is to require periodic audits of their accounts. To ease the task of auditing banks, regulators typically require them to follow industry and regulatory standards in their business practices. Applying this same approach to cyberbanking would necessitate placing limits on "permissible" cyberbanking business practices. Although such restraints make the regulators' task easier, they would not be consistent with allowing banks to experiment with new ways of operating that might achieve significant cost savings.

On the other hand, permitting unhindered adoption of new ways of banking via cybertechnologies might encourage some bank managers to engage in riskier practices. In addition, entry into banking-related businesses via, say, the Internet could greatly increase the potential for widespread illiquidity, or even insolvencies, if the businesses are based on poorly implemented plans conceived by entrepreneurs unskilled in the arts of banking. Many people could lose their savings as a result, and society as a whole could bear significant costs.

Thus, the decisions about whether or how to regulate cyberbanking technologies involve the same types of trade-offs that bank regulators have always faced. The main difference is that in the new cyberworld, governmental bodies charged with pursuing the traditional goals of bank regulation must keep up with an ever more rapidly changing financial environment.

3. What are the rationales for regulating cyberbanking? The reasons for contemplating regulation of cyberbanking mirror those typically offered for regulating traditional banking activities: preventing illiquidity, limiting insolvencies, promoting efficiency, and protecting consumers. An important issue is whether new cybertechnologies, such as smart cards, digital cash, and online banking, pose unique problems, including greater security concerns and increased potential for bank fraud, that may justify special regulation. Nevertheless, regulators contemplating restrictions on cyberbanking are likely to face trade-offs among their broad regulatory objectives that are similar to those they face in regulating traditional banking activities.

Electronic Money and Monetary Policy

As we shall discuss in detail in Chapter 17, for the past century most nations have entrusted central banking institutions with the task of determining the quantity of money in circulation. By varying the quantity of money, central banks can affect market interest rates, aggregate expenditures, and total income and employment. Thus, central banks can conduct *monetary policy* in an effort to influence overall economic performance. The advent of digital cash, however, raises an important question: Could the widespread use of digital cash complicate central banks' efforts to conduct monetary policy?

Real Money versus Virtual Money—Does It Matter?

Digital cash stored on smart cards and transferred among computers has two characteristics that distinguish it from the currency and coins that people have traditionally used. First, instead of being made of paper and metal, it consists of software stored on microchips. Second, instead of being issued by the government, it is issued by private firms. Consequently, digital cash can have a bearing on the ability of central banks to regulate the total quantity of money only if either or both of these distinguishing features constitute a dramatic departure from the *status quo*.

Let's begin by contemplating whether the *form* that money takes should make any difference for monetary policy. Consider the $100 bill, which is one of the most popular forms of money in the world. Several weeks each year, the U.S. Bureau of Engraving and Printing prints $100 bills around the clock, bundles them into shrink-wrapped packages containing 4,000 notes each ($400,000 per package), and ships them to Federal Reserve banks for distribution.

In 1991, in the first alteration of U.S. paper currency since 1957, the Bureau of Engraving and Printing began threading metallized plastic strips indicating every bill's official denomination through each bill it printed. This change was intended to stop the practice of bleaching out the printing on $1 bills, then reproducing them as $100 bills on color copiers. The plastic strip does not show up on carbon copies of the bills. (It also glows red under ultraviolet light.) The portrait of Benjamin Franklin that appears on $100 bills was enlarged and moved off-center. There was some concern at the U.S. Treasury that the public might not accept these changes. Nevertheless, even though the plastic strip was clearly visible near the Federal Reserve Board seal printed on each bill and the enlarged Franklin portrait noticeably changed the look of $100 bills, there was no drop in usage of the bills. In fact, worldwide usage of $100 bills increased substantially after 1991.

By 2000, the Treasury had made similar changes in the $5, $10, $20, and $50 bills; in particular, the portraits of Abraham Lincoln, Alexander Hamilton, Andrew Jackson, and Ulysses Grant were enlarged and moved off-center. Even though this and other changes made the bills look much different, people used the bills as before.

This experience provides an important message. Changes in the form of money, in and of themselves, have no implications for monetary policy. As long as there is no change in the purchasing power of the money that people use, they will use whatever money is most convenient, as long as it is widely acceptable in exchange. For example, as long as $20 bills are easy to use and widely accepted by others, people do not particularly care what they look like. Likewise, as long as digital cash is a simple-to-use and generally accepted form of money, the fact that it is an invisible software algorithm is unlikely to make a difference to most people.

The Big Issue: Who Will Issue Digital Cash?

Whether money takes the form of coins, paper, or deposits makes little difference to officials who are charged with conducting monetary policy, as long as it does not interfere with their ability to control the total *quantity* of money in circulation. It is this issue that makes policymakers somewhat nervous about digital cash.

If the Federal Reserve and other central banks desire to control, or at least to influence, the quantity of money in circulation, it is helpful for them to have direct and/or indirect oversight over the process by which money is placed into circulation. Let's begin by thinking about whether current private issuers of money—banks that issue checkable deposits—care about the way they "create" money. Then we shall think about why the Federal Reserve might care whether the ability to issue money extends beyond traditional banking institutions.

Digital Cash from Banks' Perspective: A Technological Change Only

To a bank, e-money is just a new way to conduct an old business. This business, which we shall discuss in detail in Chapter 12, is profiting from taking in funds in the form of deposits and lending those funds to others at higher interest rates.

To a traditional banking institution, funds that its customers download onto smart cards are no different than funds they withdraw from ATMs and hold as government-issued paper currency. Otherwise, idle balances in checking accounts—which can also be accessed by smart cards if bank customers use their smart cards as debit cards—are balances that banks can lend to others. Thus, funds that bank customers hold on deposit and access for electronic debiting via their smart-card microprocessors are available for bank lending just as traditional checking funds are. Banks can do this by making traditional loans with terms that loan officers and borrowers negotiate in bank offices. In some cases, however, the entire process might be digital: deposits accessed digitally via smart cards could effectively be "on loan" to bank customers who apply for and receive loans online.

Whether funds held on bank-issued smart cards find their way to bank borrowers through long-established or high-tech lending channels does not matter to banks. All they care about is that they earn maximum profits from undertaking their bread-and-butter business operations. To traditional banking institutions, digital cash simply amounts to a new way of raising funds. Whether those funds come from checking accounts that people can use to buy goods, services, or assets or from balances accessed with smart cards really makes no difference to banks, as long as they profit from either activity.

Digital Cash Issued by Nonbanking Institutions: A Revolutionary Change It is conceivable, however, that traditional banking institutions, such as commercial banks, savings institutions, and credit unions, will not be the only ones issuing digital cash. To a central bank such as the Federal Reserve, this is the *fundamental* monetary policy issue posed by the development of e-money. Like banks and their customers, the Federal Reserve does not particularly care what form money takes. Nevertheless, it does have some reason to be concerned about who has the power to issue money.

The Entry of Greenbacks To see why this is so, it is helpful to consider a critical historical period in U.S. monetary history, the Civil War of 1861–1865. Figure 2-3 displays the components of the U.S. money stock in 1861, which totaled $538 million. Demand deposits at banks accounted for well over half of the quantity of money in that year, but nearly all the remainder of the money stock consisted of banknotes issued by state-chartered banks. Only about 3 percent of the quantity of money had been issued by the federal government.

After the formation of the Confederacy, there were two separate moneys: U.S. dollars and Confederate dollars. Both the Union and the Confederate government issued large quantities of paper currency to pay their wartime expenditures. The end of the war left the Confederate currency worthless. The surviving Union was in a quandary about what to do with the paper currency, known as "Greenbacks" because of the distinctive color, that now was a major part of the quantity of money in the United States and was not backed by gold. Determining how to deal with these Greenbacks became a central issue for the next several years. Figure 2-4 displays estimates of the components of the nation's $1.6 billion money stock in 1866. As the figure indicates, Greenbacks had replaced banknotes in second place among types of money held by the public and accounted for exactly a third of the quantity of money.

Figure 2-3
The Composition of the Quantity of Money in 1861.

At the beginning of the U.S. Civil War, the quantity of money was composed almost solely of privately issued bank deposits and banknotes. Government currency was a very small portion of the total amount of money in circulation in the United States.

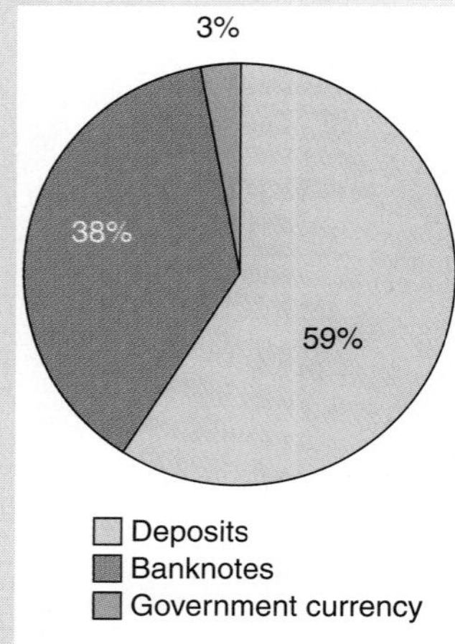

SOURCE: Richard H. Timberlake, *Monetary Policy in the United States: An Intellectual and Institutional History* (Chicago: University of Chicago Press, 1993).

A National Banking System By the end of the Civil War, another fundamental change had occurred: a significant shift from deposits and notes issued by state-chartered banks to those issued by nationally chartered banks. Naturally, part of this shift resulted from the financial devastation of many state-chartered banks in Confederate states that had been ravaged by war. Another key factor accounting for the change, however, was the passage of the National Banking Act of 1863 and subsequent amendments, which placed a special 10 percent tax on notes issued by state banks. This tax made the issue of state banknotes unprofitable. The federal government had considerable regulatory powers over nationally chartered banks. As Figure 2-5 shows, by the end of 1865 the amount of notes and demand deposits at national banks exceeded the total quantity at state banks. By 1868, in a dramatic example of how war and a policy change can combine to alter fortunes, there were over eighteen times more notes and deposits at national banks than at state banks. Thus, two significant changes occurred between 1861 and 1868: the federal government got into the business of issuing currency, and national banks regulated by the federal government issued most of the rest of the nation's circulating money.

These events set the stage for today's monetary system in the United States, because they laid the foundation for direct government issuance of circulating money and for indirect government control over bank-issued money via a federally regulated banking system. As we shall discuss in greater detail in Chapter 17, the formation of the Federal Reserve System was a natural outgrowth of this development. Since its founding in 1913, the Federal Reserve has had the power to influence the quantity of bank-issued money—demand deposits and other checkable deposits—via its ability to regulate the ability of private banks to issue deposits.

Technology and Accounts That Function as Money Although, on net, technology has improved the efficiency of the financial system, it has also complicated the Federal Reserve's efforts to influence, or perhaps even to try to control, the amount of privately issued money. For instance, the advent of computers and ATMs in the 1970s permitted people to transfer balances from noncheckable savings and time deposits into their checking accounts simply by pushing buttons. The result, as we discussed in Chapter 1, was that savings and time deposit funds came much closer to being "money" than they had been previously.

In principle, anyone can issue digital-cash accounts. Even if the government were to decide that only traditional banking institutions that fall under the Federal Reserve's regulatory umbrella can issue smart cards, what is to stop other firms from setting up e-money accounts over the Internet? That is, what is to stop firms that technically are not "banks" from issuing Internet-based digital "checking accounts" that function as money? Presumably, one answer is that Congress could pass laws prohibiting such accounts, and the Federal Reserve and other bank regulators would police the Internet to ensure that only traditional banks subject to government regulation issue such accounts.

Another possible answer, however, is that ultimately nothing may be able to stop a host of firms from pecking away at legal loopholes and eventually finding a way to essentially enter the banking business by issuing e-money accounts. Balances stored in these digital-cash accounts would be as much a part of the nation's quantity of circulating money as government currency and checkable deposits at traditional banks. As a result, the Federal Reserve's task of measuring and regulating this quantity would become much more complicated. In this way, the new cybereconomy has the potential to profoundly alter monetary affairs in the United States and, indeed, worldwide. We shall return to this theme throughout the remainder of this book, because this potential development, more than any other, may be the *truly* fundamental change brought about by the use of digital cash.

Figure 2-4
The Composition of the Quantity of Money in 1866.

Following the Civil War, government currency amounted to a third of the quantity of money in the United States.

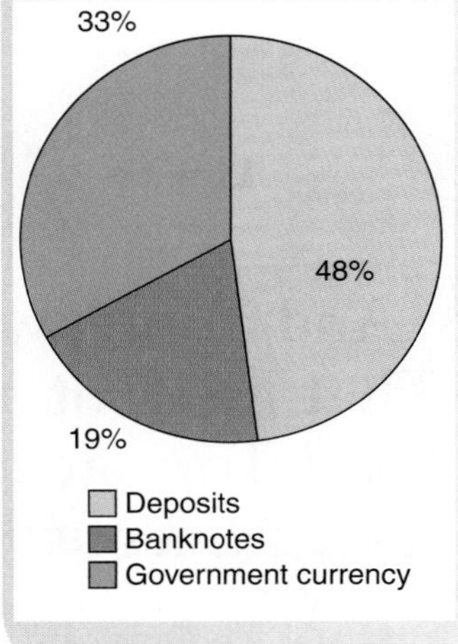

SOURCE: Richard H. Timberlake, *Monetary Policy in the United States: An Intellectual and Institutional History* (Chicago: University of Chicago Press, 1993).

Figure 2-5
Notes and Deposits at State and National Banks, 1860–1868.

The state banking system that had existed before the Civil War was largely replaced by a national banking system by the conclusion of the war.

SOURCE: Richard H. Timberlake, *Monetary Policy in the United States: An Intellectual and Institutional History* (Chicago: University of Chicago Press, 1993).

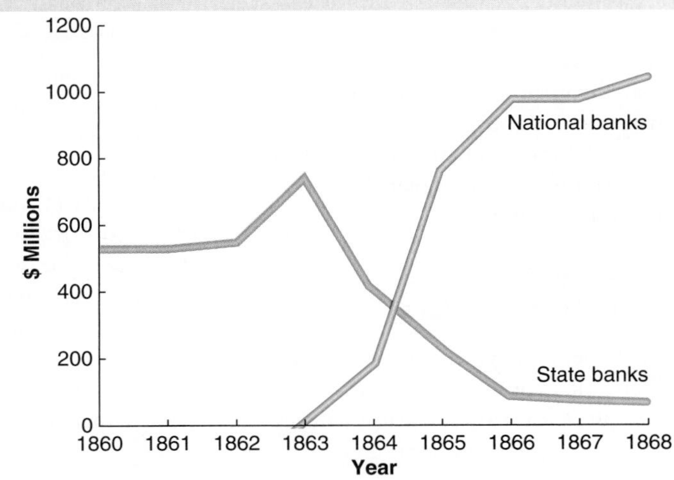

4. Does e-money matter for monetary policy? To an individual who uses physical cash, checking deposits, or digital cash, the form of money does not matter as much as its convenience and acceptability in exchange. In addition, a traditional banking institution is more concerned about whether its activity of raising funds and lending them out at higher interest rates is profitable than it is about whether it raises the funds by issuing checking accounts or smart cards. To the Federal Reserve or another central bank, the form that money takes is only a concern if the new form of money, such as digital cash, can be issued by new institutions that are not subject to the rules intended to assist the central bank in controlling the total amount of circulating money.

Link to **Management**

And You Always Thought That Most of Your Debit-Card Transactions Were Instantaneous

The security mechanisms used by debit-card systems make these systems somewhat more cumbersome than paper currency and coins. Issuers of smart cards are hoping that eventually the implied costs of debit-card transactions will convince retailers that smart cards are a more effective means of payment, because the bulk of transactions take place instantaneously.

Many users of debit cards do not realize that the majority of debit-card transactions do not occur immediately when retailers scan the cards. For a variety of reasons, most funds transfers initiated by scans of debit cards are delayed for several hours, and sometimes for a day or two.

Factors That Delay and Drive Up the Costs of Debit-Card Transfers

When a cardholder presents a typical debit card to a retailer, the retailer's electronic cash register automatically routes a request for authorization to the issuing bank. After checking the cardholder's account number against a file of lost or stolen cards and verifying that funds are available in the customer's account, the bank sends confirmation of payment authorization.

This authorization system enhances the security of the system to both the cardholder (perhaps the person trying to make a purchase stole the card) and the retailer (bank authorization guarantees receipt of funds). Nevertheless, the telecommunication costs of standard online authorizations normally range from 8 cents to 15 cents per transaction, which is much higher than the per-transaction cost of paper currency and coins.

Most Debit-Card Transactions Are *Offline*

Retailers who strive for speed in delivering goods and services—such as grocery stores and fast-food restaurants—do not want other customers to stand in line waiting while a customer provides personal identification numbers and employees await payment authorizations. For this reason, as Figure 2-6 indicates, the majority of debit-card transactions actually take place offline. Many retailers simply store transactions during the day or even for a couple of days. Then the retailers transmit requests for payment from banks during off-hours—just as they do with the checks their customers write.

Figure 2-6
Total U.S. Debit-Card Transactions.

The use of debit cards has grown at a fast pace in recent years. Nevertheless, the majority of debit-card transactions take place offline instead of online.

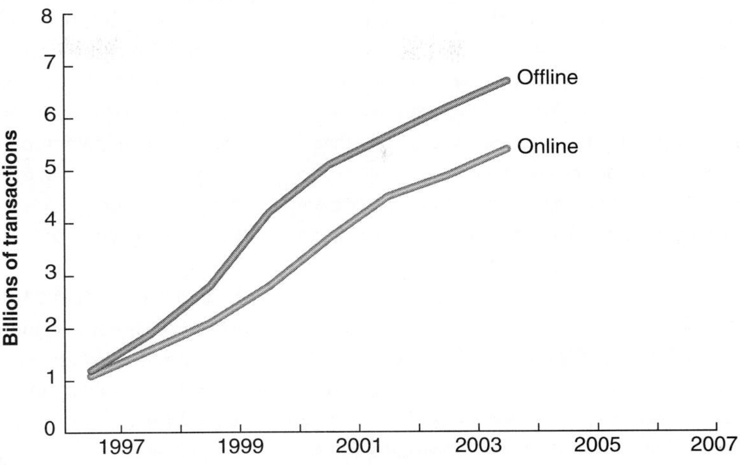

SOURCE: Bank for International Settlements and authors' estimates.

Hence, even though parties to transactions transmit payment authorization messages and funds transfers associated with debit cards electronically, only a minority of these transmissions are instantaneous. In contrast to smart-card and other digital-cash transactions, debit-card transactions more often than not entail a delayed exchange of funds to finalize purchases. This exposes firms to delays and costs that are similar to, although typically somewhat lower than, the delays and costs they face when they accept checks from their customers.

Research Project

Develop a list of the relative advantages and disadvantages of debit cards versus smart cards as payment instruments. Evaluate which of these characteristics is likely to prove most important in determining whether debit cards or smart cards emerge as the dominant means of electronic payment in the years to come.

Web Resources

1. What features of debit cards should consumers keep in mind as they use these cards? The National Consumers League provides a review of the issues at http://www.nclnet.org/debitbro.htm.

2. What are some of the pros and cons of debit cards? For a listing provided by Bankrate.com, go to http://www.bankrate.com/brm/green/atm/atm2a.asp.

Chapter Summary

1. The Distinction between Stored-Value Cards and Smart Cards: Consumers can use stored-value cards to maintain balances of electronic money that they can use to purchase specific goods or services. Stored-value cards are most often used in closed systems operated by a single business or institution, but in an open, online system, they can function as debit cards. Smart cards contain computer microchips that permit them to communicate directly with other computers to process software programs containing algorithms that store and transmit cash. In contrast to stored-value cards, smart cards can transfer funds anonymously.

2. The Security of Digital Cash: Counterfeiting and theft are potential problems with digital cash, just as they are for physical currency and coins. Special security problems of digital cash are the threat of infection by computer viruses and the potential for monetary breakdowns caused by power outages or hardware malfunctions.

3. The Rationales for Regulating Cyberbanking: The traditional justifications for regulating traditional banking activities—preventing illiquidity, limiting insolvencies, promoting efficiency, and protecting consumers—are the same rationales commonly offered for restricting cyberbanking. Some observers also argue that unique security concerns and an increased potential for bank fraud justify special regulation of cyberbanking. In any event, however, cyberbanking regulators are likely to face trade-offs among regulatory objectives that are similar to those they experience in traditional regulation of banking institutions.

4. E-Money and Monetary Policy: To private individuals who use money and private institutions that issue it, the form of money does not matter as much as its convenience and general acceptability in exchange. To a central bank such as the Federal Reserve, however, electronic forms of money could complicate its ability to control the amount of money in circulation if they can be issued by institutions not subject to its monetary regulations.

Questions and Problems

(Answers to odd-numbered questions and problems may be found on the Web at http://money.swcollege.com under "Student Resources.")

1. The state of New Jersey has what many experts have called the most widely counterfeited driver's license in the world. Partly to combat this problem, recently the state's government contemplated offering a new driver's license called "Access NJ." The proposed plastic card would contain a microprocessor. The programming on the microprocessor would allow the holder to store and transfer funds in payment for public services (such as public transportation), authenticate state certification to bear firearms or to hunt, download public benefits from authorized computer terminals, and obtain entry into public buildings. Based on the discussion of e-money systems in this chapter, what kind of system did the New Jersey government contemplate introducing? Explain your reasoning.

2. Critics of the New Jersey government's proposal discussed in question 1 worry that the Access NJ card might allow the government to create databases of personal information about the state's citizens, which it could then disseminate without their consent. Based on the description of the card in question 1, do you believe this concern might be legitimate? Do you think that "personal privacy" is also likely to be a general concern about smart cards used primarily for storing and transferring digital cash? Why or why not?

3. In what ways is a smart card a "more flexible" payment instrument than a stored-value card? Explain.

4. Most consumers are also taxpayers. To protect honest taxpayers from efforts by others who try to evade taxes, the federal government imposes bank reporting requirements designed to limit *money laundering,* or the funneling of cash into and out of bank accounts for purposes of hiding taxable transactions (as well as otherwise illegal exchanges). For instance, banks have to report to the federal government any funds transfer of $10,000 or more that an individual initiates. A key governmental concern about smart cards is that they may enable tax dodgers to avoid this reporting requirement, thereby inducing a rise in money laundering. Based on what you learned about smart cards in this chapter, does this seem to you to be a legitimate concern? Take a stand, and support your answer.

5. When discussing the pros and cons of e-money systems, a Federal Reserve economist argued that "the current paper-based system doesn't have much to recommend it, other than it works great, is cheap, reliable, and we trust it." Use this statement for evaluating the relative merits of e-money versus the currently dominant system based on using physical currency and checks for retail transactions.

6. In what ways might bank fraud be easier to perpetrate using online banking methods instead of traditional banking practices? Explain.

7. In what ways is digital cash more convenient to use than physical cash? Explain.

8. In what ways is digital cash less secure than physical cash? Explain.

9. How might greater competition in providing means of payment generate efficiency gains for the economy? Be specific.

10. How might greater competition in providing means of payment complicate monetary policy? Be specific.

Before the Test

Test your understanding of the material covered in this chapter by taking the Chapter 2 interactive quiz at http://money.swcollege.com.

Online Application

Internet URL: http://www.firstib.com

Title: First Internet Bank of Indiana

Navigation: Go directly to the above URL.

Application: Perform the following operations, and answer the following questions:

1. Click on "Contact," then click on "Find Answers." What issues arise with online banking that do not arise at traditional banks? In what ways are these advantages or disadvantages for Internet banks?

2. Back up to the "Personal Accounts" page and review the personal banking services that First Internet Bank provides. Then back up again and click on "Business Accounts" and review those services. Can you think of any basic banking services traditionally available from bricks-and-mortar banks that this Internet bank does not provide?

For Group Study and Analysis: Divide the class into two groups, and have both groups compare the online banking services and interest rates available from First Internet Bank of Indiana and another Internet bank, Nexity Bank of Birmingham, Alabama (http://www.nexitybank.com). Reconvene the class, and discuss factors that might contribute to different approaches at these two Internet banks.

Selected References and Further Reading

Bank for International Settlements. *Security of Electronic Money.* Basel, Switzerland: 1996.

Board of Governors of the Federal Reserve System. *Report to the Congress on the Application of the Electronic Fund Transfer Act to Electronic Stored-Value Products.* Washington, D.C.: March 1997.

Committee on Payment and Settlement Systems. "Survey of Electronic Money Developments." Bank for International Settlements, May 2000.

Cronin, Mary J., ed. *Banking and Finance on the Internet.* New York: John Wiley & Sons, 1998.

DeYoung, Robert. "The Financial Performance of Pure Play Internet Banks." Federal Reserve Bank of Chicago *Economic Perspectives* (First Quarter 2001): 60–75.

European Central Bank. *Report on Electronic Money.* Frankfurt, Germany: August 1998.

Furst, Karen, William Lang, and Daniel Nolle. "Who Offers Internet Banking?" Special Studies on Technology and

Banking, Office of the Comptroller of the Currency, *Quarterly Journal* 19 (June 2000): 27–46.

Group of Ten. *Electronic Money: Consumer Protection, Law Enforcement, Supervisory and Cross-Border Issues*. Report of the Working Party on Electronic Money, April 1997.

Mester, Loretta. "Changes in the Use of Electronic Means of Payment." Federal Reserve Bank of Philadelphia *Business Review* (Fourth Quarter 2001): 10–12.

Schreft, Stacey L. "Clicking with Dollars: How Consumers Can Pay for Purchases from E-tailers." Federal Reserve Bank of Kansas City *Economic Review* 87 (First Quarter 2002): 37–64.

———. "Looking Forward: The Role for Government in Regulating Electronic Cash." Federal Reserve Bank of Kansas City *Economic Review* 82 (Fourth Quarter 1997): 59–84.

Sheehan, Kevin P. "Electronic Cash." *FDIC Banking Review* 11 (1998): 1–8.

MoneyXtra

moneyxtra!

Log on to the MoneyXtra Web site now (**http://moneyxtra.swcollege.com**) for additional learning resources such as practice quizzes, case studies, readings, and additional economic applications.

Chapter 3

Financial Markets, Instruments, and Institutions

In nations such as Brazil, Colombia, Paraguay, and Peru, price-level-adjusted mortgages, or PLAMs, are commonly used to finance home purchases. Unlike traditional fixed-rate mortgages, for which nominal monthly payments are fixed, or adjustable-rate mortgages, for which monthly payments vary with changes in market interest rates, under a PLAM the real *monthly payments are constant over the life of the loan. That is, nominal monthly payments adjust automatically to variations in the price level so that the real value of each month's payment is the same. As a result, PLAMs are most clearly desirable to residents of nations with particularly high inflation rates.*

In the United States, PLAMs have not been very popular for two reasons. For one thing, U.S. inflation rates have been relatively low in recent years. For another, it is not always clear how U.S. tax laws and loan disclosure rules and related regulations would apply to PLAMs.

Another nontraditional mortgage, which does shows signs of catching on in the United States, is the reverse mortgage, *available to people aged sixty-two and older. This type of mortgage permits older individuals to borrow against the equity accumulated in their homes. Instead of the normal arrangement in which a borrower makes monthly payments to a mortgage lender, the lender issuing a reverse mortgage makes monthly payments to the borrower until the house is sold or the borrower dies. At that time, all equity in the house reverts to the mortgage lender. Although reverse mortgages have existed since the 1960s, as the portion of the American population aged sixty-two and older has grown, the incentive to enter into reverse mortgages has increased. Consequently, the market for reverse mortgages, which already involves billions of dollars, is growing rapidly.*

Fundamental Issues

1. What is the main economic function of financial markets?
2. What are primary and secondary markets for financial instruments, and what distinguishes money markets from capital markets?
3. What are the key financial instruments of the money and capital markets?
4. Why has automated financial trading grown, and what are its implications for world financial markets?
5. Why do financial intermediaries exist, and what accounts for international financial intermediation?
6. What are the main types of financial institutions?

Fixed-rate mortgages, adjustable-rate mortgages, PLAMs, and reverse mortgages are just a few of the vast array of *financial instruments*. In this chapter, you will learn about financial instruments and the markets in which they are traded.

Saving and Investment in a Global Economy

As we discuss below, *financial markets* help direct financial resources from the owners of these resources to those who require them to finance productive activities. The owners of financial resources are individuals who accumulate resources rather than consuming them each year. These people are savers of financial resources. When other individuals or businesses use financial resources to finance productive endeavors, they invest these resources. These two groups—those who save and those who invest—interact in financial markets as follows:

- **Saving.** The key economic function of financial markets is to channel saving to productive investment. **Saving** is forgone consumption. Thus, when an individual does not spend all after-tax income received within a given year, that individual has saved some of her money income.
- **Investment.** Savers, however, do not want their savings to sit idly in money balances (currency and non-interest-bearing demand deposits) if there are alternatives that yield positive returns. Typically, such alternatives exist. The reason is that other individuals or firms normally engage in **investment,** or additions to the stock of capital goods. **Capital goods** are goods that may be used to produce other goods or services in the future.

Investment in capital goods can require significant financial resources, so individuals and firms that invest often must borrow funds or sell ownership shares via initial public offerings or issues of new shares. They obtain these funds from savers with a promise to return the borrowed funds on some future date. Those who invest also promise *interest,* or payments for the use of funds borrowed from savers. They finance these interest payments using revenues from the production that their new capital goods make possible.

Savers are the ultimate *lenders* in our economy. Many of the *borrowers* are firms or individuals who wish to undertake investment. Some individuals, of course, borrow to finance current consumption. Nevertheless, the main reasons for lending and borrowing are that savers desire future interest income on the savings that they hold today, while most borrowers desire to finance investment projects that they expect to yield returns in the future.

Saving: Forgone consumption.

Investment: Additions to the stock of capital goods.

Capital goods: Goods that may be used to produce other goods or services in the future.

1. What is the main economic function of financial markets? The main economic role of financial markets is to direct saving to those who wish to make capital investments, or purchases of capital goods that may be used to produce additional goods and services in the future.

Financial Markets and Instruments

Financial markets facilitate the lending of funds from saving to those who wish to undertake investments. Those who wish to borrow to finance investment projects sell IOUs to savers, as Figure 3-1 illustrates. Financial markets are markets for these IOUs, which can have many forms. The various forms of IOUs are known as **financial instruments.** Such instruments, which are also called **securities,** are claims that those who lend their savings have on the future incomes of the borrowers who use those funds for investment.

When we think of "instruments," we may think of tools such as a surgeon's scalpel. We refer to financial claims as "instruments" because they also are tools, though they are in the form of paper (or electronic) documents. Yet just as a surgeon's instruments can be used to perform delicate tasks, individuals and firms can use financial instruments to undertake crucial exchanges of financial resources. They can also use financial instruments to help reduce risks of financial loss.

Financial markets can be categorized in two basic ways. One distinguishes between *primary* and *secondary* markets by separating types of financial markets depending on whether or not they are markets for newly issued instruments. The other distinguishes between *money* and *capital* markets, depending on the maturities of the instruments that are traded in the markets. The **maturity** of an instrument is the time from the date of issue until final principal and interest payments are due to its holders. Maturities of less than a year are **short-term maturities,** maturities in excess of ten years are long-term maturities, and maturities ranging from one to ten years are **intermediate-term maturities.**

Financial instruments: Claims that those who lend their savings have on the future incomes of the borrowers who use those funds for investment.

Securities: Financial instruments.

Maturity: The time until final principal and interest payments are due to the holders of a financial instrument.

Short-term maturity: Maturity of less than one year.

Intermediate-term maturity: Maturity between one year and ten years.

Primary market: A financial market in which newly issued financial instruments are purchased and sold.

Primary and Secondary Financial Markets

One way of categorizing the many financial markets is to distinguish between primary and secondary financial markets.

PRIMARY MARKETS A **primary market** is a financial market in which newly issued financial instruments are purchased and sold. For instance, a newly formed business that wishes to sell shares of ownership (commonly called

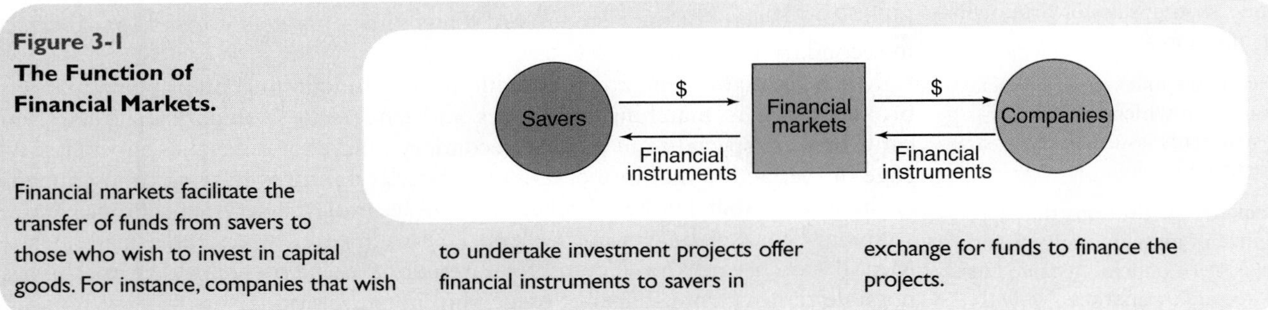

Figure 3-1
The Function of Financial Markets.

Financial markets facilitate the transfer of funds from savers to those who wish to invest in capital goods. For instance, companies that wish to undertake investment projects offer financial instruments to savers in exchange for funds to finance the projects.

"stocks") offers these shares for sale in a primary financial market. Likewise, when the U.S. Treasury issues new Treasury bonds to fund some of the public debt (which increases when the federal government spends more than its revenues), the Treasury sells these instruments in a primary market.

The first attempt by a business to issue ownership shares to the public in the primary market is called an *initial public offering (IPO)*. Although businesses could attempt to manage an IPO on their own, many rely on the assistance of **investment banks.** These institutions specialize in marketing initial ownership shares offered by new businesses. An investment bank typically *underwrites* such issues, meaning that the investment bank guarantees the business's initial fixed share price. Essentially, the investment bank temporarily purchases the shares of the business. Then it attempts to resell them in the primary market at a slightly higher price. The investment bank keeps the difference between the purchase price and the resale price (often 10 percent) as a profit.

On the Web
What are the prices for the latest IPO filings? To view a directory of the most recent IPOs, visit IPO Central at Hoover's Online at http://www.hoovers.com.

Secondary Markets Most financial instruments sold in primary markets have maturities ranging from several months to many years. Shares of ownership in firms have no set maturities. Firms in principle can last "forever," if they are going concerns. Bonds issued by the U.S. Treasury have fixed maturities in excess of ten years. Yet at some point after the initial purchase of such ownership shares or bonds, but before their maturity dates, the original purchaser may not wish to hold them any longer. Then that original owner may sell them in a **secondary market,** which is simply a market for financial instruments that were issued at some point in the past.

Secondary markets contribute to the efficient functioning of primary markets, because the ability to buy or sell previously issued financial instruments makes these instruments much more liquid than they would otherwise be. For instance, persons will be much more likely to buy ownership shares in a fledgling company if they know that there is a readily available market where they can sell the shares if they later wish to access their funds or become dissatisfied with the company's performance.

There are a variety of active secondary markets for financial instruments, including secondary markets for U.S. Treasury securities, shares of ownership in corporations, and state and municipal bonds. Now there are also secondary markets for many consumer credit obligations and for business, mortgage, and consumer loans of financial institutions. For instance, each year banks package billions of dollars of their credit-card loans into separate securities that they sell in secondary markets.

Much as investment bankers facilitate the functioning of primary markets, **brokers** assist in matching borrowers and lenders in secondary markets. Typically, brokers specialize in a single secondary market and develop expert knowledge of the factors that influence risks, costs, and returns relating to instruments exchanged in that market. Brokers receive fees for the services they provide to secondary market buyers and sellers. For instance, a broker at a firm such as Merrill Lynch earns fee income for attempting to help clients earn the highest possible returns from shares of ownership in corporations.

Investment banks: Institutions that specialize in marketing and underwriting sales of firm ownership shares.

Secondary market: A financial market in which financial instruments issued in the past are traded.

Brokers: Institutions that specialize in matching buyers and sellers of financial instruments in secondary markets.

Money Markets and Capital Markets

As discussed in more detail below, financial instruments come in a variety of maturities. For instance, there are three-month Treasury bills and twenty-year Treasury bonds. Banks and other depository financial institutions issue six-month certificates of deposit and two-and-a-half-year time deposits.

Firms, banks, and individuals trade these and other instruments in many different financial markets. Economists and traders themselves have adopted the convention of classifying markets into two broad groups based on the maturities of the financial instruments exchanged in the markets. As we shall discuss in the next chapter, the maturities of financial instruments influence their interest yields. Thus, separating financial markets by maturity is a way of grouping together sets of markets whose interest rates tend to be most closely linked.

Money markets: Markets for financial instruments with maturities of less than one year.

Federal funds market: The money market in which banks borrow from and lend to each other deposits that they hold at Federal Reserve banks.

Capital markets: Markets for financial instruments with maturities of one year or more.

MONEY MARKETS The term **money markets** refers to markets for financial instruments with short-term maturities of less than one year. The money markets include markets for short-maturity Treasury securities, including three- and six-month Treasury bills. They also include markets for bank six-month certificates of deposit, which include most of the large certificates of deposit included in the M3 measure of money discussed in Chapter 1.

The market for repurchase agreements is also a money market. Nearly all repurchase agreements have relatively short maturities. Indeed, as we noted in Chapter 1, many repurchase agreements have one-day maturities.

Banks do a significant amount of trading in the market for repurchase agreements. In addition, they lend to each other directly in a money market known as the **federal funds market.** In this private market, banks borrow from and lend to each other deposits that they hold at Federal Reserve banks. This is why it is called a market for "federal" funds, even though the funds actually belong to the lending banks themselves. Federal funds are discussed in more detail in Chapter 4.

Money market trading typically is very active, with many buyers and sellers entering the market with offers each day. As a result, money market instruments tend to be liquid. Because there are so many potential buyers, a seller of an instrument in this market can usually find someone who is willing to buy that instrument at a mutually agreeable price.

CAPITAL MARKETS Markets for financial instruments with maturities of one year or more are called **capital markets.** The reason for this name is that instruments with such long maturities are likely to be associated directly with funding capital investment projects.

There are several different capital markets. Stock shares of ownership in businesses and bonds issued by corporations are traded in separate capital markets. So are longer-term securities issued by the U.S. Treasury and agencies of the U.S. government, state and local municipal securities, home mortgages, and bank commercial and consumer loans.

Trading in capital markets can be very active, but on a given day relatively fewer buyers and sellers generally interact in these markets than in the money markets. As a consequence, capital market instruments are less liquid than money market instruments.

2. What are primary and secondary markets for financial instruments, and what distinguishes money markets from capital markets? Primary markets are markets where newly issued financial instruments are purchased and sold. Secondary markets are markets where previously issued financial instruments are traded. Money markets are markets where financial instruments with maturities of less than one year are traded. Instruments with maturities equal to or more than a year are traded in capital markets.

Money Market Instruments

Each of the many types of financial instruments has its own special set of characteristics. The most straightforward way of categorizing these instruments, however, is according to their maturities.

Money market instruments have maturities shorter than one year. As we mentioned, because they are so widely traded, money market instruments typically are more liquid than capital market instruments. Most also are less risky because of their shorter terms to maturity. Fewer "bad" things can happen within, say, three months than can occur during a span of twenty years. Thus, market traders usually have fewer risk concerns about a corporation's three-month commercial paper than about a twenty-year corporate bond.

Because of their high liquidity and relatively low risk, money market instruments are widely held and traded by banks and other depository institutions. Large corporations and individuals hold and exchange these instruments as well. Figure 3-2 displays the relative magnitudes of outstanding issues of money market instruments.

Figure 3-2
Money Market Instruments Outstanding.

Treasury bills, commercial paper, and certificates of deposit are the predominant instruments traded in the money markets.

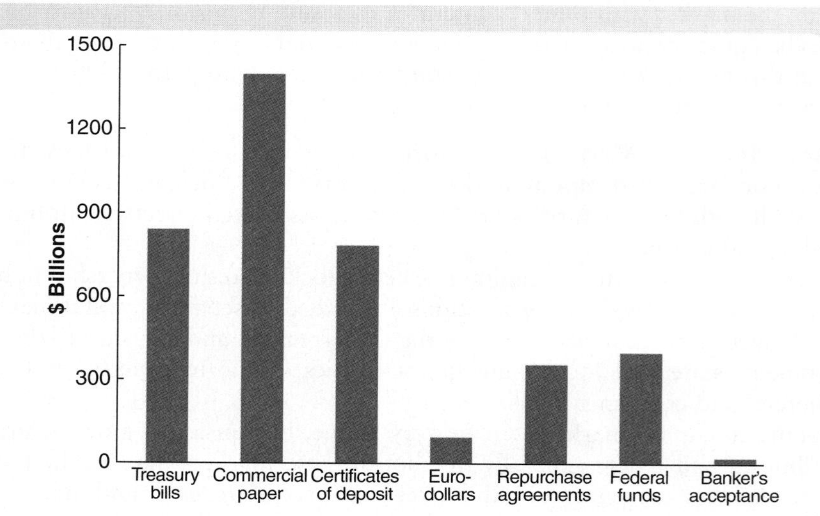

SOURCES: Board of Governors of the Federal Reserve System, *Federal Reserve Bulletin* and HG(301) *Statistical Release*, July 2002.

TREASURY BILLS The U.S. government issues financial instruments called *Treasury securities.* These are U.S. government debt obligations that are exchanged in both the money markets and the capital markets. **Treasury bills (T-bills)** are government-issued financial instruments with maturities of less than a year, so they are money market instruments. Traders widely view T-bills as very safe assets. After all, if the government decides that it needs to pay them off, it can always raise taxes. It is this taxing authority of the government that causes most individuals to regard T-bills as having extremely low risk.

Since 1998, the federal government has issued T-bills with minimum denominations of $1,000. Each successive T-bill denomination is in $5,000 increments. T-bills have terms to maturity of 91 days (three months), 182 days (six months), and 52 weeks (twelve months). The government sells T-bills at discounts from the face-value denominations. T-bills are negotiable instruments, which means that the bearer of a T-bill can sell the bill in the secondary market.

COMMERCIAL PAPER Banks, corporations, and finance companies often need to obtain short-term funding. One way to obtain such funds is to issue **commercial paper,** which is a short-term debt instrument. For businesses, commercial paper has become an important substitute for borrowing directly from banks.

Issuers typically offer commercial paper in maturities from 2 to 270 days. Most issuers sell commercial paper at a discount, just as the Treasury sells T-bills. Some commercial paper instruments offer coupon returns, however.

Typically, only the most creditworthy banks and corporations are able to sell commercial paper to finance short-term debts. Nevertheless, Moody's and Standard and Poor's assign credit ratings to different issuers. Consequently, commercial paper issues of some companies may have higher market yields than those of others because of differences in risk perceptions.

CERTIFICATES OF DEPOSIT Banks also raise short-term funds by issuing **certificates of deposit (CDs).** Most CDs are short-term time deposits with maturities of six months, although banks also issue CDs with longer maturities. At one time, CDs were *nonnegotiable,* meaning that the original purchasers could not sell them without incurring interest penalties. Since 1961, however, banks have issued *negotiable CDs.* They now are traded actively in a secondary money market.

EURODOLLARS As you learned in Chapter 1, dollar-denominated deposits in banks located outside the United States are called Eurodollar deposits. These deposits may be in foreign banks or in foreign branches of U.S. banks. Many of these deposits are negotiable. In effect, a Eurodollar deposit amounts to a type of CD that is held outside the United States.

REPURCHASE AGREEMENTS As defined in Chapter 1, a repurchase agreement is a contract to sell a financial asset with the understanding that the seller will buy back the asset at a later date and, typically, at a higher price. This means that effectively the seller of the asset *borrows* from the buyer. Thus, a repurchase agreement amounts to a very short term loan. Most repurchase agreements have maturities ranging between one and fourteen days. Banks and large corporations are active traders in the market for repurchase agreements.

FEDERAL FUNDS When banks borrow from or lend to one another, the funds that they trade are federal funds. These funds are privately owned but are held on deposit at Federal Reserve banks. Many federal funds loans have maturities

Treasury bills (T-bills): Short-term debt obligations of the federal government issued with maturities of three, six, or twelve months.

Commercial paper: A short-term debt instrument issued by businesses in lieu of borrowing from banks.

Certificates of deposit (CDs): Time deposits issued by banks and other depository institutions. Many CDs are negotiable instruments that are traded in secondary markets.

Banker's acceptance: A bank loan typically used by a company to finance storage or shipment of goods.

Equities: Shares of ownership, such as corporate stock, issued by business firms.

Dividends: Periodic payments to holders of corporate equities.

of one day, though maturities of a week or two are not uncommon. The interest rate at which federal funds are exchanged is the *federal funds rate.* As you will learn in Chapter 20, the federal funds rate is a closely watched indicator of Federal Reserve monetary policy.

BANKER'S ACCEPTANCES A **banker's acceptance** is a bank loan that typically is used by a company to finance storage or shipment of goods. These instruments commonly arise from international trade arrangements. They are traded in secondary money markets.

Capital Market Instruments

The maturities of capital market instruments exceed one year. Financial instruments with both intermediate-term (one to ten years) maturities and long-term (more than ten years) maturities are included in this category.

Capital market instruments generally are regarded as somewhat more risky than money market instruments. They also are less liquid than money market instruments. Figure 3-3 shows the relative outstanding amounts of various types of capital market instruments.

Have stock prices generally risen or fallen in recent months? Take a look at the recent performance of the S&P stock price index via EconData Online.

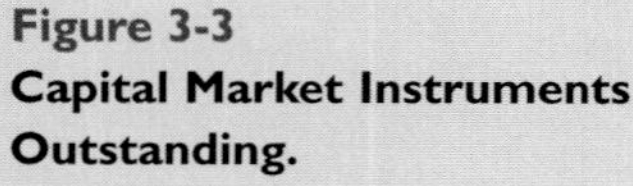
http://moneyxtra.swcollege.com

EQUITIES Business **equities** are shares of ownership, such as *common stock,* that corporations issue. Owners of equities are *residual claimants* on the income and net worth of a corporation. This means that all other holders of the corporation's debt must be paid before the equity owners. The key advantage of equity ownership, however, is that the rate of return on equities varies with the profitability of the firm. Equities typically offer **dividends,** which are periodic payments to holders that are related to the corporation's profits.

Because corporations are ongoing concerns as long as they remain profitable, the equities that they issue have no stated maturities. Hence, equities are long-term financial instruments and are classified among capital market instruments.

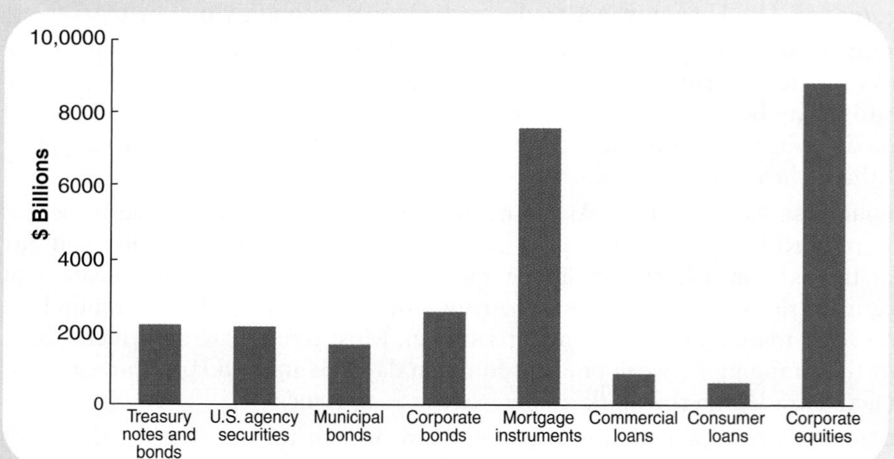

Figure 3-3
Capital Market Instruments Outstanding.

Corporate equities, mortgage instruments, and Treasury notes and bonds are key instruments of the capital markets.

SOURCES: Board of Governors of the Federal Reserve System, *Federal Reserve Bulletin* and HG(301) *Statistical Release*, July 2002.

Common Stock Equity shares most commonly are issued in two forms: common stock and preferred stock. Ownership of **common stock** entitles the shareholder to have some direct say about how the company conducts its business. As a common stock owner, the shareholder is entitled to attend meetings where shareholders can vote in elections for a company's board of directors and have some input concerning matters such as management strategy. (Shareholders do not have to attend meetings to vote.)

The fact that owners of common stock are the *residual claimants* means that if a company goes bankrupt, they are the last in line for any remaining assets of the firm. These residual assets could very well have less value than the stated value of the company's stock. Hence, owners of common stock take on more default risk than any other creditors of the company. For this reason they are granted the greatest say in management.

The potential liability of a stockholder, however, is limited to the value of the individual's shareholdings. Hence, if a company goes bankrupt, the most that a stockholder can lose is the funds that he or she has allocated to its shares.

Preferred Stock Holders of **preferred stock** have no voting rights. They sacrifice this power to influence the company's management in exchange for a guarantee that they will receive any dividends that the company may pay to stockholders. And if the company is forced into bankruptcy, preferred stockholders have first claim on any residual value of the firm after other creditors have been paid.

Stock Exchanges Corporate equity shares are traded on **stock exchanges,** which are organized physical locations that function as marketplaces for stocks. Members of stock exchanges function both as brokers and as dealers. As brokers they trade on behalf of others, and as dealers they trade on their own accounts.

There are several stock exchanges in the United States. The oldest and largest is the New York Stock Exchange (NYSE), which began in 1792. Roughly half of the stock trading in the United States is done on the NYSE. Shares of more than 3,000 companies, including many of the largest U.S. corporations, are traded there. The number of membership positions in the NYSE, called "seats," is fixed at 1,366. Over 500 of these seats are owned by securities firms. About a third of these firms are Exchange *specialists,* which are responsible for laying out and honoring basic ground rules for orderly trading activity in the Exchange. Figure 3-4 (p. 60) explains how to read NYSE data published in the *Wall Street Journal.*

Over-the-Counter Stocks In recent years a number of corporations have chosen not to be listed on the organized exchanges. Shares in these corporations are **over-the-counter (OTC) stocks** that are traded in decentralized markets. OTC trading volumes have increased in recent years as more OTC stocks are traded on electronic networks that link traders around the world.

In the United States, most OTC stocks are traded on the **National Association of Securities Dealers Automated Quotation (Nasdaq)** system. In February 1971, Nasdaq was launched as a tiny network of 100 or so securities firms linked by \$25 million worth of interconnected "desktop devices" to trade about 2,800 OTC stocks. At that time, trading in the rest of the financial world was done largely through phone calls, and stock prices were often distributed by runners on foot. Indeed, the screens displaying the OTC stock prices on Nasdaq's

Common stock: Shares of corporate ownership that entitle the owner to vote on management issues but offer no guarantees of dividends or of market value in the event of corporate bankruptcy.

Preferred stock: Shares of corporate ownership that entail no voting rights but entitle the owner to dividends if any are paid by the corporation and to any residual value of the corporation after other creditors have been paid.

Stock exchanges: Organized marketplaces for corporate equities and bonds.

Over-the-counter (OTC) stocks: Equity shares offered by companies that do not meet listing requirements for major stock exchanges, or choose not to be listed there, and instead are traded in decentralized markets.

National Association of Securities Dealers Automated Quotation (Nasdaq): The electronic network over which most over-the-counter stocks are traded.

On the Web

What are the latest innovations at Nasdaq? To find out, visit the National Association of Securities Dealers at http://www.nasd.com.

Figure 3-4
Reading Stock Quotations.

Each day the *Wall Street Journal* reports New York Stock Exchange and American Stock Exchange stock prices using the format shown here. To understand how to read published stock quotes, consider the information for each column in the quote for the common stock of Bank of America.

52-WEEK HI	52-WEEK LO	STOCK (SYM)	DIV	YLD %	PE	VOL 100s	CLOSE	NET CHG
2.88	1	Bancol ADS **CIB**	.10e	5.2	...	25	1.93	0.08
26.89	24.64	BcpSoCap **BXSA** n	2.04	7.8	...	349	26.30	−0.10
22.21	13.45	Bncpsouth **BXS**	.60	3.1	14	1102	19.46	−0.14
39.98	25.01	Bandag **BDG**	1.26	3.9	15	544	32.33	0.35
34.21	22.30	Bandag A **BDGA**	1.26	4.4	13	60	28.40	0.15
77.09	50.25	BankAm **BAC**	2.40	3.5	15	81651	68.39	3.14

52 Week Hi: Highest dollar price of a share of Bank of America common stock during the past 52 weeks, which was $77.09.

52 Week Lo: Lowest dollar price of a share of Bank of America common stock during the past 52 weeks, which was $50.25.

Stock: Corporate name of Bank of America.

Sym: Symbol identifying Bank of America, which is BAC.

Div: Annual dollar dividend per share, which was $2.40 per share.

Yld %: Stock yield measured as the annual dividend as a percentage of the closing price for the day, which was $2.40 divided by $68.39 times 100, or approximately 3.5%.

PE: Ratio of stock price to the annual earnings per share, which was equal to 15 for Bank of America.

Vol 100s: Hundreds of Bank of America shares traded this day, or 8,165,100 shares.

Close: Price of Bank of America shares at day's end, or $68.39 per share.

Net Chg: Dollar change in price of Bank of America shares relative to previous day's trading, which was an increase of $3.14.

"desktop devices" were not even known as computer screens—appropriately, because the devices did not actually compute anything. The system simply displayed stock quotes and the phone number of the broker to call to trade. Today, the Nasdaq market links about 500 dealers via true computers, and the market is home to nearly 5,500 stocks, including those of such companies as Microsoft, Intel, and Cisco.

On the Web
What are important issues to keep in mind when building a bond portfolio? Learn more about bond investments at http://www.investinginbonds.com/.

Corporate bonds: Long-term debt instruments of corporations.

Corporate Bonds Corporations may wish to fund capital expansions by borrowing instead of by issuing stock. One way to borrow is by issuing **corporate bonds,** which are long-term debt instruments of corporations. A typical corporate bond pays a fixed amount of interest twice each year until maturity. Some corporate bonds are *convertible,* meaning that the holder has the right to convert them into a certain number of equity shares prior to maturity. Corporations that offer such a convertibility feature usually do so to make the bonds more attractive to potential buyers.

Treasury notes: Treasury securities with maturities ranging from one to ten years.

Treasury Notes and Bonds The U.S. Treasury issues two categories of financial instruments with maturities of more than one year. These are Treasury notes and Treasury bonds. **Treasury notes** have maturities ranging from one to ten years. **Treasury bonds** have maturities of ten years or more. Both notes and bonds have minimum denominations of $1,000. The Treasury sells most notes and bonds at auctions.

Treasury bonds: Treasury securities with maturities of ten years or more.

SECURITIES OF U.S. GOVERNMENT AGENCIES These are long-term debt instruments issued by a variety of federal agencies. For instance, one agency called the General National Mortgage Association (GNMA, or "Ginnie Mae") issues securities backed by the value of household mortgages that it holds.

Municipal bonds: Long-term debt instruments issued by state and local governments.

MUNICIPAL BONDS Long-term securities issued by state and local governments are called **municipal bonds.** An attractive feature of these bonds for many holders is that the interest payments the holders receive typically are tax-free. Consequently, the stated interest rates on municipal bonds are lower than the rates on corporate bonds.

Mortgage loans: Long-term loans to individual homeowners or to businesses for purchases of land and buildings.

Mortgage-backed securities: Financial instruments whose return is based on the underlying returns on mortgage loans.

MORTGAGE LOANS AND MORTGAGE-BACKED SECURITIES Long-term loans to individual homeowners or to businesses for purchases of land and buildings are **mortgage loans.** Most mortgage loans are made initially by savings banks, savings and loan associations, and commercial banks.

These depository institutions sell many of the mortgage loans that they initiate to other institutions in a secondary market. The purchasing institutions, which include GNMA and other governmental or quasi-governmental agencies, fund their mortgage purchases by issuing **mortgage-backed securities.** These are financial instruments whose returns are derived from the underlying returns on the mortgage loans held by the issuer, such as GNMA. The existence of secondary markets for mortgage-backed securities makes mortgage loans more liquid than they would otherwise be.

Commercial loans: Long-term loans made by banks to businesses.

Consumer loans: Long-term loans made by banks and other institutions to individuals.

COMMERCIAL AND CONSUMER LOANS Long-term loans made by banks to businesses are **commercial loans.** Long-term loans that banks and other institutions, such as finance companies, make to individuals are **consumer loans.** Until recently, there were not many secondary markets for these loans, so they traditionally have been the most illiquid capital market instruments. As we shall discuss in Chapter 13, however, banks have worked in recent years to increase the liquidity of the loans that they make.

3. What are the key financial instruments of the money and capital markets? The most important money and capital market instruments are U.S. Treasury securities (bills, notes, and bonds), corporate equities (common and preferred stock), consumer debt instruments (mortgage loans and consumer loans), and corporate debt instruments (commercial paper, corporate bonds, and commercial loans).

The Cybertrading Revolution and Its International Ramifications

New technologies have fundamentally altered the way that many people trade financial instruments. The result has been a growing "internationalization" of financial trading.

Electronic Securities Trading

moneyxtra!

Another Perspective

For a more detailed discussion of the role of ECNs, see the Chapter 3 reading, entitled "The Emergence of Electronic Communications Networks in the U.S. Equity Markets," by James McAndrews and Chris Stefanadis of the Federal Reserve Bank of New York.

http://moneyxtra.swcollege.com

Electronic trading began in the mid-1990s with just a few Internet addresses, such as www.etrade.com, www.schwab.com, and www.lombard.com. These Web sites offered something never before available: the capability to buy shares of stock online. (Some Web-based stock-trading systems specialize in providing trade-execution services to so-called institutional investors; see *Cyber Focus: The Growing Role of Electronic Communications Networks in U.S. Stock Markets.*)

Lower Fees Trading online offers several advantages, including low brokerage fees. For instance, buying 100 shares of stock in International Business Machines (IBM) from a traditional brokerage firm entails fees in the neighborhood of $100, whereas online brokers typically charge $10—or even less—for the transaction. The result has been predictable: online securities trading has taken off.

Speed Counts Online trading is faster as well as less expensive. Anyone can reach Internet-based brokerage accounts from any computer with a secure Web browser. Today, literally at one's fingertips are hundreds of sites offering investment research sources and trading capabilities—all of which help make the Web a logical fit with the fast-paced, high-tech world of Wall Street. After a typical Internet trader punches in an ID and account password, she often has access to a package of services that might otherwise be quite costly if purchased separately, such as portfolio tracking and a database containing information about such things as companies' market capitalization and earnings growth. After conducting market research, the Internet trader can scan her portfolio of holdings, search for key information on companies whose stock she owns or is interested in, and send a request to buy or sell stock, all in a few minutes. (Trading stocks on the Internet has become a full-time job for some individuals; see on page 64 *Management Focus: Does "Day Trading" Pay?*)

Some Brokerage Firms Benefit Internet trading also provides payoffs for the brokerage firms that offer it. Most Wall Street discount brokers now accept Internet-generated orders. Internet-based brokerage firms can get by with less printed marketing material to send to clients, smaller customer-service staffs, and fewer physical branches.

Direct Offering to Savers Many companies, such as Ford Motor Company and IBM, now issue commercial paper directly to savers through interactive online services. On screen, commercial paper traders can see the issuer, maturity, settlement date, yield, ratings, and trading instructions. Typically, a commercial paper exchange can be completed in as little as eight seconds, although it can take longer if the two sides bargain about the price or yield. If the trader wishes to bargain, the computer program usually gives customers about a half-minute to decide whether to take the yield offered or to counter with a lower yield. At the conclusion of a transaction, the computer automatically thanks the saver and logs the time of the exchange.

Internet trading in commercial paper began in early 1996. By the end of that year, commercial paper trading volumes had surpassed $100 million per day. Current daily volumes average hundreds of millions of dollars.

GLOBAL | POLICY | CYBER Focus | MANAGEMENT

The Growing Role of Electronic Communications Networks in U.S. Stock Markets

About a third of the average daily transaction volume on Nasdaq is processed on *electronic communications networks (ECNs),* which are Internet-based auction networks linking buyers and sellers of stocks around the world.

The Advantages of Executing Stock Trades via ECNs

Moving stock trading to the Internet offers several advantages for investors. One is the ability to trade more hours each day. The two largest ECNs, Instinet and Island, are open 24 hours per day.

ECNs also offer investors the ability to consider stocks from multiple exchanges simultaneously. Instinet, for instance, lists stocks from sixteen different exchanges. Island lists stocks from both Nasdaq and the New York Stock Exchange.

Another advantage is that ECNs arguably offer investors more transparency than traditional stock markets. New York Stock Exchange specialists have exclusive access to information concerning all buy and sell orders that come to the trading floor for their stocks. In contrast, even though individual investors must have an account with a broker-dealer subscriber before their orders can be routed to an ECN for execution, anyone can access an ECN system using a personal computer, laptop computer, or any other Internet-ready device. Any interested party can look up buy and sell orders for any Nasdaq stocks at ECN Web sites.

The Emerging Trading Platform of Choice for Institutional Investors

So far ECNs do not offer their services directly to private individuals. Instead, ECNs specialize in executing trades on behalf of so-called *institutional investors,* such as equity funds and pension funds. For institutional investors, a major attraction of ECNs is that trades executed on an ECN are anonymous. ECN transaction records list only the price and the amount traded, not the trader's identity. This protects institutional investors from a practice called "front running," in which traders somehow learn that an institutional investor plans to buy or sell stock and trade in advance in an effort to profit from small price changes that might result from the institutional investor's later transaction.

ECNs typically charge brokers fees ranging from $1 per trade to $1 per hundred shares traded, which is significantly below the fees charged by the traditional order-execution systems employed by broker-dealers. This is why more than a third of all stock trades now take place on ECNs, even though they have only been in existence since 1992.

FOR CRITICAL ANALYSIS: Why do you suppose that so much stock trading still takes place on physical trading floors instead of the Internet?

International Cybertrading

What are CORES, MATIF, and CATS? CORES, or the Computer-Assisted Order Routing and Execution System, is a completely automated system based in Tokyo that links buyers and sellers of government securities, corporate bonds, and equity shares. MATIF, or the Marché à Terme International de France, is an analogous system located in Paris. CATS, the Toronto-based Computer-Assisted Trading System, performs the same basic functions. These trading systems, plus others in such locales as Denmark, Singapore, Sweden, the United Kingdom, and the United States, share the common feature that they permit traders in financial markets to place orders for purchases and sales of securities via computers.

On the Web
How has MATIF adjusted to the increasing integration of European financial markets? To learn the answer to this question, visit MATIF at http://www.matif.fr.

GLOBAL POLICY CYBER **MANAGEMENT Focus**

Does "Day Trading" Pay?

Some Internet traders, known as *day traders,* conduct numerous securities trades each day with a primary goal of earning a living through the profits derived from their activities. Many day traders buy and sell securities from their homes, but a number also engage in their trading activities at so-called *day trading firms,* which offer day traders access to services such as real-time data feeds and up-to-the-minute news links for monthly fees ranging from $50 to in excess of $600. Day trading firms also charge day traders commissions ranging from $15 to $25 per trade. Traders who use these services must take these costs into account when calculating their profits.

Figure 3-5 shows the trading revenues day traders at such firms must earn each month to break even under alternative fee structures. For instance, if a day trader who pays a day trading firm just $50 a month and a commission of $14.95 per trade engages in fifty trades per day, he must earn net revenues of $15,000 on his trades just to cover his explicit costs.

Unfortunately for some day traders, as well as for others who trade frequently online, evidence indicates that people who engage in more stock purchases and sales tend to earn lower overall returns on their portfolios. Terrance Odean and Brad Barber of the University of California at Davis studied the trading behavior and earnings of more than 1,600 investors who switched from phone-based trading through brokers to online trading in the 1990s. They found that the average returns on the stock portfolios of these individuals declined from about 2 percent above the market average to about 3 percent below the market average. Odean and Barber blamed this decline on the more active and speculative purchases and sales of stocks that occurred when people started trading online. In other words, some online traders may have a tendency to act impulsively, resulting in more trading, hasty decision making, and lower earnings.

FOR CRITICAL ANALYSIS: Why might some people desire to engage in day trading even though they may earn below-average returns as a consequence?

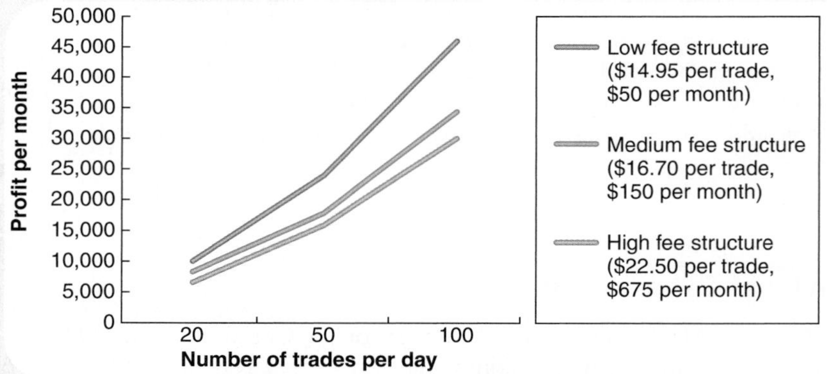

Figure 3-5 Monthly Revenues That Day Traders Using Services of Day Trading Firms Must Earn to Break Even.

This chart plots the monthly trading revenues that a day trader must earn based on alternative fees and daily trading volumes.

SOURCE: Securities and Exchange Commission.

MECHANICS OF AUTOMATED FINANCIAL TRADING Each automated trading system has its own unique characteristics, but in general computer-connected traders use system-specific software programs to access information on current market terms on a number of financial instruments. The software displays on the trader's computer screen the best bid and offer with the amounts involved, the most recent sale price and quantity traded, and related spot market prices for reference. The trader may then use the computer's keyboard to interact with the system and make trades via appropriate commands.

Automated trading has made possible nearly seamless, around-the-clock securities trading. When financial markets open in Tokyo, Hong Kong, Australia, and Singapore, it is evening of the previous day in New York and Chicago. At this time, a trader in Tokyo, for instance, may see an acceptable asking price for a financial instrument in New York and initiate a transaction to purchase the instrument. If the instrument is a U.S. Treasury security, then ownership is transferred and payment settled the next business day in the United States. A transaction arranged, for instance, on Wednesday in Tokyo—Tuesday night in New York—would settle on Thursday in New York, about a day and a half later.

POLICY ISSUES OF GLOBALIZED CYBERTRADING The globalization of financial markets brought about by automated trading has raised two problems for policymakers. One concerns how rules for securities trading on various national trading systems should be adapted to the new global trading environment. Nations with more demanding requirements for trading on their securities exchanges may incur fewer risks to their systems as trading becomes more globalized. At the same time, however, their exchanges may lose business to nations with less stringent rules.

On the Web
What regulatory issues are currently being pursued by the United Kingdom's Financial Services Authority? You can find out by visiting the FSA at http://www.fsa.gov.uk/.

A second concern for policymakers is that automated trading across borders has the potential to exacerbate financial crises. As we shall discuss in greater depth in Chapter 5, international cybertrading also increases the speed at which traders can sell one nation's financial instruments and reallocate funds to holdings of instruments issued by another nation. Thus, traders located far from the scene can respond very quickly to financial uncertainties in a country or region. Although this capability is advantageous for individual traders, there may be drawbacks for the countries experiencing such uncertainties. For instance, if many traders respond to greater uncertainty about a country's financial prospects by liquidating their holdings of financial instruments issued by that country, the result can be a collapse in the prices of those instruments. Thus, cybertrading can increase the swiftness with which financial uncertainty gives way to financial crisis. It can also increase the speed with which a financial crisis in one nation or region spills over into another.

4. Why has automated financial trading grown, and what are its implications for world financial markets? Although cybertrading of financial instruments may tempt some people to buy and sell with a frequency that actually reduces their average returns, an increasing number of individuals trade stocks and bonds via Internet brokers and other automated trading systems because of their convenience and lower costs. Cybertrading across national borders raises two fundamental policy issues. One is the potential mismatch of national regulatory responses to cybertrading. The other is the potential for widespread use of automated trading across national borders to heighten national or regional financial uncertainties and to speed the transmission of financial crises from one country or region to another.

Financial intermediation: Indirect finance through the services of an institutional "middleman" that channels funds from savers to those who ultimately make capital investments.

Domestic and International Financial Intermediation

When a saver allocates funds to a company by purchasing a newly issued corporate bond, she effectively lends directly to the company. That is, she takes part in *directly financing* the capital investment that the company wishes to undertake.

But the process of financing business investment is not always so direct. Consider, for instance, a situation in which the saver also holds a long-term time deposit with a bank. The bank can use these funds, together with those of other depositors, to purchase the same company's corporate bonds. In this instance, the saver has *indirectly financed* business capital investment. The bank, in turn, has *intermediated* the financing of the investment.

Figure 3-6 below illustrates the distinction between direct and indirect finance. In the case of direct finance, the process does not involve a financial intermediary such as a bank. A saver lends directly to parties who invest. In the case of indirect finance, however, some other institution allocates the funds of savers to those who wish to invest in capital.

This latter process of indirect finance, in which an institution stands between savers and ultimate borrowers, is **financial intermediation.** The institutions that serve as the "middlemen" in this process are *financial intermediaries*. They exist solely to channel the funds of savers to ultimate borrowers.

Asymmetric Information

Why do many savers choose to hold their funds at a financial intermediary instead of lending them directly? Most economists agree that one key reason is *asymmetric information* in financial markets.

Suppose, for instance, that a resident of Seattle, Washington, has an opportunity to purchase a relatively high-yield municipal bond issued by a town in New

Figure 3-6
Indirect Finance through Financial Intermediaries.

Those savers who exchange funds for the financial instruments of companies in financial markets undertake *direct finance* of the capital investments of those companies. Financial intermediaries make *indirect finance* possible by issuing their own financial instruments and using the funds that they obtain from savers to finance capital investments of businesses.

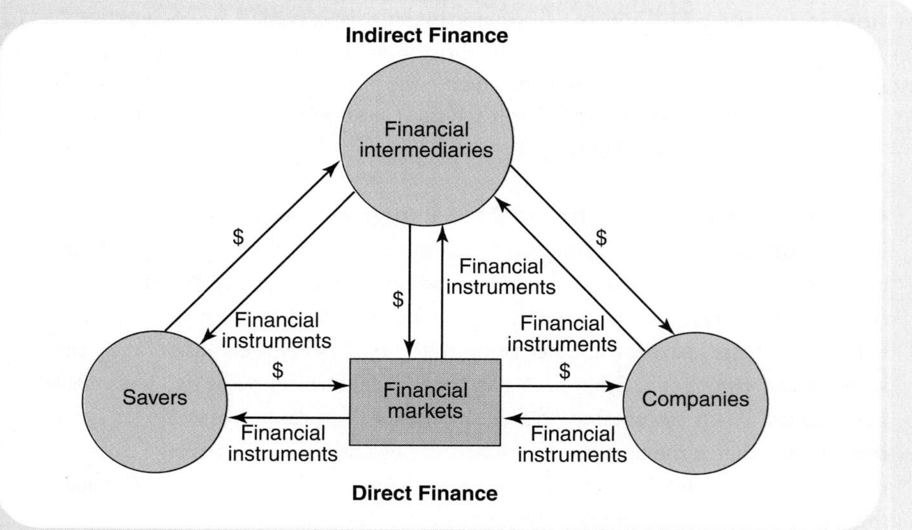

Jersey. One reason that the municipal bond may have a relatively high yield is that the town issuing the bond intends to direct the funds it raises to a risky investment project. For instance, the town may be planning to use the funds to build a convention-center hotel and auditorium complex that has uncertain financial prospects. Unless the Seattle resident happens to be an expert on the economics of municipal convention centers, he likely will find it difficult to evaluate the true riskiness of the municipal bond. This makes it hard for him to compare the yield on this bond with yields on alternative financial instruments.

In contrast, the New Jersey town issuing the municipal bond likely has considerable information about the prospects for its convention center. On the one hand, the prospects may be very good for its long-term financial success. Perhaps the city has hard evidence that it can expect significant earnings from the project. On the other hand, the program may have been launched primarily for the short-term political gains that the mayor and town council expect to reap from pleasing owners of construction companies and other town businesspersons. Either way, the town issuing the municipal bond has information about its risk that the Seattle resident does not possess. Whenever one party in a financial transaction has information not possessed by the other party, **asymmetric information** exists.

Asymmetric information: Information possessed by one party to a financial transaction but not by the other party.

Adverse selection: The problem that those who desire to issue financial instruments are most likely to use the funds they receive for unworthy, high-risk projects.

Moral hazard: The possibility that a borrower may engage in more risky behavior after a loan has been made.

ADVERSE SELECTION In the situation just described, the New Jersey town has information that the Seattle resident will not have when contemplating whether to purchase the town's municipal bond. Suppose the town's leaders know at the outset that the long-term prospects for the convention center are poor, but they think voters like the idea. In this circumstance, the town's leaders know that their bond may have *adverse,* or unfavorable, implications for those who purchase it. This aspect of asymmetric information is called **adverse selection;** it refers to the potential for those who desire funds for undeserving projects to be the most likely to wish to borrow funds or to issue debt instruments. Because people such as the Seattle resident know that the adverse-selection problem exists, they may be less willing to lend to or hold debt instruments issued by those seeking to finance otherwise high-quality projects.

MORAL HAZARD Now suppose that the leaders of the town issuing the municipal bond have every reason to believe the convention center they have planned will be a long-term financial success. After the town sells the bonds, however, an electoral turnover takes place, and the new town leaders double the size of the convention center, almost ensuring that it will fail to be profitable over the long run. This action increases the risk that bondholders will not receive the promised yields on the town's municipal bond. This possibility that a borrower may behave in a way that increases risk after a loan has been made or a debt instrument has been purchased is **moral hazard.** In other words, after a financial transaction has taken place, a borrower may undertake actions that raise the riskiness of the financial instrument that the borrower has already issued, thereby acting "immorally" from the perspective of the lender.

To test your understanding of asymmetric-information concepts, contemplate the problems that a government faces when it acts as a financial intermediary by providing deposit insurance to banks. Go to the Chapter 3 Case Study, entitled "Asymmetric Information and Deposit Insurance."
http://moneyxtra.swcollege.com

One way for the Seattle resident to deal with the adverse-selection and moral-hazard problems he faces is to make several trips to assess and then to monitor the New Jersey town's convention-center project. By acquiring as much hands-on information as possible, the Seattle bondholder could reduce the informational asymmetry he experiences concerning the municipal bond's prospects. This

Economies of scale: The reduction in the average cost of fund management that can be achieved by pooling savings together and spreading management costs across many people.

International financial diversification: The process of spreading portfolio risk by holding both U.S.-issued and foreign-issued financial instruments.

endeavor would be very costly, however. The Seattle bondholder would have to pay the direct costs of making the trips and would also incur opportunity costs, because all the time he devoted to information collecting could be used in other ways.

Benefits of Financial Intermediation

A fundamental reason for the existence of financial intermediaries is to collect information on behalf of savers so that they will not have to incur these direct and opportunity costs. Financial intermediaries cannot completely eliminate the adverse-selection and moral-hazard problems resulting from asymmetric information. Nevertheless, they can reduce these problems by specializing in gathering information about the likely prospects of financial instruments and monitoring the performance of those who issue such instruments.

Economies of Scale

Another key reason for the existence of financial intermediaries is **economies of scale,** or the reduction in average operating costs that can be achieved as a financial trader's scale of operations increases. Some financial intermediaries assist people in pooling their funds, thereby increasing the amount of funds that are saved. Pooling allows an intermediary to manage a larger amount of funds, thereby reducing average fund management costs below those that people would incur if they managed their savings individually. If intermediaries can manage funds for many savers at a lower average cost than all the savers would face if they managed their funds alone, then financial economies of scale exist. Several financial institutions, such as mutual funds and pension funds, owe their existence in large part to their ability to realize such cost reductions on behalf of individual savers.

Financial Intermediation across National Boundaries

Instead of buying a bond issued by a New Jersey municipality, the Seattle resident in our example might contemplate purchasing a bond issued by a municipality located across the border in Canada. The U.S. saver might wish to hold bonds issued by a Canadian city for several reasons. One reason might be to earn an anticipated higher return.

Another reason might be to avoid risks specific to the United States by allocating a portion of savings to Canadian municipal bonds. More broadly, the saver's goal might be to achieve overall risk reductions via **international financial diversification,** or holding bonds issued in various nations and thereby spreading portfolio risks across both U.S.-issued *and* foreign-issued financial instruments.

International Financial Intermediation Rather than buying U.S. and Canadian municipal bonds, our Seattle resident might decide to allocate part of his savings to a global bond mutual fund, thereby becoming a participant in the process of *international financial intermediation.* This is the indirect finance of capital investment across national borders by financial intermediaries such as banks, investment companies, and pension funds.

The rationales for international financial intermediation are the same as the justifications for domestic intermediation. For the Seattle-based U.S. saver, for example, evaluating the riskiness of Canadian bonds presents asymmetric-information problems that are probably at least as severe as those associated with assessing the riskiness of U.S. bonds. By allocating a portion of his total savings to a global bond mutual fund operated, say, by an investment company, the saver assigns that company the task of judging and tracking the prospects and performances of bond issuers around the world. In exchange for this service, the saver pays the investment company management fees.

ECONOMIES OF SCALE AND GLOBAL BANKING The Eurocurrency markets are at the center of international banking activities. Very few nations' capital investment projects are purely domestically financed. Even in the United States, non-U.S. banks finance a part of investment. Today, the largest U.S.-based multinational corporations on average have accounts with more foreign banks than U.S. banks.

Furthermore, as Table 3-1 indicates, the world's largest banks are not necessarily located in the United States. Most of the largest banking institutions, sometimes called *megabanks,* are based in Europe and Japan. These megabanks take in deposits and lend throughout the world. They report their profits and pay taxes in their home nations, but otherwise they are truly international banking institutions.

One possible reason that megabanks exist is economies of scale, or a reduction in average operating costs as a bank's size increases. Some economists argue that a particular form of economies of scale may help explain the megabank phenomenon: *economies of scale in information processing.* According to these economists, because many companies now have operations that span the globe, banks must also have worldwide offices to assess and monitor the creditworthiness of these companies. Having an international presence, they argue, allows banks to address asymmetric-information problems at lower average cost than they could if they were purely domestic intermediaries. Thus, this explanation of the megabank phenomenon hinges on the existence of *both* asymmetric information *and* economies of scale in international banking operations.

Table 3-1 The World's Largest Banks

Bank	Country	Assets ($ Billions)
Mizuho Holdings Tokyo	Japan	$1,281
Citigroup Inc.	United States	1,051
Sumitomo Mitsui Bank	Japan	924
Mitsubishi Tokyo Financial Group	Japan	855
Deutsche Bank	Germany	815
Allianz AG	Germany	805
UBS AG	Switzerland	754
BNP Paribas Group	France	735
HSBC Holdings PLC	United Kingdom	695
J. P. Morgan Chase	United States	639

SOURCE: *American Banker,* July 12, 2002.

5. Why do financial intermediaries exist, and what accounts for international financial intermediation? A key reason that financial intermediaries exist is to address problems arising from asymmetric information. One such problem is adverse selection, or the potential for the least creditworthy borrowers to be the most likely to seek to issue financial instruments. Another is moral hazard, or the possibility that an initially creditworthy borrower may undertake actions that reduce its creditworthiness after receiving funds from a lender. A further reason for the existence of financial intermediaries is the existence of economies of scale, or the ability to spread costs of managing funds across large numbers of savers. A potential justification for international financial intermediation by global banking enterprises is that they may experience economies of scale in information processing by spreading their credit evaluation and monitoring operations across the world.

Financial Institutions

Financial circumstances for various firms and individuals can vary widely. This is why there are so many different kinds of financial instruments and markets. Likewise, asymmetric information can exist in financial markets in a variety of ways. In large measure this helps explain why many different types of firms serve as financial intermediaries. These firms typically are called *financial institutions.*

Insurance Companies

On the Web
What has been the recent financial performance of property-casualty insurers? Find out by visiting the Insurance Information Institute at http://www.iii.org.

Insurance companies specialize in trying to limit the adverse-selection and moral-hazard problems unique to efforts to insure against possible future risks of loss. They issue *policies,* which are promises to reimburse the holder for damages suffered as the result of a "bad" event, such as an auto accident. Certainly, individuals could insure others. But such direct insurance usually is limited to informal agreements. For instance, parents often stand ready to lend financial assistance to their young-adult children who experience "bad" events, so in a sense they offer insurance. But parents also have a lot of information about their children's behavior that others do not have. Most of us, therefore, ultimately turn to insurance companies that specialize in dealing with the asymmetric-information problems associated with insuring risks.

There are two basic kinds of insurance companies. *Life insurance companies* charge premiums for policies that insure people against the financial consequences associated with death. They also offer specialized policies called **annuities,** which are financial instruments that guarantee the holder fixed or variable payments at some future date. *Property and casualty insurers* insure risks relating to property damage and liabilities arising from injuries or deaths caused by accidents or adverse natural events. Property and casualty insurance companies offer policies that insure individuals and businesses against possible property damages or other financial losses resulting from injuries or deaths sustained as a result of accidents, adverse weather, earthquakes, and so on.

Annuities: Financial instruments that guarantee the holder fixed or variable payments at some future date.

Pension Funds

Pension funds: Institutions that specialize in managing funds that individuals save for retirement.

Mutual fund: A mix of financial instruments managed on behalf of shareholders by investment companies that charge fees for their services.

Pension funds are institutions that specialize in managing funds that individuals put away as a "nest egg" for when they retire from their jobs and careers. Part of the compensation of many workers is in the form of employer contributions to such funds.

The key specialty of pension funds is creating financial instruments called *pension annuities*, which are similar to the annuities offered by life insurance companies. But life insurance annuities usually are intended as supplements to a person's income at some fixed point in the future, whether or not the person is working at the time. In contrast, pension annuities apply only to the future event of retirement. Most people regard pension annuities as their main sources of income after retirement.

Why do people use the services of pension funds instead of saving on their own? One reason certainly is asymmetric information: those who operate pension funds may be better informed about financial instruments and markets than individual savers. But the existence of economies of scale is probably a more important reason. Many people would find it very costly to monitor the instruments that they hold on a day-by-day basis throughout their lives. Pension funds do this for many people at the same time, thereby spreading the costs across large numbers of individuals.

Mutual Funds

A **mutual fund** is a mix of redeemable instruments, called "shares" in the fund. These shares are claims on the returns on financial instruments held by the fund, which typically include equities, bonds, government securities, and mortgage-backed securities.

On the Web
How can one choose from among the many mutual funds? Learn more about how investors make this decision by clicking on "Other Investments" and selecting "Mutual Funds" at http://www.investorguide.com.

Mutual funds are usually operated by investment companies, which charge shareholders fees to manage the funds. The popularity of mutual funds increased considerably during the 1970s and 1980s. During those two decades, the assets held in these funds grew by a factor of over sixty times the initial level. Indeed, today more than 7,000 mutual funds are in operation.

Like pension funds, mutual funds take advantage of financial economies of scale. Mutual fund shareholders typically pay lower fees to investment companies than they might have to pay brokers to handle their funds on a personal basis. The reason is that mutual fund managers can spread the costs of managing shareholders' funds across all the shareholders.

Depository Financial Institutions

Another type of financial institution that deals with problems arising from asymmetric information is a *depository financial institution* or, for short, a *depository institution*. As we discussed in Chapter 1, one key characteristic of a depository institution is that its liabilities include various deposits, such as time, savings, or checking accounts. But most depository institutions also deal with asymmetric-information problems specific to loan markets.

Commercial banks: Depository financial institutions that issue checking deposits and specialize in making commercial loans.

Savings and loan association: A type of depository institution that has traditionally specialized in mortgage lending.

Savings bank: Another type of depository institution that has specialized in mortgage lending.

Credit union: A type of depository institution that accepts deposits from and makes loans to only a group of individuals who are eligible for membership.

Finance company: A financial institution that specializes in making loans to relatively high-risk individuals and businesses.

COMMERCIAL BANKS Financial firms known as **commercial banks** are depository financial institutions that specialize in sizing up the risk characteristics of loan applicants. They collect information about the creditworthiness of individuals and businesses that desire loans and seek to limit their exposure to adverse-selection difficulties. In addition, commercial banks keep tabs on the customers to which they lend, thereby limiting the risks arising from moral hazard.

SAVINGS BANKS AND SAVINGS AND LOAN ASSOCIATIONS Residential housing accounts for a large portion of capital investment in the United States. **Savings and loan associations** and **savings banks** are depository institutions that traditionally have specialized in extending mortgage loans to individuals who wish to purchase homes. These institutions also face asymmetric-information difficulties. A person who wants a mortgage loan may or may not be a good risk for a loan. That person also may or may not be tempted to become a bad risk after receiving the loan. Thus, there are adverse-selection and moral-hazard problems specific to mortgage lending.

CREDIT UNIONS A **credit union** is a depository institution that accepts deposits from and makes loans to only a closed group of individuals. In the past, a credit union's services were usually available only to people employed by a business with which the credit union was affiliated. As we shall discuss in Chapter 11, however, in recent years credit unions have significantly expanded the "closed groups" eligible for membership. Credit unions typically have specialized in making consumer loans, though some have branched into the mortgage-loan business.

Finance Companies

A **finance company** also specializes in making loans to individuals and businesses. Finance companies, however, do not offer deposits. Instead, they use the funds invested by their owners or raised through issuing other instruments to finance loans to individuals and small businesses. Many finance companies specialize in making loans that depository institutions regard as too risky.

Government-Sponsored Financial Institutions

The federal government also operates or subsidizes some of the largest financial institutions in the United States. Among these are the Federal Financing Bank, which coordinates federal and federally assisted borrowing, and the Banks for Cooperatives, Federal Intermediate Credit Banks, and Federal Land Banks, which are supervised directly or indirectly by the Farm Credit Administration.

The government also sponsors four institutions that support housing markets: the Federal National Mortgage Association (FNMA, or "Fannie Mae"), the General National Mortgage Association (GNMA, or "Ginnie Mae"), the Federal Home Loan Banks (FHLBs), and the Federal Home Loan Mortgage Corporation (FHLMC, or "Freddie Mac"). These agencies make mortgage markets more liquid by buying mortgages with funds that they raise by selling mortgage-backed securities.

We shall have much more to say about this latter group of government-sponsored financial institutions in Chapter 10. Before you can learn more about the economics of both governmentally sponsored and private financial institutions, however, you must learn more about financial markets. We begin in the next chapter by discussing interest rates and the calculation of interest yields on various types of financial instruments.

6. What are the main types of financial institutions? These include depository institutions such as commercial banks, savings banks and savings and loan associations, and credit unions. Other important financial institutions include insurance companies, pension funds, mutual funds, and finance companies. Brokers, investment banks, and various government-sponsored institutions round out the main groupings of financial institutions.

Link to Management

Shifting Mortgages into Reverse Gear

Under the terms of a reverse mortgage, an individual who already owns his or her home receives payments from a lender based on a sum equal to all or a portion of the borrower's equity ownership of the house. When the individual sells the house or dies, the lender receives this amount as a lump-sum payment from the borrower or his or her heirs.

A Booming Financial Market

During the late 1990s, reverse mortgages got a bad name when a few lenders were accused of taking advantage of elderly people by using misleading sales pitches. For a while some media outlets even classified reverse mortgages as products marketed by so-called predatory lenders—a catchall term for financial companies that stretch the truth when marketing their services.

By the early 2000s, however, the market for reverse mortgages was growing by leaps and bounds. At a number of major mortgage lenders, annual growth rates for reverse mortgages have exceeded 50 percent since 2000. Undoubtedly, one key factor contributing to this big growth spurt has been the increase in the number of homeowners who meet the minimum age requirement of sixty-two. Many such individuals have been attracted by the ability to supplement their monthly incomes with stipends from reverse mortgages.

Who Bears the Downside Risks of Reverse Mortgages?

Some state and federal banking regulators worry that another factor may also be contributing to the rapid growth of reverse mortgages. A reverse mortgage is a type of *nonrecourse loan,* in which the lender does not have the legal right to hold the borrower responsible for the entire amount of the loan. For this reason, banking regulators traditionally have enforced rules sharply restricting the portion of total loans that financial institutions can issue as nonrecourse loans.

In the case of a reverse mortgage, the borrower (or the borrower's heir) is responsible only for transmitting the current market value of the house

Continued on next page

Link to Management, continued

to the lender. Therefore, if the market value when the house is sold or the borrower dies turns out to be lower than the value when the loan was made, the borrower (or heir) does not have to come up with the difference. Only the lender loses if the value of the house declines between the time the lender makes the loan and the time the borrower sells the house or dies.

Reallocating Risks in the Market for Reverse Mortgages

In years past, mortgage lenders' worries about the downside risk discouraged them from offering reverse mortgages. This reluctance to issue reverse mortgages helped depress the growth of the primary market for these instruments. It also made reverse mortgages relatively illiquid, so the secondary market for reverse mortgages had trouble even getting off the ground.

Beginning in the late 1990s, however, the U.S. government got involved in the reverse-mortgage business. The Federal Housing Administration (FHA) began offering the Home Equity Conversion Mortgage Program. Under this program, the FHA provides insurance against reverse-mortgage losses, thereby transferring the risk of loss to taxpayers. Shortly thereafter, the Federal National Mortgage Association ("Fannie Mae"; see Chapter 10), a quasi-public company, also began offering reverse mortgages. It also began purchasing reverse mortgages in the secondary mortgage market, which rapidly became much more liquid. Thus, government sponsorship of reverse mortgages has done much to improve the fortunes of the market for these capital market instruments.

Research Project

Evaluate how factors such as loan fees and tax rules can influence a borrower's decision about whether to enter into a reverse mortgage. In addition, consider what might happen if the market values of houses fell nationwide. Under current rules, who bears many of the risks associated with the potential for a broad decline in house prices? Who would incur the resulting losses, and how would these losses be paid?

Web Resources

1. For more general information about reverse mortgages, visit the Web site of the AARP (formerly the American Association of Retired Persons) devoted to this topic, http://www.reverse.org, or go to the home page of the National Reverse Mortgage Lenders Association, http://www.reversemortgage.org.

2. How much do monthly payments from a reverse mortgage vary depending on the borrower's age, the market value of the borrower's home, and other factors? To find out, go to http://www.rmaarp.com, and use the AARP's reverse-mortgage loan calculator to evaluate various possibilities.

Chapter Summary

1. The Main Economic Function of Financial Markets: Financial markets channel funds of savers to those individuals and businesses that wish to make capital investments.

2. Primary and Secondary Markets, and Money and Capital Markets: Primary markets are financial markets where newly issued financial instruments are bought and sold. Secondary markets are markets where individuals and firms exchange previously issued financial instruments. Money markets are financial markets where individuals and firms exchange financial instruments with maturities under one year. Capital markets are markets for instruments with maturities equal to or greater than one year.

3. The Main Types of Financial Instruments: The most important money market instruments are U.S. Treasury bills, commercial paper, bank certificates of deposit, Eurodollar deposits, and federal funds loans. Key capital market instruments include business equities, corporate bonds, U.S. Treasury notes and bonds and other securities issued by federal government agencies, municipal bonds, mortgage loans, and consumer and commercial loans.

4. Automated Trading of Financial Instruments: Many individuals regard cybertrading via Internet brokers and other automated trading systems as more convenient and less costly than using the services of traditional brokers or exchanges. This has spurred the growth of cybertrading, both within and among nations. Cross-border exchange of financial instruments using automated trading systems has provoked divergent regulatory responses from different nations. International cybertrading also heightens the speed at which savers can shift funds among national markets. Potentially, this can increase the speed with which financial crises take place and with which they spill over onto other world markets.

5. Financial Intermediaries: Financial intermediaries help to reduce problems stemming from the existence of asymmetric information in financial transactions. Asymmetric information can lead to adverse-selection and moral-hazard problems. Financial intermediaries may also permit savers to benefit from economies of scale, which is the ability to reduce the average costs of managing funds by pooling funds and spreading costs across many savers.

6. The Main Types of Financial Institutions: One main grouping is depository institutions, which include commercial banks, savings banks and savings and loan associations, and credit unions. In addition, there are insurance companies, pension funds, mutual funds, and finance companies, brokers, investment banks, and government-sponsored institutions such as the Federal Financing Bank, agricultural credit institutions, and mortgage-financing institutions.

Questions and Problems

(Answers to odd-numbered questions and problems may be found on the Web at http://money.swcollege.com under "Student Resources.")

1. In your view, what are the relative advantages of holding common stock instead of preferrd stock? Explain.

2. What are the disadvantages of holding common instead of preferred stock? Explain.

3. How could "impulsive" traders of stocks over the Internet find themselves earning lower net returns on their portfolios of financial instruments, even if on average they hold the same basic portfolios from month to month as more traditional traders? [Hint: Remember that people pay broker's fees when they trade.]

4. In the 1990s, many pension funds and mutual funds offered U.S. savers special portfolios composed only of financial instruments issued by companies and governments located in other nations. In 1997 and 1998, many savers who held these portfolios earned very low, and sometimes negative, returns. In contrast, most people who allocated

100 percent of their savings to U.S. financial instruments earned higher returns. Does this experience mean that international financial diversification is a mistake? Explain your reasoning.

5. A few years ago, a Florida county commissioner and her husband, a Washington lobbyist, were indicted for securities law violations. Allegedly, they sought to improve the terms under which the county could issue new municipal bonds. Suppose this information had not come to light and had made the municipal bonds riskier than they might otherwise have seemed to potential buyers. Would this have been an example of adverse selection or of moral hazard? Explain your reasoning.

6. Commercial banks make various loans, such as loans to businesses, but they also issue a variety of deposits, such as checking accounts. In the absence of asymmetric-information problems in lending, do you believe that commercial banks might cease to exist? Or would there still be a place for commercial banks? Explain your reasoning.

7. Both life insurance companies and pension plans issue annuities. Nevertheless they are generally regarded as fundamentally different types of financial intermediaries. Why? Explain your reasoning.

8. During the early years following the formation of the United States, its first Treasury secretary, Alexander Hamilton, worked hard to develop conditions in which secondary financial markets could emerge and grow. Based on this chapter's discussion, can you rationalize Hamilton's actions?

9. Commercial and savings banks issue loans and hold other financial instruments that yield interest returns. These banks pass some of this interest income on to their depositors through the interest rates that they pay on deposits that they issue. Bank deposits also are federally insured. Mutual fund shares, in contrast, are not federally insured. Would you expect that mutual fund shares would pay higher or lower returns to shareholders, as compared with rates of return on bank deposits? Explain your reasoning.

10. In what ways is competition among stock exchanges beneficial for traders and for companies that issue stocks? What gains might emerge if the United States had only one stock exchange? What factors might motivate U.S. stock exchanges to consider merging?

Before the Test

Test your understanding of the material covered in this chapter by taking the Chapter 3 interactive quiz at http://money.swcollege.com.

Online Application

Internet URL: http://www.nyse.com/

Title: The New York Stock Exchange: How the NYSE Operates

Navigation: Begin at the URL listed above. In the left margin, click on "About the NYSE" and then "Education," followed by "Educational Publications." Then click on "You and the Investment World." Next, click on Chapter 3: How the NYSE Operates.

Application: Read the chapter, and answer the following questions.

1. According to the article, the price of a seat on the NYSE currently can sell for more than $1 million. Why do you suppose that someone would be willing to pay this much for a seat? [Hint: Think about the potential ways that someone could generate earnings from holding an NYSE seat.]

2. List the key functions of a stock exchange specialist. Why is the cybertechnology called the "Point-of-Sale Display Book" likely to be particularly useful for a specialist?

For Group Study and Analysis: Divide the class into groups, and have each group examine and discuss the description of how NYSE trades are executed. Ask each group to list the various points at which Internet trading may be a more efficient way to execute a trade than trading via a traditional brokerage firm. Then go through these lists as a class, and discuss the following issue: What people in the NYSE cannot be replaced by cybertechnologies?

Selected References and Further Reading

First Boston Corporation. *Handbook of Securities of the United States Government and Federal Agencies.* Published every second year.

Geisst, Charles. *Wall Street—A History.* New York: Oxford University Press, 1997.

McAndrews, James, and Chris Stefandis. "The Consolidation of European Stock Exchanges." Federal Reserve Bank of New York *Current Issues in Economics and Finance* 8 (June 2002).

Stigum, Marcia. *The Money Market.* 3d ed. Homewood, Ill.: Dow-Jones-Irwin, 1990.

MoneyXtra

moneyxtra! Log on to the MoneyXtra Web site now (**http://moneyxtra.swcollege.com**) for additional learning resources such as practice quizzes, case studies, readings, and additional economic applications.

Unit II
Financial Markets, Instruments, and Institutions

CONTENTS

Chapter 4

Interest Rates

Fundamental Issues

1. Why must we compute different interest yields?
2. How does risk cause market interest rates to differ?
3. Why do market interest rates vary with differences in financial instruments' terms to maturity?
4. What is the real interest rate?
5. How are interest yields on bonds issued in different countries related?
6. What interest rates are the key indicators of financial market conditions?

During the summer of 2000, the market interest rate for ten-year Treasury bonds fell below the interest rate for three-month U.S. Treasury bills for the first time since 1989. This relatively uncommon event set off alarm bells among economists. In years past, when interest rates on short-maturity financial instruments fell below interest rates on longer-maturity instruments, business downturns often occurred sometime within the next six to eighteen months.

By the spring of 2001, the ten-year Treasury bond rate was back above the three-month Treasury bill rate. Nevertheless, within a few months a broad U.S. economic slowdown had begun. Although the terrorist attack on New York and Washington, D.C., in September 2001 contributed to a sharp deepening of the business downturn, some economists expressed the view that a slump would have taken place in any event. One economic forecaster went so far as to claim that a recession had been foreordained by the preceding reversal of the normal pattern of interest rates for financial instruments with different terms to maturity. Once this interest rate reversal took place, he claimed, at least a mild slowdown was an unavoidable result.

When certain economists use terms such as "foreordained," it is tempting to wonder if they are relying on spiritualistic notions of predestination instead of logical thinking. It turns out, however, that patterns in differences between interest rates on relatively long-term financial instruments and interest rates on shorter-maturity instruments really do aid in forecasting the future state of the U.S. economy. To understand why, you must learn more about the relationships among interest rates on different types of financial instruments, which is a major topic of this chapter.

Calculating Interest Yields

By holding financial instruments, such as loans or bonds, savers and financial institutions extend credit to those individuals or firms that issue the instruments. The amount of credit extended is the **principal** amount of the loan or the bond. Those who hold financial instruments do so because they receive payments from the issuers in the form of **interest.** The percentage return earned is the **interest rate.** For a simple-interest, one-year loan, for instance, the interest rate is equal to the ratio of total interest during the year to the principal of the loan. That is, the interest rate is equal to the amount of interest divided by the loan principal.

The interest return from holding a financial instrument is its yield to the owner. Hence, this interest return is often called the *interest yield* of a financial instrument.

Principal: The amount of credit extended when one makes a loan or purchases a bond.

Interest: The payment, or yield, received in exchange for extending credit by holding any financial instrument.

Interest rate: The percentage return, or percentage yield, earned by the holder of a financial instrument.

Coupon return: A fixed interest return that a bond yields each year.

Nominal yield: The coupon return on a bond divided by the bond's face value.

Current yield: The coupon return on a bond divided by the bond's market price.

Different Concepts of Interest Yields

There are different ways to think about the interest yields on financial instruments. The most important are the nominal yield, current yield, and yield to maturity.

NOMINAL YIELD Suppose that a bond is issued in an amount of $10,000 with an agreement to pay $600 in interest every year. The annual payment of $600 is the bond's annual **coupon return.** This is simply the fixed amount of interest that the bond yields each year. It is called a coupon return because many bonds actually have coupons that represent titles to interest yields.

The **nominal yield** on a bond is equal to

$$r_N = C/F,$$

where r_N is the nominal yield, C is the coupon return, and F is the face amount of the bond. The annual nominal yield of the $10,000 bond with a $600 coupon return is equal to $600/$10,000 = 0.06, or 6 percent.

CURRENT YIELD The current secondary market price of a bond typically is not the face value of the bond. Bonds often sell in secondary markets at prices that differ from their face values. For this reason, those contemplating a bond purchase often are interested in the **current yield** of a bond. This is equal to

$$r_C = C/P,$$

where r_C denotes the current yield, C is the coupon return, and P is the current market price of the bond.

For instance, the current market price of a bond with a face value of $10,000 might be $9,000. If the coupon return on the bond is $600 per year, then the annual current yield on this bond is equal to $600/$9,000 = 0.067, or 6.7 percent.

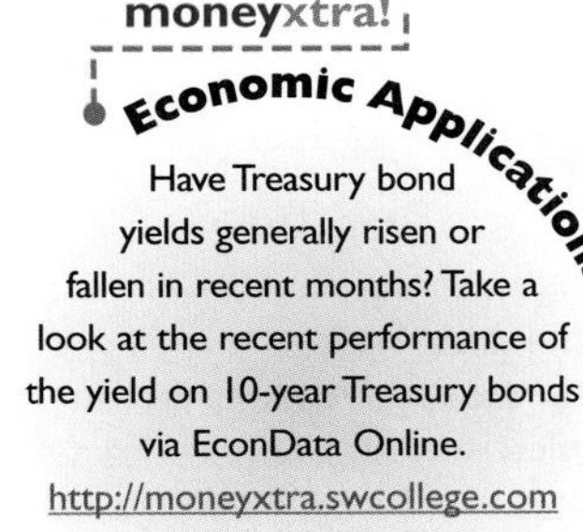

Yield to maturity: The rate of return on a bond if it is held until it matures, which reflects the market price of the bond, the bond's coupon return, and any capital gain from holding the bond to maturity.

Capital gain: An increase in the value of a financial instrument at the time it is sold as compared with its market value at the date it was purchased.

Discounted present value: The value today of a payment to be received at a future date.

YIELD TO MATURITY A bond's **yield to maturity** is the rate of return if the bond is held until maturity. Calculating this yield can be complicated, however, because the bond's market price and its face value normally differ.

Typically, bonds are sold at a *discount,* meaning that a bond's selling price is below its face value. Hence, other things being equal, the bondholder receives an automatic capital gain if the bond is held to maturity. A **capital gain** occurs when the value of a financial asset at the time it is redeemed or sold is higher than its market value when it was purchased. At the same time, the bond pays a coupon return. The yield to maturity must account for both the capital gain and the coupon returns that a bond yields to its owner.

Calculating Discounted Present Value

To understand the interplay between coupon returns and capital gains in calculating bond yields, consider a specific example—a bond whose maturity is three years. The bond's face value is $10,000. Its annual coupon return is $600. Hence, its nominal yield per year is $600/$10,000 = 0.06, or 6 percent.

DISCOUNTED PRESENT VALUE To compute the yield to maturity on this bond, we need to determine its market price. Note that the bond's owner receives three payments: $600 after the first year, $600 after the second year, and $10,600 (the principal plus the third year's interest) after the third year. And so the amount that the buyer will be willing to pay for this bond must equal the value of these payments from the buyer's perspective at the time she purchases the bond.

Today's value of payments to be received at future dates is the **discounted present value** of those payments. Discounted present value is a key financial concept, because it enables us to determine how much a future sum is worth to us from the perspective of today, given current market interest rates. As Table 4-1 shows, the future value of a dollar falls more quickly at higher interest rates. This means that the present value of payments a bond's owner will receive also declines as interest rates increase, thereby reducing the amount that a buyer would be willing to pay for the bond. Consequently, you must understand how to calculate the discounted present value of a future payment before you can understand how to compute bond prices.

In the case of our example of a specific bond with a face value of $10,000 and three annual payments of $600 each, suppose that the prevailing market interest rate is $r = 0.05$, or 5 percent. Consider the first year's return on the bond, which is $600. Note that saving $571.43 for one year at an interest rate of 5 percent would yield an amount of $571.43 (the initial amount) plus 0.05 times $571.43 (the interest), or $571.43 times the factor 1.05. But this works out to be $600. This means that from today's perspective, a $600 payment one year from now at a market interest rate of 5 percent is worth $571.43. Consequently, $571.43 is the discounted present value of $600 a year from now at the interest rate of 5 percent. This amount is equal to the future payment of $600 divided by the sum, 1 + 0.05, or $600/(1.05) = $571.43. This implies that a formula for calculating the discounted present value of a payment to be received one year from now is

Discounted present value = payment one year from now/(1 + r).

On the Web

For additional review of present value, go to http://teachmefinance.com, and click on "Time Value of Money."

Table 4-1 Present Values of a Future Dollar

This table shows how much a dollar received a given number of years in the future would be worth today at different rates of interest. For instance, at an interest rate of 8 percent, a dollar to be received 25 years from now would have a value of less than 15 cents, and a dollar to be received 50 years from now is worth about 2 cents.

	Compounded Annual Interest Rate				
Year	3%	5%	8%	10%	20%
1	.971	.952	.926	.909	.833
2	.943	.907	.857	.826	.694
3	.915	.864	.794	.751	.578
4	.889	.823	.735	.683	.482
5	.863	.784	.681	.620	.402
6	.838	.746	.630	.564	.335
7	.813	.711	.583	.513	.279
8	.789	.677	.540	.466	.233
9	.766	.645	.500	.424	.194
10	.744	.614	.463	.385	.162
15	.642	.481	.315	.239	.0649
20	.554	.377	.215	.148	.0261
25	.478	.295	.146	.0923	.0105
30	.412	.231	.0994	.0573	.00421
40	.307	.142	.0460	.0221	.000680
50	.228	.087	.0213	.00852	.000109

But the bond also pays \$600 two years after the time of purchase. Note that at a market rate of interest of 5 percent, holding \$544.22 for two years would yield \$600. The reason is that if we begin with \$544.22 and save it for a year, the accumulated saving after the year will be equal to \$544.22 times 1.05, or \$571.43. If we save \$571.43 for another year, then we end up with \$571.43 times 1.05, or \$600. This tells us that the discounted present value of \$600 to be received two years from now is equal to $\$600/[(1.05)(1.05)] = \$600/(1.05)^2 = \$544.22$.

From the logic of this calculation, we can see that a general formula for computing the discounted present value of a payment to be received n years in the future is

$$\text{Discounted present value} = \text{payment } n \text{ years from now}/(1 + r)^n.$$

In our two-year example, $n = 2$, $r = 0.05$, and the payment two years from now is \$600.

At the end of the third year, the buyer of the three-year bond receives the principal of \$10,000 and a final \$600 interest payment. We can calculate the discounted present value of this amount using the formula above:

$$\begin{array}{l}\text{Discounted present}\\ \text{value of \$10,600}\\ \text{three years hence}\end{array} = \$10{,}600/(1.05)^3 = \$9{,}156.68.$$

On the Web
To calculate present value on the Internet, go to http://rigel.mfm.com/support/manuals/ebrd/EBRDm177.htm.

Perpetuity: A bond with an infinite term to maturity.

Thus, today's value of the \$10,600 that the bondholder will receive when the three-year bond matures is \$9,156.68. (People who win lotteries must take discounted present value into account when they have a choice between cash up front or payments over several years; see *Management Focus: Accepting Millions of Dollars in Lottery Winnings Can Be a Chore.*)

THE MARKET PRICE OF A BOND We now can calculate the market value, or price, of this three-year bond. The price is how much the buyer would perceive the bond to be worth at the purchase date, given a market interest rate of 5 percent. (Remember that the bond pays an annual coupon of \$600 for three years.) This is the sum of the discounted present values of the payments received in each of the three years. Using the calculations that we have done above, this is

$$\begin{aligned}\text{Price of three-year bond} &= \$600/(1.05) + \$600/(1.05)^2 + \$10{,}600/(1.05)^3 \\ &= \$571.43 + \$544.22 + \$9{,}156.68 \\ &= \$10{,}272.33.\end{aligned}$$

Thus, \$10,272.33 is the market value of the three-year bond with an annual coupon return of \$600 and a face value of \$10,000 when the market interest rate is 5 percent.

Calculating the Yield to Maturity

So what is the yield to maturity on this bond, if it is purchased for \$10,272.33? To figure this out, we could write our formula above in a different way:

$$\$10{,}272.33 = \$600/(1 + r_m) + \$600/(1 + r_m)^2 + \$10{,}600/(1 + r_m)^3,$$

where r_m represents the yield to maturity for the bond. We already know that the value for r_m that fits this expression is 0.05. Hence, the yield to maturity for this bond with a price of \$10,272.33 is 5 percent (the market interest rate).

It is easy for us to see that 5 percent is the yield to maturity because we constructed the problem with simple numbers. But note that if the market price on the left-hand side of the equation were to rise from \$10,272.33 to some larger number, the value for r_m would have to fall somewhat. Calculating r_m requires solving a cubic equation! For this reason, traders use programmed calculators or bond yield tables when evaluating yields to maturity on long-term bonds.

YIELDS ON NONMATURING BONDS Some financial instruments never mature. For instance, one instrument issued by the British government, a *consol,* pays a fixed coupon return forever. When the bearer dies, she can pass this instrument on to her heir, who receives the coupon return each year during his lifetime.

Such a financial instrument is a perpetual bond, or **perpetuity.** This is simply a bond that never matures. It turns out that the discounted present value of the coupon returns on a perpetuity is easy to calculate. It is equal to the coupon return divided by the market interest rate. For instance, if the annual coupon return is equal to an amount C and the annual interest rate is r, then the price of a perpetuity is

$$\text{Perpetuity price} = C/r.$$

We let you prove this for yourself in problem 1 at the end of the chapter.

GLOBAL | POLICY | CYBER | MANAGEMENT Focus

Accepting Millions of Dollars in Lottery Winnings Can Be a Chore

Suppose that you have just won the Wisconsin Powerball jackpot. This is exciting news, but now you are confronted with a choice: Should you opt to accept $195 million paid in annual installments of $7.8 million over 25 years, or should you choose a lump-sum payment of $104 million instead?

What you have to do is compare an immediate payment of $104 million with the discounted present value of $7.8 million to be received every year for 25 years. Take a look at Table 4-2, which shows that the discounted value of these future payments is $115.4 million at an interest rate of 5 percent. At an interest rate of 8 percent, however, the present value of the payments is only $90.3 million.

Thus, the key to your decision is what you expect market interest returns to be over the next 25 years. At the time one recent winner won the lottery and faced this decision, most bonds were offering annual returns ranging from 7 to 8 percent, and average (though riskier) returns on shares of stock were much higher. The winner chose to accept the lump sum of $104 million.

For Critical Analysis: Why is the present value of the annual lottery payments higher at lower interest rates?

Table 4-2 The Discounted Present Value of $7.8 Million Per Year for 25 Years at Alternative Rates of Interest

	Interest Rate				
	3%	5%	8%	10%	20%
Present value	$139,900,000	$115,400,000	$90,300,000	$77,900,000	$46,300,000

This simple formula illustrates an important fact:

Prices of existing bonds are inversely related to changing market interest rates.

Suppose that the fixed coupon return is $500 per year. If the market interest rate is 5 percent, then the price of the perpetuity is equal to $500/(0.05) = $10,000. But if the interest rate rises to 6 percent, then the perpetuity's price equals $500/(0.06) = $8,333.33. A rise in the interest rate causes the bond's price to decline.

This makes sense. When the market interest rate rises, the discounted present value of each year's coupon return declines. But the bond's price is the sum of the discounted present values of all years' coupon returns. Hence, the bond's price must fall.

Consols are not especially commonplace today. But recall that corporate equities also have no maturity date. Equities, therefore, are a type of perpetuity. Indeed, we might think of the annual dividend on a share of stock as the "coupon return" and the annual rate of return derived from the share as the "interest rate." Then the dividend divided by the stock's annual rate of return will give a rough approximation of the share price. This is only an approximation because stock dividends typically are not constant over time and rates of return on shares typically vary from year to year.

Coupon yield equivalent: An annualized T-bill rate that can be compared with annual yields on other financial instruments.

YIELDS ON TREASURY BILLS Table 4-3 displays interest rates on money market instruments such as federal funds, commercial paper, bank certificates of deposit, and Treasury bills (T-bills).

The published T-bill rates are based on a fictitious 360-day year. They are calculated from the equation

$$r_T = [(F - P)/P](360/n),$$

where r_T is the T-bill rate, F is the face value, P is the price paid, and n is the number of days to maturity.

Consider the 13-week (3-month, or 91-day) T-bill rate of 1.62 percent. The face value of a T-bill is \$10,000, so F in the equation is equal to \$10,000. The number of days to maturity, n, is equal to 91. The average price at which T-bills sold at this date was \$9,959.22. Using the formula then gives us

$$\begin{aligned} r_T &= [(F - P)/P](360/n) \\ &= [(\$10{,}000 - \$9{,}959.22)/\$9{,}959.22](360/91) \\ &= (\$40.78/\$9{,}959.22)(3.96) \\ &= 0.0162. \end{aligned}$$

Thus, the published T-bill yield was 1.62 percent.

Of course, a year really lasts 365 days. A T-bill yield based on the true 365-day year is called the **coupon yield equivalent.** This is an annualized T-bill rate

Table 4-3 Interest Rates on Money Market Instruments

Federal funds	1.74%
Commercial paper	
Nonfinancial	
1-month	1.71
2-month	1.70
3-month	1.68
Financial	
1-month	1.70
2-month	1.70
3-month	1.68
Certificates of deposit (secondary market)	
1-month	1.74
3-month	1.70
6-month	1.69
Eurodollar deposits (London)	
1-month	1.73
3-month	1.70
6-month	1.69
U.S. Treasury bills (secondary market)	
1-month	1.69
3-month	1.62
6-month	1.57

SOURCE: Board of Governors of the Federal Reserve System, G.13 (415) *Statistical Release*, August 7, 2002.

that can be compared with annual yields on other financial instruments. To calculate the coupon yield equivalent, we use the formula

$$r_E = [(F - P)/P](365/n),$$

where r_E is the coupon yield equivalent for the T-bill. Hence, the coupon yield equivalent corresponding to the published yield of 1.62 percent in Table 4-3 would have been

$$\begin{aligned} r_E &= [(\$10{,}000 - \$9{,}959.22)/\$9{,}959.22](365/91) \\ &= (\$40.78/\$9{,}959.22)(4.01) \\ &= 0.0164. \end{aligned}$$

The coupon yield equivalent for this T-bill is 1.64 percent. It is higher than the published yield of 1.62 percent because it takes into account the actual number of days in the year.

Traders have a practical use for the formula for the coupon yield equivalent. They use it to determine the yields associated with quoted prices on T-bills being traded in the secondary T-bill market. For instance, suppose that an individual holds a 13-week T-bill for 30 days but then offers to sell it at a price of $9,950. To figure out the yield over the remaining 61 days to maturity, a potential buyer would use the coupon yield equivalent formula. He would set P equal to $9,950 and n equal to 61:

$$\begin{aligned} r_E &= [(F - P)/P](365/n) \\ &= [(\$10{,}000 - \$9{,}950)/\$9{,}950](365/61) \\ &= (\$50/\$9{,}950)(5.98) \\ &= 0.0301. \end{aligned}$$

This means that the approximate annual yield on this T-bill at the quoted price would be 3.01 percent. The purchaser can compare this yield with those on other available instruments. Then he can decide if he wishes to pay a price of $9,950.

On the Web
How can a person keep track of U.S. interest rates from day to day? One way is to view statistics made available by the Federal Reserve at http://www.federalreserve.gov/releases. At this site, click on "Selected Interest Rates: Daily Update."

1. Why must we compute different interest yields? The reason is that interest yields differ depending on the basis of comparison for evaluating the yield and on the period of time that a financial instrument will be held. This leads to a variety of different concepts of interest yields and several different ways to calculate these yields.

The Risk Structure of Interest Rates

Scanning through the interest rates in Table 4-3 indicates that market interest rates differ across financial instruments. Two key factors account for such differences in market rates. One is the term to maturity. The other is risk. Following standard practice, we consider each separately. In reality, however, the two factors together cause market interest rates for different instruments to differ.

The **risk structure of interest rates** refers to the relationship among yields on financial instruments that have the *same maturity* but differ on the basis of default risk, liquidity, and tax considerations.

Risk structure of interest rates: The relationship among yields on financial instruments that have the same maturity but differ because of variations in default risk, liquidity, and tax rates.

Default risk: The chance that an individual or a firm that issues a financial instrument may be unable to honor its obligations to repay the principal and/or to make interest payments.

Risk premium: The amount by which one instrument's yield exceeds the yield of another instrument as a result of the first instrument being riskier and less liquid than the second.

Investment-grade securities: Bonds with relatively low default risk.

Junk bonds: Bonds with relatively high default risk.

Default Risk

There is always a possibility that an individual or a firm that issues a financial instrument may be unable to honor its obligations to pay off the principal and/or interest. This means that any bond is subject to some degree of **default risk.**

The U.S. government has the power to raise taxes to pay off its bonds. If needed, it could even print money to do so. For U.S. Treasury securities, therefore, default risk is very small. The chance of default on a newly issued twenty-year Treasury bond, for instance, is meager, if not virtually zero.

But consider a twenty-year corporate bond. Even if the company that issues it today has a very solid credit rating, there is always a chance that the company's fortunes could change within a few years. Ten or fifteen years from now the company could be near bankruptcy. And so the perceived default risk for the corporate bond is greater than for the twenty-year Treasury bond. As a result, individuals and firms will hold corporate bonds as well as Treasury bonds only if the corporate bond pays a sufficiently higher return to compensate for the greater risk of default.

The Risk Premium The amount by which the corporate bond rate exceeds the Treasury bond rate because of greater default risk is the corporate bond's **risk premium.** Suppose that just before the company issues twenty-year bonds, word spreads that prospects for one of its products have worsened. Then those who were contemplating purchasing its bonds will not do so unless the company offers an even higher interest rate relative to the twenty-year Treasury bond rate. The risk premium on the bond will rise because the chance that the company may default is greater than it was before the news.

On the Web
What do various bond ratings mean? Learn the answer to this question at Standard & Poor's Web site, http://www.standardandpoors.com. Go to "Resource Center," and click on "Ratings Definitions" and then "Issue Credit Ratings."

Rating Securities Default risk clearly is an important consideration in bond purchases. Two predominant institutions that rate the risks of bonds are Standard and Poor's Corporation and Moody's Investors Services. Just as professors assign students grades for their relative performances, Standard and Poor's and Moody's rate the relative default risks of bonds issued by corporations.

These institutions assign several grades so as to differentiate low, medium, and high risks. Yet both use two broad risk categories. **Investment-grade securities** are those judged to have a fairly low risk of default.

So-called **junk bonds** have significantly greater default risk. Naturally, the risk premiums for junk bonds are larger than those for investment-grade securities. One person's junk, of course, is another's treasure. To an individual who very much dislikes risk, junk bonds truly are "junk"—hence, the name "junk bonds." But to someone who desires high yields and is willing to take on risk, junk bonds are worth holding.

Liquidity

Another reason that corporate bond rates exceed interest rates on U.S. Treasury bonds of identical maturities is that traders regard corporate bonds as less liquid financial instruments. Recall that the secondary market for Treasury securities is well developed and typically has much trading activity. This means that the holder of a Treasury bond knows that the bond will be easy to sell if desired.

The secondary market for corporate bonds, however, is not always so active. Sometimes many who wish to sell corporate bonds enter the secondary market only to find that few stand ready to buy. Hence, a corporate bond may be more difficult to "unload" for cash at a later date. For this reason a corporate bond is less liquid than a U.S. Treasury bond.

This means that (all other factors held constant) bondholders typically will require a higher interest rate on corporate bonds, relative to the rate on a Treasury bond of the same maturity. The higher corporate bond rate compensates the bondholders for the chance that they will have more trouble selling the corporate bonds at a future date.

THE LIQUIDITY PREMIUM Thus, a difference in default risk is not the only reason that bond rates may diverge. There is also a *liquidity premium* that accounts in part for the difference between interest rates on two bonds with identical maturities.

Distinguishing between risk and liquidity premiums would be a difficult proposition, however. For instance, junk bonds are less liquid than investment-grade securities because the secondary market for the latter typically is more active. But a key reason there is less secondary market trading of junk bonds is that fewer individuals are willing to incur risk by holding them. Clearly, default risk and liquidity interact in determining bond interest rate differences.

LIQUIDITY AND RISK Hence, the term *risk premium* typically is used broadly to characterize interest rate differences resulting from *both* default risk and liquidity considerations. When people refer to a risk premium on one bond relative to another, they really are talking about a difference that arises because one bond has a higher risk of default *and* is less liquid.

Figure 4-1 displays the average annual yields on long-term U.S. Treasury bonds, the highest-rated long-term investment-grade securities (Moody's Aaa),

Figure 4-1
Long-Term Bond Yields.

As compared with corporate bonds, Treasury bonds have lower default risk and greater liquidity. Consequently, Treasury bonds consistently have lower yields. Furthermore, the highest-rated investment-grade corporate bonds (Moody's Aaa) have lower default risk, as compared with medium-rated investment-grade corporate bonds (Moody's Baa), and the highest-rated corporate bonds also have lower yields.

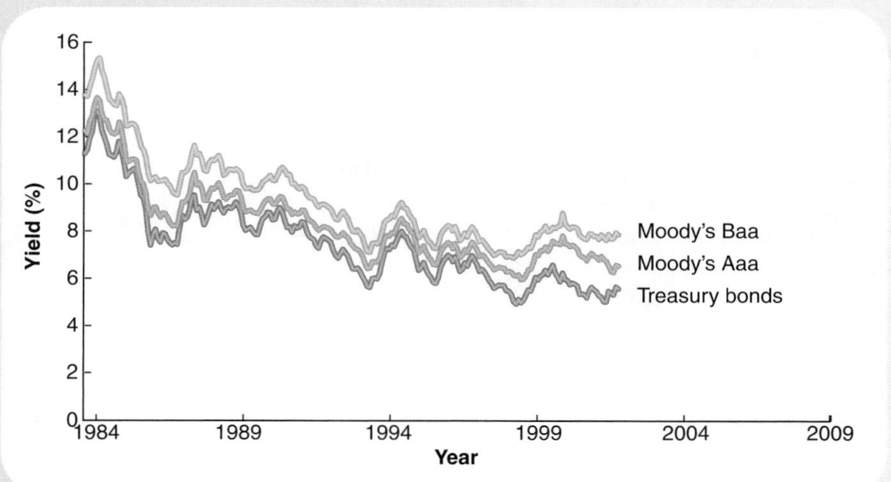

SOURCE: Board of Governors of the Federal Reserve System, *Federal Reserve Bulletin*, various issues.

and medium-rated investment-grade securities (Moody's Baa). All three are plotted on a monthly basis since 1984. The interest yields on both classes of corporate bonds always are greater than the yield on Treasury bonds. The reason is that Treasury bonds have much lower default risk and are very liquid. Likewise, the presence of a risk premium is apparent in a comparison of the rates on medium- versus highly rated corporate bonds.

Tax Considerations

A final reason that bonds with identical maturities may have different interest yields is that tax laws treat some bonds differently than others. Individuals typically are not required to pay either federal or state taxes on interest earnings from municipal bonds. This means that the pre-tax and after-tax yields on municipal bonds are identical. But interest earnings on Treasury bonds are subject to federal taxation, which depresses their after-tax yields.

For this reason, higher pre-tax interest rates are required to induce individuals to hold both Treasury bonds and municipal bonds simultaneously. As a result, pre-tax (market) Treasury bond yields tend to exceed yields on municipal bonds, as shown in Figure 4-2.

2. How does risk cause market interest rates to differ? Differences in degrees of default risk and liquidity result in risk premiums that must be present in the yields on financial instruments. Risk premiums differ across instruments, which is one key reason that yields differ. The different rates at which some instruments are taxed also cause their market rates to diverge.

Figure 4-2
Municipal and Treasury Bond Yields.

Interest earnings from municipal bonds are exempt from federal taxation, but interest earnings on Treasury bonds are subject to federal taxation. Consequently, Treasury bond yields exceed the yields on municipal bonds.

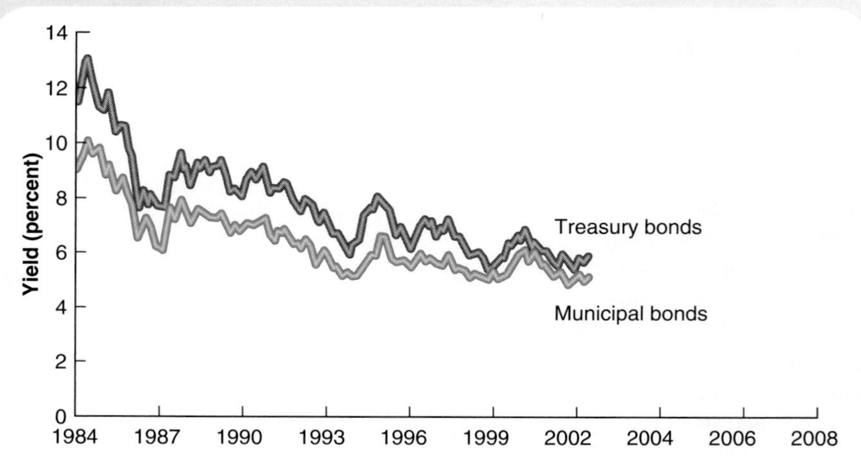

SOURCE: Board of Governors of the Federal Reserve System, *Federal Reserve Bulletin*, various issues.

The Term Structure of Interest Rates

The **term structure of interest rates** refers to the relationship among yields on financial instruments that possess the *same risk, liquidity, and tax characteristics* but have differing terms to maturity. Even if bonds with different maturities are identical in every other respect, their yields typically diverge.

Term structure of interest rates: The relationship among yields on financial instruments with identical risk, liquidity, and tax characteristics but differing terms to maturity.

Yield curve: A chart depicting the relationship among yields on bonds that differ only in their terms to maturity.

Inverted yield curve: A downward-sloping yield curve.

Segmented markets theory: A theory of the term structure of interest rates that views bonds with differing maturities as nonsubstitutable, so their yields differ because they are determined in separate markets.

The Yield Curve

This divergence of interest yields across different terms to maturity is easily seen by plotting a **yield curve.** This is a chart that depicts the relationship among yields on similar bonds with different terms to maturity. Figure 4-3 shows a typical yield curve for Treasury securities.

The yield curve in Figure 4-3 slopes upward. This is the normal shape of a yield curve. Interest yields usually are greater as the term to maturity increases. But sometimes yield curves are downward sloping. This happened, for instance, in the late 1970s. When the yield curve slopes downward, it is said to be an **inverted yield curve.** In such a situation, interest yields decline as the term to maturity rises.

Why isn't the yield curve simply horizontal? That is, why do interest yields vary with the term to maturity? Economists have offered three basic theories that seek to address this question. These are the segmented markets theory, the expectations theory, and the preferred habitat theory.

Segmented Markets Theory

According to the **segmented markets theory** of the term structure of interest rates, bonds with differing terms to maturity are not perfectly substitutable. As a result, they are traded in separate markets. Each market determines its own unique yield.

Figure 4-3
The Yield Curve.

This is a typical, mostly upward-sloping historical yield curve for U.S. Treasury securities.

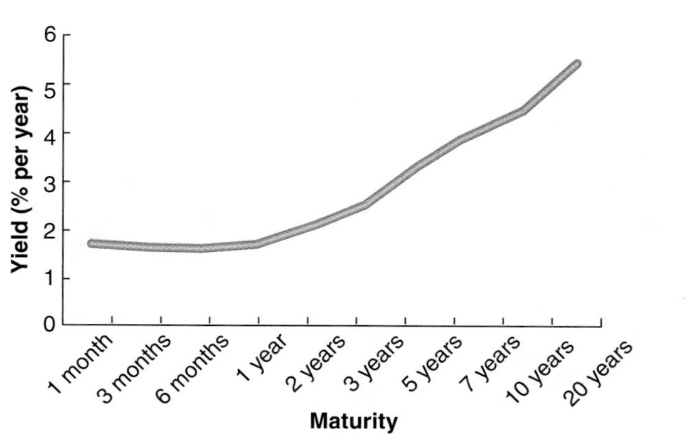

SOURCE: Federal Reserve H.15 Statistical Release, August 8, 2002.

MATCHING MATURITIES For instance, depository institutions such as commercial banks issue time deposits with relatively short terms to maturity of one to three years. They often wish to "match" these deposits with assets such as Treasury bonds with similar one- to three-year maturities, so they buy such Treasuries. Pension funds, in contrast, issue pension liabilities with much longer terms to maturity. Consequently, it is natural that they should wish to hold Treasury bonds with ten- to twenty-year maturities. According to the segmented markets theory, bond yields will reflect such differences in trading patterns.

For instance, suppose that initially the yields across Treasury bonds with differing maturities are the same. If banks decide to hold more Treasury bonds with one- to three-year maturities, however, the demand for such bonds will rise, causing an increase in their market price. As a result, the market yield on the Treasury bonds will fall. If all other factors are unchanged, the yields on Treasury bonds with one- to three-year maturities will be lower than those on Treasury bonds with ten- to twenty-year maturities. That is, market yields will differ across terms to maturity, just as we see when we plot yield curves. Indeed, in this example the yield curve slopes upward.

A nice feature of the segmented markets theory is that it can explain why the yield curve is not horizontal. It also provides a ready explanation for an upward- or downward-sloping yield curve: the slope will depend on differences in conditions in markets for shorter- versus longer-term financial instruments.

DRAWBACKS OF THE SEGMENTED MARKETS THEORY But simplicity is not always a virtue. There are two difficulties with the segmented markets theory. One is that the theory assumes that Treasury bonds with different maturities are not perfect substitutes, yet yields on Treasury bonds tend to move together. This can be seen in Figure 4-4, which depicts the yields on one-year, five-year, and twenty-year Treasury securities since 1984. If Treasury bonds with different maturities were

Figure 4-4
Treasury Security Yields.

The yields on Treasury securities tend to be higher for longer maturities. Nevertheless, the yields on Treasury securities with different maturities tend to move together over time.

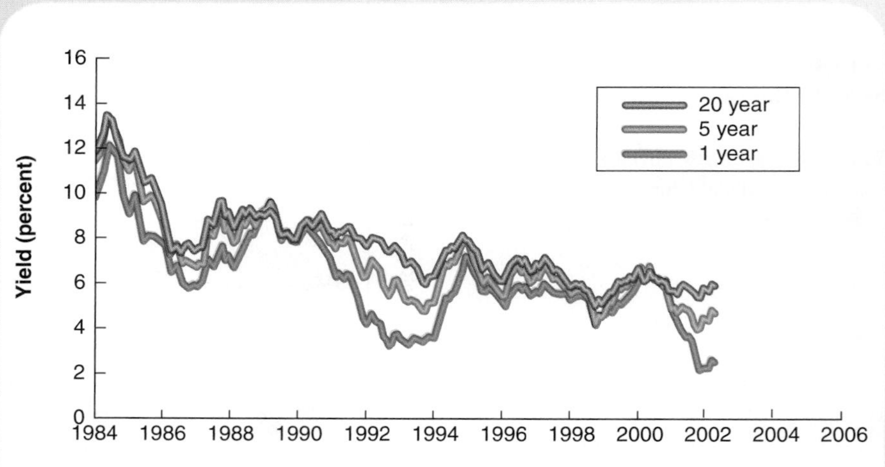

SOURCES: Board of Governors of the Federal Reserve System, *Federal Reserve Bulletin* (various issues) and G.13 (415) *Statistical Release*.

not substitutable, then there would be no reason that their yields should be related. But they clearly are.

A second problem with the segmented markets theory is that it does not explain why the yield curve should have any natural tendency to slope either upward or downward over its entire range. Yet historically the yield curve typically has sloped upward. Over long periods, downward-sloping yield curves are relatively rare occurrences. But when a yield curve does slope downward, it typically does so over most, if not all, of its range.

Expectations theory: A theory of the term structure of interest rates that views bonds with differing maturities as perfect substitutes, so their yields differ only because short-term interest rates are expected to rise or fall.

Expectations Theory

The **expectations theory** addresses the first difficulty with the segmented markets theory. It explains how expectations about future yields can cause yields on instruments with different maturities to move together. In addition, it can provide insight into why the yield curve may systematically slope upward or downward.

moneyxtra!

Economic Applications

Has the yield curve recently become steeper or more shallow? Take a look at changes in the spread between short- and long-term interest rates via EconData Online.

http://moneyxtra.swcollege.com

CHOOSING BETWEEN BONDS WITH DIFFERING MATURITIES The essential elements of the expectations theory can be understood by considering a situation in which an individual saver faces a two-year planning horizon. The saver has two alternatives. One is to place funds in a two-year bond for the two years. This bond yields an annual interest rate of R. The other alternative is for the saver to hold one-year bonds for each of the two years. Under this alternative, the saver would place funds in a one-year bond for the first year at an interest rate of r_1. Then, during the second year, the saver would place the principal plus the interest accumulated during the first year in another one-year bond. At the beginning of the two periods, when the saver must make her decision, she expects that the interest rate on the one-year bond during the second year will be r_2^e.

Holding Either Bond This individual will be willing to hold *either* one-year or two-year bonds only if she anticipates that her rate of return across the two years will be the same. This is true if

$$R = (r_1 + r_2^e)/2.$$

That is, the annual interest rate on the two-year bond, R, must equal the average expected annual interest rate from holding one-year bonds, $(r_1 + r_2^e)$. If the two-year bond rate falls below this expected average of one-year rates, then the saver will hold only one-year bonds. But if the two-year bond rate is above this expected average of one-year rates, then the saver will hold only two-year bonds. Consequently, the above condition must be met in the bond markets to induce this saver and others to hold bonds of both maturities.

The Yield Curve's Slope Suppose that the one-year bond pays $r_1 = 0.02$ during the first year and is expected to yield $r_2^e = 0.04$ during the second year. Then the two-year bond rate, R, will be the average of 0.02 and 0.04, which is $(0.02 + 0.04)/2 = 0.03$. Panel (a) of Figure 4-5 on page 94 shows the yield curve for this example. The *actual* interest yield for the one-year bond is $r_1 = 0.02$, or 2 percent. For the two-year bond, the interest yield is higher, at $R = 0.03$, or 3 percent. Therefore, the yield curve relating bonds with one- and two-year maturities slopes upward.

Now suppose that for some reason savers anticipate that one-year bond rates will fall sharply. Specifically, suppose that the expectation of the one-year bond

Figure 4-5
Sample Yield Curves for the Expectations Theory.

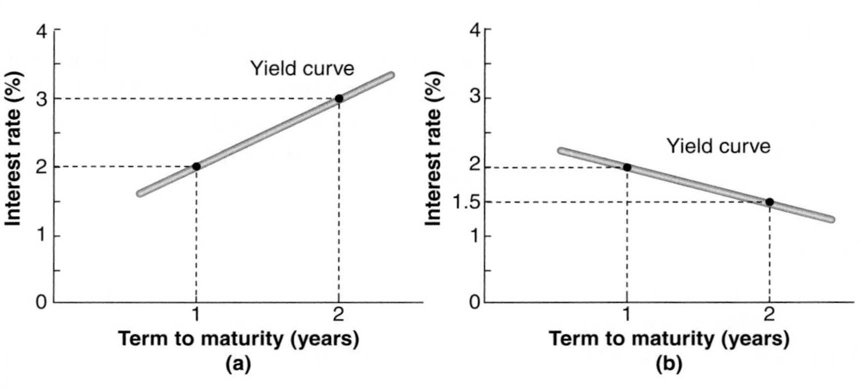

Panel (a) shows an upward-sloping yield curve that arises under the expectations theory of the term structure of interest rates if the one-year bond rate is expected to rise from 2 percent to 4 percent; then the two-year bond rate is the average of the current and expected one-year bond rates, or 3 percent. Panel (b) displays a downward-sloping yield curve that results if the one-year bond rate is expected to fall from 2 percent to 1 percent; then the two-year bond rate is the average of the current and expected one-year bond rates, or 1.5 percent.

rate during the second period falls to $r_2^e = 0.01$ (or 1 percent). If the one-year bond rate is still $r_1 = 0.02$, then the two-year bond rate must change to induce savers to be willing to hold either one- or two-year bonds. The new two-year bond rate will have to be

$$R = (r_1 + r_2^e)/2 = (0.02 + 0.01)/2 = 0.015.$$

The two-year bond now will yield 1.5 percent per year. Panel (b) of Figure 4-5 shows the new yield curve for one- and two-year bonds. It slopes downward.

What has changed to cause the yield curve to be downward sloping, or inverted? Previously, the one-year bond rate was expected to *rise* from 2 percent to 4 percent. This caused the yield curve in panel (a) of Figure 4-5 to slope upward. But now the one-year bond rate is expected to *fall* from 2 percent to 1 percent. This causes the yield curve's slope to be "inverted," as in panel (b). The yield curve now slopes downward.

Strengths and Weaknesses of the Expectations Theory Clearly, the expectations theory is not as simple as the segmented markets theory. Nevertheless, it has a very important virtue: it potentially can explain why yield curves slope upward or downward. An upward-sloping yield curve indicates a general expectation by savers that short-term interest rates will rise. A downward-sloping yield curve indicates a general expectation that short-term interest rates will decline.

There is a problem with the expectations theory, however. Yield curves usually slope upward. According to the expectations theory, this would imply that savers almost *always* expect short-term interest rates to rise. But over long periods interest rates typically are as likely to fall as they are to rise. This means that the expectations theory cannot be a full theory of the term structure of interest rates.

The Preferred Habitat Theory

Preferred habitat theory: A theory of the term structure of interest rates that views bonds as imperfectly substitutable, so yields on longer-term bonds must be greater than those on shorter-term bonds even if short-term interest rates are not expected to rise or fall.

Term premium: An amount by which the yield on a long-term bond must exceed the yield on a short-term bond to make individuals willing to hold either bond if they expect short-term bond yields to remain unchanged.

The **preferred habitat theory** combines elements of the segmented markets theory and the expectations theory. According to the segmented markets theory, bonds whose maturities differ are not at all substitutable. The expectations theory, in contrast, assumes that bonds with different maturities are *perfect* substitutes. This is why savers will hold both one- and two-year bonds only if their expected returns are equal.

According to the preferred habitat theory, bonds with different maturities are substitutable, but only imperfectly. Under this theory, savers generally have a slight preference to hold bonds with shorter maturities. Recall from Chapter 3 that money market trading is broader and more active than trading in capital markets. Consequently, money market instruments—bonds with shorter maturities—are more liquid instruments. This greater liquidity of short-term bonds can make them somewhat more attractive to savers than longer-term bonds. Hence, savers can "prefer the habitat" of money markets just as animals prefer their own special habitat, or locations, in the wild.

THE TERM PREMIUM To induce savers to hold longer-term bonds, the returns on those bonds actually must slightly *exceed* the returns on shorter-term bonds. That is, savers need to earn a **term premium** on longer-term bonds. This compensates savers for holding long-term bonds as well as short-term bonds.

Consequently, the preferred habitat theory modifies the expectations hypothesis by adding a term premium. Using our two-year example, the rate on the two-year bond now would be

$$R = TP + [(r_1 + r_2^e)/2],$$

where TP is the term premium for the two-year bond.

For instance, suppose that $r_1 = r_2^e = 0.02$, so savers expect that the one-year bond rate will remain at 2 percent for both years. Suppose also that savers have a strong preference to hold one-year bonds, so the term premium is $TP = 0.005$, or 0.5 percent. This 0.5 percent premium in the long-term yield is needed to induce savers to hold two-year bonds as well as one-year bonds. The two-year bond rate would be

$$\begin{aligned} R &= TP + [(r_1 + r_2^e)/2] \\ &= 0.005 + [(0.02 + 0.02)/2] \\ &= 0.005 + 0.02 = 0.025. \end{aligned}$$

So, under these conditions, the two-year bond rate is equal to 2.5 percent even though the one-year bond rate is expected to remain at 2 percent over both years. This implies that the yield curve relating the yields on one- and two-year bonds slopes upward, as shown in panel (a) of Figure 4-6 on the next page. The yield curve slopes upward even though the one-year bond rate is not expected to rise. Hence, over a long period in which interest rates are equally likely to rise or fall, the yield curve typically will have a positive slope.

EXPLAINING CHANGES IN THE SLOPE OF THE YIELD CURVE Now suppose that all the numbers in our example stay the same except for the expectation of the one-year bond rate for the second year. Let's suppose that savers expect the one-year

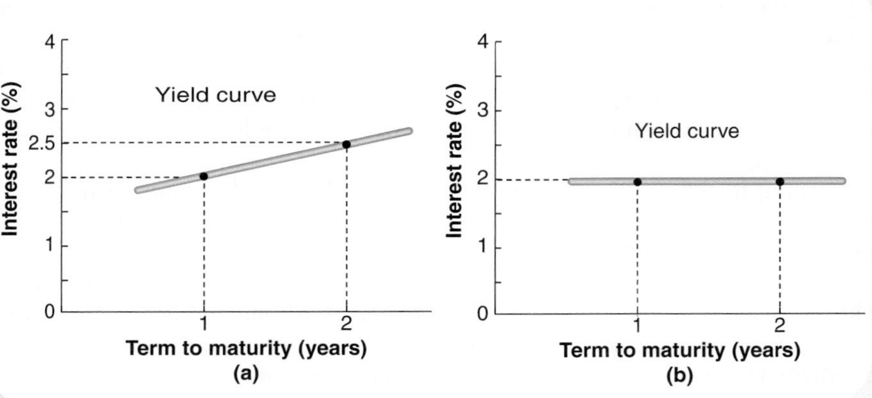

Figure 4-6
Sample Yield Curves for the Preferred Habitat Theory.

Panel (a) shows an upward-sloping yield curve that arises under the preferred habitat theory of the term structure of interest rates if there is a 0.5 percent term premium and if the one-year bond rate is expected to remain unchanged at its current level of 2 percent; then the two-year bond rate is the sum of the term premium and the average of the current and expected one-year bond rates, or 0,5 percent + 2 percent = 2.5 percent. Panel (b) displays a horizontal yield curve that results if the one-year bond rate is expected to fall from 2 percent to 1 percent; then the two-year bond rate is the sum of the term premium and the average of the current and expected one-year bond rates, or 0.5 percent + 1.5 percent = 2 percent.

bond rate to fall from 2 percent in the first year to 1 percent in the second. Then the preferred habitat theory predicts that the two-year bond rate will be

$$\begin{aligned} R &= TP + [(r_1 + r_2^e)/2] \\ &= 0.005 + [(0.02 + 0.01)/2] \\ &= 0.005 + 0.015 = 0.02. \end{aligned}$$

Hence, the one- and two-year bond rates will be equal. The yield curve will be horizontal, as in panel (b) of Figure 4-6.

This means that in our example, the only way that the yield curve could slope downward would be if the one-year bond rate were expected to fall from 2 percent to *below* 1 percent. In contrast, if the one-year bond rate were expected to fall only "a little," say, from 2 percent to 1.75 percent, the yield curve would still slope upward.

For a practical example contemplating why interest rates on short- and longer-term financial instruments might differ, go to the Chapter 4 Case Study, entitled "Did Mortgage Lenders Make a Killing in 2001 and 2002?"
http://www.moneyxtra.swcollege.com

The preferred habitat theory predicts that the yield curve will typically slope upward. This squares with the real-world facts. The theory also predicts that the yield curve will slope downward only in situations in which short-term interest rates are expected to decline sharply. Such situations can arise from time to time over long periods, but they nevertheless are relatively rare. Therefore, inverted yield curves should be observed infrequently. This is what we observe.

One feature of the preferred habitat theory is that it enables us to infer general interest rate expectations simply by looking at a yield curve. On the one hand, if we see that a yield curve for Treasury securities is nearly horizontal or inverted, then we can surmise that most savers believe that rates on T-bills are likely to decline. On the other hand, if we observe a very steeply sloped yield curve for Treasury securities, then we can determine that most savers expect that T-bill rates are likely to rise. In the intermediate situation in which most savers do not expect short-term interest rates to change, then, in contrast to the expectations theory's prediction of a horizontal yield curve, the preferred habitat theory indicates that we should observe a Treasury security yield curve with a fairly shallow, upward slope. In fact, this is typically what we see.

3. Why do market interest rates vary with differences in financial instruments' terms to maturity? Yields across maturities will not be equal for two reasons. One is expectations that short-term rates may rise or fall. Another is that short-term financial instruments generally are more liquid and less risky than longer-term instruments. Hence, a term premium is needed to induce individuals to be indifferent between holding either long-term or short-term instruments.

Nominal versus Real Rates of Interest

To this point, we have discussed interest rates only in *current-dollar* terms. There is a problem with this, however. Inflation can erode the value of interest received when a financial instrument matures. Any individual must take this into account when evaluating how much to save.

For instance, suppose that a saver can earn a stated current-dollar interest rate, or **nominal interest rate,** of $r = 0.04$ (4 percent) on each dollar that he allocates to a one-year bond. Suppose also that the saver expects that prices of goods and services will rise by a factor of $\pi^e = 0.02$ (2 percent) during the coming year, where π^e is the expected rate of inflation. This is the rate of inflation that he expects to face. Such inflation will reduce the amount of goods and services that his interest return will permit him to purchase.

Thus, although the saver earns positive interest on the bond, he anticipates that inflation will eat away at that interest at the rate π^e. Hence, the **real interest rate** that this saver anticipates, or his expected inflation-adjusted interest rate, is *approximately* equal to

$$r^r = r - \pi^e = 0.04 - 0.02 = 0.02,$$

where r^r denotes the real interest rate. In terms of what his savings can buy, this saver actually anticipates earning only 2 percent on his one-year bond.

The real interest rate is crucial for determining *how much* the individual desires to save. The reason is that saving is forgone consumption. This individual is likely to give up more consumption now if the real rate of return on saving is larger. This means that the real interest rate is a crucial determinant of the saving in the nation where this saver is a citizen. Countries with high nominal interest rates often experience very low saving rates because expected inflation is so high. Indeed, U.S. interest rates reached double-digit levels in the 1970s, but expected inflation was also in double digits. During some intervals in that decade, real interest rates were *negative,* which strongly discouraged saving. (Today investors can purchase inflation-indexed Treasury securities, and some economists believe that yields on these financial instruments can help predict movements in overall stock prices; see on the following page *Management Focus: What Can Yields on Treasury Inflation-Indexed Securities Tell Us about U.S. Stock Prices?*)

Nominal interest rate: A rate of return in current-dollar terms that does not reflect anticipated inflation.

Real interest rate: The anticipated rate of return from holding a financial instrument after taking into account the extent to which inflation is expected to reduce the amount of goods and services that this return could be used to buy.

GLOBAL POLICY CYBER **MANAGEMENT Focus**

What Can Yields on Treasury Inflation-Indexed Securities Tell Us about U.S. Stock Prices?

On January, 29, 1997, the U.S. Department of the Treasury auctioned its first "real interest rate" bonds, or Treasury Inflation-Indexed Securities (TIIS), which are structured so that the value of the principal is adjusted for inflation each day, using changes in the consumer price index as a benchmark. Thus, the principal for a TIIS grows at the rate of inflation and maintains its real value. Every six months, the Treasury issues a fixed-rate coupon payment based on the revised principal amount. Because the fixed-rate coupon rises in proportion to the increase in principal, the interest rate remains at a constant real level. At maturity, the principal is returned to the investor fully adjusted for inflation or deflation.

TIIS Yields and Real Interest Rates

Because a TIIS offers a guaranteed real rate of return, the real yield on this instrument provides a good indication of the annual real return required to induce investors to hold these financial instruments. In addition, U.S. Treasury securities are widely viewed as essentially free of default risk. Hence, the TIIS yield approximates the *riskless* real rate of interest.

Because investments in the bond market must compete with direct business investments, the TIIS yield also provides a good indication of the average anticipated real rate of return on capital allocated to productive business ventures. Therefore, an increase in the market TIIS yield over time means that investors anticipate that they could earn a higher real return from using their funds to buy shares in business enterprises, so a higher TIIS yield is required to induce them to hold these securities instead. By way of contrast, a decrease in the market TIIS yield implies that investors anticipate that the real return on funds allocated to productive businesses will be lower in the future.

An Indicator of Overall Stock Market Performance?

Figure 4-7 displays both a market TIIS yield and the Nasdaq Composite Index, a measure of average prices of equity shares traded on the Nasdaq exchange, since early 1998. Stock prices tend to reflect investors' expectations of future rates of return. Consequently, movements in the TIIS yield and the Nasdaq Composite Index are closely related.

Note that sharp swings in the TIIS yield tend to precede big move-

For purposes of deciding how to allocate saving among alternative financial instruments, however, an individual saver is safe in comparing current-dollar, or nominal, yields. The reason is that to calculate the real yield on each instrument, the saver would subtract the same expected inflation rate π^e from each instrument's annual nominal yield. If the nominal yield on one instrument exceeds the nominal yield on the other, then so will its real yield.

4. What is the real interest rate? This is the anticipated inflation-adjusted yield on a financial instrument. The real interest rate is equal to the current-dollar yield less the expected rate of inflation.

ments in the Nasdaq Composite Index. One interpretation of this pattern is that the TIIS yield adjusts quickly to changes in investors' anticipations of the future *average* real rate of return across the economy. Share prices, by way of contrast, adjust on a stock-by-stock basis, as investors sort out which companies' rates of return will tend to be higher or lower than the economy-wide average. Hence, a lagged adjustment in stock price indexes, such as the Nasdaq Composite Index, can occur. As a result, the TIIS yield may have some promise as an indicator of overall stock market performance.

FOR CRITICAL ANALYSIS: Under what circumstances could a trader earn profits?

Figure 4-7
Market Yields on Treasury Inflation-Indexed Securities and the Nasdaq Composite Index.

There has been a close relationship between the yield on the U.S. Treasury's inflation-indexed bonds and the overall performance of Nasdaq-traded stocks.

SOURCE: William Emmons, "Expectations and Fundamentals," Federal Reserve Bank of St. Louis *Monetary Trends*, July 2001.

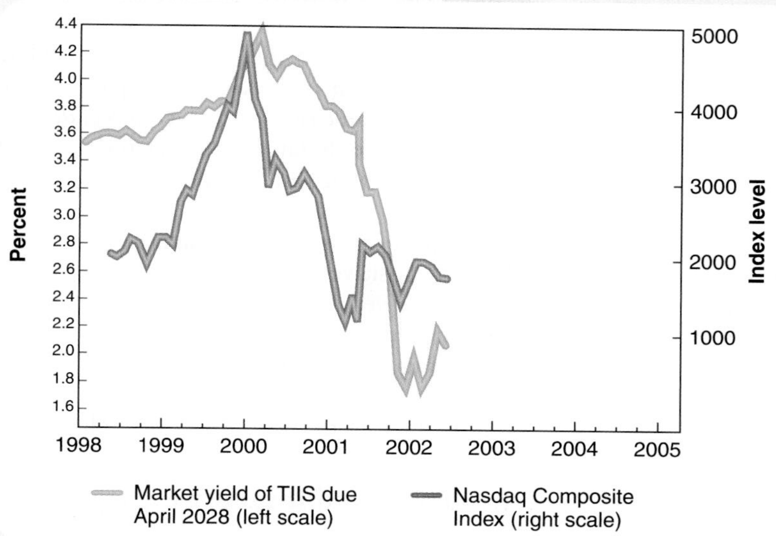

Interest Rates in an Interdependent World

The financial instruments held by U.S. residents are not limited to those issued by U.S. local, state, or federal governments or by U.S. corporations. Many U.S. citizens, businesses, and financial institutions also hold bonds issued by foreign governments and foreign businesses. Such bonds are not denominated in U.S. dollars. Instead, they are denominated in the currency of the nation of origin.

For instance, suppose that an American bank is considering holding U.S. Treasury bonds or bonds issued by the government of Japan. The bonds have the same maturity. In addition, the bank views both bonds as possessing equally low risk. And so, holding other factors constant, it might view the bonds as perfect substitutes. Yet the U.S. Treasury bond has an annual interest yield of r_{US} that

moneyxtra!
Another Perspective

Learn more about Treasury Inflation-Indexed Securities by using the Web-based Chapter 4 reading, entitled "The Information Content of Treasury Inflation-Indexed Securities," by William Emmons of the Federal Reserve Bank of St. Louis.

http://moneyxtra.swcollege.com

Exchange rate: The value of one currency in terms of another.

Depreciation: A decline in the value of one currency relative to another.

Appreciation: A rise in the value of one currency relative to another.

applies to the *dollar* denomination of the bond. In contrast, the Japanese bond has a lower annual interest yield of r_J that applies to the *yen* denomination of the bond.

The Exchange Rate, Depreciation, and Appreciation

How does the bank evaluate this situation? First, it must account for the different currency denominations of the bond. To do this, the bank must take into account the dollar-yen **exchange rate.** This is the dollar price of the yen, measured in dollars per yen.

Suppose that the current dollar-yen exchange rate is \$0.01 per yen, or $S = \$0.01/\text{yen}$, where S denotes the current exchange rate. (Hence, \$1 = 100 yen.) Note that if S were to increase, say, to a value of \$0.015, more dollars would be required to obtain one yen. This would mean that the dollar would lose some of its value relative to the yen. When the dollar loses value relative to the currency of another country, such as the Japanese yen, then the dollar **depreciates.** Hence, a *rise* in the value of S implies a *depreciation* of the value of the dollar relative to the yen. But if the dollar depreciates relative to the yen, then the yen has **appreciated** relative to the dollar. The yen's dollar value increases with a rise in the exchange rate S.

Suppose that the dollar depreciates relative to the yen at a rate s over time. Here, a positive value of s indicates a positive *rate of depreciation* of the dollar versus the yen. This would imply a fall in the value of the dollar relative to the yen. Indeed, between 1985 and 1995, the dollar depreciated relative to the yen at an average rate of 9 percent per year. Then, between 1995 and 2001, the dollar appreciated relative to the yen at an average rate of 8 percent per year. We shall discuss factors that can result in such exchange rate movements in Chapter 6.

International Interest Parity

Now let's think about the decision faced by our hypothetical bank. If it holds the dollar-denominated U.S. Treasury bond, then its total return is simply the interest return r_{US}. But if the bank holds the Japanese government bond, then it earns interest at the rate r_J. In addition, however, it anticipates that the dollar value of the yen-denominated bond will rise at an expected rate of s^e.

This bank—as well as others making a similar decision—will be willing to hold either American or Japanese government bonds only if the anticipated returns on the two are equal. This will be true when

$$r_{US} = r_J + s^e.$$

To induce holdings of *both* the American and the Japanese bonds, the U.S. Treasury bond rate must equal the Japanese government bond rate plus the rate at which the dollar is expected to depreciate relative to the yen.

This condition is very commonsensical. If the yen is appreciating relative to the dollar, then the dollar is depreciating relative to the yen. This means that for a dollar-denominated U.S. Treasury bond to yield a return comparable to the return on a Japanese bond, the U.S. bond's yield must be higher to compensate for any expected depreciation in the dollar relative to the yen. If s^e is positive, then potential holders of the bonds anticipate that the yen will appreciate and the dollar will depreciate. The U.S. Treasury bond's interest yield must be greater than the yield on the Japanese government bond to make up for this expected depreciation of the dollar. The amount by which the U.S. Treasury bond yield will exceed the Japanese government bond yield is equal to the rate at which the dollar is expected to depreciate relative to the yen, or s^e.

The technical name for this condition is **uncovered interest parity.** This condition applies to interest yields on bonds with identical risks and terms to maturity that are denominated in different national currencies. It is called "uncovered" interest parity because it does not arise from foreign exchange transactions that "cover" risks. According to the uncovered interest parity condition, the bond denominated in the currency that is expected to depreciate must have the higher of the two interest rates. The yield of the bond denominated in the currency that is expected to depreciate must exceed the other bond's yield by the rate at which the currency is expected to depreciate. We shall explore uncovered interest parity in greater detail in Chapter 9, where we shall also investigate *covered interest parity.*

Uncovered interest parity: A relationship between interest rates on bonds that are similar in all respects other than that they are denominated in different nations' currencies. According to this condition, the yield on the bond denominated in the currency that holders anticipate will depreciate must exceed the yield on the other bond by the rate at which the currency is expected to depreciate.

Federal funds rate: A short-term (usually overnight) interest rate on interbank loans in the United States.

5. How are interest yields on bonds issued in different countries related? As long as the bonds share other common characteristics, uncovered interest parity will hold. This means that the yield on the bond denominated in a currency that holders anticipate will depreciate must pay a yield that exceeds the other bond's yield by the expected rate of currency depreciation.

Key Interest Rates in the Global Economy

There are many financial markets. Hence, there are many interest rates. Three are especially important as "barometers" of conditions in financial markets.

The Federal Funds Rate

One of these key interest rates is at the shortest end of the maturity spectrum. It is the **federal funds rate,** or the market rate on interbank loans. As you learned in Chapter 3, such loans are known as "federal funds" only because banks make the loans by transferring reserves that they hold at Federal Reserve banks. Most of these loans have maturities of one or two days, so these are very short-term loans. Indeed, some federal funds loans have effective maturities of only a few hours.

Because the federal funds rate is a ready measure of the price that banks must pay to raise funds, the Federal Reserve often uses it as a yardstick for gauging the effects of its policies. Consequently, the federal funds rate is a closely watched indicator of the Federal Reserve's intentions.

The "federal funds rate" is really an average of rates across banks. Some banks pay lower interest rates to borrow federal funds than others because they are better credit risks. In addition, some very large banks both borrow and lend federal funds, even during the same day. These banks act as *dealers* in the federal funds

Prime rate: The interest rate that American banks charge on loans to the most creditworthy business borrowers.

market. They profit from lending federal funds at rates that slightly exceed the rates at which they borrow federal funds. Brokers also are active in the federal funds market. They match banks that need to borrow federal funds with other depository institutions that are willing to lend.

The Prime Rate

The **prime rate** is the rate that banks charge on short-term loans that they make to the most creditworthy business borrowers. These are the borrowers with the lowest perceived risk of default. Many other lending rates are based on the prime rate, so it is a key indicator of conditions in loan markets.

Figure 4-8 displays the behavior of the prime rate since 1940. Note that until the 1970s the prime rate showed little variation. Since then, however, the prime rate has been less rigid. There are two likely explanations for this. One is that interest rates generally have been more volatile since the beginning of the 1970s. Another is that nationwide competition among banks has increased since that time. As a result, banks have adjusted the prime rate more quickly to variations in other market interest rates. In addition, they have also begun to lend to their truly "best" customers at rates below the benchmark prime rate.

On the Web
What is the current prime rate? View this information, as well as data on many other market interest rates, in the Federal Reserve's H15 *Statistical Release,* at http://www.federalreserve.gov/releases/H15/update.

The London Interbank Offer Rate (LIBOR)

In international financial markets, bonds and deposits are denominated in a variety of currencies and pay interest yields that apply to these various currency denominations. Comparing interest yields can become complicated for those who

Figure 4-8
The Prime Rate.

The prime rate has been more volatile since the 1970s, although it has been less variable in recent years.

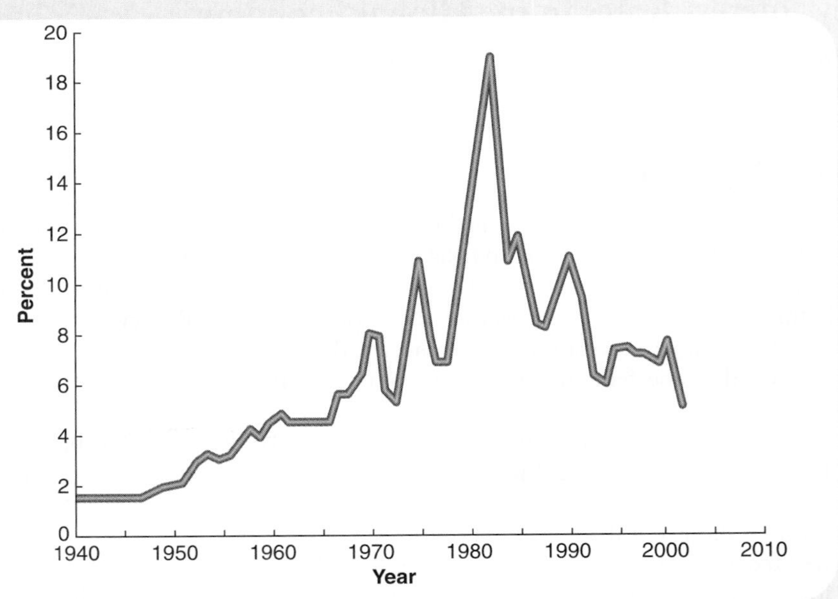

SOURCES: *2000 Economic Report of the President* and *Federal Reserve Bulletin,* various issues.

Link to Policy

Does the Yield Curve Predict Recessions?

As you learned in this chapter, a yield curve depicts interest rates for bonds with similar risk features but differing terms to maturity. Usually, yield curves slope upward. Nevertheless, sometimes short-term interest rates are close to or even above long-term interest rates, causing the yield curve to be nearly flat or even inverted and downward sloping. It is in these situations that a number of economists believe yield curves are indicative of looming business downturns.

The Slope of the Yield Curve and Economic Performance

There are two rationales for why a flat or downward-sloping yield curve might indicate that an economic slowdown is in the offing. One is that a flattened or inverted yield curve might result from tighter Federal Reserve monetary policy actions that push up short-term interest rates without bringing about immediate increases in longer-term interest rates (see Chapter 20). Such Fed actions typically aim to put a damper on economic activity, so a shallower or even downward-sloping yield curve might precede a business recession as a result. For instance, a significant Fed tightening in the late 1970s contributed to an inversion of the yield curve in 1979 that preceded a sharp recession in 1981 and 1982.

The expectations theory of the term structure of interest rates points to another reason that a decline in the slope of the yield curve might be a precursor of falling economic activity. A flat or inverted yield curve may indicate that people generally anticipate lower future short-term interest rates. To the extent that expectations of reduced real rates of return on business investment projects are associated with an anticipation of lower future interest rates, a flat or inverted yield curve might signal that businesspersons are likely to cut back on investment, which could lead to a more generalized falloff in business activity.

Post Hoc, Ergo Propter Hoc?

Economists sometimes use the Latin phrase *post hoc, ergo propter hoc,* which means "after this, therefore because of this," to describe the logical fallacy of ascribing a causal role to a particular occurrence just because it happens to precede another event. There is good reason to worry that associating recessions with the slope of the yield curve may suffer from this fallacy.

During business expansions, businesses' demand for short-term credit tends to increase because improving economic conditions naturally encourage firms to add to their working capital as they endeavor to ramp up production. This increased demand for credit, however, tends to push up short-term interest rates relative to longer-term interest rates. As a consequence, it is possible for the slope of the yield curve to decline during business expansions without necessarily implying that a recession is on the horizon. For several years after 1961, for instance, the yield curve was relatively shallow and even became inverted for a time. No recession took place until 1969, however. On the one hand, one might say that there was simply a long lag before the recession occurred. On the other hand, it is also arguable that a flattened or inverted yield curve is really associated with a business expansion. In principle, recessions that follow could occur simply as a natural course of the nation's business cycle.

Is the Yield Curve's Slope a Good Predictor of Business Downturns?

Economists have subjected the relationship between the slope of the yield curve and business activity to considerable study in recent years. Although they do not claim to fully understand the relationship, there is now general agreement on one thing: for

Continued on next page

Link to the Policy, continued

whatever reason, a flattened or inverted yield curve is definitely a good predictor of recessions.

One way that economists use the slope of the yield curve to predict recessions is by including measures of the slope in statistical models used to predict the probability of a business downturn. Figure 4-9 shows estimates of the probability of a recession based on the difference between the ten-year Treasury bond rate and the three-month T-bill rate and the difference between the twenty-year Aaa corporate bond rate and the three-month T-bill rate. A narrowing of those differences or a negative value tends to push up the probability of a recession shortly before a recession actually occurs. A number of studies have found that the slope of the yield curve is the single best indicator of whether a recession may be in the offing.

Economic policymakers rarely base their own forecasts of economic performance solely on the shape of the yield curve. Using the yield curve's slope to supplement policy forecasts offers one big advantage, however: it is relatively quick and simple to do. In addition, if forecasts using a more sophisticated approach indicate that a recession is on the horizon, policymakers can feel more confident in that conclusion if the yield curve is also flattening or inverting. Using this information, policymakers may be able to respond more quickly to the potential for a recession by implementing policies intended to reduce its severity.

Research Project

How do delays in information about the state of the economy complicate policymakers' efforts to stabilize business cycles? In what ways might policymakers make concrete use of the yield curve's slope to assist them in responding more rapidly to the threat of a recession?

Web Resources

1. How do economists use the yield curve to predict recessions? Find out more by reading a Federal Reserve Bank of New York summary of this approach to recession forecasting at http://www.ny.frb.org/rmaghome/curr_iss/ci2-7.pdf.

2. To learn more about the rationale for a relationship between the yield curve's slope and business activity, read a discussion of the topic by Campbell Harvey of Duke University at http://www.newyorkfed.org/rmaghome/staff_rp/2001/Sr/134pdf.

Figure 4-9
Estimated Probabilities of a Recession Based on Spreads between Long-Term Bond Rates and Three-Month Treasury Bill Rates.

Statistical models using the spreads between the ten-year Treasury bond rate and the three-month T-bill rate and between the rate on corporate bonds with twenty or more years to maturity and the three-month T-bill rate produce estimated probabilities of a recession. These estimated probabilities tend to increase before a recession actually takes place.

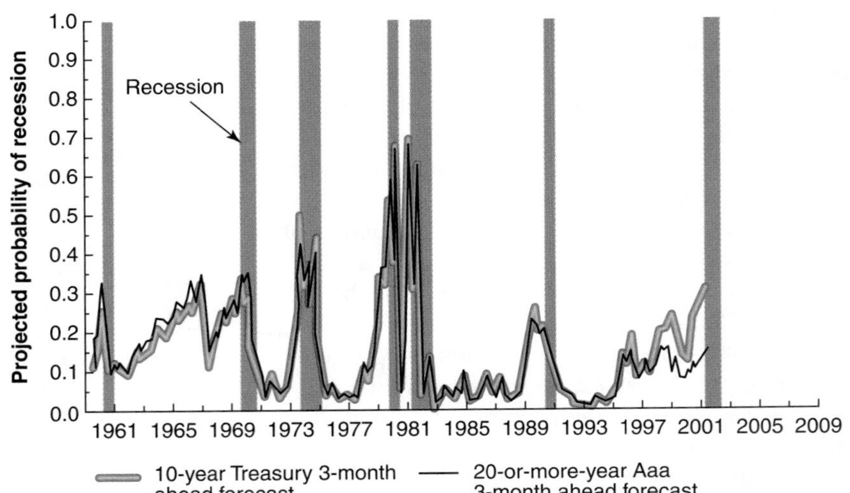

SOURCE: Christopher Neely, "What Is the Slope of the Yield Curve Telling Us?" Federal Reserve Bank of St. Louis *Monetary Trends*, August 2000.

trade such instruments. This is particularly true in **Eurocurrency markets.** These are markets for bonds, loans, and deposits denominated in currencies of given nations yet held and traded outside those nations' borders. The market for Eurodollar deposits is an example of a Eurocurrency market.

Eurocurrency markets: Markets for bonds, loans, and deposits denominated in the currency of a given nation but held and traded outside that nation's borders.

To assist in comparing interest rates in Eurocurrency markets, traders have adopted the convention of quoting rates on such bonds, loans, and deposits using a single interest rate as a benchmark. This benchmark rate is the **London Interbank Offer Rate,** or **LIBOR.** LIBOR is the interest rate at which six large London banks stand willing to lend to or borrow from each other when market trading opens on a given day.

London Interbank Offer Rate (LIBOR): The interest rate on interbank loans traded among six large London banks.

In a sense, LIBOR is the international equivalent of the American federal funds rate. It is a rough measure of the cost of funds to London banks that are especially active in international financial markets. Consequently, it is a useful barometer of conditions in those markets. Rates on Eurocurrency bonds, loans, and deposits therefore are measured as "markups" or "markdowns" from LIBOR. For instance, a Eurocurrency bond rate may be quoted as "LIBOR plus one percent." This indicates that if LIBOR currently is 5 percent, then the Eurocurrency bond rate in question is equal to 6 percent.

We shall have more to say about these key interest rates and how to interpret their movements in later chapters. In the next chapter, however, we shall provide a more detailed look at the wide variety of financial instruments in today's economy. This will set the stage for a fuller analysis of how financial institutions and the economy are affected by variations in the interest yields of these instruments.

6. What interest rates are the key indicators of financial market conditions? The three most widely watched interest rates are the federal funds rate, the prime rate, and the London Interbank Offer Rate (LIBOR).

Chapter Summary

1. Computing Different Interest Yields: Any interest yield must have a basis of comparison, such as the principal of a loan, face value of a bond, or market price of either a loan or a bond. Furthermore, the effective yield on any financial instrument depends on the remaining number of days, weeks, or months until it matures. All these factors affect the calculation of alternative yields on financial instruments. Hence, different yields must be considered.

2. Risk and Market Interest Rates: Risky and fairly illiquid financial instruments will be held when other less risky and more liquid instruments are available only if risk premiums are included in their yields. Therefore, yields on riskier and fairly illiquid instruments typically are higher than the yields of the other instruments.

3. Market Interest Rates and Different Terms to Maturity: Interest yields differ based on term to maturity for two reasons. One is that yields on longer-term financial instruments depend on expectations about yields on shorter-term instruments. Another is that longer-term instruments typically are less liquid and more risky. Consequently, longer-term financial instruments are more likely to be held if they have a somewhat higher yield than shorter-term instruments.

4. The Real Interest Rate: This is the nominal interest rate minus the expected rate of inflation. It provides a measure of the extent to which inflation is anticipated to reduce the purchasing power of interest earnings on financial instruments.

5. Relating Interest Yields on Bonds Issued in Different Countries: For those bonds that are identical in all respects other than that they are denominated in different nations' currencies, yields are related through the uncovered interest parity condition. This says that a bond denominated in a currency whose value is expected to depreciate must offer a yield that is higher than the yield on the other bond. The difference in yields will equal the expected rate of currency depreciation.

6. Key Interest Rate Indicators of Financial Market Conditions: The federal funds rate is a measure of the immediate cost of funds for American banks and is an important indicator of Federal Reserve monetary policy. The prime rate is a barometer of aggregate loan market conditions and is a base for other lending rates. The London Interbank Offer Rate (LIBOR) is the basis for interest rate quotes on many internationally traded financial instruments.

Questions and Problems

(Answers to odd-numbered questions and problems may be found on the Web at http://money.swcollege.com under "Student Resources.")

1. The formula for the price of a consol with an annual coupon return of C is C/r. Note that the discounted present value of C dollars received each year forever is equal to the infinite sum,

$$P = C/(1 + r) + C/(1 + r)^2 + C/(1 + r)^3 + C/(1 + r)^4 + \cdots$$

The amount P should be the price that the bearer of the consol would be willing to pay to hold this instrument. And so P should equal C/r. Prove that this is true. [Hint: Try multiplying the equation above by the factor $1/(1 + r)$. Then subtract the resulting equation from the equation above. Then solve for P.]

2. Explain why bond prices and interest rates are inversely related, holding all other factors unchanged.

3. Suppose that an individual holds a 26-week (182-day) T-bill for 80 days but then offers to sell it to you at a price of $9,850. The face value of the T-bill is $10,000. What is the T-bill's yield over the remaining 102 days before it will mature?

4. Suppose that an individual holds a 13-week (91-day) T-bill for a number of days but then offers to sell it to you at a price of $9,920. The coupon equivalent yield for the T-bill, which has a face value of $10,000, is 5.84 percent. How many days remain before this bill matures?

5. A nation's yield curve slopes downward. Explain what this implies, according to the preferred habitat theory of the term structure of interest rates.

6. Suppose that the three-month T-bill rate is 5.4 percent. The term premium for a six-month T-bill is equal to 0.1 percent, and the current rate on a six-month T-bill is 5.6 percent. According to the basic theory of the term structure of interest rates, what is the expected three-month T-bill rate for three months from now?

7. Most federal funds loans among banks have an overnight maturity. Typically, the overnight federal funds rate exceeds the three-month T-bill rate. Does this mean that the yield curve spanning maturities from one day to three months is normally inverted, or can you think of another possible reason for this observation? [Hint: There is a slight risk that a bank may default, or at least have a liquidity crunch, on any given day.]

8. Suppose that a U.S. Treasury bill has an annualized yield of 6.5 percent. A German government bill with the same maturity and equal risk characteristics has an annualized yield of 5.5 percent. Which country's currency is expected to *depreciate*? What is the expected rate of depreciation of this nation's currency?

9. A Malaysian government bond has an annualized yield of 12.25 percent. A U.S. Treasury bond with the same maturity has a yield of only 5.85 percent, however. Is it necessarily the case that the Malaysian currency (the ringgit) is expected to depreciate, or could there be another possible explanation for the difference in the yields? Justify your answer.

10. The real interest rate on a Treasury bond is 3 percent. The anticipated inflation rate is 4.5 percent. What is the Treasury bond's approximate nominal interest rate?

Before the Test

Test your understanding of the material covered in this chapter by taking the Chapter 4 interactive quiz at http://money.swcollege.com.

Online Application

Internet URL: http://www.federalreserve.gov/

Title: Selected Interest Rates—Board of Governors of the Federal Reserve System

Navigation: Begin at the Federal Reserve Board's home page above. Click on "Economic Research and Data," and then click on "Statistics: Releases and Historical Data."

Application: Follow the remaining instructions, and use data reported about selected interest rates to answer the following questions:

1. Next to the "Daily Release" heading beside "H.15," click on "Daily Update." Does the yield curve for Treasury securities (look at the rates under "Treasury Constant Maturities") have an upward slope? If so, is the slope relatively steep or shallow? Is the yield curve nearly flat or even inverted? Based on your answers to these questions, can you make any rough inferences about general expectations about the future behavior of short-term interest rates on Treasury securities?

2. At the same location, take a look at the yields on corporate bonds, and compare these with longer-term Treasury bond yields. Which rates are higher? Is this because of the term structure of interest rates or the risk structure of interest rates? Explain your reasoning.

For Group Study and Analysis: Go back to previous screen. Next to the "Monthly Release" heading beside "G.13," click on "Releases." Divide into groups, with each group assigned a different monthly release. Have each procure an identical overhead transparency plotting yield against maturity. Have each group plot a yield curve for Treasury securities (using the same "Treasury Constant Maturities" yield data referred to in question 1 above). Then superimpose these transparencies on an overhead projector to get a picture of how the yield curve has shifted and/or twisted over time. Discuss factors that may have led to recent changes in the position and/or shape of the yield curve.

Selected References and Further Reading

Ayuso, J., A. G. Haldane, and F. Restoy. "Volatility Transmission along the Money Market Yield Curve." *Weltwirtschaftliches Archiv (Review of World Economics)* 133 (1997): 56–75.

Clayton, Gary, and Christopher Spivey. *The Time Value of Money*. Philadelphia: W. B. Saunders, 1978.

Cook, Timothy, and Thomas Hahn. "Interest Rate Expectations and the Slope of the Money Market Yield Curve." Federal Reserve Bank of Richmond *Economic Review* 76 (September/October 1990): 3–26.

Fisher, Irving. *The Theory of Interest*. New York: Augustus M. Kelley, 1965.

Mehra, Yash. "The Bond Rate and Actual Future Inflation." Federal Reserve Bank of Richmond *Economic Review* 84 (Spring 1998): 27–47.

Rudebusch, Glenn. "Federal Funds Interest Rate Targeting, Rational Expectations, and the Term Structure." *Journal of Monetary Economics* 35 (1995): 245–274.

MoneyXtra

moneyxtra! Log on to the MoneyXtra Web site now (**http://moneyxtra.swcollege.com**) for additional learning resources such as practice quizzes, case studies, readings, and additional economic applications.

Chapter

A World Market?—
International Financial Integration

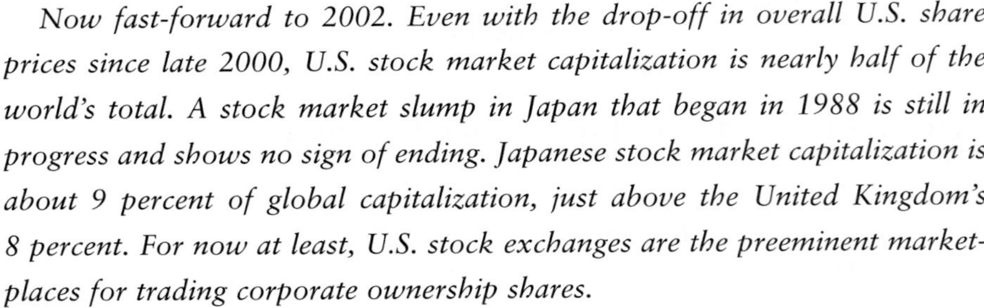

It is the fall of 1987, and even though U.S. stock prices have been on an upswing, the owners of the New York Stock Exchange and other major U.S. stock exchanges are expressing deep concerns about the even larger relative growth of Japanese stock markets. At one time, U.S. stock market capitalization eclipsed the total value of Japanese shares, but now Japan's stock markets account for more than 40 percent of the world's total stock market capitalization. U.S. markets are now just the world's second largest, with a 28 percent share.

Now fast-forward to 2002. Even with the drop-off in overall U.S. share prices since late 2000, U.S. stock market capitalization is nearly half of the world's total. A stock market slump in Japan that began in 1988 is still in progress and shows no sign of ending. Japanese stock market capitalization is about 9 percent of global capitalization, just above the United Kingdom's 8 percent. For now at least, U.S. stock exchanges are the preeminent marketplaces for trading corporate ownership shares.

Fundamental Issues

1. What is international financial integration?
2. How have cybertechnologies contributed to international financial integration?
3. What are capital controls?
4. What are vehicle currencies?
5. How do national banking systems differ?

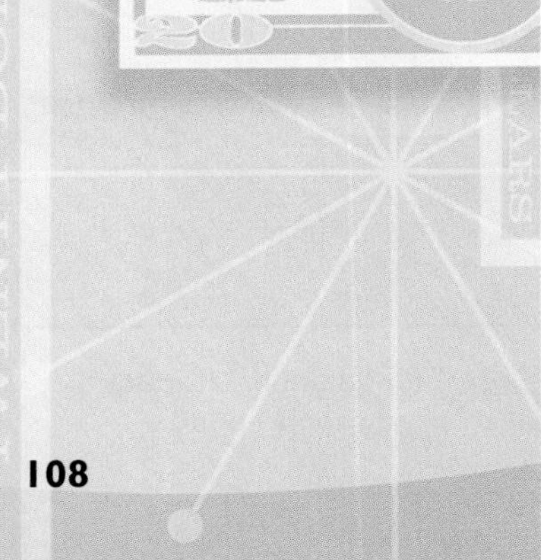

Changes in share prices provide part of the explanation for relative shrinkages or expansions of national stock markets. Another important factor is the ability of investors to shift their stock holdings between countries. Today the world's stock markets, as well as markets for bonds and other financial assets, are much more open to international investors than they were in the 1980s. The globalization of financial markets has serious implications for policymaking both at home and abroad. In this chapter you will examine whether or not we are truly in a world market.

International Money and Capital Markets

Until the 1980s, it was possible to examine the recent performance and future prospects of U.S. financial markets with relatively little immediate consideration of events in financial markets in Japan, Germany, the United Kingdom, or Russia (then part of the Soviet Union). Today, however, any evaluation of U.S. market conditions must take into account what is happening in markets abroad.

This is so because today we live in a world with relatively *high capital mobility.* **Capital mobility** refers to the ability to shift funds across borders for the purpose of purchasing financial instruments issued abroad. When capital mobility is high, savers can move funds across borders to aim for the highest available returns in light of the potential risks. Thus, a stock market boom in the United States can induce savers around the world to shift funds from London and Tokyo stock markets to those located in New York. Indeed, this appears to have occurred in recent years. In like manner, a Russian bond market crash can cause savers across the globe to move funds to the "safe haven" of the U.S. bond market, as took place in the late 1990s.

To evaluate these global market linkages, we begin by considering international money and capital markets. **International money markets** are the markets for cross-border exchanges of financial instruments with maturities of less than one year. **International capital markets** involve cross-border trades of instruments with maturities of at least one year.

Capital mobility: The extent to which savers can move funds across national borders for the purpose of buying financial instruments issued in other countries.

International money markets: Markets for cross-border exchange of financial instruments with maturities of less than one year.

International capital markets: Markets for cross-border exchange of financial instruments that have maturities of a year or more.

International Money Markets

Although a number of different types of instruments are traded in international money markets, foreign exchange instruments predominate. The daily activity on the world's foreign exchange markets exceeds $1 trillion. Often the daily volume exceeds the amount of total reserves of the world's central banks. In the United States alone, foreign exchange trading averages close to $500 billion per day. This amount is more than 70 percent of the *total assets* of the Federal Reserve System.

MEASURING TRADING VOLUMES IN INTERNATIONAL MONEY MARKETS A number of instruments other than foreign exchange instruments are also traded in international money markets. Some economists include *international derivative securities,* or securities whose returns are derived from the returns on other internationally traded instruments, among international money market instruments. There is some debate, however, concerning whether markets for derivatives should be considered alongside traditional money markets. The approach used by most economists, which we shall also adopt in this text, is to treat derivatives markets as separate from both the international money markets and the international capital markets. We shall discuss derivatives in depth in Chapter 8.

Transactions among large banks dominate trading in the international money market. Thus, we can use bank reports of their cross-border asset and liability positions to estimate the size of the market. Table 5-1 on the following page displays data for banks' cross-border positions. Reporting banks had over $20 trillion in both outstanding assets and liabilities. The total change in these positions during a recent year was close to $1 trillion.

On the Web

Where can one find a full discussion of worldwide international financial market developments? One place to check is the Annual Report of the Bank for International Settlements. Go to http://www.bis.org, click on "Publications and Statistics," and then "Regular Publications." Click on "Annual Report" and download the appropriate chapter.

Table 5-1 Cross-Border Positions of Major World Banks (Exchange-Rate-Adjusted Changes)

	Assets ($ Billions)	
	December 2001	Estimated Change in Year 2001
Industrial Countries	$ 9,183.2	$548.6
U.S. Dollar	3,894.8	283.9
Other Currencies	5,288.4	264.7
All Other Countries	2,299.5	302.3
Total	$11,482.7	$850.9
	Liabilities	
Industrial Countries	$ 9,040.1	$352.2
U.S. Dollar	4,136.9	193.7
Other Currencies	4,903.2	158.5
All Other Countries	2,122.3	404.7
Total	$11,162.4	$756.9

SOURCE: Bank for International Settlements, *International Banking and Financial Market Developments*, June 2002, and authors' estimates.

On the Web
Recent information on Eurocurrency markets may be obtained via the publication *Euromoney* at http://www.euromoney.com. Go to this Website, select "Markets and Products," and then search for recent articles relating to the market or instrument you wish to learn more about.

Table 5-1 also highlights the predominance of the banks of industrialized countries in the international money market. Cross-border positions of these banks comprise almost 80 percent of the total. The importance of the U.S. dollar is also apparent. More than one-third of the outstanding positions are denominated in dollars.

The Eurocurrency Markets The bulk of the world's money market activity takes place in the *Eurocurrency markets*. A Eurocurrency asset or liability is a bank asset or liability denominated in a currency other than that of the nation in which the asset or liability is physically located. For instance, a *Eurodollar deposit* is a bank deposit denominated in U.S. dollars, but located in a bank outside the United States.

The Eurocurrency markets are markets where banks and other institutions borrow and lend Eurocurrency assets or liabilities. These markets permit companies to raise funds in other nations. This is particularly useful for multinational firms. For instance, a German multinational company may issue commercial paper denominated in dollars in London. Thus, the Eurocurrency markets give the German company the capability to borrow from lenders that it would have difficulty connecting with in Germany's domestic financial markets. This is an example of the issuance of **Eurocommercial paper,** which is a short-term debt instrument issued by a firm and denominated in a currency other than that of the country where the firm is located. Each year, firms issue about $100 billion in Eurocommercial paper.

Eurocommercial paper: A short-term debt instrument issued by a firm and denominated in a currency other than that of the country where the firm is located.

London is the center of trading in the Eurocurrency markets, which are dominated by borrowing and lending activities among the world's largest banks. The most important money market instruments traded in the Eurocurrency market are **Eurocurrency deposits,** which are bank deposits denominated in currencies other than the currency of the nation where the deposits are located. The old

Eurocurrency deposits: Bank deposits denominated in the currency of one nation but located in a different nation.

Soviet Union's dollar-denominated (Eurodollar) deposits in London and Paris, for example, were Eurocurrency deposits. Today, however, bank deposits denominated in currencies from all over the world—including British pounds, European Monetary Union euros, and Japanese yen—are classified as Eurocurrency deposits. These deposits are a key source of funds for banks heavily involved in multinational lending.

On the Web
How did the London Stock Exchange evolve from a seventeenth-century joint stock company to one of the world's largest stock exchanges? Read a brief history at http://www.londonstockexchange.com. Under the heading "Home," select "About Us," then click on "History."

International Capital Markets

Most international bank loans are for terms exceeding a year. Hence, cross-border bank loans are international capital market instruments, as are internationally traded notes and bonds. Between 1986 and 2003, total trading activity in international capital markets increased by $1.5 trillion, or more than 3,000 percent. Activity in the international loan market, which accounts for just under a fifth of international capital market trading, has increased by 400 percent since the mid-1980s. Growth in international securities activity has been even greater. During the same period, the value of internationally traded securities outstanding has risen by nearly 500 percent.

Companies enter the Eurocurrency markets to raise funds in other nations or to issue notes and bonds denominated in other currencies. **Euronotes** are medium-term debt instruments issued in a currency other than that of the country where the notes are issued. These instruments typically have a longer term than Eurocommercial paper and a shorter term than **Eurobonds,** which are long-term debt instruments issued in a currency other than that of the country where the bonds are issued. For instance, if a Canadian business issues Canadian-dollar-denominated twenty-year bonds in London, then it has issued a Eurobond. More than $400 billion in Euronotes and $600 billion in Eurobonds are issued in the international capital markets.

International Financial Integration

The growth in the international money and capital markets raises a natural question: To what extent has there been movement toward a single world market for financial instruments?

Euronotes: Medium-term debt instruments issued in a currency other than that of the country where the instruments are issued.

Eurobonds: Long-term debt instruments issued in a currency other than that of the country where the instruments are issued.

INTERNATIONAL FINANCIAL INTEGRATION Certainly, as we will see at the end of this chapter, the world's stock markets are so many and varied that no one can convincingly argue that there is currently one world market for stocks. Nevertheless, many economists would agree that **international financial integration,** which is a process by which national financial markets become more similar in structure and function and more interrelated, is under way in most parts of the world.

International financial integration: A process through which financial markets of various nations become more alike and more interconnected.

As we noted earlier, the Eurocurrency markets have become a central connection between the financial markets of nations. Depository institutions can use the Eurocurrency markets to gather deposit funds and redirect them to activities in nations beyond the country of origin. As a result, the Eurocurrency markets are now the focus of world *arbitrage*. **Arbitrage** is the process of buying an asset at a given price in one market and profiting by selling it at a higher price in another market.

Arbitrage: Purchasing an asset at the current price in one market and profiting by selling it at a higher price in another market.

To see how arbitrage can take place across national borders, envision a situation in which the interest yields on dollar-denominated assets held in the United

moneyxtra!
Economic Applications
How are financial markets performing in other nations? Take a look at the sample data file downloads available from Global Financial Data, Inc. via Corporate Finance Online.
http://moneyxtra.swcollege.com

States decline. This induces many individuals and corporations that hold such assets to shift them to Eurodollar deposits in London, Paris, and other locations outside North America. It also encourages a number of traders to convert their dollar-denominated assets to assets denominated in other nations' currencies. As a result, interest yields on assets denominated in currencies other than the dollar ultimately will have to adjust. The result, as discussed in Chapter 4, is international interest *parity*. Arbitrage in the interconnected Eurocurrency markets is the crucial mechanism by which international interest parity is maintained.

EUROPEAN FINANCIAL INTEGRATION VERSUS ASIAN DISINTEGRATION? Fully integrated financial markets would effectively function as a single market. Although the growth of Eurocurrency markets together with recent developments in communications and computing technology has speeded the process toward integration, complete integration on a worldwide basis has not yet occurred. National financial markets do not yet behave as one, but they do increasingly react to the same events.

Two opposing developments have influenced the degree of worldwide financial integration in recent years. One is the European Monetary Union (EMU), which began on January 1, 1999. A key objective of the EMU is the development of a "single market" for financial instruments issued by all participating nations. To pursue this goal, several nations that joined the EMU, such as Italy, Spain, and Portugal, have modernized their stock and bond markets and opened them more fully to traders from abroad. As a result, traders have greater opportunities to arbitrage both across European financial markets and among markets located inside and outside Europe.

At the same time, however, the Asian financial crises that occurred in the late 1990s slowed the pace of worldwide financial integration. Indeed, in some parts of Asia, such as Indonesia and Malaysia, there may have been a regression away from more integrated financial markets. Nevertheless, there is good reason to anticipate that these events were temporary impediments to continuing integration of world financial markets.

1. What is international financial integration? International financial integration is the gradual movement toward more similar and more interconnected national financial markets, in part via the continuing development of international money and capital markets. Integration permits traders to engage in arbitrage across financial markets located in different countries. Although events in Asia in the late 1990s slowed the pace of international financial integration, the European Monetary Union has helped to maintain the trend toward increased integration of world financial markets.

Cybertechnologies and International Financial Integration

Even though progress toward greater international financial integration experiences ebbs and flows, the intensified adoption of cybertechnologies in recent years suggests that the gradual movement toward increased integration will continue. This does not mean that business practices and governmental rules cannot slow down the adoption of cybertrading and other innovations that tend to open world financial markets to arbitrage. It does mean, however, that ultimately the efforts of sophisticated traders to break down national barriers are likely to prove unstoppable. (For many people, secular legality does not overcome spiritually based rules against consuming certain financial services across otherwise open borders, but now online banking is breaking down this barrier as well; see on page 114 *Cyber Focus: Making Islamic Financial Services Available on the Internet.*)

Technology and International Financial Integration

Paper currency and coins circulate among buyers and sellers via physical transfer. The same is true of checks, although payment intermediaries must also physically handle these means of payment. For both types of payment, people, trucks, or planes typically carry funds physically across national borders. This makes controlling cross-border flows of funds a potentially expensive proposition—security guards must be hired, border checkpoints must be established, and so on. Nevertheless, in principle a national government can, if it wishes, impose restrictions on currency, coins, checks, and other physical means of payment to try to influence the extent to which savers can engage in arbitrage across the nation's borders.

Electrons Are Hard to Stop Restraining the cross-border flows of funds via cybertechnologies, however, is not so simple. To see why, let's think about how electronic systems work. The assembly language of a computer interprets a basic machine language—codes consisting of a string of zeros (for "off") and ones (for "on")—and software repackages these machine-language codes into forms that human beings can understand and manipulate. Computers store coded information magnetically, on tapes, on hard or floppy disks, or, in the most recent generations of computers, on optical storage devices. Using phone lines or fiber-optic cables, we can transfer the information stored magnetically or optically on our computer to any other computer. As long as it can receive electronic impulses—data transmissions along waves of electrons bumping into each other along a pathway that physicists call the electromagnetic spectrum—a computer can receive all those zeros and ones and then store them magnetically and/or optically.

We do not really require physical connections like phone lines or fiber-optic cables to transmit the data electronically. We can also beam signals using cell phones or satellites. As long as someone inside a warm building in Antarctica has a computer and a sufficiently powerful transmitter/receiver, he or she can send or receive computer data files via satellite connections to virtually any location on the planet. Thus, stopping or slowing financial exchange along any national border is a tall order when financial cybertechnologies are available to people on both sides of the border.

Varying Speeds of Cybertechnology Adoption Although the technology exists for transferring funds electronically from any place in the world to another, the availability of that cybertechnology is far from uniform. U.S. and European financial institutions have led the way in the adoption of electronic trading and banking. Although banks in parts of Asia and Africa have been issuing smart

GLOBAL POLICY CYBER Focus MANAGEMENT

Making Islamic Financial Services Available on the Internet

The Islamic legal code, called the Shariah, forbids the world's approximately 1.2 billion Muslims from entering into financial contracts that entail payments of interest. The Shariah generally requires Muslims to enter into financial contracts that grant payments based on shares of ownership. Naturally, this rules out dealings with most conventional financial institutions.

Currently, more than 25 million Muslims are online, and by 2005 that number should exceed 125 million. Consequently, most observers expect an upsurge in Web sites offering financial services geared toward Muslims.

These sites are likely to follow the example of London-based IslamiQ.com, which has existed since early 2000 under the guidance of a Shariah board comprised of four Middle Eastern scholars. At this site, which offers services in both English and Arabic, Islamic believers can obtain information on financial institutions that comply with the Shariah. Companion sites are IslamiQstocks.com and IslamiQmoney.com, which provide real-time quotes from global stock exchanges and information and links to Islamic banking, finance, and insurance products and services.

For Critical Analysis: Which of the financial markets active in non-Islamic countries is most likely to satisfy the spiritual code of conduct laid out in the Shariah?

cards for some time, in other respects they lag behind in adopting cybertechnologies that Western banks have embraced.

Although Asian banks made big investments in computer hardware during the 1980s, they sometimes fail to put their computer technology to good use. Throughout much of Asia, bank employees make business decisions using fewer computer systems than their European and North American counterparts. Current estimates are that Asian banks spend less than half as much as European and North American banks on global electronic management systems. In general, Asian banks are several years behind in developing and implementing electronic systems for preventing and detecting fraud, monitoring loan performance, and keeping track of security portfolios.

For instance, consider a typical Japanese bank branch, which closes at 3:00 each afternoon. Loan officers at the branch still require loan approvals to bear red-ink stamps that have served for centuries in lieu of pen-and-ink signatures. An employee at the branch is only half as likely as a typical U.S. bank branch employee to have a networked desktop computer. As a result, Japanese banks' computer systems are underutilized by their employees. In addition, some electronic systems are hard for customers to use. Even today, some Japanese banks turn off their automated teller machines during nighttime hours. Few Japanese depositors have access to online banking, and savers engage in automated securities trading at far below the U.S. rate.

Thus, financial institutions and markets in much of Asia and Africa have some catching up to do. The same is true of most South American financial institutions and markets. (Online banking has caught on quickly in Brazil, however; see *Cyber Focus: Attracting New Banking Customers via the Internet in Brazil.*) In

GLOBAL POLICY **CYBER Focus** MANAGEMENT

Attracting New Banking Customers via the Internet in Brazil

Only about a fourth of Brazil's 170 million residents have bank accounts. The remainder of the Brazilian population is "unbanked." They purchase no banking services and conduct nearly all of their transactions with cash.

A number of Brazilian banks have opted to go online in an effort to attract new customers. This has posed a challenge, though, because only about 5 percent of Brazilians have Internet access. To address this problem, one institution, Banco Bradesco, began selling basic personal computers to all employees and current and new customers for $43 per month for a total of 24 months. In a nation where *monthly* interest rates on credit-card purchases are about 12 percent, this monthly payment plan was a tremendous bargain, and Banco Bradesco's computers were a big hit with both its employees and its customers.

The bank, which was the third bank in the world to offer online banking services, also provides limited free access to the Internet as part of the deal. In addition, it has transformed its Web site into a portal where customers can connect to more than 300 online retailers, buy and sell stocks, invest in mutual funds, and apply for credit cards. People who cannot afford to buy Banco Bradesco's computers can shop online at kiosks it has installed in its 2,500 branches. The bank's services also are available through cellular phones and Web TV.

Other Brazilian banks, such as Banco Itau and Banco Unibanco, are striving to keep pace by offering Internet-related deals to their own customers. Banco Itau purchased a 12 percent share of America Online's Latin American unit so that it can offer its customers unlimited free Internet access. Banco Unibanco also provides free access to entice new customers, and it offers a special credit-card product called "e-card," which customers can use to make payments for goods and services purchased on the Internet.

For Critical Analysis: What might motivate Brazilian banks to try to expand online access for both existing and new customers?

some nations in these regions, it is not always clear that the governments want to catch up. Some, in fact, have openly attempted to shift their financial systems into reverse gear by trying to impede the use of online trading and banking systems by making certain electronic (as well as physical) transmissions of financial data illegal.

2. How have cybertechnologies contributed to international financial integration? Electronic flows of data for placement in any computer's memory-storage system can be transferred via phone lines, fiber-optic cables, or wireless transmission. The advent of cybertechnologies has made it difficult for nations to enforce physical barriers to flows of funds across geographic boundaries. Various parts of the world are adopting electronic banking and trading systems at different speeds. Currently, financial institutions of Asia, Africa, and South America are lagging behind banks in Europe and North America in adopting cybertechnologies.

Capital controls: Legal restrictions on the ability of a nation's residents to hold and trade assets denominated in foreign currencies.

Putting a Lid on Open Financial Markets: Capital Controls

Limits that countries place on the flows of funds across their borders are known as **capital controls.** Traditionally, national governments impose capital controls in the form of restrictions on their citizenry's holdings of currencies or financial assets issued by other nations. They may also restrict the ability of their nations' residents to move their own currencies or financial assets abroad.

moneyxtra!

Another Perspective

Learn much more about purposes of and experiences with capital controls by going to the Chapter 5 reading entitled, "An Introduction to Capital Controls," by Christopher Neely of the Federal Reserve Bank of St. Louis.
http://moneyxtra.swcollege.com

The Rationale for Capital Controls A key purpose of capital controls is to insulate a nation's financial system from sudden shifts of funds across its borders. Consider the example of Malaysia, whose government imposed capital controls in September 1998. In 1997 and 1998, Malaysia had experienced a financial crisis when many Malaysian and foreign savers lost confidence in the country's ability to make good on its various commitments to repay loans denominated in U.S. dollars. When savers moved funds out of Malaysia, the country found itself in a real bind, because fewer foreign-denominated funds were available for use in making the promised loan payments. Inducing foreign savers to keep their funds in Malaysia would have required much higher interest rates, which the Malaysians felt would harm the local economy. Thus, in an effort to avoid economic pain at home, the Malaysian government enacted capital controls. It prohibited Malaysian citizens from trading the national currency, the ringgit, abroad and required them to move any ringgit held offshore back into Malaysia within a month's time. The Malaysian government barred Malaysian banks from selling ringgit to foreign banks and announced that foreign firms selling shares in Malaysia would be barred from exporting the proceeds for a year. It also required all Malaysian exports to be settled in foreign currency.

Malaysia is far from being a rare case. It is only a recent example. In fact, at one time or another every nation has imposed some type of restriction on the flow of capital. Indeed, nearly every government on the planet currently has some kind of restriction in place. Nevertheless, the trend from the 1970s through the end of the twentieth century was a gradual reduction in the use of capital controls, as countries that previously had a host of restrictions on cross-border funds trading—for example, France, Italy, Hong Kong, the United States—pared back the restrictions.

The Asian economic crisis of the late 1990s altered perspectives on capital controls, however. By the end of the 1990s, a number of nations were contemplating reimposing capital controls. Some of the world's top economists, such as Paul Krugman of Princeton University, even offered qualified support for imposing temporary controls in "emergency situations."

Can Capital Controls Work in a Cyberworld? In a world with financial cybertechnologies, however, imposing capital controls is much more costly than in years past. Indeed, some observers question whether democratic governments can enforce capital controls without fundamental restraints on basic freedoms that are inconsistent with most notions of what "democratic government" is supposed to mean.

Contemplate, for instance, your task if you were charged with enforcing capital controls in today's financial environment. In addition to establishing security details at every major airport, train station, and/or ship harbor, to effectively enforce a typical set of capital controls you would have to train and unleash squads of "cyberpolice" to monitor the computer storage and data interchange systems of every financial firm in the country. Since an intelligent citizenry might find a way around the controls via funds transferals using smart cards or other electronic payments media, you would also have to put the cyberpolice to work monitoring telephone lines and cell phone systems. Of course, once you had gone to the trouble to put this kind of enforcement system into place, you might be tempted to have your cyberpolice eavesdrop on what people were saying about you in their phone calls and e-mail messages.

Thus, effective enforcement of capital controls in a cyberworld would require transforming a nation into something resembling a police state. In fact, most observers believe that not just any police state can enforce capital controls. It would take a *highly efficient* police state—probably one that does intercept and read e-mail messages—to do the job. It seems unlikely that elected governments would be able to justify this type of policing. For this reason, many economists conclude that as cybertechnologies continue to proliferate, capital controls will be increasingly hard for democratic governments to impose.

moneyxtra! Online Case Study

To consider the issues a financial services company faces when deciding whether to offer Internet services in a country where capital controls are often implemented, go to the Chapter 5 Case Study, entitled "Banking on the Chinese Internet".
http://moneyxtra.swcollege.com

3. What are capital controls? Capital controls are governmental restrictions on flows of funds across a nation's borders. Cybertechnologies make enforcing capital controls more difficult, unless a government can marshal complete control over all computer links. Technical improvements in wireless transmission of data make it increasingly unlikely that a government will be able to prohibit all cross-border flows of funds, however.

Vehicle Currencies

If people from around the world continue to interact in increasingly integrated financial markets, what currencies will they use to buy and sell financial instruments? Money market and capital market instruments are denominated in a number of currencies. Most financial instruments, however, are denominated in a few key national currencies, known as **vehicle currencies,** or commonly accepted currencies used worldwide to denominate international financial instruments. For instance, a company in Thailand may issue a bond denominated in U.S. dollars that is subsequently purchased by a European saver. In this instance, the U.S. dollar serves as a vehicle currency. The bond exchange is denominated in U.S. dollars even though no party to the transaction is located in the United States or uses dollars as a medium of exchange.

The Dollar's Traditional Predominance

Vehicle currency: A commonly accepted currency that is used to denominate a transaction that does not take place in the nation that issues the currency.

Just as the automobile is a primary vehicle of transportation, during the initial decades after World War II the dollar was the main "vehicle" for completing international transactions. Even today, almost 70 percent of U.S. paper currency and coins circulate abroad. The dollar serves as a vehicle currency even for relatively small transactions that people typically use paper currency and coins to finance.

Challenges to the Dollar's Preeminence

After the late 1970s, the Japanese yen and the German deutsche mark challenged the dollar's preeminent role as a vehicle currency. Prior to the adoption of the euro in the European Monetary Union in 2001 and 2002, about 40 percent of paper currency and coins denominated in deutsche marks circulated outside Germany. For Japan, the comparable figure is approximately 10 percent. Although these percentages are below the 70 percent figure for U.S. paper currency and coins, they indicate that other currencies besides the dollar are also desirable means of payment outside their nations of origin.

Nevertheless, the U.S. dollar's position as the world's primary vehicle currency has not yet been seriously threatened. Table 5-2 presents evidence on overall utilization of the three leading vehicle currencies, the dollar, the euro, and the yen. The U.S. dollar remains the dominant vehicle currency: It is used to denominate more than 50 percent of banks' cross-border positions and well over one-third of international bond and note issues.

Could the euro eventually rival the dollar in world financial markets? A recent study by Federal Reserve economist Michael Leahy indicates that the answer may be yes. Leahy examined the likely effect of the euro's introduction on the dollar holdings of European residents and concluded that these dollar holdings might decline as much as 35 percent, thereby significantly reducing the dollar's current use in international exchange.

4. What are vehicle currencies? These are currencies commonly used in financial transactions among people who reside outside the countries from which the currencies are issued. Currently, the U.S. dollar is the predominant vehicle currency, although both the Japanese yen and the European Monetary Union's euro function as vehicle currencies in some parts of the world. The euro could eventually rival the dollar's preeminent vehicle-currency status.

Table 5-2 Share of the Market Held by Leading Vehicle Currencies

	Banks' Cross-Border Positions in Foreign Currencies		
	Assets	Liabilities	International Bonds and Notes
U.S. Dollar	65.3%	68.1%	51.1%
Euro	17.6	12.9	31.9
Japanese Yen	5.2	5.2	5.5
All Other	11.9	13.8	11.5

SOURCE: Bank for International Settlements, *International Banking and Financial Market Developments*, June 2002, and authors' estimates.

Banking around the Globe

Banks participate in financial markets, and as those markets have become more integrated, banks have had to adjust. By the 1990s a typical U.S.-based multinational company maintained accounts with at least as many banks outside the United States as it had with U.S.-based banking institutions. Likewise, individuals and companies located in other nations increasingly retain the services of banks based elsewhere, including large U.S. banks with overseas offices. This trend has led banks around the globe to become more "international" in scope.

Nevertheless, in many respects the business of banking varies from country to country. Banking has evolved differently in every nation. As a result, each country has its own distinctive national banking system. In some nations, banks are the predominant type of financial intermediary. In others, however, banks constitute only a part of a very diverse financial system. In addition, the structure of banking markets varies across nations. Some countries have only a few large banks. Others, such as the United States, have relatively large numbers of banks distributed across various size categories ranging from very small banks to global behemoths. The legal rules that circumscribe bank interactions with household and business customers also differ from country to country. So does the tax treatment of bank accounts by national governments.

Bank versus Market Finance

One significant way in which national banking systems differ is that in some countries banks are the predominant means by which firms finance their working capital needs, while in others companies rely to a much greater extent on market finance. For example, companies located in the United Kingdom, Germany, and Japan finance significantly greater portions of their investment expenditures with bank loans as compared with U.S.-based companies. British businesses raise more than two-thirds of their funds from bank borrowings. In Germany and Japan, the portions are about one-half and close to two-thirds, respectively. In contrast, U.S. companies typically raise less than one-third of their funds by borrowing from banks.

This difference helps explain why banks in Germany and Japan more than doubled in size between 1970 and 2003. Banks in the United Kingdom grew at a slower pace. Nevertheless, their central role in British finance allowed British banks to grow at a faster pace than U.S. banks, whose overall size, adjusted for inflation, failed to change notably between 1970 and 2003.

Cross-Country Variations in Bank Market Structure

Each nation's banking system also has a distinctive *market structure*—the organization of the loan and deposit markets in which banking institutions interact. The extent of potential rivalry among banks, which economists sometimes measure as the portion of total deposits concentrated among a nation's largest banks, varies considerably from country to country. In Belgium, Denmark, France, Italy, Luxembourg, Portugal, Spain, and the United Kingdom, the five largest banks have at least a third of the deposits of their nation's residents. The five largest banks in Greece and the Netherlands have more than three-fourths of their nation's total deposits. The top five U.S. banks, by way of contrast, have about one-fifth of the deposits of U.S. residents. About a third of total assets—cash, securities, and loans—are held by the top ten U.S. banks, while the top ten German, Japanese, and British banks possess about two-thirds of all bank assets in those nations.

The degree of banking competition within a nation also depends on how open the nation's borders are to rivalry from foreign-based banking operations. By the early 1990s, foreign banks were making many loans to U.S. individuals and firms, but had barely penetrated the German and Japanese loan markets. This lack of foreign competition has undoubtedly played a role in producing the high levels of bank asset concentration in Germany and Japan. Recently, however, U.S. banks, investment banks, and brokerage firms have made stronger inroads into banking markets in both nations.

On the Web
What is so "secret" about accounts with Swiss banks? To get more details, go to http://www.swconsult.ch/chbanks/faq.htm, and click on "Frequently Asked Questions—Swiss Banking."

Banking Secrecy and Taxation

Another way in which banking systems differ is that general principles of accounting and transparency, or openness to public scrutiny, vary across countries. In some nations, banks make frequent, detailed reports that are open to the public. In others, reports on banks' conditions are often slow to appear and hard to decipher when they do.

SECRECY THAT PROTECTS DEPOSITORS In some nations, banks must keep some information secret. According to Swiss law, a banker who betrays the secret of a depositor serves up to six months of jail time and incurs fines as high as 50,000 Swiss francs (about $32,000). In 1993, however, the Swiss government responded to international concerns about money laundering by waiving the secrecy provisions in specific criminal cases. Swiss banks can still refuse to provide deposit information to tax authorities, however. Consequently, Swiss bank accounts are a tax haven, which has contributed to Switzerland's status as a center of world banking activity.

In the western hemisphere, the South American country of Uruguay has sought to duplicate Switzerland's success. Under Uruguayan law, banks cannot reveal data concerning deposit ownership, and bank deposits cannot be taxed. This has induced many residents of other South American nations to hold deposits in Uruguayan banks. Today, foreign-owned deposits account for more than one-third of the funds held in Uruguayan banks.

Holders of bank accounts in other countries can be subjected to public scrutiny. U.S. banks, for example must report interest earnings of their depositors, because the U.S. government taxes those earnings. Banks also must provide special reports to the federal government if they make particularly large transfers on behalf of their customers. To avoid taxes or make payments without public knowledge, U.S. citizens must resort to cash holdings and cash-based transactions—or obtain bank accounts in locales such as Uruguay, Switzerland, Luxembourg, and Liechtenstein.

SECRECY THAT PROTECTS BANKERS Another reason that banks may be secretive is to hide their own problems. U.S. banks have been among the most open in the

Link to the
Global Economy

Will Stock Markets outside the United States Ever Catch Up?

Figure 5-1 indicates that about three-fourths of the approximately $34 trillion in funds allocated to stocks worldwide are traded in developed nations. About $16.5 trillion, or nearly one-half, of these funds are allocated to U.S. stock markets.

Features of National Stock Exchanges

Stock markets differ in several ways. U.S. stock exchanges, discussed in Chapter 3, list mainly the shares of companies based in the United States. Stock markets in the United Kingdom have always had more of an international mix.

Mirroring U.S. stock exchanges, Japan's stock markets list mostly shares of domestic Japanese companies (more than 2,000 in all). In contrast to the United States, though, where individual and independent institutional investors own sizable portions of companies' shares, there is considerable cross-ownership of corporate shares in Japan. For instance, a Japanese auto company typically owns a large portion of the shares of a major steel producer. This pattern of cross-ownership limits the scope for corporate takeovers, which are much more common in the United States.

Stock Trading in Emerging Economies

An important development in recent years has been the growth of stock exchanges in a number of the world's emerging economies. Today such geographically dispersed locations as Nepal, Ukraine, Nigeria, and Bermuda have active stock exchanges. These and other emerging-economy stock exchanges now account for about 9 percent of world stock market capitalization.

A stock market's capitalization does not necessarily indicate anything about the typical size of the companies whose shares are traded there, as panel (a) of Figure 5-2 indicates. On average, the companies in markets in Switzerland and the Netherlands, are considerably larger than the companies in other nations' markets. Even though these two countries have relatively small exchanges, large companies' shares are traded there.

Figure 5-1
Shares of World Stock Market Capitalization

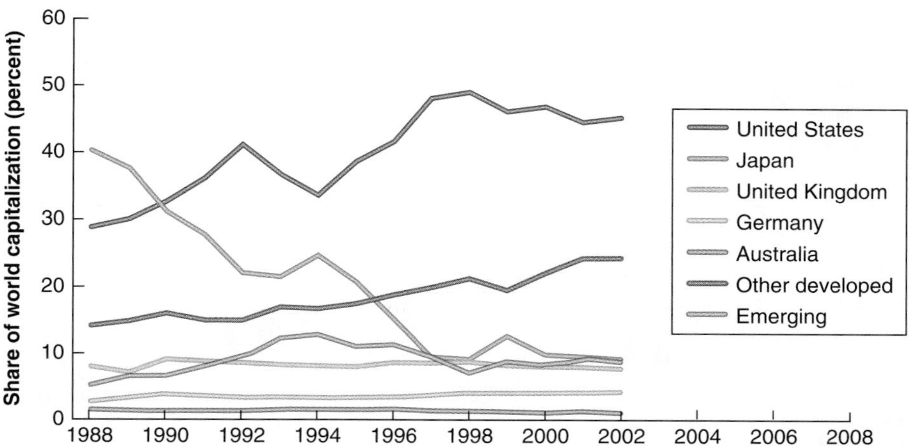

SOURCE: Standard & Poor's, *Emerging Stock Markets Factbook 2002* and authors' estimates.

Continued on next page

Link to the Global Economy, continued

Panel (b) of Figure 5-2 shows recent annual returns from holding shares in various nations' stock markets. Comparing the market performances for the countries in panel (b) with the relative market sizes in Figure 5-1 indicates that the markets with the largest overall capitalization have not necessarily been the best-performing markets.

Research Project

Why are the relative size of a nation's stock market and the average return on shares traded in that market not necessarily related? What factors are likely to have the greatest influence on the price of a share of stock?

Web Resource

How are different stock markets around the globe performing? To track recent movements in stock indexes of various world markets, go to the home page of *The Economist* magazine (http://www.economist.com) and click on "Markets and Data." Click on a national stock exchange to view charts and summaries of recent stock price information.

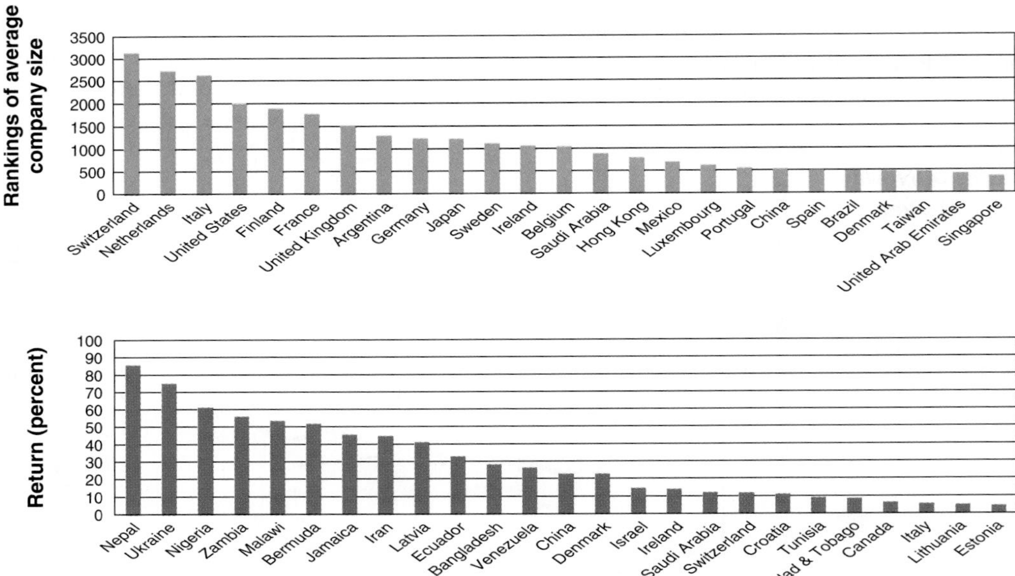

Figure 5-2
Average Company Size and Performances in National Stock Markets.

Panel (a) indicates the variation in the average sizes of companies whose shares are traded in national stock markets. Panel (b) shows how much the average percentage change in stock prices varies across stock markets.

SOURCE: Standard & Poor's, *Emerging Stock Markets Factbook 2002.*

world, because they face stiff reporting requirements established by both banking regulators and securities regulators.

In contrast, Asian banks provide the least data about their conditions. Those interested in obtaining current information about Asian banks' bad loans or exposure to world trouble spots typically cannot obtain it from the banks. Critics argue that this helps explain the Asian financial boom of the early 1990s and the big financial collapse that followed in the late 1990s. In the early part of the decade, they argue, savers from all over the world became overly optimistic about Asian financial prospects in large part because only Asian lenders and borrowers knew for sure the state of borrowers' overall creditworthiness. This helped fuel a big run-up in bank stock prices and more generally in the prices of Asian bonds and other financial instruments. Then, after markets collapsed toward the end of the decade, the lack of information from banks made it difficult for savers to believe that the worst was over. Thus, bank secrecy intensified the asymmetric-information problem that savers already faced. Many savers were unwilling to direct their funds back into Asian financial markets for several years thereafter.

5. How do national banking systems differ? One key characteristic that distinguishes national banking systems is the degree to which firms finance their operations via bank loans versus direct placement of debt instruments in financial markets. A second difference is in bank market structures. In some nations, a few relatively large banks dominate national loan and deposit markets, whereas in others a number of banks compete in these markets. Finally, countries have different laws regarding secrecy of bank accounts and their tax treatment and about open public reporting by bank managers and owners.

Chapter Summary

1. International Financial Integration: This refers to the gradual movement toward more similar and interrelated national markets for financial instruments, which make it easier for traders to conduct arbitrage across national borders. Recent economic and financial problems in Asia have slowed the pace of international financial integration there, but the European Monetary Union has speeded the process in other parts of the world.

2. Cybertechnologies and International Financial Integration: Data stored in any computer's memory system can be transferred to another computer via phone lines, fiber-optic cables, or wireless transmission. The ability to send electronic messages makes restrictions on flows of funds across geographic boundaries difficult to enforce. Although the pace at which cybertechnologies are being adopted around the world is swift overall, financial systems in Asia, Africa, and South America lag behind Europe and North America in adopting cybertechnology.

3. Capital Controls: These are legal restraints that governments impose on flows of funds across national borders. The use of cybertechnologies complicates the enforcement of capital controls, provided that governments do not have the capability to centralize control of all cybertechnology links. Widespread adoption of recent developments in wireless data transmission would make it nearly impossible for a government to prohibit all cross-border flows of funds.

4. Vehicle Currencies: Vehicle currencies are currencies used to denominate a transaction that does not include the nation that issues the currency. The U.S. dollar is the world's primary vehicle currency. The European Monetary Union's euro and the Japanese yen are the next two predominant vehicle currencies. The euro may eventually compete with the dollar's preeminent vehicle-currency position.

5. How National Banking Systems Differ: One key factor distinguishing national banking systems is the extent to which companies raise funds through bank loans versus direct issuance of debt instruments and equity shares in financial markets. A second factor is that in some countries a few large banks dominate national loan and deposit markets, whereas in others a number of banks compete. Finally, different laws regarding secrecy of bank accounts and their tax treatment and concerning open public reporting by banks can produce differences in the functioning of national banking markets.

Questions and Problems

(Answers to odd-numbered questions and problems may be found on the Web at http://money.swcollege.com under "Student Resources.")

1. Identify each of the following financial instruments as either an international stock share, an international bond, a Eurocurrency deposit, a Euronote, a Eurobond, or Eurocommercial paper.

- **a.** An Argentine company offers a five-year debt instrument for sale to international savers.
- **b.** The government of Russia offers a ten-year debt instrument, denominated in U.S. dollars, for sale in the London securities market.
- **c.** Bank of America lends a pound-denominated deposit to Royal Bank of Canada.
- **d.** A Mexican firm offers shares of its stock for sale to international savers.
- **e.** The government of Australia offers a twenty-year debt instrument, denominated in U.S. dollars, for sale in the French securities market.

2. Suppose that an individual can sell municipal bonds in Country A and then use the proceeds to buy municipal bonds issued in Country B. She then sells shares of automotive stock in Country B but finds that it is difficult to use the proceeds from that sale to purchase either automotive stocks or municipal bonds in Country C, because she must first obtain special trading registration permits that allow her to buy and sell financial instruments in Country C. Which countries in this example have more integrated financial markets? Explain.

3. Why is it easier for funds to flow across national borders via cybertechnologies than with cash or checks? Explain in your own words.

4. Are capital controls ever justifiable? Or do they require indefensible government infringements on individual liberties? Take a stand, and support your answer.

5. In your view, do emerging cybertechnologies make it easier or more difficult, on net, for repressive governments to effectively impose capital controls? Explain your reasoning.

6. Can you think of any ways that the U.S. government benefits from the U.S. dollar's role as the world's predominant vehicle currency? [Hint: Remember that the U.S. Treasury and the Federal Reserve pay no interest on currency.]

7. Do U.S. banks gain from the dollar's preeminence in international exchange? Explain.

8. How might the relative size and openness of a nation's financial markets affect the international circulation of its currency? Why?

9. From a bank customer's perspective, what difference does it make if a national banking system has highly concentrated banking markets? Explain your reasoning.

10. In your view, are there circumstances in which bank secrecy is justifiable? Can you think of circumstances under which it might be justified? Take a stand, and support your answer.

Before the Test

Test your understanding of the material covered in this chapter by taking the Chapter 5 interactive quiz at http://money.swcollege.com.

Online Application

Internet URL: http://www.ustreas.gov/fincen/html

Title: Financial Crimes Enforcement Network (FinCEN)

Navigation: Begin at FinCEN's home page above and click on "Law Enforcement" for a pop-up menu.

Applications: Follow the instructions below, and answer the associated questions.

1. Click on "Strategic Analysis," and read the short article about how FinCEN tracks illegal money flows. Then go back to the home page and click on "International overview" to read about cross-border money laundering. What is "money laundering," and how does FinCEN try to address cross-border money laundering?

2. Go back to the home page, and under the "Law Enforcement" pop-up menu click on "HIFCA Designations." What is an HIFCA? Why might there be a "jurisdiction problem" in a world in which cyberpayments are widespread?

For Group Study and Analysis: After reviewing the FinCEN Web site, divide the class into groups, and ask each group to come up with one possible way to launder money successfully using one of the e-money technologies discussed in Chapter 2. Get the class back together as a single group, and then discuss ways in which FinCEN and other government enforcement agencies—which have to think like criminals to stop their activities—might try to combat the money-laundering techniques that the groups have proposed.

Selected References and Further Reading

Bank for International Settlements. *Annual Report.* Published annually.

Bauer, Paul, and Rhonda Ullman. "Understanding the Wash Cycle." Federal Reserve Bank of Cleveland *Economic Commentary,* September 15, 2000.

Feldstein, Martin, and Charles Horioka. "Domestic Saving and International Capital Flows." *The Economic Journal* 90 (June 1980): 314–329.

Fisher, Stanley. *Capital Account Liberalization and the Role of the IMF.* International Monetary Fund, September 1997.

Frankel, Jeffrey. "Quantifying International Capital Mobility in the 1980's." In Dilip Das, ed., *International Finance: Contemporary Issues,* pp. 27–53. New York: Routledge, 1993.

French, Kenneth, and James Poterba. "Investor Diversification and International Equity Markets." *American Economic Review Papers and Proceedings* 81 no. 2 (May 1991): 222–226.

Frieden, Jeffrey. *Banking on the World.* Oxford: Blackwell, 1989.

Giovannini, Alberto, and Colin Mayer, eds. *European Financial Integration.* Cambridge: Cambridge University Press, 1991.

International Finance Corporation. *Emerging Stock Markets Factbook.* Published annually.

Leahy, Michael. "The Dollar as an Official Reserve Currency under EMU." *Open Economies Review* 7 (1996): 371–390.

Marston, Richard. *International Financial Integration.* New York: Cambridge University Press, 1997.

MoneyXtra

moneyxtra! Log on to the MoneyXtra Web site now (**http://moneyxtra.swcollege.com**) for additional learning resources such as practice quizzes, case studies, readings, and additional economic applications.

Chapter 6

Foreign Exchange Markets

Fundamental Issues

1. What are foreign exchange markets?
2. What determines exchange rates?
3. What distinguishes nominal and real exchange rates?
4. What is purchasing power parity, and is it useful as a guide to movements in exchange rates?

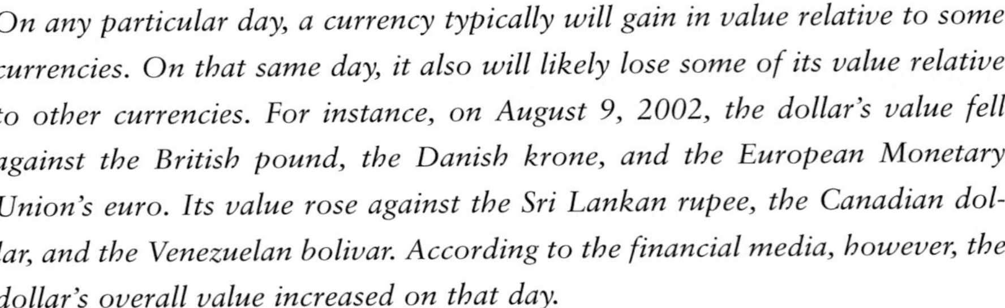

On any particular day, a currency typically will gain in value relative to some currencies. On that same day, it also will likely lose some of its value relative to other currencies. For instance, on August 9, 2002, the dollar's value fell against the British pound, the Danish krone, and the European Monetary Union's euro. Its value rose against the Sri Lankan rupee, the Canadian dollar, and the Venezuelan bolivar. According to the financial media, however, the dollar's overall value increased on that day.

Thus, the exchange value of a country's currency can rise relative to some national currencies even as it falls relative to others. Nevertheless, there are ways of determining what has happened to the overall, *global market valuation of a nation's currency. This is why headlines can state that the "value of the dollar" has recently risen or fallen even though the valuation of the dollar may now be higher relative to some currencies and lower relative to others.*

How can we make a judgment about the overall value of a nation's currency? Before you can answer this question, you must first learn about exchange rates and their determination in the world's foreign exchange markets.

Exchange Rates and the Market for Foreign Exchange

The growth rate in U.S. trading in **foreign exchange,** or exchange of various currencies, has been about 13 percent per year since the early 1990s. By 2003, the average *daily* foreign exchange trading volume in the United States exceeded $550 billion. The large majority of foreign exchange transactions involve the U.S. dollar, but significant volumes of trading are devoted to

Foreign exchange: Exchange of currencies issued by different countries.

exchanges involving the European Monetary Union's euro, the Japanese yen, the British pound, and the Swiss franc.

Banks are heavily involved in foreign exchange trading. Nearly all banks trade currencies, but the business is largely dominated by U.S. money-center banks, such as Citibank, J. P. Morgan Chase, and Bank of America, and a few European banks such as Deutsche Bank and ABN Amro. These five banks alone typically account for over one-fourth of the transactions in the U.S. **foreign exchange market,** which is a system of private banks, foreign exchange brokers and dealers, and central banks through which households, businesses, and governments buy and sell currencies.

Foreign exchange market: A system of private banks, foreign exchange brokers and dealers, and central banks through which households, businesses, and governments purchase and sell currencies of various nations.

Exchange rate: The price of one nation's currency in terms of another.

Spot market: A market for contracts requiring the immediate sale or purchase of an asset.

Spot exchange rate: The spot-market price of a currency indicating how much of one country's currency must be given up in immediate exchange for a unit of another nation's currency.

Foreign Exchange Markets and Spot Exchange Rates

Why do banks and other intermediaries, households, firms, governments, and central banks trade such large volumes of foreign exchange? Let's consider an example. A Japanese child greatly enjoys playing with Legos, the classic plastic building-block toys. Therefore, the child's mother decides to buy a large Lego playset for his next birthday. Even though Legos are made in Denmark, at the nearest toy store the price of the playset is posted in yen, the currency that the mother carries in her handbag or holds in her checking account. Thus, her payment to the toy store is denominated in yen, even though the Danish company pays its workers' wages and its owners' dividends in *kroner* (or "crowns;" singular *krone*), the Danish currency.

To make its kroner payments, the Lego company must convert Japanese yen payments for its toys into the Danish currency. It deposits the yen into its bank accounts and has its banks convert the yen into kroner in the foreign exchange market. How many kroner is the yen worth? Said in a different way, what is the value of the yen in terms of kroner? The market **exchange rate,** which expresses the value of one currency in terms of another, gives us the answer to this question.

When most of us think of an institution such as the foreign exchange market, we envision frantic traders on a trading floor. But in the case of Lego's yen-krone transfers, its banks very quietly make its foreign exchange transactions. In addition, these transactions are likely made by the banks with which it does business *within* Japan. Therefore, yen never actually physically flow out of Japan to Lego's headquarters in Denmark. Only Lego toys cross borders.

In fact, the physical flow of currencies among nations is an insignificant portion of total trading in foreign exchange markets. Cross-border movements of physical currencies and coins typically arise from activities such as tourism or illegal exchanges. The instruments most commonly traded in foreign exchange markets are foreign-currency-denominated bonds, stocks, and bank deposits.

Because there are so many different kinds of financial instruments, there are a number of foreign exchange markets. The Lego example above illustrates a *spot-market* currency exchange. Any **spot market** is a market for immediate purchase and delivery of a financial instrument. In the spot foreign exchange market, "immediate delivery" means that transferal occurs within no more than three days.

The **spot exchange rate** is the spot-market price of a currency, measured in the number of units of another currency that must be given up to purchase a unit of that currency. Table 6-1 displays spot exchange rates for foreign exchange transactions at about noon Eastern time, which are available each day on the Web site of the Federal Reserve Bank of New York. Thus, the spot exchange rates listed in Table 6-1 apply to large transactions. Those engaging in smaller spot foreign exchange trades, such as tourists, typically face less favorable rates.

Appreciation versus Depreciation

Table 6-1 displays two versions of the spot exchange rate. The first, the *U.S. dollar equivalent,* tells how many U.S. dollars one must give in exchange for one unit of foreign currency. For instance, Table 6-1 indicates that on August 8, 2002, the U.S. dollar equivalent for the South African rand was 0.0959 dollars per rand. This means that an individual would have to provide 0.0959 U.S. dollars to obtain 1.0 rand in the New York spot foreign exchange market.

It so happens that on August 9, the U.S. dollar equivalent for the rand fell slightly, to 0.0955 $/rand. Thus, on August 9, a person had to give 0.0004 fewer U.S. dollars in exchange for the South African rand. As noted in Chapter 4, this decline in the dollar price of the rand indicates that there was a dollar *appreciation* between August 8 and August 9. The dollar gained in value relative to the rand.

Table 6-1 also lists figures for *currency per U.S. dollar.* On August 8, 2002, the spot exchange rate quoted in this unit of measurement was 10.4320 rand per 1.0

Table 6-1 Exchange Rates

Country	Monetary Unit	U.S. Dollar Equivalent	Currency per U.S. Dollar
European Monetary Union	Euro	0.9653	1.0359
Australia	Dollar	0.5331	1.8758
Brazil	Real	0.3419	2.9245
Canada	Dollar	0.6322	1.5818
China, People's Republic of	Yuan	0.1208	8.2767
Denmark	Krone	0.1299	7.6975
Hong Kong	Dollar	0.1282	7.8000
India	Rupee	0.0205	48.6800
Japan	Yen	0.0083	121.0400
Malaysia	Ringgit	0.2632	3.8000
Mexico	Peso	0.1026	9.7475
New Zealand	Dollar	0.4550	2.1978
Norway	Krone	0.1292	7.7400
Singapore	Dollar	0.5647	1.7710
South Africa	Rand	0.0959	10.4320
South Korea	Won	0.0008	1,206.7000
Sri Lanka	Rupee	0.0104	96.2000
Sweden	Krona	0.1036	9.6500
Switzerland	Franc	0.6602	1.5146
Taiwan	N.T. dollar	0.0295	33.8500
Thailand	Baht	0.0216	42.4600
United Kingdom	Pound	1.5278	0.6545
Venezuela	Bolivar	0.0008	1,356.0000

SOURCE: Federal Reserve Bank of New York, August 8, 2002.

U.S. dollar. This amount is the reciprocal of the U.S.-dollar-equivalent rate for the rand: 1/(0.0959 dollars per rand) = 10.4320 rand per dollar. On August 9, the currency-per-U.S.-dollar rate rose to 10.4700 rand per dollar, which is the reciprocal of the U.S.-dollar-equivalent rate for that day: 1/(0.0955 dollars per rand) = 10.4700. This rise in the currency-per-U.S.-dollar rate for the rand means that an individual had to give up more rand to obtain dollars on August 9 than on August 8. Hence, there was a rand *depreciation* between August 8 and August 9, meaning that the rand lost value relative to the dollar. (The bulk of the activity in foreign exchange markets involves large sums exchanged among banks and large nonfinancial firms, but individuals contribute to foreign exchange market trading through tourism and cross-border retail purchases. Increasingly, foreign currency conversions for online retail transactions are becoming commonplace; see on the following page *Cyber Focus: Simplifying Cross-Border Retailing via Multicurrency Payment Processing.*)

moneyxtra!
Economic Applications
What is the current dollar value of another nation's currency? Find out via the Universal Currency Calculator available through Corporate Finance Online.
http://www.moneyxtra.swcollege.com

1. What are foreign exchange markets? Foreign exchange markets are the systems through which people exchange one nation's currency for the currency of another nation. Most transactions in foreign exchange markets entail exchanges of foreign-currency-denominated bonds and deposits. The actual movement of currency from one country to another is a relatively insignificant feature of activity in the foreign exchange market.

The Demand for and Supply of Currencies and the Equilibrium Exchange Rate

The preceding description of foreign exchange markets omitted one important question: What actually determines the exchange rates of the various currencies? As we will see, the interactions between demand and supply in the foreign exchange markets determine the *equilibrium* exchange rates that prevail in those markets.

The Demand for a Currency

The primary international role of a currency is to facilitate trade among nations. Consequently, the demand for a currency is *derived* from the demand for the goods, services, and assets that residents of other countries use the currency to purchase. Let's contemplate two countries, the United Kingdom and the United States. The demand for pounds stems from U.S. residents' demand for British goods, services, and pound-denominated assets. If U.S. consumers' demand for British goods increases, then there is a rise in the demand for pounds to purchase the British goods. The price that U.S. consumers have to pay for the pounds is the prevailing U.S.-dollar-per-pound exchange rate.

THE CURRENCY DEMAND SCHEDULE Figure 6-1 on page 131 illustrates the demand relationship in the market for British pounds. An appreciation of the dollar relative to the pound leads to a reduction in the U.S.-dollar-per-pound

GLOBAL POLICY CYBER Focus MANAGEMENT

Simplifying Cross-Border Retailing via Multicurrency Payment Processing

Imagine that it is 2016, and complete Internet connectivity exists across the globe, and retailers in nations from India to Finland, Ghana, and Ecuador have established Web sites for marketing their products. The manager of a Chicago gift shop has been scouring the Internet for something different to market in her physical establishment and on her company's Web site. She decides to purchase copper pots, jars, and jugs handcrafted in the village of Setipokhari, located in the Himalayan foothills of Nepal. At the Web site operated by a metalworking cooperative in Setipokhari, she can click a button that automatically translates product descriptions into English and converts copperware prices to dollars. The manager enters her commercial credit-card number and submits her order. The credit-card transaction is automatically processed in dollars, but payment is made to the seller's bank in the Nepalese currency, the rupee.

This scenario could prove feasible much earlier than 2016. The copperware handcrafted in the Nepalese village of Setipokhari is already marketed on the Web. Furthermore, a company called Planet Payment is already well on the way to making multicurrency conversions possible for facilitating cross-border online Web sales. Planet Payment has already signed up about 300 merchants in thirty countries to develop multilingual versions of their Web sites. The company also offers software that automatically converts prices in local currencies to other countries' currencies at the exchange rate prevailing at the moment the customer submits an Internet order.

Planet Payment also offers a facility for multicurrency processing of credit-card transactions conducted over the Internet. Payments are automatically routed among a network of international banks that translate payment debits to buyers' accounts and payment credits to sellers' accounts. Both debits and credits take place in the respective local currencies, however, so a transaction that once required an advance exchange of foreign currencies before it could take place can now bundle together a purchase and an exchange of currencies simultaneously.

For Critical Analysis: If the rupee value of the U.S. dollar rises considerably just before a U.S. customer submits an order on a site using a system such as the one operated by Planet Payment, thereby changing the terms of the transaction with a Nepalese seller, will the U.S. customer be more or less likely to click on the "order submit" button with her mouse?

exchange rate, because fewer dollars are necessary to purchase each pound. The reasoning behind the downward slope of the demand curve is that as the dollar appreciates relative to the pound, British goods become relatively less expensive for U.S. consumers to purchase. As a result, U.S. consumers choose to buy more British goods and therefore require more British pounds. Thus, there is a negative relationship between the price of the pound—the dollar-pound exchange rate—and the quantity of pounds demanded. This means that a change in the exchange rate brings about a *movement along* the demand curve. If the dollar appreciates relative to the pound—a fall in the dollar-pound exchange rate—the result is a movement down along the demand curve, as shown by the movement from point *A* to point *B* in Figure 6-1. The appreciation of the dollar relative to the pound brings about an increase in the quantity of pounds demanded.

Figure 6-1
Demand for the Pound.

The demand schedule for the pound depicts the relationship between the exchange rate and the quantity of pounds demanded. A reduction in the exchange rate from S_A to S_B indicates an appreciation of the U.S. dollar relative to the British pound, which makes British goods and services relatively less expensive for U.S. consumers. As a result, U.S. residents increase the quantity of pounds they wish to purchase with dollars, from Q_A to Q_B.

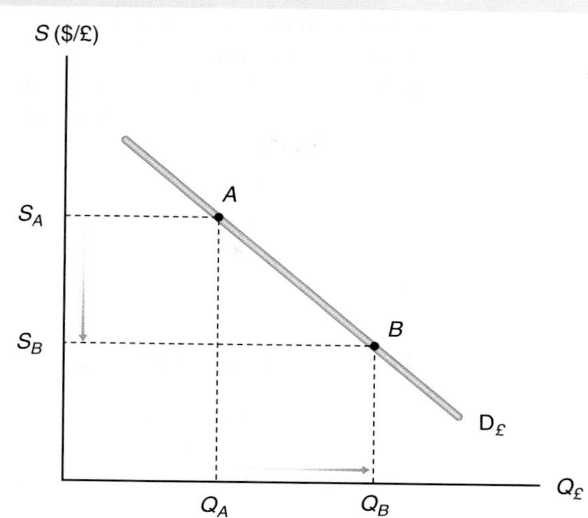

A CHANGE IN CURRENCY DEMAND Suppose that U.S. consumers' tastes for goods manufactured in the United Kingdom change so that they demand more British goods at any given exchange rate. This is a *change in the demand* for the pound that, as shown in Figure 6-2, is reflected by a *shift* in the demand schedule. The rightward shift of the demand schedule in Figure 6-2 illustrates an increase in the demand for the pound. A leftward shift would depict a decrease in the demand for the pound.

Figure 6-2
An Increase in Currency Demand.

A rise in the demand for British goods and services by U.S. residents causes an increase in the quantity of pounds demanded at any given exchange rate. Thus, the pound demand schedule shifts rightward, from $D_£$ to $D'_£$.

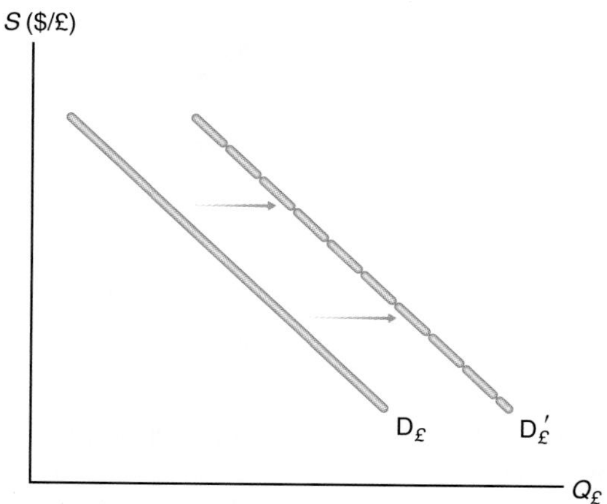

The demand for a currency is a derived demand, so the various factors that cause a change in the demand for a currency are the same factors that cause a change in the foreign demand for a country's goods, services, and assets. They include such factors as variations in foreign residents' tastes and preferences, changes in the incomes of foreign residents, and the extent to which other nations restrict imports. Thus, the increase in the demand for the pound illustrated in Figure 6-2 might stem from a shift in U.S. consumers' tastes and preferences for goods produced in Britain, a rise in U.S. incomes, or a relaxation of previously existing restrictions that had limited U.S. imports of British goods, services, or assets.

The Supply of a Currency

Now consider British consumers' demand for U.S. dollars, owing to their demand for U.S. goods, services, and assets. When British consumers purchase U.S. dollars to buy U.S. goods, they exchange pounds for dollars. As a result, there is a rise in the quantity of pounds supplied in the foreign exchange market. Thus, the British demand for dollars also represents the supply of pounds.

The Currency Supply Schedule Figure 6-3 depicts the relationship between the British demand for dollars, shown in panel (a), and the British supply of pounds, illustrated in panel (b). In panel (a), if the pound appreciates (a decrease in the pound-dollar exchange rate), then U.S. goods are relatively less expensive for British consumers to purchase. As a result, British consumers wish to buy

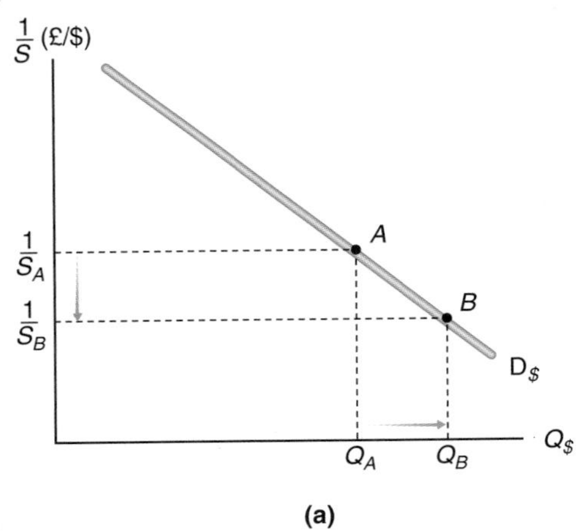

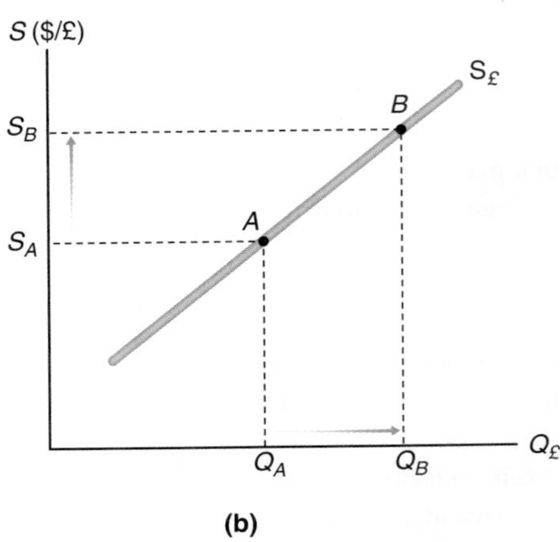

Figure 6-3
The Currency Supply Schedule.

Panel (a) shows the demand for U.S. dollars by British residents. A fall in the pound-dollar exchange rate induces an increase in the quantity of dollars demanded, shown by the movement from point *A* to point *B*. As British residents use more pounds to purchase dollars, they supply a larger quantity of pounds. Thus, as panel (b) illustrates, the corresponding rise in the dollar-pound exchange rate implies an increase in the quantity of pounds supplied for dollars in the foreign exchange market. The pound supply schedule slopes upward.

more U.S. goods, which requires them to purchase more U.S. dollars. Thus, there is an increase in the quantity of U.S. dollars demanded, shown by the movement from point *A* to point *B* in panel (a).

Panel (b) of Figure 6-3 shows an equivalent way to depict this relationship. When the pound appreciates, the dollar-pound exchange rate rises. As British consumers increase the quantity of dollars that they purchase, they exchange their pounds for dollars, so the quantity of pounds supplied increases. Hence, there is a positive relationship between the dollar-pound exchange rate and the quantity of pounds supplied, which is shown as the upward-sloping supply schedule in panel (b). The movement from point *A* to point *B* on this currency supply schedule represents an increase in the quantity of pounds supplied in response to an appreciation of the value of the pound relative to the dollar.

A CHANGE IN CURRENCY SUPPLY If British consumers reduce their desired consumption of U.S. goods at any given exchange rate, then there is a decrease in the demand for the dollar. British consumers cut back on their purchases of dollars used to facilitate their purchases of U.S. goods, thereby reducing the quantity supplied of pounds at any given exchange rate. This constitutes a *fall in the supply* of pounds, which is depicted by a leftward shift of the pound supply schedule in Figure 6-4 In contrast, an increase in the supply of pounds would correspond to a rightward shift of the supply schedule.

A change in the supply of a currency is caused by the same factors that induce a change in a country's demand for a foreign country's goods, services, and assets. These include changes in the tastes and preferences of its consumers, changes in its consumers' incomes, and alterations of existing import restrictions. For instance, the fall in the supply of pounds shown in Figure 6-4 might result from a reduced interest in U.S. goods by British consumers, a general decline in British income levels, or stiffened restrictions on British imports from the United States.

Figure 6-4
A Reduction in Currency Supply.

If British residents reduce their desired consumption of U.S. goods and services, then they supply fewer pounds in exchange for dollars at any given exchange rate. Thus, the currency supply schedule shifts leftward from $S_£$ to $S_£'$.

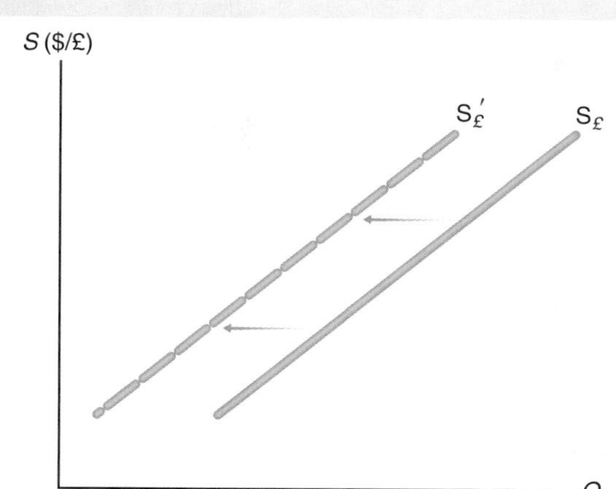

The Equilibrium Exchange Rate

In an equilibrium situation in the foreign exchange market, British residents supply an amount of pounds that is equal to the quantity of pounds demanded by U.S. residents. The exchange rate adjusts until this condition is satisfied. Thus, the *equilibrium exchange rate* is the rate at which the quantity of a currency demanded is equal to the quantity supplied. At the equilibrium exchange rate, the foreign exchange market *clears,* meaning that the quantity of the currency demanded is exactly equal to the quantity supplied.

FOREIGN EXCHANGE MARKET EQUILIBRIUM Figure 6-5 shows the point of equilibrium for the foreign exchange market as point *E*, at which the equilibrium spot exchange rate is S_E, and the equilibrium quantity of pounds exchanged is Q_E. At the exchange rate S_A, the exchange rate is at a level above its equilibrium value, and the quantity of pounds demanded by U.S. residents is equal to Q_1. The quantity of pounds supplied by British residents at the above-equilibrium exchange rate S_A, however, is equal to Q_2. Thus, the quantity of pounds supplied, Q_2, exceeds the quantity demanded, Q_1. The difference $Q_2 - Q_1$ is an excess quantity of pounds supplied in the foreign exchange market. Sellers of pounds will bid down the exchange rate until the pound depreciates to the point at which there is no excess quantity supplied. This is true at point *E*.

At the below-equilibrium exchange rate S_B, the quantity demanded is Q_2, which exceeds the quantity supplied, Q_1. In this case, the pound's value will appreciate until there is no excess quantity demanded, once again at point *E*. The foreign exchange market remains in equilibrium at this point unless some factor induces one or both of the schedules to shift.

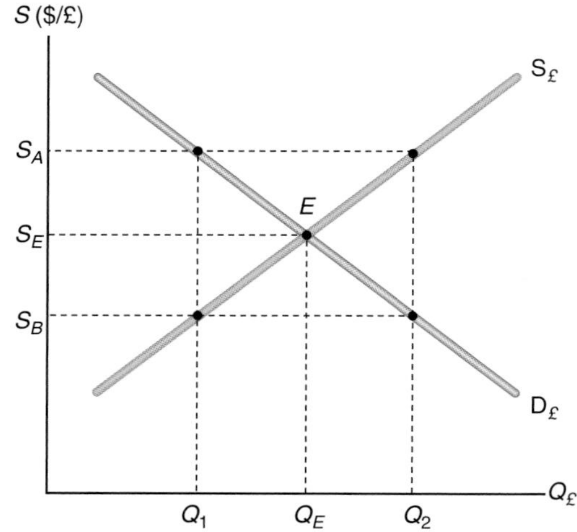

Figure 6-5
Foreign Exchange Market Equilibrium.

At the exchange rate S_E, the quantity of pounds supplied by British residents is equal to the quantity of pounds demanded by U.S. residents. At the above-equilibrium exchange rate S_A, there is an excess quantity of pounds supplied, so the exchange rate will be bid downward toward its equilibrium level (the dollar's value will appreciate relative to the pound). At the below-equilibrium exchange rate S_B, there is an excess quantity of pounds demanded, so the exchange rate will be bid upward toward its equilibrium level (the dollar's value will depreciate relative to the pound).

CHANGES IN THE EQUILIBRIUM EXCHANGE RATE To see how the equilibrium exchange rate might rise, consider Figure 6-6. In both panel (a) and panel (b), the initial equilibrium is at point E, where the equilibrium exchange rate is S_E and the equilibrium quantity of pounds traded is Q_E. Panel (a) illustrates the effects of an increase in the demand for British goods by U.S. consumers. This induces a rise in the demand for pounds, so the currency demand schedule shifts rightward. At the initial equilibrium exchange rate S_E, there is now an excess quantity of pounds demanded. Thus, the exchange rate must rise to a new equilibrium value S_E' at point E', which means that the pound appreciates in value relative to the dollar. Note that the appreciation of the pound relative to the dollar makes British goods relatively more expensive to U.S. consumers, who reduce desired purchases of British goods due to this change in the exchange rate. As a result, the quantity of pounds demanded declines somewhat, but at point E' the equilibrium quantity of pounds traded has increased, on net, from Q_E to Q_E'.

Panel (b) of Figure 6-6 illustrates another way that the equilibrium exchange rate can increase. If British residents cut back on their purchases of U.S. goods, then they supply fewer pounds in exchange for dollars. As a result, the currency supply schedule shifts leftward. At the initial equilibrium exchange rate S_E, therefore, there is now an excess quantity of pounds demanded. To clear the market, the exchange rate must rise to S_E' at point E'. Once again, the pound appreciates relative to the dollar. This causes a reduction in the equilibrium quantity of pounds demanded, so the equilibrium volume of pounds traded falls.

On the Web

Where are data on the exchange value of the U.S. dollar relative to the major currencies of the world? One place to look is at the monthly and daily data series provided by the Federal Reserve Bank of St. Louis at http://www.research.stlouisfed.org/fred/data/exchange.html.

Figure 6-6
An Increase in the Equilibrium Exchange Rate.

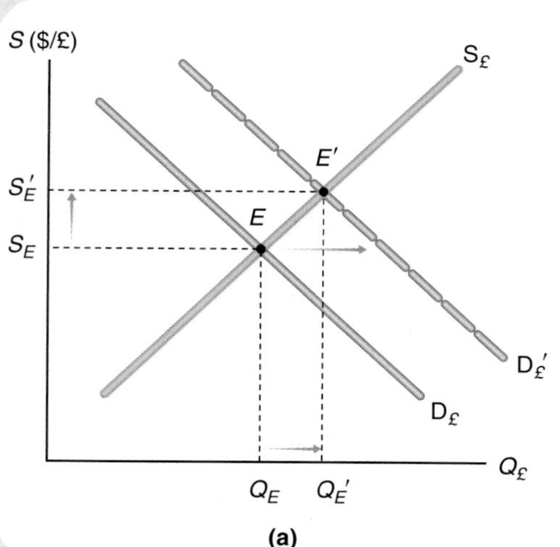

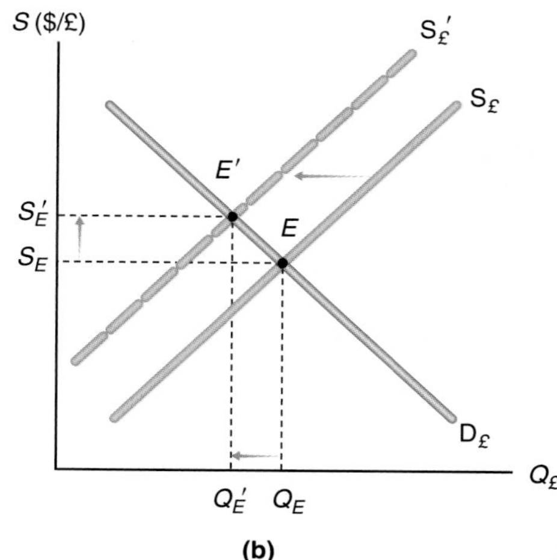

In panel (a), an increase in the demand for British goods by U.S. residents causes the pound demand schedule to shift rightward. At the initial equilibrium exchange rate S_E, there is now an excess quantity of pounds demanded, so the exchange rate is bid upward toward a new equilibrium value equal to S_E'. Panel (b) illustrates the effect of a reduction in the British demand for U.S. goods that entails a reduction in the supply of pounds by British residents. At the initial equilibrium exchange rate S_E, there is now an excess quantity of pounds demanded, so the exchange rate is bid upward toward a new equilibrium value equal to S_E'. Thus, both examples illustrate a depreciation of the dollar relative to the pound.

2. What determines exchange rates? The interaction between the demand for a currency and the supply of the currency determines the equilibrium exchange rate for that currency relative to another. The equilibrium exchange rate is the exchange rate at which the quantity of a currency demanded is equal to the quantity supplied. Changes in the equilibrium exchange rate occur as a result of variations in the demand for or the supply of a currency.

moneyxtra!

Another Perspective

To evaluate how foreign economic growth can affect the exchange value of the dollar, go to the Chapter 6 reading, entitled "Foreign Economic Growth and the Dollar," by Owen Humpage of the Federal Reserve Bank of Cleveland.

http://www. moneyxtra.swcollege.com

Purchasing Power Parity

From time to time, policymakers and financial media commentators argue that the currency of one nation is "undervalued" or that the currency of some other nation is "overvalued." Unfortunately, it is not always clear what they mean. Often policymakers and commentators are unclear about exactly how they have reached their conclusions, making it difficult to judge the validity of their claims.

Traditionally, economists have approached the issue of whether a currency's value is "too low" or "too high," meaning that some adjustment is likely to occur in the market, by studying the behavior of *real exchange rates,* which take into account how the exchange rates observed to clear markets today relate to relative differences in nations' overall prices of goods and services. Given a theory of how real exchange rates are determined, economists define an **overvalued currency** as a currency that has a current market value higher than the theory predicts, implying that the currency is likely to experience a depreciation. In contrast, an **undervalued currency** is a currency whose value is weaker than predicted by the theory, indicating that it is likely to appreciate in value.

To judge whether a currency is over- or undervalued, economists often use the theory of *purchasing power parity.* Before we explain this theory, however, you must first understand real exchange rates.

Overvalued currency: A currency whose present market-determined value is higher than the value predicted by an economic theory or model.

Undervalued currency: A currency whose present market-determined value is lower than that predicted by an economic theory or model.

Nominal exchange rate: An exchange rate that is unadjusted for changes in the two nations' price levels.

Real exchange rate: An exchange rate that has been adjusted for differences between two nations' price levels, thereby yielding the implied rate of exchange of goods and services between those nations.

Real Exchange Rates

The exchange rates displayed in Table 6-1 on page 128 are **nominal exchange rates,** which tell us today's market value of our own currency in exchange for a foreign currency. These exchange rates do not reflect changes in price levels in the two nations, however. If we are interested in the amount of foreign goods and services that our currency will buy, then we must take into account the **real exchange rate,** which adjusts the nominal exchange rate for changes in the nations' price levels and thereby measures the *purchasing power of the domestic goods and services in exchange for foreign goods and services.* To know how much of another country's goods and services we can obtain by trading our own nation's goods and services, using our own currency as a medium of exchange in the transaction, we must know the value of the real exchange rate.

Nominal Currency Depreciation To see why the real exchange rate matters, consider the bilateral exchange relationship between the United States and Brazil between 2001 and 2002. In August 2001, the currency-per-U.S.-dollar spot exchange rate for the Brazilian real was 2.467 reals per dollar. By August 2002, the real's value had declined, and the exchange rate was equal to 3.090 reals per dollar.

Both of these exchange rates are nominal exchange rates. The rate of appreciation of the U.S. dollar relative to the Brazilian real between August 2001 and August 2002 was equal to $[(3.090 - 2.467)/2.467] \times 100$, which is equal to 25.3 percent. This means that in August 2002 more than 25 percent more reals—one real to begin with, plus one-fourth more reals after the exchange rate change—were needed to buy a dollar in the foreign exchange market than had been necessary in August 2001.

THE REAL EXCHANGE RATE AND REAL CURRENCY DEPRECIATION Clearly, the significant decline in the value of the real relative to the dollar had the immediate effects of making Brazilian goods and services effectively cheaper for U.S. consumers to purchase and U.S. goods and services more expensive from the perspective of Brazilian consumers. Something else also happened between 2001 and 2002. Brazil had a higher inflation rate than the United States. The annual rate of consumer price inflation in Brazil was about 6.8 percent, compared with only about 1.6 percent in the United States.

These relative inflation differences matter because changes in the prices of goods and services alter the effective prices that Brazilian residents pay for U.S. goods and services and that U.S. residents pay for Brazilian goods and services. To see how, let's take August 2001 as the starting point for comparing the relative purchasing power of the two countries' goods and services. Thus, let's set the consumer price index equal to 100 in both countries at that point in time. This means that by August 2002 the Brazilian consumer price index was equal to 106.8, while the U.S. consumer price index was equal to 101.6.

To measure the real exchange rate between Brazil and the United States in August 2001, we multiply the nominal exchange rate at that time, 2.467 reals per U.S. dollar, by the ratio of the U.S. consumer price index to the Brazilian price index, 100/100, to get 2.467. Thus, by choosing August 2001 as our starting point, we have defined the nominal and real exchange rates at that point as being equivalent.

To calculate the real exchange rate for August 2002, we multiply the nominal exchange rate at that time, 3.090 reals per U.S. dollar, by the ratio of the U.S. consumer price index to the Brazilian price index, 101.6/106.8, which yields 2.940. This implies that the *real rate of appreciation* for the dollar was equal to $[(2.940 - 2.467)/2.467] \times 100 = 19.2$ percent. This calculated real rate of dollar appreciation was slightly lower than the nominal appreciation rate of 25.3 percent, because the relatively higher Brazilian inflation rate implied somewhat higher prices of Brazilian goods and services relative to U.S. goods and services. Thus, the relatively higher inflation in Brazil slightly offset the large nominal appreciation in the dollar's value that took place in that year.

3. What distinguishes nominal and real exchange rates? A nominal exchange rate is the observed rate at which a nation's currency trades in foreign exchange markets for units of the currency of another country. Nominal exchange rates do not take into account changes in the price levels across nations. A real exchange rate adjusts the nominal exchange rate for changes in the nations' price levels. Hence, real exchange rates measure the purchasing power of a nation's goods and services in exchange for the goods and services of other nations.

Purchasing power parity (PPP): A condition that states that if international arbitrage is unhindered, the price of a good or service in one nation should be the same as the exchange-rate-adjusted price of the same good or service in another nation.

A Theory of Real and Nominal Exchange Rates: Purchasing Power Parity

The first, and oldest, theory of exchange rates, which many economists still use to gauge whether currencies are over- or undervalued in the marketplace, is the theory of *purchasing power parity.* One reason this theory has proved so popular is that it is easy to understand. Another reason is that it is easy to apply. As you will learn, the simplicity of purchasing power parity may or may not be a virtue. Indeed, generations of economists have literally spent centuries debating the relevance of the theory and its applicability to issues of public policy in the sphere of international economic relations.

In its most basic form, the idea of **purchasing power parity (PPP)** is that, in the absence of factors such as costs of transportation, cross-country tax differentials, and trade restrictions, homogeneous goods and services that are tradable across national borders should have the same price in two countries after converting their prices into a common currency. For this reason, economists often refer to this basic concept of purchasing power parity as the *law of one price.*

To illustrate the law of one price, suppose that the market price of a high-grade golden delicious apple is US$0.50 in Detroit, Michigan. The market price of the same quality and type of apple in Windsor, Ontario, is C$0.75. This would imply that the dollar-equivalent exchange rate should be US$0.50/C$0.75 = 0.667 U.S. dollar per Canadian dollar. Using this rate, we can convert the Canadian dollar price of the apple in Windsor to a U.S. dollar price of US$0.50 (C$0.75 × 0.67 US$/C$ = US$0.50). Therefore, the apple has the same price in Windsor as it does in Detroit after adjusting for the exchange rate.

ARBITRAGE AND PURCHASING POWER PARITY If, in our apple-exchange example, the exchange rate were not 0.67 US$/C$, then an arbitrage opportunity would exist. Suppose the exchange rate is equal to 0.72 US$/C$. Then the U.S. dollar price of a golden delicious apple in Windsor would be C$0.75 × 0.72 US$/C$ = US$0.54. A Canadian apple arbitrageur who can buy many apples in Detroit for US$0.50 per apple, place them on a large truck, and drive them a short distance to Windsor to sell for C$0.75 each (US$0.54 in U.S. dollars at the 0.72 US$/C$ exchange rate) will earn a profit of US$0.04 per apple. Thus, if the arbitrageur can move 10,000 apples from Detroit to Windsor to sell in Canada, the profit will be $400, ignoring the relatively small transportation costs.

If a sufficient number of people engage in this sort of arbitrage activity, then the result will be a flow of apples from Detroit to Windsor. The exchange of Canadian dollars for U.S. dollars on the foreign exchange market thereby will cause an increase in the demand for U.S. dollars relative to Canadian dollars. The three markets (Detroit apple market, Windsor apple market, and foreign exchange market) will experience adjustments. The outflow of apples from Detroit will generate an increase in the price of apples in Detroit. The inflow of apples to Windsor will cause a decrease in the price of apples in Windsor.

If a number of apples and other goods and services are arbitraged in response to the misaligned exchange rate, then the demand for U.S. dollars will increase relative to Canadian dollars. This will cause the value of the U.S. dollar to appreciate relative to the Canadian dollar. All of these adjustments, which result from the arbitrage activity, will tend to equalize the (same currency) prices of traded goods and services, thereby removing any further scope for profiting from cross-border arbitrage.

ABSOLUTE PURCHASING POWER PARITY This analysis of the relationship between prices and exchange rates implies the condition of *absolute purchasing power parity,* which we can formalize in the following manner. Let's define S to be the U.S.-dollar-equivalent exchange rate of the Canadian dollar, P to be the price of golden delicious apples in the United States, and P^* to be the price of golden delicious apples in Canada. Then we can express absolute PPP as

$$P = S \times P^*.$$

In words, the U.S. price of apples should equal the Canadian price times the spot exchange rate. Thus, in our example, if the U.S. dollar–Canadian dollar exchange rate is 0.667 U.S. dollars per Canadian dollar and the Canadian price of apples is C$0.75 per apple, then the U.S. dollar price of apples should equal US$0.50.

A Theory of the Exchange Rate If *all* goods and services are fully and freely tradable across U.S. and Canadian borders, then absolute PPP will hold for all goods. In this instance, we can interpret P as the overall price level of U.S. goods and services and P^* as the overall price level of Canadian goods and services. Note that in this instance, we can rearrange the absolute PPP relationship to solve for the spot exchange rate:

$$S = P/P^*.$$

That is, when absolute PPP holds for all goods and services, the spot exchange rate equals the U.S. price level divided by the Canadian price level. Thus, absolute PPP is a theory of exchange rate determination: if absolute PPP holds, then the spot exchange rate should equal the ratio of the price levels of the two nations. Hence, the demand and supply schedules in foreign exchange markets should move to positions yielding this exchange rate.

Some Limitations It is a big jump from golden delicious apples to all goods and services, however. To apply the concept of absolute PPP to exchange rate determination, our simplifying assumptions of no transportation costs, no tax differentials, and no trade restrictions that we used in our apple-exchange example must be met in the real world. This is highly unlikely to be true. After all, loading 10,000 or more apples into a truck is a costly endeavor, apple sales might be subject to different tax rates in Canada and the United States, or one of the two nations could have legal restraints on apple trade. Certainly, we might expect transportation expenses, different tax treatment, or trade restrictions to apply for a number of other goods even if they do not have significant effects in the national markets for apples.

Furthermore, even if transportation costs, tax differences, and trade restrictions are insignificant, we still would anticipate problems in applying absolute PPP to all goods and services of two nations. The reason is that people in the two nations may consume different sets of goods and services. As an extreme example, imagine that the typical U.S. consumer buys apples and pears, but the typical Canadian consumer buys apples and oranges. If these are the only goods consumed in each nation, then using overall price levels for the two nations to make a statement about exchange rate determination would be a mistake. The price levels for the

On the Web

Where can you learn more about recent PPP facts and figures? Try going to http://pacific.commerce.ubc.ca/xr. Under the heading "Surveys," click on "What Is Purchasing Power Parity?"

two nations would be based on the prices of different goods, meaning that the arbitrage argument that lies behind the absolute PPP condition could not apply. Arbitrage could not really relate the prices of both sets of goods, so we would be mistaken to infer an exchange rate from the absolute PPP relationship.

Absolute PPP and the Real Exchange Rate Another way to see why absolute PPP is unlikely to hold in the real world is to recall how we calculate a real exchange rate: we multiply the spot exchange rate, S, by the relative price levels for the two countries, P^*/P, so the real exchange rate is equal to

$$S \times (P^*/P).$$

If absolute PPP holds, however, then $S = P/P^*$, so the real exchange rate is equal to

$$S \times (P^*/P) = (P/P^*) \times (P^*/P) = 1.$$

A real exchange rate equal to 1 means that one unit of goods and services in a country, such as the United States, always exchanges one-for-one with a unit of goods and services in another country, such as Canada. Thus, absolute PPP implies that the real exchange rate is always equal to 1. If people in different countries consume goods and services in different proportions, however, it is highly unlikely that this will be so.

RELATIVE PURCHASING POWER PARITY Not surprisingly, using absolute PPP as a theory of exchange rate determination is not very useful. For this reason, economists often use a different benchmark that is known as *relative purchasing power parity*. Relative PPP relates *proportionate changes* in exchange rates to relative *changes* in countries' price levels.

We can use the expression for absolute PPP to derive the relative version of PPP. Let's denote the percentage change of a variable by placing the characters "$\%\Delta$" (percentage change in) in front of the variable. Then, for example, $\%\Delta P$ would represent the proportionate change in the price level for a period. By calculating the change of each variable in the equation for absolute PPP, we can express relative PPP as

$$\%\Delta S = \%\Delta P - \%\Delta P^*.$$

Thus, relative PPP implies that the percentage change in an exchange rate equals the difference between the percentage changes in the countries' price levels. The percentage changes in the nations' price levels for a given interval are their inflation rates, denoted π and π^*. Thus, we can express relative PPP as

$$\%\Delta S = \pi - \pi^*.$$

According to relative PPP, therefore, the appreciation or depreciation of a currency is equal to the difference between the two nations' inflation rates.

How does relative PPP do as a theoretical predictor of actual exchange rate changes? Most studies indicate that relative PPP performs better than absolute PPP, but relative PPP typically is not a very good theory for predicting exchange rate movements over periods of less than a few years. Our earlier example of the 25 percent depreciation of the Brazilian real relative to the U.S. dollar between 2001 and 2002, even though the Brazilian inflation rate exceeded the U.S. inflation rate by only 5.2 percentage points, is a case in point.

Relative PPP often does perform better over short-run intervals for countries that experience episodes of very high inflation. This is true because during such episodes, price changes typically are the dominant influence on the value of the domestic currency. Over short-run intervals, however, factors other than relative price levels or inflation rates can have significant effects on exchange rates. Thus, neither version of PPP works particularly well for explaining short-term exchange rate variations.

Purchasing Power Parity as a Long-Run Determinant of Exchange Rates Economists have long recognized the factors that limit their ability to use PPP as a complete theory of exchange rate determination. Nevertheless, the logic of the law of one price has led most economists to believe that, given sufficient time, exchange rates should *eventually* adjust to values consistent with PPP, at least in its relative form.

Random-Walk Exchange Rates In the 1970s and 1980s, however, study after study found that it was difficult to rule out the possibility that real exchange rates follow a "random walk." This meant that if some event, such as an abrupt, temporary change in the price level in one nation, were to occur, the real exchange rate would move to a new level. The real exchange rate would tend to stay at this new level until the next unexpected, short-lived event took place to "bump" it to another level. As we already noted, absolute PPP implies that the real exchange rate should tend toward the value of 1. As we discussed, relative PPP is less restrictive. Nonetheless, if relative PPP holds, it turns out that the real exchange rate should tend toward a *constant* value (but not necessarily a value of 1). If the real exchange rate were to follow a random walk, however, then as time passes it would not necessarily settle down to a constant value. Thus, random-walk behavior of real exchange rates was strong evidence against PPP.

By the mid-1980s, the PPP doctrine was in such doubt that *The Economist* magazine developed an initially satirical measure of PPP called the "Big Mac Index." The idea was that McDonald's Big Mac sandwich has the same basket of ingredients in all world locations, so if the law of one price holds, the exchange-rate-adjusted price of a Big Mac should be the same everywhere. In fact, however, from year to year the Big Mac guide to exchange rates does relatively poorly (see on the next page *Global Focus: PPP Packed into a Sesame Seed Bun*).

To contemplate the limitations of purchasing power parity for managers, go to the Chapter 6 Case Study, entitled "Purchasing Power Parity as a Business Guide?"
http://moneyxtra.swcollege.com

Saving PPP? In the 1990s, new rounds of research on real exchange rates evaluated the possibility that earlier studies were biased because they considered only a few countries or relatively short spans of time. Looking at insufficient observations of the real exchange rate might make short-term variations in the real exchange rate look like random-walk movements when in fact they were simply movements of real exchange rates toward levels consistent with PPP. One set of studies, therefore, examined large numbers of countries' real exchange rates simultaneously, thereby evaluating PPP with massive amounts of cross-country data. These studies consistently found little evidence of random-walk behavior of exchange rates. Recently, however, a debate has arisen about whether this "cross-country approach" to evaluating PPP suffers from its own special difficulties.

This has led other researchers to concentrate on real-exchange-rate behavior over long time periods, spanning from six decades to as long as nearly seven

text continues on page 145

GLOBAL Focus | POLICY | CYBER | MANAGEMENT

PPP Packed into a Sesame Seed Bun

Among businesspersons, the most popular version of PPP is the Big Mac Index from *The Economist* magazine. The 2002 version of the Big Mac Index appears in Table 6-2.

Table 6-2 shows that the price of a Big Mac in the United States is \$2.49, whereas the price of a Big Mac in Japan is ¥262. Using the equation for absolute PPP, $S = P/P^*$ (P^* = U.S. price), the implied exchange rate is 105¥/\$, which is shown in the third column. The fourth column gives the actual value of the yen-dollar exchange rate at the time, 130¥/\$. The true, market-determined value of the dollar relative to the yen is higher than the value implied by absolute PPP. The Big Mac Index, therefore, indicates that the yen is undervalued relative to the dollar. We can express this undervaluation as the percentage difference between the implied value of the dollar according to the Big Mac PPP measure and the market value. This works out to be 19 percent for the yen. Hence, according to the Big Mac measure of PPP, the yen should appreciate relative to the dollar.

How does the Big Mac perform as a guide to exchange rate movements? In the short run, the index certainly is not an accurate predictor of exchange rates. The index performs better in the long run, but most of the adjustment to PPP occurs through price changes.

Table 6-2 The Big Mac Index

	Big Mac prices in local currency	Big Mac prices in dollars	Implied PPP* of the dollar	Actual dollar exchange rate 4/23/02	Under(−)/over(+) valuation against the dollar, %
United States†	\$2.49	2.49	-	-	-
Argentina	Peso 2.50	0.78	1.00	3.13	-68
Australia	A\$3.00	1.62	1.20	1.86	-35
Brazil	*Real* 3.60	1.55	1.45	2.34	-38
Britain	£1.99	2.88	1.25‡	1.45‡	+16
Canada	C\$3.33	2.12	1.34	1.57	-15
Chile	Peso 1,400	2.16	562	655	-14
China	Yuan 10.50	1.27	4.22	8.28	-49
Czech Rep	Koruna 56.28	1.66	22.6	34.0	-33
Denmark	DKr24.75	2.96	9.94	8.38	+19
Euro area	€2.67	2.37	0.93§	0.89§	-5
Hong Kong	HK\$11.20	1.40	4.50	7.80	-42
Hungary	Forint 459	1.69	184	272	-32
Indonesia	Rupiah 16,000	1.71	6,426	9,430	-32
Israel	Shekel 12.00	2.51	4.82	4.79	+1
Japan	¥262	2.01	105	130	-19
Malaysia	M\$5.04	1.33	2.02	3.8	-47
Mexico	Peso 21.90	2.37	8.80	9.28	-5
New Zealand	NZ\$3.95	1.77	1.59	2.24	-29
Peru	New Sol 8.50	2.48	3.41	3.43	-1
Philippines	Peso 65.00	1.28	26.1	51.0	-49
Poland	Zloty 5.90	1.46	2.37	4.04	-41
Russia	Rouble 39.00	1.25	15.7	31.2	-50
Singapore	S\$3.30	1.81	1.33	1.82	-27
South Africa	Rand 9.70	0.87	3.90	10.9	-64
South Korea	Won 3,100	2.36	1,245	1,304	-5
Sweden	SKr26.00	2.52	10.4	10.3	+1
Switzerland	SFr6.30	3.81	2.53	1.66	+53
Taiwan	NT\$70.00	2.01	28.1	34.8	-19
Thailand	Baht 55.00	1.27	22.1	43.3	-49
Turkey	Lira 4,000,000	3.06	1,606,426	1,324,500	+21
Venezuela	Bolivar 2,500	2.92	1,004	857	+17

*Purchasing power parity; local price divided by price in the United States.
†Average of New York, Chicago, San Francisco, and Atlanta. ‡Dollars per pound. §Dollars per euro.

SOURCES: McDonald's; *The Economist.*

FOR CRITICAL ANALYSIS: Studies have found that the Big Mac Index is closely related to several other more elaborate measures of PPP, so some economists have concluded that the Big Mac Index is a surprisingly good longer-term indicator of PPP valuations of exchange rates. What does the predictive performance of the Big Mac Index imply about the likely usefulness of absolute PPP as a *shorter-term* measure of currency under- or overvaluation?

centuries. The idea is that if PPP holds, it must hold on average over such long intervals. Indeed, these studies find strong evidence that, given sufficient time, real exchange rates tend to settle down at constant long-term levels predicted by the PPP doctrine. These studies conclude that a reason there is so little evidence in favor of PPP over shorter-term periods is that departures from PPP take so long to disappear. For example, if some temporary factor causes the real exchange rate to move above the level consistent with PPP, these studies of long-run horizons indicate that it typically takes between three and seven years for the real exchange rate to get halfway back to its PPP level. If these more recent studies are correct, PPP is truly a long-run determinant of exchange rates. This may help explain why *The Economist*'s Big Mac Index has performed better when evaluated over intervals of several years, even though it consistently fails to fit exchange rates on a year-to-year basis.

4. What is purchasing power parity, and is it useful as a guide to movements in exchange rates? Purchasing power parity is a theory of the relationship between the prices of traded goods and services and the exchange rate. Economists have used two key versions of PPP to try to understand how exchange rates are determined. Absolute PPP relates price levels to the nominal exchange rate. Relative PPP relates inflation rates to exchange rate appreciation or depreciation. Because people in different countries consume various baskets of goods and services, relative PPP has the greatest potential as an approach to exchange rate determination. Nevertheless, most evidence indicates that even relative PPP is at best a long-run guide to understanding how exchange rates are determined.

Link to Policy

Measuring the Overall Value of the Dollar—Effective Exchange Rates

Bilateral exchange rates are the rates of exchange at which currencies actually trade in foreign exchange markets—the value of one currency relative to another. To evaluate overall movements in the value of a nation's currency, economists use effective exchange rates, which are measures of a currency's relative value based on bilateral market exchange rates relating that currency to the currencies of several other nations.

Currency Baskets

Measuring the value of a currency against every other currency in the world is impractical, so when constructing a currency's effective exchange rate, economists take into account only those currencies that they judge to be most important. Which currencies are "important" depends on the particular application. If a policymaker wishes to know how changes in the value of the dollar will affect U.S. imports and exports, then the effective exchange rate for the dollar certainly should include the bilateral exchange rates of the largest trading partners of the United States.

Continued on next page

Link to Policy, continued

The currencies whose bilateral exchange rates are included when constructing an effective exchange rate compose what economists call a *currency basket*. For example, if a policymaker wants to know how changes in the value of the dollar may affect U.S. trade with nations of the European Monetary Union (EMU), Canada, and Japan, then the effective exchange rate should take into account the bilateral exchange rates of the dollar relative to the EMU euro, the Canadian dollar, and the Japanese yen.

Effective exchange rates are *weighted averages* of bilateral exchange rates, in which the weights reflect the relative importance of each currency in the currency basket. The more important currencies in the currency basket receive greater weights than those comprising smaller portions of the basket.

For instance, to determine the weights of the euro, Canadian dollar, and Japanese yen in the currency basket for an effective exchange rate for the dollar, a policymaker might determine that during 2001 U.S. trade (the sum of exports and imports) with EMU nations amounted to $300 billion, trade with Canada was $300 billion, and trade with Japan was $200 billion. Hence, total trade with all three regions combined was $800 billion. Proportionate shares of this total, expressed as decimal fractions, therefore were 0.375 for the EMU, 0.375 for Canada, and 0.250 for Japan. The policymaker could then use these trade weights to construct an effective exchange rate for the dollar, relative to these nations, for 2001.

Calculating Effective Exchange Rates

To calculate an effective exchange rate, let's assume that the policymaker is interested in evaluating the overall change in the dollar's value relative to the euro, the Canadian dollar, and the yen between April 2001 and April 2002. Columns (a) and (b) of Table 6-3 display the currency-per-U.S.-dollar exchange rates for these currencies in these months.

Given the effective-exchange-rate weights implied by the trade shares of the three trading partners, the next step in constructing the effective exchange rate is to construct measures of each bilateral exchange rate relative to the initial exchange rate in April 2001. We show calculations of these measures in columns (c) and (d) of Table 6-3. Naturally, the April 2001 exchange rates are 100 percent of their own values—hence, the values of 100 for each currency in column (c). Column (d) indicates that the April 2002 euro-per-dollar exchange rate was 103.7 percent above its April 2001 value. The April 2002 Canadian-dollar-per-U.S.-dollar exchange rate was 106.8 percent greater than its April 2001 value, and the April 2002 yen-per-dollar exchange rate was 89.7 percent of its April 2001 value. Hence, the yen appreciated relative to the dollar while the Canadian dollar and euro both depreciated slightly.

What Changes in Effective Exchange Rates Mean

Now we can use the data in columns (c) and (d) of Table 6-3 to calculate effective exchange rates for April 2001 and April 2002. For April 2001, our starting point for comparing the year-to-year change in the effective value of the dollar relative to these three currencies, the calculation is very simple. The effective exchange rate for April 2001

Table 6-3 Currency-per-U.S.-Dollar Exchange Rates and Relative Values of Currencies of Major U.S. Trading Partners

	(a) April 2001	(b) April 2002	(c) (a) ÷ (a) × 100	(d) (b) ÷ (a) × 100
Canadian dollar	1.47	1.57	100%	106.8%
EMU euro	1.08	1.12	100	103.7
Japanese yen	117	105	100	89.7

SOURCE: Federal Reserve Bank of New York.

is simply equal to the sum of each currency's portfolio weight times the value of 100 displayed for each currency in column (c) of the table, or (0.375)(100) + (0.375)(100) + (0.250)(100) = 100. Hence, the effective exchange rate for our starting point, or *base period*, of comparison equals 100. Now let's calculate the effective exchange rate for April 2002 by adding together each currency's portfolio weight times its column (d) value in Table 6-3, or (0.375)(106.8) + (0.375)(103.7) + (0.250)(89.7) = 101.4. Comparing this April 2002 effective exchange rate to the April 2001 effective exchange rate of 100 indicates that in April 2002 the dollar's value was 101.4 percent of its April 2001 value. Because the value of the effective exchange rate rose, the dollar *appreciated*, on average, relative to the weighted shares of the three currencies. The percentage appreciation of the dollar relative to this particular basket of currencies was equal to 1.4 percent (101.4 − 100 = 1.4).

The Federal Reserve publishes a nominal and real (price-level-adjusted) effective exchange rate for the U.S. dollar in the *Federal Reserve Bulletin*, and the International Monetary Fund publishes multilateral-weighted effective exchange rates in its monthly bulletin *International Financial Statistics*. These and other national and multinational policymakers use effective exchange rates to judge the overall performance of currencies in foreign exchange markets.

Research Project

What are some potential pitfalls that can arise if policy decisions are based on effective exchange rate indexes? For instance, what if policymakers rely on an effective exchange rate constructed using a base year from the 1980s or 1990s? How can policymakers address this and other possible drawbacks associated with effective exchange rates they might use as measures of the overall values of national currencies?

Web Resources

1. What are the current values of nominal and real effective exchange rates for the U.S. dollar? Find out at the Federal Reserve's H.10 Release: Foreign Exchange Rates Summary, at http://www.federalreserve.gov/releases/H10/Summary/.

2. How have real purchasing powers of various national currencies changed in recent years? To find out, take a look at the International Monetary Fund's World Economic Outlook data appendix by going to http://www.imf.org. Click on "Publications," then type "World Economic Outlook" next to "Search by Title," and click search. Next, click on the most recent issue, and then click on "Link to Text."

Chapter Summary

1. The Foreign Exchange Markets: These markets are systems through which individuals, companies, and governments exchange one nation's currency for the currency of another nation. The spot exchange rate is the rate at which people agree to trade currencies to be delivered immediately, typically in the form of foreign-currency-denominated bonds or bank deposits. Actual trades of currency and coins constitute a very small portion of total activity in foreign exchange markets.

2. Determining the Value of a Currency: The interaction of the forces of supply and demand in the foreign exchange market determines the value of a currency. The equilibrium spot exchange rate is the exchange rate at which the total desired quantity of a currency for immediate delivery is equal to the total quantity of the currency supplied. Variations in the equilibrium exchange rate occur as a result of changes in the demand for or the supply of a currency.

3. Distinguishing Nominal and Real Exchange Rates: The equilibrium rate of exchange of one nation's currency in the foreign exchange market is the nominal exchange rate. The nominal exchange rate does not take into account changes in the price levels across nations. The real exchange rate adjusts the nominal exchange rate for price-level changes.

Consequently, a real exchange rate measures the purchasing power of a nation's goods and services in exchange for the goods and services of another country.

4. Purchasing Power Parity and Its Usefulness for Predicting Exchange Rates: In its simplest form, known as the law of one price, purchasing power parity implies that the exchange-rate-adjusted price of a tradable good in one nation should equal the price of that good in another nation. There are two versions of PPP as an approach to understanding how exchange rates are determined. Absolute PPP relates the price levels of two countries to the exchange rate. Relative PPP relates two nations' inflation rates to the rate of change in the exchange rate. Most evidence indicates that neither approach is particularly useful as a short-run guide to exchange rate movements. Relative PPP may be a useful guide to exchange rates over long-run horizons, however.

Questions and Problems

(Answers to odd-numbered questions and problems may be found on the Web at http://money.swcollege.com under "Student Resources.")

1. Suppose that on Thursday the U.S.-dollar-equivalent exchange rate of the Brazilian *real* (the name of the Brazilian currency) was 0.3325. On Friday this value fell to 0.3262. Did the Brazilian real appreciate or depreciate relative to the U.S. dollar?

2. In question 1, what was the percentage appreciation/depreciation of the real?

Use the data in the table below to answer questions 3, 4, and 5.

3. In 1994, what was the nominal spot exchange rate for the Canadian dollar relative to the Japanese yen? What was the nominal exchange rate between these two currencies in 2004?

4. What was the real exchange rate for the U.S. dollar relative to the Japanese yen in 1994? In 2004? Did the U.S. dollar experience a real appreciation or depreciation relative to the yen between 1994 and 2004?

5. What was the real exchange rate for the U.S. dollar relative to the Canadian dollar in 1994? In 2004? Did the U.S. dollar experience a real appreciation or depreciation relative to the Canadian dollar between 1994 and 2004?

6. Suppose that the current U.S.-dollar-equivalent exchange rate between the Hungarian forint and the U.S. dollar is equal to 0.005. A change in the demand for the forint results in a rise in this value to 0.006. Did the demand for the forint rise or fall, assuming that the supply schedule did not shift? Use a diagram of the market for forint to explain your reasoning.

7. Suppose that at present, the U.S.-dollar-equivalent value of the Slovakian koruna is 0.0216. At this exchange rate, however, U.S. residents interested in purchasing koruna with U.S. dollars cannot find a sufficient number of Slovakian residents willing to provide koruna in exchange. What must happen to the exchange rate, and why? Use a diagram to assist in explaining your answer.

8. Initially, the currency-per-U.S.-dollar exchange rate relating the value of the Mexican peso was equal to 13.0. Then there was a sharp drop-off in the U.S. demand for Mexican-produced goods and services. At the same time, residents of Mexico sharply increased their desired consumption of U.S.-manufactured goods. Use a diagram to assist in explaining the likely effects of these events on the value of the peso.

9. Suppose the Swiss franc price of a dollar was 1.6341 Sfr/$ in 1990 and 1.4322 Sfr/$ in 2005. The price index for Switzerland (1990 = 100) is 128.11 in 2005, and the price index for the United States (1990 = 100) is 111.86 in 2005. According to absolute PPP, is the dollar over- or undervalued, relative to the Swiss franc in 2005? Considering this information, would you expect the dollar to appreciate or depreciate? By what percentage?

	1994 Spot Exchange Rate	2004 Spot Exchange Rate	1994 Consumer Price Index	2004 Consumer Price Index
Japan	$0.0073/yen	$0.0092/yen	100	105.8
Canada	$0.867/C$	$0.651/C$	100	129.8
U.S.			100	119.0

10. Using the data provided in question 9, was the dollar over- or undervalued in 2005 according to relative PPP? Considering this information, would you expect the dollar to appreciate or depreciate and by how much (in percentage terms)?

Before the Test

Test your understanding of the material covered in this chapter by taking the Chapter 6 interactive quiz at http://money.swcollege.com.

Online Application

Internet URLs: http://www.oecd.org/statistics and http://www.federalreserve.gov/releases/h10/Hist

Titles: Purchasing Power Parities and Exchange Rates

Navigation: First go to the home page of OECD statistics (http://www.oecd.org/statistics). Click on "Short-Term Economic Statistics," and then under the heading "Exchange Rate Statistics,"click on "Purchasing Power Parity Statistics," and then on "Purchasing Power Parities for OECD Countries." Print this document. Next, go to the Federal Reserve Board's home page (http://www.federalreserve. gov), and click on "Economic Research and Data," then click on "Statistics: Releases and Historical Data." Under H.10, click on "Daily Update," and "Historical Data."

Application: Use the reports to apply PPP.

1. The first set of columns in the OECD table gives the currency-per-U.S.-dollar exchange rates consistent with PPP. The Federal Reserve Board provides data on actual exchange rates. Select a nation in the OECD's PPP table, and compare the exchange rates predicted by PPP for a selected year in the table with *actual* exchange rates. During the year you selected, did PPP indicate that this nation's currency was over- or undervalued?

2. Look over the nation's exchange rates in the Federal Reserve's H.10 release for all five years in the OECD table. Were the actual exchange rates consistent with PPP over this five-year period?

For Group Study and Analysis: Assign questions 1 and 2 to several groups, each of which will examine the data for a different country. Discuss possible reasons why PPP may apply better for some countries than for others.

Selected References and Further Reading

Cumby, Robert E. "Forecasting Exchange Rates and Relative Prices with the Hamburger Standard: Is What You Want What You Get with McParity?" *NBER Working Paper, 5675* (July 1996).

Frankel, Jeffrey, and Andrew Rose. "A Panel Project on Purchasing Power Parity: Mean Reversion within and between Countries." *Journal of International Economics* 40 (May 1996): 209–224.

Lothian, James, and Mark Taylor. "Real Exchange Rate Behavior: The Recent Float from the Perspective of the Past Two Centuries." *Journal of Political Economy* 104 (June 1996): 488–509.

O'Connell, Paul. "The Overvaluation of Purchasing Power Parity." *Journal of International Economics* 44 (February 1998): 1–19.

Pakko, Michael, and Patricia Pollard. "For Here or to Go? Purchasing Power Parity and the Big Mac." *Federal Reserve Bank of St. Louis Review* 78 (January/February 1996): 3–22.

Rogoff, Kenneth. "The Purchasing Power Parity Puzzle." *Journal of Economic Literature* 34 (June 1995): 647–668.

Taylor, Mark. "The Economics of Exchange Rates." *Journal of Economic Literature* 33 (March 1995): 13–47.

MoneyXtra

moneyxtra! Log on to the MoneyXtra Web site now (http://moneyxtra.swcollege.com) for additional learning resources such as practice quizzes, case studies, readings, and additional economic applications.

Chapter 7

Finding the Best Mix of Financial Instruments—The Theory of Portfolio Choice

Fundamental Issues

1. What is a financial portfolio?
2. What are the key determinants of portfolio choice?
3. What is the distinction between idiosyncratic risk and market risk?
4. How does holding international financial instruments make a portfolio more diversified?
5. What are the special risks of holding international financial instruments?

The portion of U.S. residents who own shares of stock in corporations has grown considerably. The fraction of the population owning at least some shares of stock, called the stock market participation rate, *is about 50 percent today—up from just over 32 percent at the beginning of 1990.*

Some economists speculated that this increase in the stock market participation rate may have been partly responsible for the upsurge in stock prices during the 1990s. Their idea was that the increase in the number of stockholders spread overall stock market risks over a larger number of investors, causing the rate of return necessary to compensate shareholders for those risks to decline and thereby helping to boost the market prices of shares.

Nevertheless, the fraction of stocks held by the richest 10 percent of U.S. households has remained unchanged at about four-fifths of all shares outstanding since the beginning of the 1990s. Even though more U.S. residents are holding stocks, rich people still own most of the shares of stock in the United States and thereby also continue to bear most of the risks associated with stockholding. Thus, it is unlikely that there was significant spreading of stock market risks across the population as the stock market participation rate increased. Although more people own stock than before, most of these relatively new stockholders do not own very many shares.

What determines the portion of stocks that individuals hold among their total financial assets? To answer this question, you must learn about the theory of portfolio choice.

Financial Instrument Portfolios

Wealth: An individual's total resources.

In the preceding four chapters, you have learned about various types of financial instruments, about the ways in which market interest rates are related, about international connections among financial markets, and about how exchange rates are determined. In this chapter we shall combine these concepts to contemplate how savers allocate their wealth among the broad array of financial instruments available in today's world.

Saving and Wealth

When people add to their holdings of financial instruments, they *save*. All their holdings of financial instruments are part of their total *wealth*. Before we proceed further, it is important to understand the distinction between these two concepts.

Saving As we discussed in Chapter 3, saving is the act of forgoing consumption. Setting aside a portion of income earned during the most recent week or month can permit an individual to expand his or her capability to consume in the future—provided that the amount the individual saves retains or, better yet, increases in value over time.

Saving is a *flow*. That is, it is an amount that a person *adds* to savings accumulated in previous weeks and months. Thus, economists measure saving as the amount added to an individual's total accumulated savings from one point in time to another.

Wealth A person's **wealth** consists of all the resources owned by that individual. An individual who saves a portion of her or his income each month adds to *accumulated savings* at the end of each month. For most people, accumulated savings constitute a large portion of total wealth. Economists often broaden the definition of wealth to include nonfinancial resources, such as durable goods that have a current market value. They also often include *human capital*, which is the amount of knowledge and training possessed by an individual. People can transform their human capital into income and thereby can use human capital to accumulate more financial wealth. Certainly, bankers recognize this when they contemplate making loans. They are more likely to make a loan to a college graduate who is in every other way identical to a person without a college degree, because they realize that the college graduate possesses additional human capital.

Nevertheless, a person cannot trade durable goods or human capital directly for stocks, corporate bonds, or Treasury securities. In this chapter, we shall focus our attention on the part of wealth that people hold as financial instruments. This is their *financial wealth*, or their accumulated financial savings. Financial wealth is a *stock*, meaning that we measure a person's wealth at a point in time. Wealth is a snapshot at a specific point in time. It is the amount of total savings the person has accumulated as of a particular date.

Financial Portfolios

A key reason that most people forgo consumption is so that they can expand their capability to consume in the future. At some later time in their lives, they hope to be able to direct accumulated savings to future expenditures on items

Portfolio: The group of financial instruments held by an individual, which together make up the individual's financial wealth.

such as a bigger or better home for themselves and their families, higher education for their children, or perhaps more "frivolous" expenditures such as a European vacation or an Alaskan cruise.

To be able to make the greatest possible future expenditures, however, people must find ways to retain the value of their financial wealth. Indeed, they must find ways to expand their financial wealth as much as possible given the circumstances that they face. As you learned in Chapter 4, holdings of financial instruments yield rates of return. Thus, directing saving to purchases of interest-bearing financial instruments is a fundamental saving allocation for most individuals who wish to increase their future spending potential as much as they can.

The set of financial instruments that an individual possesses at a given point in time is his financial **portfolio.** These holdings constitute the individual's allocation of his financial wealth. Given that an individual's objective is to be able to use this portfolio to finance future consumption, choosing the "best" mix of financial instruments is a fundamental issue for any saver. The *theory of portfolio choice* provides insights into the manner in which savers identify the financial instruments that they should hold in their portfolios.

1. What is a financial portfolio? A financial portfolio is the set of financial instruments currently owned by an individual. This combined portfolio is the individual's financial wealth, and one key way that an individual saves is by adding to an existing financial portfolio, thereby expanding financial wealth.

Fundamental Determinants of Portfolio Choice

Figure 7-1 displays the aggregate portfolio allocations of U.S. households. As you can see, U.S. households hold a number of different types of assets in their portfolios. The percentage allocations to various assets in Figure 7-1 tell us something about the average portfolio of a typical U.S. household. The portfolios of individual households vary widely, however. Why is this so? To answer this question, let's begin by thinking about the factors that influence portfolio choice.

Wealth

Naturally, a key determinant of any individual's portfolio of financial assets is the person's total wealth. To understand why this is so, imagine two different college students. Both are females, have similar intellectual capabilities, maintain the same grade point average, live in the same apartment complex, and major in the same subject. They have nearly identical course schedules, and they even have similar tastes in music, movies, and sports. The main way they differ, however, is their wealth. After paying tuition and fees for the current semester, one student has $1,500 in financial wealth. The other has financial wealth equal to $150,000.

At the end of last week, the less wealthy student had $750 in a checking account at a bank and $750 in a savings account. The wealthier student had $25,000 in a checking account with the same bank. In addition, she had $125,000 in savings deposits.

Figure 7-1
Aggregate Portfolio Allocations of U.S. Households.

The majority of U.S. household wealth is allocated to pension funds and equity holdings.

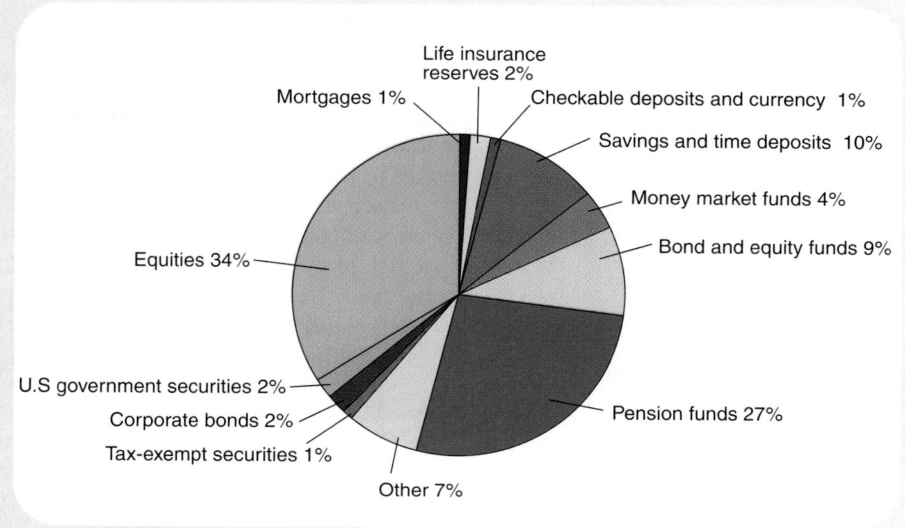

SOURCE: *Flow-of-Funds Accounts,* Board of Governors of the Federal Reserve System, June, 2002.

Now think about each student's reaction to receiving identical cash windfalls of $1,500 this week. Both students, we shall assume, are thrifty individuals who want to save these windfalls. Undoubtedly, they will allocate the new funds differently, however, because their total wealth and current portfolio allocations are significantly different. Let's suppose that the less wealthy student chooses to place $500 in her bank checking account and the remaining $1,000 in her bank savings account. In contrast, the wealthier student adds $100 to her checking deposits and $1,400 to her savings deposits. (To simplify, we assume that these are the only savings options either student considers in the near term.)

THE WEALTH ELASTICITY OF ASSET DEMAND In our example, the less wealthy student experienced a doubling of her financial wealth. That is, her financial wealth increased by 100 percent. She responded by increasing the size of her checking account holdings by 67 percent (the $500 addition to her initial $750 checking balance) and by raising her savings account balance by 133 percent (the $1,000 addition to her initial $750 savings balance). These figures tell us something about the *sensitivity* of each desired asset allocation to the change in wealth that she experienced. Economists call this sensitivity the **wealth elasticity of demand,** which is the percentage change in the quantity of an asset demanded divided by a given percentage change in wealth. Thus, the less wealthy individual's wealth elasticity of demand for bank checking deposits is equal to 67 percent divided by 100 percent, or 0.67. Her wealth elasticity of demand for savings deposits is equal to 133 percent divided by 100 percent, or 1.33.

Wealth elasticity of demand: The percentage change in the quantity of an asset demanded by an individual divided by a given percentage change in the individual's wealth.

The wealthier student experienced a much smaller percentage increase in wealth equal to 1 percent ($1,500 is 1 percent of $150,000). She increased her checking account balance by 0.4 percent ($100 is 0.4 percent of $25,000), so her

Necessity asset: An asset with a wealth elasticity of demand less than 1, which implies that an individual increases holdings of the asset less than proportionately in response to a given proportionate increase in wealth.

Luxury asset: An asset with a wealth elasticity of demand greater than 1, which indicates that an individual raises holdings of the asset more than proportionately in response to a given proportionate increase in wealth.

wealth elasticity of demand for checking deposits is equal to 0.4 (0.4 percent divided by 1 percent). Her savings deposits rose by 1.12 percent ($1,400 is 1.12 percent of $125,000), so her wealth elasticity of demand for savings deposits is equal to 1.12 (1.12 percent divided by 1 percent).

As we might expect, the students responded to their $1,500 windfalls by making very different *absolute* dollar allocations between the two types of bank accounts. The sensitivities of their demands for assets also differ, with the less wealthy student showing greater sensitivity in her demand for both checking and savings deposits in response to a proportionate increase in her wealth. This is a normal observation. Wealth elasticities of demand for any asset tend to be larger for less wealthy individuals. Because they have less wealth to begin with, they tend to allocate relatively higher shares of wealth increases to all their asset holdings, as compared with the way wealthier individuals would allocate an identical wealth increase.

NECESSITY ASSETS VERSUS LUXURY ASSETS For both students, however, the wealth elasticity of demand for checking deposits is less than 1. This indicates that the students regard checking deposits as a **necessity asset,** meaning that they feel they must have a checking account on hand (for buying groceries, paying rent, and so on), but will increase their holdings of this asset less than proportionately as their wealth increases. Furthermore, at sufficiently high levels of wealth people typically reach a point at which they add proportionately little to their holdings of necessity assets, as is the case for the wealthier of the two students in our example.

An asset is a **luxury asset** when people respond to a rise in their wealth by increasing their demand for the asset more than proportionately. The wealth elasticity of demand for savings deposits is greater than 1 for both students, indicating that both regard savings accounts as luxury assets.

This example illustrates two important facts about portfolio choice. First, greater wealth tends to lead an individual to increase her holdings of any financial asset. Second, the proportionate increase in the quantity of a financial instrument that a person holds following an increase in her wealth depends on her wealth elasticity of demand for the instrument. Her wealth elasticity of demand, in turn, depends both on her total wealth and on whether she regards the asset as a necessity asset or a luxury asset.

Expected Asset Returns

Suppose that someone offers to sell you two financial instruments. Both are equally susceptible to variations in their market values, and both are equally likely to be salable in secondary markets if you should desire to convert them into cash in a hurry. They differ in only one respect: one asset has a higher expected return than the other.

Our guess is that you would find this choice to be a "no-brainer." Why? The reason is that the asset with the higher expected return will permit you to engage in higher expected consumption of goods and services in the future.

On the Web
How can a trader assess expected returns on financial assets? Use The Hedgehog's financial calculators to answer this question at http://hedge-hog.com.

A number of factors influence the expected return on a financial instrument. As you learned in Chapter 4, one is the instrument's anticipated nominal yield. Another is the extent to which governments tax the nominal returns on the instrument. Furthermore, the anticipated inflation rate affects the real yield that one anticipates earning by holding the instrument to maturity. In addition, if the financial instrument is denominated in a foreign currency, then the expected rate of appreciation or depreciation affects the expected return.

Asset Liquidity

In fact, financial instruments have a number of characteristics that typically distinguish them. For example, suppose that two financial instruments have the same expected return. Indeed, they are identical in all other respects as well, except for one. This one distinguishing feature is that market trading volumes for one instrument usually are higher than for the second instrument.

This means that if the person who owns the second instrument wishes to exchange it for cash, perhaps because of a family emergency that requires a significant expenditure of funds, he has a lower chance of getting an offer to buy the instrument. Hence, the second instrument has less *liquidity*. As a result, holding it instead of the first instrument that is exchanged in a market with greater trading volumes is less desirable.

Of course, as we discussed in Chapter 4, it is unlikely that the two instruments would have the same expected returns for very long. People would opt to purchase the more liquid instrument, thereby increasing the demand for that instrument and pushing up its market price. This would tend to reduce its yield relative to that of the less liquid instrument. Indeed, this happened in the market for U.S. Treasury securities in the fall of 1998, when trading volumes for Treasury bonds with 28 and 29 years remaining to maturity fell off sharply relative to volumes of trading for 30-year-maturity Treasury bonds. As a result, people who previously had actively traded Treasury bonds maturing in 28 and 29 years became skittish about continuing to hold the bonds. Market demand for the bonds dropped off, and the yield on 30-year bonds dropped below the yields on bonds maturing in 28 and 29 years. (As discussed in Chapter 4, longer bonds normally carry greater yields.) This is a real-world example of how liquidity is an important determinant of portfolio choice—and market yields.

Information Costs

In Chapter 3, we noted that asymmetric information—information possessed by those who issue financial instruments that is not available to those who buy them—helps explain why financial intermediaries exist. Asymmetric information is also a key factor influencing portfolio choice. The reason is that it is costly for buyers of financial instruments to try to overcome informational asymmetries. Doing so requires obtaining reports about the prospects of issuers, spending time evaluating those reports, and reaching conclusions about the trustworthiness of the information they contain. All these activities entail both explicit and opportunity costs.

Thus, financial instruments for which information is more readily available are, holding all other factors equal, more desirable for inclusion in a portfolio. Holding such instruments reduces the costs of managing the portfolio, thereby raising the overall expected net return on the portfolio as a whole.

Risk aversion: The preference, other things being equal, to hold assets whose returns exhibit less variability.

Asset Risk

Another crucial factor influencing portfolio choice is the relative riskiness of alternative financial instruments. Most savers are **risk-averse,** meaning that if all other characteristics of financial instruments are the same, savers prefer to hold the financial instrument with the least potential for swings in its yield and, consequently, its price. Of course, some people enjoy taking risks. Nevertheless, most people prefer to reduce their risks of loss whenever possible.

On the Web
How can an investor keep up with scheduled initial public offerings and news of mergers and acquisitions? One approach is to visit The Online Investor at http://theonlineinvestor.com.

Asset Return Risks To see how risk can influence a person's choice between competing financial instruments, consider a situation in which a new company has an initial public offering. Stock market analysts have determined that there is a 50 percent chance that the company's shares will yield a 5 percent annual return and a 50 percent chance that they will yield a 7 percent annual return. Therefore, the expected annual return from purchasing the new company's shares is the average of the two returns, or 6 percent.

At the same time, another new company is also issuing shares for the first time. Analysts forecast that there is a 50 percent chance that its shares will yield an annual return of 12 percent. There is also a 50 percent chance that the annual return will turn out to be 0 percent. Consequently, the expected annual return from purchasing this company's shares is also the average of these returns, or 6 percent.

Given this choice, a risk-averse saver will prefer to buy shares issued by the first company, because there is less potential deviation of actual returns from the expected returns of its shares compared with the second company. Even though the expected returns for both companies are the same, the return offered by the first company's shares tends to exhibit greater *stability.* This makes its shares less risky financial instruments.

Measuring Risk Table 7-1 summarizes the various factors that can affect the choice of which financial instruments to hold. Savers know their own financial wealth and can make forecasts of average returns. In addition, savers know the information costs that they face, and data about trading volumes are readily available in financial publications. But how can savers measure the riskiness of financial instruments?

Because assets that have returns with greater potential deviations from expected returns are riskier, a natural measure of asset risk is the *statistical variance.* This is a summary statistic that indicates how widely actual values of an asset's return tend to vary relative to the expected return. Thus, a financial instrument

Table 7-1 Factors That Influence Portfolio Choice

Factor	Effect of an Increase in Factor on Desired Asset Holdings
Wealth	Increase
Expected asset return	Increase
Asset liquidity	Increase
Information costs	Decrease
Asset risk	Decrease

whose return has a larger statistical variance is judged to be riskier than one that has the same expected return but with a smaller statistical variance.

As we discuss below, this approach to measuring risk leads naturally to the application of *mean-variance analysis*, or the evaluation of trade-offs between financial assets' expected returns and variances of returns, to the portfolio-choice problem. First, however, let's consider how savers' concern about risk can induce them to hold a *mix* of different kinds of financial instruments. (Today banks have developed Web-based tools that help wealthy clients understand the trade-offs between average return and risk in their asset portfolios; see on the next page *Cyber Focus: Using the Web to Help Rich Clients Understand Their Portfolios.*)

On the Web
What are the basic issues concerning personal investment choices? Contemplate this question further at http://www.maxinvest.com.

2. What are the key determinants of portfolio choice? Other things being equal, savers will prefer to hold more of a given financial instrument (1) if they experience an increase in their wealth, (2) if the instrument's expected return rises, (3) if the savers are risk-averse and the riskiness of the instrument's return declines, (4) if the instrument's market liquidity increases, and (5) if the costs of acquiring information about the instrument fall.

The Gains from Domestic and International Diversification

Figure 7-1 on page 151 shows that U.S. households possess a wide array of financial instruments. Some of these instruments have higher expected returns than others, and some are riskier. Indeed, it is possible that some instruments have lower expected returns and greater risk than others. How could this be true if risk-averse individuals prefer to hold financial instruments with higher expected returns and lower riskiness? The answer is that savers can benefit from *diversifying* their portfolios, thereby reducing their *overall* portfolio risk. Sometimes achieving such overall risk reduction can require holding financial instruments that individually have lower expected returns and greater inherent riskiness.

Idiosyncratic Risk versus Market Risk

There is risk in holding any financial instrument. The bottom could drop out from under stock prices on any given day. A hedge fund collapse could take down a closely linked corporation, making its commercial paper worthless. In 1996, a political stalemate led to a perception that the U.S. government might suspend payments on its debts, so for a time traders perceived even Treasury securities as somewhat risky.

Financial economists view the risk of any financial instrument as separable into two components: *idiosyncratic risk* and *market risk*. Holding a mix of financial assets can help reduce the first type of risk but cannot offset the second type.

Idiosyncratic risk: Risk that is unique to a particular financial instrument; also known as *nonsystematic risk*.

IDIOSYNCRATIC RISK The first form of risk, **idiosyncratic risk** (sometimes called *nonsystematic risk*), is risk that is unique to a specific financial instrument. For example, shares of stock issued by a new company that specializes in security

GLOBAL | POLICY | CYBER Focus | MANAGEMENT

Using the Web to Help Rich Clients Understand Their Portfolios

In the days before J.P. Morgan Bank merged with Chase Manhattan Bank to become today's J.P. Morgan Chase, the stand-alone J.P. Morgan Bank was known for its efforts to attract the rich with so-called private-banking arrangements. Qualifying customers met with bankers in lavish offices with amenities such as leather armchairs, grandfather clocks, and polished brass lamps. Each year, on the anniversary of establishing their accounts, favored customers were honored in the bank's private dining room at tables set with engraved menus. To be a favored customer, one had to maintain a personal account with a balance of at least $5 million.

Today many other banks have lowered the bar for what it takes to be considered a big private customer to only about $1 million or so. A single trust account can generate up to $10,000 per year in fee income for a bank. This is why some banks are willing to incur annual expenses of $3,000 to $4,000 per employee to try to transform tellers and branch managers into private-banking specialists.

Nowadays, private-banking customers are less impressed by fancy office furniture. Instead, customers are looking for detailed information about their accounts that is also easily comprehended at a glance. At Northern Trust, private-banking customers have access to a Web-based reporting system called FundDimensions. This Internet-accessed program displays various aspects of an individual's account portfolios in multicolor graphics, which can transmit quick, visual understanding of the elements of market and idiosyncratic risks associated with the portfolios.

Northern Trust worked with a Toronto-based software company to develop this tool just for its rich clients. Funds in private-banking accounts at the bank total well over $1 trillion and generate millions of dollars in interest and fee income for the bank. Consequently, the bank considered the development of this Internet software tool well worth the expense.

For Critical Analysis: Why might wealthy clients especially value Internet reporting systems that they can read and understand in just a few moments?

encryption for e-money trades are subject to very special risks. For instance, there is always the possibility that the encryption codes, which are crucial to the company's future performance, have an undetected flaw that a capable computer hacker will discover in the near future. Or it may be that a key individual involved in developing the encryption software is a disgruntled employee who may leave for another job. Perhaps the company's encryption software will turn out to be particularly susceptible to a new computer virus. Perhaps the company's prospectus provides misleading information that has not yet been discovered by the Securities and Exchange Commission.

These and a number of other factors specific to this e-money security company could cause the value of its shares to fall in the marketplace at some future date. The risk of such company-specific events occurring is the idiosyncratic risk associated with shares of stock issued by the company.

On the Web
How does the Securities and Exchange Commission seek to limit the risks faced by individual investors? Explore this issue at the SEC's Web site, http://www.sec.gov/investor/alerts.shtml.

Idiosyncratic risk is not necessarily company specific. It could apply to all e-money security companies. For example, it is possible that all such companies, including this specific firm, have jumped the gun, entering the e-money encryption market before people are ready to buy e-money security services. As a result, near-term performances of such companies could turn out to be very poor. As a result, the returns on shares in these companies might be much lower than expected.

Even though each of these scenarios is possible, and even though this makes holding shares of stock in the e-money security company risky, a saver can offset the risk through **diversification,** or holding a mix of financial instruments that have returns that typically do not move in the same direction simultaneously. As a result, the saver can reduce overall portfolio risk even though the financial instruments of specific issuers are individually risky.

Diversification: Holding a mix of financial instruments with returns that normally do not move together.

Market risk: Risk that is common to all financial assets within a portfolio; also called *systematic risk*.

To see how a saver can do this, note that a person who wishes to hold shares in the specific e-money security company could opt to hold shares in several other e-money security firms as well. Then, if the encryption software of an individual company turns out to be easy for a hacker to decrypt, if a key employee leaves a firm, if software is susceptible to a virus, or if a firm's managers commit fraud, solid performances by other e-money security firms will generate strong returns that will offset this one weak performance.

In addition, the saver could hold financial instruments issued by providers of traditional payment technologies, such as makers of automated teller machines, producers of check-processing technology, or even private firms that make coins for the Treasury Department. Then, if e-money security technology turns out to be an idea ahead of its time as far as market performance is concerned, continued solid performances by producers of traditional payment systems will yield returns that will compensate for low returns from the shares issued by the e-money security companies.

Market Risk The other component of the risk of any financial instrument is **market risk** (also called *systematic risk*), or risk coming from the entire system. This is risk that all financial assets in a portfolio share in common, perhaps because of general variations in common economic conditions that influence all issuers of financial instruments.

Because market risk is common to all financial instruments within a portfolio, diversification cannot reduce the overall market risk of the portfolio. Hence, savers cannot reduce market risk by altering the mix of financial instruments that they hold. Savers can, however, try to avoid holding financial instruments with returns that largely move with returns of other instruments in their portfolios, thereby allowing them to reap the fullest possible benefits of diversification.

moneyxtra!

Another Perspective

Read about the special problems that financial institutions face in managing their portfolio risks in the Chapter 7 reading, entitled "The Challenges of Risk Management in Diversified Financial Companies," by Christine Cumming and Beverly Hirtle of the Federal Reserve Bank of New York.
http://moneyxtra.swcollege.com

For instance, banking tends to be a cyclical business. When economic performance is weak, the returns on bank shares tend to fall, and when the economy is doing well, the returns on bank shares tend to rise. (The amount of risk banks take on in their lending can have a major bearing on their overall performance; see on the following page *Management Focus: Banks Try to Make Up Their Minds—Do They Want Low-Risk Customers, High-Risk Customers, or Both?*) This is true of many other businesses, such as the automobile industry. Thus, the returns on stocks of banks, automobile manufacturers, and many other companies tend to move together during the course of economic cycles. A saver may wish to hold shares in stocks that move *countercyclically,* such as shares of companies that specialize in retraining unemployed workers, to help insulate the overall portfolio return from the market risk of economic fluctuations.

GLOBAL POLICY CYBER **MANAGEMENT Focus**

Banks Try to Make Up Their Minds—Do They Want Low-Risk Customers, High-Risk Customers, or Both?

About two-thirds of the assets of commercial banks are loans. When bank managers attempt to assess the overall riskiness of their assets, therefore, loans receive most of their attention.

Prime Loans versus Subprime Loans

Recall from Chapter 4 that the *prime rate* is the interest rate that banks charge on short-term loans extended to the most creditworthy business borrowers. You might think that banks would scramble to compete for such borrowers. Indeed, they do. In recent years, however, they have also engaged in heavy competition for so-called *subprime loans*, or loans extended to those borrowers who just barely meet the banks' qualifications to receive loans. Figure 7-2 shows that in the market for mortgage loans, the amount of subprime lending has increased considerably since the mid-1990s.

Why have many banks been seeking to lend to the *least* creditworthy borrowers? The answer is that the market interest rates on these loans are significantly higher than the prime rate. If both prime and subprime borrowers fully repay both loan principal and interest, then sub-

Figure 7-2
Subprime Mortgage Lending.

The amount of subprime mortgage lending has increased significantly since the mid-1990s.

SOURCE: Federal Deposit Insurance Corporation.

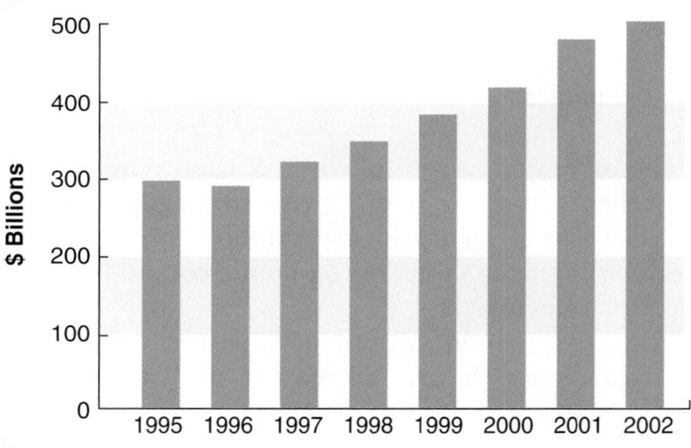

3. What is the distinction between idiosyncratic risk and market risk? Idiosyncratic risk is risk that is specific to a financial instrument. Market risk, in contrast, is risk that stems from general factors affecting the returns of all financial instruments. Holding a diversified portfolio of financial instruments with counterbalancing idiosyncratic risk characteristics reduces the overall portfolio risk because their returns tend to move in offsetting directions.

prime loans are unambiguously more profitable for banks.

Forgotten Benefits of Diversification

The problem, of course, is that, other things being equal, subprime borrowers are less creditworthy and thereby are less likely to provide full and timely payment of loans. This does not necessarily mean that a bank's overall portfolio risk rises if it increases its subprime lending relative to its loans to highly creditworthy customers. After all, it is at least conceivable that borrowers who appear most creditworthy overall might be more likely than subprime borrowers to default on their obligations if some kind of specific events were to occur. For instance, terrorists might attack the operations of the nation's highest-quality borrowers without having direct effects on the income-earning activities of lower-quality borrowers.

Hence, banks could potentially reap diversification benefits from making loans to borrowers with various degrees of creditworthiness. By the early 2000s, however, a few banking institutions were suffering because they had oversold themselves on the income-enhancing benefits of making subprime loans and had apparently forgotten about the diversification benefits of lending to high-creditworthy customers as well as subprime customers.

A good example was Providian Bank, a so-called monoline institution that had developed a niche in specializing almost completely in making loans through credit cards. By the late 1990s, the bank had discovered that it could earn significant profits by issuing credit cards mostly to relatively less creditworthy individuals and charging very high rates of interest. When U.S. economic activity dipped in 2001, however, these individuals began to default at a much more rapid pace than did more creditworthy borrowers. As a consequence, Providian's portfolio returns dropped rapidly, and the bank learned that there was a significant price to pay for its failure to diversify lending across different groups of borrowers.

For Critical Analysis: Given that all banks face a trade-off between average earnings and risks when they make loans, why might any bank try to specialize primarily in making one type of loan?

Portfolio Diversification within and across Borders

Market risk is not equal across financial instruments. The returns from holding some financial instruments may be more susceptible to nondiversifiable market risk than are the returns of other instruments. A natural question then is how a saver can identify financial instruments with mostly idiosyncratic risks that can be offset via portfolio diversification.

Identifying Assets with Diversifiable Risks Savers will shy away from a financial instrument whose risk stems primarily from market risk, because they cannot mitigate that risk through diversification. Financial economists try to judge a financial instrument's market risk via a measure called **beta** (the Greek symbol β), which is the sensitivity of the financial instrument's expected return to changes in the complete set of financial instruments. For instance, the beta value for a share of stock in an e-money security company measures the percentage increase in the value of the stock generated by a 1 percent rise in the value of all shares in the stock market as a whole. For example, if a 1 percent increase in the

Beta: A measure of the sensitivity of a financial instrument's expected return to changes in the value of all financial instruments in a market portfolio; calculated as the percentage change in the value of a financial instrument resulting from a 1 percent change in the value of all financial instruments in the portfolio.

For a concrete application of the concepts of market risk and idiosyncratic risk, go to the Chapter 7 Case Study, entitled "Portfolio Diversification via Bank Branching or a Merger?"
http://moneyxtra.swcollege.com

value of all shares traded in the stock market is accompanied by a 2 percent rise in the value of the shares of the e-money security company, then the value of beta for that company's stock is equal to 2. If the result is only a 1 percent rise in the value of the company's shares, then the value of beta is equal to 1, indicating half as much systematic risk as a beta of 2.

Savers prefer financial instruments with lower values of beta, because these instruments possess more *diversifiable* risk that the savers can reduce by holding diversified portfolios. Thus, if confronted with a choice between two financial instruments with equal expected returns, liquidity, and information costs, savers will choose the financial instrument with the lower beta value.

International Portfolio Diversification Although financial instruments from other nations may be held for various reasons including the pursuit of arbitrage profits, a fundamental rationale for holding internationally issued financial instruments is *international portfolio diversification.* Recall that market risk arises from common factors influencing the returns of financial instruments in a saver's portfolio. A key common factor is overall economic performance. A nationwide U.S. recession, for instance, tends to reduce the returns of most U.S. financial instruments, which makes aggregate economic performance an important source of market risk for a U.S. saver's portfolio.

In today's more financially integrated world, however, savers can regard even the risk of an overall U.S. economic downturn as somewhat diversifiable. Certainly, the United States is the world's largest economy, so a U.S. recession potentially can slow the economic growth rates of its major world trading partners. Nevertheless, it is not uncommon for an Asian economic expansion to take place in the midst of a U.S. recession, as occurred in the early 1990s. Indeed, U.S. savers who held financial instruments issued by companies and governments of many Asian nations during the early 1990s earned less volatile overall portfolio returns than U.S. savers who held only U.S. financial instruments. Likewise, Asian savers who held European and U.S. financial instruments in the later 1990s insulated themselves somewhat against the considerable variability of returns on Asian financial instruments during the sharp Asian downturn during this period.

moneyxtra!
Economic Applications

Are stock returns in different countries diverging or converging? For links to the stock markets of various nations, go to Corporate Finance Online.
http://moneyxtra.swcollege.com

Thus, in a truly integrated world financial system, the scope for market risk would be limited to broad global risk factors. Savers in an integrated system could regard even national economic variability as a form of idiosyncratic risk. As we discussed in Chapter 6, however, we still do not live in a world of fully integrated financial markets. Nonetheless, savers around the globe can increasingly diversify against country-specific risks.

4. How does holding international financial instruments make a portfolio more diversified? If national financial markets were completely unrelated, then a key source of nondiversifiable market risk would be national economic factors that influence financial instrument returns. If savers can purchase financial instruments of other nations, however, then national sources of risk become more idiosyncratic and, consequently, diversifiable. In a completely integrated world financial system, market risk would arise only from common global factors that affect the returns of all financial instruments.

Risks of Holding International Financial Instruments

Economics is often called the "dismal science," because a fundamental implication of economic analysis is that every facet of human experience involves tradeoffs. This is no less true of international portfolio diversification. Holding international financial instruments helps limit a portfolio's exposure to purely national risk factors. At the same time, however, holding international financial instruments exposes the portfolio to other types of risks known as *foreign exchange risks* and *country risk*.

Foreign exchange risk: The potential for the value of a foreign-currency-denominated financial instrument to vary because of exchange rate fluctuations.

Transaction risk: A foreign exchange risk arising from the possibility that the proceeds from trading a financial instrument may change as a result of exchange rate variations.

Translation risk: A foreign exchange risk resulting from altered home-currency values of foreign-currency-denominated financial instruments caused by fluctuations in exchange rates.

Economic risk: A foreign exchange risk that stems from the possibility that exchange rate movements can affect the discounted present value of future streams of income.

FOREIGN EXCHANGE RISKS As displayed in Table 7-2, a saver faces three basic types of **foreign exchange risk,** which is the prospect that the value of a foreign-currency-denominated financial instrument will change as a result of exchange rate variations. One type of foreign exchange risk is **transaction risk,** which is the risk that the proceeds from exchanging a financial instrument may change. Typically, transaction risk arises when a saver commits to a foreign-currency-denominated asset exchange at some future date. This exposes the saver to a change in the expected return on the transaction caused by a change in the exchange rate during the intervening period.

Another type of foreign exchange risk is **translation risk.** This risk arises when the values of foreign-currency-denominated financial instruments are converted into a single currency value. To see how translation risk can arise, consider the balance sheet of a multinational corporation based in the United States. Because the company does business in so many locations around the world, its assets and liabilities are denominated in a number of currencies. At the end of the company's fiscal year, when it is time to report the company's net worth to shareholders and regulators, its accountants must express the value of all assets and liabilities in terms of U.S. dollars. Fluctuations in the value of the dollar relative to other currencies before the reporting date induce variations in the dollar values of the assets and liabilities outside the United States, thereby influencing the reported net worth of the company.

The third type of foreign exchange risk is **economic risk,** which is the prospect that exchange rate variations can affect the discounted present value of future streams of income. For a saver, economic risk arises when exchange rate changes affect the present value of earnings from financial instrument holdings. For a company, economic risk arises when movements in exchange rates influence the present value of the firm's earnings, thereby affecting the long-term ability of the firm to compete.

Table 7-2 Types of Foreign Exchange Risk

Type of Risk	How Risk Exposure Arises
Transaction risk	Commitment to a future transaction denominated in a foreign currency
Translation risk	Conversion of values of foreign-currency-denominated assets and liabilities into home-currency units
Economic risk	Changes in underlying asset returns and, thus, discounted future income streams, resulting from exchange rate variations

Country risk: The potential for returns on international financial instruments to vary because of uncertainties concerning possible changes in political and economic conditions within a nation.

Exchange rate variations may have positive or negative effects on the prospects faced by a saver or a company. Nevertheless, risk-averse savers and managers typically wish to avoid foreign exchange risks to the extent possible. International portfolio diversification is one way to try to reduce exposure to foreign exchange risks. By holding a broad portfolio of international financial instruments, for example, a saver is somewhat insulated from foreign exchange risks, because adverse effects of depreciation of one country's currency may be offset somewhat by the implied appreciation of the currency of another country. Likewise, owning plants and offices in various countries can help a firm avoid some of the foreign exchange risks it would face if all its plants and offices were located in a single country. As we shall discuss in Chapter 8, it is also possible to *hedge*, or offset, exposure to many foreign exchange risks by using derivative securities.

Country Risk In addition to foreign exchange risks, holding international financial instruments exposes savers to **country risk,** which is the prospect of variations in returns generated by uncertainties about the political and economic environments of nations. For instance, governments with considerable amounts of external debt could, when faced with tough economic times, seek to postpone debt payments or possibly even default on some of their foreign debts. In times of economic or political difficulties, governments have been known to take over foreign-owned factories and offices or to outlaw flows of funds across their borders.

Thus, a nation's prospects for economic and political stability influence the perceived riskiness of the securities issued by its government and of the bills, notes, bonds, and stocks of companies that do business in that country. Naturally, country risk is particularly difficult to measure. Determining the degree of country risk of a government bond can entail trying to forecast the outcomes of elections, the potential for internal political turmoil, and the likelihood of border disputes becoming all-out war. The market prices of a nation's financial instruments respond quickly to good or bad news about the country's economic and political prospects, thereby exposing holders of the instruments to risks.

To a large extent, country risk is idiosyncratic. This means that savers can attempt to reduce the extent of country risk by holding a diversified portfolio containing international assets from a broad range of locations. Thus, the adverse effects of turbulent political times in one part of the world may be counterbalanced by the positive effects of peace and tranquillity in other regions.

5. What are the special risks of holding international financial instruments? One is foreign exchange risk, which arises in three forms: (1) transaction risk, which is the risk that the proceeds from holding a financial instrument may change because of exchange rate variations; (2) translation risk, which is the risk owing to varying home-currency values of foreign-currency-denominated instruments in the presence of exchange rate fluctuations; and (3) economic risk, which is the risk that exchange rate variations may affect the discounted present value of streams of returns from financial instrument holdings. The second type of risk is country risk, which is the risk of variations in returns on financial instruments owing to nation-specific economic and political factors.

Link to
Management

Why Is Stockholding Still So Highly Concentrated among the Rich?

As Figure 7-3 indicates, the U.S. stock market participation rate has increased considerably since 1990. At the same time, however, the portion of stocks held by the richest 10 percent of households in the United States has remained between 78 percent and 82 percent.

Information Costs and Income Risk

Hui Guo of the Federal Reserve Bank of St. Louis suggests that there are three reasons that half of all households still own no stocks and that so many households that do own stocks hold so few shares. One is that small investors may face relatively high costs of collecting information about stocks. An unwillingness to incur these costs may dissuade them from holding many shares.

Another reason is that people who are not rich depend on labor earnings as their primary source of income. Hence, they face considerable risks during economic downturns. After all, stock prices tend to fall during downturns, and people are also more likely to face pay cuts, layoffs, or job terminations. Consequently, Guo suggests, working people tend to allocate the bulk of their savings to assets that are relatively safer than stocks.

Refusing to Bet the House on the Stock Market?

Finally, Guo argues that for most households, ownership of a house constitutes the bulk of total wealth. Because house prices are so volatile, Guo suggests, households tend to manage the rest of their wealth very conservatively and that likely means holding fewer shares of stock.

In Figure 7-4, the "wealth percentiles" along the horizontal axis range from those with the least wealth, on the left, to those with the greatest wealth, on the right. People in the lowest percentiles own minuscule amounts of either real estate or corporate stocks, but those in the middle percentiles allocate relatively large shares of their wealth to ownership of real estate. Only at the upper end of the wealth distribution do people hold relatively large shares of their wealth as stocks, while holding less as real estate.

Figure 7-3
The Stock Market Participation Rate and the Share of Stocks Held by the Richest 10 Percent of Stockholders.

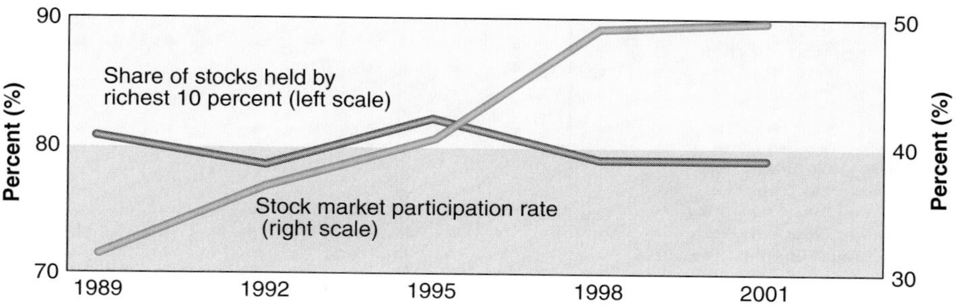

In recent years, the percentage of U.S. households holding shares of corporate stock has increased considerably. Nevertheless, the portion of shares of stock held by the wealthiest 10 percent of households has remained fairly stable.

SOURCES: Hui Guo, "Stockholding Is Still Highly Concentrated," Federal Reserve Bank of St. Louis *National Economic Trends*, June 2001; Federal Reserve *Survey of Consumer Finances* (various issues), Board of Governors of the Federal Reserve System; and authors' estimates.

Continued on next page

Link to Management, continued

RESEARCH PROJECT

In some emerging nations, such as Egypt, as much as 90 percent of housing and other real estate is not legally registered with national policymakers. How might these and other data problems complicate efforts to compare household wealth allocations across countries? How might economists get around these difficulties to study international differences in how households allocate their wealth?

WEB RESOURCES

1. What Federal Reserve resources concerning households' allocations of wealth are available on the Web? Take a look at the index to the Fed's Survey of Consumer Finances at http://www.federalreserve.gov/pubs/oss/oss2/scfindex.html.

2. How do the wealth allocations of U.S. households differ from those of households in the United Kingdom? Learn more about this by visiting the Web site of the British Household Panel Survey's 2001 conference at http://www.iser.essex.ac.uk/activities/bhps-2001, where you can click on "Paper Download" and then download (in PDF format) a study of this subject by James Banks, Richard Blundell, and James Smith entitled "Wealth Portfolios in the U.K. and the U.S."

Figure 7-4
Portions of Household Assets Allocated to Stocks and Real Estate, by Wealth Percentile.

People in the middle portion of the wealth distribution tend to allocate a relatively large share of their wealth to holdings of real estate. In contrast, wealthier people tend to hold larger portions of their wealth in stocks.

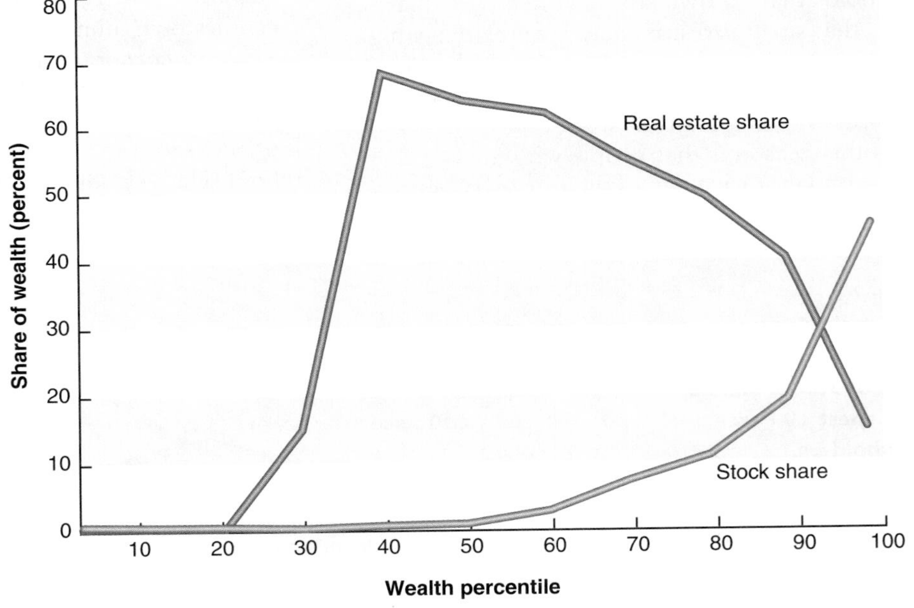

SOURCES: Joseph Tracey and Henry Schneider, "Stocks in the Household Portfolio," Federal Reserve Bank of New York *Current Issues in Economics and Finance* 7 (April 4, 2001); Federal Reserve *Survey of Consumer Finances* (various issues), Board of Governors of the Federal Reserve System.

Chapter Summary

1. Financial Portfolios: A financial portfolio is the complete group of financial instruments that an individual holds at a point in time. These holdings constitute the individual's financial wealth, which the individual can increase by allocating saving to purchases of additional financial instruments.

2. The Key Determinants of Portfolio Choice: One key factor that influences portfolio decisions of savers is their wealth. Another is the expected return from holding the instrument. A third is the riskiness of the instrument's return, and a fourth is the market liquidity of the instrument. Finally, the costs of acquiring information influence savers' choices of financial instruments to hold in their portfolios.

3. The Distinction between Idiosyncratic Risk and Market Risk: Idiosyncratic risk is risk that is specific to a given financial instrument, whereas market risk arises from factors that influence the returns of all financial instruments. A saver can reduce the overall riskiness of a portfolio by holding a diversified portfolio of instruments with offsetting idiosyncratic risk characteristics, so that their returns tend to move in opposite directions.

4. How Holding International Financial Instruments Makes a Portfolio More Diversified: If international financial markets were completely separate, then a key source of nondiversifiable market risk would be national economic factors that influence financial instrument returns. If savers can purchase financial instruments of other nations, however, then national sources of risk become more idiosyncratic and, consequently, diversifiable. In a completely integrated world financial system, market risk would arise only from common global factors that affect the returns of all financial instruments.

5. Special Risks of Holding International Financial Instruments: Two categories of risk apply specifically to international financial instruments. One is foreign exchange risks. The first type of foreign exchange risk is transaction risk, which is the risk that the returns from holding financial instrumens may vary because of exchange rate changes. The second type of foreign exchange risk is translation risk, which is the risk resulting from fluctuations in home-currency values of foreign-currency-denominated instruments caused by exchange rate movements. The third type of foreign exchange risk is economic risk, which is the risk that exchange rate changes can influence the discounted present value of returns from holding financial instruments. The second category of risks from holding international financial instruments is country risk. This is the risk of varying returns on financial instruments caused by country-specific economic and political factors.

Questions and Problems

(Answers to odd-numbered questions and problems may be found on the Web at http://money.swcollege.com under "Student Resources.")

1. Suppose that an individual's wealth increases by 2 percent. Listed below are the individual's percentage increases in holdings of certain financial instruments. Calculate this individual's wealth elasticity of demand for each instrument and identify the instrument as either a necessity asset or a luxury asset for this individual.

- **a.** Treasury bills: +1.4 percent
- **b.** Treasury bonds: +3.0 percent
- **c.** Corporate stock: +1.8 percent

2. Even though asset risk and market liquidity are separate determinants of portfolio choice, in actual practice it can sometimes be very difficult to disentangle the separate effects of these factors on household portfolio allocations. Explain why this is so. [Hint: As an example, consider the fact that trading of high-risk, so-called junk bonds dropped off considerably in the late 1990s at the same time that the perceived riskiness of those bonds increased sharply.]

3. Explain why a saver can diversify against idiosyncratic risks. Then explain why market risks are nondiversifiable.

4. In your view, which of the following risks is nondiversifiable in today's financial system? For those that you believe to be diversifiable, give an example of how you might diversify against this risk in your own portfolio (assuming you have the resources to do so).

- **a.** The risk that a sharp downturn in the wool industry will cause a drop in the share prices of major wool producers.

b. The risk that a political revolution will topple the leader of an African nation, causing the nation to default on its bonds.

c. The risk that a sharp rise in world energy prices will cause a global economic downturn.

5. In 1998, the Federal Reserve helped arrange a privately funded bailout of Long-Term Capital Management, a large hedge fund based in Connecticut. Many market participants interpreted this as a signal that the Federal Reserve considered such hedge funds "too big to fail." If you had been considering holding shares in a large hedge fund, how would this action have influenced your decision about whether to hold hedge fund shares instead of alternative financial instruments? Explain your reasoning.

6. Bonds A and B have equal maturities and expected returns, and both have similar daily market trading volumes. Savers have identical information about both bonds. The variance of bond A's return is higher than the variance of the return on bond B. Bond B, however, has a higher beta value than bond A. For a risk-averse saver, is holding one bond preferable to holding the other, if all other factors are the same? Explain.

7. Stock X has a lower risk premium, measured against a risk-free rate, and a lower beta than stock Y. Both have the same expected return, and costs of acquiring information about the two bonds are not significantly different. Other things also being equal, and assuming that savers are risk-averse, is holding one stock preferable to holding the other? Explain.

8. You have been made chief financial officer for an equities fund that has significant holdings in winter sportswear companies. Provide some suggestions for how the equities fund might diversify its risks by using new funds it has raised to add to its existing stock holdings. Justify your choices.

9. A large multinational firm has determined that its year-end balance sheet shows a negative net worth in one country but a positive net worth in another country. Explain how this might occur, assuming that the company holds a number of assets and liabilities valued in more than one currency.

10. As part of a strategy to diversify internationally, a U.S. money market fund holds a number of stocks and bonds denominated in various other currencies. Periodically, it also adjusts its international asset holdings by purchasing and selling international financial instruments. Discuss the pros and cons of this strategy.

Before the Test

Test your understanding of the material covered in this chapter by taking the Chapter 7 interactive quiz at http://money.swcollege.com.

Online Application

Internet URL: http://cme.com

Title: The Chicago Mercantile Exchange (CME)

Navigation: Begin with the CME home page (http://cme.com). Click on "About CME," and then, from the left-hand menu, click on "Sharehold/Member."

Application: Read the discussion, and then answer the following questions:

1. Click on "Membership Prices." What was the last price at which a full CME membership traded? Why would someone be willing to pay that much to have the right to execute a trade on the CME?

2. Based on what you have learned about prices of financial instruments, if you were contemplating allocating some of your wealth to purchasing a CME membership—which you would regard as an asset within your overall portfolio of assets—what factors do you think might determine the price of a membership? [Hint: Imagine holding this membership for a number of years and earning an annual return each year, and then think about how to price the anticipated stream of returns from a CME membership.]

For Group Study and Analysis: Divide into groups, and discuss what factors might cause the price of a CME membership to *vary*. After the class reassembles, discuss the various factors that groups have identified as likely determinants of the riskiness of owning a CME membership.

Selected References and Further Reading

Elton, Edwin, and Martin Gruber. "Modern Portfolio Theory, 1950 to Date." *Journal of Banking and Finance* 21 (December 1997): 1743–1759.

Fama, Eugene. "Multifactor Portfolio Efficiency and Multifactor Asset Pricing." *Journal of Financial and Quantitative Analysis* 31 (1996): 441–465.

Markowitz, Harry. *Portfolio Selection.* New Haven: Yale University Press, 1959.

Sarkar, Asani, and Kai Li. "Should U.S. Investors Hold Foreign Stocks?" Federal Reserve Bank of New York *Current Issues in Economics and Finance* 6 (March 2000).

Szego, Giorgio. *Portfolio Theory with Application to Bank Asset Management.* New York: Academic Press, 1980.

Tracy, Joseph, and Henry Schneider. "Stocks in the Household Portfolio: A Look Back at the 1990s." Federal Reserve Bank of New York *Current Issues in Economics and Finance* 7 (April 2001).

Wei, K. C. John. "An Asset-Pricing Theory Unifying the CAPM and APT." *Journal of Finance* 43 (September 1988): 881–892.

MoneyXtra

moneyxtra! Log on to the MoneyXtra Web site now (http://moneyxtra.swcollege.com) for additional learning resources such as practice quizzes, case studies, readings, and additional economic applications.

Chapter

Managing Risks in the Global Economy—Derivative Securities

Fundamental Issues

1. What are interest rate risk, financial instrument duration, and derivative securities?
2. What are forward and futures contracts, and how can they be used to limit risks?
3. What are options, and how can they be used to reduce foreign exchange risk exposure?
4. What are swaps, and how are they used to hedge against risks?
5. What are the key risks of derivative securities, and what regulations govern derivatives trading?

It was autumn in Greenwich, Connecticut, and the leaves of many of the city's trees had already taken on a golden tint. At a Greenwich financial firm called Long-Term Capital Management (LTCM), however, the situation had become black. The firm's managing partners, who included a former Federal Reserve Board governor, a former Salomon Brothers vice president, and two Nobel-Prize-winning financial economists, had just lost nearly all the shareholders' equity in the firm. The total loss had been estimated at more than $4 billion, and the partners had accepted a $3.5 billion bailout financed by private banks but brokered by the Federal Reserve Bank of New York.

LTCM had experienced losses on derivative instruments—securities with returns derived from the returns on other securities—that it had used to hedge bets that it had made about future interest rate movements. The specific derivative instruments that had brought down the firm were interest rate swaps. *LTCM's partners had made bets that returns on European and U.S. stocks and bonds would always revert to a "long-term norm." Instead, the Asian financial crisis of 1997–1998 had induced investors around the world to engage in a "flight to quality" by purchasing large volumes of U.S. bonds and stocks, thereby persistently pushing the prices of those instruments above previous long-term norms. As a result, the returns on U.S. bonds had stayed well below long-term norms for weeks longer than LTCM had anticipated. What had looked like safe bets with interest rate swaps suddenly had turned out to be disastrous gambles.*

Why did LTCM think that by using interest rate swaps it could earn profits if interest rates and stock and bond prices were consistent with "long-term norms"? Was there anything unusual about this financial institution's use of interest rate swaps? What are the characteristics of derivative instruments? What other kinds of derivative securities do financial and nonfinancial firms most commonly hold? To learn the answers to these questions, you must learn about interest yields, interest rate risk, and derivative securities.

Interest Rate Risk, Duration, and Derivative Securities

In Chapter 4 we explained how to compute interest yields and discussed how interest rates and market prices of financial instruments are related. As Figure 8-1 indicates, interest rates can be volatile over time. This means that the market values of financial instruments also can vary considerably. As a result, anyone holding such instruments incurs an inherent risk.

Interest Rate Risk

A key issue that anyone who holds financial instruments must face is that such instruments are risky. One source of risk, of course, is the risk of default. Another, however, is the chance that the market value of an instrument will vary as interest rates change. This type of risk is called **interest rate risk.**

Interest rate risk: The possibility that the market value of a financial instrument will change as interest rates vary.

Figure 8-1
Selected Interest Rates.

Interest rates can vary considerably over time. This exposes owners of financial instruments to the risk of capital losses.

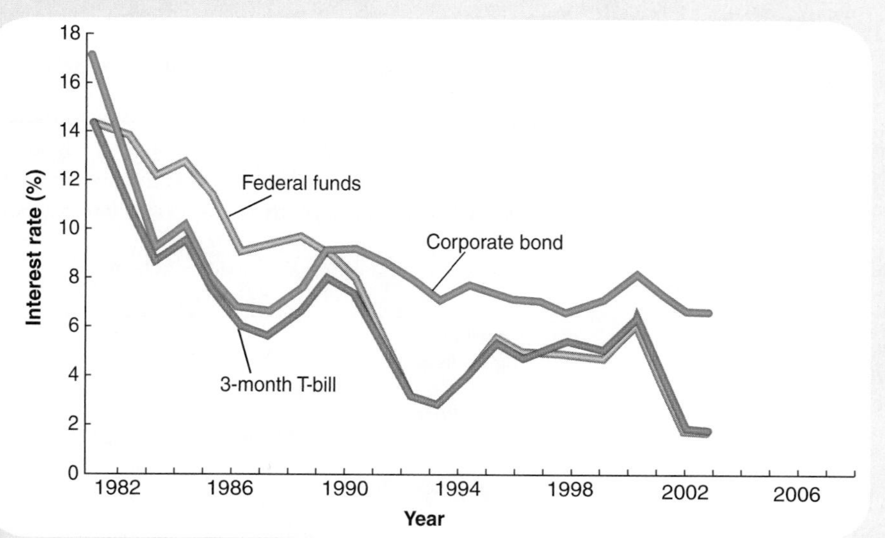

SOURCES: *Economic Report of the President, 2002;* and *Economic Indicator.*

Zero-coupon bonds: Bonds that pay lump-sum amounts at maturity.

Capital loss: A decline in the market value of a financial instrument at the time it is sold as compared with its market value at the time it was purchased.

As we discussed in Chapter 4, bond prices and interest yields are interdependent, and the effective yield on an instrument such as a Treasury bill depends on the time remaining until the instrument matures. It follows that how much bond prices vary in response to interest rate changes depends in part on the time remaining until the bond matures. The price of a bond, of course, is the market value of the bond. Hence, the extent to which a bond's value varies as interest rates change depends on the time until the bond matures. This, in turn, implies that the interest rate risk of the bond will depend on how far off the bond's maturity date is.

TERM TO MATURITY AND INTEREST RATE RISK To better understand why time to maturity matters for interest rate risk, consider an example of two very simple bonds. One pays $10,000 after a single year. The other pays $10,000 after the passage of two years. Such bonds are known as **zero-coupon bonds** because they pay lump-sum amounts at maturity.

Table 8-1 calculates the prices of the two bonds for market interest rates of 7 percent and 8 percent. A rise in the market interest rate from 7 percent to 8 percent causes the price of each bond to decline. Holders of the bonds would incur **capital losses,** meaning that the market value of their bond holdings will fall.

The calculations in Table 8-1 show that the percentage capital loss on the two-year bond is 1.8 percent, which is twice the 0.9 percent capital loss on the one-year bond. The reason is that the rise in the market interest rate from 7 percent to 8 percent applies across two years for the two-year bond. But the same interest rate rise affects the one-year bond's price just for the bond's one-year lifetime.

This simple example illustrates that a bond's *lifetime* plays a key role in determining the proportionate capital loss incurred when market interest rates rise.

Table 8-1 Effects of an Interest Rate Increase on the Market Prices of Two Zero-Coupon Bonds

This example illustrates that the prices of bonds with longer maturities fall in greater proportion following an expected rise in the market interest rate. Consequently, bonds with longer lifetimes have greater exposure to interest rate risk.

	One-Year $10,000 Zero-Coupon Bond	Two-Year $10,000 Zero-Coupon Bond
Bond Price at 8% Rate	$10,000/(1.08) = $9,259.26	$10,000/(1.08)^2 = $8,573.39
Bond Price at 7% Rate	$10,000/(1.07) = $9,345.79	$10,000/(1.07)^2 = $8,734.39
Dollar Price Change	−$86.53	−$161.00
Percentage Price Change	(−$86.53/$9,345.79) × 100 = −0.9%	(−$161.00/$8,734.39) × 100 = −1.8%

Bonds with longer terms to maturity are susceptible to greater risk of capital loss. Thus, bonds with longer lifetimes have greater exposure to interest rate risk.

FREQUENCY OF COUPON RETURNS AND INTEREST RATE RISK Another key factor influencing interest rate risk is how often bonds pay coupon returns. For instance, think about a zero-coupon bond that pays $10,000 to the bearer after two years, as compared with a bond that pays a stream of $10,000 at quarterly intervals ($1,250 per quarter for eight quarters) over two years. The bearer of the latter bond receives returns on the bond much more quickly. Hence, if market interest rates rise, the effective capital loss on the bond that pays out quarterly coupon returns will be lower, even though both bonds have the same two-year maturity.

Interest rate risk poses both rewards and challenges to an individual or firm. The rewards arise if the individual or company finds ways to profit from increases in financial instruments' market values following reductions in market interest rates. The challenges entail balancing the potential for such capital gains against the possibility of *capital losses* that will be incurred if market interest rates rise, thereby reducing the market values of financial instruments.

FINANCIAL INSTRUMENT DURATION Thus, *two* factors influence interest rate risk. One is term to maturity, or a bond's lifetime. The other is how often a bond pays returns to the holder. To assess interest rate risk, bond traders need to be able to measure these factors together. They do this using a concept called **duration.** This is a measure of the average time required to receive all payments of principal and interest.

On the Web

Where on the Web can a person learn how to calculate duration? One place to check is the Financial Pipeline home page, http://www.finpipe.com. Click on "Bonds" in the left-hand margin, then click on "Valuing Bonds," and under "Related Articles," click on "Duration."

Strategies for Limiting Interest Rate Risk

Various strategies can be used to limit exposure to interest rate risk. One approach might be to hold mostly short-term financial instruments. Financial instruments with short-term maturities, as we noted earlier, have lower risk of capital losses when interest rates rise as compared with instruments of longer maturity. A more sophisticated strategy might be to hold bonds with shorter durations. This takes into account both the maturity of the financial instrument and the frequency of payments received.

There are three problems with both strategies, however. One is that if the yield curve slopes upward, long-duration instruments are more likely to provide greater returns. This is so because if all other factors are unchanged, duration rises with the term to maturity. The longer the term to maturity, the higher the interest yield when the yield curve exhibits its normal shape. Thus, holding only short-duration instruments constitutes a low-return strategy.

Second, continually selling and repurchasing—"rolling over"—short-term instruments can be costly. Traders would incur both opportunity costs of time spent on this activity and direct costs in expending effort. Furthermore, rolling over instruments with short terms to maturity entails potentially significant exposure to **reinvestment risk.** This is the possibility that market yields will decline by the time the short-term instrument matures. In that case, a trader could have earned a higher net yield by holding longer-term instruments instead.

Duration: A measure of the average time during which all payments of principal and interest on a financial instrument are made.

Reinvestment risk: The possibility that available yields on short-term financial instruments may decline, so that holdings of longer-term instruments might be preferable.

Furthermore, holding only short-maturity instruments sacrifices benefits that traders can gain from *portfolio diversification.* As we discussed in Chapter 7, diversification entails spreading risks across holdings of financial instruments with different characteristics. Portfolio diversification can also help reduce interest rate risk. For instance, short-term yields may fall at the same time that long-term yields are rising. Thus, placing funds in a portfolio consisting only of short-term instruments could lead to a lower return than one could otherwise earn by holding a broader mix of instruments. If traders allocate their funds to a portfolio including longer-term instruments, then the rise in yields on these instruments helps offset the effect on the total portfolio return from declines in short-term yields.

Hedging and Derivative Securities

In light of the drawbacks of holding primarily shorter-maturity, low-duration financial instruments, individuals, companies, and banks have developed an alternative strategy for addressing interest rate risk. This is *hedging* against risk. The fundamental instruments for engaging in hedging are *derivative securities.*

HEDGING To reduce interest rate risk on a portfolio, it is possible to use other instruments to **hedge,** or engage in a countervailing financial trading strategy that reduces interest rate risk in the underlying portfolio. A *perfect hedge* fully eliminates these risks. Hedging strategies can also help reduce, or even fully offset, the *foreign exchange risks* that we discussed in Chapter 7.

Market interest and exchange rate conditions can vary from one hour to the next. Consequently, holders of financial instruments must meet two key requirements to hedge interest rate risk and foreign exchange risks. One is sufficient *flexibility* to adapt to various situations that one might face. Another is the capability to conduct necessary transactions *rapidly.* The desire to find hedging strategies that combine both flexibility and speed has led to the development of sophisticated instruments called *derivative securities,* or "derivatives."

DERIVATIVE SECURITIES A **derivative security** is any financial instrument whose return is linked to, or derived from, the returns of other financial instruments. Derivatives trading has increased dramatically worldwide since the 1980s. Indeed, between 1995 and 2003 alone, the "notional value" of derivatives (the value based on underlying market values of the financial instruments) held by U.S. banks increased by over 350 percent, to more than $50 trillion, as bank managers found ways to use derivative securities in hedging strategies. By way of contrast, in 1986, banks held less than $1.5 trillion in derivative securities.

At the same time, however, a number of banks and other derivatives traders determined that they could earn significant short-run profits by speculating with derivative securities. Some traders learned, however, that derivatives speculations can turn out to be wrong. The results were sizable speculative losses, the most notable of which we tabulate in Table 8-2. Particularly dramatic among these were the 1994 loss of over $1.5 billion by Orange County, California, and the 1995 loss of about $1.4 billion by Britain's Barings Bank. The broader consequences of these losses were layoffs for Orange County employees and the collapse of Barings Bank.

Hedge: A financial strategy that reduces the risk of capital losses arising from interest rate or currency risks.

Derivative securities: Financial instruments whose returns depend on the returns of other financial instruments.

Table 8-2 Major Derivatives Losses since 1990

A number of companies and municipalities have experienced multimillion-dollar losses from derivatives.

Estimate of Loss	Company/Municipality	Primary Derivatives
$50 million	First Boston	Options
$260 million	Volkswagen	Currency futures
$100 million	Cargill Fund	Mortgage derivatives
$157 million	Procter & Gamble	Currency futures
$100 million	Florida State Treasury	Mortgage derivatives
$20 million	Gibson Greeting Cards	Swaps
$35 million	Dell Computer	Swaps and options
$20 million	Paramount Communications	Swaps
$150 million	Glaxo, Inc.	Mortgage derivatives
$1,500 million	Orange County, California	Mortgage derivatives
$50 million	Capital Corp. Credit Union	Mortgage derivatives
$195 million	Wisconsin Investment Funds	Swaps
$25 million	Escambia County, Florida	Mortgage derivatives
$1,400 million	Barings Bank, UK	Stock index futures
$65 million	PacifiCorp	Currency options
$83 million	Bank of Tokyo-Mitsubishi	Swaps and options
$689 million	United Bank of Switzerland	Stock index futures
$720 million	Deutsche Bank	Swaps and options
$149 million	NatWest Bank	Swaps and options
$3,500 million	Long-Term Capital Management	Swaps
$691 million	Allied Irish Banks	Currency options

The derivatives-related losses summarized in Table 8-2 captured media attention and caused many to question the trillions of dollars of derivatives trading by individuals, companies, and banks. As we have noted, however, most traders use derivatives to *hedge* against risks. Thus, you may wonder how it is that so many have lost so much by trading these instruments. To understand how this can happen, you must first have a better understanding of what derivative securities are and how people can use them both to hedge *and* to gamble. As you will see, it is derivatives *gambles* that most often lead to big losses—and, for some, to sizable profits.

1. What are interest rate risk, financial instrument duration, and derivative securities? Interest rate risk is the chance that the prices of financial instruments may vary because of unexpected movements in market interest rates. The two key determinants of interest rate risk are the maturity and frequency of returns on financial instruments. Instruments of longer maturities and with less frequent returns, which therefore have longer durations, or average periods necessary to receive all principal and interest payments, possess greater interest rate risk. Derivative securities are financial instruments whose returns are based on the returns of other financial instruments. Traders may use derivative securities to hedge against interest rate and foreign exchange risks. They may also use derivatives to try to earn profits based on speculations about future movements in interest rates and exchange rates.

Forward contract: A contract requiring delivery of a financial instrument at a specified price on a certain date.

Interest-rate forward contract: A contract committing the issuer to sell a financial instrument at a given interest rate as of a specific date.

Forward and Futures Contracts

There are several categories of derivative securities. The characteristic that they all share is that their returns stem from returns on other financial instruments. In addition, traders may use them for hedging or in speculative strategies.

Forward Contracts

An important example of a derivative security is a **forward contract,** which is a contract requiring delivery of a commodity or a financial instrument at a specific price on a particular date. The delivery price of the financial instrument depends in part on the market value of the financial instrument, which means that the value of the forward contract itself is *derived from* the instrument's market price. This is why a forward contract is a derivative security.

HEDGING WITH FORWARD CONTRACTS To hedge against interest rate risk, financial market traders can use a particular type of forward contract. Called an **interest-rate forward contract,** it guarantees the future sale of a financial instrument at a specified interest rate as of a specific date.

To see how an interest-rate forward contract can be a *perfect* hedge for two parties to such a contract, consider an example. Suppose that a Paris bank is sure that next year it will receive 10 million euros in future interest and principal payments from very creditworthy customers who have borrowed from the bank. As part of a new strategy, the bank's managers have decided to reduce the bank's lending next year and to place half that amount, or 5 million euros, in default-risk-free five-year notes issued by the nations within the European Monetary Union (EMU). The bank's managers wish to guarantee that at this time next year the bank will still be earning the current market interest yield on the European government notes, which we shall suppose is equal to 5 percent. At the same time, a Tokyo bank's securities portfolio contains several million euros worth of five-year European government notes that will mature in three years. The Tokyo bank's managers believe that market interest rates may rise above 5 percent during the next three years, which would imply a fall in the prices of the notes, causing the bank to incur a capital loss on its euro-denominated note holdings.

To try to hedge against the risks that they face, the Paris and Tokyo banks negotiate an interest-rate forward contract. The Paris bank agrees to purchase five-year European government notes valued at 5 million euros *one year from now* at a price that would yield the 5 percent interest yield currently in effect for those notes. The Paris bank thereby guarantees that it will earn today's 5 percent market rate a year from now. The Tokyo bank also relieves itself of the risk of capital loss within the next year on a significant portion of its portfolio of five-year European government notes. This is because the contract guarantees the Tokyo bank that the price of the notes will be consistent with a 5 percent yield in the following year.

SPECULATION WITH FORWARD CONTRACTS In this example, the banks use derivative securities as hedging instruments to protect their portfolios from risks of loss. This does not, however, rule out the possibility that traders may use derivative securities for purposes of risky speculation in the pursuit of profits.

How Attempts to Hedge Can Amount to Risky Speculation To understand how derivatives transactions may *increase* overall risk, let's slightly change the conditions of the example. Suppose now that the Paris bank's managers believe that the interest cost of their bank's funds, which currently averages 4 percent, is likely to be lower by this time next year. Their belief, however, is not consistent with the widespread views of other financial market participants, who generally expect a significant increase in the average funding costs Paris banks will face during the next year. Nevertheless, the Paris bank's managers are so sure that their expectation will turn out to be correct that they are willing to enter into the interest-rate forward contract with the Tokyo bank that we discussed above.

Recall that this contract commits the Paris bank to buy the European government notes at a price consistent with the *current* market yield of 5 percent. This means that if the expectation that banks' average interest funding costs will rise significantly by the following year is correct, then the net interest profit that the Paris bank will earn on the European government notes will be much lower next year than the bank's managers currently *speculate* that it will be. For example, if banks' average funding costs rise as high as 5 percent or more, then the net profit that the Paris bank will earn on its EMU notes will turn out to be zero or below. Thus, to the extent that the consensus forecast of higher bank funding costs indicates a strong likelihood that this actually will occur, the Paris bank will have negotiated a speculative contract and added to its overall risk.

This example indicates that while financial market traders can use derivative securities to hedge against risks, they also can use them to engage in speculation. If speculations fail to pay off, then parties to derivative contracts can lose. Where did all the "lost" funds tabulated in Table 8-2 end up? The answer is that the funds did not evaporate. Instead, they fell into the possession of individuals, businesses, financial institutions, and government agencies that made the right choices in their own speculative strategies. For instance, in our example if the Paris bank's managers turn out to be incorrect in their anticipation of a fall in average bank funding costs, then the Paris bank will experience losses from the interest-rate forward contract. The "lost" funds will flow to the Tokyo bank, which will be able to remove the EMU notes from its portfolio at a 5 percent yield, and hence at an above-market price, in the following year.

Both a Winner and a Loser This leads us to the following conclusion about losses in trading forward contracts and other derivatives transactions:

> **For each "loser" in derivatives speculation, there must also be a "winner" on the other side of the transaction.**

From society's perspective, gains and losses from derivatives speculation must, in a purely accounting sense, "cancel out." As we shall discuss below, however, this does not imply that governments have been unconcerned about the potential for broader fallout from large derivatives losses.

SHORT AND LONG POSITIONS IN FORWARD CONTRACTS In the example of an interest-rate forward contract between Paris and Tokyo banks, the Paris bank agreed to purchase European government notes in the following year at a price consistent with the current market yield. In the terminology of forward contracts, the Paris bank took a **long position**, meaning that the bank is obliged to *purchase*

Long position: An obligation to purchase a financial instrument at a given price and at a specific time.

Short position: An obligation to sell a financial instrument at a given price and at a specific time.

Forward currency contract: A forward contract calling for delivery of foreign currency, or financial instruments denominated in a foreign currency, at a specific exchange rate on a certain date.

the European government notes next year at a fixed yield. By way of contrast, the Tokyo bank selling the notes took a **short position,** meaning that the bank must *sell* the European government notes the following year at the contracted price. By entering into the forward contract, however, the Tokyo bank's managers were able to remove the European government notes from their portfolio more quickly, thus avoiding incurring a capital loss if market yields were to rise.

Covering a Foreign Exchange Transaction with a Forward Contract Individuals, firms, and banks also use forward contracts to hedge against foreign exchange risks. They do this by using **forward currency contracts,** which require delivery of foreign currency or a foreign-currency-denominated financial instrument at a specified exchange rate on a particular date.

To see how a forward currency contract can be used to hedge against foreign exchange risk, think about the situation faced by a multinational firm that has promised, after considerable bargaining, to purchase some equipment from a foreign supplier for delivery three months from now. The multinational firm's managers know that the company will have to make a payment to the supplier that is denominated in the supplier's national currency. In addition, however, the firm's managers realize that there is a possibility that the foreign currency could rise in value during the next three months, which would effectively raise the price the firm would have to pay for the equipment when the payment date arrives. To eliminate the risk of this occurrence, the managers can enter into a forward currency contract in which they agree to purchase the required amount of foreign currency at the currently prevailing three-month *forward exchange rate,* which is the exchange rate on foreign exchange to be delivered three months from now. By doing this, the managers ensure that the firm will pay the agreed price for the equipment, so all its hard bargaining will not have been in vain.

The market for forward contracts may be limited by two factors: (1) difficulties in setting the terms of the contracts and (2) default risk. Parties to forward contracts must agree to specific contract terms. Sometimes it is hard for two parties to do this. In our example, we simply assumed that the multinational firm could reach mutually satisfying terms with another party. In reality, reaching an agreement on the terms of forward contracts can be a complex undertaking.

Default risk also somewhat deters the use of forward contracts. In our banking example with interest-rate forward contracts, the Paris bank might be better off defaulting on the contract if its funding costs rise sharply within a year's time. (It is rare for banks to fail to follow through on forward contracts or other interbank financial transactions, but such defaults have been known to occur.) This risk could make the Tokyo bank less likely to agree to the terms of the contract. Such potential incentives for default make interest-rate forward contracts riskier and less liquid, thereby restraining trading volumes somewhat.

Futures Contracts

One disadvantage with forward contracts is that they are not "standardized." They tend to share similar features, but parties to a contract must work out the specific terms. This can take much time and effort.

Like a forward contract, a **futures contract** is an agreement by one party to deliver to another a quantity of a commodity or financial instrument at a specific future date. In contrast to forward contracts, however, futures contracts specify *standardized* quantities and terms of exchange. Futures contracts specify in advance the amounts to be traded and the guidelines for transactions. Because futures contracts are standardized, parties do not have to spend time working out the contract terms.

Futures contract: An agreement to deliver to another a given amount of a standardized commodity or financial instrument at a designated future date.

Interest rate future: A contract to buy or sell a standardized denomination of a specific financial instrument at a given price at a certain date in the future.

Stock index future: An agreement to deliver, on a specified date, a portfolio of stocks represented by a stock price index.

Holders of futures experience profits or losses on the contracts at any time before the contracts expire. This is because futures contracts require daily cash-flow settlements. In contrast, profits or losses occur only at the expiration date of a forward contract, which requires settlement at maturity.

The futures exchange is an organized market that simplifies the task of selling futures contracts, thereby making them highly liquid. Consequently, futures trading has grown much more rapidly than trading in forward contracts. Nevertheless, derivatives trading outside public futures exchanges is hardly "small potatoes"; the estimated annual value of worldwide forward contracts and other derivatives transactions amounts to nearly $130 trillion, or nearly twelve times the amount of *annual* U.S. nominal national income.

INTEREST RATE FUTURES Contracts requiring delivery of standard quantities of a financial instrument at a specified price and rate of return and on a certain date are **interest rate futures.** Traders undertake transactions in these contracts at the Chicago Board of Trade (CBOT) futures exchange and other exchanges around the world. Each exchange establishes requirements that parties to such a transaction must meet. The financial instruments of futures contracts usually are U.S. Treasury bonds and other government bonds. For instance, a trader may enter into a five-year U.S. Treasury note futures contract, which constitutes an agreement to purchase or sell U.S. Treasury notes in standard denominations of $100,000.

STOCK INDEX FUTURES Standardized agreements to deliver, on a specified date, a portfolio of stocks represented by a stock price index are **stock index futures.** For example, in the case of Standard and Poor's (S&P) 500 futures traded at the Chicago Mercantile Exchange, the stock portfolio is representative of the market value of the 500 companies listed in the S&P index. Likewise, Nikkei-225 Stock Average futures are based on a portfolio of 225 stocks traded on the Tokyo Stock Exchange. In 1995, a series of bad bets, made by a poorly supervised manager, about Nikkei-225 futures traded in the Singapore International Monetary Exchange (Simex) led to the downfall of Barings Bank, a 233-year-old British institution.

To see how to calculate the value of a futures contract, let's consider an example involving an S&P 500 index futures contract. Computing the dollar value of such a contract requires multiplying the current market price of the futures contract times $500. For instance, if the S&P 500 futures price is 400, then the value of the contract is equal to $200,000. If an individual takes a *short position* with an S&P 500 futures contract, she agrees to deliver a cash amount of $500 times whatever the futures price turns out to be at the date in the contract. The party

Currency future: An agreement to deliver to another a standardized quantity of a specific nation's currency at a designated future date.

on the other end of the transaction, in contrast, takes a long position and agrees to pay 400 times $500 for this contract today. Assume that when the date arrives, the market price of the futures contract is equal to 500. Therefore, the contract has a dollar value of $250,000, so the individual in the short position loses $50,000 and the buyer in the long position gains $50,000. The buyer in the long position has paid $200,000 for the $250,000 cash payment that the seller in the short position is obligated to make.

CURRENCY FUTURES Futures contracts entailing the future delivery of national currencies are **currency futures.** Currency futures contracts, like other futures, entail daily cash-flow settlements, whereas currency forward contracts entail a single settlement only at the date of maturity. As a result, the market prices of forward and futures contracts usually differ. In addition, futures contracts typically involve smaller currency denominations as compared with forward contracts. Large banking institutions and corporations that transmit large volumes of foreign currencies in their normal business operations are the primary users of forward contracts. Individuals and smaller firms that wish to undertake hedging or speculative strategies typically trade currency futures instead.

Hedging with Currency Futures As we discussed in Chapter 7, exchange rate movements cause those who trade in international financial markets to face risks arising from variations in asset prices. They also experience interest rate risks arising from interest rate volatility. Let's consider how traders confront this additional source of risk.

How can currency futures be used to hedge against foreign exchange risk? Suppose that a British firm has a franchise operation in the United States. The firm's managers anticipate that the current year's profits from this operation will be $3 million, which they plan to convert to British pounds. If the dollar depreciates relative to the pound during the year, then the pound-denominated value of the $3 million will be lower at year's end. That is, the British firm's exposure to translation risk would cause it to lose part of its dollar-denominated profits from its U.S. operation. To hedge against this risk, the firm's managers can take a long position via a pound future that expires in September. As the firm's dollar-denominated profit earnings decline in value relative to the British pound, the pound-denominated value of the firm's September future will rise, thereby offsetting, at least partially, the effect of the dollar's depreciation against the pound.

Reducing translation risk requires the firm to establish a margin account with a futures broker. The firm posts an *initial margin* (sometimes called the *bond performance requirement*) in this account by paying a small portion of the total value of the futures that the broker will purchase on the firm's behalf. Typically, the initial margin is less than 2 percent of the total value of the futures purchased. During the year, the firm must maintain a maintenance margin (sometimes called the *minimum bond performance requirement*), which is a minimum balance that must remain in its account with the futures broker. The broker and the firm also establish a *mark-to-market* procedure for applying the futures contract gains and losses to the firm's account at the close of each trading day.

Consider Figure 8-2, which displays the currency futures price quotes for British pounds that a firm can view at the Web site of the Chicago Mercantile Exchange (**http://www.cme.com**). Suppose that the market price for a September

Figure 8-2
Currency Futures Prices for the British Pound.

The Chicago Mercantile Exchange reports futures prices using the format shown above. To understand how to read published currency futures quotes, consider the information for each column.

MTH/ STRIKE	OPEN	---SESSION--- HIGH	LOW	LAST	SETT	PT CHGE	EST VOL	---PRIOR DAY--- SETT	VOL	INT
SEP02	1.5264	1.5266	1.5176	1.5264	----	−58	2518	1.5204	6260	31094
DEC02	1.5190	1.5190	1.5080	1.5114	----	−56	40	1.5174	26	596
MAR03	----	----	----		----	−56		1.5084		
JUN03	----	----	----		----	−56		1.4994		
TOTAL							EST. VOL	VOL		OPEN INT
TOTAL							2558	6286		31730

Mth/Strike:	Maturing month.
Open:	Price of futures contract at the opening of business. On this day, a contract for 62,500 pounds for September 2002 began trading at $1.5264 per pound.
High:	Highest price of the futures contract reached during the day; $1.5266 per pound on this day.
Low:	Lowest price of the futures contract reached during the day; $1.5176 per pound on this day.
Last:	Price of the last futures contract at the close of business on this day; $1.5264 per pound.
Pt. Chge:	Change in price during the day.
Est.Vol.:	Approximate number of pound futures transactions during the day.
Prior Day Sett.:	Price of the contract at market close the previous day.
Prior Day Vol.:	Volume of futures contracts traded the previous day.
Prior Day Int.:	Number of contracts outstanding on the previous trading day.

pound future is 1.5264 dollars per pound, as shown in Figure 8-2. The standard size of a pound future is 62,500 pounds. If the current spot exchange rate is 1.5290 dollars per pound, then the firm purchases an amount of pound futures equal to ($3 million/$1.5290 per pound)/62,500 pounds, which is approximately equal to 31. Therefore, purchasing 31 standard pound futures contracts provides the best possible futures hedge for the British firm. Note that with a $2,000 initial margin per contract, the firm's initial margin is 31 × $2,000 = $62,000. Thus, for a $3 million futures account, the firm must post only $62,000 in its margin account with its broker.

Daily Futures Settlement To illustrate the daily settlement process of a typical futures contract, let's extend our example by supposing that on the first trading day the market closes at a futures price of $1.5284 per pound, so that the firm's 31 pound futures appreciate. To keep things simple, let's also assume that the firm pays no brokerage fees. On the first day, the firm earns a profit equal to ($1.5284 per pound − $1.529 per pound) × 62,500 pounds × 31 = $3,875. The firm's margin account thereby rises from $62,000 (the initial margin) to $62,000 + $3,875 = $65,875.

If the closing futures price on the second trading day drops to $1.5254 per pound, then the firm experiences a dollar loss on the pound futures equal to ($1.5254 per pound − $1.5284 per pound) × 62,500 pounds × 31 = −$5,812.50. The firm's margin account thereby falls from $65,875 to $65,875 − $5,812.50 = $60,062.50.

Now suppose that the futures price rises to \$1.5294 per pound on the third trading day. Then the firm earns a dollar profit equal to (\$1.5294 per pound −\$1.5254 per pound) × 62,500 pounds × 31 = \$7,750, and the firm's margin account thereby rises from \$60,062.50 to \$60,062.50 + \$7,750 = \$67,812.50.

Note how the set of 31 futures contracts serves as a hedging instrument for the British firm. If during the course of the year the pound appreciates against the dollar, then the firm's realized pound-denominated value of profits from its U.S. franchise operation declines, so each dollar of profits from those operations has a smaller pound-equivalent value at the end of the year. As the pound appreciates against the dollar, however, the British company's futures margin position improves, thereby offsetting some or all of the firm's translation risk exposure.

(Some companies lack the expertise to hedge foreign exchange risks by trading currency futures and other types of derivatives, but now there are online firms that offer to manage these risks for a fee; see *Cyber Focus: Make Your Online Trades in Dollars and Leave the Hedging to Us.*)

Option: A financial contract giving the owner the right to buy or sell an underlying financial instrument at a certain price within a specific period of time.

Exercise price: The price at which the holder of an option has the right to buy or sell a financial instrument; also known as the *strike price.*

Call option: An option contract giving the owner the right to purchase a financial instrument at a specific price.

Put option: An option contract giving the owner the right to sell a financial instrument at a specific price.

American option: An option that allows the holder to buy or sell a security any time before or including the date at which the contract expires.

European option: An option that allows the holder to buy or sell a financial instrument only on the day that the contract expires.

Futures options: Options to buy or sell futures contracts.

2. What are forward and futures contracts, and how can they be used to limit risks? Forward contracts are agreements to provide commodities or financial instruments on future dates and at specific prices. Futures contracts are similar agreements, but the quantities of commodities or financial instruments exchanged via futures contracts are standardized. Individuals, companies, and banks can use forward and futures contracts to ensure interest rate or exchange rate responses of derivatives returns that tend to offset variations of returns on other asset holdings. This reduces net exposures to interest rate risk and to foreign exchange risks.

Options

Another type of derivative instrument is an **option,** which is a financial contract giving the holder the right to purchase or sell an underlying financial instrument at a given price. The holder of this right is not required to buy or sell, but has the *option* to do so. The given price at which the holder of an option can exercise the right to purchase or sell a financial instrument is the option's **exercise price,** which traders also call the *strike price.*

Types of Option Contracts

Call options allow the holder to *purchase* a financial instrument at the exercise price. **Put options** allow the buyer to *sell* a financial instrument at the exercise price. In addition, traders call an option granting the holder the right to exercise the right of purchase or sale at any time before or including the date at which the contract expires an **American option.** They call an option that allows the holder to exercise the right of purchase or sale *only* on the date that the contract expires a **European option.**

Stock Options and Futures Options Many individuals and firms use options to hedge against risks owing to variations in interest rates or stock prices. To do this, they trade **futures options,** which are options to buy or sell stock

GLOBAL | POLICY | CYBER Focus | MANAGEMENT

Make Your Online Trades in Dollars and Leave the Hedging to Us

As discussed in Chapter 2, various online payments methods are emerging. Nevertheless, U.S. firms that sell goods and services on the Internet continue to allow their U.S. and foreign customers to make the bulk of their payments with credit cards. Customers who reside in other nations, however, may encounter difficulties with foreign exchange risk. For one thing, by the time foreign residents have finished searching through a seller's online catalog, filled out an order form at the appropriate Web page, and clicked the "submit order" button, the rates of exchange for their currencies relative to the U.S. dollar may have changed. Moreover, for transactions finalized using credit cards, exchange rates almost certainly will have changed by the time credit-card companies such as Visa and MasterCard have processed the transactions. Thus, foreign residents who wish to purchase items online face foreign exchange risks, which can reduce their incentives to shop at the Web sites of U.S. firms.

Many U.S. companies have concluded that the solution to this problem is to offer online shoppers using credit cards the opportunity to purchase items with their own currencies. To do this, the U.S. sellers must post prices expressed in foreign currencies. In this way, foreign consumers will know what charges will show up on their credit-card bills.

The problem is that if U.S. firms were to charge prices expressed in yen, euros, or other currencies, they would be taking on all the risks of exchange rate fluctuations caused by delays in settling credit-card transactions. Hedging these risks would require the U.S. firms either to learn how to trade currency futures and options or to pay banks hefty fees to arrange currency swaps or forward contracts.

Now the U.S. firms have another alternative. A company called E4X, Inc., now makes it possible for client firms to display prices on their Web sites in as many as twenty-six currencies. E4X installs a software program at a client firm's Web site that permits its customers to select a currency from a set that appears in a drop-down menu. Prices in a given currency are based on predetermined exchange rates that E4X guarantees to hedge using currency derivatives.

In exchange for this service, E4X charges its client firms commissions ranging between 1.5 and 3 percent of their foreign sales. The size of the commission rate varies directly with the length of time that a client wishes the prices in the drop-down menu to remain unchanged. Naturally, the hedging costs that E4X incurs by engaging in derivatives transactions behind the scene increase if it must guarantee fixed prices in foreign currencies for longer periods.

For Critical Analysis: Why can't U.S. Web sellers feel safe in assuming that foreign Internet shoppers will just arrange to hedge foreign exchange risks on their own?

index futures or interest rate futures, and **stock options,** which are options to buy or sell shares in corporations.

Trading volumes in the stock index futures market have risen considerably since the 1980s. Paralleling this growth has been broadened trading in the futures options market. In fact, today more options on stock index futures—essentially derivatives of derivatives—are traded than options based on actual stocks.

Stock options: Options to buy or sell firm equity shares.

Currency option: A contract granting the holder the right to buy or sell a given amount of a nation's currency at a certain price within a specific period of time.

Currency Options Contracts that give the owner the right to buy or sell a fixed amount of a given currency at a specified exchange rate at a certain time are **currency options.** Currency put options grant the holder the right to sell an amount of currency, while currency call options grant the holder the right to purchase an amount of currency. Multinational corporations can purchase currency options directly from banks via *over-the-counter* contracts and can also purchase them in organized exchanges.

Using Option Contracts to Reduce Exposure to Foreign Exchange Risks

moneyxtra!

Another Perspective

Sometimes firms have to adjust their portfolios of underlying assets to hedge against swings in the values of their option contracts. To read about how they do this, go to the Chapter 8 reading, entitled "Issues in Hedging Options Positions," by Saikat Nandi and Daniel Waggoner of the Federal Reserve Bank of Atlanta.

http://moneyxtra.swcollege.com

The best way to understand how to use options to hedge against foreign exchange risks is by considering an example. Let's evaluate how currency call options help to limit losses and provide profit opportunities for a fictitious U.S. importer.

Let's consider how a U.S. importer buying 2 million euros worth of finished goods for an agreed-upon December payment might hedge against foreign exchange risk using a currency call option. If the current spot rate is $0.990 per euro, then the 2 million euros are equal to $1,980,000. To hedge against an unanticipated change in the exchange rate between now and December, the importer purchases December euro call options.

Figure 8-3 displays currency option quotes that the importer can locate at the Web site of the Chicago Mercantile Exchange (**http://www.cme.com**). At an exercise price of $1.070 in Figure 8-3, the upper limit on the dollar cost of the imported goods is $2,140,000. In Figure 8-3, a December option with this exercise price has a *premium* of $0.0020 per euro, which is the effective cost of purchasing the contract. Consequently, one contract for the standard amount of 62,500 euros requires an expenditure of $125. Covering the 2 million euros in standard allotments of 62,500 euros requires exactly 32 contracts, for a total expenditure, or *total premium,* of 32 × $125 = $4,000.

Once the importer purchases the 32 option contracts for $4,000, if the dollar depreciates above $1.070 per euro, and if we ignore exercise fees that the contract might specify, then the importer would choose to exercise the option. For example, if the dollar depreciates to an exchange rate of $1.090 per euro, then it costs the importer $2,180,000 to obtain 2 million euros in the spot market. The exchange rate change increases the importer's costs by $2,180,000 − $1,980,000 = $200,000. Exercising the option and obtaining the 2 million euros at the exercise price of $1.070 per euro, or at a total dollar expenditure of $2,140,000, thereby saves $40,000. Considering the premium that the importer paid for the options, the importer comes out ahead by an amount equal to $40,000 − $4,000 = $36,000.

Note that the firm did not fully hedge against losses if the spot exchange rate turns out to be $1.090 per euro, because the firm pays a total of $2,140,000 + $4,000 = $2,144,000 using its option contracts. This is $164,000 more than the $1,980,000 that the firm would have had to pay if the exchange rate had remained at its initial value of $0.990 per euro. Hence, the firm still incurs a net loss of $164,000 as a result of a rise in the exchange rate from $0.990 per euro to $1.070 per euro. Nevertheless, this is better than the $200,000 loss it would otherwise have incurred without the currency options.

A spot exchange rate of $1.070 per euro is just one possible outcome, however. Figure 8-4 on the next page illustrates the limited loss and potential profit

Figure 8-3
Currency Options Prices for the Euro.

The Chicago Mercantile Exchange reports currency options prices on the Internet using the format shown above. To understand how to read published currency options quotes, consider the information for each column.

MTH/ STRIKE	OPEN	---SESSION--- HIGH	LOW	LAST	SETT	PT CHGE	EST VOL	---PRIOR DAY--- SETT	VOL	INT
ZC DEC02 EUROFX OPTIONS CALL										
1030	.00530	.00530	.00520	.00520	.00500	+5	10	.00450	22	201
1040	----	----	----	----	.00380	+3	1	.00350		190
1050	----	----	----	----	.00390	+2		.00280	93	337
1060	----	----	----	----	.00240	+1		.00230	9	1210
1070	.00200	.00200	.00200	.00200	.00200	UNCH	5	.00200	48	721
970	.02150	.02150	.02080A	.02120B	.02040	+19	5	.01850	170	229
980	.01640	.01640	.01640	.01640	.01640	+16	5	.01480	43	1471
990	.01350	.01350	.01350	.01350	.01300	+12	5	.01180	25	855
TOTAL							EST. VOL	VOL		OPEN INT
TOTAL							4305	3369		53327
ZC DEC02 EUROFX OPTIONS PUT										
900	.00340	.00340	.00300	.00300	.00350	−8	11	.00430	11	396
910	.00480	.00480	.00480	.00480	.00490	−11	7	.00600	17	184
920	.00650	.00660	.00650	.00660	.00680	−14	10	.00820		491
TOTAL							EST. VOL	VOL		OPEN INT
TOTAL							1182	2237		38763

Mth/Strike: Month of maturity and various exercise (or strike) exchange rates of option contracts on 62,500 euros.

Open: Price of options contract at the opening of business. On this day, a call option contract of 62,500 euros for December 2002 with an exercise exchange rate of 1.070 began trading at $0.0020 per option.

High: Highest price of option contracts reached during the day.

Low: Lowest price of option contracts reached during the day.

Last: Price of the last option contract at the close of business.

Pt. Chge: Change in price during the day.

Est. Vol.: Approximate number of euro options transactions during the day.

Prior Day Sett.: Price of the contract at market close the previous day.

Prior Day Vol.: Volume of options contracts traded the previous day.

Prior Day Int.: Number of contracts outstanding on the previous trading day.

resulting from the importer's call options for a range of values of the spot exchange rate. The maximum net loss that the importer can experience is the total premium of $4,000 for the 32 option contracts. Below the strike exchange rate of $1.070 per euro, the importer is "out of the money," meaning that the firm cannot exercise the options. If the spot exchange rate rises to $1.070 per euro, however, then the importer can exercise the options. At this strike exchange rate, the importer is "at the money." Above the strike exchange rate, the firm is "in the money," meaning that it earns gross receipts that begin to offset the premium it paid for the options.

If the spot exchange rate rises to $1.072 per euro, then the gross earnings from exercising the option increase to $4,000, which exactly recoups the total premium of $4,000. Hence, the spot exchange rate of $1.072 per euro is the *break-even point* for the importer's option contracts. If the spot exchange rate rises above $1.072 per euro, then the importer earns net profits from its options; that is, its gross earnings exceed the total premium paid for the option contracts. Note that if the spot exchange rate turns out to be $1.090 per euro in Figure 8-4, then

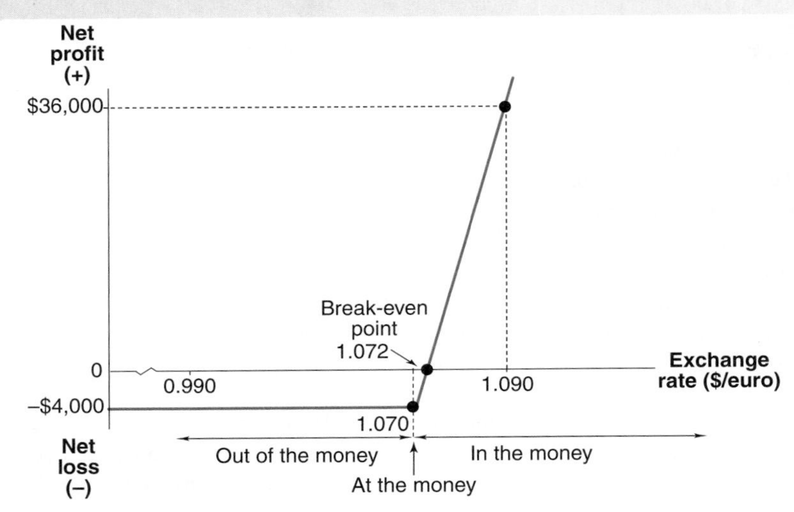

Figure 8-4
Potential Profit and Limited Loss from a Call Option.

At a per-contract premium of $0.0020 per euro, each 62,500-euro contract entails a premium expenditure of $125, so the holder of the options pays the total premium of 32 × $125 = $4,000. The maximum loss that the holder can incur on the options is limited to this amount. At or above the exercise exchange rate of $1.070 per euro, the holder may exercise the options and recoup at least a portion of the premiums paid for the options. At the spot exchange rate of $1.072 per euro, the holder's earnings from exercising the options just cover the total premiums paid. At a higher spot exchange rate, the holder earns a net profit. For example, at the spot exchange rate of $1.090 per euro, the holder earns a net profit of $36,000.

the importer's net gain from the option contracts is equal to ($1.090 per euro − $1.072 per euro) × 2,000,000 euros = $36,000, which is the amount we calculated previously.

3. What are options, and how can they be used to reduce foreign exchange risk exposure? Options are contracts that permit the owner to buy or sell a financial instrument at a certain price within a specific interval. Traders and all participants in foreign-currency-denominated contracts can use currency options to respond to a currency appreciation or depreciation by buying or selling the currency and earning net returns that are higher than those they would otherwise have achieved.

Swaps

Swaps are financial contracts in which parties to the transactions exchange *flows* of payments. Typically, these are flows of interest payments or payments denominated in foreign currencies.

Swap: A contract entailing an exchange of payment flows between two parties.

Interest rate swap: A contractual exchange of one set of interest payments for another.

Interest Rate Swaps

An **interest rate swap** is an important type of swap in international financial markets. Under this contract, one party commits itself to exchange a set of interest payments that it is scheduled to receive for a different set of interest payments owed to another party.

Financial market traders can use interest rate swaps to reduce their exposure to interest rate risk. For instance, a company holding a portfolio consisting primarily of long-duration financial instruments might engage in an interest rate swap for a stream of interest returns on a portfolio consisting mainly of shorter-duration instruments. This strategy could reduce the overall interest rate risk that the company faces.

Currency swap: An exchange of payment flows denominated in different currencies.

Currency Swaps

Another key swap contract is a **currency swap,** which is an exchange of payment flows denominated in different currencies. Figure 8-5 illustrates a currency swap, in which we suppose that Ford Motor Company earns a flow of Japanese-yen-denominated revenues from auto sales in Japan, while Honda earns dollar revenues from selling autos in the United States. Ford pays dollar dividends and interest to its owners and bondholders, and Honda pays yen-denominated dividends and interest to its owners and bondholders. Therefore, Ford and Honda could, in principle, use a currency swap as a mechanism for trading their yen and dollar earnings for the purpose of paying income streams to their stockholders and bondholders.

There are various types of interest rate and currency swaps. The most common swap is the *plain vanilla swap* (sometimes called a *bullet swap*), in which two parties to the swap arrangement agree simply to trade streams of payments to which each is entitled. Other swap contracts are more sophisticated. For instance, a *forward swap* delays the actual swap transaction for a period ranging from a

Figure 8-5
A Sample Currency Swap.

Ford Motor Company receives yen-denominated earnings from selling automobiles in Japan, and Honda receives dollar-denominated earnings from selling autos in the United States. The two companies could use a currency swap contract to trade their yen- and dollar-denominated earnings to make payments to holders of their stocks and bonds.

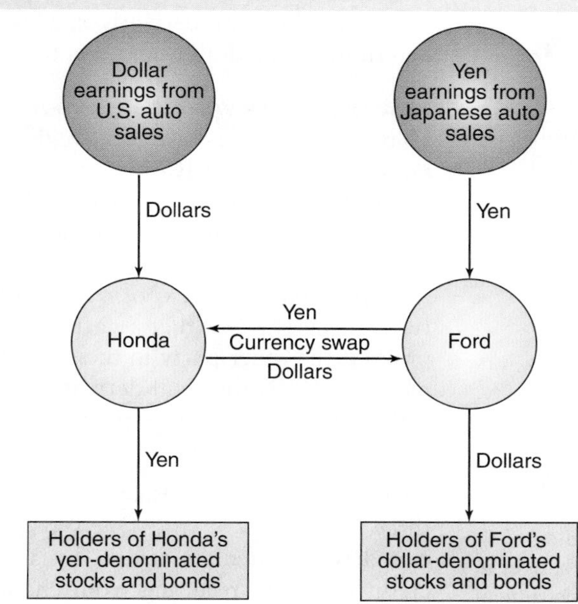

few days to a few years. A *swap option* (sometimes called a *swaption*) grants the owner the right to enter into a swap when the swap's market price reaches an exercise or strike price. Determining the effective returns on these and other derivatives of swaps can be fairly complicated. This has led to the emergence of a group of financial economists who call themselves "financial engineers" and who seek to develop methods for computing the appropriate market prices of these derivative securities. (More businesses than ever are using derivatives; see *Management Focus: Just How Much Do U.S. Businesses Really Use Derivatives?)*

4. What are swaps, and how are they used to hedge against risks? A swap is an exchange of payment flows between two parties. Traders typically engage in swaps of promised streams of interest payments or of flows of payments denominated in foreign currencies. Trading flows of payments derived from portfolios with differing maturities can help reduce interest rate risk, and trading foreign-currency-denominated payment flows can reduce foreign exchange risk exposures.

Derivative Risk and Regulation

Table 8-2 on page 173 shows that those who trade derivatives can incur big, and sometimes even huge, losses. Clearly, trading in derivative securities is not a risk-free endeavor.

Derivatives Risk

To think about factors influencing a firm's choice among alternative derivative instruments, go to the Chapter 8 Case Study, entitled "Too Many Derivatives from Which to Choose?"
http://www.moneyxtra.swcollege.com

Financial engineers also seek to identify and measure the risks that traders incur by speculating with derivatives. This is a challenging task, partly because simply determining the dollar amounts of derivatives trading can be difficult.

Measuring Derivatives Risks A widely used measure of aggregate derivatives volume, which some use as a rough measure of exposure to derivatives risk, is the *notional value* of derivatives, or the amount of principal that serves as a basis for computing streams of payments. The estimated notional value of derivative contracts worldwide in 2003 was nearly $130 trillion, up from just over $43.2 trillion in 1996.

Replacement cost exposure is another popular measure of derivatives-related risk. This is the cost that a party to a derivatives contract faces at current market prices if the other party in the derivative contract defaults before contract settlement. In 1992, the total derivatives replacement cost exposure of U.S. commercial banks amounted to 4 percent of their assets. By 1997 this figure had risen to 8 percent. Today it exceeds 10 percent.

Derivative credit risk: Risk stemming from the potential default by a party in a derivative contract or from unexpected changes in credit exposure because of changes in the market yields of instruments on which derivative yields depend.

Types of Derivatives Risks By holding derivatives, firms expose themselves to three basic types of risk. One type is **derivative credit risk.** This is the risk associated with potential default by a contract party or an unexpected change in credit exposure resulting from changes in the market prices of the underlying instruments on which derivative yields depend. The replacement-cost-exposure measure focuses on this form of derivatives risk.

GLOBAL POLICY CYBER MANAGEMENT Focus

Just How Much Do U.S. Businesses Really Use Derivatives?

To try to learn more about just how commonplace derivatives are for nonfinancial companies, Gordon Bodnar, Gregory Hayt, and Richard Marston conducted a survey of a large set of U.S. firms. They found that exactly half of the companies used derivatives. Of these, more than 90 percent indicated that their use of these instruments had recently increased

Among the largest firms surveyed, 83 percent reported that they used derivatives. This percentage dropped to 45 percent among medium-sized firms and to 12 percent among small firms. Derivatives were used by 48 percent of the manufacturing companies surveyed, and 42 percent of the service firms.

Managing exposure to foreign exchange risk was an important application of derivatives for 83 percent of the surveyed firms. The majority indicated that they hedge less than 25 percent of their perceived risk exposure. Only about a third reported hedging 75 percent or more of their total exposure to foreign exchange risks. The survey indicated that more than 80 percent of currency derivatives used by companies are forward and futures contracts. Firms reported that they used currency swaps somewhat more frequently than currency options.

For Critical Analysis: Does the survey provide any support for the argument that there are economies of scale (that is, lower costs for larger firms) in the use of derivatives?

Another type of risk is **derivative market risk,** which is the risk of potential losses stemming from unexpected glitches in the payments system or unusual price changes at the time of settlement. Such events can cause derivative traders' liquidity levels to drop and can slow their normal efforts to adjust their derivatives holdings, thereby exposing them to risks of loss. For instance, a multinational firm may decide to execute a currency option before an anticipated unfavorable price movement, but when it tries to do so, it finds that a critical computer link is temporarily "down," thereby causing it to experience a loss when the price changes. In like manner, the price of an underlying asset in a derivatives transaction might fluctuate unexpectedly at the last moment before settlement, also causing the holder to incur a loss.

Finally, derivatives traders must confront **derivative operating risk,** or the risk of loss owing to unwise management. Many of the notable derivatives losses summarized in Table 8-2 on page 173 resulted from situations in which firm managers incorrectly valued derivatives and discovered their errors only at settlement. Institutions such as Bankers Trust, which settled several lawsuits concerning derivatives trading that it performed on behalf of client firms, had problems due to inadequate internal controls. These resulted in poorly supervised trading by mid-level managers, who were accused of mispricing derivatives and of misleading the bank's clients about the risk exposures they faced by holding derivatives.

As individuals, banks, and companies have become more adept at finding ways to use various derivatives for both hedging and speculation, the markets for these instruments have continued to grow around the world. So have some of the losses that have arisen when institutions have done a poor job of managing their

Derivative market risk: Risk arising from unanticipated changes in derivatives market liquidity or from failures in payments systems.

Derivative operating risk: Risk owing to a lack of adequate management controls or from managerial inexperience with derivative securities.

risks. This potential for loss has begun to capture the attention of the world's financial regulators. Many regulators have been endeavoring for the past several years to do a better job of assessing both the benefits and the costs associated with derivatives.

Should Derivatives Trading Be Subjected to Greater Regulation?

Recall from Chapter 2 that bank regulators seek to attain four fundamental goals:

1. Increased bank efficiency
2. Limited risk of bank illiquidity
3. Reduced potential for bank insolvency
4. Protection of consumers of banking services

So far, bank regulators and other financial regulators have concluded that derivatives trading makes banks and financial markets more efficient. In addition, they have noted that the multimillion-dollar losses that have captured so much media attention over the years pale in significance next to the tens of trillions of dollars of worldwide derivatives trading that takes place each year.

To this point, therefore, most financial regulators have been hesitant to impose direct restrictions on derivatives trading by banks and others. Instead, as you will learn in Chapter 15, they have tried to induce individuals, companies, and banks to fully report their derivatives activities. For instance, in 1998 the U.S. Securities and Exchange Commission began requiring most large banks and about 500 other publicly traded companies to disclose estimates of their derivatives risks. The idea behind this requirement was that public information about high derivatives risks would reduce the affected firms' market values, giving them an incentive to reduce their derivatives risks voluntarily.

Another major effort to regulate derivatives has come from the U.S. Financial Accounting Standards Board (FASB—pronounced "fazbee"). In 1998, this regulatory body decided to change U.S. accounting standards to require banks and companies to report on how the market values of their derivatives holdings affect the net-worth positions that they report to shareholders. Today financial and nonfinancial firms must attempt to provide regular assessments of their derivatives risk exposure in their financial reports.

5. What are the key risks of derivative securities, and what regulations govern derivatives trading? Derivatives credit risk is the potential for default or unanticipated changes in the prices of securities from which derivatives' returns are derived. Derivatives market risk is the possibility of losses caused by payment-system breakdowns or unusual price changes at settlement. Derivatives operating risks are the potential losses caused by poor management of trading positions. At present, derivatives are subject to limited regulation in the United States, most of which is confined to reporting requirements that exceed those of most other locales.

Link to Management

Following the Money in Derivatives Markets

When a group of large banks provided Long-Term Capital Management with a $3.5 billion rescue in the fall of 1998, many people were surprised that the institution had entered into so many interest rate swaps. When most people think of derivative securities, they tend to focus on exchange-traded derivative instruments, which include futures and options traded in organized exchanges. Indeed, the value of derivatives traded in organized exchanges has grown in recent years. As Figure 8-6 indicates, global derivatives trading in organized exchanges now amounts to more than $18 trillion—considerably more than in 1990.

Figure 8-6
Values of Derivatives Traded in Organized Exchanges and Over-the-Counter.

Total derivatives trading has soared in recent years, with most of the growth occurring in trading of over-the-counter derivatives.

SOURCES: Donald Mathieson and Garry Schinasi, *et al., International Capital Markets: Developments, Prospects and Policy Issues,* August 2001, International Monetary Fund; BIS Global OTC Derivatives Market Semi-Annual Reports; BIS International Banking and Financial Market Developments.

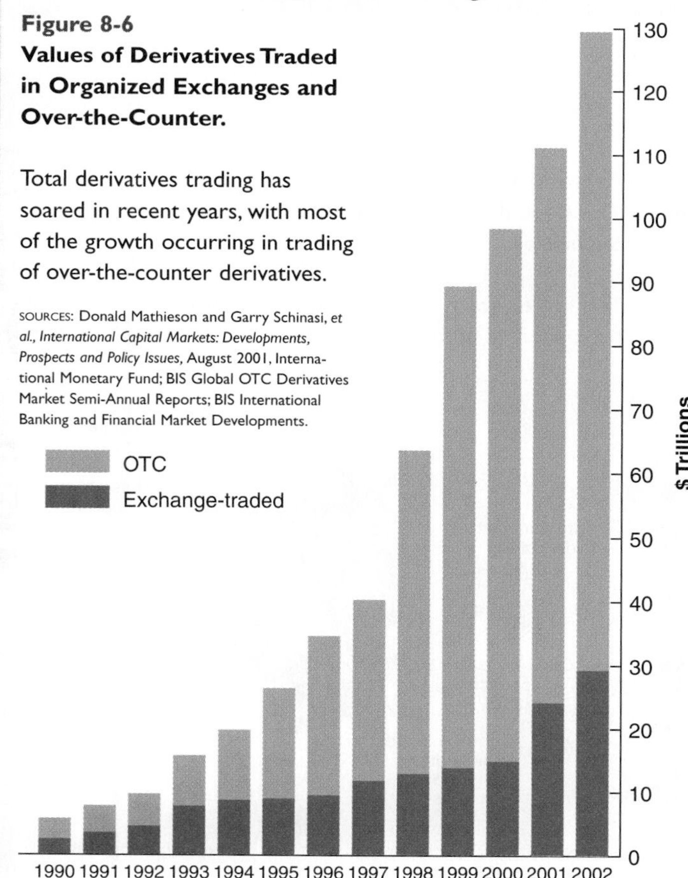

Over-the-Counter Derivatives

Nevertheless, as Figure 8-6 shows, exchange-traded derivatives transactions are dwarfed by trades of *over-the-counter (OTC) derivatives instruments,* which are contractual arrangements negotiated between parties without the use of organized exchanges. OTC derivative instruments account for almost 85 percent of global derivatives securities, and they include instruments such as forward contracts, OTC options, and swaps. Hence, the interest rate swaps that helped bring down LTCM were OTC derivatives.

As you can see in Figure 8-7, LTCM's use of interest rate swaps reflected the significant trading of these types of derivatives throughout the global financial system. Furthermore, the use of interest rate swaps continued to increase following the LTCM disaster.

The Current Distribution of Derivative Securities

Figure 8-8 displays the present worldwide allocation of total derivative securities, including both exchange-traded and OTC derivatives. Today, interest rate swaps account for about 43 percent of the total value of all derivative securities. The next most commonly used derivative securities are currency forward contracts, which also are OTC derivatives and account for about 9 percent of total derivatives.

It is natural to think of the Chicago Mercantile Exchange and the London International Futures and Options Exchange as major locations where individuals and firms trade derivative securities. Although they are important derivatives trading centers, the futures and options traded there are only a fraction of

Continued on next page

Link to Management, continued

the total value of derivatives held around the world.

Research Project

What factors influence whether a firm hedges risks using a forward contract, a swap, a future, or an option? Why are financial institutions more likely to trade forward contracts and swaps, while nonfinanical firms are more likely to trade futures and options? Are the answers to these two questions related, and if so, how?

Web Resources

1. What are the most recent figures for global exchange-traded and OTC-traded derivative instruments? To find out, go to the home page of the Bank for International Settlements at http://www.bis.org, and in the drop-down menu under "Publications and Statistics," click on "International Financial Statistics," and then click on "Derivatives Statistics."

2. How heavily are U.S. banks using derivative securities? To find out, go to the Office of the Comptroller of the Currency, at http://www.occ.treas.gov. In the left-hand column, click on "News Releases," and then scroll down to the latest edition of the "OCC Derivatives Report."

Figure 8-7
The Value of Interest Rate Swaps Relative to the Value of OTC Derivatives.

Interest rate swaps account for a steadily growing proportion of OTC derivatives. The dollar amount of interest rate swaps is now more than half of the total global holdings of OTC derivatives.

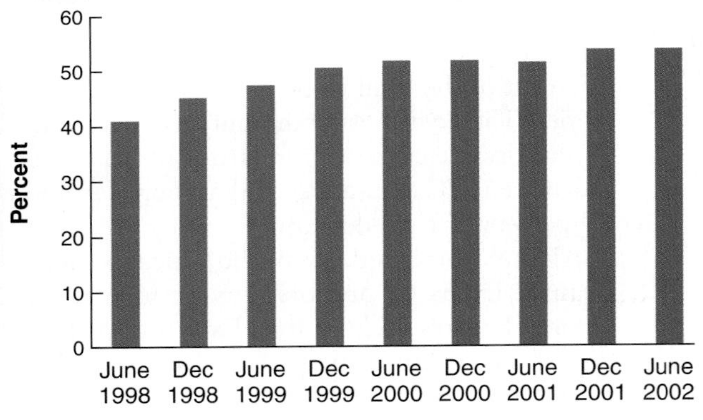

SOURCES: Donald Mathieson and Garry Schinasi, *et al., International Capital Markets: Developments, Prospects and Policy Issues*, August 2001, International Monetary Fund; BIS Global OTC Derivatives Market Semi-Annual Reports; BIS International Banking and Financial Market Developments.

Figure 8-8
The Global Distribution of Holdings of Derivative Securities.

This figure displays the overall distribution of derivative securities traded on both organized exchanges and over-the-counter.

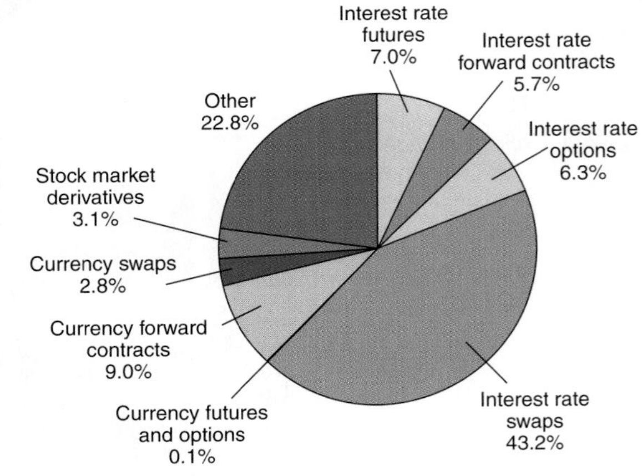

SOURCES: BIS Global OTC Derivatives Market Semi-Annual Reports; BIS International Banking and Financial Market Developments.

Chapter Summary

1. Interest Rate Risk, Financial Instrument Duration, and Derivatives: Interest rate risk is the potential for prices of financial instruments to vary because of unanticipated changes in interest rates. The two key factors influencing interest rate risk are the maturity and frequency of returns on financial instruments. Instruments of shorter maturities and with more frequent returns have shorter durations, or average periods necessary to receive all principal and interest payments. Such shorter-duration instruments possess lower interest rate risk. Derivative securities are financial instruments with returns derived from the returns of other financial instruments. Traders can use derivative securities to hedge against interest rate and foreign exchange risks. They can also employ derivatives to engage in profitable or unprofitable speculations about future movements in interest rates and exchange rates.

2. Forward and Futures Contracts, and How They Can Be Used to Limit Risks: A forward contract is a commitment to provide commodities or financial instruments on a future date and at a specified price. A futures contract is a similar instrument, but futures contracts specify standardized quantities of commodities or instruments. Traders can use forward and futures contracts to establish flows of returns based on interest rate or exchange rate movements that tend to counter variations of returns on other asset holdings. The result is a net reduction in exposure to interest rate risk or to foreign exchange risks.

3. Options and How They Can Be Used to Reduce Foreign Exchange Risk Exposure: Options are financial contracts granting the owner the right to purchase or sell a financial instrument at a certain price within a specific period. Traders can use currency options to respond to a currency appreciation or depreciation by buying or selling the currency at a prearranged exchange rate. This can allow them to earn higher net returns.

4. Swaps and How They Are Used to Hedge against Risks: A swap is an agreement between two parties to exchange payment flows, such as streams of promised interest payments or flows of foreign-currency-denominated payments. Exchanging flows of payments derived from portfolios with differing maturities can help reduce interest rate risk, and trading payment flows denominated in different currencies can reduce foreign exchange risk exposure.

5. Key Risks of Derivative Securities and Derivatives-Trading Regulations: Derivatives credit risk is the possibility of default or of unanticipated changes in the prices of securities from which derivatives' returns are derived. Derivatives market risk is the potential for losses stemming from payment-system glitches or unusual price changes at settlement. Derivatives operating risks are the risks of losses resulting from bad management of trading positions. Most derivatives regulation takes place in the United States, where banks and corporations face stiffer reporting requirements than in other nations.

Questions and Problems

(Answers to odd-numbered questions and problems may be found on the Web at http://money.swcollege.com under "Student Resources.")

1. What is interest rate risk?

2. Explain why a financial instrument's duration influences the degree of interest rate risk incurred by holding the instrument.

3. Explain why the losses displayed in Table 8-2 on page 173 are private losses and not social losses.

4. How does a currency futures contract differ from a forward currency contract?

5. Banks make heavy use of forward contracts, while individual and corporate traders tend to use futures contracts. Can you think of a reason why this is the case? [Hint: Think about the drawbacks of forward contracts as compared with futures contracts and why these might pose less of a problem for banks.]

6. Why is a stock futures option a "derivative of a derivative"? Explain briefly.

7. Suppose that a bank has flows of future payments and receipts denominated in foreign currencies. Evaluate the pros and cons of using currency options or currency swaps to reduce foreign exchange risks associated with these forthcoming payments and receipts. [Hint: Think about the relative costs of the two hedging instruments, and contemplate the problems of finding a partner in a swap arrangement.]

8. Banks are heavily involved in trading currency swaps. In light of your answer to question 7, explain why this makes sense.

9. Evaluate the usefulness of the notional value of derivatives as compared with their replacement cost exposure as measures of overall risk exposure to derivatives.

10. Of the three types of derivatives risks, which would you expect to be most common? Least common? Why?

Before the Test

Test your understanding of the material covered in this chapter by taking the Chapter 8 interactive quiz at http://money.swcollege.com.

Online Application

Internet URL: http://asx.com.au

Title: Australian Stock Exchange Derivatives

Navigation: Begin at the above Web site.

Application: Follow the directions below, and answer the related questions.

1. Go to "About ASX," choose "Publications," and download the booklet entitled "What Is a Derivative?" Read the text. What is a warrant? What makes a warrant different from a basic option contract?

2. Back up to the opening page. Then click on "Understanding Margin Obligations" and download the booklet. Based on the discussion in the booklet, explain in your own words, without any equations or formulas, what a margin is and how it generally is calculated. How do people typically meet margin requirements?

For Group Study and Analysis: The second page of the booklet entitled "What Is a Derivative?" describes "covered call writing" as a simple and common strategy for earning extra income from existing holdings of stock. Split the class into four groups that are assigned to examine how this strategy is likely to pan out under the following scenarios: bull market, steady market, bear market, market collapse. Have each group determine whether covered call writing functions as a hedging or a speculative strategy in each scenario.

Selected References and Further Reading

Abken, Peter. "Beyond Plain Vanilla: A Taxonomy of Swaps." Federal Reserve Bank of Atlanta, *Financial Derivatives: New Instruments and Their Uses,* December 1993, pp. 51–69.

_______. "Globalization of Stock, Futures, and Options Markets." Federal Reserve Bank of Atlanta, *Financial Derivatives: New Instruments and Their Uses,* December 1993, pp. 3–24.

Abken, Peter, and Milind Shrikhande. "The Role of Currency Derivatives in Internationally Diversified Portfolios." Federal Reserve Bank of Atlanta *Economic Review* 82 (Third Quarter 1997): 34–59.

Cohen, Hugh. "Beyond Duration: Measuring Interest Rate Exposure." Federal Reserve Bank of Atlanta, *Financial Derivatives: New Instruments and Their Uses,* December 1993, pp. 130–138.

Fieleke, Norman. "The Rise of the Foreign Currency Futures Market." *New England Economic Review,* March/April 1985, pp. 38–47.

Gilbert, R. Alton. "Implications of Netting Arrangements for Bank Risk in Foreign Exchange Transactions." Federal Reserve Bank of St. Louis *Review,* January/February 1992, pp. 3–16.

Haubrich, Joseph. "Swaps and the Swaps Yield Curve." Federal Reserve Bank of Cleveland *Economic Commentary,* December 2001.

Kawaller, Ira G., Paul D. Koch, and Timothy W. Koch. "The Relationship between the S&P 500 Index and S&P 500 Index Futures Prices." Federal Reserve Bank of Atlanta, *Financial Derivatives: New Instruments and Their Uses,* December 1993, pp. 40–48.

Koprianov, Anatoli. "Derivatives Debacles: Case Studies of Large Losses in Derivatives Markets." Federal Reserve Bank of Richmond *Economic Quarterly*, Fall 1995, pp. 1–40.

Lopez, Jose. "Financial Instruments for Mitigating Credit Risk." Federal Reserve Bank of San Francisco *Economic* Letter, No. 2001-34, November 23, 2001.

Nandi, Saikat, and Daniel Waggoner. "Issues in Hedging Options." Federal Reserve Bank of Atlanta *Economic Review* (First Quarter 2000): 24–39.

Wall, Larry D., and John J. Pringle. "Interest Rate Swaps: A Review of the Issues." Federal Reserve Bank of Atlanta, *Financial Derivatives: New Instruments and Their Uses,* December 1993, pp. 70–85.

MoneyXtra

moneyxtra! Log on to the MoneyXtra Web site now (http://moneyxtra.swcollege.com) for additional learning resources such as practice quizzes, case studies, readings, and additional economic applications.

Chapter 9

Efficient Markets and International Interest Parity

Fundamental Issues

1. What is the distinction between adaptive and rational expectations?
2. What is the efficient-markets hypothesis?
3. How are the prices of financial instruments determined in efficient markets?
4. What is the forward exchange market?
5. What is covered interest parity?
6. What is foreign exchange market efficiency?

Suppose that you are a financial officer of a company that wishes to set aside several million dollars for use six months from now. You are considering purchasing either six-month-maturity U.S. Treasury bills or analogous short-term instruments issued by the British government, which are called "gilts." U.S. T-bills offer a 5 percent annualized interest return, and British gilts pay an annualized interest return of 4 percent. In your view, which currently is shared by most others, the U.S. dollar is likely to depreciate by more than 1 percent during the next year. This means that if your company were to sell dollars for pounds in the foreign exchange market, it could earn a 4 percent interest return on the pounds during the year. Then it could convert the pounds back to dollars and earn an additional dollar return, as a result of the dollar's depreciation of more than 1 percent in the meantime. Hence, your company's total anticipated return from holding gilts would be greater than the 5 percent annual interest return that could be earned from holding T-bills.

Of course, if others in the United States really do share your view on the anticipated returns on T-bills and gilts, all U.S. companies and individuals facing a similar choice will also choose to hold gilts. But if everyone does this, the demand for pounds in the foreign exchange market will increase, driving up today's rate of exchange of dollars for pounds and immediately making it more expensive to acquire pounds to purchase gilts. In addition, if everyone begins shifting funds away from the U.S. T-bill market, T-bill prices should decline, and the interest yields on T-bills should rise. Furthermore, the increased demand for British gilts should cause gilt prices to rise and gilt interest yields to decline.

This basic economic reasoning implies that the current incentive for your company to hold its funds in gilts instead of T-bills is likely to last only a short time. The possibility of earning an "excess return" on gilts relative to T-bills should be fleeting. As long as markets for T-bills, gilts, and foreign exchange adjust speedily to changes in traders' expectations and resulting flows of funds, opportunities to earn such excess returns should also be relatively rare. Nevertheless, there is considerable evidence that excess returns are available to companies and individuals who transfer funds among national bond markets via currency conversions in foreign exchange markets. Excess returns appear to be frequently available in both developed and less-developed countries, and sometimes those opportunities are available for relatively long stretches of time.

As you will learn in this chapter, if effective rates of return reflecting anticipated changes in exchange rates equalize for similar bonds of different nations, then the *uncovered interest parity* condition is satisfied. After you read this chapter, you will understand why the potential to earn excess returns from converting one currency to another and holding bonds abroad provides some evidence that the world's financial markets are not entirely *efficient,* even in the world's most developed nations.

The Rational Expectations Hypothesis

In preceding chapters, you have learned how interest rates and financial instrument prices are determined in a number of markets, including domestic bond and stock markets and markets for foreign currencies. In addition, you have learned how individuals, companies, and banks allocate asset portfolios in light of risks. Furthermore, you have learned how they can hedge against many of these risks by using derivative securities.

When people make decisions about holding financial instruments, however, they face a very fundamental source of uncertainty: no one knows exactly what will transpire in the future. Although traders have a good idea how markets will determine the prices and returns on those instruments days, weeks, or months from now, they do not know for sure what the demand and supply conditions will be. Thus, the decisions they make *today* are based on their best guesses about future events. As they compare prices, returns, and risks of instruments in the present, they must form *expectations* about likely *future* instrument prices and returns. Then, based on these expectations, traders determine their desired purchases or sales of financial instruments. Thus, expectations influence the demands for and supplies of financial instruments and, hence, play a part in determining the prices of and returns on those instruments.

Expectations of Market Values of Financial Instruments

If economists are to understand how market prices of and returns on financial instruments are determined, they must have a good understanding of how individuals, companies, and banks form their expectations. A key element of *modern* financial economics that separates it from past study of how market prices and returns arise is a greater effort to clarify the role that the *expectations formation process* plays in determining current prices and returns. Modern economists have developed clear-cut hypotheses for how people forecast future market prices and returns, and they incorporate these hypotheses into their theories of the determination of current prices of and returns on financial instruments. As you will learn in Chapter 24, they have also applied these hypotheses to try to develop a broader understanding of how expectations affect the overall performance of the economy.

In this chapter, we shall focus on how economists have applied different hypotheses in their effort to understand the role of expectations in financial markets. Economists have considered two fundamental hypotheses about how people form expectations. One is the hypothesis of *adaptive expectations*. The other is the *rational expectations hypothesis,* which has come to dominate modern economic thinking. Our first goal, therefore, is to explain why this is so.

Adaptive Expectations

Many of the choices that we make each day depend on our anticipations of future events. Should you take a course next term with an instructor known to cover simpler material and award higher-than-average grades, or should you wait until the following term when the course will be taught by a tougher instructor who also has a reputation for being more up-to-date? Should you purchase a new printer for your computer today, or do you expect that it might be available at a sale price by the end of next month?

Clearly, to make any decisions that have future consequences, you must act on forecasts that you make based on whatever information you currently possess. Such information includes the prices of goods, services, and financial assets that you purchase in your own town or city, market prices that you see posted in local and national media, and information that you can glean from reports on regional or national television news programs.

How can you use such information to infer the prospects for future returns on bonds or future stock prices? How can you forecast future exchange rates for national currencies? At a more mundane level, how do you forecast the price of a sweater a couple of weeks from now so that you can decide whether to buy one today or wait until then? Most likely, you would have trouble providing a detailed, scientific answer to any of these questions, which all entail answering how you form your own expectations about future prices and returns. Certainly, it is improbable that you engage in any formal statistical analysis or use a computer to make your forecasts. You probably just do the best that you can given the information available to you. You make your own "best guess."

But what is a person's best guess of the price of a share of stock next year? Simply saying that an individual does the best that he or she can with limited information is not a very precise statement. As you have learned, economists need to be very specific about their assumptions when they construct theories of how market prices and returns are determined. For this reason, in recent years they have developed precise conceptions about alternative processes by which people form expectations.

ADAPTIVE EXPECTATIONS PROCESSES One way to make an inference about the likely future price of a financial instrument is to do so "adaptively." The easiest way to understand what this means is to consider an example. Imagine that a friend, or perhaps even a pollster, asks you for your forecast of the rate of return on a share of stock in an e-commerce company a year from now. How would you come up with an answer?

One approach might be to collect data on the company's rate of return in recent weeks, months, and (if it has existed that long) years. You then could plot these data on a chart and make a rough drawing of the "trend line" along these points and beyond. The point on your trend line one year out from the present date would then be your forecast of the company's rate of return a year from now.

If you have completed a statistics course, you might adopt a more sophisticated approach. You could use statistical techniques to determine the specific equation for the trend line that best fits the data you have collected. This equation would enable you to give a predicted value, or forecast, of the company's rate of return for a given time, including a year from now.

Either of these forecasting methods would require you to sacrifice time and effort to collect a considerable amount of data on the company's rate of return. If you do not wish to incur this opportunity cost to make a sophisticated forecast of the company's likely future return, then you could choose a simpler method. For instance, you might just guess that next year's rate of return will turn out to be an average of the company's returns over the past three years. Even simpler, you might guess that next year's return will turn out to be similar to the return during the past year.

Each of the above forecasting methods is an example of an **adaptive expectations** process, meaning that each method uses only *past information.* Drawing a rough trend line, using statistical techniques to calculate an exact trend line, computing a three-year average, or just extrapolating from the current rate of return share the common feature that past data formed the sole basis for the forecast. This reliance on past data only makes the forecast an *adaptive forecast.*

DRAWBACKS OF ADAPTIVE EXPECTATIONS Perhaps one of the methods just described seems close to the way you think you make your own forecasts. Nevertheless, many economists reject the idea of adaptive expectations. One reason for this negative judgment is that if people really did use adaptive expectations, they would often make forecasts that they realize in advance should turn out to be wrong. If people relied only on past data to form their expectations, they would have to ignore new information, such as reports of the emergence of a host of new competitors that might erode the rate of return of the e-commerce company in our example. This means that an economic theory based on the hypothesis of adaptive expectations would yield forecasts of market prices and returns that consistently ignored information relevant to the actual determination of those prices and returns in the future. Thus, any economic theory based on

Adaptive expectations: Expectations that are based only on information from the past up to the present.

Rational expectations hypothesis: The idea that individuals form expectations based on all available past and current information and on a basic understanding of how markets function.

adaptive expectations will be internally inconsistent because the people whose behavior the model attempts to mimic would behave inconsistently.

Another troublesome aspect of the hypothesis is that there is no way to say, in advance, which adaptive expectations process is "best." Among an infinite number of possible adaptive expectations which one should we include in a theory of the determination of market prices and returns? There is no good way to answer this question.

Rational Expectations

In the 1970s, economists began to confront the quandary that adaptive expectations posed for evaluating theories of the determination of prices of goods, services, and financial instruments. Basic statistical approaches to forecasting prices and returns seemed to fit adaptive expectations. Nevertheless, for the reasons we have just discussed, using adaptive forecasts seemed both arbitrary and inconsistent.

In 1969, an Indiana University economist named John Muth proposed an alternative way to think about how people form expectations. Then future Nobel laureate Robert Lucas of the University of Chicago and others followed up on Muth's idea to develop a possibly better way to think about how people forecast future prices of goods, services, and financial instruments. As we shall discuss in Chapter 24, one of Lucas's key interests was understanding how people forecast the overall price level and inflation. Nonetheless, financial economists quickly recognized that the new approach had important implications for understanding financial markets.

The approach to expectations that Muth, Lucas, and others developed is called the **rational expectations hypothesis.** According to this hypothesis, an individual makes the best possible forecast of a market price or return using all available *past and current* information *and* drawing on an understanding of what factors affect the price or return. In contrast to an adaptive forecast, which only looks backward because it is based on past information, a rational forecast also looks forward while taking into account past information as well.

Thus, the distinction between adaptive and rational expectations can be summarized as follows:

> **An *adaptive* expectation is based only on past information. In contrast, a *rational* expectation takes into account both past and current information, plus an understanding of how the economy functions.**

ADVANTAGES OF THE RATIONAL EXPECTATIONS HYPOTHESIS Because the rational expectations hypothesis does not impose artificial constraints on how people use information, it is a more general theory of expectations formation than adaptive expectations. Whereas an adaptive expectations process uses only past information, the rational expectations hypothesis states that if an individual can improve upon an adaptive forecast, then that is what the individual will do.

It is important to recognize that even though rational expectations generally will be better than adaptive expectations, they will not always be correct. Rationally formed forecasts of market prices and returns are better, on average, than adaptive forecasts. *Actual* prices and returns, however, can still turn out to be much higher or lower than people rationally predicted.

ARE THERE LIMITS ON RATIONALITY? The rational expectations hypothesis poses a couple of conceptual problems of its own. One is that the hypothesis is very broad, so broad that incorporating it fully into a theory can prove challenging. A related difficulty is that the hypothesis indicates that each person acts on her or his rationally formed expectation of market prices and returns. This means that *realized* market prices and returns will depend on how all individuals form their expectations. If each person realizes that the expectations of others play a role in affecting actual market prices and returns, does this mean that each person should attempt to forecast others' forecasts?

Representative-agent assumption: The assumption that every trader in the marketplace can obtain the same information and has the same basic view of how the market operates.

To get around these problems, economists often use two simplifying assumptions when they construct models that include rational expectations. First, under the **representative-agent assumption,** an economic model presumes that each person in the marketplace has access to the same information and has the same conception of how the market works. This gets around the issue of different expectations across individuals in the market. The representative-agent assumption also dodges the problem of individuals worrying about others' forecasts, because by assumption each person's forecast is the same.

The second assumption is that people in the marketplace understand how the market functions. That is, an economist using the rational expectations hypothesis typically assumes that the people whose behavior the model tries to describe behave *as if* they understand that the economy works according to the economist's own theory. This assumption boils down to presuming that the people in an economic model *know the model.*

1. What is the distinction between adaptive and rational expectations? An adaptive expectation is formed using only past information. In contrast, a rationally formed expectation is based on past and current information and on an understanding of how market prices and returns are determined.

Efficient Markets

Those who wish to trade assets use past and current market prices in an effort to determine the likely future returns from holding the assets. They do this using their understanding of how the market values of financial assets are determined. Under the rational expectations hypothesis, therefore, *current* prices of financial assets should reflect the fact that traders form their expectations of future returns rationally. This has led economists to develop a theory of the determination of market prices and returns that explains how people use current information and rationally formed forecasts of future market prices and returns when they determine their demands for and supplies of financial instruments. This theory is called the *efficient-markets hypothesis* of market prices and returns.

Rational Expectations and Financial Asset Returns

You learned in Chapter 4 that bond prices are inversely related to interest rates. To demonstrate this inverse relationship, we considered perpetual bonds that pay an infinite stream of coupon returns. To calculate the price that someone would

Efficient-markets hypothesis: A theory that stems from the application of the rational expectations hypothesis to financial markets. It states that equilibrium prices of and returns on financial instruments should reflect all past and current information plus traders' understanding of how market prices and returns are determined.

be willing to pay for such a bond, we summed up the discounted present value of the stream of coupon returns. To compute the discounted present value of each year's coupon return, we used the current market interest rate. But what if the market interest rate might vary from year to year? Then the price of the bond would actually equal the *expected* discounted present value of the stream of coupon returns, based on people's *expectations* of future market interest rates.

Let's think about how we might apply the rational expectations hypothesis to this more realistic view of how bond prices are determined. Under the rational expectations hypothesis, an optimal forecast reflects all available past *and* current information as well as an understanding of how the relevant variable is determined. In the case of an interest return, therefore, the rational expectations hypothesis indicates that the expected future market interest rates used in bond-price calculations are rational forecasts of future interest returns by those who purchase and hold financial assets.

As a result, the price of a perpetual bond would equal the rationally anticipated discounted present value of the sum of future coupon returns. The market price thereby would incorporate rationally formed expectations.

The Efficient-Markets Hypothesis

This reasoning forms the basis for the **efficient-markets hypothesis,** which states that prices of financial assets should reflect all available information, including traders' understanding of how financial markets determine asset prices. As applied to the perpetual bond we studied in Chapter 4, the theory indicates that the current price of a bond should be equal to the rational forecast of the discounted value of the sum of coupon returns yielded by the bond.

More generally, the efficient-markets theory says that the price of *any* asset should reflect the rational forecast of the asset's returns. Consequently, the market price of any financial instrument, whether it is a share of stock, a corporate bond, or a derivative security, should reflect a recognition of all available information by those who trade the instrument. If the market price of the financial instrument were to fail to reflect all such information, that would imply that the market for that instrument functions inefficiently, because traders could earn higher returns if they accounted for the unused information.

2. What is the efficient-markets hypothesis? According to the efficient-markets hypothesis, the market price of a financial asset should reflect all available information in that market. This is so because the demand for and supply of an asset, such as a bond, will take into account rationally formed expectations of future prices of the asset. Traders form these expectations, in turn, in light of all information in their possession.

Financial Instrument Prices in Efficient Markets

The efficient-markets hypothesis has three key implications. First, it indicates that there should be a definite relationship between the market price or the return on a financial instrument and traders' expectation of the market price or return. Second, it implies that some factors are likely to cause greater movements in prices or returns than others. Finally, the hypothesis has an important prediction about efforts by traders to earn higher-than-average rates of return.

The Expected Price of a Financial Instrument

The efficient-markets hypothesis is based on the rational expectations hypothesis. Thus, it implies that a person's best guess of the price of an asset should take into account everything that people know about factors that influence the asset's price.

INDIVIDUAL FORECASTS AND AVERAGE PRICES OF FINANCIAL INSTRUMENTS The factors that determine the price of a financial instrument are all those that traders know will affect the demand for and supply of that instrument. They likely will include such factors as the wealth and income levels of all traders, changes in the riskiness, liquidity, and tax treatment of the instrument, and so on. Of course, those who buy and sell financial instruments cannot perfectly predict future values of all these factors.

Nevertheless, to make the best decisions about the quantities of a financial instrument to buy or sell, each trader must form his or her own best estimates of these factors. This allows each trader to make his or her own *individual forecast* of the market price of a financial instrument. Let's call this individual price forecast P^f. This is the individual forecast of the market price of the financial instrument based on a typical trader's information about current and past market prices and understanding of how the market determines the instrument's price.

Now let's think about the average market price of the instrument, which technically is called the *expected,* or *mean value,* of the market price, denoted P^e. This is the *true* average price of the financial instrument, taking into account the way that random factors can influence the market demand for and market supply of the instrument. The behavior of these random factors depends on the true *distributions of probabilities* for what these factors will turn out to be in the future. Because the average market price P^e reflects these distributions of probabilities for the market as a whole, economists call the true average price the *market expectation* of the financial instrument's price.

Under the efficient-markets hypothesis, each trader does her or his best to form an individual forecast of the market price, P^f, taking into account all relevant information. In turn, "all relevant information" includes the factors that ultimately affect the market price, *including* the scope for random factors to affect the market demand for and market supply of the financial instrument. This means that the forecast of any particular trader should typically be as good, on average, as the market price expectation, P^e. If an individual trader's forecast of the market price were consistently worse than the true average price, then the trader would seek better information and improve her or his forecasting performance.

Hence, when all traders form their individual forecasts rationally, their forecasts typically will correspond to the average market price. That is, it will be true that $P^f = P^e$. The best individual forecast will equal the expected, or average, market price of the financial asset.

ACTUAL AND FORECAST PRICES OF FINANCIAL INSTRUMENTS Of course, it is a rare event for any forecast to be exactly on the mark. Thus, the *actual* price of a financial instrument, denoted P, usually will reflect random factors that cause market demand and supply to change in ways that traders could not have completely anticipated in advance. Thus, the market price will turn out to equal its average price, P^e, plus an unpredictable random component, which we shall call ε. That is, the market price is equal to

$$P = P^e + \varepsilon.$$

Thus, the difference between the actual market price of a financial instrument and its average value, $P - P^e$, arises from the unpredictable random component, ε, which in turn stems from random factors influencing the demand for and supply of the financial instrument.

As noted above, according to the rational expectations hypothesis an individual forecast of the financial instrument's price will equal the market expectation of the price, or the average price, so that $P^f = P^e$. This means that another way to express the true market price of a financial instrument is

$$P = P^f + \varepsilon.$$

Thus, the market price is equal to the typical *trader's* price forecast plus an unpredictable random element that the trader lacks information to forecast.

Implications for Variations in Financial Instrument Prices

The final equation above is very simple, but it has two important implications. The first is that the market price of a financial instrument reflects traders' best forecasts of the instrument's price given the information available to them. In other words, the actual market price can differ from a typical trader's forecast only because of factors that traders cannot systematically predict.

Thus, the efficient-markets hypothesis indicates that there are two reasons that prices of financial instruments might change. One is that unpredictable, random events can occur. These can cause the demand for or supply of financial instruments to vary unexpectedly, inducing an unanticipated change in the price.

Such unanticipated price variations are likely to be short term in nature, however. The reason is that if they resulted from factors that caused *persistent* changes in the demand for or supply of financial instruments, traders would be able to forecast these factors. Thus, another way that financial instrument prices can change is because of *predictable* changes in the underlying demand for and supply of the instruments. These predictable factors, which financial economists often call the *fundamental* determinants of the market price, or simply the *fundamentals,* are those which traders incorporate into their individual forecasts of the market price, P^f. Fundamental, predictable determinants of the market price also determine the average price, P^e.

In the absence of short-term, unpredictable variations in the price of a financial instrument—that is, if ε has a value of zero—the price of a financial instrument will vary only because of variations in the fundamentals, so that $P = P^e = P^f$. In an efficient market, the true market price will equal the expected market price that people can forecast given the information available to them. If this condition did not hold, then traders would fail to take into account all available information about the fundamental determinants of variations in the market prices of financial instruments. As a result, they would earn lower returns than they would earn if they used all information in their possession.

Can People Beat the Market?

Recognition that failure to use all available information about factors that cause market prices to vary would result in lower returns than traders could otherwise earn leads to another key implication of the efficient-markets hypothesis:

> **In an efficient financial market, there should be no unexploited opportunities for traders to earn higher returns.**

If such opportunities existed, then a number of traders would seek to profit from buying or selling greater quantities of a given financial instrument. This would cause the market price of the instrument to change.

What direction would the instrument's price move? The answer is that it would adjust to its efficient-market price, which would reflect the rational forecasts of individual traders. Rational expectations in the market would induce trading that would yield this efficient-market price.

Does this mean that no trader could ever earn profits from trading bonds? The answer clearly must be no, otherwise people would not earn their livelihoods by speculating in financial markets. Nevertheless, the efficient-markets hypothesis does indicate that speculators should not be able to earn profits from taking advantage of unused information for very long. Any unexploited information will be quickly recognized by a sufficient number of traders that market prices and returns will adjust quickly. Profits from such trades may be significant, but they will also be fleeting. (This does not rule out the possibility that traders who have access to more information than others can earn profits; see on the following page *Policy Focus: The Demise of the Thirty-Year Treasury Bond—Insider Trading or a Bureaucratic Comedy?*)

According to the efficient-markets hypothesis, therefore, people cannot "beat the market." They cannot consistently earn above-average returns from holding either stocks or bonds issued by domestic companies or governments. In addition, they cannot earn above-average returns from holding financial instruments issued internationally. We turn next to some key implications of this latter conclusion.

3. How are the prices of financial instruments determined in efficient markets? The efficient-markets hypothesis implies that individual forecasts of the market price of a financial instrument should be the same as the average price of the instrument, because otherwise individual traders would not efficiently use all information in their possession. Furthermore, the actual market price of an instrument will equal its average price plus an unpredictable component, which will be the same as a typical trader's individual forecast of the market price plus the unpredictable component of the price. This means that on average no individual trader should be able to do a better job of predicting an instrument's actual price than any other trader. Thus, in an efficient market no single trader should systematically be able to earn higher returns than other traders.

GLOBAL POLICY Focus CYBER MANAGEMENT

The Demise of the Thirty-Year Treasury Bond—Insider Trading or a Bureaucratic Comedy?

On Wednesday, October 31, 2001, the U.S. Treasury Department accidentally created a Halloween monster. It made two big mistakes, and as a consequence, it lost considerable credibility with private securities firms on Wall Street.

Both of the Treasury's mistakes occurred as it prepared to formally announce that it was immediately discontinuing the issuance of thirty-year government bonds. For years, the thirty-year Treasury bond had been a key vehicle for U.S. government borrowing. Beginning in the late 1990s, the Treasury had made it clear that it planned to phase out the bonds. Financial markets did not know exactly when that would happen, but the Treasury had settled on announcing the formal discontinuance of the bond on October 31.

The morning of that day, Treasury officials conducted a 9 A.M. news briefing intended solely for media representatives. Officials told the reporters that the information about the bond's demise would be public as of 10 A.M. and that as a courtesy they were being informed in advance to give them time to write their stories. Officials failed to check the credentials of everyone who attended the meeting, however, and one of those individuals was a financial consultant who did not understand that this early news of the bond's end was "embargoed" until 10 A.M. After the briefing ended just before 9:30 A.M., the consultant called some of his clients and relayed the news.

Shortly before the formal public release of the information at 10 A.M., bond prices jumped as many traders began betting that bond investors who could no longer hold thirty-year bonds would begin shifting some of their funds to stocks, thereby causing bond rates to decline. If not for a second mistake, the Treasury could easily have argued that the consultant had helped his clients profit from **insider information.** The second mistake was that the Treasury had accidentally posted the public announcement of the thirty-year bond's demise on its Web site at 9:49 A.M. Almost immediately, several news wire services noticed the announcement on the Web site and began to file reports. Hence, although some traders may have earned profits on insider information gleaned from the consultant's release, it is also possible that some traders earned profits simply because they were paying close attention to the Treasury's own Web site.

For Critical Analysis: Why might it be in the Treasury's interest to give the media advance notice of major policy actions such as the elimination of a type of bond?

Insider information: Information that is not available to the public.

To learn more about U.S. rules regarding insider trading, see the Chapter 9 reading entitled, "The Insider Trading Debate," by Jie Hu and Thomas Noe from the Federal Reserve Bank of Atlanta. http://moneyxtra.swcollege.com

The Forward Exchange Market and Covered Interest Parity

The concept of market efficiency does not apply just to financial asset prices and interest rates that are determined in a nation's domestic financial markets. It may also be extended to markets for financial assets that are traded internationally, such as bonds and national currencies. This means that, ultimately, currency exchange rates, national interest rates, and expectations all must be related.

The Forward Exchange Market

As a first step toward understanding these international relationships, let's begin by examining the forward market for foreign currencies. In Chapter 6, we discussed *spot* foreign exchange markets, which determine spot exchange rates for national currencies that traders deliver immediately. As you learned in Chapter 8, however, individuals, companies, and banks may wish to enter into *forward currency contracts* in which they agree to deliver a quantity of a foreign currency at a specified exchange rate on a future date. The exchange rate specified in the forward contract is called the *forward exchange rate,* and it is determined in a **forward exchange market,** which is a market for forward delivery of foreign currency. (Financial institutions engage in large volumes of trading in the forward exchange market, and many of the world's largest banks are gradually shifting their spot and forward currency transactions to the Internet; on the next page see *Cyber Focus: Foreign Exchange Trading Moves Online.*)

COVERING FOREIGN EXCHANGE RISK WITH A FORWARD CURRENCY CONTRACT Table 9-1 on page 207 lists exchange rates for several currencies, as reported on a sample date by the Federal Reserve Bank of New York. Included are three-month and six-month forward exchange rates for the European euro and the Japanese yen. To see how a forward currency contract can be used to hedge against foreign exchange risk, let's consider a hypothetical example. Suppose that a U.S. book retailer has agreed to purchase €1 million in books from a Belgian-based company three months from now. During the intervening time, the spot dollar-euro exchange rate is unlikely to remain at its current level. If the U.S. book retailer waits until the books arrive in the United States to obtain euros in the spot market to pay for the books, then there is a good chance it will end up paying more dollars to purchase them at the agreed-upon price in euros. Thus, the U.S. company faces a foreign exchange risk exposure in this transaction.

Let's suppose that the three-month forward exchange rate is equal to the rate displayed in Table 9-1, which is 0.9656 \$/€. To ensure a fixed *dollar* price of the €1 million in Belgian books, the U.S. bookseller can enter into a three-month forward currency contract at this exchange rate. The U.S. company can purchase €1 million in the forward exchange market for the euro at this rate, meaning that it will receive €1 million in exchange for \$965,600 three months from now. Thus, the U.S. company removes all uncertainty about the dollar price it will pay for the books, which will be \$965,600. By removing this uncertainty, the U.S. bookseller *covers* the foreign exchange transaction, meaning that it completely hedges against the risk of exchange rate movements during the coming three months.

On the Web
Where on the Internet can one find daily updates of euro and yen forward exchange rates relative to the U.S. dollar? One place to check is the Federal Reserve Bank of New York's daily 10 A.M. foreign exchange statistical release located at http://www.ny.frb.org/pihome/statistics/forex10.shtml.

RELATING THE FORWARD EXCHANGE RATE TO THE SPOT EXCHANGE RATE In Table 9-1, the forward exchange rate is equal to 0.9656 \$/€, but the spot exchange rate is equal to 0.9695 \$/€. In this situation, in which the euro forward exchange rate is less than the euro spot exchange rate, economists say that the euro trades at a **forward discount.** When the forward exchange rate of a currency is greater than the spot exchange rate, the currency trades at a **forward premium.** Economists often express the forward premium or discount in a *standardized* form by computing it as a percentage of the spot exchange rate and expressing it as an annual figure. They use the following formula:

$$\text{Standard forward premium or discount} = (F_N - S)/S \times (12/N) \times 100,$$

where F_N is the forward exchange rate, S is the spot exchange rate, and N is the number of months of the forward contract. The first term in this standardized measure, $(F_N - S)/S$, is the forward premium or discount, which is the difference

Forward exchange market: The market for currency to be delivered at a future date via forward currency contracts.

Forward discount: A negative value for the difference between the forward exchange rate and the spot exchange rate divided by the spot exchange rate.

Forward premium: A positive value for the difference between the forward exchange rate and the spot exchange rate divided by the spot exchange rate.

GLOBAL | POLICY | CYBER Focus | MANAGEMENT

Foreign Exchange Trading Moves Online

An alliance of fifteen worldwide foreign exchange dealers, including Bank of America, operates FXall.com, a Web-based currency-trading site linking multinational corporations, institutional investors, and investment funds that wish to trade currencies in spot and forward markets. The FXall.com exchange permits traders to enter offers to buy or sell currencies online. The Web exchange then executes the orders automatically. A competing online currency exchange, Currenex.com, links traders to the foreign exchange operations of twenty-five major banks, such as AM Amro.

Foreign exchange dealers affiliated with these Web sites do not use their systems to trade with each other. Instead, the sites are virtual locations where banks' clients gain immediate access to banks' quotes in a competitive auction environment and obtain speedier settlement of transactions. About 15 percent of foreign exchange trading in spot and forward markets already takes place online, and some forecasts indicate that this percentage could double within the next five years.

Increasingly, online trading is also catching on with those who buy and sell currency derivatives. For instance, the Deutsche Bourse and the London International Futures and Options Exchange, the two key European futures and options exchanges that compete with the Chicago Mercantile Exchange and the Chicago Board of Trade, have begun merging their operations. The two European exchanges are considering maintaining separate trading centers and linking the existing exchanges via the Internet. Indeed, some industry experts anticipate that within a few years most trading in derivative securities will take place on the Internet.

For Critical Analysis: What might foreign exchange traders gain from arranging and completing transactions online instead of through traditional channels?

between the forward exchange rate and the spot exchange rate relative to the spot exchange rate. The second part, $12/N$, annualizes the forward premium by dividing by the number of months of the contract and then multiplying by 12 to express the forward premium on an annual basis. Economists multiply this annualized forward premium by 100 to express it as a percentage. In our example, the standard forward premium or discount is

$$(F_N - S)/S \times (12/N) \times 100 = [(0.9656 - 0.9695)/0.9695] \times (12/3) \times 100$$
$$= -1.61 \text{ percent.}$$

Because the computed value is negative, the forward *discount* for the euro relative to the dollar is equal to 1.61 percent.

4. What is the forward exchange market? The forward exchange market is the market for currency to be delivered at a future date via forward currency contracts. The interaction between demand and supply in this market determines the equilibrium forward exchange rate. If the current forward exchange rate exceeds the spot exchange rate determined in the spot market for the currency, then there is a forward premium. A forward discount exists if the forward exchange rate is less than the spot exchange rate.

Table 9-1 Exchange Rates

Country	Monetary Unit	U.S. Dollar Equivalent	Currency per U.S. Dollar
European Monetary Union	Euro	0.9695	1.0315
3-month forward		0.9656	1.0356
6-month forward		0.9616	1.0399
Australia	Dollar	0.5354	1.8678
Brazil	Real	0.3350	2.9850
Canada	Dollar	0.6351	1.5746
China, P.R.	Yuan	0.1208	8.2766
Denmark	Krone	0.1305	7.6615
Hong Kong	Dollar	0.1282	7.8000
India	Rupee	0.0205	48.6700
Japan	Yen	0.0083	120.4300
3-month forward		0.0083	119.9000
6-month forward		0.0084	119.4100
Malaysia	Ringgit	0.2632	3.8000
Mexico	Peso	0.1025	9.7570
New Zealand	Dollar	0.4578	2.1844
Norway	Krone	0.1300	7.6925
Singapore	Dollar	0.5669	1.7640
South Africa	Rand	0.0955	10.4700
South Korea	Won	0.0008	1,203.5000
Sri Lanka	Rupee	0.0104	96.2300
Sweden	Krona	0.1044	9.5775
Switzerland	Franc	0.6644	1.5051
Taiwan	N.T. dollar	0.0296	33.7700
Thailand	Baht	0.0236	42.3900
United Kingdom	Pound	1.5235	0.6564
Venezuela	Bolivar	0.0007	1,361.0000

SOURCE: Federal Reserve Bank of New York, August 9, 2002.

The Forward Exchange Market and Covered Interest Parity

In Chapter 6 you learned about absolute and relative purchasing power parity, which can arise from arbitrage across national markets for goods and services. Arbitrage can also take place across national financial markets, as traders attempt to earn profits by buying and selling financial instruments issued by individuals, companies, or governments of various nations.

For example, suppose the interest rate on a U.S. financial instrument is 4.1 percent. At the same time, the interest rate on a European Monetary Union (EMU) financial instrument with the same riskiness, liquidity, tax treatment, and term to maturity is 5.6 percent. Could a U.S. saver profit from shifting funds from the United States to the EMU? The answer depends on whether the realized return on the EMU financial instrument is greater than the realized return on the U.S. financial instrument. Comparing the realized returns, in turn, requires taking into account how covered interest returns (returns completely hedged against

Covered interest parity: A prediction that the interest rate on one nation's financial instrument should approximately equal the interest rate on a similar instrument in another nation plus the forward premium, or the difference between the forward exchange rate and the spot exchange rate divided by the spot exchange rate.

foreign exchange risk) on holdings of the EMU financial instrument depend on forward and spot exchange rates. Thus, forward exchange rates, spot exchange rates, and national interest rates ultimately must be taken into account by anyone who seeks arbitrage profits from trading financial instruments internationally.

ALTERNATIVE SAVING CHOICES Let's suppose, for instance, that a U.S. resident has two alternatives. One is to purchase a one-period, dollar-denominated bond that has a market interest yield of r_{US}. After one year, the U.S. resident will have accumulated $1 + r_{US}$ dollars for each dollar saved.

The other saving option is to use each dollar to buy EMU euros at the spot exchange rate of S dollars per euro, thereby obtaining $1/S$ euros with each dollar. Then the U.S. resident would use the $1/S$ euros to buy a one-year EMU bond that pays the rate r_E. After a year, the person will have accumulated $(1/S)(1 + r_E)$ *euros*. When the U.S. resident buys the EMU bond, however, we assume that at the same time he sells this quantity of euros in the forward market at the forward exchange rate of F dollars per euro. This "covers" him against risk of exchange rate changes by ensuring that the effective gross return on the EMU bond will be $(F/S)(1 + r_E)$.

COVERED INTEREST PARITY The returns on the two bonds will be the same, so there will be no incentive for U.S. savers to arbitrage across the U.S. and EMU financial markets, if

$$1 + r_{US} = (F/S)(1 + r_E).$$

Now we can use the algebra fact that

$$F/S = (S/S) + (F - S)/S = 1 + (F - S)/S$$

to rewrite the condition as

$$1 + r_{US} = [1 + (F - S)/S](1 + r_E).$$

Now we can cross-multiply the right-hand side to get

$$1 + r_{US} = 1 + (F - S)/S + r_E + [r_E \times (F - S)/S].$$

Because r_E and $(F - S)/S$ are both typically small fractions, their product is approximately equal to zero. [For example, if r_E is 0.056 and $(F - S)/S$ is -0.047, then their product is equal to -0.0026, which is very close to zero.] Making this approximation and subtracting 1 from both sides yields

$$r_{US} = r_E + (F - S)/S.$$

This last equation is called the **covered interest parity** condition. As we noted earlier, the quantity $(F - S)/S$ is the forward premium or discount, so the condition of covered interest parity says that the interest rate on a U.S. bond should approximately equal the interest rate on the foreign EMU bond plus the forward premium or discount.

If this condition failed to hold, then U.S. savers could engage in *covered interest arbitrage* by cashing in U.S. financial instruments and purchasing EMU financial instruments. This activity would tend to push national interest rates toward levels consistent with the covered interest arbitrage condition.

5. What is covered interest parity? Covered interest parity is a condition that arises if individuals hedge international financial transactions using forward currency contracts. It states that the interest rate in one nation equals the sum of another nation's interest rate and the forward premium or discount. The forward premium or discount is the difference between the forward exchange rate and the spot exchange rate divided by the spot exchange rate, so covered interest parity relates national interest rates and exchange rates. If covered interest parity does not hold, then savers can earn covered interest arbitrage profits by shifting funds between nations. These movements of funds then tend to move national interest rates and exchange rates toward values consistent with covered interest parity.

Foreign Exchange Market Efficiency

In an efficient market, traders use all available information and an understanding of the determinants of market prices and returns. If foreign exchange markets are efficient, it follows that returns on internationally traded financial instruments should reflect all information possessed by those who trade these instruments. To evaluate whether foreign exchange markets are efficient, therefore, we must consider how savers' expectations of future exchange rate movements influence the returns on internationally traded instruments.

Uncovered Interest Arbitrage

As we have discussed, covered interest arbitrage—covering the foreign exchange risk associated with financial instrument transactions across national borders—leads to the covered interest parity condition. Under covered interest parity, the interest rate on a financial instrument in one nation equals the interest rate on the equivalent instrument in another country plus the forward premium. What happens, however, if people do not cover their exposure to foreign exchange risks?

Someone might choose not to use a forward currency contract to hedge against foreign exchange risks, for instance, because the transaction is too small to warrant the trouble to set up a forward contract. Indeed, a typical forward currency contract has a denomination of at least $1 million. Hence, the individual might decide to use a different hedging instrument (see Chapter 8) or might choose not to hedge the transaction at all.

UNCOVERED INTEREST PARITY In our example, we considered a U.S. saver with a choice between a U.S. financial instrument and an EMU financial instrument with equivalent riskiness, tax treatment, liquidity, and term to maturity. Let's consider the same example, but assume that the U.S. saver does not purchase a forward exchange contract or hedge the foreign exchange risk in any other way, so the transaction is *uncovered*.

In this case, the U.S. saver again anticipates a *dollar*-denominated interest return of r_{US} by holding a U.S. financial instrument to maturity or a *euro*-denominated interest return of r_E by holding an equivalent EMU financial instrument to maturity. To the U.S. saver, however, what matters in choosing between the two instruments is the anticipated *dollar* value of the return on the EMU instrument. This is equal to $r_E + s^e$, where s^e denotes the rate at which the dollar is expected to depreciate (or, if s^e is negative, appreciate) relative to the euro. If s^e is positive, then the U.S. saver anticipates that the dollar will depreciate in value relative to the euro and will wish for the U.S. instrument's interest rate to be higher than the rate on the EMU instrument to compensate for this expected depreciation of the dollar.

moneyxtra!

Online Case Study

To consider why traders respond to deviations from uncovered interest parity by engaging in arbitrage that tends to push interest rates and exchange rates toward this parity condition, go to the Chapter 9 Case Study, entitled "Engaging in Foreign Exchange Market Arbitrage."

http://moneyxtra.swcollege.com

Thus, this U.S. saver will be indifferent between holding U.S. or EMU instruments only if the anticipated returns are equal. This will be true when

$$r_{US} = r_E + s^e.$$

If the U.S. interest rate is less than the EMU interest rate plus the expected rate of dollar depreciation, then U.S. savers who do not cover their transactions will allocate more savings to EMU financial instruments. If the U.S. interest rate is greater than the EMU rate plus the anticipated depreciation rate of the dollar, then U.S. savers will allocate fewer savings to EMU financial instruments. In theory, shifts of funds in this pursuit of *uncovered arbitrage* profits will tend to push both interest rates to levels consistent with equality between the U.S. interest rate and the sum of the EMU interest rate and the expected rate of dollar depreciation.

As we briefly discussed in Chapter 4, this equality is called *uncovered interest parity.* It is called "uncovered" interest parity because it does not arise from foreign exchange transactions that cover risks.

Risk and Uncovered Interest Parity The uncovered purchase of a foreign financial instrument exposes a U.S. saver to foreign exchange risks because the saver's expectation about currency depreciation or appreciation during the term to maturity may turn out to be incorrect. In this instance, the realized return on the foreign financial instrument would differ from the anticipated return.

If the value of a nation's currency is highly variable, then predicting its future value is difficult. This makes allocating a portion of one's wealth to holdings of foreign financial instruments a much riskier proposition. Consequently, borrowers located in nations with volatile currency values may have to offer higher interest returns to induce savers to purchase the financial instruments they issue. In this instance, it may be appropriate to include a risk premium in the uncovered interest parity condition. The risk premium is the increase in the return offered on a financial instrument to compensate individuals for the additional foreign exchange risk they undertake in uncovered transactions.

For instance, if the U.S. dollar's exchange value becomes more volatile and less predictable, then the uncovered interest parity condition may be expressed as

$$r_{US} = r_E + s^e + RP,$$

where RP is the risk premium that compensates savers for holding U.S. financial instruments instead of equivalent EMU instruments. In this situation, the differential between the U.S. interest rate and the EMU interest rate should equal the expected depreciation of the dollar relative to the euro plus the risk premium.

Foreign Exchange Market Efficiency

Note that the two international interest parity conditions discussed above provide two reasons why the interest rate for a U.S. financial instrument might be higher than the interest rate on an otherwise identical EMU instrument. One reason, provided by the *covered* interest parity condition, is the presence of a forward premium in the forward exchange market, so that the differential between the U.S. interest rate and the EMU interest rate is equal to

$$r_{US} - r_E = (F - S)/S.$$

The other reason is implied by the *uncovered* interest parity condition:

$$r_{US} - r_E = s^e.$$

This condition indicates that, in the absence of a risk premium, the amount by which the U.S. interest rate exceeds the EMU interest rate should be the expected rate of depreciation of the dollar relative to the euro.

SIMULTANEOUS INTEREST PARITIES The only way that both of these interest parity conditions are satisfied is if the right-hand terms in both are equal, or if

$$(F - S)/S = s^e.$$

This relationship states that the forward premium (or discount) for the euro relative to the dollar is equal to the rate at which the dollar is expected to depreciate (appreciate) relative to the euro in the spot foreign exchange market. Let's denote the expected future spot exchange rate at the time that a forward currency contract settles as S^e. It follows that the expected rate of dollar depreciation during the term of the contract, s^e, is equal to the expected change in the spot exchange rate, $S^e - S$, divided by the current spot exchange rate, S. Thus, $s^e = (S^e - S)/S$. If both covered and uncovered interest parity hold true, then

$$(F - S)/S = (S^e - S)/S,$$

or

$$F = S^e.$$

Thus, if both interest parity conditions are satisfied in the marketplace, the forward exchange rate is equal to the anticipated spot exchange rate at the time of settlement of the forward currency contract.

MARKET EFFICIENCY If this last equality is not satisfied, and the forward exchange rate differs from the expected future spot exchange rate, then financial market traders perceive an arbitrage opportunity. In an *efficient market,* of course, such opportunities should be very fleeting. Market expectations and prices should adjust speedily to eliminate the potential for arbitrage profits. Thus, **foreign exchange market efficiency** exists when the forward exchange rate is a good predictor—often called an "unbiased predictor"—of the future spot exchange rate, meaning that on average the forward exchange rate turns out to equal the future spot exchange rate. Therefore, when the foreign exchange market is efficient, forward exchange rates should adjust to the point at which the forward premium is equal to the expected rate of currency depreciation. Under the

Foreign exchange market efficiency: A situation in which the equilibrium spot and forward exchange rates adjust to reflect all available information, in which case the forward premium is equal to the expected rate of currency depreciation plus any risk premium. This, in turn, implies that the forward exchange rate on average predicts the expected future spot exchange rate.

Fisher equation: An equation stating that the nominal interest rate equals the sum of the real interest rate and the expected inflation rate.

rational expectations hypothesis, the expected rate of currency depreciation should be the rational forecast of the rate of depreciation, or the forecast of depreciation based on all available information and an understanding of how exchange rates are determined.

Real Interest Parity

As we discussed in Chapter 5, most economists believe that international financial markets are becoming more integrated. One reason that the concept of foreign exchange market efficiency is of practical interest is that efficiency of foreign exchange markets indicates that national markets are more broadly integrated.

The covered and uncovered interest parity conditions, however, relate *nominal* interest rate differentials to spot and forward exchange rates and expected spot exchange rates. Over shorter-term horizons, when changes in inflation may be relatively small, the effects of different national inflation rates may have little effect on saving flows. Nevertheless, saving decisions are more likely to respond to overall price changes over longer time horizons. Thus, over longer intervals savers' decisions about financial instrument allocations are likely to be motivated by real interest rate differentials instead of *nominal* differentials.

THE FISHER EQUATION Recall from Chapter 4 that the real interest rate is approximately equal to the nominal interest rate less the expected inflation rate, or

$$\rho = r - \pi^e$$

where ρ is the real interest rate and π^e is the expected rate of inflation. If we rearrange this expression for the real interest rate, we can write it as

$$r = \rho + \pi^e.$$

This relationship, often called the **Fisher equation** after the famous economist Irving Fisher who used it early in the twentieth century, states that the nominal interest rate equals the real interest rate plus the expected rate of inflation.

For example, suppose that the real rate of interest for a one-year period is 2.5 percent. The Fisher equation indicates that if the expected inflation rate is 3 percent, then savers will require a nominal return equal to the sum of these two amounts, or 5.5 percent, to ensure that they earn the market real interest rate.

COMBINING RELATIVE PURCHASING POWER PARITY AND UNCOVERED INTEREST PARITY Chapter 6 examined relative purchasing power parity, which relates inflation rates of two nations (denoted π^e and π^{*e}) to the percentage change in the spot exchange rate for their currencies. If savers anticipate that relative purchasing power parity will hold, then that implies that the following condition should be satisfied:

$$\pi^e - \pi^{*e} = s^e.$$

That is, if relative purchasing power parity holds, the expected difference between the two nations' inflation rates will equal the expected rate of currency depreciation.

Recall that if uncovered interest parity holds, and if there is no risk premium, then it will also be the case that

$$r - r^* = s^e,$$

so that the differential between the two nations' interest rates equals the expected rate of currency depreciation. If we put the above equations together, we get

$$\pi^e - \pi^{*e} = r - r^*.$$

Finally, we can rearrange to obtain the following relationship:

$$r - \pi^e = r^* - \pi^{*e}.$$

This says that if both relative purchasing power parity and uncovered interest parity hold true, then the real interest rate in one country, $\rho = r - \pi^e$, equals the real interest rate in the other country, $\rho^* = r^* - \pi^{*e}$.

This is called the **real interest parity** condition, under which real interest returns on equivalent financial instruments of two nations are equal. Given the way we have obtained it, real interest parity is a condition that requires both relative purchasing power parity and uncovered interest parity to hold.

Real interest parity: An equality between two nations' real interest rates that arises if both uncovered interest parity and relative purchasing power parity are satisfied.

Real Interest Parity as an Indicator of International Integration

Recall that uncovered interest parity is more likely to hold if financial markets are more integrated so that savers can take advantage of opportunities for uncovered interest arbitrage. At the same time, relative purchasing power parity is more likely to hold if markets for goods and services are also more open to arbitrage.

It follows that if real interest parity holds true, then international financial and goods markets are likely to be integrated. Work by Richard Marston of the University of Pennsylvania has shown that real interest differentials tend to be relatively small, particularly among the most developed, open economies. This provides some indication that some national markets are fairly highly integrated.

6. What is foreign exchange market efficiency? Foreign exchange markets are efficient if savers cannot persistently earn higher returns by shifting holdings of financial instruments across national borders. Foreign exchange market efficiency requires that the forward premium, or the difference between the forward and spot exchange rates divided by the spot exchange rate, equal the expected rate of currency depreciation. This efficiency condition holds if both the covered and uncovered interest parity conditions are satisfied. If real interest parity holds, then uncovered interest parity and relative purchasing power parity both hold true, implying a high degree of integration of national financial markets.

Link to the
Global Economy

Excess Returns and Uncovered Interest Parity

In this chapter you learned about the uncovered interest parity condition. If this condition is satisfied, the interest rate on a U.S. bond, r, should equal the interest rate on a foreign bond, r*, plus the rate at which the domestic currency is anticipated to depreciate during the period that the two bonds mature, s^e.

Breakdowns of Uncovered Interest Parity and Excess Returns

What happens if the uncovered interest parity condition fails to hold? In this situation, the expected rate of domestic currency depreciation is greater than the differential between the U.S. and foreign bonds, so s^e exceeds the difference between r and r^*.

This means that rather than simply holding the U.S. bond and earning the rate r, a U.S. resident can anticipate earning more by converting dollars to the foreign currency, holding foreign bonds and earning the rate r^*, and then obtaining more dollars per unit of foreign currency after the foreign bond matures and the domestic currency depreciates. In this way, the U.S. resident could earn an "excess return" equal to $s^e - (r - r^*)$. For instance, if the expected rate of depreciation of the dollar relative to the euro is 2 percent, the annual return on a U.S. bond is 6 percent, and the annual return on a German bond is 5 percent, then the excess return equals 2 percent − (6 percent − 5 percent) = 1 percent.

Evidence on Excess Returns

Traditionally, economists have argued that U.S. residents should have less ability to earn excess returns from holding bonds of nations that have the most developed and open financial markets. For this reason, we might expect that measured excess returns from holding bonds of more developed nations should be relatively smaller than those from holding bonds of less-developed, emerging nations.

Figure 9-1 displays estimates of excess returns during the 1990s from a study by Robert Flood of the International Monetary Fund and Andrew Rose of the University of California at Berkeley. As you can see, it is not readily apparent that larger excess returns have been available to U.S. residents who have held bonds issued in nations with emerging economies. For instance, the excess returns available from holding Indonesian bonds have tended to be no greater than those available from holding Italian bonds. Likewise, excess returns from holding bonds issued in the Czech Republic are comparable to those available from holding bonds issued in the United Kingdom.

Although U.S. residents can sometimes earn significant excess returns by holding bonds of other nations, Flood and Rose determined that *average* excess returns from many countries are not very large. Even though the figure indicates that the uncovered interest parity condition is rarely satisfied at any given point in time, over longer-run periods excess returns tend to disappear. Interestingly, this appears to be as true for emerging nations as it is for highly developed countries. Even though foreign exchange markets are not fully efficient in less-developed countries, apparently foreign exchange markets in these nations are not significantly less efficient than those in the developed countries.

Research Project

Uncovered interest parity relates to general market expectations of future spot exchange rates. Given that expectations are subjective, how can economists try to determine the magnitudes of excess returns or whether, on average, the uncovered interest parity condition is satisfied? In what ways can economists try to measure exchange rate expectations? What are the advantages and disadvantages of alternative approaches?

Web Resources

1. Where are data for annual interest rates and exchange rates for a variety of nations? One place to find this information is by going to the International Monetary Fund's home page at http://www.imf.org, clicking on "Publications," then typing in "World Economic Outlook" in the search window. Select the most recent issue of *World Economic Outlook,* which includes a downloadable data appendix.

2. Where can data for a number of countries be found? One place to look for information about exchange rates for more than fifty currencies is Pacific Exchange Rate Service, at http://pacific.commerce.ubc.ca/xr/.

Figure 9-1
Estimates of Excess Returns on International Bond Trading.

These charts display annualized monthly or quarterly excess returns (in basis points, or hundredths of a percentage point) for various nations. These excess returns are estimated expected percentage changes in the exchange rate minus interest rate differentials.

SOURCE: Robert Flood and Andrew Rose, "Uncovered Interest Parity in Crisis: The Interest Rate Defense of the 1990s," Center for Economic Policy Research Discussion Paper No. 2943, September 2001.

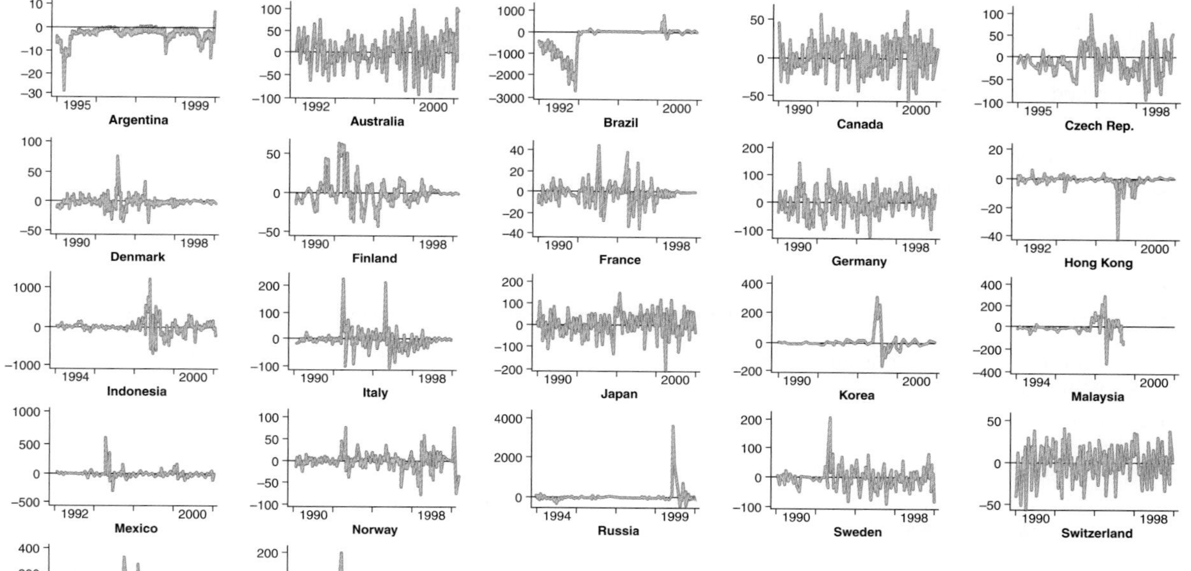

Chapter Summary

1. The Distinction between Adaptive and Rational Expectations: An expectation that is formed adaptively is based only on past information. A rational expectation is formed using all available past and current information and relying on an understanding of how markets determine prices.

2. The Efficient-Markets Hypothesis: The efficient-markets hypothesis indicates that the market price of a financial asset should reflect all available information in that market. It should also reflect rational expectations about the price of the asset on the part of those who wish to buy and sell the asset.

3. Financial Instrument Prices in an Efficient Market: Under the efficient-markets hypothesis, the realized market price of a financial instrument will equal its average price plus an unpredictable component. Thus, on average no individual trader should be better able to predict an instrument's actual price than any other trader. It follows that in an efficient market no single trader can systematically earn higher returns than other traders.

4. The Forward Exchange Market: The forward exchange market is the market for contracts calling for deliveries of currencies at future dates. Demand and supply in the forward exchange market determines the forward exchange rate. If the difference between the forward exchange rate and the spot exchange rate divided by the spot exchange rate has a positive value, there is a forward premium. If this quantity has a negative value, there is a forward discount.

5. Covered Interest Parity: If savers hedge international holdings of financial instruments by hedging with forward currency contracts, then they can earn arbitrage profits if the interest rate in one nation is different from the sum of another nation's interest rate and the forward premium. Their efforts to earn covered arbitrage profits result in equality of the interest rate in one nation with the other's interest rate plus the forward premium, which is the covered interest parity condition.

6. Foreign Exchange Market Efficiency: The foreign exchange market efficiency condition stems from combining covered interest parity with uncovered interest parity. It states that the forward premium, should be equal to the expected rate of currency depreciation. This implies that the forward exchange rate should, on average, predict the future spot exchange rate in efficient foreign exchange markets. Combining uncovered interest parity with relative purchasing power parity also indicates that real interest parity, or equality of national real interest rates, should hold true if international financial markets are integrated.

Questions and Problems

(Answers to odd-numbered questions and problems may be found on the Web at **http://money.swcollege.com** under "Student Resources.")

1. Explain the distinction between an adaptive expectation and a rational expectation. Could there ever be a circumstance in which the two are the same?

2. In your view, what are the two strongest arguments in favor of the rational expectations hypothesis? What are the two strongest arguments against it?

3. Which hypothesis is more "general," in that it could still be correct even if the other were not: the rational expectations hypothesis or the efficient-markets hypothesis?

4. Explain the distinction between the fundamental determinants of a financial instrument's price and factors that are not "fundamental" but can still induce short-term price variations.

5. In your view, would the efficient-market hypothesis be valid if illegal insider trading were widespread? Explain.

6. What is the difference between covered and uncovered interest arbitrage?

7. Suppose that the interest rate on a Japanese bond is greater than the sum of the interest rate on an equivalent Australian bond plus the forward premium for the Japanese yen relative to the Australian dollar. Predict how covered interest arbitrage will affect Japanese and Australian interest rates and the forward and spot exchange rates (measured in yen per dollar).

8. Explain how covered interest parity and uncovered interest parity differ.

9. Could the covered interest parity condition be met if the uncovered interest parity condition is not also satisfied? Why or why not?

10. Other things being equal, in a world of highly integrated financial markets but less integrated markets for goods and services, is real interest parity more or less likely to hold true, as compared with covered interest parity? Explain.

Before the Test

Test your understanding of the material covered in this chapter by taking the Chapter 9 interactive quiz at http://money.swcollege.com.

Online Application

You can track exchange rates each day by clicking into the Federal Reserve Bank of New York's home page.

Internet URL: http://www. ny.frb.org

Title: The Federal Reserve Bank of New York—10 A.M. Midpoint Foreign Exchange Rates

Navigation: Start at the Federal Reserve Bank of New York's home page (listed above). Select "Statistics," then click on "Foreign Exchange 10:00 a.m. Rates."

Application: For each day during a given week (or month), choose a currency from those listed and keep track of its value relative to the dollar.

1. Based on your tabulations, try to predict the value of the currency at the end of the week *following* your data collections. Use any information you may have, or just do your best without any additional information. How far off was your prediction?

2. According to the efficient-markets theory, would you anticipate that daily access to additional information, over and above the information you used to make your forecast, would lead to an improvement in your ability to forecast the value of your currency? Indeed, if you were to become an "expert" on foreign exchange markets, would the theory indicate that you should be able to earn higher profits on average, as compared with equally well-informed traders, by trading on your forecasts? Explain your reasoning.

For Group Study and Analysis: Divide the class into groups, and have each group use data for the dollar's value during the previous week to form a group "consensus forecast" of the dollar's exchange value at the end of the next week. Record each group's forecast. Then evaluate in class how well each group did, and discuss factors that may have led each group to overestimate or underestimate the dollar's value. Discuss whether these factors were "systematic" or "unsystematic" in nature.

Selected References and Further Reading

Frankel, Jeffrey, Sergio Schmukler, and Luis Servén. "Global Transmission of Interest Rates." World Bank Conference on Currency Regimes, June 2000 (http://www.worldbank.org/lacconference).

Froot, Kenneth, and Jeffrey Frankel. "Forward Discount Bias: Is It an Exchange Risk Premium?" *Quarterly Journal of Economics* 104 (1989): 139–161.

MacDonald, Ronald, and Mark Taylor. "Exchange Rate Economics: A Survey." *IMF Staff Papers* 39 (March 1996): 1–47.

Marston, Richard. *International Financial Integration.* Cambridge: Cambridge University Press, 1995.

Taylor, Mark. "Covered Interest Parity: A High-Frequency, High-Quality Data Study." *Economica* 54 (November 1987): 429–438.

———. "The Economics of Exchange Rates." *Journal of Economic Literature* 43 (March 1995): 13–47.

MoneyXtra

moneyxtra! Log on to the MoneyXtra Web site now (http://moneyxtra.swcollege.com) for additional learning resources such as practice quizzes, case studies, readings, and additional economic applications.

Chapter 10

Nondepository Financial Institutions

Fundamental Issues

1. What do securities market institutions do, and how does the government regulate these institutions?
2. What do insurance companies do, and who regulates their activities?
3. How are pension funds structured, and why have they grown?
4. What is the special role of finance companies?
5. How do mutual funds and hedge funds differ?

As the U.S. economy slid into a recession in 2001, a number of observers including the chair of the Federal Reserve's Board of Governors, noticed a potential and disturbing parallel with the experience of the Japanese economy a decade earlier. During a big housing boom in the 1980s, Japanese households and businesses became overloaded with debts, and Japanese financial institutions, which had financed those debts with the assistance of $3 billion in annual government housing subsidies, were dragged down. In many ways, the United States experienced an analogous housing boom in the 1990s. Nationwide housing prices increased at an unprecedented rate of nearly 20 percent during that decade. Prices in hot real estate markets such as Silicon Valley rose by more than 60 percent. The source of anxiety for some economists in the early 2000s was that the U.S. housing boom was at least partly propped up by Japan-like government subsidies and easy loan terms made possible by the widespread assumption that the government would pick up the tab for any defaults.

In the United States, two government-sponsored financial institutions are at the epicenter of governmental involvement in real estate markets. The Federal National Mortgage Association (FNMA, or "Fannie Mae") and the Federal Home Loan Mortgage Corporation (FHLMC, or "Freddie Mac") are privately owned but receive various implicit and explicit subsidies, such as tax breaks and an emergency line of credit from the U.S. Treasury. These Washington-based financial institutions do not actually issue mortgages themselves. Instead, the institutions purchase mortgages from lenders and repackage them *into tradable securities; by setting underwriting standards for the loans they purchase, Fannie Mae and Freddie Mac can significantly influence the size and shape of the market. By making good use of nearly $11 billion in annual explicit and implicit taxpayer subsidies, these institutions have expanded their role and now finance more than 45 percent of the current U.S. mortgage debt.*

A growing number of economists are concerned that Fannie Mae and Freddie Mac may have contributed to an artificial expansion of the U.S. housing market that has drawn funds away from more productive uses. If so, a big housing bust could take place, leaving U.S. households, businesses, financial institutions, and taxpayers stuck with billions of dollars in bad debts. If this were to happen, some economists worry, U.S. residents could find themselves mimicking the experience of residents of Japan during the 1990s and 2000s, with no choice but to allocate resources to paying off old debts instead of contributing to future economic growth.

Government sponsorship of some U.S. financial institutions is not new. Since the United States was formed more than two centuries ago, federal and state governments have sought to influence allocations of funds among the nation's privately owned financial institutions. In this chapter you will learn about both private and government-sponsored institutions and their role in the national and global financial system.

Because we shall devote considerable space to depository institutions in later chapters, this chapter will focus on *nondepository institutions*—institutions that do not issue checking and savings deposits. The various nondepository financial institutions in the United States provide a broad array of financial services. Some, called *securities market institutions*, specialize in intermediating risks in securities markets, while others, known as *insurance companies*, insure individuals and firms against risks of future losses. Other financial institutions called *pension funds* offer pension plans that provide retirement security income to workers. Financial institutions called *finance companies* make loans to individuals and firms that commercial banks, savings banks, and credit unions might deem uncreditworthy, while others known as *mutual funds* provide specialized portfolio management skills.

Securities Market Institutions

When business firms issue new shares of stock or offer to sell new bonds, these firms and those who contemplate buying their securities face two asymmetric-information problems. One stems from adverse selection. Some firms that issue new securities may have an incentive to do so because they are strapped for cash and teetering on the edge of financial disaster. Those considering buying new

Securities underwriting: A guarantee by an investment bank that a firm that issues new stocks or bonds will receive a specified minimum price per share of stock or per bond.

Firm commitment underwriting: An investment banking arrangement in which the investment bank purchases and distributes to dealers and other purchasers all securities offered by a business.

Standby commitment underwriting: An investment banking arrangement in which the investment bank earns commissions for helping the issuing firm sell its securities under the guarantee that the investment bank will purchase for resale any initially unsold securities.

Best efforts deal: An investment banking arrangement in which the investment bank has an option to buy a portion of the issuing firm's securities but is not required to do so.

stock or bonds recognize this possibility and need to be able to identify creditworthy firms. The firms themselves recognize this and need a way to signal their creditworthiness to potential purchasers of their securities. Securities market institutions such as investment banks and securities brokers and dealers help provide this signal by intermediating firms' securities.

Securities market institutions also assist in minimizing moral-hazard problems that arise when firms that are successful in raising funds via security issues might have an incentive to misuse those funds. By monitoring the performances of issuing firms, these institutions assure stock- and bondholders that the firms maintain their creditworthiness. This ensures that the shares of stock or the bonds of issuing firms remain liquid instruments that retain the risk characteristics that they possessed when the firms first issued them.

Investment Banks

As discussed in Chapter 3, investment banks are financial institutions that serve as intermediaries between businesses that issue stocks and bonds and those that purchase those securities. Typically, investment banks specialize in **securities underwriting,** which means that they guarantee that the issuing firm will receive a specified minimum price per share of stock or per bond.

Under **firm commitment underwriting,** an investment bank actually purchases the new securities offered by a business and then distributes them to dealers and other buyers. The investment bank seeks to profit from the spread between the price it pays the issuing firm and the actual price that others pay for the securities. In contrast, under **standby commitment underwriting** an investment bank earns commissions for helping the issuing firm sell its securities and agrees only to purchase any securities that remain unsold after the initial sale. It then seeks to find buyers for those remaining securities.

Another possible arrangement is for the investment bank to act solely as an *agent* for the issuing firm. The firm then pays the investment bank commissions for its marketing services. Under such an arrangement, which is called a **best efforts deal,** the investment bank usually has an option to buy a portion of the issuing firm's securities, but it is not obligated to exercise that option. Best efforts deals were much more common in the nineteenth and early twentieth centuries than they have been in recent decades. Nowadays these arrangements tend to arise when the securities of the issuing firms are regarded as highly risky instruments.

Securities Brokers and Dealers

Although some financial firms are either brokers or dealers, in many cases a firm that acts as a broker is also a dealer. As discussed in Chapter 3, a *broker* specializes in matching buyers and sellers in secondary financial markets. Brokers receive commissions and fees as payment for their services. A *dealer,* in contrast, sells securities from its own portfolio and seeks to profit by buying low and selling high. *Broker-dealers* engage in both businesses. Most major Wall Street brokerage firms are broker-dealers, trading both on behalf of customers and on their own accounts.

TYPES OF BROKERS When any broker makes securities trades on a customer's behalf, it acts as the customer's *agent*. This means that the broker makes the trade in place of the customer but must act as the customer wishes. A *full-service broker* offers a range of other financial services, including consultations about what financial instruments to buy or sell and other financial planning advice. The only service that a *discount broker* offers is making securities trades for clients.

One type of discount broker is a *share broker,* which bases its commission charges on the volume of shares that it trades on a customer's behalf. In contrast, a *value broker* charges commissions that are a percentage of the dollar value of each transaction. For those who wish to trade sizable volumes of securities, a share broker's services entail lower cost. Those who typically trade small numbers of shares gain from using the services of a value broker.

As we noted in Chapter 3, Internet brokers have made major inroads in the brokerage business. This has increased competition among both new Internet brokers and more established brokerage firms that have also sought to stake a claim to the growing Internet stock trading. Many brokers have responded by setting fixed fees for customers who desire only that brokers execute trades on their behalf. Commission charges increasingly apply only to traditional broker-client relationships in which the broker also offers stock information and trading advice to a client.

Over-the-counter (OTC) broker-dealer: A broker-dealer that trades shares of stock that are not listed on organized stock exchanges.

Specialists: Stock exchange members that are charged with trading on their own accounts to prevent dramatic movements in stock prices.

Limit orders: Instructions from other stock exchange members to specialists to execute stock trades at specific prices.

OVER-THE-COUNTER (OTC) BROKER-DEALERS Another type of broker, an **over-the-counter (OTC) broker-dealer,** specializes in trading shares of stock that are not listed on organized stock exchanges. Such OTC stocks are traded in decentralized markets linking OTC broker-dealers. As noted earlier, OTC stocks typically are those of smaller companies that do not meet listing requirements for the New York Stock Exchange.

Although OTC stock trading falls outside the rules of the centralized exchanges, it still must meet standards set by the *National Association of Securities Dealers (NASD)*. This self-regulating group of OTC broker-dealers also operates the *NASD Automated Quotation system (Nasdaq)*. As noted in Chapter 3, Nasdaq began as a national market system of computer and telephone links between OTC broker-dealers. Today it also connects traditional stock exchanges such as the American Stock Exchange, which merged with Nasdaq in 1998.

SPECIALISTS Some broker-dealers perform special roles in securities markets. These **specialists** are members of stock exchanges that are responsible for preventing wide swings in stock prices. They do this by adding to or reducing their own holdings of stock to counteract major changes in demand or supply conditions.

Specialists are responsible for executing specific trades called **limit orders.** These are instructions from other stock exchange members to execute trades when stock prices reach certain levels. For instance, when a share price is equal to \$25, a specialist might receive a limit order to sell a given amount of shares on the ordering broker's behalf if the share price slips to \$23. Only if the share price reaches \$23 would the specialist make the trade. But if the share price does hit \$23, the specialist is bound by the rules of the exchange to do so. In return for this service, the specialist receives a commission from the ordering broker.

As brokers place limit orders, specialists list them in ledgers called *specialist's books*. A given specialist's ledger details the specialist's own holdings of securities

Securities and Exchange Commission (SEC): A group of five presidentially appointed members whose mandate is to enforce rules governing securities trading.

Prospectus: A formal written offer to sell securities.

and the sequence of limit orders received from other brokers. If the specialist's book contains an unexecuted limit order, then the specialist cannot trade securities on its own account at the limit order price *until* it executes the limit order first. From time to time this restriction can force the specialist to forgo earnings. The limit order commissions compensate the specialist for this sacrifice.

Regulation of Securities Market Institutions

All securities market institutions must meet regulations established by the **Securities and Exchange Commission (SEC).** Congress created the SEC in the *Securities Exchange Act of 1934*. The SEC is composed of five commissioners appointed by the president of the United States on a rotating basis to five-year terms. The president names one of these individuals as chair of the SEC.

The SEC's mandate is to enforce both the 1934 act and the *Securities Act of 1933*. The 1933 act requires that all securities for sale be registered and that detailed information about each security be disclosed in a **prospectus,** or formal written offer to sell securities. The 1934 act requires securities market institutions to refrain from manipulating stock and bond prices. In light of these requirements, the SEC establishes and enforces a number of rules that govern securities trading. It also oversees and approves rules established by groups such as the NASD. (Recently, determining who to regulate has not been a simple issue for the Securities and Exchange Commission; see *Policy Focus: The SEC Asks, "What Is a Broker?"*)

1. What do securities market institutions do, and how does the government regulate these institutions? Investment banks underwrite and market new stock and bonds that corporations issue. Brokers trade securities on behalf of clients, and dealers trade on their own accounts. The Securities and Exchange Commission regulates the activities of these firms.

Insurance Institutions

As we discussed in Chapter 3, insurance companies are financial institutions that specialize in trying to limit adverse-selection and moral-hazard problems arising from insurance against future losses. The policies that they issue are promises to repay the policyholder if such a future loss occurs. In return, insurance companies receive premiums from owners of the policies, who are called policyholders. The companies set aside most of these premiums as *reserves* from which payments are made to policyholders who experience losses. Reserves are composed of securities and cash. The remaining portion of the premiums is the companies' revenues.

Dealing with Asymmetric-Information Problems in Insurance

Most insurance policies have a number of common features. Companies design these features to reduce the extent of the problems that they face in light of asymmetric information. After all, those who apply for insurance know much more

GLOBAL POLICY Focus CYBER MANAGEMENT

The SEC Asks, "What Is a Broker?"

The role of a broker in financial markets is to bring together buyers and sellers of financial instruments. Until recently, identifying institutions that function as brokers has not been particularly difficult. Under the SEC Act of 1934, a broker is someone "engaged in the business" of "effecting securities transactions." Essential activities, such as holding customer securities and handling trades on customers' behalf, are indicators that a firm is a broker. Traditionally, a firm that acts as a broker has established a physical office, registered for oversight by the SEC, and begun matching those interested in selling securities with those that express an interest in purchasing them.

In addition, however, the SEC has taken the position that the law also applies to nearly anyone who performs services on behalf of a broker in exchange for "transaction-based compensation." This stance has raised a host of issues for companies that operate financial Web sites. In the early years of the Internet, Web portals such as America Online, Compuserve, and Microsoft's MSN network provided advertising links to the sites of online brokers. As part of an effort to ensure that their advertising paid off, online brokers began working out arrangements in which the brokers made payments to these and other Web portals only when advertising links connected them with customers who actually executed trades.

Initially, the SEC approved such arrangements as long as the fees earned by the financial portals were not directly tied to the size of a customer's trade order to a broker. Receiving one-time fees for blocks of new customer orders, for instance, did not subject a financial portal to SEC regulation.

Recently, however, online brokers have begun paying some portals fees for each new account generated by customers' use of Web links. Some brokers and portals have even discussed arrangements in which portals would receive compensation for each *transaction* that results when customers link to online brokerage sites.

The SEC has been hesitant to approve such deals and thereby exempt financial portals from the normal requirement to register as brokers. The act of receiving compensation for arranging and executing securities trades is a simple criterion to use in determining who is a "broker." Exempting financial portals on the Web would immediately create a "gray area" in the definition of what constitutes a broker.

FOR CRITICAL ANALYSIS: For purposes of regulating online financial transactions, could the meaning of "broker" be redefined in a way that would exempt Web financial portals from the requirement to register with the SEC as brokers?

about their risks of loss than do the insurance companies, and those who receive insurance can do the most to limit the risks of such losses.

LIMITING ADVERSE SELECTION One way that insurance companies seek to reduce the adverse-selection problem is by restricting the availability of insurance. Insurance companies will not sell every available policy to every individual. For instance, suppose that an individual has a spouse and four children but no life insurance. This person then learns of impending death from an illness for which there is no cure. If the individual cares about the spouse and children, then the person has every incentive after learning of the illness to purchase a life insurance policy. If the insurer would permit a person in such a situation to buy such a policy, then the insurer also would be taking on a 100 percent probability of a claim that would amount to more than the premiums it would collect from that

Deductible: A fixed amount of an insured loss that a policyholder must pay before the insurer is obliged to make payments.

Coinsurance: An insurance policy feature that requires a policyholder to pay a fixed percentage of a loss above a deductible.

individual. No insurance company could stay in business for very long if it made its policies available to all who might like to buy them.

Insurers also deal with the adverse-selection problem by limiting how much insurance any one individual or firm can buy. To reduce their exposure to losses from policies taken out by applicants who may know that they have life-shortening conditions, insurers typically place limits on the dollar amount of coverage that individuals may purchase. In addition, insurance companies typically require policyholders who purchase large life insurance policies or who decide to increase their current policy coverages significantly to undergo blood tests or other physical examinations, such as a heart treadmill stress test.

Limiting Moral Hazard in Insurance Another feature of insurance policies is that they contain provisions that restrict the behavior of policyholders. These provisions are intended to reduce the extent of the moral-hazard problem that insurers also face.

As noted above, limiting the amount of insurance can counter the adverse-selection problem. It can also reduce the extent of some moral-hazard problems. For example, if a company that operates agricultural grain elevators could insure them for more than they are worth, then it would have little incentive to operate the elevators safely by keeping flammable liquids or spark-producing equipment away from them. Consequently, the risk of an explosion would increase—and so would the insurer's chances of making payments on losses. Hence, insurers typically limit policy coverages to the maximum possible losses that policyholders could incur.

One key weapon against moral-hazard problems is an insurance company's ability to cancel insurance because of "bad behavior" by a policyholder. Most insurance policies include a clause threatening cancellation if the policyholder develops a record of reckless behavior after the policy has been issued.

Insurance companies also combat the moral-hazard problem by offering policies with *deductible* and *coinsurance* features. A **deductible** is a fixed amount of a loss that a policyholder must pay before the insurance company must provide promised payments. For example, if a homeowner's child throws a rock through a $400 picture window in the insured house and the homeowner's policy has a $200 deductible against such a loss, then the homeowner is required to pay $200 of the cost of replacing the window. The insurance company pays the remaining $200. The presence of the deductible feature gives the homeowner an incentive to lecture the child about throwing rocks, thereby reducing the risk that the homeowner and the insurer will incur such a loss. This feature of the policy also gives the homeowner a reason to monitor the child's behavior.

Coinsurance is a feature that requires the policyholder to pay a fixed percentage of any loss above the specified deductible. In the example of the broken picture window, a policy with a coinsurance feature might require that the policyholder pay 10 percent of the loss over the $200 deductible. In this case, the homeowner's total loss would be $220—the $200 deductible plus 10 percent of the additional $200 loss ($20). This coinsurance feature gives the homeowner an added incentive to keep rocks from flying from the child's hands.

Determining Policy Premiums The essential principle of insurance is the pooling of risks of loss that might be incurred by individual members of a large group. Even though all members of the group might experience a loss at any time, only a small number will actually incur a loss. For example, suppose that over any one-year period, on average, two of every 10,000 retail businesses experience a major fire that destroys a retail outlet. The risk of fire damage, however, may be distributed across all 10,000 businesses, so that each pays 1/10,000 of the annual loss expected to be incurred by two of them. When the actual losses occur, sufficient funds will be on hand to reimburse the two businesses that, on average, experience fires.

Insurance companies use this type of statistical approach to computing policy premiums. They rely on **actuaries,** who specialize in using statistical and mathematical principles to calculate premiums sufficient to cover expected losses to policyholders. The premiums that are just sufficient to cover expected insured losses are called *actuarially fair* insurance premiums. Actuaries also assist in estimating the value of the insurance company, which is never known for certain because the company's losses—and consequently its liabilities—are subject to risk.

Premiums on insurance policies actually are somewhat higher than the actuarially fair premiums. As with any market price, the market premium for an insurance policy is influenced by revenue and cost conditions faced by insurers. For instance, in times when interest rates are low, insurance premiums tend to rise. The reason is that companies' loss reserves earn interest, so if market rates are low, the companies must bolster reserves and maintain profits by raising premiums.

Actuary: An individual who specializes in using mathematical and statistical principles to calculate insurance premiums and to estimate an insurance company's net worth.

Whole life policy: A life insurance policy whose benefits are payable to a beneficiary whenever the insured person's death occurs and that accumulates a cash value that the policyholder may acquire prior to his or her death.

Level premium policy: A whole life insurance policy under which an insurance company charges fixed premium payments throughout the life of the insured individual.

Life Insurance

Usually, in any given year, about 400 million life insurance policies are in effect in the United States. (Some people carry multiple policies.) Life insurance companies typically classify policies into separate categories. *Ordinary* life policies in amounts of $1,000 or more and *industrial* life policies in amounts less than $1,000 cover individuals. *Group* life policies cover a number of people under terms specified by a master contract that applies to all who are covered. Finally, *credit* life policies insure a borrower against loan foreclosure in the event of death before full payment of the loan. Figure 10-1 shows the distribution of these policies.

Most policies that life insurance companies issue guarantee payments to a designated beneficiary, such as a spouse or child, when the insured individual dies. Actuaries determine the actuarially fair premiums for life insurance policies using historical experience on probabilities of death at various ages. Because life expectancies across many policyholders are predictable, life insurance companies have a good idea how many benefits they will need to pay out in future years. Thus, the companies typically feel secure holding relatively illiquid long-term corporate bonds and stocks as sizable components of their portfolio of financial instruments.

WHOLE VERSUS TERM LIFE INSURANCE There are two basic types of life insurance policies. Under a **whole life policy,** a benefit is payable at the death of the insured, and the policy has an accumulated cash value that the policyholder may acquire before death. Whole life policies come in two forms: a **level premium policy,** in which the insurance company charges fixed premium payments throughout the life of the insured individual, and a **limited payment policy,** in which the insured individual pays premiums only for a fixed number of years and is insured during

Figure 10-1
The Distribution of Life Insurance Policies.

Ordinary and group insurance policies account for the bulk of life insurance policies in the United States.

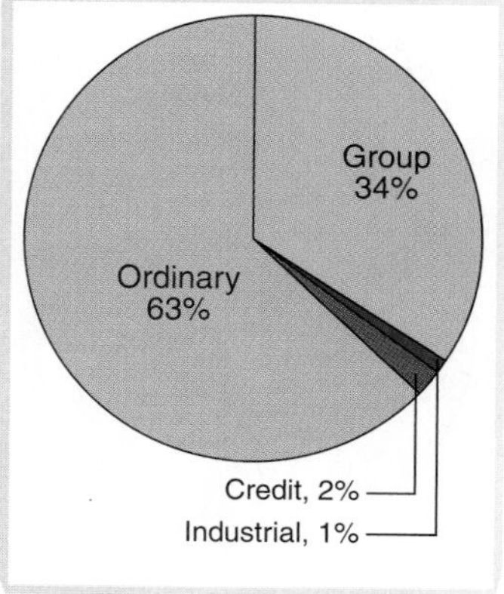

Percentages are rounded to the nearest whole percent.
SOURCE: A.M. Best, 2002.

Limited payment policy: A whole life insurance policy under which an insured individual pays premiums only for a fixed number of years and is insured during and after the payment period.

Term life policy: A life insurance policy under which an individual is insured only during a limited period that the policy is in effect.

Fixed annuity: A financial instrument, typically issued by an insurance company, that pays regular, constant installments to the owner beginning at a specific future date.

and after each payment period. Both kinds of whole life policies typically have a *cash surrender value,* meaning that after a specific date the policyholder can exchange the policy for a lump-sum amount. Hence, for some people whole life policies are saving instruments.

The other basic type of life insurance policy is a **term life policy.** Under this kind of policy, an individual is insured only during a limited period that the policy is in effect. Premiums for term life policies depend on the age of the insured person and typically increase each year that the policy renews because as the individual ages, the chance of death increases. Nevertheless, term life policies typically have lower premiums over an average life span than whole life policies. The reason is that a term life policy has no cash surrender value and thus no additional savings component. The premium therefore reflects only the risks that the insurer takes on by providing the policy.

ANNUITIES Life insurers may guarantee payments to beneficiaries in the form of a lump sum or an annuity, which is a stream of payments over a period or perhaps until the death of the beneficiary. There are two types of annuities. A **fixed annuity** makes payments to the holder in regular installments of constant dollar amounts beginning at a specific future time. With a **variable annuity,** the payouts that the holder receives depend on the value of the underlying portfolio of assets that the insurance company uses to fund the payouts.

Figure 10-2
The Distribution of Property-Casualty Premiums by Line of Business.

Premiums for policies covering autos account for nearly half of the total premium volumes of property-casualty insurers.

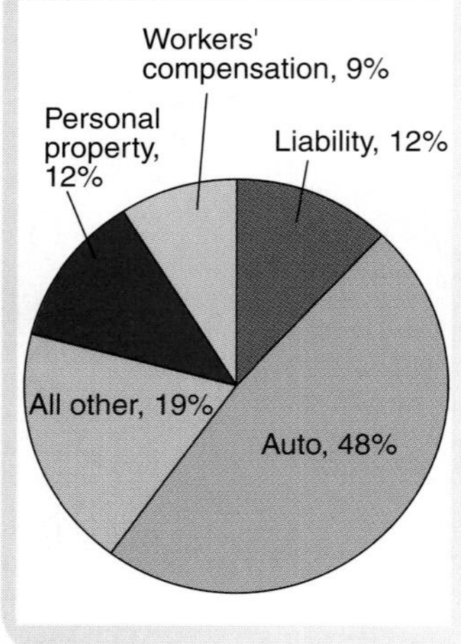

Percentages are rounded to the nearest whole percent.
SOURCE: Insurance Information Institute, 2002.

Property-Casualty Insurance

Insurance against property and casualty losses covers a variety of contingencies. Property-casualty companies issue property policies covering losses stemming from accidental or fire damage to autos, buildings, boats, ships, crops, furnaces, factory equipment, and so on. Policies also cover losses resulting from injuries or deaths due to accidents. Businesses cover their employees through policies offered in the form of workers' compensation insurance. Finally, property-casualty companies also offer policies covering liabilities stemming from automobile accidents, poorly designed or produced products, or medical malpractice. Figure 10-2 shows premiums by line of business for all property-casualty insurance companies.

Because property-casualty companies insure against such a variety of types of losses, actuaries for these companies treat each line of business separately for premium calculations. Furthermore, the varied nature of these lines of business makes it more difficult for property-casualty insurers to be certain of likely payouts to insured individuals and firms. For this reason, property-casualty insurance companies usually hold much more diversified portfolios of financial instruments, as compared with the portfolios of life insurance companies.

Regulation of Insurance Companies

Although insurance companies must meet the terms of a number of federal laws and regulations, the primary supervisory authorities for life insurance companies are in each of the fifty states. Insurers must meet not only the minimal standards established by the state where they are incorporated but also standards set by states where they sell policies. This means that companies doing business in all states must meet the minimal standards specified by the toughest state regulator.

2. What do insurance companies do, and who regulates their activities? Insurance companies offer policies that are financial guarantees to cover losses of life and property. They use a variety of techniques to minimize significant adverse-selection and moral-hazard problems inherent in insurance. Individual states regulate insurance companies, so the toughest state regulators can affect nationwide industry standards.

moneyxtra!

Online Case Study

To evaluate a major challenge facing property-casualty insurance companies today, go to the Chapter 10 Case Study, entitled "Insurers Face Facts as Customers Self-Insure More of Their Risks."

http://moneyxtra.swcollege.com

Pension Funds

As Figure 10-3 indicates, the share of financial institution assets held in pension funds has grown steadily since the 1950s. There are two likely reasons for this relative growth of pension funds. One is the gradual aging of the baby boom generation. Most "baby boomers" began working in the 1960s and 1970s. As they have aged, their incomes and, consequently, their contributions to pension funds have risen. Another reason is that pension funds have become more popular savings vehicles for many people. This is true both because pension funds have made pension arrangements more flexible over time and because most pension income is tax-deferred, meaning that contributions and earnings are not taxable until individuals begin drawing on accumulated pension savings.

Variable annuity: A financial instrument, typically issued by an insurance company, that beginning on a specific future date pays the owner a stream of returns that depends on the value of an underlying portfolio of assets.

Types of Pensions

Any pension is an arrangement in which an employer agrees to provide benefits to retired employees, usually in the form of annuities. Pensions may be **contributory pensions,** meaning that both the employer and the employee contribute to the pension fund, or **noncontributory pensions,** meaning that only the employer contributes.

Contributory pensions: Pensions funded by both employer and employee contributions.

Noncontributory pensions: Pensions funded solely by employers.

ALTERNATIVE PENSION BENEFIT ARRANGEMENTS There are two basic types of pension plans. With a *defined-contribution plan,* a person receives pension benefits that are based on total pension contributions during working years. With a

Figure 10-3
Pension Funds' Share of Financial Institution Assets.

The share of total assets of all financial institutions held by pension funds has increased steadily since the 1950s.

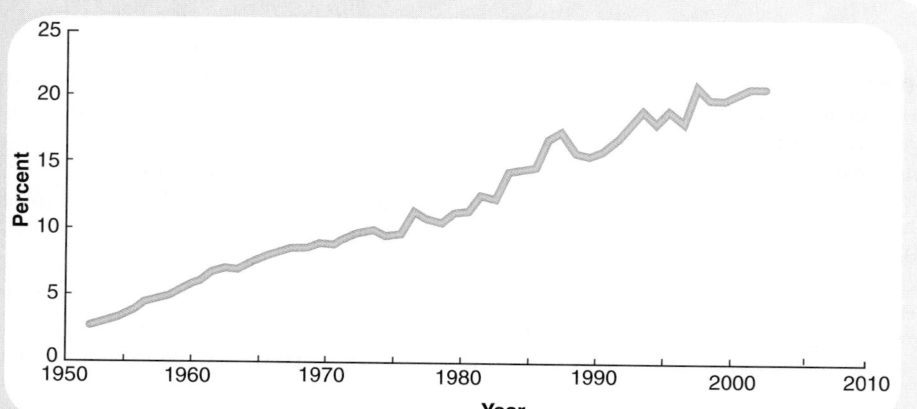

SOURCE: *Flow-of-Funds Accounts,* Board of Governors of the Federal Reserve System, various issues.

Terminally funded pensions: Pensions that must be fully funded by the date that an employee retires.

Pay-as-you-go pensions: Pensions that are not fully funded when employees retire.

Single-employer pensions: Pensions that are established by an employer only for its own employees and are nontransferable to other employers.

Multi-employer pensions: Pensions whose accumulations and benefit rights may be transferred from one employer to another.

defined-benefits plan, future benefits are set in advance. Thus, for defined-benefits plans a key issue is determining whether benefits will be completely funded at retirement.

ALTERNATIVE PENSION FUNDING ARRANGEMENTS There are also two essential approaches to funding pensions. **Terminally funded pensions** are fully funded for the payment of benefits to an employee beginning at the employee's retirement date. When an employee covered by such a pension will receive retirement benefits from his employer even if he leaves the employer prior to the retirement date, the employee is said to be *vested*. For instance, a teacher who is vested in a state teachers' pension fund will receive benefits upon retirement even if he leaves the public school system and teaches at a private school before retirement.

Some employers offer **pay-as-you-go pensions,** in which pensions are not fully funded when employees retire. Instead, the employer funds pension benefits for current retirees out of current earnings produced by current (nonretired) workers. Some employers operate pension plans that combine terminal funding with pay-as-you-go funding provisions.

TRANSFERABILITY OF PENSION FUNDS **Single-employer pensions** are established by an employer only for its own employees. Funding and benefits for such pensions are nontransferable. When an employee leaves to take another job, accumulated pension funds cannot be shifted into the new employer's pension plan.

In contrast, under **multi-employer pensions** employees may transfer accumulated funds and benefit rights when they change jobs. (This is called pension *portability*.) Multi-employer pensions typically apply to a specific industry, however. For instance, many colleges and professors contribute to TIAA-CREF, which is a multi-employer pension fund for colleges and universities. But accumulations and benefit rights from that plan generally are not transferable if a professor leaves a college to enter private industry or government service. (Yet all accumulations up to that point are fully vested and available as annuities.)

Pension Fund Insurance and Regulation

Many pension funds have insurance to cover the contingency that they will be unable to honor their obligations to make future payments to retirees. Such funds operate under legal contracts that are mutually binding on both the pension fund and the insurer. Other pension funds that are not insured typically fund their benefits under a *trust* agreement, in which a neutral party, called the *trustee,* administers the distribution of benefits to retirees.

In 1974, concerns about the solvency of some pension funds led Congress to pass the *Employment Retirement Income Security Act (ERISA)*. This act and subsequent amendments set out federal rules for disclosure of pension information, funding arrangements, and vesting provisions. It also created the *Pension Benefit Guaranty Corporation (PBGC),* which provides federal insurance for all pensions with tax-deferred benefits, which are the bulk of pensions in the United States.

On the Web

How did the federal government get involved in guaranteeing defined-benefits pension plans? To learn more about the history of the Pension Benefit Guaranty Corporation, go to http://www.pbgc.gov, click on "About PBGC," and then click on "Our Organization" and "Mission Statement." After reading text, click on "Strategic Plan."

3. How are pension funds structured, and why have they grown?
Noncontributory pension funds accumulate via funding provided solely by employers, whereas contributory pension funds also are funded by employees. Some pensions have terminal funding, which requires that they be fully funded by the time the employees retire, while pay-as-you-go pensions are funded out of the firm's current earnings. Pension funds have grown significantly because of the aging of the baby boom generation, the growing flexibility of the funds, and the tax deferments permitted by law.

Government Credit Agencies

The Pension Benefit Guaranty Corporation is one example of several federal government agencies that provide financial services. Government agencies and other government-sponsored institutions are involved in a number of financial markets.

As discussed in Chapter 3, most government credit agencies, such as the General National Mortgage Association (GNMA, or "Ginnie Mae"), the Federal National Mortgage Association (FNMA, or "Fannie Mae"), and the Federal Home Loan Mortgage Corporation (FHLMC, or "Freddie Mac"), make mortgage markets more liquid by selling mortgage-backed securities and purchasing mortgages. The Federal Housing Administration (FHA), the Department of Housing and Urban Development (HUD), and the Veterans Administration (VA) also assist eligible individuals in purchasing homes by making mortgage loans directly to those individuals or by subsidizing and guaranteeing loans that they receive from private lenders.

The federal government also operates the Farm Credit System, which makes loans to farmers. Such loans are guaranteed by the Farmer's Home Administration. The Student Loan Marketing Association is a government-assisted agency that purchases student loans that are guaranteed by the Department of Education.

In addition, the Federal Housing Finance Board governs a system of twelve Federal Home Loan Banks, which provide government-subsidized financing of loans for residential housing and community development.

In recent years key members of Congress have discussed curtailing many of the loan guarantees relating to programs for farmers, students, and veterans. But the greatest potential threat to taxpayers probably lies in the underfunded pensions insured by the Pension Benefit Guaranty Corporation. (By law, the PBGC cannot deny insurance to most pension funds and can impose only limited restrictions on underfunded pension funds; as a result, its liabilities far exceed its assets.) As members of the baby boom generation gradually reach retirement age early in the twenty-first century, pension fund payouts will escalate. Unless efforts are made to offset the multibillion-dollar negative net worth of the PBGC, U.S. taxpayers almost certainly will find themselves bailing out a number of underfunded private pension plans.

On the Web
What path did the FNMA follow to become such a sprawling financial institution? For an overview of the FNMA's history, visit Fannie Mae's home page at http://www.fanniemae.com. Click on "About Fannie Mae," then on "Understanding Fannie Mae."

Finance Companies

Finance companies traditionally have specialized in lending to businesses and individuals that are of insufficient size or creditworthiness to issue financial instruments in the money or capital markets or to borrow from other lenders

Business finance companies: Finance companies that typically specialize in making loans to small businesses.

Consumer finance companies: Finance companies that specialize in making loans to individuals for the purchase of durable goods or for home improvements.

Sales finance companies: Finance companies that specialize in making loans to individuals for the purchase of items from specific retailers or manufacturers.

Load funds: Mutual funds marketed by brokers who receive commissions based on the returns of the funds.

such as commercial banks. **Business finance companies** typically make loans to small businesses. In many instances they extend credit by saving the small businesses the trouble of collecting accounts that have not yet been paid. A business finance company often purchases accounts receivable, or receivables, owed to a small firm at a discount below the face value. For example, suppose that a small business has $51,000 in receivables. Of these, the business reasonably expects to collect $50,000. One way to finance continued operations might be for the business to sell the $51,000 in receivables to a finance company at a price of $46,000. The finance company makes a profit on this arrangement when it collects the $4,000 in easily collectible debts and some of the $1,000 in debts that the small business has already written off.

Other finance companies specialize in offering financial services to individuals. **Consumer finance companies** make loans enabling individuals to purchase durable goods such as home appliances or furniture or to make improvements to existing homes. **Sales finance companies** make loans to individuals planning to purchase items from specific retailers or manufacturers, such as Sears or Ford Motor Company.

Finance companies finance their operations by issuing debt in the form of commercial paper and bonds and through the sale of equity shares. Many also borrow from commercial banks.

4. What is the special role of finance companies? Finance companies typically specialize in lending to consumers and firms whose creditworthiness or size sometimes precludes them from qualifying for loans from depository institutions such as commercial banks.

Mutual Funds and Hedge Funds

As noted in Chapter 3, mutual funds are portfolios of financial instruments managed by investment companies on behalf of shareholders. These investment companies charge fees to manage the funds. Before the 1960s, most mutual funds specialized in stock portfolios, but in subsequent years many added bonds to their portfolios. During the 1970s, money market mutual funds also became popular as interest rates on large-denomination financial instruments outstripped regulated rates on deposit accounts at commercial banks and other depository financial institutions. Figure 10-4 depicts the growing relative importance of stock and bond and money market mutual funds since the middle of the twentieth century.

Types of Mutual Funds

Mutual funds can be categorized along two dimensions. **Load funds** are mutual funds that generally are marketed by brokers. Returns on such funds are reduced by commission rates paid to the brokers. Investment companies market

Figure 10-4
Mutual Fund Growth.

The relative shares of total assets of all financial institutions held by stock and bond and money market mutual funds have risen rapidly since the 1970s.

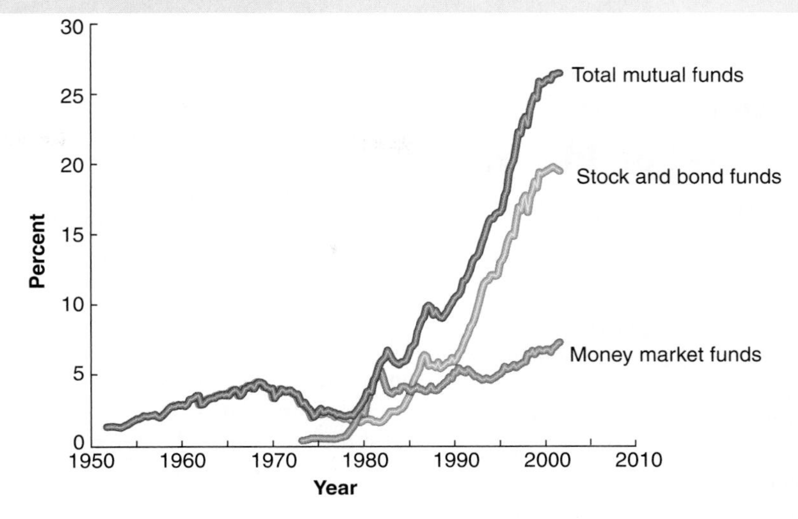

SOURCE: *Flow-of-Funds Accounts*, Board of Governors of the Federal Reserve System, various issues.

no-load funds directly to the public, so there are no commission charges on such funds, which charge annual management fees to shareholders (as do load funds).

Some mutual funds are **closed-end funds,** which sell shares in an initial offering. The shares in closed-end funds cannot be redeemed but may be sold to others much like stocks. The shares' market values vary with the market values of the pools of financial instruments held by the mutual funds. In contrast, shares of an **open-end fund** are redeemable at any time at a price based on the market value of the mix of financial instruments held by the fund. Because shares of open-end funds are redeemable, they are more liquid than those offered by closed-end funds. (Increasingly, people are holding stocks indirectly via shares in stock mutual funds; see on the next page *Management Focus: Stock Mutual Funds—For Many, a Key Link to the Stock Market.*)

Nearly all mutual funds are public companies. Consequently, they must register with the SEC, which requires mutual funds to issue prospectuses and performance reports. Making performance information public helps prospective shareholders compare rates of return and risk of the myriad mutual funds available.

No-load funds: Mutual funds that investment companies market directly to the public and that charge management fees instead of brokerage commissions.

Closed-end funds: Mutual funds that sell nonredeemable shares whose market values vary with the market values of the underlying mix of financial instruments held by the mutual funds.

Open-end funds: Mutual funds whose shares are redeemable at any time at prices based on the market values of the mix of financial instruments held by such funds.

Hedge Funds

On September 23, 1998, the world learned that on the previous evening, the Federal Reserve Bank of New York had helped arrange a privately funded, $3.5 billion "bailout" of Long-Term Capital Management (LTCM). LTCM was a *hedge*

GLOBAL POLICY CYBER **MANAGEMENT Focus**

Stock Mutual Funds—For Many, a Key Link to the Stock Market

Many people do not own shares of stock directly. Instead, they own them indirectly. Traditionally, most indirect stockholding of U.S. households has been through the accumulation of shares in pension funds. More recently, however, a growing number of individuals are owning stocks indirectly by holding shares in stock mutual funds.

As shown in Figure 10-5, the percentage of all stock assets held in mutual funds has nearly tripled since 1990. John Duca of the Federal Reserve Bank of Dallas suggests that much of the growth has resulted from liberalized rules for individual retirement accounts (IRAs) that permit these accounts to be managed by mutual funds. Changes in the tax laws and heightened concerns about long-term job security have also probably spurred individuals to invest the time required to learn how to structure IRAs within stock mutual funds.

IRAs cannot account for all of the growth in the percentage of stock owned through stock mutual funds, however. Duca argues that one reason non-IRA stockholdings of stock mutual funds grew during the 1990s was that the booming job market forced many employers to offer more investment alternatives in their thrift plans to attract and retain employees. Another factor was a general decline in the overall fees charged by managers of stock mutual funds, which tended to raise the net return on holding shares in these funds.

For Critical Analysis: Why don't the U.S. residents who hold about one out of every four dollars in stocks indirectly through stock mutual funds simply buy stocks outright?

Figure 10-5
Shares of Stock Assets Held via Stock Mutual Funds.

Since the early 1980s, an increasing share of households' stockholding is through stock mutual funds.

SOURCE: John Duca, "The Democratization of America's Capital Markets," Federal Reserve Bank of Dallas *Economic and Financial Review,* Second Quarter 2001, pp. 10–19; authors' estimates.

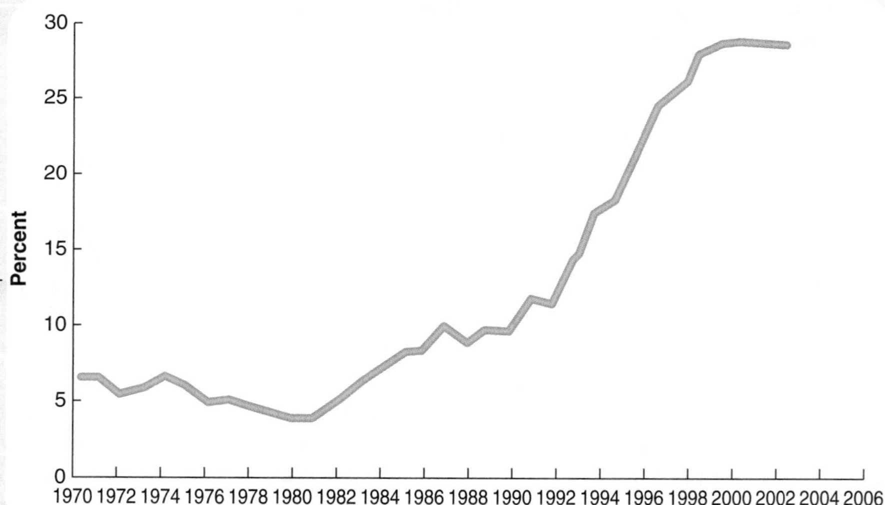

fund with twenty-five financial economists with Ph.D.'s on its payroll, including two who had received the Nobel Prize in economics. The leading firms in the bailout were Goldman Sachs, Merrill Lynch, J. P. Morgan, and United Bank of Switzerland. These institutions and several others effectively took over the operations of LTCM.

Hedge funds: Limited partnerships that, like mutual funds, manage portfolios of assets on behalf of savers, but with very limited governmental oversight as compared with mutual funds.

Among the several remarkable aspects of this event was that many people had little idea what a hedge fund was, let alone how it could lose so much money so fast. In a sense, hedge funds are a type of mutual fund. Indeed, some observers call hedge funds "unregulated mutual funds for the affluent." The key distinction is that a **hedge fund** typically is established as a limited partnership, rather than a public company; thus, these financial intermediaries avoid being regulated by the SEC. Hedge funds also charge higher fees, often 20 percent of the profits they make for investors, than mutual funds. They also typically offer higher average returns. At the same time, hedge funds tend to take on greater portfolio risk, so their returns often are more variable. Consequently, the term *hedge fund* often is something of a misnomer because some hedge funds actually offer relatively risky, unhedged returns.

moneyxtra!

Another Perspective

For a more detailed discussion of hedge funds, use the Chapter 10 reading entitled "The Truth about Hedge Funds," by William Osterberg and James Thomson of the Federal Reserve Bank of Cleveland. http://moneyxtra.swcollege.com

Hedge funds have been in existence since the 1940s. Today there are about 3,000 hedge funds holding more than $300 billion in total assets. Between 1994 and 2003, hedge fund assets more than doubled.

One reason that classifying hedge funds can be difficult is that their management strategies vary widely. Some call themselves *macro funds;* they earn profits by speculating within particular bond markets or making bets on changes in exchange rates. Other hedge funds specialize in speculating about events such as mergers or bankruptcies. Others simply make bets in stock markets.

5. How do mutual funds and hedge funds differ? Mutual funds are public companies that differ across two dimensions. One is whether they entail commission payments to those who market the funds (load funds) or simply require management fees (no-load funds). The other is whether the shares of the funds are redeemable upon demand (open-end funds) or are nonredeemable and can be sold only in secondary markets (closed-end funds). Most hedge funds are private companies that typically are operated as limited partnerships subject to little or no government regulation.

On the Web

What financial strategies do hedge funds pursue? To find out, visit the Hedge Fund Association at http://thehfa.org, click on "About Hedge Funds," and then scroll down to Hedge Fund Strategies."

Link to Policy

Are Fannie Mae and Freddie Mac Out of Control?

Figure 10-6 displays the growth of the total mortgage holdings of Fannie Mae and Freddie Mac. Even the trillions of dollars in mortgage assets owned by these institutions somewhat understate their involvement in the U.S. financial system, however. In the summer of 1999, several trade associations and institutions established a group called FM Watch. Their self-enunciated goal was to prevent Fannie Mae and other government-sponsored enterprises (GSEs) from encroaching on marketplaces that had traditionally been the province of private institutions.

The Spreading Tentacles of the GSEs

When it was formed, FM Watch had a major task just to keep an eye on the areas into which GSEs were already expanding their operations. For instance, in an effort to establish a foothold in the growing market for Web-based real estate services, Fannie Mae had funded the development of the software application that powers hundreds of lenders' online mortgage systems, which now process about 10 percent of the new mortgages that Fannie Mae acquires each year. Fannie Mae had also entered into an entangled alliance with a generally unprofitable Web-based mortgage originator called LendingTree. The GSE advanced a $2.5 million credit line to the firm at a rate that LendingTree's competitors complained was below the market rates that they faced.

In the area of subprime lending, or loans to lower-quality borrowers (see Chapter 7), Freddie Mac had already agreed to assist in transforming more than $400 million of subprime loans originated by Norwest Mortgage Corporation and almost $850 million in subprime mortage lending by Countrywide Credit Industries. Today roughly half of the originators of subprime loans sell at least a portion of their loans to Freddie Mac and other GSEs.

Table 10-1 shows the top ten debt issues during the recent heyday of debt accumulation. By the beginning of 2001, Fannie Mae and Freddie Mac had accounted for five of the top ten debt issues in U.S. history.

Branching into New Markets and Entering into New Forms of Competition

By the early 2000s, Fannie Mae and Freddie Mac were even purchasing their own mortgage-backed securities in secondary markets. The two GSEs defended these "buybacks," arguing that all they were doing was helping to boost the demand for the securities and helping to push down their yields, thereby contributing to lower mortgage rates. Critics, however, pointed out that the buybacks also put underlying mortgage risks back on the balance sheets of the GSEs, when the point of their issuance of mortgage-backed securities is supposed to be to redistribute those risks through the private sector of the economy. The buybacks also put Fannie Mae

Figure 10-6
Total Mortgage Assets of the Federal National Mortgage Association and the Federal Home Loan Mortgage Corporation.

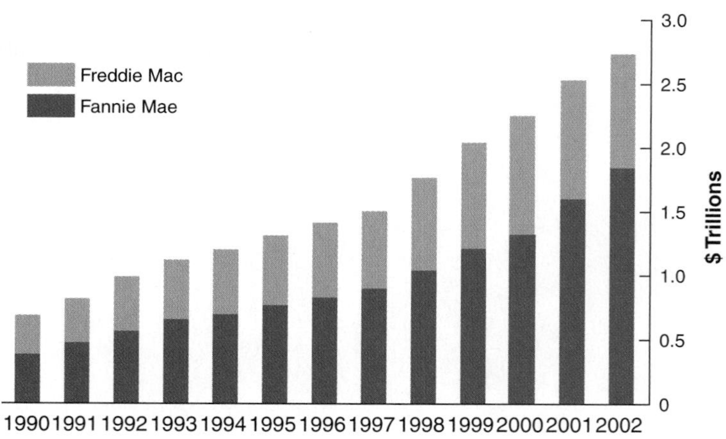

and Freddie Mac in direct competition with private firms that arbitrage risks in secondary markets.

Recently, Fannie Mae and Freddie Mac have even begun to compete with private banks, savings institutions, and credit unions. The two big GSEs now sell debt securities, called "Investment Notes" but strikingly similar to bank certificates of deposit, directly to consumers.

The two big GSEs also compete with insurance companies. Traditionally, mortgage life and disability insurance policies have been the domain of private insurers, but since the late 1990s, the government has authorized the GSEs to offer such policies to first-time home buyers.

Setting a Pattern for Other GSEs?

Some economists worry that Fannie Mae and Freddie Mac are setting a bad example that other GSEs are only too eager to follow. Since 1996, the Federal Agricultural Mortgage Corporation (or "Farmer Mac") has increased its financing for agricultural loans, most of them originated by small rural banks, by more than 400 percent, to a total amount in excess of $3 billion. Another issuer of mortgage-backed securities, the General National Mortgage Association (GNMA, or "Ginnie Mae"), has recently made efforts to end its status as purely a government agency so that it can also "privatize" while maintaining its access to government credit guarantees. Some members of Congress have supported Ginnie Mae's efforts, arguing that Fannie Mae and Freddie Mac "need more competition" from other GSEs.

Some observers have concluded that GSEs have become so important that they are "politically immune" from cautious oversight. Indeed, by 2002 the efforts of FM Watch to lobby against further expansion by the GSEs were in disarray, in large part because some FM Watch members themselves had decided to enter into lucrative deals with Fannie Mae and Freddie Mac. Nevertheless, beginning in the summer of 2002, these GSEs came under tougher supervision by the Office of Federal Housing Enterprise Oversight, which now has implemented a complex system of regulations intended to help reduce the risk of financial meltdowns at the two huge institutions.

Table 10-1 The Top Ten Debt Issues of the 1990s and Early 2000s.

Fannie Mae and Freddie Mac accounted for five of the top ten debt issues.

Issuer	$ Billions
Fannie Mae	$11.5
Fannie Mae	10.0
Deutsche Telekom	9.5
Ford	8.6
Fannie Mae	8.0
AT&T	8.0
RJR Holdings Capital	6.1
WorldCom	6.1
Freddie Mac	6.0
Freddie Mac	6.0

SOURCE: Office of Federal Housing Enterprise Oversight.

Research Project

How might the existence of Fannie Mae and Freddie Mac help to make the mortgage market more liquid? If their activities do contribute to greater liquidity of the mortgage market, how could this bring about lower mortgage rates? Is there any way that the activities of these GSEs might affect the volatility of mortgage lending or of mortgage rates?

Web Resources

1. What are the most recent examples of Fannie Mae's and Freddie Mac's involvement in financial markets outside the traditional boundaries of their mortgage-related activities? Take a look at recent issues of "The GSE Report," which is available at the home page of FM Watch, http://www.fmwatch.org.

2. In what ways does the federal Department of Housing and Urban Development oversee and supervise the activities of Fannie Mae and Freddie Mac? Find out at http://www.hud.gov/offices/hsg/gsc/gse.cfm.

Chapter Summary

1. Securities Market Institutions: These are investment banks, brokers, and dealers. Investment banks help to guarantee securities offerings of firms by underwriting those securities, meaning that they buy or have options to buy those securities. Brokers make securities market trades for their customers, and dealers seek to profit from buying instruments at low prices and selling them at higher prices. Most of the largest brokerage firms are also dealers. The main government agency that regulates these institutions is the Securities and Exchange Commission, which requires them to register with the government, disclose information about their activities, and follow prescribed trading rules.

2. Insurance Companies: These financial institutions intermediate significant asymmetric-information problems associated with providing financial guarantees against possible future contingencies. Insurance companies tend to specialize either in life insurance or in property-casualty insurance. States are the chief regulators of these companies' activities.

3. Pension Funds: These institutions manage the retirement savings of many employed U.S. residents. The accumulations in noncontributory pension funds come only from employers, but in contributory pension funds employees also can add to their pension savings. Terminally funded pensions have sufficient savings accumulated to fully pay benefits to employees when they reach retirement, whereas pay-as-you-go pension funds depend on current earnings of employers to fund benefit payments to current retirees. As the baby boom generation has matured, pension funds have grown dramatically. Also contributing to this growth have been the growing flexibility of pension plans and the deferment of taxes on current allocations.

4. Finance Companies: These financial institutions have found their niche in lending to borrowers that are either too small or too uncreditworthy to qualify to issue their own debt instruments or to borrow from other financial institutions such as commercial banks.

5. Mutual Funds and Hedge Funds: Mutual funds, which are public companies that pool savings of shareholders for the purchase of a mix of financial instruments, differ across two dimensions. Commission payments to marketers of load funds reduce shareholders' returns, whereas those who hold shares in no-load funds simply pay fixed management fees. Closed-end funds do not permit shareholders to redeem their shares at current market values, while open-end funds do permit such redemptions. Hedge funds are limited partnerships that are not public companies and hence are relatively unregulated institutions, despite their propensity to experience significant losses in recent years.

Questions and Problems

(Answers to odd-numbered questions and problems may be found on the Web at **http://money.swcollege.com** under "Student Resources.")

1. Explain why best efforts deals in investment banking now apply primarily for firms whose creditworthiness has not yet been proved, whereas firm commitment underwriting is common for firms with proven track records. In light of your explanation, can you also hypothesize why best efforts deals are much less common today than they were in the past?

2. What is the difference between a broker and a dealer? Why do you suppose that firms commonly do both kinds of business?

3. What would a broker-dealer give up to be a specialist? What would such a firm gain? In light of your answers, can you surmise why firms that trade large volumes of securities each day are especially likely to be specialists?

4. Many insurance companies will not extend life insurance to individuals who have received treatment for depression. Why do you suppose that companies have this restriction in their life insurance policies?

5. Contrast the pros and cons, from a consumer's standpoint, of term versus whole life insurance.

6. As we discussed, the Pension Benefit Guaranty Corporation (PBGC) insures all pensions with tax-deferred contributions. Some critics believe that the creation of the PBGC helped encourage the growth of pensions and, more specifically, growth in the share of pay-as-you-go pensions. Does this argument make sense to you? Explain your reasoning.

7. A number of small-town banks in rural areas complain that they are at a competitive disadvantage when farmers consider borrowing from them or from the government-supported Farm Credit System. In your view, does this argument have any merit? Explain.

8. A number of economists have predicted that after the bulk of the baby boomers retire and begin drawing on pensions, there will be a big wave of sell-offs of financial assets as pension funds convert assets to cash to fund pension payouts to retirees. Included would be sales of mortgage-backed securities issued by government-backed agencies. These economists think that the likely result will be a big decline in the market value of these securities. Assuming that this prediction turns out to be true, are FNMA securities truly "risk-free" for those who hold them? [Hint: Consider who bears the risk of FNMA securities.]

9. Evaluate the various factors that an individual saver must take into account when choosing among mutual funds. In light of the discussions of mutual funds in this chapter and of portfolio management in Chapter 7, should a wealthy saver hold shares in more than one mutual fund? Explain your reasoning.

10. Some hedge funds are officially based outside the United States, in locales such as the Caribbean islands. This has led many to question whether expanding federal regulations to include the activities of hedge funds would have much effect because many funds based in the United States could respond by simply moving their operations offshore. In light of this argument, do you believe hedge funds should nonetheless be subjected to greater governmental oversight? Why or why not?

Before the Test

Test your understanding of the material covered in this chapter by taking the Chapter 10 interactive quiz at http://money.swcollege.com.

Online Application

Internet URL: http://www.mfea.com

Title: Mutual Fund Investor's Center: Education Alliance

Navigation: Begin at the home page of the Mutual Fund Investor's Center (**http://www.mfea.com**). Select "Investment Strategies," and from the drop-down menu click on "Asset Allocation." Then click on "Model Portfolios."

Application: Read the article, and then answer the following questions:

1. Based on the discussion of "Aggressive Growth Funds," would you anticipate that the returns earned by these mutual funds are typically more or less variable than the returns on most other mutual funds? Why?

2. Based on the discussion of "Money Market Mutual Funds," would you anticipate that the returns earned by these mutual funds are typically higher or lower than the returns on most other mutual funds? Why?

For Group Study and Analysis: Separate into groups, and ask each group to rate the relative expected return and risk that it would anticipate for each type of mutual fund discussed in the article. Compare the groups' ratings. Then compare them with those provided in the table at the conclusion of the article.

Selected References and Further Reading

Ackert, Lucy, and Bryan Church. "Competitiveness and Price Setting in Dealer Markets." Federal Reserve Bank of Atlanta *Economic Review,* Third Quarter 1998, pp. 4–11.

American Council of Life Insurance. *Life Insurance Fact Book*. Published annually.

Brewer, Elija, Hesna Genay, William E. Jackson, and Paula Worthington. "Performance and Access to Government Guarantees: The Case of Small Business Investment Companies." Federal Reserve Bank of Chicago *Economic Perspectives* 20 (September/October 1996): 2–15.

Fortune, Peter. "Mutual Funds, Part I: Reshaping the American Financial System." Federal Reserve Bank of Boston *New England Economic Review,* July/August 1997, pp. 45–72.

_______. "Mutual Funds, Part II: Fund Flows and Security Returns." Federal Reserve Bank of Boston *New England Economic Review,* January/February 1998, pp. 3–22.

Insurance Information Institute. *The Fact Book*. Published annually.

Marquis, Milton. "What's Different about Banks—Still?" Federal Reserve Bank of San Francisco *Economic Letter,* No. 2001–09, April 6, 2001.

Robinson, Kenneth, and Eric F. J. Ochel. "Banks and Mutual Funds." Federal Reserve Bank of Dallas *Financial Industry Studies*, December 1993.

Sigalla, Fiona. "Insurance: A Risk to the Economy?" Federal Reserve Bank of Dallas *Southwest Economy,* July/August 2002, pp. 1–6.

Simons, Katerina. "Risk-Adjusted Performance of Mutual Funds." Federal Reserve Bank of Boston *New England Economic Review,* September/October 1998, pp. 33–48.

MoneyXtra

moneyxtra! Log on to the MoneyXtra Web site now (http://moneyxtra.swcollege.com) for additional learning resources such as practice quizzes, case studies, readings, and additional economic applications.

Unit III
Depository Financial Institutions

CONTENTS

Chapter 11

Depository Financial Institutions

Fundamental Issues

1. What are the historical origins of modern banking institutions?
2. How did today's segmented groupings of depository institutions arise?
3. What are the key assets of commercial banks?
4. What are the key liabilities of commercial banks?
5. How do savings institutions differ from commercial banks?
6. How do credit unions raise and allocate their funds?

Suppose that you are contemplating opening checking and savings accounts at a depository institution. You also anticipate applying for a credit card, and perhaps a loan, within the next year or two. As you shop around, you discover that the average interest rate that credit unions charge on credit cards is usually at least four percentage points lower than the average rate on a bank credit card. Credit unions also typically charge an average of at least two percentage points less than banks to make new-car loans.

Furthermore, credit unions pay an average yield nearly a full percentage point higher than the average yield paid by commercial banks on money market savings accounts. On certificates of deposit, credit unions normally pay an average yield about half a percentage point in excess of the average yield offered by banks. About 70 percent of credit unions offer free checking without regard to balance, as compared with only about 30 percent of banks.

Finally, credit unions are even a better deal for people who are irresponsible in handling their funds. On average, credit unions charge just over $2 less than banks for a bounced check.

Given all these advantages that the nation's more than 10,000 credit unions have over commercial banks, why are total assets at banks about twelve times larger than the aggregate assets of credit unions? To answer this question, you must understand what distinguishes commercial banks from credit unions. This is one of the several issues concerning depository financial institutions that this chapter addresses.

The Origins and Global Development of Depository Institutions

Bullion: Uncoined gold or silver used as money.

Fractional-reserve banking: A system in which banks hold reserves equal to less than the amount of total deposits.

Depository financial institutions have existed since the days of the earliest human civilizations. Consequently, their evolution has spanned the time that organized societies have inhabited the earth.

Goldsmith Bankers

As discussed in Chapter 1, inconveniences associated with barter ultimately led people to use commodities, particularly gold and silver, as money. Both metals were relatively scarce and highly valued. Both were easy to divide into units of various sizes so that people could make change.

GOLDSMITHS AND BULLION In the earliest times, people used uncoined gold and silver, known as **bullion,** to make transactions, but the purity of bullion often is not readily discernible, so its users were exposed to asymmetric-information problems. Goldsmiths specialized in reducing the extent of these asymmetric-information problems. Parties to a transaction would pay a goldsmith to weigh bullion and to assess its purity. Many goldsmiths would issue the holder of bullion a certificate attesting to the bullion's weight and gold or silver content. Other goldsmiths went a step further. To provide the holder of bullion with ready proof of the bullion's weight and purity, they produced standardized weights of gold or silver that they imprinted with a seal of authenticity. These standardized units were the earliest *coins*.

BULLION DEPOSITS AND FRACTIONAL-RESERVE BANKING Eventually, some goldsmiths simplified the process further by issuing paper notes indicating that the bearers held gold or silver of given weights and purities on deposit with the goldsmiths. Then the bearers of these notes could transfer the notes to others in exchange for goods and services. These notes were the first *paper money.* The gold and silver held on deposit with goldsmiths were the first *bank deposits.* Indeed, by providing depository services, these goldsmiths became the first bankers.

Once goldsmiths became depository institutions, it was only a matter of time before they took the final step toward modern banking by becoming lenders. Goldsmiths began to notice that withdrawals of bullion relative to new bullion deposits were fairly predictable. Therefore, as long as the goldsmiths held *reserves* of gold and silver to cover expected bullion withdrawals, they could lend paper notes in excess of the amounts of bullion that they actually kept on hand. They could charge interest on the loans by requiring repayment in bullion in excess of the value of the notes that they issued.

By lending funds in excess of the reserves of money (gold and silver bullion) that they actually possessed, these goldsmith-bankers developed the earliest form of **fractional-reserve banking.** As long as economic conditions were stable and the goldsmiths managed their accounts wisely, those who held the goldsmiths' notes would be satisfied with this arrangement. But in bad times or in instances when a few goldsmiths overextended themselves, many noteholders might show up at the same time demanding the gold or silver bullion. These were the earliest "bank runs," and if too many noteholders demanded bullion at the same time, the businesses of the goldsmith-bankers failed. Bearers of the notes would discover the notes were nearly worthless pieces of paper.

The Roots of Modern Banking

The first goldsmith-bankers cannot be traced with certainty to any specific time or place. There is evidence that such activities took place in Mesopotamia sometime during the first millennium B.C. In ancient Greece goldsmith operations existed in Delphi, Didyma, and Olympia at least as early as the seventh century B.C. By the sixth century B.C., banking was a well-developed feature of the economy of Athens.

Banking also arose elsewhere in the Mediterranean world, in cities such as Jerusalem, and further east in Persia. Banking facilitated trade because merchants who shipped goods to faraway locations typically needed loans to fund their operations. After receiving payment from the purchasers of their goods, the merchants then would repay those who had provided loan financing. These lenders became known as *merchant bankers*. Merchant banking ultimately became a linchpin of the trade linking the principalities of the Roman Empire.

The Italian Merchant Bankers The modern term *bank* derives from the merchants' bench, or *banco,* on which money changed hands in the marketplaces of medieval Italy. The term *bankruptcy* refers to the "breaking of the bench" that occurred when an Italian merchant banker overextended, then experienced a run on his notes, and failed. Most Italian merchant bankers avoided this fate, however. Indeed, during the medieval period of the twelfth and thirteenth centuries A.D. merchant bankers flourished throughout Italy.

By the time of the Italian Renaissance during the fifteenth and sixteenth centuries, merchant bankers such as the Medici family of Florence had accumulated enormous wealth and political power. Although these Italian merchant bankers directed some of their wealth to financing the fabulous art of masters such as Michelangelo and Leonardo da Vinci, ultimately they squandered much of it by building armies and conducting wars over territory and riches.

The Advent of Modern Banking While most of the Italian merchant bankers quarreled, those originally from the Lombardy region of Italy worked to maintain their merchant banking operations in other European locales, such as London and Berlin. In London, the Italian merchant bankers became such an important fixture that the city's financial dealings were centered around Lombard Street, which remains the financial heart of the city today. The German central bank, the Deutsche Bundesbank, called one interest rate at which it lent funds to private banks the *Lombard rate.* Even after the Italian city-states fell into political disarray, Italian merchant bankers hailing from Genoa financed the activities of the rising Hapsburg Empire of seventeenth- and eighteenth-century Europe.

Others in Europe eventually copied the banking practices of the Italian merchant bankers, however. The banking business took on three key features. First, as in the days of the earliest goldsmiths, banks took deposits from customers and maintained accounts on their behalf. Second, banks managed payments on behalf of customers by collecting and paying checks, notes, and other "banking currency." Finally, like the merchant banks of old, these modern banks provided advances to customers in the form of loans. The interest on these loans and the fees that banks charged for accounting and deposit services were the banks' sources of revenues and, ultimately, profits.

1. What are the historical origins of modern banking institutions?
Banks originated in the earliest civilizations as depositories for gold and silver. They evolved into merchant banking firms in medieval Italy. These firms, like modern banks, maintained deposit accounts for, processed payments on behalf of, and made loans to their customers.

Early American Banking

Naturally, before the American Revolution (1775–1783), British banking firms financed most trading between the American colonies and Britain. When the rebellion against British rule cut the ties to British banking firms, the former colonies were left in a financial bind. Although a few finance companies operated by Americans existed when the Revolution began in 1775, there were no independent banks on American soil. This complicated wartime financing, and the Continental Congress had to borrow from governments and bankers in France, Holland, and Spain and to issue currency in the form of Continental dollars, or *Continentals*. By the end of the war in 1783, the Continental Congress had printed so many Continentals that each was worth one five-hundredth (1/500th) of its face value.

PRIVATE VERSUS PUBLIC BANKING IN THE NEW REPUBLIC In 1781 Robert Morris, a Philadelphia financier, spearheaded the establishment of the Bank of North America. This bank was chartered by the Continental Congress and was the first nationally chartered bank on the North American continent. After 1783, however, the Philadelphia-based bank operated under a Pennsylvania charter, though for a time other states, including New York and Massachusetts, granted it charters as well. The national government's role in banking expanded after the individual states formally joined the United States of America. Alexander Hamilton, the first secretary of the Treasury of the new federal republic, looked to the Bank of North America as an example of how to establish a federally chartered bank, which he proposed as the First Bank of the United States. President George Washington sided with his Treasury secretary and permitted the bill authorizing a twenty-year charter for the First Bank to become law. Washington's action set the precedent for a **dual banking system,** in which American banks could receive either federal or state charters.

Dual banking system: A regulatory structure in which either states or the federal government can grant bank charters.

THE SECOND BANK OF THE UNITED STATES When the charter of the First Bank of the United States expired in 1811, Congress did not renew the charter. This arguably was not a good decision. Congress declared war on Britain the next year and found itself without a ready means of financing the war effort. This experience convinced Congress to issue a twenty-year federal charter for the Second Bank of the United States in 1816.

A dual banking system with one large national bank and many smaller state banks continued through 1836. But in 1819 many people in emerging states such as Kentucky and Tennessee blamed the Second Bank for a financial panic that brought ruin to many farmers and landholders. Among those who developed a deep distrust of the Second Bank was President Andrew Jackson, who vetoed an 1832 bill authorizing recharter of the Second Bank. After winning reelection in that year, Jackson removed all federal government deposits from the Second Bank and placed them with state banks. The Second Bank ceased to exist four years later. For twenty-six years, the federal government's direct involvement in banking was suspended.

The Free-Banking Period

From 1837 until 1863, there were two types of banks. One group consisted of banks operated by or on behalf of the state governments. As we noted in Chapter 2, the other group consisted of private banks incorporated under free-banking laws enacted in a number of states, including New York, Michigan, Wisconsin, and Alabama. Historians and economists now call this the *free-banking era* of American history.

Traditional historical accounts of the free-banking era focused on the so-called wildcat banks—unscrupulous operations that printed notes that they never intended to redeem (see Chapter 2)—and on the prevalence of counterfeiting. Indeed, by the end of the 1860s, more than 5,000 separate types of counterfeit notes were in circulation.

In recent decades, however, many historians and economists have reexamined the free-banking period in light of hard evidence that they have unearthed from the accounting ledgers of free banks and state examiners. This evidence indicates that in many states, "free banks" were not very free. Several states required banks to hold risky bonds that the states themselves issued. They also enacted laws prohibiting banks from branching within states or across state lines.

In states that subjected free banks to fewer restrictions of this type, instability was less pronounced. Some states, and notably New York, subjected free banks to state audits to assure depositors that the banks were soundly managed. In such states the notes of free banks were quite safe, and very few depositors experienced losses. Furthermore, bank failures and closings in other states with less soundly structured arrangements typically did not cause difficulties for free banks in states with better designed free-banking laws.

Consequently, the mainstream view among today's economic historians is that free banking ultimately might have been a more successful experiment if events had followed a different course. But the Civil War permanently altered the course of American banking, much as it forever changed the political landscape.

The Two-Tiered Banking System

In 1863 Congress passed the National Banking Act, which granted federal charters to a number of banks (all within the Union states) and, as amended in 1864, imposed a federal tax on all notes issued by state banks (mostly based in Confederate states). This act also imposed reserve requirements on the deposits of banks and prohibited **branch banking,** or the operation of more than one depository institution office in alternative geographic locations, by state-chartered banks. It also required national banks to back their notes by posting government bonds with the Comptroller of the Currency, a U.S. Treasury official who was designated the chief supervisor of national banks.

The National Banking Act had far-reaching consequences for American banking. First, it ended the free-banking experiment. Second, for the first time in the nation's history, the federal government became directly involved in the affairs of most of the nation's banks. Third, the act laid the groundwork for today's *two-tiered* system of both state and nationally chartered banks. Dual banking became a permanent feature of the American scene.

Branch banking: A depository institution organizational structure in which institutions operate offices at a number of geographic locations.

Mutual ownership: A depository institution organizational structure in which depositors own the institution.

The Rise of Thrift Institutions

In the fifth century B.C., Xenophon, a Greek soldier and historian, proposed the formation of a publicly owned goldsmith institution for the city-state of Athens. He envisioned the mutual sharing of interest returns by all citizens of the city. Xenophon's dream was not realized, but it foreshadowed the development of **mutual ownership** of savings institutions, or the ownership of such institutions by all depositors. In an echo of Xenophon's idea, in 1697 Daniel Defoe, the author of *Robinson Crusoe,* proposed the formation of mutually owned institutions to promote saving among working-class and poor individuals in England. A number of years later, in 1765, the first institution of this type was established in England. By the early 1800s, such institutions had spread to Scotland and the United States, where they became known as *savings banks.* These were the first so-called *thrift institutions.*

A related type of savings institution also arose in England. This was the "building society," in which individuals pooled their savings to make loans to society members, who then used the funds to finance the construction of new homes. In 1831 a Philadelphia group formed the first American building society, which was called a *savings and loan association.* Within a couple of decades, most savings and loan associations were accepting deposits from the general public, and the number of such associations expanded dramatically throughout the remainder of the nineteenth century. By the 1930s both savings banks and savings and loan associations had become the mainstay lenders in the market for residential mortgages. Today, we refer to savings and loan associations and savings banks collectively as savings institutions.

Credit unions began in Germany and Italy in the mid-nineteenth century. They were cooperative institutions serving closed memberships of individuals with common interests. Some credit unions were associated with churches, while others had memberships drawn from fraternal orders. Most, however, drew their members from employees of specific firms. Credit unions first appeared in Canada at the start of the twentieth century, and the first U.S. credit union was set up in 1909.

Until the late 1980s, savings institutions and credit unions were commonly grouped together in the broad category of *thrift institutions.* By the early 1990s, however, many savings institutions in the United States had failed, while most credit unions remained solvent. Because of their differing performances and prospects, the collective term *thrift institutions* is not used as widely as in the past to refer to these two groups of institutions.

Bank run: An unexpected series of cash withdrawals at a depository institution that can induce its failure.

Segmented Banking in the Twentieth Century

Like the Civil War, the Great Depression of the 1930s was a defining period for American depository institutions. Congress responded to the events of the Great Depression by involving the federal government even more directly in the affairs of commercial banks, savings institutions, and credit unions.

BANK RUNS One key event associated with the Great Depression was a series of bank failures and **bank runs,** or widespread deposit withdrawals at banks that often induced their failure, throughout much of the United States. Congress responded with legislation intended to sharply restrict the ability of banks to undertake risky activities. In 1933 Congress passed the Glass-Steagall Act, which separated commercial and investment banking. This legislation, which was significantly scaled back in 1999 (see Chapters 14 and 15), also prohibited commercial banks from paying interest on checking deposits, authorized the regulation of interest on bank savings deposits, and enacted an elaborate system of federal insurance of bank deposits under the administration of the Federal Deposit Insurance Corporation.

EXTENSIVE FEDERAL REGULATION Another problem during the Great Depression was that real estate values fell sharply as many people halted their mortgage payments. This led to widespread foreclosures on mortgage loans by savings institutions and of consumer loans by credit unions. But such foreclosures left the thrift institutions holding properties with depressed values, causing many savings institutions to declare bankruptcy. Congress responded with a series of laws intended to shore up the shaky thrift industry; this legislation included the Home Owners Loan Act of 1933, which established a federal charter for savings institutions, and the National Housing Act of 1934, which created a system of deposit insurance for savings institutions. In 1934 Congress also enacted the Federal Credit Union Act, which authorized federal charters for credit unions.

Consequently, within a very short interval in the 1930s, the U.S. government became closely involved in the business practices of all depository financial institutions. The government regulated interest rates, restricted banking practices, and insured bank and thrift institution deposits. Federal laws also formally segmented depository institutions into formal categories: commercial banks, savings institutions, and credit unions. Essentially, these congressional actions solidified the separate categories of depository institutions that remain with us today.

2. How did today's segmented groupings of depository institutions arise? The dual, or combined state and federal, structure of U.S. banking has its roots in decisions that the first Congress and President Washington made in the first years of the republic. After later experiments with free banking at the state level, Congress reinstituted dual banking during the Civil War. Savings institutions and credit unions have always had specialized niches, but Congress solidified the distinctions among commercial banks, savings institutions, and credit unions in a series of laws passed in the 1930s.

Commercial Banks

A commercial bank is a depository institution that faces few legal restrictions on its powers to lend to businesses and can legally issue checking deposits from which holders may write unlimited numbers of checks. There currently are more than 8,000 commercial banks in the United States, and they are the predominant depository financial institutions in the country. (In Utah, an institution that technically is not a commercial bank is thriving by mimicking the functions of commercial banks; see on the following page *Policy Focus: Looking to Become a Financial Center? Create a New Kind of Depository Institution.*)

Asset: Anything owned by a person or business that has a market value.

Commercial and industrial (C&I) loans: Loans that commercial banks and other depository institutions make to businesses.

Commercial Bank Assets

For any individual or firm, including a banking firm, an **asset** is any item legally owned by that person or business that has a market value. For instance, when a commercial bank makes a loan to a business, that loan represents a legal obligation of the business to repay the loan principal and interest to the lending bank within a specified period. Consequently, the loan is an asset of the bank.

Table 11-1 lists the *combined* total assets of *all* domestically chartered commercial banks in the United States. Three important classifications of assets are listed in Table 11-1. We consider each in turn.

LOANS A key reason for the existence of banks is that they specialize in handling asymmetric-information problems in lending markets. Because lending is the bread-and-butter business of commercial banks, loans compose the predominant category of assets held by commercial banks. There are four important loan categories.

Commercial and Industrial Loans Those loans that commercial banks and other depository institutions make to businesses are **commercial and industrial (C&I) loans.** Businesses use funding from C&I loans to meet day-to-day cash

Table 11-1 Commercial Bank Assets ($ Billions), July 31, 2002

Commercial & industrial loans	$ 990.2	14.8%
Consumer loans	568.7	8.5%
Real estate loans	1,878.7	28.0%
Interbank loans	305.9	4.6%
Other loans	284.1	4.2%
Total loans	$4,027.6	60.1%
U.S. government securities	$ 932.2	13.9%
Other securities	683.9	10.2%
Total securities	$1,616.1	24.1%
Cash assets	$ 304.7	4.5%
Other assets	$ 755.0	11.3%
Total assets	**$6,703.4**	**100.0%**

SOURCE: Board of Governors of the Federal Reserve System, H.8 (510) *Statistical Release.*

GLOBAL | POLICY Focus | CYBER | MANAGEMENT

Looking to Become a Financial Center? Create a New Kind of Depository Institution

Since 1995, assets held by various forms of financial intermediaries in the state of Utah have multiplied by a factor of almost fifty. Financial institutions in other western states, such as California, are scrambling to find ways to induce customers not to move their funds to Salt Lake City and other Utah locales.

What lies behind this development is a special kind of "nonbank bank" that is unique to Utah, called an *industrial loan corporation,* or *ILC.* These institutions first arose in the state in the 1920s, when they specialized in lending to fledgling companies trying to establish niches in then-unproven western U.S. markets. When some of those markets boomed, so did the fortunes of many of the Utah ILCs.

Today the deposits of ILCs are federally insured, but federal laws exempt them from many of the regulatory burdens faced by commercial banks, savings institutions, and credit unions. Although ILCs must submit to basic safety and soundness examinations to maintain their access to federal deposit insurance, they are able to avoid a number of other forms of federal regulatory oversight. As a consequence, ILCs can engage in certain types of businesses that are out of bounds for traditional depository institutions, even though ILCs offer the same basic depository and lending services. For instance, ILCs are able to operate direct-mail services in all fifty U.S. states without federal supervision of their interstate activities.

Not all ILCs operating today are home-grown Utah institutions. The two largest ILCs are operated by Merrill Lynch and American Express, and several other companies including General Electric and BMW also own ILCs. Microsoft and Wal-Mart have explored the possibility of opening their own ILCs in Utah. At present, ILCs appear to be a back-door approach for nondepository financial institutions and nonfinancial firms to enter the traditional domains of depository institutions. Providing an environment where ILCs can flourish has also enabled Utah to emerge as a financial center in the western United States.

For Critical Analysis: How might exemptions from certain forms of federal regulation assist Utah's ILCs in their efforts to attract customers from traditional depository institutions located in other parts of the United States?

needs or to finance purchases of plants and equipment. Businesses typically must secure C&I loans with **collateral,** or assets that a borrower pledges as security in the event it fails to fulfill its obligation to repay the principal and interest on a loan. A lending bank may seize the collateral, or a portion of it, in the event of nonpayment. Though many C&I loans require collateral, it is not uncommon for some C&I loans to extremely creditworthy borrowers to be uncollateralized.

All told, C&I loans account for almost 15 percent of total bank assets. Such loans have varying degrees of default risk and liquidity. In recent years banks have worked hard to increase the liquidity of their C&I loan holdings, as we shall discuss in greater detail in Chapter 13.

Collateral: Assets that a borrower pledges as security in case it should fail to repay the principal or interest on a loan.

Consumer Loans Commercial banks also extend credit to individuals. These loans are *consumer loans.* About a third of such loans typically finance purchases of automobiles. Many individuals also obtain consumer loans for the purchase of mobile homes, durable consumer goods such as household appliances, or materials for home improvements.

Banks typically issue consumer loans for purchase of autos or mobile homes in the form of **installment credit.** Under an installment credit agreement, the individual borrower agrees to repay the principal and interest in equal periodic payments. Payment schedules for consumer loans typically span one to five years. Interest rates on these loans usually are fixed and initially are set relative to the prime rate or an index of capital market rates, such as an index of Treasury rates. Some consumer loans, however, have adjustable interest rates.

Included among consumer loans is **revolving credit,** which refers to bank lending to individuals up to some preset limit, or ceiling. Under a revolving credit agreement, consumers have automatic approval to borrow as long as they do not exceed their specified credit ceilings. They also may pay off their loan balance at any time. Credit cards are the most widely used form of consumer revolving credit.

Real Estate Loans A third major type of bank lending consists of *real estate loans,* which are loans that banks make to finance purchases of real property, buildings, and fixtures (items permanently attached to real estate) by businesses and individuals. Banks make the bulk of their real estate loans to businesses. In the 1980s and 1990s, real estate lending became a relatively more important business for commercial banks. The share of total commercial bank assets held as real estate loans rose from around 17 percent in 1985 to the 28 percent figure in Table 11-1 on page 247. Much of the growth in real estate lending has been fueled by increases in *home equity loans,* which are loans to individual property owners that are secured by the owners' shares of title to real estate.

Interbank (Federal Funds) Loans As discussed earlier, banks extend interbank loans in the federal funds market. Most federal funds loans have one-day maturities, but some, called **term federal funds,** have maturities exceeding one day. Banks typically lend these funds in large-denomination units ranging from $200,000 to well over $1,000,000 per loan. Although large banks both lend and borrow federal funds, smaller banks are predominantly federal funds lenders.

SECURITIES *U.S. government securities,* including Treasury bills, notes, and bonds, are a key type of security held by commercial banks. Commercial bank holdings of these securities account for nearly 14 percent of all assets. The other group of securities is *state and municipal bonds.* These make up the bulk of the "other securities" category in Table 11-1, or about 10 percent of bank assets.

CASH ASSETS The most liquid assets that banks hold are **cash assets,** which are the bank assets that function as media of exchange. One component of cash assets is **vault cash,** which is currency that commercial banks hold at their offices to meet depositors' needs for cash withdrawals on a day-to-day basis. Vault cash typically accounts for nearly 2 percent of total bank assets.

A second type of cash asset is **reserve deposits** at Federal Reserve banks. These are checking accounts that commercial banks hold with the Federal Reserve bank in their geographic district. Reserve deposits usually account for about 1 percent of total bank assets. Banks write checks out of or wire-transfer funds from these reserve deposit accounts when they make federal funds loans, purchase repurchase agreements, or buy securities. Funds held as reserve deposits also count toward meeting the Federal Reserve's legal reserve requirements.

Installment credit: Loans to individual consumers that entail periodic repayments of principal and interest.

Revolving credit: Loans to individuals that permit them to borrow automatically up to specified limits and to repay the balance of the loan at any time.

Term federal funds: Interbank loans with maturities exceeding one day.

Cash assets: Depository institution assets that function as media of exchange.

Vault cash: Currency that a depository institution holds on location to honor cash withdrawals by depositors.

Reserve deposits: Deposit accounts that depository institutions maintain at Federal Reserve banks.

Correspondent balances: Deposit accounts that banks hold with other banks.

Cash items in process of collection: Checks deposited with a bank for immediate credit but not yet cleared for final payment to the bank; usually referred to simply as "cash items."

Liability: A legally enforceable claim on the assets of a business or individual.

Net worth: The excess of assets over liabilities, or equity capital.

Equity capital: The excess of assets over liabilities, or net worth.

A third form of cash asset is **correspondent balances,** which normally account for another 1 percent of bank assets. These are funds that banks hold on deposit with other private commercial banks called *correspondents.*

The final type of cash asset is **cash items in process of collection** or, more simply, "cash items." These are checks or other cash drafts that the bank lists as deposited for immediate credit but that the bank may need to cancel if payment on the items is not received. Whenever you deposit or cash a personal or payroll check at a bank, the bank lists that check as a cash item until it "clears" and the bank has received payment on the check from the issuer's financial institution. Cash items in process of collection usually amount to about 1.5 percent of total commercial bank assets.

3. What are the key assets of commercial banks? Bank assets fall into three main categories: loans, securities, and cash assets. Loans include commercial and industrial loans, real estate loans, consumer loans, and very short-term loans that banks make in the federal funds market or through purchases of repurchase agreements. Securities include U.S. government securities and municipal and state bonds. Cash assets include vault cash, reserve deposits at Federal Reserve banks, correspondent balances, and cash items in the process of collection.

On the Web

Do you want to keep up on the latest news about events affecting the banking industry? If so, read the "Daily Newsbytes" at the American Bankers Association home page, http://www.aba.com.

Trends in Bank Asset Allocations Figure 11-1 plots the shares of bank assets allocated to cash assets, securities, and all other assets (loans and miscellaneous other assets) at various intervals since 1961. As the figure indicates, there has been a general downward trend in relative holdings of cash assets.

A similar downward trend also existed for bank security holdings until the later 1980s. The portion of bank assets held as securities began to drift upward in 1986 and then rose sharply in early 1991. The reason was that between 1990 and 1992 banks curtailed lending fairly dramatically. As you can see in Figure 11-1, "other assets," nearly all of which were loans, declined during this period as the portion of assets allocated to securities increased. Many economists have classified this period as a *credit crunch,* in which banks are willing to lend only to their most creditworthy customers (we shall have more to say about the causes of this crunch in Chapter 14).

Commercial Bank Liabilities and Equity Capital

Any **liability** is the dollar value of a legal claim on the assets of an individual or business at a given point in time. In the case of a bank loan to a business, the business legally owes funds to the bank, so the loan is a liability of the business. But banks have liabilities as well. For instance, if you have a checking or savings deposit at a bank, then the bank owes you the funds in the account. While you regard the deposit as an asset, the bank views it as a liability.

If you were to add up estimates of your own assets and liabilities and subtract liabilities from assets, you would come up with an estimate of your **net worth,** or the net amount of total funds that you owe to no one. A synonym for net worth is **equity capital.** A commercial bank's equity capital is its net worth, or the amount by which its assets exceed its liabilities.

Figure 11-1 Commercial Bank Asset Allocations.

During the past four decades, there has been a general downward trend in commercial banks' holdings of cash assets relative to total assets. Over the same period, there has been a general upward trend in proportionate holdings of loans and other assets. The portion of assets held as securities increased in the early 1990s, when banks noticeably reduced lending in favor of security holdings.

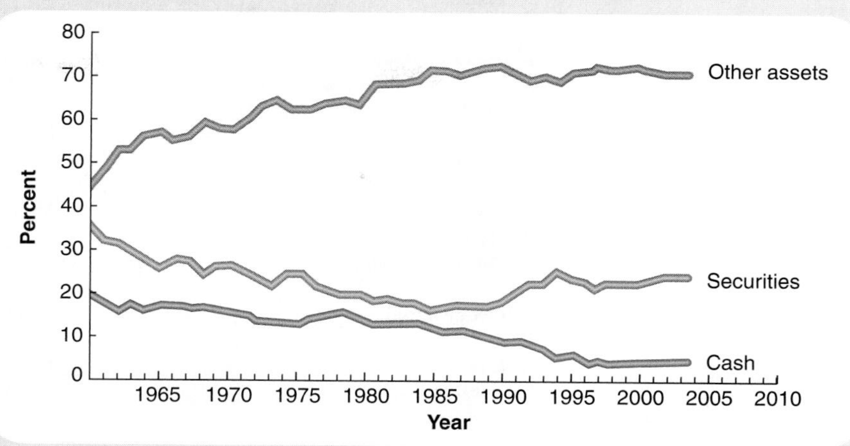

SOURCE: *Federal Reserve Bulletin* and *H.8(510) Statistical Release*, Board of Governors of the Federal Reserve System, various issues.

Table 11-2 on the next page lists the *combined* total liabilities and equity capital of *all* domestically chartered commercial banks in the United States. Note that the dollar amount of total liabilities and equity capital in Table 11-2 is exactly equal to the dollar amount of total assets in Table 11-1 on page 247. This illustrates an important accounting definition: total bank assets must always equal the sum of total liabilities and equity capital.

NONCONTROLLABLE LIABILITIES Bankers typically classify their liabilities into two categories: noncontrollable and controllable. The term **noncontrollable liabilities** is something of a misnomer in that a bank certainly could decide not to issue any particular liability. The idea behind this term, however, is that once a bank issues one of these liabilities to a customer, the *customer*, and not the bank, has considerable discretion concerning how large the customer's deposit holdings will be. It is in this sense that a bank regards such a liability as "noncontrollable."

There are four key types of noncontrollable liabilities. One is *transactions deposits*, which, as discussed in Chapter 1, include demand deposits and other checkable deposits such as NOW (negotiable order of withdrawal) accounts. Demand deposits are non-interest-bearing accounts, while banks pay market interest rates on other checkable deposits. Transactions deposits account for almost 10 percent of total bank liabilities and equity capital.

Two other noncontrollable liabilities are *savings deposits* and *small-denomination time deposits*. Savings deposits account for more than 41 percent of total bank liabilities and equity capital. Included among savings deposits are passbook and statement savings accounts typically held by small savers and money market deposit accounts usually held in somewhat larger denominations. Savings deposits have no set maturities. In contrast, small-denomination time deposits have fixed maturities. They have denominations under $100,000.

Noncontrollable liabilities: Liabilities whose dollar amounts bank customers largely determine once banks have issued the liabilities to them.

Table 11-2 **Commercial Bank Liabilities and Equity Capital ($ Billions), July 31, 2002**

Transactions deposits	$ 635.8	9.5%
Small time and savings deposits	2,765.9	41.3%
Large time deposits	1,051.1	15.6%
Total deposits	$4,452.8	66.4%
Borrowings from banks	$ 393.5	5.9%
Other borrowings	897.2	13.4%
Total borrowings	$1,290.7	19.3%
Other liabilities	$ 423.6	6.3%
Equity capital*	$ 536.3	8.0%*
Total liabilities & equity	**$6,703.4**	**100.0%**

*Authors' estimate.

SOURCE: Board of Governors of the Federal Reserve System, *H.8 (510) Statistical Release.*

The last noncontrollable liability is *deferred availability cash items.* These represent payments by banks to other parties that the banks have not yet made but have promised to make or that the banks have made but which have not yet "cleared." Deferred availability cash items are included among the "other liabilities" in Table 11-2.

CONTROLLABLE LIABILITIES AND EQUITY CAPITAL Bankers refer to the remaining liabilities that they issue as **controllable liabilities.** These are liabilities whose amounts the bankers themselves can more readily determine on a monthly, weekly, or even daily basis.

Controllable liabilities: Liabilities whose dollar amounts banks can directly manage.

Large-Denomination Time Deposits Banks raise a significant amount of funds by issuing *large-denomination time deposits.* Many of these are *large-denomination certificates of deposit (CDs)* issued as controllable liabilities. These CDs have denominations above $100,000 and typically fund a significant amount of banks' short-term lending operations. Large CDs pay market interest rates, and many are negotiable. Banks and other depository institutions issue large CDs in a variety of maturities, but most large negotiable CDs have six-month terms and trade actively in the money markets. Banks issue CDs in groups when they feel the timing is best, and banks also determine the denominations of the CDs. All told, large CDs and other large-denomination time deposits account for over 15 percent of bank liabilities and equity capital. (Large banks commonly arrange large CDs through brokers, and lately small banks have become more active in this market; see *Management Focus: Brokered Deposits Catch On at Small Banks.*)

Purchased funds: Very short-term bank borrowings in the money market.

Purchased Funds Bankers often refer to another set of controllable liabilities as **purchased funds.** These are very short-term borrowings in the money market. The most important type of purchased funds is *interbank (federal funds) borrowings,* or commercial bank borrowings from other banks in the federal funds market, which typically account for nearly 6 percent of total bank liabilities and equity capital.

GLOBAL POLICY CYBER MANAGEMENT Focus

Brokered Deposits Catch On at Small Banks

Small commercial banks throughout the United States ran into a big problem beginning in the mid-1990s. The economy was growing, so loan demand was on an upsurge. But in the quiet towns and villages where the banks were located, deposit growth was not keeping pace.

This left small commercial banks with a choice. Either they could remain satisfied with fair to middling growth of their balance sheets, or they could find another source of deposit funds. Since the late 1990s, an increasing number of smaller banks have opted to search for deposit funds outside their communities. Many of these banks are relying upon *brokered deposits*. These are CDs that are marketed regionally or even nationally. As shown in Figure 11-2, brokered deposits at banks with less than $1 billion in assets have increased noticeably during the past few years.

This trend has been somewhat worrisome to bank regulators. The reason is that in regional and national markets, the CDs of small banks compete directly with those issued by larger institutions. Consequently, small banks typically must pay higher rates on brokered deposits compared with the rates they pay in their local communities. Thus, even though acquiring brokered deposits helps the balance sheets of small banks become larger, it also tends to raise their average funding costs.

FOR CRITICAL ANALYSIS: How might the use of brokered deposits expose small commercial banks to greater risks?

Figure 11-2

Brokered Deposits at Small U.S. Commercial Banks.

Banks with total assets of less than $1 billion are increasingly using brokered deposits.

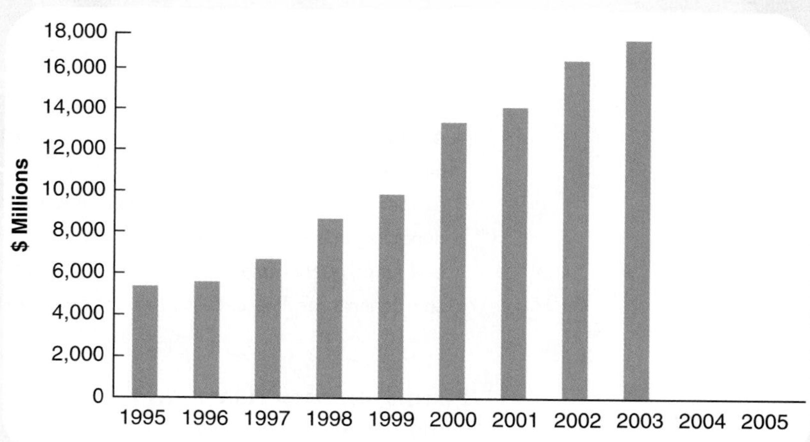

SOURCE: Federal Deposit Insurance Corporation, *Statistics on Banking*, various issues; authors' estimates.

Other Borrowings Three other kinds of purchased funds are included in the "other borrowings" category in Table 11-2. These are *sales of repurchase agreements, borrowings from the Federal Reserve,* and *Eurodollar liabilities*. When a bank sells securities under an agreement to repurchase the securities at a later time and to pay an interest yield on the transaction, it borrows for the length of the agreement. Consequently, sales of repurchase agreements are liabilities. Likewise, banks that borrow federal funds thereby issue new controllable liabilities.

Subordinated notes and debentures: Capital market instruments with maturities in excess of one year that banks issue with the provision that depositors have primary claim to bank assets in the event of failure.

All federally insured commercial banks have the privilege of applying for loans from the Federal Reserve bank in their geographic district. The Federal Reserve permits banks to borrow to meet seasonal fluctuations resulting from agricultural or construction cycles, and it lends to banks during times of acute financial distress that have made the banks illiquid but not bankrupt.

Many large CDs and repurchase agreement sales are dollar-denominated liabilities that banks issue outside U.S. borders. Consequently, these are Eurodollar liabilities of banks, which we discussed earlier in Chapter 3. Eurodollar liabilities are also included in the "other borrowings" category in Table 11-2.

The final kinds of controllable liabilities that banks issue are **subordinated notes and debentures.** These are capital market instruments with maturities in excess of one year. Many are similar to corporate bonds. But all banks issue subordinated notes and debentures with the understanding that those who hold them will have *subordinated claims* in the event of bank failures. This means that if a bank fails, holders of its subordinated notes and debentures will receive no payments until all depositors at the bank have received the funds from their accounts. These commercial bank liabilities are a portion of the "other liabilities" category in Table 11-2 on page 252.

The equity capital of a bank is the excess of total assets over total liabilities. For the banking system as a whole, we estimate that equity capital amounts to about 8 percent of all bank liabilities and capital. The Federal Reserve reports equity capital infrequently, so we must rely on estimates for this figure.

To contemplate the kinds of management issues that banks face as they allocate their assets and liabilities, use the Chapter 11 Case Study, entitled "Getting Control of the Balance Sheet."
http://moneyxtra.swcollege.com

4. What are the key liabilities of commercial banks? Noncontrollable bank liabilities are demand deposits, other checkable deposits, savings deposits, and small-denomination time deposits. Controllable bank liabilities are large-denomination time deposits such as large CDs, purchased funds including sales of repurchase agreements, federal funds borrowings, or borrowings from the Federal Reserve, and subordinated notes and debentures. The excess of assets over liabilities is a bank's equity capital, or net worth.

Trends in Bank Liabilities and Equity Capital Figure 11-3 depicts the shares of total bank liabilities and equity capital accounted for by total deposits, other liabilities, and equity capital at various dates since 1961. "Other liabilities" include both purchased funds and subordinated notes and debentures.

As the figure makes clear, until recently the general trend has been toward reduced dependence by banks on deposit funding. There has also been a slight upward trend in equity capital. The use of purchased funds and subordinated notes and debentures increased through the 1960s, 1970s, and early 1980s, then increased considerably during the 1990s, and then dropped slightly in early 2000s.

On the Web

Where can one find the quickest links to banks on the Internet? The answer is AAAdir, located at http://www.aaadir.com. This site has links to more than 3,500 banking institutions and over 1,000 credit unions.

Savings Institutions

Like commercial banks, savings institutions issue transactions deposits. Savings institutions differ from commercial banks mainly in the way they allocate their assets. Traditionally, these institutions have also faced a number of regulations designed especially for them.

Figure 11-3
Commercial Bank Liabilities and Equity Capital.

Since the 1960s, there has been an overall decline in commercial banks' reliance on deposit funds. During the 1990s, banks increasingly funded their operations with purchased funds and other liabilities, until a slight dropoff took place in recent years. They also gradually increased their equity positions.

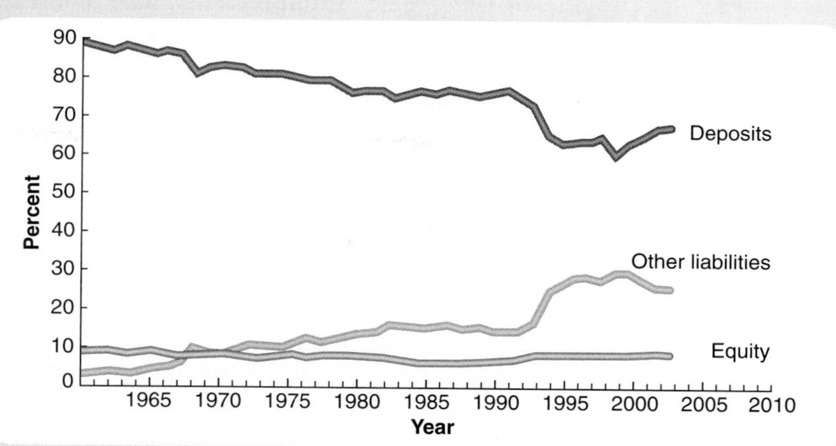

SOURCES: *Federal Reserve Bulletin* and *H.8(510) Statistical Release,* Board of Governors of the Federal Reserve System, various issues.

A Diminished Industry

Over the last decades, savings institutions have experienced serious problems. Between 1986 and 1991, savings institutions as a whole failed to earn a net profit. The scope of the problems of the savings institution industry is displayed in Figure 11-4, which plots the total deposits at these institutions since early 1988. Total deposits at savings institutions have declined from nearly $1 trillion in the spring of 1988 to today's level of just under $600 billion. Furthermore, even though the general savings institution collapse had ended by the beginning

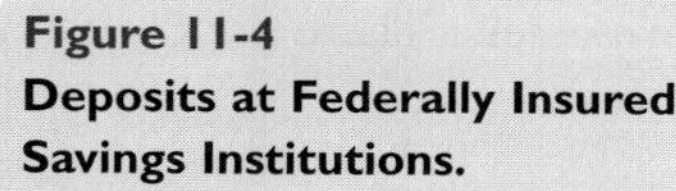

Figure 11-4
Deposits at Federally Insured Savings Institutions.

In spite of a recent recovery, deposits at savings institutions have fallen on net by over 40 percent since the end of the 1980s.

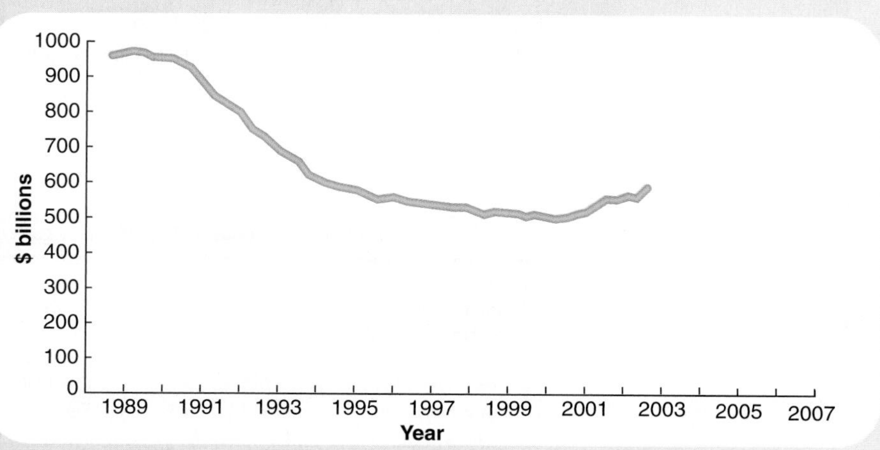

SOURCES: *Federal Reserve Bulletin,* Board of Governors of the Federal Reserve System; and *Quarterly Financial Results and Conditions of the Thrift Industry,* Office of Thrift Supervision, various issues.

of 1993, these institutions continued to lose deposits at an average rate of nearly $3 billion each month. If this pace had continued, savings institutions would have ceased to exist by the second decade of this century.

What happened? There is no single answer to this question. Some savings institutions failed because of fraudulent business practices. Some failed because of economic circumstances beyond their control. Nevertheless, as we shall discuss in Chapter 14, most economists concur that the main reason that so many savings institutions disappeared was that federal regulations and deposit insurance combined to produce a significant moral-hazard problem. Their exposure to interest rate risk had already made savings institutions very fragile by the end of the 1970s, and then regulatory changes in the 1980s encouraged savings institution managers to undertake riskier activities. Their customers' deposits were federally insured, yet the premiums that savings institutions paid on their deposits were unrelated to the risks that they incurred. The result was a crisis that engulfed a very large number of savings banks and savings and loan associations. In the end, federal regulators seized and sold over $400 billion in savings institution assets. The ultimate loss to taxpayers in funding insured deposits lost by these institutions amounted to over $200 billion, or enough to fund much of the federal government's deficit for any year in the 1980s and early 1990s. As a consequence of these problems, the savings institution industry today is much smaller than it once was.

Assets and Liabilities of Savings Institutions

Table 11-3 lists the *combined* assets and liabilities of *all* 2,000 federally insured savings institutions. Comparison of these institutions' assets and liabilities with those of commercial banks in Tables 11-1 and 11-2 shows some vague similarities. Both types of depository institutions issue deposits and depend on deposit funds in similar proportion to finance their activities. From Table 11-2, about 66 percent of commercial banks' liabilities and net worth is in deposit liabilities; Table 11-3 shows a 58 percent figure for savings institutions. Both kinds of institutions also make loans and hold securities and cash assets. There are dramatic differences, however, in the institutions' *asset allocations*.

Table 11-3 Assets and Liabilities of Savings Institutions ($ Billions)

Cash and securities	$173.8	17.4%	Total deposits	$582.5	58.4%
Mortgage loans	540.3	54.2%	Government borrowings	193.7	19.4%
Mortgage-backed securities	89.6	9.0%	Other borrowings	101.3	10.2%
Commercial loans	31.0	3.1%	Other liabilities	33.2	3.3%
Consumer loans	66.2	6.6%	Equity capital	87.0	8.7%
Other assets	96.8	9.7%			
Total assets	**$997.7**	**100.0%**	**Total equity & liabilities**	**$997.7**	**100.0%**

SOURCE: *Quarterly Financial Results and Conditions of the Thrift Industry*, Office of Thrift Supervision, May 2002.

MORTGAGE LOANS From Table 11-3, we can see that the clearly dominant asset category for savings institutions is mortgage lending, which accounts for about 54 percent of total savings institution assets.

A mortgage loan finances a purchase of real estate such as a tract of land or a structure such as a house. The borrower of a mortgage loan has the right to use the property while the mortgage is in effect. In return, the borrower must make regular payments of principal and interest.

Savings banks and savings and loan associations have always specialized in mortgage lending. Traditionally, this specialty has been their strength as well as their great weakness. It has been a strength because savings institutions have developed techniques for dealing with adverse-selection and moral-hazard problems that are endemic to mortgage lending. Savings institutions thereby have a managerial advantage over other potential competitors in this business.

The mortgage lending specialty of savings institutions has been a weakness because of the *interest rate risk* inherent in mortgage lending. Home mortgage loans typically have terms to maturity ranging from fifteen to thirty years. This means that when a savings institution grants a thirty-year mortgage loan at a fixed rate of 8 percent, it takes a chance that the rates that it must pay on its deposits and other liabilities will stay sufficiently below 8 percent to permit a long-term profit on the mortgage. Many savings institutions made exactly this bet in the early 1970s before adjustable-rate mortgages had become common. Then they watched in the late 1970s as market interest rates on deposits rose above the rates they were earning on their fixed-rate mortgage loans!

MORTGAGE-BACKED SECURITIES As discussed in Chapter 3, a mortgage-backed security is a title to a share in the principal and interest earnings from a group of mortgages with similar characteristics, such as nearly identical default risks and the same terms to maturity. Many mortgage-backed securities are issued by government-sponsored agencies, such as the General National Mortgage Association (GNMA) or the Federal National Mortgage Association (FNMA).

An institution such as the FNMA usually purchases mortgage loans from the savings institutions that initiated the loans. Typically, it pays the initiating institution fees to continue to collect principal and interest payments on its behalf. It *pools,* or segregates, the mortgage loans that it owns into groupings with like characteristics. It then sells mortgage-backed securities with yields based on the principal and interest payments derived from the underlying pools of loans.

Savings institutions themselves usually buy large numbers of mortgage-backed securities. As Table 11-3 indicates, savings institutions' holdings of mortgage-backed securities amount to 9 percent of their total assets. Consequently, these institutions allocate a total of 63 percent of their assets to mortgage-related activities.

OTHER LOANS AND ASSETS Legislation passed by Congress in the early 1980s gave savings institutions the legal power to make commercial and consumer loans within specified limits. Most savings institutions have not reached those limits, however. Together, commercial and consumer loans amount to less than 10 percent of their assets.

Like commercial banks, savings institutions hold cash assets. They also hold U.S. government securities and state and municipal bonds. Together these assets amount to about 17 percent of the total assets of savings institutions.

5. How do savings institutions differ from commercial banks? The fundamental difference between savings institutions and commercial banks is that savings institutions are much more specialized in mortgage-related lending, and a much larger portion of their security holdings is devoted to mortgage-backed securities.

Credit Unions

On the Web
How does a credit union get started? To learn more about how to form a credit union, go to the home page of the National Credit Union Administration at http://ncua.gov and click on "About Credit Unions." Then click on "How to Start a Credit Union."

There are more than 10,000 federally insured credit unions in the United States, serving over 70 million members. Table 11-4 shows the combined assets and liabilities of all federally insured credit unions, which make up 97 percent of the total number of these depository institutions.

Credit unions normally are relatively uncomplicated institutions. Share deposits of members account for more than 85 percent of liabilities and net worth of these institutions, and loans to members compose two-thirds of all credit union assets. Unlike commercial banks, credit unions are nonprofit institutions. Credit unions also differ from other depository institutions in that they take in deposits from members only and lend only to members. Most surveys show that credit unions charge 10 to 25 percent less than banks for car loans, credit cards, and unsecured personal loans and pay one-half to one percentage point higher yields on deposits.

Defining the Limits of Credit Union Membership

The Federal Credit Union Act of 1934 limited membership in these depository institutions to "groups having a common bond of occupation or association, or to groups within a well-defined neighborhood, community, or rural district." Congress designed this Depression-era law to ensure that low-income customers shunned by banks would nonetheless be able to obtain bank-like services at reasonable rates. Qualifying for membership in a credit union required an individual to meet legal criteria specific to that credit union. Credit union membership rules typically required an individual to be associated with a particular business or occupation.

Two benefits were associated with membership restrictions. One was that they usually limited the credit unions' clienteles to people who had steady incomes.

Table 11-4 Assets and Liabilities and Equity at Federally Insured Credit Unions ($ Billions)

Loans	$271.5	66.0%	Share deposits	$356.9	86.8%
Securities	100.7	24.5%	Other liabilities & equity	54.5	13.2%
Cash assets	25.8	6.3%			
Other assets	13.4	3.2%			
Total assets	**$411.4**	**100.0%**	**Total liabilities & equity**	**$411.4**	**100.0%**

SOURCE: *Statistics for Federally Insured Credit Unions,* National Credit Union Administration, March 2002.

Thus, credit unions had access to thrifty savers who provided funds that credit unions could then lend to other members who were more creditworthy than the average personal-loan customer of a commercial bank. Because the loans required less monitoring, credit unions could keep costs low. The reduced risks and lower costs that credit unions faced enabled them to pay higher rates on deposits and charge lower rates on loans.

Second, when Congress established membership rules for credit unions, it "compensated" credit unions for the restriction by exempting them from most types of taxation faced by commercial banks. This tax exemption is another factor that gave credit unions a significant cost advantage over commercial banks and many savings institutions.

Conservative No Longer?

In July 1998, Congress changed the definition of a credit union to "a viable alternative retail bank." It directed the National Credit Union Administration (NCUA), the chief federal regulator, to define a "local, well-defined community" for credit union membership. The NCUA responded by developing criteria that directed any credit union seeking to serve a county of less than 300,000 people to cite evidence of "interaction" or "common interests" in the target community, such as the existence of local festivals or area newspapers.

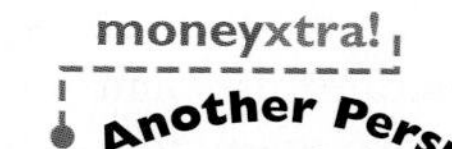

To learn more about the issues posed by recent changes in credit union membership rules, see the Chapter 11 reading, entitled "Credit Unions and the Common Bond," by William Emmons and Frank Schmid of the Federal Reserve Bank of St. Louis.
http://moneyxtra.swcollege.com

Under these new definitions, credit unions are beginning to serve members who look more like the traditional household customers of commercial banks. As a result, credit unions have begun to grapple with problems faced by banks. For instance, credit unions have faced important risk issues in recent years. Some credit unions have run into significant difficulties as they have sought to increase their returns through derivatives speculation. At various times in the past, this has led regulators to contemplate significant changes in the structure of the federal insurance for credit unions.

6. How do credit unions raise and allocate their funds? Nearly all the funds raised by credit unions come from share deposits that they issue to members. They allocate the majority of their funds to loans and the remainder to securities and cash. Until fairly recently, credit union deposit-taking and lending activities were restricted to narrowly defined memberships. Today, however, the criteria for credit union membership are so broadly defined that credit unions are likely to more closely resemble commercial banks in the future.

Link to Policy

Trying to Draw a Line on What Credit Unions Can and Cannot Do to Compete with Commercial Banks

How can credit unions consistently offer better deals on loan and deposit rates and lower fees on services than are offered by commercial banks? One reason is that a credit union is a nonprofit cooperative institution, so it does not necessarily seek to maximize profits. Instead, a credit union's managers typically strive to generate sufficient revenues to cover expenses while also maintaining the safety and soundness of the institution.

Another reason is that the federal government gives credit unions a fundamental tax advantage: because they are nonprofit cooperatives, credit unions are exempt from federal taxes. The U.S. Treasury estimates that this exemption will save credit unions around the country between $13.7 billion and $16.2 billion during the period from 2000 to 2009. Hence, even if they sought to maximize profits, credit unions would have a significant advantage over banks in setting their rates on loans and deposits and in pricing their services.

Defining the "Common Bond"

Because credit unions can offer better interest rates and prices than those offered by profit-maximizing commercial banks subject to federal taxation, many consumers have an incentive to try to join a credit union, and currently more than 70 million U.S. residents are credit union members. Not everyone can join a credit union, however. The Federal Credit Union Act of 1934 limits membership in the cooperatives to "groups having a common bond of occupation or association, or to groups within a well-defined neighborhood, community, or rural district." Until 1982, the National Credit Union Administration (NCUA) interpreted an occupational "common bond" to mean that the members of a single credit union must have a single employer. Since then, the NCUA has interpreted the law as meaning that employees of different companies can have a common bond if they are located in the same general area.

Before the 1990s, commercial bankers were irritated about this policy change, but they did not actively fight its legality until 1996. As Figure 11-5 shows, in 1996 assets at credit unions increased significantly as a percentage of assets at commercial banks, which became worried about competition from the tax-exempt cooperatives. In late 1996, the American Bankers Association convinced a federal judge to impose an injunction on credit unions' efforts to expand their memberships beyond common bonds with specific employers. The judge called the NCUA a "rogue agency" and threatened to make credit unions around the country disband some of their newly recruited members. Ultimately, Congress defused the issue in favor of credit unions by passing the 1998 Credit Union Membership Access Act. That law legalized "multiple common bonds" at credit unions by allowing several groups to join together in a single credit union as long as no single group has more than 3,000 members. Nevertheless, for a time credit unions backpedaled their efforts to expand their memberships.

How Many "Common Bonds" Should a Credit Union's Members Have?

Recently, the move to broaden memberships has led to another uptick in the relative size of credit unions as compared with commercial banks, as shown in Figure 11-5. Since 1999, the NCUA has actively assisted credit unions in developing multiple common bonds via so-called field of membership rules.

According to the American Bankers Association, these rules, which the NCUA actively supports by helping credit unions establish multiple common bonds, effectively allows credit unions to bypass

Figure 11-5
Assets of Credit Unions as a Percentage of Assets at Commercial Banks.

Credit unions' combined assets rose noticeably relative to total assets of commercial banks in 1996 and again in 2001. In both years, commercial banks filed legal challenges to credit unions' efforts to broaden their memberships.

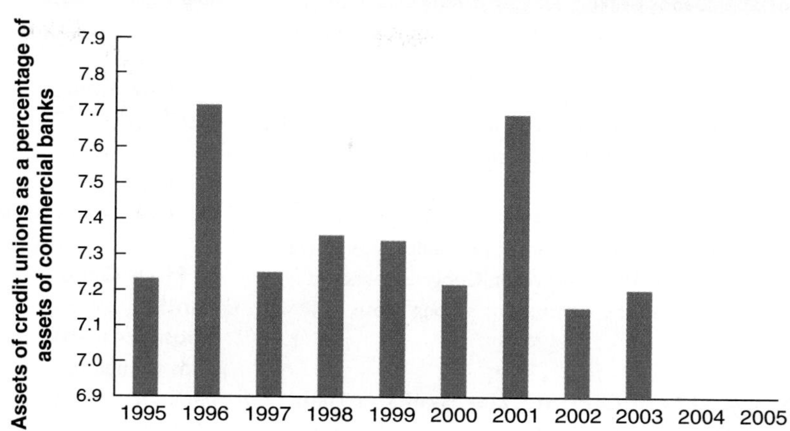

SOURCES: National Credit Union Administration; and Federal Deposit Insurance Corporation, *Statistics on Banking*, various issues; authors' estimates.

the 1998 law's 3,000-member limit. The reason is that the NCUA does not count retirees and family members of the common-bond group as members, even though their acceptance as members definitely expands credit unions' memberships. So far, however, the courts have not accepted the view that the NCUA is improperly interpreting the law.

An Emerging Issue: Can Credit Unions Make Commercial Loans?

Another source of friction has been the recent effort by credit unions to engage in business lending, which naturally intrudes directly on the turf of commercial banks. Currently, credit unions can make loans to members who operate small businesses yet still qualify for a common-bond membership in some way. Today, credit unions' share of business lending is a paltry fraction of 1 percent of total commercial loans. Fewer than a hundred of the more than 10,000 credit unions have even made such loans.

Nevertheless, business lending by credit unions is likely to increase as credit union memberships grow. In addition, special community charters make it easier for some credit unions to admit businesses as members, and more and more credit unions are switching to these charters. In the early 2000s, the NCUA even began pressing Congress to amend the federal credit union charter to remove all caps on commercial lending—an action that is likely to irritate the commercial banking industry even further.

Research Project

What is the rationale for the common-bond requirement for membership in a credit union? What are the trade-offs associated with this requirement, tax-exempt status, and the legal lines of business available to credit unions? Do commercial banks have a legitimate argument that credit unions have an "unfair advantage" in competing for deposit and loan customers?

Web Resources

1. How easy is it for a credit union to take advantage of the NCUA's field-of-membership rules for establishing multiple common bonds? Take a look at the Web page from which credit unions can download application forms on the Internet at http://www.ncua.gov/org/NCUAgovLink.htm.

2. Where are data on credit unions on the Web? Go to the home page of the NCUA at http://www.ncua.gov, click on "Credit Union Data," and then click on "Call Report Data Files Under FOIA (Freedom of Information Act)." At this page, you can download and unzip various data files concerning the overall status of the credit union industry.

Chapter Summary

1. The Historical Origins of Modern Banking Institutions: Deposit-taking, lending institutions have existed since the earliest human civilizations. Modern versions of these institutions originated with the merchant bankers of medieval Italy. Since that time, depository institutions have specialized in maintaining deposit accounts for, processing payments on behalf of, and making loans to their customers.

2. Why Depository Institutions Are Segmented: Commercial banks, savings institutions, and credit unions have always specialized. In the 1930s, however, Congress enacted legislation that strengthened the distinctions among these institutions.

3. The Key Assets of Commercial Banks: These include loans such as commercial and industrial, real estate, and consumer loans; securities such as U.S. government bonds; and cash assets such as vault cash and reserve deposits held at the Federal Reserve.

4. The Key Liabilities of Commercial Banks: These include so-called noncontrollable liabilities such as checking, savings, and small-denomination time deposits and controllable liabilities such as certificates of deposit and federal funds borrowings.

5. How Savings Institutions Differ from Commercial Banks: The key difference is that savings institutions have specialized much more narrowly in mortgage-related activities. Key activities include mortgage lending and holding mortgage-backed securities.

6. How Credit Unions Raise and Allocate Their Funds: Almost all of credit union funds come from share deposits of members. Credit unions lend the majority of these funds to members. In the past, credit union membership was limited to specific occupations, but legislation enacted in the 1990s significantly broadened the scope of eligible credit union members. Thus, in the future credit unions undoubtedly will come to look more like commercial banks.

Questions and Problems

(Answers to odd-numbered questions and problems may be found on the Web at **http://money.swcollege.com** under "Student Resources.")

1. Explain why it was natural in early times for goldsmiths to become bankers.

2. Which types of modern bank assets do you think might be similar to those on the balance sheets of Italian merchant bankers? What bank assets might truly be "new"?

3. Explain the difference between an asset and a liability.

4. Based on the data in Tables 11-1 and 11-2, would you expect that bank assets or bank liabilities would tend to have longer maturities, on average? Do you think that this could pose any problems for bank managers?

5. Based on the data in Table 11-3, would you expect that savings institution assets or liabilities would have longer average maturities? Explain your reasoning. Discuss the enhanced problems that this maturity "mismatch" poses for managers of savings institutions. How do these problems compare with those faced by commercial banks (see question 4)?

6. Derivative instruments (covered in Chapter 8) do not appear anywhere in the balance sheets discussed in this chapter. Yet many depository institutions are active derivatives traders. Explain why derivatives are absent from depository institution balance sheets.

7. In light of your answers to questions 4 and 5, why do you suppose that depository institutions use derivatives? In answering this question, draw from what you also learned in Chapter 8 about the uses of derivative securities.

8. Based on the total asset figures in Tables 11-1, 11-2, and 11-3, how much larger (in percentage terms) is the commercial banking industry as compared with savings institutions? As compared with credit unions?

9. What are fundamental differences between savings institutions and commercial banks? What are key similarities between the two types of depository institutions?

10. Commercial banks have contended that the broadened membership criteria for credit unions are "unfair." Do you agree? Why?

Before the Test

Test your understanding of the material covered in this chapter by taking the Chapter 11 interactive quiz at http://money.swcollege.com.

Online Application

Internet URL: http://www.ots.treas.gov

Title: Office of Thrift Supervision (OTS)

Navigation: Go to the OTS home page at the above Web site. Click on "Applications." Then click on "Application Status Reports," and then "Applications in Process Data Base."

Application: Under "Date," select "Filed Date," and within the field for the period, type in a recent period spanning at least several months. Under "Application Type," select "New Institution." Leave institution and location boxes blank, and leave all other boxes set on "All." Then click on "Search."

1. How many applications for *new* savings institutions did the OTS receive during the period you selected?

2. Now go back to Applications page, reset the "Application Type" field to "Subsidiary," and redo the search leaving all other fields the same. Were there more or fewer applications for new subsidiaries? What can you conclude about the main way that applicants seek to enlarge their presence in the savings institution industry? Is this experience consistent with the discussion in this chapter?

For Group Study and Analysis: Assign groups to use the search technique above to track applications for new savings institution charters and subsidiaries by state or region. Have the groups report back to the class. Are there any clear geographic trends in the savings institution industry?

Selected References and Further Reading

Dwyer, Gerald. "Wildcat Banking, Banking Panics, and Free Banking in the United States." Federal Reserve Bank of Atlanta *Economic Review* 81 (December 1996): 1–20.

Emmons, William, and Frank Schmid. "Membership Structure, Competition, and Occupational Credit Union Deposit Rates." Federal Reserve Bank of St. Louis *Review* 83 (January/February 2001): 41–50.

Hammond, Bray. *Banks and Politics in America*. Princeton: Princeton University Press, 1985.

Laderman, Elizabeth, and Wayne Passmore. "Is Mortgage Lending by Savings Associations Special?" Federal Reserve Bank of San Francisco *Economic Review* (no. 2, 1998): 30–45.

Srinivasan, Aruna, and B. Frank King. "Credit Union Issues." Federal Reserve Bank of Atlanta *Economic Review* 83 (1998): 32–41.

White, Eugene. *The Regulation and Reform of the American Banking System, 1900–1929*. Princeton: Princeton University Press, 1983.

Wicker, Elmus. *The Banking Panics of the Great Depression*. Cambridge: Cambridge University Press, 1996.

MoneyXtra

moneyxtra! Log on to the MoneyXtra Web site now (http://moneyxtra.swcollege.com) for additional learning resources such as practice quizzes, case studies, readings, and additional economic applications.

Chapter 12

Understanding How Banking Markets Work—

The Economics of Depository Institutions

Fundamental Issues

1. In the basic economic theory of banking markets, what are the sources of bank revenues and costs?
2. What are the loan supply and deposit demand schedules for perfectly competitive banks?
3. How are bank loan and deposit rates determined in perfectly competitive banking markets?
4. How is the interest rate on bank loans determined in a monopoly loan market?

Internet banks, which distribute all their services on the Internet instead of via physical branches, have learned that a number of consumers still have a stubborn attachment to face-to-face financial dealings. In particular, some consumers are reluctant to send funds to a bank with a physical location they have not seen. According to the president of the Internet bank Nexity.com, a prospective customer from California who happened to be in Alabama on a business trip made a special side trip to visit Nexity.com's physical office in Birmingham. He wanted to verify that the Web bank offering relatively high deposit rates at a virtual teller's window was "for real."

If the customer did a lot of shopping around for the best deals both online and offline, he probably discovered something else. The prices of banking services at Internet banks per constant quality unit*—that is, prices after adjusting for differences in deposit account features—are converging toward those of traditional bricks-and-mortar institutions. Internet banks continue to offer higher explicit deposit rates, but the average minimum balance required to open a basic interest-bearing checking account at an Internet bank is more than 15 percent larger than a traditional institution would require. On average, Internet banks do charge lower monthly fees than traditional institutions, and the minimum balances required to avoid fees are lower at Internet banks. Nevertheless, since early 2001 the average monthly fees on interest-bearing checking accounts at Internet banks have risen by more than 30 percent, and the average minimum balance necessary for zero fees has increased by more than 25 percent.*

As you will see in this chapter, there are good reasons to think that per-constant-quality-unit deposit rates should be roughly the same across banks, whether they offer their services online or offline. To understand why, you must learn about the economics of the markets for depository institution deposits and loans.

Depository Institution Revenues, Costs, and Profits

To understand issues concerning the banking industry and its regulation, it is helpful to understand the economic theory of how depository institutions make decisions and interact in markets for financial instruments that they hold as assets and issue as liabilities. This chapter explains the basic theory of banking markets. To do this, we shall apply concepts from principles of microeconomics concerning theories of firm behavior, perfect competition, and monopoly.

As you learned in Chapter 11, depository institutions typically have numerous assets and liabilities. In this chapter, however, our goal is to understand the basic economics of bank decision making. For this reason, we shall consider a very simple depository institution. We shall also simplify our terminology a little by referring to this depository institution as a "bank." Keep in mind, though, that with appropriate alterations to take into account institutional differences, the economic model we shall develop can also be used to describe the behavior of savings institutions and credit unions.

The Bank Balance Sheet

The bank we consider specializes in two tasks that we know to be essential to banking. First, it issues deposits to customers. The bank pays interest to all its depositors. Furthermore, these deposits are the only source of funds for this bank, which, for the sake of simplicity, issues no shares of stock. This is perhaps the most unrealistic assumption we shall make, but it makes our model much simpler and, therefore, easier to understand. Another assumption we make is that the deposits issued by the bank are not subject to legal reserve requirements, so the bank can lend out all the deposits it receives, if it so chooses. As we shall discuss in Chapter 20, this is a much more realistic assumption today than it was just a few years ago.

The bank uses deposit funds for its second task, which is making a specific type of loan, such as commercial loans. All the loans the bank makes are of this type, and the bank's loan customers are similar. For instance, no one customer has particularly more or less risk of default. Furthermore, all the loans have the same maturity, which we shall think of as just "one period" in length. In return for making these one-period loans, the bank receives interest payments from its borrowers.

Under these assumptions, this clearly is a very simple bank. It has one category of liabilities, deposits, and one category of assets, commercial loans. Let's suppose that, at a point in time, the total dollar amount of interest-bearing deposits at a typical bank is equal to the quantity D. This amount might, for instance, be

Balance-sheet constraint: The accounting constraint that a bank's assets cannot exceed the sum of its liabilities and net worth.

Real resource expenses: Expenses that a bank must incur in the form of explicit payments of wages and salaries to employees, explicit payments to other owners of factors of production, and opportunity costs of devoting resources of the bank's owners to that line of business rather than an alternative.

equal to $100 million. Likewise, let us denote the bank's lending as the dollar quantity L. Because banks only issue deposits and make loans, the entire amount of lending by each bank must be equal to the total amount of deposit funds it has obtained from its deposit customers. Thus, if the amount of deposits held at a bank is equal to $100 million, that is the amount that the bank can lend. This means that, in general, if the bank has received a dollar amount of deposits D and makes a dollar amount of loans L, then these two quantities must be equal, so that $L = D$. This equation, which is called the **balance-sheet constraint,** indicates that the bank's assets must equal its liabilities plus its net worth. In the case of this simplified bank balance sheet, the bank cannot issue more loans than deposits. Indeed, a bank's assets and liabilities must always be equal, so loans must equal deposits.

Bank Revenues, Costs, and Profits

Bank owners wish to earn income in the form of economic profits. The economic profits of any business, of course, are the difference between revenues and economic costs, which include both explicit costs and implicit opportunity costs a firm incurs by being in its chosen line of business instead of an alternative line of business. Let's consider the revenues and economic costs of a typical bank.

Bank Revenues The simple bank we are considering has a single source of revenues: the interest it receives from its commercial and industrial lending activities. Suppose that the one-period interest rate on loans made by a typical bank is equal to a rate r_L. Then the bank's total interest earnings, or *total revenues,* on its total quantity of one-period loans must equal $TR = r_L \times L$.

For instance, if the bank extends $100 million in commercial and industrial loans and the one-period loan interest rate it receives per dollar lent is $0.06 in interest per $1.00 in loans, or 0.06 (6 percent), then the bank's total interest earned for the period is equal to 0.06 × $100 million, or $6 million. This amount is the total revenues, $TR = r_L \times L =$ $6 million, received by the bank for that period.

Bank Costs Any bank incurs three basic types of expenses, or costs:

1. **Explicit interest expenses** To raise funds to use in its lending activities—that is, to have any possibility of earning revenues from making loans—the bank must issue deposits. The bank also compensates its depositors by paying them interest. If the one-period interest rate that a typical bank pays is equal to r_D, then the total deposit interest expense that the bank incurs during a given period is equal to $r_D \times D$. For example, if the one-period deposit interest rate is $0.03 per $1.00 in deposits, or 0.03 (3 percent), and the amount of deposits it issues during a period is $100 million, then the bank's interest expense for that period is equal to 0.03 × $100 million, or $3 million.

2. **Real resource expenses for deposits** Banks cannot rake in deposits without using real resources, however. Banks must draw on the talents and efforts of their employees. The bank must hire tellers to take in deposits and managers to supervise these employees. Furthermore, these people require office supplies, computer equipment, and other furnishings to accomplish these tasks. Hence, in addition to deposit interest expenses, banks also incur **real resource expenses.** Real resource expenses include *explicit costs* that the bank must

incur in its day-to-day operations. Employees must be paid wages and salaries, and other factors of production must be purchased or leased if the bank is to perform its operations effectively and maximize profits.

In addition, the bank incurs *opportunity costs:* it could be devoting its factors of production to alternative uses, so it incurs an implicit real opportunity cost. Real resource costs for any firm include both explicit and opportunity costs, which together constitute what economists call *economic costs*. The same is true for banking.

When the bank issues more deposits, it must clear more checks, hire more tellers, and so on. Thus, the total real resource cost associated with the bank's deposit activities varies directly with the total amount of deposits issued by the bank, because as the amount of deposits issued increases, the bank's total real deposit resource expenses incurred also increase.

3. **Real resource expenses for loans** Making loans also requires that the bank incur real resource expenses. The total real resource cost of making loans rises with the amount of loans made. When the bank makes more loans, it must, for example, hire more credit analysts and loan managers. Consequently, the bank's total real resource expenses increase as its dollar amount of lending rises.

The total economic costs for a typical bank are equal to the sum of three components: total deposit interest expense, total real resource costs incurred in servicing its customers' deposit accounts, and total real resource expenses incurred in making and processing loans. All three increase as the bank increases its operations and expands its balance sheet, so the total economic costs of banking vary directly with the amounts of bank loans and deposits.

Bank Profits As for any firm, a bank's economic profits equal total revenues less total economic costs. For the typical bank we are considering, therefore, profits equal loan interest revenues minus total economic costs. Because economic costs have three components, profits must equal loan interest revenues less deposit expenses, real deposit resource costs, and real loan resource costs.

On the Web

Do you want to keep up with news on the latest factors affecting bank revenues and costs? If so, click on the free articles available daily from American Banker at http://www.americanbanker.com.

This tells us some very important facts about depository institution behavior. First of all, interest rates clearly are very important to banks because they affect both the banks' revenues and their expenses. A commonplace view is that banks benefit from higher interest rates. Nevertheless, if both the interest rate earned on loans and the interest rate paid on deposits increase, then a bank's revenues and its costs both increase, and the bank's economic profits may rise, fall, or remain the same. Holding all other things constant, a bank's profits rise from a general increase in interest rates only if loan rates rise more than deposit rates.

In addition, expenditures on real resources must also be very important to banks. Banking is not just a business of making loans at "high" interest rates and taking in deposit funds at "low" interest rates to earn the highest possible profit—though this certainly is a key objective in banking. Loans must be made by bank employees using other factors of production, and deposits must be issued and services provided by other bank employees using other factors of production. Expenses on all these resources have a major bearing on the profitability of banks.

1. In the basic economic theory of banking markets, what are the sources of bank revenues and costs? The basic theory of banking markets focuses on the fundamental markets in which banks interact, which are the markets for loans and deposits. The source of revenues for banks in these markets is interest revenues on loans. Bank costs have three components: deposit interest expense, real resource costs incurred in providing deposit-related services, and real resource costs incurred in extending and monitoring loans.

A Competitive Theory of Banking

How banks attempt to maximize profits depends crucially on the market environment in which they find themselves. In most of this chapter, we shall assume that banking markets are *perfectly competitive*. This means that each individual bank is one of *many* banks issuing deposits and making commercial and industrial loans. In addition, each bank's customers view it as no better or worse than any of the other banks in the markets for its deposits and loans. Consequently, bank customers perceive that the deposits banks issue and the loans they extend are *homogeneous*. Finally, every bank has access to the same technologies for employing people and other factors of production in its banking tasks. No single bank has better access to banking technologies or to factors of bank deposit and loan production than any other bank.

moneyxtra! Another Perspective

For more background on factors contributing to a competitive environment for depository institutions, go to the Chapter 12 reading entitled "Bank Competition in the New Economy," by Mark Guzman of the Federal Reserve Bank of Dallas.

http://moneyxtra.swcollege.com

Marginal Revenue, Marginal Cost, and Profit Maximization

Any bank, whether or not it operates in perfectly competitive loan and deposit markets, must decide the dollar volume of deposits to issue and how much lending to do. It does so with an aim to maximize its economic profits. In turn, a bank's profits are maximized when the bank lends to the point at which the last dollar of deposits raised by the bank and lent to a loan customer yields zero economic profit to the bank. The reason is that if the economic profit earned on the last dollar lent were positive, it would be more profitable for the bank to lend another dollar of deposit funds. If the economic profit earned on the last dollar lent were negative—meaning that lending that last dollar reduces the bank's profits—the bank's profits could be increased by lending one less dollar of deposit funds.

The Marginal Revenue Schedule Therefore, bank profit maximization requires that each bank make loans to the point at which the additional revenue earned on the last dollar of loans made to its customers is just equal to the additional costs incurred on that last dollar it lends. The additional revenue earned on the last additional dollar of loans is a bank's **marginal revenue** ***(MR)***. For a bank, whose revenues and loans are measured in dollar terms, units of measurement for marginal revenue are dollars per dollar ($/$). Hence, marginal revenue for a bank is measured as fractions, which we can convert to percentages. Under perfect competition, the amount of lending by an individual bank is so small relative to the total amount of lending by all banks that an individual bank cannot affect the market loan rate. Hence, for a given bank, marginal revenue is equal to the interest rate earned on the next dollar lent, which is the market loan inter-

Marginal revenue: The gain in total revenues resulting from a one-unit increase in production of a good or service; for a bank, the addition to its revenues from adding an additional dollar of loan assets.

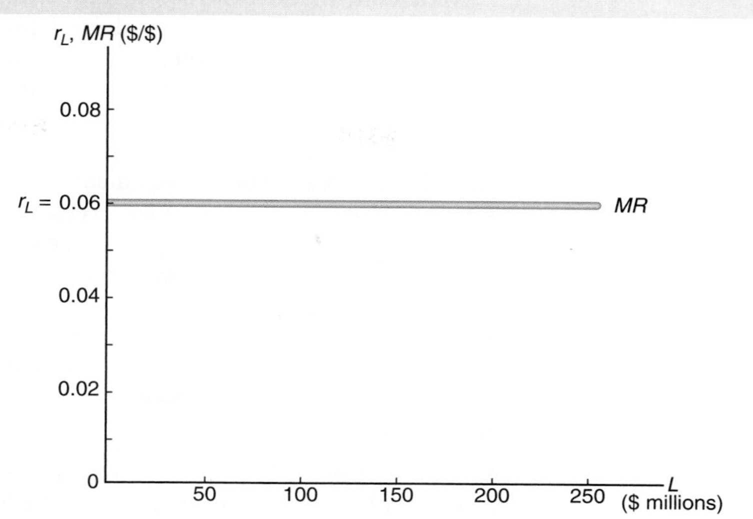

Figure 12-1
A Perfectly Competitive Bank's Marginal Revenue Schedule.

The additional revenue earned on the last additional dollar of lending by a bank is the bank's marginal revenue. In a perfectly competitive banking market, the amount of lending by an individual bank is so small relative to total loans by all banks that the individual bank cannot affect the market loan rate. Hence, for a given bank marginal revenue is equal to the interest rate earned on the next dollar lent, which is the market loan interest rate, r_L. The bank's marginal revenue schedule, *MR*, is horizontal at this loan rate, indicating that the bank's marginal revenue is equal to r_L irrespective of the volume of lending by the bank.

est rate, r_L. As shown in Figure 12-1, this means that the bank's *marginal revenue schedule,* which displays all combinations of marginal revenue and dollar amounts of lending, is horizontal at the market loan rate, so that $MR = r_L$. Each bank's marginal revenue is constant and equal to the market loan rate no matter how many loans it extends.

Marginal cost: The addition to the total cost generated by a one-unit increase in production of a good or service; for a bank, the addition to total cost from obtaining an additional dollar of deposits to lend, which is the sum of marginal deposit interest expense, marginal deposit resource costs, and marginal loan resource costs.

THE MARGINAL COST SCHEDULE Recall that a bank's total economic cost is the sum of three components: total deposit interest expense, total deposit resource costs, and total loan resource costs. It follows that a bank's **marginal cost** (*MC*), which is the addition to the bank's total cost from obtaining an additional dollar of deposits to lend, must also be the sum of three types of marginal costs: marginal deposit interest expense, marginal deposit resource costs, and marginal loan resource costs.

Marginal Deposit Interest Expense The marginal deposit interest expense incurred by a bank is the additional interest it pays per dollar of deposits. As long as the deposit market is perfectly competitive, so that actions of the individual bank cannot affect the market deposit interest rate, r_D, this market interest rate is the marginal interest expense that the bank must incur per dollar of deposits it uses to make loans. For example, panel (a) of Figure 12-2 on page 271 plots a marginal interest expense schedule for the bank if the market deposit rate is 3 percent. It is horizontal at $r_D = \$0.03/\$1.00 = 0.03$, meaning that no matter how many dollars in deposits are issued by the bank, the marginal interest expense the bank incurs is constant and equal to this market deposit rate.

We assume that, as is true for most firms, the relevant range of the short-run marginal deposit resource cost schedule for a typical bank, labeled MC_D, slopes upward against the total quantity of deposits issued by the bank, as shown in panel (b) of Figure 12-2. This means that as the bank issues more deposits, the additional dollar cost, per dollar of deposits, of providing teller services and clearing checks rises in the short run. For example, panel (b) of Figure 12-2 indicates that the real resource cost incurred on the 100 millionth dollar of deposits is equal to \$0.02 of real resource expenses per \$1.00 of deposits, or 0.02 (2 percent), while for the 150 millionth dollar it is \$0.03 per \$1.00, or 0.03 (3 percent).

Likewise, the relevant range of the marginal loan resource cost schedule, MC_L, slopes upward against the quantity of loans made by the bank. For instance, panel (c) of Figure 12-2 shows that the 100 millionth dollar of loans costs a typical bank \$0.01 worth of real resource expenses per \$1.00 of loans, or 0.01 (1 percent), while the 150 millionth dollar of loans costs the bank \$0.02 per \$1.00 of loans, or 0.02 (2 percent).

A Bank's Marginal Cost Schedule Panel (d) of Figure 12-2 shows the construction of the bank's marginal cost schedule. By definition, total marginal cost for the bank, denoted MC, is the sum of the bank's marginal interest expense, its marginal deposit resource cost, and its marginal loan resource cost. Thus, total marginal cost is given by $MC = r_D + MC_D + MC_L$, which means that the bank's marginal cost schedule is the sum of the schedules in panels (a), (b), and (c). For the 100 millionth dollar of deposits, marginal deposit interest expense is, from panel (a), equal to the market deposit rate, r_D = \$0.03/\$1.00 = 0.03, and marginal deposit resource cost, as shown in panel (b), equals \$0.02/\$1.00 = 0.02. From the bank's balance-sheet constraint, we know that if the bank has \$100 million in deposits, it also has \$100 million in loans. Therefore, we also know, from panel (c), that the bank incurs a marginal loan resource cost of \$0.01/\$1.00 = 0.01. Adding these three marginal expense components together, we deduce that, for the 100 millionth dollar of lending done by this bank, its marginal cost is equal to (\$0.03 + \$0.02 + \$0.01) per \$1.00, or \$0.06/\$1.00 = 0.06 (6 percent).

By similar reasoning, we can determine that for the 150 millionth dollar lent by the bank, the marginal cost is equal to (\$0.03 + \$0.03 + \$0.02) per \$1.00, or \$0.08/\$1.00 = 0.08 (8 percent). Hence, we have determined two combinations of marginal cost and total lending by the bank that lie on its total marginal cost *(MC)* schedule shown in panel (d). This marginal cost schedule is upward sloping, because the deposit and loan marginal resource cost schedules are upward sloping.

PROFIT MAXIMIZATION AND THE BANK'S LOAN SUPPLY SCHEDULE We can now determine how many dollars in loans this bank will desire to make if its goal is to maximize its profits. Figure 12-3 on page 272 shows the determination of the profit-maximizing quantity of lending by the bank. As we discussed earlier, to maximize its total profits the bank extends loans to the point at which marginal revenue ($MR = r_L = 0.06$) is equal to total marginal cost ($MC = r_D + MC_D + MC_L$). This equality occurs at the point at which the bank's marginal revenue schedule intersects its marginal cost schedule, which is the single point at which $MR = MC = 0.06$, at \$100 million. Hence, the profit-maximizing amount of lending by the bank is \$100 million when the market loan interest rate is equal to 0.06 (6 percent).

Figure 12-2
Marginal Cost for a Perfectly Competitive Bank.

Panel (a) depicts a bank's marginal interest expense schedule if the market deposit rate is $r_D = 0.03$ (3 percent) and the bank is perfectly competitive. Panel (b) shows the bank's marginal deposit resource cost (MC_D) schedule, which slopes upward. Panel (c) displays the bank's marginal loan resource cost (MC_L) schedule, which also slopes upward. Panel (d) shows the sum of the marginal costs displayed in panels (a), (b), and (c), which is the bank's total marginal cost schedule, MC.

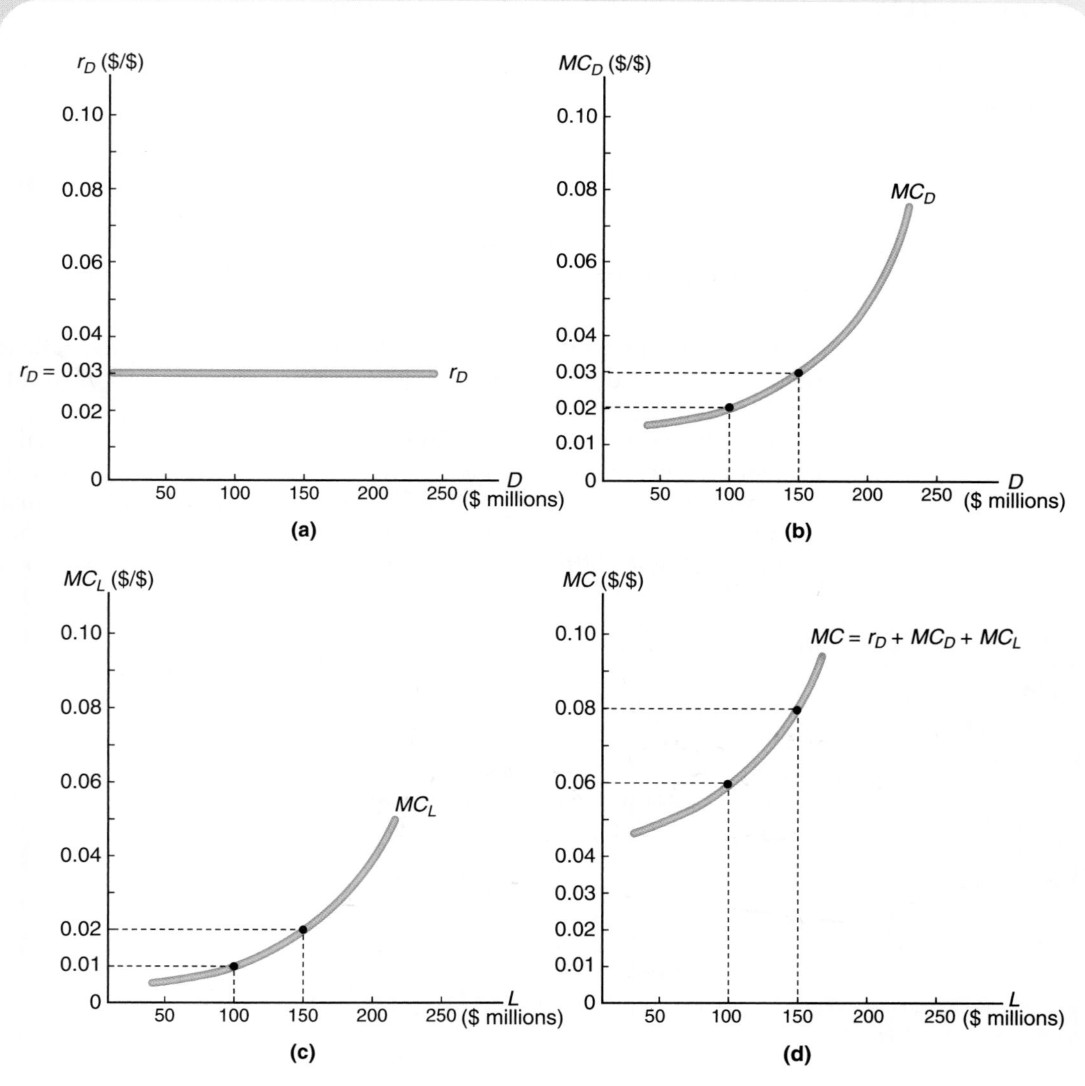

Figure 12-3
Profit-Maximizing Lending at a Perfectly Competitive Bank.

To maximize its profits, a perfectly competitive bank lends to the point at which marginal revenue ($MR = r_L = 0.06$) is equal to marginal cost ($MC = r_D + MC_D + MC_L = 0.06$), which occurs at a quantity of loans equal to \$100 million.

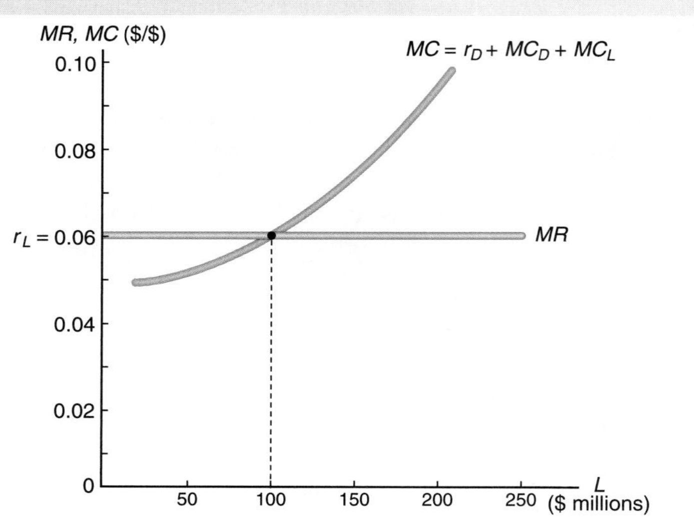

What will this bank do if the market loan interest rate changes, holding all other factors, including the market deposit rate, constant? Specifically, let us consider in Figure 12-4 what happens if the market loan rate rises to $r_L = 0.08$ (8 percent). Before the rise in the loan rate, when the loan rate was equal to 0.06 (6 percent), the profit-maximizing quantity of lending was \$100 million. The rise in the loan rate to a new level of 0.08, however, results in a higher marginal revenue for any given amount of lending the bank might undertake; that is, the marginal revenue schedule shifts upward, as shown in Figure 12-4. This means that the

Figure 12-4
A Perfectly Competitive Bank's Loan Supply Schedule.

An increase in the market loan rate from $r_L^1 = 0.06$ to $r_L^2 = 0.08$ causes the marginal revenue schedule for an individual bank to shift upward, inducing the bank to move along the marginal cost schedule and increase its lending to a new profit-maximizing level of \$150 million. Thus, over most of its range the marginal cost schedule, $MC = r_D + MC_D + MC_L$, is the bank's loan supply schedule.

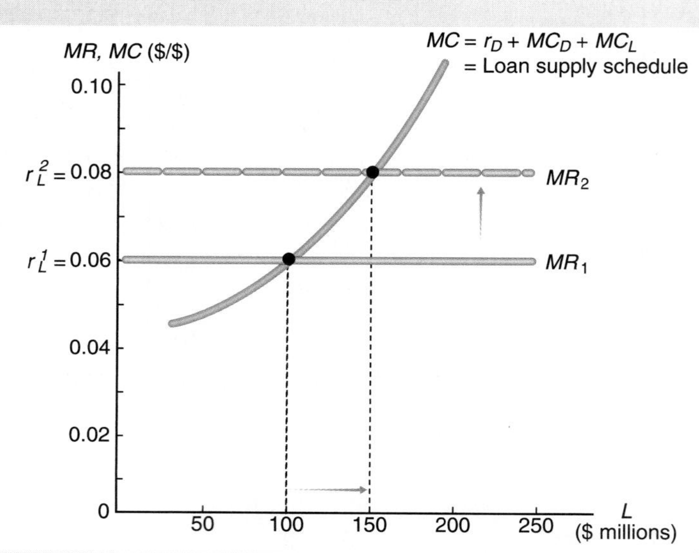

profit-maximizing level of lending must rise to a higher level corresponding to a new point at which marginal revenue equals marginal cost, or where $MR = MC = 0.08$. At this new point, as Figure 12-4 indicates, the profit-maximizing quantity of loans for this bank is equal to \$150 million.

Note that, in Figure 12-4, a rise in the market loan rate (from 0.06 to 0.08) causes the bank to move along its marginal cost schedule from one initial profit-maximizing loan quantity (\$100 million) to another (\$150 million). Points along the marginal cost schedule tell us combinations of loan rates and loan quantities that maximize the bank's profits. In other words, the bank's marginal cost schedule tells us the profit-maximizing quantities of loans that the bank will supply at different loan interest rates. This means that over most of its length the marginal cost schedule is the perfectly competitive bank's *loan supply schedule.* A rise in the market loan rate induces the bank to supply more loans along this schedule. If the market loan rate were to fall again, the bank would choose to supply fewer loans.

PROFIT MAXIMIZATION AND THE BANK'S DEPOSIT DEMAND SCHEDULE Now that we have determined that the profit-maximizing quantity of loans at a loan rate of 6 percent is \$100 million, it is tempting to deduce from the balance-sheet constraint that, obviously, this must also be the profit-maximizing quantity of deposits at this loan rate. Likewise, because the profit-maximizing amount of lending at a loan rate of 8 percent is \$150 million, that amount must be the profit-maximizing quantity of deposits at that higher loan rate. Indeed, these are the correct answers, as we shall see. It turns out, however, that we can say much more than this about the choices the bank will make.

A bank's profits are maximized when $r_L = r_D + MC_D + MC_L$. If we subtract MC_D and MC_L from both sides of this equation, we get $r_L - MC_D - MC_L = r_D$, or

$$r_D = r_L - MC_D - MC_L.$$

Thus, when the typical bank's profits are maximized, it must be true that the interest rate the bank pays on its deposits is equal to the interest rate it earns on loans less the sum of the marginal deposit and loan resource costs. Recall that the interest rate on deposits on the left-hand side of the above equation is the marginal interest expense incurred by the bank. The difference on the right-hand side of this equation is the loan rate, or the bank's constant marginal revenue, less the combination of marginal loan and deposit resource costs. We call the difference on the right-hand side of this equation the *net marginal revenue* that the bank earns on an additional dollar of deposits it issues. Hence, the equation says that a bank maximizes profits by issuing deposits up to the point at which marginal deposit interest expense—the deposit interest rate—is equal to the net marginal revenue the bank earns by using the last dollar of deposits issued to make a loan.

Figure 12-5 on the next page shows the bank's profit-maximizing deposit choice under the assumption that the market deposit rate, r_D, is equal to 0.03 (3 percent). Also drawn in Figure 12-5 is a downward-sloping schedule depicting the bank's net marginal revenue from deposits, $r_L - MC_D - MC_L$. To derive this schedule, we assume that, as in our initial example, the market loan rate is 0.06 (6 percent), and we subtract from this constant loan rate the marginal loan and deposit resource costs at each possible level of deposits issued by the bank. For example, as in Figure 12-2, the bank's marginal deposit resource cost is 0.02 for

Figure 12-5
The Profit-Maximizing Deposit Level.

An individual bank's net marginal revenue from issuing deposits is equal to $r_L - MC_D - MC_L$. To maximize its profit, the bank issues deposits to the point at which this net marginal revenue is equal to the marginal interest expense of deposits, which is equal to the deposit rate, $r_D = 0.03$. Thus, for this bank the profit-maximizing deposit level is equal to $100 million.

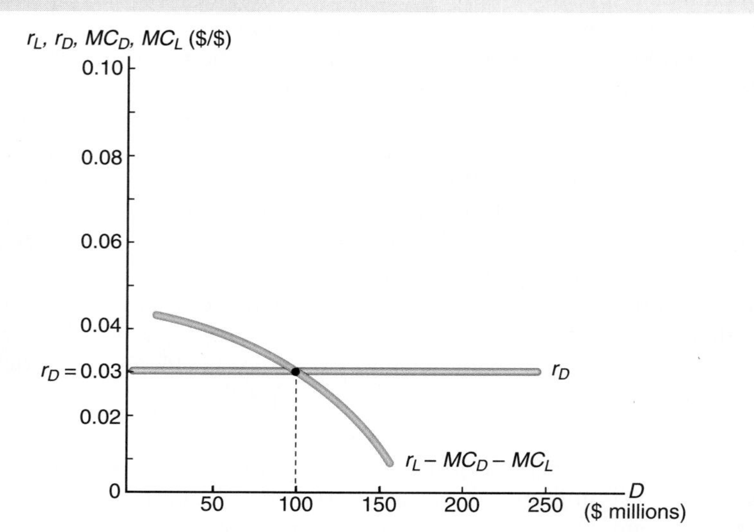

the 100 millionth dollar of deposits. Likewise, its marginal loan resource cost is 0.01 for the 100 millionth dollar of loans, which, from the bank's balance-sheet constraint, corresponds to the 100 millionth dollar of deposits. Subtracting 0.02 and 0.01 from the loan rate of 0.06, we have 0.03 as the bank's net marginal revenue from deposits, $r_L - MC_D - MC_L$.

Figure 12-5 indicates that the profit-maximizing quantity of deposits for a market loan rate of 0.06 and a market deposit rate of 0.03 is equal to $100 million. At this quantity of deposits, the bank's marginal interest expense, r_D, is equal to its net marginal revenue, $r_L - MC_D - MC_L$, and the bank's profits are maximized. Thus, the profit-maximizing quantity of deposits for the bank equals $100 million.

Figure 12-6 shows that if the deposit rate falls to 0.02, then the bank's marginal interest expense declines. As a result, marginal interest expense equals net marginal revenue at a higher quantity of deposits. The bank's new profit-maximizing quantity of deposits at this lower deposit rate of 0.02 is equal to $150 million. Thus, the fall in the market deposit rate causes the bank to increase its *quantity of deposits demanded.* This means that, over most of its range, the bank's net deposit marginal revenue, $r_L - MC_D - MC_L$, is the bank's *deposit demand schedule.* As the market deposit rate falls, the bank demands more deposits along this schedule. If the market deposit rate were to rise again, then the bank would decrease the quantity of deposits demanded.

2. What are the loan supply and deposit demand schedules for perfectly competitive banks? To maximize its economic profits, a bank lends to the point at which marginal revenue (the market loan rate) equals total marginal cost,

Figure 12-6
A Perfectly Competitive Bank's Deposit Demand Schedule.

A decrease in the market deposit rate from $r_D^1 = 0.03$ to $r_D^2 = 0.02$ causes the marginal interest expense for an individual bank to decline, inducing the bank to move along the net marginal revenue schedule and increase its deposit level to a new profit-maximizing quantity of $150 million. Thus, over most of its range the net marginal revenue schedule, $r_L - MC_D - MC_L$, is the bank's deposit demand schedule.

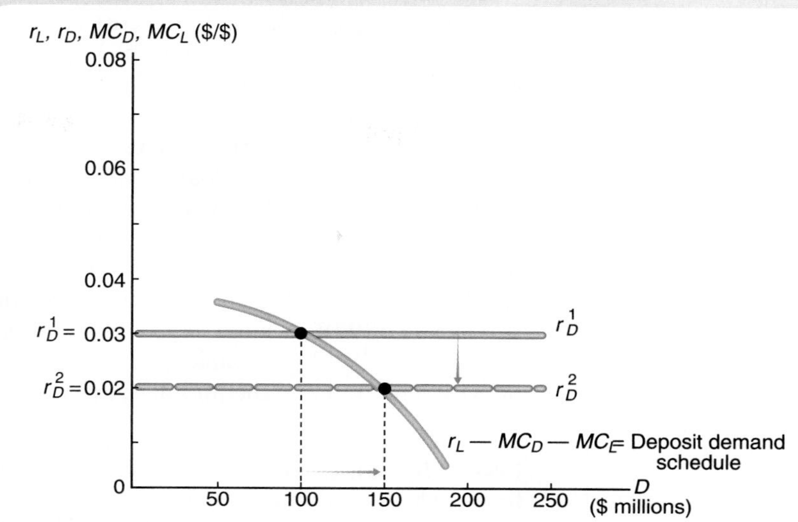

which equals the sum of the market deposit rate, the marginal resource cost of lending, and the marginal resource cost of deposits. Thus, as the loan rate changes, the bank varies its lending along its marginal cost schedule, which means that over most of its range the upward-sloping marginal cost schedule is the bank's loan supply schedule. In addition, profit maximization requires a bank to issue deposits to the point at which the interest rate on deposits is equal to the net marginal revenue from lending, which is the market loan rate minus the marginal resource costs of loans and deposits. As the deposit rate varies, therefore, the bank changes its deposits along the net marginal revenue schedule, which means that this downward-sloping schedule is the bank's deposit demand schedule.

A Competitive Market for Loans

We now turn our attention to how market interest rates on loans and deposits actually get determined. In a perfectly competitive market, these interest rates are determined by the interaction of the forces of market demand and supply.

THE MARKET LOAN SUPPLY SCHEDULE In the market for bank loans, the sellers of loans are banks. Hence, banks supply loans. The borrowers of loans are their customers who demand loans.

In a competitive market for any good or service, the market supply schedule is simply the horizontal summation of the supply schedules for all producers of that good or service. That is, we can sum the quantities producers desire to supply at each possible price to obtain a set of price-quantity combinations that constitute a total market supply schedule.

The same is true for a market with perfectly competitive banks. As we showed in Figure 12-4, a bank's marginal cost schedule is its loan supply schedule. In Figure 12-7, we reproduce the typical bank's loan supply schedule for the case in which the market deposit rate is equal to 0.03. When the interest rate on loans is equal to 0.06, this individual bank desires to supply $100 million in loans.

In a perfectly competitive market, numerous other banks also supply loans. Consequently, the *market loan supply schedule* (L^s) is the sum of the total quantities of lending by all banks in the loan market at every possible loan interest rate. As shown in Figure 12-7, the remaining banks in the loan market desire to supply $9,900 million in loans at a loan rate of 0.06 and $14,850 million in loans at a loan rate of 0.08 Hence, the total quantity of loans supplied by all banks at a loan rate of 0.06 is equal to $10,000 million, or $10 billion. The total quantity of loans supplied by all banks at a loan rate of 0.08 is equal to $15,000 million, or $15 billion. The schedule denoted L^s, therefore, is the market loan supply schedule.

LOAN MARKET EQUILIBRIUM Banks make loans to individual households and firms, which economists refer to collectively as the *nonbank public*. Each household and firm has its own loan demand schedule, which, via the law of demand, slopes downward. We can sum the quantities of loans demanded by the nonbank public at any given loan interest rate to construct the market loan demand schedule (L^d), such as the one depicted in panel (a) of Figure 12-8.

The Equilibrium Loan Rate Also shown in panel (a) of Figure 12-8 is a situation of *loan market equilibrium*. In equilibrium, the quantity of loans demanded by the nonbank public is equal to the quantity of loans supplied by banks. The

Figure 12-7
The Market Loan Supply Schedule.

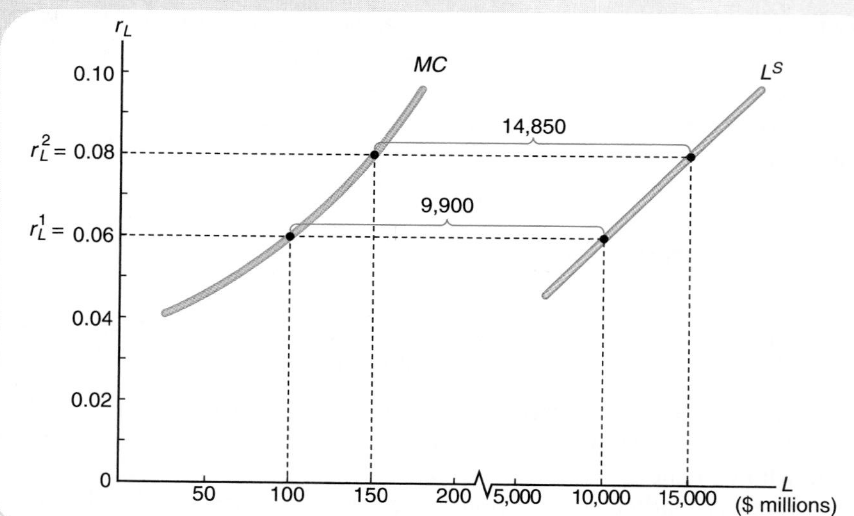

The market loan supply schedule depicts the total quantity of loans supplied by all banks in the loan market at any given loan interest rate. For example, if the loan rate is equal to $r_L^1 = 0.06$, then an individual bank supplies $100 million in loans, while remaining banks supply a total of $9,900 million in loans, so that total lending is equal to $10,000 million, or $10 billion. If the loan rate rises to $r_L^2 = 0.08$, the individual bank increases its lending to $150 million, while remaining banks increase their total lending to $14,850 million, so that total lending by all banks rises to $15,000 million, or $15 billion.

Figure 12-8 Equilibrium in a Perfectly Competitive Loan Market.

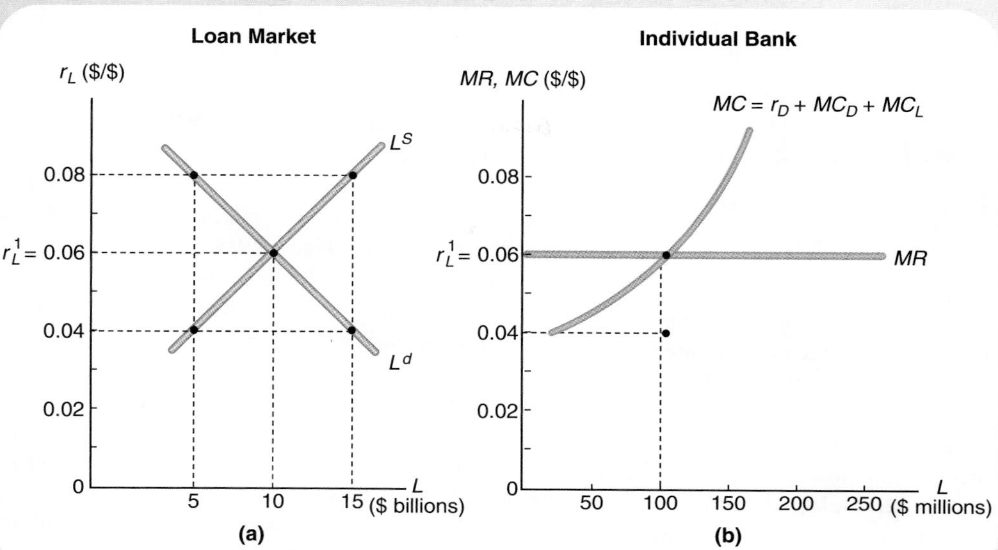

In equilibrium, the quantity of loans demanded by the nonbank public is equal to the quantity of loans supplied by banks, which is $10 billion in panel (a). If the loan rate were equal to 0.08, then there would be an excess quantity of loans supplied by banks, and banks would bid the loan rate down to its equilibrium value of $r_L^1 = 0.06$. In contrast, if the loan rate were equal to 0.04, then there would be an excess quantity of loans demanded by borrowers, and borrowers would bid the loan rate up to its equilibrium value. At the equilibrium loan rate of $r_L^1 = 0.06$, the individual bank in panel (b) maximizes profits by supplying $100 million in loans.

equilibrium quantity of loans demanded and supplied is $10 billion. The loan interest rate adjusts until this condition is satisfied. For instance, if the interest rate were equal to 0.08, there would be an excess quantity of loans supplied—which we could alternatively call surplus lending—by banks. The loan rate would be bid downward until this loan surplus was eliminated. In contrast, if the loan rate were equal to 0.04, there would be an excess quantity of loans demanded—a shortage of loans. In this event, the loan rate would be bid upward until the shortage of loans was eliminated. The equilibrium interest rate on loans, which is 0.06 in panel (a) of Figure 12-8, is the single loan interest rate at which the equilibrium quantity of lending is attained.

Equilibrium for a Bank Panel (b) of Figure 12-8 shows the lending decision at a typical bank in this market. If the market loan rate is 0.06, the bank desires to make $100 million in loans. Why does the individual bank take the market loan rate of 0.06 as "given"? Perhaps the best way to visualize why this is so is to imagine what would happen if the bank made no loans at all. The amount of lending would be reduced by only $100 million, which is very small in relation to the total amount of lending of $10 billion. Thus, the loss of this bank's presence from the banking system would scarcely be noticeable. By itself, this bank cannot influence the market loan rate. It takes the market loan rate as given. (A business downturn typically alters loan demand and the market loan rate; see on page 278 *Policy Focus: Explaining Declining Bank Lending in the Early 2000s.*)

GLOBAL | POLICY Focus | CYBER | MANAGEMENT

Explaining Declining Bank Lending in the Early 2000s

As the U.S. economy's performance leveled off and then settled into recession during 2001, banks toughened their lending standards. At the same time, there was a noticeable drop in bank lending. Some observers complained that overly burdensome bank regulations were responsible for tougher lending standards and reduced loans. They further argued that the stifling effects of regulation were contributing to the recession by cutting businesses off from credit that was available at lower market interest rates.

Regulators and bankers responded that the real culprit behind the reduced lending *and* the drop in market loan rates was the recession itself. During a downturn in economic activity, consumer and business confidence typically declines. The result is often a fall in the demand for loans. Figure 12-9 traces the effects of a decrease in the demand for loans. At any given loan interest rate, including the initial equilibrium loan rate, there is a decline in the quantity of loans demanded by individuals and firms.

Applying the basic competitive theory of banking indicates that a decrease in the demand for loans, shown in panel (a) of Figure 12-9 as a leftward shift of the market loan demand schedule, from L^d to $L^{d\prime}$, results in an excess quantity of loans supplied at the old equilibrium loan rate, 0.06. Consequently, the original equilibrium quantity of loans demanded and supplied, \$10 billion, is no longer the equilibrium amount of lending. To obtain more loans, competing bank lenders must make lower loan rate bids. As the loan rate is bid downward, the surplus of loans is eliminated, and the quantity of loans demanded now is equal to the quantity of loans supplied at a new equilibrium loan interest rate of 0.05.

As the loan interest rate is bid downward, each bank is willing to supply a smaller quantity of loans, as shown in panel (b) of Figure 12-9. The fall in the market loan rate, from 0.06 to 0.05, induces the individual bank to reduce its quantity of loans supplied from \$100 million to \$80 million. This movement along the bank's loan supply schedule in panel (b) mirrors the *movement along* the market loan supply schedule in panel (a) of Figure 12-9. This bank and all other banks in the market reduce the quantity of loans supplied until a new market equilibrium is attained at a total quantity of

A Competitive Market for Deposits

In the loan market, banks are sellers, and borrowers are buyers. Hence, banks supply loans, and borrowers demand loans. In contrast, in the deposit market, banks are the buyers, so they demand deposit funds for use in making loans. Their deposit customers are the sellers of deposits who supply their funds to banks.

THE MARKET DEPOSIT DEMAND SCHEDULE In the market for any particular good or service, the market demand schedule is the horizontal summation of the demand schedules of all agents that wish to purchase the good or service in question. This basic relationship also extends to the market for bank deposits, in which it is banks that demand deposit funds from their customers.

As we saw in Figure 12-6 on page 275, an individual bank's net marginal revenue, $r_L - MC_D - MC_L$, is that bank's deposit demand schedule. In Figure 12-10 on page 280, we reproduce the typical bank's deposit demand schedule from Figure 12-6, which we derived given a market loan rate of 0.06. If the market deposit rate is equal to 0.03, then the individual bank demands \$100 million in deposits.

Figure 12-9
Effects of a Decrease in the Nonbank Public's Demand for Loans.

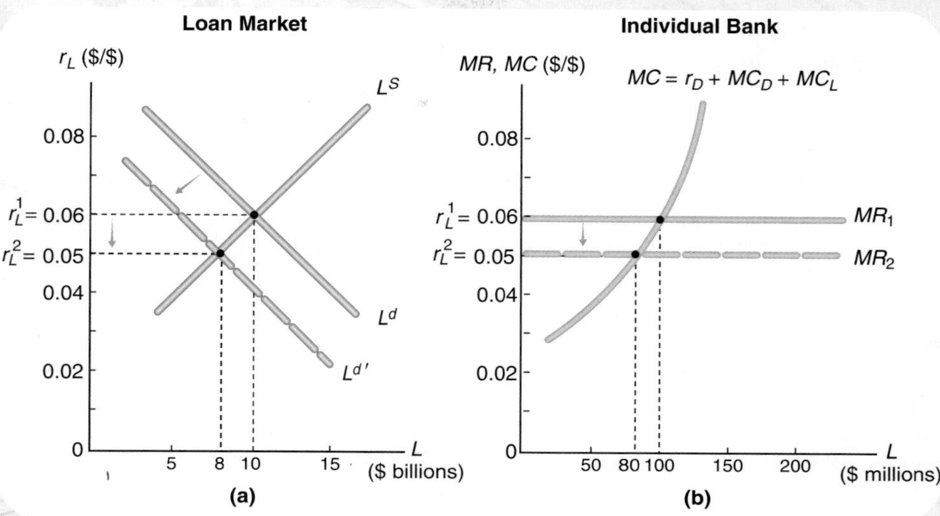

Panel (a) shows that a decrease in the demand for loans generates a leftward shift of the market loan demand schedule. As a result, there is an excess quantity of loans supplied at the initial equilibrium loan rate, $r_L^1 = 0.06$. Those banks that wish to lend bid down the loan rate to a new equilibrium value of $r_L^2 = 0.05$, and the equilibrium quantity of loans falls to $8 billion. For the individual bank, as shown in panel (b), the decline in the market loan rate induces a decrease in the profit-maximizing quantity of loans, from $100 million to $80 million.

loans supplied of $8 billion. As you can see, in a competitive loan market, a decrease in loan demand during an economic downturn naturally leads to decreases in both the amount of loans that banks make and the market interest rate on loans. Tougher regulations are not necessarily responsible.

For Critical Analysis: If loan demand had remained unchanged during the early 2000s and harsher regulations had significantly pushed up banks' resource costs of lending, what would have happened to the market loan rate?

If the deposit rate falls to 0.02, then the bank demands $150 million in deposits. To derive the total market deposit demand schedule, we must include the quantities of deposits demanded by all other banks. If the market deposit rate is equal to 0.03, all other banks wish to issue $9,900 million in deposits. The total quantity of deposits demanded at a deposit rate of 0.03, therefore, is equal to $10,000 million, or $10 billion. If the deposit rate declines to 0.02, however, then all other banks demand a total of $13,850 million in deposits, so the total amount of deposits demanded by all banks is equal to $14,000 million, or $14 billion. Thus, the schedule denoted as D^d in Figure 12-10 is the *market deposit demand schedule.*

On the Web
What are current market equilibrium rates on bank deposits such as certificates of deposit? To find out, go to the Web site of Bank Rate Monitor, http://www.bankrate.com, and click on "CDs/Savings" in the left-hand margin. Note that you can also select various loan categories to check on prevailing interest rates in bank loan markets.

Deposit Market Equilibrium Households and firms are willing to supply more deposits to banks as the market deposit interest rate paid by banks increases. Hence, the *market deposit supply schedule* (D^s) of the nonbank public slopes upward. A possible market deposit supply schedule is depicted in panel (a) of Figure 12-11 on the following page.

Figure 12-10
The Market Deposit Demand Schedule.

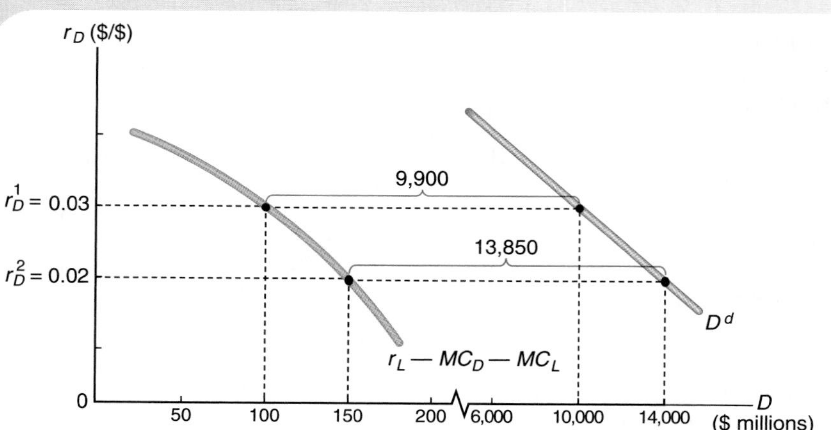

The market deposit demand schedule depicts the total quantity of deposits demanded by all banks in the deposit market at any given deposit interest rate. For instance, if the deposit rate is equal to $r_D^1 = 0.03$, then an individual bank issues $100 million in deposits, while remaining banks issue a total of $9,900 million in deposits, so that total deposits equal $10,000 million, or $10 billion. If the deposit rate declines to $r_D^2 = 0.02$, then the individual bank increases the amount of deposits it issues to $150 million, while remaining banks increase the total quantity of deposit funds they demand to $13,850 million, so that the total amount of deposits demanded by all banks rises to $14,000 million, or $14 billion.

Figure 12-11 also displays a possible equilibrium situation in the market for bank deposits. This occurs when the quantity of deposits demanded by banks equals the quantity of deposits supplied by the nonbank public. In panel (a) of Figure 12-11, the equilibrium quantity of deposits demanded and supplied is $10

Figure 12-11
Equilibrium in a Perfectly Competitive Deposit Market.

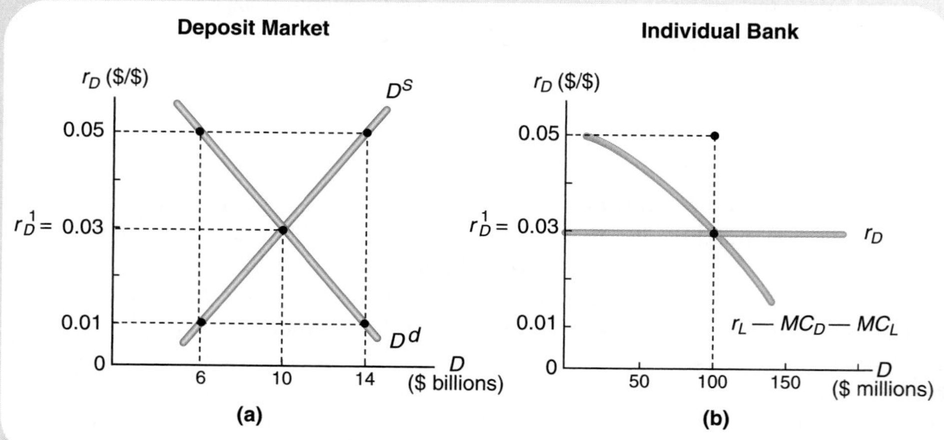

In equilibrium, the quantity of deposits supplied by the nonbank public is equal to the quantity of deposits demanded by banks, which is $10 billion in panel (a). If the deposit rate were equal to 0.05, then there would be an excess quantity of deposits supplied by the nonbank public, who would bid the deposit rate down to its equilibrium value of $r_D^1 = 0.03$. By way of contrast, if the deposit rate were equal to 0.01, then there would be an excess quantity of deposits demanded by banks, and banks would bid the deposit rate up to its equilibrium value. At the equilibrium loan rate of $r_D^1 =$ 0.03, the individual bank issues $100 million in deposits, as shown in panel (b).

billion. The interest rate on deposits adjusts until deposit market equilibrium is attained. On the one hand, if the deposit interest rate were equal to 0.05, there would be an excess quantity of deposits supplied by the nonbank public, or a surplus of deposits. Depositors competing for interest earnings would bid the deposit rate downward until the surplus was eliminated. On the other hand, if the deposit rate were equal to 0.01, there would be an excess quantity of deposits demanded by banks, or a shortage of deposits. In this event, the competing banks would bid the deposit rate upward until there was no longer a shortage of deposits. The equilibrium interest rate on deposits—0.03 in panel (a) of Figure 12-11—is the rate at which there is no surplus or shortage of deposits, given the positions of the deposit demand and supply schedules. Panel (b) of Figure 12-11 shows the decision of an individual bank about how many dollars in deposits it should obtain. It knows that its demand for deposits is an insignificant part of the total demand for deposits, so it takes the market deposit rate of 0.03 as given. (An economic downturn ultimately tends to reduce bank profits because it tends to reduce the public's supply of deposits to banks at the same time that it generates a falloff in the public's loan demand; see on page 282 *Management Focus: Why a Recession Is Tough on Banks.*)

Consider how to apply the competitive theory of banking to international issues by going to the Chapter 12 Case Study, entitled "Opening Banking Markets to International Competition."
http://moneyxtra.swcollege.com

3. How are bank loan and deposit rates determined in perfectly competitive banking markets? The basic theory of perfect competition in banking markets indicates that the equilibrium interest rate on bank loans is the rate at which the quantity of loans demanded by the public is equal to the quantity of loans supplied by banks. The equilibrium interest rate on bank deposits is the rate at which the quantity of deposits supplied by the public is equal to the quantity of deposits demanded by banks. Changes in either the market loan rate or the market deposit rate arise from variations in demand or supply in these markets.

Imperfect Competition in Banking?

As we shall discuss in detail in Chapter 13, a number of economists question whether the model of competitive banking that we have used throughout this chapter really does a good job of describing real-world banking markets. As we shall see in Chapter 14, there are several reasons that the assumptions of perfect competition may not readily apply to the banking industry. Perhaps the most important of these is that, for a number of reasons, laws and regulations have limited freedom of entry and exit in banking. If existing banks are protected from rivalry by other banks, then competitive loan or deposit markets will not exist. That is, at least some banking markets could be **imperfectly competitive markets,** in which banks can strategically set their own loan or deposit rates to maximize their individual profits.

Imperfectly competitive market: A market in which conditions for perfect competition, such as freedom of entry and exit, fail to hold, so banks can set their own loan or deposit rates to maximize their individual profits.

Monopoly: A market environment in which only a single firm, or a group of firms collectively coordinating their actions, produces a good or service; in banking, a situation in which only one bank or a coordinating group of banks lends and takes in deposits.

Let's consider what differences would arise in the case of a banking **monopoly,** or a bank market structure in which there is only one bank in a market or just a few banks that jointly seek to maximize their profits. To see these differences, we

GLOBAL POLICY CYBER **MANAGEMENT Focus**

Why a Recession Is Tough on Banks

Panel (a) of Figure 12-12 shows that as U.S. economic activity leveled off in the late 1990s and then declined in the early 2000s, banks' average *net interest margin*—the difference between the rates of return on their assets, such as loans, and their liabilities, such as deposits—narrowed considerably. During the onset of the recession, market loan rates had already dropped. Simultaneously, banks were under pressure to keep their deposit rates from declining.

The weakening economy caused incomes to stagnate and even decline. Naturally, the result was a decline in the amounts of deposit funds supplied to banks. Figure 12-12 uses the basic theory of perfect competition in bank deposit markets to predict the effects of a decrease in the supply of deposits by firms and households. In panel (b) of Figure 12-12, there is a leftward shift of the market deposit supply schedule, from D^s to $D^{s\prime}$, and there is now an excess quantity of deposits demanded at the old equilibrium deposit rate, 0.03. As a result, the original equilibrium quantity of deposits demanded and supplied, \$14 billion, is no longer the equilibrium amount of deposits. As the interest rate on deposits is bid upward, the shortage of deposits is eliminated at a new equilibrium deposit interest rate of 0.04.

Following this rise in the market deposit interest rate, each bank, such as the bank illustrated in panel (c) of Figure 12-12, demands a smaller quantity of deposits. As the market deposit rate rises from 0.03 to 0.04, the bank reduces its quantity of deposits demanded from \$100 million to \$80 million. This movement along the bank's deposit demand schedule in panel (c) mirrors the movement along the market deposit demand schedule in panel (b). This bank and all other banks in the market decrease the quantity of deposits demanded until a new market equilibrium is attained at a total amount of deposits supplied of \$8 billion. During a recession, therefore, there can be pressure for banks to boost their deposit rates even as market loan rates are falling. The result is a narrowing in the differential between loan and deposit rates, which panel (a) shows is exactly what happened in the United States. Naturally, this makes a significant dent in bank profits.

FOR CRITICAL ANALYSIS: Why is banking often called a "procyclical industry"?

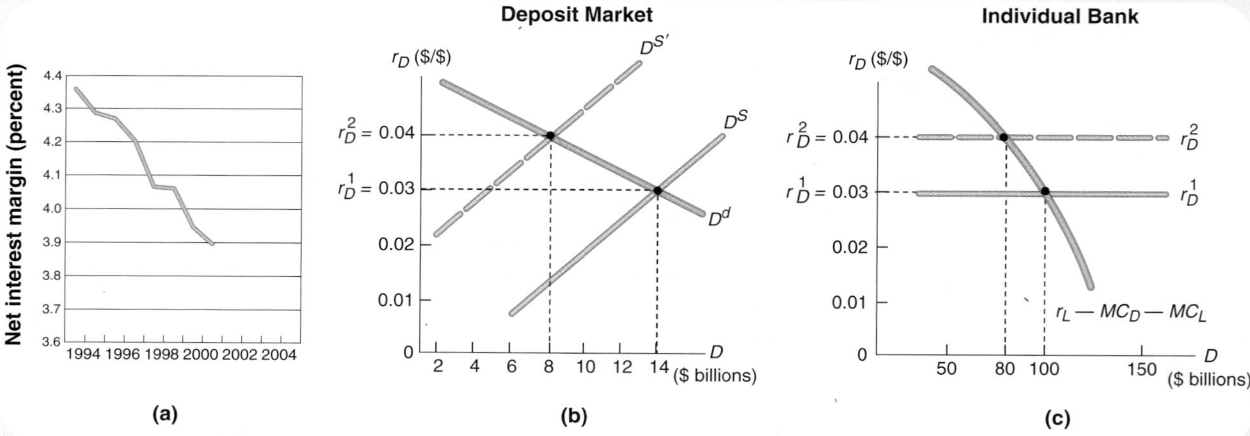

Figure 12-12 Effects of a Decrease in the Nonbank Public's Supply of Deposits.

shall focus on the effects of monopolistic banking in the market for loans. As shown in Figure 12-13, if there is only one monopoly bank in the loan market, then this bank alone faces the market loan demand schedule. This means that the bank's marginal revenue is not constant because the bank can influence the quantity of loans it makes by changing its loan rate, thereby altering the additional revenue it receives for each additional dollar of loans it makes. Indeed, as the bank lowers its loan rate, its marginal revenue from lending declines and lies below the loan rate it charges; hence, the monopoly bank's marginal revenue (*MR*) schedule slopes downward and lies below the market loan demand schedule, as shown in Figure 12-13.

Profit Maximization

To maximize its profits, the bank makes loans up to the point at which marginal revenue equals marginal cost. Thus, the bank extends loans to the point at which the marginal revenue schedule, *MR*, crosses the marginal cost schedule, $MC = r_D + MC_D + MC_L$. At this point, as depicted in Figure 12-13, the bank desires to make $L^* = \$5$ billion in loans. If the bank were to lend less than this, then its marginal revenue from lending would exceed the marginal cost it incurs, meaning that the additional revenue received from making more loans would be greater than the additional cost it would incur from increasing its lending. Hence, the bank could increase its profits by increasing the amount of loans toward \$5 billion. If the bank were to make loans beyond this level, it would find that the additional cost it incurred would be greater than the additional revenue earned. Consequently, it would reduce its lending back toward \$5 billion to increase its profits.

Figure 12-13
A Monopoly Loan Market.

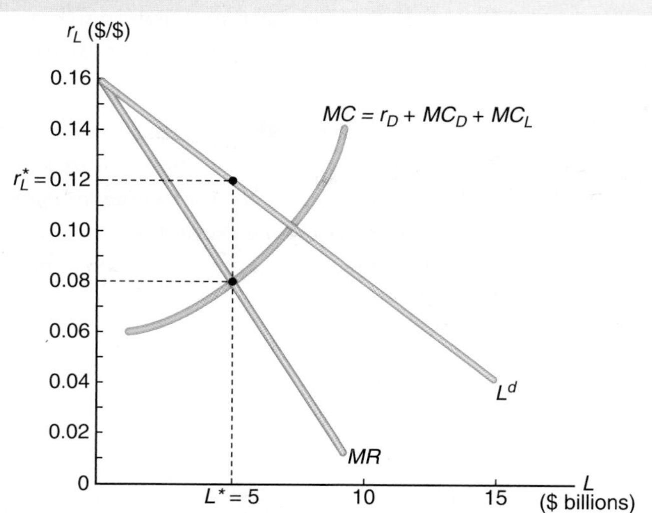

If there is only one bank in the loan market, or if all the banks in the market are able to coordinate in pursuit of maximum joint profits, then there is a loan market monopolist that alone faces the market loan demand schedule. As the monopolist reduces its loan rate, it can influence its marginal revenue from lending, which is the downward-sloping *MR* schedule. To maximize its profit, the monopolist lends to the point at which marginal revenue is equal to marginal cost (L^* = \$5 billion). It then charges the maximum loan rate that borrowers are willing to pay, which is $r_L^* = 0.12$ (12 percent).

The Monopoly Loan Rate

If the bank is truly a monopoly bank, then $5 billion will be the total quantity of loans available to borrowers in this market. What interest rate will borrowers have to pay for this amount of loans? Under perfect competition, the market loan interest rate is determined by the interaction of the forces of supply and demand. Under a bank monopoly, however, there is no longer a *market* supply schedule. Instead, the single bank determines its profit-maximizing amount of lending based solely on its own marginal revenue and cost conditions.

Consequently, the monopoly bank charges the highest loan rate that borrowers are willing to pay for the amount of loans the bank has chosen to extend to them. As we can see in Figure 12-13, if the amount of lending by the bank is $5 billion, then, according to the market loan demand schedule, the nonbank public is willing and able to pay a loan rate $r_L^* = 0.12$, or 12 percent. This, then, is the market loan rate charged by the monopoly bank.

On the Web
How much are national borders being opened to global competition in financial services? To keep track of the latest developments concerning this issue, visit the home page of the World Trade Organization at http://www.wto.org, and click on "Search." Under "Search the rest of the WTO website," type in "financial services" and review the most recent documents that the WTO has posted.

Today, there are more than 8,000 commercial banks in the United States, not including the many credit unions and savings institutions that compete, directly or indirectly, with commercial banks in loan and deposit markets. Just a decade ago, there were more than 12,000 commercial banks. Nevertheless, many economists have argued that imperfectly competitive banking markets may have been the rule rather than the exception in the United States, at least until fairly recently. As we shall discuss in Chapters 14 and 15, one reason for this may have been domestic regulations that stifled direct rivalry among commercial banks, credit unions, and savings banks and tended to shield individual institutions from competition outside their own locales.

Such competition-stifling regulations have existed in other parts of the world as well. Southeast Asia is a notable example. Nevertheless, internal barriers to banking competition have been breaking down in both the United States and Europe. Furthermore, external barriers have been weakening as well, thereby opening up the possibility of greater *international* competition in banking.

4. How is the interest rate on bank loans determined in a monopoly loan market? A monopoly bank or a group of banks that coordinate lending decisions faces the market demand for loans. The monopoly lender makes loans to the point where the marginal revenue from loans equals the total marginal cost of lending and then charges the loan rate that the public is willing and able to pay for this amount of loans.

Link to **Management**

Does the Theory of Perfect Competition Apply to Online Banking?

According to the theory of perfectly competitive banking, depository institutions in competitive markets should pay the same interest rate on deposits. Figure 12-14 displays recent index measures of average rates paid on twelve-month certificates of deposit offered online by Internet banks as compared with traditional bank competitors. The figure indicates that the rate paid by Internet banks on online deposits is almost 20 percent higher than the average rates offered by their traditional banking rivals. It is difficult to imagine that competition would not prevail in a financial system with more than 8,000 commercial banks. Is Figure 12-14 a repudiation of the theory of how competitive banking markets operate?

Higher Teaser Rates in the Short Run . . .

The answer is that the direct comparison of deposit rates in Figure 12-14 fails to take several factors into account. First, the comparison is based on data collected during the early 2000s, when Internet banks were still in the process of trying to overcome significant hurdles to establishing a foothold in banking markets. Consider that in 2000, a study of the business plans of British Internet banks found that together they intended to attract 3.5 million customers by the end of 2002, even though only about 2 million new consumers of banking services were likely to emerge in the United Kingdom. To have succeeded in accomplishing their goals, the British Internet banks would have had to attract every one of those new banking consumers and to steal away 1.5 million others from established British banking institutions.

By definition, Internet banks begin as new institutions with no customers. To be successful in establishing a market foothold, these institutions have to recruit customers rapidly. At a number of Internet banks, however, providing reliable service has turned out to be a challenge. An Internet user may become mildly irritated when a retailer's Web site is unavailable because a server crashes, but a bank customer who is counting on making a transfer to close a financial deal in thirty minutes will view such an event as disastrous.

In addition, Internet banks have struggled to offer the full range of banking products that customers can obtain from bricks-and-mortar banks. As an inducement for households and businesses to establish accounts, Internet banks can offer virtual safety deposit boxes for their customers' financial data, but they cannot match traditional banks' offers to provide low-cost access to physical safety deposit boxes. To obtain certain banking services, such as quotes on loan rates, some customers may feel that just making a phone call is quicker and easier than locating a Web page containing the desired information. In many respects, therefore, certain *quality* aspects of Internet banks' services are inferior to those offered by traditional banking rivals.

. . . But Competitive Rates in the Long Run

One of the main rationales for establishing Internet banks was that owners anticipated profiting from the big cost advantages they had over traditional bricks-and-mortar competitors. With their lower costs, owners and managers of the Internet banks felt, they could attract numerous customers from existing institutions by paying higher deposit rates and charging lower fees and still earn significant profits.

In the end, Internet banks quickly discovered that the higher interest rates they paid on deposits

Continued on next page

Link to Management, continued

Figure 12-14
Index Measures of Interest Rates Offered on Online Bank Deposits.

Internet banks typically offer interest rates on certificates of deposit that are well above the average rates paid by traditional banking institutions.

SOURCE: Office of the Comptroller of the Currency.

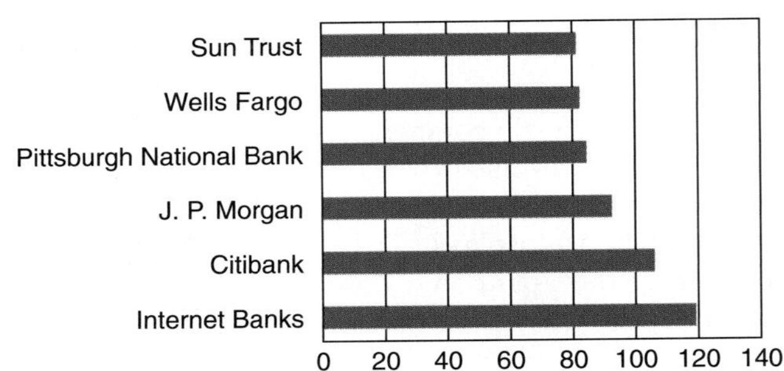

resulted in very narrow differentials between loan interest revenues and deposit interest costs. To remain profitable, many Internet banks began to push up fees and raise minimum-balance requirements to maintain zero-fee accounts. Taking into account these changes, the deposit rates that Internet banks offered their customers began to converge, on a constant-quality-unit basis, with the deposit rates paid by traditional bricks-and-mortar banks. At the same time, as traditional banks have moved more of their operations online, their resource costs have dropped, which has allowed them to boost their deposit rates somewhat. In the end, it appears that the overall prices that Internet banks and traditional banks pay customers for the use of their deposit funds have, after adjusting for quality differences, moved toward equalization, just as the theory of perfect competition suggests should have occurred.

Research Project

If the financial products and services of banks are sufficiently distinguishable, then they really amount to different brands, or heterogeneous versions of similar but identifiably different products. In this situation, the theory of perfect competition no longer applies. Are there any other theories of rivalry among many firms in the same market that could be applied in this instance? If so, what are the predictions of these theories about whether there could be lasting differences between the interest rates and prices of Internet banks and their bricks-and-mortar rivals?

Web Resources

1. What is the current status of online banking in the United States? For the latest summaries and reports, go to the home page of the Office of the Comptroller of the Currency (http://www.occ.treas.gov), and in the left margin click on "Electronic Banking."

2. How can traditional banking firms best compete with Internet banks on the Web? For one perspective on this issue, download an IBM Global Services Study entitled "Internet Strategies for Traditional Retail Banks" at http://www-3.ibm.com/e-business/resource/pdf/30287.pdf.

Chapter Summary

1. Sources of Bank Revenues and Costs in the Basic Economic Theory of Banking Markets: The basic theory of banking markets considers the key markets in which banks interact, which are the loan and deposit markets. Banks earn revenues through interest income on loans they extend in the loan market. They incur costs in the form of deposit interest expense, real resource costs incurred in providing deposit-related services, and real resource costs incurred in extending and monitoring loans.

2. The Loan Supply and Deposit Demand Schedules for Perfectly Competitive Banks: Profit maximization requires a bank to lend to the point at which the market loan rate is equal to total marginal cost, which is the sum of the market deposit rate, the marginal resource cost of lending, and the marginal resource cost of deposits. As the loan rate varies, therefore, the bank alters the quantity of loans along its marginal cost schedule, which means that over most of its range the upward-sloping marginal cost schedule is the bank's loan supply schedule. In addition, to maximize its economic profit, a bank issues deposits to the point at which the interest rate on deposits equals the net marginal revenue from lending, which is the market loan rate minus the marginal resource costs of loans and deposits. Hence, as the deposit rate changes, the bank varies its deposits along the net marginal revenue schedule, which means that this downward-sloping schedule is the bank's deposit demand schedule.

3. How Bank Loan and Deposit Rates Are Determined in Perfectly Competitive Banking Markets: According to the basic theory of perfect competition in banking markets, the equilibrium interest rate on bank loans is the interest rate at which the quantity of loans supplied by banks equals the quantity of loans demanded by the public. The theory also indicates that the equilibrium interest rate on bank deposits is the interest rate at which the quantity of deposits demanded by banks equals the quantity of deposits supplied by the public. Changes in demand or supply in either market induce variations in either the market loan rate or the market deposit rate.

4. How the Interest Rate on Bank Loans Is Determined in a Monopoly Loan Market: A monopoly bank or coordinating group of banks faces the entire market demand for loans. The monopoly lender makes loans to the point where the marginal revenue from loans equals the total marginal cost of lending. Then the monopoly lender charges the loan rate that the public is willing and able to pay for this amount of loans.

Questions and Problems

(Answers to odd-numbered questions and problems may be found on the Web at http://money.swcollege.com under "Student Resources.")

1. Suppose that, at its current levels of loans and deposits, a bank that holds loans as its only assets and issues deposits as its only liabilities finds that its marginal resource cost of loans is $0.01 per dollar of lending and that its marginal resource cost of deposits is $0.03 per dollar of deposits. The present market interest rate on deposits is 4 percent. If the banking system is perfectly competitive, and if this bank is maximizing its profits, what is the market interest rate on loans?

2. A bank in a perfectly competitive banking system finds that its marginal resource cost of loans is equal to $0.02 per dollar of lending. Its marginal resource cost of deposits is $0.04 per dollar of deposits. The market interest rate on deposits is 3 percent, and the market interest rate on loans is 10 percent. Is this bank maximizing its profits? How can you tell?

3. Should the bank discussed in question 2 increase or decrease its lending? Should the bank increase or decrease its deposits? Draw diagrams to help explain your answers.

4. Suppose that there is a decrease in the nonbank public's demand for bank loans. Assume that the banking system is perfectly competitive. Trace through the effects of this reduction in loan demand, both in the market for loans and with respect to an individual bank.

5. Suppose that all banks in an unregulated, perfectly competitive banking system find that they must pay higher wages to all their employees.

a. Explain the effects of this wage increase on the loan market behavior of an individual bank and on full loan market equilibrium. Use diagrams to assist in explaining your answer.

b. Explain the effects of this wage increase on the deposit market behavior of an individual bank and on full deposit market equilibrium. Use diagrams to assist in explaining your answer.

6. Suppose that in a competitive banking system we observe the equilibrium bank loan rate increase, from 7 percent to 8 percent, while the equilibrium bank deposit rate simultaneously falls, from 4 percent to 3 percent. If the marginal resource cost of loans is unchanged, what has likely happened to the marginal resource cost of deposits? Explain.

7. Suppose that a monopoly bank finds that it must pay higher wages to all its employees. Use a diagram to explain what the effects would be on the amount of loans made by this bank and on the loan interest rate the bank charges.

8. For years, a bank located in a geographically remote community has been the single provider of funds for mortgage loans. Now, however, many residents have access to the Internet and have learned how to obtain mortgage loans from banks located some distance away. Use the model of a monopoly bank to explain the immediate effects on the bank's profit-maximizing lending and loan rate.

9. Consider the following model of the bank deposit market:

Market deposit demand schedule: $D^d = 50 - (500 \times r_D)$

Market deposit supply schedule: $D^s = 10 + (300 \times r_D)$

a. Draw a rough diagram of the market deposit demand and supply schedules.

b. Solve for the equilibrium deposit rate and quantity of deposits.

10. Consider the following model of the bank loan market:

Market loan demand schedule: $L^d = 43 - (200 \times r_L)$

Market loan supply schedule: $L^s = 16 + (100 \times r_L)$

a. Draw a rough diagram of the market loan demand and supply schedules.

b. Solve for the equilibrium loan rate and quantity of deposits.

Before the Test

Test your understanding of the material covered in this chapter by taking the Chapter 12 interactive quiz at http://money.swcollege.com.

Online Application

Internet URL: http://www.fdic.gov

Title: The FDIC Quarterly Banking Profile

Navigation: Go to the FDIC's home page at the above Internet URL. Click on "Quarterly Banking Profiles." From the top menu bar, select "Quarterly Banking Profile" and click on "Commercial Bank Section."

Application: Read the following sections of the report for the most recent quarter, and answer the related questions:

1. Read the section that discusses U.S. banks' average net interest margin, and click on the most recent link relating to the net interest margin. Within the basic banking market framework we developed in this chapter, what factors could account for recent changes in the net interest margin? What factors might the basic theory leave out that could also explain the net interest margin?

2. Now read the section of the report that discusses bank lending exposure to foreign borrowers, and click on the latest link on this topic. Is there any recent trend in lending abroad by U.S. banks? What factors might account for this trend?

For Group Study and Analysis: Split the class into groups, and assign each group to review a separate portion of the FDIC's Quarterly Banking Profile. Have each group evaluate the aspects of banking data reviewed in the report that are or are not consistent with the basic banking market theory of this chapter. How might the theory be extended to take into account real-world factors not in the model?

Selected References and Further Reading

Baltensperger, Ernst. "Alternative Approaches to the Theory of the Banking Firm." *Journal of Monetary Economics* 6 (January 1980): 1–37.

Cosimano, Thomas, Connel Fullenkamp, and Richard Sheehan. "An Examination of Retail Deposit Rate Setting by Large Financial Institutions." University of Notre Dame, 2002.

Elyasiani, Elyas, Kenneth Kopecky, and David VanHoose. "Costs of Adjustment, Portfolio Separation, and the Dynamic Behavior of Bank Loans and Deposits." *Journal of Money, Credit, and Banking* 27 (November 1995, Part 1): 955–974.

Freixas, Xavier, and Jean-Charles Rochet. *Microeconomics of Banking*. Cambridge, Mass.: MIT Press, 1997.

Santomero, Anthony. "Modeling the Banking Firm: A Survey." *Journal of Money, Credit, and Banking* 16 (November 1984, Part 2): 576–603.

VanHoose, David. "Deregulation and Oligopolistic Rivalry in Bank Deposit Markets." *Journal of Banking and Finance* 12 (September 1988): 379–388.

MoneyXtra

moneyxtra!

Log on to the MoneyXtra Web site now (**http://moneyxtra.swcollege.com**) for additional learning resources such as practice quizzes, case studies, readings, and additional economic applications.

Chapter 13

The Business of Banking—
Depository Institution Management and Performance

Fundamental Issues

1. What are the key sources of depository institution revenues and costs?

2. What are common measures of depository institution profitability?

3. How has the philosophy of depository institution management evolved?

4. What is the main determinant of depository institution performance?

In the 1960s, many called banking a "3-6-3 business." They claimed that each workday bankers obtained funds at 3 percent interest, spent 6 hours lending the funds out to local individuals and companies and buying low-risk Treasury securities, and then headed to the golf course by 3 P.M.

Then the 1970s and 1980s arrived. Interest rates rose dramatically and became much more volatile. By the time banks' interest expenses stabilized in the late 1980s, banking had become a very different line of work. Only nimble, creative bankers willing to consider raising funds and lending in national and global markets could survive. The name of the game had become risk management, and banking specialists developed new theories of how to balance lending risks with interest rate risks on deposits and other sources of funds.

This trend continued into the 1990s. Bankers developed new ways to address lending risks, including a very direct approach—completely removing risks from their balance sheets. In their first foray in this direction, bankers developed methods for selling many of their loans to other investors. This left banks with the less risky task of collecting payments and transferring the funds, less fees for performing this service, to those investors. The investors, in turn, assumed the risks of loan delinquencies and defaults that banks had previously borne.

By the early 2000s, bankers were well on their way to implementing a less cumbersome method of transferring loan risks. They began using credit derivatives, *financial instruments with returns that depend on the underlying credit risks of loans. Under the terms of a credit derivative contract, failure of a bor-*

rower to pay off a loan is a "credit event" that requires the contract counterparties to cover the risk. To many bankers, credit derivatives began to look like a ticket to a return to the "3-6-3" days of low risks and an easier life.

Banks and other depository institutions face special types of risks to their profitability not encountered by nonfinancial firms or even by other financial institutions. In this chapter you will learn about sources of depository institution profitability, review theories of how these institutions should manage their risks, consider factors that affect their profitability, and evaluate their recent performance.

Interest income: Interest revenues that depository institutions derive from their holdings of loans and securities.

Noninterest income: Revenues that depository institutions earn from sources other than interest income, such as trading profits or fees that they charge for services that they provide their customers.

Basic Issues in Depository Institution Management

As we discussed in Chapter 11, banks, savings institutions, and credit unions specialize in various ways. Nevertheless, the fundamental economics of these depository institutions is very similar. All depository institutions incur the same basic kinds of expenses, and all derive earnings from similar, if not always identical, types of operations. The profits that they earn, of course, are the excess of revenues over costs. We begin our discussion of the economics of depository institutions by evaluating how to judge their performances in the marketplace.

Sources of Depository Institution Revenues

Banks measure their *revenues,* or incomes, as *flows* over time. For instance, a depository institution can track its interest income from loans and securities over a month, a quarter, or a year. Most depository institutions report quarterly and annual income flows.

Interest Income As you learned in Chapter 12, interest earnings on assets such as commercial and industrial loans are a key factor influencing the economic behavior of banks. The interest earnings that depository institutions derive from their loans and securities are the institutions' **interest income.** To see how interest income is a *flow* of earnings over time, consider an example in which a bank makes a $15,000 loan to an individual to help finance the purchase of a new car. The loan is a $15,000 asset for the bank at the moment it is made. If the auto loan is a typical installment loan, then the borrower will make monthly payments of principal and interest. This interest income is part of the bank's total revenues.

As Figure 13-1 shows, interest income accounts for roughly two-thirds of the revenues of commercial banks. It also represents the bulk of income to savings institutions and credit unions.

Figure 13-1
Sources of Commercial Bank Revenues.

Noninterest income has become a more important source of bank revenues in recent years, although the majority of bank revenues continues to flow from their interest earnings.

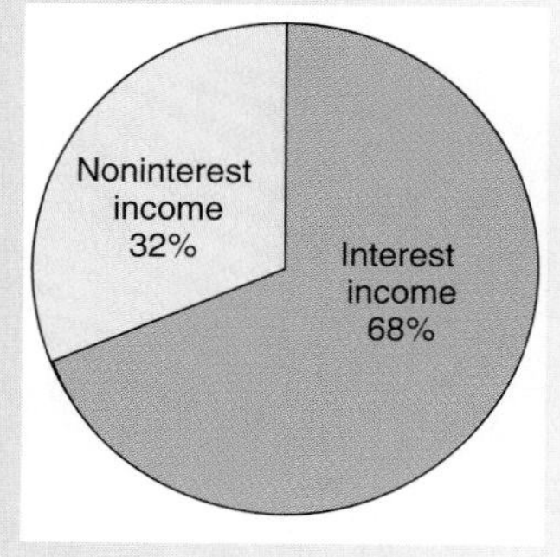

SOURCE: Federal Deposit Insurance Corporation.

Noninterest Income As Figure 13-1 indicates, commercial banks earn about 32 percent of their revenues as **noninterest income.** Noninterest income includes all income from sources other than interest income and is generated in several ways. One way that many depository institutions generate noninterest income is by selling some of the loans that they have made to other financial institutions—often at a higher market value. In addition, such loan sales commonly include an arrangement in which the depository institution selling the loans continues to maintain the loan accounts on behalf of the purchaser. That is, it continues to manage and process payments and expenses relating to the loans even though those loans are off its books. In return for such services, the depository institution charges fees to the loan purchaser. These loan management fees are a source of noninterest income.

Trading Income Depository institutions also generate noninterest income from trading in derivative instruments such as futures, options, or swaps. As discussed in Chapter 8, derivatives trading is often intended to *hedge* against risks. Such trading typically generates few revenues because depository institutions design hedges to avoid capital losses, thereby eliminating profit opportunities as well. Nevertheless, depository institutions also engage in speculative derivatives trading that can generate income (and losses!).

Income from Customer Fees *Deposit fee income,* the income that depository institutions earn by charging fees for their depository services, has been a growing source of noninterest income. Many depository institutions now charge many of their customers fees for printing checks, clearing checks, making cash withdrawals above a certain number per month, and making transfers between accounts. Today, most commercial banks charge a fee to use automated teller machines (ATMs), whereas in 1989 only a fifth of banks charged such a fee.

Some banks have even experimented with charging fees when customers with small accounts do business with human tellers at their branches. For example, in the mid-1990s First Chicago Bank began charging a $3 teller fee to account holders with checking balances under $2,500 or a combined checking/saving balance less than $15,000. As justification, the bank pointed out that, in a given year, a $500 checking account would usually yield $25 in interest income and $100 in fee income to the bank. But if the account holder were to make eight ATM transactions and four teller transactions per month, maintaining the account would cost the bank $216. Hence, the bank claimed it would lose $91 per year on such an account. For a checking account with a balance of over $5,000, the bank would earn a net profit of $314.

Naturally, account holders do not like deposit fees, and their complaints get a lot of media attention. But in the big picture of depository institution revenues, deposit fees are small potatoes. Such fees account for only about 4½ to 5 percent of the total revenues of commercial banks. Nevertheless, fees typically account for 15 to 25 percent of total noninterest income. The total estimated deposit fee income earned by commercial banks in 2003 was more than $30 billion—greater than four times the amount of fee income that banks earned in 1985. Deposit fees promise to continue to rise as a share of the noninterest income that banks and other depository institutions earn.

Costs of Depository Institution Operations

The basic economic theory of banking markets that we considered in Chapter 12 included both interest expenses and real resource expenses as key components of depository institution costs. The reason that this theory included both kinds of expenses is that they are of nearly equal importance to depository institutions.

INTEREST EXPENSES Depository institution managers issue deposits and other liabilities to raise the funds that they allocate to income-generating assets. To attract funds, depository institutions must pay interest on these liabilities, and this **interest expense** is a major component of depository institution costs. As shown in Figure 13-2, interest expense accounts for 31 percent of the total costs incurred by commercial banks. Typically, this percentage is approximately the same for savings institutions and credit unions as well.

Interest expense: The portion of depository institution costs incurred through payments of interest to holders of the institutions' liabilities.

EXPENSES FOR LOAN LOSS PROVISIONS Banking is a risky business because borrowers default on their loans from time to time. Consequently, depository institutions earmark part of their cash assets as **loan loss reserves.** This portion of their cash assets is held as available liquidity that the banks will recognize as depleted in the event that loan defaults actually occur.

Loan loss reserves: An amount of cash assets that depository institutions hold as liquidity that they expect to be depleted as a result of loan defaults.

From year to year, depository institutions must add to their loan loss reserves as loan defaults cause them to decline. These additions are **loan loss provisions,** and they constitute an expense for depository institutions. That is, they are funds that depository institutions must spend to make up for loan defaults that are an unavoidable part of their lending operations. Figure 13-2 shows that loan loss provisions account for about 12 percent of expenses by commercial banks.

Loan loss provisions: An expense that depository institutions incur when they allocate funds to loan loss reserves.

REAL RESOURCE EXPENSES Like any other kind of firm, a depository institution must use traditional factors of production—labor, capital, and land—in its operations. It must pay wages and salaries to its employees, purchase or lease capital goods such as bank branch buildings and computer equipment, and pay rental fees for the use of land on which its offices and branches are situated.

Figure 13-2 indicates that expenses on real resources amount to over half of total costs for commercial banks. Clearly, real resource expenditures are not a trivial portion of total depository institution costs. In recent years many depository institutions have sought to cut these expenses, often by reducing their employment of human resources.

Figure 13-2
Commercial Bank Expenses.

Over half of the expenses of commercial banks are noninterest expenses on real resources such as labor and capital goods. Interest expenses on deposit funds and purchased funds account for nearly all remaining expenses, although expenses on loan loss provisions typically account for a small portion of total bank costs.

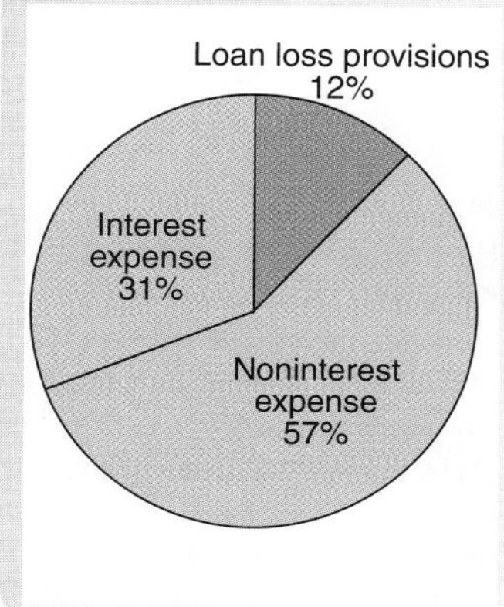

SOURCE: Federal Deposit Insurance Corporation.

1. What are the key sources of depository institution revenues and costs? The predominant source of revenues for a typical depository institution is interest income. A secondary source is noninterest income, of which a growing portion is deposit fee income. The two main types of costs that depository institutions incur are interest expenses and real resource expenses. A third key cost is expenses arising from provisions for loan loss reserves.

Measuring Depository Institution Profitability

A depository institution's *profit,* or net income, is the dollar amount by which its combined interest and noninterest income exceeds its total costs. The dollar amount of profit by itself does not always tell us much, however. To see this, suppose that you are told that an unnamed bank earned $10 million in profit last year. This seems like a lot. And it would be if the bank had only $100 million in assets, because then the bank would have earned an average *rate* of profit of 10

Return on assets: A depository institution's profit as a percentage of its total assets.

Return on equity: A depository institution's profit as a percentage of its equity capital.

percent relative to its base of assets. But if the bank had *$10 billion* in assets, a dollar profit of $10 million would be minuscule; its rate of profit relative to its assets would be only 0.1 percent. Consequently, to make better judgments about how to rate a depository institution's profitability relative to others, we need to compare its absolute profit with some measure of the depository institution's size.

RETURN ON ASSETS There are two key measures of depository institution profitability that permit such comparisons. One is **return on assets,** which is absolute dollar profit as a percentage of the dollar value of the depository institution's assets. We can compute return on assets using the following formula:

$$\text{Percentage return on assets} = \frac{\text{absolute profit}}{\text{total assets}} \times 100.$$

For the case of a bank with $1 billion ($1,000 million) in assets earning an annual profit of $10 million, the return on assets is equal to the ratio $10 million/$1,000 million multiplied by a factor of 100, or 1 percent. For the bank with assets of $10 billion ($10,000 million) and an annual profit of $10 million, the return on assets is equal to the ratio $10 million/$10,000 million multiplied by 100, or 0.1 percent. The return-on-assets measure of profitability makes clear that in this example the smaller bank is much more profitable than the larger bank.

RETURN ON EQUITY Another common measure of depository institution profitability is **return on equity.** This is the absolute profit of a depository institution as a percentage of the depository institution's equity capital. To compute return on equity, we use the following formula:

$$\text{Percentage return on equity} = \frac{\text{absolute profit}}{\text{equity capital}} \times 100.$$

Suppose that a small bank has $70 million in equity capital and earns a profit of $10 million during a given year. Then its return on equity for the year is equal to the ratio $10 million/$70 million multiplied by 100, or about 14.3 percent. During the same year, a larger bank with $800 million in equity capital earns a profit of $130 million, so its return on equity is equal to the ratio $130 million/$800 million multiplied by 100, or 16.3 percent. Based on this return-on-equity measure, the larger bank has outperformed the smaller bank.

Figure 13-3 shows how commercial banks have performed since 1990 based on both their average return on assets and their average return on equity. Banks' returns on assets and equity rose in the early 1990s and leveled off thereafter.

On the Web
How are U.S. banks performing? Keep tabs on various banking performance measures at the Web site of the Federal Deposit Insurance Corporation, http://www.fdic.gov. Under "Bank Data" in the left-hand margin, click on "Statistical," and then click on "Statistics on Banking" to review the latest quarter's bank performance data.

NET INTEREST MARGIN Return on assets and return on equity are *retrospective* measures of profitability, meaning that we can calculate them after the fact. Once we know a depository institution's profit and the amount of its assets or equity capital for a recent period, we can compute either profitability measure. Then we can try to judge how well the institution has performed in the near past.

But suppose that we are trying to gauge a depository institution's *current* or likely *future* profitability performance. Although recent figures on return on assets and return on equity might give us some basis for estimating the institution's pres-

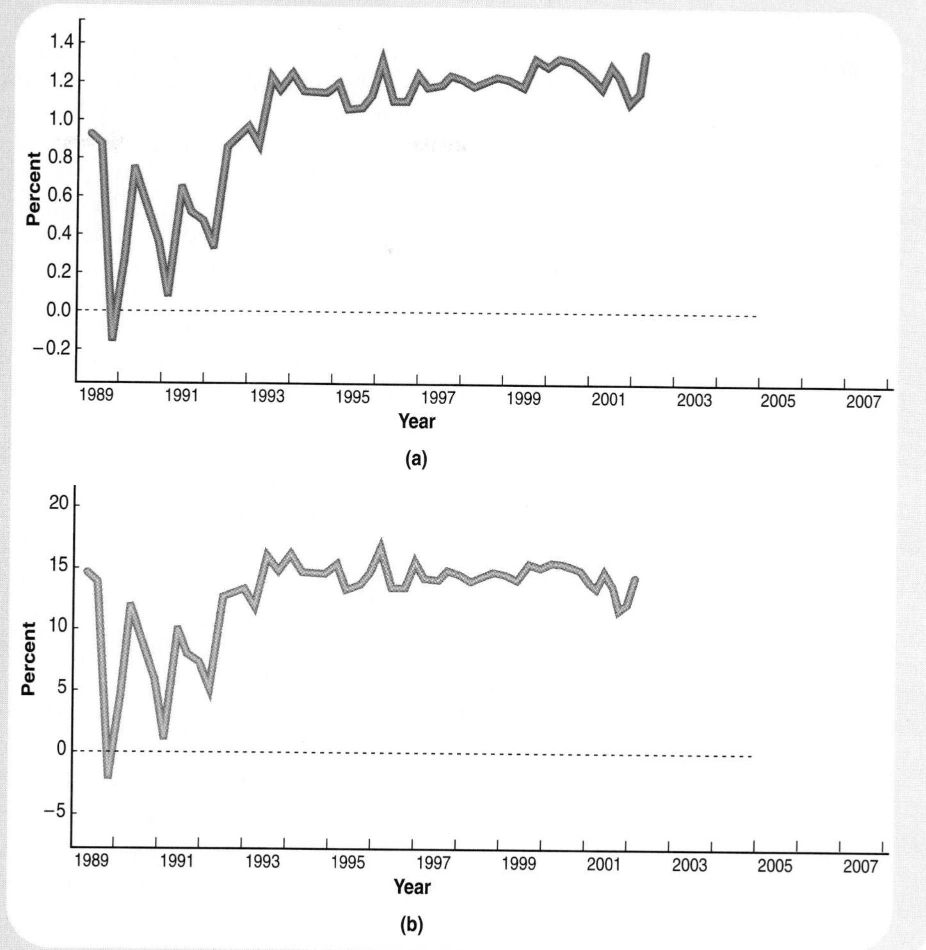

Figure 13-3
Commercial Banks' Average Returns on Assets and Equity.

Panel (a) shows that the average return on assets of commercial banks rose in the early 1990s and then leveled off, and panel (b) shows that this was also true of the average return on equity. Both measures of bank profitability were much more volatile in the early 1990s than they have been since.

SOURCE: Federal Deposit Insurance Corporation.

ent or future profitability, it would be nice to have a more *prospective,* or forward-looking, indicator of profitability. This would be especially true for a bank stockholder who is trying to assess the current performance of the bank's managers.

The most common prospective indicator of a depository institution's profitability is called the **net interest margin.** This is the difference between a depository institution's interest income and interest expenses as a percentage of total assets. We can calculate net interest margin as follows:

$$\text{Net interest margin} = \frac{\text{interest income} - \text{interest expenses}}{\text{total assets}} \times 100.$$

Because interest income is such a large portion of depository institution revenues while interest expenses represent a significant portion of costs, net interest margin is an indicator of current and future performance. A depository institution's exact

Net interest margin: The difference between a depository institution's interest income and interest expenses as a percentage of total assets.

moneyxtra!

Online Case Study

To contemplate an example of a situation in which it is important to understand the various measures of bank performance, go to the Chapter 13 Case Study, entitled "Market Share versus Profits in Banking."
http://moneyxtra.swcollege.com

net interest margin can be computed retrospectively by looking at past interest income, interest expenses, and assets. But the future net interest margin for a depository institution can also be approximated using current data.

To see how this may be done, consider an example. During the year just past, a bank's net interest margin, calculated by computing the difference between interest income and expenses as a percentage of the bank's total assets, was 3.3 percent. During the most recent quarter, however, the bank's average interest earned on loans and securities was 8.2 percent, while the average interest rate that it paid to borrow funds and issue deposit liabilities and raise equity funds was 5.4 percent. Assuming that the bank can maintain this most recent level of performance across all assets and liabilities, then the *prospective* net interest margin is simply the difference between 8.2 percent and 5.4 percent, or 2.8 percent. This would indicate that, relative to last year, this bank's performance for the current year is deteriorating.

To see how the net interest margin often proves to be a useful indicator of depository institution profitability in the near future, consider the following figures for the 1990s and early 2000s. The average net interest margin at commercial banks gradually increased during the early 1990s by nearly one-half of a percentage point. This rise in the net interest margin preceded the sharp increase in return on equity shown for that time in Figure 13-3. By 2000 the net interest margin had leveled off and begun to decline, as had the returns on assets and equity shown in Figure 13-3 before a recovery by 2001.

2. What are common measures of depository institution profitability? One typical profitability measure is return on assets, which is profit as a percentage of total assets. Another is return on equity, or profit as a percentage of equity capital. A profitability measure that people often use to assess the current and future prospects of a depository institution is its net interest margin, which is the difference between the depository institution's interest income and interest expenses as a percentage of total assets.

Theories of Bank Management

Certainly, the state of the economy, the stability of financial markets and interest rates, and other factors affecting depository institution costs and revenues can have significant effects on depository institution profitability. For reasons that we discuss later in the chapter, however, many economists believe the quality of any given depository institution's management is the most crucial factor influencing the institution's performance.

The Evolution of Depository Institution Management Philosophy

There is no single "right" way to operate a commercial bank or other depository financial institution. Indeed, there are several competing theories of depository institution management.

The Real Bills Doctrine The Italian merchant bankers discussed in Chapter 11 found that they faced a fundamental trade-off between earnings and liquidity. If a merchant bank made loans to Mediterranean traders who could repay the loans very quickly, then the bank could feel secure that it would maintain a ready stock of cash assets. Such loans would not only make the bank more liquid but would also reduce the riskiness of its portfolio of loans. The problem was that high-liquidity, low-risk loans also yielded low returns to the bank. The Italian merchant bankers tried to balance liquidity, risk, and return by making short-term loans to traders who needed them to finance transporting goods to another location for sale. There were risks of damage or loss in Mediterranean storms, but if the traders could offer proof of insurance and of ready buyers at the goods' destinations, then the banks could feel fairly confident of repayment of such loans.

Real bills doctrine: A bank management philosophy that calls for lending primarily to borrowers who will use the funds to finance production or shipping of physical goods, thereby ensuring speedy repayment of the loans.

Self-Liquidating Loans Banks also began to make loans to finance the production of goods, knowing that they would receive payment when the goods were produced and sold. Loans to finance the transportation or production of goods came to be called *self-liquidating loans,* because the likelihood of repayment was so high that the banks could regard them as highly liquid. Later, as other banks across Europe adopted this approach to lending, the term *real bills* came to be used for these loans, because banks viewed the loans as bills of credit that were claims on the resources whose transit the loans were used to finance. As a result, the bank management philosophy of lending to finance production or shipping of goods came to be known as the **real bills doctrine.**

A Self-Defeating Approach There are two difficulties with the real bills doctrine. First, if banks restrict themselves to the most short-term, highly liquid loans, then they also must accept lower returns on their lending, because more liquid loans normally carry lower risk. The second difficulty arises if all banks follow the real bills doctrine simultaneously and an economic downturn occurs. If producers and traders who otherwise would like to borrow find that the demand for their goods has fallen, then they will be unable to convince banks to lend to them. After all, such loans will not appear to banks to be self-liquidating. But if banks follow the real bills doctrine and choose not to lend, their borrowers' businesses most likely will fail, reinforcing the economic—and banking—downturn.

One way to try to salvage the real bills doctrine is to create a *central bank* that would stand ready to lend to banks when economic downturns reduce the liquidity of bank loans. Thus, the central bank would act as a *lender of last resort* during bad times. It would ensure liquidity of the banking system as a whole and thereby permit banks to follow the real bills doctrine. Although we shall see in Chapter 26 that today many economists question whether this is the fundamental rationale for central banking, it was in the minds of many who designed the Federal Reserve System in the early 1900s.

The Shiftability Theory In light of the problems that the real bills doctrine posed for earnings and for liquidity during economic downturns, many banks adopted a compromise position. They still made self-liquidating loans when feasible, but they also began to make longer-term loans with higher default risk. To balance the liquidity loss and greater risk, banks used some of their available funds to acquire low-risk securities such as government securities and commercial

Secondary reserves: Securities that depository institutions can easily convert to cash in the event that such a need arises.

Primary reserves: Cash assets.

Shiftability theory: A management approach in which depository institutions hold a mix of illiquid loans and more liquid securities that act as a secondary reserve held as a contingency against potential liquidity problems.

Anticipated-income approach: A depository institution management philosophy that calls for depository institutions to make loans more liquid by issuing them as installment loans that generate income in the form of periodic payments of interest and principal.

Conversion-of-funds approach: A depository institution management philosophy under which managers try to fund assets of specific maturities by issuing liabilities with like maturities.

Asset-liability management approach: A depository institution management philosophy that emphasizes the simultaneous determination of both the asset and the liability sides of the institution's balance sheet.

paper. Banks regarded these securities as **secondary reserves** that could easily be converted into cash if some borrowers defaulted as depositors sought to withdraw some of their funds. These secondary reserves of securities supplemented the traditional **primary reserves** of cash assets that the banks held.

This approach to "shifting" bank asset allocations to attain a different balance among earnings, liquidity, and risk became known as the **shiftability theory** of bank management. It was the original justification for the modern management strategy in which depository institutions hold a mix of long-term loans, short-term loans, and liquid securities.

Many U.S. depository institutions had adopted the shiftability theory by the end of the 1920s. But the stock market crash of 1929 and the subsequent years of the Great Depression exposed a fundamental difficulty with this approach. The problem was that even high-liquidity securities with low default risk were subject to significant interest rate risks. Securities prices plummeted at the outset of the Great Depression, so securities did not turn out to be such an effective counterbalance to longer-term, higher-risk lending after all. A number of banks (over one-third of those then in existence) failed during the Great Depression years.

THE ANTICIPATED-INCOME APPROACH After World War II, depository institution managers developed a way to make their loans more liquid. Adopting the **anticipated-income approach** to depository institution management, they made a larger number of loans as installment loans. As we discussed in Chapter 11, with these loans borrowers repay the principal and interest in installments.

This approach to loan management automatically made the loan portfolios of depository institutions more liquid. Because depository institutions receive continuous streams of payments from borrowers, the anticipated-income approach effectively made many more loans "self-liquidating" in a manner that the Italian merchant bankers of old could not have imagined. Even long-term installment loans now could generate month-to-month cash liquidity.

THE CONVERSION-OF-FUNDS APPROACH The anticipated-income approach was a breakthrough in depository institution management and continues to be widely used today. But, in the 1960s and 1970s, depository institutions sought to find ways to better manage all items on their balance sheets. This led to the **conversion-of-funds approach** to management, in which depository institution managers tried to fund assets of given maturities with sources of funds with maturities of similar length.

For example, under this approach a commercial bank manager contemplating an expansion of short-term business lending would fund new loans by issuing short-term deposits. This would ensure that the bank's net interest margin would be fixed over the short end of the maturity spectrum, thereby protecting the profitability of its short-term loan portfolio from interest rate risk.

Modern Asset-Liability Management

The conversion-of-funds approach to depository institution management was the last step to the modern approach. Today, depository institution managers actively follow an **asset-liability management approach,** which entails the coordination of all balance-sheet items so as to maximize the profitability of the depository institution. The problem, however, is figuring out how to coordinate asset-liability choices. How should a depository institution decide which short-term or long-term loans to make, which securities to hold and at what maturities, how much cash to keep on hand, how many certificates of deposit (CDs) to issue and at what maturities, how much overnight or term federal funds borrowing to do, and so on? The modern answer to this question is for depository institution managers to try to mix and match maturities while simultaneously choosing which assets to hold and which liabilities to issue in light of the interest rate risks that they face. (Sometimes the question is how to take advantage of a profitable lending opportunity with the assistance of other banks; see on the next page *Global Focus: What If Individual Borrowers Are Too Big for One Bank?*)

Gap management: A technique of depository institution asset-liability management that focuses on the difference ("gap") between the quantity of assets subject to significant interest rate risk and the amount of liabilities subject to such risk.

GAP MANAGEMENT One technique that many depository institution managers have developed to help them manage both sides of their balance sheets simultaneously is **gap management.** This asset-liability management technique focuses on the difference, or "gap," between the amount of assets subject to significant interest rate risk ("rate-sensitive" assets such as federal funds loans and money market securities) and the quantity of liabilities subject to such risk ("rate-sensitive" liabilities such as sales of repurchase agreements or short-maturity CDs). If the gap is positive, then rate-sensitive assets exceed rate-sensitive liabilities. In this case a rise in market interest rates will tend to raise the depository institution's net interest margin, because its earnings from its rate-sensitive asset holdings will rise by more than its expenses on the smaller quantity of rate-sensitive liabilities. In contrast, a negative gap would yield the opposite effect on the institution's net interest margin if interest rates were to rise.

It follows that a depository institution manager who expects market interest rates to rise will prefer to maintain a positive gap. In contrast, a manager who anticipates a decline in interest rates will want a negative gap. Alternatively, either manager could attempt to insulate the institution's income from the effects of market interest rate changes by maintaining a "zero gap" by matching the institution's amount of rate-sensitive assets by an equal quantity of rate-sensitive liabilities.

Many depository institution managers today do not look just at the overall gap for their institution. They also compute gaps at various maturities. For instance, depository institutions typically have negative gaps at short maturities of three months or less, because they issue checking and other deposits, to which customers have immediate access, but use those liabilities to fund longer-term assets. At maturities longer than three months, most depository institutions have positive gaps between rate-sensitive assets and liabilities. By monitoring gaps at different maturities, a manager can better gauge the institution's exposures to interest rate risk across the term structure of its assets and liabilities.

DURATION GAP ANALYSIS A more sophisticated gap-management method, which many banks have adopted in recent years, is to apply the concept of *duration* when conducting gap management. As you learned in Chapter 8, the duration of a financial instrument within a bank's portfolio of assets is a measure of the average time during which the bank receives all payments of principal and interest on the instrument. Likewise, the duration of a financial instrument, such as a deposit, that the bank issues as a liability is a measure of the average interval within which the bank makes payments on its liabilities.

GLOBAL Focus | POLICY | CYBER | MANAGEMENT

What If Individual Borrowers Are Too Big for One Bank?

Even though 95 percent of the U.S. banking industry's business is within U.S. borders, many U.S. companies are now multinational conglomerates with globe-spanning operations. The situation is similar in Europe and Japan. Some companies are so large that their credit needs dwarf the capability of any bank to serve as sole lender.

Banks have responded to this situation by developing a market in **syndicated loans,** which are loans pieced together by groups of banks. Typically, one or two banks arrange a syndicated loan, in return for syndication-management fees. These lead banks line up a group, or *syndicate,* of banks that fund portions of the total amount of the loan, earning interest just as they would on any other loan they extend. Often, however, shares of a syndicated loan are marketable instruments, meaning that participating banks under some circumstances can sell their shares of the loan to other banks.

Panel (a) of Figure 13-4 shows how the worldwide amount of syndicated lending has grown in recent years. Comparing panel (b) of the figure with panel (c), you can see that the relative role of syndicated loans in worldwide financing of corporation operations has increased dramatically. The share of total new corporate financing accounted for by syndicated loans rose from about 33 percent in 1992 to 52 percent in 2002.

For Critical Analysis: Would you expect the market for corporate bonds or for bank syndicated loans to be more liquid? Why?

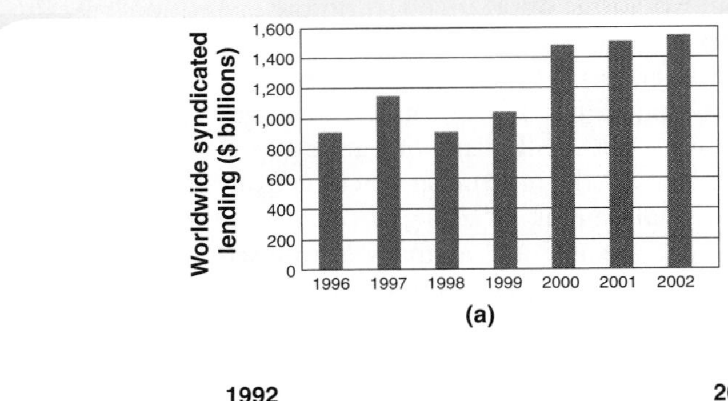

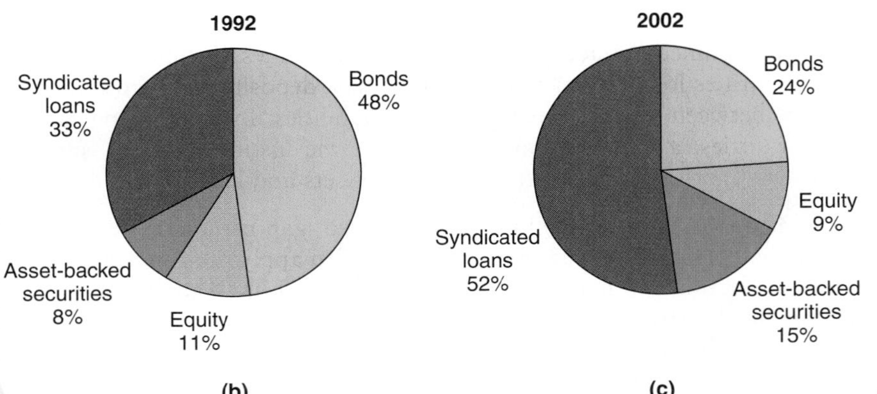

Figure 13-4
Bank Syndicated Lending in Total and As a Share of Total Corporate Financing.

As shown in panel (a), global syndicated lending by banks has jumped in the early 2000s. A comparison of panels (b) and (c) indicates that the relative role of syndicated loans in corporate financing has increased significantly.

SOURCE: Bank for International Settlements, *Quarterly Banking Profile*, various issues.

Syndicated loan: A loan arranged by one or two banks but funded by these and other banks.

To assess a bank's overall exposure to interest rate risk, its managers can use *duration gap analysis*. They do this by calculating an average duration for *all* of the bank's assets and an average duration for *all* of its liabilities. The difference between the average asset duration and the average liability duration is the bank's **duration gap.** If the bank's duration gap is positive and its managers anticipate a rise in market interest rates, then the managers can seek a higher net interest return by trying to reconfigure the bank's mix of terms to maturity for its assets and liabilities to achieve a negative duration gap. By way of contrast, if managers anticipate a decline in market interest rates, then a positive duration gap is an appropriate asset-liability structure. (In recent years, banks have experimented with using hardware and software to balance asset-liability risks; see on page 302 *Cyber Focus: The Danger of Managing Banks with Computers Instead of People.*)

Duration gap: The average duration of a depository institution's assets minus the average duration of its liabilities.

Market structure: The organization of the loan and deposit markets in which depository institutions interact.

Market concentration: The degree to which the few largest depository institutions dominate loan and deposit markets.

3. How has the philosophy of depository institution management evolved? The fundamental trade-off that depository institutions face is between earnings and liquidity. The real bills doctrine sought to achieve both higher earnings and higher liquidity through lending only for projects that would yield quick and sure returns. Because relatively few such lending opportunities are available, over the years depository institution managers have developed a number of competing approaches to the earnings-liquidity trade-off. In recent years, the asset-liability management approach, which uses gap-management techniques to address interest rate risk while striving for high earnings and liquidity, has become predominant.

An Evolving Depository Institution Market Structure

As noted above, interest income constitutes a large portion of depository institution revenues. How are market interest rates determined for bank loans and deposits? As you learned in Chapter 12, the answer to this question depends very much on whether banking markets are perfectly or imperfectly competitive. Thus, depository institution **market structure,** which refers to the organization of the markets in which depository institutions interact, can influence bank profitability.

A traditional issue has been how and why the degree of **market concentration**—the extent to which the few largest depository institutions dominate loan and deposit markets—affects the behavior of depository institutions. Market concentration can be measured in several ways, but the most straightforward is to look at the market shares of the largest few depository institutions. Typically, if the three or four largest institutions together have a large fraction of total loans or deposits, say, 70 percent or more, then the market is said to be relatively concentrated. But if the three or four largest institutions have a combined market share that is much smaller, then the degree competition is likely much greater.

Perfect Competition versus Monopoly

Economists typically regard perfect competition as the optimal market structure. The reason is that if rivalry among depository institutions pushes loan and deposit rates closely in line with the costs of providing loans and issuing deposits,

GLOBAL POLICY CYBER Focus MANAGEMENT

The Danger of Managing Banks with Computers Instead of People

By the late 1990s, many depository institution managers were convinced that they had figured out how to deal with credit risks. They assigned the analysis of the risks of their loan portfolios to computers. Actually, they assigned the task to sophisticated statistical models, which computers could operate more efficiently than people.

The Model-Based Approach to Credit-Risk Management

In mid-1997, J.P. Morgan (which has since merged with Chase Manhattan Bank to become J.P. Morgan Chase) announced that Standard & Poor's, Moody's Investors Service, Price Waterhouse, and several other credit-rating institutions would cosponsor the bank's new credit-risk management system, called *CreditMetrics*. The model was one of several *value-at-risk models* that depository institution managers began to use in the 1990s. A **value-at-risk model** is a statistical framework for evaluating how changes in interest rates and financial instrument prices are likely to affect the overall value of a portfolio of financial assets.

Within a few months, CreditMetrics, which includes a historical database that indicates the statistical likelihood of credit-rating changes, loan default likelihoods, and default recovery rates among different types of loans, became the industry standard for measuring risks associated with traditional loans, as well as credit derivatives and other derivatives such as swaps. J.P. Morgan embarked on a campaign to convince national banking regulators to loosen what it and other banks regarded as overly rigid supervisory restrictions on bank lending.

The bank argued that with CreditMetrics, any bank could examine how volatile loan values have been in the past and use that information to estimate volatility within markets for various types of loans. The computer model also allowed banks to use portfolio theory (see Chapter 7) to develop separate estimates for risks arising from a general tendency for loan markets to move together (*market risk*) or for specific loan markets to exhibit trends that differ from broader performance in all loan markets (*idiosyncratic risk*). CreditMetrics, therefore, is intended to give bank managers a more accurate picture of whether bad loans to one country or industry are likely to go hand-in-hand with bad loans to

consumers pay and receive interest rates just sufficient to cover those costs. As a result, they are not in any way forced to pay loan rates that are "too high" or to earn deposit rates that are "too low," given the actual costs that depository institutions incur in providing financial intermediation services. In fact, under perfect competition depository institutions earn no more than a **normal profit,** or a profit just sufficient to compensate owners for holding equity shares in depository institutions instead of directing their funds to other enterprises.

Value-at-risk model: A statistical framework for evaluating how changes in interest rates and financial instrument prices are likely to affect the overall value of a portfolio of financial assets.

Normal profit: A profit level just sufficient to compensate depository institution owners for holding equity shares in the depository institution instead of purchasing ownership shares of other enterprises.

At the opposite extreme from pure competition is the market structure of *pure monopoly.* In this case, a loan or deposit market is dominated by a single depository institution or by a *cartel,* or small group of institutions that effectively coordinate their actions to jointly maximize profits.

The Consequences of Monopoly

Figure 13-5 on page 304 illustrates what happens if one or a few banks sufficiently dominate loan and deposit markets to set loan rates monopolistically rather than competitively. As a simplification, the figure is drawn under the another, thereby enabling banks to spread their lending risks more wisely across industries and countries.

Is Lending an Art or a Science?

CreditMetrics possessed some acknowledged limitations, such as limited historical data about expected loan losses after default. The designers of the model used estimates provided in research papers that examined a few major U.S. industries. These estimates did not admit the possibility of a sharp, sustained change in loan risk such as the Asian crisis of the late 1990s and the longest Japanese economic downturn since World War II, a Russian debt default, and significant economic problems in Brazil, all of which took place in 1998 and 1999.

As a result, J.P. Morgan and other banks that used CreditMetrics found that the model essentially broke down after the middle of 1998 as business conditions proved far more unstable than the model had forecast. Indeed, by basing its decisions on CreditMetrics, J.P. Morgan lost over $100 million in the third quarter of 1998. Bankers Trust and BankAmerica, which also used value-at-risk models, lost hundreds of millions of dollars. According to one observer, "The senior bankers got their noses up against the computer screens and didn't step back to look at what was going on in the real world. . . . They began to believe in their models, but the assumptions were wrong." Managers who had used CreditMetrics and other value-at-risk models responded that over the long run, their models normally should have been statistically accurate and that eventually the models' estimates of credit risk would reflect actual risks. Critics, however, pointed out that it takes only a few days of substantial loan losses to bring down a big bank.

In the end, banks' experience with the Asian crisis proved invaluable. Although depository institutions continue to rely on CreditMetrics and other value-at-risk models to provide a "big-picture" look at the riskiness of their loan portfolios, recently they have adopted safeguards. Now more human beings are looking over the shoulders of those running the computer programs. Thus, when the U.S. economy began to sink during 2001, banks were relying on more than value-at-risk models to guide their lending decisions. Hence, they did not experience loan losses as significant as those that had occurred three years earlier.

For Critical Analysis: Why is it important for banks to develop estimates of market risk and idiosyncratic risk in loan markets?

assumption that a bank's marginal resource costs (as in Chapter 12, denoted MC_L and MC_D) do not vary with the amount of loans that the bank extends. As a result, the bank's total marginal cost of lending is constant and equal to its total average cost (AC) of operating in the loan market. In addition, we assume that all banks face the same marginal and average cost of lending, $r_D + MC_L + MC_D$.

Competition versus Monopoly Under these assumptions, each bank has the same horizontal marginal cost schedule shown in Figure 13-5. Recall that under perfect competition, each bank's loan supply schedule is its total marginal cost schedule. Thus, the total marginal cost schedule, MC 5 rD 1 MCL 1 MCD, is the market loan supply schedule under perfect competition for this simplified situation. The competitive market loan rate, at which the quantity of loans demanded is equal to the quantity of loans supplied, is equal to rL1. The equilibrium quantity of loans is equal to L1.

By way of contrast, if the banks in this market form a joint monopoly (keeping the same marginal cost curves), then together they face the market loan demand schedule and the associated marginal revenue schedule, labeled MR. This

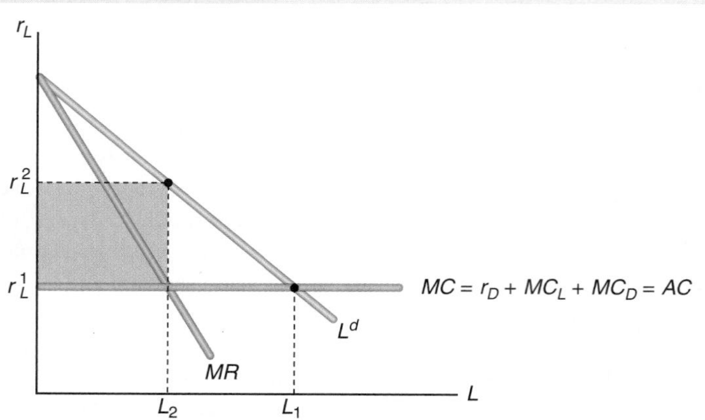

Figure 13-5
Monopolistic versus Perfectly Competitive Loan Markets.

This figure assumes that banks' marginal resource costs are constant, identical across banks, and invariant to changes in market structure. Under perfect competition, the total marginal cost schedule, $MC = r_D + MC_L + MC_D$, is the market loan supply schedule. The competitive market loan rate is r_L^1, the equilibrium quantity of loans is L_1, and in a long-run equilibrium banks earn zero economic profits. If a banking cartel successfully achieves a market monopoly, however, then together the cartel faces the market loan demand schedule and the associated marginal revenue schedule. Then the profit-maximizing loan rate is r_L^2, the quantity of loans is L_2, and the supranormal profits earned by the monopoly are equal to the shaded area.

monopoly lending coalition then maximizes its profits by making loans up to the point at which marginal revenue equals the total marginal cost of lending and charging a loan rate that customers are willing and able to pay. Consequently, the profit-maximizing amount of lending under monopoly is equal to L_2, and the loan rate is equal to r_L^2.

Supranormal Profits of Monopoly One implication of Figure 13-5, therefore, is that customers of banks in a monopoly loan market will pay more interest for fewer loans as compared with the case of perfect competition. Another is that banks that act as a single lending monopoly earn **supranormal profits.** These are profit levels above the normal profits necessary simply to induce depository institution owners to direct their funds to the banking business instead of some other endeavor. Under perfect competition, Figure 13-5 indicates that the market loan rate is equal to r_L^1, which is just equal to the average cost of lending, so banks earn zero economic profits. That is, banks in a perfectly competitive market earn accounting profits sufficient to compensate the owners for choosing to allocate their funds to the banking business. By way of contrast, the difference between the monopoly loan rate, r_L^2, and average cost times the monopoly loan quantity, which is the shaded area in Figure 13-5, is the amount of supranormal profits earned by bank owners.

Supranormal profits: Levels of profit above those required to induce depository institution owners to hold shares of ownership in those institutions instead of shares of other businesses.

In 1982 Stephen Rhoades, an economist at the Federal Reserve Board in Washington, attempted to measure the effects of monopoly power among commercial banks in loan markets in 1978. He found that monopoly power caused total bank lending to be 14 percent lower than it would otherwise have been under pure competition. Rhoades also estimated that banks earned supranormal profits. He concluded that bank profit levels in 1978 were over $1 billion, or about 13 percent, more than they would otherwise have been in purely competitive banking markets.

Structure-conduct-performance (SCP) model: A theory of depository institution market structure in which the structure of loan and deposit markets influences the behavior (conduct) of depository institutions in those markets, thereby affecting their performance.

Does Market Concentration Matter?

As we shall discuss in Chapters 14 and 15, many barriers to greater rivalry in banking markets have fallen in recent years, so a lot has changed since 1978. Yet some economists argue that unrestricted rivalry among depository institutions ultimately can lead to too much market concentration. Such concentration, they contend, feeds on itself and leads to anticompetitive behavior by commercial banks and other financial institutions. Thus, there is a natural tendency for unrestricted rivalry among banks to lead to more, rather than less, monopoly power.

The Structure-Conduct-Performance Model Those who subscribe to this view base their evaluation on the **structure-conduct-performance (SCP) model** of depository institution market structure. Figure 13-6 illustrates the basic reasoning of this theory. According to the SCP model, the *structure* of a financial market influences the *conduct* of the institutions in the market. Their conduct, in turn, determines the *performance* of those institutions.

The basic prediction of the SCP theory is that more concentrated loan and deposit markets lead to monopoly power, which as a result yields higher loan rates, lower deposit rates, and supranormal depository institution profits. This prediction causes proponents of the SCP model to prescribe an active role for governmental oversight of depository institution markets. According to SCP proponents, government regulators need to ensure that greater rivalry in banking markets does not lead to the gobbling up of small competitors by larger institutions.

Figure 13-6
The Structure-Conduct-Performance Model.

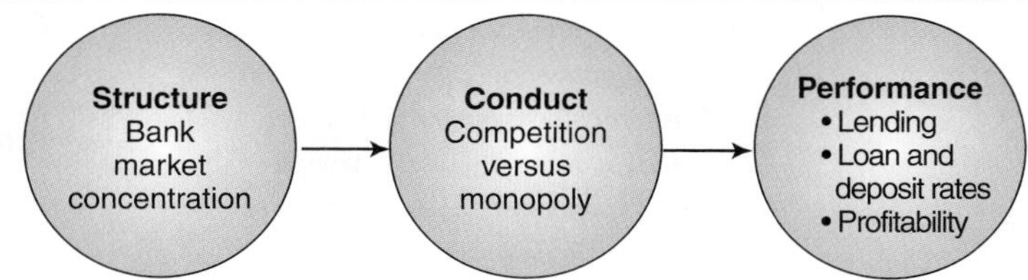

According to the structure-conduct-performance model, bank market structure can be measured by the concentration of banking markets (for instance, the combined market share of the few largest banks in a market). Bank market structure, in turn, determines whether banks conduct themselves competitively or monopolistically. Bank market conduct then determines the performance of banks, as measured, for instance, by the amount of lending, loan and deposit rates, and profitability.

Efficient structure theory: A theory of depository institution market structure in which greater market concentration and higher depository institution profits arise from the fact that a few depository institutions can operate more efficiently in loan and deposit markets as compared with a large number of institutions.

The Efficient Structure Theory On the other side are economists who promote the **efficient structure theory** of depository institution market structure. Figure 13-7 depicts their line of reasoning. According to this view, greater market concentration arises from the fact that a few depository institutions can operate more efficiently in loan and deposit markets as compared with a large number of institutions. They can do so because they can spread their costs over large computer, branching, and managerial networks.

In the past, this argument has been based in part on the idea of *economies of scale*. As discussed in Chapter 3, economies of scale refer to the ability to reduce average costs by pooling together financial resources. By pooling together ever-larger amounts of resources, efficient structure theorists argue, larger institutions can provide their services at lower costs than their competitors. The result is lower lending rates and higher deposit rates, so consumers are better off. But the reward to the more efficient institutions is *higher* profits. Consequently, the efficient structure theory, like the SCP model, predicts that greater concentration should yield greater profitability. But according to some who promote the efficient structure view, these higher profits stem from the greater efficiency of larger firms that dominate financial markets.

Recent Evidence on the Market Structure Debate

So who is correct about the effects of unrestricted rivalry on depository institution market structure and performance? Recent work looking at the relationship between commercial bank market concentration and profitability has cast a little more light on the broader debate between SCP proponents and efficient structure theorists.

Figure 13-7
The Efficient Structure Theory.

According to the efficient structure theory, any banking organization grows only as long as it remains cost-efficient. Furthermore, banks that can provide their services at lower cost are more profitable institutions and naturally gain market share as a result. Consequently, the structure of banking markets and the performance of banks in those markets depend on cost efficiencies that banks can achieve.

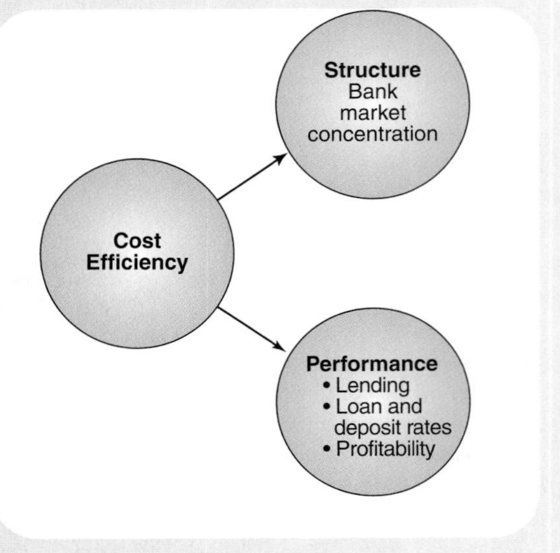

In a recent study, Allen Berger of the Federal Reserve Board's economic staff analyzed extensive data on 4,800 commercial banks for each year of the 1980s. Berger defined local loan and deposit markets based on Metropolitan Statistical Areas (MSAs) defined by the U.S. Census Bureau and on non-MSA counties. He used batteries of statistical tests to determine how market concentration related to bank profits and used a variety of tests to try to determine which theory received more support from the data. Berger reached the conclusion that there is little evidence that the SCP model fits the real world, except perhaps in a much more limited form. There is evidence that large commercial banks earn higher profits because they are successful in gaining sufficient market shares to differentiate themselves from rivals. This, he concludes, gives them some monopoly power. They are able to use this monopoly power to earn some supranormal profits.

moneyxtra!

Another Perspective

Consider why some economists have recently proposed that some social gains may be associated with monopoly power in banking by going to the Chapter 13 reading, entitled "Competition among Banks: Good or Bad," by Nicola Cetorelli of the Federal Reserve Bank of Chicago.
http://moneyxtra.swcollege.com

The efficient structure theory's emphasis on economies of scale also did not hold up to the statistical tests that Berger conducted. What Berger found was that a somewhat altered version of the efficient structure theory seemed to explain banks' performances into the 1990s. According to this variation on the efficient structure hypothesis, what really counts is the efficiency of the management of a commercial bank, irrespective of the bank's absolute size or its market share. Well-run banks earn higher profits. Banks whose managers do not do a good job of controlling costs can sometimes still become large banks, but these banks tend to earn lower profits. In general, however, more efficiently operated banks do capture larger market shares. As the efficient structure theory predicts, this is because they are better at what they do.

Surely, this conclusion would not surprise too many depository institution managers. These people must confront the real world of business decisions about lending operations and the provision of deposit services that economic theorists do not see. At this point, however, a consensus seems to be emerging among *both* economists *and* bankers: what really matters most for the performance of depository institutions, from the perspectives of their owners, managers, *and* customers, is how well they are operated.

4. What is the main determinant of depository institution performance? Although there is limited evidence that loan and deposit market concentration influences depository institution profitability by affecting the degrees of competition and monopoly power, recent evidence indicates that the overriding factor determining profitability is the capability of a depository institution's managers.

Link to **Management**

Will Credit Derivatives Allow Banks to Get Out of the Risk Business?

As Figure 13-8 shows, since the mid-1990s there has been a significant increase in the volumes of funds that U.S. banks have allocated to **credit derivatives,** which are financial instruments whose returns are derived from the underlying credit risks of loans. U.S. banks' holdings of credit derivatives account for more than half of the worldwide total value, which is estimated to be nearly $800 billion in 2003.

How Credit Derivatives Work

The mechanics of a credit derivative transaction can be complex, but the basic idea is relatively simple. For instance, the most popular credit derivative is a **default swap,** in which the seller of the swap, sometimes called a *credit protection seller,* agrees to take over the face value of a debt if the borrower should default. In return, the seller collects a fee from the counterparty, called a *credit protection buyer.* Thus, if a bank's managers think that the bank has taken on too much risk of default in a big loan to a single client, they can buy credit protection by using a default swap to reduce the bank's risk exposure. The credit protection seller in the transaction takes on this risk in exchange for the payment of a regular fee from the bank. In the event of a default, the credit protection seller reimburses the bank for its losses. Such an arrangement does not hurt the bank's standing with its clients, because borrowers are not even informed of the existence of most credit derivative contracts.

Credit derivatives: Financial instruments that have returns based on loan credit risks.

Default swap: A credit derivative that requires the seller to assume the face value of a debt in the event of default.

Panels (a) and (b) of Figure 13-9 show the distribution of credit protection sellers and buyers in the market for credit derivatives. Although banks account for 47 percent of credit protection sales, they are the predominant buyers of credit protection, accounting for about 63 percent of total purchases of credit protection via derivatives. In principle, this has enabled banks to shift significant amounts of their lending risks to other sellers of credit protection, such as insurance companies, which account for only about 7 percent of the total credit protection purchased but for 23 percent of the total credit protection sold.

Are Credit Derivatives All They Are Cracked Up to Be?

Why would a credit protection seller be willing to take on the default risk associated with a loan? One reason is that, as in the case of debt issued by developing nations, some other bank may wish to diversify its own portfolio. By agreeing to take on part of the risks of loans that have been originated by other banks, this institution can diversify its portfolio without actually going to the trouble to initiate or provide loans to such nations.

Nevertheless, loan defaults in the late 1990s and early 2000s showed that sellers and buyers of credit derivatives could sometimes disagree on how to define "default," particularly in the case of governments. For example, in 1998 the Russian government defaulted on its domestic debts but maintained payments on most foreign debts. Buyers and sellers of swaps immediately wound up in court, arguing over whether the Russian government had truly "defaulted." Likewise, when an Indiana life insurance company called Conseco decided to "restructure" $2.8 billion in debts in 2001, banks that had made loans to the insurer demanded payment from credit derivative counterparties that had issued credit protection for Conseco's loans. These counterparties, however, declared that a debt "restructuring" was not the same as an outright default and declined to pay up.

Such events have made some banking analysts question whether credit derivatives truly insulate banks from risks associated with their lending.

Banking regulators also are less willing to regard credit derivatives as true "credit protection" for banks, and this regulatory stance could cause the growth of the market for credit derivatives to slow.

Research Project

The valuations of most derivatives fluctuate whenever the price of another financial instrument changes in a financial market. Do many loans trade in secondary markets, so that their values change from week to week or day to day? How does this complicate the structure of credit derivatives? Why might counterparties to credit derivatives naturally disagree about when one party must pay the other?

Web Resources

1. How many derivatives do U.S. banks have on hand at present? To find the latest information and data, go to the home page of the Office of the Comptroller of the Currency at http://www.occ.treas.gov; click on "Publications," and then in the left-hand margin, click on "Qtrly. Derivatives Fact Sheet."

2. Just how many derivatives are in use around the globe? Get the latest data by going to the home page of the Bank for International Settlements at http://www.bis.org; click on "Publications and Statistics," then click on "Regular Publications," and then click on "Regular OTC Derivatives Market Statistics."

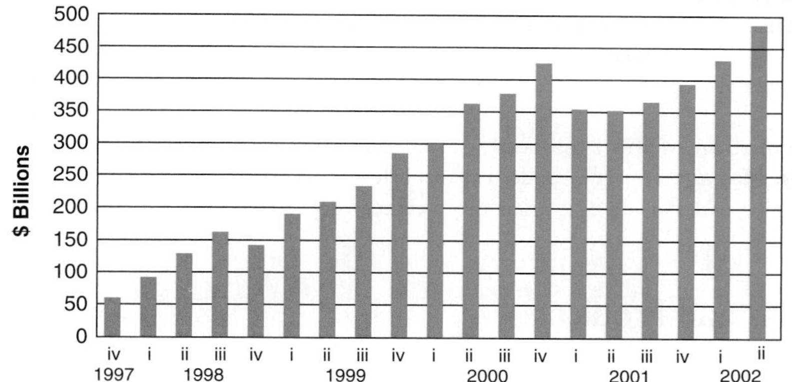

Figure 13-8
Notional Value of Credit Derivatives Held by U.S. Banks.
The notional value of credit derivatives increased throughout the latter part of the 1990s before dropping off slightly during the economic downturn that began in 2001.
SOURCE: Office of the Comptroller of the Currency, *Bank Derivatives Report*, various issues.

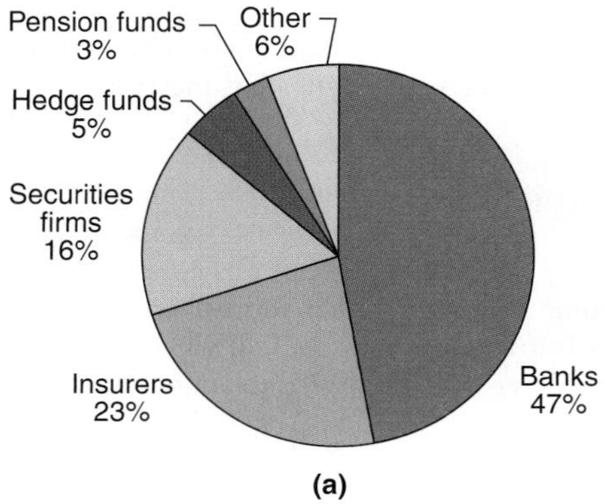

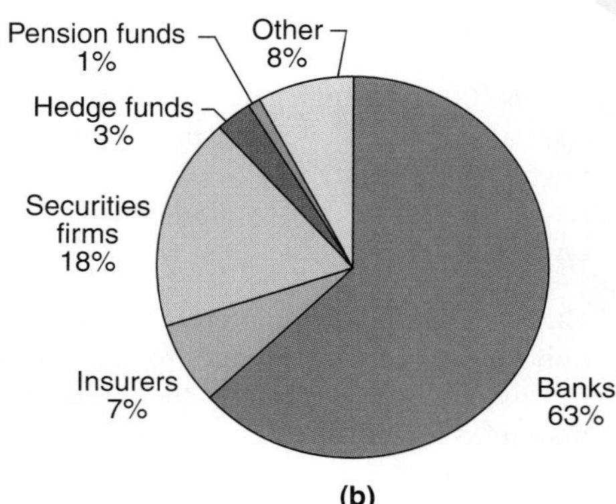

Figure 13-9
Global Distribution of the Notional Value of Credit Derivatives among Contract Counterparties.
Various types of financial institutions both sell and buy risk protection via credit derivatives. Panel (a) shows the distribution of credit protection sold by financial institutions using credit derivatives, and panel (b) displays the distribution of purchases of credit protection. Pension funds, hedge funds, and insurers tend to be net sellers of credit protection.
SOURCE: Bank for International Settlements.

Chapter Summary

1. Key Sources of Depository Institution Revenues and Costs: The main source of revenues for depository institutions is interest income derived from interest that they earn on loans and securities. The other revenue source is non-interest income, which includes fee income and trading profits. The two main sources of costs incurred by depository institutions are interest expenses on liabilities that they issue and real resource expenses for the use of productive factors such as labor, capital, and land. A third expenditure is provisions for loan loss reserves.

2. Common Measures of Depository Institution Profitability: Two commonly used measures are return on assets, or profit as a percentage of total assets, and return on equity, which is profit as a percentage of equity capital. Another measure that analysts often use to assess the near-term and future profitability of a depository institution is its net interest margin, which is the difference between interest income and interest expense as a percentage of total assets.

3. The Evolution of the Philosophy of Depository Institution Management: Under the real bills doctrine that was popular until the end of the nineteenth century, depository institutions tried to make only the most liquid loans. The shiftability theory dictated achieving more liquidity by holding securities, thereby allowing institutions to make less liquid loans. The anticipated-income approach led to the growth of installment loans as a means of generating liquidity via periodic payments of principal and interest. Under the conversion-of-funds approach, depository institution managers sought to fund assets with liabilities with similar maturities. The modern asset-liability approach, in contrast, typically permits gaps to develop between asset and liability positions at different maturities, although such gaps may be eliminated as a means of hedging against interest rate risk.

4. The Main Determinant of a Depository Institution's Profitability: At present, there is broad agreement that although short-term factors such as changes in the overall economic climate can have large effects on profitability, as can the structure of the market in which a depository institution operates, most evidence indicates that the key factor determining a given institution's profit performance is the quality of its management.

Questions and Problems

(Answers to odd-numbered questions and problems may be found on the Web at http://money.swcollege.com under "Student Resources.")

1. In 2002, the aggregate return on assets for all commercial banks in the United States was just over 1 percent, and the return on equity was nearly 15 percent. Explain why the return on equity typically is so much greater than the return on assets.

2. In recent years noninterest income has become a more important source of revenues for depository institutions. Discuss how this may affect the usefulness of net interest margin as an indicator of depository institution profitability.

3. Some have argued that if depository institutions had not given up their strict adherence to the real bills doctrine, they would ultimately have ceased to exist. Evaluate this argument.

4. In your view, what is the biggest drawback of the shiftability theory of bank management?

5. Explain why it makes sense that the fee income of banks has increased substantially in recent years.

6. Suppose that a commercial bank has a negative gap at maturities of twelve months or less but a positive gap at maturities exceeding twelve months. If the yield curve (recall this concept from Chapter 4) *rotates* in such a way that short-term interest rates rise while longer-term interest rates fall, what is likely to happen to the bank's profitability? Explain your reasoning.

7. How does derivatives trading complicate the evaluation of the overall performance of, and the prospects for, depository institutions?

8. Suppose that a bank loan market is dominated by a small group of large banks that work together to maximize their joint profitability. Use a diagram to illustrate why cutting costs is consistent with increasing the banks' profits.

9. In light of your answer to question 8, explain why proponents of the structure-conduct-performance model caution that unhindered bank mergers ultimately could be costly to consumers.

10. Profitability sometimes is greater at the larger institutions in specific loan and deposit markets. Discuss alternative ways that structure-conduct-performance model proponents and efficient structure theorists would probably explain such observations.

Before the Test

Test your understanding of the material covered in this chapter by taking the Chapter 13 interactive quiz at http://money.swcollege.com.

Online Application

Internet URL: http://www. fdic.gov

Title: Historical Statistics on Banking

Navigation: Begin at the FDIC's Web site at the above address. Under "Bank Data" in the left-hand margin, click on "Historical," and then click on "Historical Statistics on Banking." Finally, click on "Commercial Bank Reports."

Application: Follow the instructions, and answer the questions.

1. Under "Geographical Area," select "United States," and in the "Select Report" section, go to "Financial Data-Income Statement" and click on "CB04: Net Income." Beginning with the most recent year, and at ten-year intervals going back to 1966, calculate the ratio of noninterest income to total income (which you can calculate by adding together interest income and noninterest income). Do you see a trend? If so, discuss why it may exist.

2. Go back to the "Select Report" section, and click on "CB07: Noninterest Income and Noninterest Expense." Beginning with the most recent year. and at ten-year intervals going back to 1966, calculate the ratio of fee income to noninterest income. Do you see a trend? If so, discuss why it may exist.

For Group Study and Analysis: Form groups, and have each group examine the report entitled "Interest Income of Insured Commercial Banks" in the "Select Report." In the "State" box, click on "United States." Have each group make a determination about the most notable recent change in the various sources of commercial bank interest income. In addition, have each group examine the loan interest income from foreign sources relative to loan interest income from domestic sources and then report about whether they see any evidence that the U.S. banking industry as a whole is significantly more involved in international lending than in past years.

Selected References and Further Reading

Bank for International Settlements. *On the Use of Information and Risk Management by International Banks.* Basel, Switzerland: October 1998.

Berger, Allen. "The Profit-Structure Relationship in Banking—Tests of Market-Power and Efficient-Structure Hypotheses." *Journal of Money, Credit, and Banking* 27 (May 1995): 404–431.

Berger, Allen, and Timothy Hannan. "The Efficiency Cost of Market Power in the Banking Industry: A Test of the 'Quiet Life' and Related Hypotheses." *Review of Economics and Statistics* 80 (August 1998): 454–465.

Emmons, William, and Frank Schmid. "Bank Competition and Concentration: Do Credit Unions Matter?" Federal Reserve Bank of St. Louis *Review* 82 (May/June 2000): 29–42.

Federal Reserve System Task Force on Internal Credit Risk Models. "Credit Risk Models at Major U.S. Banking Institutions: Current State of the Art and Implications for Assessments of Capital Adequacy." Washington, D.C.: May 1998.

Guzman, Mark. "Bank Competition in the New Economy." Federal Reserve Bank of Dallas *Southwest Economy,* March/April 2001, pp. 1–9.

Kimball, Ralph. "Economic Profit and Performance Measurement in Banking." Federal Reserve Bank of Boston *New England Economic Review,* July/August 1998, pp. 35–53.

_______. "Innovations in Performance Measurement in Banking." Federal Reserve Bank of Boston *New England Economic Review,* May/June 1997, pp. 3–22.

Rhoades, Stephen. "Welfare Loss, Redistribution Effect, and Restriction of Output due to Monopoly in Banking." *Journal of Monetary Economics* 9 (January 1982): 375–387.

Simons, Katerina. "Value at Risk—New Approaches to Risk Management." Federal Reserve Bank of Boston *New England Economic Review,* September/October 1996, pp. 3–14.

Stiroh, Kevin, and Jennifer Poole. "Explaining the Rising Concentration of Banking Assets in the 1990s." Federal Reserve Bank of New York *Current Issues in Economics and Finance* 6 (August 2000).

Wall, Larry, and Timothy Koch. "Bank Loan-Loss Accounting: A Review of Theoretical and Empirical Evidence." Federal Reserve Bank of Atlanta *Economic Review,* Second Quarter 2000, pp. 1–19.

MoneyXtra

moneyxtra! Log on to the MoneyXtra Web site now (http://moneyxtra.swcollege.com) for additional learning resources such as practice quizzes, case studies, readings, and additional economic applications.

Chapter 14

Foundations of Depository Institution Regulation

After the Federal Deposit Insurance Corporation (FDIC), the government agency that provides federal deposit insurance to banks and savings institutions, was created in 1933, its first act was to study bank failures between 1864 and 1934. FDIC economists found that the average cost of such failures per dollar of deposits (up to a limit of $5,000, or more than $50,000 in today's dollars) was about one-fourth of 1 percent. These figures indicated that the FDIC should charge depository institutions an annual deposit insurance premium, *or annual charge for deposit insurance, of one-fourth of 1 percent for each dollar of deposits.*

Nevertheless, the FDIC's first director, Leo Crowley, convinced Congress that this deposit insurance premium rate would be too high to make bankers enthusiastic about the new federal system. He also argued that the new federal banking regulations imposed when the FDIC was established would reduce depository institution failures relative to historical levels. Following Crowley's recommendation, Congress specified an initial deposit insurance premium of 0.083 percent, or one-twelfth of 1 percent.

Fifty-four years would pass before the FDIC would increase this premium rate. After hundreds of savings institutions collapsed in the 1980s, FDIC economists of the early 1990s looked over the experience of past years and settled on a base insurance premium rate for savings institutions that was very close to one-fourth of 1 percent—almost exactly what FDIC economists of the 1930s had first suggested would be appropriate. Nevertheless, today more than 95 percent of all depository institutions pay a premium rate even lower than Leo Crowley recommended in 1934. These depository institutions

Fundamental Issues

1. In what ways did laws adopted in the 1930s exert long-term effects on the U.S. banking industry?
2. How did deposit interest rate ceilings ultimately help to spur depository institution deregulation in the 1980s?
3. Why does the provision of federal deposit insurance help to justify federal regulation of depository institutions?
4. How has the federal government sought to reduce the FDIC's exposure to losses?
5. How did the Financial Services Modernization Act of 1999 alter the structure of U.S. bank regulation and supervision?
6. Do national bank regulators coordinate their policies?

continue to face an implicit cost because they must submit to federal oversight and supervision, but they pay no explicit deposit premiums at all.

Why is it that most depository institutions do not pay premiums for federal deposit insurance? Why does the existence of deposit insurance help to justify the complex web of federal banking regulations? Why does the federal government insure deposits in the first place? This chapter addresses these and other questions about the current regulatory environment faced by depository institutions.

The Evolution of U.S. Depository Institution Regulation

We discussed the traditional rationales for government regulation of depository financial institutions in Chapter 2. They are as follows:

1. **Maintaining depository institution liquidity.** Any depository institution without sufficient cash on hand to meet the needs of its depositors suffers from *illiquidity* that inconveniences its customers. Illiquidity throughout the banking system threatens the smooth flow of payments for goods and services and can have negative consequences for the broader economy.
2. **Assuring bank solvency by limiting failures.** A depository institution is *insolvent* if the value of its assets falls below the value of its liabilities so that the value of its *equity,* or net worth, is negative. A fundamental purpose of regulatory supervision of depository institutions is to reduce the likelihood of insolvency and the resulting failure of a depository institution to remain a going concern.
3. **Promoting an efficient financial system.** A banking system that is most cost efficient economizes on the real resources that a nation commits to the services that banking institutions provide, thereby freeing up the largest possible amount of remaining resources for other social uses. Thus, another key goal of depository institution regulation is to promote an environment in which these institutions can provide their services at the lowest possible cost.
4. **Protecting consumers.** *Asymmetric information* can make it difficult for consumers to make informed choices in their dealings with depository institutions. In some instances, unscrupulous depository institution managers might be able to use asymmetric information to their advantage, thereby subjecting consumers to contract terms that some might regard as "unfair." For this reason, in most countries consumer protection is another fundamental goal of bank regulation.

As also noted in Chapter 2, one of the great challenges of regulating depository institutions is balancing these goals. The evolution of U.S. depository institution regulation reflects the government's "balancing act" in the face of potentially conflicting objectives. Complicating the U.S. regulatory effort have been programs that the federal government itself has adopted, including the public insurance of most deposits issued by private depository institutions.

Federal Regulation: 1933–1970

The federal government's involvement in banking dates to the earliest days of the United States. Nevertheless, the federal government's role was relatively limited until the twentieth century. In response to the economic hardships of the Great Depression, in the 1930s Congress initiated a series of measures that dramatically increased the federal government's role in the affairs of depository financial institutions. The *McFadden Act* of 1927, which restricted nationally chartered banks to branching only according to state laws, already had done much to limit the scope for competition among banks. Nevertheless, many in Congress blamed the large number of bank failures of the early 1930s—about 2,000 per year between 1929 and 1933—on "destructive competition" in banking. Congress therefore set out to reduce the scope for competition and to make the federal government a "traffic cop" overseeing the nation's channels of financial commerce.

The Banking Act of 1933, otherwise known as the *Glass-Steagall Act,* created the Federal Deposit Insurance Corporation (FDIC), which supervises the nation's taxpayer-guaranteed deposit insurance system for commercial banks and savings institutions. The legislation also separated commercial and investment banking and placed interest rate ceilings on checking deposits of commercial banks. In short, the Glass-Steagall Act formally made the federal government the legal supervisor of the activities undertaken by depository institutions.

FEDERAL DEPOSIT INSURANCE Under the terms of the Glass-Steagall Act, the FDIC initially supervised a "Temporary Deposit Insurance Fund." Both the FDIC and its fund became more permanent fixtures of the nation's banking system in early 1935.

As part of the *National Housing Act* of 1934, Congress also set up a separate system of federal deposit insurance for savings institutions under the supervision of a Federal Home Loan Bank System that Congress had created in the *Federal Home Loan Bank Act* of 1932. The Federal Home Loan Bank Board governed the Federal Home Loan Bank System.

Credit unions also have federal deposit insurance. The National Credit Union Administration (NCUA), which Congress established in 1970, supervises this deposit insurance system. Instead of paying annual premiums to the NCUA's National Credit Union Share Insurance Fund, credit unions deposit 1 percent of their deposits with the NCUA fund. (Note that this 1 percent is a total *stock* of deposits, not to be confused with an annual *flow* assessment such as the FDIC's annual risk-based bank and savings institutions insurance fees.)

THE SEPARATION OF COMMERCIAL AND INVESTMENT BANKING Some commercial banks that failed at the outset of the Great Depression were also heavily involved in securities underwriting (see the discussion of investment banking in Chapter 3). To many observers at that time, it appeared that such activities had entailed significant risk for those banks and had contributed to highly visible failures that had reduced the public's confidence in the banking system. This lack of confidence, many argued, helped to fuel the banking panics that followed. Consequently, a key provision of the 1933 Glass-Steagall Act was the prohibition of securities underwriting by commercial banks or any other depository institutions.

Interstate branching: The operation of banking offices in more than one state.

Intrastate branching: The operation of banking offices anywhere within a state.

Branching Restrictions The Glass-Steagall Act also amended the 1927 McFadden Act in ways that further discouraged nationally chartered banks from attempting to open branch offices in states other than those in which their home offices were located. This made nationwide or even regional branching impossible without the explicit permission of both the state of a bank's origin and the state in which the bank wished to branch. For a number of years, very few states were willing to allow such arrangements. Consequently, **interstate branching,** or the opening of banking offices in more than one state, effectively was illegal.

Indeed, until the 1970s many states made branching a difficult proposition even *within* their boundaries. These states restricted even **intrastate branching,** permitting banks to open branch offices only within their home counties, or perhaps in adjacent counties. Some *unit banking* states went even further, preventing banks from operating any branch offices whatsoever. Only recently have most U.S. states permitted unlimited branching within their borders.

In spite of the various state regulations inhibiting branching, banks found ways to expand their branch networks considerably over the years. Indeed, the number of bank branches in the United States grew significantly during past decades even as the number of banks remained steady and, in recent years, began to decline.

Interest Rate Regulation The Glass-Steagall Act of 1933 also prohibited the payment of interest on demand deposits at commercial banks, which until the 1970s were the only form of checking deposits in the United States. The rationale for this provision was that if banks had to pay market interest rates on demand deposits when economic times were good, then they would be forced to search for high-interest assets that also entailed significant risks. Following an economic downturn, such risky assets would lose their market values. Then banks would lose liquidity and be unable to honor depositors' requests for funds. The result would be banking panics, such as those the country had experienced between 1929 and 1933. Those who framed the 1933 legislation sought to eliminate interest on checking deposits as a means of inhibiting such "destructive competition."

In addition, the Glass-Steagall Act authorized the Federal Reserve to place interest rate ceilings on bank savings and time deposits. The Federal Reserve imposed such ceilings through a rule it called Regulation Q. These "Reg-Q" ceilings, as they were called, remained in place until the 1980s. One Glass-Steagall interest ceiling, a zero-interest restriction on business demand deposits, remains in effect today.

Until the 1960s such interest rate ceilings applied only to commercial bank deposits. But under the terms of the Interest Rate Adjustment Act of 1966, similar ceilings constrained interest rates on savings and time deposits at savings institutions. The result of the imposition of these ceilings was the "Credit Crunch of 1966." When market interest rates rose well above the deposit rate ceilings at banks and savings institutions, depositors removed many of their funds from these institutions and used those funds to purchase alternative financial instruments, such as Treasury bills. This left depository institutions with fewer funds to lend. They responded by cutting back on loans, so otherwise creditworthy individuals and businesses were unable to obtain loans. Congress responded by raising the minimum T-bill denomination from $1,000 to $10,000, thereby inhibiting the ability of small savers to shift their funds in this manner. This action was not reversed until 1998.

1. In what ways did laws adopted in the 1930s exert long-term effects on the U.S. banking industry? The Glass-Steagall Act of 1933 had far-reaching effects on the depository institution industry. It strengthened interstate-branching restrictions and established the first federal deposit insurance fund, which laid the foundation for the establishment of the Federal Deposit Insurance Corporation. In addition, the legislation authorized ceilings on bank interest rates, including the zero-interest restriction on business demand deposits still in force today.

The Experiment with Partial Deregulation: 1971–1989

By the end of the 1960s, it had become apparent that interest rate regulations were likely to cause periodic **disintermediation.** During these intervals, other market interest rates rose sufficiently to induce savers to withdraw their funds from depository institutions and other financial intermediaries and use them to purchase financial instruments with higher, unregulated yields. The problem for depository institutions was that even when other market interest rates fell back to previous levels, former customers did not necessarily redeposit their funds. Rather than return to depository institutions to intermediate the savings-investment process, these former customers purchased financial instruments directly—hence the term *disintermediation.* The problems of the depository institutions were worsened by technological advances in information processing that had made it easier for other institutions to offer depository services.

THE DEPOSITORY INSTITUTIONS DEREGULATION AND MONETARY CONTROL ACT OF 1980 In 1980, Congress took steps to improve the ability of depository institutions to compete for funds. It reduced some of the regulatory constraints on banks, savings institutions, and credit unions by enacting the *Depository Institutions Deregulation and Monetary Control Act (DIDMCA).* The act contained three provisions that greatly improved the competitive position of all depository institutions. First, it set up a six-year phaseout of all interest rate ceilings that these institutions faced. Second, beginning in 1981, it permitted all depository institutions nationwide to offer negotiable-order-of-withdrawal (NOW) accounts, which essentially were interest-bearing checking deposits. Third, the DIDMCA increased federal deposit insurance coverage from $40,000 per deposit account to $100,000. Notably, *Congress raised this limit without increasing the insurance premiums that depository institutions had to pay to the FDIC.*

The DIDMCA also had some special benefits for savings institutions and credit unions. Savings institutions were allowed to make consumer loans, purchase commercial paper up to a limit of 20 percent of total assets, and issue credit cards. Credit unions could now make residential and real estate loans. These changes permitted more direct competition among savings institutions, credit unions, and commercial banks.

On the Web
How is federal deposit insurance administered? To find out, go to http://www.fdic.gov.

Disintermediation: A situation in which customers of depository institutions withdraw funds from their deposit accounts and use these funds to purchase financial instruments directly.

The DIDMCA of 1980 was a complicated piece of legislation. Although in the above respects it deregulated depository institutions, in other ways it increased their federal regulatory burdens. For instance, it required all federally insured depository institutions to meet reserve requirements established and maintained by the Federal Reserve on transactions deposits (demand deposits and NOW account deposits). It also required depository institutions to pay the Federal Reserve for check-clearing and wire-transfer services that they chose to use. Before the DIDMCA, only commercial banks that were members of the Federal Reserve System had to hold reserves with Federal Reserve banks, and these institutions had received Fed services without charge. The advantage of the DIDMCA for Fed member banks was that it effectively reduced their reserve requirements. For institutions that previously had not been required to hold reserves with the Fed, the advantages were access to Fed services (albeit at a cost) and the authorization to apply to Federal Reserve banks for loans when they faced liquidity difficulties.

On net, therefore, the DIDMCA did two things. Without doubt, it significantly deregulated depository institutions. Yet, at the same time, by placing all these institutions under the regulatory umbrella of the Federal Reserve System, a quasi agency of the U.S. government, and dramatically raising federal deposit insurance coverage, the DIDMCA effectively *increased* the federal government's stake in these institutions. Consequently, the DIDMCA only *partially* deregulated depository institutions. In several ways it enlarged the federal government's role in the industry.

The Garn–St Germain Act of 1982 In 1982, Congress passed another important piece of legislation that became known as the *Garn–St Germain Act.* One feature of this act was the authorization of *money market deposit accounts.* As noted in Chapter 1, these are savings deposits that offer market interest rates and a limited number of transfers each year. Within two years after their mid-1982 introduction, these accounts accumulated to almost $400 billion at all depository institutions. Undoubtedly, depository institutions won back some of their previous depositors, because shares in investment companies' money market mutual funds, which had grown at the depository institutions' expense during the 1970s, declined by nearly $50 billion during the same period. But most of the funds were deposited by people who already had savings accounts at depository institutions. These individuals simply moved their funds to money market deposit accounts to earn higher yields. As a result, many depository institutions found themselves incurring significantly greater interest expenses for only slightly larger volumes of deposits.

The other key elements of the Garn–St Germain Act attempted to address a festering problem. Since the 1970s the combined net worth of all savings institutions had declined precipitously. Some economists, such as Edward Kane of Boston College, used market value measures that indicated that much of the industry was technically bankrupt by the early 1970s. Even without taking into account the market values of their assets, by the middle of 1980 one-third of all savings institutions, with over a third of the total assets of such institutions, were operating at losses. To try to help savings institutions compete more effectively with other depository institutions, the Garn–St Germain Act increased the

DIDMCA limit on consumer loans and commercial paper, authorized savings institutions to make commercial real estate loans, and gave these institutions the power to purchase "unsecured loans," including low-rated, "junk" bonds, discussed in Chapter 4.

Finally, to further the process of closing troubled banks and savings institutions, the Garn–St Germain Act gave the FDIC broad powers to permit such institutions to merge with healthier partners, even across state lines. In retrospect, this provision of the legislation may have been the most successful. Many blame the Garn–St Germain Act for spurring the savings institution crisis that mushroomed a few years hence. Nevertheless, in later years the FDIC found itself putting its expanded powers to much greater use than Congress could have imagined when it passed the 1982 law.

2. How did deposit interest rate ceilings ultimately help to spur depository institution deregulation in the 1980s? Legal ceilings on deposit interest rates placed depository institutions at a competitive disadvantage whenever other market interest rates rose well above the ceilings, inducing depositors to withdraw their funds in search of higher yields. This so soured the fortunes of banks and savings institutions that Congress felt obliged to reduce the regulatory burdens that they faced in the laws that it passed in 1980 and 1982.

Deposit Insurance: The Big Regulatory Complication

In the United States, depository institution regulators face a major complication: the bulk of the deposits of nearly all depository institutions are insured by the federal government.

Deposit Insurance and Moral Hazard

Until recently, a key feature of the U.S. deposit insurance system was that depository institutions paid flat amounts for federal deposit insurance irrespective of their risks. In addition, all depository institutions are eligible for such insurance as long as they meet certain minimal standards.

THE MORAL-HAZARD PROBLEM OF DEPOSIT INSURANCE Recall from Chapter 10 that private insurance companies use a number of techniques to protect themselves from the fundamental *moral-hazard* problem of insurance. The difficulty is that once an individual or business receives insurance coverage, the covered person or firm may be tempted to behave more recklessly. After all, once one is insured, the expected personal cost arising from losses that might result from reckless behavior will be lower.

The existence of federal deposit insurance likewise can lead depository institution managers to make riskier choices than they might otherwise. This means that federal deposit insurance can expose the entire depository institution industry to significant moral-hazard problems.

Too-big-to-fail policy: A regulatory policy that protects the largest depository institutions from failure solely because regulators believe that such failure could undermine the public's confidence in the financial system.

Regulation as a Partial Solution The potential solution to the moral-hazard problem that arises from federal deposit insurance is depository institution regulation. By conducting periodic examinations of insured institutions and by issuing and enforcing rules for prudent management, depository institution regulators can reduce the scope for widespread moral-hazard difficulties. (Regulation consumes social resources, though, and someone must provide these resources; see *Management Focus: Paying to Be Regulated.*)

As we have seen, deposits at U.S. depository institutions have not always been federally insured. Once the U.S. government extended such insurance, however, the extent of federal regulation of depository institutions increased markedly.

Too Big to Fail? Deposit insurance covers deposits only up to certain limits, but what happens when deposits exceed those limits? The answer may depend on the size of the depository institution. In 1982, a large bank named Penn Square failed because declining energy prices had caused the market values of energy-related loans that the bank had extended to fall dramatically. Penn Square had close financial dealings with a number of other institutions, including Continental Illinois Bank, which was based in Chicago and at the time was the nation's seventh largest commercial bank. Continental Illinois had purchased over $1 billion of Penn Square's energy loans and soon found itself on the same slippery slope toward bankruptcy.

It is difficult for a large bank to keep such problems secret. When word of Continental Illinois's problems began to spread, it became the victim of an electronic bank run. Depositors whose account balances exceeded the $100,000 limit for deposit insurance coverage made wire transfers out of their accounts at the bank, causing it to lose over $10 billion in deposits within a two-month period in the spring of 1984. The bank offered above-market interest rates in an effort to induce individuals and firms to purchase its certificates of deposit, and it sold billions of dollars of its assets, but to little avail. By May of 1984, the FDIC decided to bail out Continental Illinois by purchasing over $2 billion in subordinated notes from the bank. In addition, the Federal Reserve Bank of Chicago extended long-term credit to the bank.

These actions by the FDIC and the Federal Reserve to keep the bank from failing were unprecedented in that they protected uninsured depositors of the bank as well as those whose funds were covered by federal guarantees. In September of 1984, the comptroller of the currency, the chief regulator of national banks, announced to Congress that he and his staff had decided that the eleven largest national banks in the United States were "too big to fail." This **too-big-to-fail policy** had its intended effect of shoring up public confidence in the nation's banking system. Ultimately, the other federal banking regulators, the Federal Reserve and the FDIC, implicitly adopted the same policy.

The Savings Institutions Crisis In the late 1980s and early 1990s, banking regulators sought to shore up the position of commercial banks for two reasons. One reason was that bank ratios of equity to assets had sunk to low levels in any event. A second reason, however, was that regulators wanted to avoid a commercial banking collapse analogous to the one that had just engulfed many U.S. savings institutions. The latter collapse was staggering in its own right: between the mid-1980s and 1990, more than half of all savings institutions—almost 1,500

GLOBAL | POLICY | CYBER | **MANAGEMENT Focus**

Paying to Be Regulated

When a regulatory agency examines a bank, it dispatches a group of examiners to the location. They spend a few days looking over the bank's accounting data, interviewing the bank's managers, and evaluating its performance in the areas of capital adequacy, asset quality, management, earnings, and liquidity. This process yields a "CAMEL" (the acronym for capital-assets-management-earnings-liquidity) rating for the bank. A CAMEL rating of 1 or 2 indicates that the examiners regard the institution as healthy. A rating of 3 causes the regulatory agency to place the institution on its "watch list," and a rating of 4 or 5 indicates that the examiners consider the institution to be in serious trouble.

The Assessment System

Conducting a bank examination incurs costs for allocating the full-time use of bank examiners' expertise and time, transporting the examiners to the institution's location, and housing them during the period of the examination. Somehow regulatory agencies must generate revenues to cover these costs.

The regulated institutions themselves provide these revenues through "assessments" imposed by the regulatory agencies. The Office of the Comptroller of the Currency (OCC), for instance, imposes semiannual assessments on the national banks it regulates. The OCC charges higher assessment rates to larger banks. A bank with $2 million in assets pays an OCC assessment of about $10,000 per year, and a bank with $20 million in assets pays an annual assessment of more than $17,000.

In the early 2000s, the OCC found itself facing a dilemma. Because the U.S. economy had leveled off and even contracted, bank assets had also stopped growing and had even shrunk slightly. As a result, the agency's flow of revenues to fund bank examinations began to decline even as the expenses entailed in conducting examinations continued to increase.

Small Banks Confront Big Assessment Increases

The OCC decided to increase its assessments. The agency raised assessments on small national banks by more than 60 percent while pushing up assessments for large national banks by only 26 percent. Small banks complained that singling them out for higher increases was unjustified. They contended that because larger banks typically have more complicated operations involving credit cards, subprime loans, and derivative securities, the OCC should have raised the assessments for large banks by a greater amount. The OCC responded that transportation and housing for the examiners—not the complexity of a bank's operations—account for most of the cost of a bank examination. Those costs tend to be higher for small banks, which are often in more remote communities. This, the OCC explained, is why small banks were singled out for bigger increases in their assessments.

For Critical Analysis: If a bank regulatory agency's revenues fail to cover its costs—which happens from time to time—who pays the difference? (Hint: The OCC is part of the Department of the Treasury, and the Treasury's budget is funded by congressional appropriations.)

institutions—failed outright or were closed by regulators. A similar collapse of the commercial banking industry would have been a real catastrophe.

What caused the savings institution crisis? Certainly, the cumulative effects of high and variable interest rates during the 1970s had driven up interest expenses at savings institutions even as their interest incomes remained relatively fixed. This exposure to interest rate risks had already pushed many savings institutions to the brink of insolvency by the end of the 1970s. In addition, increased competition stemming from deregulation in the early 1980s compressed the profit margins at many institutions that already were trying to overcome managerial inexperience with new lines of business permitted under the Garn–St Germain Act. Furthermore, a major decline in oil prices slashed real estate prices and mortgage values in the southwestern United States, where livelihoods depended heavily on energy-related industries. Finally, there was outright fraud at some institutions.

Most economists agree, however, that the crisis was really caused by two related factors: *moral hazard* and *regulatory failure*. By insuring the deposits of savings institutions, the government gave the managers of these institutions an incentive to undertake riskier activities. The deregulation provisions of the 1980 DIDMCA and 1982 Garn–St Germain Act added to these incentives. As discussed earlier in this chapter, a key rationale for regulation is to minimize this moral-hazard problem. In the case of savings institutions in the 1980s, regulation failed to perform this function. Indeed, otherwise well-meaning congressional actions largely induced the great savings institution debacle of the 1980s and 1990s.

3. Why does the provision of federal deposit insurance help to justify federal regulation of depository institutions? Providing deposit insurance exposes the federal government to the moral-hazard problem that managers of depository institutions will respond by making riskier decisions. A way to try to prevent more reckless behavior by depository institution managers is to subject them to regulatory examination and supervision.

Reregulation versus Deregulation in the Late 1980s and Early 1990s

By early 1987 the savings institution deposit insurance fund was technically insolvent. Yet not until 1989 did Congress pass legislation to deal with the savings institution crisis.

THE FINANCIAL INSTITUTIONS REFORM, RECOVERY, AND ENFORCEMENT ACT OF 1989 The 1989 legislation specified means of enforcing broad governmental mandates to accomplish the recovery objective. Consequently, Congress called the legislation the *Financial Institutions Reform, Recovery, and Enforcement Act (FIRREA)*.

Although the FIRREA left the Federal Home Loan Bank System largely intact, it dismantled the Federal Home Loan Bank Board. As a new regulator for savings institutions, the FIRREA created the Office of Thrift Supervision (OTS) within the Treasury Department. The legislation also created a Federal Housing Finance Board to supervise the operations of the Federal Home Loan Bank System but gave this board meager regulatory responsibilities. The FIRREA reassigned the supervision of the savings institution deposit fund to the FDIC; it continued the traditional separation of bank and savings institution deposit funds, however. One FDIC fund, the **Bank Insurance Fund (BIF)**, covers commercial banks; another, the **Savings Association Insurance Fund (SAIF)**, provides federal deposit insurance to savings institutions.

Bank Insurance Fund (BIF): The FDIC's fund that covers insured deposits of commercial banks.

Savings Association Insurance Fund (SAIF): The FDIC's fund that covers insured deposits of savings institutions.

To shore up the SAIF, the FIRREA gave the FDIC broadened authority to try to recover asset values of insolvent savings institutions, and it authorized tax-financed funding of savings institution "resolutions," which Congress found to be a nicer word than "closings." The FIRREA specified that funding for such resolutions was to be handled through the Treasury Department and another new agency, the Resolution Finance Corporation (RFC). Yet another agency, the Resolution Trust Corporation (RTC), handled the day-to-day aspects of closing down insolvent savings institutions. The FIRREA set 1992 as a target date for the completion of the duties of the RFC and RTC, but these agencies did not go out of business until 1994.

Another set of provisions in the FIRREA reversed the deregulation thrust of the DIDMCA and the Garn–St Germain Act. The FIRREA prohibited savings institutions from holding junk bonds (high-interest, high-risk bonds), and it toughened the limitations on commercial real estate lending.

THE FDIC IMPROVEMENT ACT OF 1991 The FIRREA basically was a stopgap effort to deal with old problems. In contrast, the *FDIC Improvement Act (FDICIA)* of 1991 represented a forward-looking effort. By passing this legislation, Congress sought to reform various aspects of depository institution regulation and to revamp specific elements of federal deposit insurance. The FDICIA of 1991 did a number of things:

1. Established regulatory responses to banks failing to meet capital standards.
2. Established a regulatory system of **structured early intervention and resolution (SEIR)**, under which the FDIC has authority to intervene much more quickly in the affairs of a depository institution that may generate losses for either the BIF or the SAIF.
3. Required the FDIC to set up a clear set of rules for determining when a depository institution's net worth reaches a sufficiently low level that it must be closed.
4. Authorized the FDIC to shore up both the BIF and the SAIF by setting **deposit insurance premiums,** or annual charges to depository institutions for depository insurance. high enough to increase both insurance funds.
5. Restricted the extent to which the Federal Reserve can lend to undercapitalized depository institutions.
6. Required bank regulators to treat troubled large banks under the same timetables and procedures that they apply to small banks that are failing.
7. Mandated a system of **risk-based deposit insurance premiums,** under which the premiums that depository institutions pay the FDIC to fund the BIF and the SAIF depend on the institutions' degrees of capitalization.

Structured early intervention and resolution (SEIR): A regulatory system, established by the FDIC Improvement Act of 1991, that authorizes the FDIC to intervene quickly in the management of a depository institution that currently threatens to cause losses for the federal deposit insurance funds.

Deposit insurance premium: The price that depository institutions pay to the FDIC's insurance fund in exchange for a guarantee of federal insurance of covered deposits that they issue.

Risk-based deposit insurance premiums: Premiums that depository institutions pay the FDIC based on the varying degrees to which they are capitalized and on the differing risk factors that they exhibit.

The Great Regulatory Experiment: Capital Requirements

At the same time that the federal government sought to bolster the FDIC's deposit insurance funds, it developed a new framework for seeking to reduce the potential for failure of individual depository institutions. This new approach focused attention on depository institutions' equity capital positions.

Capital requirements: Minimum equity capital standards that regulators impose upon depository institutions.

Risk-based capital requirements: Regulatory capital standards that account for risk factors that distinguish different depository institutions.

Risk-adjusted assets: A weighted average of bank assets that regulators compute to account for risk differences across types of assets.

On the Web

What types of regulatory issues are currently attracting the attention of international banking supervisors? To stay up-to-date, go to the home page of the Bank for International Settlements (http://www.bis.org), and click on "Basel Committee, publications" to view a listing of the committee's recent reports on issues in bank regulation.

Capital Requirements

A depository institution's equity capital represents a "cushion" against losses to depositors, who have the first crack at getting back their funds if an institution should fail. Holders of equity shares, in contrast, are the last in line for funds in such an event. For this reason, depository institution regulators—and in particular the FDIC as the supervisor of federal deposit insurance—regard capital as the first line of defense against depositor losses in the event of a failure. In recent years this has led regulators to impose **capital requirements,** or enforced minimum standards for depository institution equity capital.

Although various requirements on depository institution equity capital positions had existed prior to the 1980s, it was not until Congress passed the *International Lending Supervision Act* of 1983 that regulators began efforts to impose relatively uniform standards for depository institutions. A provision of this legislation authorized the Federal Reserve, the Office of the Comptroller of the Currency (OCC), and the FDIC to determine and supervise capital requirements for commercial banks. In 1985, these three regulators set up a system of capital requirements using two measures of capital. The narrower measure essentially included most equity shares and loan loss reserves (see Chapter 13), and the broader measure added remaining equity shares and subordinated debt—long-term bond issues by depository institutions. The regulators then required banks to meet a two-tiered requirement involving ratios of the capital measures to assets.

The imposition of these capital standards helped end a gradual decline in bank capitalization that had begun in the 1960s (see Figure 11-3 in Chapter 11). Nevertheless, a commonly recognized problem with simple ratios of capital to assets was that they treated any two banks with the same dollar-denominated capital and asset positions as identical. In fact, however, one bank might have made huge loans to a developing country on the verge of default while the other might have maintained a well-diversified portfolio of high-quality loans and safe securities. Consequently, simple ratios mainly affect the mix of liabilities and equity capital of depository institutions. Influencing this mix might make sense if regulators care only about *liquidity risks,* or risks associated with loss of liquidity resulting from unexpected deposit withdrawals. Using simple capital ratios alone, however, would fail to account for differences in *credit risks,* or risks relating to the quality of assets, among depository institutions.

ESTABLISHING RISK-BASED CAPITAL REQUIREMENTS In 1988, the Basel Committee on Banking Supervision—senior representatives of bank supervisory authorities of the United States and eleven other industrialized nations whose activities are based at the Bank for International Settlements in Basel, Switzerland—announced a system of **risk-based capital requirements.** This system was intended to factor risk characteristics into the computation of required capital standards. Under this system, which applies to most banks in the developed world, institutions compute ratios of capital in relation to **risk-adjusted assets.** This figure is a weighted average of all the bank's assets, in which the weights account for risk differences across types of assets.

The safest assets, which regulators traditionally have perceived to be cash assets, U.S. Treasury securities, and fully government-guaranteed GNMA mortgage-backed securities, receive a zero weight and hence do not count at all in the computation of risk-adjusted assets. Assets that regulators view as having a slight possibility of default, such as interbank deposits, municipal bonds, and partially government-guaranteed FNMA mortgage-backed securities, receive a weight of 20 percent. Riskier assets such as first home mortgages receive a weight of 50 percent. All other loans and securities receive a 100 percent weight. In addition, regulators compute "credit exposure dollar equivalents" for banking activities such as derivatives trading that do not appear as assets or liabilities on banks' balance sheets. These typically also receive a 100 percent weight. Then regulators add up all the weighted dollar amounts to get a bank's total risk-adjusted asset figure. This amount is the denominator of the capital ratios that banks have to compute.

Under the Basel capital standards, banks calculate two ratios of capital relative to risk-adjusted assets, based on separate "tiers" of bank capital. The first, "Tier 1 capital," or **core capital,** consists of common shareholders' equity plus retained earnings (income not paid out to shareholders). Regulators have defined a bank's **total capital** as core capital plus "Tier 2 capital," or **supplementary capital.** This latter measure includes some types of preferred stock and most types of subordinated debt.

Since 1989, the regulations have called for the ratio of core capital to risk-adjusted assets to exceed 4 percent and the ratio of total capital to risk-adjusted assets to be greater than 8 percent. In addition, the regulators imposed a simple-ratio standard in which the ratio of total capital to *unadjusted total assets* must exceed 4 percent. Thus, this structure of capital requirements sought to address both liquidity risk and credit risk.

Core capital: Defined by current capital requirements as shareholders' equity plus retained earnings.

Total capital: Under currently imposed bank capital requirements, the sum of core capital and supplementary capital.

Supplementary capital: Under standards currently used to calculate required capital, a measure that includes certain preferred stock and most subordinated debt.

CALCULATING RISK-BASED CAPITAL REQUIREMENTS To see how these original capital requirements worked, consider a very simple example of two banks. One has $1 million in cash, $2 million in U.S. Treasury securities, and $10 million in commercial loans, so its total assets equal $13 million. It has $0.5 million in common stockholders' equity and retained earnings and $0.5 million in subordinated debt. Hence, its core capital is $0.5 million, and its total capital is $1 million. The $3 million in cash and Treasury securities do not count toward the bank's risk-adjusted assets. Its $10 million in commercial loans count 100 percent, so its total risk-adjusted assets equal $10 million. Consequently, its ratio of core capital to risk-adjusted assets is equal to $0.5 million/$10 million, or 5 percent. Its ratio of total capital to risk-adjusted assets is equal to $1 million/$10 million, or 10 percent. Its unadjusted capital ratio is $1 million/$13 million, or about 7.6 percent. Thus, this bank meets all required capital standards.

Now consider a bank with $0.5 million in cash, $0.5 million in securities, and $12 million in commercial loans. Like the first bank, this one has $13 million in assets on its balance sheet. In contrast, however, it has sufficient off-balance-sheet activities to merit a "credit exposure dollar equivalent" rating of $3 million. Like the first bank, this bank also has $0.5 million in core capital and $0.5 million in supplementary capital. Consequently, the second bank's unadjusted capital ratio, like that of the first bank, is equal to 7.6 percent. Yet the second bank clearly is a riskier bank, because it has more loans and undertakes off-balance-sheet activities. This shows up in the current capital requirement calculations. The second bank's $1 million in cash and securities do not count toward its risk-adjusted

moneyxtra!

Another Perspective

Evaluate the details of a proposal for using subordinated debt as a key component of market-oriented bank regulation by going to the Chapter 14 reading from the Federal Reserve Bank of Chicago, entitled "Subordinated Debt as Bank Capital: A Proposal for Regulatory Reform," by Douglas Evanoff and Larry Wall.

http://moneyxtra.swcollege.com

assets, but its $12 million in commercial loans and $3 million in "credit exposure dollar equivalents" from its off-balance-sheet activities count fully, giving it a risk-adjusted asset total of $15 million. This bank's ratio of core capital to risk-adjusted assets then is $0.5 million/$15 million, or 3.3 percent. Its ratio of total capital to risk-adjusted assets is $1 million/$15 million, or 6.7 percent. Thus, even though it has the same actual assets and capital as the first bank, the second bank fails both the 4 percent and the 8 percent capital standards that apply to core capital and total capital, respectively.

The Effects of Capital Requirements

After announcing the new capital standards, banking regulators phased them in gradually through the end of 1992. A number of banks failed to meet the three ratio requirements. In particular, banks often failed the 4 percent simple-ratio requirement even when they met the risk-adjusted ratio standards. To adjust to the requirements, banks could have issued new stock or cut back on lending. Banks' stock prices tend to decline sharply, however, whenever they announce that they plan to issue new shares. This tendency may have discouraged many banks from issuing new stock and induced them to cut back on issuing new loans instead. By chance, an economic downturn that depressed the demand for loans also occurred in 1990 and 1991.

These two factors together—reduced issuance of loans in response to higher capital standards for banks and decreased loan demand—may have acted together to cause a significant cutback in bank lending between 1990 and 1992. Panel (a) of Figure 14-1 uses the competitive banking model developed in Chapter 12 to illustrate the initial effects of these events. The imposition of capital requirements raised the marginal cost of lending at many banks, thereby causing them to reduce their supply of loans. Thus, the market loan supply schedule shifts leftward, from L^s to $L^{s\prime}$. At the same time, the demand for loans by households and businesses declined somewhat during the economic downturn, as depicted by the leftward shift in the loan demand schedule from L^d to $L^{d\prime}$ in panel (a). We can predict that the result should have been a reduction in the quantity of loans issued by banks and, if the fall in loan supply exceeded the decline in loan demand, a reduction in lending and a rise in the equilibrium loan rate.

Refer back to Figure 11-1 on page 251, and you will see that commercial bank lending did indeed fall off noticeably in the early 1990s. Panel (b) of Figure 14-1 shows how the spread between interest rates on short-term personal loans charged by small and large banks and the two-year Treasury note rate increased significantly following the adoption of risk-based capital requirements, whether the banks were classified as well-capitalized or undercapitalized.

As Figure 14-2 on the following page indicates, however, the adoption of the risk-based capital standards nevertheless had the longer-run effect on aggregate equity positions of U.S. commercial banks that regulators had hoped to achieve. For the first time in almost fifty years, the ratio of equity to assets rose, beginning in 1990. Figure 14-2 shows that the adoption of the new capital standards may have ended a 150-year downward trend in the overall equity ratio at commercial banks. Furthermore, as market interest rates declined in the late 1990s, the cost of meeting capital requirements declined at banks, inducing a recovery in lending and a decline in the loan rate–Treasury note rate spread.

Figure 14-1
Predicted and Actual Loan Rate Effects of the Imposition of Capital Requirements.

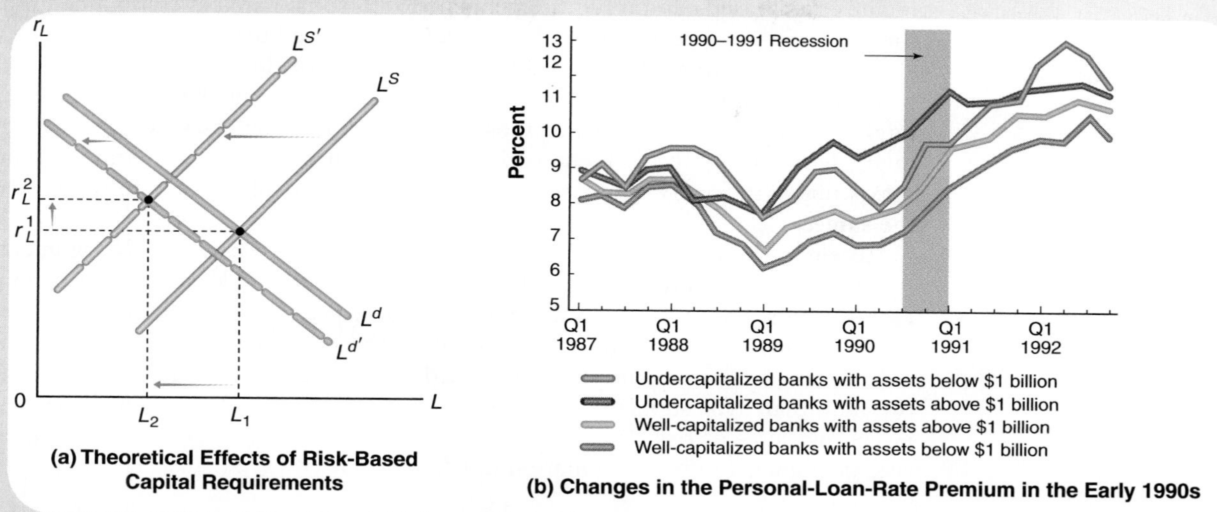

Panel (a) indicates that capital requirements that treat loans as risky assets raise the marginal cost of lending for each bank in the loan market, so the market loan supply schedule shifts leftward. In the face of a recession, there is also a fall in loan demand, so the equilibrium quantity of loans definitely falls. The market loan rate rises on net if the reduction in loan supply outweighs the fall in loan demand. Panel (b) indicates that the interest rate on personal loans did indeed rise relative to the two-year Treasury note rate at banks of all sizes and capitalization levels.

SOURCE [panel (b)]: Cara Lown and Stavros Peristiani, "The Behavior of Consumer Loan Rates during the 1990 Credit Slowdown," *Journal of Banking and Finance* 20 (December 1996): 1673–1694.

Figure 14-2
Equity as a Percentage of Bank Assets in the United States, 1840–Present.

U.S. bank equity ratios fell considerably between the mid-nineteenth and the mid-twentieth century. More recently, they have risen slightly.

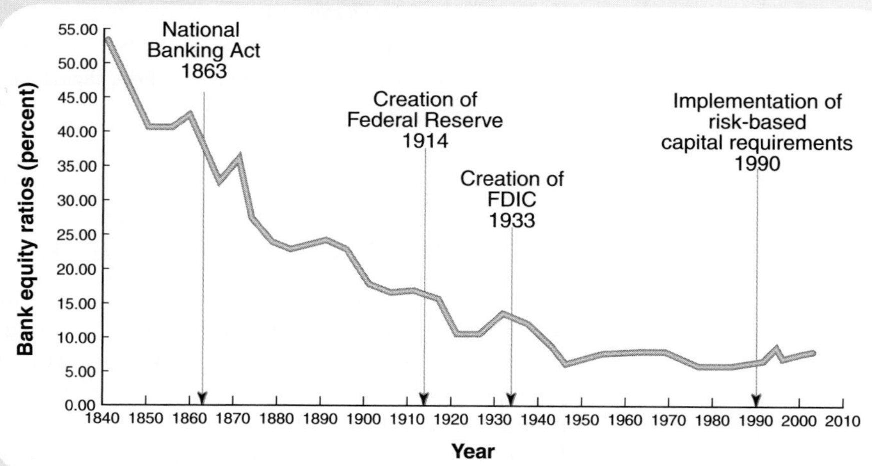

SOURCES: Allen N. Berger, Richard J. Herring, and Giorgio P. Szego, "The Role of Capital in Financial Institutions," *Journal of Banking and Finance* 19 (June 1995); and Federal Deposit Insurance Corporation.

New Capital Requirements for the 2000s?

When the Basel Committee on Banking Supervision first proposed and implemented risk-based capital requirements in 1989, some bankers complained that the risk weights were arbitrary. The bankers contended that banks with balance sheets that were treated identically for the purpose of the 1989 capital requirements could actually have very different degrees of risk. One bank, for instance, might make loans only to the most creditworthy businesses, while another might lend to highly risky enterprises, yet for purposes of calculating capital ratios under the 1989 standards the banks' loan portfolios were to be treated the same.

Recently, the Basel Committee announced that it agreed with this argument. By 2005, the committee plans to have in place modified risk weights for capital requirements that will include a greater-than-100-percent risk weighting for low-quality loans. It also intends to try to take into account *operational risks,* such as risks arising from computer failure, poor documentation, or fraud. Furthermore, the new plan will supplement numerical capital ratios with so-called market-based measures of risk. We shall explore the possible role of such market-based risk assessments in bank regulation in Chapter 15.

4. How has the federal government sought to reduce the FDIC's exposure to losses? Legislation enacted in 1989 and in 1991 established clear rules that the FDIC must follow to identify potential risks to the federal deposit insurance funds. These laws also specify actions that the FDIC can take to enforce its efforts to limit the risk of depository institution failures, including closure of weak institutions. An additional feature of the legislation was the authorization of risk-based deposit insurance premiums. To induce banks to restrain their risk of loss and failure, regulators have developed narrow and broad measures of bank capital and a measure of assets that adjusts for differences in risk across groups of assets. The regulators have set mimimum requirements for the ratios of the two capital measures relative to the measure of risk-adjusted assets. Banks must meet these capital standards or face greater supervision or perhaps even closure.

The Current Regulatory Framework

Of the various banking laws reviewed in this chapter, the most far-reaching was the Glass-Steagall Act of 1933. For sixty-seven years, this legislation provided the structure for U.S. financial intermediation. Nevertheless, within a few years of its passage, bills were introduced in nearly every Congress to amend or even to repeal various aspects of the act. Senator Carter Glass himself decided that the law was overly restrictive and introduced bills aimed at modifying it. Year after year, however, efforts to loosen some of the restraints of the act failed to advance to law. Finally, in 1999, Congress reached a consensus that the Glass-Steagall Act had outlived its usefulness.

The Financial Services Modernization Act of 1999

The law that Congress passed, the *Financial Services Modernization Act of 1999*, also called the *Gramm-Leach-Bliley Act,* swept away a number of Glass-Steagall's provisions. The two key provisions of the new law were the following:

1. Securities firms and insurance companies are permitted to own commercial banks.
2. Banks are empowered to underwrite insurance and securities, including shares of stock.

Was the Gramm-Leach-Bliley Act a good idea, or was it bad public policy? To review alternative perspectives on this debate and make your own judgment, go to EconDebate Online. http://moneyxtra.swcollege.com

Thus, securities brokers and dealers, investment banks, and insurance companies can now compete directly with commercial banks. In addition, commercial banks can compete directly with traditional insurers, brokers and dealers, and investment banks.

Undoubtedly, as the 2000s continue to unfold, the Gramm-Leach-Bliley Act will pave the way for major changes in U.S. financial intermediation. More commercial banks, securities firms, and insurers are likely to form financial conglomerates. Some financial firms may retain their individual identities but work more closely together. For instance, some insurers may package and manage insurance products that banks will market to their customers, and the two types of institutions will share the revenues from these activities. We shall explore more fully the ramifications that the Gramm-Leach-Bliley Act may have for commercial banks in Chapter 15. The new law also has important implications for how U.S. banking regulation and supervision are likely to be conducted in the future.

Effect of the 1999 Law on the Regulation and Supervision of Commercial Banks

The present regulatory structure for commercial banks stems in part from the dual banking system that emerged after the Civil War. The Office of the Comptroller of the Currency (OCC) has always been the primary regulator of national (federally chartered) banks, and the OCC continues in this capacity today. Under the Banking Act of 1935, which you will learn in Chapter 17 significantly restructured the Federal Reserve, by 1937 all federally insured state banks either had to join the Federal Reserve System and be regulated and supervised by the Fed or had to subject themselves to regulatory supervision from the FDIC. This produced a trilateral federal regulatory structure. The OCC regulates national banks, the Federal Reserve regulates state banks that are members of the Federal Reserve System, and the FDIC regulates state banks that do not opt to be members of the Federal Reserve System.

On the Web
How many types of regulations do banks face? For an A–Z listing of Federal Reserve Regulations, go to the home page of the Federal Reserve Bank of New York (http://www.ny.frb.org), and click on "Banking Information" in the left-hand margin. Then click on "Regulatory & Legal Matters." Finally, click on "A Guide to Federal Reserve Regulations" (http://www.ny.frb.org/pihome/regs.html).

THE BASIC BANK REGULATORY STRUCTURE This commercial bank regulatory structure, therefore, has existed for over sixty years. The only "wrinkle" was the establishment of the Federal Reserve as the chief regulator of *bank holding companies,* some of which own national banks or state banks that are not Federal Reserve member banks. But the three regulatory bodies have worked out lines of authority that apply to such situations.

Each of the three commercial bank regulators retains staff accountants, statisticians, and economists. These individuals examine and audit the books of the banks that they regulate, collect and analyze data from specific institutions and for all institutions combined, and evaluate the effectiveness of current or proposed regulatory policies. Of the roughly 8,000 commercial banks, about 2,000 are national banks that the OCC regulates. Of the 6,000 or so state-chartered banks, about 900 are Federal Reserve members and thereby fall under the Fed's regulatory umbrella. The FDIC currently has oversight responsibilities for over 5,000 commercial banks.

On the Web
How do bank examiners at various U.S. regulatory agencies coordinate their activities? To find out, visit the Web site of the Federal Financial Institutions Examination Council, http://www.ffiec.gov.

BANKING REGULATION AND SUPERVISION UNDER THE GRAMM-LEACH-BLILEY ACT
From the perspective of individual banks, the Gramm-Leach-Bliley Act did not alter the basic trilateral structure of banking regulation. In one respect, however, the act split supervisory authority between the Federal Reserve and the OCC. In a compromise worked out with the two regulators, Congress gave the Fed and the OCC the authority to veto each other's decisions to grant new powers to commercial banks under their respective regulatory jurisdictions. This means that these two bank regulators will be forced to cooperate in determining whether commercial banks may create subsidiaries that act as investment banks, brokers, or insurers.

Nevertheless, the Gramm-Leach-Bliley Act left the Fed solely in charge of supervising bank holding companies. This means that the Fed is the ultimate regulator of multiservice conglomerates such as Citigroup. In an important sense, therefore, the Gramm-Leach-Bliley Act makes the Fed the preeminent banking regulator. The Fed has the authority to permit bank holding companies to branch out into various lines of business—securities underwriting, insurance, and the like—without any input from other banking regulators. (For some financial institutions, establishing a multiservice conglomerate is a quick way to vault into the ranks of top U.S. banks; see *Policy Focus: A Quick Route into the Top Ten within U.S. Banking.*)

Regulation and Supervision of Savings Institutions

To contemplate the pros and cons of a recent proposal to consolidate the U.S. Treasury's regulation of bank and savings institutions, see the Chapter 14 Case Study, entitled "Time to Combine the OCC and the OTS?"
http://moneyxtra.swcollege.com

The Gramm-Leach-Bliley Act had fewer implications for the regulation and supervision of savings institutions. Under a provision of the 1989 Financial Institutions Reform, Recovery, and Enforcement Act, the main federal regulator of savings institutions remains the Office of Thrift Supervision (OTS). The OTS is a bureau within the Treasury Department, and its relationship to nationally chartered savings institutions mirrors the OCC's relationship to nationally chartered commercial banks in many respects.

Nevertheless, in some ways the authority of the OTS is limited. Feeling somewhat "burned" by the regulatory breakdowns that occurred during the savings institution crisis of the 1980s, in 1989 Congress gave the FDIC the power to overrule the OTS in some instances. For instance, the FDIC can close OTS-regulated institutions or withdraw federal deposit insurance from such institutions even in the face of OTS objections. At the same time, Congress reduced the likelihood of such squabbles by also making the heads of the OCC and OTS members of the five-person board of directors of the FDIC.

GLOBAL | POLICY Focus | CYBER | MANAGEMENT

A Quick Route into the Top Ten within U.S. Banking

To implement the Gramm-Leach-Bliley Act, in 2000 the Federal Reserve established *financial holding companies (FHCs)*. These are umbrella organizations, regulated by the Fed, that can own banks, insurance companies, and securities firms. Initially, only large banking institutions such as Citibank applied to become FHCs.

In February 2001, however, MetLife became an FHC. MetLife is one of the nation's largest life insurance companies. The company also operates securities brokerage firms and sells mutual funds and retirement plans.

Since becoming an FHC, MetLife has also become a banking institution. Indeed, it became one of the top ten "banking institutions" in the United States the very day the Federal Reserve granted it status as an FHC—the speediest advance ever by a single institution into the list of the nation's top ten banks. As you can see in Table 14-1, based on total assets MetLife is currently the seventh-largest banking institution.

For Critical Analysis: People often disagree about whether financial institutions should be ranked by their assets, their equity, or their earnings. How has the Gramm-Leach-Bliley Act further complicated efforts to rank the largest banks?

Table 14-1 The Ten Largest U.S. Banking Institutions

These were the ten top banking companies as of 2002.

	Assets ($ Billions)
Citigroup, Inc.	$1,051
J. P. Morgan Chase	694
Bank of America	622
Wachovia	330
Wells Fargo & Co.	308
Bank One	269
Metlife, Inc.	257
Taunus	227
Washington Mutual	208
FleetBoston	204

SOURCE: *American Banker.*

Under the Gramm-Leach-Bliley Act, state authorities continue to regulate state-chartered savings institutions. Nevertheless, nearly all such institutions are federally insured. The OTS does not have supervisory authority over state-chartered savings institutions, but these institutions must meet standards established by the FDIC. Consequently, state-chartered savings institutions ultimately must meet federally mandated standards and effectively must satisfy FDIC regulations.

Regulation and Supervision of Credit Unions

The Gramm-Leach-Bliley Act had very little to say about the structure of federal regulation and supervision of credit unions. Under the terms of earlier laws, the key federal regulator of credit unions is the National Credit Union Administration (NCUA). A board of three individuals governs this government agency, which has sole responsibility for chartering, insuring, supervising, and examining federally chartered credit unions. The NCUA administers the National Credit Union Share Insurance Fund, and most state-chartered credit unions contribute to and are covered by this insurance fund. Although state regulatory bodies have immediate supervisory responsibilities for such state-chartered institutions, those covered by the NCUA's insurance program must meet the standards that it sets for coverage. Because the NCUA's fund covers all federally insured credit unions, the FDIC plays no role in the supervision or regulation of credit unions.

Indeed, those who have advocated streamlining the regulatory environment faced by commercial banks often point to the NCUA as a possible model for a simplified bank regulatory structure. Those who favor maintaining the status quo for commercial bank regulation respond that even though there are more credit unions than commercial banks, the amount of dollars involved in the two industries differs dramatically. After all, the assets of all credit unions combined amount to less than one-tenth of the assets of commercial banks, and the latter institutions have played more dominant and varied roles in the nation's financial system. This, goes the counterargument, helps to justify the more complex web of regulators and regulations that commercial banks face. We should note, however, that this counterargument may lose some of its force in the future, because the NCUA currently is contemplating the imposition of capital requirements, as well as other bank-type regulations, on the credit unions that it regulates.

5. How did the Financial Services Modernization Act of 1999 alter the structure of U.S. bank regulation and supervision? Since the 1930s, commercial banks have had three regulators: (1) the Office of the Comptroller of the Currency (OCC), which supervises nationally chartered banks, (2) the Federal Reserve, which supervises state-chartered banks that are members of the Federal Reserve System (Fed), and the Federal Deposit Insurance Corporation (FDIC), which supervises the remaining state-chartered banks. The Financial Services Modernization Act, or Gramm-Leach-Bliley Act, of 1999 altered the U.S. financial landscape by allowing direct ties between and rivalry among commercial banks, securities firms, and insurance companies. This required modifying the structure of federal banking supervision, and Congress gave the Fed primary authority over umbrella, multibank companies that own both banks and other financial firms. The Fed and the OCC share authority to determine what types of financial firms individual banks may own. The Gramm-Leach-Bliley Act did little to alter the basic structure of federal regulation of savings institutions, which are supervised by the Office of Thrift Supervision (OTS), or of credit unions, which are supervised by the National Credit Union Administration (NCUA).

International Dimensions of Bank Regulation

Countries do not always share the same cultures, languages, or political systems. One thing that countries all over the world do have in common, however, is their recent propensity to experience major banking catastrophes.

The Global Epidemic of Bank Failures

In the United States, the final bill for the government-arranged bailout of the nation's savings and loan industry during the early 1990s totaled at least $200 billion, or just over 2 percent of the total national output for a single year. But this is a drop in the bucket compared with the banking problems that other countries have faced in recent years. For example, efforts by Argentina's government to recover from a banking crisis in the early 1980s probably cost more than half of that country's single-year gross domestic product. Today the country is again struggling with banking instability.

BANK TROUBLES IN THE WEST . . . As banking systems in some locales such as the United States rebounded in the 1990s, conditions worsened in many other regions of the Western world, including Scandinavia. Between 1992 and 1993, Norway's government effectively purchased over half of the nation's banking system to keep it financially afloat, and in 1992 the government of Sweden took control of two of the country's four largest banking institutions. Eastern Europe experienced even worse problems. In 1996, Bulgaria's banking system imploded and had to be rescued by the country's government. Today, nearly a third of the loans issued by banks in the Czech Republic and in Slovakia are "nonperforming," meaning that the banks will be unlikely to recover significant portions of the principal amounts of the loans.

Other parts of the Western world also slid into crisis. Since 1994, Venezuela has spent over 25 percent of its national output for one year repairing its banking system. The cost of Mexico's 1995 banking collapse, which the Mexican government is still dealing with today, has been estimated at nearly 15 percent of that country's output for a given year.

. . . AND MAJOR BANKING PROBLEMS IN THE EAST The biggest problems, however, have arisen in East Asia. By 1997, South Korea's banking system teetered on bankruptcy, as more than 10 percent of all loans by that country's banks—nearly $25 billion, or the combined market value of all South Korean banks—were nonperforming, In that same year, banking systems collapsed in Indonesia, Malaysia, and Thailand.

On the Web
How is South Korea's financial system structured? Learn more about South Korean banking by visiting the home page of the Bank of Korea at http://www.bok.or.kr. First, select the English-language version at the upper right. Then click on "Financial System."

Today, banking conditions have improved somewhat in these Southeast Asian nations. Nevertheless, national banking systems throughout Asia continue to be troubled. In India, nearly a fifth of the loans extended by twenty-seven government-owned banks are nonperforming. The Bank of China estimates that about the same portion of Chinese bank loans also are nonperforming.

Even in Japan, more than $250 billion in bank loans soured in 1995 alone when home mortgage companies known as *jusen* went bankrupt following a collapse in Japanese real estate prices. Within just a few years, the Japanese banking system was reeling, as banks faced a cumulative total of more than *$600 billion* in bad loans to clean up. One bit of market "fallout" from these problems has been the *Japan premium.* Since the late 1990s, Japanese banks have had to pay 0.20 to 0.25 percentage points more for interbank loans, as compared with U.S., British, German, and other Western banks. A little over two-tenths of a percentage point may not seem like much until one takes into account the hundreds of billions of dollars of worldwide money market funds that Japanese banks must raise. For each billion-dollar increment of fund-raising in global money markets, a 0.20 percent "Japan premium" translates into an additional $2 million that Japanese banks must pay for funds. This extra funding cost, of course, has placed Japanese banks at a considerable competitive disadvantage in international lending markets.

Regulatory arbitrage: The act of trying to avoid regulations imposed by banking authorities in one's home country by moving offices and funds to countries with less constraining regulations.

A Big World with Relatively Few Healthy Banks The International Monetary Fund (IMF) estimates that since 1980, 133 of 181 IMF member nations have suffered banking problems that it judges to be "significant." Moody's Investors Service, which rates the riskiness of banks in 61 nations on a scale ranging from A (best risk) to E (worst risk), has determined that 31 countries have "average banks" that rate D or E. Banks in the A and B categories are concentrated in countries within the European Monetary Union, the United States, and the United Kingdom.

Why have so many countries' banking systems faltered in recent decades? There are two basic viewpoints on this issue. One is that banking is an inherently unstable business whose fortunes ebb and flow with the performances of national economies. From this perspective, government regulation and "safety nets," such as deposit insurance or "last-resort" governmental lending agencies, must be put in place to prevent periodic banking collapses from taking place.

Another argument, however, is that governmental safety nets themselves may be responsible for recent banking crises. According to this view, if bankers know that governments stand ready to bail them out if their "bets" turn sour, then they have every incentive to make highly profitable loans whose yields include hefty risk premiums. Thus, goes this argument, banking safety nets create moral-hazard problems for taxpayers, who ultimately must back up governmental guarantees.

International Linkages and Bank Regulation

The declining strength of banking and other financial markets around the world in recent years has had significant implications for banking policies in the United States and elsewhere.

Limiting Regulatory Arbitrage One special area of concern for banking regulators has been the potential for banks to engage in **regulatory arbitrage.** Through this process, banks try to escape the effects of regulations imposed by authorities in their home nations by shifting operations and funds to offices in locales where regulatory constraints are less substantial.

To avoid the potential for regulatory arbitrage by U.S. banks, U.S. banking regulators have sought to coordinate their policies with those of banking regulators in other developed nations. For instance, in 1988 the Federal Reserve, the FDIC, and the OCC joined with banking regulators of most major nations to develop and implement the risk-based capital requirements described earlier in the chapter. The idea behind this internationally coordinated policymaking was that if all banks in such nations as Germany, Japan, the United Kingdom, and the United States had to meet the same basic capital requirements, then the banks would face similar constraints. In addition to limiting the scope for regulatory arbitrage, therefore, this coordinated action was aimed to ensure that major banks would not face competitive advantages or disadvantages in international competition for loans and deposits.

The Limitations of International Coordination When the banking regulators gathered at the Bank for International Settlements in Basel, Switzerland, to announce the coordinated system of risk-based capital requirements, they viewed the event as a watershed in international coordination of banking policies. Ultimately, nearly forty nations signed on to what became known as the "Basel Accord" on risk-based capital standards. In the end, however, national enforcement of the standards has varied so widely that "coordination" has never been achieved.

Undeniably, the Basel capital standards had a significant effect on international banking. Consider, for instance, their initial impact on Japanese banking. During the 1980s, Japanese banks had emerged as global powerhouses, establishing major presences as lenders in Africa, Asia, Europe, the Middle East, South America, Mexico, and even the United States. In 1995, several of the top ten banks in the world were based in Japan. By 1998, however, Japanese banks were shutting down offices all around the globe. One reason, noted earlier, was the sharp rise in nonperforming loans at these banks. Other key reasons for the worldwide cutback by Japanese banks were the declining value of the yen in late 1996 and 1997, the simultaneous decline in Japanese stock market prices, *and*, notably, the Basel capital standards. The 1997 surge in the dollar's value, which swelled the *yen* values of dollar-denominated loans that Japanese banks had extended outside Japan, sharply increased the *yen*-denominated value of loans for purposes of computing the capital requirements of Japanese banks.

Since 1997, a number of large Japanese banks have barely held sufficient capital to meet the risk-adjusted capital ratio requirement of 8 percent. Because their share values also have declined in the Japanese stock market, capital ratios of Japanese banks have been squeezed from both directions: rising values of yen assets and declining values of yen-denominated capital measures. They have had no choice but to reduce their presence in global lending markets. Indeed, a few large banks have sold some of their loans, in what some analysts call an ongoing "fire sale." Eventually, a number of these banks have merged to form new Japanese megabanks that are less internationally active than Japanese banks were in the 1980s.

Large banks throughout Asia have faced similar difficulties. This has left Asian banking regulators with a stark choice: they can strictly enforce the Basel capital requirements and promote a rapid erosion in the global competitive positions of their nations' banks, or they can relax their enforcement of the capital standards to give their banks some "breathing room." Most regulators, including those in Japan, have chosen the latter course. As a result, banks in Western Europe and the United States today face tougher capital standards than those enforced by banking regulators in most other nations. Even though almost forty nations have "officially" adopted the Basel requirements, less than half that number strictly enforce the capital standards.

6. Do national bank regulators coordinate their policies? The Basel capital standards were determined after considerable consultation among banking regulators of major industrialized nations. In this sense they reflected international coordination of regulatory policies. In recent years, however, national regulators have differed in their interpretation and enforcement of the Basel capital requirements.

Link to Policy

If Deposit Insurance Is Not a Free Lunch, Why Do So Many Financial Institutions Want a Seat at the Table?

In years past, the Federal Deposit Insurance Corporation has paid out billions of dollars from the insurance funds it maintains from collections of insurance premiums from depository institutions. Table 14-2 shows the FDIC's largest payouts to resolve individual failures of depository institutions since 1980. As the table indicates, the FDIC's failure resolution costs can vary considerably across institutions of different sizes. Sometimes large portions of an institution's assets are lost to a failure, but in other instances the FDIC manages to contain the losses to a smaller portion of the assets.

The Big Drop-off in Deposit Insurance Premiums

Something else that once varied noticeably across depository institutions was the deposit insurance premium rate they paid to the FDIC. Panel (a) of Table 14-3 displays the insurance premiums the FDIC charged in early 1993 when it first implemented risk-based deposit insurance under the terms of the 1991 FDIC Improvement Act. The FDIC established three broad categories based on depository institutions' capital ratios and defined them as "well capitalized," "adequately capitalized," and "undercapitalized." Within each category were three additional classifications, labeled A, B, and C, that the FDIC determined based on aspects of an institution's risk positions that are unrelated to its level of capitalization. Well-capitalized depository institutions that fell into classification A were those that the FDIC viewed as least risky and subject to the lowest insurance premium rate of 0.23 percent, or very close to the one-fourth of 1 percent first suggested by FDIC economists in 1934.

Panel (b) of the table displays today's deposit insurance premium rates. Even though the official premium rate for undercapitalized, group C institutions is 0.27 percent, very few institutions pay a premium this high. Since the late 1990s, the deposit insurance fund has exceeded 1.25 percent of total institution deposits (the upper limit set by Congress on the dollar amount that the insurance fund can contain), and nearly all depository institutions have been classified as well-capitalized, group A institutions. Thus, the base insurance premium for most of the U.S. banking industry has been zero.

Table 14-2 The FDIC's Most Costly Failure Resolutions since 1980

Depository Institution	Assets ($ Billions)	Failure Date	FDIC Resolution Cost ($ Billions)
First Republic Bank (Dallas)	$33.5	July 1988	$3.9
MCorp (Dallas)	15.7	February 1989	2.8
Continental Illinois (Chicago)	33.6	May 1984	1.1
Texas American (Fort Worth)	4.8	July 1989	1.1
First City Bancorp (Houston)	4.8	April 1988	1.1
Bank of New England (Boston)	21.8	January 1991	0.9
Goldome FSB (Buffalo)	8.7	May 1988	0.8
New York Bank for Savings (NYC)	3.4	March 1982	0.8
1st National Bank of Keystone (WV)	1.1	September 1999	0.8
Crossland Savings Bank (Brooklyn)	7.3	January 1992	0.7
Superior Bank (Illinois)	2.3	July 2001	0.6

The Rush to Obtain Zero-Rate Deposit Insurance Coverage

As traditional broker-dealers such as Merrill Lynch & Co. and Salomon Smith Barney have taken advantage of the opportunity to blend financial services offered by the

1999 Gramm-Leach-Bliley Act, the zero premium rate for deposit insurance has emerged as a major issue. In the early 2000s, both institutions created "money market sweep accounts." These accounts automatically shifted funds back and forth between clients' uninsured money market accounts and multiple, federally insured accounts at commercial banks owned by the institutions or associated with umbrella holding companies. The result was that an individual customer with a previously uninsured money market account immediately received as much as $600,000 in deposit insurance coverage.

The actions of these institutions alone increased the total amount of insured deposits in the banking system by more than $50 billion. Because deposit insurance premiums were zero for the banks associated with both Merrill Lynch and Salomon Smith Barney, the institutions were able to provide their customers with deposit insurance at no explicit cost.

Is It Past Time for Reform?

In response to these developments, the FDIC has proposed a series of changes to the U.S. deposit insurance system. One proposal is to charge a flat insurance premium but rebate a portion of the premium to well-managed, highly capitalized institutions, thereby returning to a risk-based premium system. Another proposal is to eliminate the 1.25 percent threshold for the ratio of total FDIC reserves to insured deposits. To make the proposal more palatable to depository institutions, the FDIC has also proposed increasing the per-account coverage limit from $100,000 to $200,000 and eventually indexing deposit insurance coverage to inflation. The FDIC is also exploring the possibility of transferring some of its risk to so-called *reinsurance companies,* which are private insurers that would offer the FDIC itself insurance coverage in the event of unexpectedly large deposit insurance losses.

In the meantime, the FDIC has established a backup plan for increasing deposit insurance premiums if the total amount of funds available falls below 1.25 percent of insured deposits. The proposed premium rate is 0.23 percent of insured deposits—once again very close to the one-fourth of 1 percent rate first proposed back in 1934.

Table 14-3 FDIC Risk-Based Deposit Insurance Premiums, 1993 versus Today

(a) January 1, 1993

	Risk Classification		
	A	B	C
Well Capitalized	0.23	0.26	0.29
Adequately Capitalized	0.26	0.29	0.30
Undercapitalized	0.29	0.30	0.31

(b) Today

	Risk Classification		
	A	B	C
Well Capitalized	0.00	0.00	0.00
Adequately Capitalized	0.03	0.10	0.24
Undercapitalized	0.10	0.24	0.27

Note: All premiums are percentages of insured deposits.

SOURCE: Federal Deposit Insurance Corporation.

Research Project

The FDIC has argued that reinsurance would help it determine market-based premiums for the deposit insurance coverage that it offers to banks and savings institutions. Evaluate the merits of this argument.

Web Resources

1. What are some of the key issues involved in efforts to reform federal deposit insurance? Go to the FDIC's home page at http://www.fdic.gov; under "Deposit Insurance," click on "Insurance Funds & Assessments." Then click on the link to "Reform of Deposit Insurance."

2. What is the FDIC's formal proposal for reform? Follow the first two steps above, and then click on "Recommendations for Deposit Insurance Reform" to download a summary of the FDIC's proposals.

Chapter Summary

1. The Long-Term Effects of Banking Laws Adopted in the 1930s: The Glass-Steagall Act of 1933 toughened interstate-branching restrictions and put limits on linkages between banking and other financial services. The act also laid the foundation for the establishment of the Federal Deposit Insurance Corporation and authorized ceilings on bank interest rates, including today's zero-interest restriction on business demand deposits.

2. How Deposit Interest Rate Ceilings Spurred Deregulation: During periods when other market interest rates rose well above the legal ceiling rates on deposits, disintermediation occurred as depositors withdrew funds to place them in instruments with higher yields. Ultimately, in the 1980s the threat that disintermediation posed to depository institutions led Congress to pass laws that significantly deregulated depository institutions.

3. Deposit Insurance as a Justification for Federal Regulation: Because a large portion of the deposits at depository institutions receives federal insurance guarantees, depository institution managers may be induced to make riskier asset and liability choices. Hence, federal deposit insurance exposes the government (taxpayers) to a significant moral-hazard problem. Monitoring insured institutions via periodic examinations and providing enforceable supervisory rules that managers must follow are means that governmental regulators can use to reduce the magnitude of the moral-hazard problem.

4. How the Federal Government Has Sought to Reduce the FDIC's Exposure to Losses: In 1989 and in 1991, Congress passed laws that set out strict procedures that the FDIC must follow to identify potential risks to the federal deposit insurance funds. The laws authorize the FDIC to enforce its efforts to limit the risk of depository institution failures by closing particularly troubled institutions. The legislation also authorized risk-based deposit insurance premiums. In an effort to directly constrain the riskiness of banks, regulators have defined two measures of bank capital. Then they examine ratios of these measures relative to a risk-adjusted measure of a bank's assets. Failure of a bank to maintain ratios that regulators deem sufficient can result in more regulatory supervision or possibly even closure of the bank.

5. The Financial Services Modernization Act of 1999 and the Structure of U.S. Bank Regulation and Supervision: Supervision of the activities of commercial banks is split among three regulators. The Office of the Comptroller of the Currency (OCC) supervises nationally chartered banks, while the Federal Reserve supervises state-chartered banks that are members of the Federal Reserve System (Fed). The Federal Deposit Insurance Corporation (FDIC) supervises state-chartered banks that are not members of the Federal Reserve System. The Financial Services Modernization Act, or Gramm-Leach-Bliley Act, of 1999 permits direct linkages between banks and other financial firms. Thus, the Gramm-Leach-Bliley Act changed the structure of federal banking supervision. It requires the Fed and the OCC to jointly decide what types of financial firms individual banks may own. Nevertheless, it made the Fed the primary regulator of umbrella corporations that own both banks and other financial firms, thereby centralizing considerable regulatory authority with the Fed. The Gramm-Leach-Bliley Act did not fundamentally change the basic structure of federal regulation of savings institutions, which are supervised by the Office of Thrift Supervision (OTS), or of credit unions, which are supervised by the National Credit Union Administration (NCUA).

6. International Coordination of Bank Regulatory Policies: Bank regulators of major developed economies established the Basel capital standards following considerable consultation. Thus, the implementation of bank capital requirements reflected international policy coordination. During the past several years, however, national regulators have interpreted and enforced the Basel capital requirements differently.

Questions and Problems

(Answers to odd-numbered questions and problems may be found on the Web at http://money.swcollege.com under "Student Resources.")

1. Many economists believe that markets should be as free and unregulated as possible. Yet a number of these same economists have been critical of federal depository institution regulations that they perceive as having been too "lax" in past years. What might account for these apparently contradictory positions?

2. Disintermediation has commonly occurred during intervals when many individuals and firms that in the past had been able to get bank loans found that banks no longer were willing to lend. Explain why this makes sense.

3. Economists have found that banks that were judged too big to fail in the late 1980s sometimes could pay lower interest rates on their large certificates of deposit. Explain why this might have happened.

4. Because the FDIC's insurance funds are judged to be "fully capitalized," nearly all depository institutions pay no deposit insurance premiums. In your view, is this a desirable situation, given that regulatory supervision continues and capital requirements remain in force? Take a stand, and support your answer.

5. Suppose that a depository institution has $20 million in cash assets and U.S. Treasury securities. It also has $5 million in GNMA mortgage-backed securities and $10 million in FNMA mortgage-backed securities. It has $48 million in mortgage loans outstanding. It is not involved in any off-balance-sheet activities. If its core capital is $2 million and its total capital is $3 million, would this depository institution meet the capital requirements established in 1989? Show your work and explain.

6. In 2004, a Danish bank has total assets of 1,000 million kroner. Of these assets, 80 percent are loans to businesses, and the remainder are holdings of cash assets and government securities. The bank engages in derivatives trading that Danish regulators, who strictly follow the 1989 Basel capital standards, assign a credit equivalence exposure value of 400 million kroner. The bank's equity capital amounts to 100 million kroner, and the bank has no subordinated debt. Does the bank meet current capital requirements? Show your work and explain.

7. Economists usually use the term *regulatory arbitrage* to refer to international banking activities. Given the current structure of depository institution regulation in the United States, could U.S. depository institutions potentially engage in regulatory arbitrage within U.S. borders? Explain. [Hint: There are three federal commercial banking regulators and federal and state regulators of savings institutions and credit unions.]

8. Explain why purely domestic considerations can make it difficult for national banking regulators to abide by international agreements to coordinate regulatory policies.

9. Shortly after the Gramm-Leach-Bliley Act passed, a number of financial institutions rushed to establish umbrella companies merging banking, insurance, mutual funds, and securities firms under a single corporate structure. By 2002, however, several of the new corporations were already "spinning off" some of these lines of business into separate firms specializing in particular activities. Does this imply that the legislation was misguided? Take a stand, and explain your reasoning.

10. As noted in this chapter, in 2005 the new Basel capital requirements will attempt to account for operational risks relating to equipment failures and managerial errors or fraud. Bankers have complained that attempts to "quantify" these risks will be so judgmental that capital ratios will become too subjective to provide meaningful ratings of a bank's capital adequacy. Evaluate this argument.

Before the Test

Test your understanding of the material covered in this chapter by taking the Chapter 14 interactive quiz at http://money.swcollege.com.

Online Application

Internet URL: http://www.fdic. gov

Title: FDIC Rules and Regulations

Navigation: Begin at the home page of the FDIC given above. In the left margin, click on "Laws & Regs." Then click on "FDIC Law, Regulations, and Related Acts." Next, click on "6000 Bank Holding Company Act."

Application: Follow the instructions, and answer the corresponding questions.

1. Under "Sec. 2: Definitions," click on "(c) Bank Definition." According to the Bank Holding Company Act, what is a "bank"? Does this definition correspond to the definition provided in Chapter 11? In what ways is it more specific or more general? Explain.

2. Back up to the table of contents, and under "Sec. 3: Acquisition of Bank Shares and Assets," click on "(d) Interstate Banking." Under the original Bank Holding Company Act, are federal or state laws binding on the permitted extent of interstate branching?

For Group Study and Analysis: Divide into groups, and have each group assign its members to review various sections of the Bank Holding Company Act and determine what types of institutions a bank holding company may own. In class, have each group report back its findings about allowable activities of bank holding companies. Based on these findings, to what extent can banking and various financial services be combined under this law?

Selected References and Further Reading

Barth, James. *The Great Savings and Loan Debacle.* Washington, D.C.: American Enterprise Institute Press, 1991.

Benston, George, and George Kaufman. "Deposit Insurance Reform in the FDIC Improvement Act: The Experience to Date." Federal Reserve Bank of Chicago *Economic Perspectives* 22 (Second Quarter 1998): 2–20.

Berger, Allen, Richard Herring, and Giorgio Szego. "The Role of Capital in Financial Institutions." *Journal of Banking and Finance* 19 (June 1995): 393–430.

Kopecky, Kenneth, and David VanHoose. "A Model of the Monetary Sector with and without Capital Requirements." Temple University and Baylor University, 2001.

Lindgren, Carl-Johan, Gillian Garcia, and Matthew Saal. *Bank Soundness and Macroeconomic Policy.* Washington, D.C.: International Monetary Fund, 1996.

Lown, Cara, and Stavros Peristiani. "The Behavior of Consumer Loan Rates during the 1990 Credit Slowdown." *Journal of Banking and Finance* 20 (December 1996): 1673–1694.

O'Hara, Maureen, and Wayne Shaw. "Deposit Insurance and Wealth Effects: The Value of Being 'Too Big to Fail.'" *Journal of Finance* 45 (December 1990): 1587–1600.

Thomson, James. "Who Benefits from Increasing the Federal Deposit Insurance Limit?" Federal Reserve Bank of Cleveland *Economic Commentary,* September 15, 2001.

White, Lawrence J. *The S&L Debacle: Public Policy Lessons for Bank and Thrift Regulation.* New York: Oxford University Press, 1991.

MoneyXtra

moneyxtra! Log on to the MoneyXtra Web site now (http://moneyxtra.swcollege.com) for additional learning resources such as practice quizzes, case studies, readings, and additional economic applications.

Chapter 15

Economic Consequences of Depository Institution Regulation

Today, the Office of the Comptroller of the Currency, the Federal Deposit Insurance Corporation, the Federal Reserve System, the Office of Thrift Supervision, and the National Credit Union Administration employ thousands of individuals to examine and supervise the operations of depository institutions. Each year these agencies together spend billions of dollars to pay the salaries of the people who conduct periodic on-site examinations that delve into the safety and soundness of individual commercial banks, savings institutions, and credit unions.

Some economists wonder if banking regulators really need all these employees. They envision a time when just a few employees at each regulatory agency will be able to surf the Internet for data, plug the information into computer-based economic models of factors that contribute to bank failures, and decide at their desks whether it is time to put pressure on a depository institution to shape up or close down. The data that would make this possible, these economists argue, are market yields on certain bank liabilities that regulators would require depository institutions to issue. Yields on these liabilities would, the economists contend, indicate market perceptions of the status of individual institutions, which could fulfill the same role as traditional safety and soundness examinations. In this brave new world of bank regulation, on-site examinations would no longer take place, so armies of examiners would no longer be necessary.

Fundamental Issues

1. Will interstate banking make depository institutions more cost-efficient?
2. Are depository institution mergers undesirable?
3. Do banking and commerce mix?
4. How has off-balance-sheet banking complicated the task of regulating depository institutions?
5. What are the benefits and costs of financial consumer-protection laws?

So far bank regulators have not given up on old-style visits to depository institutions by squads of examiners. In fact, in recent years the menu of issues that examiners must contemplate as they evaluate the performance of banks, savings institutions, and credit unions has lengthened. In this chapter you will learn about current issues in the regulation of depository institutions, including why a growing number of economists advocate substituting market yields on certain bank liabilities for detailed examinations of banks' balance sheets and income statements.

Economies of Scale and Scope: Does Bank Size Matter?

In recent years, the number of commercial bank branches in the United States has increased even as the total number of banks has declined. All told, depository financial institutions (including both banks and savings institutions) insured by the Federal Deposit Insurance Corporation (FDIC) operate nearly 70,000 branches in the United States. Prior to 1996 only about 50 of these were interstate branches, and they existed only as a result of specific historical exceptions to the general prohibitions on interstate banking discussed in Chapter 14. A few had existed before the passage of laws restricting interstate branching arrangements. Others served military installations and received special exemptions as a result. In other cases, regulators had permitted interstate branches to facilitate the mergers of failing depository institutions with healthier institutions located in different states.

The Current Status of Interstate Banking

During the 1970s and 1980s, various constituencies began to argue in favor of lifting the ban on interstate branching. They included some states, which believed interstate branching would lead to capital inflows for their states; people living in metropolitan areas spanning more than one state, who felt it would add convenience and flexibility; and many depository institutions, which argued that it would enable them to achieve more geographic diversification and take advantage of technological developments to market their products nationwide.

Legal Considerations Standing in the way of interstate banking were two key pieces of legislation left over from the early part of the twentieth century. The 1927 McFadden Act left it to the states to determine whether national banks could branch across state lines. The 1933 Glass-Steagall Act had toughened this restriction, effectively making interstate branching illegal unless states voluntarily opened themselves to branching by banks based in other states. This effectively meant that all fifty states would have to coordinate if full interstate banking were to become feasible throughout the nation.

It took several decades, but by the early 1990s the states had made significant progress in this direction largely by permitting banking corporations to acquire banks across state lines. Initially, many states required *reciprocity* from other states. For instance, Missouri would agree to let a bank based in Illinois acquire a Missouri-based bank only if Illinois would allow Missouri banks to acquire Illinois banks. By the mid-1990s, roughly half of all states had worked out such reciprocity arrangements with other states. Several of the remaining states permitted acquisitions under an open invitation for reciprocity from any other state. A number had no reciprocity requirement. Consequently, the nation entered the 1990s with a crazy quilt of interstate banking arrangements stemming from laws enacted several decades before.

Passage of the *Interstate Banking and Branching Efficiency Act of 1994* initiated a change in this situation beginning in 1997. Under this legislation, an umbrella banking corporation is able to own a depository institution anywhere in the United States. The legislation allows holding companies to consolidate into a single, multistate bank, thereby saving the holding companies the expense of setting up legally distinct institutions with separate boards of directors and officers in each state where they have branches.

CONSOLIDATION OF DEPOSITORY INSTITUTIONS Many commentators hailed the 1994 legislation as a precursor to truly sweeping changes in the structure of U.S. banking. Several observers predicted that within a few years the number of commercial banks would fall from about 10,000 to fewer than 4,000 or 5,000. They also predicted that large depository institutions would become even larger as they swallowed up smaller banking organizations around the country, thereby consolidating existing banking operations among fewer institutions. There is now some evidence supporting these predictions. Most noticeably, the number of U.S. banks has declined by about 20 percent since the Interstate Banking Act's passage.

Cross-Border Deposits In states that have opened their borders to interstate acquisitions of banking offices, the shares of deposits held by out-of-state depository institutions have increased considerably in recent years. By the early 2000s, citizens of the "average" state who owned deposits at commercial banks held one-fourth of their deposits in depository institutions based in states outside their own. In extreme cases, such as Arizona, Washington, and Nevada, residents with commercial bank deposits held over 80 percent of their deposits with banks headquartered in other states.

Furthermore, the largest banks really have been getting bigger. Before 1960, the largest 50 banks in the United States issued fewer than 40 percent of all bank deposits, and the largest 100 banks issued less than half of all deposits. Today, the largest 100 banks together account for two-thirds of all bank deposits. The largest 50 banks issue *over* half of all deposits.

Limits on Consolidation Nevertheless, there are also good reasons to question just how dramatic banking consolidation may be as interstate banking restrictions wither away. One point that is easy to overlook is just how effectively depository institutions already had sidestepped the McFadden Act and Glass-Steagall Act by forming multistate umbrella banking corporations. Furthermore, as discussed in Chapter 13, it pays for banks to get bigger and bigger only if there are unlimited economies of scale so that larger banks experience lower average operating expenses. Yet most studies have found that economies of scale are not particularly significant in banking. Certainly, the absolute number of depository institutions will decline dramatically in coming years. Much of this decline, however, will likely occur simply because multistate umbrella companies can drop the names of all the separate institutions that laws have required that they incorporate. How much further these holding companies may expand their acquisitions of existing depository institutions remains to be seen. A key issue will be whether further acquisitions make the holding companies and their subsidiaries more cost-efficient.

Cost Efficiencies from Interstate Mergers

Recall from Chapter 13 that one perspective on depository institution market structure and its implications is offered by *efficient structure theory.* It indicates that the consolidation of banking resources that may result from interstate banking could generate more cost efficiency. If true, this might be a significant benefit from interstate banking arrangements.

As discussed in Chapter 13 and noted above, however, the efficient structure theory's earlier reliance on economies of scale as the source of cost savings from mergers is not supported by real-world data. In recent years, most proponents of the efficient structure theory—and, indeed, depository institution owners and managers themselves—have contended that the main cost savings from mergers should arise from greater managerial efficiency. According to this argument, interstate consolidations of depository institutions should help cut the size of administrative bureaucracies by eliminating duplicative layers of management.

In the early 1990s, studies by Aruna Srinivasan of the Federal Reserve Bank of Atlanta, both alone and with Larry Wall of the same bank, cast doubt on how big such cost savings were likely to be. In their joint work, Srinivasan and Wall found little evidence that mergers significantly reduced banks' expenses. In her separate study, Srinivasan found some evidence that larger banks created by mergers were able to reduce salary expenses by eliminating redundant management and staff positions, as predicted by efficient structure theorists. But she also found that these savings were typically offset by increased expenses on other aspects of the banks' operations, such as information systems and marketing.

Of course, to get around past interstate banking restrictions, multistate umbrella corporations had to incur significant expenses in setting up organizational structures to meet the requirements of various state laws. Under interstate banking, many of these artificial structures are not needed. Consequently, a movement toward interstate banking undoubtedly must save on some expenses. Studies of bank mergers in the latter part of the 1990s, after interstate banking was legalized, support this conclusion. They find that the cost savings from bank mergers in the 1990s were more than double those realized in the 1980s. Mergers after 1992 reduced the merging banks' expenses by more than 30 percent, as compared with an average cost reduction of 15 percent from mergers between the early 1980s and 1992.

1. Will interstate banking make depository institutions more cost-efficient? A large number of bank mergers have taken place since the 1980s. Many merging institutions claimed that they would realize significant cost savings. The evidence is that efficiency gains from bank mergers were relatively modest during the 1980s and early 1990s. The 1994 federal legislation legalizing interstate banking beginning in 1997 set off a wave of merger activity, and the cost savings from these mergers have been relatively higher.

Depository Institution Market Concentration and Performance

In the late 1990s, an unprecedented amount of bank merger activity occurred. During 1997 and 1998, so many bank mergers took place that some people began to joke that eventually there would be just one commercial bank for the Fed, the FDIC, and the Office of the Comptroller of the Currency to regulate. The only issue, they opined, was what name the surviving bank would go by.

Without exception, merging banks mentioned potential cost-efficiency gains as a key justification for combining their operations. As noted above, however, studies of earlier mergers began to indicate that merger-related reductions in average operating costs may have been small for a number of banks. As the merger wave of the 1990s progressed, therefore, a number of merging banks began to mention another potential advantage of banking consolidation, which they often referred to as "revenue enhancement." That is, another rationale for bank mergers is that they may lead to higher average earnings.

Concentration and Performance

Customers of depository institutions are directly concerned with the prices they must pay for services, the interest rates they must pay on loans, and the interest yields they receive on deposits. As we discussed in Chapter 13, a theory that competes with the efficient structure theory is the traditional *structure-conduct-performance (SCP) model* of depository institution markets. This model predicts that more heavily concentrated market structures lead to higher loan interest rates and lower deposit rates. The SCP model also indicates that customers of depository institutions in more concentrated markets usually must pay higher fees for the services provided by these institutions. Thus, the SCP model implies that bank mergers yield "revenue enhancements" for merging banks.

HIGHER LOAN RATES AND LOWER DEPOSIT RATES As we also noted in Chapter 13, recent studies have provided at best very limited real-world support for the SCP model's prediction that greater loan and deposit market concentration leads to higher depository institution profits. Research during the past decade by Allen Berger and Timothy Hannan, both on the Federal Reserve Board staff, has indicated that the SCP model's prediction about the effects of concentration on interest rates and fees may be more relevant. The reduced rivalry among institutions caused by increased concentration in loan and deposit markets apparently does give those institutions greater monopoly power. One result, as the monopoly bank model discussed in Chapter 12 predicts, is higher loan rates. Other outcomes of monopoly power are higher fees for banking services and lower deposit rates.

HELPING OUT RIVALS? Interestingly, Katerina Simons and Joanna Stavins of the Federal Reserve Bank of Boston have provided evidence that the banks that experience the greatest revenue enhancements from mergers are the rivals of the merging banks. These researchers hypothesize that the greater market concentration resulting from mergers typically has two immediate effects. The first is increased monopoly power for the fewer rivals in the affected market. The second effect, however, typically is a reduction in service quality on the part of the merged institutions. Quality of customer service often declines as managers struggle to develop new operational procedures that may conflict with those previously used at one or both of the merged institutions. Managers of merged banks typically try to reap cost-efficiency gains by firing or laying off employees, but this hurts employee morale. Another common managerial aim is to adopt a common "corporate culture," even though the cultures of the merged institutions may differ dramatically. In the midst of this short-term internal turmoil, Simons and Stavins conclude, service quality of the merged institutions suffers, making it difficult for the institution created by the merger to cut deposit rates. In contrast, quality of service at rival institutions is unaffected by the merger, so these rivals can take full advantage of reduced competition to pay lower rates to their deposit customers.

Defining Depository Institution Markets

As discussed above, the top 50 and top 100 depository institutions have become larger, and interstate banking promises to increase the trend toward more consolidation of banking resources. In light of the evidence we have reviewed, does this mean that because of increased interstate banking consumers ultimately will have to pay more for loans and services while receiving less for their deposits?

IDENTIFYING "LOCAL MARKETS" To answer this question, the first thing to recognize is that what matters to an individual consumer—such as you—is not whether the top 50 or top 100 banks are getting larger, or even smaller. The SCP model indicates that a key factor affecting the market interest rate that you might have to pay on an auto loan in your location, or perhaps the market interest rate that you might receive on a NOW account at a depository institution in your area, is the extent of loan and deposit market concentration in your *local market*. Indeed, when depository institution regulators and the antitrust authorities review plans for mergers among institutions, they consider the effects that such mergers might have on local rivalry.

Unfortunately, there is no good way to define geographic loan and deposit markets for purposes of measuring the extent of market rivalry. Depository institution regulators define such markets on a case-by-case basis when institutions apply for permission to merge. Most economists—including those who assist regulators in evaluating the likely effects of mergers—approximate local banking markets in towns and cities using *metropolitan statistical areas* as defined by the government for census purposes. For rural areas economists typically assume that *nonmetropolitan counties* are the relevant geographic markets.

LOCAL CONCENTRATION—LITTLE CHANGED Interestingly, although large banks have generally become bigger on a national basis, at these local levels the concentration of banking resources has varied extremely little during the past twenty-five years. For instance, in 1976 the three largest banking organizations in a typical U.S. metropolitan statistical area issued a little over 68 percent of deposits, compared with just under 67 percent of deposits today. In nonmetropolitan counties, the extent of concentration was—and is—much higher: in 1976, the three largest depository institutions in a typical nonmetropolitan county issued about 90 percent of the deposits; at present, this figure hovers around 89 percent.

It is not apparent from these figures that changes in interstate—or intrastate—competition have had much influence on the average extent of depository institution rivalry in local banking markets. Most economists interpret this evidence as an indication that interstate banking is likely to have little effect on consumer interest rates and fees. For whatever reason, this and other changes in banking arrangements during past years do not seem to have much effect on local market conditions. It may be that there is some "natural" level of rivalry that loan and deposit markets can support at local levels.

Is All Banking "Local"? A former Speaker of the U.S. House of Representatives once said that "all politics are local." In light of its use of metropolitan statistical areas and nonmetropolitan counties when evaluating bank mergers, regulatory policy seems predicated on the idea that "all banking is local."

In fact, today both bankers and regulators recognize that this is not true for a number of banks, including some of the very largest. Indeed, some of the most important rivals of the largest banks are banks based in other countries. Table 15-1 lists foreign banks with the largest amounts of U.S. assets. Their parent banks compete globally to raise deposit funds and to lend to multinational firms. Table 15-1 highlights why using only the metropolitan statistical area or nonmetropolitan county immediately surrounding the bank's headquarters could be highly misleading.

2. Are depository institution mergers undesirable? Mergers between or among depository institutions that compete within the same local market make the market more concentrated, which can lead to higher loan rates and fees and lower deposit rates for depository institution customers in that market. Mergers that take place across markets, however, such as mergers that form multinational institutions or that permit the allocation of greater resources to online banking activities could actually generate greater rivalry in some banking markets.

Table 15-1 Foreign Banks with the Most U.S. Assets

Bank	Country	Assets ($ Billions)
Deutsche Bank AG	Germany	$104.5
Stichting Prioriteit ABN-AMRO Bank	Netherlands	70.7
Societe Generale	France	69.4
Bank of Tokyo-Mitsubishi	Japan	64.1
Union Bank of Switzerland	Switzerland	46.4
Bank of Montreal	Canada	44.5
Banque Nationale de Paris	France	42.8
HSBC Holding PLC	United Kingdom	34.2
Industrial Bank of Japan	Japan	25.3
WestDeutsche Landesbank	Germany	24.2

SOURCE: *American Banker*, 2002.

Universal banking: A banking environment in which banks face few, if any, restrictions on their powers to offer a full range of financial services and to own shares of stock in corporations.

Banking and Other Lines of Commerce

When the English Parliament passed a law establishing the Bank of England in 1694, a key provision of the act was a prohibition on the bank's ability to sell nonfinancial products. Members of Parliament feared that the Bank of England would use its financial resources to compete with other businesses. The 1933 Glass-Steagall Act in the United States reflected some of these same concerns, but the 1999 Gramm-Leach-Bliley Act reflected a determination that perhaps they were not quite so worrisome after all. What are the pros and cons of separating commercial banking from other forms of commerce?

Universal versus Restricted Banking

An important feature separating national banking systems is the degree to which they allow **universal banking,** under which there are few, if any, limits on the power of banks to offer a wide range of financial services and to own corporate stock. In Germany, the United Kingdom, and several other European nations, universal banking is the norm. Japanese banks face greater restrictions on their activities than do European banks, but many Japanese banks have unrestricted authority to underwrite stocks and bonds.

In the United States, the Glass-Steagall Act prohibited universal banking from 1933 until 1999. A fundamental justification for this U.S. prohibition of universal banking was that shares of stock typically are riskier financial instruments than government securities and municipal bonds. The objective of the Glass-Steagall Act was to establish a "firewall" between commercial and investment banking, thereby insulating commercial banks from risks generated by stock market volatility.

Nevertheless, over the years U.S. banks found legal loopholes that enabled them to engage in limited investment banking functions. In 1987, J.P. Morgan found a big loophole in Section 20 of the Glass-Steagall Act, which states that a bank may not be affiliated with any firm "engaged principally" in underwriting and dealing in firm securities. J.P. Morgan, Bankers Trust, and Citicorp quickly set up "Section 20 affiliates" to engage in the equities business in a limited fashion. At that time, the Federal Reserve sanctioned these subsidiaries on condition that they earn no more than 5 percent of their revenues from securities. By 1999, the Fed had raised the limit to 25 percent, and a number of U.S. banks had established investment banking operations. This set the stage for passage of the Gramm-Leach-Bliley Financial Services Modernization Act that eliminated fixed constraints on the extent of commercial banks' investment banking activities.

Arguments against Universal Banking A traditional concern about universal banking has been that it might promote conflicts of interest. For example, a bank that purchases a stake in a new cybertrading firm might prefer for that firm's share price to remain high. The bank might try to induce its customers to purchase the company's shares, or it might buy shares in the company for portfolios that it manages on behalf of clients, even though owning the shares might not be in the customers' best interests. The bank might even cut back on its lending to a rival Internet company.

Finally, those opposed to universal banking argue that it would be a mistake to let a few large banks own large portions of common stock in U.S. companies. This concentration of financial resources, they have contended, would give bank owners too much power over the U.S. business environment.

JUSTIFICATIONS FOR UNIVERSAL BANKING Those who favor universal banking argue that holding shares of ownership in commercial firms gives banks insider information, or knowledge about the internal operations of firms normally available to inside directors and officers but not widely available to the general public. Having such knowledge could make it easier for banks to evaluate and monitor these firms' creditworthiness, thereby reducing bank costs. Banks with inside information might also be less likely to force companies into bankruptcy because the banks would be able to distinguish near-term liquidity shortfalls from longer-term solvency threats. Some favoring universal banking contend that it could limit market expectations of bankruptcies, thereby lowering firm borrowing costs. The experience of a U.S. subsidiary of the German company Metallgesellschaft AG casts some doubt on this claim, however. In late 1993 and early 1994, the U.S. subsidiary had large derivatives losses that the parent company hid from banks that owned its shares. Losses grew to 3.4 billion deutsche marks before German banks with holdings in the company learned about the situation.

Another justification for universal banking is the possibility that holding individually risky shares of stock may, nonetheless, help a bank to *reduce* its overall risk of loss. For example, according to this argument, during a period when stock returns rise but many bond yields or returns on loans fall, holding stock could reduce the riskiness of a bank's full asset portfolio.

EVIDENCE FROM LIMITED U.S. BANK SECURITIES ACTIVITIES Can economists make any forecasts about how the U.S. banking industry will fare under the more nearly universal banking permitted by the Gramm-Leach-Bliley Act of 1999? One study, by Simon Kwan of the Federal Reserve Bank of San Francisco, documented the real-world existence of universal banking trade-offs by investigating the performance of the Section 20 investment banking affiliates of U.S. banks. In support of those opposed to universal banking, Kwan found that securities trading by banks' Section 20 affiliates was more profitable but riskier than their commercial banking activities. The securities-underwriting activities in which Section 20 affiliates engaged were also riskier than traditional commercial banking activities. They also turned out to be less profitable.

Nevertheless, Kwan found that banks did reap diversification benefits from their Section 20 affiliates. This was especially true for large banks that perform an active role as primary dealers of government securities. For these banks, there was a significant negative correlation between the returns from their Section 20 affiliates and the returns from traditional commercial banking activities. Thus, when traditional banking activities tended to yield lower returns, the higher returns of the banks' Section 20 affiliates tended to compensate for the resulting earnings falloff. Kwan found, however, that the diversification benefits of Section 20 affiliates were much more limited for banks that are not primary dealers in the government securities market, because they tended to experience greater risk in their securities trading.

Should Nonfinancial Businesses Own Depository Institutions?

In 1999, Congress decided to permit depository institutions to deal in shares of nonfinancial companies. Fairness would seem to dictate reciprocity. Nonetheless, the Gramm-Leach-Bliley Act does not permit nonfinancial businesses to own depository institutions. Why did Congress hold the line against full mixing of banking and commerce?

The Potential Problems The most obvious potential problem with businesses owning depository institutions is that some businesses might pressure the banks that they own to extend them credit. If the businesses need such additional credit because they are taking on too many risks, this would increase the possibility of insolvency of the depository institutions that they own. Depositors and other creditors of the depository institutions then would suffer. So would taxpayers, given the existence of federal deposit insurance.

A related problem is that the ownership of depository institutions by commercial firms could further expose depository institutions to the ill effects of economic downturns. Consider, for instance, what could happen if an auto manufacturer owned a large bank and a sharp recession hit. Such a recession usually causes immediate reductions in sales of new cars. Not uncommonly, the share prices of automakers plummet, and their debt issues are downgraded. If an automaker also owned a bank, then the public might lose confidence in that bank when the fortunes of its owner soured. The result could be a run on the bank. At a minimum, it would experience liquidity problems.

moneyxtra!

Another Perspective

To learn more about the issues associated with mergers between banks and nonfinancial firms, go to the Chapter 15 reading, entitled "The Separation of Banking and Commerce," by John Krainer of the Federal Reserve Bank of San Francisco.

http://moneyxtra.swcollege.com

Finally, the authority of banking regulators and the Federal Reserve System potentially would be broadened if commercial firms could own banks. If a company owns a bank, then it becomes a bank holding company and is subject to Federal Reserve oversight. Thus, the Federal Reserve could end up examining all the books of companies such as General Motors and IBM.

The Possible Gains One reason that some have proposed permitting commercial firms to own depository institutions is that this would enable the institutions to raise equity funding more easily. As a result of the risk-based capital requirements that regulators imposed in the late 1980s, many banks were strapped for capital in the 1990s. If nonfinancial firms got into the banking business, they could help recapitalize the depository institutions industry.

A related justification for letting companies own depository institutions is that the injection of their resources into depository institutions might help make U.S. banking more competitive on the international scene. As Table 15-1 on page 347 indicates, many of the world's largest banks are already established in the United States.

Finally, it is possible that depository institution customers could gain from allowing commercial firms to own banks. For instance, if companies such as Wal-Mart and Sears owned banks, then their customers could do one-stop shopping for clothing, hardware, and bank loans.

In light of these potential benefits, some observers have criticized Congress's 1999 decision to authorize universal banking without permitting commercial firms to get into the banking business. Undoubtedly, these arguments for and against letting businesses own banks are likely to receive considerable attention in the coming years as the walls separating financial institutions continue to fall.

3. Do banking and commerce mix? Key rationales favoring universal banking include potential diversification gains and lower monitoring costs. These advantages of universal banking are at least partly counterbalanced by the higher volatility of equity share values relative to values of traditional banks, the potential for conflicts of interest, and the possibility of sizable concentrations of financial resources. Full-fledged universal banking would also entail ownership of depository institutions by commercial firms, leading to additional potential for conflicts of interest, greater exposure of depository institutions to the ill effects of economic downturns, and regulatory complications. When Congress passed the Gramm-Leach-Bliley Act in 1999, it decided in favor of more nearly universal banking but ruled out permitting nonfinancial firms to own banks.

moneyxtra!

Online Case Study

Review the pros and cons of combining financial and nonfinancial firms by going to the Chapter 15 Case Study, entitled "A Brave New World of Banking."
http://moneyxtra.swcollege.com

Regulating Off-Balance-Sheet Banking

One of the most important modern developments at depository institutions has been their growing reliance on **off-balance-sheet banking,** which involves activities that generate income outside the institutions' balance sheets. The growth in these activities has prompted regulators to reconsider many long-standing approaches that they had previously taken to examining and supervising depository institutions.

Securitization and Loan Commitments

Two of the key off-balance-sheet activities of depository institutions are *securitization* and *loan commitments.* **Securitization** is the pooling of loans into groups that share similar characteristics and risks for sale via asset-backed-security arrangements. A **loan commitment** is a depository institution's promise to make a loan up to some specified limit under a contracted interest rate and within a given interval.

Neither of these activities appears on a depository institution's balance sheet. When an institution securitizes a loan, by definition it has sold the loan and removed it from its asset portfolio. Likewise, a loan commitment is not a loan until the depository institution must honor the commitment. Nevertheless, these off-balance-sheet activities yield income to depository institutions. They can also complicate the tasks that regulators face. In the case of securitization, there can also be some benefits for regulators.

Off-balance-sheet banking: Bank activities that earn income without expanding the assets and liabilities that the banks report on their balance sheets.

Securitization: The process of pooling loans with similar risk characteristics and selling the loan pool in the form of a tradable financial instrument.

Loan commitment: A lending arrangement in which a depository institution promises to extend credit up to some predetermined limit at a contracted interest rate and within a given period of time.

SECURITIZATION AND "MARKING TO MARKET" Securitization has made it feasible for depository institutions to earn fee income for originating, servicing, and insuring loans while selling them to others. Depository institutions issue two basic kinds of asset-backed securities. One type, illustrated in Figure 15-1 (p. 352), is a *pass-through security.* When a depository institution issues this type of asset-backed security, it passes interest and principal payments that it receives from borrowers through to holders of securities on a proportionate basis. For example, holders of a specific asset-backed security collateralized by a depository institution's holdings of credit-card debts might receive 80 percent of the interest

Figure 15-1
Asset Securitization via a "Pass-Through" Arrangement.

A depository institution receives interest and principal payments from borrowers of loans that it originates. It then issues securities backed by these loans through a trust department and an underwriter, and investors purchase the securities. The interest and principal payments from the loans are forwarded to a trustee, who passes through to the securities investors a portion of those payments as an interest payment on the asset-backed securities.

SOURCE: Thomas Boemio and Gerald Edwards, Jr., "Asset Securitization: A Supervisory Perspective," *Federal Reserve Bulletin* (1989).

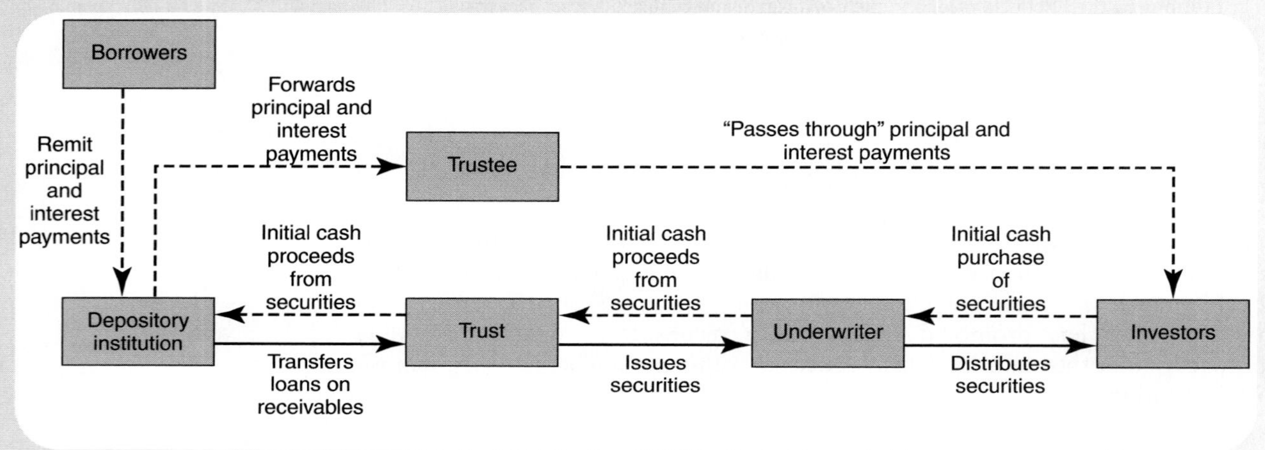

and principal payments paid by credit-card customers to the depository institution. To compensate the depository institution for the service it provides in monitoring the underlying pool of loans and making payments to the holders of the pass-through securities, these holders pay fees to the depository institution.

Another type of asset-backed security is called a *pay-through security.* Under this type of securitization arrangement, the interest and principal payments from an underlying pool of loans are held by the depository institution, which reallocates them into two or more separate sets of securities that have different payment and maturity structures.

A *collateralized mortgage obligation (CMO)* is a type of pay-through security. Under a CMO, principal and interest payments from the underlying pool of loans at the depository institution go first to holders of the CMOs with the earliest dates of maturity. Once those payments are "paid through," holders of later maturing CMOs receive their payments from the depository institution, and so on. Holders of the CMOs pay fees to the depository institution for handling the paperwork associated with this arrangement.

Securitization benefits depository institutions by shifting the default risks and interest rate risks of some loans to others. It also generates stable sources of fee income for the institutions. For this reason, depository institution regulators generally have raised few concerns about securitization.

In fact, a key advantage of securitization for regulators is that it gives them up-to-date information on market values of many types of bank loans. Regulators can determine market prices of loans that depository institutions have recently sold in secondary markets. They can then use these prices as indications of the market values of similar loans that depository institutions do *not* choose to sell in secondary markets. This practice of valuing a depository institution's assets at current market values is known as "marking loans to market," or **market value accounting.** This approach to measuring the values of depository institutions' assets contrasts with traditional **historical value accounting,** in which an institution records the initial value of a loan or security and then carries this value in its books until the loan is repaid or the security is redeemed.

Regulators prefer market value accounting because it provides a more accurate assessment of the solvency of a depository institution. In recent years a number of proposals have surfaced that would authorize the FDIC and other regulators to require depository institutions to switch to market value accounting or at least to report market values of assets alongside historical values on a periodic basis. Most of these proposals have not advanced in the face of the opposition of depository institutions, which argue that market value accounting would be prohibitively expensive. The institutions also typically argue that market values fluctuate so much that they can provide misleading information about the long-term values of assets. Nevertheless, regulators have continued to use prices of securitized assets as important information for assessing the solvency of the institutions that they examine and supervise.

Market value accounting: An accounting procedure in which a depository institution (or its regulator) values its assets in terms of the approximate market prices at which those assets would currently sell in secondary markets.

Historical value accounting: A traditional accounting procedure in which a depository institution's assets are always valued at their original values.

Revolving credit commitments: Loan commitments that permit borrowers to borrow and repay as often as they wish within an interval in which the commitment is binding on a depository institution.

Confirmed credit lines: Depository institution commitments to provide an individual or a business with a fixed amount of credit upon demand within some short-term interval.

LOAN COMMITMENTS AND RISK As Figure 15-2 on the following page shows, commitment lending grew significantly in the 1980s before leveling off in the 1990s and 2000s. During the 1970s, loans made under commitment accounted for only about 20 percent of total bank loans. Today, more than two-thirds of loans that banks extend are commitment loans.

With a typical loan commitment, a bank and a prospective borrower agree to terms, which specify a limit on how much credit the borrower can get from the bank (the borrower's "line of credit"), what the loan interest rate will be or how it will be determined, and the fee that the borrower must pay for any unused portion of the line of credit. This arrangement yields benefits for both the bank and the borrower. The borrower has a guarantee of credit at a given interest rate whenever it is needed within the specified period. The bank receives interest income on the portion of the credit line that is drawn upon by the borrower and noninterest fee income on the unused portion.

Under a *fixed-rate loan commitment,* the interest rate on any credit that a depository institution extends is set at a predetermined level. In contrast, a *floating-rate loan commitment* ties the loan rate to another market interest rate, such as the prime loan rate or the London Interbank Offer Rate discussed in Chapter 4. Most loan commitments of either type are **revolving credit commitments.** These allow borrowers to borrow and repay as desired, very much like revolving credit agreements for charge cards. Other loan commitments are **confirmed credit lines,** which normally are agreements for a bank to provide a fixed amount of credit upon demand within some short-term interval.

The growth of loan commitments has raised two types of concerns for bank regulators. One is that some banks might overextend themselves by making too many commitments, thereby creating liquidity problems. A related concern is

Figure 15-2
Growth in the Share of Commitment Lending.

This chart shows the portion of total commercial and industrial loans with maturities of less than a year that commercial banks made under commitment. The loan-commitment share of bank lending increased considerably during the 1980s before leveling off in recent years.

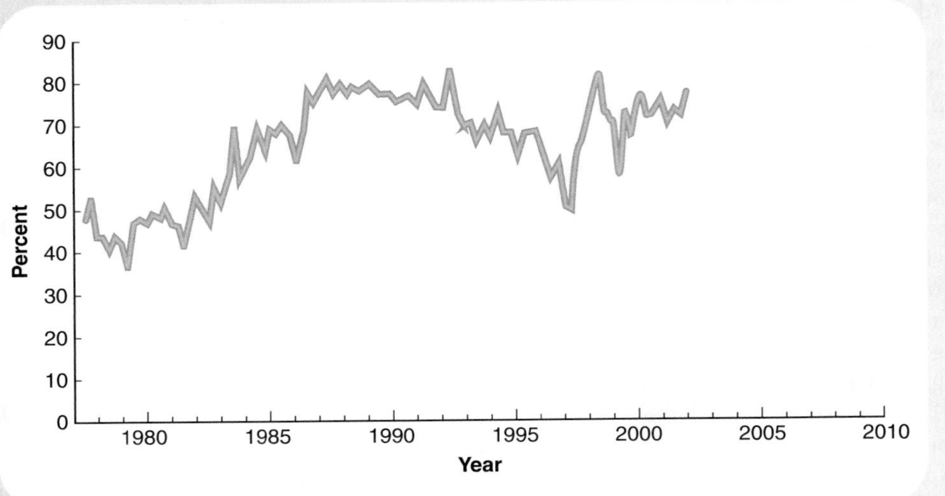

SOURCES: John Duca and David VanHoose, "Loan Commitments and Optimal Monetary Policy," *Journal of Money, Credit, and Banking* 22 (May 1990): 178–194; and Board of Governors of the Federal Reserve System, *Federal Reserve Bulletin*, various issues.

that a few banks might extend commitment loans to overly risky borrowers, thereby placing themselves at risk. So far commitment lending does not appear to have caused many difficulties of this type. Nevertheless, the inclusion of loan commitments in the computation of risk-adjusted assets in capital ratio calculations reflects regulators' concerns about such risks.

Derivatives

Recall from Chapter 8 that derivatives are financial instruments whose returns are derived from the yields on other securities. Examples of derivatives include forward, futures, option, and swap contracts. As discussed in Chapter 13, depository institutions have made greater use of derivative instruments in recent years. A few have tried to establish derivatives trading and management as a major line of business.

Because the values of derivative instruments stem from the values of other assets, measuring depository institutions' participation in the markets for derivatives is a difficult proposition. One possible measure is called the *notional value* of derivatives, which is the total amount of principal upon which interest payments stemming from derivatives are based. The notional value of commercial bank derivatives holdings grew from $1.4 trillion to $8.6 trillion between 1986 and 1992. By 2003 this figure had risen to more than $50 trillion.

Another measure of bank involvement with derivatives is called the *replacement cost credit exposure,* which is the cost that a party to a derivatives contract would face at current market prices if the counterparty to the contract were to default before settlement of the contract. In 1992, the total derivatives replacement cost credit exposure of commercial banks amounted to about 5 percent of their assets. By 2003 this figure had risen to 12 percent. Clearly, by either measure banks are much more heavily involved in derivatives operations.

REGULATING DERIVATIVES TRADING As we discussed in Chapter 8, depository institutions expose themselves to three basic types of risks when they hold and trade derivatives:

1. **Derivative credit risks.** The risks generated by the potential default of a contract counterparty or by the possibility of an unanticipated change in credit exposure caused by variations in market prices of underlying instruments on which derivative returns depend.
2. **Derivative market risks.** The risks of potential losses resulting from market liquidity reductions, payment-system breakdowns or unusual price changes at the time of settlement, or cross-market spillover effects.
3. **Derivative operating risks.** The risks owing to the possibility of misguided supervision and oversight of derivatives holdings and trading by depository institution managers.

Certainly, depository institutions themselves have strong incentives to keep tight rein on these risks. Nevertheless, the existence of federal deposit insurance weakens managers' and owners' incentives to contain derivatives risks. For this reason, depository institution regulators evaluate derivatives risks as part of their supervisory efforts.

Regulators have viewed the growth of derivatives trading by depository institutions as a positive development in some respects but as a real area of concern in other respects. On the one hand, derivatives permit depository institutions to hedge against a variety of interest rate and currency risks. In this regard, regulators have even promoted the use of derivatives by depository institutions.

On the other hand, a number of depository institutions have failed to maintain adequate internal controls over their derivatives operations and to develop appropriate techniques for valuing derivatives contracts. This, in turn, has complicated the task of examining and supervising depository institutions. Regulators now must be well versed in valuation methods for derivatives, and they must double-check the adequacy of the management methods that the institutions adopt for their derivatives operations. Derivatives are fairly new to most bank examiners just as they are relatively new to bankers, and so regulators themselves have had a lot to learn.

4. How has off-balance-sheet banking complicated the task of regulating depository institutions? Although securitization generally exposes depository institutions to reduced risks and helps regulators evaluate market values of loans, greater commitment lending has the potential to expose institutions to more liquidity and solvency risks. Derivatives trading has its own unique risks, of which perhaps the most important is the risk of inadequate internal management controls.

Consumer-Protection Regulations

Throughout history many leading U.S. citizens have mistrusted banks. Thomas Jefferson said that they were more dangerous than standing armies. When Andrew Jackson lost considerable personal wealth to banks from foreclosed loans after suffering big losses on land speculation, he made bank-bashing a favorite political pastime. More recently, members of Congress have heeded the calls of many of their constituents by passing legislation intended to protect consumers from possible misbehavior by managers of banks and other depository financial institutions.

There are bad people in all walks of life just as there is a bad apple in every barrel. Certainly, there have been unscrupulous bank managers in the past, and some probably are sitting behind desks around the country as you read these words. Should the government attempt to protect us from such individuals? Can it?

The first of these questions calls for an opinion. Whether or not the government *should* try to protect us from depository institutions, the fact is that political leaders presumably have acted upon the desires of many citizens by attempting to do so. The question of whether the government *can* protect citizens at least has the potential to be answered based on factual evidence. Certainly, if the government expends sufficient resources enforcing efforts to stop unsavory bankers from gouging consumers, such gouging will ultimately decline.

Basic Consumer-Protection Regulations

Congress has enacted several consumer-protection laws applying to depository institutions, and various governmental agencies seek to enforce them. Before we discuss their provisions, however, let's contemplate why such laws exist.

THE RATIONALE FOR PROTECTING CONSUMERS Why can't people just protect themselves? After all, rarely has a lender forced a borrower to sign a loan contract. One key rationale for consumer-protection laws and regulations relies on the problem of asymmetric information. Just as a lender has trouble identifying a creditworthy borrower, a prospective borrower can struggle to find a dependable and honest lender. Indeed, a borrower faces both adverse-selection and moral-hazard problems. An adverse-selection problem arises because unscrupulous lenders have the greatest incentive to disguise their credit terms to make them look more attractive than the honest terms quoted by more trustworthy lenders. A moral-hazard problem arises because after a lender grants credit, there is always a chance that the lender may attempt to reinterpret the loan contract in ways that are more favorable to the lender than the interpretation offered before the borrower entered into the contract.

THE SCOPE OF CONSUMER PROTECTION VIA REGULATION The *Consumer Credit Protection Act (CCPA) of 1968* is the foundation for much of the government's effort to protect consumers from costs that they might otherwise incur because of these problems of asymmetric information. This legislation requires that institutions provide every applicant for consumer credit with the specific dollar amount of finance charges and with annual percentage interest rates computed on the unpaid amount of the total quantity of a loan. Under the law, all institutions must make this information available so that consumers can make direct comparisons across institutions as they shop for credit. This provision of the CCPA attempts to reduce the extent of the adverse-selection problem that consumers face with respect to information. Other provisions bind lenders to the terms that they give consumers, thereby addressing the moral-hazard problem.

A difficulty with the CCPA was that it did not anticipate complications that arose when adjustable-rate mortgages became popular in the 1970s. A provision of the Depository Institutions Deregulation and Monetary Control Act of 1980 amended the CCPA to account for variable-rate loans. It requires potential lenders to construct hypothetical fixed- and variable-rate examples that enable prospective borrowers to compare the amounts that they might pay depending upon which type of loan they choose.

The CCPA applies to all financial institutions that extend credit. It also covers all loan applicants irrespective of their race, ethnicity, gender, or age. In recent years, however, these applicant characteristics have been the subject of much interest in the consumer-protection area.

Redlining: A practice under which some depository institution managers allegedly have refused to lend to individuals or businesses located in particular geographic areas.

Banking Regulation and Race, Ethnicity, Gender, and Age

A major policy issue in recent years has been the extent to which depository institutions may treat customers differently based on their race, gender, ethnicity, or age. Congress has enacted laws addressing this issue. Furthermore, Congress has charged depository institution regulators with monitoring and enforcing these laws.

REDLINING One way that depository institutions allegedly have discriminated against specific groups is by refusing to provide loans to individuals or businesses located in specific geographic areas. Such a practice is called **redlining;** the name refers figuratively to incidents in which depository institution managers supposedly used red ink to outline certain areas on maps as ineligible for loans. Managers allegedly would instruct lending officers to deny loans to anyone located in such areas or to applicants for mortgage or real estate loans intended to purchase properties there.

Note that redlining is not necessarily a form of racial, ethnic, or gender discrimination, although it might effectively be used as a means of such discrimination if redlined areas were predominantly occupied, say, by African American or Hispanic households or by female-owned businesses. Nevertheless, the basic allegation is that redlining, if it occurs, discriminates against individuals simply because of where they live or operate their businesses. In the case of mortgage redlining, the depository institutions that redline would effectively discriminate against the owners of properties within redlined regions. Those outside the area who wished to buy the properties would also feel victimized by discrimination because they would experience difficulties obtaining credit to purchase these properties.

ANTIDISCRIMINATION LAWS Depository institutions must meet requirements established by three key antidiscrimination laws. The first of these is the *Equal Credit Opportunity Act (ECOA) of 1975*. This legislation broadened some of the CCPA's provisions by outlawing retaliation by a lender against a borrower who insists upon rights granted by the CCPA, by applying CCPA provisions to many business and commercial transactions, and by extending consumer lending protections in a variety of ways. But the ECOA's novel feature was its prohibition of lending discrimination on the basis of an applicant's race, color, religion, national origin, gender, age, or marital status.

On the Web
How do banks go about complying with the Home Mortgage Disclosure Act? To find out, take a look at the Federal Financial Institutions Examination Council's "Guide to HMDA Reporting" at http://www.ffiec.gov/hmda/pdf/guide.pdf.

Because of concerns about widespread allegations of mortgage redlining by some depository institutions, Congress also passed the *Home Mortgage Disclosure Act (HMDA)* in 1975. This legislation requires depository institutions to report information about mortgage loan applications and lending decisions. It also requires depository institution regulators to collect and analyze this information.

Then, in 1977, Congress passed the now-controversial *Community Reinvestment Act (CRA),* which added considerably to the reporting requirements that the HMDA had imposed on depository institutions. The basic paperwork required from each depository institution under the CRA includes the following:

1. A statement listing the types of loans that the institution is willing to make.
2. Acceptable evidence that the institution's board of directors reviews this statement at least once each year.
3. A map showing the boundaries of the communities in which the institution lends.
4. A visible notice to customers advising them of the CRA.
5. A CRA file open for review by any member of the public who would like to read it.
6. Implementation of a "CRA planning process" supported by a full analysis of the geographic distributions of the institution's major lines of business.
7. Collection of complete data concerning lending applications, acceptances, and denials.
8. Analysis of how these data relate to the characteristics of the populations in the areas where the institution lends.

Under the CRA, depository institution regulators are to aim to achieve twelve separate objectives relating to redlining and other forms of lending discrimination. For instance, regulators are supposed to use the data that institutions report to evaluate each institution's record of lending to various groups of the populations that it serves. Furthermore, the CRA requires that regulators examine institutions and provide them with ratings of their performances in meeting the credit needs of all groups. All major regulators have attempted to coordinate their CRA ratings schemes so that all institutions receive roughly similar CRA examinations. (Depository institutions do not have to make loans or provide services directly to customers to comply with key CRA requirements; see *Management Focus: Banks Find a Creative Way to Comply with the Community Reinvestment Act.*)

Benefits and Drawbacks of Consumer-Protection Regulations

Presumably, the consumer-protection laws that Congress has put in place would not exist if many citizens did not believe that they were beneficial. Nevertheless, any law can produce unexpected complications. Therefore, it is not surprising

GLOBAL POLICY CYBER **MANAGEMENT Focus**

Banks Find a Creative Way to Comply with the Community Reinvestment Act

Under one provision of the Community Reinvestment Act, banks with more than $250 million of assets are examined to determine whether their commitments to low- and moderate-income communities are "adequate" in three respects: lending, securities investment, and service. Lending is the dominant factor, but direct bank holdings of securities related to low- and moderate-income communities count for 25 percent of a bank's overall score. At smaller banks not subject to the three-part test, CRA-related investments can often mean the difference between a "satisfactory" and an "outstanding" rating.

Federal regulators consider a security investment to be CRA-related if the securities primarily promote community development. For example, the Office of the Comptroller of the Currency (OCC) has determined that a mortgage-backed security qualifies for meeting the CRA's requirements if the entire security primarily funds affordable housing for low- or moderate-income individuals.

The OCC and other banking regulators have said that both direct and *indirect* investments qualify as CRA-related. This decision led to the development of a private mutual fund called the CRA Qualified Investment Fund. This mutual fund specializes in finding securities that satisfy CRA requirements, documenting compliance with the CRA, and allocating the securities to specific banks. At present, the mutual fund invests primarily in securities backed by single- and multifamily mortgages and in taxable municipal bonds issued to finance community development projects.

To participate in the CRA Qualified Investment Fund, a depository institution must hold a minimum of $250,000 in shares in the fund. So far banks in fifteen states are participating, and their shares earn the fund's average rate of return, which is based on the returns on the underlying CRA-qualifying securities. In addition, the banks go a long way toward satisfying their CRA requirements without having to go to the trouble of locating low- and moderate-income individuals who desire loans or other banking services.

For Critical Analysis: What are the pros and cons of allowing banks to meet the CRA requirements through arrangements such as those offered by the CRA Qualified Investment Fund?

that consumer-protection laws that apply to depository institutions have both benefits and costs for society.

Benefits of Consumer-Protection Regulations The most obvious benefits of consumer-protection regulations are that they reduce the extent of potential adverse-selection and moral-hazard problems faced by depository institution customers. By requiring institutions to make comparable quotes of loan terms, these laws confound the ability of unsavory managers to mislead loan applicants. The laws also make it more difficult for depository institutions to alter their interpretations of loan terms after customers are bound to agreements.

Consumer-protection laws also give customers of depository institutions legal recourse if they are treated unjustly by lenders. In addition, the laws follow in the tradition of many civil rights laws by attempting to assure equal treatment of all loan applicants irrespective of their race, gender, ethnicity, age, or other characteristics.

GLOBAL POLICY CYBER Focus MANAGEMENT

Internet Banks Confront Consumer-Protection Regulations

An emerging issue in enforcing the Community Reinvestment Act is how to define the "service area" of a bank that operates exclusively in cyberspace. Some banks that market their services solely on the Web, such as Atlanta-based Netbank.com, have reached agreements with regulators to serve low- and middle-income communities within specific regions near the buildings that house their management offices. Others, such as Houston-based Compubank.com, were able to gain designations as "limited-purpose banks" with scaled-down CRA obligations in exchange for promises to lend directly to minority-owned businesses and to provide those businesses with computers that would allow them to access the bank's services online.

As Internet banks begin to gain competitive footholds in markets outside the immediate geographic vicinities of their offices, they are coming under increasing pressure to meet CRA requirements everywhere their customers are located. Already, consumer groups are contending that an Internet bank should have to regard any regions where it makes loans as its "service area." At present, exactly what this might mean is unclear. Under a literal interpretation of the law, an Internet bank based in, say, Indiana could find itself developing "CRA planning processes" that encompass such far-flung locales as Pullman, Washington, and Clanton, Alabama. After all, if borrowers in those locales successfully point and click their way to a loan from the bank, then its "service area" extends a considerable distance from its Indiana office. So will its obligation to compile paperwork to satisfy the CRA's requirements.

FOR CRITICAL ANALYSIS: Who ultimately pays the costs of CRA enforcement and compliance: banks, consumers, or both?

COSTS OF CONSUMER-PROTECTION LAWS Several costs are associated with consumer-protection regulations in banking. The most glaring are the explicit costs associated with meeting the reporting requirements of the various laws that Congress has passed. Some of this expense undoubtedly leads to higher loan interest rates and higher fees for consumers.

Enforcing consumer-protection laws such as the CRA is also a costly undertaking. Considerable regulatory resources, most of which are taxpayer financed, go into monitoring, analyzing, and investigating possible instances of anticonsumer or discriminatory behavior by depository institutions. Depository institutions also face considerable costs in complying with the provisions of the CRA. Federal banking regulators have calculated that depository institutions together expend 1.25 million hours a year on compliance, which translates into an estimated dollar cost of \$35.4 million a year. Individual institutions with more than \$250 million of assets typically spend 500 to 635 hours a year complying with the CRA, and smaller institutions devote 50 to 200 hours a year.

Some critics argue that banking regulators overenforce the CRA. A study of the more than 16,000 CRA examinations of small banks and savings institutions from 1990 to 1999 found that only three institutions had failed to comply. This led Congress to push for a reduction in the number of CRA compliance reviews for smaller depository institutions. (Internet banks face particular complications in trying to comply with the CRA's provisions; see *Cyber Focus: Internet Banks Confront Consumer-Protection Regulations*.)

5. What are the benefits and costs of financial consumer-protection laws? Consumer-protection laws benefit depository institution customers by reducing the extent to which they face adverse-selection and moral-hazard problems when they apply for and agree to loans. The laws also help ensure that depository institutions treat individuals equally irrespective of their gender, ethnicity, race, age, or other characteristics. These laws can, however, be costly to administer and enforce. They can also generate large paperwork expenses for regulated institutions.

Link to Policy

Could Financial Markets Guide Bank Regulation?

Depository institution supervision is a costly activity for society. Considerable social resources are required to employ and transport armies of bank examiners to conduct frequent on-site inspections of income statements and balance sheets. In recent years, regulators themselves have been exploring alternatives to direct examination and supervision.

Market-Based Regulation

An alternative that has received considerable attention is **market-based regulation,** or regulation based in part on market measures of bank risk. One key measure that a number of financial economists have contemplated is the market value of bank debt instruments. As discussed in Chapter 14, *subordinated debt instruments* are an important liability of banks and are included by regulators in one measure of bank capital. These are long-term bonds that banks issue to raise funds in the capital markets. The basic idea of market-based regulation is to use the market prices of depository institutions' subordinated debt as a fundamental indicator of the riskiness of the institutions' activities.

A fundamental assumption of this approach is that private market traders of depository institutions' debt securities have good information about the institution risks. Another presumption is that the market for depository institution debt instruments is efficient, so that these risks are fully reflected in the market prices of the securities. Thus, financial economists have sought to determine if the yields on depository institution debt securities closely track accounting measures of the issuers' risk characteristics commonly used by bank examiners. A number of studies in the late 1990s and early 2000s found considerable evidence that this was the case for large banks' debt securities, thereby lending credence to the idea that regulatory enforcement could be linked to movements in market yields on depository institution debt instruments. With this approach, governments could realize significant resource savings because they could pay a few regulators to track market yields instead of paying large numbers of examiners to do the job.

Do Regulators Have an Informational Advantage?

Market-based regulation has some obvious drawbacks. One is that not all depository institutions issue subordinated debt. This is particularly true

Market-based regulation: Regulation that uses observable measures of depository institution risk as guidelines for supervisory enforcement.

Continued on next page

Link to Policy, continued

of smaller depository institutions in the United States and other developed nations. In emerging economies where financial markets are less developed, the lack of bank access to debt markets makes the proposal for market-based regulation a tough sell. Indeed, following the Asian crisis in the late 1990s, the International Monetary Fund, central bankers, and private bankers alike called for more U.S.-style, hands-on examination and supervision in many countries that previously had relied on private markets to discipline their banks. The argument then was that financial markets in many emerging economies are too inefficient for market yields to fully reflect bank risks.

In addition, many of the debt securities issued by depository institutions are traded relatively infrequently, so even in developed financial systems, markets for these securities typically are relatively less liquid than many other financial markets. Those who promote market-based regulation recognize this point and include, as part of their proposals, the requirement that all depository institutions issue debt securities. This requirement would ensure that market participants and regulators alike could track every institution's securities and that the market would be sufficiently liquid that yields would adequately reflect the underlying riskiness of the institutions.

A third, and perhaps most fundamental, difficulty is that the direct examination of depository institutions' income statements and balance sheets may give regulators an informational advantage over private financial market traders. A 2001 study by Robert DeYoung of the Federal Reserve Bank of Chicago, William Lang of the Office of the Comptroller of the Currency, and Mark Flannery and Sorin Sorescu (the authors of an earlier study that provided some support for market-based regulation) found that government regulatory examinations of large national banks provided significant information about the banks' riskiness that debt yields failed to reflect for periods as long as several months—plenty of time for a bank's fortunes to collapse and induce failure.

Thus, the current research on depository institution debt yields as guidelines for regulatory enforcement provides only limited support for the idea. Although yields of depository institution debt securities appear to reflect the riskiness of the institutions, they may do so only after relatively lengthy intervals. Of course, regulators themselves could reduce these intervals by immediately publicizing the results of examinations rather than keeping the information private. Nevertheless, this would still argue for employing large numbers of examiners to conduct frequent examinations, thereby weakening a key argument favoring market-based regulation, which is the possibility of reducing or eliminating direct examinations.

Research Project

What are the fundamental pros and cons associated with using yields on subordinated debt to implement a market-based approach to bank regulation? Why is it so difficult to evaluate whether this specific proposal would improve bank regulation?

Web Resource

What are the details of the proposal to use subordinated debt yields as a guide for bank regulation? Find out by going to the home page of the Federal Reserve Bank of Chicago (http://www.chicagofed.org), click on "Publications and Educational Resources," click on "Research Publications," and then click on "Economic Perspectives." Next, click on "2001" and then, under "First Quarter," click on "Market Discipline and Subordinated Debt: A Review of Some Salient Issues," by Robert Bliss.

Chapter Summary

1. Interstate Banking and Depository Institution Efficiency: Bank mergers became increasingly common in the 1980s and early 1990s, but economists typically found that relatively small cost savings resulted. The Interstate Banking and Branching Efficiency Act of 1994 removed nearly all barriers to interstate banking beginning in 1997. This promised the potential for achieving enhanced efficiencies through mergers, and recent evidence indicates that in fact the cost savings from bank mergers have indeed been more significant.

2. The Effects of Depository Institution Mergers: Depository institution mergers within the same local market make the market more concentrated. Theory indicates that the resulting increase in monopoly power can generate higher loan rates and fees and lower deposit rates for customers of depository institutions. Cross-market mergers that create multinational institutions or that permit greater investment in cybertechnologies may generate greater rivalry in some banking markets.

3. Universal Banking: The main justifications for universal banking are that it may yield diversification gains and lower monitoring costs for depository institutions. Nevertheless, these potential advantages are partly offset by the greater variability of equity returns relative to returns on traditional depository institution assets, possible conflicts of interest, and the potential for significant concentration of financial resources. Truly universal banking would also open up ownership of depository institutions to commercial firms. This could lead to additional potential for conflicts of interest, greater exposure of depository institutions to the ill effects of economic downturns, and involvement of bank regulators in the affairs of commercial firms. Thus, it does not appear that fully universal banking in the United States is inevitable, though the recent trend of gradually increasing linkages between banks and financial and nonfinancial firms likely will continue.

4. Regulatory Complications Arising from Off-Balance-Sheet Banking: Securitization simplifies the task of regulators by removing risky loans from depository institutions' balance sheets. In contrast, loan commitments expose institutions to greater liquidity risks and to potential default risks. In recent years the rapid growth of derivatives trading by depository institutions has exposed them to new types of risks, and regulators have had to adjust their examination and supervision procedures in light of these risks.

5. The Benefits and Costs of Financial Consumer-Protection Laws: Such laws help reduce the extent of adverse-selection problems that consumers might otherwise face if confronted with loan interest rate calculations that are difficult to compare, and the laws decrease somewhat a moral-hazard problem arising from the possibility that a lender might attempt to reinterpret loan contract terms before the consumer has repaid the loan. These laws are costly for depository institutions to abide by because they require so much paperwork from the institutions. The laws are also costly to enforce.

Questions and Problems

(Answers to odd-numbered questions and problems may be found on the Web at http://money.swcollege.com under "Student Resources.")

1. Explain in your own words why the growth of umbrella corporations owning banks in more than one state during the 1980s may have made the effects of the 1994 law deregulating interstate branching more muted than they might otherwise have been.

2. Why was the number of depository institutions likely to fall after the legalization of interstate banking even if multistate umbrella corporations did not acquire any more institutions based in other states? Explain your reasoning.

3. Discuss circumstances in which widespread depository institution mergers could actually increase rivalry in banking markets.

4. What competitive advantages do you believe a large bank is likely to have over a small bank? What advantages do you think a small bank has over a large bank? Explain your reasoning.

5. In your view, who most likely gains from interstate banking? Support your answer.

6. On net, is universal banking a good or bad idea? Take a stand, and support your answer.

7. Many observers believe that as depository institution managers become more adept with derivatives operations, most risks associated with their involvement in derivatives will dissipate. Do you agree with this assessment?

8. Some depository institution managers have proposed that the federal government should pay the costs that the institutions currently bear in complying with consumer-protection laws. Can you see any reasonable economic basis to support such a proposal? Explain.

9. In what ways could a bank loan officer who reviews Internet loan applications continue to practice discrimination against particular groups?

10. Discuss the pros and cons of market-based regulation of depository institutions.

Before the Test

Test your understanding of the material covered in this chapter by taking the Chapter 15 interactive quiz at http://money.swcollege.com.

Online Application

Internet URL: http://www.occ. treas.gov

Title: Community Reinvestment Act Regulations

Navigation: Start at the home page of the Office of the Comptroller of the Currency (OCC) given above. In the left margin, click on "Regulatory Information." Scroll down, and then click on CRA Regulations.

Application: Follow the instructions, and answer the associated questions.

1. Click on "25.22 Lending Test." Make a list of the criteria that the OCC evaluates in testing whether a national bank has met the CRA's lending standards. In your view, what is the main objective of the OCC's lending test?

2. Go back to previous page and click on "25.24 Service Test." Make a list of the criteria that the OCC evaluates in testing whether a national bank has met the CRA's service standards. In your view, what is the main objective of the OCC's service test?

For Group Study and Analysis: Divide the class into groups. Have each group pretend that it is a board of directors for a new bank that is making a proposal for a national charter. To obtain a charter, the new bank must meet CRA standards established by the OCC. Have each group read "25.27 Strategic Plan" at the above Web site, and assign each group to draft its own "strategic plan" for the new bank it is proposing. Reconvene the class, and have each group report on the plan it has drafted. Compare the plans. Which CRA features did each group emphasize? Do the OCC's standards appear to push new banks toward developing similar strategic plans for CRA compliance?

Selected References and Further Reading

Avery, Robert, Raphael Bostic, and Glenn Canner. "The Profitability of CRA–Related Lending." Federal Reserve Bank of Cleveland *Economic Commentary,* November 2000.

Berger, Allen, and Timothy Hannan. "The Price-Concentration Relationship in Banking." *Review of Economics and Statistics* 71 (May 1989): 291–299.

Black, Harold, M. Cary Collins, and Ken Cyree. "Do Black-Owned Banks Discriminate against Black Borrowers?" *Journal of Financial Services Research* 11 (1997): 189–204.

Bliss, Robert. "Market Discipline and Subordinated Debt: A Review of Some Salient Issues." Federal Reserve Bank of Chicago *Economic Perspectives,* First Quarter 2001, pp. 24–45.

Bostic, Raphael, and Glenn Canner. "Do Minority-Owned Banks Treat Minorities Better? An Empirical Test of the Cultural Affinity Hypothesis." Board of Governors of the Federal Reserve System, December 1997.

Calomiris, Charles, Charles Kahn, and Stanley Longhofer. "Housing-Finance Intervention and Private Incentives: Helping Minorities and the Poor." *Journal of Money, Credit, and Banking* 26 (August 1994): 634–678.

DeYoung, Robert, Mark Flannery, William Lang, and Sorin Sorescu. "The Informational Advantage of Specialized Monitors: The Case of Bank Examiners." Federal Reserve Bank of Chicago Working Paper Series, #WP-98-4, August 1998.

Estrella, Arthur, Sangkyun Park, and Stavros Peristiani. "Capital Ratios as Predictors of Bank Failure." Federal Reserve Bank of New York *Economic Policy Review,* July 2000, pp. 33–52.

Flannery, Mark, and Sorin Sorescu. "Evidence of Bank Market Discipline in Subordinated Debenture Yields: 1983–1991." *Journal of Finance* 51 (September 1996): 1347–1377.

Krainer, John. "The Separation of Banking and Commerce." Federal Reserve Bank of San Francisco *Economic Review,* 2000, pp. 15–25.

Kwan, Simon. "Securities Activities by Commercial Banking Firms' Section 20 Subsidiaries: Risk, Return, and Diversification Benefits." Paper presented at Federal Reserve Bank of Chicago Conference on Bank Structure and Competition, May 1998.

Robinson, Kenneth. "Banks Venture into New Territory." Federal Reserve Bank of Dallas *Economic and Financial Policy Review* 1 (2002): 1–14.

Simons, Katerina, and Joanna Stavins. "Has Antitrust Policy in Banking Become Obsolete?" Federal Reserve Bank of Boston *Economic Review,* March/April 1998, pp. 13–26.

Srinivasan, Aruna. "Are There Cost Savings from Bank Mergers?" Federal Reserve Bank of Atlanta *Economic Review* 77 (March/April 1992): 17–28.

Srinivasan, Aruna, and Larry Wall. "Cost Savings Associated with Bank Mergers." Federal Reserve Bank of Atlanta Working Paper 92-2, February 1992.

MoneyXtra

moneyxtra! Log on to the MoneyXtra Web site now (http://moneyxtra.swcollege.com) for additional learning resources such as practice quizzes, case studies, readings, and additional economic applications.

Unit IV
Central Banking, Monetary Policy, and the Federal Reserve System

CONTENTS

Chapter 16

Why Money and Banking Go Together—

Depository Institutions and Money

Fundamental Issues

1. How does a change in total depository institution reserves cause a multiple expansion effect on the deposit liabilities of these institutions?
2. What are Federal Reserve open market operations?
3. What is the money multiplier, and why is it important?
4. What factors influence the money multiplier?
5. What is the credit multiplier?
6. How will electronic money affect the money supply process?

At one time, investors around the globe rushed to check the financial media for the latest weekly report on the value of M1 measures of the quantity of money in circulation in the United States, Europe, and Japan. Often the latest annualized growth rates of M1 in these nations would be the subject of headlines. Financial economists and forecasters would scramble to try to explain the latest blip in the growth rates of these monetary aggregates. Typically, they would analyze components of so-called M1 multipliers*—factors multiplied times measures of currency and bank reserves to determine the overall quantity of money in circulation—for clues to why, say, M1 dropped in Japan even as it jumped in the United States.*

Central banks still tabulate monetary aggregates and publish weekly reports of values and growth rates of M1 and various other measures of the money stock. Yet, while media attention has been focused on how central bank policies affect interest rates, a worldwide trend has developed with little fanfare. Although central banks continue to compute and release data on M1, they most often examine another monetary aggregate—M2—for indications of overall levels of national liquidity. One reason for this change is that M2 measures of money have appeared to be more closely related to economic performance in most nations. Another reason, however, is that M2 multipliers *linking M2 to currency and reserves that central banks can control have been more stable than M1 multipliers in recent years. Thus, central banks are more confident that variations in M2 will serve as useful indicators of the broader effects of their policy actions.*

Why are measures of money in circulation multiples of the amount of currency and reserves in a nation? What factors influence the relationships between monetary aggregates and the total level of currency and reserves that central banks can directly influence? In this chapter you will learn the answers to these questions, which will help you understand why M2 has tended to eclipse M1 as central banks' preferred measure of the quantity of money in circulation.

Reserve Requirements and Deposit Expansion

Depository institutions are "special" financial institutions in one key respect: they issue transactions deposits—demand deposits and negotiable-order-of-withdrawal (NOW) accounts. These deposits, as you learned in Chapter 1, are fundamental components of the most common measures of the quantity of money in our economy. Hence, depository institutions represent the crucial link between policies to influence the quantity of money and the actual effects that these policies have on that quantity. Our goal in this chapter is to explain how depository institutions perform this role.

Required Reserves and Depository Institution Balance Sheets

As we discussed in Chapter 11, the main liabilities of depository institutions are deposit accounts, such as transactions deposit (checking) accounts. Depository institution assets are loans, securities, and cash assets. A portion of cash assets is composed of vault cash and reserve deposits held at Federal Reserve banks, even though neither reserves at the Fed nor vault cash yields interest to depository institutions.

Traditionally, a key reason that depository institutions hold cash in their vaults or on deposit at the Fed is that they are *required* to do so. Recall from Chapter 14 that the Depository Institutions Deregulation and Monetary Control Act of 1980 gave the Federal Reserve the authority to place reserve requirements on all federally insured depository institutions that offer transactions accounts. The Federal Reserve establishes its reserve requirements using **required reserve ratios,** which are fractions of transactions deposit balances that depository institutions legally must maintain either as deposits with Federal Reserve banks or as vault cash. At present the Federal Reserve subjects most transactions deposits to a required reserve ratio of 10 percent. Thus, for every $10 of transactions deposits at a depository institution, the institution must hold $1 on deposit with a Federal Reserve bank and/or in its vault. Ignoring any other complications—and in the real world, as we discuss in Chapter 20, there is an important complication known as *sweep accounts*—if the institution issues $1,000 million ($1 billion) in transactions deposits, then it is obliged to hold total reserves of $100 million. This total amount of legally mandated cash reserve holdings constitutes the institution's **required reserves.**

Required reserve ratios: Fractions of transactions deposit balances that the Federal Reserve mandates that depository institutions maintain either as deposits with Federal Reserve banks or as vault cash.

Required reserves: Legally mandated reserve holdings at depository institutions, which are proportional to the dollar amounts of transactions accounts.

Depository Institution Balance Sheets and T-Accounts The existence of this reserve requirement implies that a single depository institution can use any new transactions deposit funds to make new loans or buy new securities only to

Excess reserves: Depository institutions' cash balances at Federal Reserve banks or in the institutions' vaults that exceed the amount that they must hold to meet legal requirements.

Total reserves: The total balances that depository institutions hold on deposit with Federal Reserve banks or as vault cash.

T-account: A side-by-side listing of the assets and liabilities of a business such as a depository institution.

the extent that it has cash reserves above the required level. That is, the depository institution can lend or purchase securities only if it possesses **excess reserves,** or reserves in excess of reserves that it must hold to meet reserve requirements.

Consider a depository institution with $1,000 million in transactions deposit liabilities. To make our example a little more concrete, we'll assume that this depository institution is based in Boston. To simplify, however, we assume that the institution has no other liabilities nor any equity capital. If it holds all these funds as cash assets, then it has total cash reserves of $1,000 million. For simplicity we shall refer to the institution's total cash reserves as **total reserves.** In Figure 16-1 we display this institution's assets and liabilities inside a **T-account,** which is just a listing of the assets of the depository institution alongside its liabilities. You saw the equivalent of T-accounts in Chapter 11 when we discussed the assets and liabilities of commercial banks, savings institutions, and credit unions. As we discussed in Chapter 11, a depository institution's assets must be matched exactly by the sum of its liabilities and equity capital. Consequently, this depository institution's total reserves of $1,000 million exactly balance with its transactions deposit liabilities of $1,000 million. Because T-accounts display such a balancing of assets and liabilities, they are also often called *balance sheets.*

As Figure 16-1 indicates, this depository institution's required reserves are $100 million, or 10 percent of its transactions deposits of $1,000 million. This means that its excess reserves are $900 million, or the amount by which its total reserves of $1,000 million exceed the institution's legal reserve requirement of $100 million.

A "Loaned-Up" Depository Institution Excess reserves earn no interest income for the depository institution. Therefore, no profit-maximizing depository institution would permit itself to remain in the situation shown in Figure 16-1 for very long. The Boston institution's managers will allocate the institution's $900 million in excess reserves to alternative uses, such as holdings of loans and securities.

Figure 16-2 shows the result of such a managerial reallocation of the depository institution's assets. Once the managers have used all available excess reserves to make loans or to buy securities, then the institution is said to be fully "loaned up," meaning that it has expanded its loans and other interest-bearing assets as fully as possible in view of the required reserve ratio that it faces. For a fully loaned-up institution, excess reserves are equal to zero, and total reserves equal required reserves, as in Figure 16-2. Once this depository institution's managers have allocated all excess reserves to loans and securities, the institution's excess reserves fall to zero, and its total reserves decline to the level of its required reserves, or $100 million.

Figure 16-1
T-Account for the Boston Depository Institution.

Assets		Liabilities	
Total reserves	$1,000 million	Transactions deposits	$1,000 million
Required reserves ($100 million)			
Excess reserves ($900 million)			

Figure 16-2
T-Account for the Boston Depository Institution When It Is Fully Loaned Up.

Assets		Liabilities	
Total reserves	$ 100 million	Transactions deposits	$1,000 million
Required reserves			
($100 million)			
Excess reserves			
($0)			
Loans & securities	$ 900 million		
Total:	$1,000 million	Total:	$1,000 million

The Deposit Expansion Process

The Boston-based depository institution that we have envisioned is only one of thousands of such institutions throughout the United States. To understand how its indirect interactions with these other institutions in the face of transactions by the Federal Reserve can influence the total quantity of deposits in *all* institutions combined, let's expand our example.

How a Reserve Increase Affects a Single Depository Institution Suppose that a New York securities dealer has a transactions deposit account at the Boston-based depository institution that we considered above. Let's suppose that the Federal Reserve Bank of New York buys $100 million in U.S. government securities from the securities dealer. Then the dealer receives $100 million from that Federal Reserve bank, which it places in its transactions account at the depository institution that we considered in Figures 16-1 and 16-2.

As shown in Figure 16-2, before the dealer's transaction with the New York Federal Reserve Bank, the Boston institution had $1,000 million in transactions deposit liabilities, $100 million in total reserves, and $900 million in loans and securities. Figure 16-3 displays the situation faced by this depository institution after the dealer's transaction with the Fed. Because $100 million in new funds have flowed into the dealer's transactions deposit account with the depository institution, the institution now has $100 million in new cash reserves, or total reserves of $200 million. But the depository institution also has $1,100 million in transactions deposit liabilities, so its required reserves have risen from $100 million to $110 million (10 percent of the $1,100 million in total transactions

Figure 16-3
Boston Depository Institution's T-Account after New York Securities Dealer's Transaction.

Assets		Liabilities	
Total reserves	$ 200 million	Transactions deposits	$1,100 million
Required reserves			
($110 million)			
Excess reserves			
($90 million)			
Loans & securities	$ 900 million		
Total:	$1,100 million	Total:	$1,100 million

deposits). Because the institution has $200 million in total reserves but faces a reserve requirement of $110 million, it has $90 million in excess reserves. As a result of its customer's transaction with the New York Federal Reserve Bank, the Boston depository institution is no longer fully loaned up.

The managers of this depository institution have an additional $90 million in excess reserves that they may either lend or use to buy securities. Figure 16-4 shows the T-account for the Boston institution after its managers have reallocated its assets so that the institution once again is fully loaned up. When this position is reattained, the institution's excess reserves again equal zero, and its total reserves equal its required reserves, which now are equal to $110 million. The amount of loans and securities has expanded to $990 million, so the institution's total assets remain equal to $1,100, which is the same as the amount of its total transactions deposit liabilities.

How a Reserve Increase Spills from One Institution to Others Note in Figure 16-4 that for the Boston depository institution, the $100 million transaction between the securities dealer and the Federal Reserve Bank of New York has led to a $10 million expansion of total reserves, from $100 million to $110 million, and a $90 million expansion of loans and securities, from $900 million to $990 million. Yet this cannot be the conclusion of the story for all depository institutions. The reason is that when the Boston institution extends more loans and buys more securities, the recipients of the $90 million in new loans and funds that it pays for securities now have $90 million in funds that *they* may deposit in transactions deposit accounts at the depository institutions where they maintain such accounts.

To make this point more concrete, let's suppose that the Boston depository institution expanded its combined loan and security assets simply by buying $90 million in government securities from a securities dealer based in Chicago. Furthermore let's suppose that the Boston depository institution makes payment by transferring the $90 million directly into the Chicago securities dealer's transactions deposit account in a Chicago-based depository institution. Figure 16-5 shows only the *changes* faced by the Chicago institution after this second transaction occurs. Its transactions deposit liabilities have *increased* by $90 million, so its required reserves have *risen* by $9 million (10 percent of the $90 million in new deposits). Hence, the Chicago depository institution now has $81 million in new excess reserves that *its* managers may use to make new loans or to buy new securities.

Figure 16-4
Boston Depository Institution's T-Account after It Once Again Is Fully Loaned Up.

Assets		Liabilities	
Total reserves	$ 110 million	Transactions deposits	$1,100 million
Required reserves ($110 million)			
Excess reserves ($0)			
Loans & securities	$ 990 million		
Total:	$1,100 million	Total:	$1,100 million

Figure 16-5
Chicago Depository Institution's T-Account Changes after Second Security Purchase.

Assets		Liabilities	
Total reserves	+$90 million	Transactions deposits	+$90 million
Required reserves (+$9 million)			
Excess reserves (+$81 million)			
Total:	+$90 million	Total:	+$90 million

Suppose that the Chicago-based depository institution makes a loan of $81 million to a Milwaukee-based company. Then, as shown in Figure 16-6, this means that in the end the Chicago institution's total reserves expand by only the required amount, or $9 million. Its total assets rise by $90 million, or the amount of the increase in deposits caused by the security transaction between the Boston-based depository institution and the Chicago securities dealer.

THE ULTIMATE CHAIN REACTION: AGGREGATE DEPOSIT EXPANSION Yet our story *still* is not finished. When the Milwaukee company spends the $81 million that it borrows to purchase a needed piece of equipment, its payment for this equipment will show up in the account that the equipment manufacturer has at some other depository institution, perhaps in Minneapolis. This causes the reserve requirement at this new institution to rise by 10 percent of $81 million, or $8.1 million, leaving it with $72.9 million in new excess reserves that it can use to make new loans or to purchase new securities.

Indeed, this process of redepositing followed by further lending and security purchases by depository institutions continues through a long line of institutions and their deposit customers. Table 16-1 on the next page shows how our story works out if we continue it to its ultimate conclusion. Eventually, required reserves at *all* depository institutions will rise by $100 million. Loans and securities at *all* institutions will rise by $900 million. Total transactions deposits at *all* institutions ultimately will increase by $1,000 million, or $1 billion. (We shall explain shortly how we know that these total changes are correct; for the moment, take our word for these numbers.)

Figure 16-6
Chicago Depository Institution's T-Account Changes after It Once Again Is Fully Loaned Up.

Assets		Liabilities	
Total reserves	+$ 9 million	Transactions deposits	+$90 million
Required reserves (+$9 million)			
Excess reserves (+$0)			
Loans & securities	+ $81 million		
Total:	+$90 million	Total:	+$90 million

Table 16-1 The Ultimate Effects Stemming from the Federal Reserve Bank of New York's $100 Million Security Transaction

Depository Institution	Increase in Required Reserves	Increase in Loans and Securities	Increase in Transactions Deposits
Boston	$ 10.0 million	$ 90.0 million	$ 100 million
Chicago	9.0 million	81.0 million	90 million
Minneapolis	8.1 million	72.9 million	81 million
All other depository institutions	72.9 million	656.1 million	729 million
All Depository Institutions Combined	**$100.0 million**	**$900.0 million**	**$1,000 million**

This example illustrates how a Federal Reserve Bank of New York transaction with a single securities dealer can cause transactions deposits across all depository institutions to expand by *more* than the amount of the transaction. In the example, a $100 million reserve injection via the purchase of securities by the New York Federal Reserve Bank has resulted in a tenfold increase in total transactions deposits, to $1,000 million. (At one time, much of this deposit expansion required banks to clear large numbers of physical checks, but now efforts are under way to clear many checks electronically; see *Cyber Focus: Replacing Check Clearing with Interbank Internet Payments Networks.*)

1. How does a change in total depository institution reserves cause a multiple expansion effect on the deposit liabilities of these institutions? An increase in excess reserves induces the institution that receives the reserves to increase its lending or security holdings. The funds that it lends or uses to purchase securities typically are redeposited at other depository institutions, which can also expand their lending and security holdings. The result is a multiple expansion of deposits in the banking system.

THE FEDERAL RESERVE'S ROLE IN DEPOSIT EXPANSION The key to the multiple expansion of deposits that occurred in our example was the Federal Reserve's injection of $100 million in *new* reserves. What would have happened if, instead of the Federal Reserve Bank of New York, some other securities dealer had bought the securities from the dealer who had the account at the Boston depository institution? Then that other dealer would have transferred funds out of an account at some other depository institution. Deposits would again rise at the Boston depository institution, as in our previous example. But deposits would fall by an equal amount at another institution, which would then have to *reduce* its holdings of loans and securities. As a result, the initial $100 million increase in reserves at the Boston depository institution would be matched by a $100 million reduction in reserves at another depository institution. A simple *transfer* of funds *within* the banking system would occur, with no multiple expansion of deposits.

GLOBAL | POLICY | CYBER Focus | MANAGEMENT

Replacing Check Clearing with Interbank Internet Payments Networks

Because check clearing is such a resource-intensive process, depository institutions have long sought to reduce the numbers of checks they have to clear. Since the 1970s, depository institutions have operated *automated clearing houses (ACHs),* which are facilities that electronically interchange credits and debits among commercial banks, savings banks, and credit unions.

Moving the remaining check transactions to ACHs has been hindered by the fact that ACHs can only transfer payments. To keep track of information about what the payments are for, depository institutions using ACHs must maintain separate record-keeping systems analogous to those they use to track checks. This limits the resource savings that depository institutions can hope to achieve from inducing customers to switch from checks to electronic payments.

Now depository institutions are hoping to bypass ACHs by moving many transactions currently conducted with checks to Internet payments systems, which can securely transfer both funds *and* transaction information among institutions. Already two major Internet networks are linking large U.S. banks. Bank of America, Bank One, and Citibank are part of an Internet payments network operated by Xign Corporation, and J.P. Morgan Chase, Bank of New York, and Wells Fargo are members of another group operating the Web-based Electronic Payments Network through the New York Clearing House Association.

Both networks provide banks with code numbers that they and their customers can use instead of detailed account information when they transfer funds and payment information within the network. Like check-clearing administrators, the central offices of the networks keep them operating smoothly, but because fund and information transfers are virtual, the use of these networks eliminates all the paper associated with traditional check clearing.

For Critical Analysis: Do depository institutions necessarily have an advantage over other firms in transmitting payments within Internet networks?

The Fed, Electronic Impulses, and Deposit Expansion

Why does the Federal Reserve's involvement in a transaction make such a difference? The reason is that the Federal Reserve is the single institution empowered to create depository institution reserves. When the Federal Reserve Bank of New York buys a security from a dealer, it produces reserves that previously had not existed in the banking system. This ultimately leads to the expansion of deposits summarized in Table 16-1.

Open market operations: Federal Reserve purchases or sales of securities.

Open market purchase: A Federal Reserve purchase of a security, which increases total reserves at depository institutions and thereby raises the size of the monetary base.

Open market sale: A Federal Reserve sale of a security, which reduces total reserves of depository institutions and thereby reduces the size of the monetary base.

Federal Reserve Open Market Operations

When the Federal Reserve buys or sells securities in the money or capital markets, it engages in **open market operations.** In the example above, in which the New York Federal Reserve Bank purchased $100 million in securities from a New York securities dealer, we considered the effects of an **open market purchase.** In contrast, if the transaction had involved an **open market sale,** the Federal Reserve Bank of New York would have sold U.S. government securities to the dealer.

Figure 16-7
T-Accounts for a Federal Reserve Open Market Purchase.

Open Market Purchase			
Federal Reserve		**Boston Depository Institution**	
Assets	**Liabilities**	**Assets**	**Liabilities**
Securities +$100 million	Reserve deposits +$100 million	Reserve deposits +$100 million	Transactions deposits +$100 million

How the Fed Conducts an Open Market Purchase To better understand the mechanics of a Federal Reserve open market purchase, let's consider what must have occurred to initiate the first step of our example above. Figure 16-7 displays T-accounts for both the Federal Reserve and the Boston-based depository institution. When the New York Federal Reserve Bank purchases securities from a New York dealer with a transactions deposit account at the Boston institution, it typically makes a *wire transfer,* which is a transfer of funds—via computer—from the Fed directly to the Boston bank account of the dealer receiving the funds. The wire transfer, which in this case is known as a *book-entry security* transaction (see Chapter 18 for more details), digitally transfers ownership of the securities from the dealer to the Federal Reserve. Consequently, the Boston-based depository institution gains $100 million in reserve assets, while the Federal Reserve increases its reserve deposit liabilities by $100 million. But the Federal Reserve gains a matching $100 million in new assets—the securities that it has purchased from the New York dealer.

Thus, a Fed wire transfer of funds used to purchase securities is the action that causes the Boston institution's transactions deposits to rise by $100 million in the first place. Where do these funds come from? The answer is that the Fed creates them. Note that the Fed does not have to start a printing press to create the funds. It simply enters numbers into data files and then transmits the data to a receiving bank. The Fed effectively alters the quantity of money in circulation by transmitting *electronic impulses.*

On the Web
What open market operations has the Federal Reserve Bank of New York undertaken today? Go to http://www.ny.frb.org/ and click on "News & Events," and then click on "Open Market Operations."

Open Market Sales What happens if the Federal Reserve *sells* $100 million in securities to a dealer with a transactions deposit account at the Boston depository institution? As shown in Figure 16-8, the answer is that such an open market sale of securities has exactly the opposite T-account effects as those stemming from an open market purchase. Whether the dealer pays the Federal Reserve for the securities by writing a check or transferring funds directly, the dealer's transactions deposits at the Boston institution decline by $100 million. This causes the Boston institution's reserve deposits with the Federal Reserve to fall by this amount.

Figure 16-8
T-Accounts for a Federal Reserve Open Market Sale.

Open Market Sale			
Federal Reserve		**Boston Depository Institution**	
Assets	**Liabilities**	**Assets**	**Liabilities**
Securities −$100 million	Reserve deposits −$100 million	Reserve deposits −$100 million	Transactions deposits −$100 million

At the Federal Reserve, the sale of securities causes its total assets to shrink by \$100 million. Balancing this reduction in the Federal Reserve's assets is the decline in reserve deposits of depository institutions. Such an open market sale effectively *removes* reserves from the banking system.

2. What are Federal Reserve open market operations? Open market operations are the purchases or sales of U.S. government securities by the Federal Reserve. Typically, the Fed purchases securities by wiring funds to the account of the dealer from whom the purchase is made. Open market purchases increase the total reserves of depository institutions. Open market sales reduce the total reserves of depository institutions.

How the Fed Expands and Contracts Total Deposits

We now have developed the key concepts that are needed to understand how the Federal Reserve influences the total quantity of deposits in the nation's banking system. Now let's see how to determine the *amounts* by which the Fed's actions can potentially expand, or contract, the total quantity of deposits at the country's depository institutions.

EXPANDING TOTAL DEPOSITS Consider the example of an open market purchase of \$100 million in securities by the Federal Reserve Bank of New York. The immediate effect of this purchase is an increase in total reserves in the banking system—specifically, at the Boston depository institution—of \$100 million. Let's call a change in total reserves ΔTR, where the Greek letter delta (Δ) indicates a change in a variable. Then the direct effect of the open market purchase is a reserve increase equal to $\Delta TR = +\$100$ million.

Recall that we have assumed throughout our example that the legal required reserve ratio is equal to 10 percent, or 0.10. Let's denote this ratio as $rr_D = 0.10$. In addition, let's denote the change in deposits in the banking system by ΔD. This means that any change in required reserves (RR) in the banking system, ΔRR, is equal to $rr_D \times \Delta D$, because the level of required reserves equals $rr_D \times D$, where rr_D is the constant required reserve ratio.

Finally, remember that we assumed that the Boston-based depository institution and all other depository institutions desire to be fully loaned up, meaning that they prefer to hold no excess reserves. That means that the amount by which required reserves change matches the change in total reserves, or $\Delta RR = \Delta TR$.

Putting all this together tells us that

$$rr_D \times \Delta D = \Delta TR.$$

Now let's divide both sides of this equation by rr_D to get an expression for the change in deposits:

$$\frac{rr_D \times \Delta D}{rr_D} = \frac{\Delta TR}{rr_D}$$

or

$$\Delta D = (1/rr_D) \times \Delta TR.$$

Deposit expansion multiplier: A number that tells how much aggregate transactions deposits at all depository institutions will change in response to a change in total reserves of these institutions.

This final expression tells us that the change in deposits equals a factor $1/rr_D$ times a change in total reserves. In our example, $rr_D = 0.10$, so $1/rr_D = 10$. Hence, a change in reserves causes a tenfold increase in deposits. This explains our claim in Table 16-1 that a \$100 million increase in total reserves caused by an open market purchase ultimately causes deposits at all depository institutions to expand by \$1,000 million, or by ten times the amount of the reserve increase. We determine this amount simply by using the expression just developed:

$$\Delta D = (1/rr_D) \times \Delta TR = (10) \times (+\$100 \text{ million}) = +\$1{,}000 \text{ million}.$$

The factor $1/rr_D$ is called the **deposit expansion multiplier** because it tells us how much deposits in the banking system can rise or fall as a result of an increase or decrease of reserves by the Federal Reserve. In our example, the value of the deposit expansion multiplier is $1/rr_D = 1/(0.10) = 10$.

CONTRACTING TOTAL DEPOSITS An open market sale of U.S. government securities by the Fed would have the opposite effect on total deposits, as we can see by using the expression for deposit expansion. A \$100 million sale of securities by the Federal Reserve causes reserves in the banking system to decline, so $\Delta TR = -\$100$ million in the case of an open market sale. Then, using our expression for ΔD, we have

$$\Delta D = (1/rr_D) \times \Delta TR = (10) \times (-\$100 \text{ million}) = -\$1{,}000 \text{ million}.$$

Whereas a Federal Reserve open market purchase induces a multiple expansion of deposits in the banking system, a Federal Reserve open market sale causes a multiple *contraction* of deposits.

Deposit Expansion and the Money Multiplier

As we discussed in Chapter 1, the amount of transactions deposits in the banking system is a key component of the *monetary aggregates,* or measures of the total quantity of money in circulation in the economy. This means that we have almost explained how the Federal Reserve can influence the nation's money stock.

We are not quite finished, however. Another key component of any monetary aggregate is the amount of *currency*—the government-produced paper money and coins that we use in simple hand-to-hand transactions. Currency typically constitutes more than 40 percent of the M1 measure of money. This is such a large portion that we cannot simply ignore it. Certainly, the Federal Reserve cannot ignore it because the Fed is the institution that supervises the distribution of this currency. If you have any dollar bills handy, take a look at one; you will see "Federal Reserve Note" printed prominently on the bill. (Many of these Federal Reserve notes circulate outside the United States; see *Policy Focus: Oh, Where Have All Those Dollars Gone?*)

Depository Institution Reserves, the Monetary Base, and Money

As we discussed in Chapter 1, the narrowest monetary aggregate is the amount of money produced directly by the government, or the *monetary base.* The monetary base, MB, is the amount of currency, C, plus the total quantity of reserves in the banking system, TR, or

GLOBAL | POLICY **Focus** | CYBER | MANAGEMENT

Oh, Where Have All Those Dollars Gone?

When the Federal Reserve analyzes the holdings of U.S. currency, it typically discovers that more than 80 percent of all the paper notes it has issued are hard to find. A portion—most estimates indicate something in the neighborhood of 5 percent—can be accounted for by the underground economy where illicit drug and weapons deals take place. The remaining dollars are circulating abroad, particularly in developing countries, such as Russia and the nations of Latin America. Look at the estimated value of American currency in circulation outside the United States in Figure 16-9. In many developing countries, the dollar has become the currency standard.

Consider how this has benefited the U.S. government. The almost \$500 billion of U.S. currency circulating abroad is equivalent to an interest-free loan from the rest of the world. This is a form of seigniorage, a concept you were introduced to in Chapter 1. The Federal Reserve estimates that the U.S. government garners savings of between \$15 billion and \$20 billion a year from this seigniorage. This is the amount of interest that taxpayers would otherwise have to pay on a \$500 billion loan.

FOR CRITICAL ANALYSIS: Under what circumstances would a foreign resident choose to hold dollars, rather than local currency?

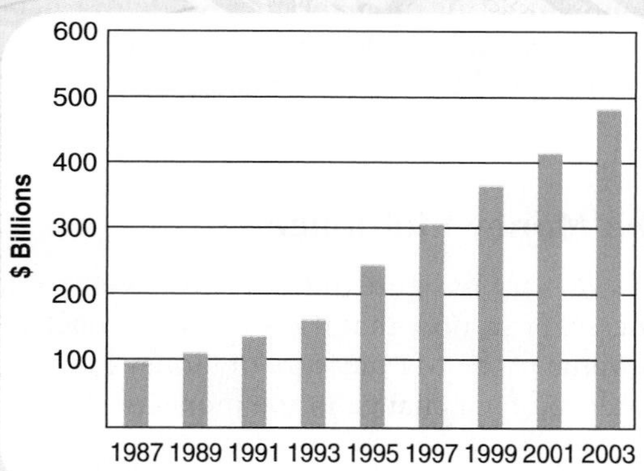

Figure 16-9
The Estimated Value of U.S. Currency in Circulation outside the United States.

The amount of U.S. dollars circulating outside U.S. borders has grown steadily in recent years.

SOURCES: Peter Porter and Ruth Judson, "The Location of U.S. Currency: How Much Is Abroad?" Board of Governors of the Federal Reserve System, October 18, 1995; authors' estimates.

$$MB = C + TR.$$

We already know that if depository institutions hold no excess reserves, then $TR = RR = rr_D \times D$. Let's also assume that consumers and businesses desire to hold a fraction c of transactions deposits as currency. It then follows that $C = c \times D$, so that the expression for the monetary base, when we make these substitutions, can be written as

$$MB = (c \times D) + (rr_D \times D) = (c + rr_D) \times D.$$

Hence, we can express the monetary base as the sum of the desired currency ratio and required reserve ratio multiplied times the amount of transactions deposits in the banking system.

A broader monetary aggregate, and the one on which we shall focus our attention, is M1. Recall from Chapter 1 that M1 is equal to the sum of currency and transactions deposits, or

$$\text{M1} = C + D.$$

Because $C = c \times D$, we can rewrite the expression for M1 as

$$\text{M1} = (c \times D) + D = (c + 1) \times D.$$

Now if we divide by MB, we get

$$\frac{\text{M1}}{MB} = \frac{(c + 1) \times D}{MB} = \frac{(c + 1) \times D}{(c + rr_D) \times D} = \frac{c + 1}{c + rr_D}.$$

If we multiply both sides of this equation by MB, we get

$$\text{M1} = \frac{c + 1}{c + rr_D} \times MB,$$

which then is an expression for the quantity of money given the value of the monetary base and the ratios c and rr_D. This expression tells us that:

> **Once the Federal Reserve determines the size of the monetary base, the amount of the monetary aggregate M1 depends upon the required reserve ratio rr_D and the desired ratio of currency to transactions deposits for consumers and businesses given by c.**

The Money Multiplier

Now let's try to figure out how this algebra relates to the basic deposit expansion process. First, note that if c and rr_D are unchanged, then the above expression for the value of the M1 measure of money indicates that a change in the money stock is induced by a change in the monetary base, or

$$\Delta\text{M1} = \frac{c + 1}{c + rr_D} \times \Delta MB.$$

Because rr_D is less than one, the factor multiplied by ΔMB in this new expression is greater than one. This means that a change in the monetary base has a *multiple* effect on the quantity of money. In fact, if we define a "money multiplier" m_M to be equal to the factor $(c + 1)/(c + rr_D)$, then we can write a final expression relating a change in the monetary base to a resulting change in the quantity of money:

$$\Delta\text{M1} = m_M \times \Delta MB.$$

Money multiplier: A number that tells how much the quantity of money will change in response to a change in the monetary base.

The **money multiplier,** m_M, is a number that tells us the size of the effect of a change in the monetary base on the quantity of money. To get an idea of roughly how large this multiplier might be, let's suppose that the desired ratio of currency holdings relative to deposits, c, equals 0.25. Then the value of the money multiplier would be $m_M = (c + 1)/(c + rr_D) = (0.25 + 1)/(0.25 + 0.10) =$

1.25/0.35, which is equal to approximately 3.6. Consequently, an increase in the monetary base would raise the total quantity of money by just over three and one-half times.

Recall that in our earlier example we came up with a deposit expansion multiplier that was equal to 10. Why is the money multiplier in this example only a third of that size? The reason is that the earlier example ignored the existence of currency. If securities dealers, businesses, and consumers desire to hold some cash in the form of currency, then each time a depository institution purchases new securities from dealers or makes new loans to businesses or consumers, some funds must leave the banking system in the form of currency holdings. At every step of the deposit expansion process, therefore, fewer funds are redeposited in depository institutions, leaving fewer funds for the institutions to use for security purchases or loans. As a result, the multiplier's value must be smaller when currency accounts for part of the quantity of money.

Federal Reserve Policymaking and the Money Multiplier

Because of the deposit expansion process, the Federal Reserve cannot control monetary aggregates such as M1 directly. What it can do, however, is change the amount of reserves at depository institutions to influence such a monetary aggregate. Because the monetary base, MB, is the sum of currency, C, and total reserves, TR, it follows that the only way that the monetary base can change is if the Federal Reserve changes the quantity of currency, the amount of reserves, or both currency and reserves. Typically, the Federal Reserve does not use variations in the stock of currency to influence the total quantity of money. But it can, and does, conduct open market purchases to increase total reserves or open market sales to reduce total reserves. An open market purchase increases the monetary base and thereby causes a multiple increase in the quantity of money. An open market sale decreases the monetary base and thereby causes a multiple reduction in the quantity of money.

As we shall discuss in Chapter 20, the Federal Reserve does not have to rely on open market operations to influence the quantity of money through the money multiplier process. The Federal Reserve can also try to change total reserves at depository institutions by inducing depository institutions to borrow more or fewer reserves from Federal Reserve banks' discount windows. If depository institutions' discount window borrowings increase, then total reserves, the monetary base, and the quantity of money will also increase. If depository institutions' discount window borrowings decline, then total reserves, the monetary base, and the quantity of money will also decline.

The Federal Reserve could also choose to change the quantity of money by altering the required reserve ratio, rr_D. This would change the money multiplier and thereby cause the quantity of money to rise or fall even if total reserves in the banking system were to remain unchanged. The Federal Reserve rarely changes reserve requirements, however. Typically, it relies on daily open market operations coupled with intermittent changes in its discount window policies.

3. What is the money multiplier, and why is it important? The money multiplier is a number that determines the size of the effect on the quantity of money caused by a change in the monetary base. The money multiplier is important because the Federal Reserve can influence the quantity of money only by varying the size of the monetary base. Consequently, the money multiplier determines how Federal Reserve policy actions will affect the money stock.

Extended Money and Credit Multipliers

In light of the expressions that we have developed so far in this chapter, it might be tempting to think that the Fed can simply compute money multipliers and then determine precisely how to conduct monetary policies. Unfortunately for the Fed, things are not quite so simple.

The Time-Varying Money Multiplier

One problem that the Federal Reserve faces is that the money multiplier is not constant over time. Another is that M1 is not the only monetary aggregate. Indeed, for reasons we discuss at the end of this chapter and again in Chapter 20, the Fed has relied considerably more on the broader monetary aggregate M2 in recent years.

Figure 16-10 shows estimates of the money multipliers for the M1 and M2 aggregates. The M1 multiplier is the ratio of M1 to the monetary base, while the M2 multiplier is the ratio of M2 to the monetary base. The M1 multiplier is always smaller than the M2 multiplier because M2 includes savings and time

Figure 16-10
M1 and M2 Multipliers.

Because M2 includes a number of financial assets that are not included in M1, the M2 multiplier is significantly larger than the M1 multiplier. Both money multipliers vary over time.

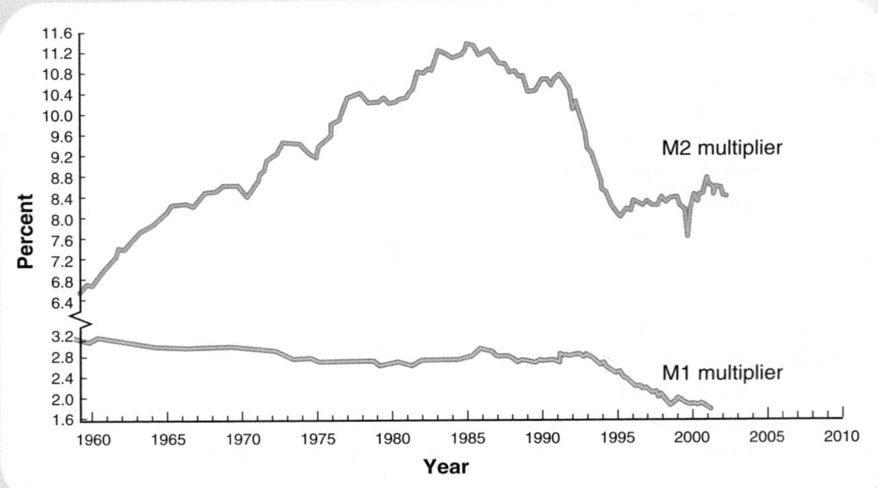

SOURCE: Federal Reserve Bank of St. Louis, *Federal Reserve Economic Data*, various issues.

deposits that are subject to an expansion process following a change in the monetary base.

Why do money multipliers vary? One reason is that the desired ratio of currency to deposits, c, is not constant. Instead, this ratio typically changes with the extent to which currency is a favored means of undertaking some types of transactions in the economy. If you look back at the expression for the M1 money multiplier that we computed above, you will see that variations in this ratio will cause the multiplier to vary as well.

Excess Reserves and the Money Multiplier

Another important real-world factor that can cause variations in money multipliers is volatility in desired holdings of excess reserves by depository institutions. Up to this point we have assumed that depository institutions always desire to be fully loaned up. This has simplified our explanation of the basics of deposit expansion and the money multiplier process, but it is not very realistic. In fact, depository institutions usually *do* voluntarily hold some excess reserves.

Reasons That Depository Institutions Hold Excess Reserves Why do depository institutions hold excess reserves, even though such reserves yield no explicit interest return? They do so because excess reserves yield an *implicit* return: if customers make unexpected deposit withdrawals, having excess reserves on hand saves depository institutions from having to bear the costs of calling in loans, selling securities, or borrowing reserve funds in order to meet their reserve requirements.

Another possible reason to hold some excess reserves is that doing so permits a depository institution to make speedy loans when good deals arise unexpectedly. If a long-standing customer with a credit line should need funds unexpectedly, it can be useful to have some on hand.

Of course, depository institutions incur an *opportunity cost* when they hold excess reserves. This is the interest return that the institutions forgo by holding cash instead of lending or purchasing securities. For this reason, depository institutions try to maintain their excess reserve holdings at levels that just cover the kinds of contingencies that they are likely to face in their own special circumstances. Nevertheless, depository institutions do hold positive, albeit small, amounts of excess reserves.

How Excess Reserves Change the Money Multiplier To see how excess reserves affect the money multiplier, let's take a last look at the money multiplier. Recall that the monetary base is $MB = C + TR$. If depository institutions hold excess reserves, then total reserves equal required reserves plus excess reserves, or $TR = RR + ER$, where ER denotes the amount of excess reserve holdings. Suppose that depository institutions desire to hold a fraction e of their transactions deposit liabilities as excess reserves. Then $ER = e \times D$, and $MB = C + TR = C + RR + ER$. Using the expressions that we have already developed, this means that the monetary base may be expressed as

$$MB = (c \times D) + (rr_D \times D) + (e \times D) = (rr_D + e + c) \times D.$$

This states that the monetary base is equal to the sum of the required reserve ratio, desired excess reserve ratio, and desired currency ratio multiplied times total transactions deposits.

Using the definitions for M1 and MB, we see that the money multiplier is equal to

$$\frac{M1}{MB} = \frac{C + D}{C + TR}.$$

Using the expressions that we have already developed, we can substitute for C and TR to rewrite the money multiplier as

$$\frac{M1}{MB} = \frac{(c + 1) \times D}{(rr_D + e + c) \times D}$$

$$= \frac{c + 1}{rr_D + e + c}.$$

The value of the multiplier now also depends on the desired ratio of excess reserve holdings to transactions deposits, e.

Note that the desired excess reserve ratio e appears in the denominator of the money multiplier. Consequently, if e increases, meaning that depository institutions desire to hold more excess reserves relative to their transactions deposit liabilities, the money multiplier gets smaller. This makes sense in the context of the deposit expansion process that underlies the multiplier. If depository institutions hold some excess reserves, then at each stage of the deposit expansion process they will make fewer loans or purchase fewer securities than they would if they did not hold excess reserves. This automatically reduces the extent to which deposits can expand in the banking system following a change in total reserves.

Excess reserve holdings of depository institutions typically are "small" relative to their total reserve holdings. In a given week, excess reserves rarely are much larger than around 1 percent of total depository institution reserve holdings. Yet excess reserve holdings also are highly variable. Figure 16-11 displays depository institutions' total holdings of excess reserves from July 1999 to July 2002. As you can see, there is significant volatility in excess reserves. This volatility contributes to variability in the money multiplier, thereby complicating the Federal Reserve's task in determining how its policies will affect monetary aggregates.

4. What factors influence the money multiplier? A key determinant of the size of the money multiplier is the amount of currency that consumers and businesses desire to hold relative to transactions deposits. Another important factor is the quantity of excess reserves that depository institutions wish to keep on hand in relation to transactions deposits. Both of these factors influence the amount of deposit expansion following changes in total reserves and, hence, the monetary base. For broader monetary aggregates such as M2, the deposit expansion process also affects savings and time deposits included in such aggregates. Therefore, desired consumer and business holdings of savings and time deposits relative to holdings of transactions deposits also affect the money multipliers for these broader monetary aggregates.

Figure 16-11
Excess Reserve Holdings of Depository Institutions.

Aggregate excess reserve balances can rise and fall considerably over time. This causes variability in the ratio of excess reserves to transactions deposits, which results in volatility in the money multiplier. Excess reserves increased dramatically following the September 2001 terrorist attacks.

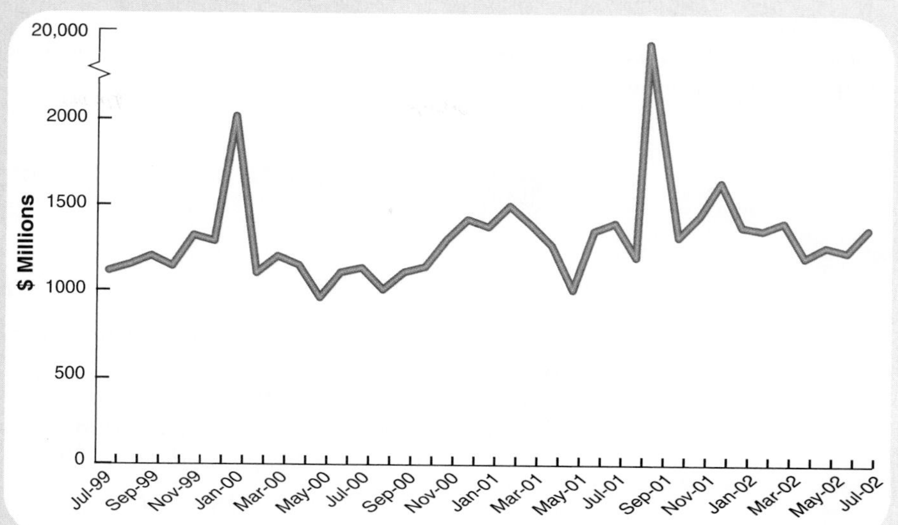

SOURCE: Board of Governors of the Federal Reserve System, H.3 (502) *Statistical Release*.

The Credit Multiplier

In recent years the Federal Reserve has not focused its attention solely on monetary aggregates as indicators of the effects of its policies. Federal Reserve officials also look at other financial variables, such as market interest rates, prices of financial instruments, and prices of some commodities such as gold.

Another variable of interest to the Federal Reserve is the total amount of credit that depository institutions extend by lending or purchasing securities. As financial intermediaries, a key function that depository institutions perform is to issue such credit to help finance purchases of goods, services, and financial assets. Because multiple deposit expansion also entails multiple expansion of loans and security holdings at depository institutions, Federal Reserve policies can affect the volume of such purchases, and consequently economic activity, by influencing the aggregate amount of credit that depository institutions extend.

Figure 16-12 on the next page displays the conceptual T-account that would apply to all depository institutions that issue transactions deposits to finance lending, securities purchases, and holdings of required and excess reserve balances. The figure indicates that because assets and liabilities must balance, the sum of loans, securities, and required and excess reserves must equal the amount of deposits. If we let L denote the dollar amount of loans and S represent the dollar quantity of securities holdings, then this means that $L + S + RR + ER = D$.

TOTAL CREDIT Now let's call the combined amount of loans and securities the *total credit* extended by depository institutions, or $L + S = TC$, where TC is the dollar amount of depository institution credit. Because the sum of loans, securities, and reserves equals deposits in the banking system (if we continue to simplify by ignoring other liabilities), then this tells us that $TC + RR + ER = D$. We can solve for total credit by subtracting RR and ER from both sides, to obtain

Figure 16-12
A Consolidated T-Account for Depository Institutions.

Assets	Liabilities
Loans (*L*)	Transactions deposits (*D*)
Securities (*S*)	
Required reserves (*RR*)	
Excess reserves (*ER*)	

$$TC = D - RR - ER.$$

Hence, total credit is equal to transactions deposits minus required and excess reserves.

Because our T-account abstracts from reality by ignoring other kinds of deposits and other depository institution assets, let's look at changes in total credit resulting from changes in deposits or in required or excess reserves:

$$\Delta TC = \Delta D - \Delta RR - \Delta ER.$$

A Bank Credit Multiplier We leave it to you in problem 8 at the end of this chapter to show that after a couple of algebra steps this equation becomes

$$\Delta TC = \frac{1 - rr_D - e}{c + rr_D + e} \times \Delta MB.$$

Consequently, a change in the monetary base is multiplied by the factor $(1 - rr_D - e)/(c + rr_D + e)$ to cause a change in total credit. This factor is the **credit multiplier,** or a number that tells us the multiple expansion effect on total depository institution credit that a change in the monetary base induces. For instance, if $rr_D = 0.10$, $c = 0.25$, and $e = 0.01$, then the value of this multiplier is $(1 - 0.10 - 0.01)/(0.25 + 0.10 + 0.01) = 0.89/0.36$, or approximately 2.47. This would indicate that each $1 increase in the monetary base would cause the amount of credit extended by depository institutions to rise by about $2.47.

We can conclude that if the Federal Reserve conducts policies, such as open market operations, that alter the monetary base, then the result must be a change in the quantities of loans and securities at depository institutions. For instance, an open market purchase that increases the monetary base raises the combined amount of lending and security holdings of depository institutions. An open market sale, in contrast, reduces total loans and security holdings of these institutions.

Note that the credit multiplier depends on the same basic factors as the money multiplier. These include the required reserve ratio rr_D, the desired ratio of consumer and business holdings of currency to transactions deposits *c*, and the desired ratio of depository institution holdings of excess reserves to transactions deposits *e*. Consequently, variations in any of these factors cause the total credit multiplier to change, just as such variations cause movements in the money multiplier.

Credit multiplier: A number that tells how much total loans and securities at depository institutions will change in response to a change in the monetary base.

Changes in the monetary base exert multiplier effects on both the quantity of money and the total amount of depository institution credit. Which of these variables should the Federal Reserve actually *try* to influence? The answer to this question depends on whether money or credit relates more closely to the volume of economic activity, an issue that we shall consider more fully in Unit V. Before we can address this issue, however, you need to learn much more about the Federal Reserve, how it conducts its policies, and how those policies can affect the extent of economic activity.

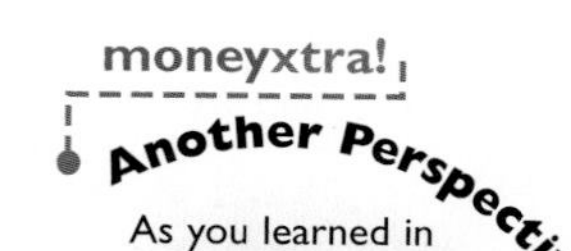

As you learned in Chapter 14, depository financial institutions face capital requirements. To consider how these requirements may affect the credit expansion process, go to the Chapter 16 reading, entitled "Does Bank Capital Matter for Monetary Transmission?" by Skander Van den Heuvel, from the Federal Reserve Bank of New York.
http://moneyxtra.swcollege.com

5. What is the credit multiplier? The credit multiplier is a number that tells how much the combined amount of loans and security holdings of depository institutions will change as a result of a change in the monetary base. Because credit expansion accompanies deposit expansion at these institutions, the credit multiplier depends on the same basic factors that influence the money multiplier.

Electronic Money and the Money Multiplier

As we have discussed in earlier chapters, and especially Chapter 2, several electronic money, or *e-money,* mechanisms are in use or under consideration at present. The use of stored-value cards is already widespread in several regions of the world. Furthermore, smart cards and online banking and payments techniques may engender growing use of *digital cash,* or funds contained in security-encrypted programs embedded in microchips or on hard drives.

How is digital cash likely to affect the process of determining the quantity of money in circulation? We can answer this question on two levels. The first focuses on the most immediate and straightforward effects of widespread adoption of digital cash, which are easier to assess. The second level leads to less clear-cut conclusions because it takes into account a number of indirect effects that the use of digital cash may have on the money supply process.

The Direct Effects of Digital Cash on the Money Supply Process

When assessing the implications of digital cash for the quantity of money in circulation, we must first recognize that the broad adoption of smart cards and other mechanisms for using digital cash will undoubtedly require a redefining of the monetary aggregates. Because digital cash will function as a medium of exchange, it ultimately will be included in the M1 definition of money. In turn, M1 is included within the broader monetary aggregates, so M2 and M3 will also include digital cash.

THE REVISED MONEY MULTIPLIER WITH DIGITAL CASH We shall denote digital cash as DC. In the coming cyberworld with digital cash, the M1 definition of money will be the sum of government-issued currency, C, privately issued digital cash, DC, and privately issued transactions deposits, D. Thus, the expression for M1 will be

$$\text{M1} = C + DC + D.$$

Let's denote the public's desired holdings of digital cash relative to transactions deposits as dc, so $DC = dc \times D$. Recognizing again that $C = c \times D$, in a cyberworld with a significant volume of digital cash in circulation, we can write the expression for the M1 definition of money as

$$\mathrm{M1} = (c + dc + 1) \times D.$$

Now we can determine an expression for the M1 money multiplier. We know that this multiplier is equal to M1/*MB*, where *MB* is the monetary base, or the amount of money issued directly by the government, which does not include privately issued digital cash. We know from our earlier discussion that we can express the monetary base as

$$MB = RR + ER + C = (rr_D + e + c) \times D.$$

Thus, in the presence of digital cash, the money multiplier is equal to

$$\frac{\mathrm{M1}}{MB} = \frac{(c + dc + 1) \times D}{(rr_D + e + c) \times D}$$

$$= \frac{c + dc + 1}{rr_D + \mathrm{e} + c}.$$

This expression indicates that, other things being equal, the widespread use of digital cash—the addition of the factor *dc* and an increase in its value as more and more people adopt digital cash—increases the money multiplier. The inclusion of *dc* in the money multiplier raises the value of the numerator, thereby pushing up the multiplier's value. Intuitively, the reason this occurs is that if people hold digital cash on smart cards, their personal computers, or other devices, then an increase in reserves in the banking system induces an expansion effect on the volume of transactions deposits, as well as on the volume of *digital cash*.

DIGITAL CASH IN THE DEPOSIT EXPANSION PROCESS To see why this is so, imagine that the Fed in a cybereconomy of the not-so-distant future buys \$1 million in government securities. Transactions deposits initially increase by \$1 million, but the initial recipient of these funds allocates a portion of this amount to both government-issued currency *and* digital cash. The depository institution of the recipient can lend out the remaining deposits less an amount that it must hold to meet its reserve requirement. The institution's lending generates a deposit at another institution, and the depositor will also allocate some of these funds to government currency *and* to digital cash. Thus, at each stage of the deposit expansion process, there is an initial "leakage" of digital cash from transactions deposits, which by itself tends to push down the money multiplier. But funds held as digital cash are included in our revised definition of the quantity of money. Therefore, at every stage of the deposit expansion process, new digital cash is "created" as e-money included in M1. On net, therefore, the overall quantity of money increases with the addition of digital cash—again, under our assumption that all other things are equal—and the multiplier linking this measure of money to the monetary base must also rise in value.

It is important to recognize, however, that the expansion of digital cash occurs via the deposit expansion process generated by an increase in bank reserves. If the Fed injects more reserves into the banking system, then this generates a multiple increase in deposits, which in turn implies an increase in digital-cash holdings as individuals shift a desired portion of funds from deposit accounts to smart cards and other digital-cash storage devices. Unlike currency holdings, however, which together with reserves are constrained by the size of the monetary base created by the government, privately issued digital cash varies directly with the extent of transactions deposit expansion.

The Indirect Effects of Digital Cash on the Money Supply Process

The preceding discussion indicates that, *other things being equal,* the *immediate* effect of the broad adoption of digital cash will be an increase in the quantity of money and a rise in the value of the money multiplier. Over time, however, we would *not* expect that other things will *remain* equal. Consequently, in the long run we would anticipate that the money multiplier implications of digital cash are unlikely to be so clear-cut.

DIGITAL CASH AS A SUBSTITUTE FOR GOVERNMENT CURRENCY To understand why, consider Table 16-2, which lists the key characteristics of checks, government-issued currency, and digital cash. Clearly, people face a trade-off in deciding whether to hold currency or checks. Checks offer greater security: if a thief steals a woman's handbag containing cash and checks, she can tell her depository institution to halt payment on all checks in the handbag, but the thief can spend all the cash he has taken because cash payments are final at the point when a transaction is made. Currency requires face-to-face contact for purchases, whereas checks can be sent through the mail. Nevertheless, not everyone will accept a check in payment for a transaction, and a check payment is not final until the check clears. Check transactions also are more expensive. In addition, currency transactions are anonymous, which may be desirable under some circumstances. After evaluating these features of currency and checks, people typically choose to hold *both* payment instruments.

On the Web
How far along are network payment systems for transmitting digital cash? To find out, go to http://ganges.cs.tcd.ie/mepeirce/project.html.

Digital Cash versus Currency and Checks If people can also use digital cash, then they will compare its features with those currently offered by currency and checks. As Table 16-2 indicates, at present the extent of the acceptability of digital cash is uncertain. Nonetheless, we are contemplating a future in which digital cash will be nearly as acceptable as government-provided currency. As for security, digital cash held on smart cards without special security features such as personal identification numbers will be as susceptible to theft as government currency. Some digital cash, however, may be held on devices, such as laptop

Table 16-2 Features of Alternative Forms of Money

Feature	Checks	Currency	Digital Cash
Security	High	Low	High(?)
Cost Per Transfer	High	Medium	Low
Payment Final, Face-to-Face	No	Yes	Yes
Payment Final, Non-Face-to-Face	No	No	Yes
Anonymity	No	Yes	Yes
Acceptability	Restricted	Wide	Uncertain at present

SOURCE: Aleksander Berentsen, "Monetary Policy Implications of Digital Money," *Kyklos* 51 (1998): 89–117.

computers or even wristwatches (Swiss watch manufacturers have already developed watches with microchips for storing digital cash), requiring an access code before a microchip containing digital cash can be accessed. Overall, therefore, digital cash is likely to be somewhat more secure than government-provided currency, though not as secure as check transactions.

Finality and Anonymity Digital-cash transactions are likely to be less costly to undertake than those involving currency or checks. People will be able to access digital cash at home on their personal computers and will not have to go to depository institution branches or automated teller machines to obtain it (although they undoubtedly will be able to do this if they wish). In addition, they will be able to send digital cash from remote locations using the Internet, and digital-cash transactions will be instantaneously final. Unlike transactions using currency, therefore, digital-cash transactions need not be conducted on a face-to-face basis. Like currency transactions, however, most digital-cash transfers will be anonymous.

In most respects, therefore, digital cash looks like a "better" means of payment than government-provided currency. Certainly, for some time to come currency will be used to purchase a number of items—canned beverages and candy in vending machines, for example. Many economists, however, believe that widespread adoption of privately issued digital cash ultimately will tend to "crowd out" government-provided currency. Eventually, even vending machines are likely to have smart-card readers.

From the perspective of the money multiplier model of the money supply process, the ultimate displacement of a large portion of government-provided currency by digital cash will reduce the value of the desired ratio of government-provided currency to transactions deposits, thereby reducing the value of c in the money multiplier expression we derived on page 388. Although this would reduce the numerator of the money multiplier, it would also reduce the denominator, and the latter effect would dominate. Therefore, a decline in the use of government-provided currency as people switch to digital cash likely will also tend to increase the money multiplier somewhat.

OTHER EFFECTS OF DIGITAL CASH ON THE MONEY SUPPLY PROCESS Table 16-2 also suggests that digital cash has some features that recommend its use relative to checks. For instance, in many circumstances making a digital-cash transaction over the Internet is likely to be more convenient and less costly than sending a check. Consequently, bank-issued digital cash may prove to be a substitute for some portion of transactions deposits. Any direct substitution of digital cash for transactions deposits, however, will affect only the composition of the quantity of money in circulation and will not directly influence the quantity of money.

In evaluating the effect of digital cash on the money supply process, we have defined the monetary base to include only government-issued money. Some economists argue that in the cybereconomy of the future, it will be more appropriate to include digital cash in the monetary base. Viewed from this perspective, the monetary base would include both government-issued and privately issued forms of money. In our discussion, however, we have followed the more traditional approach to defining the monetary base.

Online Banking and the Money Supply Process What if online banking permits people to make payments directly from their checking accounts without having to write checks? Will this affect the money supply process?

By transferring funds electronically from their transactions deposit accounts via automated bill payment and other Internet-based online payment mechanisms, people simply avoid writing paper checks. Aside from possible resource-cost savings, the economic implications of the transactions are identical to those that arise if paper checks change hands, provided that the funds are redeposited in another depository institution. If normal redepositing occurs, then the only change is that the transactions that lie behind the normal deposit expansion process are mostly electronic in nature. Effects on balance sheets are unchanged. Thus, online transmission of checking funds has no fundamental effect on the money supply process.

To contemplate the monetary policy issues raised by variability in components of the M1 and M2 multipliers, go to the Chapter 16 Case Study, entitled "Sorting among the Multipliers."
http://moneyxtra.swcollege.com

This is true, however, only if all transactions deposits from which people can transmit funds online are maintained at depository institutions. If nondepository institutions find ways to issue transactions deposits via online mechanisms such as the Internet, then these deposits will also function as money, yet they will not be subject to reserve requirements. In this event, the money multiplier effectively will rise, potentially by a sizable amount. At present, any such activities are illegal; only traditional depository institutions have the power to issue transactions deposits accessible either by check or via the Internet. As we shall discuss in subsequent chapters, central banks around the globe are struggling to determine how to address efforts to get around this legal restriction. For you to understand why central banks struggle with this issue, however, we shall have to explain the nature of central banks. We turn to this subject in the next chapter.

6. How will electronic money affect the money supply process? The direct effect of adding privately supplied digital cash as a component of monetary aggregates will be an immediate increase in the size of the money multiplier linking the government-supplied monetary base to the quantity of money in circulation. This effect likely will be enhanced over time as people substitute digital cash for government-issued currency. The money multiplier will rise substantially if nondepository institutions find ways to issue transactions deposits via online banking mechanisms, but at this point such activities are illegal.

Link to the Global Economy

M2—By and Large the Monetary Aggregate of Choice

The basic money multiplier framework we examined in this chapter applied to the M1 definition of money. In fact, however, currently most of the world's central banks use M2 as their main indicator of the quantity of money in circulation.

Extending the Multiplier Model to M2

To understand why central banks tend to focus on the M2 measure of money, let's expand the basic money multiplier framework to encompass nontransactions deposits, such as savings accounts and money market deposit accounts. Let's define M2 to equal the sum of $M1 = C + D$ and the total quantity of nontransactions deposits, N, so that $M2 = C + D + N$. Consumers and businesses desire to hold a fraction c of transactions deposits as currency. In addition, let's suppose that their desired holdings of nontransactions deposits are equal to n times their holdings of transactions deposits, so that $N = n \times D$. Thus, we can express M2 by the quantity $M2 = C + N + D = (c \times D) + (n \times D) + D = (c + n + 1) \times D$.

Suppose that the central bank sets a required reserve ratio equal to r_N for nontransactions deposits, as is true in the European Monetary Union as well as in nations such as Canada, Japan, and the United Kingdom. Then the quantity of required reserves that banks must hold relative to nontransactions deposits equals $rr_N \times N$, and the total amount of required reserves in the banking system is $RR = (rr_D \times D) + (rr_N \times N) = (rr_D \times D) + (rr_N \times n \times D)$. Consequently, the monetary base equals currency plus total reserves including both required and excess reserves, or $MB = C + RR + ER = (c \times D) + (rr_D \times D) + (rr_N \times n \times D) + (e \times D) = (c + rr_D + rr_N \times n + e) \times D$.

To obtain an expression for the money multiplier for M2, we can now divide M2 by the monetary base:

$$\frac{M2}{MB} = \frac{(c + n + 1) \times D}{(rr_D + rr_N \times n + e + c) \times D}$$

$$= \frac{c + n + 1}{rr_D + rr_N \times n + e + c}.$$

Thus, the M2 multiplier depends on the same factors that affect the M1 multplier, c, e, and rr_D, as well as the public's desired holdings of nontransactions deposits relative to transactions deposits, n, and the required reserve ratio for nontransactions deposits, rr_N.

What Makes M2 So Attractive to Central Banks

Recall that a key factor that contributes to variability in the M1 multiplier is volatility in banks' holdings of excess reserves relative to transactions deposits. Hence, an important contributor to unexpected increases or decreases in the M1 measure of money is changes in the value of e in the M1 multiplier, $(c + 1) / (rr_D + e + c)$.

The M2 multiplier includes terms involving n in the numerator and, if there is a reserve requirement for nontransactions deposits, in the denominator. Figure 16-13 displays the U.S. ratio of nontransactions deposits to transactions deposits since 1959. As you can see, this ratio, which indicates the value of n, has, aside from dips in the early 1990s and 2001, grown steadily over time. Take a look at the expression for the M2 multiplier above, and you will see that this means that the inclusion of nontransactions deposits reduces the relative contribution of the desired excess reserve ratio e in determining the size of the multiplier. This implies that the relative contribution of volatility in excess reserves to the M2 multiplier is reduced. Hence, the overall growth of n has helped provide an additional source of *stability* to the M2 multiplier as compared with the M1 multiplier.

The ratio of nontransactions deposits to transactions deposits also tends to be similarly stable in other countries. This means that in most nations, people have tended to hold gradually larger quantities of nontransactions deposits relative to transactions deposits. Since the mid-1990s, this behavior appears to have contributed to greater stability of the M2 multiplier. (Take a look back at Figure 16-10 on page 382, where you can see that the M2 multiplier has stabilized even as the M1 multiplier has dropped.) The M2 measure of money, therefore, has generally become a more reliable guide for monetary policy in the face of variations in excess reserves.

Research Project

Under what circumstances would a nation's central bank determine that M1 is more reliable than M2 as a measure of the quantity of money in circulation? Under what circumstances might a central bank conclude that it might be better off relying on a *broader* monetary aggregate that includes even more types of deposits, such as large time deposits?

Web Resources

1. How do most central banks in Europe, Japan, and the United States conduct monetary policy? To learn more about monetary policy indicators and strategies in developed nations, go to the home page of the Bank for International Settlements (http://www.bis.org). Click on "Publications and Statistics," and then click on "BIS Papers." Select paper No. 9, "Comparing monetary policy operating procedures across the United States, Japan and the euro area," by Claudio Borio.

2. What are the monetary policy approaches of central banks in emerging economies of the world? Start again at the home page of the Bank for International Settlements, and again click on "Publications and Statistics." Next, under "BIS Papers," click on "Policy Papers," and select No. 3, "The transmission mechanism of monetary policy in emerging market economies," also by Claudio Borio. For studies of specific nations, return to BIS Papers, click "Economic Papers," and select No. 47, "The implementation of monetary policy in industrial countries: a survey."

Figure 16-13
The Ratio of Nontransactions Deposits to Transactions Deposits in the United States.

As in many other nations, the ratio of nontransactions deposits relative to transactions deposits has generally risen since the 1970s.

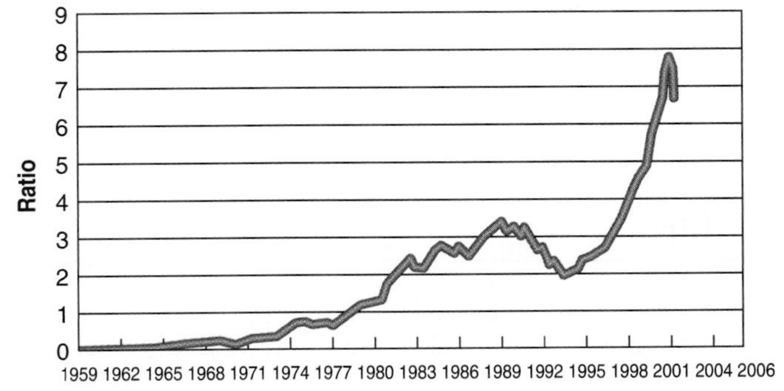

SOURCE: Board of Governors of the Federal Reserve System, H.6 (508) *Statistical Release*, various issues.

Chapter Summary

1. How a Change in Total Depository Institution Reserves Causes a Multiple Expansion Effect on Their Deposits: An increase in total reserves at one depository institution induces it to expand its lending and its holdings of securities. The recipients of these funds deposit some or all of the funds in their transactions accounts at other depository institutions, which enables those institutions to increase their loans and security holdings as well. Hence, the initial increase in reserves causes a multiple expansion of transactions deposits throughout the banking system.

2. Federal Reserve Open Market Operations: These are Federal Reserve purchases or sales of securities. An open market purchase by the Fed increases total reserves of depository institutions. An open market sale by the Fed reduces total reserves of these institutions.

3. The Money Multiplier and Its Importance: The money multiplier is a number that sums up the total amount by which the quantity of money will change in response to a change in the monetary base. This number is important because Federal Reserve policies that alter the amount of total reserves in the banking system affect the size of the monetary base. Consequently, to know how much it should change total reserves to induce a given change in the quantity of money, the Federal Reserve needs to know the size of the money multiplier.

4. Factors That Influence the Money Multiplier: Any factor that affects the extent of the deposit expansion process influences the size of the money multiplier. One important factor is the amount of currency that consumers and businesses wish to hold relative to their holdings of transactions deposits. Another is depository institutions' desired holdings of currency relative to transactions deposits. A third key factor is the required reserve ratio for transactions deposits that the Federal Reserve establishes. Finally, changes in banks' desired holdings of excess reserves influence the portion of new reserves that banks lend, thereby affecting the money multiplier.

5. The Credit Multiplier: This is a number that tells how much the total amount of credit that depository institutions extend by lending or buying securities will change in response to a change in the monetary base. Because credit expansion occurs alongside deposit expansion, the credit multiplier depends on the same basic factors that affect the money multiplier.

6. Electronic Money and the Money Supply Process: Including privately supplied digital cash as a component of monetary aggregates will have the direct effect of increasing the money multiplier relating the government-issued monetary base to the quantity of money in circulation. If people substitute digital cash for government-issued currency, however, then this effect will tend to dissipate over time. The money multiplier will rise considerably if nondepository institutions circumvent current legal restrictions on their ability to issue transactions deposits using online banking mechanisms.

Questions and Problems

(Answers to odd-numbered questions and problems may be found on the Web at http://money.swcollege.com under "Student Resources.")

1. Why is it that you cannot induce any net multiple deposit expansion in the banking system by buying a U.S. government security, yet the Federal Reserve can do so?

2. Suppose that the total liabilities of a depository institution are transactions deposits equal to $2,000 million. It has $1,650 million in loans and securities, and the required reserve ratio is 0.15. Does this institution hold any excess reserves? If so, how much?

3. A depository institution holds $150 million in required reserves and $10 million in excess reserves. Its remaining assets include $440 million in loans and $150 million in securities. If the institution's only liabilities are transactions deposits, what is the required reserve ratio?

4. Consider a world where there is no currency and depository institutions issue only transactions deposits and hold no excess reserves. The value of the money multiplier (for the M1 monetary aggregate) is equal to 4. What is the required reserve ratio? What is the total credit multiplier?

5. Explain in your own words why the money multiplier rises if consumers and businesses desire to hold less currency relative to their holdings of transactions deposits.

6. Explain why the money multiplier becomes larger if depository institutions wish to hold fewer excess reserves relative to transactions deposits that they issue.

7. Suppose that $c = 0.35$, $rr_D = 0.05$, and $e = 0.05$. In the absence of digital cash, and if banks issue only transactions deposits, what is the money multiplier for the M1 monetary aggregate? What is the total credit multiplier?

8. Show that the expression $\Delta TC = \Delta D - \Delta RR - \Delta ER$ can be rearranged into the total credit multiplier expression, $\Delta TC = [(1 - rr_D - e)/(c + rr_D + e)] \times \Delta MB$. [Hint: First write $\Delta TC = \Delta D - \Delta RR - \Delta ER = (1 - rr_D - e) \times \Delta D$. Then remember that the monetary base is $MB = C + TR = C + RR + ER = (c + rr_D + e) \times D$, so that a *change* in the monetary base is $\Delta MB = (c + rr_D + e) \times \Delta D$. Now solve this last equation for ΔD and substitute for ΔD in your expression for ΔTC.]

9. Briefly review the ways increased use of smart cards and online accounts at financial institutions may affect the money supply process. Economists continue to evaluate whether digital cash is more likely to displace government-issued currency or bank-issued checking accounts. From the standpoint of controlling the total quantity of money in circulation, does it matter? Explain your reasoning.

10. Suppose that the required reserve ratio for transactions deposits is equal to 0.05. The public's desired ratio of government-issued currency to transactions deposits is equal to 0.4, and the public's desired ratio of digital cash to transactions deposits is equal to 0.1. The M1 definition of money includes digital cash. Depository institutions desire to hold no excess reserves. The Federal Reserve engages in a $2 million open market purchase of government securities from a dealer that has an account with a New York bank. Trace through the first three steps of the deposit expansion process that results, showing what happens to depository institution holdings of reserves and to the public's holdings of transactions deposits, government currency, and digital cash at each step. Based on your work, why does it make sense that the inclusion of digital cash increases the M1 money multiplier on net, even though at each stage of the deposit expansion process the public converts a portion of transactions deposits to digital cash outside the banking system? Explain your reasoning.

Before the Test

Test your understanding of the material covered in this chapter by taking the Chapter 16 interactive quiz at http://money.swcollege.com.

Online Application

In this chapter, you learned how monetary policy actions of the Federal Reserve induce changes in total deposits in the banking system. Now let's think about monetary policy-making in a world with online checking.

Internet URL: http://www.echeck.org/overview/what.html

Title: What Is the Echeck?

Navigation: First, go to the Echeck home page (http://www.echeck.org). Click on *Overview*, and then click on *What Is Echeck*?

Application: Read the discussion, and then answer the following questions.

1. Are echecks substitutes for currency and coins, or are they substitutes for traditional paper checks? Does the answer to this question make a difference for how echecks are likely to feature in the money multiplier process?

2. Suppose that consumers and businesses widely adopt echeck technology. Would this affect the basic money multiplier model that we developed in this chapter? If so, how? If not, why not?

For Group Study and Analysis: Divide the class into groups. Have each group evaluate the likely effects of echeck adoption, as well as widespread adoption of other forms of electronic retail payment mechanisms, on both the money and credit multipliers. Re-form the class, and discuss the channels by which adoption of electronic moneys will potentially affect both multipliers.

Selected References and Further Reading

Berentsen, Aleksander. "Monetary Policy Implications of Digital Money." *Kyklos* 51 (1998): 89–117.

Bernkopf, Mark. "Electronic Cash and Monetary Policy." *FirstMonday* (Internet Journal at http://www.firstmonday.dk), 1996.

Humphrey, Thomas. "The Theory of Multiple Expansion of Deposits: What It Is and Whence It Came." Federal Reserve Bank of Richmond *Economic Review* 73 (March/April 1987): 3–11.

McAndrews, James, and William Roberds. "The Economics of Check Float." Federal Reserve Bank of Atlanta *Economic Review,* Fourth Quarter 2000, pp. 17–27.

Osterberg, William, and James Thomson. "Bank Notes and Stored-Value Cards: Stepping Lightly into the Past." Federal Reserve Bank of Cleveland *Economic Commentary,* September 1, 1998.

Roberds, William. "What's Really New about the New Forms of Retail Payment?" Federal Reserve Bank of Atlanta *Economic Review,* First Quarter 1997, pp. 32–45.

Stevens, Ed. "Electronic Money and the Future of Central Banks." Federal Reserve Bank of Cleveland *Economic Commentary,* March 1, 2002.

Tanaka, Tatsuo. "Possible Economic Consequences of Digital Cash." *FirstMonday* (Internet Journal at http://www.firstmonday.dk), 1996.

MoneyXtra

moneyxtra! Log on to the MoneyXtra Web site now (http://moneyxtra.swcollege.com) for additional learning resources such as practice quizzes, case studies, readings, and additional economic applications.

Chapter 17

Central Banking and the Federal Reserve System

History undoubtedly will record September 11, 2001, the date of the terrorist attacks on New York City and Washington, D.C., as the darkest day for the United States since December 7, 1941, when the Japanese Navy attacked Pearl Harbor. About 500 fewer lives were lost at Pearl Harbor, however. In addition to the human tragedy, whereas the 1941 attack damaged or eliminated much of the U.S. Navy's Pacific Fleet, the 2001 attack primarily succeeded in destroying prime U.S. office space in New York City. A Federal Reserve economist estimated that the total office space lost in the destruction of the World Trade Center complex was roughly equivalent to the entire amount of office space available in downtown Dallas, Texas.

The attack was also a major short-term blow to the U.S. financial system. Several major bond traders had offices and employees at the World Trade Center, and many of the facilities of the top payments-processing bank in the United States were located there. Key communications networks branched from satellite dishes and radio towers atop the two towers, so communication links among numerous financial institutions were severed when the buildings collapsed.

Within minutes of the New York attacks, Federal Reserve officials were at work trying to minimize the financial fallout from the attacks. They contacted managers of U.S. banks and brokerage and bond-trading firms and rapidly arranged emergency injections of liquidity. Fed officials also established rapid communications with their counterparts in Europe and Canada. To help assure that the European Central Bank, the Bank of England, and the Bank of Canada could advance emergency dollar-denominated loans to U.S. branches

Fundamental Issues

1. What were the first central banking institutions, and how did central banking initially develop in the United States?
2. Where did responsibilities for monetary and banking policies rest in the absence of a U.S. central bank in the nineteenth and early twentieth centuries?
3. What motivated Congress to establish the Federal Reserve System?
4. Why did Congress restructure the Federal Reserve in 1935?
5. Who makes the key policy decisions at the Federal Reserve?

of European and Canadian banks, the Fed arranged to temporarily swap more than $50 billion for euros, pounds, and Canadian dollars. Thanks to the Fed's quick action, the U.S. financial system shuddered on September 11, 2001, but it did not collapse.

The founders of the Federal Reserve System could never have anticipated the advent of terrorism in the late twentieth and early twenty-first century. Nevertheless, they did envision that situations might arise in which speedy policy reactions by a central banking institution could prevent financial collapse. In this chapter you will learn more about this and other rationales for central banks in today's global economy.

The Central Banking Experience

On the Web
What induced Sweden to establish the world's first central bank? Learn more about the history of the Riksbank by going to its English-language home page at http://www.riksbank.com. Then click on "History."

The world's first central bank was the Swedish Sveriges Riksbank (known as the Risens Standers Bank until 1867), which was established in 1668. The Swedish parliament, the Riksdag, gave a special commission the responsibility of managing the Sveriges Riksbank, which initially did not issue money. By 1701, however, the Riksbank had authority to issue "transfer notes" that basically functioned as a form of currency, and in 1789 the Riksdag established a National Debt Office that formally issued Swedish government currency. The Riksbank Act of 1897 made the Riksbank the only legal issuer of Swedish currency.

The second central bank was the Bank of England, which the English Parliament established in 1694. Parliament gave the Bank of England the power to issue currency notes redeemable in silver, and these notes circulated alongside notes issued by the government and private finance companies.

Expanding the Central Bank Population

As late as 1800, the Riksbank and the Bank of England were the only central banks. Indeed, the total number of central banks worldwide remained a single digit as late as 1873. Figure 17-1 shows that a significant increase in the number of central banks took place beginning in the late nineteenth century and especially during the latter part of the twentieth century. A portion of this growth stemmed from the establishment of central banks by former colonial states that achieved independence and developed their own currencies. (The number of central bank employees varies dramatically across countries; see on page 400 *Global Focus: Does Russia's Central Bank Really Need So Many Employees?*)

The European System of Central Banks In January 1999, the central banks of eleven European nations—Austria, Belgium, Finland, France, Germany, Ireland, Italy, Luxembourg, the Netherlands, Portugal, and Spain—formed the *European System of Central Banks.* Almost two years later, the Bank of Greece joined the system. The six-member executive board for this system is based at the *European Central Bank (ECB),* the hub of the European System of Central Banks located in Frankfurt, Germany. All final operating and policy decisions for the system, however, ultimately must be approved by an eighteen-member governing

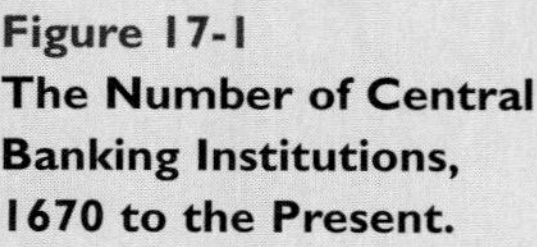

Figure 17-1
The Number of Central Banking Institutions, 1670 to the Present.

The twentieth century witnessed considerable growth in the number of central banks.

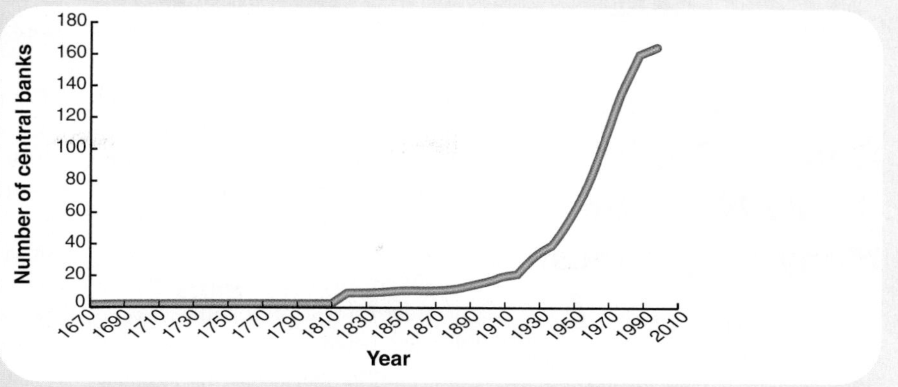

SOURCE: Forrest Capie, Charles Goodhart, and Norbert Schnadt, "The Development of Central Banking," in Capie et al., eds., *The Future of Central Banking: The Tercentenary Symposium of the Bank of England* (Cambridge: Cambridge University Press, 1994), pp. 1–231, and authors' estimates.

council composed of the executive board in Frankfurt and the governors of the twelve national central banks. Thus, each member nation plays a role in determining the policies of the European Central Bank.

This combination of centralized and decentralized decision making has its roots on the other side of the Atlantic Ocean, where another initially loose federation of states wrestled with money and banking problems for well over a century before settling on a unique central banking system. Ironically, this arrangement, the U.S. Federal Reserve System, was constructed in the early twentieth century following years of careful study of European central banking institutions. Hence, there is a circularity in the history of central banking institutions, with the early European experience forming the basis for U.S. central banking, which in turn has served as a model for today's European institutional structure.

The Origins of U.S. Central Banking, 1791–1836

Today U.S. residents take for granted that the Federal Reserve is responsible for managing the nation's monetary affairs. Yet the Federal Reserve has been the U.S. central banking institution for only a little over a third of the nation's history. During nearly half of the U.S. republic's existence, there was no formal central bank. Consequently, you must first understand the historical background that led to the creation and development of the Fed.

Because the original thirteen states that composed the United States were settled mainly by English immigrants, their customs and legal precedents largely reflected those of England. These states, therefore, looked to British practices as a guide to developing banking institutions for the federal government that they initiated in 1791. The center of British arrangements was the Bank of England, which Parliament had established in 1694. This central bank was the main depository of the British government and also served as a key lender to the government, particularly during times of war. Ultimately, the Bank of England also became a

GLOBAL Focus | POLICY | CYBER | MANAGEMENT

Does Russia's Central Bank Really Need So Many Employees?

The Central Bank of Russia has in excess of 90,000 people on its staff, or more than 15 percent of the total estimated number of central bank employees on planet Earth. As Figure 17-2 indicates, Russia's central bank employment, including workers at all government-related financial enterprises coordinated by the Central Bank of Russia, translates into nearly 62 employees for every 100,000 people within the entire Russian population. This is about twice as many per 100,000 people as are employed by the Bank of Greece, which has the second-highest total in the world. Even though China's central bank has about 150,000 employees, on a per capita basis Russia still has more than four times as many central bank employees.

Does Russia really require so many people to operate its central bank? Economists who specialize in the study of central banking institutions strongly suspect that the answer is no. Undoubtedly, the Central Bank of Russia has had trouble breaking away from the socialist hiring practices of the Communist regimes that formerly governed the country.

Of course, many economists also wonder if the central banks of France, Belgium, Germany, and Italy truly require so many employees now that many traditional central banking functions are coordinated by the European Central Bank. Those four European countries alone have about 43,000 central bank employees, as compared with the 24,000 people that the Federal Reserve employs to coordinate banking and monetary policies for the entire United States.

For Critical Analysis: Why might a central bank require thousands of employees to perform its various functions?

On the Web
How is the Central Bank of Russia coordinating its continuing transition to modern central banking? Follow its progress at http://www.cbr.ru/eng/.

Figure 17-2
Central Bank Employees Per 100,000 Residents for Selected Nations.

Relative to the size of of its population, Russia has more than twice as many employees on the staff of its central bank as the Bank of Greece, the central bank with the second-largest number of employees per 100,000 residents.

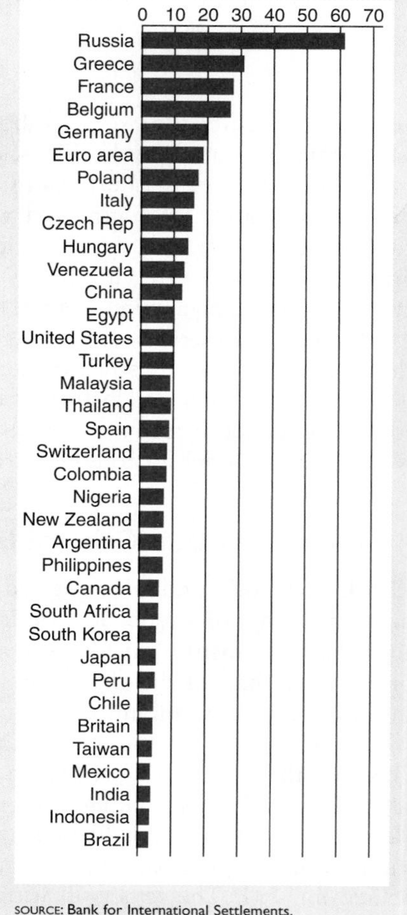

SOURCE: Bank for International Settlements.

central depository for other private banks of the British Empire. From this position the Bank of England effectively was able to establish and enforce policies that other banks felt obliged to follow.

The Bank of North America In 1781, when Robert Morris lobbied the Continental Congress to approve a **charter** (official banking license) for the Bank of North America, he and his supporters regarded the Bank of England as an example to emulate. Morris based many features of the charter of the Bank of North America on the original charter of the Bank of England. He and others who placed their funds in the Bank of North America also had high hopes that it might emerge as a central bank.

Charter: A governmental license to open and operate a bank.

Although the Bank of North America generally was conservatively managed and successful, it never rose to the stature of a central bank for several reasons. One was that the U.S. banking and financial systems were very small compared with those of the British Empire. Another was that U.S. financial markets were very decentralized. Finally, although the Continental Congress granted the Bank of North America a charter, it did not give the bank any special powers beyond those of the few other state-chartered banks of the time.

The First Bank of the United States When Alexander Hamilton, the new nation's first Treasury secretary, contemplated the establishment of the first U.S. central bank, he reviewed the history of the Bank of North America. Hamilton's ambition, however, was for the United States to have a central bank that would rival the Bank of England in power and influence. Toward this end, Hamilton convinced the U.S. Congress to establish a Bank of the United States modeled very much along the lines of the Bank of England.

In 1791, Congress granted the First Bank of the United States a twenty-year federal charter and authorized the U.S. Treasury to purchase a fixed amount of the First Bank's equity shares and to hold deposits at the First Bank. It also authorized the First Bank to open branches throughout the nation and to issue its own currency notes that the federal government would accept as payments for internal taxes, foreign tariffs, and fees for government services.

During its twenty years of existence, the First Bank generally was a stable and profitable institution. Nevertheless, Congress did not renew its charter in 1811, largely because of concerns that foreigners had acquired too many of its shares and that the First Bank might accumulate sufficient resources to influence the affairs of state banks. Indeed, by 1810 the directors of the First Bank had begun to recognize that they could reduce the overall volume of credit in the banking system by requesting that state banks redeem their notes with the gold reserves that backed those notes. In a sense this was the early-nineteenth-century equivalent of an open market sale by today's Fed, as discussed in Chapter 16. Although Hamilton had hoped that the First Bank would ultimately develop such financial power, Congress was unwilling to let the First Bank develop into a central banking institution capable of exercising such authority over the nation's banking and monetary affairs.

The Second Bank of the United States Just as the charter of the First Bank of the United States expired, the nation became embroiled in several disputes with Britain. During the resulting War of 1812, the U.S. Treasury found itself without an agent to assist it in raising funds to finance its wartime expenditures. The Treasury also lacked a central depository for the funds that it was able to raise. Furthermore, a significant period of inflation occurred after the conclusion of the war. These events together convinced President James Madison to recommend that Congress grant a federal charter to a Second Bank of the United States. Congress authorized a charter that would span the period 1816–1836. It also modeled the Second Bank closely upon the structure of the First Bank. The nation now seemed ready for a central banking institution.

By 1823, when Nicholas Biddle became the Second Bank's president, the bank was well on the way to becoming such an institution. In that year the Second Bank held almost half of all the specie (monetary gold and silver) in the nation. Like the First Bank, it had found that it could influence national credit conditions by choosing when and to what extent to redeem state bank notes for the specie that backed them. Under Biddle's direction, the Second Bank liked to think of itself as a benevolent institution, or in Biddle's own words, "the enemy of none, but the common friend of all."

Nevertheless, in 1836, the Second Bank officially closed its doors—political missteps by Biddle and the vehement opposition of President Andrew Jackson had led to its demise.

1. What were the first central banking institutions, and how did central banking initially develop in the United States? The world's first central banks were in Sweden and England. Subsequently, other central banks were established in Europe, where today several nations have formed the European System of Central Banks. Although neither the First nor the Second Bank of the United States possessed the extensive monetary policy or bank regulatory powers of today's Federal Reserve, both in various respects represented the first central banking institutions of the United States. Both institutions had the capability to affect the rest of the U.S. banking system, and the Second Bank used this capability at various times.

Policy and Politics without a Central Bank, 1837–1912

Following the demise of the Second Bank of the United States, the U.S. Treasury again found itself without a central financial agent. It also was forced to find state-chartered banks with which to deposit its funds. The state banks that it chose became known as "pet banks," because banks that the Treasury did not select felt slighted.

The Free-Banking Period Whether or not they were "pets," state banks faced neither federally chartered competition nor federal regulation for over two decades after the closure of the Second Bank. In a number of states, however, the degree of loan and deposit market rivalry among state-chartered banks actually increased with the advent of "free banking." As discussed in Chapter 2, the free-banking period lasted until the Civil War. During this interval, each state had its own banking rules, and many states permitted relatively open competition among banks.

What did the U.S. Treasury do during this period without the assistance of a central banking institution? Essentially, after several years of trial and error the Treasury figured out how to get along without a central bank. By 1846 an "Independent Treasury System" was in operation. Under this system, the Treasury

Department issued notes that were close substitutes for money, and in 1847 it conducted the first open market operation in U.S. history when it repurchased outstanding securities that it had used to help finance the Mexican War (1846–1848). The Treasury made several more repurchases of outstanding securities during the next several years. Although the main justification was to reduce the size of the Treasury's outstanding debt, the Treasury tried to time several of its open market purchases during the late 1840s and early 1850s to stabilize national money and credit conditions.

In the autumn of 1857, however, a major banking panic occurred. Although this episode was muted and short-lived by the standards of some later financial crises, the Treasury's failure to offset the effects of the panic and the subsequent economic downturn had important political repercussions.

The Civil War, Greenbacks, and National Banking Most modern historians identify 1857 as the point at which the nation's steady drift toward sectionalism switched to a rushing current pushing toward violent hostility. In December 1860, South Carolina announced its secession from the United States, and within a few short months, other southern states had joined it in forming the Confederacy. By the middle of April 1861, Fort Sumter had fallen and the Civil War had begun. At this point, as we discussed in Chapter 2, the federal government issued an insignificant portion of the money in circulation.

The National Banking Act of 1863 encouraged most existing state banks to switch to new federal charters to qualify as depositories of Treasury funds. This legislation also established the first system of national reserve requirements. The 1865 amendment to the law adding a tax on the notes issued by state-chartered banks encouraged many state banks to switch to national charters and also induced a number of banks to offer more demand deposits instead of issuing notes. In these respects the National Banking Act laid the foundation for today's Federal Reserve System and transactions-deposit-based banking system even though the birth of the Federal Reserve was still a half-century in the future.

Panic and Resumption of the Gold Standard By 1866, government-issued currency accounted for a third of the quantity of money in circulation in the United States. Yet the nation had no central banking institution to manage its monetary affairs. Again, it was up to the U.S. Treasury to do the job.

In 1873 a severe panic struck the nation's banking and financial markets. This event followed a precipitous decline in the quantities of money and credit that the Treasury made little effort to offset. The magnitude of the panic was significant and added fuel to a great national debate over what to do about the Greenbacks still in circulation. When Congress authorized the creation of Greenbacks—which were not backed by gold—during the Civil War (see Chapter 2), it had promised to remove them from circulation after the war ended. But to citizens of western and southern states, this would mean a further reduction in the amounts of money and credit available for their use. Many citizens of these states began a movement to keep the Greenbacks in circulation, and some even argued for increasing the number of Greenbacks.

Despite a loss at the polls in 1874 that stemmed in part from their stand in favor of redeeming the Greenbacks and returning to a full gold standard, an

Free silver: A late-nineteenth-century idea for unlimited coinage of silver to meet the monetary needs of a growing U.S. economy.

outgoing Republican congressional majority passed the *Resumption Act of 1875*. This law committed the federal government to return to a full gold standard by 1879. After the 1876 election returned the Republicans to power, the Greenback movement splintered.

POPULISM, FREE SILVER, AND BIMETALISM Although the Greenback movement had lost the battle, its members continued the fight to increase the quantity of money in circulation. A new political movement known as populism arose and ultimately led to the formation of the Populist Party in 1892. Many adherents to this movement adopted a new monetary proposal: **free silver,** or the unlimited coinage of silver as needed by the expanding U.S. economy. The idea was to allow the quantities of money and credit to grow through *bimetalism*. As discussed in Chapter 1, this is the simultaneous use of gold and silver as commodity standards.

According to the free silver proponents, Congress had committed the "Crime of 1873" by passing a law that ended the legal coinage of silver dollars. By 1890, the populist and free silver forces had made enough of an impression on Republican gold-standard adherents that the Republicans gave in and passed the *Sherman Silver Act,* which authorized the Treasury to purchase silver and to issue dollars backed by silver.

The timing turned out to be bad, however. In 1893 another banking panic occurred. Gold's value rose, and the market price of silver fell. Suddenly, the Treasury found itself with large stocks of low-priced silver. This did not seem to be a good time to issue money backed by silver, so Congress immediately repealed the Sherman Silver Act.

This set the stage for the final showdown over bimetalism. In a speech during the presidential campaign of 1896, Democratic candidate William Jennings Bryan accused Republican gold-standard proponent William McKinley of attempting to crush working people under the weight of the gold standard. In the most famous line from this speech, Bryan adopted a biblical allusion and declared, "You shall not press down upon the brow of labor this cross of thorns, you shall not crucify mankind upon a cross of gold." Nevertheless, Bryan lost this election, which was just one of his four failed attempts at the presidency.

2. Where did responsibilities for monetary and banking policies rest in the absence of a U.S. central bank in the nineteenth and early twentieth centuries? Until the Civil War, individual states determined their own banking policies. After the Civil War, the federal government established the national banking system and assumed a larger role in determining policies that affected banks. During this period with no central banking institution, the U.S. Treasury functioned as the nation's monetary policy institution.

PRELUDE TO THE FEDERAL RESERVE After the Panic of 1893, which in many respects was even worse than the 1873 panic, even those who favored the gold standard began to believe that some type of monetary reform might be in order. This belief was reinforced in 1907 when yet another financial panic occurred. A conglomerate corporation known as Knickerbocker Trust attempted to corner stock in a company called United Copper. When its effort failed, Knickerbocker's own stock price collapsed. This convinced many stock traders on Wall Street that the stocks of other conglomerates would also plummet. In what economists call a *self-fulfilling* prophecy, the traders' simultaneous efforts to sell off shares in these companies *caused* the market prices of their stocks to fall.

Ultimately, Treasury secretary George Cortelyou worked out a combined public and private "bailout" of several Wall Street banks and trusts. Cortelyou entrusted $25 million in public funds to the private use of J. P. Morgan, who made loans to rescue the most financially healthy institutions on Wall Street. Morgan also arranged private funding of $25 million for further lending to prop up these institutions, and the panic finally ended.

After the Panic of 1907 had ended, President Theodore Roosevelt and members of Congress agreed that the nation should consider the creation of some type of central bank. The following year, Congress passed the *Aldrich-Vreeland Act,* which gave the Treasury secretary emergency powers to issue currency in the event of an emerging crisis that threatened to become a more widespread panic. The Aldrich-Vreeland Act also established a National Monetary Commission that was charged with developing a concrete plan for a U.S. central bank. Senator Nelson Aldrich led this commission, and the plan that it developed served as the basis for a bill that was pieced together in 1911 by Senators Carter Glass and Robert Owen. This bill became the *Federal Reserve Act of 1913*.

Federal Reserve banks: The twelve central banking institutions that oversee regional activities of the Federal Reserve System.

Federal Reserve districts: The twelve geographic regions of the Federal Reserve System.

Origins and Evolution of the Fed

The Federal Reserve Act created the *Federal Reserve System* of central banking institutions. It called for this system to be supervised by a *Federal Reserve Board* composed of the Treasury secretary, the comptroller of the currency, and five additional members appointed by the president and confirmed by the Senate to ten-year terms. The Federal Reserve System, which today we often call the "Fed," was a kind of cooperative arrangement linking consumers, businesses, banks, and the federal government. At the heart of the system were twelve **Federal Reserve banks,** which were located in major cities in geographic regions called **Federal Reserve districts.** A private bank could opt to join the system by purchasing ownership shares in the Federal Reserve bank in its district. This would entitle it to some say in the selection of the board of directors of the Federal Reserve bank and to check-clearing services and other banking services that the district bank would provide.

To keep the Fed from being simply a "bankers' club," however, Congress required that the majority of each Federal Reserve bank's board of directors be composed of individuals representing interests of consumers and nonfinancial businesses. Furthermore, Congress placed the Federal Reserve Board in Washington, D.C, expressly to supervise the activities of the system of Federal Reserve banks.

Congress charged the Fed with three tasks:

1. To develop and supervise the distribution of a national currency, which the Fed was to stand ready to supply in quantities necessary to help avert budding financial panics.

2. To establish a nationally coordinated system of check-clearing and collection services.

3. To process the federal government's financial accounts and to serve as the central depository for government funds.

moneyxtra!

Another Perspective

To learn how the Federal Reserve assists the federal government in its financial affairs, go to the Chapter 17 reading, entitled "The Federal Reserve Banks as Fiscal Agents and Depositories of the United States," by Paula Hillery and Stephen Thompson of the Board of Governors of the Federal Reserve System.

http://moneyxtra.swcollege.com

3. What motivated Congress to establish the Federal Reserve System? The key reason that Congress created the Federal Reserve System was to ensure that a central bank would be available to provide monetary resources in sufficient amounts to avert potential banking and financial panics. Another congressional objective was to provide an institution that could centralize the clearing of payments across the nation. Congress also wanted the government to have a central depository for its funds.

The Early Fed, 1913–1935

As the Federal Reserve began its operations, it was constrained in two fundamental ways. First, the Federal Reserve Act seemed to be very specific about how the Fed could try to avert panics by lending to endangered institutions. The legislation required the Fed to lend funds through a specific mechanism called *rediscounting*. To borrow from a Federal Reserve bank, a private bank that was a Federal Reserve System member would have to post collateral in the form of discount bonds with low default risk. The Fed then would lend by purchasing these bonds at a further discount, hence "rediscounting" the bonds. The percentage of the additional discount was the Fed's **discount rate,** or the effective interest rate that the Fed would charge for its loan to the bank.

A second constraint stemmed from something important that the Federal Reserve Act *failed* to spell out in detail, namely, how powers were to be distributed *within* the Federal Reserve System. Although the legislation gave the Federal Reserve Board supervisory functions within the system, it did not give the Board the power to dictate policies to the individual Federal Reserve banks. The Board at best could try to muster systemwide coordination. Such efforts were not always successful, and much of the time the Federal Reserve banks conducted their own regional policies.

THE HESITANT FED The outbreak of World War I in 1914 presented an immediate complication for the Fed. The war severely strained international flows of gold and currencies and threatened the stability of U.S. financial markets. Under the emergency provision of the Aldrich-Vreeland Act, Treasury Secretary William McAdoo, who was also a Federal Reserve Board member, arranged for the national and state banks to issue currency to help sustain the quantities of money and credit. McAdoo also insisted that the Federal Reserve purchase Treasury securities at very low yields. By the conclusion of hostilities in late 1918, the U.S. money stock had risen by about 70 percent. During the war other Federal Reserve Board members objected to McAdoo's policies, and he responded by threatening to invoke further emergency Treasury powers, including taking full control of all banking reserves. This gave the other Board members little choice but to acquiesce.

After the war the center of power within the Federal Reserve System shifted from the Treasury to the Federal Reserve bank presidents. This occurred largely through the efforts of Benjamin Strong, the president of the Federal Reserve Bank of New York. He had numerous political friends and important connections with

Discount rate: The rate of interest that the Federal Reserve charges to lend to a depository institution.

J. P. Morgan and other financial leaders. Strong initiated the Fed's first open market operations, which led to conflicts with Board members who objected to this policy innovation. Nevertheless, Strong emerged as the dominant figure in the Federal Reserve System until he died in 1928. In October of the following year, the stock market crashed. In the midst of the continuing power vacuum created by Strong's death, no leading figure appeared at the Fed to coordinate a response to the crisis.

Board of Governors of the Federal Reserve System: A group of seven individuals appointed by the president and confirmed by the Senate that, under the terms of the Banking Act of 1935, has key policymaking responsibilities within the Federal Reserve System.

THE GREAT DEPRESSION AND REFORM OF THE FED The Fed's initial response to the panic of late 1929 was to release more reserves into the banking system. As bank failures multiplied, however, Board members hesitated to bail out banks that they viewed as insolvent rather than simply illiquid. In retrospect, it is easy to see that they missed the point: the entire banking system had become illiquid, and only the Fed could have provided the liquidity that was necessary. In the end the Fed failed in this fundamental task that Congress had given it in 1913.

By 1933, a third of all the commercial banks in the United States had failed. Furthermore, the quantity of money had declined by about a third. The nation's banking and monetary system shrank, and the nation's economic activity shrank as well. The banking crisis reinforced the business downturn, and the economic decline reinforced the financial collapse. The nation had fallen into what we now call the *Great Depression* of the 1930s.

Restructuring the Fed In the area of money and banking arrangements, Congress responded to the Great Depression in two ways. First, it passed the Glass-Steagall Act and other related banking legislation that we discussed in Chapter 14. Second, Congress passed the *Banking Act of 1935*. In many respects this legislation really amounted to a new "Federal Reserve Act," because it fundamentally restructured the Federal Reserve System.

A key provision of the Banking Act of 1935 was the centralization of internal Fed authority in Washington, D.C. But Congress no longer trusted the Federal Reserve Board as specified in the original Federal Reserve Act. Instead, Congress replaced that body with a new seven-member **Board of Governors of the Federal Reserve System.** Congress designated the Board of Governors as the key policymaking body within the Fed. To shield the Board from executive branch pressures, Congress excluded the Treasury secretary and the comptroller of the currency from Board governor positions. Instead, Congress required that the president appoint and that the Senate confirm all seven governors. It also specified that no more than four of the seven governors could belong to a single political party. Congress also lengthened the term of each governor to fourteen years and established a system of overlapping terms in which the president would have the opportunity to appoint a new governor every two years.

New Lines of Authority In a further effort to centralize internal Fed policymaking authority, the 1935 legislation created the offices of chair and vice chair of the Board of Governors. These offices would be held by governors appointed by the president to four-year renewable terms. The new law gave the chair, the vice chair, and the remainder of the Board of Governors the authority to determine reserve requirements within ranges established by the law. It also gave the Board of Governors the authority to approve the discount rates set by the Federal Reserve banks.

Federal Open Market Committee (FOMC): A group composed of the seven governors and five of the twelve Federal Reserve bank presidents that determines how to conduct the Fed's open market operations.

Finally, the Banking Act of 1935 established the **Federal Open Market Committee (FOMC),** which is composed of the seven governors and five of the twelve Federal Reserve bank presidents. Congress gave the FOMC the authority to determine the strategies and tactics of the Fed's open market operations. As we discuss later in this chapter, the FOMC is the key day-to-day policymaking authority within today's Federal Reserve System.

LESSONS FOR EUROPE? Today's European System of Central Banks (ESCB) clearly regards the U.S. Federal Reserve System as something of a "role model." The ESCB's executive board of six individuals based in Frankfurt is analogous to the Fed's Board of Governors in Washington, and its governing council is analogous to the Fed's Federal Open Market Committee.

Nevertheless, in some respects the ESCB has more in common with the pre-1935 Federal Reserve System than with today's Fed. The twelve national central bank governors have a majority in the ESCB's eighteen-member governing council, and a coalition of ten of these governors could potentially overrule the executive board, effectively dictating policy for the ESCB as a whole. Some observers worry that in the event of a major economic downturn, competing regional interests could lead to a policy paralysis at the ESCB analogous to the inaction of the Fed in the 1930s.

On the Web

How is the European System of Central Banks structured? Learn more about this central banking system by going to the European Central Bank's home page at http://www.ecb.int and then clicking on "About ECB."

Like the pre-1935 Federal Reserve Board, the European Central Bank in Frankfurt also has no lender-of-last-resort authority. This power is held by the individual central banks or, in some instances, by national banking supervisors. Thus, a regional banking panic in Europe would have to be addressed by national authorities, and their actions might potentially be in conflict with the broader, Europe-wide goals of the European Central Bank.

For these reasons, a number of economists have contended that it is already time for the countries in the European Monetary Union to reform their central banking system. In their view, these nations have failed to take into account the hard lesson that the United States learned in the 1930s, which is that too much decentralization can be a mistake. (The European System of Central Banks has struggled just to coordinate its internal communications; see *Global Focus: Multilingual Monetary Musings in Europe*.)

4. Why did Congress restructure the Federal Reserve in 1935? A key defect of the original Federal Reserve Act of 1913 was that it did not spell out the lines of authority for Fed policymaking. This caused internal dissension within the Fed that complicated its ability to respond to crises such as the 1929 stock market crash and the subsequent financial panics. Congress also perceived that including Treasury officials on the Federal Reserve Board gave the executive branch of the federal government too much clout, so it sought to reduce the extent of the Treasury's influence on internal Fed policymaking.

The Evolution of the Modern Fed

In many respects the Banking Act of 1935 created a new institution. It created new offices with clearly defined responsibilities, and it centered the Fed's powers in the Board of Governors and its chair. But the legislation still left many points

GLOBAL Focus | POLICY | CYBER | MANAGEMENT

Multilingual Monetary Musings in Europe

The label "Confidential" or "Highly Confidential" commonly appears at the top of the cover page of internal Federal Reserve reports and memoranda. Within the ESCB, communicating the same idea—that internal central bank deliberations are not intended for public distribution—could well encompass the entire title page because there would have to be a label in every language spoken by residents of nations that are part of the European Monetary Union.

Being a Terminologist at the ECB Is a Tough Job, but Someone Has to Do It

Although most discussions by the eighteen-member governing board of the ESCB take place in English, translators stand ready at all meetings in case debate becomes so heated that governors lapse into their native tongues. The translators, who operate out of the language-services department of the European Central Bank (ECB), also spend considerable time translating both internal documents and reports intended for external distribution.

One member of the language-services department is a "terminologist" who specializes in figuring out what to do with words such as "vigilance," which to an English-speaking central banker most often refers to being on the watch for inflation. The Italian version of the word, however, refers specifically to banking supervision. In Finnish, the right word for "vigilance" depends on the position of the word in a sentence. In Greek, the word is impossible to translate unless the context is clearly specified.

A Justification for Expanding the ECB's Staff

During its first year of operation, the ECB's language-services department had a staff of twenty people. By the early 2000s, however, these employees were overwhelmed. Demands on their time for oral and written translations had become unbearable.

Since 2000, the ECB has more than doubled the department's staff. In addition, it has created another separate department of "legal-linguistic specialists" who work full-time to prepare ECB legal documents for distribution in all of the European Monetary Union's various native languages.

FOR CRITICAL ANALYSIS: Under what circumstances could linguistic miscommunications actually result in monetary policy mistakes?

unaddressed, including the proper relationship between the Fed and the Treasury, the full extent of the chair's authority, and the ultimate economic goals that the Fed should pursue. Much of the Fed's history since 1935 reflects its efforts to deal with these issues.

THE FED'S FIGHT FOR INDEPENDENCE The first leader of the new Federal Reserve System was a former Utah banker named Marriner Eccles. President Franklin Roosevelt appointed Eccles to the original Federal Reserve Board in 1934, and Eccles was instrumental in helping design and promote the reforms that Congress adopted in the Banking Act of 1935. He then served as chair of the Board of Governors until 1948. The original Federal Reserve Board building at 21st and C Streets in Washington, D.C., now bears his name because later Fed insiders credited Eccles with rescuing the Fed from "disgrace" following its performance between 1929 and 1933.

Working for the U.S. Treasury During most of Eccles's time as chair, however, the Federal Reserve essentially functioned as an unofficial unit of the Treasury

Federal Reserve–Treasury Accord: A 1951 agreement that dissociated the Fed from a previous policy of pegging Treasury bill rates at artificially low levels.

Free reserves: Total excess reserves at depository institutions minus the total amount of reserves that depository institutions have borrowed from the Fed.

Department. This was particularly true during World War II, when the Fed's open market operations were geared toward maintaining high and stable prices for Treasury securities to assist the government's efforts to raise the funds needed to finance wartime expenditures. The Fed did this by buying and selling securities as needed to "peg" Treasury bill (T-bill) yields at relatively low levels.

The Fight for Fed Independence After World War II ended, the Treasury pressured the Fed to continue this policy. The Fed, however, had become convinced that inflation, which had begun to heat up with the outbreak of the Korean conflict, would get out of control if it continued pegging T-bill yields. Behind the scenes, Fed officials successfully negotiated a settlement with the Treasury, which President Harry Truman grudgingly approved in 1951. This settlement is now called the **Federal Reserve–Treasury Accord,** or more simply "the Accord." The Accord was a joint agreement that the Fed could minimize the extent to which it "monetized" the public debt by purchasing securities as needed to keep market yields low.

Henceforth, the Fed has regarded itself as an *independent* institution *within* the government. Later presidents and Congresses would test the Fed's self-interpretation of its proper role "within the government."

"LEANING AGAINST THE WIND" In 1953 William McChesney Martin, one of the chief negotiators of the Accord, was appointed Board chair—a position he would hold until 1970. Shortly after the beginning of his long tenure, Martin announced that the Fed's purpose "is to lean against the winds of deflation or inflation, whichever way they are blowing." Later he offered an alternative description of the Fed's job of containing inflationary pressures caused by short-term overexpansion of the economy: the Fed's role, he said, "is to take away the punch bowl just when the party gets going."

During much of Martin's time at the helm, the Fed sought to stabilize the level of **free reserves,** or the difference between the total amount of excess reserves and the total quantity of reserves borrowed from the Fed's discount window. The idea behind this policy was that if banks' holdings of excess reserves were high relative to their borrowings from the Fed, then it would be easier for them to lend. In contrast, if banks were short on excess reserves relative to reserves that they owed the Fed, their ability to extend new loans to consumers and businesses would be more contained. Hence, conducting open market operations with an aim to keeping the amount of free reserves relatively stable would ensure that credit conditions would be neither too loose nor too tight.

The growing U.S. involvement in the Vietnam conflict (1964–1973) complicated the Fed's policymaking through the end of the 1960s. When President Lyndon Johnson decided in 1965 to expand the U.S. commitment of ground forces to Vietnam without increasing taxes to pay the expenses, the Fed faced renewed pressures from the president and the Treasury to keep U.S. Treasury bond yields low. At one point President Johnson summoned Martin to his Texas ranch and lectured him on the dangers of raising interest rates.

By 1968, President Johnson had decided that additional taxes would be required to fund the military expenses that the government was incurring. But by then the inflation rate had reached 5 percent, which at that time in the United

States was perceived as relatively high. In 1969, when Richard Nixon assumed the presidency, the inflation rate exceeded 6 percent.

The Technocratic Fed In 1970 President Nixon appointed a new Fed chair, Arthur Burns, a Columbia University economics professor and former adviser to President Dwight Eisenhower. Under Burns, the Federal Reserve attempted to take a more scientific approach to policymaking. The Board of Governors assigned a number of staff economists the task of developing reliable measures of monetary aggregates. Then it systematically began to frame its policymaking within the perspective of the likely effects on such aggregates as M1 and M2.

During Martin's term at the Fed, banks had begun to lend reserves in the federal funds market. By the time Burns became the Fed chief, the federal funds rate had become a widely recognized indicator of credit market conditions. A rise in the federal funds rate indicated a tightening of credit market conditions, while a fall in the federal funds rate signaled a loosening. Under Burns, however, the Fed began to use the federal funds rate as more than a policy indicator. Indeed, the Fed began to tailor its open market operations to move the federal funds rate to levels that it felt were consistent with its goals for magnitudes of the monetary aggregates. Although the Fed continued to pay close attention to the effects that its policies had on the spectrum of interest rates on other financial instruments, for the first time it also began to pay attention to the effects on the quantity of money.

Early in Burns's tenure at the Fed, the link between the dollar and gold was broken. In August 1971, President Nixon formally announced the end of the gold standard that had existed—at least officially—during most years since 1879. Although the United States had suspended its formal adherence to the gold standard during crises such as the Great Depression, this announcement finally severed entirely the tie between money and gold. Burns and other Fed officials now found themselves truly charged with anchoring the nation's currency system solely to confidence in the Fed's policymaking. This, to Burns and the Fed, was a key rationale for trying to aim Fed policies at stabilizing monetary aggregates as well as credit market conditions.

Inflation and Monetary Targeting Despite Burns's effort to cultivate a reputation as an "inflation fighter" during his eight-year stint as Board chair, the inflation rate was higher, at 8 percent, when he completed his second term. In addition, suspicions mounted that during President Nixon's 1972 reelection campaign Burns might have conspired explicitly or implicitly to stimulate the economy through loosened Fed policies. This alleged effort to help Nixon's reelection prospects, critics charged, added further to inflationary pressures caused in large measure by sharp rises in oil prices that occurred during and after 1973.

In 1978 President Jimmy Carter appointed G. William Miller as the new chair of the Fed's Board of Governors. During Miller's brief tenure of seventeen months, the inflation rate rose into double digits. In July 1979, Miller became the Treasury secretary. President Carter then appointed Paul Volcker, a long-time Fed insider and then president of the Federal Reserve Bank of New York, as the new Fed chief.

Within three months after assuming the top job at the Fed, Volcker had agreed to a new approach to monetary policy. Under the new approach, the Fed would attempt to stabilize the growth of the monetary aggregates while de-emphasizing interest rate stability. The result, not surprisingly, was that interest rates became much more volatile. What was a surprise was that the monetary aggregates actually became more variable as well. Nevertheless, on net interest rates rose and money growth slowed. Inflation was contained.

In 1982 the Fed discontinued its experiment with trying to stabilize the monetary aggregates. Its rationale was that the relationship between the aggregates and economic activity had broken down. Indeed, as we shall discuss in Chapter 20, this did occur. Fed critics, however, charged that the Fed had never really made an honest effort to contain monetary variability. They viewed the abandonment of the new approach as further evidence that the Fed was not serious about controlling the monetary aggregates.

Today's Middle-of-the-Road Fed Since 1987, the Fed has adopted yet another approach to conducting monetary policy: it attempts to stabilize the federal funds rate at a target value. In this respect, the policymaking of today's Fed is similar to the approach of the Fed under Arthur Burns. The Fed has been more successful in containing inflation in recent years, however. We shall examine recent experience with interest rate targeting in Chapter 27.

Since 1987 Alan Greenspan has been chair of the Fed's Board of Governors. To date, fewer complications have arisen during Greenspan's time in this position than occurred under several of his predecessors. Yet, within the Fed, there have been some significant changes in the way policies are formulated and implemented, which we shall also discuss in Chapter 27.

The Structure of the Fed

When Congress created the Federal Reserve in 1913 and revamped its structure in 1935, it was very mindful of traditional U.S. suspicions of the motives of central bankers and distrust of centralized authority. For this reason, Congress sought to construct a decentralized central banking institution that would be responsive to the concerns of U.S. citizens. At the same time, however, Congress recognized that a central bank should be operated by people who possess essential levels of competence in banking and finance. This meant that Congress needed to find a way to ensure that leaders of the Federal Reserve had banking and monetary policy experience. The somewhat convoluted structure of the Federal Reserve System reflects congressional efforts to trade off these conflicting objectives.

The Board of Governors

The seven Fed governors have several responsibilities. As noted above, the governors must authorize any discount rate change, and they also have the authority to set required reserve ratios within ranges established by law. In addition, the Board has oversight authority over the Federal Reserve district banks.

As noted in Chapter 14, the Fed is a key banking regulator charged with examining and supervising all state-chartered commercial banks that are members of the Federal Reserve System. The Fed also regulates the activities of bank holding companies and approves or disapproves proposed depository institution mergers, which invariably entail changes in the structure of a bank holding company.

On the Web: The Fed on the Net

What is going on at the Fed? Find a wealth of information about the Fed on the Internet, courtesy of the Fed itself. Following are Internet home page addresses for the Fed's Board of Governors and all twelve Federal Reserve banks:

Federal Reserve Source	Internet URL
Board of Governors	http://federalreserve.gov
Federal Reserve Bank of Atlanta	http://www.frbatlanta.org
Federal Reserve Bank of Boston	http://www.bos.frb.org
Federal Reserve Bank of Chicago	http://www.chicagofed.org
Federal Reserve Bank of Cleveland	http://www.clev.frb.org
Federal Reserve Bank of Dallas	http://www.dallasfed.org
Federal Reserve Bank of Kansas City	http://www.kc.frb.org
Federal Reserve Bank of Minneapolis	http://minneapolisfed.org
Federal Reserve Bank of New York	http://www.ny.frb.org
Federal Reserve Bank of Philadelphia	http://www.phil.frb.org
Federal Reserve Bank of Richmond	http://www.rich.frb.org
Federal Reserve Bank of San Francisco	http://www.frbsf.org
Federal Reserve Bank of St. Louis	http://www.stls.frb.org

The various consumer-protection laws discussed in Chapter 15 also require enforcement actions by the Board of Governors. Consequently, the Board issues regulations intended to induce depository institutions to comply with the provisions of these laws.

All seven Board governors are automatic members of the twelve-member Federal Open Market Committee. The FOMC sets policy for the Fed's open market operations, so the numerical superiority of the Board relative to the other FOMC members gives the Board considerable authority over the day-to-day conduct of monetary policy. The FOMC also oversees Fed trading in foreign exchange markets, so the Board also has major influence over the Fed's international operations.

Because the Board of Governors has so many responsibilities, the various governors typically specialize in specific areas of policymaking. Normally, one governor will have key responsibilities in bank regulation, while another specializes in foreign exchange operations. The Board also has standing and *ad hoc* subcommittees in these and other areas of its responsibilities. These subcommittees consider policy issues and then make recommendations to the full Board.

The Federal Reserve Banks

Each Federal Reserve bank is a federally chartered corporation that has a sphere of influence largely confined to its own Federal Reserve district. Figure 17-3 on the next page shows the locations of the Federal Reserve district banks.

Figure 17-4 on the following page illustrates the overall organizational structure of the Federal Reserve System. Member banks within each of the twelve districts own the equity shares of the Federal Reserve bank of their district. Ownership of these shares entitles these member banks to elect six of the nine members of the board of directors of their Federal Reserve bank. Three of the six directors elected by member banks must be bankers from small, medium-sized,

Figure 17-3
Federal Reserve District Banks.

This figure shows the locations of the twelve Federal Reserve banks and their geographic districts.

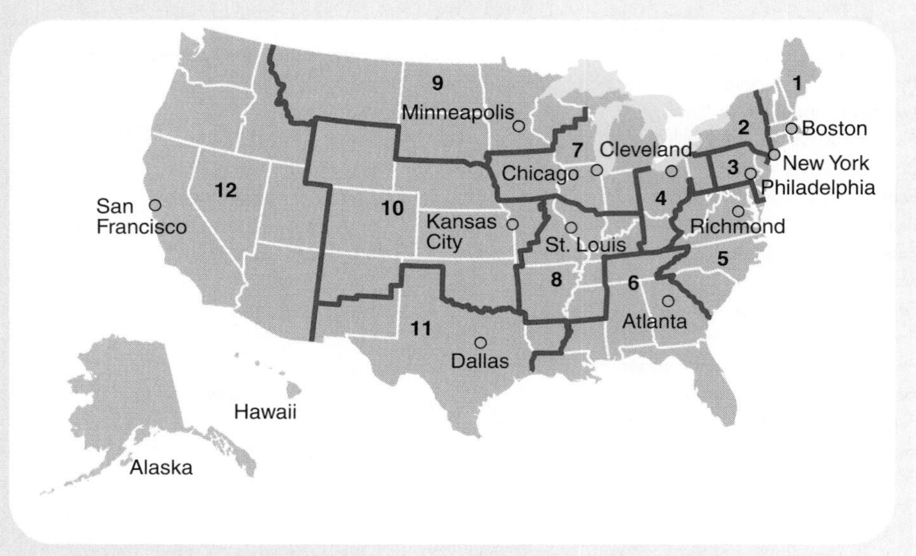

SOURCE: *Federal Reserve Bulletin*, various issues.

and large banks. The other three typically represent the interests of business or agriculture. The Board of Governors appoints the remaining three directors of each Federal Reserve bank. These directors cannot have banking connections, and the Board designates one member of this Board-appointed group as the chair of the board of directors of the Federal Reserve bank. Each Federal Reserve bank director serves for three years, and the terms are staggered so that a new director in each of the three categories is elected or appointed each year.

A key function of each Federal Reserve bank is to process electronic and nonelectronic clearings of payments. Together, then, the Federal Reserve banks and

Figure 17-4
Organizational Structure of the Federal Reserve System.

The Federal Reserve's organizational structure reflects a mixture of centralized and decentralized policymaking.

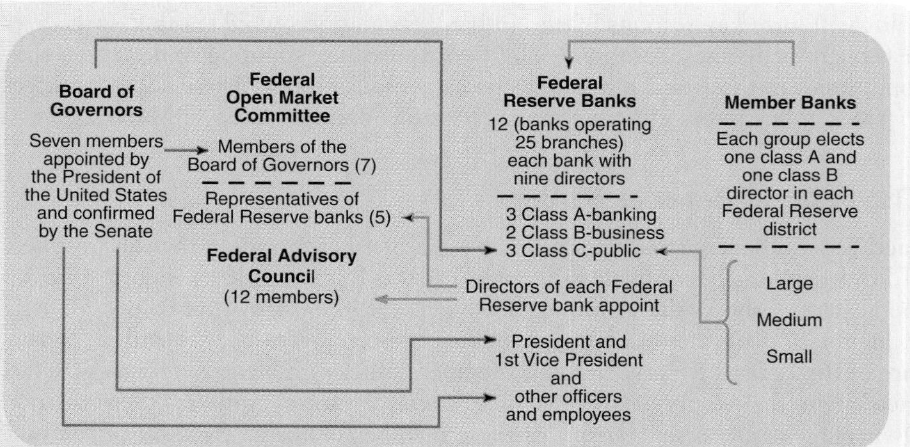

SOURCE: Board of Governors of the Federal Reserve System.

their twenty-five branches truly represent a "system" that routes payments from senders of funds to the ultimate receivers.

Although we commonly speak of the "Fed's discount window," in fact each Federal Reserve bank operates its own lending facility. Furthermore, each has its own rules and regulations for discount window lending, although these are fairly similar across the twelve district banks. Since 2002, in all districts the discount rate has been set at 1 percentage point above the market federal funds rate.

Each Federal Reserve bank president is appointed by the bank's board of directors. The presidents are chief operating officers of the district banks. All twelve presidents also have input into deliberations of the FOMC, although only five presidents serve as voting members each year.

FOMC directive: The official written instructions from the FOMC to the head of the Trading Desk at the Federal Reserve Bank of New York.

Trading Desk: The Fed's term for the office at the Federal Reserve Bank of New York that conducts open market operations on the Fed's behalf.

The Federal Open Market Committee

As noted earlier, the FOMC is composed of the seven Federal Reserve Board governors and five of the twelve district bank presidents. Because the Federal Reserve Bank of New York implements all the Fed's open market operations and foreign exchange trading, the president of this district bank is always a voting member in the FOMC. The remaining eleven district bank presidents are separated into four groups, with a member of each group qualifying to vote in the FOMC each year on a rotating basis. The chair of the Board of Governors is automatically the FOMC chair.

The FOMC holds formal meetings eight to ten times per year. At these meetings, the voting members of the FOMC determine the wording of the **FOMC directive,** or the formal instructions to the operating officers at the Federal Reserve Bank of New York who supervise open market operations and foreign exchange trading. The supervisor of open market operations is called the head of the **Trading Desk** of the New York Federal Reserve Bank. The Trading Desk is a figurative term for the office at this district bank that engages in purchases and sales of securities on the Fed's account. The head of the Trading Desk functions as the FOMC's account manager and communicates daily with designated subcommittees of FOMC members.

moneyxtra!

Online Case Study

Consider the role of the Fed chair within the Federal Reserve System by going to the Chapter 17 Case Study, entitled "The Power of the Fed Chair."

http://moneyxtra.swcollege.com

5. Who makes the key policy decisions at the Federal Reserve? Two key groups of individuals make the important policy decisions at the Fed. One of these groups is the Fed's Board of Governors, which is composed of seven people appointed by the president and approved by the Senate. The Board of Governors approves discount rate changes, sets reserve requirements, determines regulatory policies for state-chartered commercial banks that are Fed members, and regulates the activities of bank holding companies. The other main policymaking group is the Federal Open Market Committee (FOMC). The FOMC includes the Board of Governors and five of the twelve Federal Reserve bank presidents; it establishes the Fed's intentions concerning day-to-day conduct of monetary policy through open market operations. The Fed chair automatically serves as chair of the FOMC.

Link to Policy

Federal Reserve Policy on and after September 11, 2001

The terrorist attack of September 11, 2001, was an unprecedented human tragedy. It was also an event that could have had potentially serious ramifications for the U.S. financial system. Most observers agree that the Federal Reserve's actions on that day and during the days and weeks that followed averted many of the worst of the attack's conceivable consequences.

A Wide-Open Discount Window

In normal times, Federal Reserve banks are stingy with the loans they make available at the Fed's posted discount rate. By way of contrast, on September 11 and 12, Federal Reserve banks—and especially the Federal Reserve Bank of New York—were positively bursting with generosity.

Figure 17-5 displays average weekly Fed discount window lending since June 2001. As you can see, by mid-September 2001 the Fed had advanced more than $45 billion in loans to financial institutions. This was almost 800 times the average weekly amount it had extended during the period between July and early September of that year.

Unleashing a Flood of Liquidity via Open Market Operations

The Fed made liquidity available more broadly than just through loans to individual institutions at the discount window. It also purchased large volumes of securities. Most of these were repurchase agreements, or contracts stipulating that the Fed would resell the securities within a few days or a few weeks. In this way, the Fed could temporarily inject liquidity into the financial system to help avert a severe credit crunch following the terrorist attack.

Figure 17-5
Federal Reserve Discount Window Lending since June 2001.

As this chart shows, there was a huge but brief increase in Federal Reserve loans to depository institutions during the days following the September 11, 2001 terrorist attacks.

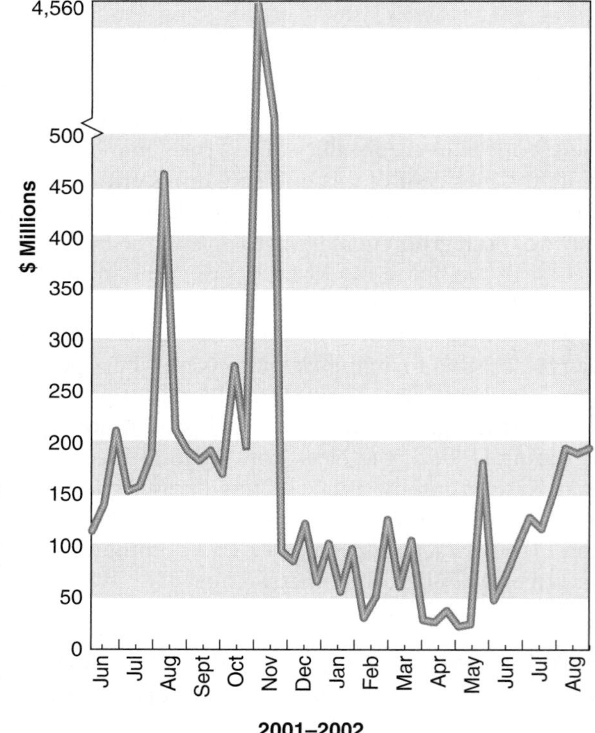

SOURCE: Board of Governors of the Federal Reserve System.

Panel (a) of Figure 17-6 compares the Federal Reserve's average holdings of repurchase agreements for the weeks from July 4 to September 5, 2001, on September 12, 2001, and on September 19, 2001. As you can see, on the day after the September 11 attack the Fed's holdings of repurchase agreements more than doubled. During the following days, the Fed sold back many of these securities. By the next week, the Fed had closed out about half of the additional repurchase agreements it had accumulated on September 12.

A Burst of Bank Reserves

As you learned in Chapter 16, an important part of the monetary base is the reserves that depository institutions hold as vault cash or on deposit with Federal Reserve banks. The two sources of reserves are loans that the Fed makes via the discount window and funds it injects via open market operations.

Panel (b) of Figure 17-6 shows that the Fed's discount window generosity and the boost in its holdings of repurchase agreements led to a huge expansion of depository institutions' reserve deposits at Federal Reserve banks. In the weeks before September 11, 2001, reserve deposits at Federal Reserve banks averaged about $19 billion, but on September 12 these deposits increased to almost $103 billion. In less than a week, however, reserve deposits at the Fed were down to close to $13 billion. By that time, what could easily have been a tremendous U.S. financial meltdown had been averted by the nation's central bank—just as the Fed's early-twentieth-century founders might have envisioned, even if none of them could have imagined the circumstances that would require a rapid response by the twenty-first-century Federal Reserve System.

Figure 17-6
Federal Reserve Holdings of Repurchase Agreements and Reserve Deposits at Federal Reserve Banks.

Panel (a) shows the large jump, relative to the average of prior weeks, in Federal Reserve holdings of repurchase agreements for the week ending September 12, 2001, the day after the terrorist attacks on New York and Washington, D.C. Panel (b) indicates the even more significant relative increase in depository institutions' reserve deposits at Federal Reserve banks during that week. This caused a substantial temporary increase in the monetary base.

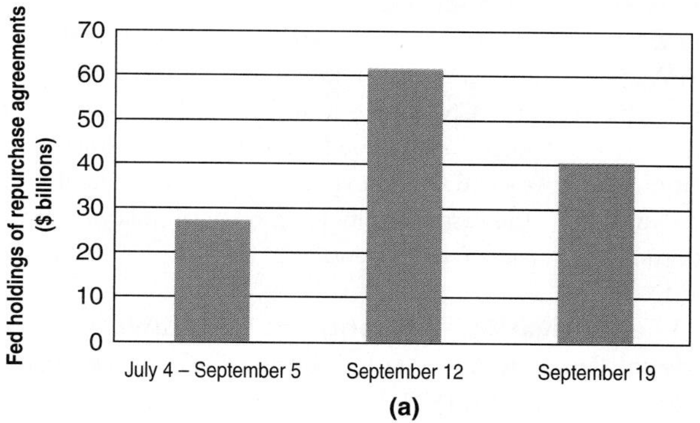

(a)

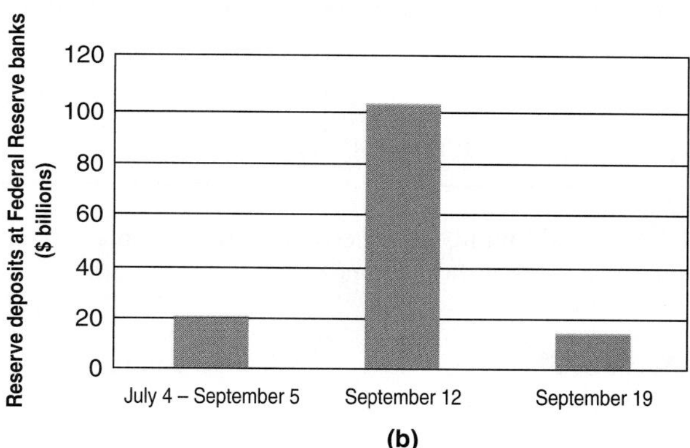

(b)

SOURCE: Board of Governors of the Federal Reserve System.

Research Project

The founders of the Federal Reserve System said that a key duty of the institution was to provide an "elastic currency" in times of crisis. What did they mean by this? Is this what the Fed did in September 2001? Have there been other instances when the Fed made sure that there was an "elastic currency"? Have there been times when the Fed has failed in this task?

Web Resources

1. How did the Fed respond to the two largest stock market crashes in history? Learn more about the 1929 and 1987 experiences in a 1987 essay by the then-president of the Federal Reserve Bank of Minneapolis at http://minneapolisfed.org/pubs/ar/ar1987.cfm.

2. Where can one find data on the discount window borrowings and reserve deposits of depository institutions? Go to the home page of the Federal Reserve's Board of Governors at http://www.federalreserve.gov, click on "Economic Research and Data, then "Statistics: Releases and Historical Data," and then select "H.4.1 Factors Affecting Bank Reserves: Releases."

Chapter Summary

1. The First Central Banking Institutions, and How U.S. Central Banking Initially Developed: Sweden and England established the first central banks. Other European nations followed suit. Today, however, the European System of Central Banks is based in part on the U.S. experience. The first U.S. central banking institutions were the First and Second Banks of the United States, which operated from 1791 to 1811 and from 1816 to 1836. Although neither developed into a full central banking institution in the modern sense, each had the ability to influence the overall volume of money and credit in the U.S. economy.

2. Responsibilities for Monetary and Banking Policies without a Central Bank in the Nineteenth and Early Twentieth Centuries: From 1837 until the Civil War, the individual states established their own banking policies, but from the Civil War onward, both the states and the federal government formulated policies regarding depository institutions. Between 1837 and the founding of the Federal Reserve in 1913, the responsibility for monetary policy rested with the U.S. Treasury Department.

3. The Motivation for Congress to Establish the Federal Reserve System: Historical experiences with banking panics in 1857, 1873, 1893, and, finally, 1907 convinced national leaders that the United States needed a central banking institution that could help stem such panics by increasing the amounts of money and credit. Congress also desired for the federal government to have its own central depository for its funds, and it wished to provide a central banking institution to help coordinate the clearing of the growing volume of payments in the nation's large industrial economy.

4. The Rationale for the 1935 Congressional Restructuring of the Federal Reserve: The Fed's lack of success in reducing the ill effects of the 1929 stock market crash and subsequent bank failures and financial panics convinced Congress that the Fed needed clearly specified lines of authority and more independence from pressures from the president and the Treasury.

5. Those Who Make the Key Policy Decisions at the Federal Reserve: Decisions concerning the discount rate, reserve requirements, and regulation of Fed member banks and bank holding companies fall within the responsibilities of the Federal Reserve's seven-member Board of Governors. Day-to-day monetary policymaking via open market purchases and sales of securities are directed by the Federal Open Market Committee (FOMC), which is composed of the Board of Governors and five Federal Reserve bank presidents. The Board chair serves as chair of the FOMC.

Questions and Problems

(Answers to odd-numbered questions and problems may be found on the Web at http://money.swcollege.com under "Student Resources.")

1. What distinguishes a central bank from a purely private bank?

2. Based on the discussion in this chapter, does it appear to you that the First and Second Banks of the United States actively conducted monetary policies? In what way could they conduct such policies, whether or not they did so on an active basis? Explain.

3. Briefly outline the history of U.S. central banking from 1791 to 1836. In your view, what were the key central banking issues during this period?

4. Given that the U.S. Treasury Department functioned without a central bank from 1837 to 1913, do you think that a central bank such as the Fed is really necessary? Support your answer.

5. Before the creation of the Federal Reserve System, monetary issues often were themes of political campaigns. Since the Fed's founding, however, such issues rarely have been discussed in campaigns. Why might this be so?

6. In what fundamental ways did the Banking Act of 1935 truly "reform" the Fed? In what ways did it leave the institution unchanged?

7. In what respects is the Fed a "private" bank? In what respects is it a government agency?

8. In what ways is the European System of Central Banks (ESCB) like today's U.S. Federal Reserve System? In what ways is it different?

9. As discussed in this chapter, a series of severe banking crises ultimately led Congress to establish the Federal Reserve System as an institution that would help prevent such crises or deal with them if they did take place. In light of the structural differences between the Fed and the ESCB, do you think that the two institutions are equally capable of carrying out this responsibility?

10. The chair of the Board of Governors has considerable authority. What are the advantages and disadvantages of placing so much power with one individual?

Before the Test

Test your understanding of the material covered in this chapter by taking the Chapter 17 interactive quiz at http://money.swcollege.com.

Online Application

Internet URL: http://www.bis.org

Title: The Bank for International Settlements

Navigation: At the above home page address, click on "About BIS." Then, in the left margin, click on "BIS Profile."

Application: Read the discussion, and answer the following questions:

1. Who owns the BIS, and what are its key functions?
2. In what ways is the BIS like a central bank? In what ways is it not a central bank?

For Group Study and Analysis: Go back to the BIS home page, and click on "Links to Central Banks." This facility provides links to a number of central banks around the world. Distribute countries (perhaps by geographic region) to groups of students to explore for information about the structure and functions of the central banks. Reconvene the entire class, and review the differences and similarities across this large set of central banks.

Selected References and Further Reading

Capie, Forrest, Charles Goodhart, Stanley Fischer, and Norbert Schnadt, eds. *The Future of Central Banking: The Tercentenary Symposium of the Bank of England.* Cambridge: Cambridge University Press, 1994.

Clarke, M. St. Clair, and D. A. Hall. *Legislative and Documentary History of the Bank of the United States.* New York: Augustus Kelley Publishers, 1967 (first published in 1832).

Giuseppi, John. *The Bank of England.* London: Evands Brothers, 1966.

Goodhart, Charles. *The Evolution of Central Banks.* Cambridge, Mass.: MIT Press, 1988.

Grieder, William. *Secrets of the Temple: How the Federal Reserve Runs the Country.* New York: Simon & Schuster, 1987.

Hammond, Bray. *Banks and Politics in America.* Princeton: Princeton University Press, 1957 and 1985.

Havrilesky, Thomas. *The Pressures on American Monetary Policy.* Boston: Kluwer, 1993.

Kettl, Donald. *Leadership at the Fed*. New Haven: Yale University Press, 1986.

Smith, Vera. *The Rationale of Central Banking*. Indianapolis: Liberty Press, 1990 (first published in 1936).

Timberlake, Richard. *Monetary Policy in the United States: An Intellectual and Institutional History.* Chicago: University of Chicago Press, 1993.

MoneyXtra

moneyxtra! Log on to the MoneyXtra Web site now (http://moneyxtra.swcollege.com) for additional learning resources such as practice quizzes, case studies, readings, and additional economic applications.

Chapter 18

The Federal Reserve and the Financial System

Imagine that you are a central bank official facing the following nightmare scenario. A major U.S. bank sells several billion yen to a Japanese bank for dollars for settlement in two days. Fund managers at the U.S. bank transfer the yen to Tokyo, only to discover too late that the Japanese bank has collapsed and will never be able to pay up. Then rumors spread through global financial markets that Japan's banks are on the verge of bankruptcy, a major U.S. bank is reeling from losses, and other U.S. banks with connections to that bank will be at risk if it fails to honor its own agreements. Immediately, other banks refuse to trade with all the affected banks or to transfer funds to complete earlier deals.

In fact, something very much like this nightmare scenario has already taken place. On June 26, 1974, Bankhaus I.D. Herstatt, a major German bank, collapsed before it could make large volumes of scheduled foreign exchange payments. Interbank settlements across the Atlantic were thrown into chaos. As word spread that a number of U.S. banks had failed to receive scheduled payments from Herstatt, other U.S. banks became reluctant to agree to payment transactions with banks suspected of trading with the German bank. Within a few hours, interbank payment flows among large U.S. depository institutions had nearly become gridlocked. Eventually, teams of accountants from private banks and central banks around the globe unraveled a complex web of interbank payment transactions. Within a couple of days, the flow of interbank payments returned to normal levels, but central bankers will never forget the day that Herstatt collapsed—or stop worrying about what might transpire if an even larger bank fails.

Fundamental Issues

1. What are the main assets and liabilities of the Fed?
2. In what ways is the Fed the government's bank?
3. What is the rationale for the Fed's role as a bank for private banks?
4. Why does the Fed play a supervisory role in the U.S. payment system?
5. In what ways do payment-system risks span national borders, and how do central banks seek to contain these risks?

Private banks process trillions of dollars of payments each day. So do central banks. Indeed, central banks themselves provide a number of payment services to private depository institutions. A key subject of this chapter is why central banks such as the Federal Reserve are in the business of processing payments and regulating the mechanisms by which private individuals, firms, and institutions settle payment transactions.

The Fed as a Central Bank

As you learned in Chapter 17, the Federal Reserve System is a complex public-policy institution. It is also a very large bank with twelve district "branches," twenty-five "sub-branches," and a "central office" in Washington, D.C. Before we get too wrapped up in the broader public-policy aspects of the Fed, let's begin by considering its banking operations.

The Fed's Balance Sheet

Each of the Federal Reserve banks has its own detailed balance sheet, as does the Board of Governors in Washington, D.C. The best way to gain a concrete understanding of the Fed's activities, however, is to examine the Fed's *consolidated balance sheet,* which is a T-account that displays the combined assets, liabilities, and equity capital for all units of the Federal Reserve System.

THE FED'S ASSETS Table 18-1 displays the Fed's consolidated balance sheet. The table displays both absolute dollar values and percentages relative to total assets and to total liabilities and net worth. You should concentrate on the percentages, because dollar amounts change considerably over time, whereas the Fed's proportionate allocations of its assets and of its liabilities and equity capital tend to remain relatively stable.

1. **Treasury securities.** U.S. Treasury securities comprise the most important category of Fed assets. The 86.1 percent figure in Table 18-1 is a typical proportionate allocation of assets to government securities. About 80 percent of these government securities are Treasury bills and notes (maturities under ten years), and the remainder are Treasury bonds (maturities exceeding ten years).
2. **U.S. agency securities.** In addition to securities issued by the U.S. Treasury, the Fed holds debt instruments issued by other U.S. government agencies. These securities account for a small and typically stable fraction of Fed assets.
3. **Discount window loans.** The Federal Reserve also lends to private depository institutions via the discount window facilities of the Federal Reserve banks. As Table 18-1 indicates, the dollar amount of discount window lending and the proportionate asset allocation to such lending are very small.
4. **Gold certificates.** These assets remain on the Fed's balance sheet as a constant reminder of the nation's former adherence to a gold standard. When the gold standard was in operation, the Treasury Department sold

Table 18-1 The Consolidated Balance Sheet of the Federal Reserve System ($ Millions, as of April 30, 2002)

Assets			Liabilities and Capital		
Asset	Dollar Amount	Percentage of Total Assets	Liability	Dollar Amount	Percentage of of Total Liabilities and Equity
U.S. Treasury securities	$581,308	86.1%	Federal Reserve notes	$613,166	90.8%
U.S. agency securities	10	—	Bank reserve deposits	27,495	4.1%
Discount window loans	72	—	U.S. Treasury deposits	5,387	0.8%
Gold and SDR certificates	13,244	2.0%	Foreign official deposits	—	—
Foreign currency reserves	14,872	2.2%	Deferred credit items	9,621	1.4%
Cash items in process of collection	9,541	1.4%	Other liabilities	11,543	1.7%
Other assets	56,221	8.3%			
			Total liabilities	667,212	98.8%
			Equity capital	8,056	1.2%
Total assets	**$675,268**	**100.0%**	**Total liabilities and capital**	**$675,268**	**100.0%**

SOURCE: Board of Governors of the Federal Reserve System, *Federal Reserve Bulletin*, July 2002.

gold to the Fed in exchange for money. The Treasury issued gold certificates to the Fed to indicate the Fed's ownership of the gold that the Treasury continued to hold in reserve. Hence, these certificates are Fed assets. As a share of total assets, however, they continue to decline over time as the absolute size of the Fed's assets increases with time.

5. Special Drawing Right (SDR) certificates. SDRs are assets issued by the International Monetary Fund (IMF), which is a financial institution that over 150 countries own and operate. In the 1970s, the IMF issued SDRs as a type of international currency intended to compensate for the declining role of gold as a basis for the world's currency system. The United States is an IMF member nation, and the Treasury owns shares in the IMF via SDRs. The Treasury financed these SDR shares by issuing a fixed dollar amount of SDR certificates to the Fed. Consequently, SDR certificates, like gold certificates, constitute a Fed asset category that continues to decline in relative importance.

6. Foreign currency reserves. The Fed maintains a portfolio of assets denominated in the currencies of other nations. A key reason that the Fed holds these foreign-currency-denominated securities and deposits is so that it can trade them when it desires to try to change the dollar's value in foreign exchange markets. We shall have more to say about this in Chapters 25 and 28.

7. Cash items in the process of collection. Finally, like any other bank (see Chapter 11), the Federal Reserve receives payments from other parties that it credits to its account but which have not yet "cleared" the payment system. Because such payments may be subject to cancellation until that time, the Fed lists them as *cash items in the process of collection.*

THE FED'S LIABILITIES AND EQUITY CAPITAL The Federal Reserve has several liabilities and its own special source of equity capital.

1. Federal Reserve notes. Over four-fifths of the Federal Reserve's total liabilities and equity capital is composed of *Federal Reserve notes.* These are the currency that the Fed issues and that we use to make most of our small purchases of goods and services. As a liability, Federal Reserve notes indicate that the Fed "owes" us something in exchange for these notes. Before the early 1930s, if you had sought to redeem a $1 Federal Reserve note at a Federal Reserve bank, you could have received gold in exchange. Now, however, you would receive a new $1 Federal Reserve note. So in what sense is this note really a liability? The answer is that if Congress were to close down the Federal Reserve System, the Fed would be liable to you for a dollar's worth of goods and services as of the time of its closure.

2. Bank reserve deposits. The second-largest liability of the Fed is reserve deposits of depository institutions. As we discussed in Chapter 16, depository institutions hold the bulk of these deposits to meet legal requirements established by the Fed. Depository institutions hold a small portion of these deposits as excess reserves, however. They often lend such reserves to one another in the federal funds market.

3. U.S. Treasury deposits. Another deposit liability of the Fed is composed of deposits of the U.S. Treasury. The Treasury draws on these funds to make payments such as purchases of goods and services or tax refunds.

4. Foreign official deposits. Foreign governments or official foreign financial institutions, including central banks such as the Bank of England or the Bank of Japan, hold dollar-denominated deposit accounts with the Fed. These are *foreign official deposits.* Many of these accounts are checking accounts, and foreign governments and central banks draw upon these accounts when they need to make dollar payments.

5. Deferred availability cash items. These are payments that the Fed has promised to another party or that it has made but which have yet to "clear."

6. Equity capital. The Fed's equity capital is composed of the ownership shares of banks that are members of the Federal Reserve System. At 1.2 percent, the Fed's equity capital is very low in relation to its assets.

1. What are the main assets and liabilities of the Fed? The primary assets of the Fed are U.S. government securities, including Treasury bills, notes, and bonds. The main liabilities are Federal Reserve notes, or currency, and reserve deposits of depository institutions.

Treasury tax and loan (TT&L) accounts: U.S. Treasury checking accounts at private depository institutions.

Fiscal agent: A term describing the Federal Reserve's role as an agent of the U.S. Treasury Department, on whose behalf the Fed issues, services, and redeems debts.

The Fed as the Government's Bank

As we noted in Chapter 17, one original rationale for the creation of the Federal Reserve System in 1913 was the government's "need" for a central bank. As the main banking institution for the U.S. government, the Fed provides depository services to the Treasury. It also performs an important role as the Treasury's *fiscal agent* in financial markets.

GOVERNMENT DEPOSITORY The U.S. Treasury holds deposits at each of the twelve Federal Reserve banks. As depositories of the Treasury, the Federal Reserve banks maintain the Treasury's accounts, clear checks drawn on those accounts, accept deposits of federal fees and taxes, and make electronic payments on the Treasury's behalf.

The Treasury also holds deposit accounts at private depository institutions. Many of these are **Treasury tax and loan (TT&L) accounts,** which are special checking accounts that the Treasury maintains with private institutions. Another key function of the Federal Reserve banks is to serve as TT&L account "go-betweens" on the Treasury's behalf. In this capacity, the Federal Reserve banks add to or draw from these TT&L accounts at other depository institutions on the Treasury's behalf to assist the Treasury in managing its cash.

Most Treasury payments to citizens and businesses flow from Federal Reserve bank deposits. The Federal Reserve banks handle payments that the Treasury disburses on a regular basis, such as Social Security benefits and salaries to federal employees, by making direct deposits into the recipients' accounts. Since 1991 the number of Fed-processed direct-deposit Treasury payments has exceeded the number of payments that the Treasury makes by check.

FISCAL AGENT The Federal Reserve functions as the key **fiscal agent** of the U.S. Treasury Department, meaning that it issues, services, and redeems debts on the Treasury's behalf. The Treasury issues debt instruments—bills, notes, and bonds—that the government uses to cover any shortfalls between its tax receipts and its expenditures on goods and services. The Treasury issues these securities at auctions. Although the Treasury announces the terms and conditions of the securities to be sold at the auctions, potential buyers submit bids for new securities to the Federal Reserve banks as well as to the Treasury's Bureau of the Public Debt. As the Treasury's fiscal agent, the Federal Reserve banks tabulate and summarize all bids and review them to ensure that they meet legal requirements. The Federal Reserve banks also issue the Treasury's securities to the purchasers and process the payments that the purchasers provide in exchange.

To facilitate the transfer of securities, the Federal Reserve banks operate two *book-entry security systems*. These are computer systems through which the Fed maintains records of Treasury sales and interest and principal payments on its securities. Most financial institutions that purchase large volumes of Treasury securities do not actually hold paper securities; instead, they maintain computerized accounts with the Fed. The Fed provides holders of these accounts with regular statements and automatically transfers interest and principal into their accounts.

When an institution wishes to sell Treasury securities to which it has title, it typically does not send paper securities to the buyer. Instead, it instructs the Federal Reserve bank that maintains its book-entry security account to transfer its title of ownership from its account to the book-entry security account of the purchasing institution. The Fed then makes the transfer electronically. Large institutions typically initiate such transfers using direct computer links with Federal Reserve banks. Smaller institutions initiate transfers by telephone using computer modems and software that the Fed has developed for this purpose.

The Federal Reserve also sells and delivers *U.S. savings bonds* on the Treasury's behalf. These are low-denomination, nonmarketable Treasury securities that are popular instruments for many small savers. The Federal Reserve also credits interest on savings bonds when holders redeem them at authorized depository institutions.

2. In what ways is the Fed the government's bank? The Fed is the main depository institution for the federal government. It also serves as the government's fiscal agent by operating the systems through which the Treasury sells new securities and makes interest and principal payments on outstanding securities.

THE FED'S INCOME AND EXPENSES One thorny issue for the Fed has been that the Treasury does not pay in full for the services that the Fed provides. Typically, the Treasury reimburses the Federal Reserve banks for only about a third of the costs that they incur in providing government depository services or acting as the Treasury's fiscal agent.

Where does the Fed get the funds to cover the unreimbursed expenses that it incurs on the Treasury's behalf? Recall that over four-fifths of the Fed's assets are U.S. government securities. These yield a steady flow of interest to the Fed and constitute its primary source of income. The Fed uses much of this income to fund its operations.

The Fed's other main source of income is the fees that it charges depository institutions for services that it provides. Since 1981 this fee income has increased steadily as the Fed has continued to charge private depository institutions for the services that it offers as a "bank for bankers."

The Fed as the Banker's Bank

Another justification that Congress provided for creating the Fed was a perceived need for a government-related institution that would centralize, oversee, and regulate the payment systems of the geographically dispersed U.S. economy. Congress also felt that such an institution was needed to function as a *lender of last resort* for depository institutions suffering temporary liquidity problems that might pose short-term threats to their individual solvency and to the broader stability of the financial system.

Externalities: Spillovers from the interactions of one set of individuals to others who otherwise are not involved in the transactions.

Negative externality: A reduction in the welfare of one individual caused by a transaction between other parties, even though the individual is not directly involved in the transaction.

Lender of last resort: An institution that is willing and able to lend to any temporarily illiquid but otherwise solvent institution to prevent its illiquid position from leading to a general loss of confidence in that institution or in others.

DO BANKS NEED A CENTRAL BANK? Congress answered "yes" to this question when it authorized the formation of the Fed. A common reason given for the Fed's role in the banking system is that private depository institutions *need* a central bank. The key rationale for such a "need" is the perception that financial markets are subject to **externalities,** or situations in which transactions between two parties can spill over to affect others. The classic externality is pollution, such as noise pollution. If you are *not* an enthusiast, say, of country-western or rap music, yet your neighbors on either side of your apartment or house enjoy purchasing and playing such music at loud volumes, then you likely suffer a **negative externality.** Even though the companies that produce and sell such music benefit from the sales and your neighbors benefit from consuming the music, you find yourself worse off as a result of the transactions between these parties.

Likewise, it is arguable that many financial transactions can generate externalities, many of which could be negative. For instance, suppose that an individual owes you money but cannot pay you until he completes a transaction with another party. If something goes awry in that other transaction, then you will be worse off even though you were not a direct party to the transaction. You experience a negative externality effect because the failure of that transaction to take place causes you to fail to get a payment that you had counted on receiving.

A key justification for a central bank, therefore, is to supervise and regulate the processes and systems by which consumers, businesses, and financial institutions exchange payments. According to this view, financial institutions "need" a central bank to keep systems by which payments are exchanged operating smoothly on a day-to-day basis and to repair any breakdowns in these systems as they occur.

LENDER OF LAST RESORT The most dramatic sort of financial breakdown is a bank run, in which large numbers of depositors lose confidence in the ability of depository institutions to retain their asset values and seek to liquidate their accounts, thereby driving large numbers of institutions into insolvency (see Chapter 2). A key justification for the formation of the Federal Reserve System was that the Fed would prevent such runs from occurring by serving as the financial system's **lender of last resort.** This is a central banking institution that stands ready to lend to any temporarily illiquid but otherwise solvent institution to prevent its illiquidity from leading to a general loss of confidence that can set off a "run on the bank."

Under the provisions of the original Federal Reserve Act, a key duty of the Fed is to provide lender-of-last-resort assistance when needed. As amended by the Banking Act of 1935, the Federal Reserve Act authorizes the Fed to lend to *anyone* if it believes doing so is necessary to prevent a financial crisis. In practice, however, the Fed restricts itself to loans to depository financial institutions that find themselves caught in temporary "liquidity crunches."

3. What is the rationale for the Fed's role as a bank for private banks? The key rationale is the possibility for negative externalities, or spillovers, that exists in the financial system. Because financial transactions among depository institutions and others are interconnected, there is a potential for bank runs and other crises. As a supervisory authority and lender of last resort, the Fed can potentially reduce the possibilities that such events might occur.

Cyberbanking, the Fed, and the U.S. Payment System

When an individual makes a transaction using currency, the transaction is final at the moment that the exchange of currency for a good, service, or asset takes place. In contrast, transactions with other means of payment, such as checks or wire transfers, are final only after depository institutions transfer funds from the account of the purchaser to the seller. Using these other means of payment, therefore, requires parties to a transaction to rely upon depository institutions as intermediaries in the nation's **payment system.** This is the institutional structure through which individuals, businesses, governments, and financial institutions make payments.

The Federal Reserve System is a significant part of the payment system of the United States. The Fed also monitors and regulates a significant portion of the payment system that it does not directly supervise and operate. Before we discuss the Fed's roles in the payment system, however, let's consider the current structure of the system.

Retail Payments

Today's payment system is a fascinating mix of old and new. As we discussed in Chapter 1, nonelectronic means of payment such as currency and checks account for about 98 percent of all transactions in the United States. At the same time, however, electronic payments account for approximately 85 percent of the *dollar value* of all transactions. This means that although U.S. residents continue to use currency and checks for the large number of low-value transactions that they make each day, they have adopted electronic payments as the primary means of conducting their less frequent but large-value transactions.

The U.S. payment system has two components. One consists of the various mechanisms for processing *retail payments,* which are funds transfers for transactions of relatively "small" value—tens of thousands of dollars or less. Consumer transactions with merchants account for the bulk of retail payments. The other component of the payment system consists of the electronic delivery systems that process large-value transactions (described later in the chapter).

Payment system: A term that refers broadly to the set of mechanisms by which consumers, businesses, governments, and financial institutions exchange payments.

NONELECTRONIC PAYMENTS In terms of number of transactions, the most popular means of retail payment in the United States are decidedly nonelectronic paper notes and coins. Such currency transactions alone make up over three-fourths of *all* U.S. transactions. Hence, the bulk of transactions in the U.S. economy remain very "low-tech." Nevertheless, currency transactions are quite small on average, so small that together they account for less than 0.5 percent of the total dollar value of all exchanges in the United States. Think of all the times you make minor purchases of such low-ticket items as candy bars or pens or pencils, and you will understand why this is the case.

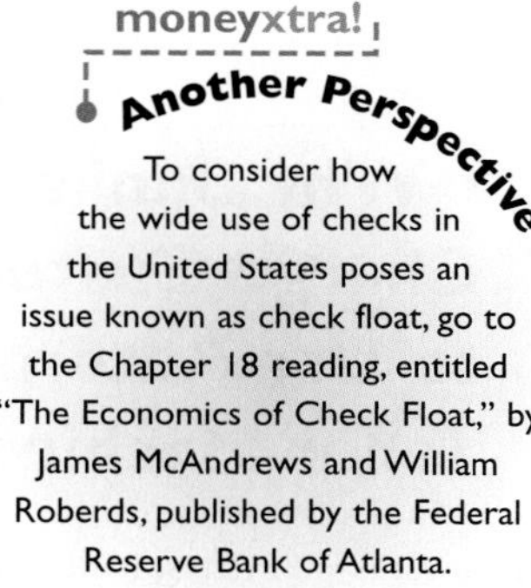

Checks are the second most popular payment medium, accounting for a little under a fifth of all transactions and just below 15 percent of the total dollar value of all exchanges. Depository institutions clear millions of checks each day, for a total of more than 65 billion in a year. This is possible because nearly all checks have magnetic ink encryptions that special machines can read. This permits the machines to sort and distribute checks automatically. They can also process information for crediting and debiting accounts. This large-scale automation of check sorting, accounting, and distribution has kept the per check cost of clearing checks very low.

Other nonelectronic means of payment include money orders, traveler's checks, and credit cards. Together these make up less than 1 percent of both the total number of transactions and the dollar value of all transactions.

CONSUMER-ORIENTED ELECTRONIC PAYMENT SYSTEMS There now are several consumer-oriented electronic payment mechanisms. Most U.S. consumers have experience using *automated teller machine (ATM) networks,* which are depository institution computer terminals activated by magnetically encoded bank cards. There are more than 150,000 ATMs in the United States. On average, consumers perform about 100,000 transactions each year at a typical ATM, for an annual total of nearly 15 billion ATM transactions. Many consumers use ATM networks to make deposits, obtain cash from checking and savings accounts, and transfer funds among accounts. A growing number of consumers also pay some of their bills using ATM networks. A recent innovation in ATM technology is the "Personal Touch" ATM, which offers visual contact with depository institution employees at another location. Using such ATM links, consumers now can apply for loans and mortgages, purchase mutual funds, and obtain information about loan and deposit terms and rates. (No consumer likes paying fees on ATM transactions, and some municipalities have even tried to eliminate them, but banks have reasons to charge these fees; see on the following page *Management Focus: Why Banks Charge Customers to Use Automated Teller Machines.*)

Automated clearing houses (ACHs) are another type of consumer-oriented electronic payment mechanism. These are computer-based clearing and settlement facilities for the interchange of credits and debits via electronic messages instead of checks. ACHs process payments within one or two days after the request for a transfer of funds. Very common ACH transfers are automatic payroll deposits, in which businesses make wage and salary payments directly into employees' deposit accounts. The federal government also makes large use of ACH facilities. The Social Security Administration distributes many payments to Social Security beneficiaries via ACH direct-deposit mechanisms. In addition, the government disperses a growing portion of welfare and food stamp payments using an *electronic benefits transfer (EBT) system.* An EBT system functions like an ACH system but looks a lot like an ATM network to welfare and food stamp beneficiaries, because they receive their welfare funds or food stamps from special cash or food stamp disbursement machines.

On the Web
How do ACH systems function? Find out by visiting the Web site of the National Automated Clearing House Association at http://www.nacha.org, where you can click on "About Us" for a summary and "Resources" for links to many other informative Web sites.

GLOBAL POLICY CYBER MANAGEMENT **Focus**

Why Banks Charge Customers to Use Automated Teller Machines

Several U.S. cities, including New York City, Newark, San Francisco, and Santa Monica, have sought to ban fees that depository institutions charge on transactions at automated teller machines. So far these and other cities have had little success in convincing courts that they have the legal authority to regulate ATM fees. Time after time state and federal courts have ruled that depository institutions can charge fees to cover the costs of providing ATM services.

In fact, this is how depository institutions use most of the revenues generated via ATM fees. As Figure 18-1 indicates, the costs of electronic information transfers on ATMs are a very small part of the total expenses associated with operating the machines. More than 40 percent of ATM fees go simply to cover the costs of maintaining the machines and replacing worn-out parts.

A particularly common fee associated with ATM use is the "ATM surcharge." This is a fee that a depository institution charges for processing a transaction using an ATM card issued by another depository institution. Expenses for processing these types of ATM transactions can range from 30 cents to well over a dollar, depending on whether the other depository institution is part of the same ATM network or uses a completely different system. It is not surprising, therefore, that depository institutions assess ATM surcharges.

FOR CRITICAL ANALYSIS: If depository institutions compete in perfectly competitive markets but cities are able to ban ATM fees and surcharges, what do you think would happen to the quantity and quality of ATMs available for use by depository institution customers in those locales?

Figure 18-1
Average Expense Allocations of ATM Fees at Depository Institutions.

This figure shows the average allocations of depository institutions' expenses on ATM machines and networks.

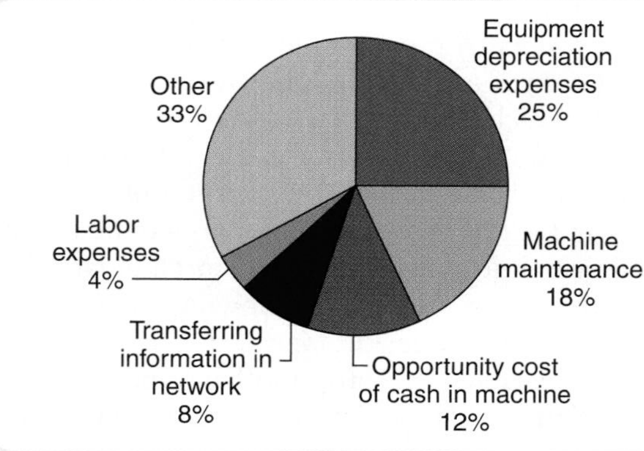

SOURCE: Office of the Comptroller of the Currency.

Point-of-sale (POS) networks: Systems in which consumers pay for retail purchases through direct deductions from their deposit accounts at depository institutions.

Since the 1970s technology has permitted the use of **point-of-sale (POS) networks.** These systems permit consumers to pay for purchases on the spot via direct deductions from their deposit accounts at depository institutions. POS networks have not developed as quickly as some observers had expected, even though most large chains of department stores and other retail outlets use networks of cash-register terminals that have the capability of processing POS payments. The costs of setting up POS systems can be significant, and it has never been clear who would be willing to incur these costs. Check-processing costs have remained so low that depository institutions have had little incentive to switch to POS networks, and retailers have had little desire to incur the cost of installing the systems. If POS networks become more widespread in the future, it is likely that it will be because consumers desire to use them—and to pay for them. Recent trends toward greater consumer use of online banking via the Internet may lead to greater consumer interest in POS networks in future years.

IS THE UNITED STATES BEHIND THE "POWER CURVE"? In Chapter 2 we discussed a number of ongoing cybertechnology developments in the U.S. financial system. In spite of these developments, however, U.S. consumers use paper-based, nonelectronic—mainly check—transactions much more than people in most other nations. As Table 18-2 indicates, the average U.S. resident made 234 such transactions each year in the mid-1990s—3 to 100 times more than residents of other nations.

Table 18-2 shows that residents of many other industrialized countries, except Italy, use electronic means of payment much more regularly than residents of the United States. One traditionally popular retail payment mechanism in many European nations is *electronic giro* systems, in which banks, post offices, and other payment intermediaries transfer funds via telephone lines or other forms of electronic communication. This eliminates the need for paper checks and for ACH networks. Europeans have also been more receptive to adopting stored-value cards, and a number of current smart-card projects are under way in European locales.

Wholesale Payments

Consumer-oriented electronic payment systems account for a growing portion of both the number and the dollar value of transactions. Yet, even though online banking, stored-value cards, and smart cards continue to make inroads,

Table 18-2 Annual Noncash Transactions Per Person in Selected Countries

Country	Number of Transactions Per Person: Paper-Based	Electronic	Percentage Electronic Payments
Switzerland	2	65	97%
Netherlands	19	128	87
Belgium	16	85	84
Denmark	24	100	81
Japan	9	31	78
Germany	36	103	74
Sweden	24	68	74
Finland	40	81	67
United Kingdom	7	58	50
France	86	71	45
Canada	76	53	41
Norway	58	40	41
Italy	23	6	20
United States	234	59	20

SOURCE: David Humphrey, Lawrence Pulley, and Jukka Vesala, "Cash, Paper, and Electronic Payments: A Cross-Country Analysis," *Journal of Money, Credit, and Banking* 28 (November 1996, Part 2): 914–939.

Large-value wire transfer systems: Payment systems such as Fedwire and CHIPS that permit the electronic transmission of large dollar sums.

Fedwire: A large-value wire transfer system operated by the Federal Reserve that is open to all depository institutions that legally must maintain required reserves with the Fed.

Clearing House Interbank Payment System (CHIPS): A large-value wire transfer system that links about ninety depository institutions and permits them to transmit large dollar sums relating primarily to foreign exchange and Eurodollar transactions.

electronically processed retail payments make up small fractions of both classifications. Currently, most payments accomplished via electronic delivery systems are *wholesale payments,* which are large-value transactions typically denominated in the hundreds of thousands or millions of dollars.

LARGE-VALUE ELECTRONIC PAYMENT SYSTEMS The delivery systems for processing wholesale payments are **large-value wire transfer systems,** which are designed and operated specifically to manage electronic transfers of large sums. Large-value wire transfer systems transfer nearly 85 percent of the value of all payments initiated by consumers, businesses, governments, and financial institutions. Nevertheless, these systems handle less than 1 percent of the total number of transactions. Clearly, they truly specialize in transferring large transactions.

In the United States, there are two key large-value wire transfer systems. One is **Fedwire,** which is operated by the Federal Reserve System. All depository institutions that must hold reserves at Federal Reserve banks have access to Fedwire, although fewer than 2,000 institutions regularly use the system. Depository institutions pay fees for the wire transfer services that Fedwire provides, and they use Fedwire mainly for two specific kinds of transfer.

One of the main uses of Fedwire is for book-entry security transactions. As discussed above, the Fed operates book-entry security systems on behalf of the Treasury. Fedwire is the means by which depository institutions pay for the securities that they purchase using these systems. The second primary use of Fedwire is for funds transfers among the reserve deposit accounts that depository institutions maintain at Federal Reserve banks. When depository institutions extend or repay federal funds loans to other depository institutions, they send the funds on Fedwire. The average Fedwire payment is over $3 million, and the total average daily payment volume on the Fedwire system is nearly $1 trillion ($1,000,000,000,000).

The other major large-value wire transfer system in the United States is the **Clearing House Interbank Payment System (CHIPS).** This is a privately owned system operated by the New York Clearing House Association, which has about ninety member depository institutions. These institutions typically transfer funds for foreign exchange and Eurodollar transactions using CHIPS, and the average value of a CHIPS transaction is more than $6 million. The average daily payment volume on CHIPS is now about $1.5 trillion.

Table 18-3 lists the world's major large-value wire transfer systems and provides estimates of the number of transactions and flows of funds on these systems, which are similar in structure to Fedwire and CHIPS. For instance, the Bank of Japan's BOJ-NET system and the European Central Bank's TARGET system are analogous to Fedwire, and the European Banking Association's Euro-1 system and the British CHAPS system perform functions similar to those provided by CHIPS.

On the Web

How many Fedwire transactions took place in the latest quarter? To track Fedwire data, go to the Federal Reserve's home page at http://www.federalreserve.gov, click on "Payment Systems," and then, under "Payment Services," click on "Fedwire and Net Settlement."

The Rationale for Fed Supervision: Payment-System Risks

Any financial transaction entails some degree of risk. When you accept a payment in currency, for instance, there is always a small chance that the bills that you receive might be counterfeit. Yet, unless you are in the habit of making large

Table 18-3 The World's Key Large-Value Wire Transfer Systems

Country/Payment System	Transactions (Millions)	Value ($ Trillions)
European Monetary Union		
TARGET	53.7	$322.8
Euro-1	28.6	51.2
Japan		
Zengin	5.0	84.9
BOJ-NET	15.9	540.9
United Kingdom		
CHAPS	27.8	58.8
United States		
Fedwire	112.4	423.9
CHIPS	60.4	311.7

SOURCES: Payment systems' statistical publications, various issues, 2002.

cash transactions, your risk of loss in a typical exchange where currency is the means of payment is fairly small. In the multimillion-dollar transactions on Fedwire and CHIPS, however, the dollar risks are much more significant. For this reason, the Federal Reserve is closely involved in monitoring and regulating CHIPS in addition to operating and supervising Fedwire.

Three types of risk arise in any payment system: *liquidity risk, credit risk,* and *systemic risk*. A key function of financial institutions and markets is to intermediate such risks. Nevertheless, as we discuss below, systemic risk may entail significant externalities for financial institutions and others who use large-value payment mechanisms. As we noted earlier, the existence of such externalities is a key rationale for the involvement of a central bank, such as the Fed, in a nation's financial system.

LIQUIDITY RISK People do not always make payments on time. The risk of loss because payments may not be received when they are due is called **liquidity risk.** Losses arising from late payments may be in the form of opportunity costs, in that the late funds could have been used for other purposes. Sometimes the losses are more explicit. For instance, late receipt of a payment may complicate one's ability to honor another financial commitment.

The existence of liquidity risk accounts in large measure for the development of large-value wire transfer systems such as Fedwire and CHIPS. Before computer technology made such electronic mechanisms possible, depository institutions had to rely on hand delivery by courier or postal services. Sometimes delays occurred that generated significant implicit or explicit costs for these institutions. Wire transfers can be initiated within minutes. Once initiated, they are almost instantaneous.

Liquidity risk: The risk of loss that may occur if a payment is not received when due.

CREDIT RISK In many transactions, one party to the transaction makes good on her end of the deal before the other party reciprocates. This means that she has effectively extended credit to the other party, thereby exposing herself to **credit risk,** or the possibility that the other party will fail to honor fully the terms of the exchange.

Credit risk: The risk of loss that might occur if one party to an exchange fails to honor the terms under which the exchange was to take place.

Systemic risk: The risk that some depository institutions may not be able to meet the terms of their credit agreements because of failures by other institutions to settle transactions that otherwise are not related.

One type of credit risk is *market risk,* which arises when one party to a financial exchange fails to honor the terms of the exchange because of some change in condition that makes fulfilling the bargain impossible. In such a situation, the two parties typically must get together and renegotiate the terms of the exchange, which causes the party that had honored its side of the bargain to incur a loss. Another form of credit risk is *delivery risk,* which is the possibility that one party in a financial transaction will fail entirely to honor the terms of the exchange. In such a situation, the other party to the transaction loses the entire value of the transfer.

Large-value wire transfer systems have elaborate rules intended to reduce participating institutions' exposures to both kinds of credit risk. These rules spell out the responsibilities of both parties to a wire transfer and the role of the system in adjudicating disputes concerning failure to settle a transaction in a timely fashion.

SYSTEMIC RISK Participants in large-value wire transfer systems are interconnected, which can cause payment flows among depository institutions to be interdependent. For instance, a bank in San Francisco anticipating a wire transfer from a New York bank at 12:30 eastern standard time (EST) may agree to wire funds to a bank in Chicago at 12:45 EST. The Chicago bank, in turn, may have committed to wire funds to a Los Angeles bank at 1:00 EST, using the funds that it expects to receive from the San Francisco bank. Thus, if the New York bank fails to deliver the funds promised at 12:30 EST to the San Francisco bank, the latter bank may send funds to Chicago at 12:45 EST that it does not really have. Furthermore, if the New York bank finds that it is unable to send the funds at all, then an entire chain of payments may occur even though the institutions involved do not have sufficient funds to cover the payments.

The risk that the New York bank will fail to settle its transaction with the bank in San Francisco is a liquidity or credit risk for the San Francisco bank. But for the Chicago and Los Angeles banks, it is **systemic risk.** This is a risk that some depository institutions, such as the Chicago and Los Angeles banks in our example, may be unable to honor credit agreements because of settlement failures in otherwise unrelated transactions. For these institutions, systemic risk is a negative externality that arises as a result of the interdependence of transactions in the payment system. It is the existence of such negative externalities that the Fed seeks to address via its supervisory role in the payment system. (Depository institutions are willing to take on liquidity, credit, and systemic risks because payments-related activities generate a large portion of their revenues; see *Management Focus: The Payoff from Payment Intermediation.*)

4. Why does the Fed play a supervisory role in the U.S. payment system? Although most transactions in the U.S. payment system involve cash or checks, the bulk of the dollar flows occur using large-value wire transfer systems. Because such systems link depository institutions in complex webs of payment flows, there is a potential for large negative externalities, or systemic risk. The Fed supervises these systems in an effort to reduce the extent of this risk.

GLOBAL | POLICY | CYBER | MANAGEMENT **Focus**

The Payoff from Payment Intermediation

As you learned in Chapter 2, a *payment intermediary* is an institution that assists the transmission of funds between a buyer and a seller. Even though payment intermediation has traditionally been a large part of the business of depository institutions, the amount that this aspect of their operations contributes to the bottom line has often been hard for economists to determine.

A study by Lawrence Radecki of the Federal Reserve Bank of New York attempted to determine banks' payoffs from providing payments-related services to their customers. Radecki studied the income statements of the twenty-five largest U.S. bank holding companies and attempted to estimate the revenues generated via three payments-related functions: funds transfers for deposit holders, credit-card payment processing, and securities payment processing. Figure 18-2 displays his estimates of the sources of operating revenues across all twenty-five banking institutions.

Radecki estimated that revenues derived from payment intermediation amounted to about 38 percent of the institutions' combined operating revenues. The banks earned about three-fourths of these payment-related revenues from providing basic funds transfers for their depositors. These services accounted for about 28 percent of operating revenues. Revenues the banks derived from processing funds transfers for credit-card and securities transactions accounted for as much as 10 percent of their total operating revenues.

For Critical Analysis: Why do banks function as both financial intermediaries and payment intermediaries?

Figure 18-2
Sources of Operating Revenues for the Top Twenty-Five U.S. Bank Holding Companies.

Revenues that banks earn from providing payments services account for a significant portion of their total revenues.

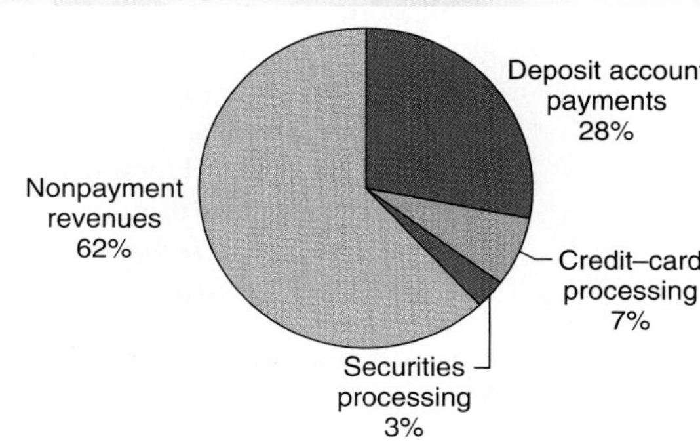

SOURCE: Lawrence Radecki, "Banks' Payment-Driven Revenues," Federal Reserve Bank of New York *Economic Policy Review* 5 (2, July 1999): 53–70.

Globally Linked Payments: Where Do Central Banks Fit In?

As noted in the opening to this chapter, systemic risk spans national borders. Thus, the Federal Reserve is not the only institution that frets over systemic risk in the payment system. Systemic risk is of concern to central banks throughout the world.

Herstatt risk: The risk of any form of loss due to payment settlement failures that occur across national borders; named after a German bank that collapsed in 1974.

International Payment Risks

When Germany's Bankhaus I.D. Herstatt collapsed on June 26, 1974, German regulators closed the bank down at 3:30 P.M. Frankfurt time—after the bank had received foreign currency payments from banks based elsewhere in Europe but *before* the bank had made dollar payments that it owed to banks in the United States. After all the accounting had been unraveled in the days following Herstatt's collapse, several U.S. banks determined that together they had lost as much as $200 million. The Herstatt episode unsettled U.S. financial markets, and several payment systems in other countries, including the United States, temporarily shut down.

HERSTATT RISK Ever since this event, bankers and central bank officials have broadly referred to international payment-system risks as **Herstatt risk.** This term describes the risk of any form of loss due to payment settlement failures that occur across national boundaries.

Herstatt risk actually encompasses two forms of risk that arise primarily from payment processing relating to foreign currency transactions between payment intermediaries based in different countries. First, Herstatt risk refers in part to the direct liquidity and credit risks that payment intermediaries take on when they agree to receive payments from institutions located in other nations in different time zones. For the U.S. banks that had to wait for millions of dollars of payments or that experienced outright losses when Herstatt collapsed in 1974, these direct payment risks turned out to be significant.

Second, and more broadly, Herstatt risk refers to the systemic risks owing to global linkages among national payment systems. Because large payment intermediaries around the globe may be separated by significant time differences, these intermediaries face the potential that events occurring in one time zone, such as the German Herstatt failure, may have broader effects on the functioning of payment systems in another time zone. In this sense, Herstatt risk constitutes an *international externality* that arguably requires the cooperative supervisory and regulatory efforts of many central banks.

THE FOREIGN EXCHANGE MARKET, HERSTATT RISK, AND NETTING ARRANGEMENTS Most cross-border payment transactions arise from trading in the world's foreign exchange markets. As a result of this trading, individual institutions experience considerable exposure to both liquidity and credit risk. Indeed, current estimates are that foreign exchange settlements account for 50 percent of the daily volume of the U.S., British, and European Monetary Union payment systems. When Herstatt failed in mid-1974, the average dollar value of a currency trade was $750,000. Today, the value of a typical currency exchange in the foreign exchange market is $10 million. Undoubtedly, the upper limit on the systemic-risk exposure arising from foreign exchange transactions is only a fraction of the $4 trillion in aggregate daily currency trading in the world's foreign exchange markets, but even a small fraction of $4 trillion is a risk of considerable magnitude.

In recent years, central banks have advised bank managers to tighten and better police their systems for internal funds transfers, promote sound risk-management practices, and set up contingency plans for crisis management. In addition, they have called upon banks to establish *netting arrangements,* in which a bank tallies its trades with another bank during the course of a day and then makes (or receives) a single payment for the net amount of each currency it owes (or is owed by) that bank at the end of the day. Netting significantly reduces the amount of payment transactions among banks. Consequently, if one institution fails to deliver, its trading partners lose only the smaller, net amount owed, not the gross value of all trades with the failed bank.

Free-rider problem: A situation in which some individuals take advantage of the fact that others are willing to pay for a jointly utilized good, such as a system of multilateral netting of foreign exchange payments.

Even before central banks began pushing for increased foreign exchange netting, banks had begun to respond to the growing liquidity and credit risks that they faced. During the 1990s, a number of banks established their own *bilateral netting* deals, which are one-to-one netting arrangements between banks. Some banks use netting services that supply proprietary computer software that keeps track of net flows of currency transactions. Accord, which is operated by the Society for Worldwide Interbank Financial Telecommunications (known as "Swift"), is an example of a bilateral netting system.

In addition, banks have set up *multilateral netting* arrangements, which extend netting deals to a number of institutions. For instance, the Exchange Clearing House, Ltd., operates a multilateral netting service for fifteen large European banks, and several large U.S. and Canadian banks operate a similar system called Multinet.

THE "FREE-RIDER PROBLEM" Multilateral netting arrangements are used jointly by the participating institutions. Setup costs are a significant portion of the cost of a multilateral netting system. Once the system has been established, the day-to-day operating costs are relatively low.

As a result, multilateral netting systems often experience a **free-rider problem,** which occurs when some participants in a joint system such as multilateral currency netting take advantage of the fact that other participants have already shouldered the burden of establishing the arrangements. In 1996, for instance, a banker was quoted as saying, "If somebody is going to go to all the trouble of setting up a clearing bank [for multilateral currency settlement] and you can join later, let him pay the expense."

The free-rider problem in foreign currency netting is a further justification offered for the involvement of central banks in the payment system. For profit-maximizing private banks, the free-rider problem reduces the incentive to incur the sizable costs of establishing a system that they know "free-riders" will benefit from in the future. In the case of currency payment netting, however, which spans national boundaries, there is a rationale for central banks to *coordinate* their efforts. Thus, the free-rider problem in international payments processing has been a major incentive for central banks to work together to contain global payment-system risks.

DEALING WITH THE FREE-RIDER PROBLEM Taking the lead in this joint central bank effort has been the *Bank for International Settlements (BIS)*. This institution, which is based in Basel, Switzerland, has functioned for several decades as a trustee for various international loan agreements and serves as an agent in miscellaneous foreign exchange markets for many of the world's central banks. Private American banks, including Citibank and J.P. Morgan, participated with governments of the Group of Ten (G10) nations—Belgium, Canada, France, Germany, Italy, Japan, the Netherlands, Sweden, the United Kingdom, and the United States—in founding the BIS in 1930, and a number of private banks continue to own shares of ownership in the BIS. The original task of the BIS was to supervise the settlement of financial claims among European nations relating to World War I. After World War II, the BIS became a central agent for clearing payments among nations participating in the European Recovery Program, which was designed to rebuild European economies after the ravages of the war.

Ultimately, the BIS developed into a clearing house providing information to the central banks of the G10 nations plus the Bank of Switzerland, the Swiss central bank. Staff members of the BIS organize periodic briefings for top G10 central banking officials and coordinate conferences for staff economists of policymaking agencies of the G10 nations. As we discussed in Chapter 14, in 1988 central banks and other banking regulators of the G10 nations adopted the *Basel Agreement* establishing common risk-based bank capital standards under the auspices of the BIS. Today the BIS also serves as a mechanism for coordinating central bank efforts to establish multilateral netting systems for international payment flows.

A recent result of these efforts is a new currency payment settlement system called the *Continuous Linked Settlement (CLS) Bank,* which was established in 1997. Although the BIS and its member central banks helped initiate the formation of the CLS Bank, thereby absorbing some of its initial setup costs, the CLS Bank is a private institution. It is formally based in the United States, but the main site of its operations is London. The CLS Bank holds currency settlement accounts with G10 central banks and other central banks around the world, and it conducts continuous daily currency settlements on behalf of the largest banks in the world. The CLS Bank formally began its operations in 2000.

Common Payment-System Standards

In an international context, difficulties in payment-system settlements may arise because of different rules and legalities applying to transactions that cross from one nation's large-value wire transfer system to a system located in another country. For example, a U.S. payment intermediary may use CHIPS to transmit a payment to a Hong Kong bank that is a member of the British CHAPS system. These two large-value wire transfer systems may have slightly different rules about settling payments. In addition, the U.S., British, and Hong Kong legal systems may also have somewhat divergent perspectives on the duties and responsibilities of parties to an exchange of funds.

To consider the issues raised by different means of settling payments, go to the Chapter 18 Case Study, entitled "Time to Eliminate Daylight Overdrafts on Fedwire?"

http://moneyxtra.swcollege.com

To address the possibility of problems arising from international cross-system payment transfers, the BIS has assisted in the development of a common set of rules called the *Lamfalussy standards.* These standards clarify the essential legal payment responsibilities of any payment intermediary that participates in a large-value wire transfer system operated within a G10 nation. Furthermore, all large-value wire transfer systems have agreed to operate within the framework of rules established under the Lamfalussy standards.

5. In what ways do payment-system risks span national borders, and how do central banks seek to contain these risks? Payments relating to foreign-exchange-market transactions account for the bulk of international payment-system risks. Bankers and central bank officials refer to these specific risks collectively as Herstatt risk. Most efforts to contain Herstatt risk focus on limiting the magnitude of risk exposures through bilateral and multilateral netting of payments among banks that actively trade currencies in the foreign exchange market. Central banks and the Bank for International Settlements have assisted in establishing net settlement systems, and these institutions have also been at the forefront of developing common standards for international payment systems.

Link to Policy

Just How Many Daylight Overdrafts Are Too Many?

Although depository institutions very rarely fail to settle their obligations on Fedwire and CHIPS, it is not at all uncommon for some institutions to send wire transfer payments when they do not have the funds on hand to cover those payments. This practice contributed to the major complications that arose when Herstatt Bank failed in 1974. Many U.S. banks had already sent payment messages on Fedwire and CHIPS assuming that they would be able to use funds coming from Herstatt to cover some of those payments.

Daylight Overdrafts

Depository institutions can do this if final settlement of payments does not occur until the conclusion of each business day. As long as institutions can settle their accounts at the end of the day, there is nothing to stop them from sending wire transfer payments even though they do not have funds to honor the payments at the time; when they do this, they overdraw their reserve deposit accounts at Federal Reserve banks. The Fed calls such Fedwire or CHIPS payment overdraws of reserve deposit accounts *daylight overdrafts*.

Panel (a) of Figure 18-3 displays the typical pattern of daylight overdrafts by a depository institution that engages in such behavior. This institution runs a steady stream of overdrafts beginning at around 10:00 A.M., so its reserve account balance at a Federal Reserve bank becomes negative shortly after that time. Just before 2:00 its total overdrafts reach their "peak," and the institution's reserve balance reaches its greatest negative value for the day. As the afternoon progresses, the institution begins to receive funds transfers from other institutions, perhaps as it borrows funds in the federal funds market. Shortly before 4:00, the institution's reserve account balance once again becomes positive.

Fed Policies to Reduce Daylight Overdrafts

Daylight overdrafts on Fedwire have exposed the Fed to sizable credit risks. In the late 1980s, peak daylight overdrafts amounted to nearly three times the size of the total reserves of all depository institutions, and it was not unusual for as many as a thousand depository institutions to overdraw their Fed deposit accounts within a given day.

In April 1994, the Fed began to charge an interest fee quoted on an annual basis, based on a 360-day year and the 18-hour days that Fedwire is open. From April 1994 until April 1995, this fee was equal to 24 *basis points* on each dollar of overdrafts above the permitted deductible, which the Fed established in recognition of the fact that some amount of overdrafts is unavoidable. Because one basis point equals 0.01 percent, this fee amounted to an annual interest charge of 24 hundredths of 1 percent.

As panel (b) of Figure 18-3 indicates, both average and peak overdrafts fell dramatically after the Fed began charging for them. In hopes of reducing daylight overdrafts even further, in April 1995 the Fed raised the fee to 27 basis points. Nevertheless, peak and average overdrafts have shown slight upward trends since 2000.

Net Payment Settlement versus Real-Time Gross Settlement

Some economists think that the real problem is that the operators of U.S. large-value payment systems permit daylight overdrafts at all. In Europe, most large-value payment systems use *real-time gross settlement*, in which a payment directly alters a bank's reserve account at the moment the system transmits the payment. In a real-time gross settlement system, daylight overdrafts cannot occur unless the operator of the system chooses to permit them. Otherwise, if a bank initiates a payment that would cause it to incur a daylight overdraft, it immediately exhausts its reserve balances; the bank

Continued on next page

Link to Policy, continued

is then required to convert other assets into cash to make good on its payment.

CHIPS uses a multilateral netting system for interbank payment clearing, as does the CLS Bank for clearing foreign-exchange-market payments. Nevertheless, both institutions now use sophisticated techniques for matching payments that considerably reduce the size of the banks' "net positions" and significantly cut the time between initiation and clearing of net interbank debts. Cybertechnologies are quickly making real-time settlement a means of limiting exposure to risks arising from daylight overdrafts. Fedwire is a real-time gross settlement system, but the Federal Reserve *chooses* to permit daylight overdrafts. This makes Fedwire more liquid but exposes the Fed to greater payment-system risks.

Research Project

Why do daylight overdrafts on Fedwire expose the Fed to credit risk? Why might the Fed nonetheless conclude that it is better to permit positive daylight overdrafts for a fee than to prohibit daylight overdrafts altogether?

Web Resources

1. What are the Fed's current policies regarding payment-system risk? Learn more about this topic by going to the Federal Reserve's home page at http://federalreserve.gov. Click on "Payment Systems," and then under "Payment Policies," click on "Payment System Risk."

2. What are the most recent volumes of Fedwire daylight overdrafts? Follow the steps above, and then click on "Daylight Overdrafts and Related Fees: April 27, 1994 to Present—Data." (Note that these are current-dollar figures based on an 18-hour trading day, whereas the data in Figure 18-3 are in 1995 dollars and are based on the 10-hour days that were relevant in the 1980s.)

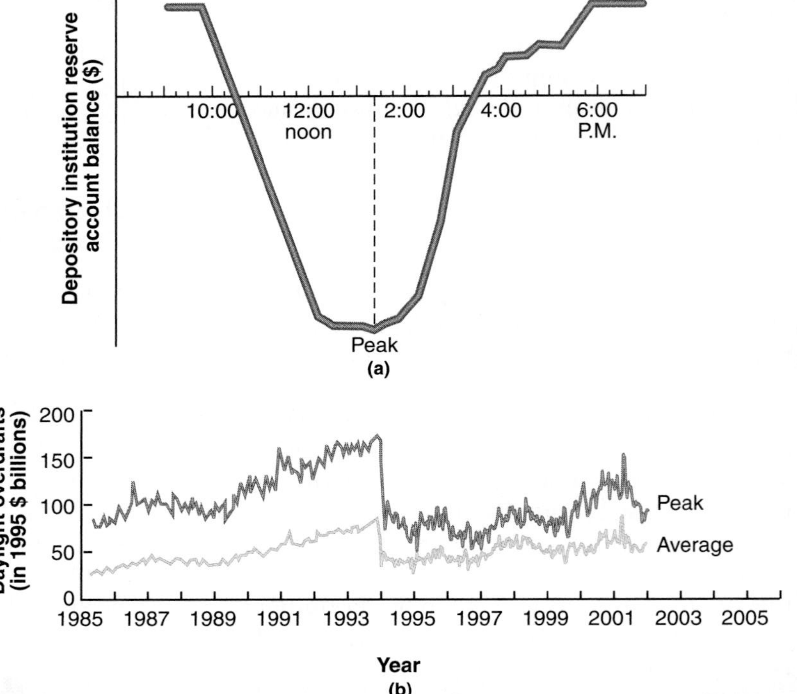

Figure 18-3
Daylight Overdrafts.

Panel (a) shows the typical pattern of daylight overdrafts for a large U.S. bank that overdraws its reserve account shortly after the regular business day begins, experiences peak overdrafts early in the afternoon, and then begins to receive funds from other sources until its reserve balance is positive by the end of the day. Panel (b) displays the average and peak volumes of reserve account overdrafts by depository institutions at all twelve Federal Reserve banks.

SOURCES: Board of Governors of the Federal Reserve System and Diana Hancock and James Wilcox, "Intraday Bank Reserve Management: The Effects of Caps and Fees on Daylight Overdrafts," *Journal of Money, Credit and Banking* 28 (2, November 1996): 870–908; Board of Governors of the Federal Reserve System.

Chapter Summary

1. The Main Assets and Liabilities of the Fed: Over four-fifths of the Fed's assets are its holdings of government securities. An even larger portion of its liabilities consists of the currency that it issues and reserve deposits of depository institutions, which together compose the monetary base.

2. Ways in Which the Fed Is the Government's Bank: The Treasury maintains large deposits with the Federal Reserve banks, which provide a number of depository services to the Treasury. In addition, the Fed issues securities on the Treasury's behalf, and it maintains book-entry security accounts through which the Treasury makes payments of interest and principal to large institutional holders of government securities.

3. The Rationale for the Fed's Role as a Bank for Private Banks: Because depository institutions are interconnected, breakdowns in transactions among a few institutions can spill over to create hardships for a large number of institutions. A key role for the Fed, therefore, is to contain the potential for such negative externalities in the financial system.

4. The Reason the Fed Plays a Supervisory Role in the U.S. Payment System: Most dollar flows in the U.S. payment system are large-value wire transfers on Fedwire and the Clearing House Interbank Payment System (CHIPS). These two systems together connect thousands of depository institutions. Although the systems increase the efficiency with which depository institutions can make transactions, they also expose the institutions to systemic risk, or the possibility of significant negative externalities arising from spillovers from a few institutions to many. The Fed monitors and supervises the payment system in an effort to contain these risks.

5. How Payment-System Risks Span National Borders, and How Central Banks Seek to Contain These Risks: Transfers of payments for foreign-exchange-market transactions generate the majority of international payment-system risks, which together are called Herstatt risk. Central banks, alone and together through the Bank for International Settlements (BIS), have promoted bilateral and multilateral netting of foreign-exchange-market payments as a key means of reducing banks' exposures to Herstatt risk. Central banks and the BIS have also pushed the development of common international standards for the world's major payment systems.

Questions and Problems

(Answers to odd-numbered questions and problems may be found on the Web at http://money.swcollege.com under "Student Resources.")

1. Explain in what sense currency is a liability of the Federal Reserve System.

2. What are the Fed's key roles as a central bank? In your view, what is the single most important role of a central bank? Could the Fed perform this role without performing its other roles? Explain your reasoning.

3. In your own words, define a negative externality. Explain how such externalities can arise in the financial system.

4. Any depository institution that is required to hold reserves with the Federal Reserve System has access to Fedwire. By way of contrast, the owners of CHIPS determine which institutions can join CHIPS and make use of its facilities; thus, the owners can require member institutions to provide information about their internal management procedures for handling risk. Some economists have speculated that these structural differences alone tend to make CHIPS a less risky large-value wire transfer system. Does this argument make sense to you? Why or why not? [Hint: Think back to the asymmetric-information problems of financial intermediation discussed in Chapter 3.]

5. Can you see any ways that the Federal Reserve's direct involvement in the U.S. payment system, via its operation of Fedwire and its own check-clearing and automated clearing house systems, assists it in its efforts to monitor and supervise the overall payment system? Explain.

6. Privately operated institutions that offer their own payment services often complain that the Fed has an "inherent competitive advantage." Sometimes they even claim that the Fed's business interest in its own payment systems can expose it to a conflict of interest in its role as a supervisor of the U.S. payment system. In your view, could these concerns have any merit? Why or why not?

7. Discuss the three basic ways that payment intermediaries are exposed to Herstatt risk arising from payments relating to foreign-exchange-market transactions. [Hint: Recall the three types of payment-system risks, and evaluate how these can arise in an international setting.]

8. Explain why net currency settlement helps reduce payment intermediaries' total exposures to Herstatt risk.

9. How can multilateral net settlement systems give rise to a free-rider problem?

10. In your view, is the free-rider problem likely to be sufficiently great to justify the involvement of central banks?

Before the Test

Test your understanding of the material covered in this chapter by taking the Chapter 18 interactive quiz at http://money.swcollege.com.

Online Application

Internet URL: http://www.chips.org

Title: The Clearing House Interbank Payment System

Navigation: Begin at the above Web site. In the left-hand margin of the CHIPS home page, click on "About Us." Then, in the "For More Information" box, select "click here" to download the PDF CHIPS brochure.

Application: Read the brochure, and answer the following questions:

1. How does CHIPS limit credit risk?

2. What types of real-time settlement procedures does CHIPS use in an effort to contain settlement risks?

For Group Study and Analysis: Divide the class into six groups. Assign each group one of the six Lamfalussy objectives, and have each group examine and summarize ways in which CHIPS has sought to meet each objective. In addition, ask each group to speculate about ways in which CHIPS still may experience problems in meeting each objective.

Selected References and Further Reading

Bank for International Settlements. *Real-Time Gross Settlement Systems.* Basel, Switzerland: March 1997.

Berger, Allen, Diana Hancock, and Jeffrey Marquardt, eds. "Payment Systems Research and Public Policy: Risk, Efficiency, and Innovation." Federal Reserve Board Conference on Payment Systems Research and Public Policy, *Journal of Money, Credit, and Banking* 28 (Special Issue, November 1996).

Chakravorti, Sujit, and Timothy McHugh. "Why Do We Use So Many Checks?" Federal Reserve Bank of Chicago *Economic Perspectives,* Third Quarter 2002, pp. 44–59.

DeBrandt, Olivier, and Philipp Hartmann. "Systemic Risk: A Survey." European Central Bank Working Paper No. 5, November 2000.

Eisenbeis, Robert. "International Settlements: A New Source of Systemic Risk?" Federal Reserve Bank of Atlanta *Economic Review* 82 (Second Quarter 1997): 44–50.

Fokerts-Landau, David, Peter Garber, and Dirk Schoenmaker. "The Reform of Wholesale Payment Systems and Its Impact on Financial Markets." *International Monetary Fund Working Paper,* #WP/96/37, April 1996.

Furfine, Craig, and Jeffrey Stehm. "Analyzing Alternative Daylight Credit Policies in Real-Time Gross Settlement Systems." *Journal of Money, Credit, and Banking* 30 (November 1998): 832–848.

Gilbert, Adam, Dara Hunt, and Kenneth Winch. "Creating an Integrated Payment System: The Evolution of Fedwire." Federal Reserve Bank of New York *Economic Policy Review,* July 1997, pp. 1–7.

Green, Edward, and Richard Todd. "Thoughts on the Fed's Role in the Payment System." Federal Reserve Bank of Minneapolis *Quarterly Review* 25 (Winter 2001): 12–27.

Hancock, Diana, and David Humphrey. "Payment Transactions, Instruments, and Systems: A Survey." *Journal of Banking and Finance* 21 (December 1997): 1573–1624.

McAndrews, James, and Samira Rajan. "The Timing and Funding of Fedwire Funds Transfers." Federal Reserve Bank of New York *Economic Policy Review,* July 2000, pp. 17–32.

Stavins, Joanna. "A Comparison of Social Costs and Benefits of Paper Check Presentment and ECP with Truncation." Federal Reserve Bank of Boston *New England Economic Review,* July/August 1997, pp. 27–44.

VanHoose, David. "Bank Behavior, Interest Rate Determination, and Monetary Policy in a Financial System with an Intraday Federal Funds Market." *Journal of Banking and Finance* 15 (April 1991): 343–365.

______. "Central Bank Policymaking in Competing Payment Systems." *Atlantic Economic Journal* 28 (June 2000): 117–139.

MoneyXtra

moneyxtra! Log on to the MoneyXtra Web site now (**http://moneyxtra.swcollege.com**) for additional learning resources such as practice quizzes, case studies, readings, and additional economic applications.

Unit V
Monetary Policy and the Economy

CONTENTS

Chapter 19

How Much Money Do People Want to Hold?—
The Demand for Money

Fundamental Issues

1. What is the Cambridge equation?
2. What are real money balances?
3. According to the inventory theory of the demand for money, what are the key factors influencing desired holdings of real money balances?
4. What do other transactions-related theories add to our understanding of the demand for money?
5. What theories explain the demand for real money balances based on money's function as a store of value?
6. What difficulties do economists face in trying to predict the overall demand for money?

How much money would you like to have on hand? The answer, of course, seems obvious: As much as possible! If this question is qualified, however, by adding the phrase "given your available income and wealth," then the answer is not so apparent. After all, you surely do not hold as much money as possible, because then you would have converted all your possessions to cash. Most of us choose to allocate only a fraction of our income or wealth to holding various forms of money, such as currency and checking deposits.

Economists have conducted hundreds of studies trying to identify the key factors that determine how much money residents of the United States and other nations desire to hold. So many studies have been conducted on this topic that economists sometimes refer to them as an "industry."

Most theories of the demand for money indicate that two key factors affecting how much money people wish to hold are the incomes that people earn and the interest rates on bonds and other financial instruments that they can hold instead of or alongside various forms of money. Nevertheless, economists have not reached a consensus about exactly how the public's total holdings of money respond to changes in incomes or interest rates. Some economists worry that it may never be possible to determine just how responsive total desired money holdings are to these key factors.

Why do so many economists study the determinants of the demand for money? Why are incomes and interest rates thought to be key factors affecting the public's desired money holdings? What aspects of the relationships between incomes and interest rates and the quantity of money demanded make it difficult for economists to agree on just how much influence these factors have on the amount of money people want to have on hand? These are the fundamental questions addressed in this chapter.

Transactions motive: The desire to hold currency and transactions deposits to use as media of exchange in planned transactions.

Portfolio motive: The desire to hold money as part of a strategy of balancing the expected rate of return on money with rates of return on other assets.

The Motives for Holding Money

When the subject of the demand for money comes up today, most economists think of the early-twentieth-century British economist John Maynard Keynes. Keynes tried to identify people's fundamental *motives* for holding coins, pieces of paper, and bank accounts that offer little or no financial return. One of these he called the **transactions motive.** This is the incentive to hold non-interest-bearing currency and non- (or low-) interest-bearing transactions deposits for use as media of exchange in planned transactions, such as buying groceries each week and paying rent and utility bills each month.

In addition, Keynes proposed a *speculative motive* for holding real money balances. The more modern term for this incentive to hold money is the **portfolio motive,** which refers to the demand for money as one item in a broad portfolio of assets, based on expected relative rates of return. The portfolio motive, therefore, relates to money's role as a store of value. (A few people are *too* motivated to obtain cash; see on the next page *Policy Focus: Confronting Counterfeit Currency.*)

In this chapter we shall consider these motives and their implications for the overall demand for money in an economy. In addition, we shall consider how economists seek to measure total desired money holdings in an economy. We shall also evaluate the predictability of the overall demand for money. As you will learn in the next chapter, there are good reasons that economists—particularly those who work at the Federal Reserve—may wish to predict the demand for money.

The Transactions Demand for Money

Following earlier economic tradition, Keynes argued that total income is a key determinant of total desired money holdings. As income rises, Keynes concluded, so does the total quantity of money demanded to satisfy the transactions motive for holding money as a medium of exchange. Let's think about why this is likely to be the case and about whether we can be more specific in predicting *exactly* how much money a person is likely to hold relative to his or her income.

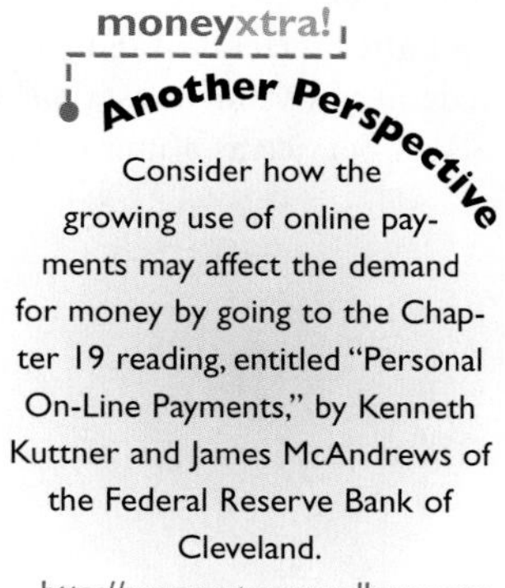

The Demand for Money as a Medium of Exchange

Several components of common measures of money, such as currency and transactions deposits, either have no interest yields or pay interest at lower rates than alternative instruments. Why would anyone hold these money assets? The reason, as we discussed in Chapter 1, is that individuals and business firms use such money assets as media of exchange.

THE CAMBRIDGE EQUATION Because people use money assets to buy other goods and services, their demand for such assets as media of exchange depends on how many purchases they plan to make. This, of course, depends on their ability to spend, which in turn depends on their incomes.

A simple way to express this idea is through a relationship called the *Cambridge equation,* which is named for economists at Cambridge University in

GLOBAL | POLICY Focus | CYBER | MANAGEMENT

Confronting Counterfeit Currency

Counterfeiting within U.S. territory first took place during colonial days; courthouse records document the trials of persons charged with manufacturing or passing counterfeit money. During the American Revolution, the British sought to undermine the fledgling colonial government by counterfeiting its Continental currency. Although the colonial government did its part to oversupply the currency, the British efforts helped push its value so low that the phrase "not worth a Continental" became a way of expressing disdain for an item's market value. At least a third of the currency in circulation in the United States during the Civil War was counterfeit, and after the end of that war, the federal government established the Secret Service as a unit of the Treasury Department and charged it with confronting and suppressing the efforts of counterfeiters.

In the past, counterfeiters designed their own versions of the engraving on legal currency notes and attempted to print their own bills. Today, counterfeiters use computers and color printers and copiers to create nearly half of all bogus notes. This approach to counterfeiting has the advantage of exactly duplicating the engraving visible on real bills but continues to suffer from difficulties in reproducing the quality of the paper used in legal currency. In addition, the printing on photocopied notes appears dull and lifeless when compared with an actual bill.

At present, the Secret Service estimates that about $400 million in phony currency circulates in the United States. In an effort to combat the use of digital technologies to produce counterfeit notes, the Treasury Department recently established the Against Digital Counterfeiting (ADC) program, which is administered by a committee made up of representatives from the Treasury, the Secret Service, the Bureau of Engraving and Printing, and the Federal Reserve. One of the main goals of the ADC program is to encourage private producers of printers and scanners to design software capable of using a preprogrammed checklist of suspicious features to halt the printing or scanning of an object. A Japanese company called Omron Electronics, for example, has developed printer driver programs that automatically halt the printing of items that have a size, color, pattern, or print quality that matches known features of several major currencies.

FOR CRITICAL ANALYSIS: What incentive do manufacturers of printers and scanners have to incorporate software capable of detecting counterfeiting efforts into the programs that operate the hardware?

England who developed it at the beginning of the twentieth century. The Cambridge equation is

$$M^d = k \times Y,$$

in which M^d is the total nominal (current-dollar) quantity of money demanded for use as a medium of exchange, Y is the total current-dollar income of consumers and businesses, and k is a fraction that represents the portion of current-dollar income that consumers and businesses wish to hold as money.

For instance, suppose that the total income of all individuals and business firms is $10 trillion, which is roughly the size of total income in the United States. Then, if consumers and businesses desire to hold 20 percent of their income as money, the value of k is 0.2, and the total quantity of money demanded is equal to $k \times Y = 0.2 \times \$10$ trillion, or $2 trillion.

1. What is the Cambridge equation? The Cambridge equation is a simple representation of the transactions theory of the demand for money. According to the Cambridge equation, people wish to hold a portion of their current-dollar income as money. Consequently, the quantity of money demanded varies directly with income.

Real money balances: The purchasing power of the quantity of money in circulation, measured as the nominal quantity of money divided by an index measure of the prices of goods and services.

THE DEMAND FOR REAL MONEY BALANCES In the form $M^d = k \times Y$, the Cambridge equation focuses on the demand for nominal, or current-dollar, money balances. When we decide how much cash to carry, however, what really matters to us is the purchasing power of the money we hold. Suppose, for instance, that you decide one morning to carry \$15 in cash to cover the purchases that you intend to make that day—say, lunch for \$10 and an afternoon snack for \$5. After you leave home, however, the price level doubles. As a result, the lunch you had intended to purchase now costs \$20, and your planned afternoon snack costs \$10. Now your \$15 will not even cover the complete lunch that you had planned, and you will have to forgo your afternoon snack. The purchasing power of your \$15 in cash is half its previous value. To purchase the same lunch and snack, you will need to double your nominal money balances to \$30. Thus, a doubling of prices requires a doubling of nominal money balances to maintain the required purchasing power for the day's expenses.

The upshot of this example is that the real purchasing power of nominal cash balances is the price-adjusted value of their money holdings, or $m = M/P$, where m denotes **real money balances**—the real purchasing power of the quantity of money in circulation—and P denotes an index of the overall prices of goods and services that people purchase using their real incomes. It turns out that the Cambridge equation can tell us something about the total demand for real money balances. To see why, let's think about *real income,* which is the real value of all individuals' current-dollar income, which we shall denote as y. This is the price-adjusted value of total real income, or $y = Y/P$. By rearranging this relationship, we can express current-dollar income as $Y = y \times P$. Thus, another way to write the Cambridge equation is

$$M^d = k \times y \times P.$$

If we divide both sides of the Cambridge equation by P, we end up with

$$M^d/P = k \times y.$$

Of course, M^d/P is the demand for real money balances, or m^d. Consequently, the Cambridge equation tells us that the demand for real money balances is

$$m^d = k \times y,$$

which means that the *real* money balances that people wish to hold are a fraction, k, of their *real* incomes. The total real purchasing power of money holdings that people desire to maintain will depend on their total real income.

2. What are real money balances? Real money balances are the purchasing power of the current-dollar value of the quantity of money that people hold. Economists measure real money balances by dividing the quantity of money in circulation by an index measure of the prices of goods and services. In the Cambridge equation, the quantity of real money balances demanded is equal to a desired fraction of real income.

Inventory theory of money demand: A theory of the demand for money that focuses on how people determine the best inventory of money to keep on hand.

The Inventory Approach to the Demand for Money

An obvious shortcoming of the basic Cambridge equation is that it fails to take into account the opportunity cost of holding money instead of other interest-bearing financial assets. Furthermore, the Cambridge equation does not allow for variations in the demand for money over time as a result of seasonal or other factors that are likely to affect individuals' spending patterns and, thus, their desired money holdings.

Money Holdings as an Inventory One way to think about a change in desired money holdings that typically occurs during a seasonal spending period such as the Christmas season is to visualize it as an *inventory adjustment*. Just as a retailer that produces filters for air conditioners typically increases the available inventories of filters to sell during spring and summer, an individual increases his cash holdings during the weeks prior to the Christmas season. That is, the individual adjusts his desired *cash inventory* in recognition that he will need more cash on hand for the increased spending he will undertake before Christmas.

In the early 1950s, William Baumol of Princeton University and James Tobin of Yale University independently developed the idea of applying *inventory theory*, or the theory of how people determine the best inventory of a good to keep on hand, to achieve a better understanding of the transactions demand for money. Their theory came to be known as the **inventory theory of money demand.** What they both discovered was that while the Cambridge equation captures the "spirit" of the transactions motive, it likely overlooks some essential elements as well.

Simplifying Assumptions of the Cash-Inventory Theory The basic theory of the transactions demand for money that Baumol and Tobin developed begins with some simplifying assumptions that capture the basic aspects of the inventory problem that people face when they try to determine how much money they should hold. One assumption is that all money holdings yield no interest return. This assumption rules out interest-bearing transactions deposits such as NOW accounts, but it is fairly straightforward to adjust the Baumol-Tobin approach to take into account interest-bearing forms of money.

A second key assumption is that people earn a fixed amount of real income, y, each period. Furthermore, people receive all income in the form of direct deposits into bond funds that yield an overall interest return equal to r. To hold money for use as a medium of exchange in planned purchases of goods and services, people must convert a portion of these bond holdings to real money balances. Making these conversions is not costless, however. Each conversion entails a fee equal to f.

Another assumption is that people buy goods and services at a constant rate. This is probably the hardest assumption to accept because it literally implies that a person is spending a fixed amount every second of every day. Although the theory can be modified to consider more realistic spending patterns, let's abstract from the "real world" to keep things as simple as possible. Figure 19-1 shows what the spending pattern of a recent college graduate with a real annual income of \$36,000 looks like if she spends her entire annual income on her apartment rent, groceries, entertainment, and other goods and services at a constant rate during a year's time. She begins the year by receiving her \$36,000 in real income as a direct deposit into her bond fund. Then she converts this amount into \$36,000 in real money balances, which she spends at a constant rate during the year. At the end of the year, she has zero real money balances remaining.

Figure 19-1
An Annual Spending Pattern with a Constant Rate of Spending.

This figure displays the spending pattern of an individual who receives her entire $36,000 annual real income payment at the beginning of the year and immediately converts it into real money balances. She then spends at a constant rate until she has no real money balances remaining at the conclusion of the year.

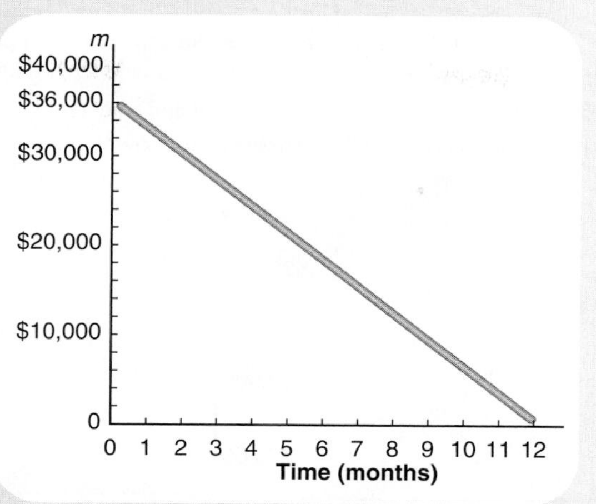

Figure 19-1 illustrates a further simplifying assumption of the Baumol-Tobin inventory theory of the demand for money, which is that people use up all their real money balances before converting any more bonds into new cash balances. To continue spending during the next year, the person whose spending pattern is depicted in Figure 19-1 will have to convert more bonds into real money balances.

Most people, of course, do not start a year with a large cash balance that they stretch out over the entire twelve months. For instance, as shown in panel (a) of Figure 19-2 on the following page, the individual whose spending pattern is depicted in Figure 19-1 might decide to finance her $36,000 in spending during the year with two $18,000 cash conversions. She could make one of these conversions at the beginning of the year and then spend at a constant rate until her money holdings are used up at the middle of the year. Then she could convert bonds into a new starting inventory of $18,000 in real money balances and spend them at a constant rate until year-end.

Panel (b) of Figure 19-2 illustrates yet another alternative. In this spending pattern, the individual chooses to make twelve (that is, monthly) cash conversions during the year. Because she knows that she will spend a total of $36,000 during the year, she converts $3,000 of bonds into real money balances at the beginning of a given month and spends at a constant rate until she needs to make a new cash conversion at the beginning of the next month.

The examples in Figure 19-2 illustrate a final assumption of the Baumol-Tobin inventory model of the demand for money: people make cash conversions in constant fractions of a year. In panel (a), for example, the individual makes a cash conversion from bonds to money every half-year. In panel (b), she makes cash conversions each twelfth of a year, or monthly.

THE AVERAGE REAL MONEY BALANCE OVER THE COURSE OF A YEAR An important implication of the spending patterns illustrated in Figures 19-1 and 19-2 is that a person's *average inventory* of real money balances depends on how often she makes cash conversions. As shown in Figure 19-1, a person who makes only

Figure 19-2
Alternative Spending Patterns.

An individual who spends a real amount of \$36,000 at a constant rate during the year might, as in panel (a), make separate \$18,000 cash conversions from her bond account at the beginning and middle of the year. Alternatively, as shown in panel (b), she might make monthly \$3,000 conversions.

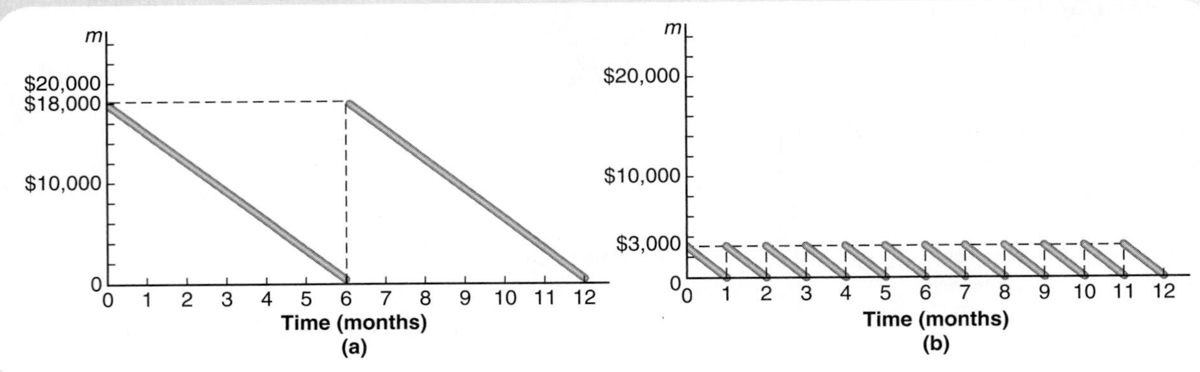

one \$36,000 cash conversion at the beginning of the year and then spends those funds at a constant rate throughout the year has an average real money balance of \$18,000. Panel (a) of Figure 19-2 shows, however, that someone who makes two cash conversions of \$18,000 at the beginning and middle of the year has an average real money balance of \$9,000. For someone who makes monthly \$3,000 cash conversions, the average money balance during the year is \$1,500.

In each case, the individual's average real money balance depends on the number of cash conversions, n, that she makes during the year. In Figure 19-1, n is equal to 1, and the individual's average money balance is equal to $(y/1)/2 =$ \$36,000/2 = \$18,000. In panel (a) of Figure 19-2, n is equal to 2, so her average money balance for the year is equal to $(y/2)/2 =$ (\$36,000/2)/2 = \$18,000/2 = \$9,000. In panel (b) of Figure 19-2, n is equal to 12, so her average money balance equals $(y/12)/2 =$ (\$36,000/12)/2 = \$3,000/2 = \$1,500. Clearly, this means that for any given number of cash conversions n, her average real money balance for the year is equal to $(y/n)/2$, or half the amount of each equally spaced cash conversion during the year.

DETERMINING THE OPTIMAL NUMBER OF CASH CONVERSIONS Let's suppose that this individual is contemplating how many cash conversions she ought to make during the year. Should $n = 1$, as in Figure 19-1, so that she makes only one conversion and stretches out her available real cash balances for the entire year? Or should $n = 2$, as in panel (a) of Figure 19-2? Or should $n = 12$, as in panel (b) of Figure 19-2? Or should she select some other value for n, such as $n = 52$, which would mean weekly cash conversions?

Minimizing the Total Cost of Holding Money The answer is that the individual should choose a number of conversions that minimizes her total cost of maintaining her inventory of real money balances over the course of the year. This cost has two components. One is the total conversion costs that she must incur during the year. Each conversion entails a fee equal to f, so her total cash-conversion cost is equal to this conversion fee, f, times the number of conversions, n, or $f \times n$. This is the upward-sloping line shown in Figure 19-3.

The other component of the individual's cost of holding money is the opportunity cost of holding real money balances during the year. This is equal to the forgone interest return, r, times the average money holding during the year, which we determined to equal $(y/n)/2 = y/(2 \times n)$. Thus, the total opportunity cost of holding money during the year is equal to $(r \times y)/(2 \times n)$. As Figure 19-3 shows, this cost steadily falls as the number of cash conversions increases. [As n becomes larger, the denominator $2 \times n$ increases, so the total opportunity cost of holding money, $(r \times y)/(2 \times n)$, declines.]

Consequently, converting bonds to cash more often during the year has two effects on the total cost of maintaining a cash inventory. Increasing the number of cash conversions raises the explicit cost of paying fees to make conversions. At the same time, however, converting bonds to cash more often reduces the opportunity cost of holding money by reducing the average amount of real money balances that a person maintains.

The Cost-Minimizing Number of Conversions The total cost of holding real money balances equals the sum of the explicit cash-conversion costs and the implicit opportunity cost of holding money. This is the vertical sum of both types of costs, which is the smooth U-shaped curve in Figure 19-3. For any given number of cash conversions, we can read up to a point on this curve and determine the total cost of holding real money balances. Naturally, an individual will choose to minimize this cost. Thus, she will choose the number of cash conversions that

Figure 19-3
The Total Cost of Maintaining a Cash Inventory.

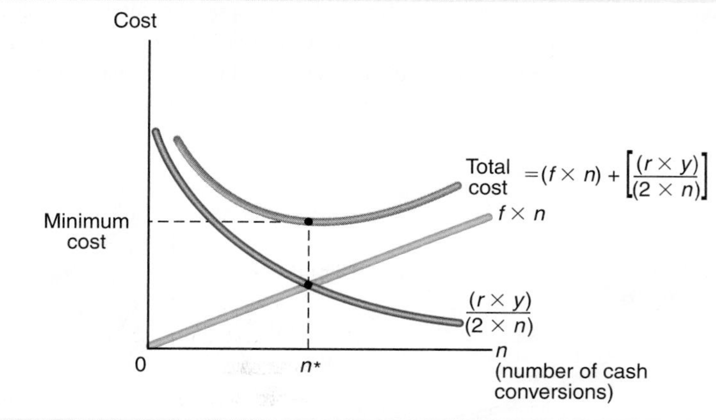

If each cash conversion that an individual makes entails a fee equal to f, and if she makes n conversions during a year, then her total cash-conversion costs for the year equal $f \times n$, which is the upward-sloping line in the figure. Her total opportunity cost of holding money during the year is equal to the forgone interest return, r, times her average money balance during the year, $y/(2 \times n)$, which is the downward-sloping curve. The total cost of holding real money balances during the year is the sum of these two curves, which is the U-shaped curve. To minimize her total cost of holding money, the individual chooses the number of cash conversions equal to n^*.

corresponds to the minimum point on the total cost curve. Problem 3 at the end of the chapter lets you work out an exact solution for the cost-minimizing number of conversions, which we denote as n^* in Figure 19-3.

Panel (a) of Figure 19-4 shows how a rise in the cash-conversion fee affects the number of cash conversions that minimizes the individual's total cost of maintaining her inventory of real money balances. A rise in the fee causes an upward rotation of the upward-sloping line giving the individual's explicit conversion costs. As a result, the total cost curve shifts upward and to the left. Hence, to minimize the costs of maintaining her money inventory, the individual should reduce her cash conversions from n^* to n^{**}.

Panel (b) of Figure 19-4 shows what happens if there is an increase in r, the interest return on bonds. This increases the opportunity cost of real money balances, which shifts the total cost curve upward and to the right. Consequently, to minimize the total cost of holding money, the individual should increase the number of cash conversions, n^* to n^{**}.

THE OPTIMAL CASH BALANCE We can now evaluate the key factors that the inventory approach predicts will influence the amount of real money balances that an individual wishes to hold. As we determined earlier, the theory indicates that the average money balance during the course of a year is equal to $(y/n)/2$, or $y/(2 \times n)$. Given the optimal number of conversions during the year, n^*, it follows that the quantity of money demanded is equal to $m^* = y/(2 \times n^*)$. This quantity clearly depends on real income. Furthermore, the optimal number of

Figure 19-4
Factors Influencing the Cost-Minimizing Number of Cash Conversions.

Panel (a) shows the effect of an increase in the conversion fee, f, on the cost-minimizing number of conversions during the year. A rise in this fee shifts the total cost curve upward and to the left. This causes the optimal number of cash conversions to decline. By way of contrast, an increase in the interest return on bonds, r, raises the opportunity cost of holding money during the year. As shown in panel (b), this causes the total cost curve to shift upward. Thus, a rise in the interest rate induces an increase in the cost-minimizing number of cash conversions during the year.

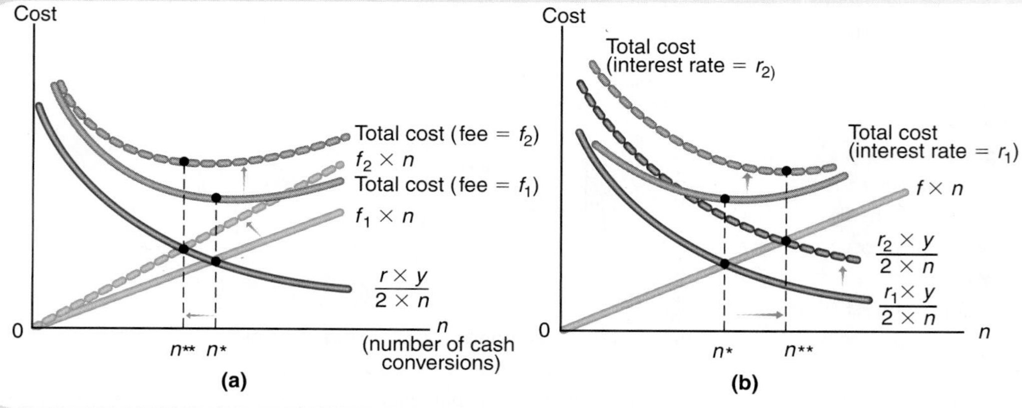

cash conversions depends on the interest rate and the cash-conversion fee, so the quantity of money demanded depends on these two factors as well.

Thus, the inventory theory of the demand for money implies that three key factors affect the amount of real money balances that an individual wishes to hold:

1. **Real income.** Although a rise in real income tends to increase the average opportunity cost of holding money and thereby raises the cost-minimizing number of conversions, the *direct* effect of an increase in real income is to raise the individual's average money balance during the year. As we ask you to show in problem 3 at the conclusion of the chapter, this direct effect dominates. A *rise in real income,* therefore, causes an *increase* in the quantity of money demanded.

2. **The interest rate.** As discussed, an increase in the interest rate on bonds raises the opportunity cost of holding an inventory of real money balances. The best way for an individual to respond to a rise in the interest rate, therefore, is to make more cash conversions and thereby reduce the average money inventory at any given point in time. Consequently, an *increase in the bond interest rate* induces a *reduction* in the quantity of money demanded.

3. **The cash-conversion fee.** As we noted earlier, an increase in the fee incurred in shifting funds from bond holdings to real money balances induces a cost-minimizing individual to cut back on the number of cash conversions. As a result, the average real money balance increases. Hence, an *increase in the cash-conversion fee* causes an *increase* in the quantity of money demanded.

As in the basic Cambridge equation approach, the inventory theory of the demand for money indicates that the quantity of money demanded depends directly on the real income people earn. In addition, however, the inventory theory also predicts that the quantity of real money balances that people wish to hold varies inversely with the nominal interest rate and directly with the explicit costs people face in shifting funds from bond holdings to cash inventories.

3. According to the inventory theory of the demand for money, what are the key factors influencing desired holdings of real money balances? The inventory theory of money demand indicates that an increase in the opportunity cost of holding money caused by a rise in a market interest rate reduces the quantity of money demanded. It also implies that the quantity of money demanded depends positively on real income and cash-conversion fees.

Alternative Transaction-Based Theories of Money Demand

Although the Baumol-Tobin inventory theory is a half-century old, it has been a key starting point for many more elaborate and more recent theories of the demand for money by individuals and businesses. This does not mean, however, that economists are in agreement that the inventory theory is the best approach to understanding the determinants of desired holdings of real money balances.

Shopping-time theory of money demand: A theory of the demand for money that focuses on money's role in helping people reduce the amount of time they spend shopping, thereby freeing up more time for leisure or work.

Cash-in-advance approach: A theory of the demand for money based on the assumption that people must have real money balances in their possession before they can purchase any goods or services.

THE SHOPPING-TIME THEORY A common criticism of the inventory approach to the demand for money is that it takes for granted that people use money. Consequently, it fails to explain why money is what people use to buy goods and services. One possible way to remedy this perceived problem is to develop an alternative theory that sets out a clear motivation for using money in transactions. The **shopping-time theory of money demand** follows this approach by providing an explanation for why money has value as a medium of exchange. As its name implies, the shopping-time theory emphasizes money's role in reducing time spent shopping, thereby freeing up time for other activities.

The shopping-time theory is based on essential microeconomic principles that you learned in your first economics course. These are that people typically like to consume goods and services but also like to have leisure time. Nevertheless, every individual faces the constraint that there are only twenty-four hours in each day. In addition, to be able to consume, people must work to earn income, and they must spend time shopping for the goods and services that they consume. Time allocated to shopping is not available for leisure or work pursuits.

One way to obtain additional time for leisure or work is to reduce the amount of time spent shopping. In the shopping-time theory of money demand, this is the fundamental role of money. Other things being equal, having more real money balances available to spend tends to reduce the amount of time that an individual must devote to shopping. As in the inventory theory of money demand, holding real money balances entails an opportunity cost of forgone interest on bonds, so the quantity of money demanded depends negatively on the interest rate. In this respect, the shopping-time theory is similar to the inventory theory.

Because the shopping-time theory emphasizes money's role in facilitating the purchase of goods and services that people consume, however, the theory differs from the inventory theory in one fundamental prediction: *real consumption* replaces real income as a key determinant of the quantity of real money balances that people wish to hold. According to the shopping-time theory, as people increase their consumption of goods and services, they increase their holdings of real money balances in an effort to cut their shopping time. Consequently, the shopping-time theory predicts that an *increase in real consumption* generates an *increase* in the quantity of money demanded. (In recent years residents of Italy have had some big incentives to use an alternative to the lira to shop for certain goods and services; see *Global Focus: Were Italian Lire Just Part of a Vast Central Banking Conspiracy?*)

THE CASH-IN-ADVANCE APPROACH A very different transaction-based approach to understanding the overall demand for money takes as "given" that money must be offered in exchange. This theory, called the **cash-in-advance approach** to money demand, starts with the presumption that people cannot buy most goods and services unless they have real money balances to spend. That is, they must have "cash in advance" of any purchases they wish to make.

Under the cash-in-advance approach to money demand, people naturally adjust the quantity of real money balances that they hold as they change the amount of time they devote to work and their resource allocations among consumption, investment in capital goods, and holdings of bonds and other financial assets. In other words, in the cash-in-advance theory the amount of money that people hold

GLOBAL Focus | POLICY | CYBER | MANAGEMENT

Were Italian Lire Just Part of a Vast Central Banking Conspiracy?

Among central banks, the Bank of Italy is in a class by itself. It is publicly incorporated but privately owned and by most measures highly economically independent, yet most studies find that it has very little political independence from the Italian government.

Seeking to Undermine an Alleged Plot against the People

According to a law professor in Guardiagrele, Italy, the reason for the Bank of Italy's unusual structure is that the institution is part of a government plot to rob common citizens by distributing new money through the Italian banking system instead of simply sending it directly to individuals in equal shares. The professor contends that the Bank of Italy thereby defrauds Italian residents by making banks the "owners" of money so that everyone else becomes "indebted" to banks.

Although most economists have a little trouble following this argument, the Italian professor has been undeterred in his efforts to undermine the conspiracy he alleges to exist within his country. After failing in an effort to sue the Bank of Italy in Italian courts, the professor hired a printer to produce several boxes full of *simecs,* a currency of his own creation. *Simec* is the Italian acronym for "econometric symbol of inducted value." The professor, who is relatively wealthy, then told every retailer in his hometown that he would repurchase every *simec* they accepted from townspeople with two lire of his own. Forty retailers accepted his offer, and within two days $40,000 worth of *simecs* were being used by the townspeople to buy goods and services. The *simecs* became so popular that within six weeks at least *2 billion simecs* were in circulation.

Like All Conspiracy Theories, This One Is Hard to Disprove

The interpretation of what happened next depends on whether one subscribes to the professor's conspiracy theory. The facts are as follows. First, the *simec* prices of goods, which previously had been half the lire price, reflecting the professor's promise to redeem every *simec* presented to him with two lire, began to rise closer to parity with lire prices. Then the town's shopkeepers who accepted *simecs* found the currency so popular that they began holding their own inventories of *simecs* alongside government-issued lire. After that, shopkeepers who did not accept *simecs* found that they were losing customers, so they filed formal complaints with the Italian government. Shortly thereafter, about a hundred members of the Italian government's Finance Guard, which prosecutes crimes such as smuggling and tax fraud, showed up in town and carted off boxes full of *simecs*. The Bank of Italy also issued a statement reminding Italians that any collection of funds within the country is "reserved to subjects authorized by law."

Nevertheless, local and regional courts determined that Italian laws covered counterfeiting of lire but did not make it illegal to issue private currencies. Judges ordered the *simecs* returned to Guardiagrele, where about 700 million remain in circulation.

At present the Italian government is appealing these decisions. In the meantime, euros have replaced lire, but the professor is promising to continue his battle against central banks by taking on the European Central Bank. To help promote his competing currency, the professor even runs his own after-Christmas sales on clothing and leather merchandise, where he rejects payments in any currency except *simecs*.

FOR CRITICAL ANALYSIS: How could the *simec* price of goods and services fall to less than double the lire price, if the Guardiagrele professor stood ready to provide two lire in exchange for each *simec*?

amounts to a *residual*—that is, a "leftover"—once they determine how much income they desire to earn given their talents and skills, how much they want to buy with that income, and how many financial assets they desire to hold.

This approach also indicates that the quantity of money demanded will depend positively on real income and negatively on the interest rate. In the cash-in-advance theory, however, real income itself depends on decisions about how much to work and choices concerning how to allocate one's earnings. As a result, the predictions about key determinants of the demand for money yielded by the cash-in-advance approach are less straightforward than those implied by the inventory and shopping-time theories. The predictions become even muddier in today's setting when people purchase many goods—called "credit goods" by those who developed the cash-in-advance approach—using credit cards or trade-credit invoicing systems. Nevertheless, many economists have found the cash-in-advance approach helpful as part of broader theories of the overall performance of an economy.

4. What do other transactions-related theories add to our understanding of the demand for money? The shopping-time theory of money demand emphasizes the role that money plays in reducing the time an individual must spend shopping for goods and services; the theory indicates that the quantity of money demanded varies directly with real consumption. The cash-in-advance approach, which relies on the idea that people must offer money in exchange for goods, services, and assets, highlights how decisions about work effort can affect money holdings.

The Portfolio Demand for Money

The transactions motive focuses on money's role as a medium of exchange. At least since the ancient Greeks, philosophers had emphasized this factor in their thinking about money. When Keynes contemplated the demand for money in the 1920s and 1930s, however, he wished to take into account another important function of money: its role as a *store of value*.

As noted at the beginning of the chapter, this led Keynes to develop a theory of the *speculative motive* for holding money arising from the interplay between interest rates and the prices of financial assets such as bonds. The modern term for this rationale for holding money is the *portfolio motive*. The idea behind the portfolio motive is that money is just one of many financial assets among which individuals can allocate their wealth. Changes in relative returns on assets, which arise from interest rate changes and movements in bond prices, induce people to adjust their desired asset allocations, thereby causing changes in money holdings.

The Keynesian Portfolio Demand for Money

People can hold accumulated wealth in a number of ways. One is to hold nonfinancial assets, such as land, residential housing, or durable goods like automobiles. Another is to hold financial assets, such as bonds, stocks, and savings accounts. Keynes also viewed money as a key part of a person's financial wealth.

MONEY, BONDS, AND FINANCIAL WEALTH To keep things simple, let's assume that an individual's real financial wealth may be allocated only between real money holdings, m, and real holdings of another financial asset called "bonds," b. The factor that distinguishes money from bonds is that the nominal price of money is always equal to 1 unit of money (for instance, \$1, 1 euro, 1 yen, etc.). In contrast, the nominal price of a bond can change over time. As a result, an individual who holds a bond earns a *capital gain* if the nominal price of the bond increases over a given interval in time or a *capital loss* if the nominal price of the bond falls during some other period. A \$1 bill of U.S. currency or a \$1 portion of a checking account at a bank has the same \$1 *nominal* value over any given interval. Consequently, people cannot earn nominal capital gains or incur nominal capital losses if they hold all their financial wealth as currency or deposit forms of money. This makes the return on real money balances inherently more stable than the return on bond holdings.

To think about how a person is likely to decide how to allocate real financial wealth between real money balances and bonds, let's suppose that at some given point in time, a person's nominal financial wealth is equal to some amount w. The individual can split this wealth between real money balances, m, which we shall assume are non-interest-bearing cash, and bond holdings, b, on which the individual earns an interest return, r. At the point in time we are considering, it must be true that the individual's financial wealth is equal to holdings of real money balances plus holdings of bonds:

$$w = m + b.$$

Because real financial wealth is constant at a point in time, it must be true that the sum of changes in money and bond holdings must equal zero, or $\Delta m + \Delta b = 0$. That is, any change in holdings of bonds, Δb, must be offset by an equal-sized change in money holdings in the opposite direction, $-\Delta m$. For example, suppose that a person who has \$10,000 in real financial wealth holds \$5,000 as real money balances and \$5,000 as bonds. If this person wishes to increase his bond holdings by \$2,000, then he must reduce his money holdings by \$2,000, leaving him with \$3,000 in cash and \$7,000 in bonds, so as to maintain the same total financial wealth of \$10,000.

THE SPECULATIVE MOTIVE Keynes recognized that allocating a fixed amount of real financial wealth between money and bonds implies a relationship between the demand for real money balances and the interest rate. Because bonds earn an explicit interest return, changes in the interest rate affect the market prices of bonds and an individual's desired bond holdings. But changing bond holdings requires altering money holdings. Consequently, interest rate variations typically will induce changes in desired holdings of money.

Interest Rate Expectations Now let's consider how a person might adjust his money and bond holdings as part of a speculative strategy involving expected changes in interest rates. Because he understands that bond prices are inversely related to the market interest rate, he recognizes that his future capital losses or gains from bond holdings depend directly on whether interest rates rise or fall in the future. Consequently, the individual will adjust his portfolio of money and bonds in light of his *anticipation* of future movements in the interest rate.

Suppose that the market interest rate rises, in the present, to a level that the individual believes is rather high. As a result, he anticipates that the interest rate will decline in the future, and, therefore, bond prices will rise. Thus, he anticipates a future capital gain on bonds that he holds as part of his financial wealth. To further increase his anticipated capital gains from bond holdings, this individual will allocate more of his financial wealth to bonds in the present. To do this, however, he must reduce his holdings of money because his financial wealth is fixed in the present. Consequently, for this individual a current rise in the market interest rate causes him to reduce his desired money holdings. His demand for money depends negatively on the market interest rate.

Suppose instead that the market interest rate falls, in the present, to levels that the individual perceives to be rather low. Therefore, he anticipates that the market interest rate will rise in the future, causing bond prices to fall and causing him to incur capital losses on his existing bond holdings. To avoid some of these anticipated future losses, he will sell bonds in the present, thereby allocating more of his fixed financial wealth to holdings of money. Hence, a current fall in the market interest rate induces him to increase the amount of money demanded. Again, the individual's demand for money is inversely related to the market interest rate.

Money Demand and the Interest Rate From this line of reasoning, Keynes concluded that the portfolio motive for holding money implies that real income is not the only determinant of money holdings. The demand for money should also depend on the nominal interest rate. Furthermore, *there should be a negative relationship between the quantity of money demanded and the interest rate.*

The modern approach to Keynes's speculative motive for holding money builds on concepts borrowed from the theory of portfolio choice discussed in Chapter 7. Indeed, the theory of portfolio choice itself began with research on the demand for money by James Tobin of Yale University in the 1950s. Tobin later won the Nobel Prize for his early work on the modern portfolio theory of money demand and its larger contribution to the modern theory of finance. This theory focuses on an individual's determination of how much money to hold in light of potential average portfolio returns and risks. In addition to Keynes's prediction that the quantity of money demanded is inversely related to the interest rate, the modern portfolio theory also predicts that the *variability* of the interest rate plays a role.

Money as a Social Store of Value: The Overlapping-Generations Approach to the Demand for Money

Keynes's speculative theory and the modern portfolio theory focus on an individual's portfolio allocation. A more recent theory emphasizing money's store-of-value property is the **overlapping-generations approach,** whose proponents view money as a means of storing and transferring wealth across time.

Overlapping-generations approach: A theory of money demand that emphasizes how societies use money as a way to store and transfer wealth across time.

A Basic Overlapping-Generations Economy Figure 19-5 depicts the essential foundations of the overlapping-generations approach. The figure illustrates successive generations of people who have two-period lifetimes. In the first period of their lives, "youth," people work and save for their retirement in the "old-age" period. People do not work in the retirement period. At the beginning

Figure 19-5
A Basic Overlapping-Generations Economy.

This figure shows the fundamental setup of the overlapping-generations approach to the demand for money. There are successive generations of people with two-period lifetimes. While one generation is in its "youth," the other is experiencing "old age." Thus, generations overlap.

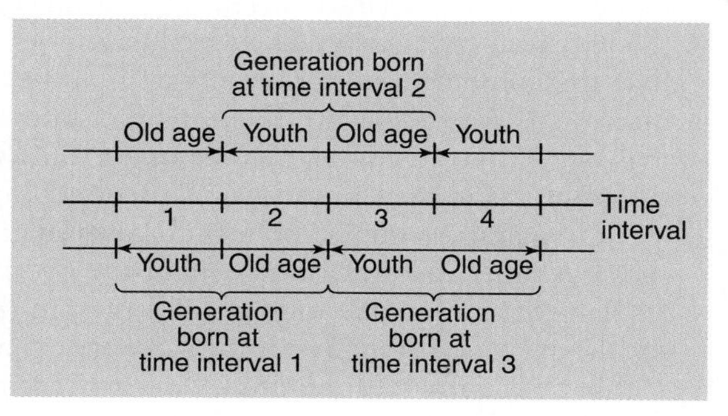

of the old-age period of one generation, another generation emerges and lives through its period of youth. Thus, in each period the economy's population includes both young and old people. Generations overlap—hence, the name of this approach to understanding the demand for money.

Let's suppose that the economy's productive capacity expands at a constant rate each period. Let's further suppose that there initially is no money in this economy. In this situation, people will have to store goods to consume when they reach retirement. The total amount of goods that they can consume during their lifetime is limited to the amount that they produce in their youth, so they must allocate these goods across their youthful and old-age periods of life. This is so even though the economy is growing, so that the youth who are working during a given generation's old-age period produce a larger amount of goods and services than the generation that preceded them was capable of producing.

MONEY IN THE OVERLAPPING-GENERATIONS ECONOMY Now let's add money to this overlapping-generations economy. During their youth, people know that they will be able to use money to purchase goods and services during their retirement years from the youthful people who will be producing these goods and services. Because the economy is growing each period, they also know that more goods and services will be available for each person to consume during his or her retirement.

As long as money is acceptable in exchange each period, people will be able to use money to buy goods and services in any period. Consequently, old-age individuals will be able to use money balances that they accumulated in their youth to purchase some of the goods and services produced by those who are currently young. Money, therefore, enables the current old-age individuals to consume a portion of the goods and services *currently produced* by youthful individuals. It turns out that in a growing economy this ability to hold and use money over time permits each generation to consume more goods and services than the generations could have consumed within their lifetimes if money did not exist.

Thus, the overlapping-generations approach to money demand emphasizes money's role as a welfare-increasing "social compact." When the foundations of the approach are expanded to include a role for financial markets, it turns out that the combined aggregate money holdings of an economy's young and old individuals depend negatively on market interest rates. In addition, money holdings depend positively on income or, in some versions of the approach, on consumption (as in the shopping-time theory discussed earlier).

Although these implications of the overlapping-generations approach replicate those of other theories, adherents of the overlapping-generations approach prefer it to others for one fundamental reason: the approach gives an explanation for the existence of money at the same time that it explains total money holdings within an economy. In addition, the approach offers a theory of why people may wish to trade goods, services, and financial assets, namely, that relative differences in the wealth positions of successive generations induce trade among generations.

5. What theories explain the demand for real money balances based on money's function as a store of value? There are two basic store-of-value theories of money demand. The modern portfolio theory views an individual's choice of what portion of wealth to hold as money as dependent primarily on the average portfolio return and the variability of that return. The overlapping-generations approach to money demand emphasizes money's role as a mechanism for storing and shifting wealth over time.

The Money Demand Schedule

Each of the theories of the demand for money emphasizes different aspects of money's role in the economy. As a result, there are some differences in the theories' predictions concerning factors that are likely to determine the demand for money. According to the inventory theory, for example, costs of converting bonds to money influence the timing of conversions and thereby affect average money holdings. In addition, the modern portfolio theory of money demand indicates that the variability of bond returns should also influence desired holdings of real money balances. These two factors do not emerge directly in the other theories.

Nevertheless, all the theories share two essential predictions:

1. An increase in the *opportunity cost* of holding money, measured as a bond rate or an average return on a bond portfolio, causes people to reduce their holdings of real money balances.

2. An increase in the size of a *scale factor* such as income, consumption, or financial wealth raises people's desired money holdings.

Because so many approaches to the demand for money agree that these factors should be important, they are the focus of most efforts to assess the real-world determinants of total desired money holdings.

The Basic Money Demand Schedule

We can capture the predicted money demand relationships using a simple diagram of a *money demand schedule,* which is a graphical depiction of the relationship between the quantity of money demanded and the nominal interest rate. A typical money demand schedule is shown in panel (a) of Figure 19-6. The downward slope of this schedule reflects the inverse relationship between the quantity of real money balances demanded and the nominal interest rate that the various money demand theories agree should exist. In addition, we label the schedule $m^d(y_1)$ to indicate that the *position* of the money demand schedule depends, according to several of the theories, on the current level of real income, such as a real income level equal to y_1.

Panel (b) of Figure 19-6 illustrates the effect of an increase in real income, from y_1 to a larger amount y_2. At any given nominal interest rate, people demand more real money balances as a result, so the money demand schedule would shift rightward, as shown in panel (b) by the shift from $m^d(y_1)$ to $m^d(y_2)$.

Identification problem: The problem that economists face in evaluating whether real-world data are consistent with the downward-sloping money demand schedule that money demand theories predict, given the fact that both money demand and money supply vary over time.

The Identification and Simultaneity Problems

To gauge the extent to which factors such as interest rates or income affect desired money holdings in the real world, economists examine actual data. To measure real money balances that people in an economy actually hold at any given time, they divide the nominal quantity of money in circulation by an index measure of the overall level of prices (see Chapter 21 for more on price indexes). Then they use statistical techniques to assess the degree to which factors such as observed interest rates and real income, consumption, and/or wealth levels help to explain observed variations in real money holdings.

THE IDENTIFICATION PROBLEM Figure 19-7 (p. 464) illustrates one problem that economists face in accomplishing this task. This is called the **identification problem** in money demand estimation, or the difficulty in assessing whether real-

Figure 19-6
A Money Demand Schedule.

Panel (a) depicts a typical money demand schedule. Because the quantity of money demanded depends inversely on a market interest rate, the money demand schedule slopes downward. Its position depends on a scale variable such as the real income level, y_1. Panel (b) illustrates the effect of an increase in real income to y_2, which is a rightward shift of the money demand schedule.

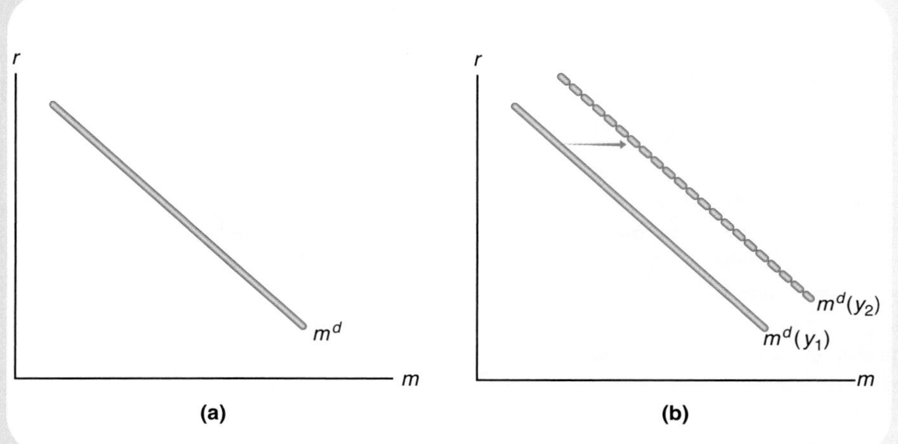

world data actually trace out a money demand schedule consistent with theory. Panel (a) shows the best possible situation for someone who wishes to "identify" a real-world money demand schedule. As we discussed in Chapter 16, we can envision the nominal quantity of money *supplied* by the Federal Reserve as equal to the product of a money multiplier times the monetary base. Let's use M^s to denote this nominal quantity of money supplied. If the aggregate price level is equal to P, then the quantity of real money balances supplied by the Fed equals M^s/P. Panel (a) of Figure 19-7 shows what happens if the Fed varies the supply of money over time (assuming no appreciable change in the price level, real income, or any other factor). As you can see, this causes a change in the equilibrium interest rate in the *market for real money balances*. The result is a movement along the money demand schedule and a neat "tracing out" of the schedule. If real-world data arose solely from changes in the supply of money, then economists would have an easy time identifying a real-world money demand schedule.

Figure 19-7
The Identification Problem.

Panel (a) indicates that if the money demand schedule is stationary, but the money supply schedule shifts rightward over time, then real-world data for interest rates and corresponding levels of real money balances trace out the money demand schedule. The identification problem arises, however, when a scale factor such as real income rises, say, from y_1 to y_2, or declines, say, from y_2 to y_3, thereby causing the rightward and leftward shifts in the money demand schedule shown in panel (b). Using real-world data for interest rates and quantities of real money balances then would identify the money supply schedule instead of the money demand schedule. An even more complicated situation is depicted in panel (c), where both the money demand schedule and the money supply schedule shift over time, so that neither schedule is identified.

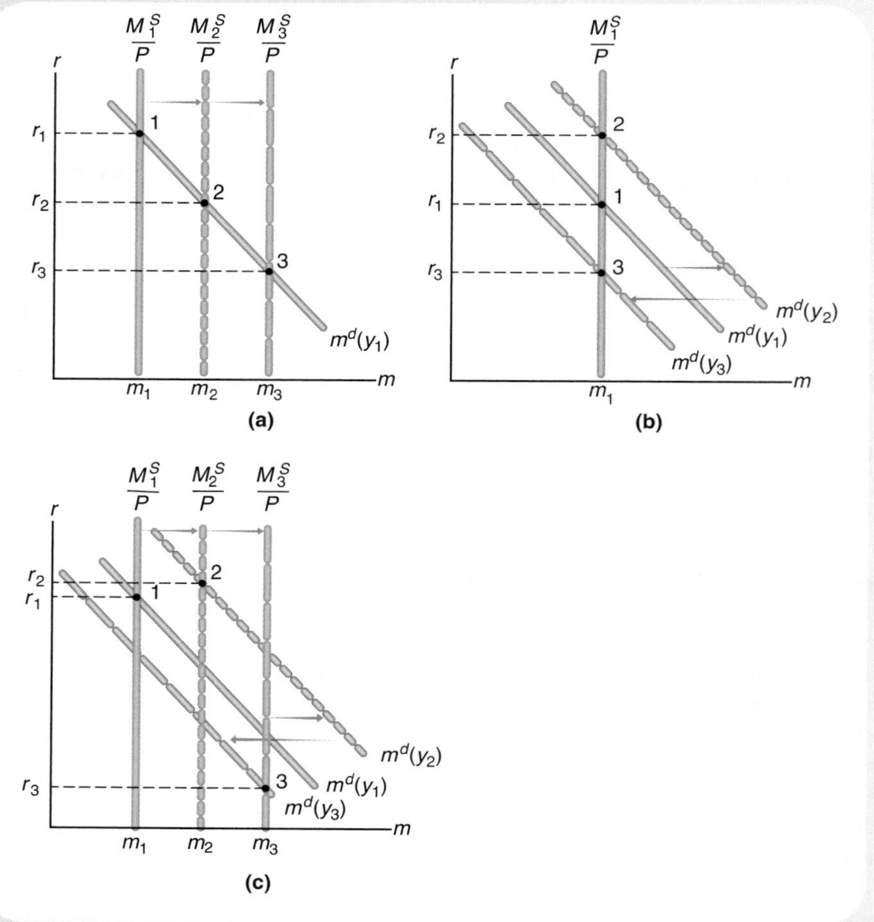

In fact, the situation depicted in panel (a) is likely to be extremely rare. One reason for this is that real income (or alternative scale factors such as consumption or wealth) can rise or fall over time, thereby causing the money demand schedule to shift to the right or left, as shown in panel (b). If an economist collected data on interest rates and real money balances alone and made a plot of these data for a period that happened to coincide with the situation depicted in panel (b), then she would actually identify the money supply schedule instead of the money demand schedule. Panel (c) depicts an even more complicated situation, in which the positions of *both* the money demand schedule *and* the money supply schedule vary over time.

The best way to account for the potential shifts in money demand and supply is for economists to take into account changes in various scale factors, such as real income, consumption, or financial wealth, when trying to identify a real-world money demand schedule. As long as at least one of these factors has no significant effect on the position of the money supply schedule, then statistical techniques should permit economists to identify a money demand relationship.

Simultaneity problem: The problem of accounting for the possibility that factors influencing the quantity of money demanded are themselves affected by how many real money balances people hold, which can complicate assessments of how well real-world observations square with theories of money demand.

The Simultaneity Problem A potentially significant problem in using real-world data to assess the key determinants of the demand for money is the **simultaneity problem,** or the possibility that factors that influence the quantity of money demanded are themselves affected by how many real money balances people hold. For example, as we shall discuss in Chapter 24, conditions in the market for real money balances ultimately affect equilibrium real national income. Thus, aggregate money holdings, interest rates, and real income actually are determined *simultaneously* in the real world. This means that statistical tests that assume that data on a scale factor such as real income are independent from observed money holdings will not yield trustworthy answers.

moneyxtra!

Online Case Study

Gain an understanding of how difficulties in predicting money can cause real-world policy problems by going to the Chapter 19 Case Study, entitled "Wrestling with Money Demand Prediction Problems at the Fed."

http://moneyxtra.swcollege.com

To deal with the simultaneity problem, economists typically use "two-stage" statistical estimation procedures. They locate data on variables that they know are likely to affect real income but are highly unlikely to be related to desired holdings of real money balances. Incorporating these data into their statistical analysis of money demand permits economists to take into account any feedback effects from desired money holdings to real income. Then, at least in principle, economists can determine the net effect the changes in real income directly exert on desired holdings of real money balances.

6. What difficulties do economists face in trying to predict the overall demand for money? Most theories of money demand agree that the quantity of money demanded should depend negatively on the interest rate and positively on income. Hence, the money demand schedule should slope downward in a graph with the interest rate measured along the vertical axis and the quantity of real money balances measured along the horizontal axis, and an increase in income should shift the schedule rightward. Attempting to estimate the position and shape of the money demand schedule with real-world data is complicated by the identification problem, which arises from the fact that variations in both money demand and money supply typically take place. Another difficulty is the simultaneity problem: changes in the demand for money can affect real income and, in turn, the interest rate, complicating the process of disentangling the independent effects of income and the interest rate on the demand for money.

Link to the
Global Economy

The Responsiveness of the Demand for Money to Income and Interest Rates

As you learned in this chapter, there are a number of theories of why the demand for money should depend on real income. The simplest is the Cambridge equation, $m^d = k \times y$. This equation implies $\%\Delta m^d = \%\Delta k + \%\Delta y$, where "$\%\Delta$" denotes the percentage change. The key assumption of the Cambridge equation is that the fraction k is constant, so $\%\Delta k = 0$. This means that it should be true that

$$\%\Delta m^d = \%\Delta y.$$

If we divide both sides by $\%\Delta y$, then

$$\frac{\%\Delta m^d}{\%\Delta y} = 1.$$

According to the Cambridge equation, therefore, the percentage change in the quantity of real money balances demanded resulting from a percentage increase in real income, which economists call the *income elasticity of the demand for money,* should equal 1. Other transactions theories tend to predict a smaller value for the income elasticity of money demand, but all theories agree that the value of the income elasticity, $\%\Delta m^d / \%\Delta y$, should be positive. The quantity of money demanded should respond directly to an increase in real income.

Global Evidence on How the Quantity of Money Demanded Responds to Changes in Income

No single study of money demand can encompass large numbers of the world's nations. Subramanian Sriram, an economist at the International Monetary Fund, reviewed 66 studies conducted during the 1990s that examined evidence on the demand for components of M1 and M2 in the United States and ten other developed nations and in nineteen less developed countries.

Panel (a) of Figure 19-8 shows how many income elasticity estimates fell within various ranges. As you can see, most of the estimates are clustered between 0.75 and 1.25. Panel (b) of the figure shows the average and median (values halfway between the highest and lowest) estimates of income elasticities of the demand for money from panel (a). In fact, all the estimates are very close to a value of 1. This may indicate that the Cambridge equation, the simplest possible approach, is not a bad approximation of the real-world demand for money.

What about Interest Rates and Money Demand?

The predictions of money demand theories about the responsiveness of money holdings to interest rate variations are less clear-cut. For instance, among the studies that Sriram reviewed, estimates of the $\%\Delta m^d / \%\Delta r$, ranged all the way from -0.02, indicating that a 1 percent rise in the interest rate would cause only a 0.02 percent decline in the quantity of money demanded, to -9, implying that money holdings would fall by 9 percent in response to a 1 percent interest rate increase. The main conclusion so far is that the interest sensitivity of money demand likely varies considerably both from country to country and over time within individual countries.

Research Project

How does the interest elasticity of money demand affect the extent to which monetary policy actions are likely to affect market interest rates? If the main way that monetary policy affects the economy is by raising or lowering interest rates and thereby retarding or stimulating total spending on goods and services, is monetary policy likely to be more or less powerful if the absolute value of the interest elasticity of money demand is smaller?

Web Resources

1. To take a look at another, more detailed study by Subramanian Sriram entitled "Survey of Literature on Demand for Money: Theoretical and Empirical Work with Special Refer-

ence to Error-Correction Models," go to the International Monetary Fund's home page (http://www.imf.org), and click on publications. Then search under the author name Sriram, and select this paper. Then click on "Full Text in PDF Format" to download a free copy.

2. What are some recent studies of the demand for money outside the United States? Follow the steps to IMF online publications above, but then search under "Demand for Money," and a page containing several recent, downloadable money demand studies will appear.

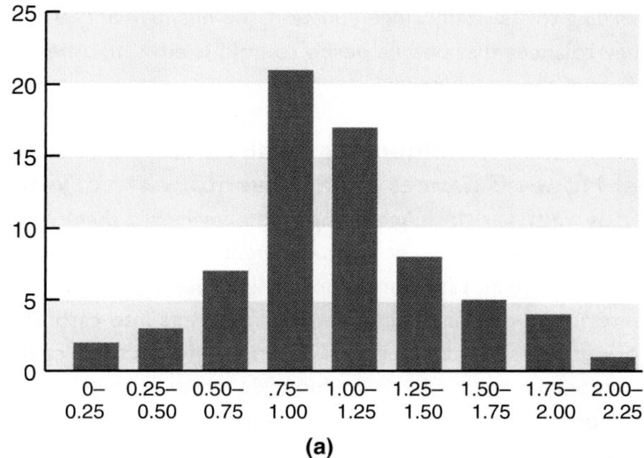

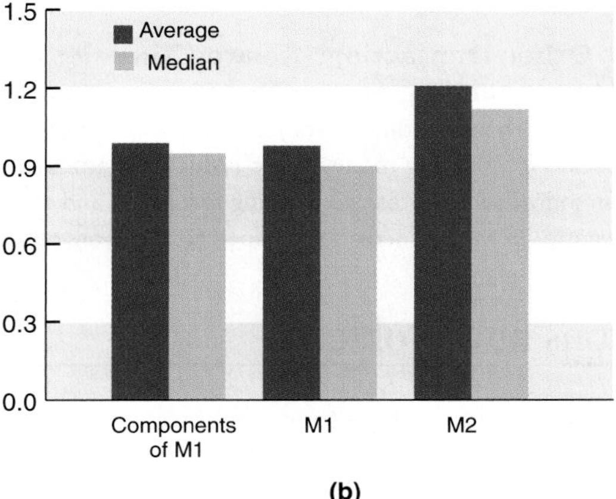

Figure 19-8
Estimated Income Elasticities of Money Demand.

Panel (a) displays the distribution of the estimated income elasticities of demand for components of M1, M1, and M2 from 66 studies covering a number of different nations. Panel (b) displays the average and median values of the income elasticity estimates from these studies.

SOURCE: Subramanian Sriram, "A Survey of Empirical Money Demand Studies," IMF Staff Papers 47 (3, 2000): 334–365.

Chapter Summary

1. The Cambridge Equation: This equation is the most basic transactions theory of the demand for money. It indicates that people desire to hold a portion of their current-dollar income as money. Therefore, the quantity of money demanded varies directly with income.

2. Real Money Balances: Real money balances are the purchasing power of the total nominal quantity of money, which economists measure by dividing the quantity of money in circulation by an index measure of the prices of goods and services. According to the Cambridge equation, the quantity of real money balances that people desire to hold is equal to a desired fraction of their real income.

3. Key Factors Influencing Desired Holdings of Real Money Balances in the Inventory Theory of Money Demand: According to the inventory theory of the demand for money, people hold inventories of real money balances to use as a medium of exchange. They adjust their inventories by converting interest-bearing assets into cash. The theory predicts that an increase in market interest rates raises the opportunity cost of holding money, thereby inducing a reduction in the quantity of money demanded. The theory also indicates that the quantity of money demanded depends positively on real income and cash-conversion fees.

4. What Other Transactions-Related Theories Add to Our Understanding of the Demand for Money: According to the shopping-time theory of money demand, which focuses on how using money helps reduce the amount of time that an individual devotes to shopping for goods and services, the quantity of money demanded depends positively on real consumption. In the cash-in-advance approach to money demand, real income remains the key scale variable, but other factors such as an individual's allocation of time between work and leisure also influence the demand for money.

5. Theories That Explain Money Demand through Money's Store-of-Value Function: The modern portfolio theory focuses on choices that people must make when they allocate their financial wealth in light of the average portfolio return and the variability of that return. The overlapping-generations approach to the theory of money demand emphasizes money's social role in allowing people to store and allocate wealth across time.

6. Difficulties Economists Face in Trying to Predict the Overall Demand for Money: Money demand theories agree that there is a negative relationship between the quantity of real money balances demanded and the interest rate; thus, the money demand schedule should slope downward in a graph with the interest rate measured along the vertical axis and the quantity of real money balances measured along the horizontal axis. Most theories also indicate that money demand is positively related to income, so a rise in income should shift the schedule rightward. The fact that both the money demand and the money supply schedules vary over time creates an identification problem that complicates efforts by economists to use real-world data to estimate the position and slope of the money demand schedule. The simultaneity problem, or the fact that changes in the demand for money can affect real income and, in turn, the interest rate, further complicates the effort to determine the separate effects of income and the interest rate on money demand.

Questions and Problems

(Answers to odd-numbered questions and problems may be found on the Web at http://money.swcollege.com under "Student Resources.")

1. Suppose that economists determine that M2 is the monetary aggregate most useful for guiding monetary policy and also determine that people desire to hold one-fourth of their current-dollar incomes in the form of money. At present, total holdings of assets included in M2 amount to $2.4 trillion. According to the Cambridge equation, what is the current-dollar level of national income? Show your work.

2. In question 1, suppose that the current value of an index of the overall prices of goods and services in the economy is equal to 1.067. What is real national income? What is the value of the level of real money balances? Show your work, and round to the nearest hundredth of a trillion dollars (that is, round to the nearest 10 billion dollars).

3. Use the inventory theory of the demand for money to work out an exact expression for the cost-minimizing number of conversions. Then use this solution in the expression for the average cash balance to determine the optimal cash balance that an individual will hold, in terms of the cash-conversion fee, the interest rate, and real income. [Hint: Note in Figure 19-3 that the number of conversions that minimizes total cost happens to correspond to the point where the upward-sloping cash-conversion cost line and the downward-sloping implicit opportunity cost curve cross. Therefore, at this point that they share in common, it must be true that $f \times n = (r \times y)/(2 \times n)$. You can solve this equation for n. Then use this solution for n in the expression for the average real money balance to solve for the individual's optimal holdings of money.]

4. Suppose that greater competition among mutual funds and depository institutions leads to a reduction in the market fee that mutual funds and depository institutions charge to convert funds from bond accounts to real money balances. Use the inventory theory of the demand for money to reason out the likely effect on total desired holdings of real money balances throughout the economy. Explain your answer.

5. The inventory theory of the demand for real money balances indicates that the level of real income is the key scale factor influencing desired money holdings. The shopping-time theory, however, indicates that *real consumption* is the appropriate scale factor. Even though they possess a lot of data on income and consumption, however, economists have had trouble determining which of these scale factors actually has the greater *independent* influence on money demand in the real world. Why do you suppose this is so? Explain.

6. Early versions of the cash-in-advance approach to the demand for money, which were developed in the 1960s, assumed that people have to use money to obtain all goods and services. By the 1980s, however, most economists using this approach felt that this assumption was unreasonable in a world with credit cards and other revolving-credit arrangements. Do you agree? How might you modify the cash-in-advance approach to make it more applicable to today's world? Explain.

7. Critics of the overlapping-generations approach to the demand for money often claim that it may help explain why money exists but does a poor job of helping economists understand the quantity of money that people currently hold. Proponents of the theory respond that it is not possible to understand present money holdings unless economists also take into account underlying reasons for the existence of money. Evaluate these positions.

8. Suppose that the money supply schedule is stationary but the money demand schedule shifts rightward and leftward over time because of variations in the public's use of technologies for making exchanges. How would this affect economists' efforts to determine the slope and position of the money demand schedule?

9. Suppose that the United States experiences a period during which the economy's money demand schedule tends to shift leftward over time. At the same time, the Federal Reserve's goal is to keep interest rates from changing, so it varies the position of the money supply schedule as required to attain this objective. Would this pose an identification problem or a simultaneity problem for a researcher interested in evaluating the demand for money using data collected during this period? Explain, using a diagram to assist.

10. Suppose that there is widespread adoption of cybertechnologies that enable people to economize on their holdings of real money balances. Use a diagram of the market for real money balances to show the effect of this development on the position of the economy's money demand schedule and on the market interest rate. Suppose, in addition, that the economy's level of real income tends to be inversely related to market interest rates. Would this pose an identification problem or a simultaneity problem for a researcher interested in evaluating the demand for money using data collected during this period? Explain, using a diagram to assist.

Before the Test

Test your understanding of the material covered in this chapter by taking the Chapter 19 interactive quiz at http://money.swcollege.com.

Online Application

Internet URL: http://research.stlouisfed.org/fred

Title: Federal Reserve Economic Data (FRED)

Navigation: Go to the Web page of the Federal Reserve Bank of St. Louis (http://www.stlouisfed.org). Under "Economic Research," click on "Economic Data—FRED."

Application: Follow the instructions below, and answer the questions:

1. Click on "Monetary Aggregates," and then click on "M2 Money Stock—1959:01." Print the M2 data so that you can have them by your side as you continue. Now go back to the "Economic Data—FRED page, and click on "Interest Rates," followed by "6-Month Treasury Constant Maturity Rate—1982.01." According to theories of the demand for money, the quantity of money demanded varies inversely with market interest rates. Reviewing the M2 and six-month Treasury security rates since 1982, does this relationship appear in the data? Based on the discussion in this chapter, can you offer some reasons for why the relationship may not be apparent in the data?

2. Go back to "Monetary Aggregates" and click on "M2 Own Rate—1979.01." Explain what these data measure. How would you expect this factor to influence the relationship between other market interest rates and the quantity of money (M2) demanded?

For Group Study and Analysis: FRED contains numerous financial data series. Break the class up into three groups assigned to examine data for M1, M2, and M3. Have each group take a look at the rest of the FRED database and determine what data might be helpful in trying to estimate the demand for the assigned monetary aggregate.

Selected References and Further Reading

Duca, John. "Should Bond Funds Be Added to M2?" *Journal of Banking and Finance* 19 (April 1995): 131–152.

Elyasiani, Elyas, and Alireza Nasseh. "The Appropriate Scale Variable in the U.S. Money Demand: An Application of Nonnested Tests of Consumption versus Income Measures." *Journal of Business and Economic Statistics* 12 (January 1994): 47–55.

Goldfeld, Stephen. "Demand for Money: Empirical Studies." In *The New Palgrave: Money,* ed. John Eatwell, Murray Milgate, and Peter Newman, pp. 131–143. New York: W. W. Norton, 1989.

Laidler, David. *The Demand for Money: Theories, Evidence, and Problems,* 4th ed. New York: HarperCollins, 1993.

Marquis, Milton. *Monetary Theory and Policy.* Minneapolis–St. Paul: West Publishing Company, 1996.

McCallum, Bennett, and Marvin Goodfriend. "Demand for Money: Theoretical Studies." In *The New Palgrave: Money,* ed. John Eatwell, Murray Milgate, and Peter Newman, pp. 117–130. New York: W. W. Norton, 1989.

Thorn, Richard, ed. *Monetary Theory and Policy: Major Contributions to Contemporary Thought.* New York: Praeger Publishers, 1976.

MoneyXtra

moneyxtra! Log on to the MoneyXtra Web site now (http://moneyxtra.swcollege.com) for additional learning resources such as practice quizzes, case studies, readings, and additional economic applications.

Chapter 20

Day-to-Day Monetary Policy—
Fed Operating Procedures

Today, many economists regard reserve requirements as an anachronism from bygone days. According to these economists, reserve requirements might be a useful stabilizing tool if central banks really desired to achieve targets for monetary aggregates that are linked to the monetary base via money multipliers with values that depend in part on required reserve ratios. Currently, however, most central banks pay relatively little attention to variations in money growth, so, in the view of these economists, reserve requirements around the world should be sharply reduced, if not eliminated.

A significant number of countries are on the way to doing just that. Although depository institutions in Germany and other nations of the European Monetary Union (EMU) face required reserve ratios of 2 percent for both transactions and nontransactions deposits, this is much lower than the normal 5–12 percent range for transactions deposits and 3–5 percent range for nontransactions deposits previously faced in Germany and other major EMU nations. The Bank of Japan requires Japanese depository institutions to set aside no more than 1.3 percent of either type of deposits as reserves. Today, the required reserve ratio for both types of deposits in the United Kingdom is only 0.35 percent, and depository institutions in Canada and New Zealand face no reserve requirements whatsoever on transactions deposits. Among developed nations, only the United States appears to be an exception to the trend toward lowering or eliminating reserve requirements. Although the Fed assesses no reserve requirement on nontransactions deposits, it continues to require U.S. depository institutions to set aside 10 percent of their transactions deposits as either vault cash or reserve deposits held with Federal Reserve banks.

Fundamental Issues

1. What are the key instruments of monetary policy?
2. What key factors affect the demand for reserves by depository institutions?
3. How do Federal Reserve policies influence the supply of reserves to depository institutions and the federal funds rate?
4. How is the federal funds rate related to other market interest rates?
5. How do Federal Reserve policies affect the quantity of money?
6. What are Federal Reserve operating procedures, and what operating procedures has the Federal Reserve used in recent years?

In fact, the effective U.S. required reserve ratio is much lower than 10 percent because many U.S. banks evade the bulk of reserve requirements. They do this by artificially reducing the size of the transactions deposit liabilities they must report to the Fed for purposes of meeting reserve requirements. They really do hold 10 percent of transactions deposits as reserves, but because the amount of transactions deposits officially on their balance sheets has shrunk, so have the amounts of reserves they must hold with the Fed. Thus, required reserves in the United States have fallen along with those held with central banks elsewhere in the developed world.

How do U.S. depository institutions evade legal reserve requirements? In what way does this complicate interpreting movements in monetary aggregates? How does the Federal Reserve conduct monetary policy if monetary aggregates are not central features of its policymaking? To be able to contemplate these questions, you must first understand how the Federal Reserve conducts monetary policy from week to week and, indeed, from day to day. Helping you gain this understanding is the purpose of the present chapter.

The Instruments of Monetary Policy

In its role as monetary policymaker, the Fed can influence the monetary base, monetary aggregates, credit flows, and, ultimately, other economic variables such as interest rates, national income, and the rate of inflation. It does so using its available monetary policy *instruments,* which are factors that the Fed can determine, at least in principle, on a day-to-day basis.

Open Market Operations

Open market operations are the key means by which the Fed conducts monetary policy each day. As we discussed in Chapter 17, the voting members of the Federal Open Market Committee (FOMC)—the seven Federal Reserve Board governors and five Federal Reserve bank presidents—determine the general strategy of open market operations at meetings that take place every six to eight weeks. They outline this strategy in the FOMC directive, which lays out the FOMC's general objectives, mandates short-term federal funds rate objectives, and establishes specific target ranges for monetary aggregates. After each meeting, the FOMC issues a brief statement to the media, which then run stories about the Fed's action or inaction and what it is likely to mean for the economy. Typically, these stories appear under headlines such as "Fed Cuts Key Interest Rate," "Fed Acts to Push Up Interest Rates," or "Fed Decides to Leave Interest Rates Alone."

The FOMC leaves it to the Federal Reserve Bank of New York's Trading Desk to implement the directive from day to day during the weeks between FOMC meetings. The media spend little time considering how the Trading Desk conducts its policies, taking it for granted that the Fed can implement the policy action that it says it plans to undertake. In this chapter, you will learn what happens behind the scenes.

THE MECHANICS OF OPEN MARKET OPERATIONS The Trading Desk's open market operations typically are confined to a one-hour interval each weekday morning. The New York Fed's Trading Desk conducts two types of open market operations. One type, called an *outright transaction,* is an open market purchase or sale in which the Fed is not obliged to resell or repurchase securities at a later date. The other kind of operation is a *repurchase-agreement transaction.* As discussed in Chapters 1 and 3, repurchase agreements are contracts that commit the seller of a security to repurchase the security at a later date. The Trading Desk often buys securities from dealers under agreements for the dealers to repurchase them at a later date. The Trading Desk also commonly uses *reverse repurchase agreements* when conducting open market sales. These are agreements for the Fed to repurchase the securities from dealers at a later time.

Table 20-1 summarizes the Fed's open market transactions during a typical year. The Trading Desk often uses outright purchases or sales when it wishes to change the aggregate level of depository institution reserves. In contrast, it normally uses repurchase agreements when its main goal is simply to stabilize the current level of reserves. Nevertheless, the Trading Desk can substitute repurchase-agreement transactions for outright purchases or sales to change the overall reserve level by appropriately mismatching repurchase-agreement transactions on a continuous basis.

A MULTIPLIER VIEW OF THE EFFECTS OF OPEN MARKET OPERATIONS As you learned in Chapter 16, open market operations that change the total amount of reserves at depository institutions cause the monetary base to change. A variation in the size of the monetary base, in turn, alters the quantities of money and credit.

Recall from Chapter 16 that a change in the quantity of money, M, induced by a change in the monetary base, MB, is equal to the money multiplier times the amount of the change in the monetary base, or

$$\Delta M = m_M \times \Delta MB,$$

where m_M is the money multiplier. In Chapter 16, we found that the value of this multiplier for M1 is $m_M = (c + 1)/(rr_D + e + c)$, where c is the public's desired holdings of currency relative to transactions deposits, rr_D is the required reserve ratio for transactions deposits, and e is the desired ratio of excess reserve holdings to transactions deposits for depository institutions. Likewise, if m_{TC} denotes

Table 20-1 Fed Open Market Transactions during 2002 ($ Millions)

Outright transactions:	
Purchases	$ 45,357
Sales and redemptions	1,429
Repurchase agreements and matched transactions:	
Purchases	4,677,597
Sales	4,715,526
Net change in Federal Reserve System open market account	5,999

SOURCE: Board of Governors of the Federal Reserve System, *Federal Reserve Bulletin,* July 2002; authors' estimates.

the value of the credit multiplier, then the amount by which all depository institutions change total credit, TC, by lending and acquiring securities, in response to a change in the monetary base is equal to

$$\Delta TC = m_{TC} \times \Delta MB.$$

In Chapter 16, we determined that the value of the total credit multiplier is $m_{TC} = (1 - rr_D - e)/(c + rr_D + e)$.

Recall that the monetary base is equal to the sum of currency, C, and total reserves, TR. But we can think of total reserves at depository institutions as arising from one of two sources. One way that depository institutions can obtain reserves from the Fed is to borrow reserves directly from the Fed's discount window. Such reserves are *borrowed reserves,* denoted BR. The primary way that depository institutions get reserves from the Fed, however, is through open market operations. These reserves, called *nonborrowed reserves,* denoted NBR, are the amount of total reserves not borrowed from the Fed. Total reserves then are the sum of borrowed reserves and nonborrowed reserves, or $TR = BR + NBR$.

Hence, open market operations cause a change in nonborrowed reserves and thereby change total reserves and the monetary base. As a result, changes in nonborrowed reserves caused by open market operations have direct multiplier effects on the quantities of money and credit. From our relationships above, the amounts of these effects on money and credit could be computed using the following equations:

$$\Delta M = m_M \times \Delta NBR$$

and

$$\Delta TC = m_{TC} \times \Delta NBR.$$

For instance, suppose that the money multiplier is equal to $m_M = 2.5$ and the credit multiplier is equal to $m_{TC} = 3$. In this instance, a \$10 million open market purchase by the Fed increases the quantity of money by \$25 million and the total amount of loans and securities held by depository institutions by \$30 million. This helps us to see why the Fed uses open market operations as its key means of conducting monetary policy, given that it can conduct such operations any day that it wishes, thereby producing desired changes in the amounts of money and credit. (Recently, the Fed has been contemplating whether a dwindling market for Treasury securities might require it to find a different financial asset to buy and sell in conducting open market operations; see *Policy Focus: What Would the Fed Do If Government Securities Were to Disappear?*)

The Discount Window

In principle, another way that the Fed can influence the quantities of money and credit is by inducing changes in depository institution borrowing at the discount window. The Fed can do this by altering the terms under which it stands willing to lend to depository institutions.

DISCOUNT WINDOW POLICY Earlier in the Fed's history, depository institutions borrowed from the Fed via a process called "discounting." A depository institution would post U.S. government securities at a Federal Reserve bank, which would increase the institution's reserve account balance by an amount smaller

GLOBAL POLICY Focus CYBER MANAGEMENT

What Would the Fed Do If Government Securities Were to Disappear?

As the federal government's budget deficit began to decline in the late 1990s, the U.S. Treasury began to cut back on issues of new Treasury bills, notes, and bonds, and it eliminated 30-year bonds entirely. The prospect of balancing the federal budget and perhaps even operating with federal surpluses meant that eventually the Treasury might redeem outstanding debt over time without replacing it. As a result, the stock of Treasury securities in the hands of the public and on the balance sheet of the Federal Reserve might dwindle away as the market for Treasury securities disappeared. This prospect induced Fed officials to launch a crash effort to figure out how to conduct monetary policy without Treasury securities to buy and sell.

Finding New Securities for Open Market Operations?

One possible Federal Reserve response to a dried-up market for Treasury bills, notes, and bonds would be to find new financial instruments to buy and sell, such as corporate stocks or bonds. Conducting open market operations with either stocks or corporate bonds, however, would leave the Fed open to accusations that it was favoring some borrowers over others and interfering with private allocations of credit. Undoubtedly, if the Fed bought and sold privately issued securities, critics would worry about such issues as whether the Fed should be purchasing the securities of a company with a spotty environmental record or whether the Fed was selling another company's securities because it had inside knowledge of a falloff in the company's growth prospects.

The Fed also considered bonds issued by foreign governments, municipal bonds, and securities issued with the full backing of the U.S. Treasury, such as mortgage-backed securities of the General National Mortgage Association. Conducting open market operations using financial instruments issued by foreign governments, municipal governments, or U.S. government agencies at least would not expose the Fed to criticism that it was favoring one private enterprise over another. Nevertheless, in some situations the Fed still might feel pressured to help foreign governments, cities or states, or federal government agencies facing funding difficulties.

A Reprieve for the Fed

Even as the Fed began to contemplate these alternatives to open market operations with Treasury securities in the early 2000s, increased federal spending and declining tax revenues pushed the federal government back into a deficit that the U.S. Treasury forecasts will last until at least 2005. Consequently, the Treasury is likely to continue issuing securities for at least a few more years. The Fed now has plenty of time to evaluate the pros and cons of alternative approaches to monetary policymaking.

For Critical Analysis: In terms of how open market operations affect the quantity of money in circulation, does it make any difference what financial asset the Fed buys or sells?

than the value of the securities. When the discount arrangement expired, the depository institution would repurchase the securities at their true value. The Federal Reserve bank would keep the difference as a "discount rate," or effective interest charge for the loan.

Today, most discount window loans are actually *advances*. The Fed simply increases the balance in the borrowing institution's reserve account and has an officer of the institution sign a promissory note. The term *discount window borrowing* remains with us, however. And the interest rate that the Fed charges for advances continues to be known as the *discount rate,* even though it is really just a lending rate.

THE DISCOUNT RATE, MONEY, AND CREDIT IN THE MULTIPLIER MODEL The main alternative to borrowing new reserves from the Fed is for a depository institution to borrow existing reserves from other depository institutions in the federal funds market. This means that a key determinant of total discount window borrowing is the difference, or *spread,* between the federal funds rate and the discount rate. As the amount by which the federal funds rate exceeds the discount rate rises or the amount by which the discount rate exceeds the federal funds rate declines, discount window borrowing becomes relatively more attractive to depository institutions.

Suppose that the Fed decides to use discount window policy as a means of increasing the quantity of money and credit. This requires reducing the discount rate relative to the federal funds rate. This causes borrowed reserves to rise by some amount, ΔBR, which results in an increase in total reserves and in the monetary base, thereby generating a multiplier effect on the quantity of money:

$$\Delta M = m_M \times \Delta BR.$$

That is, the quantity of money rises by the induced rise in borrowed reserves times the money multiplier. Likewise, the increase in borrowed reserves induces a multiplier effect on the amount of credit extended by depository institutions:

$$\Delta TC = m_{TC} \times \Delta BR.$$

This says that the total amount of loans and securities at depository institutions rises by the induced increase in borrowed reserves multiplied by the credit multiplier.

An Indirect Policy Approach Note that once the Fed induces a given change in discount window borrowing, the multiplier effects on money and credit are analogous to those generated by open market operations. Nevertheless, the effects of discount window policy are much less direct because the Fed must be able to cause the difference between the discount rate and the federal funds rate to change by just the right amount to induce the desired change in borrowing.

For almost eighty years, the Fed tended to keep the discount rate unchanged for weeks at a time, and it typically set the discount rate slightly below the federal funds rate. In 2002, however, the Fed altered the way it lends to depository institutions. It now sets the discount rate *above* the federal funds rate. This discourages depository institutions from seeking loans unless they truly face significant liquidity problems. Currently, the Fed keeps the discount rate 1 percentage point higher than the market-determined federal funds rate. Thus, if the market federal funds rate is 3 percent, the discount rate is 4 percent. If the federal funds rate increases to 3.5 percent, the Fed automatically raises the discount rate to 4.5 percent.

Theory, Not Fact In principle, the Fed could continue to use the discount rate as an instrument of monetary policy by changing the amount by which the discount rate exceeds the federal funds rate. For instance, if the Fed reduced the differential from 1 percentage point to 0.05 percentage point, this would greatly reduce depository institutions' disincentive to borrow from the Fed. As Fed lending increased in response, borrowed reserves would rise. The Fed has indicated that it does not plan to conduct monetary policy in this way, however.

Reserve Requirements

As we discussed in Chapter 14, the Depository Institutions Deregulation and Monetary Control Act of 1980 empowered the Fed to impose uniform reserve requirements on all federally insured depository institutions. Since that time the Fed has mandated that all such institutions hold reserves as fractions of their transactions deposit balances. These reserve requirements are the final key tool that the Fed has at its disposal to influence monetary and credit aggregates.

Computation of Reserve Requirements Today, the Fed's reserve requirements are fairly simple. For the first $50 million or so in transactions deposits, any depository institution must hold 3 percent as required reserves. For deposits in excess of this amount, depository institutions must hold 10 percent as reserves. Because most transactions deposits in the United States are at the largest institutions, this means that the bulk of transactions deposits are subject to the 10 percent requirement. From 1984 to 1998, depository institutions computed their required reserves by averaging their transactions deposits over a two-week *computation period.* Then they applied the Fed's required reserve ratios to this average amount of deposits and maintained an average reserve level consistent with their reserve requirement during a two-week reserve *maintenance period.* The maintenance period and computation period largely overlapped, so depository institutions' required reserves were very closely related to their current deposits.

In 1998, however, the Fed decided to return to the procedure that it had used for calculating required reserves before 1984. Under this procedure, the *computation period* precedes the *maintenance period* by several days. As a result, depository institutions have more time to determine the amounts of reserves that they will have to hold each week to meet their reserve requirements.

How Reserve Requirement Changes Affect Money and Credit To see how reserve requirements themselves might be changed to influence the amounts of money and credit, recall that the basic money multiplier is $m_M = (c + 1)/(rr_D + e + c)$ and the basic credit multiplier is $m_{TC} = (1 - rr_D - e)/(c + rr_D + e)$. A reduction in the required reserve ratio, rr_D, increases the values of both multipliers. This makes sense because if reserve requirements are lower, then depository institutions can lend more reserves at every stage of the process of deposit and credit expansion. In contrast, an increase in the required reserve ratio reduces the multipliers.

This means that changes in reserve requirements can alter the quantities of money and credit by increasing or reducing the multipliers that link money and credit to the monetary base. In principle, therefore, the Fed could try to influence the amounts of money and credit by varying its required reserve ratios. The Fed, however, rarely does this. Every change in reserve requirements necessitates alterations in planning and management by both the Fed and depository institutions. Therefore, the Fed usually changes reserve requirements as rarely as possible. Indeed, the Fed has changed reserve requirement ratios only three times since

1980, and none of these changes was for the purpose of influencing the quantities of money or credit. Furthermore, if anything, the Fed's stance on reserve requirements since the mid-1990s has further *reduced* their significance, as we discuss in *Link to Policy* on page 497.

1. What are the key instruments of monetary policy? The Fed's key tool for conducting monetary policy on a day-to-day basis is open market operations, which change the amount of nonborrowed reserves and thereby affect the monetary base and the quantities of money and credit. A secondary policy tool is discount window policy. By changing the terms by which it makes discount window loans available, the Fed can influence the amount of reserves that depository institutions borrow, which also ultimately affects the amounts of money and credit. A third, but seldom-used, tool is required reserve ratios. Changes in these ratios alter the money and credit multipliers, thereby causing variations in monetary and credit aggregates.

The Demand for Depository Institution Reserves

The money multiplier approach is useful for assessing the essential effects of changes in the Federal Reserve's monetary policy instruments. Nevertheless, it does not address several questions: How does Federal Reserve policymaking influence interest yields? How do changes in interest rates affect money holdings of consumers and businesses? To answer these questions, you must understand the factors that determine how many reserves depository institutions wish to hold.

The Federal Funds Rate and Excess Reserves

Recall from Chapter 16 that, because of the money multiplier process, depository institutions play a key role in determining the quantity of money. From the day-to-day perspective of depository institutions, the key interest rate is the federal funds rate because this is the rate at which these institutions can lend or borrow reserves from day to day to meet reserve requirements or to fund their extensions of credit through lending or purchases of securities.

The Opportunity Cost of Holding Excess Reserves As we discussed in Chapter 16, depository institutions usually maintain some holdings of reserves over and above the amounts that they must hold to meet the Fed's reserve requirements. These reserves are *excess reserves*. Normally, depository institutions hold excess reserves as a contingency against a need for cash arising, perhaps, from unanticipated deposit withdrawals or unexpected opportunities for profitable loans or security purchases.

Holding reserves as vault cash or as reserve deposits with Federal Reserve banks yields no interest return to depository institutions, however. Instead of holding such excess reserves, depository institutions can easily lend them to other institutions that wish to borrow such reserves in the federal funds market. In so doing, the lending institutions convert non-interest-bearing excess reserves into short-term loans that generate revenues and enhance profitability.

This means that the federal funds rate—the rate of interest at which depository institutions borrow from and lend to one another in the federal funds market—is the best measure of the opportunity cost of holding excess reserves. If the federal funds rate is relatively low, then the opportunity cost that depository institutions incur by holding excess reserves is relatively small, and they will be more likely to hold relatively large amounts of excess reserves. But if the federal funds rate rises significantly, the opportunity cost of holding excess reserves will increase, and depository institutions will be more likely to lend these reserves to other institutions in the federal funds market.

The Inverse Relationship between the Federal Funds Rate and Excess Reserves This reasoning implies that the demand for excess reserves by depository institutions should be *inversely related* to the federal funds rate. If the federal funds rate rises, then depository institutions will desire to hold fewer excess reserves. In contrast, if the federal funds rate falls, then depository institutions will be more willing to maintain larger balances of excess reserves.

In principle, therefore, the Federal Reserve can influence how many reserves depository institutions desire to hold even without any reserve requirements. It can do this by enacting policies that alter the federal funds rate. We shall return to this point shortly, when we discuss how the Fed supplies reserves to depository institutions.

Transactions Deposits and Required Reserves

As you learned in Chapter 16, however, required reserves constitute the predominant component of depository institution reserve holdings. As we already noted, the Fed assesses two required reserve ratios: a 3 percent ratio for just over the first $50 million in transactions deposits (the Fed adjusts this threshold upward from time to time) at each depository institution and a 10 percent ratio for all transactions deposits above this level. The 10 percent ratio applies to the bulk of transactions deposits, so we can approximate the total amount of reserves that depository institutions desire to hold to meet reserve requirements by

$$RR = rr_D \times D,$$

where RR denotes required reserves, rr_D is the required reserve ratio, and D represents the total amount of transactions deposits at depository institutions.

Suppose that the amount of transactions deposits in the banking system is equal to $430 billion. Then, with a required reserve ratio of $rr_D = 0.10$, the amount of reserves that depository institutions demand equals $RR = rr_D \times D = 0.10 \times \$430$ billion $=$ $43 billion.

Depository Institutions' Total Reserve Demand

The total reserves that depository institutions desire to hold is the sum of their desired holdings of excess reserves and the amount of reserves that they demand to meet reserve requirements established by the Fed. Because depository institutions must hold sufficient reserves to meet their reserve requirements, the *minimum* amount of reserves that they demand is equal to their required reserves. In

Reserve demand schedule: A graphical depiction of the inverse relationship between the total amount of reserves demanded by depository institutions and the federal funds rate.

Figure 20-1, this is shown as the \$43 billion amount computed above based on a required reserve ratio of $rr_D = 0.10$ and a level of transactions deposits of \$430 billion.

In addition, however, depository institutions usually hold some amount of excess reserves. As we discussed above, the amount of funds that these institutions allocate to excess reserves depends on the opportunity cost of these funds, as measured by the federal funds rate, denoted r_f in Figure 20-1. If the federal funds rate is sufficiently high, such as $r_f = 10$ percent, then the opportunity cost may be high enough that depository institutions choose to hold zero excess reserves. In this situation, their desired total reserve holdings will be equal to the minimum amount that they must hold to meet reserve requirements, or \$43 billion. This is the uppermost point of the reserve demand schedule shown in Figure 20-1.

But if the federal funds rate is lower, such as $r_f = 5$ percent, then depository institutions will perceive a reduced opportunity cost of holding excess reserves. Consequently, they will be more willing to hold such reserves as a contingency against deposit withdrawals or the possibility that profitable loan or security opportunities might arise. Figure 20-1 indicates a situation in which depository institutions are willing to hold an amount of excess reserves equal to $ER = \$2$ billion at this lower federal funds rate. At this rate, therefore, the total reserves demanded by depository institutions equal the sum of the \$43 billion that they must hold to meet their reserve requirements and the \$2 billion in excess reserves that they are willing to hold at the federal funds rate of $r_f = 5$ percent, or $TR = RR + ER = \$43 \text{ billion} + \$2 \text{ billion} = \$45 \text{ billion}$.

This analysis indicates that there is an *inverse relationship* between the federal funds rate and total reserves demanded by depository institutions. The **reserve demand schedule** in Figure 20-1 depicts this inverse relationship. This schedule,

Figure 20-1
The Demand for and Supply of Total Depository Institution Reserves.

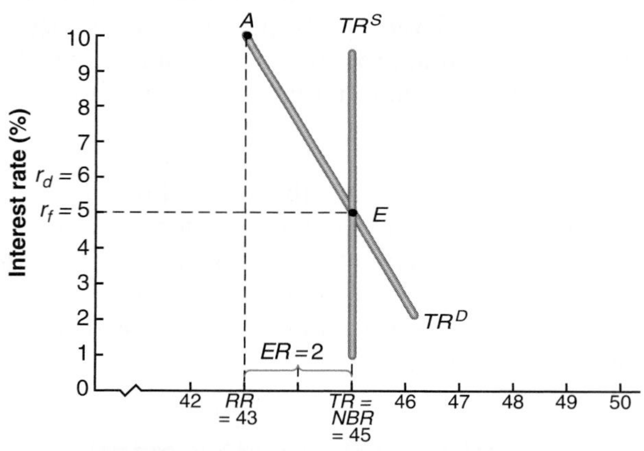

The minimum amount of reserves that depository institutions demand is the amount that they must hold to meet their reserve requirements. With a required reserve ratio of 10 percent and total transactions deposits of \$430 billion, this amount is \$43 billion. At a market federal funds rate of 5 percent, depository institutions hold \$2 billion in excess reserves, so the total quantity of reserves demanded equals \$45 billion. If the Fed supplies \$45 billion in reserves then the market federal funds rate is 5 percent at point E, and the quantity of reserves supplied equals \$45 billion.

which we denote TR^D, shows how total reserves desired by depository institutions vary with changes in the federal funds rate. Along this schedule, a rise in the federal funds rate induces depository institutions to demand fewer reserves until they reach the minimum amount needed to meet their reserve requirements. A decline in the federal funds rate, in contrast, induces depository institutions to accumulate increasingly large amounts of reserves at levels above the minimum required amount. Hence, the reserve demand schedule slopes downward.

2. What key factors affect the demand for reserves by depository institutions? Depository institutions desire to hold reserves to meet reserve requirements and as a contingency against unexpected cash needs. Consequently, the main factors affecting their desired reserve holdings are the required reserve ratio, the quantity of transactions deposits in the banking system, and the opportunity cost of holding reserves in excess of those required. The opportunity cost of holding excess reserves is the federal funds rate that institutions could earn by lending excess reserves in the federal funds market.

The Supply of Depository Institution Reserves

When Congress enacted the Federal Reserve Act of 1913, it gave the Federal Reserve System the authority to lend to depository institutions. Then, in the Banking Act of 1935, it granted the Fed the authority to conduct open market operations. Hence, these congressional actions authorized the Fed to supply reserves to the nation's depository institutions. If we want to understand the supply side of the reserves market, we must turn our attention back to the Fed.

The Discount Window and Borrowed Reserves

As we discussed earlier, one way that the Federal Reserve supplies reserves to depository institutions is through direct discount window loans to individual institutions. In principle, the Fed can alter the total volume of this lending by changing the terms under which it makes reserves available, but in actuality, the Fed rarely changes the basic rules under which it lends.

Since the Fed's 2002 policy change that places the discount rate exactly 1 percentage point above the market federal funds rate, depository institutions have had little incentive to borrow reserves from the Fed at all. This means that the amount of borrowed reserves supplied by the Fed from its discount window is typically at or very close to zero at any given time.

Open Market Operations and Nonborrowed Reserves

The key means by which the Fed supplies new reserves to depository institutions is through open market purchases of government securities. The quantity of reserves that it supplies in this way are *nonborrowed reserves, NBR*.

You will see shortly that the Federal Reserve Bank of New York's Trading Desk can influence interest rates by conducting open market operations that *change* the amount of nonborrowed reserves in the banking system. In the absence of any open market purchases or sales, however, the amount of nonborrowed reserves is a constant amount. Furthermore, this amount of nonborrowed reserves places a *lower bound* on the amount of reserves in the nation's banking system at a given point in time. These reserves can circulate among depository institutions, but the aggregate volume of reserves cannot fall below this level in the absence of open market operations by the New York Fed's Trading Desk.

On the Web
What is the current distribution of depository institution reserves? Find out the split of total reserves between borrowed and nonborrowed reserves and between required and excess reserves by viewing the Federal Reserve's H.3 *Statistical Release* at http://www.federalreserve.gov/releases/.

The Fed's Supply of Total Depository Institution Reserves

Figure 20-1 on page 480 depicts the supply schedule for total depository institution reserves. As we have discussed, the base level of reserves supplied by the Fed is the quantity of nonborrowed reserves, NBR, which the Fed has supplied through past open market purchases. Thus, the total amount of reserves supplied by the Fed cannot fall below this quantity, which in Figure 20-1 is equal to $NBR = \$45$ billion.

In the past, whenever the federal funds rate exceeded the discount rate, depository institutions borrowed additional reserves from the Fed's discount window. Suppose that at some time before 2002, the discount rate was equal to $r_d = 4.5$ percent. In that case, if the federal funds rate was less than 4.5 percent, depository institutions had no incentive to borrow reserves from the Fed. Under such circumstances, the amount of reserves supplied by the Fed was the amount of nonborrowed reserves, NBR. But if the federal funds rate was higher than the discount rate, as it usually was, then depository institutions would borrow additional reserves directly from the Fed. For instance, suppose that the federal funds rate, r_f, was 5 percent. The 0.5 percentage point spread between the federal funds rate and the discount rate might have induced institutions to *borrow* \$1 billion from the Fed's discount window. Then the amount of borrowed reserves would have been equal to $BR = \$1$ billion, and the total quantity of reserves supplied by the Fed would have been the sum of the \$44 billion in nonborrowed reserves and the \$1 billion in borrowed reserves, or $TR = NBR + BR = \$44$ billion + \$1 billion = \$45 billion.

In Figure 20-1, however, we assume that with the discount rate set above the market federal funds rate at $r_d = 6$ percent, which is how the Fed now sets the discount rate, the quantity of reserves that depository institutions borrow from the Fed is approximately \$0 billion. Therefore, the **reserve supply schedule** in Figure 20-1, which is labeled TR^S, is vertical at the level of nonborrowed reserves of $NBR = \$45$ billion. This schedule shows that the amount of reserves that the Fed supplies to depository institutions does not vary with the federal funds rate.

Reserve supply schedule: A graphical depiction of the relationship between the total amount of reserves supplied by the Fed and the federal funds rate.

Determining the Equilibrium Federal Funds Rate

The market for total depository institution reserves attains an equilibrium when the total quantity of reserves that depository institutions demand from the Federal Reserve is just equal to the total quantity of reserves that the Fed supplies through open market operations and discount window loans. When this state of balance occurs, there are no pressures for the federal funds rate to rise or to fall. The resulting federal funds rate is the *equilibrium federal funds rate*.

Figure 20-1 depicts such an equilibrium situation. The total depository institution reserve demand schedule slopes downward to the right of the minimum amount of reserves that depository institutions desire to hold to meet their reserve requirements, RR = \$43 billion. The total reserve supply schedule is vertical at the quantity of nonborrowed reserves NBR = \$45 billion. At the point where the two schedules cross, the quantity of reserves demanded by depository institutions is equal to the quantity of reserves supplied to these institutions by the Fed, at \$45 billion.

The equilibrium federal funds rate in Figure 20-1 is equal to r_f = 5 percent. At this federal funds rate, the total amount of reserves demanded by depository institutions just matches the total quantity of reserves that the Fed supplies. Hence, there are no pressures for the federal funds rate to rise or to fall. The reason is that depository institutions are satisfied holding the amount of reserves that the Fed has supplied as long as the federal funds rate is equal to 5 percent.

Figure 20-2 summarizes the factors that determine the quantities of reserves supplied and demanded. The Fed's open market operations determine the quantity of nonborrowed reserves (NBR = \$45 billion in our example). The required reserve ratio and total deposits determine the amount of required reserves (RR =

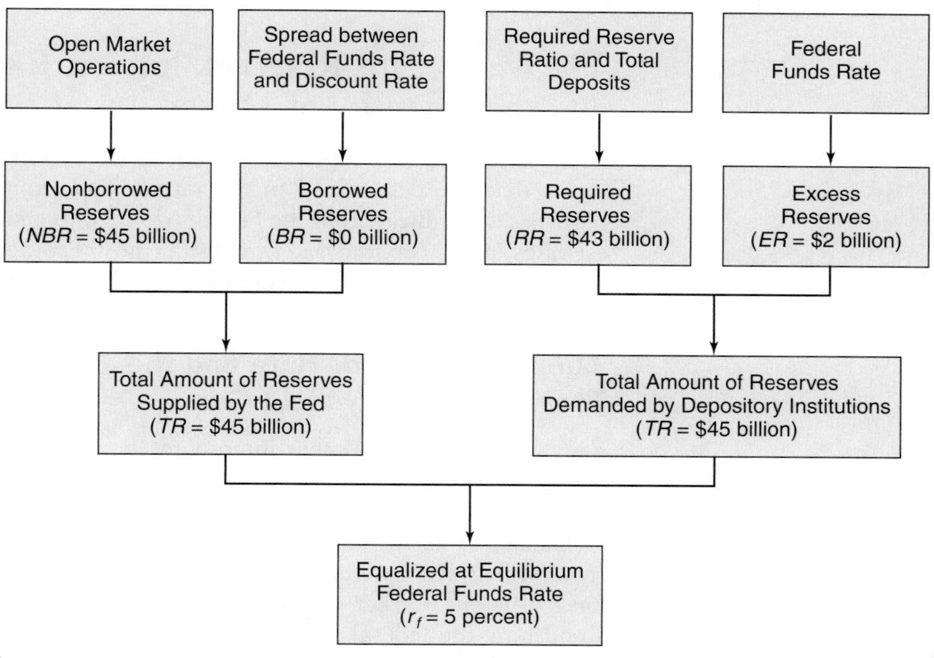

Figure 20-2 Factors That Determine the Equilibrium Federal Funds Rate.

The Fed supplies nonborrowed reserves via its open market operations. In Figure 20-1 on page 480, with the discount rate always set above the federal funds rate, no depository institutions borrow reserves from the Fed. Depository institutions hold most reserves to meet reserve requirements, and their excess reserve holdings vary with the opportunity cost of excess reserves, which is the federal funds rate. In Figure 20-1, these factors together yield \$43 billion in required reserves and \$2 billion in excess reserves. The federal funds rate adjusts to equalize the quantity of reserves supplied by the Fed and the quantity of reserves demanded by depository institutions.

\$43 billion in our example). The federal funds rate determines the opportunity cost of holding excess reserves and, consequently, the amount of excess reserve holdings of depository institutions (ER = \$2 billion). Therefore, reserve requirements, total deposits in the banking system, and the federal funds rate all influence the total amount of reserves demanded by depository institutions.

At the equilibrium federal funds rate, the total amount of reserves supplied by the Fed is equal to the total amount of reserves demanded by depository institutions. That is, the federal funds rate adjusts so that these quantities just balance. In our example, the amounts of reserves demanded and supplied are equal (TR = \$45 billion) at an equilibrium federal funds rate of $r_f = 5$ percent.

3. How do Federal Reserve policies influence the supply of reserves to depository institutions and the federal funds rate? The Fed controls the supply of reserves by determining the amount of nonborrowed reserves through open market purchases or by influencing the amount of reserves that depository institutions borrow through changes in its discount window policies. Because the equilibrium federal funds rate arises from the balancing of the quantity of reserves demanded by depository institutions with the quantity of reserves supplied by the Fed, the Fed's open market operations and discount window policies ultimately determine the value of the federal funds rate.

The Market for Reserves, Interest Rates, and the Quantity of Money

As we discussed in Chapter 4, the federal funds rate is only one of many interest yields that are determined in the money and capital markets. And yet media reports often indicate that the Fed has decided to change the *overall level* of interest rates in the economy. Let's consider how Fed actions that affect the equilibrium federal funds rate can spill over to influence other interest yields.

The Federal Funds Rate and the Treasury Security Yield Curve

Recall from Chapter 4 that interest rates on different financial instruments are related in two respects. One relationship is the *risk structure of interest rates:* financial instruments with identical terms to maturity will have different market yields as a result of different degrees of risk. The other relationship is the *term structure of interest rates:* financial instruments with similar risk features will have different market yields if they have different terms to maturity. To understand how the federal funds rate relates to the Treasury bill rate, we must take into account both of these concepts.

YIELD CURVES FOR FEDERAL FUNDS AND TREASURY SECURITIES As we discussed in Chapter 4, we can construct a *yield curve* for Treasury securities by plotting the yields that correspond to the securities' various terms of maturity, such as three months, six months, twelve months, and so on. Such a yield curve relates the interest rates on Treasury securities alone, because Treasury securities all have the same low risk. The existence of a term premium typically causes the Treasury securities yield curve to slope upward even in circumstances in which traders in financial markets do not expect interest rates to change.

We can also construct a yield curve for federal funds loans. As we noted in Chapter 3, most federal funds loans have one-day maturities, but some are *term federal funds loans* with maturities of one or more weeks. Typically, the yields on such term federal funds loans increase with the term of the loan. Consequently, the federal funds yield curve also slopes upward.

Federal funds loans, however, are riskier than Treasury securities. The government stands behind the Treasury securities that it issues with the full taxing power that it possesses. This makes defaults on such securities extremely unlikely. In contrast, most federal funds loans are unsecured transactions backed only by the ability of a borrowing depository institution to repay the loan when its one-day or multiday term ends. Although federal funds loan defaults are fairly rare, they do occur from time to time. In addition, on rare occasions parties to a federal funds transaction have disagreed on how to interpret the terms that they negotiated, and the result has been costly delays in the final settlement on the transaction.

DETERMINING THE TREASURY BILL RATE Because federal funds loans are riskier financial instruments than Treasury securities, there is a *risk premium* for any federal funds loans with maturities that match those of Treasury securities. This means that the federal funds yield curve will lie *above* the Treasury securities yield curve, as in Figure 20-3. At any term to maturity, the vertical distance between the two yield curves represents the risk premium.

Figure 20-3
Determining the Treasury Bill Rate.

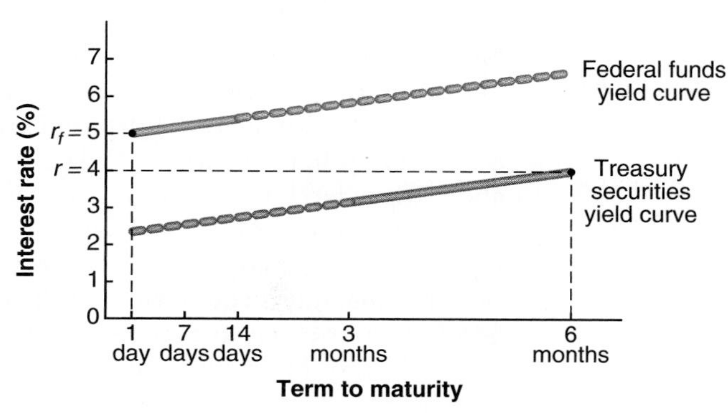

The Treasury securities yield curve typically slopes upward. Though market yields on very short Treasury maturities do not exist, they can be inferred from prices of Treasury securities that are within days of maturity—hence, the dashed portion of the Treasury securities yield curve. Likewise, the federal funds yield curve also slopes upward over maturities that range from a day to several weeks. Longer-term federal funds rates may be extrapolated from actual market rates on short-maturity federal funds loans—hence, the dashed portion of the federal funds yield curve. Federal funds are riskier than Treasury securities, so the federal funds rate typically exceeds the Treasury security rate that applies to a given maturity. Consequently, the Treasury security yield curve lies below the federal funds yield curve. If the equilibrium federal funds rate for a one-day maturity is 5 percent, then the six-month Treasury bill rate consistent with the term and risk structures of interest rates is 4 percent.

Note that the actual terms to maturity on term federal funds loans are never as lengthy as the shortest terms of Treasury bills (T-bills). Nevertheless, we can *infer* these dashed portions of both yield curves in Figure 20-3 by calculating the federal funds yields that would emerge from successively renewing federal funds loans from week to week and by examining the prices of Treasury securities that are within days of final maturity.

Once we have constructed yield curves for federal funds loans and Treasury securities, we can determine the equilibrium interest yield on a six-month T-bill, as depicted in Figure 20-3. Given an equilibrium one-day term federal funds rate of r_f = 5 percent, the six-month Treasury security rate consistent with the risk and term structures of interest rates must be equal to r = 4 percent. Because a six-month T-bill is nearly risk-free, it typically has a lower yield than a one-day federal funds loan even though the six-month T-bill has a much longer 182-day term to maturity. In the real world, however, the difference between the federal funds rate and the six-month T-bill rate normally is about 0.25 to 0.50 percentage point, rather than the 1 percentage point differential that we have chosen as a round number for our example in Figure 20-3.

4. How is the federal funds rate related to other market interest rates? Federal Reserve policies determine the supply of reserves to depository institutions and thereby influence the equilibrium federal funds rate. The risk and term structures of interest rates link the federal funds rate to other market interest rates, including Treasury security rates.

The Equilibrium Quantity of Money

Now we are in a position to evaluate all aspects of the linkage from Fed policymaking to the quantity of money. Figure 20-4 depicts this linkage from the Fed's primary policy tools to the determination of total aggregate money holdings in the economy. In panel (a), the Fed's choice of a discount rate one percentage point above the federal funds rate and of a level of nonborrowed reserves equal to NBR = \$45 billion determines the supply of total reserves to depository institutions. Given the demand for reserves by those institutions, the equilibrium federal funds rate that maintains equilibrium in the reserves market, at a total reserve level of \$45 billion, is equal to r_f = 5 percent.

Panel (b) of Figure 20-4 then shows the determination of the six-month T-bill rate. The interest yield on six-month T-bills that is consistent with the risk and term structures of interest rates depicted by the federal funds and Treasury security yield curves in panel (b) is equal to r = 4 percent. This interest yield is the opportunity cost of holding money. Panel (c) then shows the determination of the equilibrium quantity of money. From the money demand schedule, we can see that the total amount of desired money holdings at a 4 percent interest yield on six-month Treasury securities is \$1,000 billion (\$1 trillion). This, in our example, is the equilibrium quantity of money.

Of course, this is just an example. Values of the Fed's policy tools, total reserves, the federal funds rate, Treasury security rates, and the quantity of

Figure 20-4
Determining the Equilibrium Quantity of Money.

In the market for reserves, the federal funds rate adjusts to equilibrate the quantity of reserves demanded by depository institutions with the quantity of reserves supplied by the Fed at a level of \$45 billion. Given an equilibrium federal funds rate of $r_f = 5$ percent, the term and risk structures of interest rates reflected by the positions and shapes of the Treasury security and federal funds yield curves determine the equilibrium interest rate on a six-month Treasury bill, $r = 4$ percent. This interest rate is the opportunity cost of holding money. At this rate, and given their current total income, consumers and businesses choose to hold money balances of \$1,000 billion (\$1 trillion). In this instance, this is the equilibrium quantity of money.

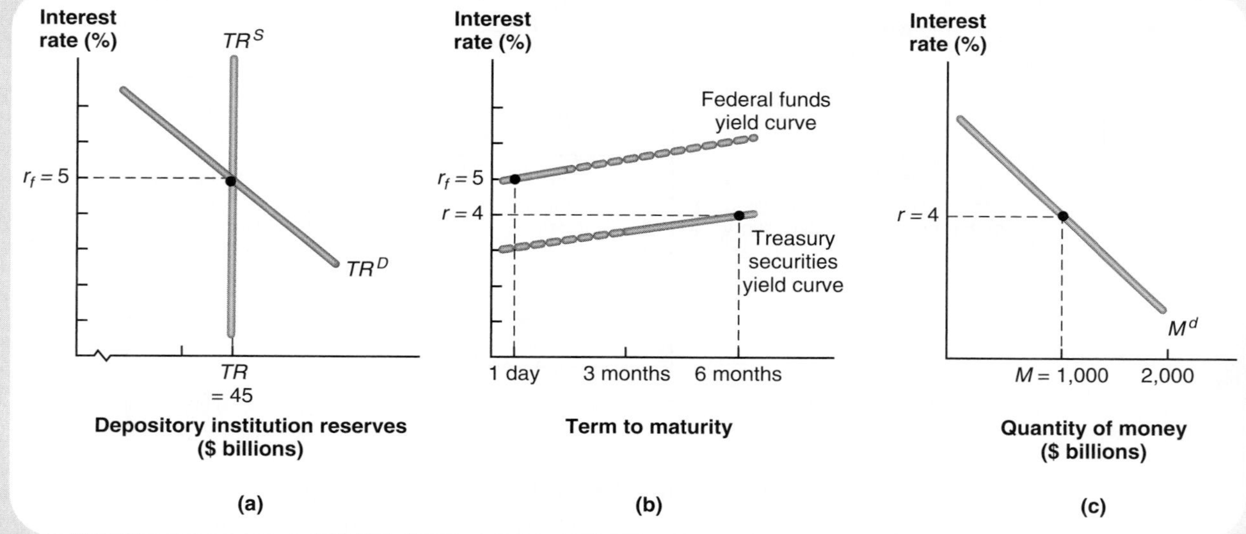

money vary from week to week and even from day to day. But Figure 20-4 shows the essential mechanics by which the Fed's policy choices relate to the final determination of the amount of money in the economy. Understanding the linkages depicted in Figure 20-4 is necessary for understanding how the Fed has conducted monetary policy in the past and how it conducts monetary policy today.

LINKING FED POLICIES IN THE MARKET FOR RESERVES TO THE QUANTITY OF MONEY Figure 20-5 on the next page uses solid arrows to chart the full policy connections that our example illustrates. Through open market operations and discount window policy, the Fed can control the total supply of reserves to depository institutions. The interaction of the Fed's supply of reserves with depository institutions' demand for reserves then determines the federal funds rate. Then the risk and term structures of interest rates, as reflected by the shapes and positions of the federal funds and Treasury security yield curves, determine the equilibrium T-bill rate that measures the opportunity cost of money holdings by consumers and businesses. Given their incomes, individuals and businesses then take into account this opportunity cost and determine the total amount of money that they desire to hold. This is the equilibrium quantity of money.

Figure 20-5
Linking Fed Policy Tools to the Quantity of Money.

This figure summarizes how Fed policy tools relate to the determination of the equilibrium quantity of money. Changes in a Fed policy instrument affect the supply of reserves and influence the equilibrium federal funds rate. Via the term and risk structures of interest rates, this induces a change in the Treasury bill rate, which alters the opportunity cost of holding money and thereby gives people the incentive to change their desired money holdings. The indirect, interest rate channel of monetary policy is indicated by the dashed arrows: Fed policy tools affect the federal funds rate, which influences the Treasury bill rate, which, in turn, affects the equilibrium quantity of money.

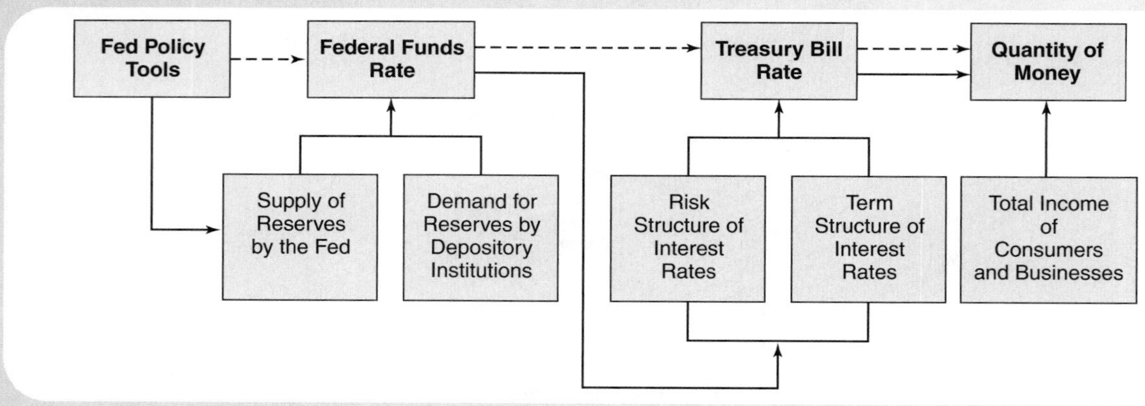

The *dashed arrows* in Figure 20-5 depict basic connections from the Fed to the quantity of money. Fed policy tools directly influence the federal funds rate, which, in turn, affects the T-bill rate. Then, given the total income of households and businesses, the T-bill rate influences their total money holdings. Consequently, the dashed arrows capture the essential *interest rate channel* through which Fed policy tools affect the quantity of money.

HOW FED POLICY ACTIONS CHANGE THE QUANTITY OF MONEY Because the Fed changes reserve requirements very infrequently, open market purchases and sales and changes in the terms of its lending to depository institutions are the primary means by which the Fed makes tactical monetary policy adjustments from day to day and week to week. Both of these policy tools exert their effects by changing the total amount of reserves that the Fed supplies to depository institutions. Such variations in the supply of total depository institution reserves cause changes in the equilibrium federal funds and T-bill rates and alterations in the quantity of money that consumers and businesses desire to hold.

To understand how the Fed can cause such changes, let's think about how a change in the supply of reserves affects interest rates and the quantity of money. Figure 20-6 illustrates the effects of an open market purchase, which increases the total quantity of reserves supplied at the current equilibrium federal funds rate. Hence, the open market purchase generates an imbalance in the market for depository institution reserves: the quantity of reserves supplied by the Fed exceeds the quantity of reserves demanded by depository institutions. Depository institutions

Figure 20-6
Inducing an Increase in the Quantity of Money.

A Fed open market purchase increases the amount of reserves, from *TR* to *TR′*, and thereby induces a decline in the equilibrium federal funds rate, from r_f to r_f'. People then expect that future federal funds rates will be lower, and so the federal funds yield curve shifts downward. Other things being equal, the risk premium between a Treasury security and a federal funds loan will remain the same at any term to maturity, so the Treasury security yield curve shifts downward, and the six-month Treasury bill rate falls from *r* to *r′*. This reduction in the opportunity cost of holding money will induce people to increase their holdings of money so the equilibrium quantity of money rises from *M* to *M′*.

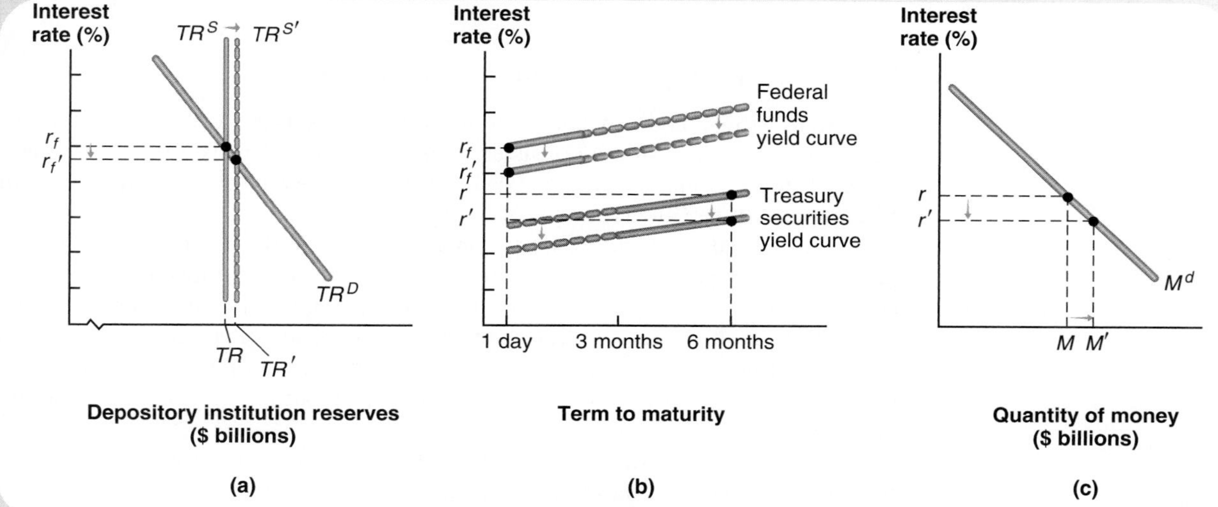

increase their excess reserve holdings only if the federal funds rate falls, causing the opportunity cost of holding excess reserves to decline. Thus, the second effect of the open market purchase is a reduction in the equilibrium federal funds rate.

The fall in the federal funds rate leads to an expected decline in the federal funds rate for future days as well. This means that expected interest rates across the term and risk structures of interest rates decrease. At a six-month term to maturity, the interest yield on a Treasury security falls. The final effect stems from the fact that this reduction in the six-month T-bill rate causes the opportunity cost of holding money to decline. As a result, individuals and businesses increase their money holdings. The open market purchase thereby causes the quantity of money to increase.

5. How do Federal Reserve policies affect the quantity of money?
Open market operations and discount rate changes alter the supply of reserves to depository institutions, thereby changing the federal funds rate. Via the risk and term structures of interest rates, such variations in the federal funds rate induce movements in the Treasury bill rate and alter the opportunity cost of holding money. This causes individuals and businesses to change the amount of money that they hold.

Federal Reserve Operating Procedures

Once a battle begins, military leaders must make a number of tactical decisions. They have to decide how to place and maneuver their land, air, and naval forces in a manner that is consistent with their overall strategic plan. Likewise, Fed officials often must vary their policy tools each day or week as they try to follow the broad strategy that they have established for a period encompassing many weeks or months. Like military officers, Fed officials must develop tactics, or day-to-day and week-to-week policy actions that are consistent with their broader strategy for monetary policy.

Monetary Policy Operating Procedures

As human beings, Fed officials sometimes make mistakes; their short-term policy decisions turn out to be inconsistent with their broader strategy for monetary policy. If the Fed makes a tactical policy mistake one day or week, it can attempt to compensate for its error the following day or week. Nevertheless, to achieve its strategic goals over many weeks or months, the Fed must follow appropriate daily and weekly tactics in its conduct of monetary policy. Indeed, a policy strategy can be defined as a *set of tactics*. For this reason, let's begin by discussing how the Fed can make tactical policy changes using its available policy tools. Once we understand how the Fed can conduct policy on a daily or weekly basis, we can then consider how it pursues broader strategies by adopting particular operating procedures for monetary policy.

Sometimes critics contend that the Fed makes too many policy decisions "by the seat of its pants." Yet the Fed typically follows predetermined *strategies* in its conduct of monetary policy. In military thinking, a strategy is the formation of broad plans for achieving an overall objective through an intended set of battlefield movements. Likewise, for the Fed, a *monetary policy strategy* is a general plan for achieving some set of economic objectives. The Fed normally tries to implement such a strategy by following an **operating procedure**, which is a self-imposed guideline for conducting monetary policy over a horizon stretching across several weeks or months. During the past thirty years, the Fed has experimented with a variety of operating procedures.

Alternative Operating Procedures for Monetary Policy

The Fed may adopt two basic types of *strategies* over periods of many weeks, months, or even years. One strategy involves focusing on target levels for depository institutions' reserves. The other strategy entails targeting an interest rate.

A Reserves-Targeting Procedure A possible approach to a reserves-targeting strategy is for the Fed to establish a target value for total reserves. Then it can conduct open market operations as needed to keep the level of total reserves at this target level.

Operating procedure: A guideline for conducting monetary policy over several weeks or months.

To understand the tactical approach that the Fed needs to follow from day to day if it pursues a reserves-targeting strategy, consider panel (a) of Figure 20-7. To keep the equilibrium level of reserves at a targeted level, the Fed must deter-

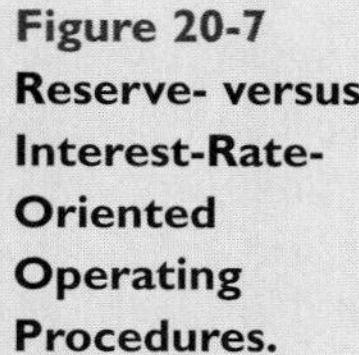

Figure 20-7 Reserve- versus Interest-Rate-Oriented Operating Procedures.

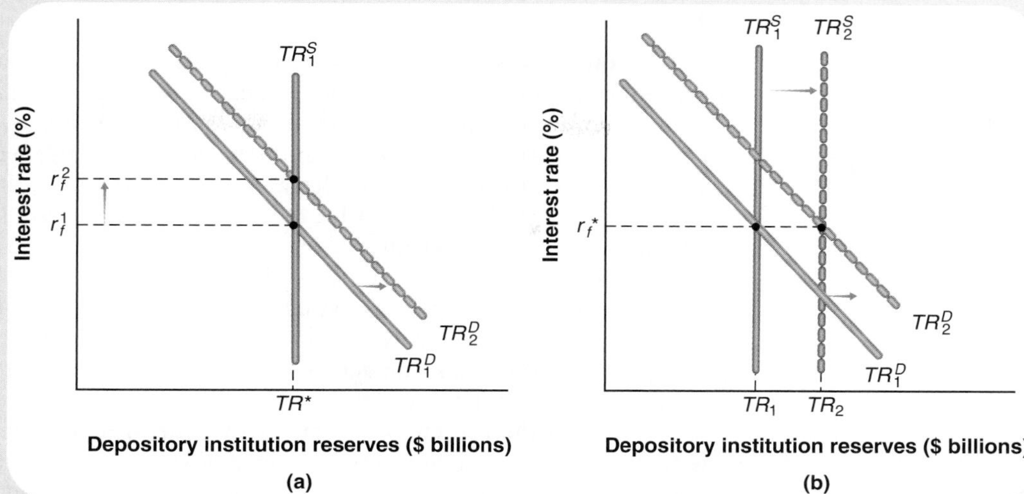

If a central bank targets bank reserves, then, as shown in panel (a), an increase in total reserve demand resulting from a rise in desired excess reserve holdings by banks requires keeping the reserve supply schedule in position to maintain the target reserve level, denoted TR^*. Hence, with a reserve-oriented operating procedure, stabilizing the level of bank reserves often entails greater variability in interest rates. Panel (b) illustrates an interest-rate-oriented operating procedure, in which the central bank sets a federal funds rate target of r_f^*. In the face of an increase in reserve demand, keeping the interbank funds rate at this target level will require an increase in the supply of reserves, which the central bank can bring about by conducting open market purchases and increasing nonborrowed reserves, thereby causing the level of bank reserves to rise from TR_1 to TR_2.

mine the likely position of total reserve demand. If the Fed forecasts that reserve demand will be TR_1^D, then to achieve a target level of total reserves denoted TR^*, it must adjust the amount of nonborrowed reserves to a level that places the reserve supply schedule at the location given by TR_1^S. If banks increase their demand for excess reserves, causing the reserve demand schedule to shift to the right, to TR_2^D, then to maintain its total reserve target the Fed must maintain the supply of reserves at TR_1^S.

Why might the Fed use such an operating procedure? One reason is that if the Fed's objective is to target the quantity of money, and if the money multiplier is relatively insensitive to interest rate changes, then keeping total reserves stable will help to stabilize the monetary base and the total quantity of money. Furthermore, such an operating procedure will automatically keep variability in interest rates from influencing the amount of reserves at depository institutions, thereby preventing volatility in the monetary base that such interest rate volatility could otherwise produce.

Note, however, that a Fed operating procedure that stabilizes total reserves tends to make interest rates more variable. In our example, for instance, we observed that the Fed had to let the federal funds rate increase to keep total reserves stabilized at the target level. As we shall discuss in Chapter 24, however, induced increases in Treasury security yields and other interest rates could cause reductions in spending flows in the economy. Consequently, a potentially negative aspect of a reserves-targeting operating procedure is that it can lead to significant interest rate volatility that translates into more variability in economic activity.

A Federal-Funds-Rate-Targeting Procedure An alternative Fed operating procedure focuses on reducing or eliminating such interest rate volatility. Panel (b) of Figure 20-7 depicts a *federal-funds-rate-targeting operating procedure.* Here, the Fed establishes a target for the federal funds rate, denoted r_f^*. If the Fed anticipates that the total reserve demand schedule will be at the position given by TR_1^D, then achieving this target for the federal funds rate requires setting the level of reserves at TR_1. Under this operating procedure, if a rise in banks' demand for excess reserves causes reserve demand to shift rightward to TR_2^D, then the Fed must *increase* the supply of reserves. It can do so by engaging in open market purchases that raise nonborrowed reserves. Hence, this operating procedure of targeting the federal funds rate achieves more stable interest rates but can produce larger variations in bank reserves.

Why might the Fed choose to target the federal funds rate? The main reason is that doing so eliminates any perceived adverse effects that interest rate variability might have on the economy. As long as the risk and term structures of interest rates are stable, targeting the federal funds rate also keeps Treasury security rates from changing, thereby stabilizing the opportunity cost of holding money. This can contribute to greater stability of the equilibrium quantity of money demanded.

Targeting the federal funds rate can have a potentially significant drawback, however. Suppose that there is variability in the demand for money by consumers and businesses arising from factors other than the opportunity cost of money, such as variations in their incomes. Because a federal-funds-rate-targeting procedure stabilizes the opportunity cost of holding money, such variations in the total demand for money translate into the maximum possible changes in the amount of money that consumers and businesses choose to hold. By stabilizing interest rates, the Fed keeps the opportunity cost of money from changing so as to help offset such swings in desired money holdings. This can make the equilibrium quantity of money demanded more volatile than it otherwise would be. If controlling the amount of money is a Fed objective, then this negative aspect of targeting the federal funds rate can make it a less desirable operating procedure. In addition, to the extent that the quantity of money influences aggregate spending—and you will learn in Chapter 22 that it does—such variability in the quantity of money could also lead to greater volatility in economic activity.

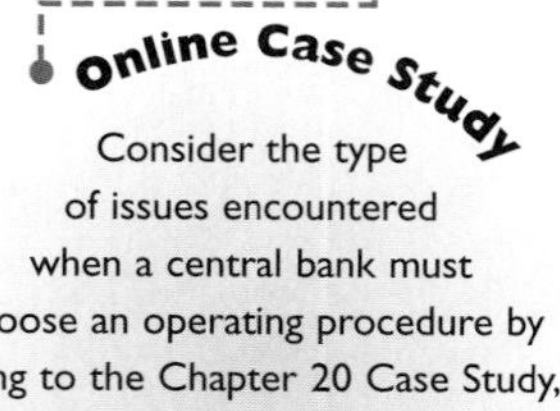

Consider the type of issues encountered when a central bank must choose an operating procedure by going to the Chapter 20 Case Study, entitled "Searching for the Best Operating Procedure."
http://moneyxtra.swcollege.com

Past and Current Federal Reserve Operating Procedures

In light of the trade-offs associated with both reserves- and interest-rate-based operating procedures, what strategies has the Fed actually used in past years? How have they worked out? The Fed has been around since 1913, but let's confine ourselves to the most recent three decades as we consider these questions.

Federal Funds Rate Targeting, 1970–1979 As we discussed briefly in Chapter 17, the Fed first began to think about its policy strategies more "scientifically" at the beginning of the 1970s. At that time, it chose to target the federal funds rate. Technically, the Fed established a "target range" for the federal funds rate, but typically its policy tactics entailed keeping the federal funds rate very close to the middle of this target range.

The Fed adopted federal funds rate targeting in an effort to achieve greater stability in the quantity of money and in economic activity. As our discussion above pointed out, however, targeting the federal funds rate poses problems in attaining these objectives if money demand becomes more variable. Unfortunately for the Fed, this is exactly what happened after the early 1970s. The Fed began to miss its monetary targets by wide margins, and the nation's income, spending, and inflation rate became more volatile. By 1979, the Fed was searching for a new operating procedure. (Since the 1970s the Federal Reserve has also struggled to determine how open it should be about its policy intentions; see on the next page *Policy Focus: Can There Be Too Much Transparency in Monetary Policy?*)

NONBORROWED RESERVES TARGETING, 1979–1982 During the 1970s, Fed critics argued that it should switch to targeting total reserves and permit the federal funds rate to vary in the marketplace. In the fall of 1979, the Fed decided to experiment with a slightly different type of reserves-based operating procedure. The Fed would try to predict how many reserves depository institutions would borrow during the coming months, and then it would determine the amount of nonborrowed reserves necessary to keep total reserves stable in light of its prediction. The Fed then treated this level of *nonborrowed reserves* as its policy target.

By aiming for a nonborrowed reserves objective, the Fed ended up allowing some variability in total reserves. This offset somewhat the negative aspect of a reserves-based procedure that we discussed above: interest rate variability. Nevertheless, interest rates were much more volatile after the Fed switched to nonborrowed reserves targeting in late 1979. Furthermore, by allowing total reserves to vary somewhat, the Fed also ended up permitting the quantity of money to vary from its target level. In the end, targeting nonborrowed reserves led to significant variations in *both* interest rates and the quantity of money.

BORROWED RESERVES TARGETING, 1982–1987 In 1982 the Fed tried an operating procedure that "split the difference" between targeting reserves and targeting the federal funds rate. It began to target the level of *borrowed reserves*. This was not really a novel policy, however. Recall from Chapter 17 that during the 1950s and 1960s the Fed tried to stabilize *free reserves,* or the difference between excess reserves and borrowed reserves. By targeting borrowed reserves, the Fed tended to stabilize free reserves, so this 1980s procedure looked a lot like a return to old-style policymaking.

In a sense it also looked like federal funds rate targeting. At this time, the Fed set the discount rate *below* the federal funds rate, and the key determinant of the amount of discount window borrowing by depository institutions was the difference between the federal funds rate and the discount rate. The way the Fed attempted to stabilize borrowed reserves was by keeping this difference stable, which, in turn, required a stable federal funds rate. And so targeting borrowed reserves also entailed keeping the federal funds rate from being excessively volatile.

Indeed, some critics of the Fed argued that the borrowed reserves procedure was really a "cover" for a return to federal funds rate targeting. A few even contended that the Fed never seriously targeted nonborrowed reserves but implicitly

GLOBAL | POLICY Focus | CYBER | MANAGEMENT

Can There Be Too Much Transparency in Monetary Policy?

Back in 1975, a Georgetown University law student filed suit against the Federal Open Market Committee. The FOMC, he alleged, was unlawfully keeping its policy directives secret for ninety days following their adoption. U.S. freedom-of-information laws, the student complained, required the Fed to make its policies more *transparent,* or open to public view.

In its response to the legal complaint, the Federal Reserve argued that an absence of FOMC secrecy could contribute to "unfair speculation" in financial markets, to "undesirable" market reactions, and to swings in interest rates that could harm the federal government's commercial interests. In the end the Fed won its case after the United States Supreme Court remanded the lawsuit to a federal appeals court that ruled that the Fed was the best judge of whether monetary policy secrecy is helpful or harmful to financial markets and the economy.

A Big Policy Reversal

During the 1980s, the Federal Reserve's attitude about the desirability of monetary policy secrecy began to shift. Although economists were able to identify possible ways that increased policy transparency could make interest rates and bond and stock prices more volatile, they also found ways that more openness could be a stabilizing factor for financial markets. These findings cast doubt on the Fed's earlier argument that releasing information about the Fed's policy intentions would necessarily have adverse effects.

By the early 1990s, Fed officials had become convinced that financial markets and the economy were more likely to benefit, on net, from greater transparency about Fed policies. In February 1994, therefore, the FOMC began to release a summary of its policy directive to the public immediately after each meeting. This summary provides information about the Fed's policy goals, specific policy actions the Fed has implemented, and how the Fed believes these actions will promote the attainment of its objectives.

Can Transparency Ever Be Bad?

In May 1999, the Fed went a step further. As part of its public statement about FOMC deliberations, the Fed began to indicate the direction it was leaning concerning *future* monetary policy actions. Whenever it made a policy change that officials regarded as significant, the Fed announced the FOMC's current "bias" in its attitude about the likely direction of future policy actions.

Over the next few months, the Fed began to perceive that its well-intentioned effort to be even more transparent had opened up a can of worms. Traders in financial markets began to treat the directives as virtual guarantees of the outcomes of subsequent FOMC meetings. Investors began to assume, for instance, that an FOMC "bias" toward a policy tightening meant that the Fed would certainly engage in a policy contraction at the next FOMC meeting, or that a "neutral bias" implied that the Fed would not alter its policy stance at the next FOMC meeting. As a consequence, Fed officials at times felt boxed in by the likely market reactions that would result if they were to act differently than a "bias" in a previous FOMC policy statement had indicated. In the end, both Fed officials and traders in financial markets agreed that announcing the FOMC's policy "bias" had increased financial market confusion about where monetary policy was heading—exactly the opposite of what the increased openness was supposed to achieve.

Thus, since 2000 FOMC statements have no longer included any indications of a "bias" toward higher or lower interest rates. Instead, the FOMC provides a more general description of how the committee views "risks" to the economy. The FOMC now only indicates its perception of whether higher inflation or a slowdown is a greater risk to the economy or whether the risks are balanced between the two. It leaves the task of guessing what that may mean about future Fed policy actions to those who trade in financial markets.

For Critical Analysis: Did the Fed's attempt to be open about the FOMC's "bias" fail because of too much policy transparency, or was it simply a communication failure?

Figure 20-8
Variability of the Federal Funds Rate and M1 Growth under Different Operating Procedures.
As shown in panel (a), federal funds rate variability rose considerably when the Fed switched from targeting the federal funds rate to targeting nonborrowed reserves in 1979 and then fell significantly when the Fed switched to targeting borrowed reserves in 1982. Panel (b) shows that the variability of money growth likewise rose after 1979 and then declined somewhat after 1982.

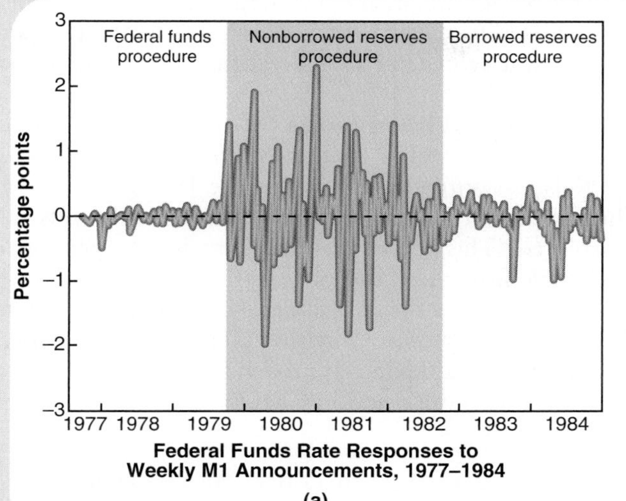

Federal Funds Rate Responses to Weekly M1 Announcements, 1977–1984
(a)

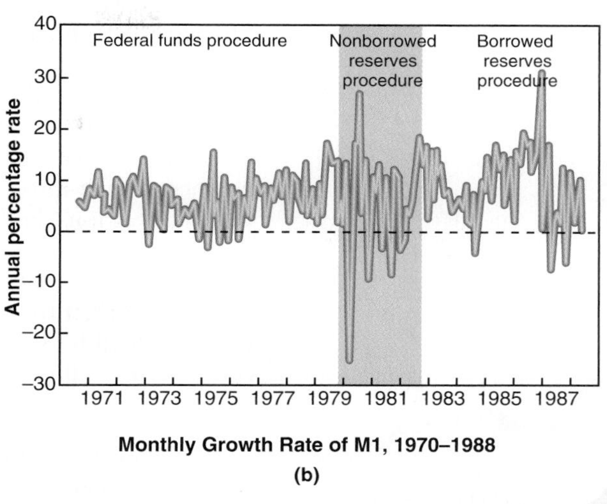

Monthly Growth Rate of M1, 1970–1988
(b)

SOURCE: Carl E. Walsh, "Issues in the Choice of Monetary Policy Operating Procedures," in *Monetary Policy for a Changing Financial Environment*, ed. William Haraf and Phillip Cagan (Washington, D.C.: AEI Press, 1990), pp. 8–37.

stabilized the federal funds rate instead. Nevertheless, a study by Thomas Cosimano and Richard Sheehan of the University of Notre Dame found strong evidence that the Fed really did use the three separate operating procedures. Their study involved sophisticated statistical analysis, but you can get a flavor for why they reached this conclusion by considering Figure 20-8, which is taken from a 1990 study by Carl Walsh of the University of California at Santa Cruz. Panel (a) shows how the equilibrium federal funds rate moved in response to Fed announcements of the size of M1. Because the Fed kept the funds rate near its target before 1979, such announcements typically had little effect on the federal funds rate. But when the Fed targeted nonborrowed reserves between 1979 and 1982, the federal funds rate varied considerably. During the period after 1982, when the Fed switched to borrowed reserves targeting, the federal funds rate varied more than it did during the period of federal funds rate targeting but less than it did during the interval of nonborrowed reserves targeting.

Panel (b) of Figure 20-8 displays the monthly growth rates for M1 between 1970 and 1987. As noted above, variability in the growth of M1 actually *increased* during the 1979–1982 interval when the Fed targeted nonborrowed reserves, as compared with the 1970s when the Fed used a federal-funds-rate-targeting procedure. During the period from 1982 to 1987, the variability of M1

On the Web
What is the Federal Reserve's *current* policy stance regarding open market operations and the federal funds rate? Find out by going to the Federal Open Market Committee's Web site at http://www.federalreserve.gov/fomc and clicking on "Minutes" for the most recent month.

growth declined slightly but was still much greater than during the 1970s. Consequently, both panels in Figure 20-8 indicate that the Fed really did use three distinctive operating procedures during the 1970s and 1980s.

Renewed Targeting of the Federal Funds Rate, 1988 to the Present In October 1987, stock prices plummeted, as many stocks lost over a third of their values in a single day. To help prevent a broader financial crisis, the Fed announced that it stood ready to provide as much liquidity as needed. It also decided to keep interest rates stable to prevent further volatility in the prices of financial instruments. To do this, it switched to a federal funds rate target once again.

From 1988 until the present, the Fed has continued to use the federal funds rate as its strategic variable of monetary policy. Its tactics, however, have differed from the approach of the 1970s. In contrast to the Fed of the 1970s, today's Fed has been much more willing to *adjust* the target value of the federal funds rate when conditions have warranted. This increased flexibility has helped offset some of the otherwise undesirable features of this policy procedure. Even former critics of the Fed have given it high marks for its willingness to change its federal funds rate target to stabilize economic activity. Only the future will tell, however, if the Fed will be able to maintain such a flexible approach to this operating procedure. We shall explore this issue in more detail in Chapter 27.

moneyxtra!

Another Perspective

To learn about all the various factors affecting bank reserve holdings in recent years, go to the Chapter 20 reading, entitled "Are U.S. Reserve Requirements Still Binding?" by Paul Bennett and Stavros Peristiani of the Federal Reserve Bank of New York.

http://moneyxtra.swcollege.com

6. What are Federal Reserve operating procedures, and what operating procedures has the Federal Reserve used in recent years?

Operating procedures are strategies that the Fed adopts to guide its open market operations and discount window policies over the course of many weeks, months, or even years. The Fed basically can choose between operating procedures that target reserves and procedures that focus on the federal funds rate. Since the 1970s, the Fed has used operating procedures that have targeted the federal funds rate, nonborrowed reserves, and borrowed reserves. Currently, the Fed targets the federal funds rate.

Link to Policy

Have Sweep Accounts Made M1 Irrelevant?

Even though the Federal Reserve's official required reserve ratio for transactions deposits is 10 percent, the *effective U.S.* required reserve ratio is much lower, because most large U.S. banks evade the bulk of reserve requirements that they otherwise would face via *sweep accounts*. These accounts shift funds from transactions deposits subject to reserve requirements to savings deposits that are exempt from reserve requirements.

How Sweep Accounts Work

In the 1970s, depository institutions began to offer automatic-transfer-service accounts, in which funds are shifted automatically from savings deposits to checking accounts whenever a customer's checking balance falls to zero. In 1993, a few large banks realized that there was no legal rule against *reversing* the flow of funds between checking and savings accounts. They began to shift funds from negotiable-order-of-withdrawal (NOW) accounts to money market deposit accounts (MMDAs), thereby reducing transactions deposits subject to reserve requirements.

The most common sweep account is called a "NOW sweep." At the beginning of a month, a bank shifts funds in excess of a predetermined minimum NOW account balance from a customer's NOW account into an MMDA. During the days that follow, if the customer's NOW account activity drives the account balance toward zero, the bank's computers automatically reallocate funds from the MMDA back to the NOW account. At the beginning of the next month, the cycle of "sweeps" begins anew.

Sweep Accounts, Reserves, and M1

Sweep accounts allow banks to reduce non-interest-bearing required reserves, thereby freeing up reserves to lend or to allocate to securities at market interest rates. As panel (a) of Figure 20-9 shows, total funds in sweep accounts (and, thus, total funds exempt from the 10 percent required reserve ratio) increased dramatically after June

Figure 20-9
Sweep Accounts and Reserves of U.S. Depository Institutions at Federal Reserve Banks.

Panel (a) depicts the growth of sweep accounts, or shifts of funds from transactions deposits subject to reserve requirements to nontransactions deposits with no legal required reserve ratios. Panel (b) shows that the effect of these sweep accounts has been a steady decline in reserve balances that depository institutions hold with Federal Reserve banks.

SOURCE: Board of Governors of the Federal Reserve System.

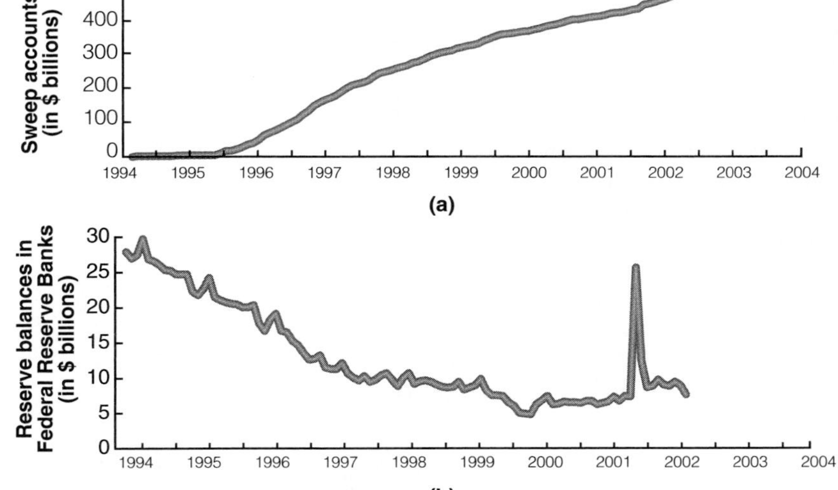

Continued on next page

Link to Policy, continued

1995. Panel (b) indicates that the result was a significant decline in the actual reserves that U.S. banks held at Federal Reserve banks.

Another important effect of sweep accounts, however, has been a significant reduction in the usefulness of M1 as an indicator of the thrust of monetary policy. Figure 20-10 shows M1 and M2 since 1959. Both monetary aggregates have grown considerably. Monetary growth cooled in the early 1990s, as evidenced by the slower increase in M2 during that period. Nevertheless, M2 did tend to *grow* along with the U.S. economy. By way of contrast, M1 underwent an outright *decline* in the mid-1990s before leveling off in the vicinity of $1 trillion, and it has stayed near this level since. The main explanation for this behavior of M1 is sweep accounts.

Today, most economists have given up on using M1 as a monetary policy indicator. Because both transactions deposits and savings deposits that are part of sweep programs are contained within M2, this monetary aggregate has remained untarnished by the advent of sweep accounts. Few economists, including those at the Fed, pay much attention to M1 anymore, because it is so distorted by sweep programs.

Research Project

Of what practical use are monetary aggregates for Federal Reserve policymaking? Should the Fed attempt to control monetary aggregates, or should it use monetary aggregates only as indicators of total liquidity in the U.S. economy? In either case, how can sweep accounts and other past, current, or potential future innovations complicate efforts to apply monetary aggregates in real-world policymaking?

Web Resources

1. For the latest data on U.S. sweep accounts, go to the Federal Reserve Bank of St. Louis's FRED database at http://research.stlouisfed.org/fred/. Then in the right-hand margin, under "Related Links" click on "Federal Reserve Board Data on Sweep Programs" where you can read an article about these programs and download data by clicking on "Monthly Sweeps Data."

2. What have been the overall effects of sweep accounts? For a good overview, go to the research page of the Federal Reserve Bank of St. Louis (http://research.stlouisfed.org), and click on "Publications." Then under "Review—Bimonthly," click on "Past Issues," and choose "January/February 2001." From this page you can download "Retail Sweep Programs and Bank Reserves," by Richard Anderson and Robert Rasche.

Figure 20-10
M1 and M2 since 1959.

Both M1 and M2 grew steadily until sweep accounts were established beginning in 1993. Since that time, M2 has continued to trend upward, but M1 declined slightly before leveling off.

SOURCES: *Economic Report of the President,* 2000; Federal Reserve's H.6(508) Statistical Release.

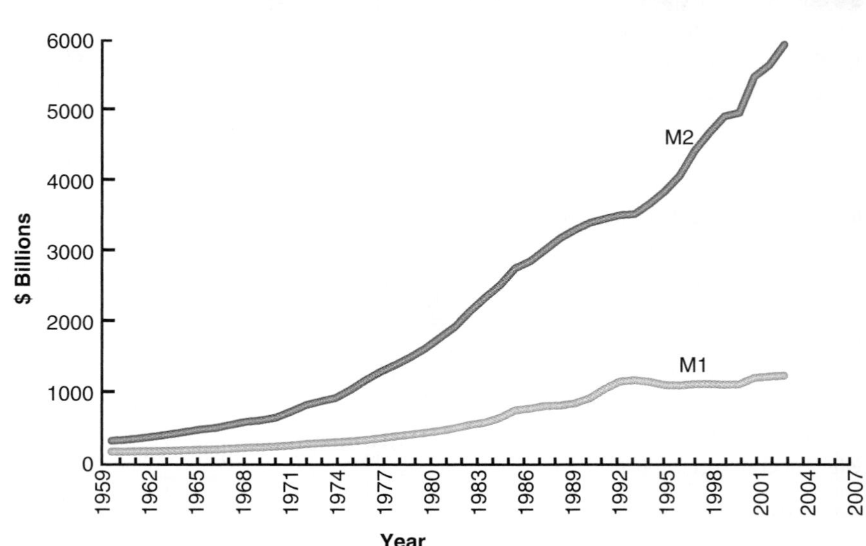

Chapter Summary

1. The Primary Tools through Which the Fed Conducts Monetary Policy: The Fed's fundamental day-to-day monetary policy instrument is open market operations. Fed purchases and sales of securities change the amount of nonborrowed reserves and thereby alter the monetary base and the quantities of money and credit. In addition, by changing the terms by which it lends reserves through the discount window, the Fed can influence the amount of reserves that depository institutions borrow, which also ultimately affects the amounts of money and credit. A third, though infrequently used, instrument is reserve requirements. Changes in the required reserve ratios alter the money and credit multipliers, thereby generating variations in monetary and credit aggregates.

2. Key Factors That Affect the Demand for Reserves by Depository Institutions: There are three determinants of depository institutions' demand for reserves. Two of these are the required reserve ratio set by the Fed and the total quantity of transactions deposits in the banking system, which together determine the amount of required reserves. The third factor is the opportunity cost to banks of holding excess reserves, which is the federal funds rate.

3. How Federal Reserve Policies Influence the Supply of Reserves to Depository Institutions and the Federal Funds Rate: The Fed's open market operations determine the amount of nonborrowed reserves in the banking system, and its discount window policies influence the amount of borrowed reserves. Consequently, through open market purchases and sales or alterations in the terms at which depository institutions may borrow from the discount window, the Fed can change the supply of reserves and affect the equilibrium federal funds rate.

4. The Linkage between the Federal Funds Rate and Other Market Interest Rates: The risk and term structures of interest rates link Treasury security rates and other interest yields to the federal funds rate, which the Fed can influence with its policy tools. Consequently, Fed policy actions that alter the federal funds rate ultimately cause other market interest rates to move in the same direction as the federal funds rate.

5. How Federal Reserve Policies Affect the Quantity of Money: Open market operations and discount rate changes vary the supply of reserves to depository institutions, thereby inducing changes in the equilibrium federal funds rate. Changes in the federal funds rate induce movements in the Treasury bill rate through the risk and term structures of interest rates. This alters the opportunity cost of holding money, thereby inducing people to adjust the amount of money that they hold.

6. Types of Federal Reserve Operating Procedures, and Operating Procedures That the Federal Reserve Has Used in Recent Years: Operating procedures are the guidelines by which the Fed pursues its broader economic goals. The Fed typically must choose between operating procedures that entail targeting reserve measures and a procedure of stabilizing or targeting the federal funds rate. In recent decades the Fed has experimented with targeting the federal funds rate, nonborrowed reserves, and borrowed reserves. Since the late 1980s, the Fed has targeted the federal funds rate but has adjusted its target for this rate more often than when it used a similar operating procedure in the 1970s.

Questions and Problems

(Answers to odd-numbered questions and problems may be found on the Web at http://money.swcollege.com under "Student Resources.")

1. Explain why an open market sale causes a change in the quantity of money by inducing a change in the monetary base instead of a change in the money multiplier.

2. What practical constraints make it impracticable for the Federal Reserve to vary reserve requirements on a weekly basis, so as to use this policy instrument as a frequent tool of monetary policy? In light of these constraints, can you think of any rationale for reserve requirements? Explain.

3. Why does the demand schedule for depository institution reserves slope downward? Explain.

4. Suppose that most of the nation's banks apply a new computerized inventory-tracking system to manage their excess reserves, thereby enabling them to reduce their excess reserves to minimal levels. Assuming no response by the Federal Reserve, what effect will this have on the equilibrium federal funds rate?

5. The Federal Reserve wishes to reduce the quantity of money but does not wish to do so by conducting open market operations. Use appropriate diagrams to explain how the Fed can accomplish its goal.

6. As we discussed, the Fed's current operating procedure is to target the federal funds rate. If the Fed wishes to reduce reserve requirements for some reason unrelated to monetary policy needs, should it buy or sell securities to keep the federal funds rate at its target level? Explain your reasoning.

7. Why is the six-month Treasury bill rate typically lower than the one-day federal funds rate even though the federal funds yield curve lies above the Treasury security yield curve?

8. Draw appropriate diagrams, and show how the Fed can push up market interest rates via an open market operation.

9. Suppose that the Fed is targeting the federal funds rate and there is an increase in the demand for money because of a rapid expansion in the economy's level of nominal income, perhaps because of rapid inflation. Keeping in mind that part of the total quantity of money is deposits subject to reserve requirements (and assuming that not all such deposits are part of sweep account programs), reason out the effect on the reserve demand schedule. Outline a policy action that will enable the Fed to keep the federal funds rate at its target value in the face of this event. Use diagrams to assist in explaining your answer.

10. As an extension to question 9, suppose that the Fed wishes to keep the quantity of money unchanged at its original level following the rise in the demand for money. Can the Fed maintain its current target for the federal funds rate? Explain.

11. The Fed currently uses an operating procedure in which it targets the federal funds rate, but it changes its target more often than in the 1970s, when it used a similar procedure. In light of the drawbacks associated with this procedure, is there any potential gain from the Fed's greater flexibility in setting the federal funds rate target? Explain your reasoning. [Hint: Think about how this approach can help "split the difference" between the gains and losses of interest rate targeting versus reserves targeting.]

Before the Test

Test your understanding of the material covered in this chapter by taking the Chapter 20 interactive quiz at http://money.swcollege.com.

Online Application

Internet URLs: http://www.stlouisfed.org and http://www.bis.org

Titles: Federal Reserve Board Data on OCD Sweep Account Programs and Bank for International Settlements

Navigation: Go to the first URL above. Then under "Economic Research," click on "Economic Data—FRED." In the right hand menu, select "Federal Reserve Board Data on Sweep Account Programs."

Application: Read the discussion, and answer the following questions:

1. What are the two types of sweep account programs? What constraints do banks face on their ability to shift funds from checkable deposits into deposits not subject to reserve requirements?

2. Click on "Monthly Sweeps Data" to observe data on the amounts most recently "swept" by U.S. banks. Based on the discussion in the article, is it correct to adjust the M1 measure of money by directly subtracting these amounts?

For Group Study and Analysis: Assign groups to various regions of the world (e.g., North America, South America, Western Europe, Eastern Europe, Asia, and Africa). Have each group go to the home page of the Bank for International Settlements (**http://www.bis.org**) and click on "Central Banks." From there, they can navigate to the Web sites of central banks worldwide. Ask each group to examine each Web site for information about reserve requirement policies and operating procedures of other central banks. Regroup, and compare notes. How forthcoming are central banks concerning their policies regarding reserve requirements and operating procedures? For those whose operating procedures can be deduced, do reserve requirements appear to be an important element?

Selected References and Further Reading

Anderson, Richard, and Robert Rasche. "Retail Sweep Programs and Bank Reserves." Federal Reserve Bank of St. Louis *Review* 83 (January/February 2001): 51–72.

Bennett, Paul, and Spence Hilton. "Falling Reserve Balances and the Federal Funds Rate." Federal Reserve Bank of New York *Current Issues in Economics and Finance* 3 (April 1997).

Clouse, James, and Douglas Elmendorf. "Declining Required Reserves and the Volatility of the Federal Funds Rate." Board of Governors of the Federal Reserve System, December 1998.

Cosimano, Thomas, and Richard Sheehan. "The Federal Reserve Operating Procedure, 1984–1990: An Empirical Analysis." *Journal of Macroeconomics* 16 (Summer 1994): 573–588.

Krainer, John. "Retail Sweeps and Reserves." Federal Reserve Bank of San Francisco *Economic Letter,* No. 2001–02, January 26, 2001.

Sellon, Gordon, Jr., and Stuart Weiner. "Monetary Policy without Reserve Requirements: Analytical Issues." Federal Reserve Bank of Kansas City *Economic Review* 81 (Fourth Quarter 1997): 5–24.

VanHoose, David, and David Humphrey. "Sweep Accounts, Reserve Management, and Interest Rate Volatility." *Journal of Economics and Business* 53 (July/August 2001): 387–404.

Walsh, Carl, E. "Issues in the Choice of Monetary Policy Operating Procedures." In *Monetary Policy for a Changing Financial Environment,* ed. William Haraf and Phillip Cagan. Washington, D.C.: AEI Press, 1990.

Wrase, Jeffrey. "Is the Fed Being Swept Out of (Monetary) Control?" Federal Reserve Bank of Philadelphia *Business Review,* November/December 1998, pp. 3–12.

MoneyXtra

moneyxtra! Log on to the MoneyXtra Web site now (http://moneyxtra.swcollege.com) for additional learning resources such as practice quizzes, case studies, readings, and additional economic applications.

Chapter

21

How Do We Know How We're Doing?—
The Macroeconomic Environment

Fundamental Issues

1. What is gross domestic product, and how is it calculated?

2. How do economists measure international transactions?

3. What is the difference between nominal GDP and real GDP?

4. What are business cycles, and what are their key features?

During the spring of 2000, average prices on the New York Stock Exchange rose by nearly 5 percent. Between June 2000 and March 2001, stock prices proceeded to fall by more than 7 percent. Within another three months, however, the average share price had jumped 5 percent once again.

To most observers, these are just typical examples of unpredictable gyrations in the values of shares traded in the stock market. Nonetheless, some economists think that important information can be gleaned from such changes in market valuations of equity shares. The amounts that investors are willing to pay for stocks, these economists argue, reflect investors' forecasts of how productive firms are likely to be the future. Consequently, stock price movements may be useful in predicting overall business productivity—how much output companies can produce using given volumes of inputs—which is a key determinant of both firms' profitability and aggregate economic growth.

The pace of productivity enhancements and the speed of economic growth have potentially important effects on more than financial market activity. Productivity growth and the growth of overall economic activity also influence the rate of joblessness and the level of prices of goods and services. In this chapter you will learn how economists gauge economic growth. In addition, you will learn about how they measure the aggregate price level and unemployment rates.

The Circular Flow of Income and Product

The previous chapter discussed the tools that the Fed uses to implement monetary policy. So far, however, we have not considered the broader effects of Fed policies. This will be the subject of the remainder of this book. In this chapter, we begin by contemplating how economists track the overall performance of the economy.

Gross domestic product (GDP): The value, tabulated using market prices, of all final goods and services produced within a nation's borders during a given period.

Gross Domestic Product

Before economists can evaluate how monetary policy actions may influence overall economic performance, they must have measures of aggregate output. These can, as we shall discuss, provide some indication, albeit imperfect, about a nation's overall standard of living.

Defining GDP The key measure of the flow of aggregate output produced in an economy is **gross domestic product (GDP)**. This is the total value, in terms of market prices, of all *final* goods and services produced within a nation's borders within a specific period, such as a month or a year. Economists avoid adding together very different items such as computer software, Internet services, orange juice, and passenger jets by summing the *dollar values* of such final goods and services. To determine these dollar values, economists must be able to multiply market prices times the quantities produced and sold. Consequently, the final goods and services included in GDP must be traded in markets.

Exclusions Gross domestic product, therefore, does not include any items provided through nonmarket transactions. Economists exclude such items as child-care, lawn-care, or other services provided by husbands or wives (or children) who stay at home rather than entering the labor force. They also leave out illegal transactions such as those associated with the illicit drug trade.

In addition, economists include only the values of *goods and services* in GDP. Consequently, they do not include the market values of stocks, bonds, or other financial assets. Brokers' fees are included, however, because they are the brokers' earnings for providing services for trading these assets.

Furthermore, economists avoid double-counting by including only the production of goods and services in their *final form* in GDP calculations for a given interval. If a computer manufacturer buys digital-versatile-disk (DVD) drives from various manufacturers to build into a personal computer during 2004 and sells the assembled computer that year, then only the sale price of the *computer* counts in GDP. The market values of the DVD drives that the company purchased before assembling the personal computer are not individually included in GDP for 2004. Doing so would double-count the production and sale of DVD drives, because their value is already included in the sale price of the computer.

Inventory Investment and Depreciation By way of contrast, suppose that we are computing GDP for 2004 at the end of the year. At that time, inventories of unassembled computer components, including DVD drives recently shipped from suppliers, are in storage at the computer manufacturer's assembling facility. In this situation, economists would count the market value of the unassembled computer components as inventory *investment* in materials used in the production process. Suppose also that the manufacturer has a number of fully assembled personal computers that have not yet been sold at the time of the GDP calculation. These produced but unsold goods would also be included in the company's inventory investment. Hence, GDP includes all inventory investment during 2004 to make sure that we total up all production during that year.

Capital consumption allowance: The total market value of capital goods that are expended during the process of production.

Circular flow diagram: A chart that depicts the economy's flows of income and product.

National income accounts: Tabulations of the values of a nation's flows of income and product.

Something else that economists tabulate as part of GDP is **capital consumption allowance,** which is the value of all equipment that is used up or worn out during the process of producing goods and services and must be replaced if the existing amount of equipment is to be maintained. As noted in Chapter 3 the total amount of productive equipment is known as *capital goods,* or goods that may be used to produce other goods and services in the future. Depreciation expense arises from allocating additional production simply to keep the current amount of capital from declining. This means that depreciation is part of a year's production of goods. Thus, it is included as part of gross investment, which is a key component of GDP.

Income Equals the Value of Product

Figure 21-1 helps to visualize why economists use GDP as the key measure of aggregate economic performance. The figure is a **circular flow diagram,** which depicts the total flows of income and product in the economy. Business firms use factor services—labor services, service flows from capital goods, service flows from land, and entrepreneurship or business know-how—to produce goods and services. Firms sell these goods and services in *product markets.* Households, which are individuals or families, purchase these goods and services using the income that they earn from providing factor services to firms. Households receive this income as wages and salaries, interest, rents, and profits. The values of factor services are determined in the *factor markets,* which are the markets for labor, capital, land, and entrepreneurship.

The circular flow diagram indicates that households purchase the product of firms—their output, or GDP—using the income that they earn from providing the factor services that firms utilize to produce GDP. The value of the circular flow in Figure 21-1, therefore, is the amount of GDP. This means that:

> **GDP is both a measure of an economy's total output and a measure of the total income of all individuals in the economy.**

This is so because the production of output is what generates the income of households. It follows that GDP is an overall measure of output *and* an overall measure of income. There are, as we shall see below, slight accounting distinctions between GDP and "national income." From a broad, conceptual perspective, however, the two concepts are equivalent.

Measuring Domestic Variables: The National Income Accounts

The circular flow diagram in Figure 21-1 implies that there are two approaches to tabulating GDP. One is to total all spending on goods and services produced and sold or counted as inventory investment. The other is to add together all the income earnings. In fact, the **national income accounts,** which are the formal calculations of the nation's income and product, reflect both of these approaches to computing GDP.

Figure 21-1
The Circular Flow of Income and Product.

Business firms make factor payments to households for the use of households' factor services. The total value of these factor payments constitutes total household income, which households spend on the goods and services that firms produce. The aggregate value of these goods and services is gross domestic product (GDP).

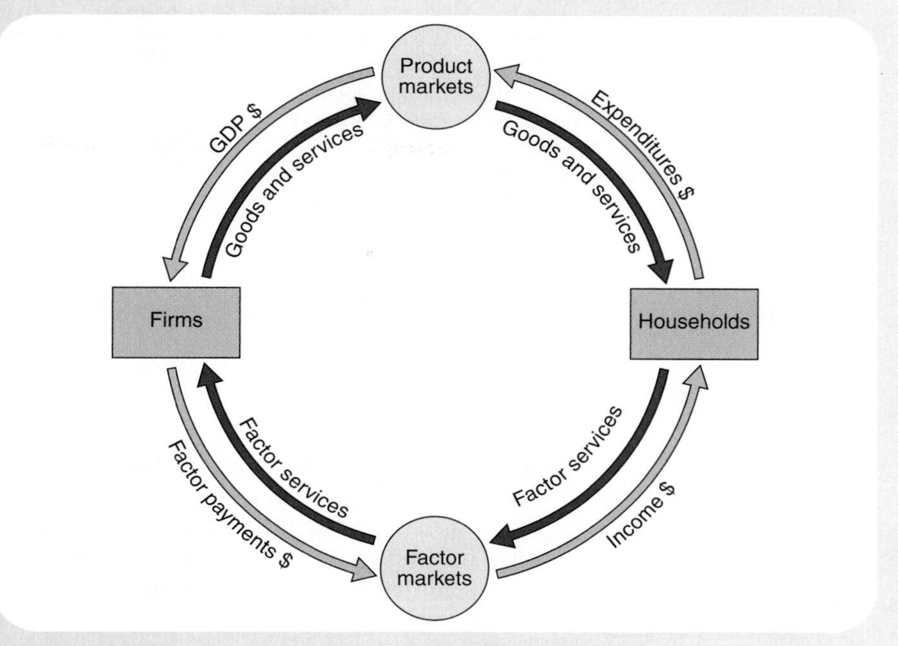

The Product Approach to Tabulating GDP

The *product approach* to GDP tabulation focuses on GDP as an output measure. Under this approach, economists add together all expenditures on final goods and services produced during a particular year. Essentially, they determine the magnitude of the flow through the product markets in the circular flow diagram.

Table 21-1 on the next page shows how to compute GDP using the product approach. There are four fundamental forms of spending on final goods and services during the year. One is **consumption spending** by households. Another is **investment spending,** which includes business spending on new capital goods, net accumulations of inventories of newly produced goods, and spending on construction—houses and apartment buildings—by households and businesses. *Gross investment* includes all investment spending during a year. Part of investment expenditures, however, is allocated toward replacement of worn-out capital, or depreciation. Thus, *net investment* is equal to gross investment minus depreciation. Economists typically regard net investment as a better indication of how much an economy's stock of capital goods grows during a year. Nonetheless, gross investment measures total spending on such goods, and for this reason it is included in GDP.

The third component of GDP is **government spending.** This is the aggregate amount of spending on goods and services by state, local, and federal governments.

The fourth type of expenditures on final goods and services is **net export spending,** which is equal to total expenditures on domestically produced goods and services by residents of other nations, less spending on foreign-produced

Consumption spending: Total purchases of goods and services by households.

Investment spending: The sum of purchases of new capital goods, spending on new residential construction, and inventory investment.

Government spending: Total state, local, and federal government expenditures on goods and services.

Net export spending: The difference between spending on domestically produced goods and services by residents of other countries and spending on foreign-produced goods and services by residents of the home country.

Table 21-1 The Product Approach to Calculating Gross Domestic Product

	1988	1993	1998	2003*
Consumption Spending	3,356.6	4,454.7	5,856.0	7,701.1
Investment Spending	821.1	955.1	1,538.7	1,831.0
Government Spending	1,036.9	1,293.0	1,538.5	2,013.2
Net Export Spending	−106.3	−60.5	−151.7	−370.5
Gross Domestic Product	5,108.3	6,642.3	8,781.5	11,174.8

Note: Amounts are in billions of dollars.
*Authors' estimates.
SOURCES: 2002 *Economic Report of the President*; *Economic Indicators* (various issues).

goods and services by domestic residents that does not constitute spending on domestic production. Since the early 1980s net export spending has been negative: expenditures by U.S. residents on foreign goods and services have exceeded foreign spending on U.S.-produced goods and services. The sum of all four types of expenditures on domestically produced final goods and services during a year is that year's GDP.

On the Web
Where are the latest data on U.S. GDP and its components? One location is the Federal Reserve Bank of St. Louis's "FRED (Federal Reserve Economic Data)" at http://research.stlouisfed.org/fred, where you can click on "Gross Domestic Product and Components."

The Income Approach to Tabulating GDP

Table 21-2 illustrates the alternative approach to computing GDP, which economists call the *income approach*. It attempts to measure the flows that run through the factor markets along the lower part of Figure 21-1. To implement the income approach, economists first add together wages and salaries, interest income, rental income, and profits of businesses to obtain the official definition of **national income,** which is the total of all factor earnings in the economy. Then economists add indirect taxes and transfer payments to businesses, which are excise and sales taxes and government subsidies that slightly depress reported income flows, to obtain *net national product*. Next, economists add the capital consumption allowance to obtain **gross national product (GNP).** Finally, they add the income earned by foreign residents from U.S.-based production net of earnings of home residents abroad. This yields GDP. Thus, GNP and GDP are different measures of a nation's output:

> **GNP includes earnings of domestic residents abroad while excluding foreign residents' earnings from domestic production. GDP excludes earnings of home residents abroad while including foreign residents' earnings from home production. Thus, GDP measures the value of all goods and services produced within a nation's borders.**

National income: The sum of all factor earnings, or net domestic product minus indirect business taxes.

Gross national product (GNP): The value, tabulated using market prices, of all final goods and services produced by a nation's residents during a given period.

Limitations of GDP

Although GDP is a very helpful indicator of a country's economic performance, it has its limitations.

Table 21-2 The Income Approach to Calculating Gross Domestic Product

	1988	1993	1998	2003*
Wages and Salaries	2,973.8	3,814.4	4,989.6	6,522.2
Interest Income	389.4	374.3	511.9	640.0
Rental Income	44.1	90.9	138.6	155.4
Business Profits	743.8	972.3	1,401.3	1,662.5
National Income	4,151.1	5,251.9	7,041.4	8,980.1
Indirect Taxes and Transfers	348.3	602.0	664.7	847.7
Net National Product	4,499.4	5,853.9	7,706.1	9,827.8
Capital Consumption Allowance	627.4	812.8	1,072.0	1,367.2
Gross National Product	5,126.8	6,666.7	8,778.1	11,195.0
Net Income Payments Abroad	−18.5	−24.4	+3.4	−20.2
Gross Domestic Product	5,108.3	6,642.3	8,781.5	11,174.8

Note: Amounts are in billions of dollars.
*Authors' estimates.
SOURCES: 2002 *Economic Report of the President*; *Economic Indicators*.

THE EXCLUSION OF NONMARKET PRODUCTION First, GDP includes only the value of goods and services traded in markets, so by definition it fails to account for *nonmarket* production, such as the household services provided by members of households themselves. This can complicate comparing an industrialized country's GDP with the GDP of an emerging nation where nonmarket production is often more important. Excluding nonmarket production can also make comparisons difficult if nations have different definitions of legal versus illegal activities. For instance, a nation where the sale of all alcoholic beverages is legal counts the value of such sales in GDP. But in a country where sales of certain alcoholic beverages are prohibited, those who sell liquor naturally will not report sales, so they are not counted in that country's GDP.

COUNTRY DIFFERENCES Even if two nations measure GDP using identical methods, cross-country comparisons are problematic unless we make some adjustments. One is to account for population differences. After all, after accounting for inflation (more on this appears later in this chapter), GDP in India usually is about three times Switzerland's GDP even though the population of India is about 125 times larger than the Swiss population. Hence, economists use *per capita GDP*—GDP divided by the number of people residing within the country—when trying to compare different countries' economic performances.

GDP IS NOT A MEASURE OF WELFARE Even though per capita GDP may be a useful benchmark for comparison, it still may not be a good measure of well-being. After all, the production of such goods as minerals, electricity, and irrigation for farming can have negative effects on the environment. Examples include the destruction of forests from strip mining, air and soil pollution from particulate emissions, and erosion. Hence, it is important to recognize that GDP is only a measure of production and a potentially useful economic indicator; it is not a welfare measure.

1. What is gross domestic product, and how is it calculated? Gross domestic product (GDP) is the market value of all final goods and services produced during a given period. Using the product approach, GDP is equal to the sum of consumption spending, investment spending, government expenditures, and net export spending. Under the income approach, GDP is equal to the sum of wages and salaries, net interest, rental income, profits, indirect taxes, and depreciation.

Measuring International Transactions: The Balance of Payments

Along with tabulating domestic flows of income and product, economists also seek to account for payment flows across a country's borders. They do this by using an accounting system called the **balance of payments accounts,** which are a complete tabulation of all the exchanges between U.S. residents and residents of all other nations. The balance of payments accounts include all transactions in goods, services, income earnings and payments, and assets by individuals, businesses, and governments across U.S. borders.

There are three separate balance of payments accounts. The first is the **current account,** which tabulates international trade and transfers of goods and services and flows of income. The second balance of payments account is the **capital account,** which tabulates all nongovernmental asset transactions. Finally, economists keep track of asset transactions involving governmental agencies in the **official settlements balance.**

In each of these accounts, economists record any cross-border exchange entailing a *payment* by a U.S. individual, business, or government agency as a deficit item. Thus, a payment is a *negative* entry, indicating that this type of transaction causes funds to flow out of the United States. In contrast, economists list any international transaction that leads to a *receipt* by a U.S. resident, company, or government agency as a *positive* entry, thereby indicating an inflow of funds into the United States.

Balance of payments accounts: A tabulation of all transactions between the residents of a nation and the residents of all other nations in the world.

Current account: The balance of payments account that tabulates international trade and transfers of goods and services and flows of income.

Capital account: The balance of payments account that records all nongovernmental international asset transactions.

Official settlements balance: A balance of payments account that records international asset transactions involving agencies of home and foreign governments.

Exports, Imports, and the Current Account

The *current account* receives the most media attention because it includes U.S. trade of goods and services. The major focus of the media typically is a *subaccount* within the current account known as the *merchandise trade balance.*

THE MERCHANDISE TRADE BALANCE Economists record all cross-border sales of *physical goods* by U.S. firms to residents of other nations as *merchandise exports,* and they tabulate the value of goods that U.S. residents purchase from foreign firms as *merchandise imports.* Table 21-3 lists dollar values of U.S. merchandise exports and imports for recent years. Exports generate receipts by U.S. residents, so they are positive entries in the table. Imports entail payments abroad by U.S. residents, so they appear as negative entries.

The final row in Table 21-3 displays the *merchandise trade balance* for each year. When the merchandise trade balance is positive, a *trade surplus* exists,

Table 21-3 The U.S. Merchandise Trade Balance ($ Millions)

	1993	1998	2003*
Merchandise Exports	+456,943	+670,416	+789,765
Merchandise Imports	−589,394	−917,112	−1,252,315
Merchandise Trade Balance	−132,451	−246,696	−462,550

*Authors' estimates.
SOURCES: *Economic Report of the President; Economic Indicators.*

meaning that U.S. residents export more goods than they import. The table indicates, however, that this has not been the case during the last decade, when U.S. merchandise imports have consistently exceeded merchandise exports. As a result, the U.S. merchandise trade balance has been significantly negative, meaning that the United States has experienced sizable *trade deficits.*

THE CURRENT ACCOUNT BALANCE In recent years, the U.S. media somewhat grudgingly have begun to recognize that the merchandise trade balance can be a misleading indicator, because the output share of industries that produce physical goods has declined. Travel, transportation, and financial services have become noticeably more important industries in the United States.

Accounting for Services Table 21-4 shows that net international service transactions are listed in the current account. The recent norm has been for U.S. residents to sell more services to residents of other nations than they buy from firms abroad. Service transactions therefore have on net yielded receipts for U.S. residents, as indicated by the positive entries for this category in the second row of Table 21-4.

Summing the first and second rows of Table 21-4 yields the *balance on goods and services,* which appears in the third row of the table. Because this balance includes *both* goods *and* services, most economists believe that it is a more useful indicator of U.S. trade performance than the merchandise trade balance. Nevertheless, the merchandise trade balance typically receives greater media attention.

As Table 21-4 indicates, there has been a deficit in the U.S. balance on goods and services for some time. Although U.S. service industries have tended to generate net receipts of funds in recent decades, their growth has not fully

On the Web
How has the U.S. balance on goods and services behaved lately? Find out by reviewing export and import data at the Federal Reserve Bank of St. Louis's "FRED (Federal Reserve Economic Data)" site at http://research.stlouisfed.org/fred.

Table 21-4 The U.S. Current Account ($ Millions)

	1993	1998	2003*
Merchandise Trade Balance	−132,451	−246,696	−462,550
Net Service Transactions	+63,660	+79,868	+83,895
Balance on Goods and Services	−68,791	−166,828	−378,655
Net Income Flow	+23,905	+7,510	+16,140
Unilateral Transfers	−37,637	−44,509	−52,858
Current Account Balance	−82,523	−203,827	−415,373

*Authors' estimates.
SOURCES: *Economic Report of the President; Economic Indicators.*

compensated for the net payments that U.S. residents have made on cross-border transactions that appear in the merchandise trade balance.

Income Flows The U.S. current account also tabulates international flows of income receipts to U.S. residents and payments abroad by U.S. individuals and firms. U.S. residents earn income on assets that they hold in other nations, and these income earnings generate positive entries in the U.S. current account. Foreign individuals and firms simultaneously earn income on assets that they own in the United States, and these flows of income from the United States to foreign residents generate negative entries in the U.S. current account. The fourth line of Table 21-4 shows the *net* income flow for each period.

Unilateral Transfers A tabulation of all *unilateral transfers* is the final component of the current account. Unilateral transfers are gifts from U.S. residents to residents or governments of other nations or gifts from foreign residents or governments to U.S. residents. Transfers from foreign residents to U.S. residents are receipts by U.S. residents and are positive entries. Transfers from U.S. residents to foreign residents are payments by U.S. residents and are negative entries. The fifth line of Table 21-4 shows total net unilateral transfers. The U.S. government provides sizable amounts of foreign aid and military transfers to other countries, so net unilateral transfers usually are negative.

The Balance on the Current Account The sum of lines 3 through 5, which appears in the final line of Table 21-4, is the *current account balance*. This is the sum of all net international flows of goods, services, income, and transfers. Since 1981 the U.S. current account balance has been negative, so during these years the United States has experienced *current account deficits*. For more than two decades U.S. residents have persistently paid out more to the rest of the world than they have received in international transactions of goods and services, income flows, and transfers.

The Capital Account, the Private Payments Balance, and the Overall Balance of Payments

To think about the pros and cons associated with relatively large current account deficits and capital account surpluses, go to the Chapter 21 Case Study, entitled "Interpreting Deficits and Surpluses in the Balance of Payments."

http://moneyxtra.swcollege.com

Changes in asset holdings by U.S. residents and residents of other nations take place in international financial markets and are recorded outside the current account. The private *capital account* tabulates asset transactions involving private individuals or companies. Asset transactions involving official governmental entities such as the U.S. Treasury or the Federal Reserve enter a third account called the *official settlements balance,* as pointed out above.

THE CAPITAL ACCOUNT AND THE PRIVATE PAYMENTS BALANCE All changes in private asset holdings by U.S. residents abroad and by foreigners in the United States appear in the capital account. U.S. acquisitions of foreign assets, such as purchases of shares of ownership of plants or equipment and purchases of securities such as bonds, are negative entries in the U.S. capital account. Foreign acquisitions of such assets within U.S. borders are positive entries.

The total of all these asset changes for individuals and businesses is the private *capital account balance*. U.S. capital account balances for recent years are listed in the second line of Table 21-5. Recently, this balance has been positive, which

Table 21-5 The U.S. Private Payments Balance ($ Millions)

	1993	1998	2003*
Current Account Balance	−82,523	−217,457	−415,373
Capital Account Balance	+11,465	+90,917	+352,111
Private Payments Balance	−71,058	−126,540	−63,262

*Authors' estimates.
SOURCES: *Economic Report of the President; Economic Indicators.*

indicates that on net U.S. residents have acquired fewer foreign assets relative to acquisitions of U.S. assets by foreign residents.

The first line of Table 21-5 shows the current account balances listed in Table 21-4. The sum of the first and second lines of Table 21-5—that is, the sum of the current account balance and the private capital account balance—is the **private payments balance.** The private payments balance gives the net total of all private exchanges between U.S. individuals and businesses and the rest of the world. Commonly, the private payments balance is referred to as the "balance of payments." Unfortunately, as we shall discuss shortly, this is a misleading term. Therefore, we shall be careful to refer to it mainly by a more proper name: the *private payments balance.*

Since the early 1980s, private U.S. individuals and businesses have made more payments to foreign residents than they have received from foreign residents, so the U.S. private payments balance has been persistently negative. This means that the United States has experienced *private payments deficits,* commonly called "balance of payments deficits."

The Official Settlements Balance and the Overall Balance of Payments

As we noted earlier, governments also make cross-border asset exchanges. Purchases of foreign assets or overseas deposits of funds by the U.S. Treasury, the Federal Reserve, or any agencies of the U.S. government are receipts that appear as negative entries in the *official settlements balance,* the last account of the balance of payments accounts. Acquisitions of U.S. assets or deposits by foreign central banks or governments are recorded as inflows and appear as positive entries in this account.

Governments and central banks of various nations also keep deposit accounts with other countries' central banks. If the U.S. Treasury or the Federal Reserve deposits additional funds with another nation's central bank, then this outflow of funds from the United States appears as a negative entry in the U.S. official settlements balance. In contrast, if foreign governments or central banks place more funds in deposit accounts at the Federal Reserve, then this inflow of funds appears as a positive entry in the U.S. official settlements balance.

The total net amount of all governmental and central bank transactions is the final amount of the official settlements balance. The second line of Table 21-6 on the following page gives recent values for the U.S. official settlements balance, which typically has been positive.

Private payments balance: The sum of the current account balance and the private capital account balance, or the net total of all private exchanges between U.S. individuals and businesses and the rest of the world.

The Statistical Discrepancy The first line of Table 21-6 carries down the private payments balance figures from Table 21-5. If all this international accounting goes well, then the sum of the first two lines of Table 21-6 should be the

Table 21-6 The Overall Balance of Payments for the United States ($ Millions)

	1993	1998	2003*
Private Payments Balance	−71,058	−126,540	−63,262
Official Settlements Balance	+69,935	+139,314	+23,050
Statistical Discrepancy	+1,123	−12,774	+40,212
Overall Balance of Payments	0	0	0

*Authors' estimates.
SOURCES: *Economic Report of the President; Economic Indicators.*

overall balance of payments, or the net of *all* transactions of U.S. individuals, businesses, and governmental agencies with all other nations of the world. In the end, however, the accounting rarely works out exactly, so there is a significant *statistical discrepancy* each period. The statistical discrepancy for each year appears in the third line of Table 21-6. One reason for this discrepancy is that errors naturally occur during the collection of the large volume of data on international transactions. Another reason is that significant numbers of illegal international exchanges, relating to such activities as the illicit drug trade or armaments shipments, cannot be recorded because those who engage in them go to great lengths to keep them secret.

The Overall Balance of Payments The fourth and final line of Table 21-6 is the overall balance of payments. This overall balance *must always equal zero,* because every transaction between a U.S. resident and a foreign resident involves both a payment and a receipt. As a result, across all the accounts such payments and receipts *must* cancel out. This means that the overall balance of payments must equal zero.

We noted earlier that it is misleading to use the term "balance of payments" to describe the private payments balance. Now you can see why. The reason is that the *overall balance of payments is always equal to zero.* The private payments balance, in contrast, may be positive (a private payments surplus) or negative (a private payments deficit). The traditional, though misleading, term for a private payments surplus is "balance of payments surplus," and the traditional term for a private payments deficit is "balance of payments deficit." These are the terms most often used by the media. Because the use of these terms is so widespread, most economists use them as well, while keeping in mind that the *true* balance of payments is the overall figure that must equal zero.

moneyxtra!

Another Perspective

Learn about an important government account that contributes to the official settlements balance when the U.S. Treasury intervenes in foreign exchange markets by using the Chapter 21 reading, entitled "The Exchange Stabilization Fund: How It Works," by William Osterberg.
http://moneyxtra.swcollege.com

An important point follows from the zero value for the overall balance of payments:

After allowing for the statistical discrepancy, the private payments balance must always be offset by the official settlements balance.

For example, if there is a private payments deficit, then the official settlements balance must be positive. If a private payments deficit occurs, then U.S. residents have paid more to residents of other countries than they received from foreign residents. But this means that other countries' governments and central banks eventually must accumulate dollars that the U.S. residents have paid, on net, to those countries. Foreign governments and central banks hold many of these dollars in deposit accounts in the United States. The result is an increase in the U.S. official settlements balance that tends to make its value positive. In the end, in the absence of statistical discrepancies, the two balances offset each other. This leads to a zero value for the overall balance of payments.

2. How do economists measure international transactions? They use the balance of payments accounts. The balance of payments accounts are composed of three accounts that tabulate exchanges between U.S. residents and residents of other nations. The current account tabulates cross-border exchanges of goods and services, unilateral transfers, and income flows. The capital account records private asset transactions, and the official settlements balance tabulates governmental asset transactions.

Accounting for Inflation: Price Deflators and Real GDP

Figure 21-2 shows that for more than forty years U.S. GDP has risen each year. Does this mean that the U.S. economy has grown without letup? The answer is no. Annual GDP has increased for two reasons. One, of course, is that in many years the economy really *has* grown. Since 1959, U.S. businesses have expanded their resources and developed innovative ways to increase their production and sale of goods and services.

During some years, however, business production has actually declined, even though GDP increased. This seemingly contradictory increase in GDP occurred because of inflation. Recall that economists calculate GDP using market prices to value the production of firms. Economy-wide price increases, therefore, increase the *measured value* of output.

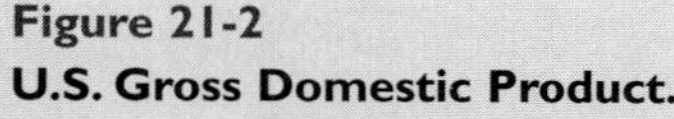

Figure 21-2
U.S. Gross Domestic Product.

The dollar value of newly produced goods and services within U.S. borders has increased each year because actual production has risen and because the price level has increased.

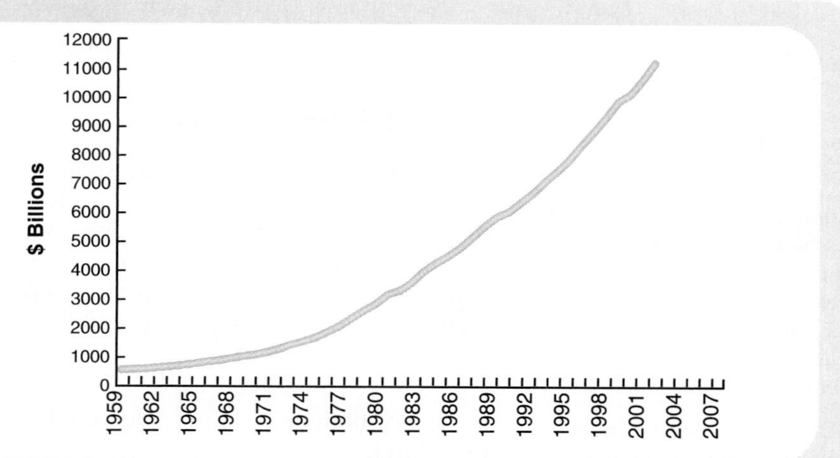

SOURCES: *Economic Report of the President*, 2002; and *Economic Indicators* (various issues).

Consequently, we cannot look at Figure 21-2 and conclude that the true production of goods and services has risen persistently in the United States. Because the United States has experienced inflation almost every year since World War II, at least some portion of the general rise in the annual GDP data displayed in the figure occurred simply because of rising prices.

Real versus Nominal GDP

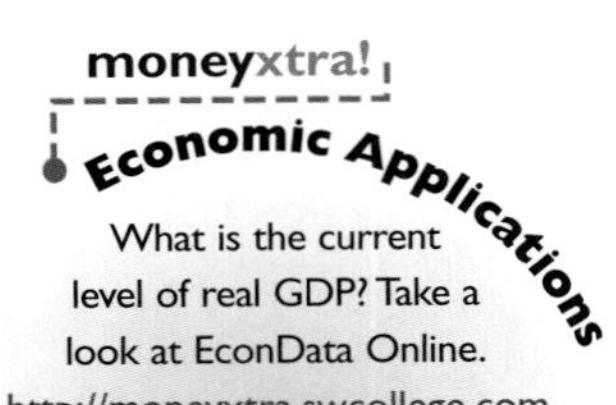

We must conclude that using unadjusted calculations of GDP in an inflationary environment would result in persistent *overstatements* of the actual volume of economic activity. If we are to make year-to-year comparisons of an economy's productive performance, therefore, we must somehow adjust GDP data to correct for the bias that inflation creates.

To see clearly why we need to adjust GDP for price changes, suppose that your employer increases your hourly wage by 100 percent. Ignoring any taxes or other deductions from your pay, your hourly income has doubled. Suppose, however, that the inflation rate also happens to equal 100 percent. This means that the prices you must pay to purchase goods and services also have doubled. Thus, your 100 percent pay raise only maintains the purchasing power of your wage—you really are no better off than you were before your wage increase.

In a like manner, if measured GDP doubles solely as a result of a 100 percent increase in the overall price level, then the total volume of economic activity really has not changed. Year-to-year comparisons of GDP thus would provide vastly distorted measures of the *real* growth in economic activity.

To deal with this potential problem of inflation-distorted GDP figures, economists have developed an inflation-adjusted measure of GDP, called **real gross domestic product,** or *real GDP.* This measure of aggregate output accounts for price changes and thereby more accurately reflects the economy's true volume of productive activity, net of any artificial increases resulting from inflation.

Economists distinguish between real GDP and unadjusted GDP by calling the unadjusted measure **nominal gross domestic product,** or *nominal GDP.* This means "GDP in name only." In other words, nominal GDP is calculated in current-dollar terms with no adjustment for effects of price changes.

Real gross domestic product (real GDP): A price-adjusted measure of aggregate output, or nominal GDP divided by the GDP price deflator.

Nominal gross domestic product (nominal GDP): The value of final production of goods and services calculated in current-dollar terms with no adjustment for effects of price changes.

GDP price deflator: A flexible-weight measure of the overall price level; equal to nominal GDP divided by real GDP.

The GDP Price Deflator

If properly calculated, real GDP should measure the economy's actual volume of production of goods and services. This implies that multiplying real GDP by a measure of the overall level of prices should yield the value of real GDP measured in current prices, which, in turn, is our definition of nominal GDP. If we let y denote real GDP and P denote a measure of the overall price level, then nominal GDP, denoted Y, thereby must be

$$Y = y \times P.$$

In words, nominal GDP should equal real GDP times a measure of the overall price level.

Indeed, the factor P is a standard measure of the price level, which economists call the **GDP price deflator,** or simply the "GDP deflator." They refer to P as a "deflator" because if we solve our expression for nominal GDP, $Y = y \times P$, for y, we get

$$y = Y/P.$$

This tells us that real GDP, y, is equal to nominal GDP, Y, adjusted by dividing, or "deflating," by the factor P. For example, suppose that nominal GDP measured in current prices, Y, is equal to \$11.49 trillion and the value of the GDP deflator, P, is equal to 3. Then real GDP can be calculated by deflating the \$11.49 trillion nominal GDP figure by a factor of one-third. To do this, we divide \$11.49 trillion by 3 to get real GDP = \$3.83 trillion.

Knowing that the GDP deflator P is equal to 3 tells us little, however, unless we also have a reference point for interpreting this value. To provide a reference point, economists define a **base year** for the GDP deflator, which is a year in which nominal GDP is equal to real GDP ($Y = y$), so that the GDP deflator's value is one ($P = 1$). Consequently, if the base year were, say, 1965, and the value of P in 2005 were equal to 3, then this would indicate that the overall level of prices tripled between 1965 and 2005.

Base year: A reference year for price-level comparisons, which is a year in which nominal GDP equals real GDP, so that the GDP deflator's value equals one.

At present, the U.S. government uses 1996 as the base year in its real GDP calculations. Panel (a) of Figure 21-3 shows the values of the GDP deflator since 1959. As you can see, the overall level of prices increased by almost a factor of 5, from 0.26 to 1.13, between 1959 and 2003. This means that in 2003 you would have needed nearly \$5 to purchase an item that cost \$1 in 1959. Alternatively stated, approximately \$5 in 2003 would have purchased the equivalent amount of goods and services that \$1 purchased in 1959.

Figure 21-3
The GDP Deflator and Real and Nominal GDP.

Panel (a) shows annual values of the GDP deflator. Panel (b) displays nominal GDP (the same chart as Figure 21-2) and real GDP. As panel (b) indicates, because real GDP accounts for the effects of price changes, it exhibits less growth from year to year.

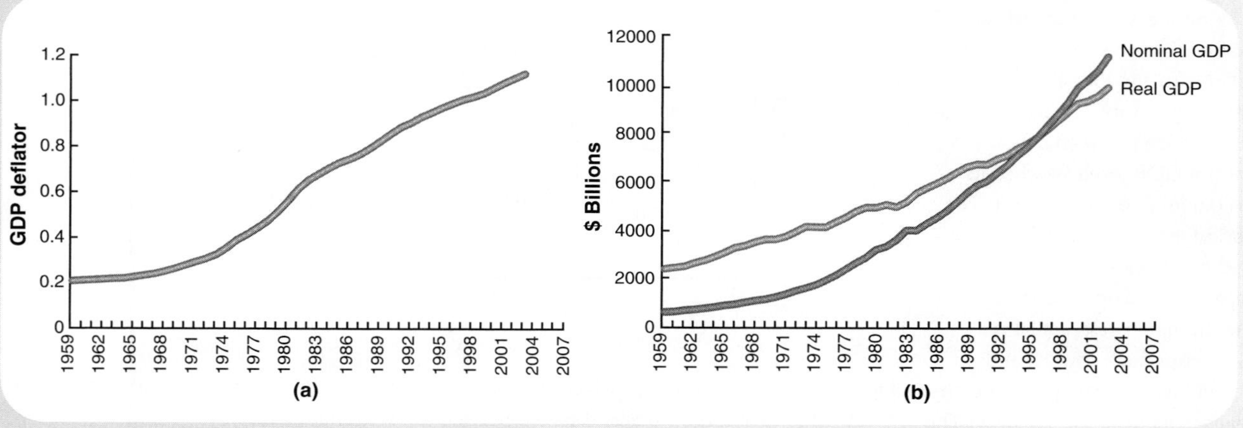

SOURCE: *Economic Report of the President*, 2002; *Economic Indicators* (various issues).

Business cycles: Variations in real GDP around its long-run growth path.

Natural GDP: The level of real GDP that is consistent with the economy's natural rate of growth.

Panel (b) of Figure 21-3 plots real and nominal GDP figures since 1959. Note that in 1996 nominal and real GDP are equal because 1996 is the base year in which $P = 1$, so $Y = y$. Clearly, adjusting for price changes has a significant effect on our interpretation of GDP data. (There are several other ways to measure changes in the overall price level; see *Policy Focus: The Alphabet Soup of Price Indexes.*)

This is why it is so important to convert nominal GDP to real GDP using the GDP price deflator. Thus:

Only real GDP data can provide useful information about true year-to-year changes in the economy's productive performance.

3. What is the difference between nominal GDP and real GDP?
Nominal GDP is the total value of newly produced goods and services computed using the prices at which they sold during the year they were produced. In contrast, real GDP is the value of final goods and services after adjusting for the effects of year-to-year price changes. The basic approach to calculating real GDP is to divide nominal GDP by the GDP deflator, which is a measure of the level of prices relative to prices for a base year.

Cycles in Economic Activity

Variations in real GDP, or a nation's real income, relative to its long-run growth path are known as **business cycles.** Figure 21-4 illustrates some key concepts associated with a complete business cycle. The dashed line in the figure shows a hypothetical growth path for **natural GDP,** which is what economists call the

Figure 21-4
A Hypothetical Business Cycle.

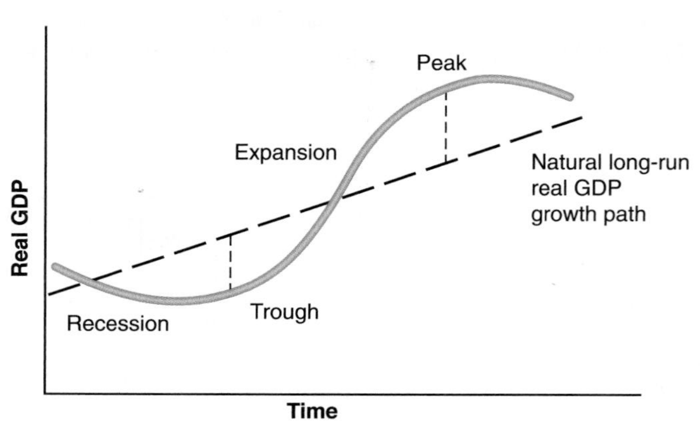

At a business-cycle trough, actual real GDP is at its lowest point relative to the long-run growth path of natural GDP, so the vertical distance between actual and natural GDP levels reaches its maximum size for the cycle. The period in which real GDP declines toward this trough is a recession. Beyond the trough of the business cycle, actual real GDP rises back toward and beyond its long-run growth path until it reaches its peak for the cycle. This period is called a business-cycle expansion. At the point at which the expansion peaks, the vertical distance between the actual real GDP growth path and the natural GDP growth path reaches its maximum size.

GLOBAL | POLICY Focus | CYBER | MANAGEMENT

The Alphabet Soup of Price Indexes

The GDP price deflator used in real GDP calculations is a *flexible-weight price index,* or a price index whose weights on various goods and services change automatically as the output of goods and services varies over time. The overall price level can also be measured using *fixed-weight price indexes,* which are calculated by selecting a fixed set of goods and services and then tracking the prices of these specific goods and services from year to year.

The CPI and the PPI

The best-known fixed-weight price index is the *consumer price index (CPI),* which is a weighted sum of prices of a full set of goods and services that the Bureau of Labor Statistics (BLS) in the U.S. Department of Labor determines a typical U.S. consumer purchases each year. The government incorporates various categories of expenditures into its weighting scheme for the CPI including a typical consumer's annual purchases of housing services and utilities, food and beverages, transportation, medical care, apparel, and entertainment. Figure 21-5 shows the current distribution of these expenditures in the computation of the CPI. All told, the BLS samples prices on about 95,000 different items. In addition, the government calculates a number of alternative consumer price indexes, such as CPIs for urban consumers, for rural consumers, and so on.

There are several other fixed-weight price indexes. One is the *producer price index (PPI),* which is a weighted average of prices of goods that the BLS determines a typical business charges for the goods and services it sells. Another is the *personal consumption expenditure (PCE)* price index, which the Bureau of Economic Analysis (BEA) in the U.S. Department of Commerce calculates as an average of two different fixed-weight price indexes based on shifting baskets of goods and services purchased by consumers each year.

Problems with Fixed-Weight Price Indexes

Although the CPI and PPI are popular measures of the overall price level, they suffer from some important drawbacks that relate to the fact that they are fixed-weight indexes. The PCE tries to deal with some of these drawbacks, but it too suffers from problems.

The most glaring problem is that relative prices of goods change over time, so people substitute among goods, changing their spending allocations. This means that the fixed weights that the BLS assigns to a "typical" consumer or producer when computing the CPI and PPI are

Continued on next page

Figure 21-5
The Distribution of Expenditures in Computing the Consumer Price Index.

The consumer price index is a weighted average of prices of a fixed set of goods and services, distributed as shown here.

SOURCE: Bureau of Labor Statistics.

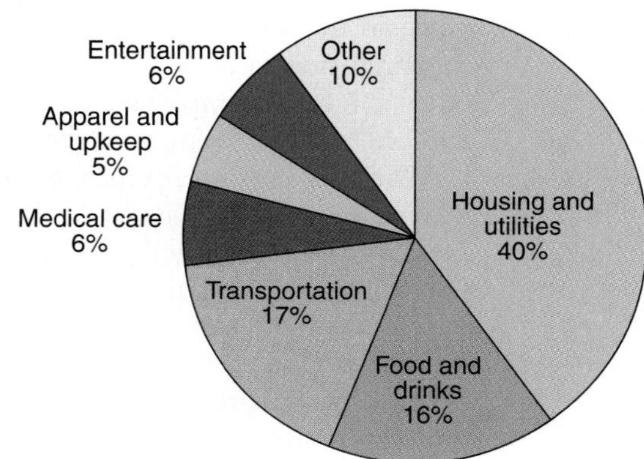

Policy Focus, continued

artificially fixed. For any truly representative consumer or producer, the weights surely must change somewhat from year to year. Using the PCE helps address this problem by calculating year-to-year price changes based on averages of weights in the two years.

Using fixed weights for price indexes also ignores the potential for *quality* changes in the goods and services that consumers buy. In addition, fixed-weight indexes suffer from various data collection problems. To calculate the CPI and PPI, the BLS collects data on *list* prices, which are the prices that businesses formally print in catalogues, price lists, and so on. In fact, however, during times when competition for business is most pressing, consumers often can get bargain prices below those in the formal price lists available to the BLS. The proliferation of discount retailers since the 1980s may have worsened this measurement problem for the CPI and PPI. Data collection problems for the PCE may be even more severe, because the BEA estimates consumer spending on goods and services by subtracting sales to businesses and governments from total sales, thereby measuring consumer spending only indirectly for purposes of constructing index weights.

Because the government uses the CPI to index Social Security, there have been many studies of the problems with calculating the CPI. Estimates in the mid-1990s indicated that the various problems added as much as 2 percentage points to official CPI inflation figures. Beginning in 1997, the BLS altered its sampling procedure for food and nonfood items and improved the accuracy of its treatment of rents and hospital and generic drug prices. As a result, the CPI inflation rate dropped by about 0.2 to 0.3 percentage point. Further calculation changes between 1998 and 2001 reduced estimated inflation by nearly 1 percentage point.

FOR CRITICAL ANALYSIS: The government has not changed past published data on the CPI. Why is this fact important to policymaking today?

level of real GDP along the long-run growth path that the economy otherwise would follow in the absence of cyclical fluctuations. The solid curve is a hypothetical growth path for *actual* GDP, which may fluctuate.

Recessions and Expansions

When actual real GDP declines, economists say that the economy experiences a phase in the business cycle called a **recession.** The National Bureau of Economic Research normally defines a recession as a recurring period of decline in total output, income, employment, and trade that lasts at least six months to a year and affects many sectors of the economy.

Recession: A decline in real GDP lasting at least two consecutive quarters, which can cause real GDP to fall below its long-run, natural level.

Trough: The point along a business cycle at which real GDP is at its lowest level relative to the long-run natural GDP level.

Depression: An especially severe recession.

When a recession reaches its low point, actual real GDP is at its lowest point relative to its natural path. At this point, therefore, the vertical distance between the natural GDP growth path and the actual growth path reaches its maximum size for the cycle. This point is the **trough** of the business cycle; at the trough, business activity is at its lowest level over the course of the entire business cycle. If the recession is severe, then actual real GDP may be well below the economy's natural level. Furthermore, if a severe recession lasts a particularly long time, then economists say that an economy experiences a **depression.** Economists often disagree about when recessions are sufficiently severe for this term to apply, but all agree that a depression occurred in the United States during the 1930s.

When actual real GDP begins to rise again, the economy enters the **expansion** phase of the business cycle. At the point where actual real GDP rises to its highest point relative to natural GDP, the business cycle is at its **peak.** The cycle then continues.

Actual business cycles are not as simple as the one illustrated in Figure 21-4. During various periods in the past, the actual path of real GDP has been much less smooth than the hypothetical path shown in the figure. Furthermore, the durations of expansions and recessions have rarely been of equal length. Table 21-7 displays the durations between troughs and peaks of the twenty-two business cycles that the United States has experienced since 1899. As the table indicates, the lengths of the expansion and recession phases of business cycles have varied considerably.

Expansion: A point along a business cycle at which actual GDP begins to rise, perhaps even above its natural, long-run level.

Peak: The point along a business cycle at which real GDP is at its highest level relative to the long-run, natural GDP level.

Unemployment and the Business Cycle

Business cycles entail movements in aggregate GDP that affect us all. For some of us, the effects of business-cycle recessions can hit especially hard when they generate job losses. By way of contrast, expansions can pave the way to brighter futures for many families as they bring about overall reductions in unemployment. (Among those who are employed around the world, the number of hours worked can vary widely; see on the following page *Global Focus: Putting in Long Hours Has a Different Meaning Depending on Where You Are.*)

Table 21-7 Business-Cycle Expansions and Contractions in the United States

			Duration in Months*		
Peak	Trough	Peak	RECESSION	EXPANSION	CYCLE
June 1899	December 1900	September 1902	18	21	39
September 1902	August 1904	May 1907	23	33	56
May 1907	June 1908	January 1910	13	19	32
January 1910	January 1912	January 1913	24	12	36
January 1913	December 1914	August 1918	23	44	67
August 1918	March 1919	January 1920	7	10	17
January 1920	July 1921	May 1923	18	22	40
May 1923	July 1924	October 1926	14	27	41
October 1926	November 1927	August 1929	13	21	34
August 1929	March 1933	May 1937	43	50	93
May 1937	June 1938	February 1945	13	80	93
February 1945	October 1945	November 1948	8	37	45
November 1948	October 1949	July 1953	11	45	56
July 1953	May 1954	August 1957	10	39	49
August 1957	April 1958	April 1960	8	24	32
April 1960	February 1961	December 1969	10	106	116
December 1969	November 1970	November 1973	11	36	47
November 1973	March 1975	January 1980	16	58	74
January 1980	July 1980	July 1981	6	12	18
July 1981	November 1982	July 1990	16	92	108
July 1990	March 1991	March 2001	8	120	128
March 2001	May 2002		14	—	—

*Cycles are measured from peak to peak.
SOURCES: National Bureau of Economic Research; *Survey of Current Business;* authors' estimates.

On the Web

Where can you find out when the National Bureau of Economic Research has determined that a recession is under way? The answer is to visit the NBER's home page at http://www.nber.org, where you can click on "Data" in the right-hand margin, then "Recessions."

GLOBAL Focus | POLICY | CYBER | MANAGEMENT

Putting in Long Hours Has a Different Meaning Depending on Where You Are

Undoubtedly, there have been times in your life—on a full-time or part-time job or even in your efforts as a student—when you have felt that you were putting in long hours of work. Exactly what it means to put in "long hours" differs around the world, however.

As you can see in Figure 21-6, the average number of hours that an individual works during an entire year can vary considerably from place to place. In the United States, the average resident works just over 1,978 hours per year. Comparing this figure with the 1,376 hours that a typical resident of Norway spends working each year indicates that on average a U.S. resident devotes the equivalent of fifteen additional 40-hour weeks to work each year relative to an individual in Norway.

Although the average U.S. resident spends more time working than a typical individual in any other developed, industrialized nation, people in some countries, such as the Czech Republic and South Korea, allocate even more of their time to work each year. A typical South Korean resident works almost 500 hours more than an average U.S. resident and nearly 1,100 hours more than a resident of Norway. This means that for every hour that an individual in Norway spends on the job, someone in South Korea is at work 50 minutes longer.

For Critical Analysis: Does the fact that a typical individual in Spain works more hours per year than an average German resident necessarily imply that the individual in Spain produces more output of a comparable good or service in that time?

Figure 21-6
Annual Hours Worked per Person in Selected Nations.

The average number of hours a worker spends on the job varies considerably across countries.

SOURCE: International Labor Organization.

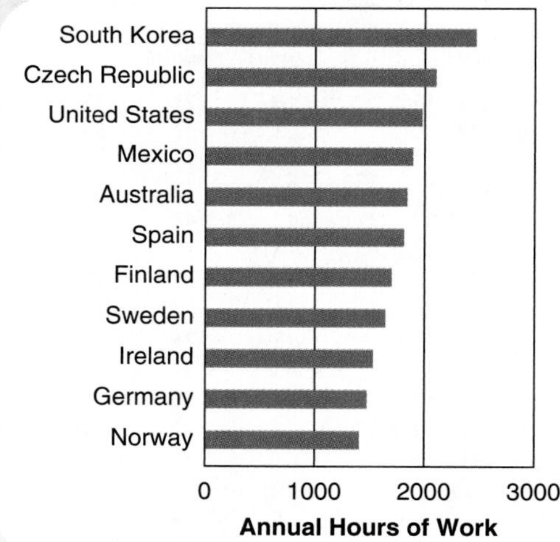

The Unemployment Rate To determine the extent of total unemployment in the U.S. economy, the government tabulates the **unemployment rate,** which is simply the percentage of the civilian labor force that is unemployed. Terminology is crucial. The civilian labor force consists of all individuals sixteen years of age to retirement who are not in the military or confined to an institution such as a hospital and who either have a job or are actively seeking a job. The number of people in the civilian labor force who are unemployed includes all who are not working yet are available for and actively seeking a job. This means that people who are not employed but who also are not actively looking for work are not included in either the civilian labor force or the ranks of the unemployed. Such *discouraged workers* are not counted in calculations of the unemployment rate.

It also is important to understand that the official unemployment rate is an *estimate.* The government does not calculate the entire labor force. On behalf of the Bureau of Labor Statistics, the Bureau of the Census conducts a monthly *Current Population Survey* covering 60,000 households in about 2,000 counties and cities across the fifty states and the District of Columbia. The BLS then uses the information from this monthly survey to calculate its estimates of the size of the labor force and the number of people in the labor force who are unemployed. It then uses these estimates to calculate the unemployment rate.

Business Cycles and the Unemployment Rate The unemployment rate varies systematically across business cycles, as Figure 21-7 on the following page shows. Recessions, the shaded periods in the figure, are accompanied by higher unemployment rates. During business-cycle expansions, in contrast, unemployment rates tend to decline.

Economists classify three components of the unemployed portion of the nation's civilian labor force. One is **frictional unemployment,** which describes the portion of the labor force consisting of people who are qualified for gainful employment but are temporarily out of work. They may be in this situation because they recently quit a job and have accepted another job that they will begin in a few weeks.

Another component of unemployment is **structural unemployment.** This refers to the portion of the civilian labor force made up of people who would like to be gainfully employed but who lack skills and other attributes necessary to obtain a job. The duration of unemployment for such individuals can stretch into months or perhaps even years.

Most economists define the ratio of those who are frictionally and structurally unemployed to the civilian labor force as the **natural rate of unemployment,** or the unemployment rate that would arise if the economy could stay on its long-run growth path. The variations in the overall unemployment rate shown in Figure 21-7 thereby would arise from changes in the third category of unemployment, called **cyclical unemployment.** This is the portion of the civilian labor force composed of those who lose their jobs because of business-cycle fluctuations.

A key issue of concern to economists inside and outside the Federal Reserve is whether the Fed can undertake policies that can influence the economy's rate of growth or smooth cyclical fluctuations in economic activity.

Unemployment rate: The percentage of the civilian labor force that is unemployed.

Frictional unemployment: The portion of total unemployment arising from the fact that a number of workers are between jobs at any given time.

Structural unemployment: The portion of total unemployment resulting from a poor match of workers' abilities and skills with current needs of employers.

Natural rate of unemployment: The portion of the unemployment rate that is accounted for by frictional and structural unemployment.

Cyclical unemployment: The portion of total unemployment resulting from business-cycle fluctuations.

Figure 21-7
Unemployment Rates and Phases of the Business Cycle.

The cyclical component of the unemployment rate increases during business-cycle downturns. As a result, the overall unemployment rate typically rises during recessions.

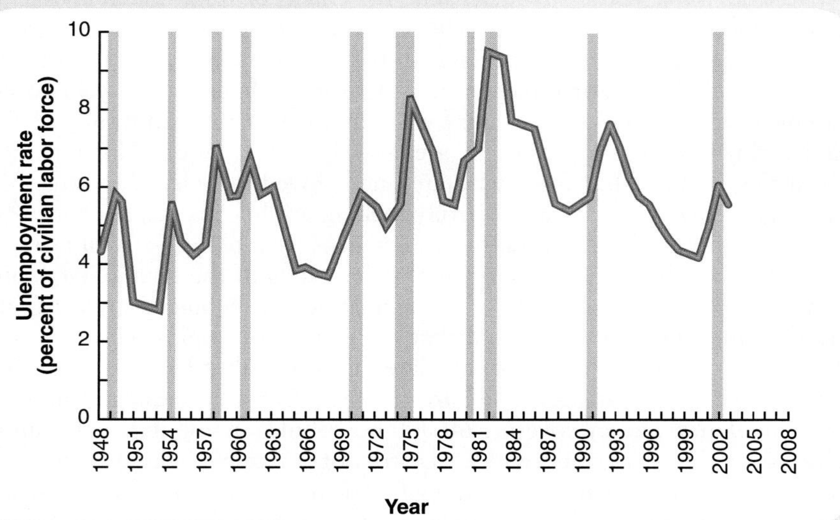

SOURCES: *Economic Report of the President,* 2002; National Bureau of Economic Research, *Economic Indicators.*

4. What are business cycles, and what are their key features? Business cycles are fluctuations in real income above or below the level that is consistent with the economy's long-run growth. Recessions occur when real income falls below its long-run level, and expansions take place when real income rises back to or even above its long-run level. Although the existence of frictional and structural unemployment implies that there is a natural unemployment rate, the overall unemployment rate has a cyclical component that rises during recessions and falls during expansions.

Link to **Management**

Does the Stock Market Forecast Business Productivity?

Like the prices of other financial assets, stock prices should be inversely related to market interest rates. Stock prices should also depend positively on anticipated annual future earnings of companies that issue equity shares, because companies will pay annual dividends to shareholders from those earnings. Companies' earnings, in turn, are positively related to business productivity, or the ability of businesses to produce a given amount of output from a fixed quantity of inputs. When business productivity increases, firms are able to produce a given volume of output at lower cost, thereby boosting both their own earnings and economic growth.

The Relationship between Productivity and Stock Prices

Because companies' current and future earnings are related to productivity, investors have good reason to keep close tabs on productivity trends when deciding how much they are willing to pay for shares of stock. Other things being equal, when investors are convinced that productivity is on an upswing, stock prices should increase. If investors have good reason to anticipate a drop-off in business productivity, then if other factors are unchanged they will tend to bid lower amounts for shares of stock, and market share prices should fall.

Because investors have strong incentives to forecast business productivity and act on their forecasts in ways that influence stock prices, some economists have suggested that movements in stock price indexes can provide good signals of future business productivity. Certainly, we do often observe a positive relationship between stock prices and business productivity. During quarters when stock prices have risen, business productivity has also tended to increase, and vice versa. This pattern often arises even when the economy's performance is flat, so it does not just reflect a response of stock prices to changing economic activity. On the surface, this relationship does seem to suggest that movements in stock prices may help firms gauge current trends in overall productivity.

Using Stock Prices to Forecast Business Productivity

But does this positive relationship between stock prices and productivity exist because investors do a particularly good job of anticipating future productivity or because investors are simply adept at reacting quickly to previously unexpected productivity increases or declines? If stock prices rise or fall because of speedy investor reactions to recent productivity movements, then stock prices are not likely to provide much information about *future* productivity trends. Instead, stock price movements would simply reflect changes in business productivity already observed in the marketplace.

To evaluate whether it is possible to use stock price measures to forecast future productivity growth, Evan Koenig, an economist at the Federal Reserve Bank of Dallas, used ratios of stock prices to firms' earnings and dividends to try to predict business productivity growth in following quarters between 1982 and 2000. His forecasting method controlled for movements in interest rates, inflation expectations, and trends in employment. As you can see in Figure 21-8, movements in ratios of stock prices to earnings and dividends yielded relatively accurate predictions of productivity growth during this period. Hence, there is some evidence that variations in stock prices really can assist in forecasting future changes in business productivity.

Research Project

Why might a firm be interested in trying to forecast future movements in productivity for the economy as a whole? Provide a list of potential reasons, and evaluate the ways an individual company might improve its own current and future profitability by successfully anticipating aggregate productivity.

Web Resources

1. What are broader economic implications of the relationship between the stock market and productivity? Find out by going to the home page of the Federal Reserve Bank of Dallas http://www.dallasfed.org, where you can click on "Publications," then "Southwest Economy." At this page, click on "2000" and download the January/February issue to read Evan Koenig's paper entitled "Productivity, the Stock Market, and Monetary Policy in the New Economy."

2. What are recent trends in U.S. business productivity? Find out by going to the home page of the Bureau of Labor Statistics (http://www.bls.gov) and clicking on "Productivity and Costs."

Figure 21-8
Actual and Predicted Productivity Growth.

Predictions of productivity growth using stock prices closely match actual growth in business productivity.

SOURCE: Evan Koenig, "Productivity, the Stock Market, and Monetary Policy in the New Economy," Federal Reserve Bank of Dallas *Southwest Economy*, January/February 2000, pp. 6–12.

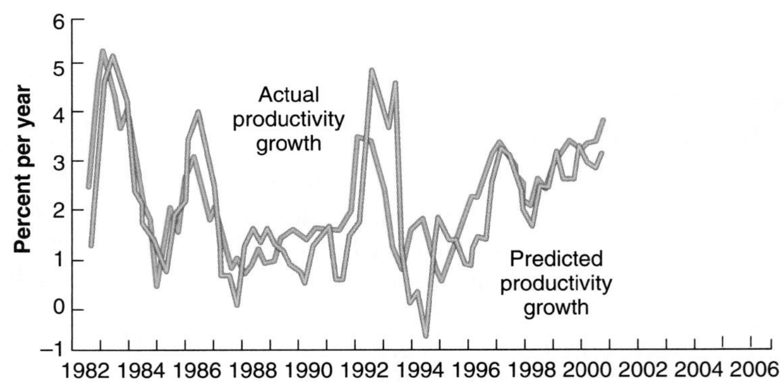

Chapter Summary

1. Gross Domestic Product and Its Computation: By definition, gross domestic product (GDP) is the total of all final goods and services produced during a given period, evaluated at market prices. The product approach to calculating GDP totals consumption spending, investment spending, government expenditures, and net export spending to obtain GDP. The income approach yields GDP as the sum of wages and salaries, net interest, rental income, profits, indirect taxes, and depreciation.

2. How Economists Measure International Transactions: The balance of payments accounts measure the values of cross-border exchanges. There are three balance of payments accounts. One, the current account, tracks international exchanges of goods and services, unilateral transfers, and income flows. Another, the capital account, tabulates private asset transactions. Finally, the official settlements balance accounts for governmental asset transactions.

3. The Difference between Nominal GDP and Real GDP: Nominal GDP is the market value of final goods and services evaluated in terms of the prices at which the goods and services were traded during the year they were produced. Real GDP, in contrast, is the value of final goods and services after taking into account the effects of price variations. We compute real GDP by dividing nominal GDP by the GDP deflator, which measures the price level relative to the price level of goods and services in a base year.

4. Business Cycles and Their Characteristics: Business cycles are variations in real income around its long-run growth path. Recessions are periods of a real income decline below its long-run level, and expansions are increases in real income to levels that for a time can exceed its long-run level. Frictional and structural unemployment exist even without business cycles, but the overall unemployment rate has a cyclical component that tends to rise during recessions and to decline during expansions.

Questions and Problems

(Answers to odd-numbered questions and problems may be found on the Web at http://money.swcollege.com under "Student Resources.")

1. In your own words, define GDP. Carefully distinguish between GDP and GNP.

2. Consider the following data ($ billions) for a given year:

Consumption spending	$8,000	Wages and salaries	$7,300
Interest income	600	Depreciation	1,400
Rental income	300	Government spending	2,200
Investment spending	2,300	Net export spending:	−450
Profits	1,900		

Calculate the following:

a. Gross domestic product

b. National income

c. Net national product

d. Indirect business taxes

3. Explain the distinction between nominal GDP and real GDP.

4. What does the merchandise trade balance measure? Why is it not necessarily a good indicator of a nation's trade position vis-à-vis other countries if the nation has relatively large service-oriented industries?

5. Explain why a nation's overall balance of payments must equal zero.

6. Consider a two-good economy. In 2003, firms in this economy produced 25 units of good *X*, which sold at a market price of $4 per unit, and 15 units of good *Y*, which sold at a market price of $4 per unit. In 2004, the economy produced the same amounts of both *X* and *Y*, but the price of good *X* rose to $6 per unit, and the price of good *Y* increased to $5 per unit. What were the values of nominal GDP in 2003 and 2004?

7. In question 6, if 2003 is the base year, what were the values of real GDP in 2003 and 2004?

8. Using your answers from questions 6 and 7 and assuming again that 2003 is the base year, what is the value of the GDP price deflator for 2003? What is the approximate value (rounded to the nearest hundredth) of the GDP price deflator for 2004? What is the approximate value (rounded to the nearest percentage point) of inflation between 2003 and 2004?

9. Suppose that the GDP deflator for the year considered in question 2 has a value of 1.42. Based on your answer to part (a) in question 2, what is real GDP for this year?

10. In light of the definitions of business-cycle troughs and peaks, explain why the trough of the business cycle in Figure 21-4 does not correspond to the lowest level of real GDP over the cycle that the figure depicts and why the peak is not at the highest level of real GDP that the figure displays.

Before the Test

Test your understanding of the material covered in this chapter by taking the Chapter 21 interactive quiz at http://money.swcollege.com.

Online Application

To view the most current information concerning the consumer price index (CPI), take a look at the home page of the Bureau of Labor Statistics. As noted in this chapter, the CPI is a fixed-weight index measure of the U.S. price level.

Internet URL: **http://stats.bls.gov:80/eag/eag.us.htm**

Title: Bureau of Labor Statistics: Economy at a Glance

Navigation: Begin at the home page of the Bureau of Labor Statistics (**http://stats.bls.gov**).

Application: Perform the indicated operations, and answer the following questions:

1. On the Bureau of Labor Statistics home page, under the heading "At a Glance Tables," click on "U.S. Economy at a Glance," and then click on "Consumer Price Index." Scan down that page, and under the heading "CPI Fact Sheets," click on "How to Use the Consumer Price Index for Escalation." Read the material at this location. Based on this discussion, what exactly does the CPI measure?

2. Back up to "U.S. Economy at a Glance." Click on the graph box and take a look at the chart. How much does the CPI appear to vary from year to year? Has it varied much within the most recent year?

Selected References and Further Reading

Clayton, Gary E., and Martin Gerhard Giesbrecht. *A Guide to Everyday Economic Statistics*. New York: McGraw-Hill, 1995.

Council of Economic Advisers. *Economic Indicators*. Washington, D.C.: U.S. Government Printing Office, various issues.

______. *Economic Report of the President*. Washington, D.C.: U.S. Government Printing Office, February 2002.

Federal Reserve Bank of Kansas City. *Policies for Long-Run Economic Growth*. 1992.

Gould, David, and Roy Ruffin. "What Determines Economic Growth?" Federal Reserve Bank of Dallas *Economic Review,* Second Quarter 1993, pp. 25–40.

International Monetary Fund. *World Economic Outlook*. Washington, D.C., October 1996.

U.S. Department of Commerce. *Survey of Current Business*. Washington, D.C., various issues.

MoneyXtra

moneyxtra! Log on to the MoneyXtra Web site now (http://moneyxtra.swcollege.com) for additional learning resources such as practice quizzes, case studies, readings, and additional economic applications.

Chapter

22

The Self-Regulating Economy—

Classical Monetary Theory

As the old saying goes, the only things that are certain in life are death and taxes. Those U.S. residents who have been alive since the 1940s might also be tempted to add inflation to this short list of life's certainties. Each year since 1949, the level of prices of goods and services in the United States has risen. During that interval, the average annual rate of increase in overall prices has been 4.1. percent. As a result, the U.S. price level is now more than 10 times higher than it was in 1946.

Something else that has grown considerably during the same period is the quantity of money in circulation. The M1 measure of the quantity of money has increased by a factor of almost 11 times, or at an annual rate of 4.3 percent, since 1946. The M2 measure is now more than 40 times greater, and its average annual growth rate since 1946 has been 6.6. percent.

Fundamental Issues

1. What are the key assumptions of classical monetary theory?
2. How are the aggregate levels of labor employment and real output of goods and services determined in the classical theory?
3. What factors determine the price level in the classical framework?
4. How are interest rates determined in classical monetary theory?
5. How is the international value of a nation's currency determined in classical monetary theory?

The simple fact that both monetary aggregates and prices have increased considerably over the years does not mean that these economic variables are necessarily related. Nevertheless, most economists believe there is good reason to expect that there should be a direct relationship between money growth and inflation. In this chapter, you will learn about how one group of economists, called the classical economists, explain this predicted co-movement between the rate of growth of the quantity of money and the rate of inflation.

Fundamental Classical Perspectives

Three assumptions underlie the classical theory of the relationship between the quantity of money in circulation and economic activity:

1. Workers, consumers, and businesspersons are motivated by rational self-interest.

2. People do not experience *money illusion.*

3. Pure competition prevails in the markets for goods and services and for factors of production.

Let's consider each of these assumptions in turn.

Rational Self-Interest

A basic assumption of the classical theory is that consumers, workers, and businesspersons desire to maximize their total satisfaction. This means that individuals attempt to achieve the highest possible overall well-being, or utility. Consequently, classical economists assume that individuals are *utility maximizers.*

Businesses operate to produce the highest net income for their owners. The net income of any business is its flow of profits. Within the classical theory, therefore, businesses are *profit maximizers.*

No Money Illusion

Consider the following example. A college student has a part-time job at a local retailer. The manager increases his hourly wage from $10.00 per hour to $10.50 per hour, or by 5 percent. Simultaneously, however, the overall level of the prices of the goods and services that the student purchases also rises by 5 percent, in large part because of sizable increases in tuition and fees at his college.

If this student responds to the 5 percent increase in his current-dollar wages by changing his behavior, then he will exhibit **money illusion.** This refers to any tendency for an individual or business to change preferred transactions of goods, services, or factors of production solely as a result of *nominal* price changes. In this example, if the student exhibits money illusion, then he will be so pleased by his 5 percent raise that he will offer to work more hours at the higher current-dollar wage. Nevertheless, in light of the 5 percent rise in his living costs, he actually is no better off in real terms than he was before his wage increase.

A basic hypothesis of classical theory is that people normally do not exhibit money illusion. According to the classical approach, when businesspersons, workers, and consumers make decisions about how much to produce, sell, or purchase, they respond only to changes in price-level-adjusted, or *real,* variables. If changes in nominal quantities do not translate into *real* changes, then individuals and businesses will not alter their desired market transactions.

Money illusion: A situation that exists when economic agents change their behavior in response to changes in nominal values, even if there are no changes in real (price-level-adjusted) values.

Pure Competition

Although classical economists recognize that monopoly firms, such as electric utilities, exist, they argue that the dominant type of market interaction among businesses in the overall economy is *pure competition.* Under pure competition, there are enough buyers and sellers of a typical good, service, or factor of production that no single buyer or seller can affect the market prices of these items.

Consequently, each buyer and seller is a price taker in purely competitive markets. The buyer or seller takes market prices as "given." That is, purchases or sales initiated by any individual buyer or seller in isolation cannot affect market prices. Only aggregate—though typically uncoordinated—purchases or sales of a good, service, or factor of production cause changes in market prices. The forces of market demand and supply, therefore, determine market prices. These prices, in turn, respond speedily to variations in market demand or market supply.

1. What are the key assumptions of classical monetary theory? The classical theory presumes that people pursue their own self-interest. It is also based on the assumption that people do not experience money illusion. Thus, in classical monetary theory, individuals realize that they are no better off with higher nominal wages if prices also are higher. Classical monetary theory also presumes that pure competition prevails in the aggregate economy. Thus, in the classical theory, there are large numbers of buyers and sellers of goods and services who cannot individually influence prices in markets for goods, services, and factors of production.

The Classical Theory of Production and Employment

Any theory of the relationship between money and the economy must provide an explanation of how many goods and services businesses produce and how many units of factors of production, such as labor, they utilize. Classical monetary theory's approach to understanding production and employment is the benchmark, or starting point of comparison, for all other theories of the relationship between the quantity of money in circulation and economic activity. It is very important, therefore, for you to strive for a complete understanding of this topic.

The Production Function

The economy-wide, or *aggregate* **production function** is a relationship between the quantities of factors of production—labor, capital, land, and entrepreneurship—employed by all firms in the economy and the total production of real output by those firms, given their current technology.

SHORT-RUN PRODUCTION The classical approach presumes that in the short run firms cannot adjust their use of capital, land, and entrepreneurship. The only variable factor of production for businesses is the quantity of labor that they employ on an hourly and weekly basis, denoted as N.

In principle, there are three ways to measure the amount of labor that firms employ. One way is simply to count the number of people employed during a given time interval. An alternative approach is to calculate the total time worked by all people employed by businesses, which is just the sum of all the hours that employees work during a period. Finally, economists can measure employment by using a combination of these two measures, known as *person-hours*.

In the short run, business firms combine labor with fixed amounts of other productive factors to produce output. Some firms, such as ice cream parlors, may

Production function: A relationship between possible quantities of factors of production, such as labor services, and the amount of output of goods and services that firms can produce with current technology.

use very simple production processes. Others, such as telecommunications-equipment manufacturers, may use complex processes to assemble components manufactured at diverse locations around the globe. The aggregate production function sums up the result of these processes as the total quantity of real output of goods and services, y, generated by employing the total quantity of labor, N:

$$y = F(N).$$

This expression says that the aggregate amount of real output in the economy is a *function* of the amount of labor employed by all firms.

Panel (a) of Figure 22-1 shows a sample aggregate production function, $F(N)$. Any point along this function indicates how much real output firms can produce for a specific quantity of labor they employ. For example, if firms employ an amount of labor equal to N_1, then the total output of goods and services, or real GDP, is equal to y_1. If firms employ a larger quantity of labor, N_2, then naturally they are able to produce a larger amount of real output. Real GDP increases to y_2.

The production function in panel (a) of Figure 22-1 is *concave,* which means that it is bowed downward. As a consequence, the *slope* of the production function—the change in output resulting from a change in employment, or "rise" divided by "run"—varies along the function. For instance, the slope of the func-

Figure 22-1
The Aggregate Production Function and the Marginal-Product-of-Labor (MP_N) Schedule.

Given a fixed stock of capital and a current state of technology, higher levels of labor employment are necessary to achieve increased production of real output. The bowed, or concave, shape of the production function in panel (a) reflects the law of diminishing marginal returns, which states that total output increases at a decreasing rate for each additional one-unit rise in employment of labor. Consequently, as shown in panel (b), the marginal product of labor declines as employment rises.

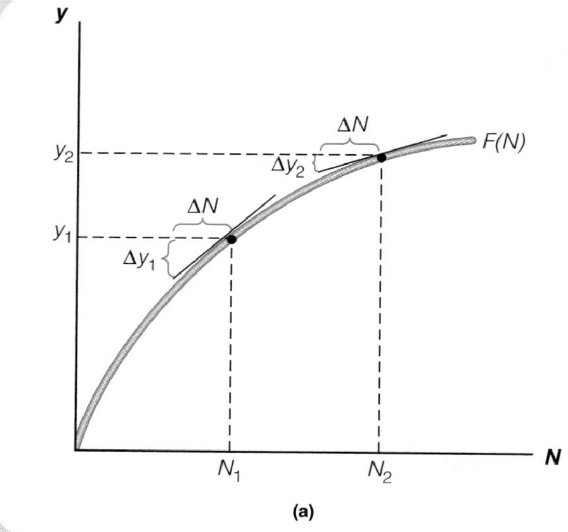

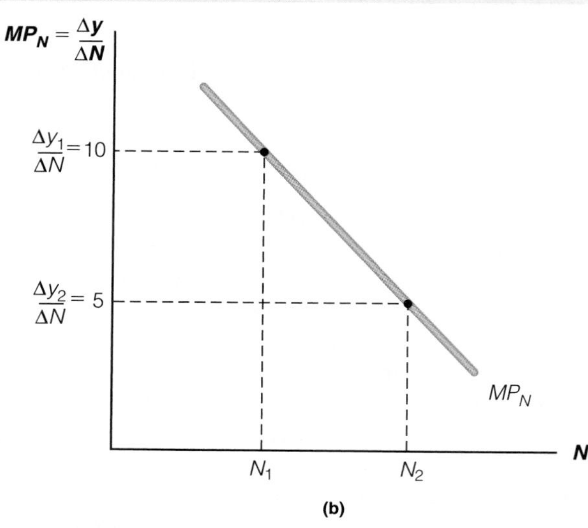

tion at the employment level N_1 is the slope of the line tangent to the function at this point, or $\Delta y_1/\Delta N$, where the symbol Δ denotes a change in a quantity. By way of contrast, at the higher employment level N_2, the same change in employment, ΔN, yields a smaller change in output, Δy_2. Thus, the slope of the production function at the level of employment N_2, which is equal to $\Delta y_2/\Delta N$, is lower than the slope of the production function at the employment level N_1.

THE MARGINAL PRODUCT OF LABOR The fact that the slope of the production function decreases as the quantity of labor employed by firms increases reflects the **law of diminishing marginal returns.** According to this law, the additional output produced by an additional unit of labor ultimately falls as additional units of labor are employed by firms. The slope of the production function, $\Delta y/\Delta N$, is by definition the additional amount of output that firms can produce by employing an additional unit of labor. This slope, therefore, is the **marginal product of labor,** or MP_N. Hence, MP_N is equal to $\Delta y/\Delta N$, or the slope of the production function at a given quantity of labor.

Law of diminishing marginal returns: The law that states that each successive addition of a unit of a factor of production, such as labor, eventually produces a smaller gain in real output produced, other factors held constant.

Marginal product of labor: The change in total output resulting from a one-unit increase in the quantity of labor employed in production.

Panel (b) of Figure 22-1 displays the marginal product of labor, which at the employment level N_1 is equal to $\Delta y_1/\Delta N$, or the slope of the production function at this level of employment level. Suppose that the value of this slope is assumed to be equal to 10. If total employment rises to N_2, then the slope of the production function declines to $\Delta y_2/\Delta N$, which is assumed to equal 5. The marginal product of labor, therefore, is lower at this higher employment level.

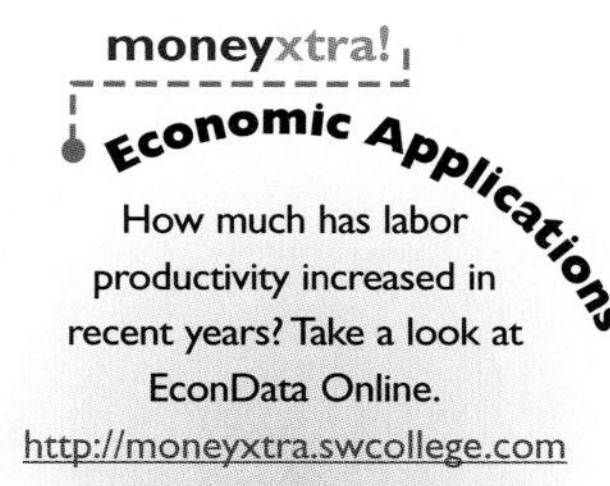

Of course, the employment levels N_1 and N_2 are just two examples. At levels of employment below N_1, the marginal product of labor must be larger than $\Delta y_1/\Delta N$. At employment levels above N_2, the marginal product of labor must be smaller than $\Delta y_2/\Delta N$. Furthermore, at successively higher employment levels between N_1 and N_2, the marginal product of labor must decline. Thus, there is a downward-sloping set of values for the marginal product of labor corresponding to the production function shown in panel (a) of Figure 22-1. This is the *marginal-product-of-labor schedule,* or MP_N *schedule,* which panel (b) displays. The MP_N schedule depicts the marginal product of labor, or slope of the production function, at any given quantity of labor. The downward slope of the MP_N schedule reflects the law of diminishing marginal returns.

Labor Demand

The marginal product of labor indicates how much more output an additional unit of labor produces, so it is a critical element in any firm's decision concerning how much labor to employ. Another fundamental factor that a firm must consider, of course, is the cost it incurs by employing another unit of labor. Profit maximization requires a firm to balance the revenue gain from the sale of the additional output produced by another labor unit against the cost of employing that unit of labor.

A FIRM'S DEMAND FOR LABOR A profit-maximizing firm produces output to the point at which its marginal revenue (MR), or additional revenue generated by producing and selling an additional unit of output, equals its marginal cost (MC), or the additional cost that it incurs in this activity. If MR were to exceed MC at a given production level, then the firm would earn a positive net profit from producing the last unit, thereby giving the firm an incentive to produce more units. If MC were to exceed MR, however, then the firm's net profit on the last unit produced would be negative, which would induce the firm to reduce its output. Thus, when $MR = MC$, the firm produces a level of output that ensures positive net profits for every unit of production up to the last unit produced. This output level thereby maximizes the firm's profit from total production of output.

The Competitive Price As we noted earlier, a central hypothesis of the classical approach is that pure competition prevails. Consequently, in the classical theory prices are market determined. No single firm can influence the market price, so each unit of output that an individual firm produces by definition yields the same marginal revenue, which is the market price. Hence, each purely competitive, profit-maximizing firm produces to the point at which

$$MR \equiv P = MC.$$

(The three-barred equals sign "≡" means that a relationship is true by definition; it is an identity.) That is, a purely competitive firm produces output to the point at which the market price, which by definition is the firm's marginal revenue, equals marginal cost.

In the short run, however, a firm's marginal cost depends on the cost it faces in employing its single variable factor of production, labor. Its labor expense is the nominal wage rate that it pays a unit of labor, denoted as W and measured in dollars per labor unit. For example, suppose that the current market wage rate is $W_1 = \$20$ per unit of labor. A firm's marginal cost is measured in dollars spent per unit of output produced. Suppose that the marginal product of labor at the firm's current output level is $MP_N = \Delta y/\Delta N = 5$ units of output per unit of labor. Then, to calculate the firm's marginal cost of producing output at the nominal wage $W_1 = \$20$ per unit of labor, we divide W_1 by MP_N, which gives $MC =$ (\$20 per unit of labor)/(5 units of output per unit of labor) = \$4 per unit of output. Marginal cost by definition is therefore equal to W/MP_N.

Thus, we can express a purely competitive firm's profit-maximizing condition, $P = MC$, as

$$P = W/MP_N.$$

Note that we can rearrange this profit-maximizing condition by dividing both sides of the condition by P, which yields the expression,

$$W/P = MP_N.$$

This expression says that another way of stating the firm's profit-maximizing condition is that the firm should hire labor to the point at which W/P, the *real wage* that the firm pays, is equal to the marginal product of labor.

Profit-Maximizing Employment of Labor Figure 22-2 illustrates this condition for two examples. One example is for the nominal wage $W_1 = \$20$ per unit of labor. Suppose that the price of the firm's output, P, is \$2 per unit. Then the real value of the nominal wage is \$20 per unit of labor divided by \$2 per unit of output, or 10 units of output per unit of labor. In other words, the \$20 wage that the firm pays each unit of labor is equivalent to a payment of 10 units of the firm's output. This is the real wage that the firm pays each unit of labor. To maximize

Figure 22-2
The Demand for Labor.

A profit-maximizing firm employs labor to the point at which the marginal product of labor is equal to the *real* wage. Consequently, with an unchanged price level, a fall in the nominal wage induces a decline in the real wage and causes an increase in the quantity of labor demanded by firms.

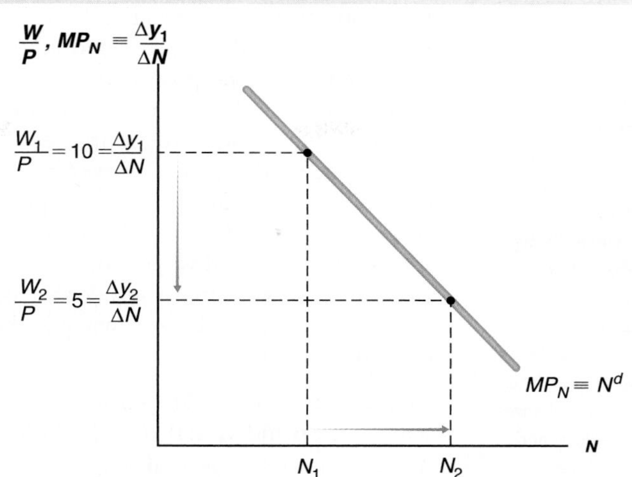

its profit, the firm therefore employs labor to the point at which the marginal product of labor is equal to 10 units of output per unit of labor and employs a total of N_1 units of labor. Thus, the firm pays the worker an amount equal to the real value of the labor that the worker provides the firm.

If the market wage rate falls to W_2 = \$10 per unit of labor, then the real wage paid by the firm will decline to \$10 per unit of labor divided by P = \$2 per unit of output, or 5 units of output per unit of labor. Hence, the firm will require the marginal product of the last unit of labor employed to equal 5 units of output, so it will raise its employment of labor to N_2 units. That is, the firm will demand more units of labor when the real market wage declines. We have now reached an important conclusion:

> **The MP_N schedule for a purely competitive firm is that firm's labor demand schedule. This schedule shows how many units of labor, *N*, the firm demands at any given real wage, *W/P*.**

Because the MP_N schedule is the labor demand schedule, we also label it N^d in Figure 22-2.

Labor Supply

Most people try to find an occupation that provides them with a feeling of satisfaction. Nonetheless, the time that people spend working is time that they could otherwise allocate to leisure activities. Thus, the value that individuals place on leisure time represents an *opportunity cost* that they incur when they devote their time to work. This is the reason that firms must pay real wages to induce people to devote large portions of their weekly schedules to work-related activities.

On the Web
What are recent trends in labor productivity in the U.S. economy? You can get these data for various sectors from the Bureau of Labor Statistics at http://stats.bls.gov/mprhome.htm. Then scroll down to "Economic News Releases" and click on "Multifactor Productivity Trends," and choose the sector of the economy you wish to examine.

On the Web
How fast are nominal wages rising in the United States? Take a look at U.S. employment cost trends by going to the home page of the Bureau of Labor Statistics at http://stats. bls.gov. Under "Wages, Earnings, and Benefits," click on "Employment Cost Index," and under "Most Requested Statistics," click on "Employment Cost Index" once more. Choose desired intervals to display percentage changes in "Civilian Workers, Wages and Salaries," and select "All Years."

MEASURING THE COMPENSATION TO LABOR: THE REAL WAGE Classical theorists focus on the *real wage* as the relevant measure of the compensation that workers receive for time that they spend laboring. The reason is that the real wage measures the purchasing power of a worker's earnings.

To understand why this is so, consider a simple example. During a full year, an individual works 40 hours per week and earns a weekly nominal wage of $500. During the year, however, the level of prices of goods and services that the person consumes *doubles*. Consequently, by the end of the year her $500 weekly wage is worth *half* as much to the worker as at the beginning of the year. Thus, it is not the nominal wage alone that matters to a worker. What the worker really cares about is how many goods and services she can use her nominal wage to purchase. This is why the real wage is the correct measure of a worker's compensation for labor time.

THE LABOR SUPPLY SCHEDULE Holding all other factors unchanged, the only way that an individual may be induced to give up some leisure time and work more hours is if the real wage increases. Because the real wage is equal to the nominal wage divided by the price level, W/P, there are two ways that the real wage can rise. One is if the nominal wage rises relative to the price level; the other is if the price level falls relative to the nominal wage.

Panel (a) of Figure 22-3 illustrates the effect on the labor supply of a rise in the nominal wage, from an initial value, W_1, to a higher value, W_2, with the price level unchanged at P_1. This causes the real wage to increase, and the quantity of labor supplied increases from N_1 to N_2 as workers respond to the higher real wage by giving up leisure time to work. Economists call this the *substitution effect* stemming from a rise in the real wage, because workers substitute labor for leisure. Note that at sufficiently high real wages, an *income effect* theoretically could arise: workers' incomes could be high enough that they would prefer to work less so that they could enjoy more leisure time. Most evidence indicates, however, that the substitution effect predominates in the aggregate. Consequently, the labor supply schedule, N^s, typically slopes upward, as displayed in the figure.

Panel (b) of Figure 22-3 shows the labor supply effect of a decline in the price level. A fall in the price level, from an initial value, P_1, to a lower level, P_2, increases the real wage that an individual earns. The effect is the same as if the nominal wage had risen with prices unchanged: individuals work more hours, so the quantity of labor supplied increases from N_1 to N_2. The diagram in panel (b) again assumes that the substitution effect generated by a rise in the real wage dominates the income effect.

The Labor Market and the Aggregate Supply Schedule

The total demand for labor is the sum of the labor demand schedules of all businesses in the economy. Likewise, the total supply of labor is the sum of the labor supply schedules of all people who participate in the economy's labor force. In the classical theory, the interactions among firms and workers through the forces of demand and supply in the labor market determine the equilibrium nominal wage and the equilibrium level of employment. (Equilibrium overall wages paid

Figure 22-3
Changes in the Real Wage and Labor Supply.

An increase in the money wage typically induces workers to give up leisure time to work. Hence, workers supply more labor as the money wage rises relative to the price level, as shown in panel (a), and so the labor supply schedule slopes upward against the real wage. A decline in the price level, from P_1 to P_2, with the money wage unchanged, also causes the real wage to rise. As a result, workers choose to supply more labor services, as shown in panel (b).

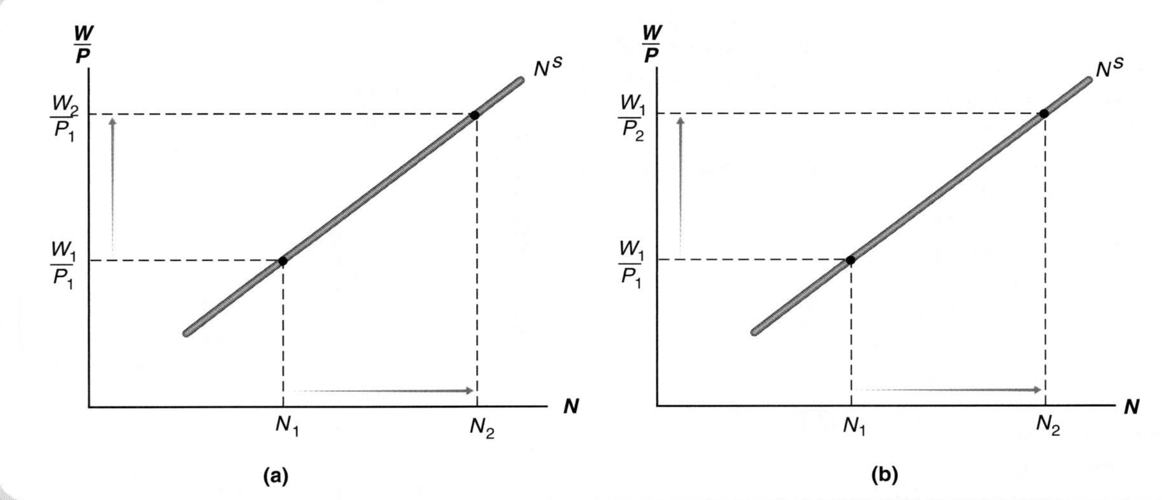

to workers, or total employee compensation including benefits, vary considerably across nations; see on the following page *Global Focus: It's All in a Day's Work—Depending on Where You Live.*) The aggregate production function then determines the aggregate level of real output produced in the economy.

The Price Level, Employment, and Real Output Figure 22-5 on page 537 depicts the determination of wages, employment, and output in the classical theory. In panel (a) an initial equilibrium *nominal wage,* W_1, arises at which the quantity of labor demanded by firms is equal to the quantity of labor supplied by workers, *given* the prevailing price level, P_1. This equilibrium quantity of labor demanded and supplied is the equilibrium employment level, N_1. The aggregate production function in panel (b) then indicates the equilibrium level of real output, y_1, that is produced with this aggregate amount of labor employed. Finally, panel (c) shows that this yields a price-level/real output combination P_1 and y_1.

The price level ultimately is determined in the aggregate market for goods and services. Nonetheless, we can consider the effects of changes in the price level on nominal wages, employment, and output via a simple, and rather extreme, example in which the price level doubles from P_1 to $2P_1$. In panel (a), this causes the real wage, which is measured along the vertical axis, to decline by a factor of two, or to half its original value. This, in turn, results in an excess quantity of labor

GLOBAL Focus | POLICY | CYBER | MANAGEMENT

It's All in a Day's Work—Depending on Where You Live

Figure 22-4 shows the average hourly costs of compensating manufacturing workers in various nations, expressed as index numbers using the compensation cost for U.S. workers as a base. Thus, the U.S. value of the index equals 100, which means that in all nations with values exceeding 100, average labor costs, including both wages and benefits, are higher than the cost of compensating a typical worker in the United States.

In this set of nations, the average cost of compensating a worker for an hour of time is highest in Germany, where a typical worker receives 36 percent more compensation per hour than a worker in the United States. Firms incur the lowest labor compensation expense in Mexico, where the hourly compensation rate is only about 11 percent of the U.S. level.

For Critical Analysis: Are the workers who earn higher rates of hourly compensation necessarily more productive than those in nations where rates of hourly compensation are lower?

Figure 22-4
Hourly Labor Costs in Manufacturing in Selected Nations.

The total compensation paid to workers varies considerably across countries.

SOURCE: U.S. Department of Labor.

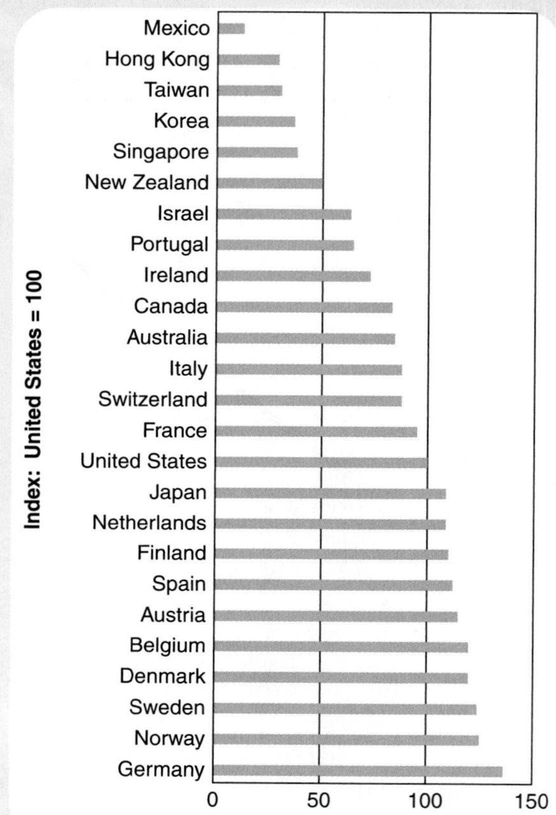

Figure 22-5
The Effects of a Doubling of the Price Level on the Equilibrium Nominal Wage, Employment, and Real Output.

If the price level doubles, then the real wage falls to half its original level in panel (a). At the lower real wage, there is an excess quantity of labor demanded. The money wage is bid upward until labor market equilibrium is reattained. Thus, equilibrium output also is unchanged, as shown in panel (b). As a result, the increase in the price level has no effect on the production of real output, implying that the aggregate supply schedule in panel (c) is vertical.

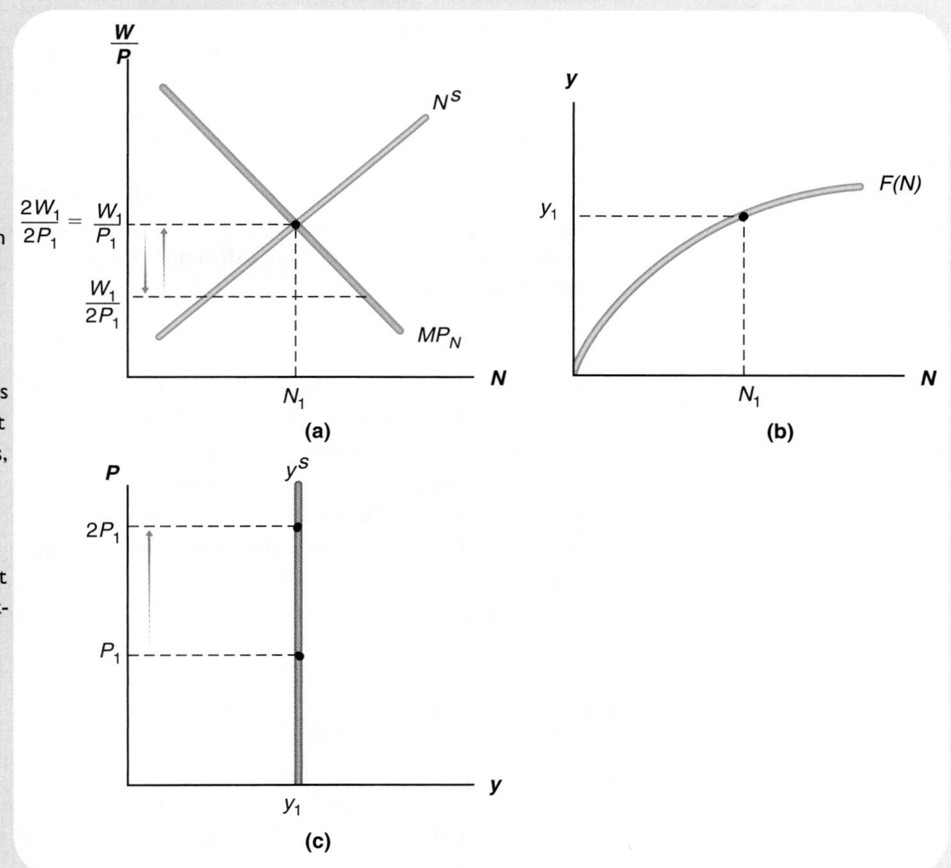

demanded, because firms now desire to hire more workers at the reduced real wage, but individuals are less willing to supply labor to firms. Firms begin to bid up the nominal wage to induce individuals to supply more labor, and eventually the real wage returns to its original level. This happens, however, only after the equilibrium nominal wage has doubled. Thus, the end result of the doubling of the price level is a doubling of the nominal wage and no change in the equilibrium employment level.

The Classical Aggregate Supply Schedule Equilibrium employment does not change when the price level doubles, so panel (b) indicates no change in real output. Nevertheless, panel (c) of Figure 22-5 displays a new price-level/real output combination, $2P_1$ and y_1. This combination, along with the original combination P_1 and y_1, lies along a schedule of price-level/real output combinations that is vertical, meaning that any given change in the price level leaves real output unchanged. This vertical schedule is the classical **aggregate supply schedule,**

Aggregate supply schedule (y^s): The combinations of various price levels and levels of real output that maintain equilibrium in the market for labor services.

which is the set of combinations of prices and real output that maintain labor market equilibrium.

Because the aggregate supply schedule is vertical, we can say that the level of real output is "supply determined." Most economists credit Jean Baptiste Say (1767–1832) with first emphasizing this point, which led to the dictum, "Supply creates its own demand." That is:

> **No matter what shape the economy's demand schedule might take, the classical theory of aggregate supply implies that equilibrium real output is determined solely by factors that influence the position of the vertical aggregate supply schedule.**

2. How are the aggregate levels of labor employment and real output of goods and services determined in the classical theory? The demand for labor stems from the marginal product of labor, which is the slope of the aggregate production function. Equilibrium employment occurs at the real wage at which the quantity of labor demanded by firms equals the quantity of labor supplied by households. Equilibrium output then is determined by the aggregate production function. According to the classical approach, a change in the price level has no effect on equilibrium employment or output, so the classical aggregate supply schedule is vertical.

Money and Aggregate Demand

Because the quantity of real output is determined by the position of the aggregate supply schedule in the classical theory, the concept of the aggregate demand for output is critical to understanding how the price level is determined in this theory.

The Aggregate Demand Schedule

The reason for this is clear if you envision any type of downward-sloping demand schedule crossing the aggregate supply schedule depicted in panel (c) of Figure 22-5. By analogy to microeconomics, it should be clear that the position of this schedule will effectively determine the equilibrium "market price," which in this case is the overall level of prices of all goods and services. This analogy to microeconomics is only a loose one, however, because the classical theory of aggregate demand and price-level determination stems from the classical theory of the *demand for money.*

THE QUANTITY THEORY OF MONEY The original classical theorists realized that money serves as a store of value, unit of account, and standard of deferred payment. Nevertheless, they viewed the medium-of-exchange property of money as the basis for explaining how much money people desire to hold. Consequently, the classical theory of the demand for money focuses on money's role as a medium of exchange. To understand how much money people desire to hold, the classical economists concentrate on explaining the demand for money for purchases of newly produced goods and services. The transactions-based theory of money demand that they developed is now known as the **quantity theory of money.**

Quantity theory of money: The theory that people hold money for transactions purposes.

The starting point for the quantity theory of money is the **equation of exchange:**

Equation of exchange: An accounting identity that states that the nominal value of all monetary transactions for final goods and services is equal to the nominal value of the output of goods and services purchased.

$$M \times V \equiv P \times y.$$

In the equation of exchange, M is the nominal quantity of money, or the current-dollar value of currency and checking deposits held by the nonbank public. The term V represents the **income velocity of money,** or the average number of times people spend each unit of money on final goods and services per unit of time. Consequently, the left-hand side of the equation of exchange is the value of current-dollar monetary payments for final goods and services. On the right-hand side of the equation, the price level for final goods and services is multiplied times the quantity of output of goods and services. This quantity is also the current-dollar value of monetary payments for final goods and services. Therefore, both sides of the equation of exchange must be identical. The equation of exchange is thus an accounting definition, or identity. It states that the product of the nominal quantity of money times the average number of times that people use money to buy goods and services ($M \times V$) must equal the market value of the goods and services that they use the money to purchase ($P \times y$).

Income velocity of money: The average number of times each unit of money is used to purchase final goods and services within an interval.

An economic identity is a truism. It is not a theory of how people make decisions. The foundation of the quantity *theory* of money is the *Cambridge equation,* which you learned about in Chapter 19. Recall that the Cambridge equation is

$$M^d = k \times Y,$$

where M^d denotes the total nominal quantity of money all people in the economy wish to hold and k is a fraction ($0 < k < 1$). The Cambridge equation, therefore, says that people desire to hold some fraction of their nominal income as money. As we discussed in Chapter 21, the nominal value of real output, $P \times y$, corresponds to the total level of nominal income, Y. Thus, the Cambridge equation may also be written as

$$M^d = k \times P \times y.$$

Thus, if $k = 0.2$, then people wish to hold 20 percent, or one-fifth, of their nominal income as money. (Of course, it is the real purchasing power of money, M/P, that people ultimately determine when they decide how much money they wish to hold, and the real purchasing power of \$1 is a lot less than it used to be; see on the next page *Policy Focus: A Dollar Really Doesn't Buy Much Anymore.*)

The Aggregate Demand Schedule We now have the essential building blocks that we need to understand how aggregate demand and the price level are determined in the classical theory. Suppose that the quantity of nominal money balances supplied through the actions of a central bank is equal to an amount M_1. In equilibrium, all individuals in the economy desire to hold this quantity of money balances, so

$$M^d = M_1.$$

The Cambridge equation then indicates that

$$M_1 = k \times P \times y.$$

GLOBAL | POLICY Focus | CYBER | MANAGEMENT

A Dollar Really Doesn't Buy Much Anymore

You have probably heard your parents or grandparents talk about the days when a dollar could buy much more than it does today. They are not making it up. Inflation dramatically eroded the purchasing power of $1 during the past century.

Figure 22-6 illustrates just how much erosion has taken place by starting with a $1 value of goods and services in 1900 and showing the market value of goods and services that a dollar bill would have been able to purchase in the years following. By 1918 a dollar was able to buy only what 40 cents would have purchased in 1900. During the Great Depression, a decline in the overall price level caused the value of a dollar to recover somewhat, so that during much of the 1930s a dollar could purchase an amount of goods and services that about 60 cents could have obtained in 1900.

Gradual inflation since the late 1930s has resulted in a steady decline in the dollar's purchasing power. Today a one-dollar bill will allow you to buy an amount of goods and services that a nickel would have purchased in 1900.

For Critical Analysis: One way to make a dollar worth approximately what it was back in 1900 might be for the government to print new U.S. currency, announce that twenty units of old currency must be traded for each unit of new currency on a particular date, and require all prices to be reduced by a factor of twenty as of that date. Would society necessarily come out ahead if the government were to do this?

Figure 22-6
The Falling Purchasing Power of a Dollar.

A dollar bill issued today buys less than what a nickel would have purchased in 1900.

SOURCE: Bureau of Labor Statistics.

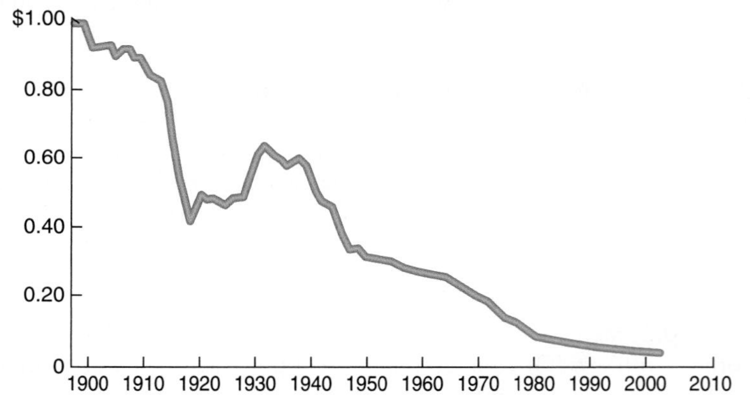

If we divide both sides of this equation by $k \times P$, we obtain

$$M_1/(k \times P) = y.$$

Reversing the two sides of this equation then leaves us with

$$y^d = M_1/(k \times P).$$

This is an equation for the economy's **aggregate demand schedule.** The aggregate demand schedule is all combinations of real output and price levels at which households are satisfied holding the available quantity of nominal money balances (M_1 in this example), given their average desired ratio of money holdings, k.

Aggregate demand schedule (y^d): The combinations of various price levels and levels of real output at which individuals are satisfied with their consumption of output and their holdings of money.

Figure 22-7 depicts the aggregate demand schedule. As the equation for the aggregate demand schedule indicates, the quantity of real output of goods and services that people wish to purchase declines as the price level rises. An increase in the price level raises nominal income and thereby induces people to raise their holdings of nominal money balances. Thus, when the price level rises from P_1 to P_2, people reduce their expenditures, and the amount of real output demanded falls from y_1 to y_2. This is a leftward *movement along* the aggregate demand schedule.

SHIFTS IN THE AGGREGATE DEMAND SCHEDULE Two factors can cause the aggregate demand schedule's position to change. One is a change in the quantity of money supplied by the government or by a central bank. As you can see by referring to the equation for the schedule, $y^d = M_1/(k \times P)$, a rise in the quantity of money to an amount larger than M_1 increases the right-hand side of the equation. As a result, the nominal purchasing power available to all individuals in the economy is higher at any given price level, and so people desire to purchase more real goods and services at any given price level. The aggregate demand schedule shifts to the right. Thus, aggregate demand *rises.* In contrast, a decline in the quantity of money shifts the aggregate demand schedule to the left, and aggregate demand *falls.*

Figure 22-7
The Classical Aggregate Demand Schedule.

The aggregate demand schedule stems from the Cambridge equation. It is negatively sloped, indicating that at higher price levels, with the nominal quantity of money and the Cambridge k unchanged, the quantity of real output demanded declines.

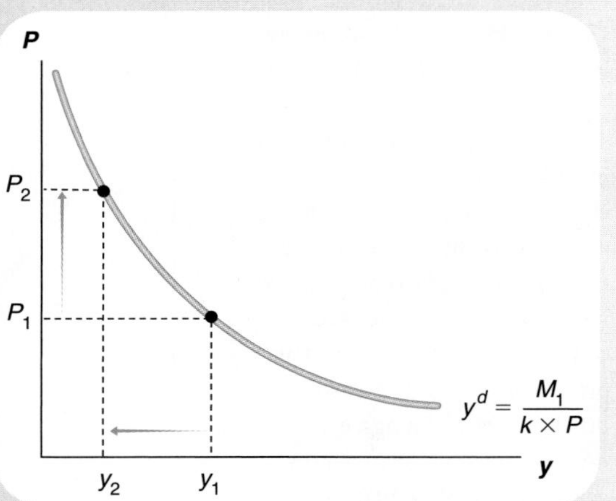

The other factor that can influence the position of the aggregate demand schedule is a change in the value of k in the Cambridge equation. For instance, suppose that a technological change, such as the widespread use of debit cards and automated teller machines at banks, reduces people's desire to keep ready cash on hand. Then the value of k declines, as people hold fewer money balances relative to their nominal income, $Y = P \times y$. Referring once more to the equation for the aggregate demand schedule, $y^d = M_1/(k \times P)$, you can see that a decline in k, because it reduces the denominator of the right-hand side of the equation, increases the total purchasing power available to individuals in the economy. Just as an increase in the quantity of money supplied causes a rise, or rightward shift outward, in the aggregate demand schedule, so does a decline in the demand for money by individuals. In contrast, a rise in money demand will induce a reduction in aggregate demand and a leftward shift in the aggregate demand schedule.

The Market for Real Output and Price-Level Determination

Figure 22-8 displays aggregate demand and aggregate supply schedules together on the same diagram. This diagram is the classical visualization of the workings of the economy's *market for real output*. Equilibrium in this market arises at the point at which the aggregate demand schedule crosses the aggregate supply schedule. At this point on the aggregate demand schedule, the quantity of output demanded equals the amount of output supplied, y_1. The *equilibrium price level* is P_1. This is the price level at which individuals are satisfied with their current money holdings and with their current rate of purchases of real goods and services.

In the output market equilibrium shown in Figure 22-8, the equation of exchange identity tells us that $M_1 \times V \equiv P_1 \times y_1$. But we also know that in equi-

Figure 22-8
Output Market Equilibrium in the Classical Model.

The equilibrium price level ensures that the amount of real output that individuals wish to purchase, given the quantity of money and the income velocity of money, is equal to the level of real output produced by firms. This price level corresponds to the point at which the aggregate demand schedule crosses the aggregate supply schedule.

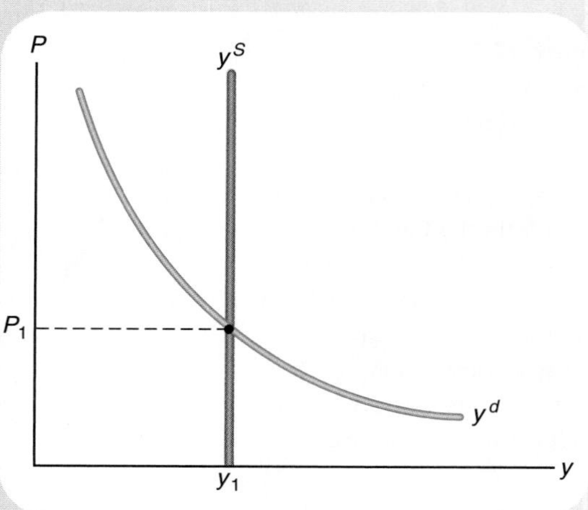

librium, the aggregate demand equation is satisfied, so $y_1 = M_1/(k \times P_1)$. If we substitute this value for real output into the equation of exchange identity, we see that

$$M_1 \times V \equiv P_1 \times M_1/(k \times P_1) = M_1/k.$$

Now, if we divide both sides of this equation by M_1, we get

$$V = 1/k.$$

This says that a key assumption of the classical theory is that the income velocity of money, or the average number of times that the quantity of money is used in exchange for real goods and services, is equal to the reciprocal of the k factor of proportionality in the Cambridge equation. Because the Cambridge equation assumes that k is constant, this tells us that the classical theory of aggregate demand and price-level determination implicitly assumes that the income velocity of money is constant. Is this a reasonable assumption? Figure 22-9 shows the behavior of the U.S. income velocity of money, which clearly has changed over time. The original classical theorists recognized that this was true, but they argued that the key factor affecting the ability of their theory to explain current and future price-level movements was the *predictability* of velocity. As long as velocity could be predicted fairly accurately, they argued, their theory would provide a reasonable explanation of price-level movements.

3. What factors determine the price level in the classical framework? In the classical theory, the aggregate demand schedule gives combinations of price levels and real output levels at which individuals are satisfied with their output consumption and money holding. The equilibrium price level adjusts to equalize the quantity of real output demanded and the supply-side-determined quantity of real output produced.

Figure 22-9
The Income Velocity of Money in the United States.

The U.S. income velocity of money using the Federal Reserve's M2 measure of money has exhibited year-to-year variability. Nevertheless, its value has remained within a relatively narrow range since the late 1950s.

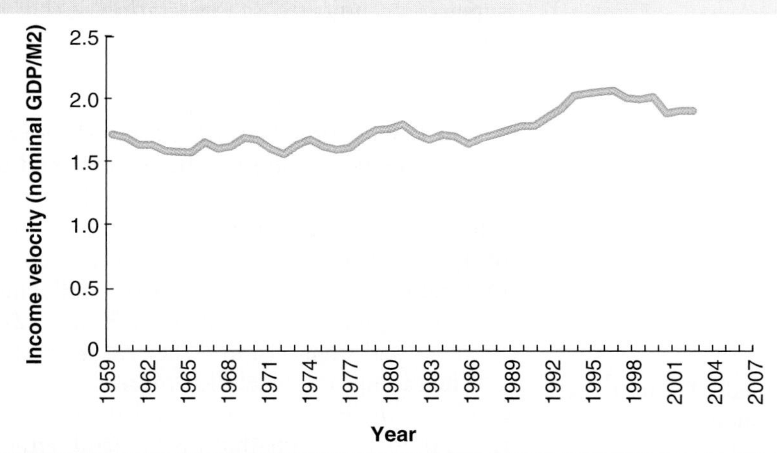

SOURCES: *Economic Report of the President*, 2002; *Economic Indicators; Federal Reserve Bulletin*, various issues.

Interest Rate Determination

Each day publications such as the *Wall Street Journal* and *The Financial Times* list interest rates on Treasury securities issued by the U.S. government, corporate bonds and commercial paper issued by firms, certificates of deposit issued by banks, and money, bond, and equity fund shares issued by mutual funds. Furthermore, these and other media outlets often run stories speculating about what effects interest rate changes may have on economic activity.

You will learn in later chapters that some theories of short-run variations in economic activity imply that interest rate variations can lead to changes in prices and output. In the classical framework, however, interest rates do not perform such a "causal" role. Instead, they adjust to equate quantities demanded and supplied in markets for credit.

The Loanable Funds Market and the Classical Theory of Interest Rate Determination

Not all income that is earned is spent. Many people save a portion of their earnings. This means that somewhere along the multiple chains of expenditures that take place in the economy, there is a *leakage* from the total flow of expenditures when people save. Yet achieving equilibrium in the market for real output means that people ultimately purchase all goods and services that businesses produce. This means that all saving ultimately must find its way back into the aggregate flow of spending on goods and services. In classical monetary theory, the role of interest rates is to ensure that this occurs in equilibrium.

SAVING AND THE REAL INTEREST RATE According to the classical approach, real saving depends on the *real interest rate*. As you learned in Chapter 4, the real rate of interest is the difference between the nominal interest rate and the expected rate of inflation. If we denote the nominal interest rate as r, and the expected inflation rate as π^e (the Greek letter pi denotes the inflation rate and the "e" superscript indicates an expectation of that rate), then the real interest rate, r^r, is equal to

$$r^r = r - \pi^e.$$

The key hypothesis of the classical theory of saving is that there is a direct relationship between the real interest rate and the amount that individuals save out of a given level of real income, holding all other factors unchanged. If the real interest rate rises, the real return on their savings rises, and people will save more of a given level of income and thereby choose to consume a smaller portion of that income. If the real interest rate falls, individuals will save less and consume more of a given level of income. Figure 22-10 illustrates this direct relationship between real saving, s, and the real interest rate, r^r.

Loanable funds: The term that classical economists use to refer to the amount of real income that households save, representing claims on real output.

The saving of households represents claims on real goods and services, so the original classical economists called these financial claims **loanable funds.** Essentially, these are funds that people lend, either via direct participation in financial markets or by using financial institutions as intermediaries. Therefore, the saving schedule, s, in Figure 22-10 is a supply schedule in the market for loanable funds

Figure 22-10
The Classical Market for Loanable Funds.

For a given level of real income, individuals save more and consume less as the real interest rate rises, so the saving schedule, *s*, which is the supply of loanable funds, slopes upward. In contrast, desired real investment spending by firms declines as the real interest rate increases. As a result, the investment schedule, *i*, slopes downward. In the absence of a government budget deficit or surplus, the equilibrium real interest rate equilibrates private investment and saving.

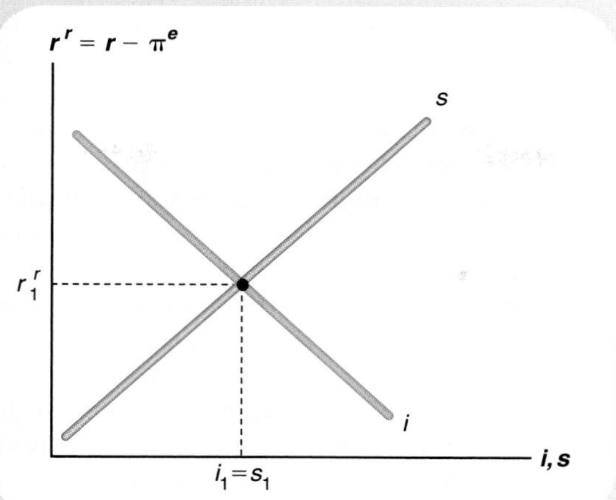

channeled through the financial markets, and the real interest rate is the price of loanable funds.

Investment and the Demand for Loanable Funds Of course, not everyone saves. At any given time, many people desire to spend more than their incomes would otherwise permit them to spend. This is especially true for owners of businesses. To be able to produce goods and services, owners of business firms often need to purchase or build expensive capital goods such as machines and factories. The required capital expenditures commonly exceed the real incomes of individuals who own these firms. For this reason, firm owners often desire to borrow funds from those who save. That is, those who *invest* in new capital equipment *demand loanable funds*. Then they use these funds to purchase capital goods. In this way, a large portion of the saving leakage from the economy's flow of spending is *reinjected* into that flow.

In the classical framework, the amount of desired investment spending depends negatively upon the real interest rate. As the real interest rate rises, the price of loanable funds for firm investment increases, and business owners respond by reducing the quantity of loanable funds demanded. As the real interest rate declines, the quantity of loanable funds demanded by firms rises. This inverse relationship between desired investment spending and the interest rate is shown as the *investment schedule,* labeled i in Figure 22-10.

The saving schedule and investment schedule cross at the real interest rate r_1^r. At this real rate of interest, the quantity of loanable funds supplied by household savers, s_1, is equal to the quantity of loanable funds demanded by business owners to fund private investment, i_1.

Fiscal policy: Actions by the government to vary its spending or taxes.

If businesses were the only source of demand for loanable funds in the economy, then r_1^r would be the *equilibrium* real rate of interest. It also would be the real interest rate at which the market for real output is in equilibrium. This would be so because at this real interest rate the equality of desired saving and desired investment would imply that all leakages from the flow of real expenditures in the form of savings would be reinjected into that flow as investment expenditures.

Business firms are not the only source of demand for loanable funds, however. The government may also be a key borrower and thus can also influence real interest rates. The government does this by conducting **fiscal policies,** or variations in government spending or taxes. If real government spending exceeds real taxes, then the government operates with a deficit that it must fund by borrowing, which in the classical model adds to the demand for loanable funds and thereby boosts the equilibrium real interest rate. By way of contrast, if the government's expenditures are less than its tax revenues, then the government saves and adds to the supply of loanable funds, which tends to reduce the equilibrium real interest rate.

On the Web
What are the current outlays and revenues of the U.S. government, and is the government currently operating with a deficit or a surplus? View the historical tables of the U.S. government's budget at http://w3.access.gpo.gov/usbudget/index.html.

Money and Interest Rates

Note that in classical theory, monetary policy plays no role in determining the real interest rate. The equilibrium real interest rate is determined solely by the real income allocations of savers and borrowers of loanable funds.

In classical theory, monetary policy actions determine the *nominal* rate of interest. Because the real interest rate is equal to the nominal interest rate minus the expected inflation rate, or $r^r = r - \pi^e$, we can express the nominal interest rate as the real interest rate plus the expected inflation rate, or $r = r^r + \pi^e$. As we discussed earlier, changes in the quantity of money cause the price level to rise, holding all other factors unchanged. Thus, according to the classical approach, a 2 percent increase in the rate of money growth will, if real GDP and velocity are unchanged, cause the price level to rise by 2 percent. Lenders and borrowers then will anticipate a sustained 2 percent inflation rate. Consequently, when they negotiate bond or loan contracts, they arrange for a nominal rate of interest that accounts for this anticipated rate of inflation. This means that, ultimately, the growth rate of the quantity of money determines the nominal interest rate. Higher money growth raises expected inflation and causes an increase in the nominal interest rate. Lower money growth reduces expected inflation and causes a decrease in the nominal interest rate.

moneyxtra!
Online Case Study
To contemplate factors that can cause the nominal interest rate to change, go to the Chapter 22 Case Study, entitled "Explaining Interest Rate Movements."
http://moneyxtra.swcollege.com

4. How are interest rates determined in classical monetary theory? The real interest rate, which is equal to the nominal interest rate minus the expected rate of inflation, adjusts to equate the quantity of loanable funds supplied (saving) with the quantity of loanable funds demanded (desired investment plus a government deficit). Higher government deficits induce a rise in the demand for loanable funds that increases the equilibrium real interest rate. Larger government surpluses push up the supply of loanable funds and generate a decrease in the equilibrium real interest rate. By changing the expected rate of inflation, the growth rate of the quantity of money determines the nominal interest rate in classical monetary theory.

Classical Monetary Theory in an Open Economy

Closed economy: An economy that operates separately from the rest of the world.

Open economy: An economy that is linked by trade with other economies of the world.

To this point, we have considered the classical theory of a **closed economy,** which functions in isolation from the rest of the world. In such an economy, either no international trade occurs or the government prohibits such trade.

Few economies are truly closed. Like most other nations of the world, the United States is increasingly becoming an **open economy,** in which international trade accounts for a significant portion of a nation's total income. In 2003, exports and imports accounted for about 11 percent and 14 percent, respectively, of U.S. GDP, as compared with 5 percent and 4 percent in 1960.

The Cornerstone of Classical Exchange Rate Theory: Purchasing Power Parity

Greater openness engenders greater interest in determinants of the exchange value of a nation's currency relative to other world currencies. As Figure 22-11 indicates, the U.S. dollar's relative value has varied considerably since the 1970s. How would a classical theorist explain these movements in the dollar's value?

First, recall from Chapter 6 that the *exchange rate* is the value of one nation's currency in terms of the currency of another nation. In the case of the U.S. dollar ($) and the European euro (€), for instance, the dollar-euro exchange rate may be calculated as the price of the euro, measured in dollars per euro. Recall that if the dollar-euro exchange rate *rises* from 0.9 $/€ to 1.0 $/€, then the dollar's value *depreciates,* meaning that a U.S. resident must give up more dollars in exchange for the euro. Hence, if *S* denotes the value of the dollar-euro exchange rate, then a *rise* in the value of *S* implies a depreciation of the value of the dollar relative to the euro. If the dollar depreciates relative to the euro, of course, then the euro experiences an *appreciation* relative to the dollar.

Figure 22-11
The Value of the Dollar.

This figure displays annual values of an index of the dollar's value relative to currencies of U.S. trading partners.

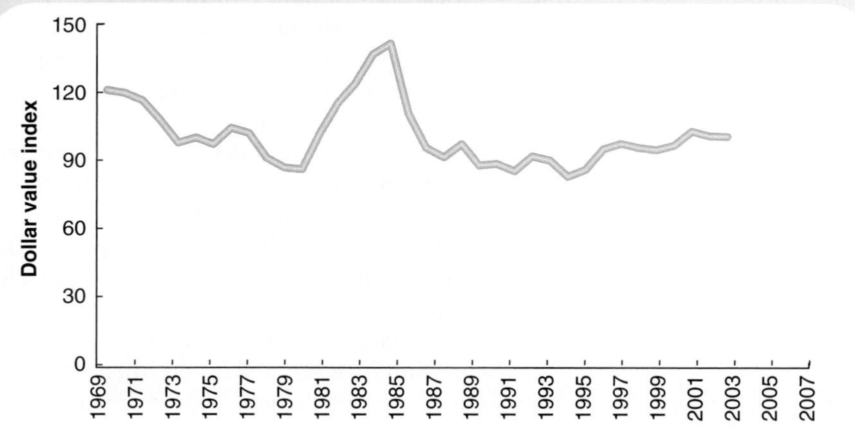

SOURCES: *Economic Report of the President,* 2002; *Federal Reserve Bulletin* (various issues).

What might cause such a dollar depreciation and euro appreciation? The key to the answer, according to the classical theory, is to be found in the concept of *purchasing power parity.* As we discussed in Chapter 6, under purchasing power parity the price of a good in one nation should be the same as the exchange-rate-adjusted price of the same good in another nation. For instance, suppose that an economics textbook sells for a euro price of $P^* = €50$ in a country in the European Monetary Union, such as Belgium. If the rate of exchange of euros for dollars is equal to $S = 0.9$ \$/€, then according to purchasing power parity the price of the same book in the United States should equal $P = P^* \times S = €50 \times 0.9$ \$/€ = \$45. Thus, under purchasing power parity, the only factor causing the prices of the textbooks in the two nations to differ is that they are measured in different currency units.

Exchange Rate Determination in the Classical System

As you learned in Chapter 6, purchasing power parity can hold only if people can freely take advantage of the opportunity to engage in international arbitrage. The original classical economists recognized that there often are limits on international arbitrage for some goods and services, but they regarded purchasing power parity as a *benchmark* for understanding how a nation's exchange rate is determined.

Figure 22-12 shows how purchasing power parity can be combined with the classical theory of price-level determination to provide an explanation for why a nation's currency might depreciate over time. The diagram in panel (a) of Figure 22-12 displays an initial equilibrium price level, denoted P_1, at the intersection of the classical aggregate demand and aggregate supply schedules. Panel (b) is a diagram of the purchasing power parity condition, $P = P^* \times S$. Recall that the intercept-slope equation for a straight line says that a variable measured along the vertical axis of a diagram is equal to an intercept plus the slope times a variable measured along the horizontal axis. Hence, the condition $P = P^* \times S$ is just the equation of a straight line in which the domestic price level, P, is measured along the vertical axis in panel (b) of Figure 22-12, and the exchange rate, S, is measured along the horizontal axis. The intercept of this equation is equal to zero, and the foreign price level, P^*, is the *slope* of the line. At the current price level in our home nation, P_1, the purchasing power parity condition yields an equilibrium exchange rate equal to S_1.

As we will see in the *Link to Policy* at the end of this chapter, classical monetary theory indicates that a likely reason for persistent inflation is consistently high growth in the quantity of money that shifts the aggregate demand schedule to the right over time. Panel (a) in Figure 22-12 shows such a rightward shift in aggregate demand that causes our home price level to rise to P_2. According to the purchasing power parity condition, if foreign prices remain unchanged at P^*, our nation's exchange rate must rise to S_2, as depicted in panel (b). If the nation under consideration is the United States, then the exchange rate S is measured in dollars per unit of foreign currency (for instance, euros). Hence, when the exchange rate rises from S_1 to S_2, U.S. residents will have to provide more dollars in exchange for euros. The value of the dollar will have *depreciated.* In other words, the classical approach predicts that persistent growth in the quantity of money in the

Figure 22-12
The Classical Approach to Exchange Rate Determination.

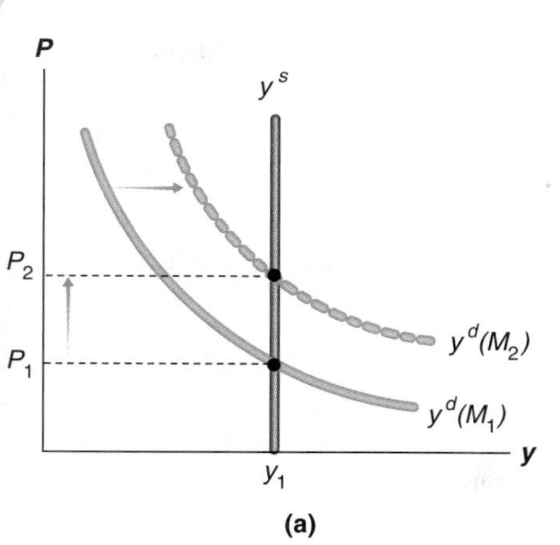

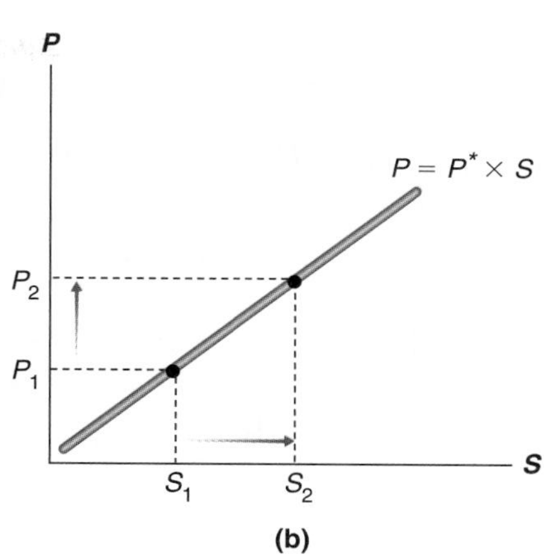

In the classical model, a nation's price level is determined in the market for real output, as in panel (a). A rise in aggregate demand caused by an increase in the nation's money stock causes an increase in the price level. According to the purchasing power parity relationship, the price level can be expressed as $P = P^* \times S$, where P^* is the foreign price level and S is the exchange rate in units of home currency per unit of foreign currency. The graph of this relationship is a straight line, as shown in panel (b). There, you can see that a rise in the price level results in an increase in the exchange rate, and so more units of home currency must be given up in exchange for units of foreign currency. Consequently, the home currency depreciates relative to the foreign currency.

United States causes a fall in the value of the dollar as well as persistent U.S. inflation.

5. How is the international value of a nation's currency determined in classical monetary theory? The value of a country's currency is its exchange rate. According to the classical approach, a key benchmark for understanding how the exchange rate is determined is the purchasing power parity condition, which states that the home price level is equal to the foreign price level times the exchange rate. Given the foreign price level and the determination of the home price level in the market for real output, the exchange rate adjusts to maintain purchasing power parity.

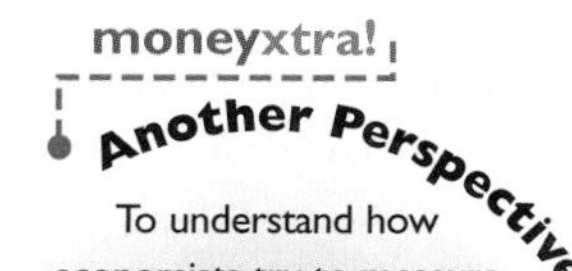

To understand how economists try to measure the long-term trend of inflation in the United States, go to the Chapter 22 reading, entitled "Comparing Measures of Core Inflation," by Todd Clark of the Federal Reserve Bank of Kansas City.
http://moneyxtra.swcollege.com

Link to Policy

Is Inflation Mainly a Monetary Phenomenon?

Panel (c) of Figure 22-13 shows annual U.S. inflation rates for the past few decades. Clearly, inflation rates have been variable. Inflation rates also have consistently been positive. The price level in the United States has risen in almost every year (also see Figure 21-3 on page 515).

Supply-Side Inflation Doesn't Fit the Facts

What could account for such persistent inflation? The classical theory provides two possible explanations. One is depicted in panel (a) of Figure 22-13, which shows a rise in the price level caused by a *fall in aggregate supply.* Thus, one conceivable rationale for persistent inflation is continual reductions in the production of real output.

Consider the factors that could cause the aggregate supply schedule to shift leftward: (1) lower labor force participation, induced perhaps by a population decline; (2) a decline in labor productivity; (3) higher marginal tax rates on wages; or (4) the provision of government benefits that give households incentives not to supply labor services to firms. Although tax rates and government benefits definitely increased overall during the latter part of the twentieth century, so did the U.S. population. More recently, the government has cut back on the provision of benefits that might reduce the labor supply. In addition, although the marginal product of labor has declined for short intervals, particularly during periods in the 1970s when the costs of complementary factors of production such as energy experienced sharp increases, labor productivity otherwise has increased, on net, since the 1950s. The overall rise in real GDP that has taken place during the past few decades tells us that population growth and productivity gains have dominated other factors. On net, therefore, the aggregate supply schedule actually has shifted *rightward,* not leftward, over time. Thus, the classical approach indicates that this *supply-side* explanation for persistent inflation *cannot* be the *true* explanation.

Money Growth and Demand-Side Inflation

According to classical monetary theory, this leaves only one other explanation for the observation of persistent inflation. This is illustrated in panel (b) of Figure 22-13. If aggregate demand increases for a given level of aggregate supply, then the price level must increase. The reason is that, at an initial price level such as P_1, people desire to purchase more real goods and services (y_2) than firms are willing and able to produce (y_1) given the currently available technology and present labor force participation rates. As a result, the rise in aggregate demand leads only to a general rise in the price level, from P_1 to P_2.

Recall that there are two possible reasons that aggregate demand might shift rightward over time. One would be persistent reductions in the demand for money, which would imply year-to-year declines in the factor of proportionality k in the Cambridge equation. Recall that k is equal to the reciprocal of velocity, so Figure 22-9 on page 543 actually plots the reciprocal of k. There have been some periods of general declines or increases in the value of k, but otherwise it has been remarkably stable. Hence, though changes in k undoubtedly have influenced the price level, from a classical perspective this cannot have been the predominant factor explaining U.S. inflation.

The other factor that classical theory indicates could cause persistent increases in aggregate demand is consistent growth of the quantity of money. Panel (d) of Figure 22-13 shows that the Federal Reserve's M2 measure of the quantity of money has exhibited persistent growth since the 1950s. *This,* most classical theorists argue, is the key explanation for the persistence of inflation. Persistent money growth, they contend, has produced persistent inflation.

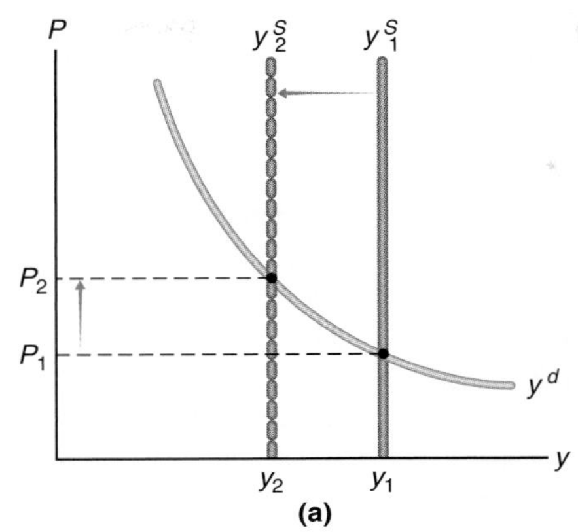

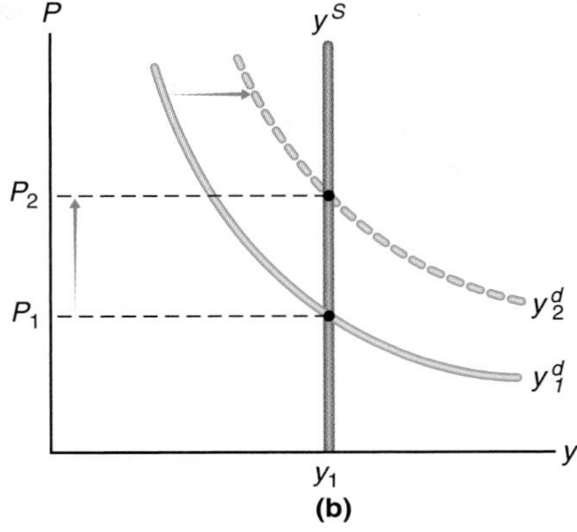

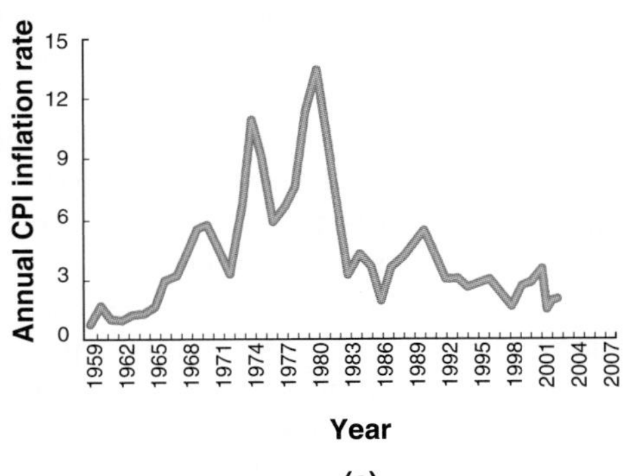

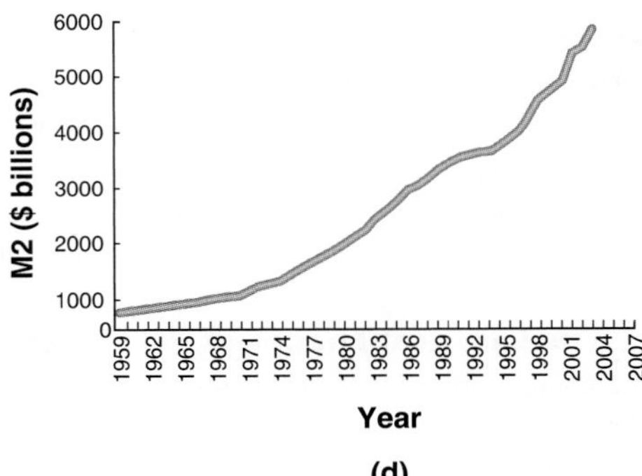

Figure 22-13
Assessing Theory and Evidence Concerning U.S. Inflation.

Panels (a) and (b) provide two possible explanations for the persistent U.S. inflation depicted in panel (c). Panel (a) shows the effects of a reduction in aggregate supply. A fall in aggregate supply can bring about a rise in the price level, but the accompanying decline in real output is inconsistent with the significant growth in real output experienced by the United States over the long term. As panel (b) shows, an increase in aggregate demand, which the classical theory indicates could result from the persistent increases in the quantity of money depicted in panel (d), could also bring about a higher price level.

SOURCES: *Economic Report of the President*, various issues; Board of Governors of the Federal Reserve System.

Research Project

Under what circumstances does classical monetary theory indicate that demand-side inflation could take place without an increase in the quantity of money? How might these circumstances arise in the real world? Would it ever be possible for demand-side inflation to take place, on net, during a period when the quantity of money declines?

Web Resource

To evaluate whether there is evidence of international relationships between money growth and inflation, go to the home page of the Federal Reserve Bank of St. Louis (http://stlouisfed.org). In the gray bar at the top, click on "Economic Research," and in the left-hand column, select "Publications." Scroll down to "International Economic Trends Quarterly." At the next page, first click on a nation's "Inflation and Prices Charts" to download figures displaying the country's recent inflation performance. Then click on "Monetary Aggregates: Short-Run Charts" to download figures showing growth rates in monetary aggregates. Then compare the charts to see if there is evidence of a direct relationship between money growth rates and inflation in various countries.

Chapter Summary

1. Key Perspectives of Classical Monetary Theory: One key presumption is that people rationally pursue their own self-interest. A second is that people do not experience money illusion, so they are not fooled by current-dollar changes that make no difference to their real incomes. The final presumption is that markets for goods, services, and factors of production are purely competitive, meaning that there are large numbers of buyers and sellers, none of whom individually can affect market prices.

2. The Determination of Employment and Output in the Classical Theory: According to the classical framework, the amount of labor employed in the economy is determined by labor market equilibrium. Real and nominal wages adjust to keep the quantity of labor supplied by workers equal to the quantity of labor demanded by firms. The equilibrium amount of real aggregate output is the amount that firms can produce with this quantity of labor, given their use of other factors of production and the technology available to them. Because the equilibrium nominal wage adjusts in equal proportion to changes in prices, employment and output are unchanged in response to price-level variations. Consequently, the classical aggregate supply schedule is vertical.

3. The Classical Theory of Price Determination: The equilibrium price level adjusts to ensure that the quantity of real output demanded is equal to the amount supplied by firms. This occurs at the point at which the aggregate demand schedule, whose position is determined by the quantity of money in circulation and the income velocity of money, crosses the classical vertical aggregate supply schedule.

4. Interest Rate Determination in the Classical Framework: According to the classical approach, the real interest rate adjusts to equalize the quantity of loanable funds supplied, or aggregate private saving, with the quantity of loanable funds demanded, or the sum of total desired private investment and the government deficit. A rise in the government's deficit increases the demand for loanable funds, thereby causing a rise in the equilibrium real interest rate. An increase in anticipated growth of the quantity of money causes expected inflation to rise, thereby increasing the nominal interest rate, which is equal to the real interest rate plus the expected inflation rate.

5. The Value of a Nation's Currency: The exchange rate is the value, or price, of one nation's currency in terms of that of another nation. The classical theory's benchmark for understanding how exchange rates are determined is purchasing power parity, which states that if international arbitrage can occur, then the price level in one nation should equal the foreign price level times the exchange rate. Once a home nation's price level is determined in its market for real output, and given the foreign price level, the home nation's exchange rate adjusts to maintain purchasing power parity. Persistent inflation in the home nation caused by excessive money growth therefore will be accompanied by persistent depreciation in, or decline in the value of, the home nation's currency.

Questions and Problems

(Answers to odd-numbered questions and problems may be found on the Web at http://money.swcollege.com under "Student Resources.")

1. Based on the classical framework, what specific factors might play a part in influencing the rate of growth in a nation's real GDP? Explain.

2. Suppose that a wave of immigration takes place during the next ten years, causing the labor force to expand. Use the classical theory to predict the effects that this would have on the equilibrium real wage, equilibrium employment, and equilibrium real GDP.

3. Based on your answer to question 2, determine the effect that a rise in immigration and a resulting increase in the labor force would have on the price level in the classical theory, holding all other factors constant. Explain your answer.

4. Suppose that a nation experiences a severe earthquake that destroys a significant portion of its capital stock. Use the classical approach to predict the effects that this would have on the equilibrium real wage, equilibrium employment, and equilibrium real GDP.

5. Based on your answer to question 4, determine the effect that destruction of part of the nation's capital stock would have on the country's price level in classical monetary theory, holding all other factors constant. Explain your answer.

6. Suppose that the increasing use of the Internet to make transactions with credit cards causes the income velocity of money to decline substantially. Use the classical approach to predict what, if any, effects this would have on the price level, real GDP, the real interest rate, and the nominal interest rate.

7. Suppose that the Cambridge k is equal to 0.20. Real GDP is equal to 5 trillion base-year dollars, and the price level is equal to 1.2 current-year dollars per base-year dollar. What is the current-dollar value of the quantity of money in circulation?

8. Explain how a nation's nominal interest rate could decline without a change in the real rate of interest, according to the classical theory. Would it be possible for the real interest rate to rise even as the nominal rate of interest declines? Explain your reasoning.

9. Suppose that the central bank of a small nation in eastern Europe keeps the quantity of money in circulation stable. Its government's budget is balanced. In addition, its income velocity of money is stable, as are conditions in its labor market. Its technology and other factors of production also have not changed. Nevertheless, the value of its currency is persistently depreciating relative to that of a country that is its major trading partner. Given the conditions this country faces, what *single* factor would the classical theory indicate must account for this steady depreciation of the small nation's currency?

10. Several governments in Africa have experienced relatively sizable deficits that they have funded in large measure by purchasing government bonds with new money printed by central banks. Apply the classical approach to explain the effects that such government actions would likely have on prices, real GDP, the real interest rate, the nominal interest rate, and the exchange rate of an African nation that finds itself in this situation.

Before the Test

Test your understanding of the material covered in this chapter by taking the Chapter 22 interactive quiz at http://money.swcollege.com.

Online Application

The Federal Reserve's "Beige Book" provides a wealth of information about the current status of U.S. labor markets. You can access this Internet locale to keep track of developments in wages, employment, and unemployment in the United States.

Internet URL: **http://federalreserve.gov/FOMC/beigebook**

Title: The Beige Book—Summary

Navigation: Begin with the Federal Reserve Board's home page (**http://www.federalreserve.gov**), and click on Monetary Policy. Then click on Beige Book to access the Beige Book home page (**http://www.federalreserve.gov/FOMC/beigebook**). Click on "Report" for the most recent available date.

Application: Read the report summary and answer the following questions:

1. Has overall employment been rising or falling during the most recent year? According to classical monetary theory, what factors might account for this pattern? Does the Beige Book summary bear out any of these theoretical explanations for changes in aggregate U.S. employment?

2. Have nominal wages been rising or falling during the most recent year? Does the Beige Book provide any information that permits you to deduce the implications for aggregate real wages?

For Group Study and Analysis: The left-hand margin of the Beige Book site lists the reports for the twelve Federal Reserve districts. Divide the class into twelve groups, and have each group develop brief summaries of the main conclusions of each report for the behavior of nominal wages, prices, employment, and output in each district. Reconvene, and compare the reports. Are there pronounced regional differences?

Selected References and Further Reading

Clark, Todd. "Comparing Measures of Core Inflation." Federal Reserve Bank of Kansas City *Economic Review,* Second Quarter 2001, pp. 6–31.

Fisher, Irving. *The Theory of Interest.* New York: Macmillan, 1930.

Hicks, John R. *Theory of Wages.* London: Macmillan, 1932.

Marshall, Alfred. *Principles of Economics.* New York: Macmillan, 1925.

Mill, John S. *Principles of Economics.* New York: Macmillan, 1848.

Say, Jean B. *A Treatise on Political Economy.* London: Longmans, 1821.

Wicksell, J. G. K. *Interest and Prices,* trans. R. F. Kahn. London: Macmillan, 1936.

MoneyXtra

moneyxtra! Log on to the MoneyXtra Web site now (http://moneyxtra.swcollege.com) for additional learning resources such as practice quizzes, case studies, readings, and additional economic applications.

Chapter 23

Money and Business Cycles—Essentials of the Keynesian System

During the 1990s, as the United States experienced its longest peacetime economic expansion, some economists and policymakers began to contemplate the possibility that the nation might have become recession-proof. The idea was that widespread investments in new information technologies might have paved the way for uninterrupted positive growth of a so-called new economy into the foreseeable future.

Of course, the recession that began in the spring of 2001 dashed these grand dreams. Ironically, its root cause was a significant drop in expenditures on the new technologies observers had claimed would make the new economy recession-proof. Business spending on computers and related hardware and software plummeted. Rippling waves spread through the rest of the U.S. economy, and real output growth declined for the first time in ten years. In a further irony, this experience with an investment-induced recession mirrored several past U.S. recessions dating from well before the advent of modern information technologies.

In this chapter, you will learn about a theory, developed by British economist John Maynard Keynes, that proposed a prominent role for fluctuations in business investment as a factor in economic cycles. Keynes formulated his theory during the Great Depression of the 1930s when the self-correcting model of the classical economists no longer seemed to fit reality. Hence, Keynes assigned a rather different role to monetary policy than it had played in classical economics. This chapter presents the traditional Keynesian system including the potential stabilizing role for monetary policy and its role in affecting the size of the trade balance.

Fundamental Issues

1. What are the key relationships implied by the circular flow of income and expenditures?
2. What are the components of aggregate desired expenditures in the basic Keynesian model?
3. How is equilibrium real income determined in the basic Keynesian model?
4. How does the basic Keynesian theory explain short-run business cycles?
5. Why does the basic Keynesian model indicate that there may be a potential stabilizing role for monetary policy?
6. How is the equilibrium trade balance determined, and what role may monetary policy play in affecting the size of the trade balance?

Aggregate Income and Expenditures

As you will learn in Chapters 24 and 25, not all economists today agree that the classical theory was as seriously flawed as Keynes perceived it to be. Nevertheless, Keynes's reformulation of monetary theory had dramatic effects on the way that economists think about the relationship between money and the economy today. For this reason, it is important for you to understand how Keynes's approach to monetary theory differed from the classical approach.

We begin our analysis of the basic Keynesian approach to the determination of national income at the same point where Keynes began. This is the circular flow of income and expenditures.

The Circular Flow of Income and Expenditures

Figure 23-1 provides a more detailed version of the circular flow diagram you saw in Chapter 21. This expanded version of the diagram displays financial flows as well as flows of taxes and expenditures by the government. In spite of the greater detail, however, one key point is the same:

The value of the flow of income to households must equal the value of the output produced by firms.

Figure 23-1
Circular Flow of Income and Expenditures.

Firms' earnings from goods and services produced and supplied through product markets ultimately flow to households, which own the firms and the factors of production. Households consume domestic goods and services, import foreign goods and services, save, and pay net taxes. The goods and services produced by firms are purchased by households, firms, the government, and foreign residents.

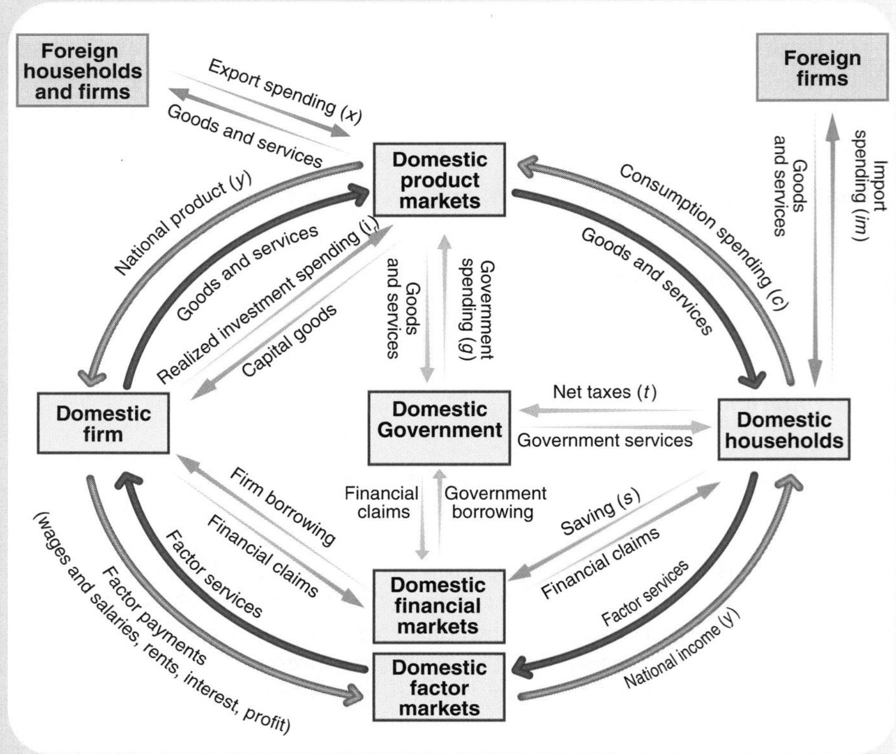

Thus, abstracting from depreciation and indirect business taxes and transfers that can differentiate their tabulations in the national income accounts, real income and real output by definition are the same.

Figure 23-1 indicates that households direct their earnings of real income, denoted y, to four uses:

1. **Real net taxes.** A portion of the real income of households goes to taxes that they pay the government. **Real net taxes,** denoted t, are the total taxes that households pay net of any **transfer payments.** These transfer payments are income redistributions that the government manages through programs such as Social Security, Temporary Aid to Needy Families, and the like. Consequently, real net taxes are the portion of tax revenues actually available to the government to spend on final goods and services.

2. **Real consumption.** Households may spend some of their real income on goods and services produced in *domestic* markets, or markets for goods and services produced in their home country. Such domestic consumption spending is called **real consumption,** denoted c.

3. **Real imports.** Households may also purchase goods and services produced in other nations. This is real import consumption, or more simply, **real imports,** denoted im.

4. **Real saving.** Households may allocate any untaxed or unspent portion of their real income earnings to **real saving,** s. Households save by purchasing financial claims issued in the economy's financial markets.

Real net taxes: The amount of real taxes paid to the government by households, net of transfer payments.

Transfer payments: Governmentally managed income redistributions.

Real consumption: The real amount of spending by households on domestically produced goods and services.

Real imports: The real flow of spending by households for the purchase of goods and services from firms in other countries.

Real saving: The amount of income that households save through financial markets.

Income identity: An identity that states that real national income equals the sum of real consumption, real saving, real net taxes, and real imports.

Real realized investment: Actual real expenditures by firms in the product markets.

The Income Identity

Because households use their total real income in these four ways, real income must, by definition, equal the sum of real consumption, real saving, real net taxes, and real imports:

$$y \equiv c + s + t + im.$$

We use the three-bar equality symbol to indicate that this relation is a truism, or identity. Because it is a truism for how real income must be allocated in the circular flow, economists call it the **income identity.**

The Product Identity

As emphasized by the classical model, owners of business firms borrow a portion of real household saving by issuing financial claims, such as stocks and bonds, in the financial markets. They use these funds saved by households to finance purchases of capital goods, as well as other goods and services, from other firms. Firms may also use these funds to finance the maintenance of inventories of produced goods that they have not yet sold. Such actual real expenditures by firms constitute **real realized investment,** denoted i_r. It is important to recognize the distinction between *realized* investment, i_r, and *desired* investment, which we denote as i. The two can—and for short periods often do—deviate from one another. This occurs whenever firms experience unintended depletions or accumulations

Real exports: The real value of goods and services produced by domestic firms and exported to other countries.

Product identity: An identity that states that real national product is the sum of real consumption, real realized investment, real government spending, and real exports.

of inventories of finished goods that are included in realized investment but which firms did not desire. As we shall discuss shortly, such unplanned changes in inventories induce firms to vary their production and thus perform a key role in achieving an equilibrium flow of real income.

Governments also borrow by issuing bonds and other financial claims to households in exchange for the use of their saving. The government uses these funds to cover its deficit, which is the difference between real government spending, g, and real net taxes, t.

Note that there are three sources of domestic spending on goods sold in domestic product markets. These are household consumption, firms' realized investment, and government spending. In addition, however, foreign residents may purchase goods and services produced by domestic firms. Such purchases from abroad are exports by domestic firms, and so they constitute the nation's **real exports,** denoted x. Adding this final type of spending on the output produced by domestic firms yields the **product identity** for the domestic economy:

$$y \equiv c + i_r + g + x.$$

Because this relationship is a truism, we again use the three-bar equality symbol.

The classical economists were well aware of these identities that the circular flow implies. Keynes, however, used them extensively in his effort to understand the nature of short-run variations in real income that business cycles generate.

1. What are the key relationships implied by the circular flow of income and expenditures? We can infer two fundamental identities from the circular flow diagram. One is the income identity, which indicates that households allocate real income to domestic consumption, saving, taxes, and import spending. The other is the product identity, which states that the real value of output of goods and services is equal to real expenditures on that output in the form of domestic consumption, realized investment, government spending, and export spending by foreign residents.

Aggregate Desired Expenditures and Equilibrium National Income

Keynes viewed the flows among households, firms, and the government, and the national income and product identities that they imply, as the building blocks necessary to construct a foundation for a theory of the relationship between money and the economy.

The Components of Aggregate Desired Expenditures

To understand how flows of spending and income relate to one another in the economy, Keynes analyzed each part of this foundation as a separate component. We shall follow his example.

HOUSEHOLD CONSUMPTION AND SAVING Because household consumption of domestic goods and services typically represents about two-thirds of total expenditures, Keynesian theory has emphasized its importance. The basic proposition of the Keynesian theory of household consumption is that the amount of such consumption depends positively upon **real disposable income,** or real income after taxes, denoted $y_d \equiv y - t$.

Note that we can rearrange the income identity, $y \equiv c + s + t + im$, by subtracting real net taxes, t, from both sides of the identity, which gives us $y - t \equiv c + s + im$. And so disposable income can be defined as $y_d \equiv c + s + im$. That is, households can allocate their after-tax income to consumption of domestic goods and services, saving, or purchases of imported goods and services.

Changes in Disposable Income Because disposable income by definition is equal to $y_d \equiv c + s + im$, it follows that a *change in* disposable income must equal

$$\Delta y_d \equiv \Delta c + \Delta s + \Delta im,$$

where the symbol Δ denotes "change in." Thus, households use any additional disposable income for additional consumption, additional saving, and additional spending on imports. If we divide both sides of this identity by Δy_d, we obtain the following relationship:

$$\frac{\Delta y_d}{\Delta y_d} = 1 \equiv \frac{\Delta c}{\Delta y_d} + \frac{\Delta s}{\Delta y_d} + \frac{\Delta im}{\Delta y_d}$$

This disposable income identity says that the sum of a change in consumption resulting from a change in disposable income ($\Delta c/\Delta y_d$), a change in saving resulting from a change in disposable income ($\Delta s/\Delta y_d$), and a change in real imports resulting from a change in disposable income ($\Delta im/\Delta y_d$) must be equal to 1.

Real disposable income: A household's real after-tax income.

Marginal Propensities Keynes called the first ratio on the right-hand side of this identity, $\Delta c/\Delta y_d$, the **marginal propensity to consume** (*MPC*), or the change in real consumption that is induced by a change in real disposable income. For instance, if $\Delta c/\Delta y_d$ is equal to a value of 0.85, then this means that a one-dollar increase in real disposable income induces households to increase their real consumption of domestically produced goods and services by 85 cents.

Marginal propensity to consume (*MPC*)**:** The additional consumption caused by an increase in disposable income; a change in consumption spending divided by a corresponding change in disposable income; the slope of the consumption function.

Keynes defined the second ratio, $\Delta s/\Delta y_d$, as the **marginal propensity to save** *(MPS)*, which is a change in real saving caused by a change in real disposable income. If $\Delta s/\Delta y_d$ is equal to 0.10, then a one-dollar rise in real disposable income will induce households to increase their real saving by 10 cents.

Marginal propensity to save (*MPS*)**:** The additional saving caused by an increase in disposable income; a change in saving divided by a corresponding change in disposable income; the slope of the saving function.

Finally, $\Delta im/\Delta y_d$ is the **marginal propensity to import** *(MPIM)*, or the additional spending on imported goods and services by households. If $\Delta im/\Delta y_d$ is equal to 0.05, then each additional dollar of real disposable income will induce households to spend 5 cents on additional imported goods and services.

Marginal propensity to import (*MPIM*)**:** The additional import expenditures stimulated by an increase in disposable income; a change in import spending divided by a corresponding change in disposable income; the slope of the import function.

The identity above says that all three marginal propensities must sum to one, or $MPC + MPS + MPIM = 1$. Consequently, the 85 cents of each new dollar of real disposable income used for domestic real consumption, the 10 cents of each additional dollar of real disposable income allocated to saving, and the 5 cents of each new dollar of real disposable income spent on imports must sum to the total 1 dollar of additional real disposable income.

The Saving Function In the Keynesian theory of household saving, a key determinant of households' annual savings flow is their disposable income. The basic idea is that as disposable income rises, households can increase their saving. This notion is captured by the function

$$s = -s_0 + (MPS \times y_d).$$

As shown in panel (a) of Figure 23-2, this is a straight-line function in its intercept-slope form, where $-s_0$ is the intercept and MPS is the slope. This *saving function* says that aggregate household saving is equal to a constant amount, $-s_0$, plus an amount that depends on disposable income, $MPS \times y_d$. Recall that $MPS \equiv \Delta s/\Delta y_d$, which is the slope of the saving function. Thus, the slope of the saving function tells us how much real saving rises with the receipt of additional real disposable income, y_d. Note that the constant intercept of the saving function, $-s_0$, is a negative number. The reason is that if disposable income were equal to zero, then households would need to draw down existing wealth to buy domestic and foreign goods. For instance, suppose that you had to make it through a semester of college with no disposable income and without any outside assistance from family members. Undoubtedly, you would have to withdraw funds from bank accounts and other accumulated wealth to buy books, food, and housing.

Hence, the basic Keynesian theory of household saving says that real domestic saving has two components. One is *induced saving*, $MPS \times y_d$, which is the saving brought about by the receipt of disposable income. The other component is *autonomous dissaving*, $-s_0$, or the amount by which households would need to draw from their wealth to make purchases of domestic consumption and foreign imports.

Figure 23-2
The Saving, Import, and Consumption Functions.

Panel (a) displays the saving function, in which the intercept $-s_0$ represents autonomous dissaving. The slope of the saving function, $MPS = \Delta s/\Delta y_d$, is the marginal propensity to save. Panel (b) shows the import function. The intercept of this function, im_0, is the amount of autonomous imports, and the slope, $MPIM = \Delta im/\Delta y_d$, is the marginal propensity to import. Finally, panel (c) shows the consumption function. Because real consumption of domestic goods and services, c, is equal to disposable income less saving and import expenditures, the intercept of the consumption function is $c_0 = s_0 - im_0$, which is autonomous consumption. The consumption function's slope is $MPC = \Delta c/\Delta y_d$, which is equal to $1 - MPS - MPIM$, or one minus the marginal propensity to save and the marginal propensity to import.

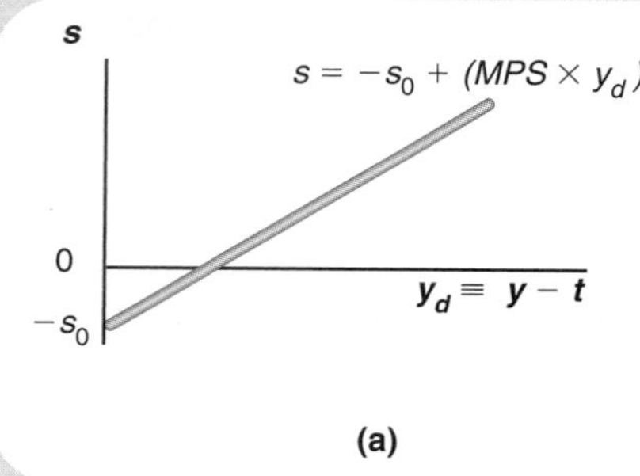

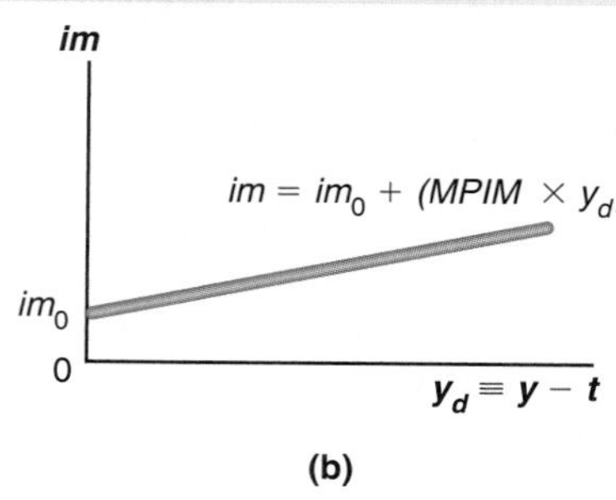

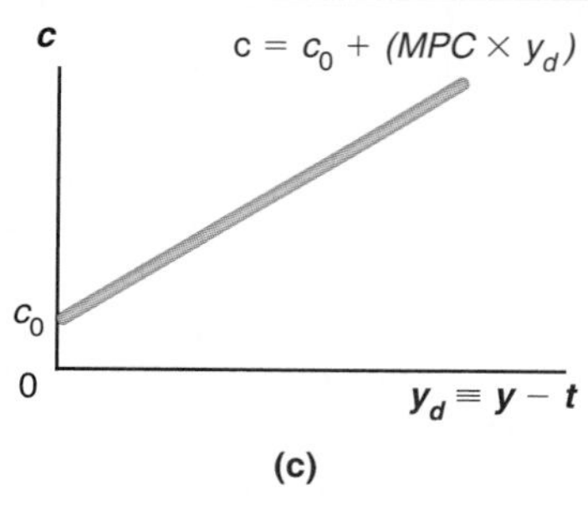

The Import Function Import expenditures also consist of autonomous and induced components. This is captured by using the straight-line *import function,*

$$im = im_0 + (MPIM \times y_d).$$

Here, im_0 denotes *autonomous import spending,* which is the amount of spending on imports by households irrespective of their total disposable income. As shown in panel (b) of Figure 23-2, im_0 is the constant intercept of the import function. The amount $MPIM \times y_d$ is *induced import spending.* This is the level of household spending on imports that is directly related to their earnings of disposable income, where the marginal propensity to import, $MPIM \equiv \Delta im/\Delta y_d$, is the slope of the import function.

The import function slopes upward. This means that growth in disposable income in the nation in which households reside will induce a rise in imports. Recall from Chapter 21 that a nation's trade balance is exports minus imports. Consequently, if exports are unchanged, a rise in a nation's real disposable income causes its trade balance to decline. We shall return to this issue later in the chapter.

Note that in this chapter we shall abstract from another important determinant of desired import spending, which is the price of foreign goods relative to the price of domestic goods. A key factor influencing this relative price is the rate of exchange between foreign and domestic currency. To keep our basic Keynesian model as simple as possible for now, however, we shall postpone further consideration of this issue until Chapter 28.

The Consumption Function Finally, we shall consider the consumption function,

$$c = c_0 + (MPC \times y_d),$$

where the slope of the consumption function is equal to $MPC \equiv \Delta c/\Delta y_d$. Note that by definition, $y_d \equiv c + s + im$, so household disposable income is split among consumption expenditures on domestically produced output, saving, and import spending. This means that the consumption, saving, and import functions must be interrelated. To see this, let's substitute the saving function, $s = -s_0 + (MPS \times y_d)$, and the import function, $im = im_0 + (MPIM \times y_d)$, into the disposable income identity to get

$$y_d = c + s + im,$$

or

$$y_d = c - s_0 + (MPS \times y_d) + im_0 + (MPIM \times y_d).$$

Note that we now have an equals sign instead of a three-bar identity symbol because our saving and import functions are hypotheses that may or may not be true. If we rearrange the last equation above and solve for c, we obtain

$$c = (s_0 - im_0) + [(1 - MPS - MPIM) \times y_d].$$

Thus, it must be true that **autonomous consumption,** the amount of household domestic consumption expenditures that would take place irrespective of disposable income, is $c_0 \equiv s_0 - im_0$, or autonomous dissaving allocated to domestic

Autonomous consumption: Household consumption spending on domestically produced goods and services that is independent of the level of real income.

consumption, less autonomous import spending. Furthermore, the marginal propensity to consume is $MPC \equiv 1 - MPS - MPIM$. Note that adding $MPS + MPIM$ to both sides of this relationship implies that $MPC + MPS + MPIM = 1$. And so, as discussed earlier, the three marginal propensities sum to 1.

FIRMS' INVESTMENT EXPENDITURES The Keynesian theory of desired investment expenditures is based on the classical approach. As in the classical loanable funds theory, desired investment, which we shall assume takes place only domestically, depends negatively on the real interest rate—the nominal interest rate minus the expected inflation rate. Therefore, as shown in panel (a) of Figure 23-3, for a given expected rate of inflation, a decline in the real interest rate from r_0^r to r_1^r causes desired real investment spending to rise from i_0 to i_1.

Panel (b) of Figure 23-3 shows another way that desired investment could rise from i_0 to i_1. Holding the real interest rate unchanged, the investment schedule itself could shift to the right, causing the same rise in desired investment. Keynes argued that such shifts in the desired investment schedule were commonplace and that they resulted from changes in firms' expectations of inflation or of future profits. The rightward shift of the investment schedule in panel (b) of Figure 23-3, for instance, could result from a general anticipation by firms of lower inflation (which would reduce the perceived real interest rate) or higher profits in the future. This would induce them to increase their total investment in capital goods, so as to expand future production, and in their inventories of finished goods, which they would expect to sell in the near future.

Panel (c) of Figure 23-3 shows that, whether induced by a fall in the real interest rate or expectations of higher future profits, an increase in desired investment would cause investment to rise at any given level of aggregate income, y. Consequently, with investment measured along the vertical axis and real income measured along the horizontal axis, a rise in desired investment implies an upward shift in a horizontal desired investment schedule, from $i = i_0$ to $i = i_1$. (Since the 1990s, a big part of business investment has been purchases of computing equipment; see on page 564 *Cyber Focus: Investing in Computing Power.*)

GOVERNMENT SPENDING AND TAXATION A number of factors can influence the levels of government spending and taxation. How much a government spends can depend on such factors as its concern about national defense and law enforcement, its desire to maintain parks, monuments, and buildings, or even purely political factors such as "pork barrel" spending to satisfy various constituencies. We shall simplify considerably by treating all these various factors as beyond the scope of our theory and assuming that real government spending on domestic output is just equal to an autonomous amount, $g = g_0$. As shown in panel (a) of Figure 23-5 (p. 565), this means that the *government spending schedule* is horizontal. If the government increases its spending on national defense or decides to build a new dam in West Virginia or an office building in Washington, D.C., the government spending schedule will shift upward by the rise in spending, to $g = g_1$, where g_1 is the new, higher level of government expenditures.

Governments have a number of possible sources of net taxes, including income taxes, sales taxes, excise taxes, and the like. The dependence of a government's income tax revenues on the level of income means that, realistically, net taxes depend on aggregate real income. Nevertheless, we again shall try to keep things

On the Web

How much does the U.S. Congress expect that it will tax and spend during the next few years? Obtain the latest printout of the Joint Committee on Taxation's "Estimates of Tax Expenditures" at the following location: http://www.house.gov/jct. Select "Click here" to continue, then click on "JCT Publications," and you will find this document among the most recent materials.

simple by assuming that net taxes are equal to a lump-sum, autonomous amount. Under this simplification, the *net tax schedule* also is horizontal, as shown in panel (b) of Figure 23-5. If the government increases net taxes from an amount $t = t_0$ to a larger amount $t = t_1$, then the net tax schedule will shift upward by the amount of the tax increase, as shown in Figure 23-5.

Figure 23-3
Factors Causing Changes in Desired Investment.

Panels (a) and (b) show two key factors that might induce an increase in desired real investment expenditures. One, illustrated in panel (a), is a decline in the real interest rate, owing to a fall in the nominal rate of interest or a rise in anticipated inflation, which would cause a movement along the investment schedule graphed against the real interest rate. Another, displayed in panel (b), follows from a shift in the investment schedule itself, so that a rise in desired investment would take place at any given real interest rate. Such a shift could arise from an increase in firms' expectations of future profitability from new investment. As panel (c) indicates, either cause of an increase in desired investment spending would lead to an upward shift in the investment schedule graphed against real income.

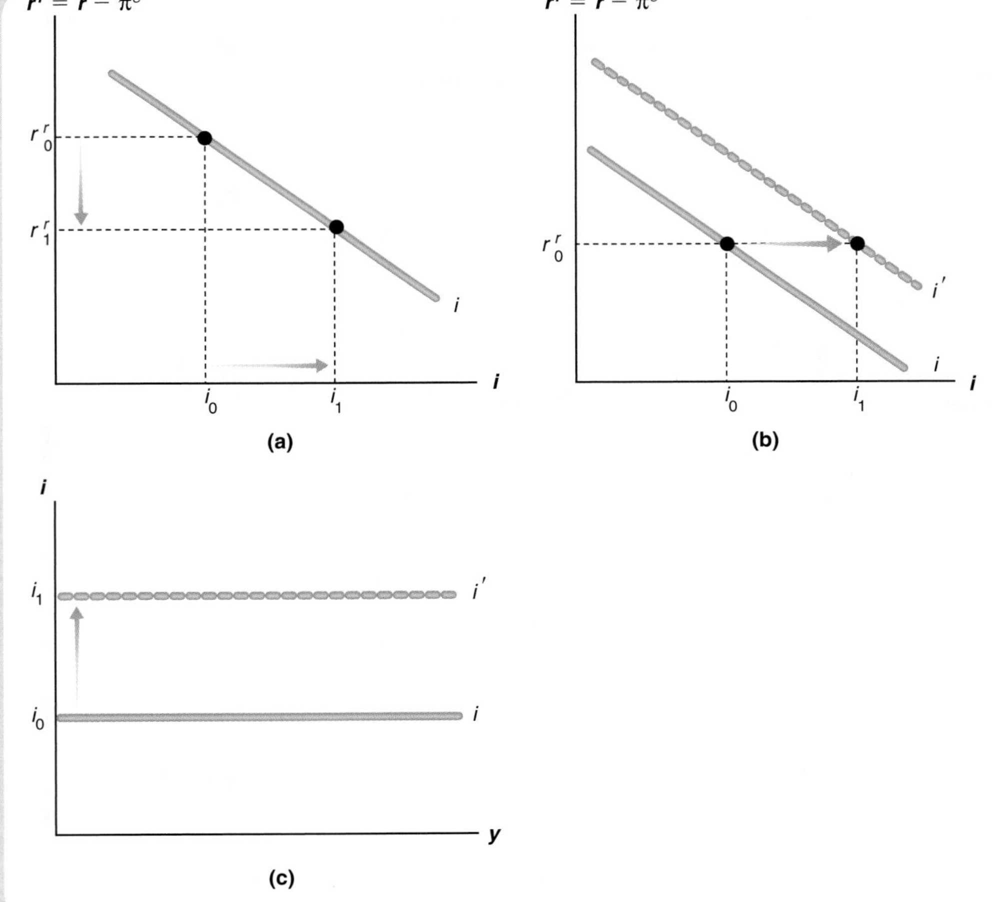

GLOBAL | POLICY | CYBER Focus | MANAGEMENT

Investing in Computing Power

Business spending on computers is a component of equipment and software investment, which in turn is a large part of total fixed investment in the U.S. National Income and Product Accounts. As Figure 23-4 shows, business spending on computers increased from about $37 billion in 1987 to nearly $120 billion in 2000 before declining somewhat in the early 2000s. Business purchases of computers typically account for about 75 percent of all computer purchases. Households buy only about 17 percent of all computers, and the government buys the remaining 8 percent. Undoubtedly, a key factor motivating businesses, households, and the government to boost their purchases of computing equipment has been the 95 percent decline in the real price of computers—the average nominal price of computers relative to the overall price level—also displayed in the figure.

All told, business purchases of computers now account for almost 9 percent of total nonresidential business fixed investment in the United States. When investment in computer software and communications technologies that link computers is included with investment in computing equipment, total investment in information technology now accounts for between 35 and 40 percent of aggregate business investment each year.

For Critical Analysis: What factors other than computer prices are likely to influence businesses' decisions about how much to invest in computers that they will use for a number of years?

Figure 23-4
U.S. Final Sales of Computers and the Real Price of Computers.

As the real price of computers has declined, sales of computers have increased. A large portion of these sales has been to companies and recorded as business investment.

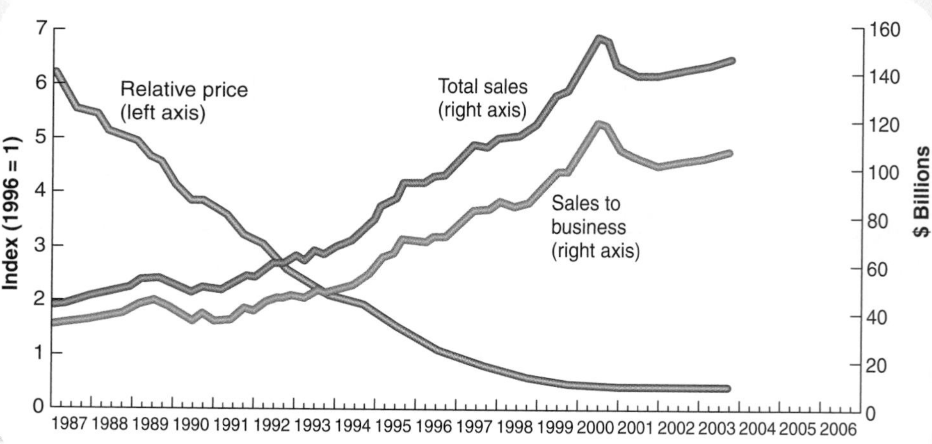

SOURCE: Michael Pakko, "Accounting for Computers," Federal Reserve Bank of St. Louis *National Economic Trends*, May 2001; authors' estimates.

Export Expenditures The final component of total spending in a nation's economy is the level of expenditures by foreign residents on the exports produced and sold by domestic firms. As we shall discuss briefly later in this chapter and in greater detail in Chapter 28, two key factors affect spending on a nation's exports. One is the real incomes of nations whose residents purchase domestically produced goods. As other nations' incomes rise, their residents desire to

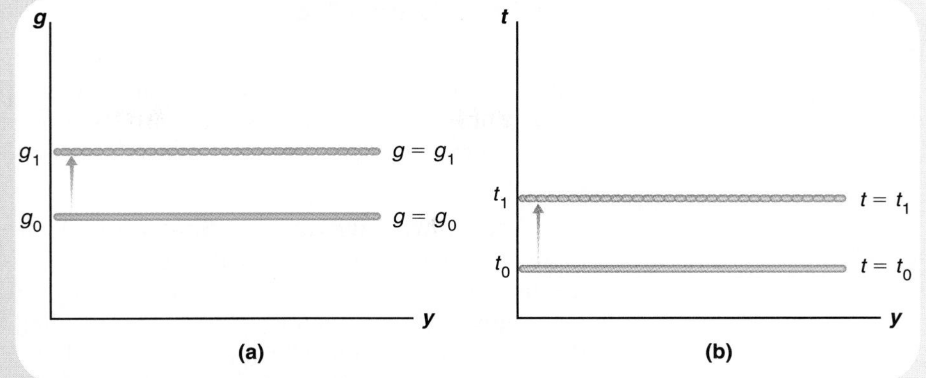

Figure 23-5
The Government Spending and Net Tax Schedules.

In the basic Keynesian model, we assume that government spending is autonomous, so the government spending schedule is horizontal, as shown in panel (a). An increase in government spending thereby causes an upward shift in this schedule. Likewise, in our basic model we assume that net taxes are autonomous, so the net tax schedule in panel (b) also is horizontal. An increase in net taxes results in an upward shift in this schedule.

purchase more domestic output. The other factor is the rate of exchange between a nation's currency and the currencies of its trading partners. For instance, if the domestic currency *depreciates,* so that fewer units of foreign currency are required to obtain domestic currency, then domestic exports become less expensive to foreigners, and they are likely to increase their spending on domestic exports.

Domestic income, *y,* has no effect on real exports, however. Consequently, the *export schedule* is horizontal, as shown in Figure 23-6. A rise in foreign nations' incomes or a depreciation of the domestic currency would cause exports to increase from an amount $x = x_0$ to a larger amount $x = x_1$. Thus, either type of change would cause the export schedule to shift upward, as shown in the figure.

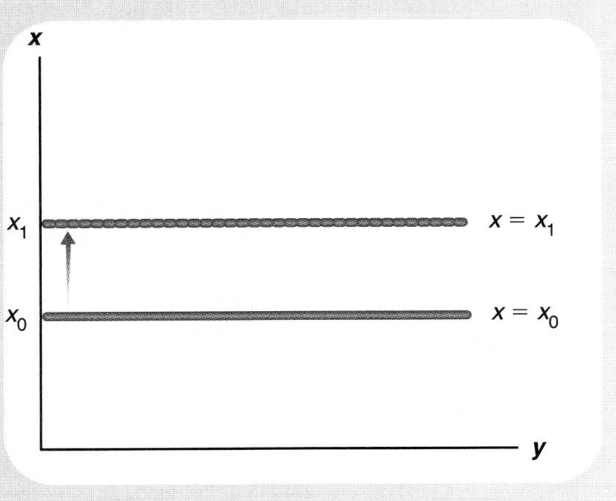

Figure 23-6
The Export Schedule.

Because foreign residents purchase domestic export goods, domestic income has no direct effect on export expenditures. Consequently, the export schedule is horizontal. If foreign incomes rise or the domestic currency's value depreciates, however, export spending will rise, causing an upward shift in the export schedule.

Putting the Pieces Together: Aggregate Expenditures and Equilibrium National Income

Total spending on domestically produced goods and services is the sum of household consumption spending, desired investment spending, government expenditures, and spending on domestic exports by residents of foreign nations. In terms of our notation, therefore, total expenditures on domestic output are equal to $c + i + g + x$.

THE AGGREGATE EXPENDITURES SCHEDULE Figure 23-7 explains how to add up these components of aggregate desired expenditures. Panel (a) of the figure sums up the purely autonomous components, which are desired investment spending, $i = i_0$, government spending, $g = g_0$, and spending on exports, $x = x_0$. This yields the horizontal schedule $i_0 + g_0 + x_0$ in panel (a).

Total spending on domestically produced goods and services also includes domestic consumption spending by households. In panel (b) of Figure 23-7, we again display the upward-sloping household consumption function, $c = c_0 + (MPC \times y_d)$. Note however, that we now recognize that disposable income, y_d, is equal to total real income, y, minus real net taxes, t. Hence, if t_0 is the current lump-sum amount of net taxes, we can substitute $y - t_0$ for y_d to get $c = c_0 + (MPC \times y)$. This implies that the consumption function is

$$c = c_0 - (MPC \times t_0) + (MPC \times y).$$

With total real income measured on the horizontal axis, the consumption function's intercept, $c_0 - (MPC \times t_0)$, takes into account the consumption-reducing effect of taxes. Its slope remains equal to the marginal propensity to consume.

Figure 23-7
Deriving the Aggregate Expenditures Schedule.

Adding together the autonomous levels of desired investment spending, government spending, and export expenditures yields the schedule $i_0 + g_0 + x_0$ in panel (a). Summing this amount with the level of consumption at each income level, given by the consumption function, yields the aggregate expenditures schedule $c + i + g + x$, as displayed in panel (b).

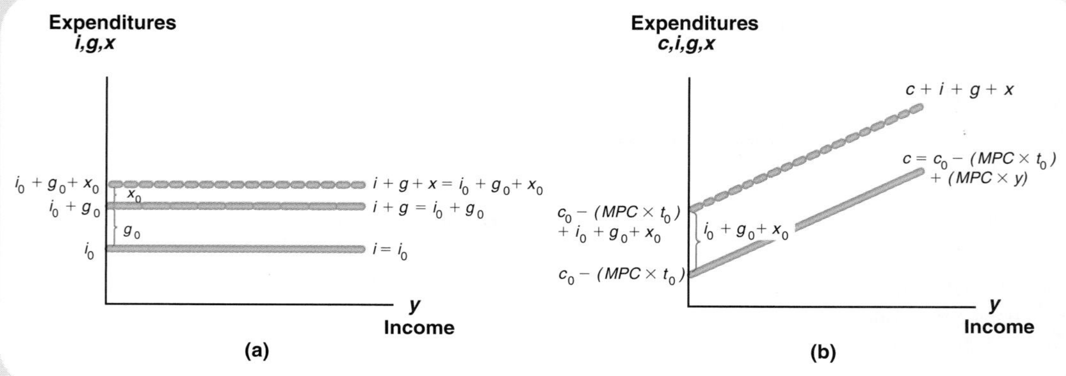

At each level of income we then add the vertical distance $i_0 + g_0 + x_0$ to the amount of consumption. This gives us the **aggregate expenditures schedule,** $c + i + g + x$. This schedule tells us how much households, firms, the government, and foreign residents combined will desire to spend on domestically produced output at any given level of domestic real income y. Its intercept is **aggregate net autonomous expenditures,** or $c_0 - (MPC \times t_0) + i_0 + g_0 + x_0$. This is total net spending on domestically produced output that is independent of the current level of total real income.

Aggregate expenditures schedule: A schedule that represents total desired expenditures by all the relevant sectors of the economy at each and every level of real national income.

Aggregate net autonomous expenditures: The sum of autonomous consumption, autonomous investment, autonomous government spending, and autonomous export spending, all of which are independent of the level of national income in the basic Keynesian model.

Because we have constructed the aggregate expenditures schedule by adding a fixed vertical distance all along the consumption function, the slope of the aggregate expenditures schedule is equal to the consumption function's slope. This slope is the marginal propensity to consume. We shall assume that the marginal propensity to save and the marginal propensity to import are relatively small fractions, so that the marginal propensity to consume is a relatively large fraction. For example, if the marginal propensity to save is equal to 0.10 and the marginal propensity to import is equal to 0.08, then the marginal propensity to consume is equal to $1 - 0.10 - 0.08 = 0.82$.

2. What are the components of aggregate desired expenditures in the basic Keynesian model? Aggregate desired expenditures are composed of household consumption of domestically produced goods and services, desired investment spending by firms, government spending, and export spending by foreigners. In the basic Keynesian model, we assume that desired investment, government spending and net taxes, and export spending are autonomous. Consumption spending, however, is positively related to disposable income. As a result, the aggregate expenditures schedule slopes upward.

Determining the Equilibrium Flow of Income and Expenditures

The detailed circular flow diagram in Figure 23-1 on page 556 depicts the relationships that must exist among the various components of total income and aggregate expenditures. While it tells us the direction of the overall flow of income and spending, however, the circular flow diagram does not tell us anything about the total *magnitude* of the flow. The flow of water along a riverbed, for instance, might run from east to west, but it could be either a trickle or a torrent. Likewise, the size of the flow of household income that ultimately flows to firms in the form of expenditures on goods and services could be meager, implying a weak economy, or it could be large, implying a robust economy.

EQUILIBRIUM REAL INCOME The *equilibrium* flow of real income is that level at which households, firms, the government, and foreign residents desire to purchase all real output that is produced and sold by domestic firms. Another way of saying the same thing is that in equilibrium, households, firms, the government, and foreign residents are satisfied with the actual flow of income and expenditures through the domestic economy. If the actual flow were to differ from the desired level, then households, firms, the government, and foreign

45-degree line: A line that cuts in half the 90-degree angle of the coordinate axes on a diagram relating real income to aggregate desired expenditures; every point on the 45-degree line could, in principle, be a point of equilibrium at which real income equals aggregate desired expenditures.

residents would have an incentive to change their expenditures, which in turn would affect the total flow of spending and income. Therefore, in equilibrium there is no tendency for the flow of real income and expenditures to change from its current level.

In light of this definition of equilibrium, we can define a nation's *equilibrium real income* as the real income level at which aggregate desired expenditures are equal to the real value of domestically produced output. The circular flow diagram tells us that the real value of output is equal to real income. Consequently, in equilibrium, real income is equal to aggregate desired expenditures, or $y = c + i + g + x$.

THE INCOME-EXPENDITURES EQUILIBRIUM Figure 23-8 depicts a schedule of all the possible combinations of real income and aggregate desired expenditures that can satisfy our definition of equilibrium. This schedule is a **45-degree line,** because it cuts in half the 90-degree angle of the coordinate axes on the diagram. At any point along this 45-degree line, the level of real income along the horizontal axis is equal to the level of aggregate desired expenditures along the vertical axis. This means that every point on the 45-degree line could, in principle, satisfy our definition of equilibrium.

Panel (a) of Figure 23-9 illustrates the determination of a single income-expenditures equilibrium. This figure superimposes Figures 23-7 and 23-8. The aggregate expenditures schedule, $c + i + g + x$, is taken from Figure 23-7. It displays all combinations of real income and desired expenditures by households, firms, the government, and foreign residents. As just discussed, the 45-degree line (Figure 23-8) displays all combinations of real income levels that could be equal to aggregate desired expenditures. Hence, the single point at which the two schedules intersect is the single point that satisfies the equilibrium condition $y = c + i + g + x$. The equilibrium level of real income at this point is denoted y_e.

Figure 23-8
The 45-Degree Line.

The economy is in equilibrium when aggregate desired expenditures equal aggregate real income. This will be true along the 45-degree line. If aggregate desired expenditures equal the amount y_1, then reading over to the 45-degree line and downward to the horizontal axis, we find that this level of total spending is equal to the aggregate income level y_1. The same is true for the higher level of expenditures y_2. Consequently, any point along the 45-degree line is a potential equilibrium point.

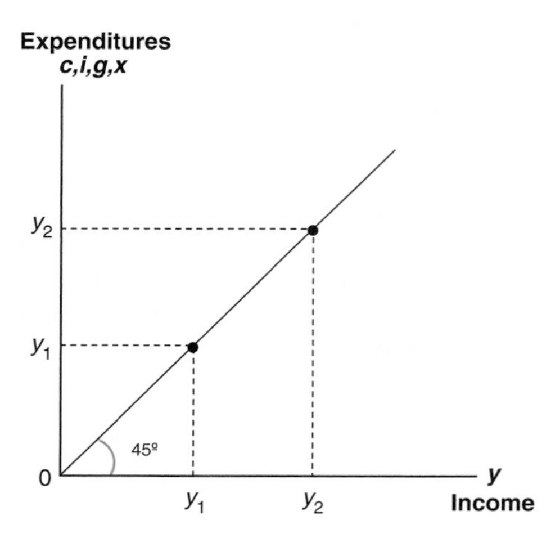

Figure 23-9
Two Approaches to Determining Equilibrium Real Income.

Equilibrium real income arises at the point at which aggregate desired real expenditures, $c + i + g + x$, equal aggregate real income. This is true at the single real income level, y_e, at which the aggregate expenditures schedule crosses the 45-degree line in panel (a). Alternatively, as shown in panel (b), equilibrium income also arises at the point at which leakages from the flow of spending on domestic output, given by $s + t + im$, equal total injections back into the spending flow, which equal $i + g + x$.

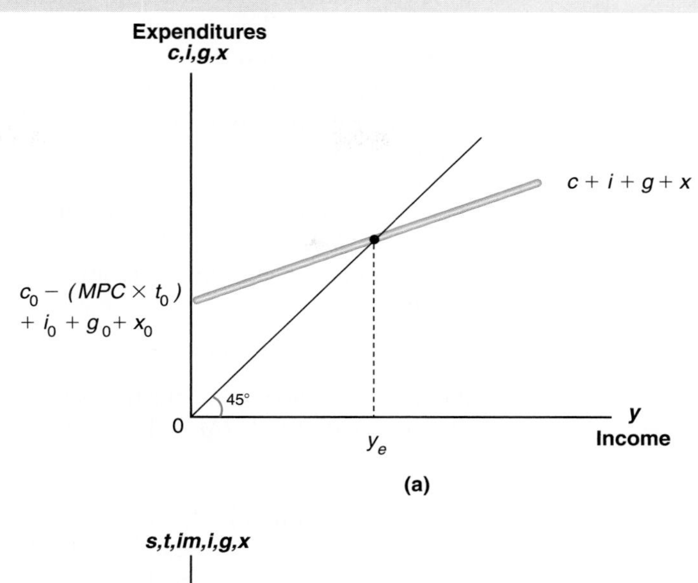

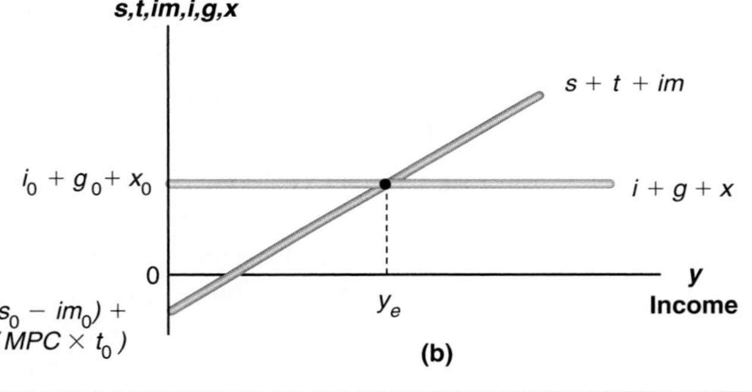

THE LEAKAGES-INJECTIONS APPROACH TO DETERMINING EQUILIBRIUM REAL INCOME There is another way to think about equilibrium. This entails substituting the real income identity, $y \equiv c + s + t + im$, for y in the equilibrium condition $y = c + i + g + x$, which gives us

$$c + s + t + im = c + i + g + x.$$

If we subtract c from both sides of this equation, we get another expression for the equilibrium condition:

$$s + t + im = i + g + x.$$

If you look back at the circular flow diagram in Figure 23-1 on page 556, you will see that the left-hand side of this new condition is the sum of all *leakages* from the flow of spending on domestic output that take place because households save, pay taxes, and purchase imports from foreign firms. The right-hand side consists of *injections* back into the flow of spending on domestically produced goods and services that take place when firms, the government, and foreign residents purchase domestically produced output. Hence, the equation says that in equilibrium, all leakages from the flow of spending ultimately are *reinjected* back into that flow.

Panel (b) of Figure 23-9 displays this alternative leakages-injections approach to determining equilibrium real income. The right-hand side of the leakages-injections equilibrium condition is described by the horizontal schedule $i_0 + g_0 + x_0$ from panel (a) of Figure 23-7. Using the saving and import functions we discussed earlier, the left-hand side of the equation, $s + t + im$, is equal to $-s_0 + (MPS \times y_d) + t_0 + im_0 + (MPIM \times y_d)$. Remembering that $y_d \equiv y - t$, where $t = t_0$ is the current lump-sum level of taxes, we can rearrange this expression in the form,

$$s + t + im = -c_0 + t_0 + [(MPS + MPIM) \times (y - t_0)].$$

Finally, by factoring out the terms relating to t_0 on the right-hand side and recalling that $MPS + MPIM = 1 - MPC$, we obtain

$$s + t + im = -c_0 + (MPC \times t_0) + [(1 - MPS) \times y],$$

which is the equation of the upward-sloping "$s + t + im$" schedule that is displayed in panel (b) of Figure 23-9. The intersection of these two schedules then determines equilibrium real income, y_e. This is the same as the equilibrium real income level determined via the income-expenditures approach in panel (a) of Figure 23-9.

THE COMPLETE DEPICTION OF EQUILIBRIUM REAL INCOME Figure 23-10 summarizes the graphical depiction of the determination of a nation's equilibrium real income flow. Households, firms, the government, and foreign residents purchase all the output produced domestically ($y = c + i + g + x$), and leakages from the spending flow ultimately are reinjected into that flow ($s + t + im = i + g + x$). From either perspective, equilibrium real income is equal to the same level, y_e.

Finally, remember that the national product identity is $y \equiv c + i_r + g + x$, where i_r is the amount of realized, or actual, investment spending by firms. In equilibrium, $y = c + i + g + x$. If we substitute the national product identity for y in this equilibrium condition, we obtain $c + i_r + g + x = c + i + g + x$ in equilibrium. After subtracting $c + g + x$ from both sides of this equation, we find a third and final way to express equilibrium:

$$i_r = i.$$

This equation says that in equilibrium firms undertake the amount of investment spending that they *desire* to undertake. That is, in equilibrium firms hold neither more nor fewer inventories of finished goods than they desire to hold.

In Figure 23-10, if real income somehow increased to y_1, above the equilibrium income level y_e, such an increase could only be temporary. The reason is that at this higher income level y_1, real income—the real value of output—would exceed the level of desired spending on output, or $y > c + i + g + x$. This would mean that realized real investment would be greater than desired investment, or $i_r > i$. Firms' inventories of unsold goods would rise above desired levels, causing the firms to cut back on production. As a result, production of new output would decline, causing the value of real output, or real income, to decline toward the equilibrium level y_e.

Figure 23-10
The Determination of Equilibrium Real Income.

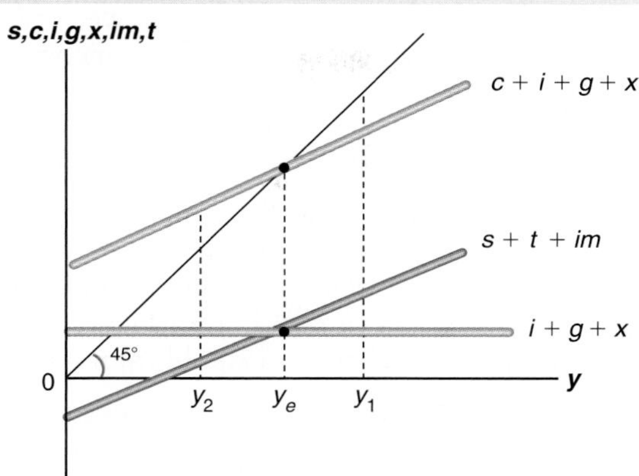

Equilibrium real income is attained both when aggregate desired expenditures, $c + i + g + x$, equal real income and when spending-flow leakages, $s + t + im$, equal spending-flow injections, $i + g + x$. At an income level above the equilibrium level of real income denoted y_e, such as the income level y_1, realized investment would exceed desired investment. Firms would cut back on production, and real income would fall back toward the equilibrium level y_e. In contrast, at an income level below the equilibrium income level, such as y_2, realized investment would be less than desired investment. Firms would increase production, and real income would rise toward the equilibrium level y_e.

In contrast, if real income were to decline to y_2, below the equilibrium income level y_e in Figure 23-10, real income would be less than the level of desired spending on output, or $y < c + i + g + x$. This would mean that realized real investment would be lower than desired investment, or $i_r < i$. Firms' inventories of unsold goods would fall below desired levels, causing the firms to increase production to add to their inventories. As a result, production of new output would increase, causing the value of real output, or real income, to rise toward the equilibrium level y_e.

3. How is equilibrium real income determined in the basic Keynesian model? In equilibrium, a nation's real income is equal to the aggregate desired expenditures on domestically produced goods and services by households, firms, the government, and foreign residents. This occurs at the point where the aggregate expenditures schedule crosses the 45-degree line, or where $y = c + i + g + x$. It also occurs at the point where leakages from the economy's overall flow of spending, $s + t + im$, equal reinjections into the flow, $i + g + x$.

Business Cycles, Equilibrium Income, and Monetary Policy

What factors could cause equilibrium real income to change, thereby generating cyclical changes in real income that we observe over business cycles? What factors account for the magnitudes of such cyclical income variations? Can governmental

Multiplier effect: The ratio of a change in the equilibrium real income to an increase in autonomous net aggregate expenditures. When the aggregate expenditures schedule shifts vertically, the equilibrium level of national income changes by a multiple of the amount of the shift.

Autonomous expenditures multiplier: A measure of the size of the multiple effect on equilibrium real income caused by a change in aggregate net autonomous expenditures; in the simple Keynesian model, the multiplier is equal to $1/(MPS + MPIM) = 1/(1 - MPC)$.

policies, including monetary policies, help to smooth out business cycles? To answer these questions, we need to consider the various implications of the basic Keynesian model of real income determination.

The Multiplier Effect and Short-Run Business Cycles

The first of these implications is called the **multiplier effect.** This is the fact that a given 1-unit change in aggregate net autonomous expenditures—a 1-unit movement in the intercept of the aggregate desired expenditures schedule $c + i + g + x$ in panel (a) of Figure 23-9 and in Figure 23-10—causes a greater-than-1-unit change in equilibrium real income in the same direction.

THE AUTONOMOUS EXPENDITURES MULTIPLIER To see how the multiplier effect occurs, let's begin with a little bit of algebra. The income-expenditures equilibrium condition is $y = c + i + g + x$. If we substitute from our consumption function, $c = c_0 - (MPC \times t_0) + (MPC \times y)$, and use our assumptions that net taxes and desired investment, government spending, and export spending are all autonomous, we can rewrite this condition as

$$y = c_0 - (MPC \times t_0) + (MPC \times y) + i_0 + g_0 + x_0.$$

Now, if we subtract $(MPC \times y)$ from both sides of this equation, we obtain

$$y - (MPC \times y) = c_0 - (MPC \times t_0) + i_0 + g_0 + x_0.$$

Finally, if we divide both sides of the above equation by $(1 - MPC)$, we get

$$y = \frac{1}{1 - MPC} [c_0 - (MPC \times t_0) + i_0 + g_0 + x_0].$$

This final expression is an equation for equilibrium real income. It tells us that equilibrium real income is equal to the ratio $1/(1 - MPC)$ times aggregate net autonomous expenditures, $c_0 - (MPC \times t_0) + i_0 + g_0 + x_0$. The ratio $1/(1 - MPC)$ is the Keynesian **autonomous expenditures multiplier,** which we shall call simply the "multiplier." This is a measure of the size of the multiplier effect on equilibrium real income caused by a change in the level of aggregate net autonomous expenditures. The marginal propensity to consume is between zero and one, so the multiplier is greater than 1. For example, if the marginal propensity to consume is equal to 0.8, then the multiplier is equal to $1/(1 - MPC) = 1/(1 - 0.8) = 1/0.2 = 5$. In this instance, a \$1 billion per year reduction in aggregate net autonomous expenditures would cause a \$5 billion decline in equilibrium real income per year.

The multiplier effect is illustrated in Figure 23-11, where the initial equilibrium is point *A*, at the level of real income y_1. Now suppose that there is an autonomous fall in investment spending, perhaps because firms anticipate lower future profits or because of a rise in the real interest rate. A decline in investment equal to Δi_0 will cause the aggregate desired expenditures schedule to shift downward by that amount. As a result, equilibrium real income falls by a larger amount, from y_1 to y_2, or Δy, at point *B*. In fact, our final equation for equilibrium real income above tells us that the exact amount of the decline in real income is equal to $\Delta y = [1/(1 - MPC)] \times \Delta i_0$. Real income will decline by the

Figure 23-11
The Multiplier Effect on Real Income Caused by a Decline in Real Investment.

A decline in real autonomous investment expenditures equal to Δi_0 causes the aggregate expenditures schedule to shift downward by that amount and induces a movement from equilibrium point *A* to equilibrium point *B*. As a result, equilibrium real income declines by a larger amount than the fall in autonomous investment, given by $\Delta y = y_1 - y_2$. The amount of the fall in equilibrium real income is equal to $\Delta y = [1/(1 - MPC)] \times \Delta i_0$.

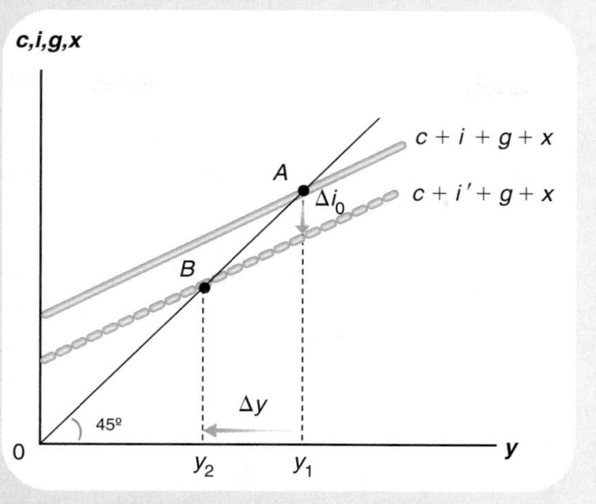

autonomous fall in investment times the autonomous spending multiplier, $1/(1 - MPC)$.

Behind the Multiplier What accounts for the multiplier effect? Consider the following example in which $MPC = 0.80$. This means that each dollar reduction in household disposable income induces a reduction in disposable income of 80 cents. If investment declines by an amount Δi_0 = \$1 billion, then firms now spend \$1 billion less than before on capital goods and inventories of finished goods. This spending reduction immediately reduces real income by \$1 billion. The result is a \$1 billion decline in disposable income, which in turn reduces household consumption spending by 80 percent of \$1 billion, or \$800,000. This reduces the real income of all firms from which households would have purchased domestically produced goods and services by \$800,000. At this point, therefore, the \$1 billion decline in investment has reduced total real income by \$1.8 billion.

The process of spending reduction is not yet complete, however. The owners and workers at the firms that have lost \$800,000 in sales and income earnings now reduce their consumption spending by 80 percent of this amount, or by 0.8 × \$800,000 = \$640,000. Furthermore, this spending reduction generates a fall in real income of \$640,000 for other firm owners and workers, who then will reduce their consumption spending by 0.8 × \$640,000 = \$512,000.

Ultimately, the total reduction in real income will equal the sum of all these declines (\$1 billion + \$800,000 + \$640,000 + \$512,000 + · · ·) in spending. As we determined earlier, if the marginal propensity to consume is equal to 0.8, the total decline in real income caused by a \$1 billion fall in investment will be equal to \$1 billion times 1/(1 − 0.8), or \$1 billion times 5, or a real income reduction of \$5 billion.

A Basic Keynesian Theory of Business Cycles

Note that a multiple decline in real income caused by an autonomous fall in investment would, if all other factors were unchanged, lead to a recession. Real income would fall relative to its long-run growth path, and equilibrium real income would not rise again until investment or some other component of aggregate net autonomous expenditures increased. The result would be a downturn in the business cycle.

Our final equation for equilibrium real income indicates that a number of factors could cause such a downturn. Any change causing a reduction in aggregate net autonomous expenditures, $c_0 - (MPC \times t_0) + i_0 + g_0 + x_0$, could induce a recession. For instance, a fall in the value of c_0 equal to Δc_0 would cause real income to decline by $\Delta c_0 \times 1/(1 - MPC)$. Recall that autonomous consumption is $c_0 \equiv s_0 - im_0$, which implies that a decline in autonomous consumption of domestically produced goods and services occurs either because people decide to save more than they did before or because they choose to purchase more imports from abroad. The result would be a fall in equilibrium real income and a recession.

In addition, a significant fall in real export spending by foreign residents could induce an economic downturn. A decline in spending on real exports equal to Δx_0 would cause real income to decline by $\Delta x_0 \times 1/(1 - MPC)$.

Finally, changes in autonomous net taxes or in government spending can also influence equilibrium real income. A rise in net taxes would reduce real income, as would a fall in government spending. The fact that the government can induce equilibrium real income to change via alterations in these *fiscal policy* variables led Keynes and his followers to propose an economic stabilization role for government.

4. How does the basic Keynesian theory explain short-run business cycles? Equilibrium real income changes are a multiple of any changes in aggregate net autonomous expenditures. Consequently, variations in autonomous spending can cause equilibrium real income to vary from a level consistent with the economy's long-run growth path. The amount by which equilibrium real income diverges from its long-run level is a multiple of the change in net autonomous expenditures.

Monetary Stabilization Policy

Although Keynes himself emphasized the role of fiscal policy and downplayed the usefulness of monetary policy for stabilizing real income over the business cycle, later economists have applied the basic Keynesian theory to consider how monetary policy might be used for this purpose.

LINKING MONETARY POLICY TO EQUILIBRIUM REAL INCOME To see how monetary policy is linked to real income in the basic Keynesian model, consider Figure 23-12. Panel (a) of the figure depicts the market for *real* depository institution reserves—that is, the price-level-adjusted quantity of total reserves in the banking system (converted to a real quantity, *tr,* by dividing current-dollar total reserves, *TR*, by the GDP deflator, *P*). As discussed in Chapter 20, below a rela-

Figure 23-12
Linking Monetary Policy to Equilibrium Real Income.

Panel (a) displays a situation of equilibrium in the market for real depository institution reserves, where the real quantity of total reserves is $tr \equiv TR/P$. Given the equilibrium federal funds rate in panel (a), the Treasury securities yield curve in panel (b) indicates the equilibrium longer-term interest rate, r_1, that is relevant to firms in making decisions about investment spending. The level of real desired investment is determined in panel (c). Adding this investment level to consumption, government spending, and export expenditures gives the position of the aggregate expenditures schedule in panel (d), which determines equilibrium real income.

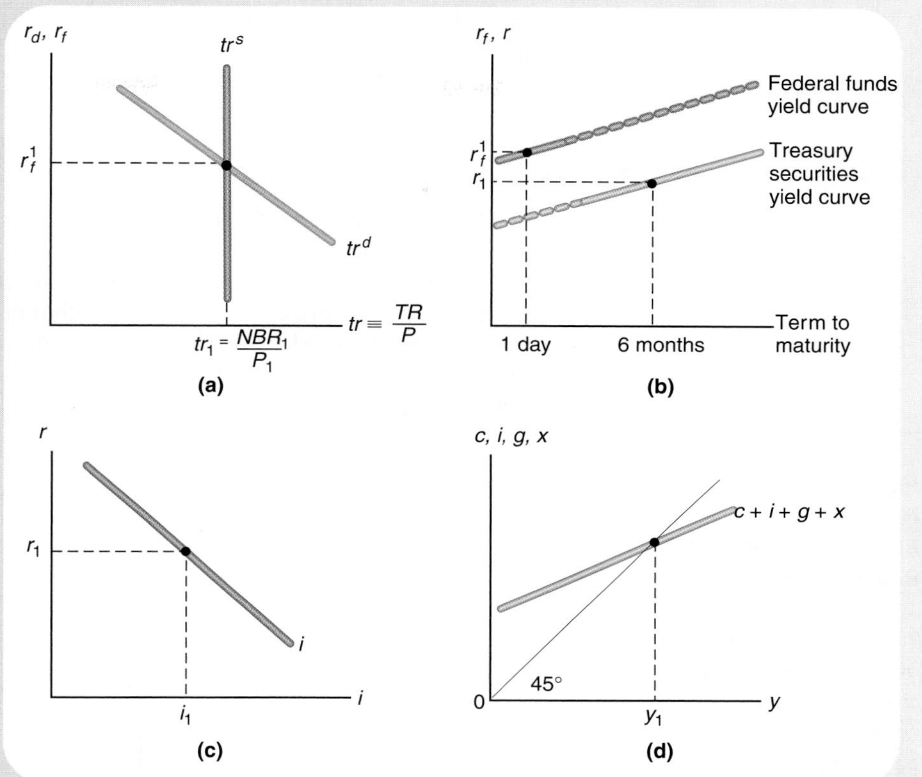

tively high threshold federal funds rate, r_f, the demand for total depository institution reserves depends negatively on the federal funds rate. Thus, the real reserve demand schedule, tr^d, slopes downward over most of its range in panel (a). The Fed influences the supply of real depository institution reserves and thereby influences the position of the supply schedule. The Federal Reserve's Trading Desk accomplishes this by using open market operations to determine the current-dollar level of nonborrowed reserves, equal to NBR_1, in panel (a). Another factor affecting the *real* supply of reserves to depository institutions, however, is the price level. In the market for real reserves, if there are no borrowed reserves, the position of the reserve supply schedule depends on the price-level-adjusted quantity of nonborrowed reserves, NBR_1/P_1, where P_1 denotes the actual current value of the price level. The crossing point of the reserve demand and supply schedules determines the equilibrium federal funds rate, r_f^1, and the equilibrium real level of total reserves in the banking system, tr_1.

Panel (b) depicts federal funds and Treasury securities yield curves that reflect the term and risk structures of interest rates that prevail for the economy. Given the equilibrium federal funds rate in panel (a), the Treasury securities yield curve implies a longer-term interest rate relevant to business investment decisions that is equal to r_1. At this interest rate, panel (c) indicates that desired investment spending is equal to i_1. Adding this level of investment expenditures to domestic consumption, government spending, and export expenditures by foreign residents yields the position of the aggregate expenditures schedule in panel (d). The result is equilibrium real income, y_1.

How Monetary Policy Can Influence Equilibrium Real Income To see how monetary policy can affect equilibrium real income, take a look at Figure 23-13, which depicts the effects of an open market purchase by the Fed under the assumption that the price level remains unchanged at P_1. The open market purchase increases the level of nonborrowed reserves to NBR_2, so that the reserve supply schedule shifts rightward in panel (a), which induces a decline in the equilibrium federal funds rate, to r_f^2.

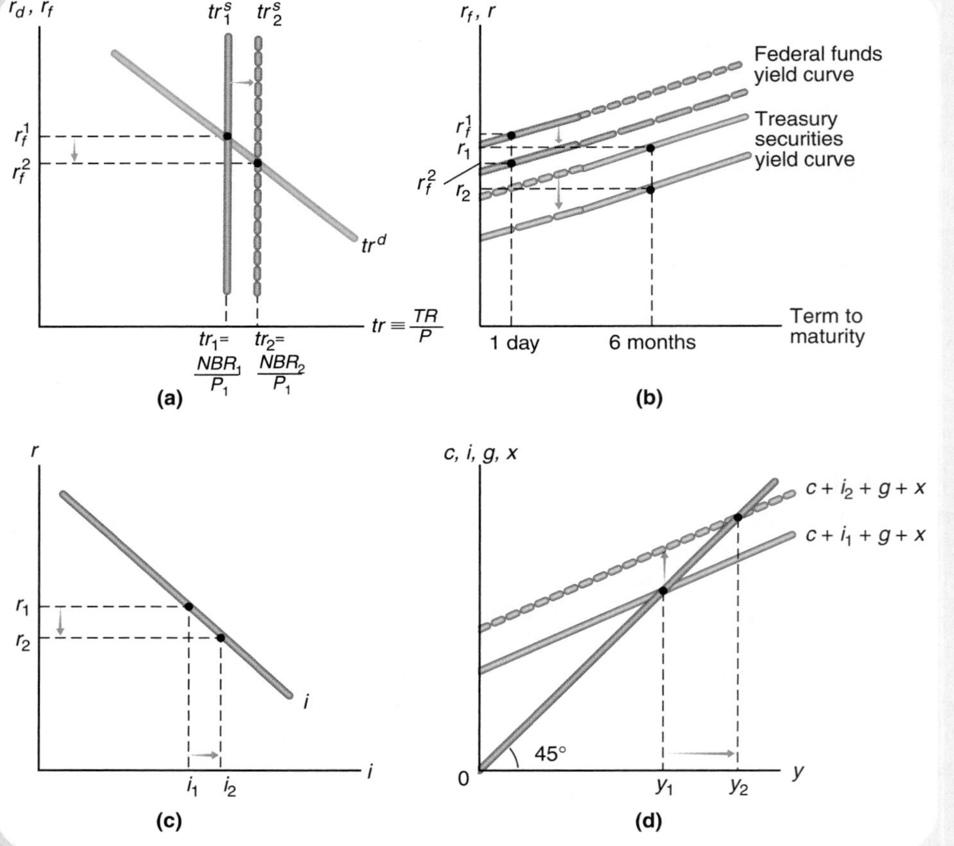

Figure 23-13
Monetary Policy Effects on Equilibrium Real Income.

Panel (a) shows the effect of an open market purchase that increases the nominal quantity of nonborrowed reserves in the banking system. With an unchanged price level, this action increases the supply of real total reserves and induces a decline in the equilibrium federal funds rate. As long as financial market traders believe that the Fed's policy action will be sustained, the federal funds and Treasury securities yield curves shift downward in panel (b). Thus, the longer-term interest rate declines, and real desired investment rises, as shown in panel (c). This causes the aggregate expenditures schedule to shift upward in panel (d), so that equilibrium real income increases.

If financial market traders interpret the Fed's policy action as one that is intended to bring about a long-lasting reduction in the equilibrium federal funds rate, then the expectations theory of the term structure of interest rates (see Chapter 4) indicates that the federal funds yield curve must shift downward in panel (b), as the expected federal funds rates for future days and weeks decrease. As long as the risk structure of interest rates remains unchanged, this also induces a downward shift in the Treasury securities yield curve. Thus, the longer-term interest rate relevant to business investment decisions decreases to r_2.

These declines in interest rates induced by the Fed's open market purchase without a change in the price level constitute the **liquidity effect** of monetary policy. It is called a liquidity effect because the open market purchase raises the overall liquidity in the economy. Depository institutions, individuals, and firms will be satisfied with the higher level of liquidity that results only if equilibrium nominal interest rates decline. Recall from Chapter 4 that interest rates and bond prices are inversely related. The rise in bond prices caused by declining interest rates discourages individuals from buying additional bonds because of their concern that future bond price declines will yield capital losses. Thus, as long as interest rates decline and bond prices increase, people will be willing to hold the larger quantity of money in circulation that results from the open market purchase.

Liquidity effect: A fall in the equilibrium nominal interest rate resulting from sustained open market purchases, holding the price level unchanged.

Interest-elastic reserve demand: Demand for depository institution reserves that is relatively sensitive to interest rate variations.

In panel (c), the decline in longer-term interest rates that influence business investment decisions generates an increase in desired investment spending, from i_1 to i_2. In turn, this increase in investment spending causes the aggregate expenditures schedule to shift upward in panel (d). As a result, equilibrium real income increases. The amount of the increase in real income, from y_1 to y_2, depends on the size of the autonomous spending multiplier, $1/(1 - MPC)$.

THE KEYNESIAN MONETARY POLICY TRANSMISSION MECHANISM The example above illustrates the *Keynesian monetary policy transmission mechanism,* which is the fundamental Keynesian explanation for how a monetary policy action is ultimately transmitted to real income. Our discussion indicates that there are two linkages by which this transmission takes place. First, an increase in nonborrowed reserves caused by an open market purchase brings about a liquidity effect that reduces equilibrium nominal interest rates. Second, a resulting general decline in interest rates causes desired investment and desired expenditures to rise. In the end, therefore, as summarized in Figure 23-14 on the next page, an expansionary monetary policy induces a rise in equilibrium real income.

According to this proposed mechanism, the amount of the effect of a monetary policy action depends on two factors. One is the size of the liquidity effect on the general level of interest rates. If the liquidity effect is large, then the ultimate effect of a monetary policy action is more likely to be sizable. If the liquidity effect is small, then the ultimate effect on real income is more likely to be negligible. The size of the liquidity effect, in turn, depends on two things:

1. **The elasticity of the demand for real depository institution reserves.** If there is a situation of relatively **interest-elastic reserve demand**—so that a given percentage change in the federal funds rate causes a relatively large proportionate change in the quantity of reserves demanded—then an open market operation induces a relatively small change in the overnight federal

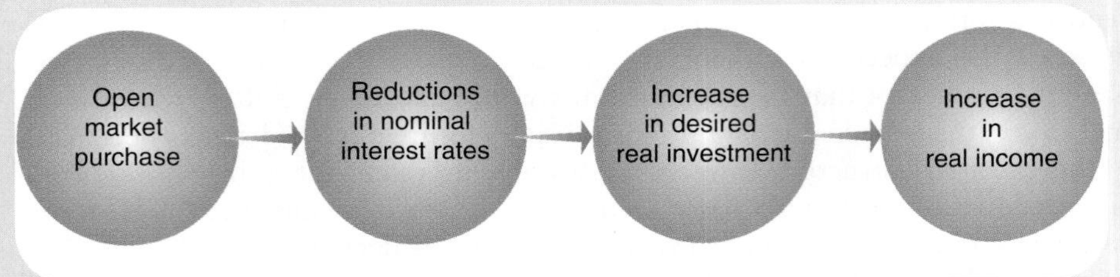

Figure 23-14 The Keynesian Transmission Mechanism of Monetary Policy.

According to the Keynesian model, an expansionary monetary policy action, such as a sustained policy of open market purchases, induces a liquidity-effect reduction in equilibrium interest rates. This in turn induces an increase in desired investment spending, which brings about a rise in equilibrium real income.

funds rate. In contrast, in a situation of relatively **interest-inelastic reserve demand**—so that a given percentage change in the federal funds rate causes a relatively small proportionate change in the quantity of reserves demanded—an open market operation induces a relatively large change in the federal funds rate. Consequently, the lower the interest elasticity of the demand for reserves, the larger will be the liquidity effect resulting from a change in the quantity of money.

2. The effects on the positions and slopes of yield curves relating short-term interest rates to longer-term interest rates that affect investment-spending choices of firms. In our example, we assumed that financial market traders perceived the monetary policy action as intended to bring about a long-lasting reduction in the equilibrium federal funds rate. Thus, they believe that the reduction in the daily federal funds rate will be sustained into the foreseeable future. If individuals and firms perceive that an expansionary monetary policy action today is likely to be reversed in the next few days or weeks, however, then yield curves are unlikely to shift very much at longer maturities. As a result, the effect of the policy action on longer-term interest rates is likely to be relatively small. (Note that this means that the *credibility* of the Fed's policy plans is very important, an issue we shall explore in detail in Chapter 26.)

Interest-inelastic reserve demand: Demand for depository institution reserves that is relatively insensitive to interest rate variations.

Interest-inelastic desired investment: Desired investment spending that is relatively insensitive to interest rate variations.

Interest-elastic desired investment: Desired investment spending that is relatively sensitive to interest rate variations.

The second factor that helps determine the amount by which a monetary policy action affects equilibrium real income is the interest elasticity of desired investment. This is the proportionate response of desired investment spending to a given percentage change in longer-term interest rates relevant to investment decisions. In a situation with relatively **interest-inelastic desired investment,** a given change in the interest rate will have a comparatively small effect on desired investment, aggregate desired expenditures, and real income. In a situation with relatively **interest-elastic desired investment,** a given change in the interest rate will have a comparatively larger effect on desired investment, aggregate desired expenditures, and real income. Therefore, the more interest-elastic desired investment spending is, the stronger the second linkage in the monetary policy transmission mechanism will be.

We can conclude that, according to the Keynesian monetary policy transmission mechanism, a constant-price increase in nonborrowed reserves via an open market purchase will cause the equilibrium level of nominal interest rates to fall, desired investment expenditures to increase, and the equilibrium level of real income to rise. A constant-price decrease in nonborrowed reserves via an open market sale will cause the equilibrium level of nominal interest rates to rise, desired investment expenditures to decline, and the equilibrium level of real income to fall. The size of the effect on real income will be larger when the demand for real depository institution reserves is relatively more interest-inelastic, when financial market participants believe the monetary policy action is intended to be long-lasting, and when desired investment spending is relatively more interest-elastic.

MONETARY POLICY AS A TOOL OF ECONOMIC STABILIZATION The example depicted in Figure 23-13 on page 576 illustrates how monetary policy might be used to help offset the cyclical effects of changes in aggregate net autonomous expenditures.

Suppose, for instance, that the real income level y_2 in the figure is the income level consistent with the economy's long-run growth path but that a reduction in aggregate net autonomous expenditures—say, a fall in autonomous export spending by foreign residents—had previously induced a decline in real income to the level y_1. A clear implication of the basic Keynesian model, which Figure 23-13 illustrates, is that expansionary open market operations can be used to push equilibrium real income back up to its long-run level. In this way, the basic Keynesian framework indicates that monetary policy may be useful for smoothing out business cycles. (The Bank of Japan has been experiencing difficulties in smoothing cycles in the Japanese economy; see on the following page *Global Focus: Is Japan Caught in a "Liquidity Trap"?*)

Whether monetary policy can really stabilize real economic activity in this manner has been one of the most widely debated issues in economics. We will devote considerable attention to it in Chapters 24 and 25. Before we explore this broad topic further, however, let's consider another issue raised by our example: Namely, can monetary policy assist in balancing a nation's international trade flows with other nations?

moneyxtra!

Online Case Study

To consider how to conduct monetary policy in the Keynesian system, go to the Chapter 23 Case Study, entitled "Using the Keynesian Transmission Mechanism of Monetary Policy.
http://moneyxtra.swcollege.com

5. Why does the basic Keynesian model indicate that there may be a potential stabilizing role for monetary policy? The basic Keynesian theory indicates that business cycles result from changes in aggregate net autonomous expenditures that induce multiplier effects on equilibrium real income, thereby pushing it alternately above and below the level consistent with an economy's long-run growth potential. The Keynesian transmission mechanism for monetary policy indicates that central bank policy actions in the market for depository institution reserves can influence short-term interest rates, thereby affecting longer-term interest rates, desired investment spending, and equilibrium real income. Thus, monetary policy actions can, at least in principle, induce changes in equilibrium real income that help smooth business cycles.

GLOBAL Focus | POLICY | CYBER | MANAGEMENT

Is Japan Caught in a "Liquidity Trap"?

Since the early 1990s, Japan has faced rising unemployment, price deflation, and sluggish growth in real income. The nation's central bank, the Bank of Japan, has responded by reducing interest rates in an effort to stimulate real expenditures. As Figure 23-15 indicates, by early 1999 short-term interest rates in Japan were virtually zero.

Keynes suggested that very low interest rates could create a *liquidity trap*, or a situation in which interest rates are so low that very few people are willing to hold bonds instead of the most liquid asset, money. Thus, a central bank effort to stimulate aggregate expenditures by boosting the quantity of money is rendered impotent by the willingness of domestic residents to hold money rather than spend it.

Evidence Favoring a Liquidity Trap

Two pieces of evidence point to the possible existence of a liquidity trap in Japan. One is the fact that interest rates in Japan have been so very low—the lowest for any major industrialized nation since the Great Depression of the 1930s.

Another piece of evidence is that even though the Bank of Japan has steadily increased bank reserves, the monetary base, and monetary aggregates, its actions have had little noticeable effect on economic activity. When the Bank of Japan has induced increases in reserves in the banking system, Japanese banks have seemed content to hold them alongside other assets that offer zero rates of return, and the Japanese public likewise has been willing to hold more cash in the form of currency and checking account balances. Thus, increases in bank reserves have not been bringing about increased spending on goods and services. Every month since the beginning of

Figure 23-15
Short-Term Interest Rates in Japan since 1990.

Interest rates have hovered near zero in Japan since 1999.

SOURCES: Michael Hutchison, "Japan's Recession: Is the Liquidity Trap Back?" Federal Reserve Bank of San Francisco *Economic Letter*, No. 2000-19, June 16, 2000; Bank of Japan.

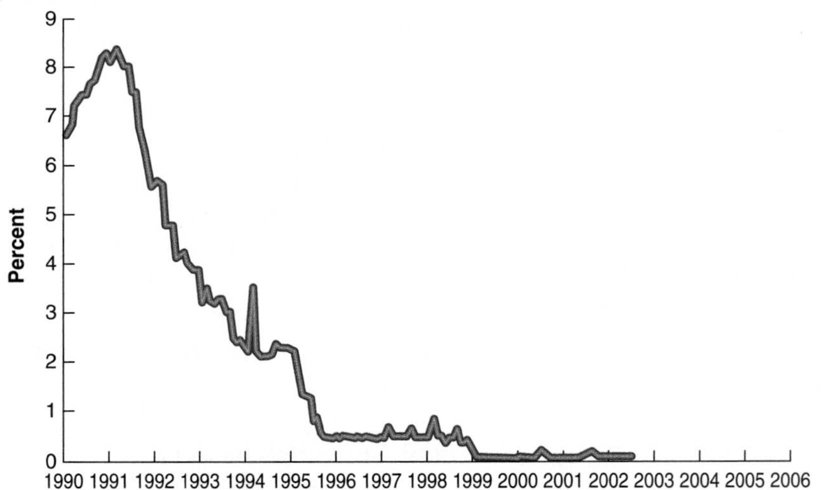

2000, Japan's M1 has grown at annual rates of 4 to 9 percent, and M2 has increased at annual rates of 2 to 4 percent, but the nation has continued to experience a series of recessions interrupted by short-lived, meager recoveries.

Is the Real Problem a Credit Crunch?

Not all economists are convinced that the Keynesian liquidity-trap story is correct. In their view, the fact that banks are holding new reserves instead of lending them out to individuals and businesses that might otherwise like to borrow at very low interest rates indicates that banks are intentionally withholding credit.

In fact, in the late 1980s and early 1990s, the value of properties that many Japanese borrowers purchased using bank loans fell below the amounts they had borrowed. This made it difficult for large numbers of borrowers to fully repay the banks. At the same time, Japanese banks suffered as the values of the shares of stock they held fell during a prolonged stock market slump. These events, some economists argue, produced a *credit crunch,* or a situation in which banks are reluctant to lend, either because they regard relatively few prospective borrowers as creditworthy or because they regard their own financial positions as too precarious to justify lending even to loan applicants who otherwise might be good credit risks. Thus, according to this credit-crunch perspective, bank pessimism, rather than extraordinarily low interest rates, is the reason the Japanese economy has remained in the doldrums since the mid-1990s.

For Critical Analysis: If the credit-crunch view of the Japanese situation is correct, can the Bank of Japan still play a role in helping to alleviate recessions?

Monetary Policy, National Income, and the Balance of Trade

It turns out that the Keynesian model does imply that, at least in principle, monetary policy can influence a nation's trade balance.

Exports, Imports, and National Income

As discussed in Chapter 21, the United States has run significant trade and current account deficits in recent years. What factors might explain such deficits? What monetary and other governmental policies might be enacted to address them? It turns out that we can apply the Keynesian model that we have just developed to give some initial answers to these questions.

The Trade Balance Schedule Recall that the balance of trade is equal to exports minus imports. Using the model developed in this chapter, we can explore factors that influence the trade balance by developing a *trade balance schedule.* Net export spending is equal to the quantity $x - im$. We assume that export spending is autonomous, so $x = x_0$, and the import function is $im = im_0 + (MPIM \times y_d)$. It follows that our measure of the trade balance is

$$\begin{aligned} x - im &= x_0 - im_0 - (MPIM \times y_d) \\ &= [x_0 - im_0 + (MPIM \times t_0)] - (MPIM \times y). \end{aligned}$$

As shown in panel (b) of Figure 23-16, this expression for the trade balance is a downward-sloping, straight-line function. We shall call this the *trade balance schedule*. The reason the trade balance schedule slopes downward is that a rise in aggregate real income raises household disposable income and stimulates higher import spending, which reduces the nation's balance of trade.

Note that a fall in autonomous exports or a rise in autonomous imports naturally would reduce the trade balance at any given level of real income. Consequently, a decline in x_0 or a rise in im_0 would reduce the intercept of the trade balance schedule, thereby *shifting* the trade balance schedule downward. In addition, a tax reduction would raise household disposable income even if total real income is unchanged, thereby worsening the trade balance. Therefore, a decline in autonomous net taxes, t_0, also reduces the value of the intercept of the trade balance schedule and shifts the schedule downward.

moneyxtra! Another Perspective

To think about factors that have contributed to relatively large trade deficits in the United States, go to the Chapter 23 reading, entitled "Is the Large U.S. Current Account Deficit Sustainable?" by Jill Holman of the Federal Reserve Bank of Kansas City.
http://moneyxtra.swcollege.com

The Equilibrium Balance of Trade Figure 23-16 illustrates the determination of the equilibrium trade balance. Panel (a) displays the income-expenditures approach to the determination of the equilibrium level of real income, y_1. We then can read off the trade balance schedule $x - im$ in panel (b) to determine the equilibrium trade balance $(x - im)_1$. As drawn, these diagrams show a situation in which there is a trade deficit, so $(x - im)_1 < 0$.

This theory of the equilibrium balance of trade can help to explain factors that cause a country to experience a trade deficit. Clearly, if all other things are unchanged, one factor that can induce a trade deficit is a high level of real income, which induces greater import spending that, in turn, reduces the trade balance. Holding other factors constant, higher growth of real output tends to improve the likelihood of running a trade deficit.

Figure 23-16
Determining the Equilibrium Trade Balance.

The trade balance is the difference between export spending and import expenditures, or $x - im$. Import expenditures rise as real income increases, so the trade balance declines with a rise in real income. Hence, the trade balance schedule slopes downward, as shown in panel (b). At a current equilibrium real income level, such as y_1, in panel (a), the equilibrium trade balance can be determined by reading off the trade balance schedule. Here, there initially is a trade deficit. To eliminate the trade deficit, policymakers might contemplate policies that would shift the trade balance schedule upward and to the right, as illustrated in panel (b).

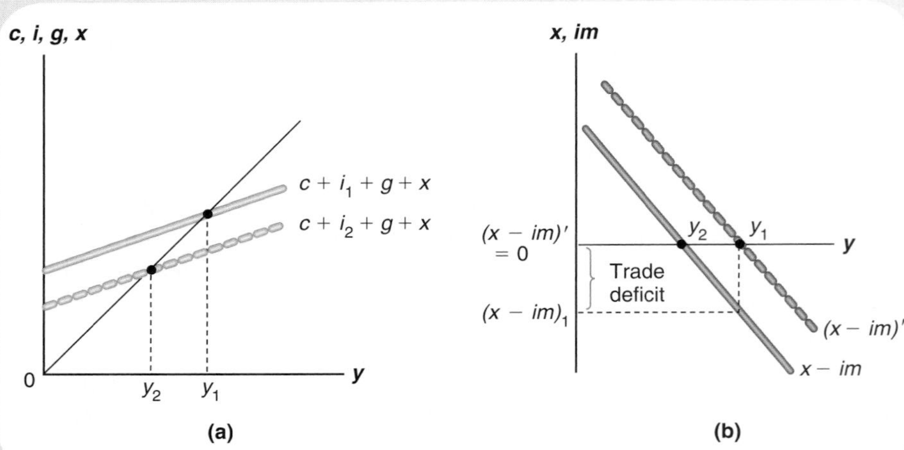

Monetary Policy and the Trade Balance

Can monetary or other governmental policies influence a nation's trade balance? Again, the Keynesian model answers a qualified "yes."

Expenditure-Switching Policies The most direct way to contemplate reducing a trade deficit is to try to induce an upward shift of the trade balance schedule. For example, if the trade balance schedule could be shifted to the position shown by the dashed schedule $(x - im)'$ in Figure 23-16 while holding equilibrium real income constant, then exports would equal imports, and the nation's trade would be balanced.

One way to try to accomplish such a shift would be to enact policies intended to increase autonomous exports and reduce autonomous imports. Economists call these **expenditure-switching policies,** because they induce home residents to reduce their purchases of foreign goods and services while giving foreign residents incentives to buy domestically produced goods and services. One direct expenditure-switching approach might be to provide subsidies to domestic industries to promote exports and to place tariffs on imports to discourage their consumption.

Expenditure-switching policies: Governmental policies, such as tariffs or subsidies, that induce an increase in export spending while reducing import spending, thereby improving a nation's trade balance.

Expenditure-reducing policies: Governmental policies, such as contractionary monetary policy actions, that reduce overall spending by home residents, thereby reducing import spending and improving a nation's trade balance.

Expenditure-Reducing Policies In principle, monetary policy could be used to achieve the same end effect on the trade balance. In the face of a sizable trade deficit, contractionary open market operations would raise the general level of interest rates, thereby discouraging investment spending and reducing aggregate expenditures, as shown by the shift to the dashed aggregate expenditures schedule in Figure 23-16. This would reduce equilibrium real income to y_2, thereby discouraging imports and achieving balanced trade along the $x - im$ schedule.

In this way, a sustained contractionary monetary policy could be used as an **expenditure-reducing policy.** Such policies induce cuts in overall domestic expenditures on all goods and services, including domestic output as well as foreign imports, in an effort to reduce a nation's trade deficit.

There is an obvious problem with using monetary policy as an expenditure-reducing means of achieving balanced trade. Although a contractionary monetary policy reduces the trade deficit, it achieves this effect at the cost of reduced real income for home residents. Thus, the basic Keynesian model indicates that achieving a trade balance via contractionary monetary policy can entail a significant price: a potentially reduced standard of living for a nation's residents.

6. How is the equilibrium trade balance determined, and what role may monetary policy play in affecting the size of the trade balance? Because import spending is positively related to disposable income, a nation's trade balance will, holding other factors unchanged, decline as its real income increases. Consequently, the equilibrium size of the trade balance varies with the equilibrium level of real income. One way to reduce a trade deficit is by instituting expenditure-switching policies that induce home residents to purchase fewer imported goods and services and to buy more domestically produced goods and services. Another approach is to use expenditure-reducing policies, such as a contractionary monetary policy, to induce lower spending on both home and foreign goods. The cost of this approach is reduced equilibrium real income at home.

Link to Policy

An Investment Recession

Most people link the recession that began in early 2001 to the terrorist attacks on New York and Washington, D.C., that took place in September of that year. The climate of uncertainty created by those attacks undoubtedly contributed to the economic downturn. Nevertheless, economists at the National Bureau of Economic Research (NBER) formally dated the onset of the recession to March 2001, six months before the attacks.

Accounting for the Decline in Aggregate Expenditures

Although determining when a recession has taken place is a "judgment call" on the part of NBER economists, in a typical recession aggregate real income *declines* for at least two quarters. In the traditional Keynesian framework, a fall in equilibrium real income takes place because of a decline in aggregate autonomous expenditures.

Economists did not have to look far to see two factors that likely contributed to a falloff in autonomous spending. Figure 23-17 displays real consumption, government spending, investment, and export expenditures since 1993. As you can see, government spending continued to grow as the recession commenced in early 2001, as did consumption, although the rate of increase in consumption began to decline at the recession's onset as the decline in real income generated a drop-off in induced consumption. Investment spending and export expenditures, which are both part of autonomous spending in the basic Keynesian model, fell just as the recession began. Hence, both of these factors contributed to bringing about the decline in U.S. real income that took place beginning in the spring of 2001.

The Main Culprit: Reduced Investment in Information Technology

A close look at Figure 23-17 indicates that export spending by foreign residents began to fall *after* the decline in U.S. investment. Although economists are still studying the role of exports in the 2001 recession, some believe that foreign exports began to fall partly *in response* to the onset of the U.S. downturn. As U.S. national income began to fall, so did import spending by U.S. residents, which dropped by 7 percent between the end of 2000 and the fall of 2001. The resulting decline in purchases of other nations' goods and services tended to depress incomes in those countries, whose residents then reduced their purchases of U.S. goods and services.

This leaves the drop in investment spending at the beginning of 2001 as the main factor that brought about the U.S. recession. This decline followed a major upswing in investment, which by 1998 had bypassed government spending as the second-largest component of aggregate expenditures on U.S. goods and services. The main factors accounting for the investment boom that ended in 2001 were purchases of equipment and software relating to information technologies, biotechnologies, and communications technologies. Figure 23-18 displays the considerable growth in investment in equipment and software from the beginning of 1993 until 2000. In the latter part of 2000, however, business purchases of equipment and software began to fall slightly, and this decline, which accelerated early in 2001, accounted for the bulk of the overall drop in investment spending that most economists agree was ultimately most responsible for bringing about the recession.

Research Project

Looking back at the components of aggregate spending on U.S. goods and services, which typically exhibits the most variation over time? In principle, could policymakers use this fact to help in forecasting and responding to recessions?

When the 2001 recession began, most members of the House and Senate agreed that either tax cuts or increases in government spending would boost aggregate spending and thereby raise real income, but they had trouble agreeing on whether to emphasize tax cuts or spending increases. Why?

WEB RESOURCE

For historical quarterly and annual data on the components of aggregate expenditures, go to the home page of the Bureau of Economic Analysis (http://www.bea.doc.gov), click on "Download the NIPA Tables," and then click on "Frequently Requested NIPA Tables," where you can select among tables displaying both nominal and real values of consumption, investment, government spending, and export expenditures as far back as 1929.

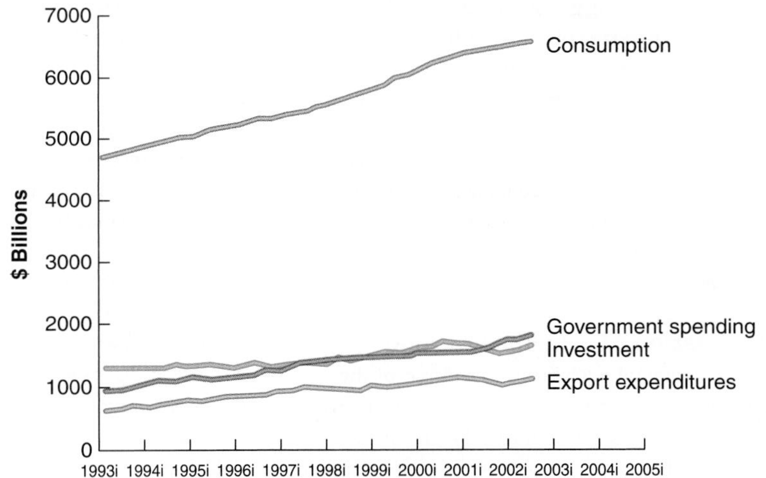

Figure 23-17
Real Consumption, Government Spending, Investment, and Exports since 1993.

Business investment expenditures leveled off in late 2000 and then dropped in early 2001, and export spending declined shortly thereafter.

SOURCE: *Economic Indicators*, various issues.

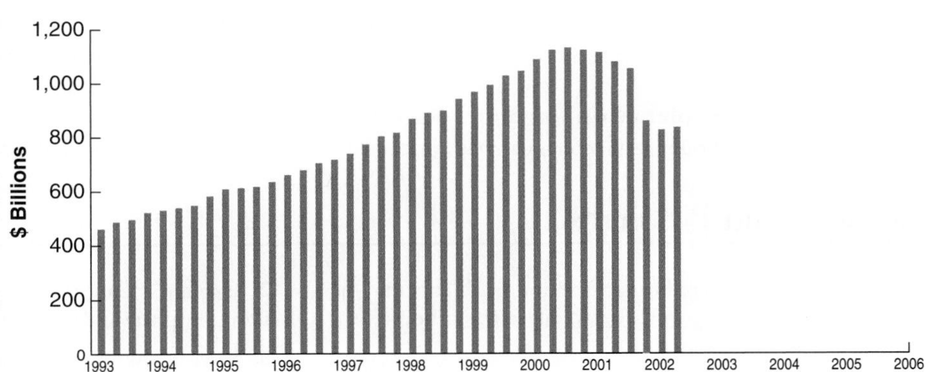

Figure 23-18
U.S. Equipment and Software Investment.

Business investment spending on equipment and software, which had risen steadily until 2000, then leveled off and abruptly declined at the end of 2000 and into 2001.

SOURCE: *Economic Indicators*, various issues.

Chapter Summary

1. The Key Relationships Implied by the Circular Flow of Income and Expenditures: One fundamental identity that can be inferred from the circular flow is the income identity. This identity says that households allocate their real income to domestic consumption, saving, taxes, and import spending. The other identity is the product identity, which states that the real value of output of goods and services is equal to real expenditures on that output in the form of household consumption, business investment, government spending, and export spending by foreign residents.

2. The Components of Aggregate Desired Expenditures in the Basic Keynesian Model: Aggregate desired expenditures are equal to the sum of household consumption of domestically produced goods and services, firms' desired investment spending, government expenditures, and export spending by foreigners. In the most basic Keynesian theory, desired investment, government spending and net taxes, and export spending are autonomous, but consumption spending is positively related to disposable income. Therefore, the aggregate expenditures schedule is upward sloping.

3. The Determination of Equilibrium Real Income: The fundamental equilibrium condition of the Keynesian model is that a nation's real income is equal to the aggregate desired expenditures on domestically produced goods and services by households, firms, the government, and foreign residents. This occurs where the aggregate expenditures schedule crosses the 45-degree line, so that $y = c + i + g + x$. It also occurs where total leakages from the economy's overall spending flow, $s + t + im$, equal reinjections, $i + g + x$.

4. The Keynesian Explanation for Short-Run Business Cycles: Equilibrium real income changes are a multiple of a change in aggregate net autonomous expenditures. As a result, changes in autonomous spending can cause equilibrium real income to vary from its long-run level. The amount by which real income diverges from the long-run level is equal to the change in aggregate net autonomous expenditures times the autonomous expenditures multiplier.

5. The Potential Stabilizing Role of Monetary Policy in the Basic Keynesian Model: According to Keynesian theory, open market operations induce changes in the federal funds rate, which, if the open market operations are expected to constitute a sustained policy, also lead to changes in longer-term interest rates that affect desired investment spending. Changes in desired investment expenditures, in turn, affect the equilibrium level of real income by changing aggregate net autonomous expenditures. Consequently, the potential exists for monetary policy to play a role in smoothing out variations in autonomous expenditures, thereby stabilizing real income and smoothing business cycles.

6. The Determination of the Equilibrium Trade Balance and the Relationship between Policies and the Trade Balance: Import spending is positively related to disposable income. Holding other factors equal, therefore, a nation's trade balance will tend to fall as its real income rises. In the event that a nation experiences a trade deficit at its current equilibrium real income level, it might improve its trade balance by implementing expenditure-switching policies, such as tariffs or subsidies, that induce domestic residents to cut back on imports while inducing foreign residents to increase their export spending. Alternatively, it could enact expenditure-reducing policies, such as a contractionary monetary policy, that generate reductions in spending on both domestically and foreign-produced goods and services.

Questions and Problems

(Answers to odd-numbered questions and problems may be found on the Web at http://money.swcollege.com under "Student Resources")

1. Refer to the circular flow diagram in Figure 23-1, and identify flows that constitute *leakages* from the economy's overall spending flow. Now identify the flows that are *reinjections* into the overall flow of expenditures. What is definitionally true of these leakages and reinjections? Explain.

2. Explain the meanings of the intercepts and slopes of the saving, import, and consumption functions.

3. In your own words, without reliance on any algebraic equations, explain why the marginal propensities to save, import, and consume domestic goods must sum to one.

4. In the simple Keynesian model, suppose that $MPS = 0.05$ and $MPC = 0.88$. What is the marginal propensity to import ($MPIM$)? If disposable income rises from \$900 billion to $1,000 billion, by how much will consumption rise? By how much will saving rise? By how much will imports rise? Is the sum of your answers equal to the change in income?

5. Explain, in your own words, the difference between desired investment and realized investment. Why are these two magnitudes equal at the equilibrium level of real income?

6. Suppose that the value of the autonomous expenditures multiplier is equal to 4. The marginal propensity to save is equal to 0.10, and the economy is open to international trade. What is the value of the marginal propensity to import? Show your work.

7. Suppose that the level of government spending is equal to $200 billion (in base-year dollars) and the level of real net taxes is equal to $100 billion. This economy is closed to international trade. In equilibrium, will saving be equal to real desired investment? Why or why not?

8. Suppose that equilibrium real income, in base-year dollars, is y = $500 billion. The consumption function is c = $50 + (0.75)$y_d$. Real net taxes are equal to $100 billion, and real government spending is equal to $125 billion.

a. What is the equilibrium level of consumption?

b. If real desired investment is equal to $10 billion, what is the amount of autonomous real exports?

9. Suppose that the Fed embarks on a policy of sustained sales of U.S. government securities. Use appropriate diagrams to evaluate the likely effects on market interest rates, desired investment expenditures, the equilibrium quantity of real money balances in circulation, and equilibrium real income, assuming that the price level remains unaffected by the Fed's policy stance.

10. Suppose that during a given interval the Fed keeps the discount rate one percentage point above the federal funds rate, leaves the required reserve ratio unaltered, and undertakes no open market operations. During the interval, however, the price level rises. Use appropriate diagrams to evaluate the likely effects of the price-level increase on market interest rates, desired investment expenditures, the equilibrium quantity of real money balances in circulation, and equilibrium real income. [Hint: Note that a rise in the price level, like a reduction in current-dollar nonborrowed reserves following open market sales as discussed in question 9, reduces the real quantity of nonborrowed reserves.]

Before the Test

Test your understanding of the material covered in this chapter by taking the Chapter 23 interactive quiz at http://money.swcollege.com.

Online Application

A quick way to keep up on the behavior of the components of GDP is via the "FRED" database made available on the Internet by the Federal Reserve Bank of St. Louis. You can use this information to understand which component of desired expenditures accounted for movements in equilibrium income.

Internet URL: **http://research.stlouisfed.org/fred/data/gdp.html**.

Title: Quarterly Gross Domestic Product and Components

Navigation: Begin at the home page of the Federal Reserve Bank of St. Louis (**http://www.stlouisfed.org**). Click on "Economic Research," and then click on "Economic Data—FRED." Then click on *Gross Domestic Product and Components.*

Application:

1. Under the heading, "Personal Income and Its Disposition (Monthly)," click on *Disposable Personal Income,* and write down disposable income for the most recent four years. Back up and click on *Personal Savings,* and write down savings data. Use these data to calculate the average propensity to save for each of these quarters.

2. Back up to *Gross Domestic Product and Components.* Now under "3 Decimal," click on *Real Gross Domestic Product in Chained 1996 Dollars.* Scan through the data since the mid-1960s. In what years did the largest variations in GDP take place? What component(s) of GDP appear to have accounted for these large movements?

For Group Study and Analysis: Divide the class into "consumption," "investment," "government-sector," and "foreign-sector" groups. Have each group evaluate the contribution of each category of spending to GDP and to its quarter-to-quarter volatility. Reconvene the class, and discuss the factors that appear to create the most variability in GDP.

Selected References and Further Readings

Branson, William. *Macroeconomic Theory and Policy.* New York: Macmillan, 1978.

Dillard, Dudley. *The Economics of John Maynard Keynes.* Englewood Cliffs, N.J.: Prentice Hall, 1948.

Hansen, Alvin. *A Guide to Keynes.* New York: Macmillan, 1953.

Hicks, John. "Mr. Keynes and the Classics: A Suggested Interpretation." *Econometrica* 5 (April 1937): 147–159.

Holman, Jill. "Is the Large U.S. Current Account Deficit Sustainable?" Federal Reserve Bank of Kansas City *Economic Review,* First Quarter 2001, pp. 5–23.

Keynes, John Maynard. *The General Theory of Employment, Interest, and Money.* New York: Harcourt Brace Jovanovich, 1964.

Klein, Lawrence. *The Keynesian Revolution,* 2d ed. New York: Macmillan, 1966.

LeKachman, Robert, ed. *Keynes and the Classics.* Boston: Heath, 1965.

Miller, Roger LeRoy, and David VanHoose. *Macroeconomics: Theories, Policies, and International Applications,* 3d ed. Cincinnati: ITP-Southwestern, 2004.

MoneyXtra

moneyxtra! Log on to the MoneyXtra Web site now (**http://moneyxtra.swcollege.com**) for additional learning resources such as practice quizzes, case studies, readings, and additional economic applications.

Chapter 24

Can Monetary Policy Have Long-Lasting Real Effects?—

Different Views on How Monetary Policy Affects the Economy

The unemployment rate in France has hovered close to or even above 10 percent for several years. In 2000, the French government decided to attack the problem directly: it cut the legal workweek from 39 hours to 35 hours for both hourly and salaried workers. Only senior managers and company executives were exempted. The government issued thousands of citations that alleged that senior managers of companies were working their employees too many hours and threatened them with fines of up to $1 million and prison terms of up to two years.

In response, French corporations began installing electronic time clocks in factory and office hallways. When workers arrived at their jobs, took coffee and lunch breaks, and departed at the end of the day, they had to swipe their ID cards through the clocks to formally record the time. To allow companies some flexibility, the government permitted employees to work more than 35 hours in some weeks, as long as they worked fewer than 35 hours in others. Workers could accumulate up to 15 hourly "work credits" in weeks when they exceeded the 35-hour threshold. Managers had to contact any worker who accumulated 15 credits and provide assistance in drawing up a plan to reduce the backlog. Any workaholics who persistently exceeded the 15-hour limit received special counseling to help them cut back on hours spent at work.

Fundamental Issues

1. What factors determine aggregate demand in the traditional Keynesian model?
2. What factors determine the shape and position of the Keynesian aggregate supply schedule?
3. According to traditional Keynesian theory, what are the price and output effects of expansionary monetary policies?
4. In what respects do modern economic theories reach similar and conflicting conclusions about the relationship between monetary policy and economic activity?

This French law, which was recently scaled back somewhat, was intended to tackle the nation's unemployment problem directly. The logic was that if companies had to cut back on hours for current employees, they would have an incentive to hire additional workers. Some economists, however, suspected that the problem in France and several other European nations was not so much a lack of rules and regulations as *too many* laws governing the conditions under which firms could hire and employ workers. Many also believed that monetary and fiscal policies and their broader effects on output and inflation had important ramifications for unemployment in France and the rest of Europe. In this chapter you will learn about the underpinnings of this potential relationship among output, inflation, and unemployment.

Aggregate Demand and Supply in the Keynesian Framework

The classical theory discussed in Chapter 22 concludes that aggregate demand depends primarily on the quantity of money supplied by a central bank such as the Federal Reserve. Hence, the quantity of money in circulation is the main determinant of the position of the aggregate demand schedule, which in the classical model is the set of real output–price level combinations for which people are satisfied holding the quantity of money supplied.

As we shall now discuss, the basic Keynesian model discussed in Chapter 23 also implies a theory of aggregate demand. In addition, the traditional Keynesian approach to understanding the relationship between money and economic activity also offers an alternative to the classical theory of aggregate supply. These competing theories yield very different implications about the capabilities of central banks to influence employment and real income levels.

Monetary Policy and the Keynesian Aggregate Demand Schedule

As we discussed in Chapter 23, the position of the reserve supply schedule in the market for real reserves depends on the price-level-adjusted quantity of nonborrowed reserves, NBR_1/P_1, where P_1 denotes the actual current value of the price level. Furthermore, as shown in panel (a) of Figure 24-1, the point where the reserve demand and supply schedules cross, labeled point A, determines the equilibrium federal funds rate, r_f^1, and the equilibrium real level of total reserves in the banking system, tr_1. Together, the term and risk structures of interest rates in financial markets then determine longer-term interest rates, such as the interest rate r_1 at point A in panel (b), that influence investment spending. Given the level of investment expenditures i_1 in panel (c), therefore, equilibrium real income is equal to y_1. In panel (d), this results in the price level–real income combination P_1 and y_1 at point A.

In Chapter 23, we focused on how monetary policy actions can influence equilibrium real income with an unchanging price level. Now let's consider how equilibrium real income responds to a change in the price level.

THE REAL BALANCE EFFECT As shown in panel (a) of Figure 24-1, a sustained rise in the price level to P_2 reduces the real value of nonborrowed reserves in the banking system and thereby shifts the reserve supply schedule leftward in the market for real depository institution reserves. The result is an increase in the equilibrium federal funds rate, to r_f^2 at point B.

Figure 24-1 Deriving the Keynesian Aggregate Demand Schedule.

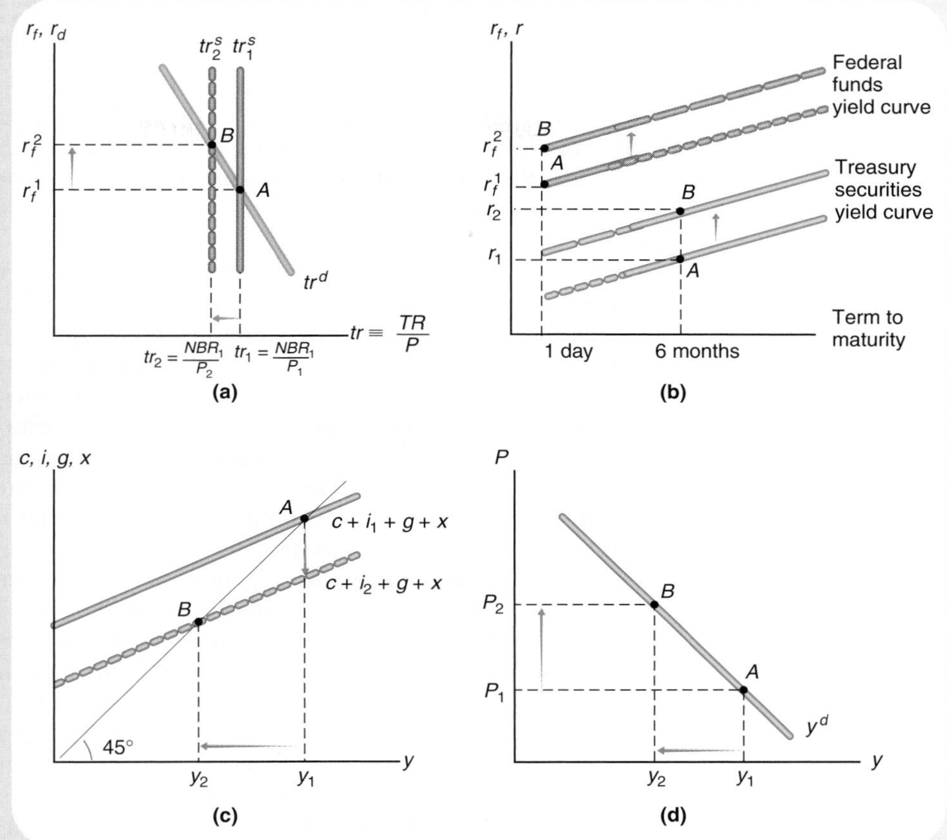

A sustained rise in the price level, from P_1 to P_2, reduces the real value of nonborrowed reserves from NBR_1/P_1 to NBR_1/P_2. Thus, the reserve supply schedule shifts leftward in panel (a). The result is a real-balance-effect increase in the equilibrium federal funds rate and, as shown in panel (b), upward shifts in the federal funds and Treasury securities yield curves. Panel (c) indicates that higher longer-term interest rates induce a decline in real desired investment spending, so equilibrium real income falls. Thus, as depicted in panel (d), the rise in the price level induces a decline in equilibrium real income. The price level–real income combinations P_1 and y_1 at the initial point A and P_2 and y_2 at the final point B in panel (d) lie along a downward-sloping aggregate demand schedule.

Because the price-level increase is sustained, financial market traders anticipate that future values of the federal funds rate will also be higher. Consequently, the expectations theory of the term structure implies that interest rates at longer terms to maturity will also increase. Thus, there is a rise in the longer-term interest rate from r_1 at point *A* in panel (b) to r_2 at point *B*. Economists call this increase in market interest rates caused by an increase in the price level the **real balance effect** because it results from a change in the real value of the nominal reserve balances generated by a change in the price level.

Real balance effect: An increase in the nominal rate of interest that results from an increase in the price level, holding total depository institution reserves unchanged.

THE AGGREGATE DEMAND SCHEDULE As shown in panel (c) of Figure 24-1, the increase in market interest rates stemming from a rise in the price level gives firms an incentive to reduce their investment spending. As a result, equilibrium real income declines from y_1 to y_2.

This generates a movement from the price level–real income combination P_1 and y_1 at point A in panel (d) to the combination P_2 and y_2 at point B. Points A and B lie along the Keynesian aggregate demand schedule, denoted y^d. Thus:

The Keynesian theory of aggregate demand stems directly from the *monetary transmission mechanism* of the basic Keynesian model. At all price-level and real income combinations along the Keynesian aggregate demand schedule, financial markets are in equilibrium, and income is equal to aggregate desired expenditures.

Monetary Policy and Aggregate Demand In Figure 24-1, we derived the aggregate demand schedule by considering only the real balance effect arising from an increase in the price level. All other factors, including monetary policy, were unchanged. This means that a change in other factors affecting the positions of the reserve demand or supply schedules, financial market yield curves, or aggregate desired expenditures would alter the position of the aggregate demand schedule. Among these are autonomous consumption, net taxes, and government spending. In the decades after Keynes, traditional interpretations of the implications of Keynesian theory emphasized the potential role of *fiscal policies*—government spending and tax policies—in influencing aggregate demand. Another key factor that can affect aggregate demand, however, is monetary policy.

For instance, suppose that the Fed embarks on a policy of open market purchases that increase the nominal quantity of nonborrowed reserves in the banking system from NBR_1 to a larger amount, NBR_2. Panel (a) of Figure 24-2 shows that at an initial real income–price level combination y_1 and P_1 at point A, the rise in nonborrowed reserves induces a rightward shift of the reserve supply schedule and a decline in the federal funds rate to r_f^2 at point B. As traders reduce their expectations of the federal funds rate for future days as well, the federal funds and Treasury securities yield curves shift down, and the longer-term interest rate relevant to investment-spending decisions falls from r_1 to r_2 in panel (b). This liquidity effect (see Chapter 23) on interest rates gives firms an incentive to increase investment spending. Thus, the aggregate expenditures schedule shifts upward in panel (c), and equilibrium real income rises, from y_1 at point A to y_2 at point B.

The new real income–price level combination y_2 and P_1 lies to the right of the original aggregate demand schedule, denoted $y^d(NBR_1)$ in panel (d). Nevertheless, this new point B in panel (d) is consistent with the financial market equilibrium points B in panels (a) and (b). In addition, it is consistent with equilibrium real income and expenditures at point B in panel (c). Because the Keynesian aggregate demand schedule is a set of real income–price level combinations that maintain equilibrium in financial markets and simultaneously equilibrate real income and aggregate desired expenditures, then point B in panel (d) must be on a *new* aggregate demand schedule. Consequently, a policy of sustained open market purchases by the Fed shifts the aggregate demand schedule to the right. This policy *increases aggregate demand.*

By way of contrast, a policy of sustained open market sales would reduce the supply of nonborrowed reserves, placing upward pressure on interest rates and, therefore, downward pressure on investment spending. Thus, open market sales

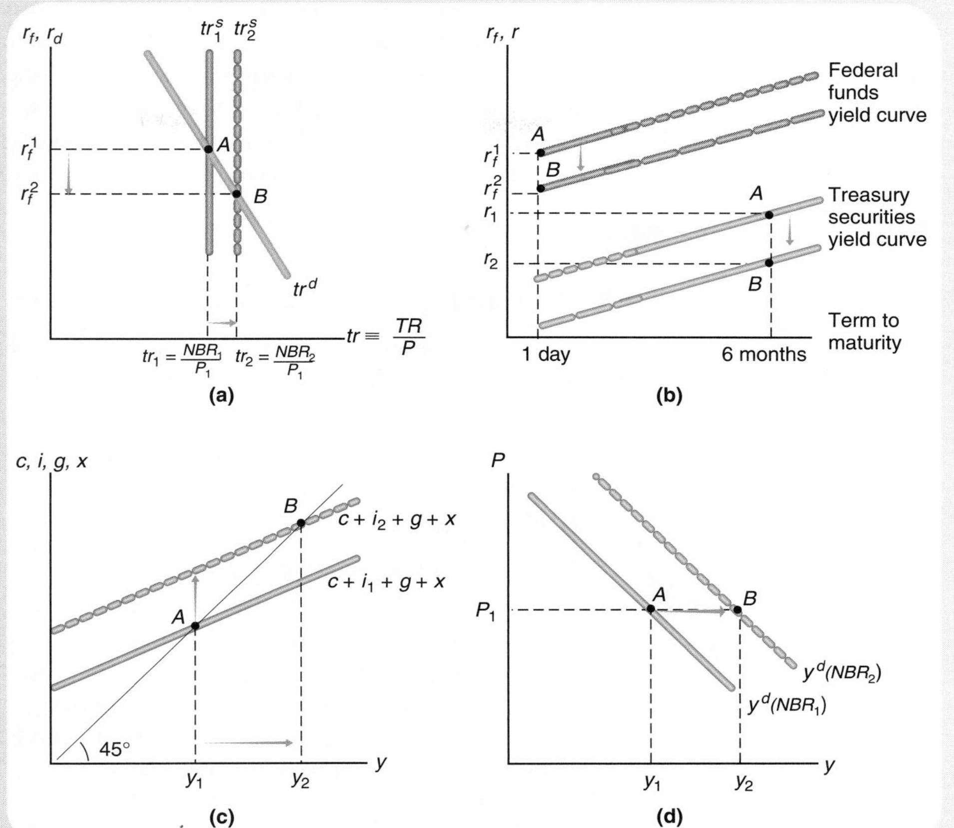

Figure 24-2
The Effect of Open Market Purchases on Aggregate Demand.

Given an unchanging price level, open market purchases increase the nominal quantity of nonborrowed reserves in the banking system from NBR_1 to NBR_2. Consequently, the reserve supply schedule shifts rightward in panel (a). The result is a liquidity-effect decrease in the equilibrium federal funds rate and, as shown in panel (b), downward shifts in the federal funds and Treasury securities yield curves. Panel (c) indicates that lower longer-term interest rates induce an increase in real desired investment spending, so equilibrium real income rises. As a result, as depicted in panel (d), there is movement to a new price level–real income combination P_1 and y_2 at a new point *B* to the right of the initial combination P_1 and y_1 at point *A*. Thus, the aggregate demand schedule shifts rightward in response to Fed open market purchases.

ultimately would cause equilibrium real income to fall at any given price level. The aggregate demand schedule would shift leftward as a result, so sustained open market sales would reduce aggregate demand.

It is important to recognize that the amount by which aggregate demand shifts as a result of a sustained change in the Fed's open market operations depends on the size of the liquidity effect that the change in nonborrowed reserves exerts and on the responsiveness of desired investment expenditures to a change in the level of interest rates. The sizes of these responses, in turn, depend on the interest elasticity of reserve demand and on the interest elasticity of desired investment. In other words, the size of the effect of a money-stock change on aggregate demand depends on the linkages of the Keynesian monetary policy transmission mechanism. As you learned in Chapter 23, the linkages in this mechanism strengthen as the demand for real depository institution reserves becomes more interest-inelastic and as desired investment spending becomes more interest-elastic.

1. What factors determine aggregate demand in the traditional Keynesian model? Any factors that influence aggregate desired expenditures affect the position of the Keynesian aggregate demand schedule. These include autonomous consumption, government spending, and taxation. In addition, however, monetary policy actions can alter interest rates and desired investment, thereby influencing the position of the Keynesian aggregate demand schedule.

Keynesian Aggregate Supply

Recall from Chapter 22 that the classical economists made three important assumptions when they examined the market for labor and derived the classical aggregate supply schedule:

1. Workers, consumers, and entrepreneurs are motivated by rational self-interest.
2. People do not experience money illusion.
3. Pure competition prevails in the markets for goods and services and for factors of production.

Proponents of the Keynesian approach to aggregate supply typically have no trouble accepting the first classical proposition. They doubt the generality of the latter two assumptions, however. They argue that because information is imperfect, in the short run people certainly have no choice but to exhibit money illusion, even if they are rationally motivated by self-interest. In addition, they contend that self-interest can induce workers and firms to set up institutional arrangements that inhibit pure competition, thereby making wages and prices less than fully flexible. We begin our discussion of the Keynesian approach to aggregate supply by considering the effects of wage stickiness. Then we discuss the implications of imperfect information for the theory of aggregate supply.

A Sticky-Wage Theory of Aggregate Supply Why might nominal wages be inflexible, or "sticky"? One possible explanation might be the existence of minimum-wage laws that place artificial floors on wages that firms can pay. In addition, organized groups of workers, such as unions, might seek to keep their nominal wages at levels that they feel are appropriate relative to other occupations. In a highly unionized economy, **explicit contracts**—legally binding contracts laying out the terms for workers' compensation, benefits, and so on—establish wages for specified periods; these contracts could also account for downward inflexibility of the nominal wage. Furthermore, a number of labor economists contend that workers and firms adopt **implicit contracts**, which are tacit agreements that firms will not reduce workers' wages when economic activity ebbs in exchange for the right not to raise wages as much when business conditions improve. Wide use of implicit contracts could make nominal wages relatively invariant to upturns and downturns of business cycles.

Explicit contracts: Contractual arrangements in which the terms of relationships between workers and firms, especially about wages, are in writing and legally binding upon both parties.

Implicit contracts: Unwritten agreements between workers and firms, concerning terms of employment such as wages, that may or may not be legally binding.

Recall from Chapter 22 that the aggregate supply schedule for an economy is the set of real output–price level combinations that maintain labor market equilibrium. To see how nominal wage inflexibility affects the nature of the aggregate supply schedule, consider Figure 24-3. Panel (a) of the figure is a labor market diagram where we measure the nominal wage on the vertical axis, panel (b) shows the aggregate production function, and panel (c) is a diagram of real output–price level combinations.

The Value of the Marginal Product of Labor To understand panel (a) in Figure 24-3, recall that we can express a purely competitive firm's profit-maximizing condition, $P = MC$ (marginal cost), as

$$P = W/MP_N,$$

where W is the nominal wage and MP_N is the marginal product of labor. If we multiply both sides of this equation by MP_N, we get $P \times MP_N = W/MP_N = (W/MP_N) \times MP_N = W$. This expression indicates that an alternative way to express the firm's profit-maximizing condition is

$$W = P \times MP_N.$$

This expression tells us that a purely competitive, profit-maximizing firm should employ labor to the point at which the money wage that the firm pays each unit

Figure 24-3
Keynesian Aggregate Supply Schedule with Wage Inflexibility.

A rise in the price level causes an increase in the value of labor's marginal product, $MP_N \times P$. As a result, the demand for labor by firms increases. If the money wage were flexible, as in the classical model, then the labor supply schedule would shift back to the left, because workers would perceive a decline in their real wage due to higher prices and respond by supplying fewer labor services at any money wage. Thus, in the classical model, equilibrium employment would remain unchanged, at N_1 at point C in panel (a). With an inflexible money wage, however, the rise in labor demand induces an increase in employment via a movement from point A to point B in panel (a), causing production of output to increase [panel (b)]. Consequently, a rise in the price level induces an increase in real output and a movement from point A to point B in panel (c), so the aggregate supply schedule slopes upward.

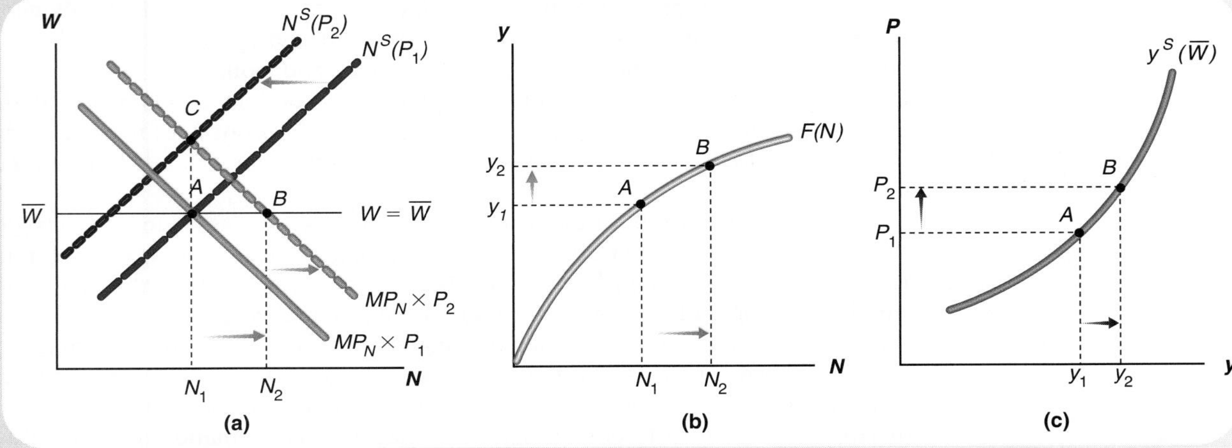

Value of the marginal product of labor: The marginal product of labor times the price of output.

of labor is equal to the price it receives for each unit of output that labor produces times the marginal product of labor. This quantity, $P \times MP_N$, is the **value of the marginal product of labor,** or VMP_N. For instance, if the market price of a firm's output is \$2 per unit of output and the marginal product of labor is 10 units of output per unit of labor, then the value of labor's marginal product is equal to the product of these two figures, or \$20 per unit of labor. As you learned in Chapter 22, the MP_N schedule generally slopes downward. Thus, $VMP_N = P \times MP_N$ is also a downward-sloping relationship known as the *value-of-marginal-product-of-labor schedule,* or VMP_N schedule. Because firms hire workers to the point at which $W = P \times MP_N$, the VMP_N schedule is a representation of firms' demand for labor.

In the classical model, given a current price level P_1, the quantity of labor supplied increases as the nominal wage increases. Thus, the labor supply normally is the dashed schedule $N^s(P_1)$ in panel (a). If the general level of nominal wages is determined by legal requirements and explicit and implicit contracts, however, the aggregate wage rate in the economy may be regarded as fixed in the short run, at $W = \overline{W}$. This means that workers supply whatever amount of labor firms demand at this nominal wage. Because the price level is P_1, then the value-of-marginal-product schedule, $MP_N \times P_1$, represents the labor demand schedule. Consequently, at the fixed nominal wage $W = \overline{W}$, the amount of labor demanded is equal to N_1 at point A in panel (a). Referring to the aggregate production function in panel (b), this yields the level of real output y_1. Consequently, at the price level P_1, the real output level consistent with equilibrium employment with a fixed nominal wage W is y_1. This is one point, labeled point A in panel (c), on the economy's aggregate supply schedule.

Sticky Wages and Aggregate Supply Now consider the effect of a rise in the price level, from P_1 to P_2. This causes the value of labor's marginal product to rise to $MP_N \times P_2$. Hence, the demand for labor increases, as shown in panel (a) of Figure 24-3. In the classical model, the labor supply would decline, from $N^s(P_1)$ to $N^s(P_2)$, because workers would recognize that the rise in the price level reduces the real wage that they earn. Thus, in the classical theory the resulting labor market equilibrium would be at point C, with no change in employment. But if nominal wages are fixed through laws and contracts, then the classical labor supply schedule no longer plays any role, and point C is not attained. Instead, the rise in labor demand leads to an increase in employment to the amount N_2, at point B in panel (a). As a result, real output rises to y_2 in panel (b). The result is a new real output–price level combination y_2 and P_2 at point B in panel (c).

Points A and B are both consistent with fixed-wage equilibrium outcomes in the labor market. Therefore, both of these points lie on an upward-sloping *Keynesian aggregate supply schedule.* Because we have derived this aggregate supply schedule under the assumption that the nominal wage is fixed at $W = \overline{W}$, we label it $y^s(\overline{W})$. Note also that the aggregate supply schedule is convex, or bowed upward. The reason is that the production function is concave, or bowed downward (due to the law of diminishing marginal returns), and so successive increases in the price level stimulate increases in labor demand and in employment that induce successively smaller gains in real output production.

Finally, because we derive the aggregate supply schedule for a *given* fixed wage, a change in the fixed nominal wage rate will require us to derive a new aggregate supply schedule. At a higher nominal wage, employment levels and, hence, corresponding output levels will always be lower. As a result, the amounts of real output corresponding to various price levels will be lower; therefore, if the fixed nominal wage increases, the aggregate supply schedule will lie to the left of its original position. A rise in the nominal wage, perhaps as a result of union demands for wage increases or from an increase in the legal minimum wage, will shift the aggregate supply schedule upward and to the left. The higher value for the fixed nominal wage will reduce aggregate supply.

AN IMPERFECT-INFORMATION THEORY OF AGGREGATE SUPPLY Keynesian proponents also disagree with the classical assumption that people never exhibit money illusion. They argue that real-world individuals live in a world of uncertainty, where information about the actual current price level is not always available and people are never fully informed about *future* events.

Anticipating the Market Wage These considerations mean that when workers decide how much labor to supply, they must base their decision on their *perception* of what the current real wage is and on their *anticipation* of what it will be during the period that they agree to work at that wage. In other words, workers must form an *expectation* of the value of the real wage that they will earn if they work at any given nominal wage that a firm offers. To do this, workers must form an expectation of the price level, which we shall denote P^e.

To see how imperfect information motivates a Keynesian theory of aggregate supply, consider Figure 24-4 on the next page. Here, we assume that there is no wage stickiness, so that nominal wages are flexible. Thus, as in the classical model, the equilibrium nominal wage is determined by the intersection of the labor demand and labor supply schedules in panel (a). If the current price level is equal to P_1, then the labor demand schedule is the value of labor's marginal product, $MP_N \times P_1$. If workers base their labor supply decisions on their expectation of the overall price level, however, then the position of the labor supply schedule depends on their price expectation. Let's suppose that the specific value of this price expectation is $P^e = P_1$, so that workers anticipate that the price level during their period of employment will be equal to P_1, and the position of the labor supply schedule is given by $N^s(P^e = P_1)$. Consequently, at point A in each panel of Figure 24-4, workers correctly anticipate the *actual* price level. Given this correct expectation, the equilibrium nominal wage in panel (a) is equal to W_1, and equilibrium employment is equal to N_1. The amount of real output produced is equal to y_1 in panel (b), and the resulting real output–price level combination is y_1 and P_1 in panel (c).

Consider, however, what occurs if the price level rises above the value P_1 that workers had expected, to a larger value equal to P_2. Because information about this change is not immediately available, workers do not instantaneously recognize that it has taken place. Thus, they maintain their price expectation at $P^e = P_1$, and the position of the labor supply schedule in panel (a) is unchanged. Firms, however, observe the rise in the prices of the products they sell and the resulting increase in the value of labor's marginal product, to $MP_N \times P_2$. Labor demand rises, and the equilibrium nominal wage rises to W_2 at point B in panel (a).

Figure 24-4
Keynesian Aggregate Supply with Imperfect Information.

If workers have imperfect information about price changes, then their price expectations can fail to reflect actual price movements. As a result, the position of the labor supply schedule does not adjust immediately to a change in the price level. An increase in the price level raises the value of labor's marginal product, $MP_N \times P$, thereby raising the demand for labor by firms and inducing a movement along the labor supply schedule from point *A* to point *B* in panel (a). As shown in panel (b), this causes an increase in the production of output. Hence, a rise in the price level induces an increase in real output and a movement from point *A* to point *B* in panel (c). The aggregate supply schedule slopes upward.

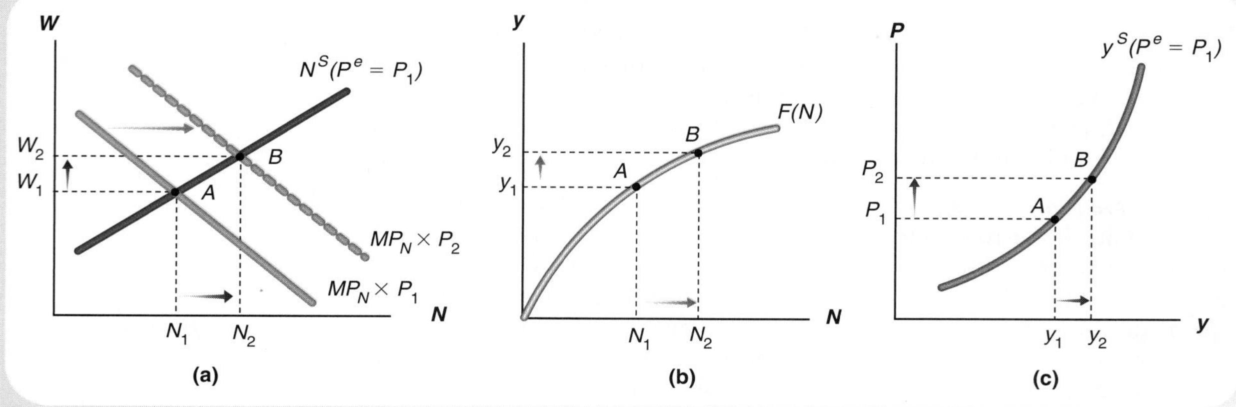

The Aggregate Supply Schedule Because workers do not have sufficient information to realize that the nominal wage has risen because of an increase in the price level, they perceive an increase in the real wage. Workers therefore supply more labor services, as shown by a movement upward along the labor supply schedule to the new equilibrium employment level N_2 at point *B*. As shown in panel (b), this rise in employment then induces an increase in real output, from y_1 to y_2. As a result, there is a new real output–price level combination, y_2 and P_2 at point *B* in panel (c), that lies above and to the right of the original combination at point *A*. The schedule containing both point *A* and point *B* is the aggregate supply schedule. We label this schedule $y^s(P^e = P_1)$, because we have derived it given this specific value for workers' expected price level.

Now consider what would happen if workers increase their price expectation. This would shift the labor supply schedule back to the left somewhat. Then we could again go through an aggregate supply derivation like the one in Figure 24-4. But for any given price level, we would plot lower employment and output levels. Consequently, the aggregate supply schedule that we would derive would lie to the left of the one in Figure 24-4. We can conclude that a rise in the expected price level would shift the aggregate supply schedule leftward. That is, higher price expectations would reduce aggregate supply.

This Keynesian aggregate supply schedule, like the one we derived for the case of inflexible nominal wages, slopes upward and has a convex, or bowed, shape. In this case, however, the rationale for the slope and shape of the aggregate supply schedule is imperfect information. As you can see, removing *either* the classical assumption of pure, unhindered determination of market wages *or* the classical presumption that workers do not experience money illusion is sufficient to produce an upward-sloping aggregate supply schedule. We may conclude that in the Keynesian model there is a positive relationship between the price level and the amount of real output produced by firms.

2. What factors determine the shape and position of the Keynesian aggregate supply schedule? There are two traditional Keynesian theories of aggregate supply, and both imply that the aggregate supply schedule slopes upward and is convex. One proposes that nominal wages are inflexible. According to this theory, a rise in nominal wages following union demands for higher wages or increases in a legal minimum wage will shift the aggregate supply schedule upward and to the left. The other theory follows from the assumption that workers have imperfect information. This theory indicates that a higher expectation of the price level shifts the aggregate supply schedule upward and leftward.

Monetary Policy in the Keynesian Market for Real Output

Let's summarize the Keynesian theories of aggregate demand and aggregate supply. The Keynesian aggregate demand schedule is the set of all combinations of real income for which financial markets are in equilibrium and aggregate desired expenditures equal real income. The aggregate demand schedule slopes downward, and its position depends on the stance of monetary policy and on other factors that influence aggregate expenditures.

The Keynesian aggregate supply schedule slopes upward, either because of nominal wage inflexibility or because workers have imperfect information concerning the price level. For the remainder of this chapter, we shall simply draw the aggregate supply schedule as upward sloping (and convex) without offering a specific rationale for the upward slope unless one is required for the issue under consideration.

Combining Aggregate Demand and Aggregate Supply

Figure 24-5 on the next page combines the two schedules on a diagram of the market for real output. They cross at point E, where the equilibrium price level, labeled P_1, is determined. Several conditions hold simultaneously at point E:

1. Because point E is on the aggregate demand schedule, aggregate desired expenditures are equal to the level of real income y_1.

2. Because point E is on the aggregate demand schedule, financial markets are in equilibrium at the current level of interest rates.

3. Because point E is on the aggregate supply schedule, workers and firms are willing and able to produce the level of real output y_1 at the price level P_1.

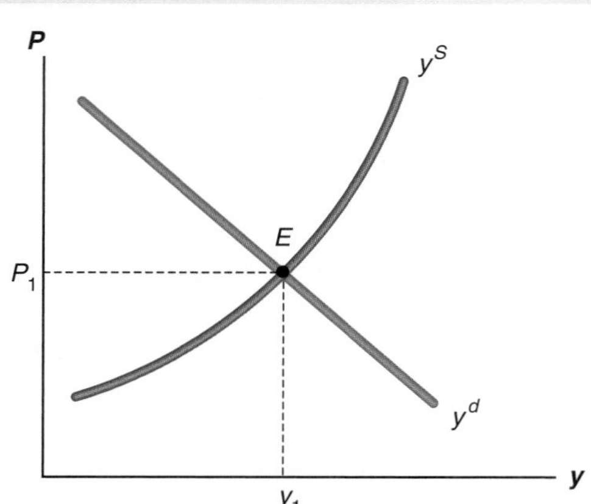

Figure 24-5
Equilibrium in the Keynesian Market for Real Output.

In the Keynesian model, the equilibrium price level and the equilibrium level of real output arise at the intersection of the aggregate demand and aggregate supply schedules. This point, denoted *E*, is on the aggregate demand schedule and corresponds to a point at which the market for depository institution reserves is in equilibrium and real income is equal to aggregate desired expenditures. At the same time, this point is on the aggregate supply schedule. At the price level corresponding to point *E*, therefore, workers and firms are willing and able to produce the equilibrium real output level.

Point *E* satisfies all these conditions given the factors that determine the positions of the aggregate demand and aggregate supply schedules. Changes in aggregate desired expenditures, which may be induced by monetary policy actions, can change the positions of the schedules and thereby alter the location of point *E*.

Monetary Policy, Prices, and Real Output

In the classical theory discussed in Chapter 22, monetary policy actions can influence aggregate demand. Because the aggregate supply schedule is vertical, however, monetary policy actions cannot affect equilibrium real output. As a result, the classical approach to monetary theory implies that money is neutral in its effects on real economic activity.

Money is *nonneutral* in the Keynesian monetary framework. To understand why this is so, consider Figure 24-6. At an initial output market equilibrium at point *E*, with the nominal quantity of nonborrowed reserves NBR_1, the aggregate demand schedule is given by $y^d(NBR_1)$, and the equilibrium price level and quantity of real output are equal to P_1 and y_1, respectively. Suppose now that the Fed embarks on a policy of sustained open market purchases and raises the amount of nonborrowed reserves in the banking system from NBR_1 to a larger amount, NBR_2. This action causes the level of interest rates to decline, thereby stimulating investment spending and pushing up real income and desired spending on real output at point *F.*

After the rightward shift in aggregate demand from $y^d(NBR_1)$ to $y^d(NBR_2)$, however, workers and firms continue to produce only the real output level y_1 at the price level P_1. They are willing and able to increase production only if the

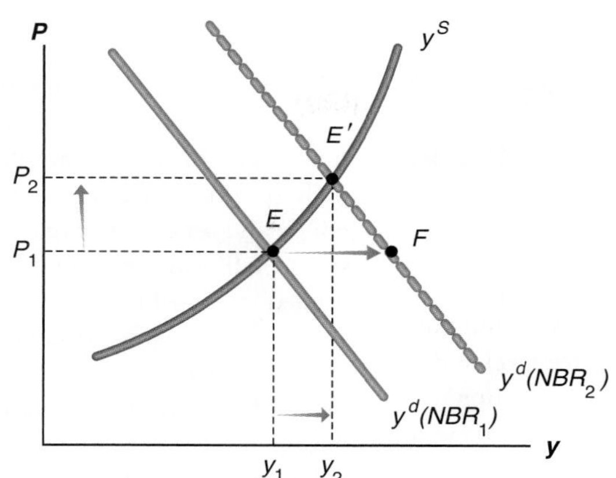

Figure 24-6
The Price-Level and Real Output Effects of Expansionary Monetary Policy.

Open market purchases by the Fed increase nonborrowed reserves and induce a rightward shift of the aggregate demand schedule by the distance $F - E$. Nevertheless, workers and firms will be willing to produce more real output only if the price level increases, as shown by an upward movement from point E to point E' along the aggregate supply schedule. On net, the expansionary monetary policy action leads to a rise in the equilibrium price level and an increase in the equilibrium level of real output.

price level rises to P_2. This induces a movement upward along the aggregate supply schedule, from point E to point E'. The rise in the price level causes a decline in the amount of real nonborrowed reserves in the banking system, so that reserve demand tends to decline somewhat in the market for real depository reserves. This causes a real balance effect that raises the level of interest rates somewhat and generates a movement back along the new aggregate demand schedule, from point F to point E', and a fall in the quantity of real output demanded, to y_2.

On net, therefore, a central bank expansion of the nominal money stock increases both the equilibrium price level *and* equilibrium real output. Because monetary policy is nonneutral in the Keynesian model, proponents of this model typically prescribe expansionary or contractionary monetary policy actions to stabilize real economic activity. The notion that the Federal Reserve and other central banks can stabilize real output—and, by implication, employment—contrasts sharply with the classical position, which contends that price-level stabilization is all that monetary policy can accomplish. (Recently, officials of the Bank of Japan have claimed that they cannot stimulate aggregate demand but that if they were to try, too much inflation would result; see on the following page *Global Focus: The Bank of Japan Tries to Have It Both Ways.*)

3. According to traditional Keynesian theory, what are the price and output effects of expansionary monetary policies? In the Keynesian aggregate demand–aggregate supply model, a Federal Reserve policy of sustained open market purchases causes an increase in aggregate demand. The results are a rise in the equilibrium price level and an increase in equilibrium real output.

GLOBAL Focus | POLICY | CYBER | MANAGEMENT

The Bank of Japan Tries to Have It Both Ways

Since the mid-1990s, the Japanese economy has experienced simultaneous declines in the price level and real output, which the traditional Keynesian theory indicates are associated with a fall in aggregate demand. Recently, the Diet, Japan's parliament, decided that it was time for the Bank of Japan to make serious efforts to halt deflation. To try to force the hand of central bank policymakers, leaders of the ruling political party within the Diet advanced a law requiring the Bank of Japan to aim for a target of positive inflation.

Officials at the Bank of Japan offered two criticisms of the proposed restriction on its activities. First, they pointed out that the central bank had already pushed up money growth to annual rates as high as 10 percent, yet prices of goods and services in Japan continued to fall. This experience, they argued, revealed that the Bank of Japan faced significant impediments to its ability to raise aggregate demand by boosting the monetary base and thereby bringing about increases in the price level and national output.

In addition, however, the officials contended that pushing up growth of the monetary base any faster would be "dangerous." What was the alleged danger? Speeding the growth of the Japanese monetary base could, they worried, pose serious inflation risks for the Japanese economy.

Members of the Japanese Diet, as well as economists around the world, were left scratching their heads. The essence of the central bank officials' argument, after all, was that they had little ability to generate increases in aggregate demand, yet felt that if they made the attempt, aggregate demand could rise so rapidly and so dramatically that dangerously high inflation might result. Officials at the Bank of Japan could not really have it both ways, but this did not stop them from making an inconsistent argument that a U.S. economist was quick to point out would have earned them zero credit in any basic money and banking course.

For Critical Analysis: If boosting the growth of the monetary base caused aggregate demand to expand sufficiently to raise the price level beyond some desired level, what could a central bank such as the Bank of Japan do to push inflation back down again?

Recent Developments in Monetary Theory

Missing from the theories we have considered was a clear explanation for how people form inflation expectations. As economists sought to develop a more complete understanding of factors that might influence business cycles, they began to recognize that how people forecast inflation is a key determinant of business-cycle peaks, troughs, and durations. This meant that economists needed to carefully consider the assumptions about expectation formation in their theories.

Rational Expectations and New Classical and Modern Keynesian Theories of Money and the Economy

During the 1970s and 1980s, economists applied the *rational expectations hypothesis* in an effort to fill this gap. Recall that under this hypothesis, an individual makes the best possible forecast of an economic variable such as the price level or inflation rate using all available past *and current* information *and* drawing on an understanding of what factors affect the economic variable. In contrast to an adaptive forecast, which only looks backward because it is based on past information, a rational forecast also looks forward while taking into account past information as well.

Fed watching: An occupation that involves developing forecasts of Federal Reserve monetary policy actions based on careful examination of the process by which the Fed appears to make its policy decisions.

THE NEW CLASSICAL APPROACH The first group of economists to incorporate the rational expectations hypothesis in theories of the relationship between monetary policy and the economy are known as *new classical economists.* Beginning in the 1970s, this group argued that expectations are so important that they should play a key role in any theory of how monetary policy influences the economy. The body of theory that they promoted returned to themes of the classical theory that we surveyed in Chapter 22, namely, that pure competition, with completely flexible wages and prices, prevails throughout the economy.

To capture the idea that people track current policies and try to forecast future policies, the new classical economists propose that the price-level expectation of workers, P^e, depends in part on their *expectation* of the level of nonborrowed reserves determined by Fed open market operations, denoted NBR^e. The Fed, of course, determines the *actual* quantity of nonborrowed reserves, NBR, which may or may not turn out to be the anticipated quantity. The kind of forecasting behavior that the new classical model proposes is known as **Fed watching.** A number of economists make a living by observing each nuance of Federal Reserve policymaking and selling forecasts of likely Fed policy actions during the coming weeks or months. Many of these professional "Fed watchers" work as independent consultants, but some are employed by banks, investment firms, and other financial services corporations. In terms of the model proposed by the new classical economists, what Fed watchers do is help people keep their forecast of monetary policy, NBR^e, as up-to-date as possible.

ANTICIPATED VERSUS UNANTICIPATED MONETARY POLICIES IN THE NEW CLASSICAL THEORY Now let's consider the new classical theory of short-run output and price-level determination, which is illustrated in Figure 24-7 on the next page. In both panels, the aggregate demand schedule slopes downward, and its position depends on actual nonborrowed reserves, NBR_1. As in the Keynesian imperfect-information theory of aggregate supply, the aggregate supply schedule slopes upward. Its position depends on people's expectation of the price level, P^e. A key determinant of the price-level expectation that people form is their anticipation of nonborrowed reserves, NBR_1^e. Thus, we label the aggregate supply schedule as $y^s(P^e\text{: } NBR_1^e)$ to indicate that its position depends on the expectation of the price level, which in turn depends on anticipated values of policy variables.

Fed watching does not always lead to correct policy anticipations. Nevertheless, in both panels we assume that initially these anticipations *are* correct, so that $NBR_1^e = NBR_1$. Consequently, $P^e = P_1$ at point E in each panel, because initially people expect the equilibrium current price level. The issue that we shall think about now is what effects policy *changes* would have on the equilibrium price level and real output, depending on whether or not people correctly anticipate them.

The Effects of Anticipated Monetary Policy Panel (a) illustrates the effects of expansionary monetary policy actions that are *correctly* anticipated. An increase in nonborrowed reserves, from NBR_1 to NBR_2, shifts the aggregate demand

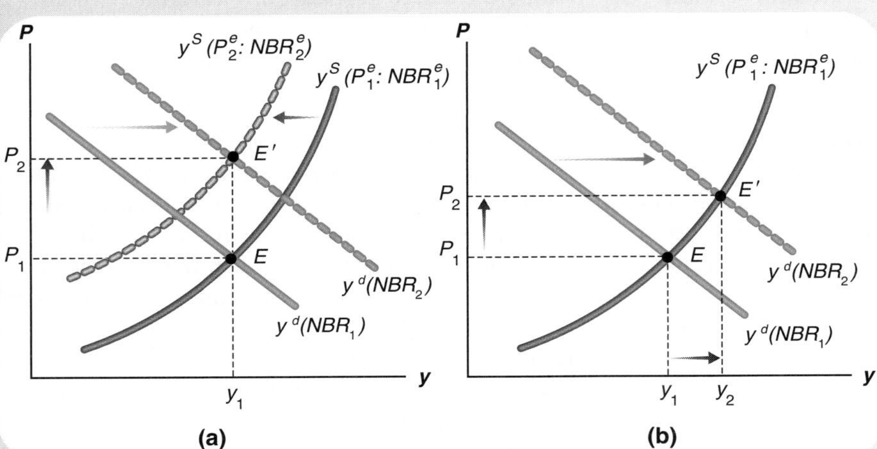

Figure 24-7 Anticipated versus Unanticipated Monetary Policy in the New Classical Model.

Expansionary monetary policy via open market purchases causes an increase in nonborrowed reserves and a rightward shift in the aggregate demand schedule. In the new classical theory, if people correctly forecast these policy actions, then they fully anticipate the increase in the price level that the policy will induce. Accordingly, in panel (a) people respond by raising their price expectation, causing a leftward shift in the aggregate supply schedule. On net, the equilibrium price level rises, but the equilibrium amount of real output remains unchanged. By way of contrast, as shown in panel (b), if this policy action is completely unanticipated, then people fail to forecast it, so their price expectations remain unchanged. Consequently, the aggregate supply schedule's position is unaltered, and the rise in aggregate demand induces increases in both the equilibrium price level and the equilibrium level of real output.

schedule rightward. If people correctly anticipate these policy actions, then they alter their nonborrowed reserves expectation to $NBR^e_2 = NBR_2$. As a result, they anticipate the rise in the price level brought about by the policy-induced increase in aggregate demand. This rise in their price expectation implies an anticipation that the real wage will fall. Workers thereby cut back on their supply of labor to firms, and firms produce less real output at any given price level. As a result, the aggregate supply schedule, y^s, shifts leftward, as shown in panel (a). At the new short-run equilibrium point, E', the equilibrium price level is higher, at P_2, but real output remains unchanged, at y_1. Correct anticipations of monetary policy effectively neutralize its effects on actual real output. Thus, correctly anticipated expansionary monetary policy actions have no real output effects, *even in the short run*. They result only in a higher price level.

The Effects of Unanticipated Monetary Policies Of course, people cannot always correctly predict monetary policies. Panel (b) of Figure 24-7 displays an expansionary monetary policy that people completely fail to anticipate. Again, the policy action is a sustained increase in nonborrowed reserves, from NBR_1 to NBR_2, which shifts the aggregate demand schedule rightward. Workers fail to anticipate the Fed's policy action, however, and expect that nonborrowed reserves will remain at NBR_1; therefore, in the short run they misperceive any rise in the nominal wage as indicating an increase in their real wage. Such a nominal wage increase occurs because a rise in the price level caused by the unanticipated increase in aggregate demand increases the demand for labor. Workers increase the quantity of labor services that they supply, so firms produce more real output. In the short run, therefore, the equilibrium price level increases, from P_1 to P_2, and equilibrium real output also increases, from y_1 to y_2, as the aggregate demand schedule shifts along the aggregate supply schedule from point E to point E'.

Policy ineffectiveness proposition: The new classical view that systematic (predictable) monetary policy actions will not have short-run effects on real quantities.

The New Classical Policy Ineffectiveness Proposition The examples in Figure 24-7 illustrate the fundamental monetary policy implication of the new classical theory. Only Fed policy actions that are not fully anticipated can affect real output in the short run. Correctly anticipated policy actions can have no effects on real output. This means that correctly anticipated actions also cannot influence employment or the unemployment rate. These conclusions form the basis for the new classical **policy ineffectiveness proposition,** which states that *systematic,* or predictable, monetary policy actions should have no short-run effects on real GDP. This means that systematic monetary policy actions also cannot influence employment and the unemployment rate, which the new classical economists argue remains at the *natural rate of unemployment.* This is the ratio of structural and frictional unemployment to the labor force (see Chapter 21), which arises under full information. Hence, in the new classical view, systematic policy actions that people can anticipate lead only to changes in the price level and the inflation rate and cannot affect the unemployment rate.

In the new classical theory, *unsystematic* policies, which people cannot always anticipate fully, can still have short-run real effects. Although these effects disappear in the long run, as in the monetarist model, in principle they can be sizable in the short run.

THE MODERN KEYNESIAN WAGE-CONTRACTING APPROACH Because new classical economists were the first to include the rational expectations hypothesis in their models of the economy, new classical theory brought about a revolution in thinking about monetary policy. Proponents of traditional Keynesian and monetarist theories of the relationship between monetary policy and economic activity have reacted in two ways to this state of affairs. One response has been to deny the relevance of the rational expectations hypothesis. The other has been to consider its implications for the traditional Keynesian and monetarist approaches.

Those who have followed the second course have sought to develop theories that include a role for rational expectations but, at the same time, admit the possibility that nominal wages may be sticky in the short run. Thus, modern Keynesian theory retains both wage stickiness and imperfect information from the traditional Keynesian model but follows the new classical theory by adopting the rational expectations hypothesis. Consequently, the modern Keynesian model adopts the new classical assumption that people make rational forecasts of the price level and the inflation rate in the face of imperfect information but forgoes the new classical assumption that purely competitive markets determine flexible nominal wages. The theory proposes that both parties to a wage contract choose a contract wage based on their rational expectations of the conditions that will prevail in the labor market during the period in which the wage contract is in force. Consequently, the modern Keynesian model of wage contracts follows the new classical theory by imposing the requirement that workers and firms act on the basis of rational forecasts.

Observational equivalence: The fact that the basic version of the modern Keynesian theory with sticky wages makes some of the same fundamental policy predictions as the new classical model that is based on pure competition with completely flexible wages.

Two key conclusions emerge from this modern Keynesian approach. The first is that in the short run nominal wage stickiness can be "rational" in light of imperfect information available at the time workers and firms reach agreements about wages. As a result, the basic sticky-wage theory of aggregate supply displayed in Figure 24-3 on page 595 can be consistent with the rational expectations hypothesis. During the period that nominal wages are fixed by contracts, monetary policy actions can have short-run effects, because these actions can induce the price level to move in directions that workers failed to anticipate when they reached wage agreements with firms.

The second conclusion, however, is that if workers can fully anticipate monetary policy actions before their wages are set, they will bargain to have their nominal wages reflect changes in the price level. Thus, completely anticipated monetary policy actions will lead to wage adjustments that leave employment unchanged, as in the classical theory discussed in Chapter 22.

OBSERVATIONALLY EQUIVALENT THEORIES The modern Keynesian approach, therefore, concludes that policies that workers and firms cannot correctly anticipate before reaching contractual agreements will affect real output and employment during the term that the agreements are binding. In contrast, fully anticipated policy actions will induce workers and firms to adjust the contract wage accordingly; hence, the policy actions will have no influence on equilibrium real output or employment.

These policy conclusions, of course, are essentially the same as the predictions of the new classical theory. This similarity between the policy predictions of the basic new classical and modern Keynesian theories is known as **observational equivalence.** Even though the two theories are based on very different assumptions—pure competition with completely flexible wages in the new classical theory versus contractual wage setting with fixed wages in the modern Keynesian model—in their most basic forms they offer very similar policy predictions. Both theories predict that real employment and output variations should occur only in the event of unanticipated changes in the price level, which economists often call price-level "misperceptions" or "surprises." In the new classical theory, price-level misperceptions could occur, for instance, when the Fed makes mistakes, is misunderstood, or is insincere in its policy announcements. In the modern Keynesian model, surprise changes in the price level could take place whenever the price level differs from the level that workers and firms anticipated when they negotiated their wage contracts. This could occur for the same reasons proposed in the new classical theory.

moneyxtra!
Online Case Study
To evaluate the implications of the new classical and modern Keynesian theories for policy secrecy, go to the Chapter 24 Case Study, entitled "Does Monetary Policy Secrecy Pay?"
http://moneyxtra.swcollege.com

New Keynesian Theory versus Real Business Cycles

In the classical and new classical theories, flexibility of wages and prices leads to rapid adjustments of real output to the level consistent with an economy's long-run growth potential, but imperfect information can allow monetary policy actions to affect real output in the short run. Modern Keynesian theory has focused its attention on wage inflexibilities, but it has reached strikingly similar conclusions.

The most recent developments in monetary theory, however, have widened the differences separating economists' views on the relationship between monetary policy and economic activity. On the one hand, one group of economists, called *new Keynesian economists,* have developed theories that emphasize the potential importance of differences, or *heterogeneities,* among households and firms, and they contend that monetary policy actions can have significant effects on real output. On the other hand, another group of economists, known as *real-business-cycle theorists,* have developed models that generally are based on the assumption of *homogeneous,* or identical, households and firms, and they conclude that little if any stabilizing role exists for monetary policy.

NEW KEYNESIANS AND STICKY PRICES Many new Keynesian theories emphasize possible sources of stickiness in the price level. If the prices of goods and services are inflexible, then this could help to explain why real output might be variable in the short run. Price stickiness also might be part of a rationale for persistence in output changes in response to temporary changes in economic conditions. Together with wage stickiness, price stickiness can also lead to real-wage rigidities that could help to explain unemployment.

Although new Keynesian theories of price stickiness differ in many respects, they typically share a couple of common features. First, these theories depart from the classical assumption of purely competitive markets for goods and services or for factors of production. Recall that in purely competitive markets, there are many buyers and sellers, there is free entry into and exit from markets, and products that firms produce and the services of factors of production are indistinguishable. New Keynesian theories, in contrast, are based on the assumption of *imperfect competition.* Thus, they consider market environments in which the number of buyers or sellers may be limited, there may be barriers to market entry or exit, or firm products or factor services may be differentiated.

The idea that imperfect competition could help to explain price rigidities was first suggested in the 1930s by an economist named Gardiner Means. His *administered pricing hypothesis* proposed that firms that are not purely competitive are able to set prices and to maintain relatively *inflexible* pricing policies over lengthy intervals. In the 1980s and 1990s, new Keynesian economists brought the administered pricing hypothesis back to life in the form of a theory called the *small-menu-cost model.* As the name indicates, the basis of the theory is the proposal that firms incur small but measurable costs, called **small menu costs,** when they change the prices that they charge their customers. These costs may include expenses entailed in printing new price tags, menus, and catalogues; costs incurred in bringing together firm managers for meetings on price changes; and costs of renegotiating business deals with customers. If firms face these costs of changing prices, then in their quest to maximize profits, they may choose to adjust prices infrequently. The resulting price stickiness can permit monetary policy actions to influence economic activity. (The growth of Internet commerce may have a bearing on the real-world applicability of the small-menu-cost model; see on the following page *Cyber Focus: Shopbots—Making the Small-Menu-Cost Model Less Relevant or Providing a New Source of Price Stickiness?*)

Small menu costs: The costs firms incur when they make price changes, such as the costs of changing prices in menus or catalogues and the costs of renegotiating agreements with customers.

NEW KEYNESIAN COORDINATION FAILURES A feature common to many new Keynesian models is *market failure,* or the failure of a private market to reach an equilibrium that reflects all the costs and benefits entailed in producing a good or providing a factor service. An example of a market failure is an *externality,* or a

GLOBAL | POLICY | CYBER Focus | MANAGEMENT

Shopbots—Making the Small-Menu-Cost Model Less Relevant or Providing a New Source of Price Stickiness?

Shopbots have been a key development in the continuing growth of Internet commerce. Consumers can use these software programs to search the Internet for the best available prices.

Shopbots as a Boon to Price Competition

Most observers have argued that shopbots will be a boon for consumers. The idea is that shopbots will enable consumers to flock to Web sites that post the lowest prices, thereby encouraging firms to keep their prices at the marginal cost of production. Any firm that markets products on the Internet will rapidly lose customers if it tries to raise its price above this level.

If this view is correct, then shopbots should help reduce the potential for firms to exercise any pricing power—a key assumption of the small-menu-cost model. Without the power to set price above marginal cost, and hence to keep prices fixed in the face of small menu costs, firms will adjust prices rapidly to changes in demand or supply conditions in the marketplace. From this standpoint, the wider use of shopbots weakens the applicability of the small-menu-cost model to a growing portion of the U.S. economy, namely Internet commerce.

Using Shopbots to Discourage Rivals

According to Hal Varian, an economist at the University of California at Berkeley, it is not so clear that shopbots will help make the economy more competitive. The reason is that there is nothing to stop firms from using shopbot programs, too. Indeed, some firms already are programming shopbots to keep tabs on the Web sites of rivals so that they can respond rapidly to price cuts by competitors. If all rivals in the marketplace follow the same strategy—and know that they do—then each firm knows that all its rivals will respond to a cut in the price of its goods by cutting their prices. At the same time, however, each firm knows that if it raises its price, no other firm is likely to follow, and it will lose its clientele as a result. Consequently, firms have *less* incentive to change their prices.

Varian argues that which outcome eventually prevails depends on whether consumers or producers move faster in spotting and responding to price differences. In his view, consumers are likely to be at a disadvantage. After all, they will unleash their shopbots only when they happen to be shopping for a specific item. In contrast, producers will keep their shopbots busy checking out rivals' prices. Many firms that sell on the Internet already engage in real-time monitoring of the Web sites of their rivals and *automatically* match any price cut.

FOR CRITICAL ANALYSIS: If the widespread use of shopbots ultimately leads to greater price stickiness, should firms' outputs be more or less variable in the face of unanticipated changes in demand for their products?

Aggregate externalities: Situations in which aggregate equilibrium in all, or at least many, markets fails to account for spillovers across markets, so that equilibrium aggregate real output, employment, and the price level all differ from their long-run, natural levels.

situation in which a private cost or benefit differs from a social cost or benefit because of spillover effects stemming from the production or consumption of a good or service. For example, noise pollution produced by booming car speakers that everyone in stalled traffic is forced to listen to is a *microeconomic* externality, or an externality that arises in a single market. New Keynesian proponents contend that there also are **aggregate externalities.** These are situations in which equilibrium in all, or at least many, markets throughout the economy fails to account for spillovers across markets, so that equilibrium aggregate real output, employment, and the price level all differ from their long-run, natural levels.

New Keynesians argue, for instance, that decisions by firms to adjust prices infrequently can produce aggregate externalities. To understand why, suppose that there is an overall decline in the demand for goods throughout the economy. When one set of firms chooses to cut their prices in the face of this fall in demand, consumers allocate more of their spending to consumption of the output of those firms, although on net the firms' production levels still will fall. This leaves fewer consumer funds available for spending on the goods produced by firms that keep their prices fixed. As a result, there is a further decline in demand at each of those fixed-price firms, thereby reinforcing their output declines. Consequently, the decisions by some firms to cut their prices have spillover effects on those firms that do not change their prices, and vice versa.

Coordination failures: Spillover effects between workers and firms, arising from movements in economic variables, that hinder efforts by individual households and firms to plan and implement their consumption, production, and pricing decisions.

Real-business-cycle theory: An approach to the theory of overall economic activity in which variations in technology are the key factors accounting for cyclical fluctuations in real output.

If the firms in this example could somehow coordinate their production and pricing decisions, then these aggregate spillover effects would be reduced. Hence, a key new Keynesian explanation for persistent responses of real output to temporary changes in economic conditions lies in the idea of **coordination failure.** This refers to the inability of workers and firms to plan and implement labor supply, production, and pricing decisions because of aggregate externalities that affect workers and firms in different ways. New Keynesians argue that the failure of workers and firms to share information and to make decisions jointly makes them particularly susceptible to such externalities and can lead to levels of real output that persistently differ from the economy's natural, long-run level.

New Keynesians contend that a key reason that coordination failures can occur is *heterogeneities* among workers and firms, or differences in how they respond to events such as Fed policy actions. Several types of heterogeneities may exist. Firms come in different sizes and use different technologies, which means that they face different costs. They also may produce differentiated products. Many firms work out wage contracts on a worker-by-worker basis, while others engage in collective bargaining with unions. In addition, workers and consumers arguably are different, too. Heterogeneities exist in workers' training and abilities and in their responsiveness to changes in real wages. Because consumer tastes vary, their responses to changes in real incomes induced by monetary policy are likely to differ. As a result of coordination failures introduced by all these heterogeneities, new Keynesians argue, it is hard to envision that monetary policy actions would not have potentially long-lasting real effects. Monetary policy, new Keynesians contend, is nonneutral.

REAL-BUSINESS-CYCLE THEORY At the opposite extreme from this perspective is an approach called **real-business-cycle theory.** As its name implies, this approach hinges on the idea that *real* factors, such as technological or productivity changes, induce cyclical fluctuations in economic activity. According to real-business-cycle theorists, the key to identifying how monetary policy relates to employment, real output, and inflation is to develop a more complete understanding of the processes that govern labor supply and firms' output production and capital investment. The reason, they argue, is that these are the factors that ultimately matter in determining employment and real output.

Figure 24-8 on the next page illustrates the key source of economic fluctuations in real-business-cycle models, which is technology shocks, or sudden variations in the technological capabilities of firms. Such sudden changes in technology cause

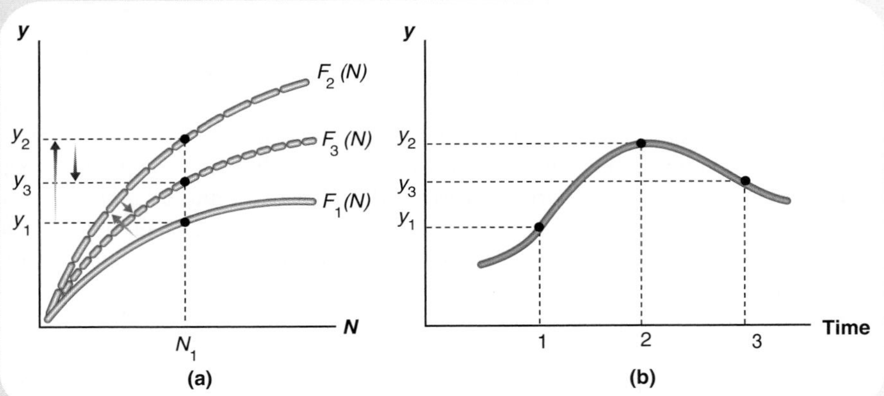

Figure 24-8
Technology Shocks and Real Output Variations.

In real-business-cycle models, variations in real output stem primarily from technology shocks, or factors that cause the aggregate production function to rotate. As shown in panel (a), at any given quantity of labor, such as N_1, such rotations in the production function will lead to variations in real output over time. Panel (b) traces the movements in real output owing to these technology shocks. As indicated, such shocks can produce cyclical movements in real output that we observe in actual business cycles.

a change in the shape and position of the aggregate production function. For instance, suppose that a spurt of new techniques for producing high-speed computer processing chips, such as occurred in the 1990s, causes a jump in the productive capacity of firms that make computers and improves the efficiency of the computers that they build. As a result, the productivity both of computer manufacturers and of all companies that use computers rises. For the economy as a whole, this yields an increase in the marginal product of labor, which translates into an increase in the slope of the aggregate production function, as shown in panel (a) of Figure 24-8. The production function rotates upward, so real output rises, from y_1 to a higher level given by y_2, and an economic expansion occurs.

Nevertheless, some technological innovations turn out to be disappointments. Implementation of a more inefficient technology will, for a time, make existing capital less productive than it was in the past. For example, suppose that computer makers switch to a just-in-time inventory system that ultimately fails to speed deliveries and, for a time, actually slows them down. As a result, aggregate productivity falls, causing the production function to rotate downward. Real output then will fall from y_2 to a lower level, y_3, as shown in panel (a).

Panel (b) indicates that these technological shocks end up producing cyclical behavior in real GDP. If we interpret the subscripts 1, 2, and 3 in panel (a) as referring to points in time, then we can plot the behavior of real GDP over time. To do this, we assume that the intervals between the two shocks we have envisioned are of equal length. The resulting diagram shows a typical business cycle with a short-run expansion followed by a short-run downturn.

MONETARY POLICY IMPLICATIONS OF REAL-BUSINESS-CYCLE MODELS In its focus on technology as the key determinant of real output, the real-business-cycle model looks a lot like a more sophisticated version of the classical model of

Chapter 22. Essentially identical firms face an aggregate production function, and their production decisions depend largely on the technology available to them. Nevertheless, real-business-cycle theory differs from the classical model in its treatment of money and the effects of monetary policy.

Recall from Chapter 22 that the classical model assumes that the quantity of money in circulation is fully controlled by a central bank such as the Fed. In contrast, in the real-business-cycle theory, the nominal quantity of money supply is determined largely by interactions between the depository financial institutions and the public. Real-business-cycle proponents contend that when people's real income rises, so does their demand for transactions services from banks (as in the Keynesian transactions motive for holding money). The banks respond by increasing their production of transactions services and, hence, deposits that are included in the nominal money stock. The total amount of bank deposit money, called **inside money** because its quantity depends on conditions within the banking system, depends on real income and is outside the control of a central bank. Indeed, the quantity of inside money adjusts automatically to changing economic conditions and performs no separate causal role with respect to any aggregate variables.

Inside money: Bank deposit money.

Outside money: Money in the form of currency and bank reserves.

Consequently, in the real-business-cycle model, inside money does not affect the price level. Only **outside money,** which is composed of currency and bank reserves that a central bank *can* control because they are determined by the central bank's policies, can influence the price level. The amount of outside money determines the level of aggregate demand. Because the real-business-cycle theory's aggregate supply schedule is vertical, the amount of outside money effectively *determines* the price level.

CURRENT AND FUTURE PROSPECTS FOR THE ALTERNATIVE THEORIES Many policymakers currently at the Fed were trained when the traditional Keynesian and monetarist theories predominated in economic thinking. Nevertheless, the new classical and modern Keynesian approaches have had a considerable effect on Fed policymaking. Most Fed officials appear to subscribe to the view that monetary policy can have powerful short-run effects because of informational imperfections and nominal wage stickiness. Nevertheless, they typically espouse the view that there is a limit on the ability of monetary policy actions to exert long-run effects on real economic activity.

The deep philosophical divisions between the new Keynesians and real-business-cycle theorists are likely to continue until either approach proves that it can provide predictions that businesspersons and policymakers can rely on to guide their decisions. At present, both approaches show some promise. On the one hand, new Keynesian economics potentially can explain price stickiness, unemployment, and persistent states of recession or expansion. On the other hand, real-business-cycle economists can provide theories that closely mimic real-world business cycles.

moneyxtra!

Another Perspective

To consider essential similarities and differences between the new Keynesian and real-business-cycle perspectives, go to the Chapter 24 reading, entitled "On Business Cycles and Countercyclical Policies," written by Marco Espinosa and Jang-Ting Guo and published by the Federal Reserve Bank of Atlanta.
http://moneyxtra.swcollege.com

In their current forms, however, both approaches cannot simultaneously be correct because they are based on fundamentally different views about the economy. Whereas the new Keynesian theory relies on imperfect competition, heterogeneities, aggregate externalities, and coordination failures, the real-business-cycle approach depends on pure competition, homogeneity, perfect markets, and rational, self-interested individuals and firms. Ultimately, some combination of the two approaches may be the wave of the future in explaining how monetary policy ultimately affects real economic activity. Already some new Keynesian theorists have begun to use techniques borrowed from real-business-cycle enthusiasts. At the same time, some proponents of real-business-cycle theory have begun to experiment with models that include sticky wages and prices. It remains to be seen if the two approaches will ever find a common ground. At present, neither theory has provided a sufficiently strong foundation to serve as a practical guide for monetary policymaking.

4. In what respects do modern economic theories reach similar and conflicting conclusions about the relationship between monetary policy and economic activity? New classical theory indicates that monetary policy can have short-run effects on real output only if Fed actions are unanticipated. The policy ineffectiveness proposition of new classical theory is that systematic, and thus predictable, monetary policies have no effects on real economic activity. Modern Keynesian theory, which differs from the new classical approach in its assumption that nominal wages are determined by contracts, reaches strikingly similar conclusions. By way of contrast, new Keynesian theories focus on price stickiness, worker and firm heterogeneities, and potential coordination failures as reasons that monetary policy may have long-lasting real effects. At the opposite extreme, however, real-business-cycle theories that examine essentially identical firms and workers indicate that monetary policy actions influence only the price level in both the short run and the long run.

Link to the Global Economy

Is Labor Market "Flexibility" a Key to Lower Unemployment?

Statutory minimum wages, rights to parental leave, mandated compensation for fired employees, plant-closing notification requirements, legal limits on hours spent on the job—all these are examples of legal restrictions that make labor markets less flexible in some nations than in others. As you have learned, how much wages and employment adjust to changes in prices and inflation influences the responses of a nation's real output and unemployment rate.

Labor Market Flexibility and Unemployment

For some time, a number of economists have argued that countries with inflexible labor markets are likely to experience higher unemployment than nations with relatively more flexible labor markets. Their hypothesis is that when firms face mandates governing how much to pay workers or limiting the scope of layoffs or dismissals, their incentive to hire workers in the first place is reduced.

Figure 24-9 provides survey evidence about companies' perceptions of their capability to adjust job-security and compensation standards of their employees; the survey used a scale ranging from zero (no flexibility) to one hundred (full flexibility). As the figure indicates, during recent years low-flexibility countries such as France and Spain have had higher average annual unemployment rates than high-flexibility nations such as Denmark and Switzerland. Thus, the figure tends to support the hypothesis that reduced labor market flexibility contributes to higher unemployment.

Lessons from the Irish and Dutch Experiences?

In recent years, two countries, Ireland and the Netherlands, have succeeded in reducing their unemployment rates. As shown in Figure 24-10, the unemployment rates in both nations have fallen sharply since the mid-1990s.

In the Netherlands, reforms first implemented in the early 1980s and maintained since have allowed

Figure 24-9
Labor Market Flexibility and Unemployment Rates in Selected Nations.

There appears to be an inverse relationship between the degree of labor market flexibility and the unemployment rate. That is, less flexible labor markets are associated with higher rates of unemployment.

SOURCE: Rafael Di Tella and Robert MacCulloch, "The Consequences of Labor Market Flexibility: Panel Evidence Based on Survey Data," Harvard Business School, November 1998.

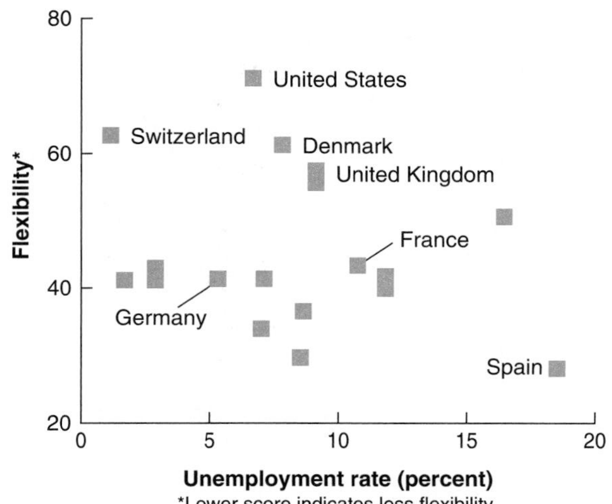

Continued on next page

Link to the Global Economy, continued

both wages and employment to adjust more flexibly to changes in economic conditions. Since the reforms were instituted, the real value of Dutch minimum wages has declined by more than 25 percent, tax rates firms pay on workers they hire have declined from 30 percent of workers' earnings to about 14 percent, and unemployment benefits have dropped from about 80 percent of a worker's wages to closer to 60 percent.

Ireland implemented similar reforms beginning in the late 1980s. The Irish government also established what it called "active labor market policies" aimed at providing workers with more job training and placement programs.

For these two countries, policies that reduce firms' costs of employing workers have led to relatively large drops in their national unemployment rates. Many economists regard them as useful case studies for understanding how increased labor market flexibility and pro-employment policies together can contribute to lower unemployment rates.

Research Project

Make a list of the factors that influence national rates of unemployment in the short run and in the long run. Which is likely to be most important in causing near-term and longer-term variations in unemployment? Explain your reasoning.

Web Resources

1. Where is the best Web site to obtain the most up-to-date inflation and unemployment data for European nations and other industrialized countries? Go to the Organization for Economic Cooperation and Development (http://www.oecd.org), click on "Statistics" at the top of the page, and then go to page 2 and click on "Latest Key Short-Term Indicators" for CPI inflation rates and unemployment rates.

2. What source provides inflation and unemployment data for developing nations? Go to the home page of the International Monetary Fund (http://www.imf.org), and click on "Publications." Under "Title," enter "World Economic Outlook," and then click on "Search" for a list containing the most recent issue.

Figure 24-10
Unemployment Rates in Ireland and the Netherlands.

After Ireland and the Netherlands implemented reforms making their labor markets more flexible, their unemployment rates declined below the average for the European Union.

SOURCES: Cedric Tille and Kei-Mu Yi, "Curbing Unemployment in Europe: Are There Lessons from Ireland and the Netherlands?" Federal Reserve Bank of New York *Current Issues in Economics and Finance* 7 (5, May 2001); Organization for Economic Cooperation and Development; authors' estimates.

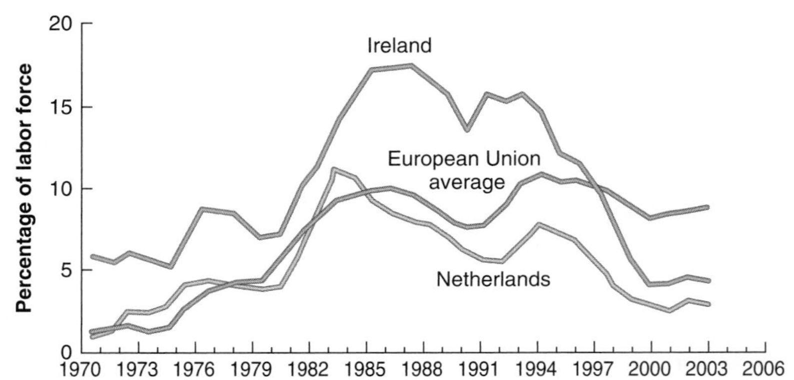

Chapter Summary

1. The Factors That Determine Aggregate Demand in the Traditional Keynesian Model: The position of the Keynesian aggregate demand schedule is affected by any factors that influence autonomous aggregate expenditures, such as autonomous consumption, government spending, and net taxes. Also included is monetary policy, which can influence the level of interest rates and desired investment spending. Consequently, monetary policy actions can affect the position of the Keynesian aggregate demand schedule.

2. The Factors That Determine the Shape and Position of the Keynesian Aggregate Supply Schedule: According to the sticky-wage and imperfect-information theories of aggregate supply, the aggregate supply schedule is upward sloping and has a convex shape. Under the sticky-wage theory, a rise in nominal wages, perhaps as a result of union demands for higher wages or an increase in a legal minimum wage, will shift the aggregate supply schedule upward and to the left. Under the imperfect-information theory, higher price-level expectations will shift the aggregate supply schedule upward and to the left.

3. The Price and Output Effects of Expansionary Monetary Policies in the Traditional Keynesian Model: According to Keynesian theory, a Fed policy of sustained open market purchases induces a rise in aggregate demand. This generates an increase in the equilibrium price level and an increase in equilibrium real output.

4. Ways in Which Modern Economic Theories Reach Similar and Conflicting Conclusions about the Relationship between Monetary Policy and Economic Activity: According to the new classical approach, only unanticipated monetary policy actions can have short-run effects on real output. A key implication of new classical theory is the policy ineffectiveness proposition, which states that systematic, and thus predictable, monetary policies cannot influence real economic activity. Modern Keynesian theory differs from the new classical approach in its assumption that nominal wages are determined by contracts, yet its key policy conclusions are strikingly similar. New Keynesian theories, however, emphasize price stickiness, worker and firm heterogeneities, and potential coordination failures, and they indicate that monetary policy may have long-lasting real effects. Real-business-cycle theories, by way of contrast, analyze the behavior of essentially identical firms and workers and conclude that monetary policy actions influence only the price level in both the short run and the long run.

Questions and Problems

(Answers to odd-numbered questions and problems may be found on the Web at http://money.swcollege.com under "Student Resources")

1. In the classical model, fiscal policy actions cannot influence aggregate demand, but in the Keynesian theory they can. Why is this so?

2. Make a list of the various factors that can cause inflation in the classical model. Then construct a similar list for the Keynesian theory. Which list is longer? Explain why this is so.

3. Why does monetary policy affect real output and the unemployment rate in the traditional Keynesian model?

4. Explain verbally, and with diagrams to the extent that they assist, why a sudden decline in price expectations shifts the short-run aggregate supply schedule downward and to the right.

5. As a follow-up to question 4, what effect would a sudden decline in price expectations have on the actual equilibrium price level, assuming that there is no change in factors that affect the aggregate demand schedule?

6. Suppose that the sudden decline in the expected price level discussed in questions 4 and 5 is accompanied by a reduction in the quantity of money in circulation. Is it possible to predict what happens to the actual equilibrium price level and quantity of real output?

7. Explain why it is so important whether monetary policy actions are or are not anticipated in the new classical theory.

8. Explain, in your own words, the concept of observational equivalence as it applies to the modern Keynesian theory and the new classical theory.

9. Use an aggregate demand–aggregate supply diagram to explain why the existence of widespread price stickiness would be extremely important in allowing monetary policy actions to influence equilibrium real output.

10. Most economists view real-business-cycle theory as more closely related to the new classical theory than to the modern Keynesian theory, even though the latter two theories are "observationally equivalent." Why is this so?

Before the Test

Test your understanding of the material covered in this chapter by taking the Chapter 24 interactive quiz at http://money.swcollege.com.

Online Application

According to the Keynesian aggregate demand–aggregate supply model, the unemployment rate should be inversely related to changes in the inflation rate, other things being equal. This application allows you to take a direct look at unemployment and inflation data to judge for yourself whether the two variables appear to be related.

Internet URL: **http://stats.bls.gov**

Title: Bureau of Labor Statistics: Economy at a Glance

Navigation: Begin at the home page of the Bureau of Labor Statistics (**http://stats.bls.gov**). Under "At a Glance Tables," click on "U.S. Economy at a Glance."

Application: Perform the indicated operations, and answer the following questions:

1. Click on "U.S. Economy at a Glance." Then scan down to "Prices," and click on "Consumer Price Index." Take a look at the solid line showing inflation in the graph box. How much has the inflation rate varied in recent years? Compare this behavior with previous years, especially the mid-1970s to the mid-1980s.

2. Back up to "Economy at a Glance," and now click on "Unemployment Rate." Take a look at the graph box. During what recent years was the unemployment rate approaching and at its peak value? Do you see any appearance of an inverse relationship between the unemployment rate and the inflation rate (question 1 above)?

For Group Study and Analysis: Divide the class into groups, and have each group search through the "Economy at a Glance" site to develop an explanation for the key factors accounting for the recent behavior of the unemployment rate. Have each group report back with its explanation. Is there any one factor that best explains the recent behavior of the unemployment rate?

Selected References and Further Reading

Espinoza-Vega, Marco, and Jang-Ting Guo. "On Business Cycles and Countercyclical Policies." Federal Reserve Bank of Atlanta *Economic Review,* Fourth Quarter 2001, pp. 1–11.

Gordon, Robert. "What Is New-Keynesian Economics?" *Journal of Economic Literature* 28 (1990): 1151–1171.

Gray, Jo Anna, and David Spencer. "Price Prediction Errors and Real Activity: A Reassessment." *Economic Inquiry* 28 (October 1990): 658–681.

Gray, Jo Anna, Magda Kandil, and David Spencer. "Does Contractual Wage Rigidity Play a Role in Determining Real Activity?" *Southern Economic Journal* 58 (1992): 1042–1057.

Laidler, David. "The Legacy of the Monetarist Controversy." Federal Reserve Bank of St. Louis *Review* 72 (March/April 1990): 49–64.

Mayer, Thomas, ed. *The Political Economy of American Monetary Policy.* Cambridge: Cambridge University Press, 1990.

Stadler, George. "Real Business Cycles." *Journal of Economic Literature* 32 (1994): 1750–1783.

MoneyXtra

moneyxtra! Log on to the MoneyXtra Web site now (**http://moneyxtra.swcollege.com**) for additional learning resources such as practice quizzes, case studies, readings, and additional economic applications.

Unit VI
Monetary Policy

CONTENTS

Chapter 25

What Should the Fed Do?—
Objectives and Targets of Monetary Policy

Fundamental Issues

1. What are the ultimate goals of monetary policy?
2. Why might a central bank use an intermediate monetary policy target?
3. What are the pros and cons of interest rates versus monetary aggregates as intermediate monetary policy targets?
4. What is the policy assignment problem?

Throughout most of the 1970s, financial news headlines revolved around what the Federal Reserve was likely to do with interest rates. Then, in 1979, the Fed shifted gears, and for about three years, reporters awaited the latest information on growth rates of monetary aggregates and whether they were close to the Fed's targets. From about 1982 until 1987, the Fed pursued a strategy that effectively returned to interest rate targeting via an indirect approach that focused on the discount window. Beginning in the late 1980s, the Fed returned once again to openly targeting interest rates.

Some economists think that the Fed could have avoided all these shifts in policymaking—and gained the side benefit of greater U.S. economic stability—by simply targeting nominal GDP. Pursuing a nominal GDP target, they claim, would automatically accomplish at least as much, in terms of stabilizing output and prices, as the Fed can manage by successfully targeting either interest rates or monetary aggregates.

Why has the Federal Reserve used so many different policy procedures since the 1970s? Why has it targeted interest rates or monetary aggregates instead of aiming directly at broader output, employment, and price goals? Would nominal GDP targeting have worked as well as its proponents claim? Answering these and related questions about monetary policymaking is the objective of this chapter.

Internal and External Objectives of Monetary Policy

Up to now, you have learned about broad theories of how monetary policy actions may influence real output, employment, and prices. You have discovered that each of these theoretical approaches has special implications for monetary policymaking.

We have not yet asked some very tough questions, however. What should the Federal Reserve and other central banks do? What goals should they seek to achieve? How should they go about pursuing those goals? In this chapter, you will learn that even if there might happen to be widespread agreement concerning the appropriate *objectives* of monetary policy, the best way to *implement* monetary policy still might not be apparent.

In this chapter, we shall begin by examining the factors that determine the **ultimate goals,** or final economic objectives, of monetary policy. Then we shall devote the bulk of the remainder of the chapter to contemplating how the Fed might go about trying to pursue these goals.

Ultimate goals: The final objectives of economic policies.

Internal Goals of Monetary Policy

In Chapters 23 and 24, we examined the factors that determine a nation's equilibrium nominal interest rate, its equilibrium real income, and its trade balance. Monetary policy actions can alter interest rates, desired investment expenditures, and equilibrium real income, thereby influencing aggregate demand and the price level. Consequently, monetary policy actions could affect a nation's economic performance, so the Fed can contemplate adopting policy strategies with an explicit intention to achieve specific national economic goals.

One aim of central banks and governments could be to achieve *internal goals,* or purely domestic policy objectives. Although the Fed might seek to achieve a number of internal goals, most economists focus on three sets of internal goals that monetary policymakers might contemplate pursuing.

INFLATION GOALS As Table 25-1 shows, a number of social costs are potentially associated with inflation and inflation variability. In light of these costs, there is a good justification for the Fed to try to maintain low (or even no) inflation. In addition, there is a strong rationale for limiting year-to-year variability in inflation rates.

moneyxtra!

Economic Applications

Should the Federal Reserve aim at a zero inflation policy? To review alternative perspectives on this debate and make your own judgment, go to EconDebate Online.
http://moneyxtra.swcollege.com

OUTPUT GOALS According to the classical, new classical, and real-business-cycle theories, there is little that monetary policymakers can do to affect real output over any time horizon, and the monetarist and modern Keynesian theories

Table 25-1 The Costs of Inflation and Inflation Variability

Type of Cost	Cause
Resources expended to economize on money holdings (more trips to banks, etc.)	Rising prices associated with inflation
Costs of changing price lists and printing menus and catalogues	Individual product/service price increases associated with inflation
Redistribution of real incomes from individuals to the government	Inflation that pushes people into higher, nonindexed nominal tax brackets
Reductions in investment, capital accumulation, and economic growth	Inflation variability that complicates business planning
Slowed pace of introduction of new and better products	Volatile price changes that reduce the efficiency of private markets
Redistribution of resources from creditors to debtors	Unexpected inflation that reduces the real values of debts

generally indicate that there is little scope for long-run output effects of monetary policies. Nonetheless, several theories indicate that unexpected changes in Fed policies can affect real output over short-run intervals. Therefore, another potential ultimate goal of economic policy might be to prevent sharp swings in real GDP relative to its natural, full-information level. Pursuing this policy goal could, according to some of the economic theories we have discussed, limit business cycles.

Employment Goals Labor is a key factor of production, and in a democratic republic workers also account for the bulk of voters. Consequently, both fiscal and monetary policymakers are likely to feel pressures to pursue policies that aim to prevent significant variability in worker unemployment rates and that might spur greater growth in real output and employment. (In recent years, a number of countries have decided that the best long-run approach to achieving their output and employment goals is to try to keep their inflation rates near preannounced targets; see *Global Focus: Inflation Targeting Gains New Adherents.*)

On the Web
What was the substance of the most recent statements to Congress by the chair of the Fed's Board of Governors? You can review the chair's testimony and report by going to the Fed's Web site at http://federalreserve.gov, where you can click on "Testimony and Speeches" in the left-hand margin. Then click on "Humphrey-Hawkins Testimony" (http://federalreserve.gov/boarddocs/hh/). Then click on "Monetary Report to the Congress."

moneyxtra! Another Perspective
To learn more about nations' experiences with inflation targeting, go to the Chapter 25 reading, entitled "Inflation Target Design: Changing Inflation Performance and Persistence in Industrial Countries," written by Pierre Siklos and published by the Federal Reserve Bank of Atlanta.
http://moneyxtra.swcollege.com

Legislated Internal Goals

Can the Fed pursue inflation, output, and employment goals simultaneously? Certainly, stabilizing output will often be consistent with an objective of stable employment and a low unemployment rate. Nonetheless, as you learned in Chapter 24, attempting to push up real output can also boost the equilibrium price level, so there may be conflicts among these objectives.

For this reason, nations sometimes choose to make economic goals explicit. In the United States, two laws lay out a course for economic policymakers. One is the *Employment Act of 1946,* which legally commits all agencies of the federal government to the objectives of "maximum employment, production, and purchasing power." Thus, the 1946 act officially seeks the highest possible employment and real output levels as well as low inflation. This legislation is silent, however, about exactly how the U.S. government should address potential tradeoffs among these goals.

In 1978, Congress established more concrete objectives when it passed the *Full Employment and Balanced Growth Act,* more commonly known as the *Humphrey-Hawkins Act.* This legislation set goals for 1983 of an unemployment rate of 3 percent and an inflation rate of 0 percent. When 1983 arrived, the problems with trying to legislate explicit objectives became apparent, however: in that year, the actual unemployment rate exceeded 9 percent, and actual inflation was about 5 percent. By the early 2000s, however, the unemployment rate had fallen to 4 percent, and the inflation rate hovered between 1 and 3 percent, both of which were closer to the 1978 targets. Nevertheless, most economists are doubtful that the natural rate of unemployment is as low as 3 percent in the United States.

External Goals of Monetary Policy

In addition to purely domestic, internal goals, a nation's central bank may also be concerned about international payment flows. Thus, policymakers at the Fed or other central banks may desire to achieve *external goals,* or objectives for

GLOBAL Focus | POLICY | CYBER | MANAGEMENT

Inflation Targeting Gains New Adherents

Several nations including New Zealand, Canada, the United Kingdom, Sweden, and Australia have stopped attempting to engage in short-run efforts to stabilize output and employment. Instead, these nations have adopted a policy approach called *inflation targeting*, which aims to keep the actual rate of inflation very close to an announced target level.

As you can see in Figure 25-1, the New Zealand and Canadian inflation-targeting efforts have done much to smooth inflation in those countries. Before New Zealand adopted its inflation-targeting approach to monetary policy in 1990, the average annual inflation rate was more than 10 percent, but since then it has been below 2 percent. Annual inflation in Canada now hovers very close to the same rate, which is noticeably below the rates of inflation the nation experienced prior to implementing inflation targeting in 1992.

A key advantage of inflation targeting is its transparency. It is easy to measure actual inflation rates and see if they fall within target ranges specified by central banks. Furthermore, if people believe that inflation will remain steady, they will feel more comfortable entering into nominal contracts that assume a stable rate of inflation. Thus, inflation targeting can provide a foundation for more consistent production and investment decisions, which in turn can contribute to greater real output and employment stability. In principle, therefore, inflation targeting can best enable central banks to achieve long-run stability of output and employment as well as greater price stability.

For Critical Analysis: Are any potential pitfalls associated with inflation targeting?

Figure 25-1
Inflation Targeting in New Zealand and Canada.

Since the central banks of New Zealand and Canada implemented inflation targeting, the two nations' inflation rates have dropped significantly and become less volatile.

SOURCES: Bank of New Zealand and Bank of Canada.

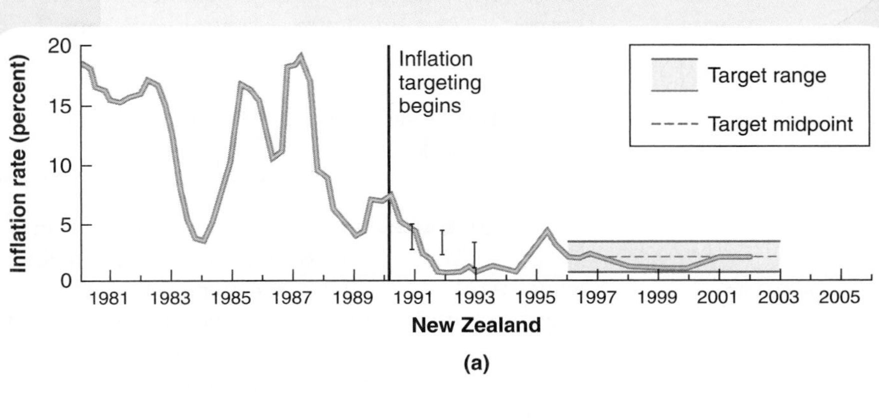

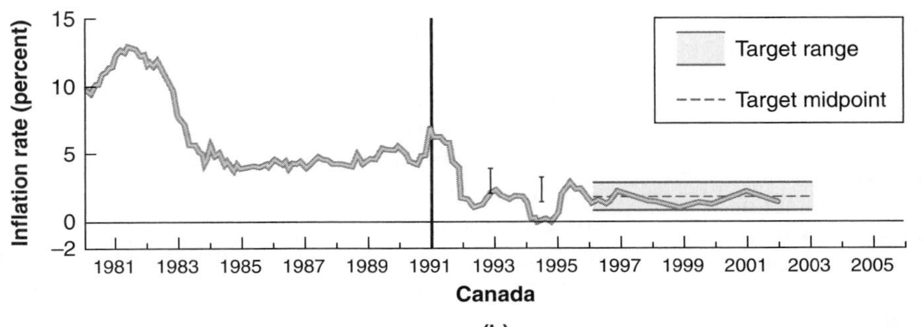

international flows of goods, services, income, and assets or for the relative values of their national currencies.

Why would a nation's residents want central bank policymakers to pursue external objectives? One reason is that international factors help determine domestic outcomes in open economies. If residents of a nation engage in significant volumes of trade with other nations, international considerations may affect the nation's ability to achieve its output, employment, and inflation objectives. Consequently, internal and external objectives may go hand in hand. Another reason, however, is that a number of a nation's citizens may have immediate interests in the international sectors of their nation's economy. They may perceive that international variables themselves—such as the nation's trade balance—should be ultimate policy goals.

INTERNATIONAL OBJECTIVES AND DOMESTIC GOALS As we discussed in Chapter 23, two factors that play a role in determining a country's aggregate desired expenditures are export expenditures on the nation's output of goods and services by residents of other nations and import spending by its own residents on foreign-produced goods and services. An increase in export expenditures increases aggregate desired expenditures, whereas a rise in import spending reduces the fraction of disposable income available for consumption of domestically produced output. Therefore, both of these international factors influence the equilibrium level of real income.

It follows that a central bank such as the Federal Reserve must consider the volumes of export and import expenditures when contemplating appropriate policy strategies. At a minimum, a central bank must account for the real income effects of trade-related expenditures that are unrelated to purely domestic influences. More broadly, however, a central bank may reach the conclusion that achieving its internal goals requires careful attention to international factors. For example, a central bank may seek to achieve balanced international trade as part of a general strategy intended to achieve its domestic output, employment, and inflation objectives.

EXTERNAL BALANCE FOR ITS OWN SAKE Central banks in most countries, however, typically regard external objectives as being separable from internal objectives. Workers and business owners in industries that export large portions of their output often push their governments to enact policies that promote exports. At the same time, workers and business owners in industries that rely on domestic sales of their output may pressure government and central bank officials to pursue policies that restrain imports. Persistent efforts by both of these interest groups could induce a nation's policymakers to seek trade balance *surpluses* as external-balance objectives.

History is replete with examples of nations that have sought to achieve persistent trade surpluses. In the seventeenth and eighteenth centuries, for example, successive generations of British citizens advocated a national policy of **mercantilism.** This school of thought holds that inflows of payments relating to international commerce and trade are a primary source of a nation's wealth. During this period, therefore, British mercantilists advocated policy actions designed to promote exports and to hinder imports. A fundamental difficulty with mercantilist thought, of course, is that if *all* countries simultaneously try to attain trade surpluses through import limitations, international commerce will likely be stymied.

Mercantilism: The idea that a primary determinant of a nation's wealth is international trade and commerce, so a nation can gain by enacting policies that spur exports while limiting imports.

Realization of this self-defeating aspect of mercantilism led to its decline in the nineteenth century. Mercantilist thought supports the goals of special interest groups in any open economy, however, so these groups still use mercantilist arguments today in an effort to pressure policymakers to maintain balanced trade, if not trade surpluses.

The interests of exporters and importers may also make exchange rate objectives part of the mix of external-balance goals. On the one hand, a reduction in the exchange value of a nation's currency effectively makes domestically produced goods less expensive to foreign residents. Thus, if export industries comprise a predominant political interest group, a country's central bank may face pressures to reduce the value of its currency. On the other hand, an increase in a currency's exchange value reduces the effective price that domestic residents pay for foreign-produced goods. Consequently, if importers have considerable political clout, a central bank may be lobbied to push up the value of the nation's currency.

In the face of potentially conflicting ultimate goals and generally vague guidance from legislators, how should central bank officials conduct monetary policies? What near-term goals should they pursue in an effort to achieve broader, ultimate economic policy objectives? These are the issues that we shall address in the remainder of this chapter and in the chapters that follow.

1. What are the ultimate goals of monetary policy? The ultimate goals of the Federal Reserve and other central banks are the final objectives of monetary policy strategies and actions. Central banks often pursue two categories of economic goals. One consists of internal objectives, which are ultimate goals for national real income, employment, and inflation. Under the terms of 1946 and 1978 legislation, the formal goals of the U.S. government and the Federal Reserve System include low and stable inflation rates, high and stable output growth, and a high and stable employment level. The other category of potential ultimate goals for a nation's monetary policy consists of external-balance objectives, which are objectives for the trade balance and other components of the balance of payments.

Intermediate Targets of Monetary Policy

As you have learned in previous chapters, nearly every approach to economics—with the exception of the classical and real-business-cycle models—indicates that monetary policy actions can potentially have short-term or even longer-term effects on real output and employment. All economic theories imply that monetary policy actions influence the price level.

Hence, central banks clearly perform important tasks. Indeed, some observers have called the chair of the Fed's Board of Governors the second-most-important person in the United States, after the president.

Intermediate Monetary Policy Targets

Although the Fed cannot control the total quantity of deposits in the banking system directly, it clearly can influence this amount by conducting open market operations—buying or selling U.S. government securities. In addition, by varying

Intermediate target: An economic variable that a central bank seeks to control because it determines that doing so is consistent with its ultimate objectives.

reserve requirements, the Fed can affect the size of the money multiplier linking a change in reserves caused by its open market operations to the total amount of money in circulation. Finally, the Fed can influence the total amount of reserves held by private banks by changing the discount rate that it charges such institutions, thereby inducing them either to increase or to reduce the amounts of reserves that they borrow from the Federal Reserve banks.

Thus, even though the Federal Reserve and other central banks of the world cannot directly "control" the quantity of money in circulation, they could use their policy instruments—in the case of the Fed, open market operations, the discount rate, and reserve requirements—to try to vary the quantity of money in a precise effort to achieve their inflation, output, and employment objectives. Nevertheless, rather than taking such a direct approach, most central banks typically have sought to achieve **intermediate targets** of monetary policy. An intermediate target is an economic variable whose value a central bank tries to control because it feels that doing so is consistent with its ultimate objectives. Such a variable is distinguishable from the central bank's ultimate policy goals but is sufficiently closely related that it can serve as a "stand-in" or "proxy" for the ultimate objectives, as indicated in Figure 25-2.

The Rationales for Intermediate Targeting

There are two rationales for using an intermediate target in monetary policy. One is that central bank officials often have difficulty reaching agreement about the ways in which monetary policy affects inflation, real output, and employment in the short and long run. The other rationale is that even if central bank policymakers could unanimously agree on how their policy actions influence economic activity, they typically possess limited information about the economy.

PROBLEMS WITH DIRECTLY PURSUING ULTIMATE POLICY GOALS As you have learned by now, there is no shortage of theories about how monetary policy actions affect inflation, real output, and employment. In any central bank, different officials often subscribe to distinctly different theoretical views, making it difficult for central bank policymakers to reach a consensus concerning the best means of attaining ultimate policy objectives.

Figure 25-2
The Intermediate Targeting Strategy for Monetary Policy.

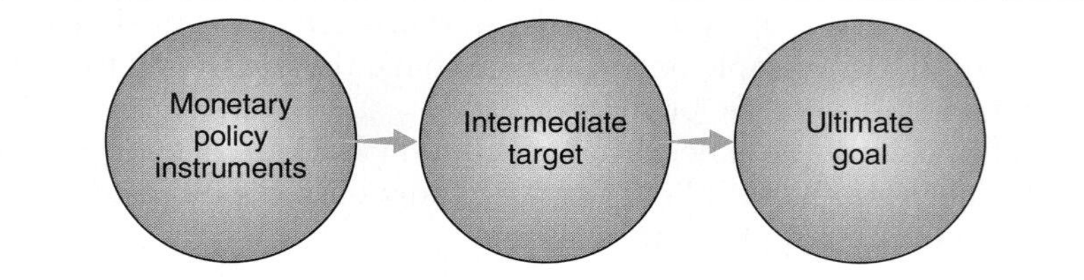

An intermediate target is a macroeconomic variable that a central bank seeks to influence as a stand-in for its ultimate goals, which are more difficult to observe or influence in the near term.

Consequently, the policymakers may *compromise* by seeking to achieve an intermediate monetary policy target. For example, as we shall discuss in more detail shortly, in the past several central banks have used the quantity of money as an intermediate target variable. Not all economic theories agree that monetary policy actions affect real output and employment, but all theories indicate that a sustained change in depository institution reserves should cause monetary aggregates and the price level to move in the same direction, if not in exactly the same proportion. Lacking agreement on any other aspect of how the monetary policy process works, central bank officials might compromise by trying to aim for a monetary objective.

Conducting Monetary Policy with Limited Information Even if all policymakers could agree on one "true" economic theory, they would still have a strong economic justification for using an intermediate monetary policy target. The reason is that central bank officials must conduct monetary policy in the absence of perfect information. Some economic variables, such as interest rates and the quantities of money or credit, can be measured day-to-day or week-to-week. Other variables, such as nominal income, can be estimated weekly but generally are known only on a monthly basis. Still others, particularly the price level, real GDP, and employment, can at best be tracked (or, in the case of real GDP, estimated) only from month to month. Even then, central bank and government statisticians often revise their calculations of these variables in the weeks following their initial release.

Consequently, current information about the central bank's ultimate policy goals—inflation, real output, and employment—typically is the least readily available. In contrast, interest rate, money, and credit data are more likely to be available for observation and use at any given moment. Nominal income data are not forthcoming as quickly as these financial data, but still generally appear more frequently than information about ultimate policy goal variables.

The notion of using an economic variable as an intermediate target follows naturally from the fact that information about other variables is more readily available than information about ultimate objectives. By aiming for an intermediate target, a central bank can more quickly discern whether it is on the way to achieving the basic intent of its policies. Otherwise, monetary policymakers might have to wait much longer to make this assessment.

Choosing an Intermediate Target Variable

A central bank that decides to use an intermediate targeting approach to conducting monetary policy must then choose an appropriate target variable. In selecting its intermediate target variable, a central bank considers several criteria.

Characteristics of Intermediate Targets To be useful, an intermediate target variable should exhibit four key attributes:

1. Frequently observable. Because information timing is a fundamental rationale for using an intermediate targeting approach, an intermediate target variable should be observable more frequently than ultimate goal variables. As we discussed above, the price level, real GDP, and employment are at best observable on a monthly basis. Consequently, the central bank is likely to choose an intermediate target variable that it can observe from week to week or even from day to day.

2. Consistency with ultimate goals. Achieving a target value for an intermediate variable should be consistent with achieving the central bank's ultimate objectives. If a central bank were to hit its chosen intermediate target successfully only to discover that it had widely missed its goals for inflation, output, and employment, then its policy strategy would have been counterproductive.

3. Definable and measurable. Defining and measuring an intermediate target variable should be a straightforward task. If a potential intermediate target variable is susceptible to redefinition because of intermittent regulatory or technological changes, then a central bank would have trouble settling on a consistent way to measure the target variable and evaluate its relationship to ultimate policy goals.

4. Controllable. The central bank should be able to readily influence the value of the intermediate target variable. Otherwise, it would be futile for the central bank to try to achieve its ultimate policy objectives by attaining its intermediate target.

THE MENU OF POTENTIAL INTERMEDIATE TARGET VARIABLES Several alternative categories of economic variables might qualify as intermediate monetary policy targets. Consequently, central banks around the globe have adopted a number of different intermediate targeting procedures over the years.

Monetary Aggregates Many nations, including Germany, the United Kingdom, and Japan, have experimented with procedures that use *monetary aggregates,* or alternative measures of the nominal quantity of money in circulation, as intermediate target variables. In the United States, the Federal Reserve in the past has targeted M1 and M2.

The basic rationale for targeting a monetary aggregate has been that various economic theories indicate that the quantity of money should help determine aggregate demand, thereby influencing the price level and, possibly, real output and employment. Thus, central banks have believed that a relationship should exist between monetary aggregates and their inflation, output, and employment objectives. Furthermore, values of monetary aggregates typically are known weekly. Finally, central banks clearly have the ability to influence monetary aggregates.

Nevertheless, central banks have had some difficulties using intermediate monetary targeting approaches. One problem has been that regulatory and technological changes have blurred the lines among various financial assets that function as money. In the United States, for instance, the Federal Reserve has redefined M1 or M2 every few years as new forms of money-like assets have emerged. The existence of more than one monetary aggregate is itself indicative of the problems in defining "money." Another problem that was particularly bothersome in the 1980s and early 1990s was a breakdown in the previously consistent relationship between the basic M1 and M2 aggregates and GDP. Furthermore, as we discussed in Chapter 20, the advent of sweep accounts in the 1990s significantly degraded the usefulness of the M1 aggregate.

Credit Aggregates Another quantitative financial target, which central banks in China and Russia have emphasized, is a *credit aggregate* target, which is a measure of the volume of lending. One type of credit aggregate is *aggregate credit,* or the total amount of all lending in an economy. A narrower credit aggregate is *total bank credit,* or total lending and securities holdings by banks. As you learned in Chapter 16, central banks can influence such measures of credit, because the expansion of bank lending accompanies the multiple expansion of bank deposit money. Thus, Fed policy instruments can affect total credit as well as the total quantity of money in circulation. Additionally, credit aggregates usually are straightforward to define and to measure, and credit data usually are observable weekly.

Credit aggregates, however, suffer from problems similar to those that monetary aggregates entail. In particular, relationships between credit measures and ultimate goals generally have been *at least* as tenuous as relationships between monetary aggregates and ultimate goals.

Interest Rates The most commonly used intermediate monetary policy target is the *price of credit,* or the nominal interest rate. Central banks can observe interest rates daily and often by the minute. In addition, central banks' policy actions can have clear-cut effects on nominal interest rates.

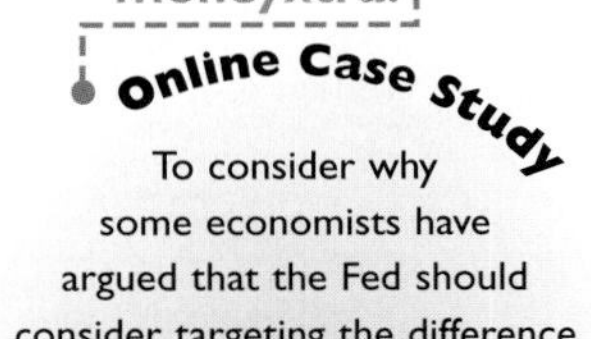

To consider why some economists have argued that the Fed should consider targeting the difference between long- and short-term interest rates, go to the Chapter 25 Case Study, entitled "Should the Fed Target the Spread?" http://moneyxtra.swcollege.com

Interest rates and economic activity are not always closely related, however. While lower interest rates can spur capital investment and economic activity, increased income raises the demand for credit and pushes nominal interest rates upward. Hence, the relationship between nominal interest rates and real income is not always predictable. In addition, there are many interest rates that central banks could consider targeting, including interest rates on financial instruments with short and long maturities.

Nominal GDP In recent years many economists have proposed that *nominal gross domestic product (GDP)* be used as a target, even though nominal GDP data are not available much more frequently than observations of real GDP and the price level. The essential argument favoring targeting nominal GDP hinges on the fact that nominal GDP by definition is equal to real GDP times the GDP price deflator. There are a number of competing theories about how monetary policy influences the price level and real output, but this definitional relationship indicates that if a central bank wishes to stabilize real output and prices, then minimizing variations in the growth rate of nominal GDP would help contain volatility in either of these ultimate goal variables. We shall illustrate this argument in the *Link to Policy* at the conclusion of the chapter.

Exchange Rates A number of central banks have used exchange rates as intermediate targets of monetary policy. This policy procedure has been particularly common in small economies open to cross-border trade and financial flows.

The rationale for exchange rate targeting is that in small countries buffeted by international events beyond their control, real GDP, employment, and inflation often depend on the exchange value of a nation's currency. Thus, central banks in these nations often conclude that their main task should be to keep the exchange rate at a level consistent with ultimate economic goals. As we shall discuss in Chapter 28, key issues then become how to determine the appropriate target for the exchange rate and what procedure to follow to keep the exchange rate close to this target level.

2. Why might a central bank use an intermediate monetary policy target? Because of limitations on the availability of data on ultimate objectives and different interpretations of how monetary policy actions influence ultimate policy goals, central banks such as the Federal Reserve sometimes adopt an intermediate target. Such an intermediate target variable should be observable with greater frequency than ultimate goal variables, easy to measure, subject to influence through monetary policy actions, and closely related to ultimate policy objectives. Possible intermediate target variables include money and credit aggregates, interest rates, nominal GDP, and exchange rates.

Interest Rate Targeting

As we discuss in Chapter 27, today most of the world's central banks, including the Federal Reserve, implement monetary policy through some type of interest-rate-targeting procedure. Let's begin our discussion of intermediate monetary targets by contemplating the pros and cons of targeting a nominal interest rate in an effort to achieve an ultimate policy goal.

Targeting the Nominal Interest Rate

Figure 25-3 explains how a central bank can choose and maintain a nominal interest rate target. In panel (d), we assume that the ultimate target for real income is equal to y^*. Suppose that inducing a level of desired investment that is consistent with attaining y^* in panel (d) requires achieving the nominal interest rate target r^*. In light of the term and risk structures of interest rates illustrated by the positions of the yield curves in panel (b), the Fed must attain the federal funds rate given by r_f^1 in panel (a). It does this by conducting open market operations, and thereby varying nonborrowed reserves, to make sure that the supply of reserves to depository institutions crosses the reserve demand schedule at point A in panel (a). As shown in panel (c), at the targeted nominal interest rate r^* and given the current price level P_1, the equilibrium quantity of real money balances is equal to M_1/P_1.

Now suppose that there are variations in the demand for real money balances, perhaps because of changes in the technology by which people make payments. For instance, a decline in the demand for real money balances, from $m_1^d(y^*)$ to $m_2^d(y^*)$, causes the quantity of real money balances demanded to decrease from M_1/P_1 to M_2/P_1 in panel (c). Because a portion of the quantity of money is held as checking accounts at depository institutions that are subject to reserve requirements, this decrease in the quantity of money demanded causes a reduction in required reserves. Thus, reserve demand decreases in panel (a). This places downward pressure on the federal funds rate, toward r_f' at point B in panel (a).

To keep interest rates from falling in response to the decline in money demand, the Fed engages in open market sales. As shown in panel (a), this policy action reduces nonborrowed reserves and shifts the reserve supply schedule leftward. As

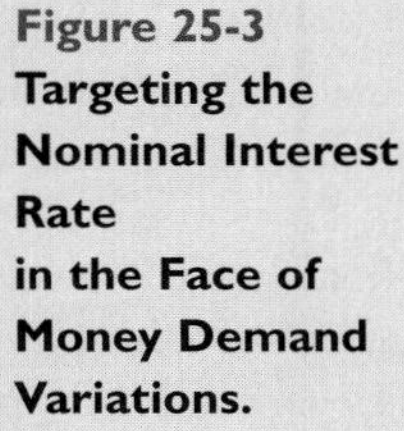

Figure 25-3 Targeting the Nominal Interest Rate in the Face of Money Demand Variations.

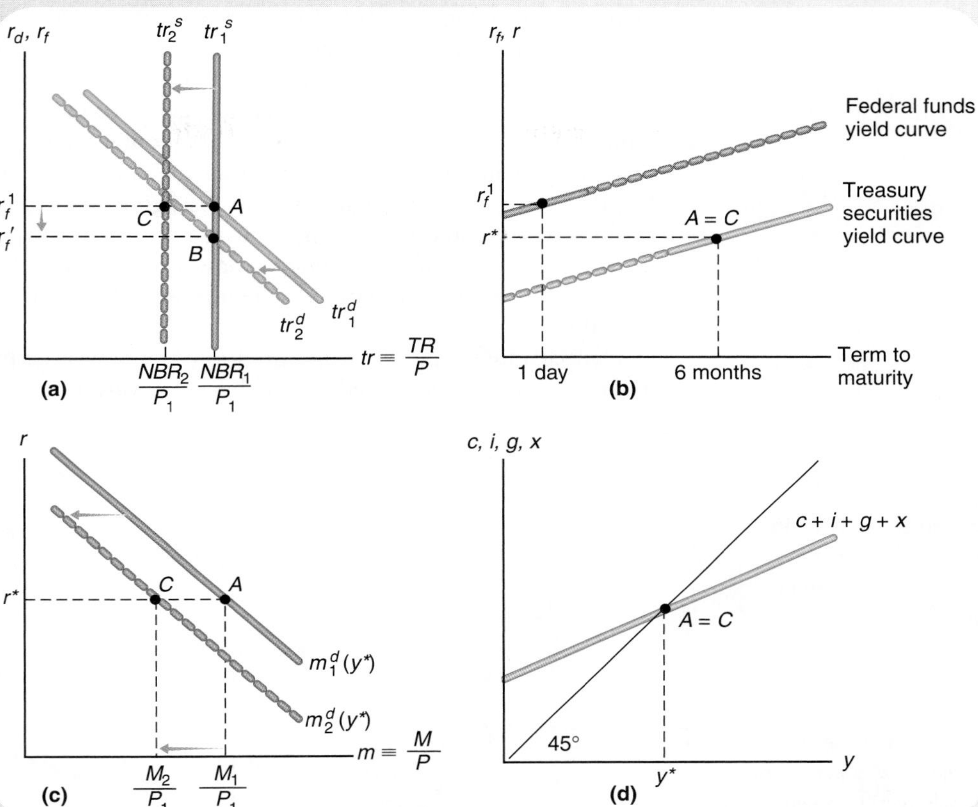

At point A in panel (d), the interest rate target r^* is consistent with the ultimate real income target y^*. If the demand for money declines, then the quantity of real money balances demanded falls in panel (c). As transactions account balances at depository institutions decline, required reserves fall, causing reserve demand to decrease in panel (a), which tends to push the federal funds rate downward toward r_f'. To keep the federal funds rate at its target value, the Fed sells securities and shifts the reserve supply schedule leftward in panel (a). This keeps the nominal interest rate at its target value of r^* in panel (b), thereby stabilizing real income at the target level y^* in panel (d).

a result, the Fed keeps the federal funds rate from changing, so the nominal interest rate stays at its target value of r^* at point C in panel (b). As a result, investment spending remains unchanged, and equilibrium real income remains at the target level of y^* in panel (d). As shown in panel (c), stabilizing the nominal interest rate permits the quantity of money in circulation to decline by the full amount of the reduction in the demand for real money balances. Permitting the quantity of money to decline, however, is consistent with attaining the Fed's ultimate income objective.

The Drawback of Interest Rate Targeting: Variations in Autonomous Expenditures

In the example depicted in Figure 25-3, adopting the nominal interest rate as an intermediate target is an appropriate monetary policy procedure. Nominal-interest-rate targeting clearly stabilizes real income in the face of variations in money demand and shifts in the demand for depository institution reserves.

Unfortunately for a central bank such as the Federal Reserve, however, other factors in the economy can also change unexpectedly. Figure 25-4, for example, illustrates the effects of variations in autonomous expenditures. Recall from Chapter 23 that a decline in autonomous consumption, investment, government spending, or exports or a rise in net taxes or autonomous import spending causes a multiple reduction in equilibrium real income. Figure 25-4 illustrates the effect of variations in any one of these autonomous expenditure components. In panel (d), the result is a downward shift in the aggregate expenditures schedule. Equilibrium real income falls from y^* at point A to y_2 at point B. Furthermore, so does the quantity of real money balances demanded, from M_1/P_1 to M_2/P_1 in panel (c), as the money demand schedule shifts leftward in response to the decline in real income.

Hence, under a policy of nominal-interest-rate targeting, the goal level of real income cannot be achieved when there are variations in autonomous expendi-

Figure 25-4 Targeting the Nominal Interest Rate in the Face of Variations in Autonomous Expenditures.

A decline in autonomous aggregate spending causes the aggregate expenditures schedule to shift downward in panel (d). As a result, the demand for money also falls, as shown in panel (c). If the central bank enacts policies that keep the interest rate at its target level of r^* in panels (a) and (b), then equilibrium real income will remain below its target level of y^*. Thus, targeting the interest rate is inconsistent with the central bank's ultimate goal in the face of variations in autonomous expenditures.

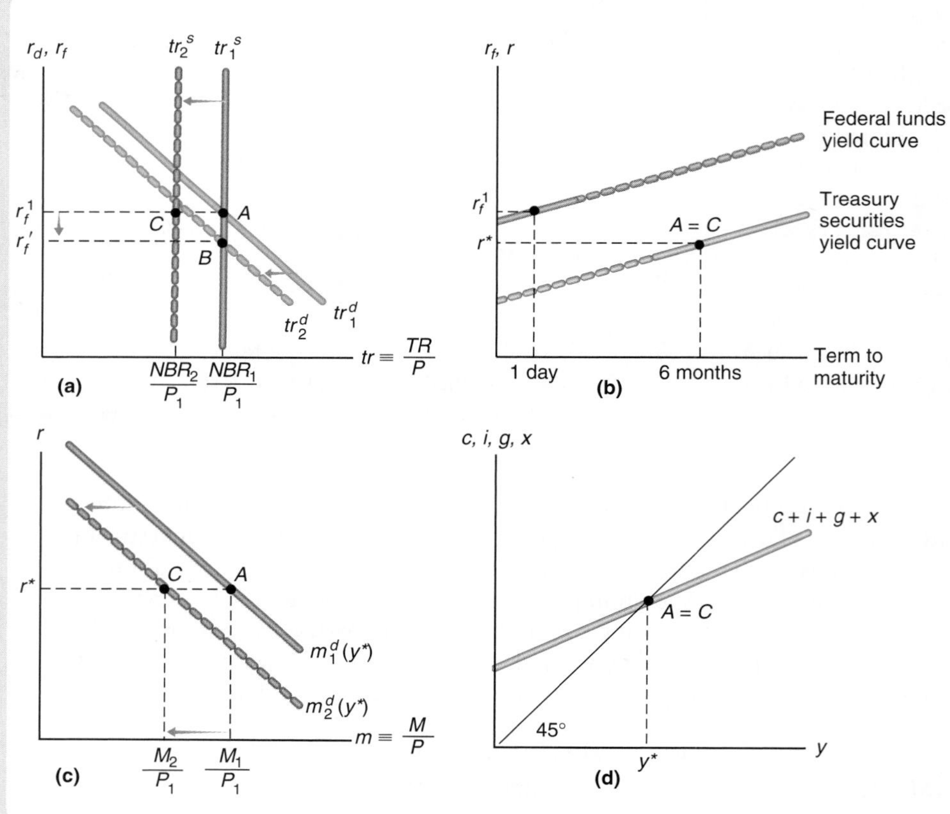

tures. Given the many potential sources of variations in autonomous expenditures, this is a potentially significant drawback of this intermediate targeting procedure. Nevertheless, as we shall discuss in greater detail in Chapter 27, in recent years the Fed has placed its near-term policy focus on interest rates.

Targeting Monetary Aggregates

What should a central bank do if there is significant volatility in aggregate desired expenditures, thereby making a nominal interest rate less attractive as an intermediate monetary policy target? One possible answer is to target a monetary aggregate instead. (A fundamental precondition, of course, is that the central bank must have confidence in the data for the monetary aggregate it chooses to target; see on the following page *Global Focus: Is the ECB's "Complex Strategy for a Complex Region" Too Complicated?*)

The Rationale for Monetary Targeting

Under a targeting procedure that focuses on a monetary aggregate, the Fed selects a target for the nominal quantity of money in circulation, denoted as M^*. Given a price level equal to P_1, therefore, the equilibrium quantity of real money balances is M^*/P_1 at point A in panel (c) in Figure 25-5 on page 633. The Fed chooses the target level for the quantity of money to achieve its ultimate goal for income, which again is equal to y^* in panel (d).

Now suppose that there is a sudden autonomous decline in export spending. This causes the aggregate expenditures schedule to shift down, which places downward pressure on equilibrium real income, from y^* at point A in panel (d) toward y_2 at point B. As a result, the money demand schedule shifts leftward. The equilibrium quantity of real money balances begins to fall toward M_2/P_1 in panel (c), and as required reserves decline, the result is a reduction in reserve demand in panel (a).

To maintain its monetary target M^*, the Fed must maintain the current level of nonborrowed reserves, thereby keeping the reserve supply schedule in an unchanged position panel (a). This action pushes down the equilibrium federal funds rate and induces downward shifts in the yield curves in panel (b). As a result, the nominal interest rate declines, from r_1 to r_2. This interest rate decline has two effects. First, it induces an increase in the quantity of money demanded, so that the equilibrium quantity of real balances rises back toward M^*/P_1 in panel (c). Thus, the policy action keeps the quantity of money at its target level. Second, it causes desired real investment to increase, which tends to offset the initial autonomous fall in export spending. In the best of all outcomes for the Fed, which is depicted in panel (d), aggregate desired spending returns to its initial level. As a result, monetary targeting maintains real income at its goal level of y^*.

Note that the key to achieving the target level of the monetary aggregate is for the Fed to permit interest rates to vary as necessary. Indeed, interest rate changes are crucial for monetary targeting to be consistent with the ultimate goal level of real income in the face of variations in autonomous expenditures.

GLOBAL Focus | POLICY | CYBER | MANAGEMENT

Is the ECB's "Complex Strategy for a Complex Region" Too Complicated?

Since it assumed its role as a policymaking institution for the European Monetary Union (EMU) in 1999, the European Central Bank (ECB) has pursued a two-pronged approach to determining appropriate monetary actions. On the one hand, its officials pay considerable attention to a broad set of leading indicators of inflation within the nations using the euro as a common currency. On the other hand, the officials also wish to keep M3, a broad measure of money that includes currency, checking and saving deposits, and both small and large time deposits, close to a level felt to be consistent with a steady rate of growth of total liquidity. In effect, the ECB has combined monetary targeting with extra policy adjustments in light of information it gleans from various additional inflation indicators.

Critics have argued that this approach to monetary policymaking is overly complicated, but the ECB officials reply that a complex strategy is required for a complex region. Nevertheless, an additional complication has arisen in recent years: the ECB has made significant mistakes in calculating the quantity of money in circulation within EMU nations. For instance, as EMU economies showed signs of slipping into recessions in 2001, the ECB maintained a restrained monetary policy because of concerns that the annual growth rate of M3 was too high above the target rate. Then, a few weeks later, an ECB report indicated that the statisticians had overcounted the components of M3. As a result, when ECB officials refrained from boosting the growth of the EMU's monetary base and pushing down market interest rates, they were working with an estimated growth rate for M3 that was nearly 1 percentage point higher than the actual rate.

ECB officials have since argued that the 2002 switchover to circulating euro currency within EMU nations will reduce the scope for errors in tabulating monetary aggregates. This has not satisfied the critics, however, who argue that the miscalculations in 2001 resulted from problems distinguishing money market funds held by EMU residents from funds held by residents of nations outside the EMU. According to the ECB's critics, it is impossible for the ECB to justify the continued use of a complicated, pseudo-monetary-targeting approach when these and other measurement errors can occur.

For Critical Analysis: Why might the ECB choose to supplement a monetary targeting approach with policy adjustments based on movements in leading indicators of inflation?

The Drawback of Monetary Targeting: Money Demand Variability

The example in Figure 25-5 illustrates the best possible outcome under monetary targeting. In that example, maintaining the quantity of money at its target level simultaneously assures the achievement of a goal level of real income.

A problem arises, however, if the demand for real money balances is variable. Consider Figure 25-6 on page 634, in which real income initially is equal to y^* at point A in panel (d). Panel (c) illustrates the effects of an autonomous rise in the demand for money, from $m_1^d(y^*)$ to $m_2^d(y^*)$, perhaps resulting from a flight to liquidity following a sharp, unexpected drop in bond and stock prices. As a result, the quantity of real money balances rises from M^*/P_1 at point A to M_2/P_1

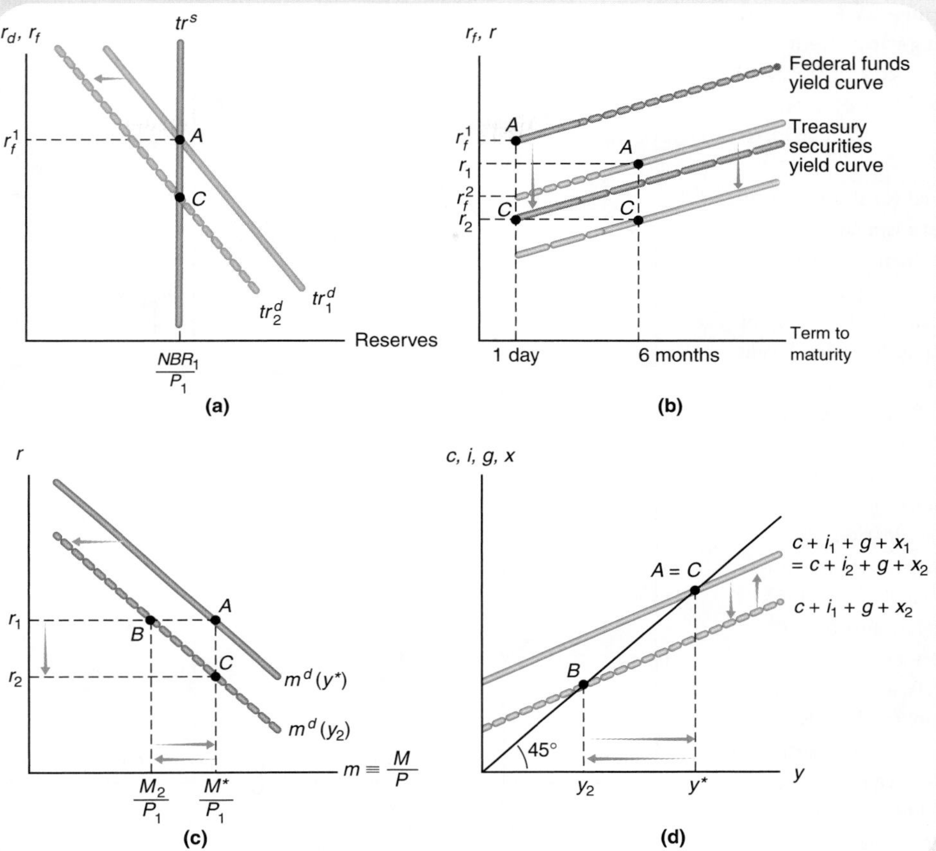

Figure 25-5 Targeting the Quantity of Money in the Face of Variations in Autonomous Expenditures.

A decline in autonomous aggregate spending, such as a fall in autonomous exports from x_1 to x_2, causes the aggregate expenditures schedule to shift downward in panel (d). As a result, the demand for money also falls, as shown in panel (c). Panel (a) indicates that the reserve demand tends to shift leftward as required reserve holdings decline with the reduction in deposits. To keep the equilibrium quantity of real money balances at M^*/P_1 in panel (c), where M^* is the monetary target, the Fed must maintain the reserve supply and allow declines in market interest rates. Thus, equilibrium rates of interest fall in panels (a) and (b). This stimulates desired investment spending, pushing equilibrium real income back toward the target level in panel (d).

at point *B*. Reattaining a quantity of money consistent with the Fed's target requires an increase in the nominal interest rate to r_2 at point C along the new money demand schedule.

In the market for real depository institution reserves, the increase in the quantity of deposit money in the banking system induces an increase in required reserves. Thus, reserve demand rises, which pushes up the equilibrium federal funds rate, from r_f^1 at point *A* in panel (a) to r_f' at point *B*. Achieving a rise in the longer-term nominal interest rate sufficient to maintain the Fed's monetary target may also require a further boost in the federal funds rate. As illustrated in panel (a), this can be achieved by maintaining the current levels of nonborrowed reserves and reserve supply, which yields the equilibrium federal funds rate r_f^2 at

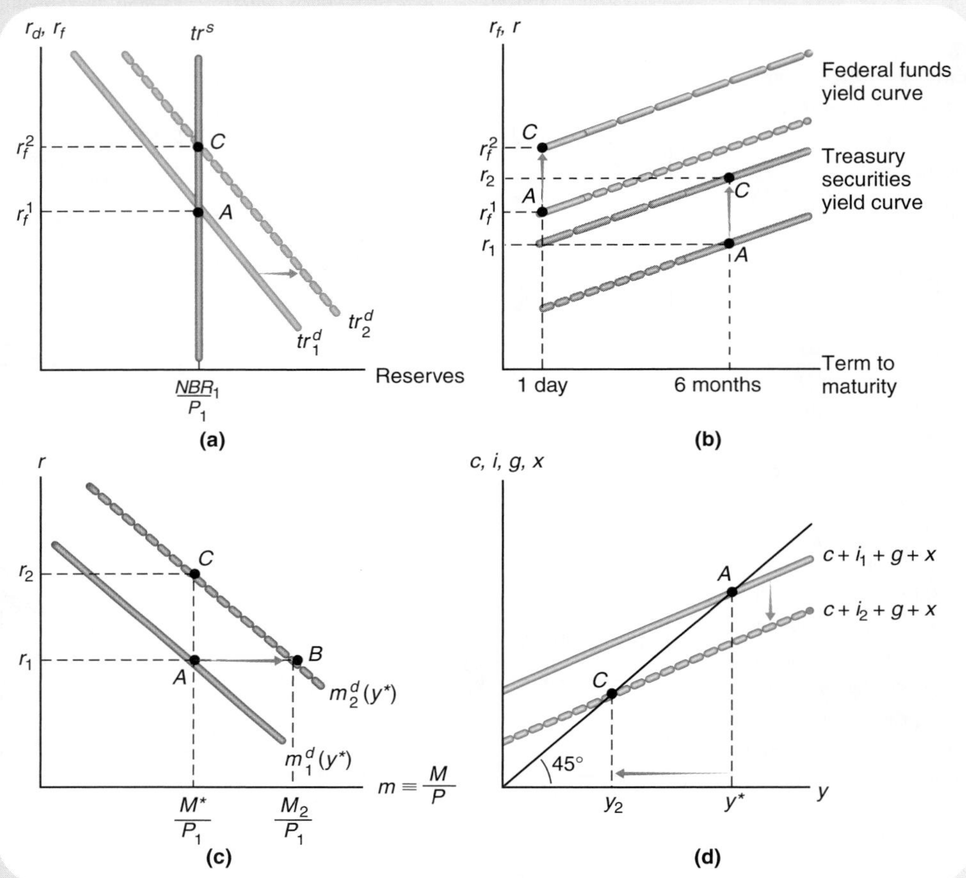

Figure 25-6 Targeting the Quantity of Money in the Face of Money Demand Variations.

Panel (c) shows that if there is a sudden rise in the demand for money, then the quantity of money balances begins to rise from the target level M^*/P_1 at point A to M_2/P_1 at point B. To keep the quantity of money at its target level, the Fed must allow market interest rates to rise, as shown in panels (a) and (b). Real money balances then fall back toward M^*/P_1 at point C in panel (c). The rise in market interest rates, however, induces a decline in desired investment spending, which causes equilibrium real income to decline below y^* in panel (d). Consequently, achieving a monetary target in the face of a rise in the demand for money is inconsistent with stabilizing real income.

point C. Panel (b) shows that this increase in the one-day federal funds rate shifts up the federal funds and Treasury securities yield curves sufficiently to raise the longer-term nominal interest rate to r_2, thereby reattaining the monetary target.

Given unchanged inflation expectations, however, the higher nominal interest rate pushes down desired investment spending. As a result, the aggregate expenditures schedule shifts downward in panel (d) of Figure 25-6, and equilibrium real income declines from y^* to y_2 at point C in panel (d). Thus, in its effort to achieve its intermediate target for a monetary aggregate in the face of an unexpected rise in the demand for money, the Fed induces a fall in equilibrium real income. Intermediate monetary targeting fails to achieve the Fed's ultimate goal for real income.

Note what would have happened if the Fed had not responded to the rise in money demand in Figure 25-6. Although the quantity of real money balances in circulation would have risen, real income would have been unaffected. Thus, if the Fed had targeted the nominal interest rate instead, the ultimate goal level of real income, y^*, would have been attained.

The fundamental point illustrated by the examples in Figures 25-3 through 25-6 was first made by William Poole of Brown University more than twenty-five years ago:

> When a central bank chooses between targeting the nominal interest rate and targeting a monetary aggregate, the key criterion the central bank should consider is the main source of variability that it faces.

If most variability is in money demand and the demand for depository institution reserves, then using the nominal interest rate as an intermediate target is preferable. In contrast, if most variability arises from changes in autonomous spending and in the position of the aggregate expenditures schedule, then targeting a monetary aggregate is a more desirable approach.

3. What are the pros and cons of interest rates versus monetary aggregates as intermediate monetary policy targets? Using a nominal interest rate as an intermediate target helps to stabilize aggregate demand if money demand is highly volatile while aggregate desired expenditures are relatively stable. In contrast, adopting a monetary target makes aggregate demand more stable if aggregate desired expenditures are variable while money demand is relatively stable.

Exchange Rate Targeting

Conducting monetary policy to keep an exchange rate fixed, with adjustments in the fixed exchange rate from time to time as required by economic conditions, is one way to use the exchange rate as an intermediate target. Another approach is to let exchange rates vary in foreign exchange markets but to intervene in those markets as needed to keep the exchange rate within a desired range. In these interventions, the central bank supports its own nation's currency by buying the currency with the currencies of other nations or, conversely, pushes down the value of its own nation's currency by selling the currency in exchange for other countries' currencies. A central bank's use of the exchange rate as a monetary policy target to achieve internal and external economic goals may be complicated, however, by its interactions with governmental authorities who determine fiscal policies.

The Assignment Problem

As we discussed in Chapter 17, governments typically delegate monetary policy responsibilities to government-appointed individuals or boards. These individuals or boards supervise and regulate private banks and manage the provision of financial services to the government. At the same time, however, elected or appointed officials of the government finance ministries or treasury departments implement policies regarding public expenditures and taxation.

Assignment problem: The problem of determining whether monetary or fiscal policymakers should assume responsibility for achieving either external-balance or internal-balance objectives.

This situation gives rise to the policy **assignment problem,** which refers to the complications that can arise in determining the appropriate policy objectives for the central bank and the finance ministry (or treasury) to pursue. In principle, each authority can conduct policies aimed at achieving a specific ultimate objective. Thus, to attain an exchange rate target, a nation's central bank can vary the monetary base, and its finance ministries can alter the composition of the government's budget.

Suppose, for instance, that the central bank and the finance ministry agree on two key economic goals for the nation for the current year: to achieve a desired level of real GDP and to maintain balanced trade with the nation's key trading partners. Hence, the nation has an internal objective (the desired GDP level) and an external objective (balanced trade). Both the central bank and the finance ministry could conduct policies intended to achieve either objective, but it would be redundant for both authorities to aim at the same objective. Instead, it makes sense for one authority to focus on the domestic objective of a desired real GDP level while the other authority aims to achieve the international objective of a balanced trade account.

But how should the responsibilities be assigned? Would it be in the nation's best interests for the central bank to aim for an exchange rate target intended to achieve the desired real GDP level while the finance ministry varies the composition of its budget in an effort to attain balanced trade? Or should the central bank seek to attain an exchange rate consistent with a trade balance, leaving the finance ministry with the responsibility for altering real GDP through its budgetary policies?

Achieving External Balance

To think about the fundamental nature of the assignment problem, let's begin by considering Figure 25-7. Point *A* in panel (a) displays an initial income-expenditure equilibrium position for an economy given a level of government spending equal to g_1. Panel (b) shows the economy's trade balance schedule (see Chapter 23). At the initial equilibrium income level y_1, there is balanced trade. That is, $x - im = 0$ at point *A* in panel (b). We shall assume that this position of balanced trade is the external-balance objective and that the central bank concentrates on achieving this goal by targeting the exchange rate.

Now consider what happens if the government increases its spending from g_1 to g_2. As shown in panel (a), the aggregate expenditures schedule shifts upward, and equilibrium real income increases. This results in a rise in import expenditures and, as indicated in panel (b), a movement along the trade balance schedule to point *B*. Thus, the nation begins to run a trade deficit equal to $(x - im)_2$. To try to reattain balanced trade, the central bank could intervene in the foreign exchange markets by selling the nation's currency. This pushes down the currency's value, thereby raising the value of the spot exchange rate from its initial level of S_1 to a higher value of S_2, as shown in panel (c). The fall in the value of the home currency encourages foreign residents to buy more domestic goods. As a result, autonomous export expenditures increase, and the trade balance schedule shifts up, eliminating the trade deficit and reattaining external balance at point C in panel (b).

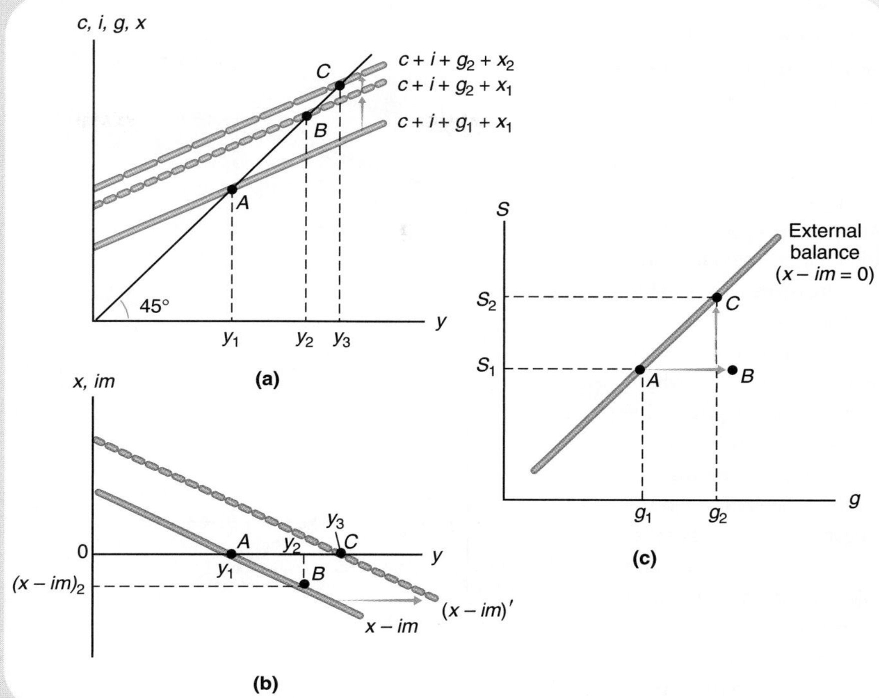

Figure 25-7
Monetary and Fiscal Policy Combinations for External Balance.

The exchange rate–government spending combination g_1 and S_1 at point *A* in panel (c) yields the equilibrium real income level y_1 at point *A* in panel (a). At this level of real income, panel (b) indicates that trade is balanced at point *A*, where $x - im = 0$. If the government increases its spending to g_2 while the exchange rate remains equal to S_1, then the aggregate expenditures schedule shifts upward in panel (a), causing an increase in equilibrium real income and a consequent trade deficit at point *B* in panel (b). To stimulate exports, the central bank increases the exchange rate so that the domestic currency depreciates. This stimulates exports and eliminates the trade deficit at point *C* in panel (b). Thus, points *A* and *C* in panel (c) lie along a set of combinations of exchange rates and government spending that maintain balanced trade. This is the external-balance schedule.

Thus, both points *A* and *C* in panel (c) of Figure 25-7 are part of a set of government spending–exchange rate combinations that maintain external balance. These combinations are the upward-sloping *external-balance schedule* in panel (c). This schedule indicates that to maintain the nation's external-balance objective of balanced trade, the central bank must increase its exchange rate target whenever the government increases its spending.

Achieving Internal Balance

In Figure 25-8 on the following page, we consider what policymakers must do to achieve *internal* balance in the face of increased government spending. At point *A* in panel (a), equilibrium real income is equal to y_1. This happens to correspond to government policymakers' real income objective, denoted y^*. If the government increases its spending, then equilibrium real income rises to y_2 at point *B*, above the target income level. As shown in panel (b), this also causes a movement along the trade balance schedule to point *B*, so that the nation begins to run a trade deficit equal to $(x - im)'$.

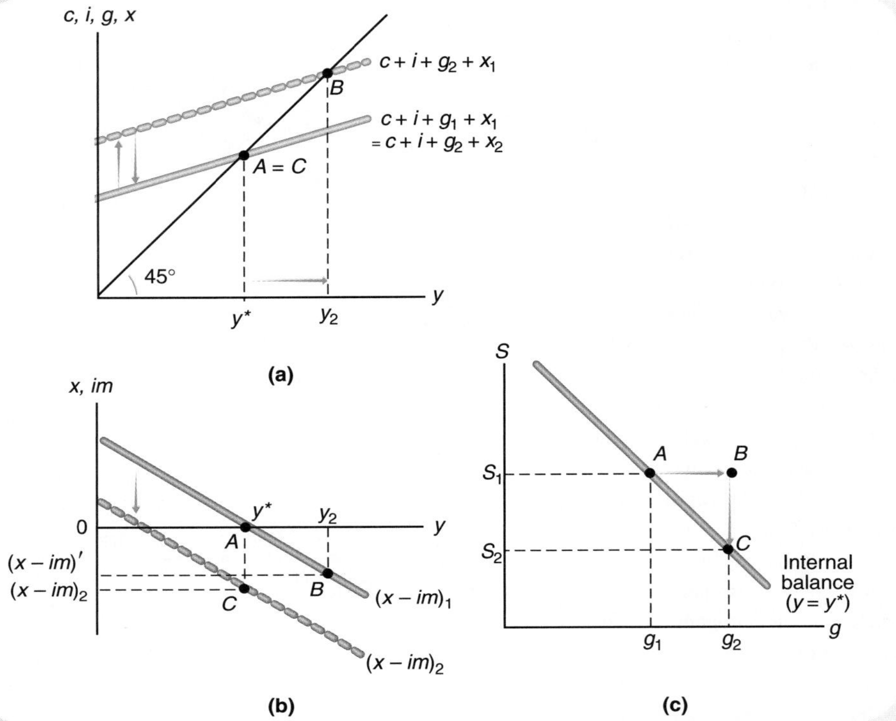

Figure 25-8
Monetary and Fiscal Policy Combinations for Internal Balance.

The exchange rate–government spending combination S_1 and g_1 at point *A* in panel (c) yields a target real income level y^* at point *A* in panel (a). At this level of real income, panel (b) indicates that trade is balanced at point *A*, where $x - im = 0$. If the government increases its spending to g_2 while the exchange rate remains equal to S_1, then the aggregate expenditures schedule shifts upward in panel (a), causing an increase in equilibrium real income and a consequent trade deficit at point *B* in panel (b). To reattain its real income target, the central bank reduces the exchange rate, so that the domestic currency appreciates. This reduces exports and widens the trade deficit at point *C* in panel (b). Nevertheless, points *A* and *C* in panel (c) lie along a set of combinations of exchange rates and government spending that maintain domestic real income at the target level. This is the internal-balance schedule.

To push the nation's economy back to a position of internal balance, the central bank must adjust its exchange rate target to reduce aggregate desired expenditures. This entails reducing the exchange rate from S_1 to S_2, so that the value of the nation's currency rises, causing autonomous export expenditures to decline. As a result, the aggregate expenditures schedule shifts back down in panel (a), and equilibrium real income returns to its original level. In panel (b), the trade balance schedule shifts downward, and the trade deficit widens, to $(x - im)_2$.

Both points *A* and *C* in panel (c) of Figure 25-8 lie along a schedule of points giving government spending–exchange rate combinations that maintain internal balance. These policy combinations comprise the downward-sloping *internal-balance schedule* in panel (c). This schedule indicates that to maintain the nation's internal-balance goal level of real income, the central bank must reduce its exchange rate target whenever the government increases its spending.

Assigning Internal and External Objectives

Panel (a) in Figure 25-9 shows both the external-balance schedule and the internal-balance schedule. The point where these schedules cross, denoted as *E,* is the only point that lies on both schedules. Thus, this point gives the single combination of the government's expenditures and the central bank's exchange rate target, denoted g^* and S^*, that can simultaneously achieve external and internal balance.

EVALUATING ALTERNATIVE ASSIGNMENTS Suppose that the government aims to achieve external balance, while the central bank seeks internal balance. Panel (a) shows what happens starting at point *A* where both government spending and the exchange rate, g_1 and S_1, are below the values consistent with both objectives. Given the exchange rate S_1, the government decreases its spending to g_2 in order to achieve balanced trade at point *B* on the external-balance schedule. To attain the goal level of real income at this lower level of government expenditures, the central bank increases its exchange rate target to S_2 at point *C* on the internal-balance schedule. Ultimately, as shown in panel (a), such back-and-forth responses by the two policymakers attain the government spending–exchange rate combination g^* and S^* at point *E*.

Now suppose that the assignment of goals is reversed: in panel (b), the government seeks to attain internal balance, while the central bank aims to achieve

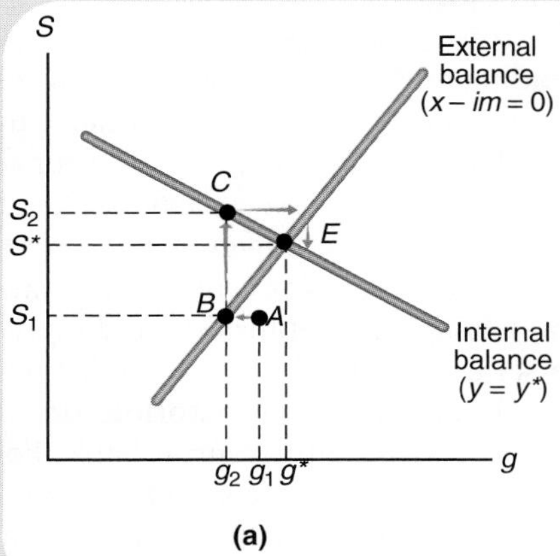

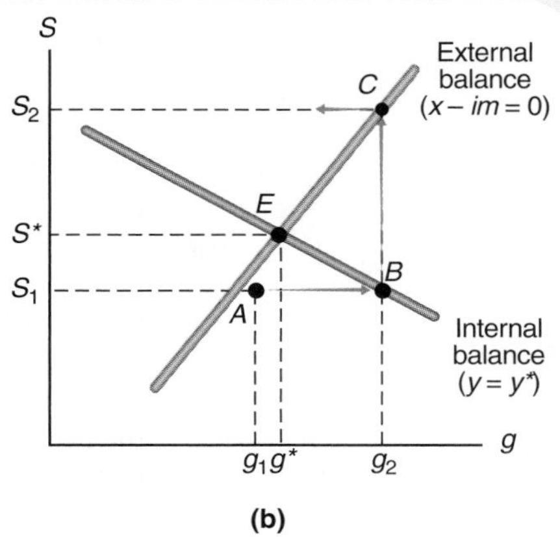

Figure 25-9
Policy Assignments for Internal and External Balance.

In panels (a) and (b), point *A* is at the same initial combination of the exchange rate and government spending. In panel (a), the government adjusts its spending in an effort to attain external balance, while the central bank sets the exchange rate to aim for internal balance. Thus, the government reduces its spending to g_2 to achieve external balance at point *B* on the external-balance schedule, which induces the central bank to raise its exchange rate target to S_2 at point *C* on the internal-balance schedule. Eventually, both policymakers settle on the policy combination g^* and S^* at point *E* consistent with both internal balance and external balance. By way of contrast, panel (b) shows what happens if the assignment of objectives is reversed, so that the government attempts to achieve internal balance while the central bank aims for external balance. Starting at point *A*, a spending increase by the government to move to point *B* on the internal-balance schedule induces the central bank to increase its exchange rate target to S_2 at point *C* on the external-balance schedule. These interactions push both policymakers farther from the best combination of policies at point *E*.

external balance. The initial point again is point *A* with the policy combination g_1 and S_1. Given the exchange rate S_1, the government increases its spending to g_2 in order to achieve its real income objective at point *B* on the internal-balance schedule. To attain balanced trade at this higher level of government expenditures, the central bank increases its exchange rate target to S_2 at point *C* on the external-balance schedule. Clearly, with this assignment of objectives, interactions between the two policymakers push government spending and the exchange rate target *farther* from g^* and S^* at point *E*.

DETERMINING THE CORRECT ASSIGNMENT In this example the appropriate policy assignment is for the government to aim for external balance and the central bank to adjust its exchange rate target to achieve internal balance. Thus, Figure 25-9 depicts a situation in which a nation's central bank can better attain domestic goals while a finance ministry can do a more creditable job of achieving international objectives. In some cases, however, it could be better for the central bank to work toward attaining international objectives while the finance ministry focuses on purely domestic goals. As you will learn in Chapter 28, the effects of central bank monetary policies on a nation's domestic performance and its private payments balance depend on whether the exchange rate floats or is fixed. Monetary policy effects also depend on how open an economy is to international trade, the extent to which financial resources can flow across national borders, how responsive import spending is to changes in real income, and how much changes in the exchange rate influence autonomous export and import expenditures. Consequently, these factors are crucial to determining the appropriate assignment of objectives.

Hence, the appropriate assignment of policy objectives varies from nation to nation, depending on the circumstances. As a result, the assignment problem can become a contentious central banking issue. A nation's central bank officials may feel confident that it would be more efficient for the government to restrict its policy interests to domestic issues, leaving the international sphere to the central bank. Government officials, however, may be reluctant to accept this assignment. It is not unusual, therefore, for central banks and government officials to squabble about these issues. Sometimes these disagreements become public spats and escalate into serious political disputes. Whether the central bank or the government officials ultimately emerge victorious depends in large part on the degree of independence possessed by the central bank. For this reason, as we shall discuss in Chapter 26, in recent years economists have devoted considerable attention to the issue of how much political and economic independence governments should grant to central bank officials.

4. What is the policy assignment problem? This is the issue of determining whether monetary or fiscal policymakers should aim their policies at internal or external goals. Under some circumstances, policies can be mismatched with ultimate goals. As a result, efforts by central banks to vary exchange rate targets and by governments to conduct fiscal policy can conflict, causing neither policymaker to achieve its ultimate economic goals.

Link to Policy

Nominal GDP Targeting—A Better Approach?

Interest rate targeting or monetary targeting intended to stabilize real income at a target level at a given price level amounts to stabilizing aggregate demand. In the real world, however, a potentially significant portion of real income variability arises as a result of variability in the aggregate supply schedule. This has led some economists to argue that nominal income targeting is preferable to targeting either an interest rate or a monetary aggregate.

Implementing a Nominal GDP Target

Panel (a) of Figure 25-10, which is based on a graphical approach to understanding nominal GDP targeting first proposed by Michael Bradley of George Washington University and Dennis Jansen of Texas A&M University, shows how nominal GDP targeting would work in the face of factors causing a decline in aggregate demand. If the central bank targets nominal GDP, it treats nominal income, $Y = P \times y$, as its intermediate target. That is, the central bank varies the quantity of money as needed to ensure that $P \times y = Y^*$ always holds, where Y^* denotes the nominal GDP target. In the panels of Figure 25-10, we assume that the target level of nominal GDP is $9,000 billion, or $9 trillion. There are many obvious price level–real income combinations that are consistent with this target, such as $P_1 = 1.5$, $y_1 = 6{,}000$; $P_2 = 2$, $y_2 = 4{,}500$; and $P_3 = 3$, $y_3 = 3{,}000$. These and all other price level–real income combinations consistent with the nominal GDP target lie along the bowed schedule (called a rectangular hyperbola) labeled $Y^* = 9{,}000$.

At point *A* in panel (a), the aggregate demand and aggregate supply schedules intersect at the equilibrium price level $P_1 = 1.5$ and the equilibrium real output level $y_1 = 6{,}000$. In addition, the natural, full-information level of output in the figure is equal to $y^* = 6{,}000$, where the long-run aggregate supply schedule, denoted y^s_{LR}, is vertical. Hence, at point *A* the market for real output is in equilibrium at the natural output level, and the nominal income target achieves this level of real output.

Now consider how the central bank responds to a decline in aggregate demand, from y^d_1 to y^d_2, which causes real income and the price level to begin to decline toward levels consistent with point *B* in panel (a). As nominal income falls, the central bank conducts open market purchases to raise aggregate demand and push nominal GDP back to its target level. Therefore, by conducting monetary policy to maintain nominal income at $Y^* = 9{,}000$, the central bank automatically stabilizes aggregate demand and achieves both its real output and its inflation goals.

Consequences of Aggregate Supply Variability

Thus, nominal GDP targeting can replicate the best outcome that nominal-interest-rate targeting or monetary targeting could achieve. The potential advantage of nominal GDP targeting is that it may reduce the inflationary consequences of aggregate supply variability, as shown in panel (b) of the figure. Suppose that there is a leftward shift in the economy's short-run and long-run aggregate supply schedules, from y^s to $y^{s\prime}$ and from y^s_{LR} to $y^{s\prime}_{LR}$, so that the natural, full-information output level falls from $y^* = 6{,}000$ to $y^{*\prime} = 4{,}500$. In the absence of any response from the central bank, the equilibrium price level would rise from $P_1 = 1.5$ toward $P' = 3$ at point C, and nominal income would begin to rise toward $Y^{*\prime} = P' \times y^{*\prime} = 3 \times 4{,}500 = 13{,}500$.

With either an interest-rate- or a money-stock-based targeting procedure that would stabilize aggregate demand, the values for the price level

Continued on next page

Link to Policy, continued

Figure 25-10
Targeting Nominal GDP.

By targeting nominal GDP at $9,000 billion ($9 trillion), a central bank ensures achievement of an equilibrium price level and equilibrium real output level at a point such as point *A* in panel (a), which lies along a set of price level–real output combinations for which $P \times y = Y^* =$ 9,000. If a fall in aggregate demand generates a decline in nominal income, the central bank can automatically stabilize both real income and the price level by automatically raising aggregate demand to push nominal income back toward the target level. A reduction in the economy's long-run output level would cause both the long-run and the short-run aggregate supply schedules to shift leftward in panel (b), and if the central bank were to stabilize aggregate demand, the long-run result would be a significant rise in the price level shown by a movement from point *A* to point *C*. If the central bank instead maintains a nominal GDP target, it reduces aggregate demand and induces a final equilibrium at point *B*, thereby limiting the rise in the equilibrium price level.

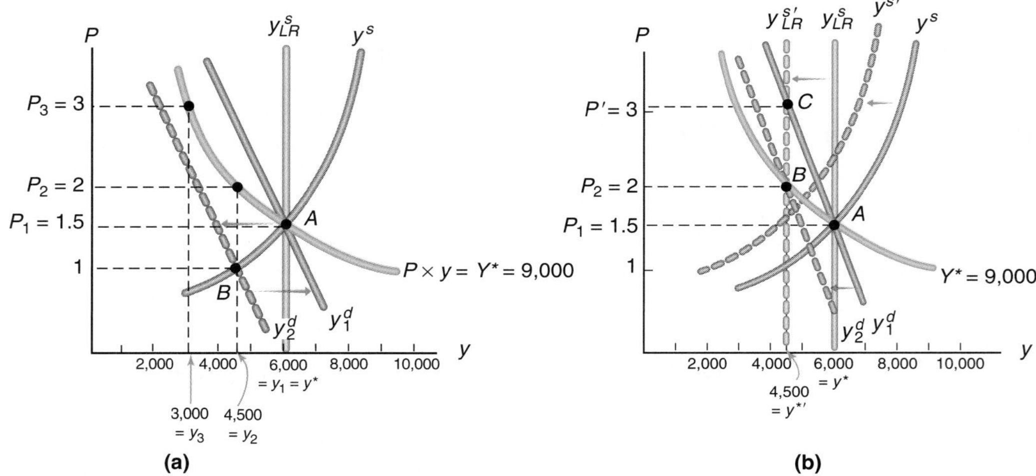

and nominal GDP would be much higher. To achieve its nominal GDP target of $Y^* = 9,000$, however, the central bank must conduct open market sales, thereby lowering aggregate demand. This yields an actual equilibrium price level equal to $P_2 = 2$ at point *B*, thereby containing the inflationary effects of the reduction in aggregate supply. Hence, nominal GDP targeting enables the central bank to come closer to its price target than it would with either interest rate or monetary targeting.

Research Project

Review the desirable characteristics of intermediate targets, and review the discussion of inflation targeting on page 621. What are the main advantages and disadvantages of targeting nominal GDP? When are nominal GDP targeting and inflation targeting equivalent policy approaches? Under what circumstances do the two policy approaches differ?

Web Resource

Where are the most up-to-date U.S. nominal GDP data on the Web? The best place to look is the site of the Bureau of Economic Analysis (http://www.bea.gov), where you can click on "GDP and Related Data." Next, click on "Select data from the NIPA Tables," then on "Download NIPA Tables," then on "Frequently Requested NIPA Tables," and finally on "Gross Domestic Product."

Chapter Summary

1. The Ultimate Goals of Monetary Policy: These are the final aims of the policy strategies and actions conducted by a central bank such as the Federal Reserve. In the United States, the 1946 Employment Act and the 1978 Humphrey-Hawkins Act established low and stable inflation, high and stable output growth, and high and stable employment as formal ultimate objectives of monetary policy. These are examples of internal objectives, which are purely domestic goals. A nation's central bank may also aim to achieve external-balance objectives, which are goals for the country's trade balance and other components of its balance of payments.

2. Why a Central Bank Might Use an Intermediate Monetary Policy Target: A central bank such as the Federal Reserve typically adopts an intermediate target because it faces limitations on the availability of data on its ultimate objectives and because its officials have different interpretations of how monetary policy actions influence these ultimate policy goals. Any intermediate target for monetary policy should be an economic variable that can be observed more frequently than ultimate goal variables. In addition, it should be straightforward to measure, controllable via monetary policy actions, and closely related to ultimate policy objectives. The menu of possible intermediate target variables includes money and credit aggregates, interest rates, nominal GDP, and exchange rates.

3. The Pros and Cons of Interest Rates versus Monetary Aggregates as Intermediate Monetary Policy Targets: On the one hand, adopting a nominal-interest-rate target makes aggregate demand more stable when money demand is highly volatile while aggregate desired expenditures are relatively stable. On the other hand, using a monetary aggregate as an intermediate target stabilizes aggregate demand when aggregate desired expenditures are variable while money demand is relatively stable.

4. The Policy Assignment Problem: The assignment problem is the problem of determining whether monetary or fiscal policymakers should concentrate on achieving an internal-balance objective such as a real income target or an external-balance objective such as balanced trade. Incorrectly assigning one of these objectives to a central bank and the other to a government fiscal authority can cause both policymakers to end up farther away from both goals.

Questions and Problems

(Answers to odd-numbered questions and problems may be found on the Web at http://money.swcollege.com under "Student Resources")

1. In your view, what should be the most important ultimate goal of monetary policy? Take a stand, and support your answer.

2. Briefly discuss the rationales for a central bank's adoption of an intermediate target. Which seems to you to be most important? Explain your reasoning.

3. List the key criteria for choosing among alternative intermediate targets of monetary policy. Does any of these seem to you to be more important than the others? Why?

4. What are the key advantages of using an interest rate as an intermediate target of monetary policy? What are the disadvantages? Explain.

5. Suppose that financial market conditions and desired money holdings by households have been relatively unstable, as compared with past years. At the same time, households' domestic consumption and import spending, firms' investment expenditures, fiscal policies, and export spending by foreign residents have been relatively stable. If you were in charge at the Fed and had to decide whether to target an interest rate or a monetary aggregate, which would you choose? Why?

6. What are the key advantages of using a monetary aggregate as an intermediate target of monetary policy? What are the disadvantages? Explain.

7. If targeting a monetary aggregate best stabilizes real income at the current price level, does this mean that real income will remain stable if the price level rises due to an aggregate supply shock?

8. In your own words, what is the basic issue associated with the assignment problem? Why is solving this problem important?

9. Redo the derivation of the external-balance schedule illustrated in Figure 25-7 under the following assumptions: (a) import spending is relatively insensitive to changes in real income, so the trade balance schedule is very shallow, and (b) a given change in the exchange rate has significant effects on autonomous exports and imports. Is the resulting external-balance schedule relatively steep or relatively shallow? Why?

10. Superimpose an external-balance schedule shaped like the one you derived in question 9 over an internal-balance schedule that has roughly a 45-degree line downward slope (this is a slope equal to –1). Reason out the correct assignment of policy goals for monetary and fiscal policy. How does the correct policy assignment compare with the assignment discussed in Figure 25-9?

Before the Test

Test your understanding of the material covered in this chapter by taking the Chapter 25 interactive quiz at http://money.swcollege.com.

Online Application

Internet URL: http://federalreserve.gov/

Title: Minutes of the Federal Open Market Committee

Navigation: Go to the above URL, the home page of the Fed's Board of Governors. Click on "Monetary Policy," click on "Federal Open Market Committee," and then click on "Meetings calendar, statements, and minutes" for the most recent data.

Application: Read the minutes for the most recent date, and answer the following questions:

1. Based on the FOMC minutes, what are the Fed's key internal objectives of monetary policy?

2. Did external objectives appear to play a role in the FOMC's most recent deliberations? If so, which external objective appeared to receive greatest weight?

For Group Study and Analysis: Have two or three separate groups of students look at FOMC minutes for different dates, with at least one of the groups looking farther back in time. Do the answers to the questions above appear to change over time? Does the Fed appear to have used an intermediate monetary policy target over the course of the last several FOMC meeting cycles? If so, what is it?

Selected References and Further Reading

Bradley, Michael, and Dennis Jansen. "Understanding Nominal GNP Targeting." Federal Reserve Bank of St. Louis *Review* 71 (November/December 1989): 31–40.

Fischer, Stanley. "Toward an Understanding of the Costs of Inflation: II." In Stanley Fischer, ed., *Indexing, Inflation, and Economic Policy,* pp. 35–69. Cambridge, Mass.: MIT Press, 1986.

Fischer, Stanley, and Franco Modigliani. "Toward an Understanding of the Real Effects and Costs of Inflation." In Stanley Fischer, ed., *Indexing, Inflation, and Economic Policy,* pp. 7–33. Cambridge, Mass.: MIT Press, 1986.

Klein, Michael, and Karen Lewis. "Learning about Intervention Target Zones." *Journal of International Economics* 35 (1993): 275–295.

Kozicki, Sharon. "How Useful Are Taylor Rules for Monetary Policy?" Federal Reserve Bank of Kansas City *Economic Review* 84 (Second Quarter 1999): 5–33.

Krugman, Paul, and Marcus Miller, eds. *Exchange Rate Targets and Currency Bands.* Cambridge, U.K.: Cambridge University Press, 1992.

Poole, William. "Optimal Choice of Monetary Policy Instruments in a Simple Stochastic Macro Model." *Quarterly Journal of Economics* 84 (May 1970): 197–216.

Svensson, Lars. "An Interpretation of Recent Research on Exchange Rate Target Zones." *Journal of Economic Perspectives* 6 (1992): 119–144.

MoneyXtra

moneyxtra! Log on to the MoneyXtra Web site now (**http://moneyxtra.swcollege.com**) for additional learning resources such as practice quizzes, case studies, readings, and additional economic applications.

Chapter 26

Rules versus Discretion in Monetary Policy

By and large, European governments have generous unemployment insurance programs. In a few nations, unemployment compensation replaces roughly 100 percent of an individual's lost wages. Several nations provide benefits for periods stretching to a year or even much longer. In some countries, an individual who still has a job and receives weekly paychecks can also receive "unemployment" compensation!

Some economists believe that if all other factors are constant, the relative generosity of national unemployment compensation systems can influence countries' inflation rates. This proposed relationship between unemployment insurance and inflation has nothing to do with potential supply-side effects on firms' labor costs and incentives for firms to produce output. Instead, the idea is that central bank officials' decisions about monetary policy actions may hinge in part on how well protected workers are from the ill effects of economic contractions.

According to this theory, if central bankers know that anti-inflationary policies they implement are less likely to harm workers—and if everyone else also knows that the central bank officials recognize this—then the officials have a greater incentive to adopt such policies to keep inflation low. Consequently, countries with more generous unemployment insurance programs should experience lower inflation, all other things being equal. Nations with relatively stingy unemployment compensation systems should experience higher annual rates of inflation.

Fundamental Issues

1. What are policy time lags, and how might they cause well-meaning monetary policymakers to destabilize the economy?
2. Why is monetary policy credibility a crucial factor in maintaining low inflation?
3. How might monetary policy credibility be achieved?
4. What is the evidence concerning the benefits of greater central bank independence?
5. Do countries necessarily gain from making their central banks more independent?

Nearly every country on the planet has experienced inflation during the past several decades. Why do central banks, which can do so much to affect aggregate demand for goods and services within their nations, allow inflation to occur? Why don't they bind themselves to zero-inflation policies, at least on average? In this chapter you will learn about potential explanations for why inflation is such a common experience throughout the world.

Time Lags in Monetary Policy and the Case for Rules

In Chapter 25, we surveyed the various ultimate and intermediate objectives that the Fed and other central banks might seek to achieve. We also discussed how they might seek to achieve those goals. As we noted in our discussion of intermediate monetary targets, one important hindrance to successful attainment of ultimate policy goals is the existence of information lags. A related problem that we shall consider in this chapter is the time that it takes central bank officials themselves to adjust their policies in response to changing circumstances. This forces policymakers to make a crucial decision that can have significant consequences: Should they alter their policies in response to each short-term change in the economy, or should they stand firm on a policy approach that they feel has the best chance of achieving their long-term goals? A key goal of this chapter is to evaluate the trade-offs that central banks face when deciding which approach to adopt.

A fundamental problem faced by any policymaker, whether it is a public utility, a college's board of trustees, or the Fed's Federal Open Market Committee, is the existence of **policy time lags.** These are the intervals between the need for a policy action and the ultimate effects of that action on an economic variable. Any policymaker faces three types of constraints on its ability to make the best policy choices that it can as quickly as such choices should be made:

1. In the presence of time lags, at any given point in time policymakers have limited information about current events.
2. Policymakers are fallible human beings who face constraints on their abilities to recognize and respond appropriately to changing circumstances, particularly in light of lags in their recognition of varying circumstances.
3. Policymakers are constrained by their lack of certainty about the timing and size of the effects of their policy actions.

Together, these constraints can slow policymakers' responses to episodes or incidents that may require speedy attention if policymakers are to attain their goals.

Time Lags in Monetary Policy

Policy time lags: The time intervals between the need for a countercyclical monetary policy action and the ultimate effects of that action on an economic variable.

There are three types of time lags in monetary policymaking: the *recognition lag,* the *response lag,* and the *transmission lag.* Let's discuss each in turn before considering their broader consequences.

The Recognition Lag As we have seen, a key problem central banks such as the Fed confront as they pursue their ultimate inflation, output, employment, and balance of payments objectives is limited current information. Not only are data on many economic variables available only on a monthly basis, but government statisticians often must revise these monthly computations as they discover measurement or calculation errors. Thus, Fed policymakers cannot always be certain that initially reported values for ultimate-goal variables are accurate. On some occasions, government statisticians have had to correct their computations of annualized GDP growth rates for given quarters by more than 50 percent!

Such data uncertainties complicate the lives of policymakers. To understand why, suppose that a nation's inflation rate increases significantly because of an unexpected rise in aggregate demand. If all other factors are unchanged, an appropriate central bank response is to cut back open market purchases, thereby reducing the growth of the supply of reserves to depository institutions. This policy action offsets the rise in aggregate demand and stems upward pressures on the price level. Given the data limitations that they face, however, central bank officials may not realize that inflation has begun to rise until a number of weeks have passed.

The time between the need for a monetary policy action and the recognition of that need is known as the **recognition lag.** As in this example, the recognition may be only a few weeks, but it can easily stretch to a few months. For instance, even if central bank officials notice the rise in the inflation rate, they may take some time to determine its causes. Some officials might speculate that temporary factors that have pushed up business costs are responsible, leading them to argue that the central bank should not take any action. Misleading signals such as this could hold up central bank action to contain aggregate-demand-induced inflation for several additional weeks.

Recognition lag: The interval that passes between the need for a countercyclical policy action and the recognition of this need by a policymaker.

Response lag: The interval between the recognition of a need for a countercyclical policy action and the actual implementation of the policy action.

Transmission lag: The interval that elapses between the implementation of an intended countercyclical policy and its ultimate effects on an economic variable.

THE RESPONSE LAG Even after policymakers conclude that altered economic circumstances call for a policy change, they may take some time to decide on the appropriate action. The **response lag** is the time between recognition of the need for a change in monetary policy and the actual implementation of a policy action.

In the United States, the response lag for monetary policy should not exceed six to eight weeks, which is the typical period between formal meetings of Federal Reserve policymakers. Indeed, the response lag could be even shorter, because Fed officials across the nation communicate each day. Nevertheless, a longer response lag is also possible if Fed officials are unable to reach a consensus about the best policy action to undertake. For instance, some Fed officials might argue for a speedy and sizable response to a perceived increase in the inflation rate, while other officials argue for a more gradual, measured response. Such disagreements among Fed officials could delay policy actions, thereby significantly lengthening the monetary policy response lag.

THE TRANSMISSION LAG Once implemented, a monetary policy action takes time to transmit its effects to overall economic activity. The time that passes before an implemented monetary policy exerts its effects on economic activity is the **transmission lag.** In earlier chapters, we have shifted schedules and discussed the effects of policy actions on real income or the price level without regard for the time it takes for such effects to occur. In fact, months may pass before the full effects of monetary policy actions are transmitted to ultimate policy goal variables. According to current estimates the average length of the monetary policy transmission lag is roughly twelve months. Thus, as a result of the combined recognition, response, and transmission lags, well over a year may elapse between the initial need for a monetary policy action and that action's final effects on the economy.

Time Lags and the Case for Monetary Policy Rules

Time lags can pose a real problem for central banks. To see why, consider Figure 26-1. The curve labeled y^a in panel (a) shows the path that real income would follow in the *absence* of any policy actions. For simplicity, we assume that the anticipated path of real income is a relatively smooth business cycle. The curve labeled y^p depicts the central bank's *planned* path for the contributions of its policy actions to real income in light of its anticipation that real income in the absence of its policies will follow the path y^a.

Successful Countercyclical Monetary Policy We assume that the central bank officials plan to pursue a *countercyclical* policy strategy by increasing their contributions to real income when they anticipate that real income will decline and reducing their contributions to real income when they expect it to rise.

At any given time, the actual level of real income in the presence of policy actions, denoted y, is the sum of y^a and y^p. Note that the figure assumes that monetary policymaking can add permanently to total real income. As we dis-

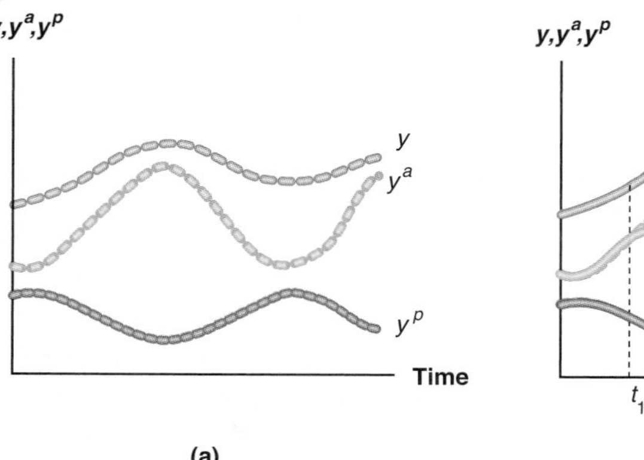

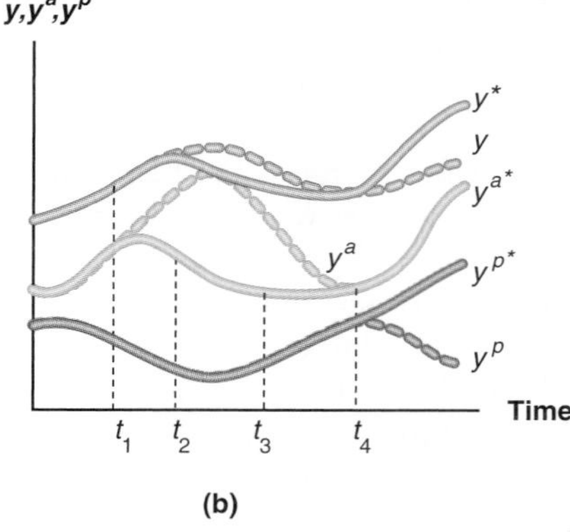

Figure 26-1
How Policy Time Lags Can Make Well-Intentioned Policy Destabilizing.

Panel (a) illustrates a possible situation in which policy actions help to stabilize real income over time. The path labeled y^a illustrates a hypothetical anticipated path for real income in the absence of policy actions. The path labeled y^p shows a planned countercyclical path for real income contributions of monetary policy, in which a policymaker reduces its contribution to real income as real income in the absence of policy is rising and increases its contribution to real income as real income in the absence of policy is declining. As a result, the path of total real income, y, is smoother than it would otherwise have been. Panel (b)

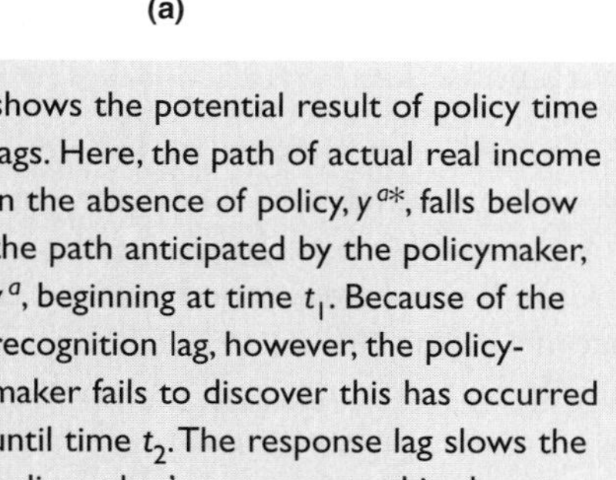

shows the potential result of policy time lags. Here, the path of actual real income in the absence of policy, y^{a*}, falls below the path anticipated by the policymaker, y^a, beginning at time t_1. Because of the recognition lag, however, the policymaker fails to discover this has occurred until time t_2. The response lag slows the policymaker's response to this change until time t_3, and the transmission lag holds up the actual effects of the policy action until time t_4. By this time, however, real income in the absence of policy has returned to its predicted path once again, so the new policy contributions to real income are procyclical and destabilizing.

cussed in Chapter 24, not all economists agree that this is so. We shall assume, however, for purposes of an illustrative example that policy can make some permanent contribution, and other diagrams in this chapter will mirror this assumption. You should keep in mind, however, that the classical, new classical, and real-business-cycle theories indicate that monetary policy can at most induce short-term variations in real income.

If the central bank successfully pursues its countercyclical policy strategy, the result is an actual path of real income, y, that is smoother than the anticipated real income path in the absence of policy actions, y^a. Thus, the central bank successfully dampens the business cycle.

How Time Lags Can Make Monetary Policy Destabilizing The same curves shown in panel (a) of Figure 26-1 appear as dashed curves in panel (b). The solid curves, however, depict actual paths that might arise in the presence of policy time lags if the central bank reacts to unexpected departures of real income from the path that it had anticipated. Panel (b) shows a temporary change in the path of real income in the absence of policy effects, denoted y^{a*}. We assume in this example that real income drops below the level that the central bank had anticipated beginning at a point in time denoted t_1. The path of real income without any policy effects then stays below its anticipated path until the time t_4, when it again returns to the anticipated path.

Visualizing the Effects of Time Lags The time that passes between t_1 and t_2 is the time interval that elapses before the central bank realizes that the actual path of real income has fallen below the anticipated path. Thus, this period is the *recognition lag*. At time t_2, central bank officials have no way of knowing that in the absence of their policy contributions real income will eventually return to the anticipated path at time t_4. Thus, in their effort to engage in countercyclical monetary policy, at time t_3 the officials decide to implement a policy action that increases the central bank's contribution to real income. The time that passes between t_2 and t_3 is the interval between the central bank's recognition of the need for a countercyclical policy change and the implementation of this intended change, or the *response lag*.

Finally, it takes time for the policy change to have an effect. In panel (b), by time t_4, the policy change finally begins to take effect following a *transmission lag* between t_3 and t_4. As a result, the contribution of monetary policy to real income increases. The actual path of policy contributions to real income, denoted y^{p*}, turns upward, whereas the central bank's *original* plan would have called for a reduction in policy contributions to real income to commence at time t_4. Yet t_4 is the point in time at which real income in the absence of policy's contribution has already *returned* to its anticipated path. In the end, the policy-influenced real income path, denoted y^*, is the sum of the y^{a*} and y^{p*} curves. As you can see, in this example the well-meaning effort of the central bank to stabilize real income actually ends up yielding a path of real income that is *more variable* than it would have been if the central bank had not reacted to the temporary fall in real income.

Thus, in this example, even though the central bank is well-meaning in its effort to conduct a countercyclical policy,

Discretionary policymaking: The act of responding to economic events as they occur, rather than in ways the policymaker might previously have planned in the absence of those events.

Policy rule: A commitment to a fixed strategy no matter what happens to other economic variables.

Time lags in recognition, response, and transmission can end up producing a *procyclical* monetary policy.

The central bank would have come closer to its objective of smoothing the business cycle if it had stuck to its original planned policy path, y^p. (As the European Union and the European Monetary Union consider adding new member nations, some economists worry that the resulting structure of the European Central Bank will lengthen the recognition and response lags of monetary policymaking; see *Global Focus: Will European Policymaking Lags Lengthen If the European Union Expands?*)

Discretion versus Rules Nobel Prize–winning economist Milton Friedman argued a half-century ago that situations such as the one illustrated in panel (b) of Figure 26-1 can be relatively common. He argued that despite their good intentions in conducting countercyclical policies, central banks nevertheless may *add* to cyclical real income fluctuations via their well-meaning attempts to dampen natural cycles. This, Friedman contended, is a basic defect of **discretionary policymaking,** or undertaking monetary policy responses on an *ad hoc* basis. In the presence of lengthy and variable policy time lags, Friedman concluded, discretionary policymaking can more often than not end up destabilizing economic activity.

For this reason, Friedman suggested that central banks adopt **policy rules.** These are policy strategies to which central banks *commit* themselves. Friedman recommended that central banks should pursue these strategies no matter what events occur. In his view, standing by a policy rule will, on average, prevent unintentional destabilizing actions by central banks themselves. With the simplest type of policy rule, a central bank neither adds to nor subtracts from its contributions to real income. For instance, the central bank would strive to maintain a constant growth rate of depository institution reserves, the monetary base, or a monetary aggregate.

moneyxtra!

Economic Applications

Should the Federal Reserve pursue a fixed policy rule? To review alternative perspectives on this debate and make your own judgment, go to EconDebate Online.
http://moneyxtra.swcollege.com

1. What are policy time lags, and how might they cause well-meaning monetary policymakers to destabilize the economy? There are three types of policy time lags: (1) the recognition lag, which is the time between the need for a monetary policy action and a central bank's realization of that need; (2) the response lag, which is the interval between the recognition of the need for an action and the actual implementation of a policy change; and (3) the transmission lag, which is the time between the implementation of a policy action and the action's ultimate effects on the economy. All told, these lags can sum to well over a year in duration. They can also lead a central bank that responds to events as they occur to enact a policy change that is procyclical, thereby destabilizing the economy. This is one argument in favor of monetary policy rules, or fixed commitments to specific monetary policy strategies.

Discretionary Monetary Policy and Inflation

In addition to an argument based on policy time lags, another argument against policy discretion has been developed by Robert Barro of Harvard University and David Gordon of Clemson University. It focuses on the likely tendency of a discretionary monetary policymaker to enact policies that are inflationary.

GLOBAL Focus | POLICY | CYBER | MANAGEMENT

Will European Policymaking Lags Lengthen If the European Union Expands?

Currently, the European Union (EU) is a collection of national economies. Nevertheless, the oft-repeated objective of the EU is to develop into a single continental economy with ever-more-coordinated monetary and fiscal policies. If, as it has contemplated, the EU expands during the next few years from 15 members to 20, and potentially to as many as 27, however, the potential for significant policy time lags to develop will also increase.

European Monetary Union Expansion: A Recipe for an Unwieldy Policymaking Process?

The European System of Central Banks is managed by an administrative council composed of a six-member executive board and the governors of the national central banks of the members of the European Monetary Union (EMU). Not all EU nations are members of the EMU, but as the EU expands, several existing and new EU members are likely to also seek membership in the EMU. In principle, therefore, if the EU increases to 27 member nations, the council governing the European System of Central Banks ultimately could have 33 members, as compared with the Federal Reserve Board's 7 governors and 12 FOMC members. Such an expansion would undoubtedly broaden the scope for disagreements in interpreting economic data, thereby increasing the recognition lag of EMU monetary policy. It could also make reaching agreement on appropriate policy actions more problematic, thereby lengthening the monetary policy response lag.

Furthermore, enlarging the EMU could widen the differences among the economies encompassed by the monetary union, thereby complicating the transmission mechanism of monetary policy. This could have the effect of lengthening the EMU monetary policy transmission lag.

Would Fiscal Coordination of an Expanded EU Be an Oxymoron?

An oxymoron is an apparent contradiction that arises when two words or terms are combined together within a single thought—for example, an "exact estimate" or an "organized mess." If monetary policymaking could become more complicated and prone to lengthier lags with a larger EMU, then that goes double—or perhaps higher orders of magnitude greater—for fiscal policymaking in an expanded EU.

The reason is that under the EU's complicated voting rules, big countries have extra votes. As a result, under most circumstances a supermajority of roughly 70 percent of all votes cast is required to pass most EU economic initiatives. As the size of the EU increases, so will the number of possible coalitions, from 32,768 for 15 EU members to about 130 million for 27 members. Naturally, this would considerably reduce the probability of passing any economic policy initiative, thereby lengthening the likely response lag for coordinated EU fiscal policy actions.

For Critical Analysis: As the EMU and EU expand, how might member nations streamline their policymaking procedures to reduce policy time lags?

A Monetary Policy Game and a Theory of Inflation

In recent years, economists have applied *game theory*—the theory of strategic interactions among individuals or institutions—to issues relating to central banking. Barro and Gordon have applied game theory to the problem of rules versus discretion in monetary policymaking. You need not have studied game theory to understand their essential argument, however. All you need to understand are concepts that we have already discussed in earlier chapters.

Capacity output: The real output that the economy could produce if all resources were employed to their utmost.

Output Market Equilibrium and Ultimate Goals of Monetary Policy

Figure 26-2 illustrates the situation that Barro and Gordon consider. They do so using the modern Keynesian theory of wage contracting. According to this theory, nominal wages are contracted at the level W_1^c, which is the market-clearing wage that workers and firms rationally expect would be determined in the labor market. Once the nominal wage is fixed, then the short-run aggregate supply schedule, $y^s(W_1^c)$ slopes upward, as we discussed in Chapter 24.

In the long run, when workers and firms are fully informed, nominal wages adjust equiproportionately with price changes. Thus, the long-run aggregate supply schedule, y_{LR}^s, is vertical at the economy's current long-run, full-information output level, denoted y_1.

Finally, the aggregate demand schedule, y_1^d, slopes downward. A possible output market equilibrium is point *A*, where all three schedules cross at the equilibrium price level P_1. Hence, point *A* depicts a situation in which the short-run equilibrium and the long-run equilibrium coincide; here the contract wage workers and firms have negotiated happens to match the nominal wage that would have arisen if the labor market had equilibrated the demand for labor with the supply of labor, as in the classical model.

In addition, Figure 26-2 also includes an output level denoted y^*. This is the ultimate output objective of the nation's central bank. A key assumption is that this target output level is *greater* than the full-information, natural output level y_1. The reason is that y^* is the **capacity output** for the economy, or the real GDP that firms could produce if labor and other productive factors were employed to their utmost. One factor that can cause the natural, full-information output level to lie below its full-capacity level is income taxes. By assessing marginal tax rates on workers' incomes, governments induce workers to supply fewer labor services

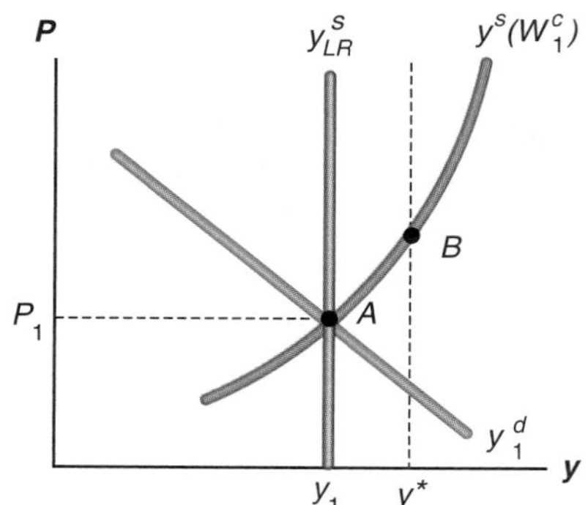

Figure 26-2
Output Market Equilibrium and Policy Goals.

A full long-run equilibrium in the market for real output arises at the point where the aggregate demand, short-run aggregate supply, and long-run aggregate supply schedules cross. At this point, denoted point *A*, the long-run, full-information output level is equal to y_1, and the equilibrium price level is equal to P_1. The capacity output level is y^*. This is an output level that workers and firms could produce but currently do not because other factors, such as income taxes and costs of regulation, reduce the long-run, full-information output level below the capacity level. The basic theory of inflationary policy proposes that policymakers would like to raise the level of output toward the capacity level but would also prefer not to increase the price level.

than they would otherwise have desired. As a result, firms produce less real output than they would otherwise have planned to produce in the absence of income taxes.

Another reason that the natural output level usually is below the capacity output level is the presence of government regulations. For instance, governments commonly institute licensing requirements that restrict entry into various industries, thereby restraining their production of goods and services. Consequently, government regulations can reduce real output relative to what it would have been in the absence of regulations.

In addition to the capacity output goal y^*, the central bank has one other ultimate objective: to minimize the inflation rate. Because the primary way a central bank can influence real output in the short run is through monetary policy actions that change the position of the aggregate demand schedule, however, the central bank faces a trade-off between its two goals. An increase in aggregate demand from point *A* in Figure 26-2 would cause a rightward movement along the short-run aggregate supply schedule, thereby raising real output toward the target y^* at point *B*. Yet a rise in aggregate demand would also cause the price level to rise, resulting in higher inflation; hence, remaining at the current equilibrium point *A* would be more desirable from the standpoint of the central bank's inflation objective. Consequently, a central bank that cares about both output and inflation goals typically would desire for aggregate demand to rise somewhat from point *A*, so as to increase real output. How much the central bank will be willing to expand aggregate demand will depend on the relative weights that the central bank assigns to its two objectives.

MONETARY POLICY DISCRETION AND INFLATION Figure 26-2 describes a situation in which there are two sets of "players" in the monetary policy game. On the one hand, to determine the setting for the contract wage W^c, workers and firms must make their best rational forecast of the price level given their understanding of the policy goals of the central bank and the output-inflation trade-off that the central bank confronts. On the other hand, the central bank must decide what action it should take to alter aggregate demand given its understanding of how workers and firms determine the contract wage.

Figure 26-3 on the following page depicts four *potential* outcomes that might arise from the interaction between workers and firm executives, who set the contract wage and thereby determine the position of the aggregate supply schedule, and the central bank, which chooses a monetary policy action that determines the position of the aggregate demand schedule. The four potential outcomes of this interaction are points *A, B, C,* and *D*. Let's consider each in turn.

Point *A* is the same initial equilibrium point that we discussed in Figure 26-2. Because it is a long-run equilibrium point, the contract wage W_1, reflects a correct expectation by workers and firms that the price level will be equal to P_1. Hence, at this initial point workers and firms produce the full-information output.

The Incentive to Raise Aggregate Demand Nevertheless, the central bank wishes to raise real output above the full-information, natural level, y_1, toward the capacity level, y^*. Thus, the central bank has an incentive to embark on a monetary policy action to raise aggregate demand from y_1^d to y_2^d in an effort to

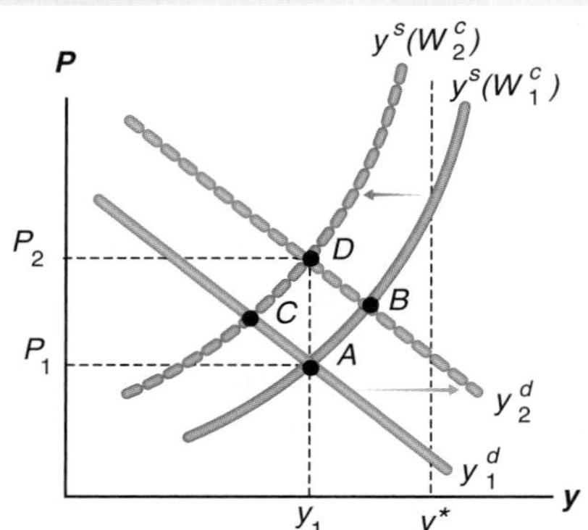

Figure 26-3
Potential and Equilibrium Outcomes of a Monetary Policy Game.

If the current equilibrium for the economy is point *A* and the central bank's goals are to raise output toward the capacity output level y^* but to keep inflation low, then splitting the difference between these conflicting objectives requires inducing a rise in aggregate demand, to point *B*. But if workers realize that prices will rise, they will bargain for higher contract wages, which shifts the aggregate supply schedule leftward. This means that if the central bank were to ignore the temptation to raise aggregate demand, the result would be higher prices and lower real output at point *C*. To avoid this, the central bank feels pressure to raise aggregate demand as workers expect. Therefore, the final equilibrium is at point *D*, with unchanged real output but a higher price level.

induce a short-run rise in real output, at point *B*. As noted earlier, a central bank would not try to push output all the way to y^*, because this would entail greater inflation. Point *B*, therefore, represents a compromise outcome for the central bank in light of the trade-off it faces: real output would rise *toward* the capacity target at the cost of *some* inflation.

Because we assume that workers and firms know the central bank's goals, however, they will not let the point *B* outcome occur. At point *B*, the price level would be higher than workers and firms anticipated when setting the contract wage W_1^c. Hence, the real wage that workers would earn at point *B* would be lower than they had bargained for, and real output would exceed the full-information, natural level that firms desire to produce. Point *B*, therefore, cannot be an equilibrium point that could arise in the monetary policy game. It would be inconsistent with the contracting strategy of workers and firms.

The Public's Response Instead, workers and firms will recognize that the central bank has an incentive to shift the aggregate demand schedule from y_1^d to y_2^d, and they respond by raising their price expectation and negotiating a higher contract wage, W_2^c. This would cause the aggregate supply schedule to shift leftward, from $y^s(W_1^c)$ to $y^s(W_2^c)$. The result is point *D* in Figure 26-3. Point *D* is consistent with the contracting strategy of workers and firms, because at this point they have chosen the contract wage optimally, taking into account the behavior they expect from the central bank. In addition, point *D* is consistent with the central bank's strategy, which is to raise aggregate demand in an attempt to increase output while keeping inflation low (even though, after the fact, the central bank would not succeed in its effort). Consequently, in contrast to point *B*, point *D* *could* be a possible equilibrium in the monetary policy game.

Given that the central bank will fail to expand real output toward the capacity goal, it might seem logical to suppose that the central bank would recognize its inability to raise output and commit itself to leaving the aggregate demand schedule at the position y_1^d. Such a commitment would constitute a policy *rule* in that the central bank would avoid responding to its incentive to try to raise real output in the short run. If workers and firms do *not* believe that the central bank would follow through on this commitment, however, then they would still raise their price expectation and negotiate an increase in the contract wage. This would cause the aggregate supply schedule to shift from $y^s(W_1^c)$ to $y^s(W_2^c)$. Thus, if the central bank followed through with a commitment to leave aggregate demand at y_1^d, point *C* would result. Point *C*, however, would be inconsistent with the central bank's strategy, because at this point inflation occurs and real output falls even *further* below the capacity objective. Therefore, point *C* could not be an equilibrium point in the monetary policy game.

Under a special circumstance, one other equilibrium point could arise in the monetary policy game. This is point *A*. *If* the central bank would commit to maintaining the aggregate demand schedule at y_1^d, and *if* workers and firms could be induced to believe that the central bank would honor that commitment, then point *A* would be maintained as the final equilibrium point. There would be no inflation, the central bank would accept its inability to raise real output toward the capacity level, and workers and firms would be satisfied at the long-run, full-information output level.

The Problem of Central Bank Credibility

Figure 26-4 is another version of Figure 26-3 that displays only the two possible equilibrium points of the monetary policy game, points *A* and *D*, so that we can focus our attention solely on these two potential outcomes. Point *A* would result

Figure 26-4
The Inflation Bias of Discretionary Monetary Policy.

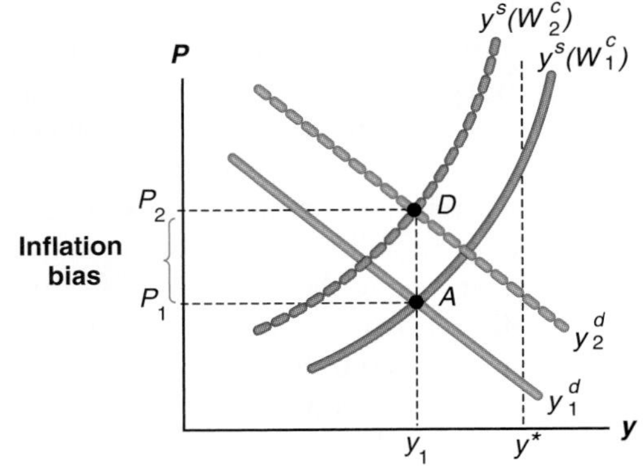

Point *A* represents a noninflationary equilibrium point of the monetary policy game that arises only if the central bank can make a credible commitment to zero inflation. In the absence of a credible zero-inflation commitment, point *D* is the equilibrium point that arises from the monetary policy game, as discussed in Figure 26-3. Hence, the increase in the price level resulting from a movement from point *A* to point *D* is an *inflation bias* resulting from discretionary monetary policy.

Policy credibility: The believability of a commitment by a central bank or governmental authority to follow specific policy rules.

Time-inconsistency problem: The policy problem that can result if a policymaker has the ability, at a future time, to alter its strategy in a way that is inconsistent both with the desires and strategies of private individuals and with its own initially announced intentions.

Inflation bias: The tendency for the economy to experience continuing inflation as a result of the time-inconsistency problem of discretionary monetary policy.

from a commitment to a monetary policy rule, so it denotes a *commitment policy equilibrium.* Point *D*, in contrast, arises from an inability or unwillingness by the central bank to make such a commitment. Point *D*, in other words, is a point of *discretionary policy equilibrium.* Thus, these two points constitute the alternative outcomes that would result from following a policy rule or pursuing discretionary policymaking.

CREDIBILITY The key determinant of which equilibrium point actually occurs is **policy credibility,** or the believability of the central bank's willingness and ability to commit to a monetary rule. If a central bank is willing and able to follow through on such a commitment, then workers and firms can believe that it will stick to its rule. The initial point *A* will remain the equilibrium of the policy game, and the economy will remain at its full-information output level without experiencing inflation. But if workers and firms doubt the central bank's willingness to honor its commitment, or if they feel that the central bank is willing but unable to do so, then this lack of policy credibility will lead to an equilibrium at point *D*.

Policy credibility is difficult to achieve in the setting that we have described because of the **time-inconsistency problem** that exists in our example. This problem is that although commitment to a policy rule yields zero inflation, as at point *A* in Figure 26-4, this commitment is inconsistent with the strategies of workers and firms if the central bank can alter its policy strategy at a later time. In our example, after workers and firms have committed to a contract wage, the central bank could attempt to expand aggregate demand, which would benefit the central bank but not the workers and firms themselves (point *B* in Figure 26-3). To protect themselves against such an alteration in policy, workers and firms increase the contract wage, thereby forcing even a central bank that might otherwise prefer to stick to a rule to expand aggregate demand to avoid a decline in real output (point *C* in Figure 26-3) . These interactions between workers and firms and the central bank result in an equilibrium at point *D* in Figure 26-4.

THE INFLATION BIAS The result of the time-inconsistency problem and the lack of policy credibility is a higher price level at point *D* as compared with point *A*. Economists call the difference between the new price level, P_2, at point *D* and the initial price level, P_1, at point *A* the **inflation bias** arising from discretionary monetary policy. This is a bias toward inflation that exists from the ability of a central bank to determine its policies in a discretionary manner when there is a time-inconsistency problem and a lack of policy credibility. The inflation bias of discretionary policy is a second reason—along with the potential for discretionary policy to be destabilizing in the presence of time lags—that many economists argue that society should find ways to dissuade central banks from using discretionary policies by making monetary policy rules credible. How society might accomplish this is our next topic. (Even a central bank that is committed to low inflation may have problems deciding just how open it should be about its internal deliberations; see *Policy Focus: To Avoid Self-Fulfilling Expectations, Should Central Banks Hide Their Forecasts?*)

2. Why is monetary policy credibility a crucial factor in maintaining low inflation? If people establish nominal contracts, then a monetary policymaker has an incentive to enact policies that will raise aggregate demand in an effort to

GLOBAL | POLICY Focus | CYBER | MANAGEMENT

To Avoid Self-Fulfilling Expectations, Should Central Banks Hide Their Forecasts?

To conduct monetary policy effectively, any central bank must develop forecasts of future economic activity. As part of these efforts, a central bank normally develops its own forecasts of inflation during the coming months. In a world where the public is watching the central bank closely to assess the credibility of its commitment to low inflation, the existence of internal inflation forecasts can pose a problem for the central bank.

The reason is that the central bank's inflation expectations affect its own policy choices, and those policy choices in turn affect the public's inflation expectations. Because the public knows that the central bank's policy decisions also depend on its forecasts of inflation, information about those inflation forecasts could directly influence the public's expectations of inflation. Of course, the inflation expectations of the public ultimately help determine the position of the economy's aggregate supply curve, thereby affecting the *actual* inflation rate that the central bank wishes to maintain at a low level.

Thus, there is the potential for expectations to be *self-fulfilling:* if the central bank releases a forecast predicting that various events will boost inflation, then the public's inflation expectations will ratchet upward, thereby *causing* higher inflation. To prevent this from happening, central banks may engage in what economists call *cheap talk*. To reduce the inflationary effects of self-fulfilling expectations, central bank officials may downgrade their own inflation estimates.

In fact, the inflation rates that central bank officials state they anticipate achieving at future dates persistently turn out to be lower than the inflation rates that actually arise. Although it is possible that central banks consistently do a poor job of forecasting inflation, it is more likely that their public pronouncements reflect an understanding of the problem of self-fulfilling expectations.

For Critical Analysis: How does the incentive for central bank officials to engage in cheap talk about their inflation forecasts complicate the public's task in assessing the credibility of the officials' anti-inflation stance?

expand real output toward its capacity level. Consequently, workers and firms negotiating wage contracts will be unlikely to believe a central bank's stated intention to limit inflation, which would reduce the purchasing power of workers' wages. As a result, workers and firms will negotiate higher wages, thereby reducing aggregate supply and causing output to fall in the absence of higher aggregate demand. This pressures the central bank into raising aggregate demand and thereby creating an inflation bias. The only way for a central bank to avoid this inflation bias would be for its commitment to low inflation to be credible to workers and firms.

Making Monetary Policy Rules Credible

It is one thing to argue that potential gains can be obtained from sticking with a monetary policy rule. It is another thing altogether to establish a mechanism for attaining such an outcome in the face of a time-inconsistency problem.

As you have learned in earlier chapters, most monetary theories indicate that money growth is a key determinant of the inflation rate. Consequently, this is the natural starting point for most discussions of how to reduce the inflation bias arising from discretionary policy. Such discussions focus on finding a way to induce a central bank to follow a policy rule and to make such a rule credible.

Constitutional Limits on Monetary Policy

Some economists, such as Milton Friedman of the Hoover Institution at Stanford University, have suggested that one way to eliminate the inflation bias would be to constrain central banks directly. This might be accomplished in the United States by amending the U.S. Constitution to require a constant annual growth rate for the quantity of money. Thus, this approach would seek to establish the credibility of a monetary policy rule by legally *requiring* the Federal Reserve, or more broadly the U.S. government, to pursue the rule.

A key problem with the constitutional amendment idea is determining the appropriate numerical rule for money growth. After all, the U.S. economy's real output growth has varied from decade to decade. Whereas a 3 percent money growth rule might have been consistent with zero inflation in the 1960s, a 2 percent money growth rule might be preferable for the current decade.

Achieving Monetary Policy Credibility by Establishing a Reputation

In the absence of such radical institutional changes, how could a central bank act on its own to make its commitments to low inflation more credible? One approach might be to establish and maintain a reputation as a "tough inflation fighter." To understand how this could enable a central bank to reduce inflation, refer back to Figure 26-3 on page 654. Recall that if the central bank honors a commitment not to raise aggregate demand in pursuit of short-term output gains but is not believed by workers and firms, then the result will be higher inflation and reduced output, which is shown in Figure 26-3 by a movement from point *A* to point *C*. If the central bank cares only about today's outcome, it will never want point *C* to occur. But if the central bank wishes to establish its reputation as an inflation fighter, then it might be willing to let the economy experience lower output at point *C* in Figure 26-3. Henceforth, its promises not to increase aggregate demand might then be credible to workers and firms.

A number of economists argue that this was what the Fed did in 1979 following the significant rise in inflation that Figure 26-5 shows took place during the preceding years. According to these economists, in 1979 and 1980 the Fed held firm to a commitment to keep aggregate demand from increasing. At first, workers and firms did not find this commitment to be credible. A sharp recession then occurred in 1980 and 1981, as a steady rise in nominal wages pushed up business costs and resulted in a reduction in real output—just as the movement from point *A* to point *C* depicts in Figure 26-3. As a result, in the years that followed, the Fed's commitment to lower inflation was credible, and actual inflation rates fell, as shown in Figure 26-5.

Figure 26-5
Annual Inflation Rates in the United States.

This figure plots annual rates of change in the consumer price index. Although average inflation has been lower since the 1980s, as compared with the end of the 1960s and the 1970s, inflation nonetheless has occurred in every single year.

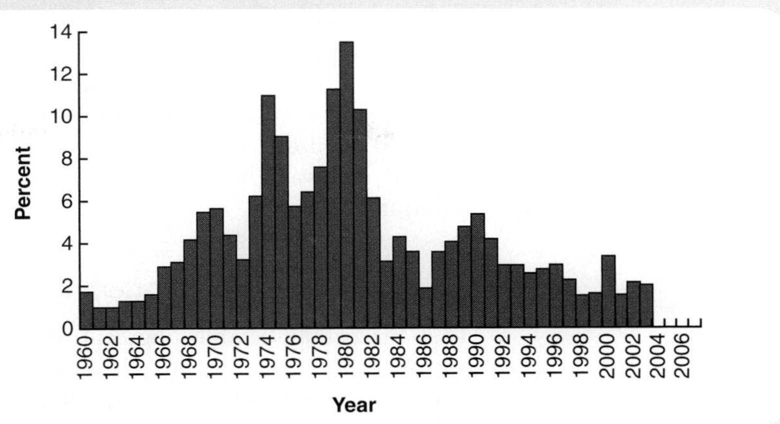

SOURCES: *Economic Report of the President*, 2002; *Economic Indicators* (various issues).

Appointing a "Conservative" Central Banker

It is easier for a central bank official to establish a reputation for being "tough" in the fight against inflation if it is well known that the official truly dislikes inflation. Some observers of the Fed's fight against inflation in the 1980s have concluded that one reason that the anti-inflation effort was so successful was President Carter's 1979 appointment of Paul Volcker, a Fed official whose dislike for inflation was well known, as the chair of the Fed's Board of Governors. The Fed's inflation-fighting reputation then was maintained, these observers argue, when President Reagan appointed Alan Greenspan, another known hawk on inflation, to that position.

The theory of the discretionary inflation bias illustrated in Figure 26-4 on page 655 indicates that appointing anti-inflation central bank officials may indeed be a way to reduce the inflation bias. A key factor influencing the size of the inflation bias is how much central bank officials dislike inflation relative to how much they desire to try to raise real output toward its capacity level. Thus, appointing a **conservative central banker,** or an individual who dislikes inflation more than the average member of society, is one way to reduce the size of the inflation bias. Such an individual would choose to expand aggregate demand by a small amount, because a rise in aggregate demand is inflationary.

Conservative central banker: A central bank official who dislikes inflation more than the average citizen in society and who therefore is less willing to induce discretionary increases in the quantity of money in an effort to achieve short-run increases in real output.

Central Banker Contracts

In recent years, several economists, including Carl Walsh of the University of California at Santa Cruz, have proposed establishing explicit **central banker contracts.** These are legally binding agreements between a government and central bank officials that provide for the officials to be punished and/or rewarded based upon the central bank's inflation performance. Research by Walsh and others has

Central banker contract: A legally binding agreement between a government and a central bank official that holds the official responsible for the nation's inflation performance.

indicated that such contracts could nearly eliminate the inflation bias of discretionary monetary policy.

In principle, a central banker contract could also reward an official with a bonus or a higher salary for maintaining low and stable prices. Although some think it is unseemly to pay central bank officials bonuses for doing the job that they are supposed to be doing in the first place, proponents of such schemes argue that this might be a small cost for society to incur in exchange for reduced inflation.

Central Bank Independence

The idea behind establishing central banker contracts is that they would make central bank officials more *accountable* for their performances. Using the contracts would not, however, rule out granting central bank officials considerable *independence* to conduct monetary policy as they see fit, while continuing to hold them responsible if inflation gets out of hand.

Indeed, many economists argue that central bank independence may be the key to maintaining low inflation rates. After all, a conservative central banker cannot establish a reputation as a tough inflation fighter if he or she is hamstrung by legal requirements to try to achieve other objectives as well, such as a low unemployment rate or a high growth rate for real output. Furthermore, even if a central banker contract holds an official accountable for a nation's inflation performance, achieving the required performance may be difficult unless the official has sufficient independence to pursue this objective in the most efficient manner.

Central bank independence has two dimensions: *political independence,* or the ability to reach decisions free of influence by the government and other outside individuals or groups, and *economic independence,* or the ability to control its own budget or to resist efforts by the government to induce the central bank to make loans to the government or to provide other forms of direct support to government policies. Hence, we can reach the following conclusion:

A truly independent central bank would be both politically and economically independent. Political independence would permit the central bank to conduct the policies that it believes to be best in the long run, without the influence of short-term political pressures. Economic independence would give the central bank the budgetary freedom to conduct these policies.

3. How might monetary policy credibility be achieved? One possible approach to achieving credibility would be to make it illegal for central banks to allow inflation to exceed a specified rate. Alternatively, central bank officials could be signed to contracts that condition their employment or salaries on their inflation performance. To help ensure that central banks would be less likely to institute inflationary policies, governments could appoint conservative central bankers who are known to have a distaste for inflation. Finally, central bankers can gain credibility by permitting output to fall in the near term as a way to convince workers of their commitment to low future inflation. This would require granting central banks sufficient independence.

Central Bank Independence: International Evidence

To evaluate the real-world effects of granting greater independence to central banks, economists have developed measures of the extent of central bank independence that take into account both its economic and its political dimensions. Then they have looked for relationships between these measures and other economic variables.

Any one nation's historical experience with central banking typically is limited. After all, each nation has only one central bank, and many countries have not changed the structures of their central banks in decades. Consequently, economists have evaluated the experiences of many countries.

Evidence Favoring Central Bank Independence

The basic theory of monetary policy discretion indicates that the degree of central bank independence might be related to a nation's inflation performance. Thus, initial studies of the economic effects of central bank independence began by examining its potential role in affecting the behavior of inflation.

CENTRAL BANK INDEPENDENCE AND INFLATION International evidence that central bank independence is related to good inflation performance has been provided by economists Alberto Alesina and Lawrence Summers, both of Harvard University. This evidence is summarized in panels (a) and (b) of Figure 26-6. In each panel, an index of central bank independence is measured along the horizontal axis of the diagram. An increase in this index indicates that a nation's central bank is more politically and/or economically independent. In the diagram in panel (a), average annual inflation rates between the mid-1950s and the late 1980s are measured along the vertical axis. The result is an *inverse relationship*

Figure 26-6
Central Bank Independence, Average Inflation, and Inflation Variability in Major Developed Nations.

As shown in panel (a), nations with more independent central banks, such as Germany, Switzerland, and the United States, have experienced lower average inflation rates as compared with countries with less independent central banks. Panel (b) shows that nations with more independent central banks also have experienced less variable rates of inflation.

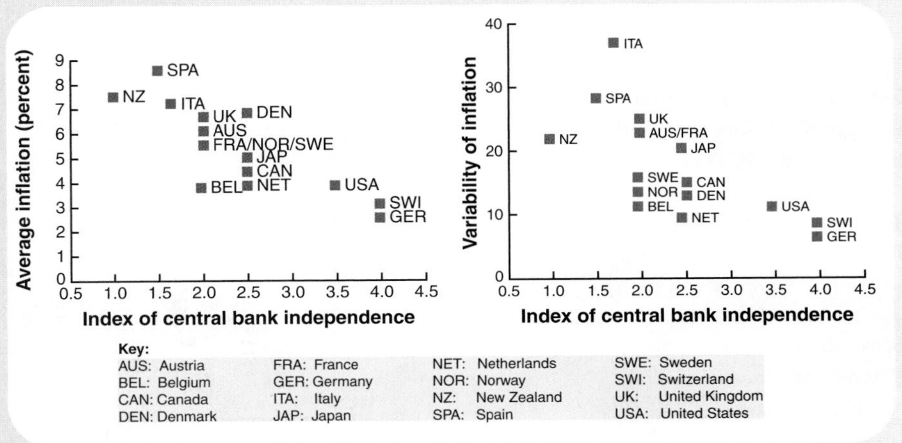

SOURCE: Alberto Alesina and Lawrence Summers, "Central Bank Independence and Macroeconomic Performance," *Journal of Money, Credit, and Banking* (May 1993): 151–162.

between central bank independence and average inflation, meaning that countries with more independent central banks tend to experience lower average inflation. Note that the two nations with the most independent central banks during this period, Germany and Switzerland, had average inflation rates of around 3 percent. The two nations with the least independent central banks, in contrast, which were New Zealand (which since has opted for a more independent central bank) and Spain (which since has joined the European Monetary Union), experienced average inflation rates that were more than twice as high.

Panel (b) of Figure 26-6 measures the variance of inflation along the vertical axis. Again there is an inverse relationship: countries with more independent central banks tend to experience less inflation volatility. Thus, increased central bank independence tends to yield more price stability as well as lower average inflation.

On the Web

Is it possible to keep track of what is going on at most of the world's central banks? You can do this by going to the home page of the Bank for International Settlements (http://www.bis.org) and clicking on "Links to Central Banks." Here, you will find links to the Web sites of many central banks.

DOES CENTRAL BANK INDEPENDENCE AFFECT REAL INCOMES? Some critics of granting central banks considerable independence have argued that the result could be worsened economic performance. If central banks concentrate too much attention on inflation, the critics argue, they will fail to smooth out business cycles. As a result, real income growth might be reduced.

Figure 26-7 provides some evidence about this issue. It plots average real GDP growth rates and the variability of these growth rates relative to an index of central bank independence for sixty countries. There is no apparent effect of central bank independence on either average GDP growth or its variability.

4. What is the evidence concerning the benefits of greater central bank independence? Most studies indicate that developed countries with more independent central banks tend to experience lower and less variable inflation. Increased central bank independence does not appear to have any adverse effects on real GDP growth in these nations.

Figure 26-7
Central Bank Independence, Average GDP Growth, and Variability of GDP Growth.

This figure shows that average GDP growth and the standard deviation of GDP growth for a large number of countries do not appear to be systematically related to an index of central bank independence.

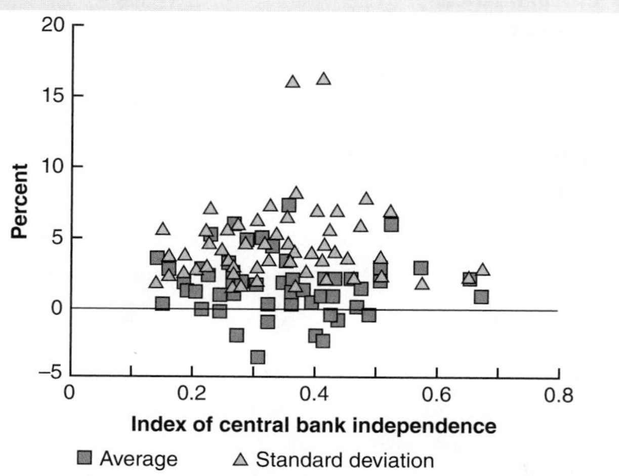

SOURCE: Carl Walsh, "Is There a Cost to Having an Independent Central Bank?" Federal Reserve Bank of San Francisco *Weekly Letter*, No. 94-05, February 4, 1994.

Some Potential Problems with Central Bank Independence

An implication of Figures 26-6 and 26-7 is that central bank independence might be a "no-lose proposition." That is, it appears to be possible to reduce the average level and variability of inflation without any apparent effects on the average level or variability of real income growth. These implications of the data convinced a number of countries to grant more independence to their central banks. Recent examples include Japan, Mexico, and Pakistan. The evidence also induced the nations that joined the European Monetary Union in 1999 to grant considerable independence to the European Central Bank.

To think about the issues involved in structuring central banks that will conduct low-inflation policies, go to the Chapter 26 Case Study, entitled "Helping to Design a Central Bank."
http://moneyxtra.swcollege.com

It remains to be seen, however, whether central bank independence is a cure-all for high and variable inflation. In spite of the apparent positive effects that greater central bank independence appears to have had in some parts of the world, there are good reasons to take a cautious view on the idea that it is a remedy for the world's inflationary ills.

CENTRAL BANK INDEPENDENCE ISN'T REALLY A "FREE LUNCH" One of the first things you learn in an economics principles course is that there is no such thing as a "free lunch." To obtain an item, people typically must give up something in exchange. There is growing evidence that the same is true of central bank independence.

As Figure 26-8 illustrates, a possible by-product of central bank independence is that a given reduction in the inflation rate may cause a greater proportionate decline in the real GDP of a country with a relatively more independent central bank. There are two possible reasons for this effect. One is that because the inflation rate tends to be lower in countries with more independent central banks, the

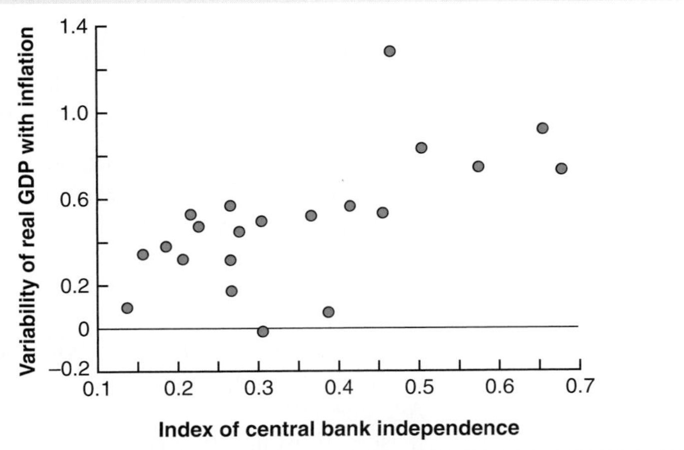

Figure 26-8
Central Bank Independence and the Inflation-Output Trade-off.

Estimates of the extent to which real GDP varies with inflation are plotted along the vertical axis of this figure. There appears to be a positive relationship between these estimates and the degree of central bank independence. This implies that a given reduction in the inflation rate may induce a greater proportionate decline in real GDP for a country that has a relatively more independent central bank.

SOURCE: Carl Walsh, "Output-Inflation Tradeoffs and Central Bank Independence," Federal Reserve Bank of San Francisco *Weekly Letter,* No. 95-31, September 22, 1995.

general level of prices naturally rises less rapidly in response to an increase in real output. This means that the short-run aggregate supply schedule is likely to be shallower in a nation with a more independent central bank. As a result, any given decline in inflation induces a larger short-run reduction in output and a corresponding increase in the unemployment rate, holding all other factors unchanged.

In addition, because inflation variability is lower in nations with more independent central banks, people have less incentive to alter the terms of their employment contracts as often. Thus, to the extent that such contracts exist, they will keep nominal wages unchanged for longer periods. They will also call for less wage indexation through cost-of-living adjustments (COLAs). This also contributes to the shallower short-run aggregate supply schedule for a nation with an independent central bank.

Consequently, the positive effects that may result from greater central bank independence—lower and less variable inflation—may have spillover effects that can influence the extent to which output and unemployment respond to changes in the inflation rate. A fall in inflation could induce a larger increase in the unemployment rate in a nation that has granted its central bank greater independence than in a nation with a less independent central bank. As a result, a relatively independent central bank may nonetheless face a problem in trying to reduce inflation: a relatively larger increase in unemployment.

Of course, this potential effect works in reverse as well. With a shallower aggregate supply curve, higher inflation causes a greater relative increase in output and associated reduction in the unemployment rate. For this reason, greater central bank independence has the interesting effect of increasing the short-term benefit of raising inflation. Thus, an independent central bank operated by officials who care about output and employment actually could face a greater temptation to push up the inflation rate in an effort to induce an increase in real income and a reduction in unemployment. This might make households and firms worry about whether even an independent central bank will hold inflation down. At least in theory, therefore, central bank independence does not necessarily make central banks more credible.

GREATER CENTRAL BANK INDEPENDENCE MAY NOT BENEFIT ALL COUNTRIES

Following the initial publication of the evidence, summarized in Figures 26-6 and 26-7, that increased central bank independence can have inflation benefits without affecting real income, other economists conducted more studies. In particular, some economists examined larger sets of countries including less-developed and emerging economies not examined in the earlier research.

As Figure 26-9 indicates, when less-developed and emerging economies are included, the implications of central bank independence become less clear-cut. Average inflation does not necessarily appear to be lower as central banks in these nations are granted greater independence. Indeed, some studies have found hints of a *positive* relationship between central bank independence and inflation in less-developed and emerging economies.

Such studies have led a number of economists to conclude that there is more to the story than central bank independence alone. It may be that greater central bank independence can have beneficial inflation effects only if certain preconditions are

Figure 26-9
Central Bank Independence and Average Inflation for a Large Set of Countries.

When less-developed and emerging economies are included in studies of central bank independence and inflation, it becomes less certain that there is a relationship between these variables.

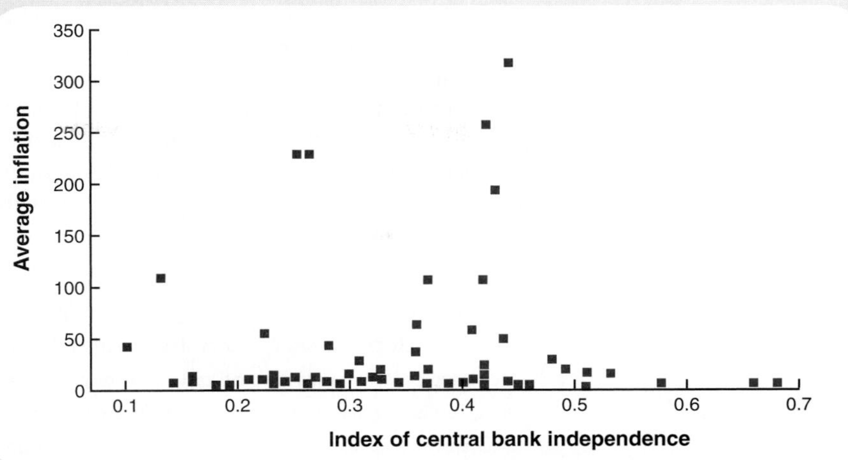

SOURCE: Roberto Chang, "Policy Credibility and the Design of Central Banks," Federal Reserve Bank of Atlanta *Economic Review* 83 (First Quarter, 1998): 4–15.

already satisfied. These may include having in place a system of well-defined property rights, bankruptcy rules, judicial adjudication, and the like, so that the ill effects of inflation are apparent to all owners of capital and other productive resources. Many less-developed and emerging economies lack these characteristics, which are commonplace in developed nations. This may help to explain why the inflation-reduction gains that developed nations experience from increased central bank independence do not appear to be shared by other countries.

CAN ECONOMISTS REALLY MEASURE CENTRAL BANK INDEPENDENCE? Economists construct indexes of central bank independence, such as those used in Figures 26-6 through 26-9, by assigning numerical weights to such factors as the degree of independence that central banks have to buy and sell bonds; to lend to banks, the government, or others; and to regulate their nation's banking system. Many studies also factor in whether central bank officials are politically appointed, the lengths of their terms of office, and so on. Typically, the numerical weight assigned to a factor such as the length of an official's term of office is arbitrary, as are the cutoff points for weighting these terms. For instance, one study might say that a term of more than ten years deserves a relatively high independence weight, while another might give a similar weight to terms in excess of eight years.

Economists may even disagree about what factors really make a central bank more independent. To some, considerable independence in regulating private banks counts as a positive factor. Others take the opposite view, seeing this as a way that a central bank might be exposed to pressures to avoid contractions that could be harmful to the national banking system.

James Forder of Balliol College in England has found that studies of the effects of central bank independence may be highly influenced by these subjective

moneyxtra!

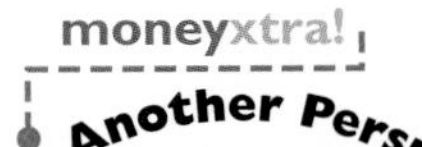

To further explore how central bank structure can influence the credibility of monetary policy, go to the Chapter 26 reading, entitled "Policy Credibility and the Design of Central Banks," by Roberto Chang of the Federal Reserve Bank of Atlanta.

http://moneyxtra.swcollege.com

choices. Thus, the conclusions of many of these studies may not be very robust—that is, they may be very sensitive to slight changes in the ways that economists have chosen to measure central bank independence.

For the moment, however, most economists remain convinced that greater central bank independence has the beneficial effect of lowering average inflation and reducing the variability of inflation. The future experience of countries that have made their central banks more independent in recent years may provide some stronger evidence one way or the other concerning the pros and cons of central bank independence.

5. Do countries necessarily gain from making their central banks more independent? Less-developed and emerging economies with more independent central banks do not appear to experience the same reductions in average inflation and inflation variability that developed nations experience. It is not as clear, therefore, that less-developed and emerging economies gain from granting more independence to central banks. In addition, there is some evidence that increased central bank independence makes the aggregate supply curve shallower. Thus, disinflationary policies may entail higher unemployment costs in countries with more independent central banks. Furthermore, inflationary policies may provide higher short-term unemployment gains, thereby making anti-inflationary policies less credible. Finally, economists do not entirely agree about how to measure central bank independence, which calls into question some of the evidence in favor of the idea.

Link to the Global Economy

Can National Unemployment Insurance Programs Substitute for Conservative Central Bankers?

By definition, a conservative central banker is more concerned than an average member of society with keeping inflation low—and less concerned than the average person with maintaining low unemployment. Being relatively less worried about the unemployment effects of monetary policy actions enables the conservative central banker to aim for smaller increases in aggregate demand over time. The result is a lower inflation bias.

But Is a Conservative Central Banker Necessary?

According to Rafael Di Tella of Harvard University and Robert MacCulloch of the London School of Economics, a nation's government may be able to bring about essentially the same outcome without necessarily having to appoint a conservative central banker. A way to do this, the authors argue, is to establish relatively generous unemployment insurance programs. If a central banker knows that workers who become unemployed as a result of tough monetary policy actions will be protected by such programs, then the central banker will have less concern about the unemployment effects of policy actions, relative to the effects on inflation. Thus, the central banker will be able to behave like a conservative central banker and concentrate more on the inflationary effects of its policy choices.

Differences in Unemployment Compensation Programs

Evaluating the relative generosity of unemployment compensation programs is complicated by significant differences in the way nations structure their programs. In the United States, for instance, individuals must be unemployed for a time before they can seek unemployment compensation, whereas some European nations provide prorated benefits to employed workers who have merely experienced reductions in their weekly hours of work. The duration of eligibility for unemployment compensation also varies across countries. Hence, Di Tella and MacCulloch developed a way to control for these differences before trying to assess the potential relationship between unemployment compensation programs and inflation across countries.

Figure 26-10 on the following page, which does *not* control for all differences in unemployment compensation schemes, plots inflation rates of various nations on the vertical axis and index measures of levels of those nations' unemployment benefits on the horizontal axis. Note that countries with relatively meager unemployment compensation levels, such as Greece and Portugal, have higher inflation rates than nations with relatively more generous unemployment insurance programs, such as Belgium and Denmark.

Consistent with the hypothesis that more generous unemployment compensation can substitute for having a conservative central banker, the figure indicates a generally inverse relationship between unemployment insurance benefits and the inflation rate. Using more sophisticated statistical analysis that took into account cross-country differences in such factors as the duration of unemployment benefits, Di Tella and MacCulloch verified that this relationship really does exist.

Research Project

What are the pros and cons of seeking to reduce inflation by providing generous unemployment insurance instead of trying to identify and appoint conservative central bankers? Could there be spillover effects relating to the unemployment rate? Why or why not?

Link to the Global Economy, continued

Figure 26-10
Inflation Rates and Unemployment Benefit Levels in Selected Nations.

There is an apparent inverse relationship between the generosity of national unemployment benefit programs and inflation rates.

SOURCE: Rafael Di Tella and Robert MacCulloch, "Unemployment Benefits as a Substitute for a Conservative Central Banker," Harvard Business School and London School of Economics, May 5, 2000.

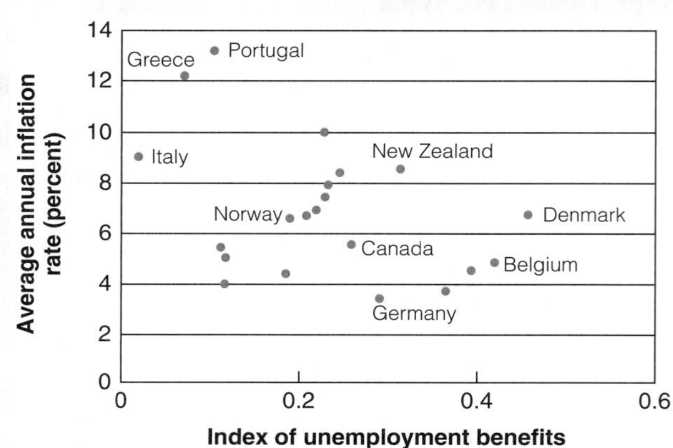

WEB RESOURCE

How much protection does unemployment insurance provide to workers in the United States? Learn more by going to the home page of the U.S. Department of Labor's Employment and Training Agency (http://www.doleta.gov), where, in the blue right-hand margin, you can click on "Unemployment Insurance."

Chapter Summary

1. Policy Time Lags, and How They Might Cause Well-Meaning Monetary Policymakers to Destabilize the Economy: Policy time lags are the intervals separating a need for a policy action and the action's eventual effects on the economy. The recognition lag is the time between the need for a Fed policy action and the Fed's realization of the need, and the response lag is the interval between the recognition of the need for an action and the actual implementation of a policy change. Finally, the transmission lag is the time between the implementation of a policy action and the action's ultimate effects on the economy. Together, these three policy time lags can amount to an interval in excess of a year. They can also cause a discretionary policymaker that reacts to changing circumstances to undertake a policy action that is procyclical, despite the policymaker's intention to enact a countercyclical policy. This potential for policy to destabilize the economy is a key argument favoring the adoption of policy rules, or fixed commitments to specific policy strategies.

2. Why Policy Credibility Is a Crucial Factor in Maintaining Low Inflation: When nominal contracts exist, a monetary policymaker can push real output toward its capacity level by increasing aggregate demand. Consequently, workers and firms that establish wage contracts will doubt the sincerity of the policymaker's commitment to restrain inflation, and they will negotiate higher wages. This will reduce aggregate supply and cause real output to decline in the absence of higher aggregate demand. To avoid this outcome, the policymaker must raise aggregate demand and create an inflation bias. To avoid this inflation bias, the policymaker would have to find a way to make the low-inflation commitment credible.

3. How Monetary Policy Credibility Might Be Achieved: A direct approach would be to make it unlawful for central banks to permit inflation in excess of a certain rate. Another approach would be to sign central bank officials to contracts that base their continued employment or their salaries on a nation's inflation outcomes. To reduce the likelihood that central banks would pursue inflationary policies, governments could appoint central banking officials who are known to dislike inflation. Finally, a central bank can gain credibility by permitting real output to decline in the short run in the face of people's doubts about its commitments to policy rules. To be able to demonstrate its commitment in this way, however, the central bank would have to be sufficiently independent from political influences.

4. The Evidence concerning the Benefits of Greater Central Bank Independence: Most studies examining developed nations that have granted various degrees of independence to their central banks find that increasing the degree of independence tends to reduce inflation rates and to make inflation rates less variable. Studies typically find that increasing central bank independence does not reduce the average growth of real GDP or make real GDP growth more variable.

5. Whether Countries Necessarily Gain from Making Their Central Banks More Independent: There is no clear evidence that less-developed and emerging economies experience reductions in average inflation and inflation variability when they grant greater independence to their central banks. Furthermore, some studies indicate that increased central bank independence tends to make the aggregate supply curve shallower, so efforts to reduce inflation may require greater short-term reductions in output and increases in unemployment rates in nations with more independent central banks. In addition, monetary policies that push up inflation may yield greater short-term unemployment reductions, making central bank monetary policies less credible. Finally, economists do not agree on the best way to measure central bank independence. This fact makes it harder to judge the strength of the evidence on this issue.

Questions and Problems

(Answers to odd-numbered questions and problems may be found on the Web at http://money.swcollege.com under "Student Resources")

1. List and define the three types of policy time lags.

2. Which of the policy time lags discussed in question 1 is likely to be least problematical for monetary policy? Explain your reasoning.

3. Which of the policy time lags discussed in question 1 is likely to be the most significant problem for monetary policy? Explain your reasoning.

4. Why can the time-inconsistency problem lead to an inflation bias when workers and firms set nominal wages in employment contracts?

5. Explain, in your own words, why a constitutional prohibition against inflation may not be a viable solution to the time-inconsistency problem.

6. Evaluate the following statement: "A real strength of performance contracts for central bankers is that they give central bankers policy discretion while subjecting them to a societal rule."

7. Explain the distinction between political and economic independence of central banks. Are both necessary for central banks truly to be independent to conduct anti-inflationary monetary policies? Why or why not?

8. In 1997, just before the European Central Bank (ECB) was established, German and French leaders argued about whether the ECB should be overseen by a committee of political leaders. French leaders supported establishment of such a group, to ensure that political leaders could steer the ECB toward policies consistent with higher economic growth for Europe. German leaders opposed the idea, which they argued would lead to higher European inflation. In light of what you have learned in this chapter, which country's leaders do you think were correct? Explain your reasoning.

9. How can an increased degree of central bank independence make a country's aggregate supply curve shallower? Why can this actually reduce the credibility of a central bank?

10. Evaluate the following statement: "According to the basic game-theoretic view of discretionary monetary policy and inflation, central bank independence alone will not necessarily restrain a central bank from pursuing inflationary policies. Thus, it should be no surprise to economists that there is no apparent relationship between the degree of central bank independence and inflation outside of the world's developed nations."

Before the Test

Test your understanding of the material covered in this chapter by taking the Chapter 26 interactive quiz at http://money.swcollege.com.

Online Applications

Internet URL: http://www.ecb.int

Title: The European Central Bank

Navigation: Open the above home page of the ECB. In the right-hand margin, click on "About ECB" and then click on "Organisation of the European System of Central Banks."

Application: Read the discussion, and answer the following questions:

1. Is price-level stabilization the ECB's only goal? Are there other goals? What are they? Explain your basis for making this statement.

2. Based on this discussion, how independent does the ECB appear to be? Compare the degree of independence of the ECB with that of the Fed. Which do you believe is more independent?

For Group Study and Analysis: In the right-hand margin, click on "Links to EU Central Banks." Assign groups to take a look at the Web sites of the members of the European System of Central Banks (keep in mind, however, that not all European nations are members of this system). Try to determine the general objectives of each of these central banks within the ESCB. Do any of these central banks appear to have policy goals that conflict with those of the ECB?

Selected References and Further Reading

Barro, Robert J. *Monetary Policy.* Cambridge, Mass.: Harvard University Press, 1990.

Cukierman, Alex. *Central Bank Strategy, Credibility, and Independence.* Cambridge, Mass.: MIT Press, 1992.

Dwyer, Gerald, Jr. "Rules and Discretion in Monetary Policy." Federal Reserve Bank of St. Louis *Review* 75 (May/June 1993): 3–14.

Forder, James. "The Case for an Independent European Central Bank: A Reassessment of Evidence and Sources." *European Journal of Political Economy* 14 (February 1998): 53–71.

Friedman, Milton. "The Effects of a Full–Employment Policy on Economic Stability: A Formal Analysis." In *Essays in Positive Economics.* Chicago: University of Chicago Press, 1953.

VanHoose, David, and Christopher Waller. "Discretion, Wage Indexation, and Inflation." *Southern Economic Journal* 58 (October 1991): 356–367.

Waller, Christopher. "Performance Contracts for Central Bankers." Federal Reserve Bank of St. Louis *Review* 77 (September/October 1995): 3–14.

Waller, Christopher, and David VanHoose. "Discretionary Monetary Policy and Socially Efficient Wage Indexation." *Quarterly Journal of Economics* 107 (November 1992): 451–460.

Walsh, Carl. "Optimal Contracts for Central Bankers." *American Economic Review* 85 (March 1995): 150–167.

MoneyXtra

moneyxtra! Log on to the MoneyXtra Web site now (**http://moneyxtra.swcollege.com**) for additional learning resources such as practice quizzes, case studies, readings, and additional economic applications.

Chapter 27

What the Fed Does—
Interest Rate Targeting and Economic Activity

From the perspective of many Europeans, it was not supposed to turn out this way. When they formally established the European Central Bank (ECB) in 1999, they expected that it would emerge as an independent world policymaker. As one of the world's most independent central banks—in some respects, the *most independent—the ECB would be free to challenge the Federal Reserve for preeminence among global central banking institutions.*

To its European critics, so far the ECB has remained well within the shadow of the Fed. Whenever the Fed has cut its federal funds rate target, the ECB has tended to respond in kind by cutting its target for the interbank rate in Europe. Likewise, the ECB has generally matched Fed target rate *increases, often point for point. Instead of conducting a truly independent, European monetary policy, say these critics, the ECB behaves like a Fed subsidiary on the other side of the Atlantic. One disparaging European commentator has even suggested that the ECB's policymaking officials should be replaced with a single individual who simply does whatever the Federal Reserve says, because that is what current officials seem to do anyway.*

Fundamental Issues

1. Why do most of the world's central banks target nominal interest rates?
2. What are base drift and price-level nonstationarity, and what accounts for these phenomena?
3. How does interest rate targeting influence the term structure of interest rates?
4. Why are accurate inflation forecasts necessary for successful implementation of the Fed's interest-rate-targeting procedure?
5. What are the international implications of interest rate targeting?

If the ECB really does adjust its interest rate targets in conjunction with the Federal Reserve's changes in its interest rate target, does this necessarily mean that the ECB is subservient to the Fed? Or could there be other explanations for the tendency of central banks to move interest rates for their economies in similar directions? Why do they use interest rate targets in the first place? When you have completed this chapter, you should be prepared to address these questions.

Interest Rate Targeting—A Global Phenomenon

When the media report on monetary policy actions undertaken by the Federal Reserve System, the European Central Bank (ECB), the Bank of Japan, or any other central bank, they rarely include an in-depth discussion of the central bank's recent operations in financial markets. Certainly, reports in the financial press typically do not talk in terms of nonborrowed reserves, the supply of or demand for reserves, or money multipliers. Even though you have learned that these concepts are part of the nuts and bolts of how monetary policy actions work, media commentators typically focus on interest rates: Will the Fed cut interest rates? Will the ECB respond in kind? Will the Bank of Japan push up rates?

Interest Rate Targeting around the Globe

The media focus on interest rates because the world's central banks have oriented their policies around interest rates. As Table 27-1 indicates, central banks frequently intervene in their nation's financial markets. They normally use open market operations or some kind of central bank lending facility to maintain a market interest rate at a target level.

Thus, *interest rate targeting* is the primary means by which the bulk of the world's central banks—and certainly those in the most developed nations—conduct monetary policy. On a daily or weekly basis, each central bank varies the supply of reserves to its nation's banking system with the intention of keeping an interest rate at or very near a target level. In turn, a central bank seeks to establish interest rate targets that are consistent with its broader objectives for its nation's economy.

Rationales for Interest Rate Targeting

Why have so many central banks decided to target interest rates? One traditional rationale for this approach emphasizes its potential to be consistent with attaining economic stability. A more recent explanation is that interest rate targeting

Table 27-1 The Frequency of Central Bank Operations and Their Policy Targets

	Frequency of Policy Operations	Central Bank Operating Target
Australia	Daily	Overnight rate
Canada	Daily	Overnight rate
European Monetary Union*	Daily	Overnight rate
Japan	At least weekly	Overnight rate
Sweden	Weekly	Overnight rate
United Kingdom	At least weekly	1- to 3-month rate
United States	Daily	Overnight rate

*Austria, Belgium, Finland, France, Germany, Greece, Ireland, Italy, Luxembourg, the Netherlands, Portugal, and Spain.

SOURCE: Claudio E.V. Borio, "The Implementation of Monetary Policy in Industrial Countries: A Survey," *Bank for International Settlements Economics Papers,* No. 47, July 1997.

may be a more credible anti-inflation policy than alternative approaches to monetary policymaking.

The Traditional Rationale for Interest Rate Targeting We discussed the traditional arguments for and against interest rate targeting in Chapter 25. Recall that this approach is more likely to be consistent with an ultimate real income objective if the main sources of variability in the economy are volatility in the demand for money and in the demand for depository institution reserves. Shifts in the money demand schedule or in reserve demand cause market interest rates to change, thereby inducing variations in desired investment spending. These changes in investment expenditures then cause equilibrium real income to deviate from the central bank's target income level.

By targeting an interest rate, a central bank automatically offsets these sources of variability in equilibrium real income. Of course, interest rate targeting exposes equilibrium real income to other sources of variability. For instance, unexpected changes in autonomous aggregate expenditures, such as a decline in autonomous consumption or in autonomous exports, can cause equilibrium real income to differ from the central bank's objective. Likewise, variability in aggregate supply can cause price-level movements that also can cause real income and the price level to vary from the central bank's goals. These sources of economic variability would normally require changes in interest rates to induce compensating adjustments in investment spending. Targeting the interest rate prevents these compensating adjustments from taking place. Consequently, according to traditional theory, interest rate targeting appears to be a good approach to monetary policy only when variations in autonomous aggregate expenditures or in aggregate supply are small and uncommon.

If this traditional perspective were the entire story, we would have to conclude that for most economies fluctuations in the demand for money and in depository institutions' reserve demands are the overriding source of volatility and that most of the world's nations rarely experience variability in either autonomous aggregate expenditures or aggregate supply. In fact, however, all countries do experience unexpected changes in autonomous aggregate expenditures from time to time. They also encounter unanticipated variations in aggregate supply, which often result from variations in the prices of important factors of production, such as oil and other commodities. Indeed, the large run-ups in oil prices during the 1970s, the significant declines in oil and commodity prices in the 1980s and 1990s, and oil-price variability in the early 2000s were important sources of economic variability in developed and emerging economies.

Consequently, the traditional argument in favor of interest rate targeting must at best be only part of the story. There must be another rationale for why so many central banks target interest rates.

On the Web

How have the world's central banks conducted interest-rate-oriented policies in recent years? For excellent overviews of monetary policy procedures of central banks, go to the home page of the Bank for International Settlements (http://www.bis.org). To learn more about central bank policies in developed nations, click on "Publications and Statistics," then on "Working Papers," and scroll down to No. 40, by Claudio Borio. To find out more about central bank policymaking in emerging economies, go back to "Publications and Statistics" and click on "BIS Papers." Then in the right-hand box, click on "Policy Papers" and scroll down to No. 5.

The Problem of Asymmetric Information in Monetary Policymaking As we discussed in Chapter 26, another problem central banks face when conducting monetary policy is that people may not believe their commitment to low-inflation policies. When people know that a central bank would like real output to be near the economy's capacity level, they anticipate that the central bank will attempt to expand aggregate demand in the short run, thereby inducing inflation. This gives workers an incentive to bargain for higher wages than they would otherwise have been willing to accept. Such wage increases, in turn, tend to shift the aggregate supply schedule upward and to the left (see Figure 26-4 on page 655). To prevent the short-run reduction in real output that would occur, the central bank engages in exactly the aggregate demand expansion that people had anticipated. Thus, this interaction between the public and the central bank leads to an *inflation bias* in monetary policy.

Why are people so often unwilling to believe a central bank's commitment to fighting inflation? For one thing, just as seeing is believing, "not seeing" can be "not believing." During his tenure as Fed chair, Alan Greenspan hardly ever passed up an opportunity to preach the virtues of price stability. Nevertheless, the price level rose in every single year of his time as chair.

Another reason a central bank's commitment to price stability may be doubted is that firms and households have incomplete knowledge of the objectives of central bank officials and, as a result, may misinterpret their policy actions. Households and firms also are imperfectly informed about the behind-the-scenes political infighting that sometimes occurs at central banks. Behind closed doors, the president, prime minister, or legislators may subject central bank officials to various types of pressures, such as threats to cut their budget or reduce their independence, unless they conduct monetary policy as the government desires. Similarly, unannounced changes in the composition of central bank governing boards or even in advisory groups may have effects that outsiders cannot observe. For all these reasons, it can be hard to discern the actual goals of central bank officials.

On the Web
What are the Fed's latest announcements? Go to the home page of the Fed's Board of Governors (http://federalreserve.gov) and click on "Press Releases." Here, you can view the latest announcements of changes in the Fed's discount rate, alterations in procedures for calculating bank reserve requirements, and other policy actions.

Even when the officials attempt to make their objectives clear, they may not succeed. As we discussed in Chapter 26, policy time lags can complicate a central bank's efforts to recognize the need for countercyclical policy actions, implement those actions, and observe their effect on economic activity. In the meantime, the public may misperceive the central bank's slow response, implementation, and transmission and policy actions as an indication of a lack of interest in countering cycles in economic activity. Furthermore, there may be an unexpected slippage in the monetary policy transmission mechanism. Thus, a central bank could enact a policy that fails to have the intended effects. Households and firms may misinterpret this policy failure as a lack of central bank commitment to stated objectives.

Thus, there is an *asymmetric-information* problem in monetary policymaking. Only central bank officials themselves really know their true aims, the political pressures they face, and the difficulties they encounter in implementing policies intended to achieve their true aims. All that people outside the central bank see is the actual policy actions and the effects of those actions.

CREDIBILITY AND THE SIGNAL-EXTRACTION PROBLEM It follows that central bank policy actions and their effects provide **monetary policy signals**, or informational messages to the public about the goals of central bank officials. Because of the asymmetric-information problem that people outside central banks face, however, the information these signals provide is not *complete*.

Monetary policy signal: An occurrence that provides information about the objectives of central bank officials.

Suppose, for example, that the Federal Reserve decides to use a monetary aggregate, such as the monetary base or M1, as its intermediate monetary policy target. The Fed announces that each quarter (every three months), it plans for the monetary aggregate to grow at an annualized rate of no more than 5 percent and no less than 3 percent. Nevertheless, during the following quarter, data indicate that the monetary aggregate grew at a rate of 8 percent. The central bank issues statements indicating that the cause was unexpected changes in the demand for money. People know that this could be true. They also know that there could be other explanations: Fed officials may wish to push up aggregate demand unexpectedly to raise real GDP, or perhaps they have given in to pressures from the president or Congress to enact this policy.

Signal-extraction problem: The problem of trying to infer a policymaker's true goals from the imperfect signal transmitted by the policymaker's actions.

Thus, policy actions are *imperfect signals* of the true intentions of central bank officials. Economists call the difficulties that people face in trying to read the true aims of policymakers from these imperfect policy signals a **signal-extraction problem.** Economic theory indicates that the best solution to the signal-extraction problem is people's best guess—which economists call their *subjective expectation*—of the true objectives that the policy signal reveals. People form this subjective expectation given their knowledge of the backgrounds of central bank officials and their understanding of the kinds of on-the-job pressures the officials are likely to face.

DOES INTEREST RATE TARGETING IMPROVE CENTRAL BANK CREDIBILITY? Now let's contemplate what factors can make policy actions better signals of central bank officials' true intentions. We can learn about the background of a central bank official such as Alan Greenspan by reading biographical sketches and following news of his activities and statements. We can keep tabs on press reports concerning interactions between central bank and government officials, such as Greenspan's traditional weekly breakfasts with the Treasury secretary. Because of the asymmetric-information problem we face, however, there is a limit to how much more information we can gather about a central bank official's activities and aims.

Something else we can do, however, is to evaluate factors that can cause a central bank to succeed or fail in attaining its stated objectives. One of these is the central bank's ability to achieve its intermediate policy goals. Recall from Chapter 25 that to be useful, an intermediate target variable should be consistent with the central bank's ultimate policy goals, frequently observable, definable and measurable, and controllable. Although limited data on monetary aggregates are available daily, central banks typically have complete information about monetary aggregates only on a weekly basis. Financial innovations and regulatory changes, such as the growth of sweep accounts since the mid-1990s, complicate the ability of central banks to define and measure monetary aggregates. Furthermore, the controllability of a monetary aggregate depends on a number of factors, such as the stability and interest elasticity of the demand for money.

By way of contrast, central banks typically have minute-by-minute access to information about market interest rates. Financial markets accurately define and precisely measure interest rates, often within hundredths of a basis point (that is, within a ten-thousandth of a percent). In addition, central banks normally have considerable ability to influence interest rates via open market operations.

Thus, by adopting an interest rate as an intermediate policy target, a central bank can make the public's signal-extraction problem less complicated. People have an easier time inferring the central bank's true objectives from its monetary policy actions. For instance, suppose that the Fed uses a monetary aggregate as

moneyxtra!

Another Perspective

To further investigate the evidence concerning Taylor rules, go to the Chapter 27 reading, entitled "How Useful Are Taylor Rules for Monetary Policy?" by Sharon Kozicki of the Federal Reserve Bank of Kansas City.

http://moneyxtra.swcollege.com

its intermediate target, as it did in the late 1970s. If the monetary aggregate grows at a faster rate than people anticipated, then they must try to figure out if this resulted from unintentional policy errors by the Fed arising from slippage in monetary control or from intentional efforts to expand aggregate demand. Given all the linkages among day-to-day policy actions, interest rates, economic activity, and money demand, reaching a conclusion about this issue is not easy. Now suppose that the Fed uses an interest rate as its intermediate policy objective. If there is a decline in this interest rate that the Fed does not reverse, then it is very unlikely that the decline was unintentional. In this way, an interest rate target provides a much clearer signal than a monetary target. (A number of economists believe that the Fed's interest rate policies imply simple rules for how it conducts monetary policy, but others are not so sure; see *Management Focus: Can Federal Reserve Policies Be Summed Up by a Single Equation?*)

As a result, interest rate targeting can make a central bank's monetary policy stance more credible than it would be otherwise. As you learned in Chapter 26, enhanced credibility improves the likelihood that a central bank can limit the inflation bias of discretionary monetary policy. Thus, even though consistency with ultimate targets is an important consideration in choosing an intermediate target, a central bank may achieve significant credibility gains from adopting an interest rate target. A number of economists believe that this is the primary reason most of the world's central banks implement monetary policies using interest rate targets. Others, however, worry that targeting an interest rate may be fundamentally inconsistent with price stability, because when a central bank targets an interest rate, it may permit the quantity of money in circulation to drift over time. We next turn our attention to this issue.

1. Why do most of the world's central banks target nominal interest rates? One possible reason is the traditional rationale, which is that interest rate targeting may be the intermediate-targeting procedure most consistent with attaining economic stability. Another rationale arises from the fact that interest rates are so visible to the public and are relatively easy for central banks to influence. As a result, interest rates are especially clear signals of central banks' monetary policy intentions. Thus, interest rate targeting may improve the credibility of monetary policymaking for many central banks.

Interest Rate Targeting, Base Drift, and the Price Level

Shortly after the Fed unofficially ended its experiment with monetary targeting in the early 1980s, Milton Friedman had the following to say about Fed policymaking:

> There is an old story about a farmer who used his barn door for target shooting. A visitor was astounded to find that each of the numerous targets on the door had a bullet hole precisely in the center of the bull's-eye. He later discovered the secret of such remarkable accuracy. Unobserved, he saw the farmer first shoot at the door and then paint the target.

GLOBAL POLICY CYBER **MANAGEMENT Focus**

Can Federal Reserve Policies Be Summed Up by a Single Equation?

In 1993, John Taylor of Stanford University proposed that the Federal Reserve sets its interest rate target based on an estimated long-run real interest rate, any current deviation of the actual inflation rate from the Fed's inflation objective, and the gap between actual real GDP and a measure of "potential" GDP under full employment of all resources. This proposed method of determining the Fed's interest rate target became known as the "Taylor rule."

The Attraction of the Taylor Rule

Since then a number of economists have conducted detailed statistical studies of data from the United States and elsewhere in an effort to determine if the behavior of the Fed and other central banks can be captured by relatively simple equations. If each central bank has its own Taylor rule for determining how to set interest rates, then in theory economists should be able to predict a central bank's policy decisions once they determine the exact form of the equation.

Many economists are wary of attempts to describe complicated behavior of an individual, business, or institution with just one equation. Nevertheless, economists studying Taylor rules have found apparently strong statistical evidence that central banks' interest rate decisions do seem to be guided by a relatively few economic factors. For instance, Robert Barro of Harvard University concluded that nearly all Federal Reserve policy actions under the guidance of Alan Greenspan after 1988 could be explained and predicted based on inflation, the unemployment rate, and changes in real GDP relative to its trend.

Is Simplicity Necessarily a Virtue?

Fitting central bank behavior into a neat equation may not be quite so simple, however. Patrick Minford, Francesco Perugini, and Naveen Srinivasan of the Cardiff Business School in London have shown that a statistical equation that looks like a Taylor rule could actually describe a relationship that has nothing to do with interest rate targeting by a central bank. They contend, for instance, that policymaking that targets a monetary aggregate can cause market interest rates to adjust in a way that looks a lot like a Taylor rule. This result occurs even though the central bank actually does nothing to intentionally smooth interest rates. Thus, economists using an estimated interest rate equation would fool themselves into believing that they had accurately described central bank efforts to target interest rates.

This argument does not necessarily imply that trying to use Taylor rules to sum up central bank decision making is misguided. Nevertheless, it does mean that economists must be cautious in their study of how central banks conduct policy. It may be a mistake to presume that statistical evidence indicating a simple relationship among interest rates and a few other economic variables undeniably supports the conclusion that a central bank intentionally aims to smooth interest rates.

For Critical Analysis: If a Taylor-rule relationship does a good job of predicting interest rates, then does it really matter whether the central bank actually engages in interest rate targeting?

> That is the precise counterpart of the way in which the Federal Reserve System hits its monetary bull's-eye. It simply repaints its target. ("The Fed Hasn't Changed Its Ways," *Wall Street Journal,* August 20, 1985)

Today, we know that when Friedman complained about "target repainting," the Fed was in the midst of a transition to its current interest-rate-targeting procedure. Nevertheless, the basic phenomenon that Friedman described, known as *base drift,* remains an issue today.

Base drift: The tendency of a measure of total depository institution reserves or a monetary aggregate to fail to adjust to a level consistent with fixed long-run average growth.

Base Drift and "Price-Level Nonstationarity"

Panel (a) of Figure 27-1 illustrates the phenomenon of **base drift.** This is a tendency for a reserve measure or a monetary aggregate—nonborrowed reserves, the monetary base, M1, etc.—to vary over time without necessarily returning to a level consistent with a single long-run average growth rate. As a result, there is no fixed trend growth rate of reserve measures or monetary aggregates. Essentially, Fed policies produce meandering growth of reserves and monetary aggregates.

Panel (a) of Figure 27-1 shows the actual drift of the M1 aggregate during the late 1970s and early 1980s, when the Fed claimed to be engaged in monetary targeting. Panel (b) illustrates how the base drift in panel (a) can take place. Suppose that at point *A* in panel (b) the Fed announces a desired growth rate for M1 of no less than 4 percent and no greater than 8 percent. The midrange of these

Figure 27-1
Base Drift.

Panel (a) shows the actual drift of the M1 monetary aggregate during the late 1970s and early 1980s, a period when the Fed claimed that its goal was to target this aggregate. Panel (b) shows how this phenomenon of base drift can occur. If the Fed permits a monetary aggregate to drift toward the upper part of its target growth range in the fourth quarter (Q) of one year and then resets its target growth ranges at the beginning of the second year, the result is base drift.

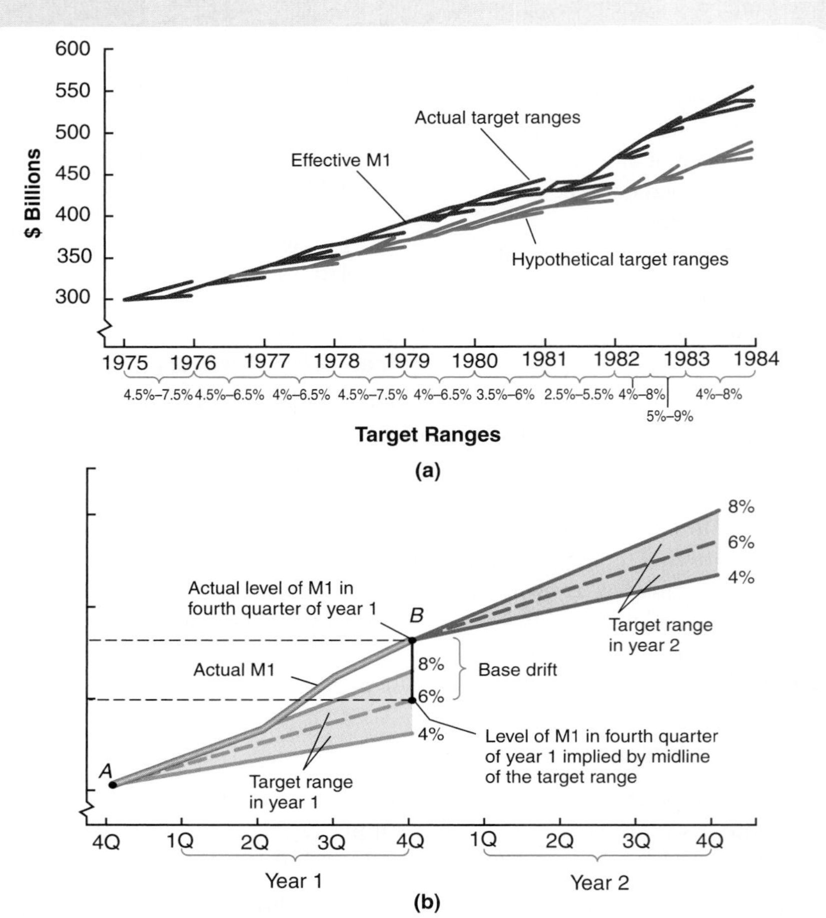

SOURCE: Alfred Broaddus and Marvin Goodfriend, "Base Drift and the Longer Run Growth of M1: Experience from a Decade of Monetary Targeting," Federal Reserve Bank of Richmond *Economic Review* 70 (November/December 1984): 3–14.

two growth rates is its announced *target* growth rate of 6 percent. During the following weeks, the Fed permits money growth to drift toward the upper part of its target growth range. Now suppose that at the next Federal Open Market Committee meeting, which occurs at the time indicated by point *B*, Fed officials reaffirm their commitment to the same target growth rate and range of permitted deviations from this target. The result, however, is *upward drift* of M1. Base drift occurs.

The phenomenon of base drift is not limited to the United States. Other central banks have followed the Fed's example in permitting drift in reserve and monetary aggregates. The drift in these aggregates has important implications for the behavior of aggregate prices in nations around the world.

As you learned in previous chapters, all the theories of the link between monetary policy and economic activity indicate that increases in reserves and monetary aggregates induce increases in aggregate demand. The resulting outward shifts in the aggregate demand schedule cause the equilibrium price level to rise.

Hence, the base drift illustrated in Figure 27-1 should invariably lead to drift in the price level as well. Indeed, base drift is associated with **price-level nonstationarity.** This term refers to a pattern of price-level changes over time in which the price level never settles down to a long-run average, or stationary, level. Instead, the price level, like depository institution reserves and monetary aggregates, drifts over time. Consistent with the pattern of M1 growth illustrated in Figure 27-1, during the past several decades the general pattern of price-level drift has been *upward.*

This leads to an important conclusion. Base drift can cause the price level to drift; that is, base drift can lead to nonstationarity of the price level, so that the price level never settles at a long-run average value. Because the general tendency has been for the price level to drift upward, inflation has occurred.

Price-level nonstationarity: Failure of the price level to adjust to a constant long-run average level; upward (or downward) drift of the price level over time.

Interest rate smoothing: Central bank efforts to attain an ultimate objective of interest rate stability.

Is Base Drift Unavoidable?

Over the years, many observers have criticized the Fed and other central banks for allowing base drift to occur. Halting base drift, they argue, is the key to eliminating inflation. For this reason, a number of economists have sought to understand why the Fed and other central banks tolerate drift of depository institution reserves and monetary aggregates.

BASE DRIFT AS A BY-PRODUCT OF INTEREST RATE SMOOTHING One potential source of base drift that economists have emphasized is the Fed's efforts to reduce interest rate variability. Economists refer to such efforts as **interest rate smoothing.**

Higher Real Income and Base Drift To see how interest rate smoothing can cause base drift, take a look at Figure 27-2 on page 680. Panel (a) shows the effects of increases in the demand for reserves by depository institutions when the Fed's goal is to keep the federal funds rate from changing. Suppose that a rise in real income induces people to hold more real money balances, so required reserves increase. Thus, real reserve demand rises from tr_1^d to tr_2^d. To maintain the federal funds rate at its initial equilibrium value of r_f^1, the Fed must increase reserve supply to eliminate upward pressure on the federal funds rate. Likewise, if reserve

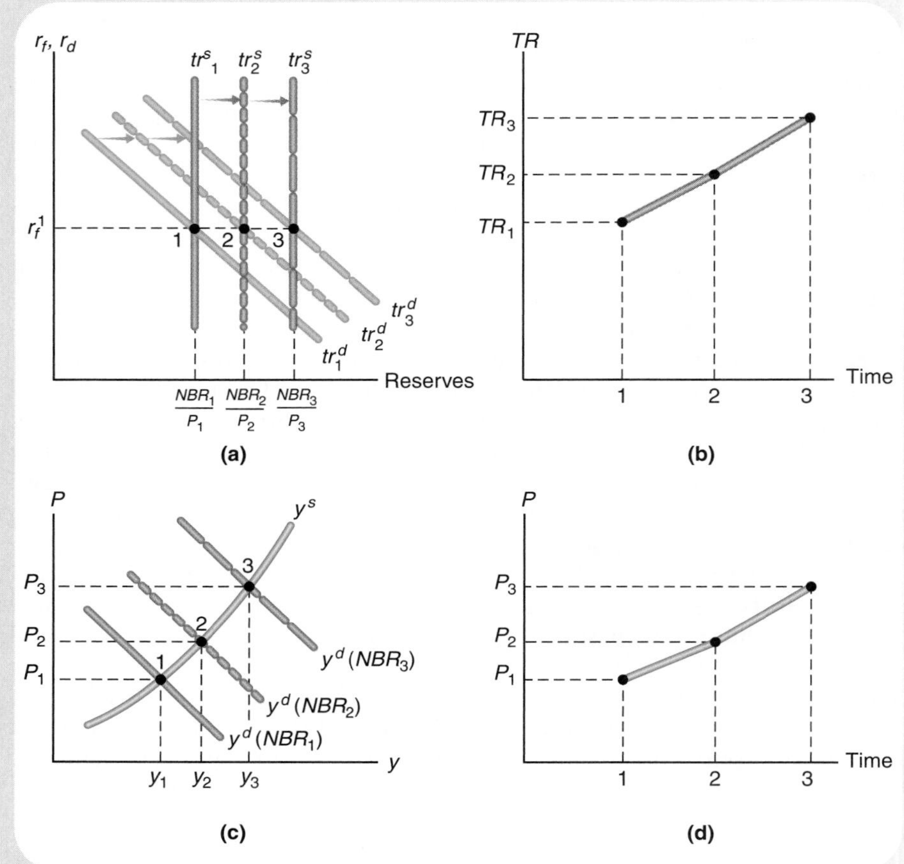

Figure 27-2
Interest Rate Smoothing, Base Drift, and Price-Level Nonstationarity.

Panel (a) depicts how the Fed must adjust nonborrowed reserves and the position of the reserve supply schedule to keep the federal funds rate unchanged in the face of back-to-back increases in reserve demand in period 2 and period 3. The result, as shown in panel (b), is upward drift in total depository institution reserves. Panel (c) shows how the Fed's policy actions in panel (a) will, in the absence of any other changes, cause aggregate demand to increase. The result, as depicted in panel (d), is upward drift of the price level, which is called price-level nonstationarity.

demand increases again a few weeks later, to tr^d_3, the Fed again must bring about an additional increase in reserve supply.

Panel (b) shows how total depository reserves adjust over time as a result of the Fed's actions to smooth interest rates. As you can see, in this example total nominal reserves (*TR*) of depository institutions drift upward. Consequently, the monetary base (total reserves plus currency) and monetary aggregates are likely to drift as well.

A Drifting Price Level Panel (c) illustrates a possible reason for the rises in real income that induced the reserve demand increases shown in panel (a). The reason is successive increases in aggregate demand, possibly generated by an increase in autonomous consumption or autonomous export spending. If the Fed had not smoothed interest rates, higher interest rates would have reduced investment spending, which would have dampened these increases in aggregate demand. Because of the Fed's interest-rate-smoothing efforts, however, aggregate demand shifts out fully in panel (c). As shown in panel (d), the result is upward drift in the price level. The price level is nonstationary because the Fed's efforts to smooth interest rates reinforce increases in aggregate demand.

This example illustrates the essential feature of an argument made by Marvin Goodfriend, a research economist at the Federal Reserve Bank of Richmond. This argument relates to the traditional drawback of targeting interest rates, namely that doing so may be inconsistent with stabilizing aggregate demand and real income (see Chapter 25). What Goodfriend showed was that smoothing interest rates entails another potential drawback: interest rate smoothing can result in base drift and price-level nonstationarity.

Does this mean that the Fed's current practice of interest rate targeting necessarily causes base drift? For Goodfriend and others, the answer to this question is definitely yes if the Fed becomes so caught up in interest rate smoothing that this objective begins to dominate its efforts. In this case, interest rate smoothing may effectively become an *ultimate* goal of Fed policy, rather than part of its intermediate-targeting procedure. When interest rate smoothing becomes a final goal of monetary policy, base drift and price-level nonstationarity result. Thus, as we shall discuss in more detail later in this chapter, a key issue when the Fed targets an interest rate is how often it should adjust its target. According to Goodfriend, failure to adjust the interest rate target in the face of changing economic conditions helps to explain base drift and nonstationary prices.

Alternative Rationales for Base Drift Does real-world experience with base drift and price-level nonstationarity imply that the Fed devotes excessive attention to limiting variability of interest rates? Some Fed critics take this position, and they may be correct. There are, however, other possible explanations of base drift that do not require central bank overattention to smoothing interest rates.

1. **Monetary targeting.** Base drift can also occur when a central bank is overzealous in seeking to target a monetary aggregate period by period. Suppose, for example, that in the current period the adoption of a payment-system innovation induces a significant fall in the demand for money. To achieve a monetary target, the Fed must induce a reduction in market interest rates by expanding depository institution reserves. This fall in interest rates, in turn, spurs desired investment spending, which induces a rise in real income—and thus an increase in aggregate demand and upward pressure on the price level. Of course, the rise in real income tends to push the demand for money back up somewhat, thereby assisting the Fed's effort to maintain its monetary target and contain the expansion in aggregate demand. Nevertheless, on net the Fed's effort to achieve its monetary target during the current period typically will push up reserves and the price level somewhat. If payment-system innovations or other unexpected events affecting money demand take place with the passage of time, then efforts to achieve a monetary target within each period can result in price-level nonstationarity.

2. **Exchange rate smoothing.** Base drift and price-level nonstationarity can also occur because of international factors. For example, consider a small nation that is completely open to international flows of funds. Recall from Chapter 4 that in this situation the *uncovered interest parity* condition should hold. Thus, the interest rate on a financial instrument issued in the

small nation, r, will equal the interest rate on an instrument with the same risks and maturity issued in another country, r^*, plus the expected rate of depreciation of the small nation's currency relative to the currency of the other country, denoted s^e. Thus, uncovered interest parity implies that $r = r^* + s^e$ or, equivalently, that $r - r^* = s^e$, so that the differential in the two nations' interest rates equals the expected rate of currency depreciation.

Now suppose that one of the key goals of the small nation's central bank is to engage in *exchange rate smoothing* by limiting variability of the exchange rate. To be successful in this task, the central bank must conduct open market operations to try to minimize expected depreciation, s^e. But keeping s^e as small as possible requires ensuring that the interest rate differential, $r - r^*$, remains very small. Hence, to smooth the exchange rate the central bank essentially must engage in interest rate smoothing. As we noted earlier, this can result in base drift and nonstationarity of the price level.

3. International interdependence. In principle, international factors can lead to base drift even when central banks do not overtly seek to smooth exchange rates. Widespread international trade causes economies to be *interdependent,* meaning that changes in prices or real income in one country can influence prices or real income in another nation. As a result, efforts to achieve domestic objectives can implicitly require exchange rate smoothing. For example, if the people in a nation import a large portion of the goods they consume from another country, then that nation's consumer prices depend on both the other country's price level and the rate of exchange of the nation's currency for the currency of the other country. Thus, reducing variability of consumer prices ultimately requires the nation's central bank to smooth exchange rates. Again, the result can be base drift and a nonstationary home price level.

Thus, there are several competing explanations for why central banks such as the Federal Reserve permit base drift and price-level nonstationarity. Too much attention to smoothing interest rates, targeting monetary aggregates, or smoothing exchange rates can lead a central bank to permit depository institution reserves, the monetary base, monetary aggregates, and the price level to wander over time.

This means that using an interest rate target to conduct monetary policy does not necessarily cause base drift and nonstationary prices. Indeed, a properly formulated interest-rate-targeting policy should limit the potential for base drift and price-level nonstationarity to occur. After all, a policy of reducing upward drift of reserves, monetary aggregates, and the price level is consistent with attaining the highest degree of central bank credibility—a key argument for targeting an interest rate in the first place.

To help reduce the potential for the price level to be nonstationary, many economists have suggested that central banks should set their interest rate targets with the explicit aim of achieving a target inflation rate. This policy of *inflation targeting* has been explicitly or implicitly pursued in several countries including Canada, New Zealand, the United Kingdom, and Sweden. Some observers believe that the Fed has implicitly pursued a type of inflation-targeting approach in recent years. Inflation targeting still permits the price level to drift upward over time, however. After all, inflation is by definition a rise in the price level over time. Completely eliminating price-level nonstationarity would require a policy of aiming for a fixed price level (at least on average) using an interest-rate-targeting approach. So far none of the world's central banks has pursued such a policy.

2. What are base drift and price-level nonstationarity, and what accounts for these phenomena? Base drift is the tendency for reserve and monetary aggregates to vary over time without ever settling down to levels consistent with a fixed long-run average growth rate. Price-level nonstationarity is the failure of the price level to adjust to a constant long-run average level. Both phenomena can result when interest rate smoothing is an ultimate goal of central banks. Period-by-period targeting of monetary aggregates can also cause price-level nonstationarity, however, as can exchange rate smoothing and other factors arising from the interdependence of nations' economies. Thus, interest rate targeting may or may not be responsible for base drift and price-level nonstationarity.

Interest Rate Targeting and the Term Structure

In Chapter 20, we discussed how the Fed influences market interest rates. Day to day the Fed focuses on the market for bank reserves. Equilibrium in this market determines the federal funds rate, or the rate on interbank loans with daily maturities. Changes in the market federal funds rate induced by the Fed's open market operations can influence interest rates on other financial instruments with different risk characteristics and longer terms to maturity, such as Treasury securities.

An interesting issue is how the Fed's interest-rate-targeting policy influences the relationship among interest rates at various terms to maturity. It turns out that in some respects day-to-day Fed policymaking using the federal funds rate can have important effects on this relationship. In other ways, however, the federal funds rate is less important than you might expect it to be.

Monetary Policy and Interest Rates

Recall from Chapter 4 that the modern theory of the term structure combines the expectations theory with the preferred habitat theory. Under the expectations theory, a longer-term interest rate is an average of current and expected future short-term interest rates. If people expect that short-term interest rates are equally likely to rise and fall, then the *yield curve*—a curve plotting interest rates at various terms to maturity—should be horizontal. But, in actual experience, yield curves typically slope upward. Thus, as indicated by the preferred habitat theory, economists typically add a *term premium* to the average of current and expected short-term rates to compute longer-term interest rates. Term premiums on longer-term instruments stem from savers' preference to hold bonds with shorter maturities. That is, savers must earn a somewhat higher return to induce them to hold longer-term instruments instead.

THE FEDERAL FUNDS RATE AS THE "ANCHOR" OF THE TERM STRUCTURE Most federal funds loans have a maturity of twenty-four hours. Consequently, the federal funds rate is at the lowest end of the maturity spectrum.

The Fed uses the federal funds rate as its day-to-day target for monetary policy. It follows from the basic theory of the term and risk structures of interest rates that the federal funds rate "pins down"—or, as economists like to put it, *anchors*—the shortest-maturity rates for yield curves of various types of financial instruments.

As you have learned, sustained open market operations that alter the targeted value of the federal funds rate change both the current twenty-four-hour term rate on federal funds and expected future values of this rate. According to the expectations theory, therefore, such Fed policy actions shift the federal funds yield curve. If risk premiums remain unchanged, this ultimately causes other yield curves, such as the Treasury securities yield curve, to shift in the same direction. In a manner of speaking, changing the target federal funds rate alters the position of the anchor for other interest rates.

Indeed, the daily federal funds rate is a very good predictor of market rates at the shorter (one- to three-month maturities) end of the maturity spectrum. A study by Glenn Rudebusch of the Federal Reserve Bank of San Francisco has credited this relationship to the Federal Reserve's policy of allowing relatively large daily deviations of the federal funds rate from the Fed's target for that rate but offsetting such deviations the following day via open market operations. As a result, financial market traders usually consider daily deviations of the federal funds rate from the target rate to be temporary. For instance, if today's funds rate appears abnormally high relative to the Fed's target rate, then traders anticipate that future daily rates will return to the target rate.

POLICY ANNOUNCEMENTS AND INTEREST RATE VARIABILITY Given the federal funds rate's role as an anchor for other interest rates, people pay close attention to Fed policies regarding its day-to-day federal funds rate target. Before February 1994, however, the Fed did not publicly announce its target. At the time of each Federal Open Market Committee (FOMC) meeting, it would make available to the public a summary of the FOMC's deliberations from the *prior* meeting several weeks earlier. Otherwise, everyone outside the Fed had to infer the target value of the federal funds rate from the Fed's actions in the market for reserves.

Naturally, when the Fed made no move to alter its federal funds rate over a lengthy period, it was relatively easy to guess the target. During times of turbulence in financial markets, however, inferring the target could be more difficult. From time to time during the 1980s, Fed officials unexpectedly altered the federal funds rate target following conference calls that took place *between* FOMC meetings. As a result, traders sometimes interpreted very short-term swings in the market for reserves as possible signs of Fed moves to change its target, when in fact the variations arose from unexpected shifts in reserve demand.

Thus, traders had to make uncertain guesses about the Fed's intentions. As a result, there was some "slippage" in the relationship between the federal funds rate "anchor" and other longer-term interest rates. Short-term fluctuations in the daily federal funds rate could thereby induce significantly larger variations in market interest rates for other financial instruments.

Since February 1994, however, the Fed has announced its federal funds rate target immediately after the FOMC has deliberated. Because traders now know for certain what the target is, they can feel more assured that any rise in funds rate variability does not represent a change in monetary policy.

Monetary policy indicator: An economic variable that gives the public an especially clear signal of the intended effects of monetary policy actions.

Efficient Markets and Indicators of Fed Policy

In light of the key role that the federal funds rate plays in influencing the general level of market interest rates, people have traditionally regarded it as an especially important signal of Fed policy. Indeed, in studies of the effects of monetary policy on the economy, many researchers have assumed that the federal funds rate is a key **monetary policy indicator,** that is, an economic variable that provides a particularly important signal of the intended effects of Fed monetary policy.

In recent years this idea has been questioned by other researchers. For instance, Michelle Garfinkel of the University of California at Irvine and Daniel Thornton of the Federal Reserve Bank of St. Louis have applied the theory of efficient markets (see Chapter 9) to this issue. They find that even though Fed open market operations directly influence the reserves market in which the federal funds rate is determined, these operations also exert speedy influences in markets for other financial instruments with longer maturities. Even before the Fed began publicly announcing its policy target, for instance, it rarely took longer than a day for other interest rates to adjust to changes in the federal funds rate.

Indeed, Garfinkel and Thornton conclude that open market operations also affect conditions in the market for one-day Treasury security *repurchase agreements*. As we discussed in Chapter 1, these are financial contracts to sell Treasury securities with a promise to repurchase them the next day. Because financial markets are so efficient, the resulting changes in interest yields on Treasury security repurchase agreements quickly influence interest rates on Treasury securities. Consequently, Treasury security rates and other shorter-term interest rates respond to Fed open market operations just as quickly as the federal funds rate does. For this reason, Garfinkel and Thornton argue that the federal funds rate is not a better monetary policy indicator than any other market interest rate. (Nevertheless, the Federal Reserve focuses its policies on the federal funds rate, so firms must forecast movements in this interest rate if they are to anticipate the future thrust of Fed policy actions; see on the next page *Management Focus: Can Firms Rely on Federal Funds Futures Prices to Predict Monetary Policy?*)

On the Web

What do the latest federal funds futures prices indicate about the market's expectation of future federal funds rates? Find out by going to the home page of the Chicago Board of Trade at http://cbot.com. Click on "Quotes Home" at the lower left, then click on "Financial Futures," and finally click on "30 Day Federal Funds."

3. How does interest rate targeting influence the term structure of interest rates? The Fed's daily target for the federal funds rate pins down, or anchors, the low-maturity end of the term structure of interest rates. Given term and risk premiums, market forces then determine other interest rates. In 1994 the Fed helped reduce slippage between the federal funds rate and other market rates by publicly announcing its target for the federal funds rate. Nevertheless, because U.S. financial markets are highly efficient, the federal funds rate is not necessarily a better indicator of Fed policy intentions than most other interest rates.

GLOBAL POLICY CYBER **MANAGEMENT Focus**

Can Firms Rely on Federal Funds Futures Prices to Predict Monetary Policy?

In October 1988 the Chicago Board of Trade (CBOT) began offering federal funds futures contracts for the average of the daily effective federal funds rate during the month of the contract. The effective federal funds rate is a weighted average of all federal funds transactions conducted by a set of federal funds brokers that make daily reports to the Federal Reserve Bank of New York. CBOT federal funds futures contracts for the current month to twenty-four months into the future are available for trading in amounts of $5 million.

Federal Funds Futures Prices as Forecasting Tools

The settlement price of a federal funds futures contract equals 100 minus the average effective federal funds rate for the month of the contract. Thus, a 30-day federal funds futures contract for January 2002 that settled at a market price of 98.255 on December 14, 2001, implied a futures rate for January of 1.745 percent (100 − 98.255).

If the futures market is efficient, then the futures rate implied by the market price of federal funds futures should on average equal the *market expectation* of the federal funds rate. Furthermore, if traders have rational expectations, the market expectation on average should equal the average value of the federal funds rate during the term of the futures contract. Of course, to form expectations about the average federal funds rate during a future period, traders must incorporate their anticipations of potential Fed actions involving the target for the federal funds rate. Because traders stand to gain or lose significant amounts if they fail to correctly anticipate Fed policy actions, some economists suggest that federal funds futures prices are a useful guide for firms interested in assessing the future course of monetary policy.

Taking into Account the Hedging Premium

Firms must use caution in interpreting futures market forecasts of the federal funds rate, however. Economists have found that the forecast of the effective federal funds rate implied by market federal funds futures prices systematically exceeds the actual effective federal funds rate. Thus, there is a positive *bias* in the futures market forecast of the federal funds rate. John Robertson and Daniel Thornton of the Federal Reserve Bank of St. Louis have estimated that this bias amounts to 3 to 4 basis points (3 to 4 hundredths of 1 percentage point) for a one-month forecast. The bias is higher with the longer forecasting horizons associated with federal funds futures maturing at future dates. Robertson and Thornton find, for instance, that the futures market forecast of the effective federal funds rate implied by futures market prices two months distant has a bias of 7 to 8 basis points.

Robertson and Thornton suggest that the likely reason for the positive bias is that market federal funds futures prices include a *hedging premium.* Large banks actively use federal funds futures to hedge against the effects that unexpected increases in the spot federal funds rate would have on the cost of funding their lending activities. To the extent that banks hedging against potential increases in the spot federal funds rate dominate market activity from day to day, there will be upward pressure on futures prices. As a result, a positive hedging premium will be factored into the effective federal funds rate implied by futures market prices.

Thus, a firm seeking to use federal funds futures prices to predict Fed actions regarding the federal funds rate must take this hedging premium into account. Otherwise, the firm will base its decisions on an overestimate of the effective federal funds rate predicted by futures market traders.

FOR CRITICAL ANALYSIS: Why would large firms contemplating sizable capital investments one or two months from now desire to have accurate forecasts of the federal funds rate thirty to sixty days in the future?

Interest Rate Targeting and the Economy

Economists generally agree that in today's highly efficient financial markets, the Fed's current policy of establishing a day-to-day target for the federal funds rate permits it to target the general level of interest rates. Nevertheless, at any given time there is rarely a consensus among economists as to what the general level of interest rates should be. In any given week, some commentators may contend that the Fed has set interest rates too high, while others argue that interest rates are too low, and still others say that interest rates are fine where they are.

How does the Fed determine its interest rate target? How does it decide the time has come to raise or lower its target? Why is this sometimes a difficult decision to make? These are the next issues we must consider.

The Fed's Balancing Act: The Liquidity Effect versus the Real-Balance Effect

To have the best chance of achieving its ultimate policy goals, a central bank must establish credibility. People must believe that it is committed to those ultimate objectives. To establish a credible interest-rate-targeting policy, however, a central bank must make clear to everyone that it stands ready to change its interest rate target as needed to attain its ultimate goals. If it holds too fast to a goal of attaining a fixed interest rate objective, then the central bank ends up smoothing interest rates. As you learned earlier, the result is drift of reserves, money, and prices. Typically, another outcome is inflation. If so, this further damages the central bank's credibility, making the pursuit of anti-inflationary policies even more difficult in the future.

This need to establish credibility may explain why you so often hear Federal Reserve officials claiming that they are on guard and ready to react to events that could lead to an upsurge in inflation. If Fed officials really desire to keep inflation very low, then it makes sense that they will wish to adjust interest rates to help maintain the credibility of their commitment to their ultimate goals.

Naturally, an issue that often arises when the Fed uses an interest rate target is what direction it should move interest rates in response to a given set of economic events. For instance, suppose that you are a member of the Fed's Board of Governors confronted with the following situation: The U.S. economy has been expanding for several years, but recent signs of weakness have led many forecasters to conclude that a recession could be just around the corner. Nevertheless, the unemployment rate is at its lowest level in more than thirty years. A recent uptick in the rate of growth of the price level could signal an upsurge in inflation. At the next FOMC meeting, should you argue for pushing up the Fed's interest rate target, for reducing it, or for taking a wait-and-see approach and leaving it unchanged?

This fictitious situation parallels the real-world situation that the Fed faced in 1999 and 2000 before it became clear in 2001 that economic activity was shrinking. To see why the situation is a potentially difficult one, recall what you learned in Chapters 23 and 24 about the liquidity effect and the real balance effect of monetary policy. Remember that the *liquidity effect* is a decline in the equilibrium nominal interest rate resulting from sustained open market purchases, given an unchanged price level. If you, as a Fed governor, wish to forestall a pending recession via a liquidity-effect reduction in interest rates that would spur investment spending and aggregate demand, then you might argue for reducing the Fed's interest rate target. But you face a problem in recommending this course of action. The ensuing rise in aggregate demand would tend to push up the price level, thereby reducing the real supply of depository institution reserves and placing upward pressure on interest rates. Keeping the interest rate target low in the face of this *real balance effect* then would require further open market purchases that ultimately would fuel further price increases. At some point in the future, therefore, the Fed would surely have to reverse itself and raise its interest rate target again.

By way of contrast, suppose that you choose to argue for raising the interest rate target. In the short run, this would induce a drop in desired investment spending, reduce aggregate demand, and stem inflationary pressures. The short-term cost, however, could be the hastening of a recession—and potentially a deeper recession.

Interest Rate Targeting and Expected Inflation

Clearly, the Fed can find itself walking a tightrope when it targets a nominal interest rate. To see why, remember from Chapter 4 that the *real interest rate* is equal to $r^r = r - \pi^e$, where r^r is the real rate of interest and π^e is the expected inflation rate. Now suppose that the Fed's interest rate target is equal to $\hat{r}$. This means that when the Fed achieves its interest rate target, the targeted nominal interest rate must be equal to the sum of the real interest rate and the expected inflation rate, or $\hat{r} = r^r + \pi^e$.

From this perspective, it is clear that the Fed can keep a nominal interest rate at the target level only if it can somehow bring about a level of the real interest rate or of the expected inflation rate that is consistent with its interest rate target. So what nominal interest rate target should the Fed aim to achieve?

Recall that most theories of the determination of the real interest rate—and certainly the classical theory we discussed in Chapter 22—imply that in the long run monetary policy actions have meager effects on real variables, including employment, the unemployment rate, real GDP, *and* the real rate of interest. Thus, beyond a short-term horizon, targeting a nominal interest rate ultimately entails aiming for a specific overall inflation expectation on the part of households and firms. That is, if the real interest rate is determined independently of monetary policy, then achieving an interest rate target equal to $\hat{r} = r^r + \pi^e$ requires inducing people to form an inflation expectation equal to the Fed's nominal interest rate target minus the real rate of interest, or $\pi^e = \hat{r} - r^r$.

This tells us something very important about a Fed policy of interest rate targeting. In the long run, the interest rate target that the Fed chooses should be consistent with attaining a specific expected inflation rate. Remember that all modern theories of economic activity that we surveyed in Chapters 23 and 24 are based on the rational expectations hypothesis. According to this hypothesis, on average people form inflation expectations consistent with the true inflation rate. Furthermore, in the long run the actual inflation rate is the average inflation rate. Consequently, we are led to an inescapable conclusion: if people form rational expectations, then in the long run the Fed's interest rate target should be consistent with the current expected inflation rate, which in turn should ultimately be consistent with the path of actual inflation.

A Credible Interest Rate Target

For instance, suppose that the real interest rate is at a long-run level of 3 percent and the current expected inflation rate is 3 percent. A nominal interest rate target value of 4 percent will be unsustainable. Indeed, people will know that trying to maintain a nominal interest rate below 6 percent will entail further expansion of aggregate demand, which will bring about further inflationary pressures. A nominal interest rate target of 5 percent, therefore, will send a clear signal to households and firms that the Fed has embarked on an inflationary policy. This low interest rate target will *reduce* the Fed's policy credibility. Only a target interest rate of 6 percent will signal households and firms that the Fed's current policy stance is credible.

Now that you are armed with this long-run perspective, put yourself back in the place of a member of the Fed's Board of Governors facing the situation of recent solid real growth but perhaps an impending recession, a historically low unemployment rate, and a recent uptick in the inflation rate. If you care about the Fed's long-term anti-inflation credibility, then the key issue you face in determining the appropriate interest rate target is what direction the inflation rate is truly headed. If the inflation rate is really about to rise, then it is time to raise the target for the nominal interest rate. If not, then holding firm at the current interest rate target may be the appropriate policy. Only if you have firm outside indications that the recent inflation uptick is temporary and that actual inflation will turn downward in the future should you argue for a reduction in the Fed's target for the nominal interest rate.

4. Why are accurate inflation forecasts necessary for successful implementation of the Fed's interest-rate-targeting procedure? The Fed and other central banks target nominal interest rates. A targeted nominal interest rate, therefore, is equal to the sum of the real interest rate and the expected inflation rate. In the long run, the real interest rate is not influenced by monetary policy. If the interest rate target is set too low in light of current expected inflation, then the Fed will lose anti-inflation credibility. Thus, the Fed's interest-rate-targeting policy must be consistent with current inflation expectations, which, if people form rational expectations, reflect the average path that inflation will actually follow.

Implications of Interest Rate Targeting for the World Economy

As Table 27-1 on page 672 indicates, many central banks target a market interest rate. As you learned in Chapter 5, however, international capital markets are very open today, which means that the international interest parity conditions discussed in Chapter 4 are more likely to hold today than in years past. One of these, the *uncovered interest parity* condition that we referred to earlier in this chapter, has some important implications for central banks' interest-rate-targeting policies.

Interest Rate Targeting, International Interest Parity, and Exchange Rates

As we noted earlier, under uncovered interest parity, the following is true:

$$r - r^* = s^e,$$

where r^* is a foreign interest rate and s^e is the expected rate of depreciation of the domestic currency. Thus, when capital flows freely and uncovered interest parity holds, the differential between the home interest rate and the foreign interest rate equals the expected rate of home currency depreciation.

Now suppose that your home country is Mexico. You are an official at the Bank of Mexico. The foreign nation is the United States, so r^* is determined via the Federal Reserve's interest-rate-targeting procedure. Because Mexico has a small economy, the Bank of Mexico cannot influence the Fed's interest rate target. U.S. and Mexican financial markets are very open to cross-border flows of financial assets, so the condition of uncovered interest parity approximately holds.

When confronted with open and efficient international financial markets, therefore, the Bank of Mexico faces a choice. One option is to set its own target in light of Mexican economic conditions and allow the actual and expected peso-dollar exchange rate to adjust until expected currency depreciation equals the resulting interest differential. Another is to try to smooth the exchange rate and thereby keep expected currency depreciation close to zero. This approach, however, essentially takes away the Bank of Mexico's freedom to independently set its own interest rate target. As we have noted in this chapter, it can also lead to upward drift in prices and a loss of policy credibility.

Indeed, during the several years leading up to 1994, the Bank of Mexico sought to maintain a steady rate of exchange rate depreciation. In a sense, this made Mexican central banking a straightforward proposition: all the Bank of Mexico had to do was to set its own interest rate target so that it maintained a nearly constant interest differential vis-à-vis U.S. interest rates. Ultimately, however, this policy of maintaining a relatively fixed interest differential became out of step with underlying conditions in the Mexican economy and financial system. In 1994, therefore, the Bank of Mexico raised its interest rate target and allowed the peso's value to adjust in foreign exchange markets. As predicted by the uncovered interest parity condition, rapid expected and actual depreciation of the peso occurred.

Is the Fed Becoming a Multinational Central Bank?

Currency board: An institution that issues currency at a fixed rate of exchange with respect to another nation's currency.

Later in the 1990s other nations—Thailand, Indonesia, Malaysia, and Brazil—had similar experiences. In an effort to avoid sharing the same fate, however, Argentina had already adopted a **currency board** arrangement. A currency board is an institution that issues a national currency at a strictly fixed rate of exchange with respect to the currency of another country. The first currency boards were established by nations that were members of the British Commonwealth, such as Hong Kong, the Cayman Islands, the Falkland Islands, and Gibraltar, which issued currency based on reserves of the British currency, the pound sterling. Singapore also has a currency board system.

In Argentina's case, its own peso was backed 100 percent by U.S. dollars. By truly fixing a one-for-one exchange rate in 1991, Argentina sought to link its financial markets to the more stable markets in the United States. When Brazil, Argentina's key trading partner, let its currency, the *real,* float in 1998, Brazilian interest rates shot up considerably. In Argentina, however, only some short-term interest rate instability occurred. Most observers believed the reason for the instability was fear that Argentina might abandon its currency board as it in fact did in 2002.

Dollarization: A country's adoption of the U.S. dollar as its sole medium of exchange, unit of account, store of value, and standard of deferred payment.

On the Web

What are the current status and future prospects of the world's currency boards? Explore this issue at Mark Bernkopf's Central Banking Resource Center at http://patriot.net/~bernkopf/, where you can click on "Currency Boards" for links to a number of resources relating to currency boards around the globe.

DOLLARIZATION: THE FED AS A MULTINATIONAL CENTRAL BANK By 1999, Argentina had begun to contemplate an even more radical change in its monetary arrangements. It was considering **dollarization,** or the abandonment of its own currency in favor of direct use of the U.S. dollar as a medium of exchange, unit of account, store of value, and standard of deferred payment. If it had implemented dollarization, Argentina would have had to import sufficient U.S. currency for people to use in hand-to-hand transactions. It also would have had to convert all Argentine financial accounts and contracts to dollars at the prevailing fixed rate of exchange.

When Argentina eliminated its currency board in 2002, the idea of an Argentinian dollarization was scuttled. Nevertheless, several Latin American nations began to consider dollarization. In 2000 Ecuador followed Panama's earlier example by dollarizing its economy. For the United States, both pros and cons are associated with the dollarization of part of Latin America. Dollarization would make it easier for U.S. companies to do business with Latin America, which accounts for about a fifth of U.S. trade.

In addition, increased use of the dollar outside the United States could create a financial windfall for the U.S. government. As we discussed in Chapter 1, governments earn *seigniorage,* the difference between the market value of money and the cost of its production, from producing money. A country such as Ecuador that dollarizes pays for the stock of U.S. dollars it needs for hand-to-hand trade by its residents by giving the U.S. government interest-bearing securities. The U.S. government then earns the interest on those securities, but as usual it does not pay interest on its currency. Currently, worldwide seigniorage is worth more than $15 billion a year to the U.S. Treasury. Dollarization by other Latin American countries undoubtedly would increase U.S. seigniorage considerably. At the same time, Fed and U.S. Treasury officials have expressed concerns about dollarization. If the Fed were to raise interest rates, say, in an effort to contain U.S. inflation, its action might be inappropriate for a dollarized Latin American economy. Thus, such a Fed action could have negative consequences outside the United States, fostering resentment and encouraging policymakers in dollarized countries to deflect blame for their economic problems onto U.S. policymakers. This could give governments of dollarized countries political cover for dodging tough decisions on appropriate economic policies within their own countries.

A Future Bipolar or Tripolar Monetary System? Emerging economies in eastern Europe have extended the idea of dollarization to the European Monetary Union's euro. Bulgaria, for instance, announced in 1999 that it might begin using the euro as its official currency. Other eastern European nations are considering the idea as well.

Some commentators have suggested that Russia should contemplate either "euro-izing" or dollarizing its economy. Dollarization might be easier to implement quickly, given that so many Russians already hold dollars. A key argument favoring adoption of the euro, however, is that Russia has relatively large trade flows with western European nations.

At present, these proposals are no more than ideas that various nations have explored. Nevertheless, in a world of interest rate targeting and internationally open financial markets, the idea of dollarization (or "euro-ization") has been one reaction to the reduced scope for relatively small countries to credibly conduct independent monetary policies.

Smaller, developing nations may or may not ultimately follow through on their dollarization ideas. Nevertheless, central banks in many of these nations gradually have sought to link their interest rate targets to those of the Fed, the European Central Bank, and, to a lesser extent in recent years, the Bank of Japan. In this way, world monetary policy interactions may become increasingly bipolar, or even tripolar, in the future. For this reason, monetary policy interactions among these three central banks have become a key focus of those interested in understanding Fed policymaking. We shall turn to this issue in the next chapter.

5. What are the international implications of interest rate targeting? In a world of very open financial markets, the uncovered interest parity condition is likely to be nearly satisfied. As a result, expected currency depreciation is approximately equal to the difference between national interest rates. This presents central banks that target interest rates in small, emerging economies with a choice. One is to target their interest rates in an effort to achieve ultimate goals at home, thereby permitting foreign exchange markets to determine how much their currencies depreciate or appreciate. The other is to try to smooth exchange rates and adjust their interest rate targets as needed, relative to those of large economies. The latter option constrains the ability to conduct independent monetary policies, so some nations have opted for currency board arrangements, in which they issue currencies that are strictly related to the currency of another major nation. Some nations have contemplated replacing their currency with another nation's currency.

Link to the Global Economy

Explaining International Interest Rate Linkages

As we discussed in Chapters 4 and 9, there are good reasons to expect that the interest rates and exchange rates of nations with few restraints on cross-border currency flows should be related through international interest parity conditions. In a world of floating exchange rates, there is no reason that the interest rates of various countries should move together, however, because movements in actual and expected exchange rates can be consistent with declining interest rates in one nation even as interest rates are increasing in another country. Nevertheless, in recent years, interest rates in several major industrialized nations have tended to move in conjunction. As you can see in Figure 27-3, the main explanation for this is that central banks have adjusted their interest rate targets in near lockstep.

Common Rationales for Similar Interest Rate Adjustments

Economists can offer at least three rationales for why central banks might choose to move their interest rate targets in similar directions over time:

1. Reactions to common events. For example, central banks might reduce interest rates simultaneously if the economies of their nations experience a temporary, worldwide oil-price shock. Because a temporary increase in global energy prices tends to push down aggregate supply within countries throughout the world, central banks may respond with similar cuts in interest rate targets intended to produce increases in aggregate demand that will stabilize real output levels.

2. Reactions to international spillovers. In some situations, economic fluctuations in one nation

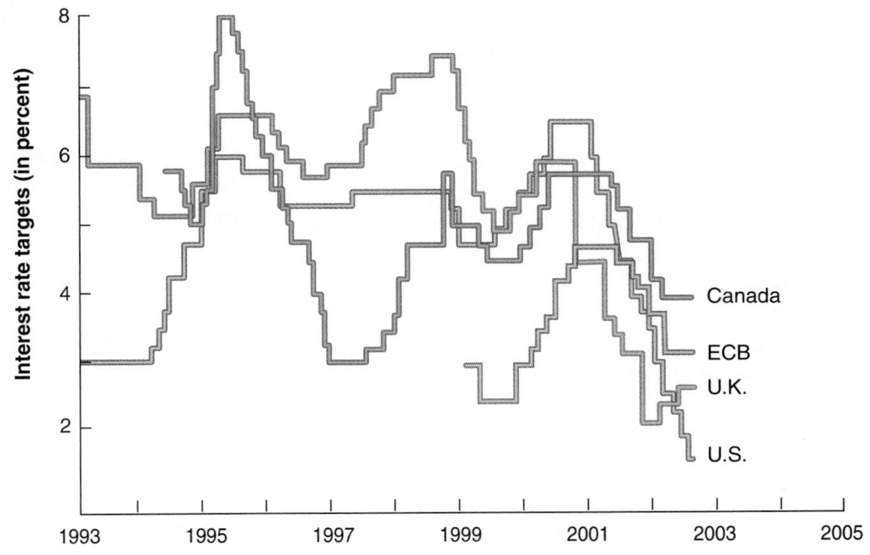

Figure 27-3
Interest Rate Targets of Major Central Banks since 1993.

Other major central banks tend to adjust their interest rate targets in conjunction with, or shortly after, a change in the federal funds rate target by the Federal Reserve.

SOURCES: Christopher Neely, "International Interest Rate Linkages," Federal Reserve Bank of St. Louis *International Economic Trends*, August 2001; Bank of Canada, Bank of England, European Central Bank, and Board of Governors of the Federal Reserve System.

Continued on next page

Link to the Global Economy, continued

may spill over to affect economic activity in other countries. A recession in the United States, for example, could cause U.S. imports from Canada, the United Kingdom, and the nations of the European Monetary Union to decline, thereby reducing the aggregate demand for goods and services in those countries. Thus, as the Federal Reserve reduces its federal funds rate target to stimulate aggregate demand in the United States, the Bank of Canada, the Bank of England, and the European Central Bank might reduce interest rates at roughly the same time in an effort to address spillover effects of the U.S. recession on their economies.

3. Smoothing exchange rates. Central banks might adjust interest rate targets in tandem to minimize swings in the exchange values of their currencies. Basic international interest parity conditions imply that if interest rates of different countries move together, actual and expected exchange rates will not change very much. If international interest rates move in equal measure, exchange rates will remain unchanged.

The Federal Reserve as "Policy Leader"

Take another look at Figure 27-3, and you will see that central banks rarely engage in equal adjustments of their interest rate targets. Thus, their actions do not appear intended to fix exchange rates. Furthermore, although target changes tend to happen at about the same time, they do not always occur simultaneously. While this leaves open the possibility of similar policy reactions to commonly experienced events, central bank decisions are also consistent with reactions to international spillovers.

During the period charted in Figure 27-3, the United States experienced a major expansion followed by a recession and gradual recovery. During this interval, the Bank of Canada, the Bank of England, and the European Central Bank often tended to follow Federal Reserve interest rate changes by implementing similar adjustments in their own target interest rates. This could be evidence of reactions by those nations to spillover effects from cyclical movements in U.S. output and prices.

In addition, however, the tendency for other nations' interest rate adjustments to lag behind those in the United States is also consistent with the notion that the Fed sometimes acts as the lead central bank of the world. According to this interpretation, the Federal Reserve pays attention mostly to factors that affect the U.S. economy and tends to be less concerned with external world economic events. Then other central banks follow the Fed's lead by adjusting their own interest rate targets.

Research Project

Some economists argue that the formation of the European Monetary Union is effectively creating an economy that rivals the United States in size. Hence, in the future the European Central Bank will be less concerned with external factors when determining its own interest rate targets. Are there reasons to agree with this perspective? To disagree? If this prediction turns out to be accurate, how are the relationship between U.S. and EMU interest rates and the behavior of the dollar-euro exchange rate likely to be affected in future years?

Web Resources

What are the current interest rate targets of major central banks? U.S. data are available by clicking on "Monetary Policy," then "Federal Open Market Committee," and then "Federal Funds Rate" at http://www.federalreserve.gov, and information on the ECB's present interest rate targets is available at http://www.ecb.int. You can find current Canadian overnight interest rate targets at http://www.bankofcanada.ca, and information about targets for interest rates in the United Kingdom is available at http://www.bankofengland.co.uk, where you can click on "Latest MPC Interest Rate Decision." To search for information about targets of other central banks, go to the home page of the Bank for International Settlements (http://www.bis.org), scroll down to "Links to Central Banks," and click on the pop-up "Central Bank Web Sites."

Chapter Summary

1. Rationales for Interest Rate Targeting by Most of the World's Central Banks: A traditional rationale for interest rate targeting is that an interest rate may be the intermediate target that is most consistent with economic stabilization. Another rationale is that interest rate targeting may help central banks maintain their anti-inflation credibility. Because interest rates are readily observable and easy for central banks to influence, they may be particularly clear signals of the objectives of monetary policy. Thus, using interest rate targets could enhance the credibility of central banks.

2. Base Drift and Price-Level Nonstationarity and Their Possible Causes: Base drift takes place whenever measures of depository institution reserves or monetary aggregates fail to adjust to levels consistent with a fixed long-run average rate of growth. Price-level nonstationarity occurs when a nation's price level drifts upward (or downward) over time without converging to a long-run average level. Central bank efforts to engage in excessive interest rate smoothing can cause base drift and price-level nonstationarity. Monetary targeting, exchange rate smoothing, and international economic interdependence can also cause base drift and price-level nonstationarity, however. For this reason, interest-rate-targeting policies are not necessarily responsible for these phenomena.

3. Interest Rate Targeting and the Term Structure of Interest Rates: The target that the Fed establishes for the twenty-four-hour federal funds rate pins down, or anchors, the low-maturity end of the term structure of interest rates. Financial markets then determine other market interest rates in light of existing term and risk premiums. Before 1994, Fed did not openly divulge its daily target for the federal funds rate, which increased uncertainty about future daily interest rates and thereby weakened somewhat the relationship between the federal funds rate and other market rates. Since 1994, the Fed has announced its target, and this has tightened the relationship. Nonetheless, U.S. financial markets are so efficient that the federal funds rate probably is not a better indicator of Fed policy objectives than most other market rates.

4. The Importance of Accurate Inflation Forecasts for Successful Implementation of Interest Rate Targeting: Any nominal interest rate that a central bank might target is equal to the sum of the real interest rate and the expected inflation rate. Because the real interest rate is not affected by monetary policy in the long run, the Fed's interest rate target must be consistent with current inflation expectations. The Fed will lose anti-inflation credibility if it sets the interest rate target too low in light of current expected inflation. In turn, if people form expectations rationally, then the expected inflation rate indicates the true average path of inflation.

5. International Implications of Interest Rate Targeting: Interest rate targeting in a world environment with very open flows of funds among national financial markets makes it more likely that the uncovered interest parity condition will be nearly satisfied. Consequently, expected currency depreciation is approximately equal to the difference between national interest rates. This limits the options of central banks in small, emerging economies. They can target interest rates to try to attain ultimate objectives and allow foreign exchange markets to determine how much their currencies depreciate or appreciate. Alternatively, they can attempt to smooth exchange rates and vary their interest rate targets relative to those of larger economies, which sharply limits their ability to conduct independent monetary policies. Given this constraint, a few nations have established currency board arrangements, in which they issue currencies at a set rate of exchange relative to the currency of another major nation. Some nations have considered dollarization, in which they replace their currency with the U.S. dollar, and others have recently contemplated replacing their currency with the European Monetary Union's euro.

Questions and Problems

(Answers to odd-numbered questions and problems may be found on the Web at http://money.swcollege.com under "Student Resources")

1. Suppose that the money multipliers relating the monetary base to M1 and M2 are highly variable, reflecting various sources of slippage from the reserves market through the term structure of interest rates to the equilibrium quantity of money. Would these conditions tend to favor targeting a monetary aggregate or an interest rate as a intermediate monetary policy target? Could money-multiplier variability tend to favor either approach from the standpoint of monetary policy credibility? Explain your reasoning for both answers.

2. Explain the basic argument for why interest rate targeting has the potential to make a Fed commitment to an anti-inflationary monetary policy more credible to the public.

3. Explain the basic concepts of base drift and price-level nonstationarity.

4. Most economists agree that price-level nonstationarity need not always accompany base drift. Explain verbally, or using graphs if they are helpful, how this could happen. Explain your reasoning. [Hint: Think about the kind of situation in which trying to make the price level stationary over time might require drift of a reserve aggregate, such as nonborrowed reserves.]

5. Under what circumstances is interest rate targeting most likely to be associated with base drift and price-level nonstationarity?

6. When is interest rate targeting least likely to induce base drift and price-level nonstationarity?

7. Suppose that a change in the twenty-year Treasury bond rate provides a signal of Fed policy intentions that is as clear as an accompanying change in the federal funds rate. What might you be able to infer about U.S. financial markets and about the relative usefulness of the federal funds rate as a key monetary policy indicator? Why?

8. In the short run, higher nominal interest rates can induce a contraction of aggregate demand and a decline in equilibrium real output. In the long run, however, higher nominal interest rates are associated with higher actual and expected inflation. Explain why this complicates the Fed's interest-rate-targeting procedure.

9. Why does the Fed depend on inflation forecasts to help it determine its interest rate targets?

10. Suppose that you are the chief of a central bank in a small developing country, and you use interest rate targeting to implement monetary policy. Large flows of financial assets and traded goods move across your borders with a large nation, and the large nation's central bank also uses an interest rate target. One of your key policy goals is to limit actual and expected changes in the rate of exchange of your currency for the currency of the large nation. Can you conduct your own monetary policy independent of the policy of the other nation's central bank? Why or why not?

Before the Test

Test your understanding of the material covered in this chapter by taking the Chapter 27 interactive quiz at http://money.swcollege.com.

Online Application

Internet URL: http://users.erols.com/kurrency/

Title: Currency Boards

Navigation: Open the above Web site. Then, under the heading "Currency Boards—General Material," click on "Introduction to Currency Boards."

Application: Read the article, and then answer the following questions:

1. What are the key features of an "orthodox" currency board?

2. In what ways has Bulgaria's currency board differed from an orthodox currency board?

For Group Study and Analysis: The article lists a number of countries that have used currency boards in the past and present. Set up groups to examine nations with currency boards in specific regions of the world. Have each group develop a list of nations in its region that have had good or poor experience with currency boards. What factors appear to influence how well a currency board works?

Selected References and Further Reading

Bernanke, Ben, Thomas Laubach, Frederic Mishkin, and Adam Posen, eds. *Inflation Targeting: Lessons from the International Experience*. Princeton, N.J.: Princeton University Press, 1999.

Cover, James, and David VanHoose. "Political Pressures, Credibility, and the Choice of the Optimal Monetary Policy Instrument." *Journal of Economics and Business,* 2001, 52 (July/August 2000): 325–341.

Daniels, Joseph, and David VanHoose. "The Nonstationarity of Money and Prices in Interdependent Economies." *Review of International Economics* 7 (February 1999): 87–101.

Garfinkel, Michelle, and Daniel Thornton. "The Information Content of the Federal Funds Rate: Is It Unique?" *Journal of Money, Credit, and Banking* 27 (August 1995): 838–847.

Goodfriend, Marvin. "Interest Rates and the Conduct of Monetary Policy." *Carnegie-Rochester Series on Public Policy* 34 (1991): 7–30.

Rudebusch, Glenn. "Federal Funds Interest Rate Targeting, Rational Expectations, and the Term Structure." *Journal of Monetary Economics* 35 (April 1995): 245–274.

Svensson, Lars. "Price-Level Targeting versus Inflation Targeting: A Free Lunch?" *Journal of Money, Credit, and Banking* 31 (August 1999): 277–295.

Walsh, Carl. "Interest Rates and Monetary Policy." Chapter 10 in *Monetary Theory and Policy.* Cambridge, Mass.: MIT Press, 1998.

MoneyXtra

moneyxtra! Log on to the MoneyXtra Web site now (**http://moneyxtra.swcollege.com**) for additional learning resources such as practice quizzes, case studies, readings, and additional economic applications.

Chapter 28

Policymaking in the World Economy—International Dimensions of Monetary Policy

Fundamental Issues

1. What are the pros and cons of fixed versus floating exchange rates?
2. What is the monetary approach to exchange rate determination?
3. What is the portfolio approach to exchange rate determination?
4. How effective are foreign-exchange-market interventions?

Inflation has been commonplace throughout the world since the end of World War II. Also typical in most nations have been tax systems that are not fully indexed to inflation. Thus, as nominal incomes of individuals and businesses have increased, so have the portions of income that they pay as taxes. In most countries, interest payments on debts are tax-deductible, but payments to shareholders are not, so companies around the globe have had an incentive to raise funds by borrowing, instead of by issuing new equity shares, as a means of reducing their inflation-boosted tax bills. As a consequence, corporate debt-equity ratios have persistently risen during the past several decades.

During the past decade, however, some nations have broken away from the inflationary tendencies of the past. Indeed, a few nations have experienced bursts of deflation. In those nations, corporate debt no longer offers significant tax advantages. Thus, companies based in those countries have been scrambling to reduce their borrowings in favor of more stock issues.

This now mixed global environment, with inflationary tendencies still present in some regions even as bursts of deflation occur in other locales, has complicated the financing choices faced by multinational corporations with operations spanning national borders. In many respects, the financial officers of these companies would have an easier time if central banks would fix exchange rates and establish a common inflationary or deflationary trend for the world as a whole. Then determining the appropriate division between debt and equity would be a less complex endeavor.

Should the world's central banks work together to aim for stable output and prices, or should they at least fix exchange rates in an effort to maintain mutually stable rates of worldwide inflation or deflation? Can central banks fix exchange rates? These are among the topics of this chapter, which considers the international aspects of monetary policy.

Fixed versus Floating Exchange Rates

As discussed in Chapter 27, some countries have abandoned central-banking arrangements in favor of currency boards. Unlike a central bank, a currency board does not have a discount window. It does not impose reserve requirements, nor does it regulate private banks. The single duty of a currency board is to issue a national currency at a fixed rate of exchange relative to the currency of another nation.

In years past, many central banks, including the Federal Reserve, sought to maintain fixed exchange rates. Since the 1970s, however, the United States and a number of other nations have permitted their exchange rates to float, meaning that global market forces determine their values.

What factors should a country take into account when choosing between fixed and floating exchange rates? We begin our exploration of the international dimensions of monetary policy by contemplating this important question.

An Argument for Fixed Exchange Rates

In a system of floating exchange rates, variations in the demand for or supply of foreign exchange cause the exchange rate to fluctuate. As we noted in Chapter 7, changes in the exchange rate can affect the market values of incomes and of financial assets that are denominated in foreign currencies. This can increase the foreign exchange risks that a nation's residents face, thereby inducing them to incur costs to avoid these risks.

Hedging Against Foreign Exchange Risk As you learned in Chapter 8, a country's residents are not defenseless in the face of foreign exchange risk. They can *hedge* against such risks, meaning that they can adopt strategies intended to offset the risk arising from exchange rate variations.

For instance, as discussed in Chapter 8, households, firms, and financial institutions can hedge against foreign exchange risks by using derivatives such as forward currency contracts, currency futures, currency options, and currency swaps. They can use forward or futures contracts to ensure that they will receive the current market forward exchange rate on the future delivery of a sum of currency. They can also use options and swaps to try to protect flows of foreign-currency-denominated earnings from fluctuations arising from exchange rate swings.

The Costs of Hedging Hedging against foreign exchange risks is not costless, however. Often, businesses and financial institutions that wish to hedge must pay for the time and talents of experts in the use of hedging strategies. Individuals must pay these experts fees and commissions. In addition, the hedging strategies themselves can sometimes entail taking potentially risky positions that expose holders of derivatives to other kinds of risk if market conditions change unexpectedly.

One common rationale for fixing exchange rates is that this policy can reduce or perhaps even eliminate hedging costs. If exchange rates are fixed, the argument goes, then the potential for exchange rate variability is greatly diminished, and households and businesses will not have to incur the costs of hedging against foreign exchange risks.

Exchange Rates as Shock Absorbers

Proponents of fixed exchange rates argue that the world's people would be better off if their governments adopted a system of completely rigid exchange rates. Indeed, taken to its logical extreme, this argument implies that we would be better off with a *single world currency.* If we all were to adopt the same currency, after all, all foreign exchange risks would be eliminated. Furthermore, people would no longer have to incur the costs of converting one currency into another. For example, today a U.S. tourist traveling from San Francisco to China must pay a fee to convert U.S. dollars to Chinese renminbi. Such fees would no longer exist if U.S. and Chinese residents all used the same currency.

Nevertheless, if a system of rigid exchange rates would be so advantageous, then why do most developed nations allow their exchange rates to be market determined? If people could gain from using a common currency, why are there so many separate currencies? Presumably, there must be potentially significant disadvantages from fixing exchange rates or from adopting a single currency. There must be a solid rationale for why so many nations have their own currencies and several countries allow their exchange rates to float. (Sometimes a nation must choose between two bad outcomes when it weighs fixed versus floating exchange rates. See *Policy Focus: Struggling to Find the Right Exchange Rate System in Poland.*)

A Rationale for Separate Currencies and Floating Exchange Rates The theory of *optimal currency areas,* which was developed by Robert Mundell of Columbia University, offers an explanation for why different nations might wish to issue separate currencies. It also explains under what circumstances people in different geographic regions, such as Colorado and Michigan, can benefit from adopting a common currency unit.

A Two-Region Example To understand the fundamental idea of an optimal currency area, consider an imaginary situation. Suppose that there is a large island whose residents have divided into two groups inhabiting separate regions of nearly identical size: region *A* and region *B*. Residents of each region specialize in producing different goods and services. Firms in region *A* manufacture garden equipment, and firms in region *B* produce digital television sets. Wages and other prices of factors of production in each region are sticky in the short run.

Households and firms in the two regions trade their goods and services across the border separating the regions, but barriers prevent the flow of people and their possessions between the regions. For instance, perhaps the residents of the regions speak different languages or have cultural, religious, or political differences that have led them to erect these barriers. In any event, these obstacles to

GLOBAL | POLICY Focus | CYBER | MANAGEMENT

Struggling to Find the Right Exchange Rate System in Poland

When the European Monetary Union launched the euro in January 1999, the National Bank of Poland linked the value of the Polish currency, the *zloty,* to a weighted average of the euro and the U.S. dollar. More weight was placed on the euro.

A Bad Match between the Euro Zone and the Zloty

During the next two years, the euro's value fell by nearly 30 percent relative to the dollar. Because the zloty was tied closely to the euro, its value also declined relative to the dollar and several other currencies. Nevertheless, two-thirds of Poland's international trade is with western Europe, where the demand for Polish exports was stagnant after 1999. Furthermore, the decline in the zloty's value did little to induce others outside western Europe, including Russians struggling with their own weak economy, to purchase Polish goods. In the meantime, Polish residents increased their spending on goods and services imported from western Europe. Consequently, Poland's current account deficit ballooned, rising from just over 4 percent of the nation's GDP to almost 8 percent.

Naturally, Poland's capital account balance soared. The problem was that most foreign capital was in the form of short-term portfolio investment—funds that Polish authorities regarded as "hot money" that could easily flow back out of the country at a moment's notice.

Back to Tough Choices for Monetary Policy

In April 2000, the National Bank of Poland decided to let the zloty float in foreign exchange markets. The currency promptly lost another 10 percent of its value relative to the dollar. Nevertheless, Polish exports remained stagnant.

This left the National Bank of Poland facing a tough decision. On the one hand, if it engaged in a monetary expansion, lower interest rates might fuel domestic demand and import spending, thereby pushing the current account deficit ever higher. On the other hand, if it implemented a contractionary monetary policy, the resulting rise in Polish interest rates would probably attract even more short-term, speculative foreign investment. Undoubtedly, some officials at the Polish central bank found themselves wishing they could return to the good old days when their main task had been to try to stabilize the zloty's value in foreign exchange markets.

For Critical Analysis: What criteria might have guided the National Bank of Poland in determining the appropriate monetary policy action with a floating zloty?

cross-border movements prevent people in the two regions from exchanging labor or other factor services. All they can do is take their final goods and services to the border to trade.

Each region has its own government. Each government, in turn, issues its own "national" currency. Therefore, to trade goods and services across the border separating the regions, people must convert their currencies at the prevailing exchange rate between the two currencies.

Adjusting to Changes in the Relative Demands for Regional Products Now envision the following event: A best-selling book on the joys of gardening induces couch potatoes across the island to turn off their televisions and begin planting. As a result, people in both regions reduce their demand for digital televisions produced in region *B* and increase their demand for the garden equipment produced in region *A*. This causes the firms in region *B* to reduce their demands for labor and other factors of production. Consequently, real income in region *B* begins to decline. Because wages are sticky, unemployment begins to rise in region *B*. Simultaneously, firms in region *A* raise their production in the face of the increased demand for garden equipment across the island. As a result, region *A* begins to run a trade surplus, and its output and employment rise.

If the rate of exchange between the regions' currencies is fixed, then the assumed short-run stickiness of wages and prices causes unemployment to persist for some time in region *B* following the changes in consumers' tastes. In the long run, of course, the price of the garden equipment manufactured in region *A* will increase, and the price of the digital televisions made in region *B* will decline, leading to a rebalancing of trade between the two regions. Until this long-run adjustment occurs, however, region *B* can experience a significant unemployment problem.

If the exchange rate is flexible, however, then the trade surplus in region *A* and the accompanying trade deficit in region *B* induce a rapid depreciation in the value of region *B*'s currency relative to the currency of region *A*. This causes an immediate fall in the effective price of region *B*'s digital televisions as perceived by residents of region *A*. At the same time, there is a quick rise in the effective price of region *A*'s garden equipment faced by residents of region *B*. As a result, trade between the two nations is balanced much more rapidly with a floating exchange rate. Furthermore, region *B*'s unemployment problem is more short-lived.

In this example, the two regions benefit from using separate currencies with a floating rate of exchange. Fixing the exchange rate—or taking the further step of adopting a single currency—would eliminate the ability of the exchange rate to adjust to changes in relative demands for the regions' goods. This would expose the regions to the possibility of chronic payments imbalances and unemployment problems.

Of course, residents of regions with separate currencies and a market-determined exchange rate face foreign exchange risks and costs of converting currency. Nevertheless, adopting individual currencies and a floating exchange rate protects the regions from unemployment dangers that arise from language, cultural, or legal barriers to worker migration.

Optimal Currency Areas Now suppose that the conditions that led to the restrictions on cross-border migration or commuting break down. Consequently, residents of region *A* can move freely to region *B* to work, and vice versa. Let's further suppose that shortly after this development, once again the demand for region *A*'s garden equipment rises and the demand for region *B*'s digital televisions declines.

Again the immediate results are a trade surplus, higher output, and higher employment in region *A* and a trade deficit, lower output, and lower employment in region *B*. As a result, some residents of region *B* find themselves without work. Now, however, these unemployed region *B* residents can migrate—or perhaps commute—to newly available jobs in region *A*. Unemployment in region *B*, therefore, is at worst a temporary phenomenon. Indeed, unemployment in both regions together is minimized in the face of such changes in the relative demands for their products.

In this example, there is no reason that the exchange rate should not be fixed, thereby permitting residents of both regions to avoid foreign exchange risks and the costs of hedging against these risks. Indeed, economists would conclude that the two regions together constitute an **optimal currency area**—a geographic area within which fixed exchange rates can be maintained without slowing regional adjustments to changing regional conditions. Furthermore, within such an optimal currency area, separate regions find it beneficial to adopt a *common currency* if the cost of converting currencies for regional trade exceeds any perceived gain from having separate currencies. Thus, if the residents of regions *A* and *B* continue to perceive sizable benefits from using separate currencies even though no barriers otherwise separate their regions, they may be willing to continue to incur the currency conversion costs that arise when they trade goods. If, however, the currency conversion costs are sufficiently large relative to the potential benefits of maintaining separate currencies, the residents of the two regions may gain, on net, from adopting a single, common currency.

Optimal currency area: A region within which fixed exchange rates can be maintained without inhibiting prompt internal adjustments of employment and output to changes in international market conditions.

RATIONALES FOR SEPARATE CURRENCIES What benefits might residents of two regions with few or no barriers to labor mobility perceive that would justify maintaining separate currencies? One might be a widespread perception that loss of a region's unique currency would entail a sacrifice of political sovereignty. If the region is a nation-state with its own cultural history that its residents associate with its currency—for instance, the United Kingdom's pound sterling and the memories it evokes of a former global empire—then convincing the residents to give up their currency could prove difficult.

LACK OF FISCAL INTEGRATION Nationalist feelings are not the only reason why a country might choose not to join others in using a single currency. National governments maintain their own budgets with their own sources of revenues and distributions of expenditures. The key source of any government's revenues is taxes. As we discussed in Chapter 1, one type of taxation is *seigniorage,* or central bank profits earned from producing money whose market value exceeds its cost of production.

Table 28-1 on the following page provides estimates of average annual rates of seigniorage relative to gross domestic product (GDP) and to government spending for selected nations between the early 1970s and the 1990s. As you can see, in several countries seigniorage has comprised less than 1 percent of GDP and less than 2 percent of government expenditures. In others, however, seigniorage has been a significant revenue source. In these nations, the government might have to undertake the politically painful task of increasing other taxes if it were to lose seigniorage following adoption of a common currency. Thus, these nations may value having a separate currency more than others.

On the Web

How do national governments manage their fiscal affairs, and to what extent do they coordinate their efforts? You can try to answer this question by surveying the links to national finance ministries available at Mark Bernkopf's central banking center at http://patriot.net/~bernkopf. To go to the Web links, click on "Ministries of Finance and Economy."

For example, suppose that our hypothetical regions *A* and *B* together constitute an optimal currency area. Consequently, the two regions can maintain a fixed exchange rate without experiencing long-term trade imbalances or unemployment. Nonetheless, if the government of region *A* depends to a much larger extent upon seigniorage as a revenue source than the government of region *B,* then region *A* may be unwilling to adopt a common currency. Thus, the two regions might keep their exchange rate fixed yet continue to use separate currencies.

Table 28-1 Average Annual Rates of Seigniorage Relative to Gross Domestic Product and Government Expenditures

Country	Seigniorage as a Percentage of GDP	Seigniorage as a Percentage of Government Spending
New Zealand	0.38	1.04
Denmark	0.39	1.05
United States	0.43	1.96
Kuwait	0.46	2.01
United Kingdom	0.47	1.28
France	0.55	1.39
Germany	0.69	2.35
Japan	0.96	5.62
Kenya	0.98	4.00
Sri Lanka	1.52	4.97
Korea	1.57	9.70
India	1.72	11.82
Spain	2.03	7.76
Colombia	2.32	17.57
Uganda	2.38	21.65
Brazil	3.04	13.71
Costa Rica	3.33	15.09
Mexico	3.72	18.97
Bolivia	3.81	19.76
Iran	4.66	15.09
Nicaragua	7.86	23.70
Yugoslavia	11.87	148.95
Israel	14.84	22.28

SOURCE: Reid Click, "Seigniorage in a Cross-Section of Countries," *Journal of Money, Credit, and Banking* 30 (May 1998): 154–171.

THE ADVANTAGE OF COMPETING CURRENCIES Another rationale for retaining separate currencies is the potential economic benefits of *currency competition.* This idea was first put forward by Frederick Hayek, a prominent economist of the mid-twentieth century. Hayek argued that a central bank may be hesitant to place too much currency in circulation if it knows that such an action will reduce the exchange value of its nation's currency relative to those of other nations, thereby inducing people to hold less of its currency and reducing its seigniorage. Competition with currencies issued by other central banks, therefore, could lead a country's central bank to hold back on inflationary money growth.

Thus, Hayek argued, having many national currencies effectively in competition with each other can be advantageous to the residents of all nations. Indeed, Hayek concluded that people ultimately could lose if governments adopted a common currency. This, he felt, would reduce the extent of currency competition and thereby remove an important check on inflation in the regions that adopted the common currency.

Does the European Monetary Union Make Economic Sense?

The theory of optimal currency areas explains why nations might wish to use different currencies and let their exchange rates float. If nations use immigration restrictions, capital controls, and the like to restrain the flow of people and other productive factors *across* their borders, then it makes sense to use their own currencies *within* their borders. Allowing the exchange rate to adjust to variations in international demand and supply conditions then permits speedier price, output, and employment adjustments to such variations. This helps to explain why residents of Argentina and Brazil, nations with somewhat different languages and cultures and hence with relatively limited cross-border movements of people and productive factors, might prefer to have their own separate currencies and to let their exchange rate vary.

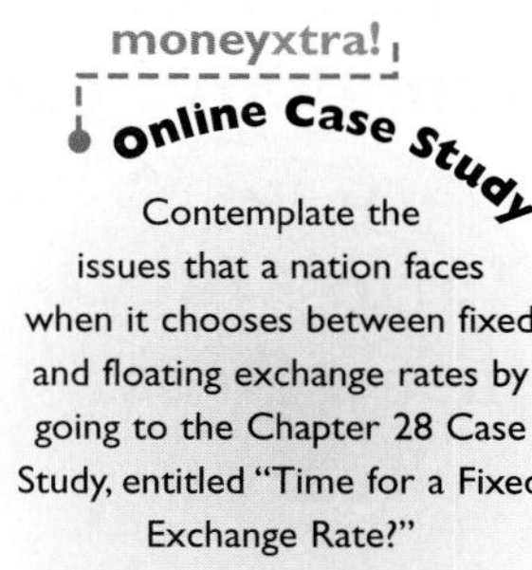

Contemplate the issues that a nation faces when it chooses between fixed and floating exchange rates by going to the Chapter 28 Case Study, entitled "Time for a Fixed Exchange Rate?"
http://moneyxtra.swcollege.com

Reducing Hedging and Conversion Costs The theory also helps to explain why residents of both Colorado and Michigan might wish to use dollars, even though they are separated by over a thousand miles. Because there is such easy mobility of labor and capital within the United States, relatively little social cost is associated with fixing a one-for-one exchange rate and adopting a common currency in the two U.S. states, as well as in the other forty-eight. By using a common currency, residents of the states also save the costs of hedging to avoid foreign exchange risks. In addition, when a Michigan resident visits relatives in Denver or when a Colorado resident buys a good listed on the Web site of a Detroit-based retailer, neither has to worry about costs of converting currencies.

Increased Mobility Finally, the theory helps to explain why nations within the European Monetary Union (EMU) adopted the euro as a common accounting unit beginning in 1999 and introduced a common currency in 2002. These nations are closely linked by trade in goods, services, and financial assets. In addition, in recent years they have somewhat reduced obstacles to flows of people and productive factors. For these reasons, adopting a common currency in EMU nations entailed fewer drawbacks than it would have just a decade or two before.

A few western European nations, such as the United Kingdom and Denmark, for now have forgone joining the EMU. There are at least two reasons for their hesitancy. Undoubtedly, one concern in the United Kingdom is the loss of the pound sterling and its historical role as a symbol of British sovereignty. Another reason is uncertainty about whether all of western Europe really constitutes an optimal currency area. Typically, comparisons of labor mobility in western Europe with those of other countries with single currencies, such as the United States and Canada, indicate that labor is much less mobile in western Europe. This implies that this portion of the world was not a strong candidate for an optimal currency area at the time the EMU was formed. (The United Kingdom continues to waffle about joining the EMU; see on p. 706 *Global Focus: The United Kingdom Practices Hard for What Turns Out to Be Just a Dress Rehearsal.*)

Nonetheless, for twelve nations—Austria, Belgium, Finland, France, Germany, Ireland, Italy, Luxembourg, the Netherlands, Portugal, and Spain in 1999 and Greece in 2001—the EMU has become a reality. These and other potential EMU members have embarked on a fascinating real-world experiment in which nations are adopting a common currency even though they fail to fully satisfy the classic criteria for an optimal currency area.

GLOBAL Focus | POLICY | CYBER | MANAGEMENT

The United Kingdom Practices Hard for What Turns Out to Be Just a Dress Rehearsal

In 1997, the government of the United Kingdom announced that it had developed five "economic tests" that it would use to determine whether the nation was ready to join the European Monetary Union (EMU). These tests involved evaluating the country's experience following the 1999 formation of the EMU to determine whether (1) the British inflation rate would fall to a level closer to the EMU average, (2) British capital investment would grow at a steady pace, (3) employment growth in the United Kingdom would remain stable, (4) London would maintain its status as a world financial center, and (5) the British economy would withstand economic shocks. By 2001, the British inflation rate had fallen to an annualized rate of about 0.5 percent, well below the EMU average inflation rate of nearly 2 percent. Domestic capital investment in the United Kingdom had remained steady, and the British unemployment rate stood at 4.7 percent, well below the average EMU unemployment rate. London's financial markets were thriving. The only unknown, given the lack of significant economic turbulence, was whether the United Kingdom could weather unexpected economic shocks that it might face if it were part of the euro zone.

Nevertheless, opinion polls consistently indicated that a large majority of the British public remained opposed to joining the EMU. As the time for the next parliamentary election approached, the government reinterpreted the five tests. Meeting the five tests would not be sufficient, the government decided. In addition, there would have to be strong evidence of "sustainability" and "durability" of the nation's ability to satisfy the five conditions. The government was careful, however, not to specify just how long the nation would have to meet the five tests before it could consider joining the euro zone. The United Kingdom had passed the test for EMU membership, yet the nation remained outside the EMU.

FOR CRITICAL ANALYSIS: What factors might explain the hesitancy of the United Kingdom to join the EMU?

Will the European Monetary Union succeed? To review alternative perspectives on this debate and make your own judgment, go to EconDebate Online.
http://moneyxtra.swcollege.com

1. What are the pros and cons of fixed versus floating exchange rates? A key drawback of floating exchange rates is the potential for foreign exchange risks generated by exchange rate variability. Fixing the exchange rate reduces the foreign exchange risks. A key problem with a fixed exchange rate, however, is that this policy eliminates the exchange rate's ability to serve as a shock absorber in the event of changing international market conditions. This is particularly true for nations with barriers to mobility of labor and other real productive factors. Such nations can benefit from adopting their own currencies and allowing exchange rates to change with evolving market forces. Furthermore, even countries within an optimal currency area may resist joining a monetary union if (1) their residents are sufficiently averse to giving up sovereignty, (2) their national governments would lose seigniorage revenues that they could not recoup via other sources of taxation, or (3) the countries fear that the loss of currency competition could remove restraints on inflationary policymaking.

Can Central Banks Peg Exchange Rates?

Even though nations continue to have their own separate currencies, a number of countries still aim to maintain fixed rates of currency exchange. These nations have determined that the costs of hedging against foreign exchange risks are greater than the costs generated by the lack of shock-absorbing adjustments in the exchange rate.

How do central banks go about trying to fix exchange rates? Can they maintain fixed rates of currency exchange? Let's try to answer these questions using the fundamental concepts that we have developed in earlier chapters.

Foreign-Exchange-Market Interventions and Exchange Rates

We must begin by developing an understanding of how central banks can attempt to influence exchange rates. To do so, central banks must become active participants in foreign exchange markets.

FOREIGN-EXCHANGE-MARKET INTERVENTION Recall from Chapter 6 that we can envision the equilibrium spot exchange rate, S, as determined by the intersection of currency demand and supply schedules. Consider point A in Figure 28-1, at which the equilibrium exchange rate for Thailand, measured in Thai *baht* per U.S. dollar, is $S_1 = 45$ baht per dollar. At this market exchange rate, the equilibrium quantity of dollars traded for baht within a given time period is equal to Q^e.

Now suppose that the Bank of Thailand, the Thai central bank, decides that an exchange rate equal to $\bar{S} = 40$ baht per dollar is preferable in light of its objectives for internal and external balance. Clearly, this preferred exchange rate is below the market exchange rate. At $\bar{S}$, therefore, the quantity of dollars

Figure 28-1
Intervening in the Foreign Exchange Market to Peg the Exchange Rate.

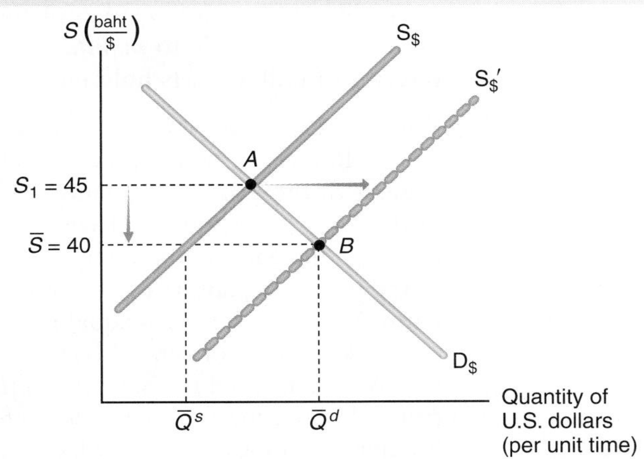

The free-market equilibrium exchange rate arises at point A in the diagram. This exchange rate is $S_1 = 45$ Thai baht per U.S. dollar. If the Bank of Thailand desires to peg the exchange rate at $\bar{S} = 40$ baht per dollar, then it must provide the excess quantity of dollars demanded, $\bar{Q}^d - \bar{Q}^s$, by selling dollar-denominated assets in exchange for baht, to yield a total quantity of baht traded for dollars within the given time interval at point B. Hence, the Bank of Thailand must reduce its foreign exchange reserves to peg the baht's value relative to the dollar.

Foreign-exchange-market intervention: A central bank purchase or sale of foreign-currency reserves in an effort to alter the value of its nation's currency.

Domestic credit: A central bank's holdings of domestic securities.

demanded in exchange for baht by currency traders, $\bar{Q}^d$, is greater than the quantity supplied, $\bar{Q}^s$. There will an excess quantity of dollars demanded by private individuals, companies, and financial institutions in the foreign exchange market at the Bank of Thailand's desired exchange rate, $\bar{S}$.

Thus, for the Bank of Thailand to be able to peg the exchange rate at $\bar{S}$, within the given period of time it must be willing and able to supply the excess quantity of dollars, which is equal to $\bar{Q}^d - \bar{Q}^s$. The Bank of Thailand therefore must sell this quantity of dollars in exchange for baht. Thus, it must use dollar-denominated assets, such as cash and securities, that it has on hand to purchase baht-denominated assets.

Let's suppose that the Bank of Thailand decides to try to peg the exchange rate at $\bar{S}$ in Figure 28-1. By selling $\bar{Q}^d - \bar{Q}^s$ in dollar-denominated assets, the Bank of Thailand conducts a **foreign-exchange-market intervention.** That is, it conducts official foreign exchange transactions, using some of its existing foreign-currency reserves—in this case, dollar-denominated assets—with an intention to alter the value of its currency. The effect of the Bank of Thailand's intervention is to shift the dollar supply schedule to the right. By purchasing baht with some of its existing reserves of dollar-denominated assets, the Bank of Thailand can thereby push the exchange rate downward, from $S_1 = 45$ baht per dollar at point A to $\bar{S} = 40$ baht per dollar at point B. It can peg the exchange rate at the desired value.

Keep in mind, however, that Figure 28-1 applies to a particular period of foreign-exchange-market trading, such as a given week in the month of February. If market conditions remain unchanged during the following week, then point A will again be the natural free-market equilibrium point, and S_1 will be the market exchange rate in the absence of actions by the Bank of Thailand. In this circumstance, the Bank of Thailand will have to repeat its intervention during this following week to keep the baht-dollar exchange rate fixed at $\bar{S}$. If the market conditions illustrated in Figure 28-1 prevail week after week, the Bank of Thailand will have to continue to draw upon its initial quantity of dollar-denominated assets. It will be able to *maintain* the exchange rate peg of $\bar{S}$ only as long as its reserves of dollar assets hold out.

Foreign-Exchange-Market Intervention and the Monetary Base Recall from Chapter 18 that the key liabilities of a central bank such as the Federal Reserve or the Bank of Thailand are the currency it issues and the reserve deposits of depository institutions. Together currency and depository institution reserves comprise the nation's *monetary base*. Thus, if the quantity of currency is equal to C and the total quantity of depository institution reserves is equal to TR, then the nation's monetary base is equal to $MB = C + TR$.

The key assets of central banks are their holdings of bonds and other securities. As you learned in Chapter 18, the bulk of these holdings are domestic securities. International economists refer to a central bank's domestic security holdings as **domestic credit,** which we denote as DC. The other securities are part of a central bank's foreign exchange reserves, denoted FER.

To keep things simple, let's suppose that, as shown in Figure 28-2, domestic and foreign securities are the only assets of a central bank and that currency and depository institution reserves are its only liabilities. (Indeed, these assets and lia-

Figure 28-2
A Simplified Central Bank Balance Sheet.

Assets	Liabilities
Domestic credit (DC)	Currency (C)
Foreign exchange reserves (FER)	Total reserves (TR)
Monetary base (MB)	Monetary base (MB)

The main assets of a central bank are domestic credit, such as domestic government securities, and foreign exchange reserves, which include holdings of foreign currencies and foreign-currency-denominated bonds. The key liabilities of a central bank are the domestic currency that it issues and the reserves of depository institutions. Viewed from either the asset side or the liability side of the balance sheet, these sum to the nation's monetary base.

bilities comprise 80 to 90 percent of the balance sheets of most central banks.) We know that the sum of the central bank's liabilities equals the monetary base. Because the central bank's assets must equal its liabilities, it follows that the sum of domestic credit and foreign exchange reserves must equal the sum of currency and total reserves of depository institutions, or the monetary base. That is, $DC + FER = C + TR = MB$. Thus, we can think of the monetary base in two ways. From the perspective of the central bank's liabilities, the monetary base is equal to currency plus total reserves of depository institutions. Viewed from the asset side of the central bank's balance sheet, the monetary base is composed of domestic credit and foreign exchange reserves.

STERILIZED VERSUS NONSTERILIZED FOREIGN-EXCHANGE-MARKET INTERVENTIONS The fact that the sum of domestic credit and foreign exchange reserves is a nation's monetary base has an important implication. Foreign-exchange-market interventions that change the quantity of foreign exchange reserves, FER, can cause the nation's monetary base to change.

For example, suppose that, as in the example illustrated in Figure 28-1 on page 707, the Bank of Thailand wishes to push the baht-dollar exchange rate below its private-market level. To do so, it must sell dollar-denominated foreign exchange reserves. Thus, FER declines. Because the monetary base is $MB = DC + FER$, then as long as domestic credit, DC, does not change, the Thai monetary base must also fall. Of course, the monetary base is also equal to $MB = C + TR$. If the Bank of Thailand keeps the stock of currency unchanged, then its sale of foreign exchange reserves also entails a reduction in total depository institutions reserves. This means that a sale of foreign exchange reserves has essentially the same immediate effect as a domestic open market sale. It reduces total reserves of depository institutions and causes the monetary base to decline.

A central bank does not have to allow interventions to affect depository institution reserves and the monetary base, however. In our example, the Bank of Thailand could engage in **sterilization** by preventing the foreign-exchange-market intervention from affecting the monetary base. In the case of a sale of foreign

Sterilization: A central bank action to prevent variations in its foreign exchange reserves from affecting the monetary base.

Monetary approach: A theory of exchange rate determination that predicts that the fundamental determination of a nation's exchange rate is the quantity of money supplied by its central bank.

exchange reserves, the Bank of Thailand can do this by simultaneously purchasing an amount of domestic securities equal to the amount of foreign-currency-denominated assets it sells. As a result, when *FER* declines, *DC* rises by an equal amount, so the Thai monetary base is unchanged.

By way of contrast, a *nonsterilized* foreign-exchange-market sale entails a reduction in foreign exchange reserves with no matching increase in domestic credit. Consequently, a nonsterilized intervention leads to a change in the monetary base.

The Monetary Approach to Evaluating the Effects of Foreign-Exchange-Market Interventions

One key perspective on the ultimate effects of foreign-exchange-market interventions on exchange rates is the **monetary approach** to exchange rate determination. It indicates that the key determinant of the equilibrium exchange rate is the quantity of money supplied by a central bank.

The Monetary Approach to Exchange Rate Determination The monetary approach to exchange rate determination has its roots in the classical monetary theory discussed in Chapter 22. Recall that classical theory is based on the assumption that purchasing power parity holds, so that

$$P = S \times P^*.$$

That is, the domestic price level, P, equals the spot exchange rate times the foreign price level, P^*. In the case of Thailand, therefore, if purchasing power parity holds, then the price level in Thailand equals the baht-dollar exchange rate times the U.S. price level.

Recall that the money-multiplier process discussed in Chapter 16 indicates that

$$M = m_M \times MB,$$

so that the quantity of money in circulation is equal to a money multiplier times the monetary base. The monetary base is $MB = DC + FER$, so we can rewrite the money-multiplier expression for the quantity of money as

$$M = m_M \times (DC + FER).$$

Finally, recall that according to classical monetary theory the quantity of money demanded is determined by the Cambridge equation:

$$M^d = k \times P \times y,$$

where k is a fraction that indicates the portion of nominal income that people desire to hold as money and $P \times y$ is nominal income, with y denoting real income, which is supply-side-determined in the classical theory.

In equilibrium, the quantity of money demanded is equal to the quantity of money supplied, so $M^d = M$, or

$$k \times P \times y = m_M \times (DC + FER).$$

Under purchasing power parity, however, $P = S \times P^*$. Thus, we can substitute $S \times P^*$ for P to get

$$k \times S \times P^* \times y = m_M \times (DC + FER).$$

Finally, we can solve this equation for S:

$$S = \frac{m_M \times (DC + FER)}{k \times P^* \times y}.$$

According to the monetary approach to exchange rate determination, the equilibrium exchange rate equals the money multiplier times the sum of domestic credit and foreign exchange reserves divided by the product of the Cambridge k, the foreign price level, and domestic real income. Thus, the monetary approach predicts that the equilibrium exchange rate will fall (the domestic currency will appreciate) if (1) the money multiplier declines, (2) the central bank reduces domestic credit, (3) the central bank reduces its foreign exchange reserves, (4) the Cambridge k increases, so that the domestic demand for money rises, (5) the foreign price level increases, or (6) domestic real income rises.

Evaluating Nonsterilized versus Sterilized Foreign-Exchange-Market Interventions Using the Monetary Approach According to the monetary approach, the exchange rate effects of foreign-exchange-market interventions depend crucially on whether or not a central bank sterilizes the interventions. In the case of a nonsterilized intervention, such as a sale of dollar-denominated assets by the Bank of Thailand, foreign exchange reserves fall without an offsetting increase in domestic credit. As a result, FER declines, and the equilibrium spot exchange rate, S, decreases. This is consistent with the foreign-exchange-market adjustment depicted in Figure 28-1 on page 707.

By way of contrast, the monetary approach implies that sterilized foreign-exchange-market interventions will not influence the equilibrium exchange rate. In the solution for S above, note that if DC increases by the same amount that FER declines, then on net the numerator remains unaltered, and the equilibrium exchange rate does not change. Thus, if the central bank engages in an open market purchase that expands domestic credit by the same amount as the reduction in its foreign exchange reserves caused by a sale of foreign-currency-denominated assets, the net effect of its actions is an unaltered exchange rate.

This means that according to the monetary approach, Figure 28-1 depicts only the effect of a nonsterilized foreign-exchange-market intervention. Thus, the monetary approach indicates that Figure 28-1 is incomplete.

Figure 28-3 on the next page depicts the modification that the monetary approach implies is necessary when the Bank of Thailand sells dollar-denominated assets to increase the supply of dollars in the foreign exchange market. This intervention tends to push the exchange rate toward $\bar{S}$ at point B. Under the monetary approach interpretation, the decline in foreign exchange reserves at the Bank of Thailand reduces the Thai money supply and thereby reduces the Thai price level. Under purchasing power parity, therefore, the exchange rate must fall to $\bar{S}$. In the absence of sterilization, this would be the end of the story.

If the Bank of Thailand purchases domestic securities to sterilize its foreign-exchange-market sale, however, point B cannot be the final equilibrium. The reason is that the resulting increase in domestic credit pushes the Thai money supply back up. At the exchange rate $\bar{S}$, Thai residents do not wish to hold the additional baht that the Bank of Thailand supplies via domestic open market operations and

Figure 28-3
Effects of a Sterilized Foreign-Exchange-Market Intervention under the Monetary Approach to Exchange Rate Determination.

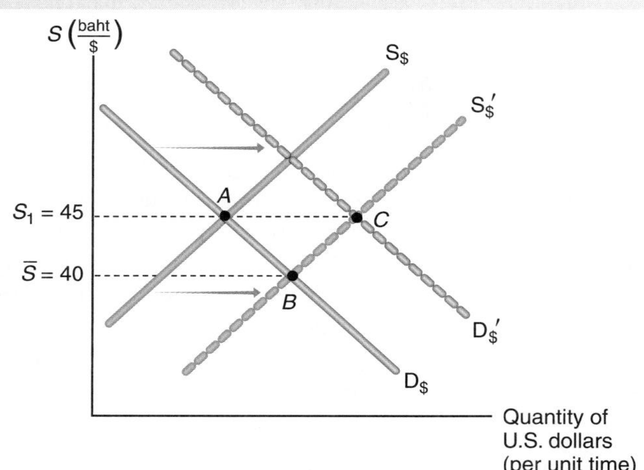

As in Figure 28-1, the sale of foreign exchange reserves by the Bank of Thailand initially reduces the Thai monetary base and money supply and shifts the dollar supply schedule rightward. If the Bank of Thailand sterilizes this intervention by purchasing domestic securities, then the Thai monetary base and money supply rise to their original levels. The monetary approach to exchange rate determination indicates that at the exchange rate $\bar{S} = 40$ baht per dollar, Thai residents will not wish to hold this amount of Thai money, so they enter the foreign exchange market seeking to purchase dollars with baht. This causes the dollar demand schedule to shift to the right, and the exchange rate returns to its original level of $S_1 = 45$ baht per dollar. Thus, according to the monetary approach, a sterilized intervention cannot influence the exchange rate.

the resulting multiple increase in deposits within the Thai banking system. Thai residents enter the foreign exchange market seeking to exchange unwanted baht for dollars, which causes the dollar demand schedule to shift rightward in Figure 28-3. The exchange rate returns to its initial equilibrium value of S_1 at point *C*. Because the Thai money supply on net is unchanged, the Thai price level also does not change. Consequently, under purchasing power parity the exchange rate remains unaltered. A sterilized foreign-exchange-market sale leaves the equilibrium exchange rate unchanged.

2. What is the monetary approach to exchange rate determination?
According to the monetary approach to exchange rate determination, nonsterilized foreign-exchange-market interventions influence exchange rates by changing the monetary base. As a result, nonsterilized interventions alter the quantity of money supplied relative to the quantity demanded, inducing an exchange rate adjustment. Sterilized foreign-exchange-market interventions, however, leave the monetary base and the money supply unchanged. Consequently, the monetary approach indicates that sterilized interventions cannot influence exchange rates.

The Portfolio Approach to Evaluating the Effects of Foreign-Exchange-Market Interventions

Portfolio approach: A theory of exchange rate determination that predicts that a nation's exchange rate adjusts to ensure that its residents are satisfied with their allocation of wealth among holdings of domestic money, domestic bonds, and foreign bonds.

The monetary approach to exchange rate determination focuses exclusively on the exchange rate's role in bringing about an equalization of the quantity of money demanded with the quantity of money supplied. The **portfolio approach** to exchange rate determination, by way of contrast, proposes a broader role for the exchange rate. According to this approach, the exchange rate adjusts to permit residents of a nation to achieve a desired allocation of *all* financial assets, including domestic and foreign bonds as well as holdings of domestic money.

THE PORTFOLIO APPROACH TO EXCHANGE RATE DETERMINATION To illustrate the basic foundation of the portfolio approach to exchange rate determination, let's suppose that all financial wealth within a nation is split among holdings of domestic money, M, domestic bonds, B, and foreign bonds, B^*. Thus, if we use the spot exchange rate, S, to value foreign bonds in terms of the domestic currency, the domestic-currency value of financial wealth, W, is

$$W \equiv M + B + (S \times B^*).$$

Thus, financial wealth by definition is equal to holdings of domestic money and bonds plus the domestic-currency value of holdings of foreign bonds. Under the portfolio approach to exchange rate determination, the exchange rate adjusts until people are satisfied with their allocation of current financial wealth among these three financial assets.

This means that as in the monetary approach to exchange rate determination, the exchange rate ultimately must settle at a level that is consistent with equalization of the quantity of money demanded with the quantity of money supplied. In addition, however, the exchange rate must adjust to ensure that the quantity of domestic bonds demanded equals the quantity of domestic bonds supplied and that the quantity of foreign bonds demanded equals the quantity of foreign bonds supplied.

THE PORTFOLIO-BALANCE EFFECT Now let's reconsider the effect of a foreign-exchange-market intervention in which the Bank of Thailand sells foreign exchange reserves in an effort to achieve a desired exchange rate $\overline{S}$ that is below the free-market exchange rate S_1. As you have seen, according to the monetary approach, the Bank of Thailand can peg the exchange rate at the below-free-market value of $\overline{S}$ only if it conducts a nonsterilized sale of dollar-denominated assets that reduces the money supply. In contrast, a sterilized intervention leaves the money supply unchanged, so the exchange rate remains unaltered at its free-market equilibrium value of S_1.

Under the portfolio approach, this is not the final effect of a sterilized intervention, however. If the Bank of Thailand sterilizes its sale of foreign exchange reserves by conducting open market purchases of bonds that keep the Thai monetary base unchanged, then its purchases of domestic bonds reduce the quantity of domestic bonds available for private exchange. At the same time, its sale of foreign exchange reserves includes sales of U.S. bonds. Hence, a sterilized foreign-exchange-market intervention is, in effect, an exchange of U.S. bonds for

Portfolio-balance effect: A fundamental prediction of the portfolio approach to exchange rate determination, in which changes in central bank holdings of domestic and foreign bonds alter the equilibrium prices at which traders are willing to hold these bonds, inducing a change in the exchange rate.

Announcement effect: A change in the exchange rate resulting from an anticipation of near-term changes in foreign-exchange-market conditions signaled by an intervention by a central bank.

Thai bonds. This means that the Bank of Thailand's sterilized intervention results in a net reduction in the demand for U.S. assets in favor of holdings of Thai assets. Obtaining the baht required to accomplish this net portfolio reshuffling of domestic and foreign bonds entails supplying dollars in the foreign exchange market. As a result, the dollar supply schedule shifts rightward as originally shown in Figure 28-1 on page 707. The exchange rate thereby declines from S_1 to $\bar{S}$ even though sterilization leaves the Thai money supply unchanged.

Hence, the portfolio approach indicates that sterilized foreign-exchange-market interventions have an exchange rate effect that is absent from the monetary approach. Economists call this a **portfolio-balance effect.** Because the portfolio approach views the exchange rate as the relative price of imperfectly substitutable bonds, changes in government or central bank holdings of bonds denominated in various currencies influence exchange rates by affecting the equilibrium prices at which traders are willing to hold these assets. For instance, in our example above, the Bank of Thailand's intervention increases the supply of domestic assets relative to foreign assets held by individuals and firms. As a result, the expected return on domestic assets falls to induce individuals and firms to readjust their portfolios in favor of domestic assets. This readjustment, in turn, requires an appreciation of the domestic currency. Thus, the portfolio-balance effect enables a central bank to induce an increase in the value of its currency by purchasing domestic bonds and selling foreign bonds.

THE ANNOUNCEMENT EFFECT The portfolio approach also indicates the possibility that an intervention can have an **announcement effect.** This effect occurs when foreign-exchange-market interventions provide currency traders with previously unknown information that alters their willingness to demand or supply currencies in the foreign exchange markets. The announcement effect can exist if a central bank's intervention clearly reveals some kind of "inside information" that traders did not have previously. Thus, a foreign-exchange-market intervention intended to induce a reduction in the exchange rate, such as the Bank of Thailand's intervention in our example, can send a signal to currency traders that the baht will appreciate relative to the dollar in the future. If currency traders believe that this appreciation will take place, then they will increase their holdings of the domestic currency, which in our example is the baht. This concerted action by currency traders then causes an actual currency appreciation. Hence, the announcement effect, like the portfolio-balance effect, induces a rise in the value of the domestic currency.

3. What is the portfolio approach to exchange rate determination?
Under the portfolio approach to exchange rates, both nonsterilized and sterilized interventions can affect exchange rates. Sterilized interventions leave the monetary base and money supply unchanged, but they change portfolio allocations between domestic and foreign financial assets. Exchange rates must change for individuals, firms, and financial institutions to be satisfied with their portfolio reallocations. Thus, sterilized interventions have portfolio-balance effects on exchange rates. Furthermore, the portfolio approach indicates that sterilized interventions can alter exchange rates through announcement effects.

Evidence on the Effects of Foreign-Exchange-Market Interventions

To be able to fix exchange rates, central banks must have the capability to peg exchange rates at values that differ from their free-market values. Thus, central banks can successfully fix exchange rates only if foreign-exchange-market interventions have independent short- and long-term effects on market exchange rates.

SHORT-RUN EFFECTS OF INTERVENTIONS As you have seen, theories of the effects of foreign-exchange-market interventions have mixed implications. On the one hand, the monetary approach indicates that only nonsterilized interventions can have even near-term effects on exchange rates. On the other hand, the portfolio approach predicts that sterilized interventions can induce portfolio-balance and announcement effects that cause exchange rates to adjust in response.

For this reason, economists have sought to evaluate the theories by examining data from real-world foreign-exchange-market interventions. Kathryn Dominguez of Harvard University and Jeffrey Frankel of the University of California at Berkeley conducted an exhaustive study of foreign-exchange-market interventions during the 1980s and early 1990s. They found evidence that both the portfolio-balance effect and the announcement effect were important during these years, especially in the late 1980s, a period when many of the world's governments conducted sizable interventions. A number of these interventions were *coordinated* actions, in which central banks cooperated in their efforts to influence exchange rates. Consequently, foreign-exchange-market interventions had their greatest potential to influence exchange rates during this period.

Dominguez and Frankel found considerable evidence that these interventions actually did affect exchange rates. Interestingly, Dominguez and Frankel found that the *announcements* of the interventions had larger effects on exchange rates than the actual magnitudes of the interventions themselves. This, they believe, provides strong evidence of announcement effects in interventions. Thus, they conclude that the data from this period provide support for the predictions of the portfolio approach, at least in the short run.

THE BIG FOREIGN-EXCHANGE-MARKET INTERVENTIONS OF THE 1980S The most significant recent episode of coordinated currency interventions took place beginning in September 1985. At the Plaza Hotel in New York, the finance ministers and central bankers of the so-called G5 nations—France, Germany, Japan, the United Kingdom, and the United States—announced that "in view of the present and prospective change in fundamentals, some orderly appreciation of the main non-dollar currencies against the dollar is desirable. We stand ready to cooperate more closely to encourage this when to do so would be helpful."

This pact among central banks became known as the Plaza Agreement. In 1987, the G5 nations reaffirmed this agreement at the Louvre Palace by adopting the Louvre Accord to continue their efforts to manage exchange rates. The official rhetoric that followed the adoption of these policy agreements and the policy actions they brought about indicated that the G5 nations believed they had largely accomplished their objective of stabilizing exchange rates at "desired" levels.

The Longer-Term Effects of Interventions Some economists, however, doubt that the central banks really achieved their objectives for more than a fleeting time. Among these doubters are Michael Bordo of Rutgers University and Anna Schwartz of the National Bureau of Economic Research. Bordo and Schwartz conducted a study in which they tabulated data on the foreign exchange interventions coordinated by the United States, Germany, and Japan between early 1985 and late 1989. Figure 28-4 displays their estimates of the combined dollar amounts of interventions by central banks and finance ministries during that period.

Based on their study of these interventions, Bordo and Schwartz reached three conclusions. First, the interventions were sporadic and highly variable. Consequently, the interventions may have *added to,* instead of reducing, foreign-exchange-market volatility and uncertainty. The result was that individuals and firms experienced unexpected changes in their wealth, as wealth was effectively transferred from some individuals and firms to others. The increased risk arising from such wealth transfers probably induced many financial market traders to increase their hedging activities. Effectively, the foreign-exchange-market interventions forced private traders to incur extra costs of hedging against the risks of unexpected central bank interventions.

Second, Bordo and Schwartz found that foreign-exchange-market interventions during the late 1980s were very small in size relative to total trading in the markets. For instance, in April 1989 total foreign exchange trading amounted to $129 *billion* per day, yet the Fed purchased only $100 *million* in marks and yen in that entire month—on a single day. Indeed, Fed purchases of marks and yen for all of 1989 amounted to about $17.7 billion, or the equivalent of less than 14

Figure 28-4
Combined U.S., German, and Japanese Interventions, February 1985–August 1989.

The total dollar amount of the foreign exchange interventions by the United States, Germany, and Japan during the late 1980s varied considerably from month to month.

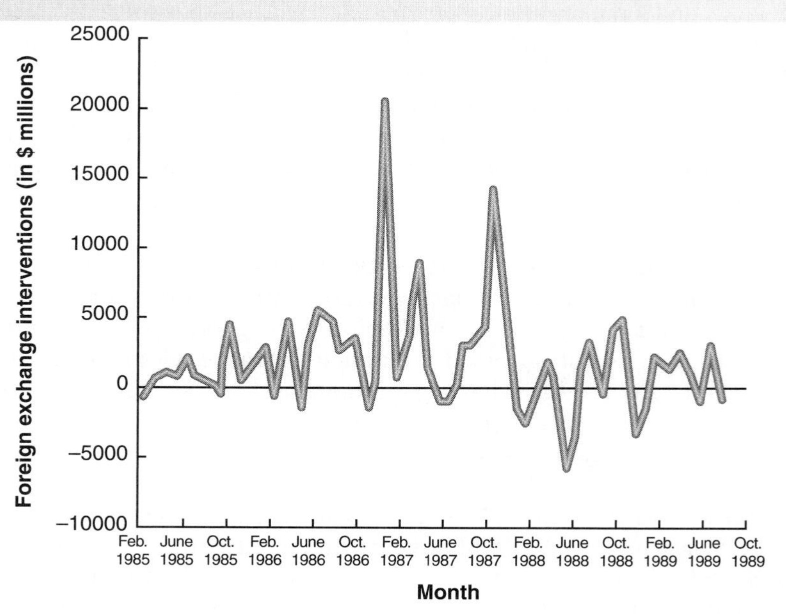

SOURCE: Michael Bordo and Anna Schwartz, "What Has Foreign Exchange Market Intervention since the Plaza Agreement Accomplished?" *Open Economies Review* 2 (1991): 39–64.

percent of foreign-exchange-market trading for an average *day* in April of that year. Given that a coalition of the world's largest central banks was able to generate only a relatively tiny volume of foreign-exchange-market trading activity during the 1985–1989 period, Bordo and Schwartz question the likelihood that central bank interventions can really have *long-lasting* effects on exchange rates.

Third, Bordo and Schwartz found that while the Federal Reserve and the Treasury together accounted for over $1 billion in realized gains from foreign exchange transactions in 1985 through 1989, the Netherlands lost 600 million Dutch guilders on dollar interventions in 1986 and 1987, and Germany reportedly lost 9 billion deutschemarks in the fourth quarter of 1987 alone. Bordo and Schwartz question the wisdom of central bank and finance ministry gambles with such large stakes, given their limited abilities to achieve exchange rate goals. In Bordo and Schwartz's view, central banks that participated in the coordinated effort to reduce the dollar's value exposed their governments, and hence their taxpaying citizens, to risks of sizable foreign exchange losses.

Nevertheless, many economists join Dominguez and Frankel in arguing that foreign exchange interventions can and do influence exchange rates from time to time. The coordinated interventions of the late 1980s, they point out, were unambiguously associated with an interval in which the value of the dollar declined. This decline, they note, continued beyond the period of active interventions, potentially implying longer-term effects.

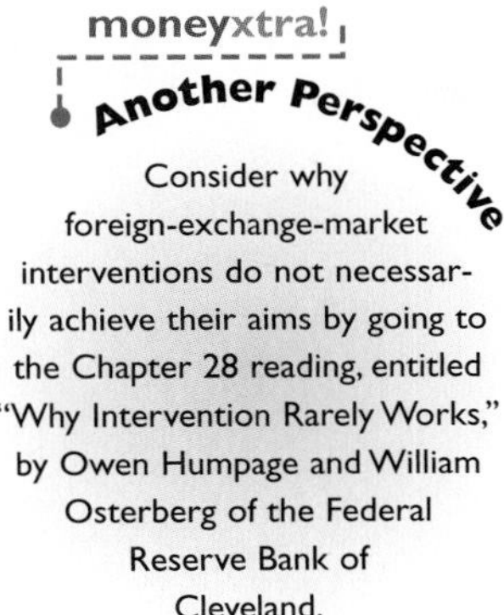

THE POSSIBLE EFFECT OF COUNTRY SIZE In spite of this view, efforts to manipulate exchange rates by central banks in developed nations, whose currencies trade actively in foreign exchange markets, have been muted since the early 1990s. Economists who doubt the ability of these central banks to influence their exchange rates, such as Bordo and Schwartz, believe that the central banks have recognized their inability to bring about long-lasting changes in exchange rates by intervening in foreign exchange markets that experience huge daily trading volumes. They note that today most efforts to peg exchange rates are undertaken by central banks in smaller, emerging economies, whose currencies trade in foreign exchange markets with low volumes of trading. Interventions in these thinner markets, they argue, are more likely to move exchange rates in directions that central banks desire.

Table 28-2 on the following page displays the exchange rate arrangements adopted by most of the world's nations. As you can see, the most developed nations have floating-exchange-rate systems. The countries that try to fix their exchange rate are among the world's smallest economies.

4. How effective are foreign-exchange-market interventions? There is some evidence that portfolio-balance and announcement effects have had short-run effects on exchange rates. This was particularly true during the period of widespread foreign exchange interventions in the 1980s. Data from this same period also indicate, however, that even coordinated central bank interventions had relatively small and fleeting effects on exchange rates. These interventions may also have added to exchange rate volatility, and they may have caused taxpayer losses owing to greater currency risks incurred by governments and central banks.

Table 28-2 Exchange Rate Arrangements around the Globe

Pegged to a Single Currency or Composite Currency Unit	Aruba, Bahamas, Bahrain, Bangladesh, Barbardos, Belize, Bhutan, Botswana, Burundi, Cape Verde, China, Comoros, Cyprus, Denmark, Egypt, El Salvador, Fiji, Iceland, Iran, Iraq, Jordan, Kuwait, Latvia, Lebanon, Lesotho, Libya, Macedonia, Malaysia, Maldives, Malta, Morocco, Myanmar, Namibia, Nepal, Netherlands Antilles, Oman, Qatar, Samoa, Saudi Arabia, Seychelles, Solomon Islands, Swaziland, Syria, Trinidad, Turkmenistan, Ukraine, United Arab Emirates, Vietnam
Crawling Peg or Crawling Bands	Bolivia, Costa Rica, Honduras, Hungary, Israel, Nicaragua, Poland, Sri Lanka, Tunisia, Turkey, Uruguay, Venezuela
Managed Float	Algeria, Azerbaijan, Argentina, Belarus, Cambodia, Croatia, Czech Republic, Dominican Republic, Ethiopia, Guatemala, Jamaica, Kenya, Kyrgyz Republic, Malawi, Nigeria, Norway, Pakistan, Paraguay, Romania, Singapore, Slovak Republic, Slovenia, Suriname, Tajikistan, Uzbekistan
Independent Float	Afghanistan, Albania, Angola, Armenia, Australia, Brazil, Canada, Chile, Colombia, Congo, Eritrea, Gambia, Ghana, Guinea, Guyana, Haiti, Indonesia, Japan, Kazakhstan, Korea, Liberia, Madagascar, Mauritius, Mexico, Moldova, Mongolia, Mozambique, New Zealand, Papua New Guinea, Peru, Philippines, Russian Federation, Rwanda, Sierra Leone, Somalia, South Africa, Sudan, Sweden, Switzerland, Tanzania, Thailand, Uganda, United Kingdom, United States, Yemen, Zambia, Zimbabwe
Exchange Arrangements with a Shared Currency	Antigua & Barbuda, Austria, Belgium, Benin, Burkina Faso, Cameroon, Central African Republic, Chad, Cote d'Ivoire, Dominica, Ecuador, Equatorial Guinea, Finland, France, Gabon, Germany, Greece, Grenada, Guinea-Bissau, Ireland, Italy, Kiribati, Luxembourg, Mali, Marshall Islands, Micronesia, Netherlands, Niger, Palau, Panama, Portugal, St. Kitts & Nevis, St. Lucia, St. Vincent & the Grenadines, San Marino, Senegal, Spain, Togo
Currency Board	Bosnia & Herzegovina, Brunei Darussalam, Bulgaria, Djibouti, Estonia, Hong Kong (China), Lithuania

SOURCE: International Monetary Fund.

Link to
Management

Inflation, Deflation, and the Choice between Debt and Equity Financing

Around the globe, corporate financial structures appear to depend in part on whether countries experience tendencies for inflation or deflation. This pattern appears to violate a fundamental starting point for the modern theory of finance, called the "Modigliani-Miller theorem," which states that for every additional unit of debt that a company issues, shareholders will simply require a higher rate of return on their equity investment to compensate for the higher risk of bankruptcy. In the simplest of worlds, this basic financial principle should hold whether the price level is rising or falling.

In the real world, however, companies pay taxes, so the choice between debt and equity financing usually does matter, sometimes substantially. The tax structures in many countries give corporate treasurers an incentive to reduce companies' tax bills by taking on more debt. By borrowing instead of issuing new equity shares, companies can reduce their after-tax capital costs and thereby increase their market value.

Another Real-World Complication: A Changing Price Level

When tax systems are not fully indexed for inflation, increases in the price level can reinforce the advantages of debt over equity. In most countries, interest payments on debt are tax-deductible, but dividend payments on equity shares are not. Thus, inflation that pushes up nominal profits and stock dividends can also push up a company's tax bill, thereby giving it an incentive to issue more debt instruments instead of additional shares of stock. Higher expected inflation also leads to higher nominal interest rates, which increase the value of debt as a "tax shelter" for a firm that wishes to raise additional funds as cheaply as possible.

Since the late 1940s, corporations around the world have been predisposed to issue debt instead of equity. Tax considerations and inflation together helped to account for this bias in favor of debt.

Recalculating the Debt-Equity Mix in a Deflationary Environment

Since the late 1990s, however, corporate treasurers in a number of countries, especially in parts of Asia, have begun to regard debt as a burden, not a shelter. The problem is that several nations have experienced deflationary episodes in recent years. Deflation, naturally, tends to depress companies' nominal earnings and to reduce nominal interest rates. This reduces the "tax-shelter" value of debt relative to equity.

Furthermore, by definition a debt instrument is a promise to repay a nominal sum at a future date. In the early and middle 1990s, many companies around the world continued to issue debt instruments as they had in years past, because they anticipated that continuing inflation would erode the value of their debt repayments. Firms in several locales experienced a rude surprise, therefore, when central banks such as the Bank of Japan and the Bank of Singapore conducted policies that led to bouts of deflation, thereby *increasing* the real value of the firms' nominal debt repayments.

Soon companies in Japan, Singapore, and other nations experiencing deflation were scrambling to pay off old debts—in many cases, financing these early debt retirements with funds raised by issuing new equity shares. Of course, a number of factors influence companies' decisions about how to finance their operations. Nevertheless, as Figure 28-5 shows, between the 1980s and 1990s, corporate ratios of debt to equity (also called *leverage ratios*) declined in several nations as their average inflation rates decreased.

Continued on next page

Link to Management, continued

Figure 28-5
Falling Inflation Rates and Debt-Equity Ratios in Selected Nations.

As average inflation rates declined in many nations between the 1980s and 1990s, so did firms' average debt-equity ratios.

SOURCES: Dale Gray and Mark Stone, "Corporate Balance Sheets and Macroeconomic Policy," *Finance and Development*, World Bank, September 1999, pp. 56–59; Stijn Claessens, Simeon Djankov, and Larry Lang, "East Asian Corporates: Growth, Financing, and Risks," World Bank, October 27, 1999; International Monetary Fund, *World Economic Outlook*, various issues.

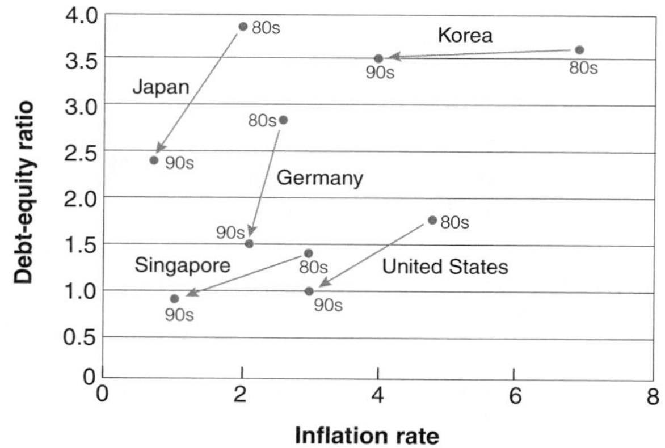

Research Project

How does deflation complicate a borrower's ability to repay previously accumulated debts? Is it likely to matter whether the deflation is anticipated or unanticipated? How might a multinational corporation's choice between debt and equity financing be influenced by the fact that it may operate in nations with very different central bank policies regarding inflation or deflation?

Web Resources

1. What are the debt-equity ratios of various U.S. industries? For these and other financial data for U.S. corporations, go to http://www.stern.nyu.edu/~adamodar/. To determine debt-equity ratios, first click on "Updated Data," then scroll down to "Capital Structure," and click on "Debt Ratio Trade Off Variables by Industry." The column "MV Debt Ratio" gives the ratio of total debt to the sum of total debt and the market value of equity. To calculate the debt-equity ratio for each industry using market values of equity, divide the ratio in the column by 1 minus that same ratio. (To calculate the ratio of debt to the book value of equity, perform the same calculation using the figures in the "BV Debt Ratio" column.)

2. Where are useful links to sources of corporate financial data? One place to start is http://www.internet-prospector.org/company.html.

Chapter Summary

1. The Pros and Cons of Fixed versus Floating Exchange Rates: The main argument against floating exchange rates is that exchange rate volatility caused by changing market forces can increase foreign exchange risks. Adopting a fixed exchange rate reduces the potential for such risks to arise, thereby saving people from having to incur costs to hedge against those risks. An important argument against fixed exchange rates is that in nations whose workers and other factors of production are relatively immobile, pegging the exchange rate removes a key source of immediate flexibility in relative prices, thereby eliminating a key means by which the nations' employment and output levels can automatically adjust to changes in international market conditions.

2. The Monetary Approach to Exchange Rate Determination: This theory of the exchange rate effects of central bank policy actions indicates that nonsterilized foreign-exchange-market interventions can affect exchange rates via changes in the monetary base. Nonsterilized interventions cause the quantity of money supplied to change relative to the quantity of money demanded, which causes the exchange rate to adjust to reattain money market equilibrium. The monetary approach indicates that sterilized foreign-exchange-market interventions cannot affect exchange rates, because sterilized interventions have no effect on the monetary base and the money supply.

3. The Portfolio Approach to Exchange Rate Determination: This theory of the exchange rate effects of foreign-exchange-market interventions predicts that both nonsterilized and sterilized interventions can influence exchange rates. According to the portfolio approach, both types of interventions alter portfolio allocations between domestic and foreign financial assets. A portfolio-balance effect thereby occurs, because the exchange rate must adjust to induce a nation's residents to be satisfied with their portfolio reallocations. In addition, the portfolio approach predicts that announcement effects can influence exchange rates as traders reallocate their portfolios in response to the signal provided by the central bank's interventions.

4. The Effectiveness of Foreign-Exchange-Market Interventions: Studies of central bank interventions in foreign exchange markets indicate that interventions exert effects on exchange rates, especially when the central banks coordinate interventions, as occurred in the 1980s. Nevertheless, there is also evidence that these effects may have been relatively small and short-lived. Foreign-exchange-market interventions may also increase the variability of exchange rates, and they may expose taxpayers to losses stemming from increased currency risks incurred by governments and central banks.

Questions and Problems

(Answers to odd-numbered questions and problems may be found on the Web at http://money.swcollege.com under "Student Resources")

1. Suppose that the residents of a particular country speak a language that most others around the world do not know. There also are legal and natural impediments to movements of other factors of production across the nation's borders. The nation's central bank maintains a fixed exchange rate. Recently, there has been a worldwide fall in the demand for the nation's primary products. Could this nation gain from letting its exchange rate float? Explain your reasoning.

2. Why might Europe benefit more fully from its adoption of a single currency if all of its residents shared at least one common language? Explain.

3. Suppose that the Bank of Thailand wishes to peg the exchange value of the baht relative to the dollar at a level above the market exchange rate. Draw a diagram of the demand for and the supply of dollars in the foreign exchange market, and explain what actions the Bank of Thailand would have to undertake to peg the baht's value.

4. Suppose that the Bank of Thailand has succeeded in pegging the baht-per-dollar exchange rate above the market exchange rate. Now the central bank decides to peg the exchange rate at a higher value. How will the Bank of Thailand do this?

5. Write out an equation for the monetary approach to the determination of the exchange rate. Suppose that domestic credit equals $400 million, foreign exchange reserves equal $200 million, the money multiplier is 2, the fraction of nominal income that individuals desire to hold as money is 20 percent, the foreign price level is 1.2, and domestic real income is $5 billion.

a. What is the quantity of domestic money in circulation?

b. What is the equilibrium exchange rate?

6. Suppose that the central bank facing the situation described in question 5, in which the monetary approach to exchange rate determination applies, conducts an unsterilized foreign-exchange-market intervention and increases foreign exchange reserves by $50 million.

a. What is the equilibrium exchange rate?

b. Does the domestic currency appreciate or depreciate?

7. Suppose that the central bank facing the situation described in question 5, in which the monetary approach to the balance of payments applies, conducts a sterilized foreign-exchange-market intervention and reduces foreign exchange reserves by $100 million.

a. What is the equilibrium exchange rate?

b. Does the domestic currency appreciate or depreciate?

8. According to the monetary approach to exchange rate determination, why should a sterilized foreign-exchange-market intervention fail to influence the value of a nation's currency?

9. Within the portfolio approach to exchange rate determination, what is the difference between the portfolio-balance effect and the announcement effect?

10. Why does the portfolio approach to exchange rate determination predict that a sterilized foreign-exchange-market intervention can influence the value of a nation's currency?

Before the Test

Test your understanding of the material covered in this chapter by taking the Chapter 28 interactive quiz at http://money.swcollege.com.

Online Application

Internet URL: http://www.ecb.int

Title: About the European Central Bank

Navigation: Begin at the above home page, and click on "About the ECB."

Application: Perform the indicated operations, and answer the accompanying questions.

1. Click on "EN" next to "Constitution of the ESCB: History—Three Stages Towards EMU," and read the article. In what ways is policymaking within the European System of Central Banks different from policymaking under the old European Monetary System?

2. Back up to "About the ECB," and click on "EN" next to "Organization of the European System of Central Banks." Read the article. What aspects of the ESCB's structure promote policy credibility?

For Group Study and Analysis: Divide the class into groups. At the page entitled "Organization of the European System of Central Banks," each group can click on "National Central Banks (NCBs)" to get links to the central banks of the European Union. Have each group explore Web sites of the central banks that are currently in the ESCB. What are the roles of the individual national central banks within the ESCB? Within their domestic economic and financial systems?

Selected References and Further Reading

Bonser-Neal, Catherine. "Does Central Bank Intervention Stabilize Exchange Rates?" Federal Reserve Bank of Kansas City *Economic Review* 81 (First Quarter, 1996): 43–57.

Bordo, Michael, and Anna Schwartz. "What Has Foreign Exchange Market Intervention since the Plaza Agreement Accomplished?" *Open Economies Review* 2 (1991): 39–64.

Dominguez, Kathryn, and Jeffrey Frankel. *Does Foreign Exchange Intervention Work?* Washington, D.C.: Institute for International Economics, 1993.

Lewis, Karen. "Are Foreign Exchange Intervention and Monetary Policy Related, and Does It Matter?" *Journal of Business* 68 (1995): 185–214.

_______. "On Occasional Monetary Policy Coordinations That Fix the Exchange Rate." *Journal of International Economics* 26 (1989): 139–155.

Mundell, Robert. "A Theory of Optimal Currency Areas." *American Economic Review* 51 (1961): 657–665.

MoneyXtra

moneyxtra! Log on to the MoneyXtra Web site now (**http://moneyxtra.swcollege.com**) for additional learning resources such as practice quizzes, case studies, readings, and additional economic applications.

GLOSSARY

Actuary: An individual who specializes in using mathematical and statistical principles to calculate insurance premiums and to estimate an insurance company's net worth.

Adaptive expectations: Expectations that are based only on information from the past up to the present.

Adverse selection: The problem that those who desire to issue financial instruments are most likely to use the funds they receive for unworthy, high-risk projects.

Aggregate demand schedule (y^d): The combinations of various price levels and levels of real output at which individuals are satisfied with their consumption of output and their holdings of money.

Aggregate expenditures schedule: A schedule that represents total desired expenditures by all the relevant sectors of the economy at each and every level of real national income.

Aggregate externalities: Situations in which aggregate equilibrium in all, or at least many, markets fails to account for spillovers across markets, so that equilibrium aggregate real output, employment, and the price level all differ from their long-run, natural levels.

Aggregate net autonomous expenditures: The sum of autonomous consumption, autonomous investment, autonomous government spending, and autonomous export spending, all of which are independent of the level of national income in the basic Keynesian model.

Aggregate supply schedule (y^s): The combinations of various price levels and levels of real output that maintain equilibrium in the market for labor services.

American option: An option that allows the holder to buy or sell a security any time before or including the date at which the contract expires.

Announcement effect: A change in the exchange rate resulting from an anticipation of near-term changes in foreign-exchange-market conditions signaled by an intervention by a central bank.

Annuities: Financial instruments that guarantee the holder fixed or variable payments at some future date.

Anticipated-income approach: A depository institution management philosophy that calls for depository institutions to make loans more liquid by issuing them as installment loans that generate income in the form of periodic payments of interest and principal.

Appreciation: A rise in the value of one currency relative to another.

Arbitrage: Purchasing an asset at the current price in one market and profiting by selling it at a higher price in another market.

Asset: Anything owned by a person or business that has a market value.

Asset-liability management approach: A depository institution management philosophy that emphasizes the simultaneous determination of both the asset and the liability sides of the institution's balance sheet.

Assignment problem: The problem of determining whether monetary or fiscal policymakers should assume responsibility for achieving either external-balance or internal-balance objectives.

Asymmetric information: Information possessed by one party to a financial transaction but not by the other party.

Automated bill payment: Direct payment of bills by depository institutions on behalf of their customers.

Automated clearinghouses: Institutions that process payments electronically on behalf of senders and receivers of those payments.

Automated-transfer-system (ATS) account: A combined interest-bearing savings account and non-interest-bearing checking account in which the former is drawn on automatically when the latter is overdrawn.

Autonomous consumption: Household consumption spending on domestically produced goods and services that is independent of the level of real income.

Autonomous expenditures multiplier: A measure of the size of the multiple effect on equilibrium real income caused by a change in aggregate net autonomous expenditures; in the simple Keynesian model, the multiplier is equal to $1/(MPS + MPIM) = 1/(1 - MPC)$.

Balance of payments accounts: A tabulation of all transactions between the residents of a nation and the residents of all other nations in the world.

Balance-sheet constraint: The accounting constraint that a bank's assets cannot exceed the sum of its liabilities and net worth.

Bank Insurance Fund (BIF): The FDIC's fund that covers insured deposits of commercial banks.

Bank run: An unexpected series of cash withdrawals at a depository institution that can induce its failure.

Banker's acceptance: A bank loan typically used by a company to finance storage or shipment of goods.

Banknotes: Privately issued paper currency.

Barter: The direct exchange of goods, services, and financial assets.

Base drift: The tendency of a measure of total depository institution reserves or a monetary aggregate to fail to adjust to a level consistent with fixed long-run average growth.

Base year: A reference year for price-level comparisons, which is a year in which nominal GDP equals real GDP, so that the GDP deflator's value equals one.

Best efforts deal: An investment banking arrangement in which the investment bank has an option to buy a portion of the issuing firm's securities but is not required to do so.

Beta: A measure of the sensitivity of a financial instrument's expected return to changes in the value of all financial instruments in a market portfolio; calculated as the percentage change in the value of a financial instrument resulting from a 1 percent change in the value of all financial instruments in the portfolio.

Bimetallic standard: A monetary system in which the value of money depends on the values of two precious metals, such as gold and silver.

Board of Governors of the Federal Reserve System: A group of seven individuals appointed by the president and confirmed by the Senate that, under the terms of the Banking Act of 1935, has key policymaking responsibilities within the Federal Reserve System.

Branch banking: A depository institution organizational structure in which institutions operate offices at a number of geographic locations.

Brokers: Institutions that specialize in matching buyers and sellers of financial instruments in secondary markets.

Bullion: Uncoined gold or silver used as money.

Business cycles: Variations in real GDP around its long-run growth path.

Business finance companies: Finance companies that typically specialize in making loans to small businesses.

Call option: An option contract giving the owner the right to purchase a financial instrument at a specific price.

Capacity output: The real output that the economy could produce if all resources were employed to their utmost.

Capital account: The balance of payments account that records all nongovernmental international asset transactions.

Capital consumption allowance: The total value of capital expended during the process of production.

Capital controls: Legal restrictions on the ability of a nation's residents to hold and trade assets denominated in foreign currencies.

Capital gain: An increase in the value of a financial instrument at the time it is sold as compared with its market value at the date it was purchased.

Capital goods: Goods that may be used to produce other goods or services in the future.

Capital loss: A decline in the market value of a financial instrument at the time it is sold as compared with its market value at the time it was purchased.

Capital markets: Markets for financial instruments with maturities of one year or more.

Capital mobility: The extent to which savers can move funds across national borders for the purpose of buying financial instruments issued in other countries.

Capital requirements: Minimum equity capital standards that regulators impose upon depository institutions.

Cash assets: Depository institution assets that function as media of exchange.

Cash items in process of collection: Checks deposited with a bank for immediate credit but not yet cleared for final payment to the bank; usually referred to simply as "cash items."

Central banker contract: A legally binding agreement between a government and a central bank official that holds the official responsible for the nation's inflation performance.

Certificates of deposit (CDs): Time deposits issued by banks and other depository institutions. Many CDs are negotiable instruments that are traded in secondary markets.

Charter: A governmental license to open and operate a bank.

Circular flow diagram: A chart that depicts the economy's flows of income and product.

Clearing House Interbank Payment System (CHIPS): A large-value wire transfer system that links about ninety depository institutions and permits them to transmit large dollar sums relating primarily to foreign exchange and Eurodollar transactions.

Closed economy: An economy that operates separately from the rest of the world.

Closed stored-value system: An e-money system in which consumers use cards containing prestored funds to buy specific goods and services offered by a single issuer of the cards.

Closed-end funds: Mutual funds that sell nonredeemable shares whose market values vary with the market values of the underlying mix of financial instruments held by the mutual funds.

Coinsurance: An insurance policy feature that requires a policyholder to pay a fixed percentage of a loss above a deductible.

Collateral: Assets that a borrower pledges as security in case it should fail to repay the principal or interest on a loan.

Commercial and industrial (C&I) loans: Loans that commercial banks and other depository institutions make to businesses.

Commercial banks: Depository financial institutions that issue checking deposits and specialize in making commercial loans.

Commercial loans: Long-term loans made by banks to businesses.

Commercial paper: A short-term debt instrument issued by businesses in lieu of borrowing from banks.

Commodity money: A good with a nonmonetary value that is also used as money.

Commodity standard: A money unit whose value is fully or partially backed by the value of some other physical good such as gold or silver.

Common stock: Shares of corporate ownership that entitle the owner to vote on management issues but offer no guarantees of dividends or of market value in the event of corporate bankruptcy.

Confirmed credit lines: Depository institution commitments to provide an individual or a business with a fixed amount of credit upon demand within some short-term interval.

Conservative central banker: A central bank official who dislikes inflation more than the average citizen in society and who therefore is less willing to induce discretionary increases in the quantity of money in an effort to achieve short-run increases in real output.

Consumer finance companies: Finance companies that specialize in making loans to individuals for the purchase of durable goods or for home improvements.

Consumer loans: Long-term loans made by banks and other institutions to individuals.

Consumption spending: Total purchases of goods and services by households.

Contributory pensions: Pensions funded by both employer and employee contributions.

Controllable liabilities: Liabilities whose dollar amounts banks can directly manage.

Conversion-of-funds approach: A depository institution management philosophy under which managers try to fund assets of specific maturities by issuing liabilities with like maturities.

Coordination failures: Spillover effects between workers and firms, arising from movements in economic variables, that hinder efforts by individual households and firms to plan and implement their consumption, production, and pricing decisions.

Core capital: Defined by current capital requirements as shareholders' equity plus retained earnings.

Corporate bonds: Long-term debt instruments of corporations.

Correspondent balances: Deposit accounts that banks hold with other banks.

Country risk: The potential for returns on international financial instruments to vary because of uncertainties concerning possible changes in political and economic conditions within a nation.

Coupon return: A fixed interest return that a bond yields each year.

Coupon yield equivalent: An annualized T-bill rate that can be compared with annual yields on other financial instruments.

Uncovered interest parity: A relationship between interest rates on bonds that are similar in all respects other than that they are denominated in different nations' currencies. According to this condition, the yield on the bond denominated in the currency that holders anticipate will depreciate must exceed the yield on the other bond by the rate at which the currency is expected to depreciate.

Credit derivatives: Financial instruments that have returns based on loan credit risks.

Credit multiplier: A number that tells how much total loans and securities at depository institutions will change in response to a change in the monetary base.

Credit risk: The risk of loss that might occur if one party to an exchange fails to honor the terms under which the exchange was to take place.

Credit union: A type of depository institution that accepts deposits from and makes loans to only a group of individuals who are eligible for membership.

Currency: Coins and paper money.

Currency board: An institution that issues currency at a fixed rate of exchange with respect to another nation's currency.

Currency future: An agreement to deliver to another a standardized quantity of a specific nation's currency at a designated future date.

Currency option: A contract granting the holder the right to buy or sell a given amount of a nation's currency at a certain price within a specific period of time.

Currency swap: An exchange of payment flows denominated in different currencies.

Current account: The balance of payments account that tabulates international trade and transfers of goods and services and flows of income.

Current yield: The coupon return on a bond divided by the bond's market price.

Cybertechnologies: Technologies that connect savers, investors, traders, producers, and governments via computer linkages.

Cyclical unemployment: The portion of total unemployment resulting from business-cycle fluctuations.

Debasement: A reduction in the amount of precious metal in a coin that the government issues as money.

Debit card: A plastic card that allows the bearer to transfer funds to a merchant's account, provided that the bearer authorizes the transfer by providing personal identification.

Deductible: A fixed amount of an insured loss that a policyholder must pay before the insurer is obliged to make payments.

Default risk: The chance that an individual or a firm that issues a financial instrument may be unable to honor its obligations to repay the principal and/or to make interest payments.

Default swap: A credit derivative that requires the seller to assume the face value of a debt in the event of default.

Demand deposits: Non-interest-bearing checking accounts.

Deposit expansion multiplier: A number that tells how much aggregate transactions deposits at all depository institutions will change in response to a change in total reserves of these institutions.

Deposit insurance premium: The price that depository institutions pay to the FDIC's insurance fund in exchange for a guarantee of federal insurance of covered deposits that they issue.

Depository financial institutions: Financial institutions that issue checking and savings deposits that are included in measures of money and that legally must hold reserves on deposit with Federal Reserve banks or in their vaults.

Depreciation: A decline in the value of one currency relative to another.

Depression: An especially severe recession.

Derivative credit risk: Risk stemming from the potential default by a party in a derivative contract or from unexpected changes in credit exposure because of changes in the market yields of instruments on which derivative yields depend.

Derivative market risk: Risk arising from unanticipated changes in derivatives market liquidity or from failures in payments systems.

Derivative operating risk: Risk owing to a lack of adequate management controls or from managerial inexperience with derivative securities.

Derivative securities: Financial instruments whose returns depend on the returns of other financial instruments.

Digital cash: Funds contained on computer software, in the form of secure algorithms, that is stored on microchips and other computer devices.

Discount rate: The rate of interest that the Federal Reserve charges to lend to a depository institution.

Discounted present value: The value today of a payment to be received at a future date.

Discretionary policymaking: The act of responding to economic events as they occur, rather than in ways the policymaker might previously have planned in the absence of those events.

Disintermediation: A situation in which customers of depository institutions withdraw funds from their deposit accounts and use these funds to purchase financial instruments directly.

Diversification: Holding a mix of financial instruments with returns that normally do not move together.

Dividends: Periodic payments to holders of corporate equities.

Dollarization: A country's adoption of the U.S. dollar as its sole medium of exchange, unit of account, store of value, and standard of deferred payment.

Domestic credit: A central bank's holdings of domestic securities.

Double coincidence of wants: The situation when two individuals are simultaneously willing and able to make a trade; a requirement for barter.

Dual banking system: A regulatory structure in which either states or the federal government can grant bank charters.

Duration: A measure of the average time during which all payments of principal and interest on a financial instrument are made.

Duration gap: The average duration of a depository institution's assets minus the average duration of its liabilities.

Economic risk: A foreign exchange risk that stems from the possibility that exchange rate movements can affect the discounted present value of future streams of income.

Economies of scale: The reduction in the average cost of fund management that can be achieved by pooling savings together and spreading management costs across many people.

Efficient structure theory: A theory of depository institution market structure in which greater market concentration and higher depository institution profits arise from the fact that a few depository institutions can operate more efficiently in loan and deposit markets as compared with a large number of institutions.

Efficient-markets hypothesis: A theory that stems from the application of the rational expectations hypothesis to financial markets. It states that equilibrium prices of and returns on financial instruments should reflect all past and current information plus traders' understanding of how market prices and returns are determined.

Electronic money (e-money): Money that people can transfer directly via electronic impulses.

Equation of exchange: An accounting identity that states that the nominal value of all monetary transactions for final goods and services is equal to the nominal value of the output of goods and services purchased.

Equities: Shares of ownership, such as corporate stock, issued by business firms.

Equity capital: The excess of assets over liabilities, or net worth.

Eurobonds: Long-term debt instruments issued in a currency other than that of the country where the instruments are issued.

Eurocommercial paper: A short-term debt instrument issued by a firm and denominated in a currency other than that of the country where the firm is located.

Eurocurrency deposits: Bank deposits denominated in the currency of one nation but located in a different nation.

Eurocurrency markets: Markets for bonds, loans, and deposits denominated in the currency of a given nation but held and traded outside that nation's borders.

Eurodollars: Dollar-denominated deposits located outside the United States.

Euronotes: Medium-term debt instruments issued in a currency other than that of the country where the instruments are issued.

European option: An option that allows the holder to buy or sell a financial instrument only on the day that the contract expires.

Excess reserves: Depository institutions' cash balances at Federal Reserve banks or in the institutions' vaults that exceed the amount that they must hold to meet legal requirements.

Exchange rate: The price of one nation's currency in terms of another.

Exercise price: The price at which the holder of an option has the right to buy or sell a financial instrument; also known as the strike price.

Expansion: A point along a business cycle at which actual GDP begins to rise, perhaps even above its natural, long-run level.

Expectations theory: A theory of the term structure of interest rates that views bonds with differing maturities as perfect substitutes, so their yields differ only because short-term interest rates are expected to rise or fall.

Expenditure-reducing policies: Governmental policies, such as contractionary monetary policy actions, that reduce overall spending by home residents, thereby reducing import spending and improving a nation's trade balance.

Expenditure-switching policies: Governmental policies, such as tariffs or subsidies, that induce an increase in export spending while reducing import spending, thereby improving a nation's trade balance.

Explicit contracts: Contractual arrangements in which the terms of relationships between workers and firms, especially about wages, are in writing and legally binding upon both parties.

Externalities: Spillovers from the interactions of one set of individuals to others who otherwise are not involved in the transactions.

Fed watching: An occupation that involves developing forecasts of Federal Reserve monetary policy actions based on careful examination of the process by which the Fed appears to make its policy decisions.

Federal funds market: The money market in which banks borrow from and lend to each other deposits that they hold at Federal Reserve banks.

Federal funds rate: A short-term (usually overnight) interest rate on interbank loans in the United States.

Federal Open Market Committee (FOMC): A group composed of the seven governors and five of the twelve Federal Reserve bank presidents that determines how to conduct the Fed's open market operations.

Federal Reserve banks: The twelve central banking institutions that oversee regional activities of the Federal Reserve System.

Federal Reserve districts: The twelve geographic regions of the Federal Reserve System.

Federal Reserve–Treasury Accord: A 1951 agreement that dissociated the Fed from a previous policy of pegging Treasury bill rates at artificially low levels.

Fedwire: A large-value wire transfer system operated by the Federal Reserve that is open to all depository institutions that legally must maintain required reserves with the Fed.

Fiat money: A token that has value only because it is accepted as money.

Finance company: A financial institution that specializes in making loans to relatively high-risk individuals and businesses.

Financial instruments: Claims that those who lend their savings have on the future incomes of the borrowers who use those funds for investment.

Financial intermediation: Indirect finance through the services of an institutional "middleman" that channels funds from savers to those who ultimately make capital investments.

Firm commitment underwriting: An investment banking arrangement in which the investment bank purchases and distributes to dealers and other purchasers all securities offered by a business.

Fiscal agent: A term describing the Federal Reserve's role as an agent of the U.S. Treasury Department, on whose behalf the Fed issues, services, and redeems debts.

Fiscal policy: Actions by the government to vary its spending or taxes.

Fisher equation: An equation stating that the nominal interest rate equals the sum of the real interest rate and the expected inflation rate.

Fixed annuity: A financial instrument, typically issued by an insurance company, that pays regular, constant installments to the owner beginning at a specific future date.

FOMC directive: The official written instructions from the FOMC to the head of the Trading Desk at the Federal Reserve Bank of New York.

Foreign exchange: Exchange of currencies issued by different countries.

Foreign exchange market: A system of private banks, foreign exchange brokers and dealers, and central banks through which households, businesses, and governments purchase and sell currencies of various nations.

Foreign exchange market efficiency: A situation in which the equilibrium spot and forward exchange rates adjust to reflect all available information, in which case the forward premium is equal to the expected rate of currency depreciation plus any risk premium. This, in turn, implies that the forward exchange rate on average predicts the expected future spot exchange rate.

Foreign exchange risk: The potential for the value of a foreign-currency-denominated financial instrument to vary because of exchange rate fluctuations.

Foreign-exchange-market intervention: A central bank purchase or sale of foreign-currency reserves in an effort to alter the value of its nation's currency.

45-degree line: A line that cuts in half the 90-degree angle of the coordinate axes on a diagram relating real income to aggregate desired expenditures; every point on the 45-degree line could, in principle, be a point of equilibrium at which real income equals aggregate desired expenditures.

Forward contract: A contract requiring delivery of a financial instrument at a specified price on a certain date.

Forward currency contract: A forward contract calling for delivery of foreign currency, or financial instruments denominated in a foreign currency, at a specific exchange rate on a certain date.

Forward discount: A negative value for the difference between the forward exchange rate and the spot exchange rate divided by the spot exchange rate.

Forward exchange market: The market for currency to be delivered at a future date via forward currency contracts.

Forward premium: A positive value for the difference between the forward exchange rate and the spot exchange rate divided by the spot exchange rate.

Fractional-reserve banking: A system in which banks hold reserves equal to less than the amount of total deposits.

Free reserves: Total excess reserves at depository institutions minus the total amount of reserves that depository institutions have borrowed from the Fed.

Free silver: A late-nineteenth-century idea for unlimited coinage of silver to meet the monetary needs of a growing U.S. economy.

Free-banking laws: Laws in force in many U.S. states between 1837 and 1861 that allowed anyone to obtain a charter authorizing banking operations.

Free-rider problem: A situation in which some individuals take advantage of the fact that others are willing to pay for a jointly utilized good, such as a system of multilateral netting of foreign exchange payments.

Frictional unemployment: The portion of total unemployment arising from the fact that a number of workers are between jobs at any given time.

Futures contract: An agreement to deliver to another a given amount of a standardized commodity or financial instrument at a designated future date.

Futures options: Options to buy or sell futures contracts.

Gap management: A technique of depository institution asset-liability management that focuses on the difference ("gap") between the quantity of assets subject to significant interest rate risk and the amount of liabilities subject to such risk.

GDP price deflator: A flexible-weight measure of the overall price level; equal to nominal GDP divided by real GDP.

Gold bullion: Within a gold standard, the amount of gold used as money.

Gold standard: A monetary system in which the value of money is linked to the value of gold.

Government spending: Total state, local, and federal government expenditures on goods and services.

Gross domestic product (GDP): The value, tabulated using market prices, of all final goods and services produced within a nation's borders during a given period.

Gross national product (GNP): The value, tabulated using market prices, of all final goods and services produced by a nation's residents during a given period.

Hedge: A financial strategy that reduces the risk of capital losses arising from interest rate or currency risks.

Hedge funds: Limited partnerships that, like mutual funds, manage portfolios of assets on behalf of savers, but with very limited governmental oversight as compared with mutual funds.

Herstatt risk: The risk of any form of loss due to payment settlement failures that occur across national borders; named after a German bank that collapsed in 1974.

Historical value accounting: A traditional accounting procedure in which a depository institution's assets are always valued at their original values.

Identification problem: The problem that economists face in evaluating whether real-world data are consistent with the downward-sloping money demand schedule that money demand theories predict, given the fact that both money demand and money supply vary over time.

Idiosyncratic risk: Risk that is unique to a particular financial instrument; also known as nonsystematic risk.

Illiquidity: A situation in which a banking institution lacks the cash assets required to meet requests for depositor withdrawals.

Imperfectly competitive market: A market in which conditions for perfect competition, such as freedom of entry and exit, fail to hold, so banks can set their own loan or deposit rates to maximize their individual profits.

Implicit contracts: Unwritten agreements between workers and firms, concerning terms of employment such as wages, that may or may not be legally binding.

Income identity: An identity that states that real national income equals the sum of real consumption, real saving, real net taxes, and real imports.

Income velocity of money: The average number of times each unit of money is used to purchase final goods and services within an interval.

Inflation bias: The tendency for the economy to experience continuing inflation as a result of the time-inconsistency problem of discretionary monetary policy.

Inside money: Bank deposit money.

Insider information: Information that is not available to the public.

Insolvency: A situation in which the value of a bank's assets falls below the value of its liabilities.

Installment credit: Loans to individual consumers that entail periodic repayments of principal and interest.

Interest expense: The portion of depository institution costs incurred through payments of interest to holders of the institutions' liabilities.

Interest income: Interest revenues that depository institutions derive from their holdings of loans and securities.

Interest rate future: A contract to buy or sell a standardized denomination of a specific financial instrument at a given price at a certain date in the future.

Interest rate risk: The possibility that the market value of a financial instrument will change as interest rates vary.

Interest rate smoothing: Central bank efforts to attain an ultimate objective of interest rate stability.

Interest rate swap: A contractual exchange of one set of interest payments for another.

Interest rate: The percentage return, or percentage yield, earned by the holder of a financial instrument.

Interest: The payment, or yield, received in exchange for extending credit by holding any financial instrument.

Interest-elastic desired investment: Desired investment spending that is relatively sensitive to interest rate variations.

Interest-elastic reserve demand: Demand for depository institution reserves that is relatively sensitive to interest rate variations.

Interest-inelastic desired investment: Desired investment spending that is relatively insensitive to interest rate variations.

Interest-inelastic reserve demand: Demand for depository institution reserves that is relatively insensitive to interest rate variations.

Interest-rate forward contract: A contract committing the issuer to sell a financial instrument at a given interest rate as of a specific date.

Intermediate target: An economic variable that a central bank seeks to control because it determines that doing so is consistent with its ultimate objectives.

Intermediate-term maturity: Maturity between one year and ten years.

International capital markets: Markets for cross-border exchange of financial instruments that have maturities of a year or more.

International financial diversification: The process of spreading portfolio risk by holding both U.S.-issued and foreign-issued financial instruments.

International financial integration: A process through which financial markets of various nations become more alike and more interconnected.

International money markets: Markets for cross-border exchange of financial instruments with maturities of less than one year.

Interstate branching: The operation of banking offices in more than one state.

Intrastate branching: The operation of banking offices anywhere within a state.

Inventory theory of money demand: A theory of the demand for money that focuses on how people determine the best inventory of money to keep on hand.

Inverted yield curve: A downward-sloping yield curve.

Investment: Additions to the stock of capital goods.

Investment banks: Institutions that specialize in marketing and underwriting sales of firm ownership shares.

Investment spending: The sum of purchases of new capital goods, spending on new residential construction, and inventory investment.

Investment-grade securities: Bonds with relatively low default risk.

Junk bonds: Bonds with relatively high default risk.

Large-denomination time deposits: Deposits with set maturities and denominations greater than or equal to $100,000.

Large-value wire transfer systems: Payment systems such as Fedwire and CHIPS that permit the electronic transmission of large dollar sums.

Law of diminishing marginal returns: The law that states that each successive addition of a unit of a factor of production, such as labor, eventually produces a smaller gain in real output produced, other factors held constant.

Lender of last resort: An institution that is willing and able to lend to any temporarily illiquid but otherwise solvent institution to prevent its illiquid position from leading to a general loss of confidence in that institution or in others.

Level premium policy: A whole life insurance policy under which an insurance company charges fixed premium payments throughout the life of the insured individual.

Liability: A legally enforceable claim on the assets of a business or individual.

Limit orders: Instructions from other stock exchange members to specialists to execute stock trades at specific prices.

Limited payment policy: A whole life insurance policy under which an insured individual pays premiums only for a fixed number of years and is insured during and after the payment period.

Liquidity: The ease with which an asset can be sold or redeemed for a known amount of cash at short notice and at low risk of loss of nominal value.

Liquidity effect: A fall in the equilibrium nominal interest rate resulting from sustained open market purchases, holding the price level unchanged.

Liquidity risk: The risk of loss that may occur if a payment is not received when due.

Load funds: Mutual funds marketed by brokers who receive commissions based on the returns of the funds.

Loan commitment: A lending arrangement in which a depository institution promises to extend credit up to some predetermined limit at a contracted interest rate and within a given period of time.

Loan loss provisions: An expense that depository institutions incur when they allocate funds to loan loss reserves.

Loan loss reserves: An amount of cash assets that depository institutions hold as liquidity that they expect to be depleted as a result of loan defaults.

Loanable funds: The term that classical economists use to refer to the amount of real income that households save, representing claims on real output.

London Interbank Offer Rate (LIBOR): The interest rate on interbank loans traded among six large London banks.

Long position: An obligation to purchase a financial instrument at a given price and at a specific time.

Luxury asset: An asset with a wealth elasticity of demand greater than 1, which indicates that an individual raises holdings of the asset more than proportionately in response to a given proportionate increase in wealth.

M1: Currency plus transactions deposits.

M2: M1 plus savings and small-denomination time deposits and balances of individual and broker-dealer money market mutual funds.

M3: M2 plus large-denomination time deposits, Eurodollars and repurchase agreements, and institution-only money market mutual funds.

Marginal cost: The addition to the total cost generated by a one-unit increase in production of a good or service; for a bank, the addition to total cost from obtaining an additional dollar of deposits to lend, which is the sum of marginal deposit interest expense, marginal deposit resource costs, and marginal loan resource costs.

Marginal product of labor: The change in total output resulting from a one-unit increase in the quantity of labor employed in production.

Marginal propensity to consume (*MPC*): The additional consumption caused by an increase in disposable income; a change in consumption spending divided by a corresponding change in disposable income; the slope of the consumption function.

Marginal propensity to import (*MPIM*): The additional import expenditures stimulated by an increase in disposable income; a change in import spending divided by a corresponding change in disposable income; the slope of the import function.

Marginal propensity to save (*MPS*): The additional saving caused by an increase in disposable income; a change in saving divided by a corresponding change in disposable income; the slope of the saving function.

Marginal revenue: The gain in total revenues resulting from a one-unit increase in production of a good or service; for a bank, the addition to its revenues from adding an additional dollar of loan assets.

Market concentration: The degree to which the few largest depository institutions dominate loan and deposit markets.

Market risk: Risk that is common to all financial assets within a portfolio; also called systematic risk.

Market structure: The organization of the loan and deposit markets in which depository institutions interact.

Market value accounting: An accounting procedure in which a depository institution (or its regulator) values its assets in terms of the approximate market prices at which those assets would currently sell in secondary markets.

Market-based regulation: Regulation that uses observable measures of depository institution risk as guidelines for supervisory enforcement.

Maturity: The time until final principal and interest payments are due to the holders of a financial instrument.

Medium of exchange: An attribute of money that permits it to be used as a means of payment.

Mercantilism: The idea that a primary determinant of a nation's wealth is international trade and commerce, so a nation can gain by enacting policies that spur exports while limiting imports.

Monetary aggregate: A grouping of assets sufficiently liquid to be defined as a measure of money.

Monetary approach: A theory of exchange rate determination that predicts that the fundamental determination of a nation's exchange rate is the quantity of money supplied by its central bank.

Monetary base: A "base" amount of money that serves as the foundation for a nation's monetary system. Under a gold standard, the amount of gold bullion; in today's fiat money system, the sum of currency in circulation plus reserves of banks and other depository institutions.

Monetary policy indicator: An economic variable that gives the public an especially clear signal of the intended effects of monetary policy actions.

Monetary policy signal: An occurrence that provides information about the objectives of central bank officials.

Money: Anything that functions as a medium of exchange, store of value, unit of account, and standard of deferred payment.

Money illusion: A situation that exists when economic agents change their behavior in response to changes in nominal values, even if there are no changes in real (price-level-adjusted) values.

Money market deposit accounts: Savings accounts with limited checking privileges.

Money market mutual funds: Pools of funds from savers that managing firms use to purchase short-term financial assets such as Treasury bills and commercial paper.

Money markets: Markets for financial instruments with maturities of less than one year.

Money multiplier: A number that tells how much the quantity of money will change in response to a change in the monetary base.

Monopoly: A market environment in which only a single firm, or a group of firms collectively coordinating their actions, produces a good or service; in banking, a situation in which only one bank or a coordinating group of banks lends and takes in deposits.

Moral hazard: The possibility that a borrower may engage in more risky behavior after a loan has been made.

Mortgage loans: Long-term loans to individual homeowners or to businesses for purchases of land and buildings.

Mortgage-backed securities: Financial instruments whose return is based on the underlying returns on mortgage loans.

Multi-employer pensions: Pensions whose accumulations and benefit rights may be transferred from one employer to another.

Multiplier effect: The ratio of a change in the equilibrium real income to an increase in autonomous net aggregate expenditures. When the aggregate expenditures schedule shifts vertically, the equilibrium level of national income changes by a multiple of the amount of the shift.

Municipal bonds: Long-term debt instruments issued by state and local governments.

Mutual fund: A mix of financial instruments managed on behalf of shareholders by investment companies that charge fees for their services.

Mutual ownership: A depository institution organizational structure in which depositors own the institution.

National Association of Securities Dealers Automated Quotation (Nasdaq): The electronic network over which most over-the-counter stocks are traded.

National income: The sum of all factor earnings, or net domestic product minus indirect business taxes.

National income accounts: Tabulations of the values of a nation's flows of income and product.

Natural GDP: The level of real GDP that is consistent with the economy's natural rate of growth.

Natural rate of unemployment: The portion of the unemployment rate that is accounted for by frictional and structural unemployment.

Necessity asset: An asset with a wealth elasticity of demand less than 1, which implies that an individual increases holdings of the asset less than proportionately in response to a given proportionate increase in wealth.

Negative externality: A reduction in the welfare of one individual caused by a transaction between other parties, even though the individual is not directly involved in the transaction.

Negotiable-order-of-withdrawal (NOW) accounts: Interest-bearing checking deposits.

Net export spending: The difference between spending on domestically produced goods and services by residents of other countries and spending on foreign-produced goods and services by residents of the home country.

Net interest margin: The difference between a depository institution's interest income and interest expenses as a percentage of total assets.

Net worth: The excess of assets over liabilities, or equity capital.

No-load funds: Mutual funds that investment companies market directly to the public and that charge management fees instead of brokerage commissions.

Nominal exchange rate: An exchange rate that is unadjusted for changes in the two nations' price levels.

Nominal gross domestic product (nominal GDP): The value of final production of goods and services calculated in current-dollar terms with no adjustment for effects of price changes.

Nominal interest rate: A rate of return in current-dollar terms that does not reflect anticipated inflation.

Nominal yield: The coupon return on a bond divided by the bond's face value.

Noncontributory pensions: Pensions funded solely by employers.

Noncontrollable liabilities: Liabilities whose dollar amounts bank customers largely determine once banks have issued the liabilities to them.

Noninterest income: Revenues that depository institutions earn from sources other than interest income, such as trading profits or fees that they charge for services that they provide their customers.

Normal profit: A profit level just sufficient to compensate depository institution owners for holding equity shares in the depository institution instead of purchasing ownership shares of other enterprises.

Observational equivalence: The fact that the basic version of the modern Keynesian theory with sticky wages makes some of the same fundamental policy predictions as the new classical model that is based on pure competition with completely flexible wages.

Off-balance-sheet banking: Bank activities that earn income without expanding the assets and liabilities that the banks report on their balance sheets.

Official settlements balance: A balance of payments account that records international asset transactions involving agencies of home and foreign governments.

Open economy: An economy that is linked by trade with other economies of the world.

Open market operations: Federal Reserve purchases or sales of securities.

Open market purchase: A Federal Reserve purchase of a security, which increases total reserves at depository institutions and thereby raises the size of the monetary base.

Open market sale: A Federal Reserve sale of a security, which reduces total reserves of depository institutions and thereby reduces the size of the monetary base.

Open smart-card system: An e-money system in which consumers use smart cards with embedded microprocessors, which may be issued by a number of institutions, to purchase goods and services offered by multiple retailers.

Open stored-value system: An e-money system in which consumers buy goods and services using cards containing prestored funds that are offered by multiple card issuers and accepted by multiple retailers.

Open-end funds: Mutual funds whose shares are redeemable at any time at prices based on the market values of the mix of financial instruments held by such funds.

Operating procedure: A guideline for conducting monetary policy over several weeks or months.

Optimal currency area: A region within which fixed exchange rates can be maintained without inhibiting prompt internal adjustments of employment and output to changes in international market conditions.

Option: A financial contract giving the owner the right to buy or sell an underlying financial instrument at a certain price within a specific period of time.

Outside money: Money in the form of currency and bank reserves.

Overlapping-generations approach: A theory of money demand that emphasizes how societies use money as a way to store and transfer wealth across time.

Over-the-counter (OTC) broker-dealer: A broker-dealer that trades shares of stock that are not listed on organized stock exchanges.

Over-the-counter (OTC) stocks: Equity shares offered by companies that do not meet listing requirements for major stock exchanges, or choose not to be listed there, and instead are traded in decentralized markets.

Overvalued currency: A currency whose present market-determined value is higher than the value predicted by an economic theory or model.

Pay-as-you-go pensions: Pensions that are not fully funded when employees retire.

Payment intermediary: An institution that facilitates the transfer of funds between buyer and seller during the course of any purchase of goods, services, or financial assets.

Payment system: A term that refers broadly to the set of mechanisms by which consumers, businesses, governments, and financial institutions exchange payments.

Peak: The point along a business cycle at which real GDP is at its highest level relative to the long-run, natural GDP level.

Pension funds: Institutions that specialize in managing funds that individuals save for retirement.

Perpetuity: A bond with an infinite term to maturity.

Point-of-sale (POS) networks: Systems in which consumers pay for retail purchases through direct deductions from their deposit accounts at depository institutions.

Point-of-sale (POS) transfer: Electronic transfer of funds from a buyer's account to the firm from which a good or service is purchased at the time the sale is made.

Policy credibility: The believability of a commitment by a central bank or governmental authority to follow specific policy rules.

Policy ineffectiveness proposition: The new classical view that systematic (predictable) monetary policy actions will not have short-run effects on real quantities.

Policy rule: A commitment to a fixed strategy no matter what happens to other economic variables.

Policy time lags: The time intervals between the need for a countercyclical monetary policy action and the ultimate effects of that action on an economic variable.

Portfolio: The group of financial instruments held by an individual, which together make up the individual's financial wealth.

Portfolio approach: A theory of exchange rate determination that predicts that a nation's exchange rate adjusts to ensure that its residents are satisfied with their allocation of wealth among holdings of domestic money, domestic bonds, and foreign bonds.

Portfolio motive: The desire to hold money as part of a strategy of balancing the expected rate of return on money with rates of return on other assets.

Portfolio-balance effect: A fundamental prediction of the portfolio approach to exchange rate determination, in which changes in central bank holdings of domestic and foreign bonds alter the equilibrium prices at which traders are willing to hold these bonds, inducing a change in the exchange rate.

Preferred habitat theory: A theory of the term structure of interest rates that views bonds as imperfectly substitutable, so yields on longer-term bonds must be greater than those on shorter-term bonds even if short-term interest rates are not expected to rise or fall.

Preferred stock: Shares of corporate ownership that entail no voting rights but entitle the owner to dividends if any are paid by the corporation and to any residual value of the corporation after other creditors have been paid.

Price-level nonstationarity: Failure of the price level to adjust to a constant long-run average level; upward (or downward) drift of the price level over time.

Primary market: A financial market in which newly issued financial instruments are purchased and sold.

Primary reserves: Cash assets.

Prime rate: The interest rate that American banks charge on loans to the most creditworthy business borrowers.

Principal: The amount of credit extended when one makes a loan or purchases a bond.

Private payments balance: The sum of the current account balance and the private capital account balance, or the net total of all private exchanges between U.S. individuals and businesses and the rest of the world.

Product identity: An identity that states that real national product is the sum of real consumption, real realized investment, real government spending, and real exports.

Production function: A relationship between possible quantities of factors of production, such as labor services, and the amount of output of goods and services that firms can produce with current technology.

Prospectus: A formal written offer to sell securities.

Purchased funds: Very short-term bank borrowings in the money market.

Purchasing power of money: The value of money in terms of the amount of real goods and services it buys.

Purchasing power parity (PPP): A condition that states that if international arbitrage is unhindered, the price of a good or service in one nation should be the same as the exchange-rate-adjusted price of the same good or service in another nation.

Put option: An option contract giving the owner the right to sell a financial instrument at a specific price.

Quantity theory of money: The theory that people hold money for transactions purposes.

Rational expectations hypothesis: The idea that individuals form expectations based on all available past and current information and on a basic understanding of how markets function.

Real balance effect: An increase in the nominal rate of interest that results from an increase in the price level, holding total depository institution reserves unchanged.

Real bills doctrine: A bank management philosophy that calls for lending primarily to borrowers who will use the funds to finance production or shipping of physical goods, thereby ensuring speedy repayment of the loans.

Real consumption: The real amount of spending by households on domestically produced goods and services.

Real disposable income: A household's real after-tax income.

Real exchange rate: An exchange rate that has been adjusted for differences between two nations' price levels, thereby yielding the implied rate of exchange of goods and services between those nations.

Real exports: The real value of goods and services produced by domestic firms and exported to other countries.

Real gross domestic product (real GDP): A price-adjusted measure of aggregate output, or nominal GDP divided by the GDP price deflator.

Real imports: The real flow of spending by households for the purchase of goods and services from firms in other countries.

Real interest parity: An equality between two nations' real interest rates that arises if both uncovered interest parity and relative purchasing power parity are satisfied.

Real interest rate: The anticipated rate of return from holding a financial instrument after taking into account the extent to which inflation is expected to reduce the amount of goods and services that this return could be used to buy.

Real money balances: The purchasing power of the quantity of money in circulation, measured as the nominal quantity of money divided by an index measure of the prices of goods and services.

Real net taxes: The amount of real taxes paid to the government by households, net of transfer payments.

Real realized investment: Actual real expenditures by firms in the product markets.

Real resource expenses: Expenses that a bank must incur in the form of explicit payments of wages and salaries to employees, explicit payments to other owners of factors of production, and opportunity costs of devoting resources of the bank's owners to that line of business rather than an alternative.

Real saving: The amount of income that households save through financial markets.

Real-business-cycle theory: An approach to the theory of overall economic activity in which variations in technology are the key factors accounting for cyclical fluctuations in real output.

Recession: A decline in real GDP lasting at least two consecutive quarters, which can cause real GDP to fall below its long-run, natural level.

Recognition lag: The interval that passes between the need for a countercyclical policy action and the recognition of this need by a policymaker.

Redlining: A practice under which some depository institution managers allegedly have refused to lend to individuals or businesses located in particular geographic areas.

Regulatory arbitrage: The act of trying to avoid regulations imposed by banking authorities in one's home country by moving offices and funds to countries with less constraining regulations.

Reinvestment risk: The possibility that available yields on short-term financial instruments may decline, so that holdings of longer-term instruments might be preferable.

Representative-agent assumption: The assumption that every trader in the marketplace can obtain the same information and has the same basic view of how the market operates.

Repurchase agreement: A contract to sell financial assets with a promise to repurchase them at a later time.

Required reserve ratios: Fractions of transactions deposit balances that the Federal Reserve mandates that depository institutions maintain either as deposits with Federal Reserve banks or as vault cash.

Required reserves: Legally mandated reserve holdings at depository institutions, which are proportional to the dollar amounts of transactions accounts.

Reserve demand schedule: A graphical depiction of the inverse relationship between the total amount of reserves demanded by depository institutions and the federal funds rate.

Reserve deposits: Deposit accounts that depository institutions maintain at Federal Reserve banks.

Reserve supply schedule: A graphical depiction of the relationship between the total amount of reserves supplied by the Fed and the federal funds rate.

Reserves: Cash held by depository institutions in their vaults or on deposit with the Federal Reserve System.

Response lag: The interval between the recognition of a need for a countercyclical policy action and the actual implementation of the policy action.

Return on assets: A depository institution's profit as a percentage of its total assets.

Return on equity: A depository institution's profit as a percentage of its equity capital.

Revolving credit: Loans to individuals that permit them to borrow automatically up to specified limits and to repay the balance of the loan at any time.

Revolving credit commitments: Loan commitments that permit borrowers to borrow and repay as often as they wish within an interval in which the commitment is binding on a depository institution.

Risk aversion: The preference, other things being equal, to hold assets whose returns exhibit less variability.

Risk premium: The amount by which one instrument's yield exceeds the yield of another instrument as a result of the first instrument being riskier and less liquid than the second.

Risk structure of interest rates: The relationship among yields on financial instruments that have the same maturity but differ because of variations in default risk, liquidity, and tax rates.

Risk-adjusted assets: A weighted average of bank assets that regulators compute to account for risk differences across types of assets.

Risk-based capital requirements: Regulatory capital standards that account for risk factors that distinguish different depository institutions.

Risk-based deposit insurance premiums: Premiums that depository institutions pay the FDIC based on the varying degrees to which they are capitalized and on the differing risk factors that they exhibit.

Sales finance companies: Finance companies that specialize in making loans to individuals for the purchase of items from specific retailers or manufacturers.

Saving: Forgone consumption.

Savings and loan association: A type of depository institution that has traditionally specialized in mortgage lending.

Savings Association Insurance Fund (SAIF): The FDIC's fund that covers insured deposits of savings institutions.

Savings bank: Another type of depository institution that has specialized in mortgage lending.

Savings deposits: Interest-bearing savings accounts without set maturities.

Secondary market: A financial market in which financial instruments issued in the past are traded.

Secondary reserves: Securities that depository institutions can easily convert to cash in the event that such a need arises.

Securities: Financial instruments.

Securities and Exchange Commission (SEC): A group of five presidentially appointed members whose mandate is to enforce rules governing securities trading.

Securities underwriting: A guarantee by an investment bank that a firm that issues new stocks or bonds will receive a specified minimum price per share of stock or per bond.

Securitization: The process of pooling loans with similar risk characteristics and selling the loan pool in the form of a tradable financial instrument.

Segmented markets theory: A theory of the term structure of interest rates that views bonds with differing maturities as nonsubstitutable, so their yields differ because they are determined in separate markets.

Seigniorage: The difference between the market value of money and the cost of its production, which is gained by the government that produces and issues the money.

Shiftability theory: A management approach in which depository institutions hold a mix of illiquid loans and more liquid securities that act as a secondary reserve held as a contingency against potential liquidity problems.

Shopping-time theory of money demand: A theory of the demand for money that focuses on money's role in helping people reduce the amount of time they spend shopping, thereby freeing up more time for leisure or work.

Short position: An obligation to sell a financial instrument at a given price and at a specific time.

Short-term maturity: Maturity of less than one year.

Signal-extraction problem: The problem of trying to infer a policymaker's true goals from the imperfect signal transmitted by the policymaker's actions.

Simultaneity problem: The problem of accounting for the possibility that factors influencing the quantity of money demanded are themselves affected by how many real money balances people hold, which can complicate assessments of how well real-world observations square with theories of money demand.

Single-employer pensions: Pensions that are established by an employer only for its own employees and are nontransferable to other employers.

Small menu costs: The costs firms incur when they make price changes, such as the costs of changing prices in menus or catalogues and the costs of renegotiating agreements with customers.

Small-denomination time deposits: Deposits with set maturities and denominations of less than $100,000.

Smart card: A card containing a microprocessor that permits storage of funds via security programming, that can communicate with other computers, and that does not require online authorization for funds transfer to occur.

Specialists: Stock exchange members that are charged with trading on their own accounts to prevent dramatic movements in stock prices.

Spot exchange rate: The spot-market price of a currency indicating how much of one country's currency must be given up in immediate exchange for a unit of another nation's currency.

Spot market: A market for contracts requiring the immediate sale or purchase of an asset.

Standard of deferred payment: An attribute of money that permits it to be used as a means of valuing future receipts in loan contracts.

Standby commitment underwriting: An investment banking arrangement in which the investment bank earns commissions for helping the issuing firm sell its securities under the guarantee that the investment bank will purchase for resale any initially unsold securities.

Sterilization: A central bank action to prevent variations in its foreign exchange reserves from affecting the monetary base.

Stock exchanges: Organized marketplaces for corporate equities and bonds.

Stock index future: An agreement to deliver, on a specified date, a portfolio of stocks represented by a stock price index.

Stock options: Options to buy or sell firm equity shares.

Store of value: An attribute of money that allows it to be held for future use without loss of value in the meantime.

Structural unemployment: The portion of total unemployment resulting from a poor match of workers' abilities and skills with current needs of employers.

Structure-conduct-performance (SCP) model: A theory of depository institution market structure in which the structure of loan and deposit markets influences the behavior (conduct) of depository institutions in those markets, thereby affecting their performance.

Structured early intervention and resolution (SEIR): A regulatory system, established by the FDIC Improvement Act of 1991, that authorizes the FDIC to intervene quickly in the management of a depository institution that currently threatens to cause losses for the federal deposit insurance funds.

Subordinated notes and debentures: Capital market instruments with maturities in excess of one year that banks issue with the provision that depositors have primary claim to bank assets in the event of failure.

Supplementary capital: Under standards currently used to calculate required capital, a measure that includes certain preferred stock and most subordinated debt.

Supranormal profits: Levels of profit above those required to induce depository institution owners to hold shares of ownership in those institutions instead of shares of other businesses.

Swap: A contract entailing an exchange of payment flows between two parties.

Syndicated loan: A loan arranged by one or two banks but funded by these and other banks.

Systemic risk: The risk that some depository institutions may not be able to meet the terms of their credit agreements because of failures by other institutions to settle transactions that otherwise are not related.

T-account: A side-by-side listing of the assets and liabilities of a business such as a depository institution.

Term federal funds: Interbank loans with maturities exceeding one day.

Term life policy: A life insurance policy under which an individual is insured only during a limited period that the policy is in effect.

Term premium: An amount by which the yield on a long-term bond must exceed the yield on a short-term bond to make individuals willing to hold either bond if they expect short-term bond yields to remain unchanged.

Term structure of interest rates: The relationship among yields on financial instruments with identical risk, liquidity, and tax characteristics but differing terms to maturity.

Terminally funded pensions: Pensions that must be fully funded by the date that an employee retires.

Time-inconsistency problem: The policy problem that can result if a policymaker has the ability, at a future time, to alter its strategy in a way that is inconsistent both with the desires and strategies of private individuals and with its own initially announced intentions.

Too-big-to-fail policy: A regulatory policy that protects the largest depository institutions from failure solely because regulators believe that such failure could undermine the public's confidence in the financial system.

Total capital: Under currently imposed bank capital requirements, the sum of core capital and supplementary capital.

Total reserves: The total balances that depository institutions hold on deposit with Federal Reserve banks or as vault cash.

Trading Desk: The Fed's term for the office at the Federal Reserve Bank of New York that conducts open market operations on the Fed's behalf.

Transaction risk: A foreign exchange risk arising from the possibility that the proceeds from trading a financial instrument may change as a result of exchange rate variations.

Transactions deposits: Checking accounts.

Transactions motive: The desire to hold currency and transactions deposits to use as media of exchange in planned transactions.

Transfer payments: Governmentally managed income redistributions.

Translation risk: A foreign exchange risk resulting from altered home-currency values of foreign-currency-denominated financial instruments caused by fluctuations in exchange rates.

Transmission lag: The interval that elapses between the implementation of an intended countercyclical policy and its ultimate effects on an economic variable.

Treasury bills (T-bills): Short-term debt obligations of the federal government issued with maturities of three, six, or twelve months.

Treasury bonds: Treasury securities with maturities of ten years or more.

Treasury notes: Treasury securities with maturities ranging from one to ten years.

Treasury tax and loan (TT&L) accounts: U.S. Treasury checking accounts at private depository institutions.

Trough: The point along a business cycle at which real GDP is at its lowest level relative to the long-run natural GDP level.

Ultimate goals: The final objectives of economic policies.

Uncovered interest parity: A relationship between interest rates on bonds that are similar in all respects other than that they are denominated in different nations' currencies. According to this condition, the yield on the bond denominated in the currency that holders anticipate will depreciate must exceed the yield on the other bond by the rate at which the currency is expected to depreciate.

Undervalued currency: A currency whose present market-determined value is lower than that predicted by an economic theory or model.

Unemployment rate: The percentage of the civilian labor force that is unemployed.

Unit of account: An attribute of money that permits it to be used as a measure of the value of goods, services, and financial assets.

Universal banking: A banking environment in which banks face few, if any, restrictions on their powers to offer a full range of financial services and to own shares of stock in corporations.

Value of the marginal product of labor: The marginal product of labor times the price of output.

Value-at-risk model: A statistical framework for evaluating how changes in interest rates and financial instrument prices are likely to affect the overall value of a portfolio of financial assets.

Variable annuity: A financial instrument, typically issued by an insurance company, that beginning on a specific future date pays the owner a stream of returns that depends on the value of an underlying portfolio of assets.

Vault cash: Currency that a depository institution holds on location to honor cash withdrawals by depositors.

Vehicle currency: A commonly accepted currency that is used to denominate a transaction that does not take place in the nation that issues the currency.

Wealth: An individual's total resources.

Wealth elasticity of demand: The percentage change in the quantity of an asset demanded by an individual divided by a given percentage change in the individual's wealth.

Whole life policy: A life insurance policy whose benefits are payable to a beneficiary whenever the insured person's death occurs and that accumulates a cash value that the policyholder may acquire prior to his or her death.

Wire transfers: Payments made via telephone lines or through fiber-optic cables.

Yield curve: A chart depicting the relationship among yields on bonds that differ only in their terms to maturity.

Yield to maturity: The rate of return on a bond if it is held until it matures, which reflects the market price of the bond, the bond's coupon return, and any capital gain from holding the bond to maturity.

Zero-coupon bonds: Bonds that pay lump-sum amounts at maturity.

INDEX

D

F

H

I

J

N

O

Q

R

S